Psychological Processes that A

Psychological research has helped to clarify how people thin... are a few of the topics relevant to critical thinking that are discussed in this book and the chapters in which they appear.

FACTORS THAT ENHANCE CRITICAL THINKING

Scientific methods and reasoning (all of Chapter 2)

Inductive, deductive, and dialectical reasoning (Chapter 8)

Reflective judgment (Chapter 8)

Creative problem solving (Chapter 8)

Algorithms, heuristics (Chapter 8)

Intelligence (Chapter 8)

Metacognition (Chapter 8)

Improving memory (Chapter 9)

Reducing negative emotions (Chapter 10)

Personality traits that foster critical thinking (Chapter 12)

Cognitive development (Chapter 13)

Role of appraisals, rethinking in coping with stress and illness (Chapter 14)

Attributions that affect feelings and behavior (Chapters 11, 16, 17)

Cognitive therapy (Chapter 16)

Independent action (Chapter 17)

BARRIERS TO CRITICAL THINKING

Psychological and cultural constraints on perception (Chapter 6)

Cognitive biases (e.g., confirmation and hindsight biases, cognitive dissonance) (Chapter 8)

Mental sets (Chapter 8)

Nonreflective judgment (Chapter 8)

Fallibility of memory (Chapter 9)

Emotional reasoning (Chapter 10)

Defense mechanisms (Chapter 12)

Cognitive distortions in mood disorders (Chapters 10, 16)

Conformity, fear of ridicule and failure (Chapter 17)

Mindlessness (Chapter 17)

Deindividuation (Chapter 17)

Diffusion of responsibility (Chapter 17)

Entrapment (Chapter 17)

Groupthink (Chapter 17)

Coersive persuasion (Chapter 17)

Prejudice and stereotypes (Chapter 18)

Ethnocentrism (Chapter 18)

PSYCHOLOGY

PSYCHOLOGY

Fifth Edition

Carole Wade
Dominican College of San Rafael

Carol Tavris

An imprint of Addison Wesley Longman, Inc.

New York • Reading, Massachusetts • Menlo Park, California • Harlow, England
Don Mills, Ontario • Sydney • Mexico City • Madrid • Amsterdam

Acquisitions Editor: Rebecca Dudley
Developmental Editor: Susan Messer
Supplements Editor: Cyndy Taylor
Marketing Manager: Jay O'Callaghan
Project Editor: Donna DeBenedictis
Text Designer: Amy Trombat
Cover Designer-Illustrator: John Odam
Graphic Art: Joanne Del Ben
Anatomical Art: Lorraine Harrison
Illustrative Art: Greg Hargreaves
Photo Researcher: Sandy Schneider
Production Manager: Alexandra Odulak
Desktop Coordinator: Joanne Del Ben
Manufacturing Manager: Hilda Koparanian
Electronic Page Makeup: Amy Trombat, Joanne Del Ben
Printer and Binder: RR Donnelley & Sons Company
Cover Printer: The Lehigh Press, Inc.

For permission to use copyrighted material, grateful acknowledgment is made to the copyright holders on pp. C1–C3, which are hereby made part of this copyright page.

Library of Congress Cataloging-in-Publication Data
Wade, Carole.
Psychology / Carole Wade, Carol Tavris. — 5th ed.
p. cm.
Includes bibliographical references and indexes.
ISBN 0-321-01129-5
1. Psychology. I. Tavris, Carol. II. Title.
BF121.W27 1998
150—dc21 97-8596
CIP

ISBN 0-321-01129-5

12345678910—DOW—00999897

Contents at a Glance

Contents

8 Thinking and Intelligence 297

9 Memory 339

12 Theories of Personality 451

13 Development over the Life Span 491

Part Five *Health and Disorder*

Boxed Features

Think About It: Puzzles of Psychology

Think About It: Issues in Popular Culture

Taking Psychology with You

To the Instructor

WHEN WE BEGAN WORK ON THE FIRST EDITION of this textbook in the mid-1980s, we had five goals, some of which were considered quite daring: (1) to make critical thinking integral to the introductory psychology course; (2) to mainstream research on culture and gender, representing psychology as the scientific study of all human beings; (3) to foster the active learning of psychology, so students would see how and why psychology is so applicable to their personal and social lives; (4) to keep "ahead of the curve" with coverage of research as psychology moves in new directions; and (5) to acknowledge forthrightly the many controversies in the field.

THINKING ABOUT CRITICAL AND CREATIVE THINKING

Our first ambition, unique to textbooks at the time, was not only to convey the basic content of psychology, but also to get students to reflect on and use what they learn—to show them what it is like to think like a psychologist. Psychology, we have always believed, is more than a body of knowledge; it is a way of approaching and analyzing the world. From the beginning, therefore, our approach has been based on **critical and creative thinking:** the understanding that knowledge is

32 Part One *An Invitation to Psychology*

AVOID EMOTIONAL REASONING Emotion has a place in critical thinking. Passionate commitment to a view can motivate a person to think boldly without fear of what others will say, to defend an unpopular idea, and to seek evidence for creative new theories. Moreover, in the absence of compassion and pity, logic and reason can lead to misguided or even destructive decisions and actions. Indeed, some of the most sadistic killers and military strategists in history have been bright, even brilliant, thinkers. But when gut feelings replace clear thinking, the results are equally dangerous. "Persecutions and wars and lynchings," observed Edward de Bono (1985), "are all a result of gut feeling."

Because our feelings seem so right, it is hard to understand that people with opposing views feel just as strongly as we do. But they usually do, which means that feelings alone are not a reliable guide to the best position. You probably already hold strong beliefs about child rearing, drugs, astrology, the causes of crime, racism, the origins of intelligence, gender differences, homosexuality, and many other issues. As you read this book, you may find yourself quarreling with findings that you dislike. Disagreement is fine; it means you are reading actively. All we ask is that you think about *why* you are disagreeing: Is it because the results conflict with an assumption you hold dear, or because the evidence is unpersuasive? Keep in mind the words of the English poet and essayist Alexander Pope: "What reason weaves, by passion is undone."

What Is Psychology? Chapter 1 33

DON'T OVERSIMPLIFY A critical thinker looks beyond the obvious, resists easy generalizations, and rejects either–or thinking. For example, is it better to feel you have control over what happens to you or to accept with tranquility whatever life serves up? Either answer oversimplifies. As we will see in Chapter 14, control has many important benefits, but sometimes it's best to "go with the flow."

Often, in a disagreement, you will hear someone *arguing by anecdote*—generalizing from a personal experience or a few examples to everyone. One crime committed by a paroled ex-convict means parole should be abolished; one friend who hates his or her school means that everybody who goes there hates it. Anecdotes are often the source of stereotyping as well: One dishonest welfare mother means they are all dishonest; one encounter with an unconventional Californian means they are all flaky. And many people make themselves miserable by generalizing from a single unfortunate event to a whole pattern of defeat: "I did poorly on this test, and now I'll never get through college or have a job or kids or anything." Critical thinkers want more evidence than one or two stories before drawing such global conclusions.

CONSIDER OTHER INTERPRETATIONS A critical thinker creatively formulates hypotheses that offer reasonable explanations of the topic at hand. The goal is to find an explanation that accounts for the most evidence with the fewest assumptions. This is called the *principle of Occam's razor,* after the fourteenth-century

Thinking Critically and Creatively About Psychological Issues

Ask questions; be willing to wonder

A Chinese man standing alone against awesome military might inspired millions during the 1989 rebellion in Tiananmen Square. Why do some people have the courage to risk their lives for their beliefs? Why do so many others go along with the crowd or mindlessly obey authority? Social psychologists probe these questions in depth, as we will see in Chapter 17.

Define your terms

People refer to intelligence all the time, but what is it exactly? Does the musical genius of a world-class violinist like Anne-Sophie Mutter count as intelligence? Is intellectual ability captured by an IQ score, or does it also include wisdom and practical "smarts"? We will consider some answers in Chapter 8.

Examine the evidence

When demonstrating "levitation," illusionists such as André Kole take advantage of the fact that people will trust the evidence of their own eyes even when such evidence is misleading, as discussed in Chapter 6.

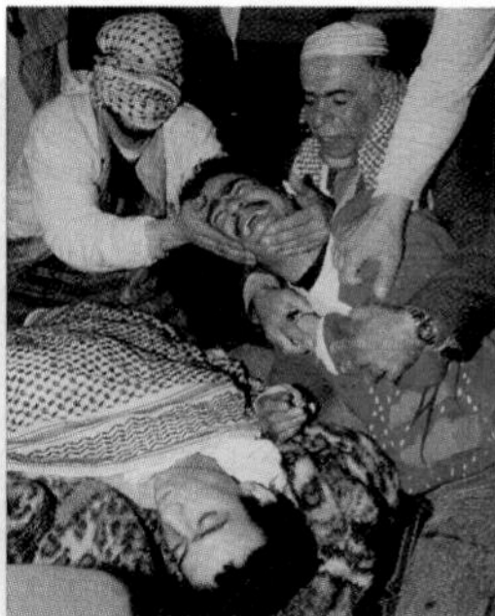

Analyze assumptions and biases

Many North Americans assume that men are "naturally" less expressive emotionally than women. But this Palestinian man, grieving over his dead son, does not fit Western stereotypes. As we will see in Chapters 10 and 18, cultural rules have a powerful influence on when, how, and to whom we express our feelings.

advanced when people resist leaping to conclusions on the basis of personal experience alone (so tempting in psychological matters), when they apply rigorous standards of evidence, and when they listen to competing views.

One of our greatest satisfactions over the years has been the success of this effort to define and implement critical thinking, and make it an integral part of the study of psychology. True critical thinking cannot be reduced to a set of rhetorical questions or to a formula for analyzing studies; it is a process of reporting and evaluating research and ideas that must be woven seamlessly into a book's narrative. In this book, we apply it to concepts that many students approach uncritically, such as astrology, "premenstrual syndrome," and the "instinctive" nature of sexuality. We also apply it to some assumptions that many psychologists have accepted unquestioningly, such as the decisive importance of childhood to later life, the hierarchical nature of motives, and the disease model of addiction. By probing beneath assumptions and presenting the most recent evidence, we hope to convey the excitement and open-ended nature of psychological research and inquiry.

The primary way we "do" critical and creative thinking is by modeling it in our evaluations of research and popular ideas. In this edition, we have tried to unify and strengthen our critical thinking approach in these ways:

A UNIFYING ICON The critical-thinking symbol of a glowing lightbulb, shown in the examples on this and the following page, is used in an integrated way—to highlight critical-thinking discussions and quiz items as well as boxes that feature critical-thinking issues.

GUIDELINES AND SIGNPOSTS The first chapter starts right off with an extended discussion of what critical thinking is and what it isn't—and why critical thought is particularly relevant to the study of psychology. This discussion describes eight guidelines to critical thinking, guidelines that we draw on throughout the text as we discuss and assess various topics. Many (though by no means all) of the critical discussions in the text are signaled by the critical-thinking symbol along with a marginal "signpost"—a provocative question that draws students into the discussion in the text. In this edition, we have explicitly identified the relevant guideline for each signpost as a headline so that students can see more easily how the guidelines are actually applied. These signposts are *not*, in themselves, illustrations of critical thinking. Rather, they serve as pointers to critical analyses in the text.

596 | Part Five *Health and Disorder*

did it. Among mental-health professionals, however, two competing and totally incompatible views of MPD currently exist. Some think it is a real disorder, common but often underdiagnosed. Others are skeptical: They think that most cases are generated by clinicians, in unwitting collusion with vulnerable and suggestible clients, and that if it exists at all it is extremely rare.

Those in the MPD-is-real camp believe the disorder originates in childhood, as a means of coping with unspeakable, continuing traumas, such as torture (Gleaves, 1996; Kluft, 1993; Ross, 1995). In this view, the trauma produces a mental "splitting"; one personality emerges to handle everyday experiences and another emerges to cope with the bad ones. MPD patients are frequently described as having lived for years with several personalities of which they were unaware, until hypnosis and other techniques in therapy revealed them. Clinicians who endorse MPD argue that diagnoses can be made more accurately now because the physiological changes that occur within each personality cannot be faked.

Those who are skeptical about MPD, however, have shown that most of the research used to support the diagnosis is seriously flawed (Merskey, 1995; Piper, 1997). A review of the claims that MPD patients have different physiological patterns associated with each personality concluded that most of the studies are anecdotal, have many methodological problems, and have failed to be replicated (Brown, 1994). Most important, research in this area has been marred by that familiar research mistake, the missing control group. When one research team corrected this flaw by comparing the EEG activity of two MPD patients with that of a normal person who merely role-played different personalities, they found EEG differences between "personalities" to be *greater* in the normal person (Coons, Milstein, & Marley, 1982). Other studies comparing MPD patients with control subjects who were merely role-playing have not found any reliable differences (Miller & Triggiano, 1992). Because normal people can create EEG changes by changing their moods, energy levels, and concentration, brain-wave activity cannot be used to verify the existence of MPD.

ASK QUESTIONS; EXAMINE THE EVIDENCE

A man charged with murder claims that one of his "other personalities" committed the crime. You are on the jury, and you know that psychologists disagree about the validity of his defense. What questions would you want to ask about this man's claim, and what evidence would help you reach a decision about it?

Clinicians and researchers who are doubtful about this diagnosis also point out that cases of MPD seem to turn up only in people who go to therapists who believe in it and are looking for it (McHugh, 1993a; Merskey, 1992, 1995; Piper, 1997; Spanos, 1996). Critics fear that clinicians who are convinced of the widespread existence of MPD may actually be creating the disorder in their clients through the power of suggestion. For example, here is the way one psychologist questioned the Hillside Strangler, Kenneth Bianchi, a man who killed more than a dozen young women:

> I've talked a bit to Ken, but I think that perhaps there might be another part of Ken that I haven't talked to, another part that maybe feels somewhat differently from the part that I've talked to. . . . And I would like that other part to come to talk to me. . . . Part, would you please come to communicate with me? (Quoted in Holmes, 1994)

Notice that the psychologist repeatedly asked Bianchi to produce another "part" of himself and even addressed the "part" directly. Before long, Bianchi was maintaining that the murders were really committed by another personality called Steve Walker. Did the psychologist in this case *permit* another personality to reveal itself, or did he actively *create* such a personality by planting the suggestion that one existed?

Proponents of the view that MPD is real and widespread often seem unaware of the difference. One of the best-known advocates of the MPD diagnosis, Richard Kluft

THINK ABOUT IT: PUZZLES OF PSYCHOLOGY Each chapter consists of one or two boxes titled "Think About It." These boxes raise psychological, social, or philosophical issues that have no easy answers; some instructors have students debate these questions in class, write short essays on them, or choose one or more for term papers. One type of Think About It box, which appears in every chapter, considers psychologically puzzling questions for the student to ponder, such as the social implications of genetic testing (Chapter 3); whether praise and high grades raise self-esteem or diminish it (Chapter 7); when and whether mental illness should permit diminished-responsibility defenses (Chapter 15); and the difference between understanding other cultures' practices and accepting them, as illustrated by the debate over female genital mutilation (Chapter 18).

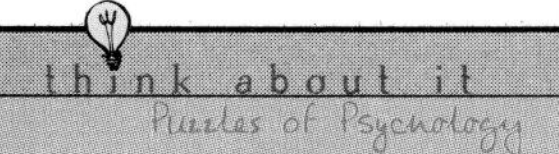

Do High Grades and Praise Raise Self-esteem?

It is popular today to blame every problem of youth, from poor academic test scores to juvenile crime, on low self-esteem. Raise self-esteem, the argument goes, and the problems will disappear. In California, a Task Force on the Social Importance of Self-esteem was convened to confirm the allegedly beneficial effects of raising self-esteem (Smelser, Vasconcellos, & Mecca, 1989). Teachers everywhere are taking this goal to heart, handing out lavish praise and high grades in hopes that students' academic performance will improve as they learn to "feel good about themselves."

One obvious result is grade inflation. In one middle school, when teachers tried to use a cutoff of a 3.5 grade point average for membership in a new academic honor society, they found that *two-thirds* of the school's 600 students were eligible, although clearly not all were doing "A" work (Celis, 1993). The teachers apparently felt obligated to give out high grades, whether the students deserved them or not. Grade inflation has infiltrated higher education, as well. In some colleges and universities, Cs, which once meant "average" or "satisfactory," are nearly extinct. (We heard about one student who was complaining about strict course requirements and said, oblivious to the irony, "Gosh, it's impossible for an average student to get an A in this class.") Pressured by parents and administrators, and worried about how students will evaluate them, many teachers go along with the trend despite their misgivings.

The problem, from a learning-theory point of view, is that to be effective, rewards must be tied to the behavior you are trying to increase. When rewards are dispensed indiscriminately, they become meaningless; they are no longer reinforcing. And when teachers praise mediocre work, that is what they are likely to get. Moreover, if a teacher gushes over work on a task that was actually easy, the hidden message may be that the child isn't very smart ("Gee, Minnie, you did a fantastic job . . . of adding two and two"). Even when the task is a challenging one, praise, if delivered too dramatically, may carry an unintended message—that the student's good work was a surprise ("Gee, Robert, you *really* did well on that paper [and who would have ever thought you could do it?]"). The result is likely to be lower, not higher, self-esteem, and reduced expectations of doing well (Kohn, 1993).

Although many people assume that self-esteem is the main ingredient of success and achievement, and its absence a major reason that children fail, there is actually no evidence to support this assumption, in spite of concerted efforts to find some (Dawes, 1994). The California task force, after reviewing virtually every study done on the relationship of self-esteem to anything (and there are thousands of them), found *no support* for any of its "intuitively correct" ideas about self-esteem (Smelser, Vasconcellos, & Mecca, 1989). Lilian Katz (1993), a professor of early childhood education, argues that "feel good about yourself" programs in schools tend to confuse self-esteem with self-involvement. Children are taught to turn their attention inward and to focus on self-gratification and self-celebration. Program after program asks children to write about such superficial things as physical attributes and consumer preferences ("What I like to watch on TV" or "What I like to eat"). In one typical curriculum she examined, Katz says, "Not once was the child asked to assume the role of producer, investigator, initiator, explorer, experimenter, wonderer, or problem-solver." Real self-esteem, Katz argues, does not come from "cheap success in a succession of trivial tasks," from phony flattery by a teacher, or from gold stars and happy faces. It emerges from effort, persistence, and the gradual acquisition of skills, and is nurtured by a teacher's genuine appreciation of the *content* of the child's work.

In recent years, studies have revealed an appalling level of illiteracy in the United States. Some high school graduates cannot read well enough to decipher a bus schedule or a warning on a nonprescription medication. Millions of people have such poor arithmetic skills that they cannot balance a checkbook or verify the change they get at the supermarket. Many students are unaware that their writing and math skills are deficient; how could they know, since they have always received high grades? The time seems right to rethink the way children are taught and schools are organized. After reading this chapter, how would you design a school system that fosters achievement, competence, and an intrinsic love of learning? What role, if any, would grades and other extrinsic reinforcers play? How would you let students know about poor performance without making them feel like failures? Think about it.

THINK ABOUT IT: ISSUES IN POPULAR CULTURE A second type of Think About It box, which appears in selected chapters, shows how psychological research might be brought to bear in critically assessing an issue that has captured the attention of the culture at large. Topics include the national furor over *The Bell Curve*, and matters of genes and IQ in general (Chapter 3); "raging hormones" and behavior (Chapter 5); "subliminal persuasion" (Chapter 6); the controversy over repressed memories of abuse (Chapter 9); the benefits and limitations of self-help books (Chapter 16); and the argument about political correctness in the use of group names (Chapter 18).

think about it

Issues in Popular Culture

Swept Away: Mob Violence and the Law

The research on people's behavior in crowds poses an interesting moral and legal issue: What is the personal responsibility of individuals who are swept away by mob violence and group pressure? Should the law treat them as harshly as it would treat persons acting alone, or is their responsibility diminished by virtue of being in a crowd? The psychology of mob violence made the news during the 1992 Los Angeles riots that followed the acquittal of four white police officers who had beaten the black motorist Rodney King. In the ensuing violence and looting, Damian Williams and three other black men attacked and nearly killed a white man, Reginald Denny. Did their anger at the acquittal of the police officers, and the understandable community outrage that followed, justify their loss of self-control? The jury that served at the men's trial seemed to think so.

In the late 1980s, British social psychologist Andrew Colman (1991a, 1991b) appeared as an expert witness in two murder trials in South Africa. In one, eight black railway workers had pleaded guilty to the murder of four black strike-breakers during a bitter industrial dispute. In the other, six black residents of an impoverished township were accused of murdering an 18-year-old black woman who was having an affair with a hated black police officer. She was "necklaced"—a tire was placed around her neck and set afire—during a community protest against the police that got out of control. The crowd danced and sang as she burned to ashes.

Colman testified about the social-psychological processes that he believed should be considered extenuating circumstances in these cases, including conformity, obedience to authority, deindividuation, and other aspects of crowd psychology. "Each of these social forces on its own," he wrote (1991b), "is powerful and can lead people to behave in ways that are not characteristic of their normal behaviour. . . . Anything that helps to explain a person's behaviour could potentially have a bearing on the moral blameworthiness of that behaviour."

Colman's testimony was not intended to acquit the defendants, who had all been found guilty, but to keep them from being executed. In this, he was successful. In the first case, only four of the eight workers were sentenced to death, and an appeals court commuted those sentences on the grounds that the psychological evidence of extenuating circumstances had not been disproved by the prosecutor. In the second case, all six defendants had their death sentences commuted to 20 months of imprisonment.

Colman regards the successful use of social-psychological findings as a breakthrough for law and justice, but other psychologists and social critics are worried that such findings could also be used to exonerate the guilty. Pumla Gobodo-Madikizela (1994), an African social scientist, interviewed some of the men accused of the necklacing and didn't find them quite so "deindividuated" after all. Some were tremendously upset, were well aware of their actions and choices, had actively debated the woman's guilt, had thought about running away, and consciously tried to rationalize their behavior. More important, she adds, "If nobody can be held culpable, it would be an open invitation to resort to vigilante justice. Surely, the thugs of the world who prefer to act in groups should be found guilty when they knowingly and willingly kill their declared 'enemies.'"

This issue alerts us to the problem, raised elsewhere this book, between understanding behavior and excusing it. Deindividuation certainly helps us understand why people in crowds do things they would never do on their own, but should they therefore be exempt from punishment? If not, what punishment is appropriate? Before you answer, you might consider that if you support a "deindividuation defense" because you sympathize with the defendants, you will need to support the same defense when you are unsympathetic to the defendants. Deindividuation may characterize a mob of oppressed people rioting to protest living conditions, but it also characterizes members of the Ku Klux Klan out on a raid, soldiers committing mass rapes in Bosnia, and the South African whites who went on bloody rampages before the 1994 elections, shooting black civilians. As Gobodo-Madikizela (1994) says, "Psychologists must separate scientific findings from our political preferences, no matter how distasteful the political consequences."

Finally, remember that in every crowd, some people don't go along; they remain individuated. During the riot in which Reginald Denny was attacked, two African-Americans, Terri Barnett and Gregory Alan Williams, rescued a white man from the same fate, and many other black people came to the aid of white and Latino passersby. Does that information affect your reaction to the deindividuation defense? We can be sure that the issue of personal responsibility and psychological understanding will return frequently in the news.

Millions remember the sight of Reginald Denny being bludgeoned by Damian Williams during the 1992 Los Angeles riots. Yet even under extreme conditions, many people retain their individuality and courage. Terri Barnett and Gregory Alan Williams were honored at City Hall for rescuing white people in danger.

Quick Quiz

If you are addicted to passing exams, try these questions:

1. What seems to be the most reasonable conclusion about the role of genes in alcoholism? (a) Without a key gene, a person cannot become alcoholic; (b) the presence of a key gene or genes will almost always cause a person to become alcoholic; (c) genes may work in combination to increase a person's vulnerability to some kinds of alcoholism.
2. Which cultural practice is associated with *low* rates of alcoholism? (a) drinking in family or group settings, (b) infrequent but binge drinking, (c) drinking as a rite of passage, (d) regarding alcohol as a sinful drink

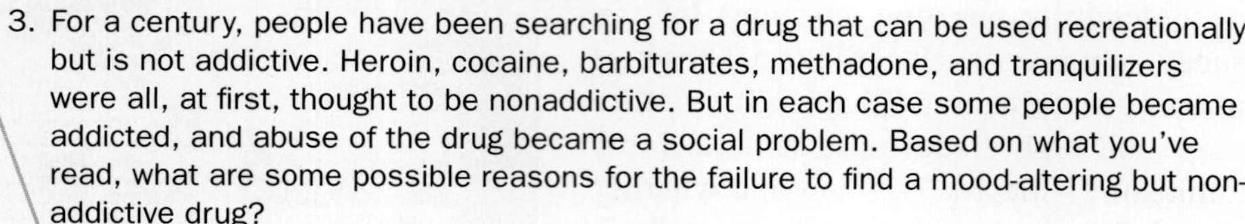

3. For a century, people have been searching for a drug that can be used recreationally but is not addictive. Heroin, cocaine, barbiturates, methadone, and tranquilizers were all, at first, thought to be nonaddictive. But in each case some people became addicted, and abuse of the drug became a social problem. Based on what you've read, what are some possible reasons for the failure to find a mood-altering but nonaddictive drug?

Answers:

1. c 2. a 3. Perhaps some people are biologically vulnerable to any mind-altering drug. Perhaps the psychological need for addiction exists in the individual and not in the chemical properties of the drug. Perhaps the chemistry of the drug is less important than the cultural practices that encourage drug abuse among some groups. If that is so, we will never find a recreational drug that has no addictive properties for *some* people.

CRITICAL-THINKING TEST QUESTIONS Many of the self-tests ("Quick Quizzes") found in each chapter include critical-thinking items that are designed to give students plenty of opportunities to practice specific critical-thinking skills. These items, identified by the critical-thinking symbol, invite the student to reflect on the implications of findings and consider how psychological principles might illuminate real-life issues. For example: What kinds of questions should a critical thinker ask about a new drug for depression? How might a hypothetical study of testosterone and hostility be improved? How might findings on working conditions and job motivation help us think critically about the reasons for an employee's habitual tardiness? Although we offer some possible responses to such questions, most of them do not have a single correct answer, and students may have valid, well-reasoned answers that differ from our own.

MAINSTREAMING CULTURE AND GENDER

At the time of our first edition, some considered our goal of mainstreaming issues of gender, ethnicity, and culture into introductory psychology quite radical—either a sop to political correctness or a fluffy and superficial fad in psychology. Today, the issue is no longer whether to include these topics, but how best to do it. From the beginning, our own answer has been to raise relevant studies about gender and culture in the main body of the text, and we continue to do so. Are there sex differences in the brain? This controversial and fascinating issue belongs in the brain chapter (Chapter 4). Do people from all cultures experience and express emotion the same way? This topic belongs in the emotion chapter (Chapter 10).

We know that topics in cultural and cross-cultural psychology are not traditionally included in introductory psychology, but we have come to believe that these topics are as important in a shrinking, culturally diverse world as is research on genetics or the brain. It is now abundantly clear that culture is not merely a superficial gloss on human behavior, but a profound influence that affects all aspects of life.

However, over the past decade, there has been a growing confusion between the scientific study of culture and the popular movement called multiculturalism. The study of culture, in our view, should increase students' understanding of what culture means, how and why ethnic and national groups differ, and why no culture is inherently superior to any other—in spite of the universal ethnocentric inclination to believe so. In some books and in many classrooms, however, multiculturalism is neither "multi" nor "cultural," but a pretext for celebrating one's own particular ethnic identity. There is a place for celebrating one's own ethnic identity! But we fear that the original reason for bringing the study of culture into psychology—to create a bigger tent that will encompass all the diversity of humankind—is in some quarters generating the construction of dozens of little separate tents.

Who is the chemical engineer, and who is the assistant? The Western stereotype holds that (1) women aren't engineers in the first place, but (2) if they are, they are Western. Actually, the engineer at this refinery is the Kuwaiti woman on the left.

Therefore, although we continue to mainstream research on culture and ethnicity where relevant throughout the book, we have retained a chapter on cultural psychology (Chapter 18) that we added in the last edition. There we address the *scientific* study of culture: problems of definition, methods of study, and interpretation of results. There too we discuss the emotionally laden subject of "political correctness" in group names; why the study of culture so often deteriorates into stereotyping and value judgments; and the sensitive matter of moral evaluations of other cultures' practices. In fact, instructors who teach in culturally diverse schools may want to assign the "Issues in Popular Culture" feature from Chapter 18 at the beginning of the course because this box concerns the psychology and politics of group names, an issue relevant to the classroom itself.

APPLICATIONS AND ACTIVE LEARNING: GETTING INVOLVED

Few disciplines have as many immediate, practical implications for individuals, groups, institutions, and society as does psychology. In our writing style and also in special features, we encourage students to get involved with what they are reading and to realize the immediate usefulness of this information. In doing so, we have taken advantage of one of the soundest findings about learning: that it requires the active encoding of material.

In this textbook, several pedagogical features in particular encourage students' active involvement in what they are reading:

GET INVOLVED Every chapter contains several exercises, new to this edition, that give students a hands-on opportunity to demonstrate for themselves what the text has described. Want to know immediately whether you have a certain gene (Chapter 3)? Want to see for yourself the power of a cultural rule for conversational distance (Chapter 18)? Want to experience right away how thoughts affect emotions

84 Part Two *Biology and Behavior*

GET INVOLVED

Ask the members of your family, one person at a time, to clasp their hands together. Include aunts and uncles, grandparents, cousins—as many biological relatives as possible. Which thumb does each person put on top?

About half of all people fold the left thumb over the right and about half fold the right thumb over the left, and these responses tend to run in families. Do your own relatives show one tendency over the other? (If your family is an adoptive one, of course, there is less chance of finding a trend.) Try the same exercise with someone else's family; do you get the same results? Even for behavior as simple as thumb folding, the details of how genes exert their effect remain uncertain (Jones, 1994).

Most human traits, even such a seemingly straightforward one as height, depend on more than one gene pair, which complicates matters enormously and makes tracking down the genetic contributions to a trait extremely difficult. Identifying even a single gene is daunting; biologist Joseph Levine and geneticist David Suzuki (1993) compared the task to searching for a particular person when all you know is that the person lives somewhere on earth. There are about 3 *billion* units of DNA (all

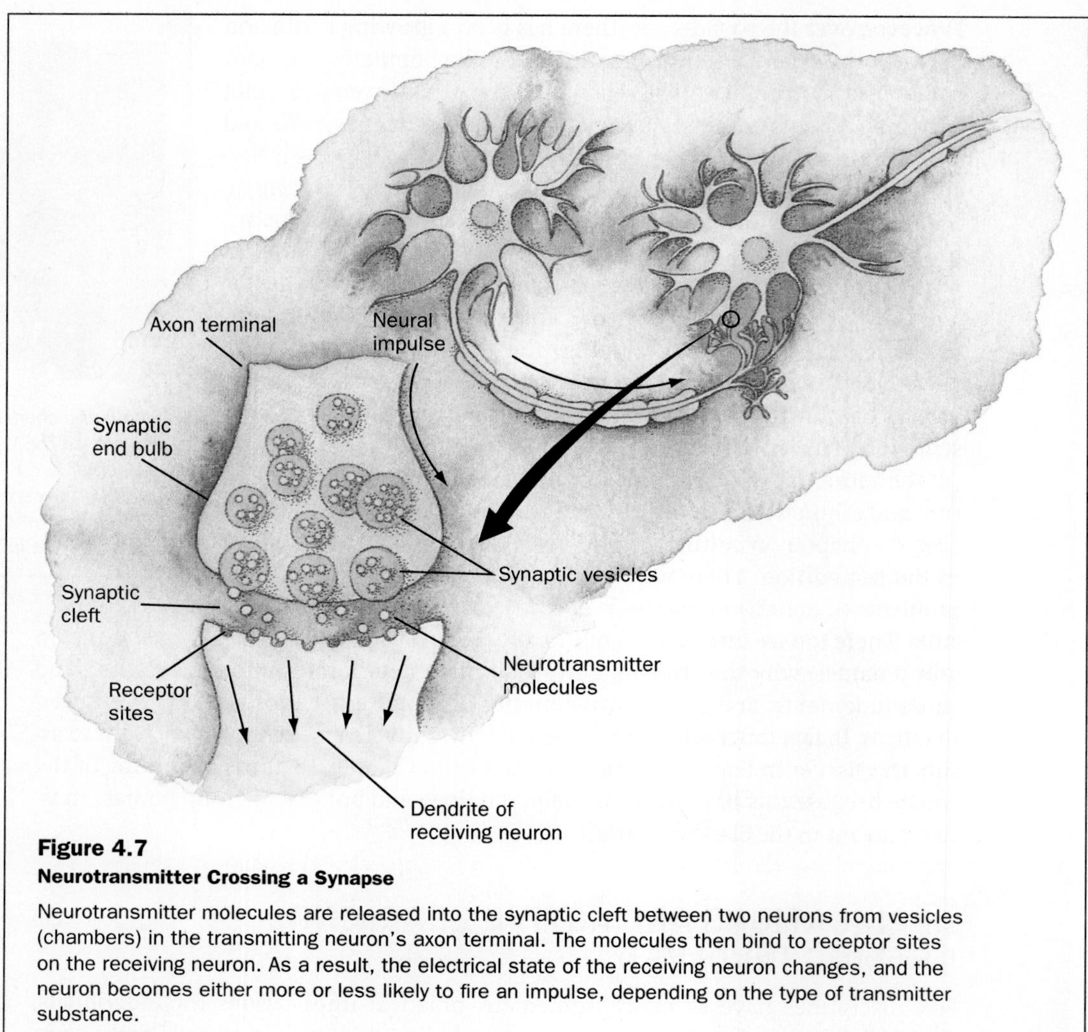

Figure 4.7
Neurotransmitter Crossing a Synapse

Neurotransmitter molecules are released into the synaptic cleft between two neurons from vesicles (chambers) in the transmitting neuron's axon terminal. The molecules then bind to receptor sites on the receiving neuron. As a result, the electrical state of the receiving neuron changes, and the neuron becomes either more or less likely to fire an impulse, depending on the type of transmitter substance.

(Chapter 10)? Some of these exercises take only a minute; others are "mini-studies" the student can do by observing or interviewing others. We think these entertaining activities make for good class assignments too because students can trade observations and responses and learn from their peers.

A COMPLETELY REVISED ART PROGRAM To help students visualize material for improved understanding and retention, this edition features new graphic illustrations of complex concepts, summary tables, models of relationships among factors, and beautiful, crystal-clear renderings of anatomical art. For example, graphic drawings show students at a glance psychology's relationship to other fields, the difference between positive and negative reinforcement, the varieties of attachment, the elements of successful therapy, how a self-fulfilling prophecy is created, and the difference between situational and dispositional attributions.

QUICK QUIZZES These periodic self-tests encourage students to check their progress, and to go back and review if necessary. They do more than just test for memorization of definitions; they tell students whether they comprehend the issues. Mindful of the common tendency to skip quizzes or to peek at the answers, we have used various formats and engaging examples to motivate students to test themselves. As we mentioned, many of the quizzes also include critical-thinking items.

We believe that the incorporation of these items makes this pedagogical feature useful for students of all abilities.

RUNNING GLOSSARY Students are enthusiastic about this feature, which defines boldfaced technical terms on the pages where they occur for handy reference and study. All entries can also be found in a cumulative glossary at the back of the book.

Other pedagogical features include chapter outlines, lists of key terms, and chapter summaries in numbered paragraph form.

In addition to these methods of increasing students' active learning and involvement, we strive to make psychology lively and relevant to their lives. We cover the many applications of research not only in the main text, as we go along, but also in a feature at the end of each chapter called **"Taking Psychology with You."** Drawing on research reported in the chapter, this feature tackles topics of practical concern, such as living with pain (Chapter 6), improving study habits (Chapter 7), becoming more creative (Chapter 8), managing anger (Chapter 10), boosting work motivation (Chapter 11), choosing a therapist (Chapter 16), avoiding the manipulations of advertisements (Chapter 17), and getting along with people of other ethnicities (Chapter 18).

Taking Psychology with You

Becoming More Creative

Take a few moments to answer these items from the Remote Associates Test. Your task is to come up with a fourth word that is associated with each item in a set of three words (Mednick, 1962). For example, an appropriate answer for the set *news–clip–wall* is *paper.* Got the idea? Now try these (the answers are given on page 336):

1. piggy–green–lash
2. surprise–line–birthday
3. mark–shelf–telephone
4. stick–maker–tennis
5. blue–cottage–cloth

Associating elements in new ways by finding a common connection among them is an important component of creativity. People who are uncreative rely on *convergent thinking,* following a particular set of steps that they think will converge on one correct solution. Once they have solved a problem, they tend to develop a mental set.

Creative people, in contrast, exercise *divergent thinking;* instead of stubbornly sticking to one tried-and-true-path, they explore some side alleys and generate several possible solutions. They come up with new hypotheses, imagine other interpretations, and look for connections that may not be immediately obvious. As a result, they are able to use familiar concepts in unexpected ways. Creative thinking can be found in the auto mechanic who invents a new tool, the mother who designs and makes her children's clothes, or the office manager who devises a clever way to streamline work flow (Richards, 1991).

Interestingly, having a high IQ does not guarantee creativity. Personality characteristics seem more important, especially these three essential ones (MacKinnon, 1962, 1968; McCrae, 1987; Schank, 1988):

• *Nonconformity.* Creative individuals are not overly concerned about what others think of them. They are willing to risk ridicule by proposing ideas that may initially appear foolish or off the mark. Geneticist Barbara McClintock's research was ignored or belittled by many for nearly 30 years. But she was sure she could show how genes move around and produce sudden changes in heredity. In 1983, McClintock was vindicated; she won the Nobel Prize. The judges called her work the second greatest genetic discovery of our time, after the discovery of the structure of DNA.

• *Curiosity.* Creative people are open to new experiences; they notice when reality contradicts expectations, and they are curious about the reason. For example, Wilhelm Roentgen, a German physicist, was studying cathode rays when he noticed a strange glow on one of his screens. Other people had seen the glow, but they ignored it because it didn't jibe with current understanding of cathode rays. Roentgen studied the glow, found it to be a new kind of radiation, and thus discovered X rays (Briggs, 1984).

• *Persistence.* This is perhaps the most important attribute of the creative person. After that imaginary lightbulb goes on over your head, you still have to work hard to make the illumination last. Or, as Thomas Edison, who invented the real lightbulb, reportedly put it, "Genius is one-tenth inspiration and nine-tenths perspiration." No invention or work of art springs forth full-blown from a person's head. There are many false starts and painful revisions along the way.

In addition to traits that foster creativity, there are *circumstances* that do. For example, the performance of students on creativity tests improved significantly after they watched a funny film or received a gift of candy, which put them in a good mood. In contrast, watching an upsetting film on concentration camps, watching a neutral film on math, or exercising to boost energy had no effect on creativity (Isen, Daubman, & Nowicki, 1987). Cheerful situations, it seems, can loosen up creative associations.

Another situational factor is the encouragement of *intrinsic* rather than *extrinsic* motivation. Intrinsic motives include a sense of accomplishment, intellectual fulfillment, the satisfaction of curiosity, and the sheer love of the activity. Extrinsic motives include a desire for money, fame, and attention, or the wish to avoid punishment. In one study, art works created for extrinsic reasons (they were commissioned by art collectors) were judged to be less creative than works done by the same artists for the intrinsic pleasure of creation. This was true whether the works were judged by the artists themselves or by judges who were "blind" to the condition under which a work had been completed. And it was true even when the person commissioning the work allowed the artist complete freedom (Amabile, Phillips, & Collins, 1993).

In another study, 72 young poets and writers created two poems. Before writing their second poems, half of the writers evaluated a list of extrinsic motives for writing (such as "The market for freelance writing is constantly expanding" and "You enjoy public recognition of your work"). The other half evaluated a list of intrinsic motives ("You like to play with words"; "You achieve new insights"). Then a panel of 12 experienced poets judged all the poems for originality and creativity, without knowing which writers had read which motives. The writers who were exposed to extrinsic reasons for writing showed a significant drop in the creativity of their second poem. Those who paid attention to intrinsic motives wrote two poems of equal quality (Amabile, 1985).

Creavitity also flourishes when people have control over how to perform a task or solve a problem; are evaluated unobtrusively, instead of being constantly observed and judged; and work independently (Amabile, 1983). And organizations encourage creativity when they let people take risks, give them plenty of time to think about problems, and welcome innovation.

In sum, if you hope to become more creative, there are two things you can do. One is to cultivate the personal qualities that lead to creativity. The other is to seek out the kinds of situations that permit you to express them.

The final Taking Psychology with You in the book is an **Epilogue,** a unique effort to show students that the vast number of seemingly disparate studies and points of view they have just read about are related. The epilogue contains two typical problems that most students can be expected to encounter, if they haven't already: the end of a love relationship and difficulties at work. We show how topics discussed in previous chapters can be applied to understanding and coping with these situations. Many instructors have told us that they find this epilogue a useful way to help students integrate the diverse approaches of contemporary psychology. Asking students to come up with research findings that might apply to other problems also makes for a good term-paper assignment.

REFLECTING NEW DIRECTIONS AND RESEARCH IN THE FIELD

Psychology is an expanding, constantly evolving enterprise. New areas of interest emerge, and suddenly research on a topic previously overlooked explodes into prominence. Accordingly, this edition features findings from three rapidly growing fields: evolutionary psychology (Chapter 3), behavioral genetics (Chapters 4 and 12), and cultural psychology (Chapter 18). Other updates in this fifth edition include:

REVISIONS OF STYLE We have purposely avoided making purely cosmetic changes, especially in the stories and examples that students enjoy. But this time we made a concerted effort to avoid a problem that often occurs in revising a book:

the tendency to add too much detail or too many exceptions to a basic conclusion. Expert reviewers, of course, tend to want students to appreciate all the complexities of their particular areas of research. However, in acknowledging areas of debate and ignorance in a particular area (such as models of memory) and in working to ensure that the research we cite is absolutely current, we keep the readers' focus on basic points and conclusions. In doing so, we hope we have achieved a balance between satisfying sophisticated reviewers without overwhelming new students of psychology.

REVISIONS OF CONTENT We have added recent, cutting-edge research in every chapter, and we reorganized some sections to make them clearer and easier to study and teach. Here are a few highlights of these changes:

- *Chapter 3 (Evolution, Genes, and Behavior)* covers new research suggesting that some arithmetic skills may be "biologically primary," a result of evolutionary demands; clarifies the differences between sociobiologists and evolutionary psychologists; and updates the research on genetic factors in human obesity and in IQ.
- *Chapter 5 (Body Rhythms and Mental States)* includes new studies of melatonin treatments for insomnia in blind people and older people, and research on light treatment and melatonin treatment for jet lag and shift workers. We have completely reorganized the section on hypnosis, summarizing what is known about its nature—what it is and what it is not—and comparing the two major theories in this area.
- *Chapter 9 (Memory)* now includes a list of the conditions under which confabulation is most likely to occur, and discusses important new findings and the latest legal developments in the recovered memory debate. We have also revised and clarified the biology section, and have added new research showing that true and false memories may activate different brain areas.
- *Chapter 12 (Theories of Personality)* includes the latest research on the Big Five model of personality, and its competitors and critics; an extended discussion and critique of projective tests; an expanded assessment of psychodynamic theories; and a summary table that integrates the four disparate theories discussed in the chapter.
- *Chapter 13 (Development Over the Life Span)*, formerly on child and adolescent development only, now includes material on adult development and life transitions, notably discussions of "the biological clock" and "the social clock"; Erik Erikson's theory of adult stages (formerly in the personality chapter); and ethical and psychological issues concerning death and dying.
- *Chapter 14 (The Psychology of Health and Well-being)* has been rewritten and revised in accordance with new developments in this field. For example, the section on emotions and health now reports the latest findings on the toxic role of hostility, the role of depression in heart disease, and how emotional inhibition can be stressful and lead to illness. The chapter critically examines the degree to which health is a matter of "mind over matter," and Taking Psychology with You reports on the practical implications of research in health psychology for coping with stress and preventing illness.
- *Chapter 15 (Psychological Disorders)* now emphasizes "vulnerability-stress" models of mental disorders, especially in depression, addiction, and schizophrenia. We have added the latest findings on the incidence of mental disorders in the

general population, and new research on the nature of brain abnormalities in obsessive-compulsive disorder and schizophrenia. We extensively revised and clarified the discussion of addiction. For example, we expanded the research on biological factors, including new findings on gender and race differences in physiological susceptibility, and added research on the role of culture and learning in addiction rates.

- *Chapter 16 (Approaches to Treatment and Therapy)* updates the discussion of therapeutic drugs, including the strong but little-known new evidence that psychotherapy is often as effective as medication for mood disorders. We have extensively revised the section on the "scientist–practitioner gap," assessing both the clinical view that research is often irrelevant to therapy and the scientific view that research is often essential to good practice. We have added findings from the Division 12 (Clinical Psychology) Task Force report on empirically validated therapies, along with a list of the specific therapies best suited to particular problems.

A detailed explanation of all deletions, additions, and changes in the fifth edition of *Psychology* is available to adopters of the previous edition, so that no one will have to guess why we made particular changes. We hope this support will make the transition from one edition to the next as painless for instructors as possible. You can obtain this description from your Longman representative or by writing to: Marketing Manager, Psychology, Addison Wesley Longman, 1185 Avenue of the Americas, New York, NY 10036.

FACING THE CONTROVERSIES

Psychology has always been full of lively, sometimes angry, debates, and we feel that students should not be sheltered from these controversies. They are what make psychology so interesting! Sociobiologists and feminist psychologists often differ strongly in their analyses of gender relations (Chapters 3 and 18). Psychodynamic clinicians and experimental psychologists differ strongly in their assumptions about memory, child development, and trauma; these differences have repercussions for, among other things, "recovered memory" therapy and the questioning of children as eyewitnesses (Chapter 9). The "scientist–practitioner gap" between researchers and psychodynamic psychotherapists is continuing to widen (Chapters 12 and 16). In this book we candidly address these and other debates, try to show why they are occurring, and suggest the kinds of questions that might lead to useful answers in each case.

SUPPLEMENTS PACKAGE

Psychology, Fifth Edition, is supported by a complete teaching package.

FOR THE INSTRUCTOR

INSTRUCTOR'S RESOURCE MANUAL This manual, written by Barbara Brown of DeKalb College, contains a wealth of teaching aids for each chapter: learning objectives, chapter outlines, lecture supplements, classroom demonstrations, and critical-thinking exercises; mini-experiments, self-test exercises and suggestions for additional readings; and an extensive guide to audiovisual materials. The IRM comes in a three-ring binder for easy reproduction of student handouts. The roomy binder also makes a great storage unit for collecting your own favorite lecture supplements and teaching materials.

TEST BANKS I & II A collaboration among Rick Fry, Peter Beckett, Margaret Gittis, and Coreena Casey at Youngstown State University, these extensive test banks feature an assortment of multiple-choice, short-answer, true/false, and essay items that test applied, factual, and conceptual knowledge. Items are referenced by learning objectives, cognitive type, topic, and skill.

TESTGEN EQ COMPUTERIZED TESTING SYSTEM This flexible, easy-to-master computer test bank includes all the test items in the two test banks. The TestGen EQ software allows you to edit existing questions and add your own items. Tests can be printed in several different formats and can include figures, such as graphs and tables. TestGen EQ is available in Macintosh and Windows formats.

LECTURE SHELL The chapter outlines of the entire text are available on disk for use in creating your own lecture outlines.

TRANSPARENCIES An Introductory Psychology Transparency Package contains 200 full-color acetates designed to accompany the text. The package features many transparencies specifically designed for large lecture halls.

PSYCHOLOGY ENCYCLOPEDIA LASERDISK IV This disk contains a wide variety of still images, animations, and video segments including both classic and contemporary footage.

MEDIA PORTFOLIO I AND II These exclusive-presentation CD-ROMs use state-of-the-art technology to provide interactive exercises, video segments, animations, and still images from many Longman introductory textbooks for easy creation of customized lecture presentations. Media Portfolio contains extensive documentation for user-friendly access.

FOR THE INSTRUCTOR AND THE STUDENT

PSYCHZONE AND WADE/TAVRIS *PSYCHOLOGY* FIFTH EDITION WEBSITE These two websites are constructed specifically to support the introductory course and contain many resources for instructors and students, including lecture updates, links to research resources, electronic transparencies, and on-line practice tests. Please contact your Longman representative for more information or visit our home page at http://longman.awl.com

SUPPLEMENTAL BOOKS FOR THE STUDENT

STUDY GUIDE Written by Tina Stern of DeKalb College, this manual has been extensively updated to reflect the new coverage in the fifth edition. It includes learning objectives, chapter outlines, critical-thinking questions illustrating important concepts in the text, practice tests with suggested answers, key-term reviews, and a "How to Study" section. New to this edition is an annotated answer key.

PSYCHOBABBLE AND BIOBUNK This collection of opinion essays, written for *The Los Angeles Times* and *The New York Times* by Carol Tavris, applies psychological research to current issues in the news. These essays may be used to encourage debate in the classroom or as a basis for student papers. Using them as models, students can write or present their own points of view on a topic, drawing on evidence from the textbook, lectures, or independent research to support their conclusions.

INTERACTIVE MEDIA FOR THE STUDENT

SUPERSHELL COMPUTERIZED TUTORIAL Created by Carolyn Meyer of Lake Sumter Community College, this interactive program helps students learn the major facts and concepts through drill and practice exercises and diagnostic feedback. SuperShell provides immediate correct answers and the text page numbers on which the material is discussed. A running score of the student's performance is maintained on the screen throughout the session. SuperShell is available for both IBM and Macintosh computers.

JOURNEY II Students are guided through a concept-building tour of the experimental method, the nervous system, learning, development, and psychological assessment with this program developed by Intentional Educations. Each module is self-contained and comes complete with step-by-step pedagogy. This program is available in Macintosh and IBM-compatible formats.

ACKNOWLEDGMENTS

Like any other cooperative effort, writing a textbook requires a support team. The following reviewers and consultants made many valuable suggestions during the development of this and previous editions of *Psychology*, and we are indebted to them for their contributions.

Benton E. Allen
Mt. San Antonio College

Susan M. Andersen
University of California, Santa Barbara

Lynn R. Anderson
Wayne State University

Emir Andrews
Memorial University of Newfoundland

Alan Auerbach
Wilfrid Laurier University

Lynn Haller Augsbach
Morehead State University

Harold Babb
Binghamton University

Brian C. Babbitt
Missouri Southern State College

MaryAnn Baenninger
Trenton State College

Patricia Barker
Schenectady County Community College

Ronald K. Barrett
Loyola Marymount University

Allan Basbaum
University of California, San Francisco

Carol Batt
Sacred Heart University

William M. Baum
University of New Hampshire

Peter A. Beckett
Youngstown State University

Bill E. Beckwith
University of North Dakota

Helen Bee
Madison, Wisconsin

David F. Berger
SUNY at Cortland

Michael Bergmire
Jefferson College

Philip J. Bersh
Temple University

Randolph Blake
Vanderbilt University

Richard Bowen
Loyola University of Chicago

Laura L. Bowman
Kent State University

Edward N. Brady
Belleville Area College

Ann Brandt-Williams
Glendale Community College

John R. Braun
University of Bridgeport

Sharon S. Brehm
SUNY at Binghamton

Sylvester Briggs
Kent State University

Gwen Briscoe
College of Mt. St. Joseph

Barbara Brown
DeKalb College

Robert C. Brown, Jr.
Georgia State University

Linda L. Brunton
Columbia State Community College

Peter R. Burzvnski
Vincennes University

Frank Calabrese
Community College of Philadelphia

Jean Caplan
Concordia University

Bernardo J. Carducci
Indiana University Southeast

Sally S. Carr
Lakeland Community College

Michael J. Catchpole
North Island College

Paul Chance
Laurel, Delaware

Herbert H. Clark
Stanford University

Job B. Clément
Daytona Beach Community College

Samuel Clement
Marianopolis College

Eva Conrad
San Bernardino Valley College

Richard L. Cook
University of Colorado

Robert Cormack
New Mexico Institute of Mining and Technology

Wendi Cross
Ohio University

Gaylen Davidson-Podgorny
Santa Rosa Junior College

Robert M. Davis
Purdue University School of Science, IUPUI

Michael William Decker
University of California, Irvine

Geri Anne Dino
Frostburg State University

Susan H. Evans
University of Southern California

Fred Fahringer
Southwest Texas State University

Ronald Finke
SUNY at Stony Brook

John H. Flowers
University of Nebraska–Lincoln

William F. Ford
Bucks County Community College

Donald G. Forgays
University of Vermont

Sheila Francis
Creighton University

Charles A. Fuller
University of California, Davis

Grace Galliano
Kennesaw State College

Mary Gauvain
Oregon State University

Ron Gerrard
SUNY at Oswego

David Gersh
Houston Community College

Jessica B. Gillooly
Glendale Community College

Margaret Gittis
Youngstown State University

Carlos Goldberg
Indiana University-Purdue University at Indianapolis

Carol Grams
Orange Coast College

Patricia Greenfield
University of California, Los Angeles

Richard A. Griggs
University of Florida

Sarmi Gulgoz
Auburn University

Jimmy G. Hale
McLennan Community College

Pryor Hale
Piedmont Virginia Community College

Len Hamilton
Rutgers University

George Hampton
University of Houston

Algea Harrison
Oakland University

Neil Helgeson
University of Texas at San Antonio

John E. Hesson
Metropolitan State College

Robert Higgins
Oakland Community College

John P. Hostetler
Albion College

Kenneth I. Howard
Northwestern University

John Hunsley
University of Ottawa

William G. Iacono
University of Minnesota

David E. Irwin
University of Illinois

James Johnson
University of North Carolina at Wilmington

Robert D. Johnson
Arkansas State University

Timothy P. Johnston
University of North Carolina at Greensboro

Susan Joslyn
University of Washington

Chadwick Karr
Portland State University

Yoshito Kawahara
San Diego Mesa College

Michael C. Kennedy
Allegheny University

Geoffrey Keppel
University of California, Berkeley

Harold O. Kiess
Framingham State College

Gary King
Rose State College

Jack Kirschenbaum
Fullerton College

Donald Kline
University of Calgary

Stephen M. Kosslyn
Harvard University

Janet E. Kuebli
St. Louis University

Michael J. Lambert
Brigham Young University

George S. Larimer
West Liberty State College

Herbert Leff
University of Vermont

Patricia Lefler
Lexington Community College

S. David Leonard
University of Georgia

Robert Levy
Indiana State University

Lewis Lieberman
Columbus College

R. Martin Lobdell
Pierce College

Walter J. Lonner
Western Washington University

Nina Lott
National University

Bonnie Lustigman
Montclair State College

Debra Moehle McCallum
University of Alabama at Birmingham

D. F. McCoy
University of Kentucky

C. Sue McCullough
Texas Woman's University

Elizabeth McDonel
University of Alabama

Susanne Wicks McKenzie
Dawson College

Mark B. McKinley
Lorain County Community College

Ronald K. McLaughlin
Juniata College

Frances K. McSweeney
Washington State University

James E. Maddux
George Mason University

Marc Marschark
University of North Carolina at Greensboro

Monique Martin
Champlain Regional College

Maty Jo Meadow
Mankato State University

Linda Mealey
College of St. Benedict

Dorothy Mercer
Eastern Kentucky University

Laura J. Metallo
Five Towns College

Denis Mitchell
University of Southern California

Timothy H. Monk
University of Pittsburgh Medical Center

Maribel Montgomery
Linn-Benton Community College

Douglas G. Mook
University of Virginia

T. Mark Morey
SUNY at Oswego

James S. Nairne
University of Texas at Arlington

Michael Nash
University of Tennessee-Knoxville

Douglas Navarick
California State University, Fullerton

Robert A. Neimever
Memphis State University

Nora Newcombe
Temple University

Linda Noble
Kennesaw State College

Keith Oatley
Ontario Institute for Studies in Education

Peter Oliver
University of Hartford

Patricia Owen-Smith
Oxford College

Elizabeth Weiss Ozorak
Allegheny College

David Page
Nazareth College

M. Carr Payne, Jr.
Georgia Institute of Technology

Dan G. Perkins
Richland College

Gregory Pezzetti
Rancho Santiago Community College

Wayne Poniewaz
University of Arkansas, Monticello

Paula M. Popovich
Ohio University

Lyman Porter
University of California, Irvine

Robert Prochnow
St. Cloud State University

Janet Proctor
Purdue University

Reginald L. Razzi
Upsala College

Sheena Rogers
University of Wisconsin-Madison

Jayne Rose
Augustana State College

Gary Ross-Reynolds
Nicholls State University

Gerald Rubin
Central Virginia Community College

Joe Rubinstein
Purdue University

Nancy Sauerman
Kirkwood Community College

H. R. Schiffman
Rutgers University

Lael Schooler
Indiana University

David A. Schroeder
University of Arkansas

Marvin Schwartz
University of Cincinnati

Shelley Schwartz
Vanier College

Joyce Segreto
Youngstown State University

Kimron Shapiro
University of Calgary

Phillip Shaver
University of California, Davis

Susan A. Shodahl
San Bernardino Valley College

Dale Simmons
Oregon State University

Art Skibbe
Appalachian State University

William P. Smotherman
SUNY at Binghamton

Samuel Snyder
North Carolina State University

Barbara A. Spellman
University of Texas at Austin

Larry R. Squire
University of California, San Diego

Tina Stern
DeKalb College

A. Stirling
John Abbott College

Milton E. Strauss
Johns Hopkins University

Judith Sugar
Colorado State University

Shelley E. Taylor
University of California, Los Angeles

Barbara Turpin
Southwest Missouri State University

Ronald J. Venhorst
Kean College of New Jersey

Wayne A. Viney
Colorado State University

Benjamin Wallace
Cleveland State University

Phyllis Walrad
Macomb Community College

Charles R. Walsmith
Bellevue Community College

Phillip Wann
Missouri Western State College

Thomas J. Weatherly
DeKalb College-Central Campus

Mary Wellman
Rhode Island University

Gary L. Wells
University of Alberta

Warner Wilson
Wright State University

Loren Wingblade
Jackson Community College

Judith K. Winters
DeKalb College

Rita S. Wolpert
Caldwell College

James M. Wood
University of Texas at El Paso

Phyllis Zee
Northwestern University Medical School

Our editorial and production teams at Longman have been superb, and we are enormously grateful to these talented people for their hard work and commitment to quality. In particular, we thank our psychology editor Rebecca Dudley, for her unwavering enthusiasm, her brilliant editorial suggestions, her stunning ability to resolve differences of opinion with grace and insight, and her practical help in helping us meet every deadline; our developmental editor Susan Messer, for her excellent ideas and editorial skills, and for expertly shepherding this complicated project from start to finish; and our absolutely indispensable project editor Donna DeBenedictis, whose sense of humor, calm manner, and brilliant organizational skills guided this project through its complicated production schedule. She has worked with us now from the beginning, and knows every word, photo, and figure in this book as well as we do. Joanne Del Ben did a wonderful job of coordinating text corrections and filling in wherever she was needed in the production process. We also thank photo researcher Sandy Schneider for her selections of photos and cartoons that illustrate so effectively abstract concepts or raise thought-provoking questions.

Our special thanks to John Odam, who created a beautiful, original cover while retaining the spirit and mystery of the previous covers by the late Saul Bass. The design team, too, was exceptional. Amy Trombat gave this fifth edition a stunning, elegant, new interior design, and art director Mary McDonnell and design manager Alice Fernandes-Brown assisted with skill and indispensable artistic contributions.

Most of all, we thank Howard Williams and Ronan O'Casey, who from the first edition to this one have bolstered us with their love, humor, and good cheer, not to mention an endless supply of freshly brewed coffee.

We have enjoyed writing this book, and we hope you will enjoy reading and using it. Your questions, comments, and reactions on the first four editions helped us make many improvements. Please let us hear from you.

CAROLE WADE
CAROL TAVRIS

To the Student

IF YOU ARE READING THIS INTRODUCTION, you are starting your introductory psychology course on the right foot. It is always a good idea to get a general picture of what you are about to read before charging forward—the better to be prepared for what you encounter on the road ahead.

Our goal in writing this book is to guide you to think critically and imaginatively about what you read, and to apply what you learn to your own life and the world around you. We ourselves have never gotten over our initial excitement about psychology, and we have done everything we can think of to make the field as absorbing for you as it is for us. However, what you bring to this book is as important as what we have written. This text will remain only a collection of pages with ink on them unless you choose to interact with its content. You won't retain much if you are just nodding along saying "hmmmmm" to yourself. The more actively you are involved in your own learning, the more successful the book and your course will be, and the more enjoyable, too.

Getting involved To encourage you to be actively involved with what you are reading and to read actively, we have included some special features:

- Every chapter contains several exercises called **"Get Involved,"** which are entertaining little experiments you can do that demonstrate what you are reading about. In Chapter 3, for instance, you can find out immediately whether you have a certain gene, in Chapter 10 we'll show you how your own thoughts affect your emotions, and in Chapter 18 you can see for yourself the power of a cultural rule for the "proper" conversational distance. Some of these exercises take only a minute; others are "mini-studies" that you can do by observing or interviewing others.

- Every chapter contains several **Quick Quizzes** that permit you to test your understanding and retention of what you have just read and your ability to apply the material to examples. Do not let the word "quiz" give you a sinking feeling. These quizzes are for your practical use and, we hope, for your enjoyment. When you can't answer a question, do not go on to the next section; pause right then and there, review what you've read, and then try again.

- Some of the Quick Quizzes contain a *critical-thinking item,* denoted by the lightbulb symbol in the margin. The answers we give for these items are only suggestions; feel free to come up with different ones. Quick Quizzes containing critical-thinking items are not really so quick; they ask you to reflect on what you have read and to apply the guidelines to critical thinking that are introduced in Chapter 1. But if you take the time to respond thoughtfully to them, we think you will get more involved with psychology, learn more, and become a more sophisticated user of psychology.

- **Critical-thinking signposts,** found in the margins and accompanied again by the critical-thinking lightbulb, indicate where critical-thinking analyses or issues appear. We hope these discussions will engage your own interest and encourage your involvement with the text. We will be telling you about many of the lively and often passionate debates that psychologists argue about—on matters of sex and sex differences, dreams, therapy, memory, and countless others—and we hope these debates will increase your involvement with the ongoing discoveries of psychology.

- In each chapter, one or two boxes called **"Think About It"** raise provocative issues in psychology that require the best of our imaginations and our ability to think critically. One such box is on **Puzzles of Psychology** that often have no easy answer, such as "Where is your 'self'?" or "Could you be a hero?" or "When does a mental disorder cause diminished responsibility?" (We hope you will have as much fun pondering these questions as we did writing about them.) Another Think About It box, **Psychology and Popular Culture,** examines pop-psych topics that appear in the news and on talk shows—and discusses what good psychological research might have to say about those topics.
- At the end of every chapter, a feature called **"Taking Psychology with You"** draws on research to suggest ways you can apply what you have just learned to everyday problems and concerns, such as how to improve your work motivation and how to get a better night's sleep, and to more serious ones, such as knowing when and how to select a psychotherapist or how to help a friend who seems suicidal.

  The very last Taking Psychology with You, at the end of this book, is an **Epilogue** that shows how you might integrate and use the findings and theories you have read about to understand events, make wise decisions, and cope with life's inevitable challenges and changes. We consider the Epilogue to be important because it suggests how you can carry psychology out of your classroom and into the rest of your life.

How to Study In our years of teaching, we have found that certain study strategies can vastly improve learning, and so we offer the following suggestions. (Reading Chapter 7, on learning, and Chapter 9, on memory, should also be helpful!)

- Start by reading the chapter title and outline to get an idea of what is in store. Browse through the chapter, looking at the pictures and reading captions and headings.
- Do not read the text the same way you might read a novel, taking in large chunks at a sitting. To get the most from your studying, we recommend that you read only a part of each chapter at a time.
- Instead of simply reading silently, try to restate what you have read in your own words at the end of each major section. Some people find it helpful to write down main points on a piece of paper or on index cards. Others prefer to recite main points aloud to someone else—or even to a patient pet. Do not count on getting by with just one reading of a chapter. Most people need to go through the material at least twice, and then review the main points several times before an exam.
- When you have finished a chapter, read the **summary.** Some students tell us they find it useful to write down their own summaries first, then compare them with the book's. Use the list of **key terms** at the end of each chapter as a checklist. Try to define and discuss each term to see how well you understand and remember it. If you need to review a term, a page number is given to tell you where it is first mentioned in the chapter.
- Every important new term in this textbook is printed in **boldface** and is defined in the margin of the page on which it appears or on the facing page. The **marginal glossary** permits you to find all key terms and concepts easily, and will help you when you study for exams. A *full glossary* also appears at the end of the book.

- The study guide, available at your bookstore, is an excellent resource to help you study the material in this book. It contains review materials, exercises, and practice tests to help you understand and apply the concepts in the book.
- If you are assigned a term project or a report, you may need to track down some references or do further reading. Throughout the book, all discussions of studies and theories are followed by one or more **citations** in parentheses like this: (Aardvark & Zymski, 1997). A citation tells you who the authors of the work are and when their paper or book was published. The full reference can then be looked up in the **bibliography** at the end of the book. At the back of the book you will also find an *author index* and a *subject index*. The author index lists the name of every author cited and the pages where each person's work is discussed. If you remember the name of a psychologist but can't recall where he or she was mentioned, look up the name in the author index. The subject index lists all the major topics mentioned in the book. If you want to review material on, say, depression—a topic discussed in several chapters—you can look up "depression" in the subject index and find each place it is mentioned.

We have done our utmost to convey our own enthusiasm about psychology, but in the end it is your efforts as much as ours that will determine whether you find psychology to be exciting or boring, and whether the field will matter in your own life. We welcome your ideas and reactions so that we will know what works for you and what doesn't. In the meantime, welcome to psychology!

CAROLE WADE
CAROL TAVRIS

About the Authors

Carole Wade earned her Ph.D. in cognitive psychology at Stanford University. She began her academic career at the University of New Mexico; was professor of psychology for ten years at San Diego Mesa College; then taught at College of Marin; and currently teaches undergraduate courses in psychology at Dominican College of San Rafael. She is coauthor, with Carol Tavris, of *Psychology in Perspective; Critical and Creative Thinking: The Case of Love and War;* and *The Longest War: Sex Differences in Perspective.* Dr. Wade has a long-standing interest in making psychology accessible to students and the general public through public lectures, workshops, general interest articles, and the electronic media. For many years she has focused her efforts on the teaching and promotion of critical-thinking skills and the enhancement of undergraduate education in psychology. She is currently chair of the APA Board of Educational Affairs's Task Force on Diversity Issues at the Precollege and Undergraduate Levels of Education in Psychology. She is also a past chair of the APA's Public Information Committee and served on the APA's Committee on Undergraduate Education and the Steering Committee for the APA's National Conference on Enhancing the Quality of Undergraduate Education. Dr. Wade is a Fellow of Divisions 1 and 2 and a member of Divisions 9 and 35 of the APA, and is a charter member of the American Psychological Society.

Carol Tavris earned her Ph.D. in the interdisciplinary program in social psychology at the University of Michigan, and ever since has sought to bring research from the many fields of psychology to the public. She is author of *The Mismeasure of Woman,* which won the 1992 Distinguished Media Contribution Award from the American Association of Applied and Preventive Psychology, and the Heritage Publications Award from Division 35 of the APA. Dr. Tavris is also the author of *Anger: The Misunderstood Emotion* and coauthor with Carole Wade of *Psychology in Perspective; Critical and Creative Thinking: The Case of Love and War;* and *The Longest War: Sex Differences in Perspective.* She has written on psychological topics for many different magazines, journals, edited books, and newspapers, notably *The Los Angeles Times* and *The New York Times.* A highly regarded lecturer, she has given keynote addresses and workshops on, among other topics, critical thinking, pseudoscience in psychology, anger, gender, and psychology and the media. She has taught in the psychology department at UCLA and at the Human Relations Center of the New School for Social Research in New York. Dr. Tavris is a Fellow of Divisions 1, 9, and 35 of the American Psychological Association and a member of Division 8; a charter Fellow of the American Psychological Society; and a Fellow of the Committee for the Scientific Investigation of Claims of the Paranormal.

PSYCHOLOGY

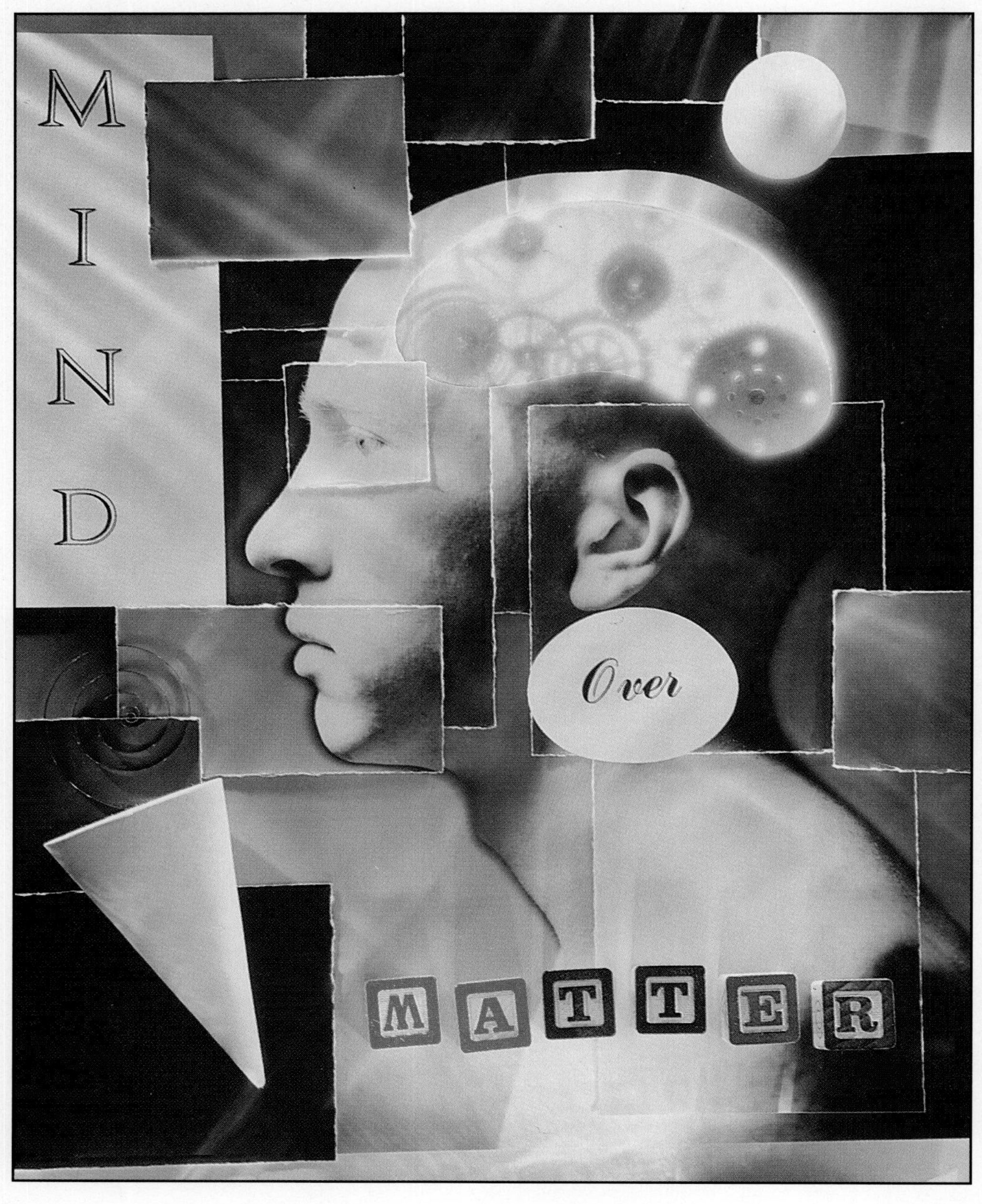

The purpose of psychology is to give us a completely
different idea of the things we know best.

— Paul Valéry

CHAPTER ONE

What Is Psychology?

Anne Frank (1929–1945)

IN 1945, A 15-YEAR-OLD JEWISH GIRL named Anne Frank died of typhus at Bergen-Belsen, a notorious Nazi death camp. She had spent the previous two years with her parents, her sister, and four other people in a cramped apartment in Amsterdam, hiding from German troops occupying Holland. Unable to go outside, the group depended entirely on Christian friends for food and other necessities. Anne, who was a gifted writer and astute observer, recorded in her diary the fears, frustrations, and inevitable clashes of people forced to live 24 hours a day in close proximity. Yet she never despaired or lost her sense of wonder at life's joys. With humor and grace, she described the pleasure of family celebrations, the thrill of first love, the excitement of growing up. Shortly before the Gestapo discovered the hideout, Anne wrote, "It's really a wonder that I haven't dropped all my ideals, because they seem so absurd and impossible to carry out. Yet I keep them, because in spite of everything I still believe that people are really good at heart. I simply can't build up my hopes on a foundation consisting of confusion, misery, and death."

Many years later, and thousands of miles away, Jeffrey Dahmer grew up in what appears to have been a fairly normal American household. As a small child, Jeffrey seemed happy and animated. Gradually, however, he drifted into a private fantasy world and began to act abnormally. He collected animal bones and carcasses, which he stored in formaldehyde-filled jars in his childhood clubhouse; he sulked alone in the woods whenever his parents fought; his eyes developed a dull and vacant look. At age 18, Jeffrey began committing a series of unspeakable crimes. Over a 13-year period, he lured 17 young men to his home and tortured, murdered, and mutilated them, keeping body parts as souvenirs and even cannibalizing one of the victims. In *A Father's Story* (1994), Jeffrey's father Lionel asked himself how his son could have become such a monster. Perhaps it was the medication his wife took during pregnancy. Perhaps he himself had been too aloof. Perhaps the parents' frequent fights and ultimate divorce were to blame. Perhaps an apparent incident of sexual abuse by a neighborhood boy had played a role. Or perhaps, the father speculated, the "potential for great evil . . . resides deep in the blood that some of us . . . may pass on to our children at birth."

How did Anne Frank, living in a world gone mad, manage to retain her love of humanity? Why did Jeffrey Dahmer, whose early life was not terribly unusual, develop bizarre urges that led him to commit gruesome acts of violence? More generally, how can we explain why some people are overwhelmed by their problems, whereas others, despite enormous difficulties, remain strong and mentally healthy? Why do some human beings pursue their dreams and others succumb to nightmares? What principles can help us understand why some of us are confident players in the game of life, while others angrily reject its basic rules?

If you have ever asked yourself such questions, welcome to the world of psychology. You are about to explore a discipline that studies the many complexities and contradictions of human behavior. Psychologists do not confine their attention to personal problems or the extremes of behavior. They take as their subject the entire spectrum of brave and cowardly, intelligent and foolish, beautiful and brutish things that human beings do. Their aim is to understand and explain how human beings—and other animals, too—learn, remember, solve problems, perceive, feel, and get along with others. They are therefore just as likely to study commonplace experiences as exceptional ones—experiences as universal and ordinary as rearing children, gossiping, remembering a shopping list, daydreaming, making love, and making a living. Most of us, after all, are neither saints nor sinners but a curious combination of positive and negative qualities. In short, psychology is not only about martyrs and murderers; it is also about you.

A MATTER OF DEFINITION

Over the years, **psychology** has been defined in various ways, but most psychologists today agree that it is the scientific study of behavior and mental processes and how they are affected by an organism's physical state, mental state, and external environment. We realize that this brief definition of psychology is a little like defining a car as a vehicle for transporting people from one place to another. Such a definition is accurate as far as it goes, but it doesn't tell you what a car looks like, how a car differs from a train or a bus, how a Ford differs from a Ferrari, or how a catalytic converter works. Similarly, to get a clear picture of what psychology is, you will need to know more about its methods, its findings, and its ways of interpreting information. Your psychology course and the rest of this textbook will give you this information.

PSYCHOLOGY AND COMMON SENSE

Let's begin by considering what psychology is *not.* First, the psychology that you are about to study bears little relation to the popular psychology ("pop psych") found in many self-help books or on TV talk shows. Serious psychology is more complex, more informative, and, we think, far more helpful. As we will see in the next chapter, its principles are based on rigorously conducted research and verifiable evidence. In recent decades, the public's appetite for psychological information has created a huge market for what R. D. Rosen (1977) called "psychobabble"—pseudoscience and quackery covered by a veneer of psychological language. Today, more than ever, when so many simplistic pop-psych ideas have filtered into public consciousness, education, and even the law, people need to know the difference between psychobabble and serious psychology, between unsupported popular opinion and documented research evidence.

Second, psychology is not just a fancy name for common sense. It is true that psychological research sometimes confirms what many people already believe to be so. When that happens, it is easy to conclude that a little intelligence and the accumulated wisdom of the ages are all you need to understand why people act as they do, and that scientific studies are a waste of time and money. Often, though, the obviousness of a psychological finding is only an illusion. Armed with the wisdom of hindsight, people may maintain that they "knew it all along" when in fact they did not.

Consider this demonstration: An instructor tells an introductory psychology class that "according to research, couples whose careers require them to live apart are more likely to divorce than other couples." Most students will claim they are not surprised; after all, as everyone knows, "out of sight, out of mind." Then, in another class, the instructor changes the report, this time saying that couples whose careers require them to live apart are *less* likely to divorce than other couples. Again, most students will claim they could have predicted the result; after all, as everyone knows, "absence makes the heart grow fonder." Both results, once they are stated, seem intuitively obvious, whether true or not, because common sense is full of contradictions (Myers, 1980). Psychologists interested in close relationships will go beyond popular folk sayings to investigate the *conditions* under which absence may or may not make the heart grow fonder. One of these conditions is the degree of emotional attachment felt by the couple before they part; absence often intensifies a bright flame but extinguishes a weak one (Brehm, 1992).

Further, psychological research often does produce surprises, findings that are not commonsensical at all. For example, according to popular belief, early experiences inevitably determine how a person turns out, for better or for worse; people speak of their "formative years" and the lifelong effects of childhood traumas. Yet, as we will see in later chapters, those formative years don't form *everything* about us. Many of our abilities and attributes change throughout life, in response to new situ-

psychology The scientific study of behavior and mental processes and how they are affected by an organism's physical state, mental state, and external environment; the term is often represented by Ψ, the Greek letter psi (usually pronounced "sy").

Psychologists study many questions that do not have obvious answers—why people dress in funny outfits, bungee-jump from hot-air balloons, develop life-threatening eating disorders, or take part in hateful mob activities, such as cross burning by the Ku Klux Klan.

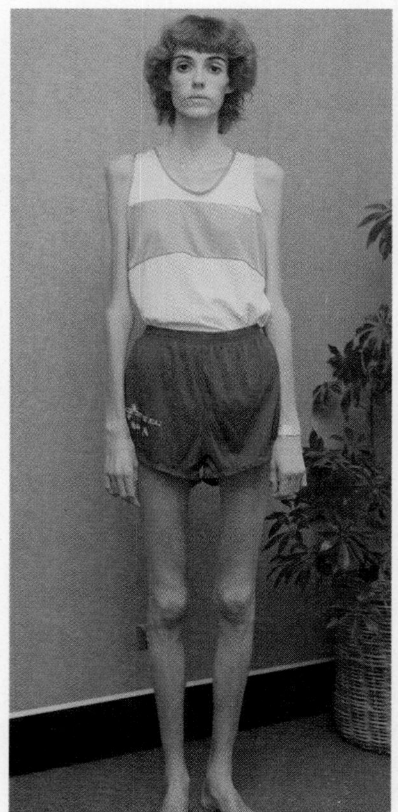

ations. Even children traumatized by abuse, neglect, or war can become happy, secure adults if their circumstances improve (Garmezy, 1991; Werner, 1989).

The finding that we may ultimately triumph over life's tragedies is reassuring, but other findings in psychology are troubling. For example, most people are willing to inflict physical harm on another person if they are told to do so by an authority figure. Even when those persons inflicting the harm are suffering emotional distress because of their actions, they obey anyway (Milgram, 1963, 1974). This disturbing discovery has important political and moral implications. To take another example: Despite all the warnings against judging a book by its cover, most people do exactly that. Good-looking individuals are more likely than others to attract dates, get jobs, and earn high pay; they even receive shorter jail sentences (Berscheid, 1985). This information is sobering for a society that considers itself to be democratic and egalitarian.

Psychology, then, may or may not confirm what you already believe about human nature, but findings do not have to be surprising to be scientifically important. Psychologists may enjoy announcing results that startle people, but they also seek to

GET INVOLVED

How reliable a guide to experience is "common sense"? For each of the following commonsense sayings, see whether you can think of another one that contradicts it. (You'll find some possible answers at the end of the chapter.)

- *Birds of a feather flock together.*
- *Haste makes waste.*
- *Actions speak louder than words.*
- *It's not whether you win or lose, it's how you play the game.*
- *You can't teach an old dog new tricks.*

extend and deepen our understanding of generally accepted facts. After all, long before the laws of gravity were discovered, people knew that an apple would fall to the ground if it dropped from a tree. But it took Isaac Newton to discover the principles that explain why the apple falls and why it travels at a particular speed while falling. Psychologists, too, strive to deepen our understanding of an already familiar world.

PSYCHOLOGY'S RELATIVES

Psychology belongs to a family of disciplines known as the social (or sometimes the behavioral) sciences. All of these sciences encourage us to analyze human problems objectively and to search for reliable patterns in behavior. Each of these disciplines teaches us to appreciate both the similarities and the differences among individuals and groups. There are also some important differences in emphasis, as we can see by comparing psychology with two other social sciences—sociology and anthropology.

Sociology is the study of groups and institutions within society, such as the family, religious institutions, the workplace, and social cliques. A sociologist might study, for example, how family roles change when women enter the paid workforce, or how and why urban gangs come into being. In general, sociologists pay less attention than psychologists do to personality traits and individual differences. One specialty, *social psychology,* falls on the border between psychology and sociology; it deals with the ways in which social groups and situations affect an individual's behavior, and vice versa.

Anthropology is concerned with the physical and cultural origins and development of the human species. Anthropologists typically focus on a large social

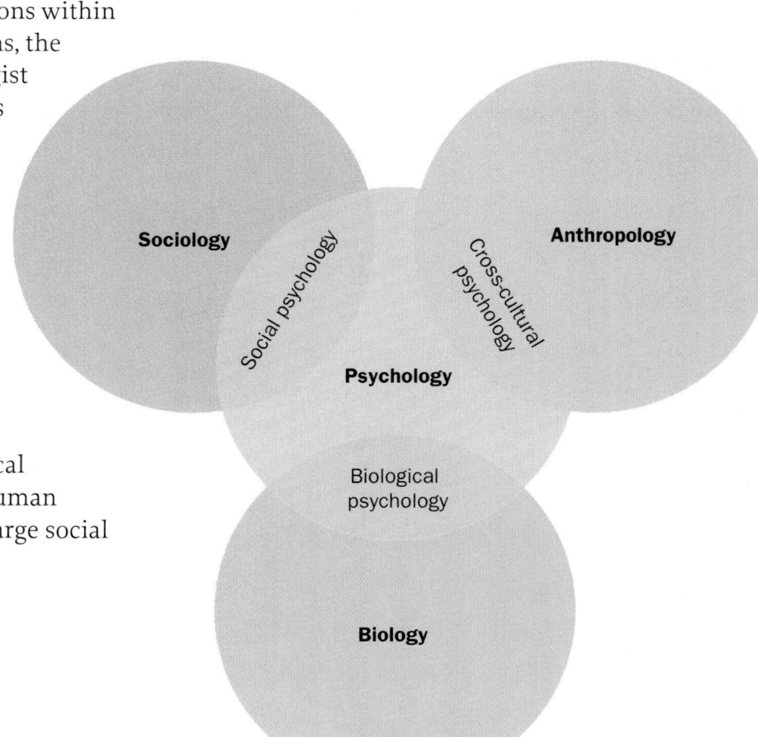

Some psychological specialties link psychology with other social and life sciences.

unit—a tribe, a community, or even an entire society. They compare customs and beliefs across different cultures, often participating in the daily lives and activities of the social group they are observing. In contrast, most psychologists study behavior only in their own society, and they study the specific behaviors or mental processes of individuals rather than the customs of entire groups. Again, the boundary between disciplines is not rigid: Some anthropologists study psychological issues, and researchers in the growing field of *cross-cultural psychology* investigate psychological differences and similarities among cultures.

Of all the social sciences, psychology relies most heavily on laboratory experiments and observations. At the same time, it is the most personal of the disciplines, focusing more than the others on the individual and his or her well-being. Psychology also makes more use of biological information than the other fields do (except for physical anthropology, which is concerned with the physical evolution of the human species). In fact, some psychologists classify psychology with the biological and life sciences rather than with the social sciences. However, whereas biologists are chiefly concerned with understanding the structure and functioning of all living things, from trees to turtles, psychologists are mainly interested in using biological research to extend their insight into human behavior and mental activities. A psychologist might study the communication of nerve cells in the brain, for example, in order to better understand learning and memory.

Psychology also has links with many other fields, including law, computer science, medicine, and business and management science. Most of the findings in this book come from research done by psychologists, but we will occasionally refer to results from related disciplines as well. When scholars and scientists cultivate only their own gardens, they may miss ways to improve their intellectual harvest. Now and then it's a good idea to glance over to see what is happening in someone else's yard.

Several research specialties straddle the boundaries between psychology and other disciplines.

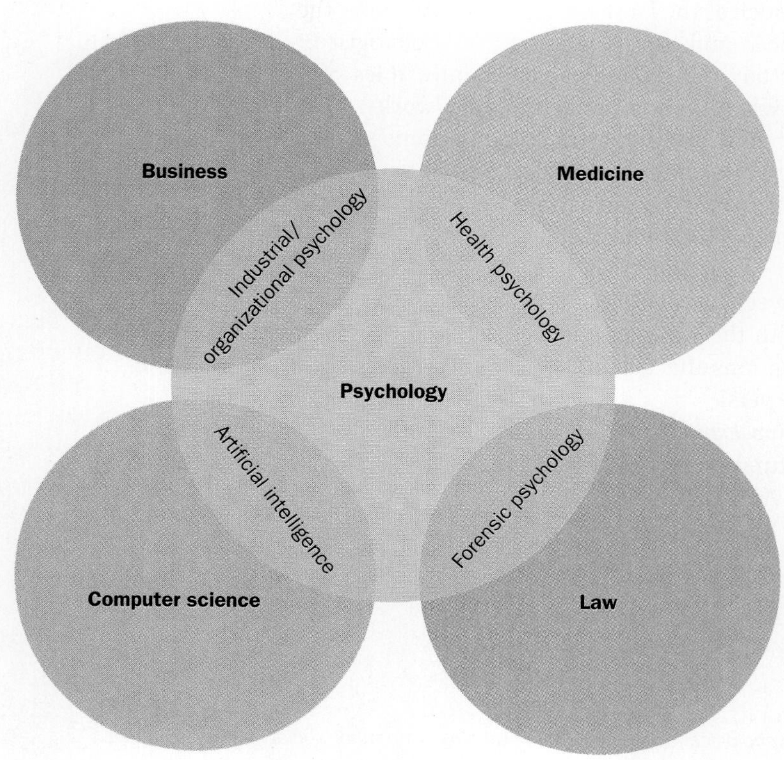

Quick Quiz

Pause now to test your understanding of the previous section. Do you have the distinctions among the various fields straight? Can you match each topic on the left with a discipline on the right?

1. How the structure of a bureaucracy affects job satisfaction
2. Sexual customs in a Polynesian society
3. The molecular structure of bodily cells
4. The effects of anxiety on IQ scores

a. biology
b. anthropology
c. psychology
d. sociology

Answers:

1. d 2. b 3. a 4. c (*Note:* This self-test does not ask you to parrot back a memorized list of definitions but rather to recognize an example of each discipline we have discussed. If you can do this, you have not merely memorized; you have understood. If you had any difficulty, we recommend that you reread the preceding section before going on.)

PSYCHOLOGY'S PAST: FROM THE ARMCHAIR TO THE LABORATORY

Most of the great thinkers of history, from Aristotle to Zoroaster, raised questions that today would be called psychological. They wanted to know how people take in information through their senses, use information to solve problems, and become motivated to act in brave or villainous ways. They wondered about the elusive nature of emotion, and whether it controls us or is something we can control. Like modern psychologists, they wanted to describe, understand, predict, and modify behavior in order to add to human knowledge and increase human happiness. But unlike modern psychologists, scholars of the past did not rely heavily on **empirical** evidence—evidence gathered by careful observation, experimentation, and measurement. Often, their observations were based simply on anecdotes or descriptions of individual cases.

This does not mean that the forerunners of modern psychology were always wrong. Even without scientific methods, the great thinkers of history often had insights and made observations that were verified by later work. Hippocrates (c. 460 B.C.–c. 377 B.C.), the ancient Greek known as the father of modern medicine, observed patients with head injuries and inferred that the brain must be the ultimate source of "our pleasures, joys, laughter, and jests as well as our sorrows, pains, griefs, and tears." And so it is. In the first century A.D., the Stoic philosophers observed that people do not become angry or sad or anxious because of actual events but because of their explanations of those events. And so they do. In the seventeenth century, the French philosopher René Descartes (1596–1650) helped promote scientific thinking by rejecting the then-common belief that human behavior is governed by unknowable forces and by searching for physical explanations of behavior. Later in the same century, the English philosopher John Locke (1643–1704) argued that the mind works by associating ideas arising from experience, a notion that continues to influence psychology today.

But without empirical methods, the forerunners of psychology also committed some terrible blunders. Even Aristotle, one of the first great philosophers to advocate the use of empirical methods, did not always use them correctly. He thought that the brain could not possibly be responsible for sensation because the brain itself feels no pain, and he concluded that the brain was simply a radiator for cooling the blood. Aristotle was absolutely right about the brain being insensitive, but he was wrong

empirical Relying on or derived from observation, experimentation, or measurement.

about the brain being a radiator and about many other things. For instance, he believed that small people have poor memories!

A good example of how prescientific psychology could lead down a blind alley comes from the early 1800s, when the theory of *phrenology* (Greek for "study of the mind") became wildly popular. Inspired by the writings and lectures of Austrian physician Joseph Gall (1758–1828), phrenologists argued that different brain areas accounted for specific character and personality traits, such as "stinginess" and "religiosity," and that such traits could be "read" from bumps on the skull. Thieves, for example, supposedly had large bumps above the ears. When phrenologists examined people with "stealing bumps" who were *not* thieves, they explained away this counterevidence by saying that other bumps on the skull represented positive traits that must be holding the person's thieving impulses in check. Phrenology was a classic pseudoscience—sheer nonsense.

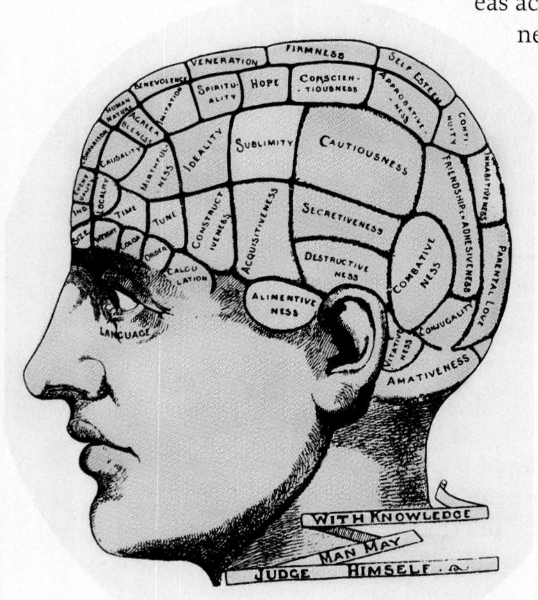

Phrenology, a nineteenth-century fad that was unsupported by any empirical evidence whatsoever, associated "skull-bumps" with character traits. On this phrenological "map," notice the tiny space allocated to self-esteem and the big hunk devoted to cautiousness!

Thus, despite some useful insights into behavior by philosophers and other scholars, psychology remained a hit-or-miss sort of business until well into the nineteenth century. It was not recognized as a separate field of study, and few formal rules guided how it was conducted.

THE BIRTH OF MODERN PSYCHOLOGY

Psychologists usually regard 1879 as the year in which psychology as a formal science was officially born. In that year, the first psychological laboratory was established, in Leipzig, Germany, by Wilhelm Wundt [VIL-helm Voont]. Wundt (1832–1920), who was trained in medicine and philosophy, was a prolific writer, turning out volume after volume on psychology, physiology, natural history, ethics, and logic. But he is especially important to psychologists because he was the first person to announce (in 1873) that he intended to make psychology a science.

Actually, psychology had many forefathers—and several foremothers, too, although their accomplishments were often unacknowledged or were even credited to others (Scarborough & Furumoto, 1987). By the time Wundt set up his laboratory, a number of individuals in Europe and North America were already doing psychological research. The Leipzig laboratory, however, was the first to be formally established and to have its results published in a scholarly journal. Although it started out as just a few rooms in an old building, it soon became the place to go for anyone who wanted to become a psychologist. Many of America's first psychologists got their training there.

Researchers in Wundt's laboratory did not study the entire gamut of topics that today's psychologists do. Most concentrated on sensation, perception, reaction times, imagery, and attention, and avoided learning, personality, and abnormal behavior. Wundt himself doubted that higher mental processes, such as abstract thinking, could be studied experimentally. He thought such topics were better understood by studying culture and natural history.

One of Wundt's favorite research methods was **trained introspection,** in which specially trained people carefully observed and analyzed their own mental experiences, including their sensations, mental images, and emotional reactions, under controlled conditions. Looking inward wasn't as easy as it sounds. Wundt's introspectors had to make 10,000 practice observations before they were allowed to participate in an actual study. Once trained, they might take as long as 20 minutes to re-

trained introspection A form of self-observation in which individuals examine and report the contents of their own consciousness.

Wilhelm Wundt (1832–1920), third from left, with co-workers.

port their inner experiences during a 1.5-second experiment. Wundt hoped that trained introspection would produce reliable, verifiable results. Ironically, although Wundt made his mark on history by declaring psychology to be an objective science, introspection was soon to be abandoned by other psychologists because it wasn't objective enough.

TWO EARLY PSYCHOLOGIES

Wundt's ideas were popularized in America in somewhat modified form by one of his students, E. B. Titchener (1867–1927), who named Wundt's approach **structuralism.** Like Wundt, American structuralists hoped to analyze sensations, images, and feelings into basic elements, much as a chemist might analyze water into hydrogen and oxygen atoms. For example, a person might be asked to listen to a metronome clicking and report exactly what he or she heard. Most people said they perceived a pattern (e.g., CLICK click click CLICK click click), even though the clicks of a metronome are actually all the same. Or a person might be asked to break down all the different components of taste when biting into an orange (sweet, tart, wet, etc.).

Despite an intensive program of research, structuralism soon went the way of the dinosaur. After you have discovered the building blocks of a particular sensation or image and how they link up, then what? Years after structuralism's demise, Wolfgang Köhler (1959) recalled how he and his colleagues had responded to it as students: "What had disturbed us was . . . the implication that human life, apparently so colorful and so intensely dynamic, is actually a frightful bore."

The structuralists' reliance on introspection also got them into hot water. To see why, imagine that you are a structuralist who wants to know what goes on in people's heads when they hear the word *triangle.* You round up some trained introspectors, say the word *triangle,* and ask them about their mental experience. Most of your respondents report a visual image of a form with three sides and three corners. Elbert, however, reports a flashing red form with equal angles, whereas Endora insists that she saw a revolving colorless form with one angle larger than the other two. Which attributes of *triangle* would you conclude were basic? This sort of conflict is exactly what occurred in structuralist studies; people disagreed. Some even claimed they could think about a triangle without forming any visual image at all (Boring, 1953).

structuralism An early psychological approach that stressed analysis of immediate experience into basic elements.

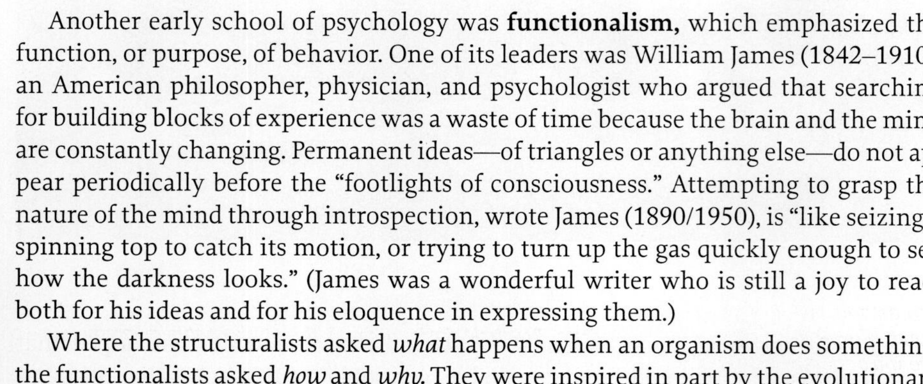

GET INVOLVED

How reliable is introspection as a method for arriving at generalizations about human experience? Find out for yourself by asking some friends what they experience mentally when asked to describe a chair. Tell them to be specific about color, shape, size, style, orientation, and so on. Which aspects of the experience do your respondents agree on, and which aspects do they report differently?

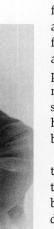

Another early school of psychology was **functionalism,** which emphasized the function, or purpose, of behavior. One of its leaders was William James (1842–1910), an American philosopher, physician, and psychologist who argued that searching for building blocks of experience was a waste of time because the brain and the mind are constantly changing. Permanent ideas—of triangles or anything else—do not appear periodically before the "footlights of consciousness." Attempting to grasp the nature of the mind through introspection, wrote James (1890/1950), is "like seizing a spinning top to catch its motion, or trying to turn up the gas quickly enough to see how the darkness looks." (James was a wonderful writer who is still a joy to read, both for his ideas and for his eloquence in expressing them.)

William James (1842–1910)

Where the structuralists asked *what* happens when an organism does something, the functionalists asked *how* and *why*. They were inspired in part by the evolutionary theories of British naturalist Charles Darwin (1809–1882). Darwin had argued that a biologist's job is not merely to describe, say, the brilliant plumage of a peacock or the drab markings of a lizard but also to figure out how these attributes enhance survival. Do they help the animal attract a mate or hide from its enemies? Similarly, the functionalists wanted to know how specific behaviors and mental processes help a person or animal adapt to the environment, so they looked for underlying causes and practical consequences of these behaviors and processes. Unlike the structuralists, they felt free to pick and choose among many methods, and they broadened the field of psychology to include the study of children, animals, religious experiences, and what James called the "stream of consciousness"—a term still used because it so beautifully describes the way thoughts flow like a river, tumbling over each other in waves, sometimes placid, sometimes turbulent.

functionalism An early psychological approach that stressed the function or purpose of behavior and consciousness.

As a school of psychology, functionalism had a short life. It lacked the kind of precise theory or program of research that inspires passion and wins recruits, and it endorsed the study of consciousness just as that concept was about to fall out of favor. Yet the functionalists' emphasis on the causes and consequences of behavior was to set the course of modern psychology.

Quick Quiz

Check your memory for the preceding section by choosing the correct response from the pair in parentheses.

1. Psychology has been a science for over (2,000/100) years.
2. The forerunners of modern psychology depended heavily on (casual observation/empirical methods).
3. Credit for founding modern psychology is generally given to (William James/Wilhelm Wundt).
4. Early psychologists who emphasized how behavior helps an organism adapt to its environment were known as (structuralists/functionalists).

Answers:

1. 100 2. casual observation 3. Wilhelm Wundt 4. functionalists

PSYCHOLOGY'S PRESENT: BEHAVIOR, BODY, MIND, AND CULTURE

Today, five major theoretical perspectives predominate in psychology: the *biological, learning, cognitive, psychodynamic,* and *sociocultural* perspectives. These approaches reflect different questions that psychologists ask about human behavior, different assumptions about how the mind works, and, most important, different kinds of explanations of why people do what they do.

We know that at this early point in your study of psychology, attempting to remember a bunch of abstract theories can be like trying to hold water in a sieve. So, as we introduce the five major perspectives (in the same order in which they are discussed more fully in this book), we will try to make them easier for you to remember by showing how they might apply to a concrete issue—the problem of violence.

The astonishing diversity of human behavior is vividly captured in Pieter Brueghel's depiction of Dutch proverbs, rhymes, and folk sayings. Psychologists approach the study of this diversity from five major perspectives.

THE BIOLOGICAL PERSPECTIVE

Many people, when they first start studying psychology, are surprised to find that psychologists are interested not only in actions and thoughts, but also in genes, hormones, and nerve cells. Yet the biological approach to psychology has been an important one from the beginning. Wilhelm Wundt's best-known work was titled *Principles of Physiological Psychology*, and for good reason: He and most other early researchers expected their science to rest on a firm foundation of anatomy and biology.

During the 1920s and 1930s, interest in mental processes and the brain flourished within *Gestalt psychology*, a movement that had begun in Germany in 1912. In German, *gestalt* means "pattern" or "configuration." The Gestalt psychologists studied how people interpret sensory information as patterns in order to acquire knowledge, and they also formulated theories of how these patterns are represented in the brain. In America, however, biological approaches to psychology languished until the 1960s, when new drugs were developed to treat mental disorders and new technologies permitted sophisticated ways of measuring brain activity. These new methods have allowed scientists to explore areas of an organism's "inner space" where no one has ventured before.

The premise behind the biological perspective in psychology is that all actions, feelings, and thoughts are associated with bodily events. Electrical impulses shoot along the intricate pathways of the nervous system. Hormones course through the bloodstream, signaling internal organs to slow down or speed up. Chemical substances flow across the tiny gaps that separate one microscopic brain cell from another. *Biological psychologists* (who sometimes call themselves *neuroscientists, neuropsychologists*, or *psychobiologists*) want to know how these bodily events interact with events in the external environment to produce perceptions, memories, and behavior. They study how biology affects the rhythms of life, perceptions of reality, the ability to learn, the experience of emotion, inborn temperaments, and vulnerability to emotional disorder. And in a popular new specialty, *evolutionary psychology*, researchers have been studying how our species' evolutionary past may help explain some of our present behaviors and psychological traits.

Biological psychologists look for the causes of self-destructive and other abnormal behavior, and of normal actions as well, in genes, brain circuits, bodily processes, and the evolutionary history of our species.

One contribution of the biological perspective has been a better understanding of how mind and body interact in illness and in health. Researchers are learning that although bodily processes can affect a person's moods and emotions, the converse is also true: Emotions, attitudes, and perceptions can influence the functioning of the immune system and thus a person's susceptibility to certain diseases. Psychobiological research has also renewed interest in the age-old debate over the relative contributions made by "nature" (genetic dispositions) and "nurture" (upbringing and environment) in the development of abilities and personality traits.

Many biological psychologists hope that their discoveries, along with those of other scientists, will help solve some of the mysteries of mental and emotional problems. Some research already suggests that many cases of impulsive, unprovoked violence may result from brain tumors, brain injuries, various diseases, or subtle neurological disorders. Dutch researchers have reported evidence, from one large family, that a genetic abnormality may explain some very unusual cases of lifelong aggression in males (Brunner, Nelen, & van Zandvoort, 1993). And damage to a part of the brain called the prefrontal cortex, caused by birth complications or child abuse, might help account for some cases of criminally violent behavior (Raine, Brennan, & Mednick, 1994).

Such findings must be interpreted with caution. People often think that the explanation for some puzzle of behavior must be *either* physical *or* psychological, and they fail to appreciate how complex the interactions between body and mind really are. But the biological approach has a useful message for us all: We cannot know ourselves if we do not know our bodies. That is why biological discoveries will be discussed in many sections of this book.

THE LEARNING PERSPECTIVE

In 1913, a psychologist named John B. Watson (1878–1958) published a paper that rocked the still-young science of psychology. In "Psychology as the Behaviorist Views It," Watson argued that if psychology were ever to be as objective as physics, chemistry, and biology, it would have to give up its preoccupation with the mind and consciousness. Psychologists, he said, should throw out introspection as a method of research and should reject such terms as *mental state, mind,* or *emotion* in explanations of behavior. They should stick to what they can observe and measure directly: acts and events taking place in the environment. In short, they should give up mentalism for **behaviorism.**

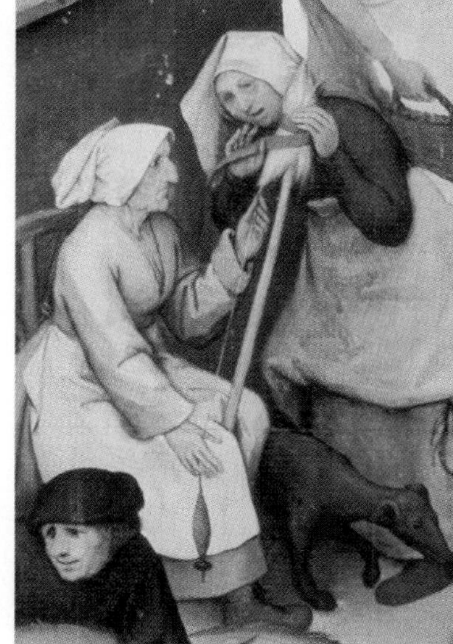

Within the learning perspective, behaviorists argue that behavior can be explained in terms of its environmental consequences. An intimate conversation with a friend, for example, brings rewarding attention from the other person.

Watson wrote approvingly of studies by the Russian physiologist Ivan Pavlov (1849–1936). Pavlov had shown that many kinds of automatic or involuntary behavior, such as salivating at the sight of food, are learned responses to specific changes, or *stimuli,* in the environment. Like Pavlov, Watson believed that basic laws of learning could explain the behavior of both human beings and animals. Later, another psychologist, B. F. Skinner (1904–1990), extended the behavioral approach, with important modifications, to voluntary acts such as turning on a light switch, riding a bike, or getting dressed. Skinner showed that the consequences of an act powerfully affect the probability of its occurring again: Acts that are followed by pleasant consequences are more likely to be repeated, whereas acts that are followed by unpleasant consequences are likely to cease.

The behavioral approach excited not only psychologists but also sociologists and political scientists. Here, at last, was a way for the social sciences to be hardheaded and earn the respect of a skeptical world. In many ways, stimulus–response or "S–R" psychology, as it was informally called, narrowed the scope of psychology. But in other ways, it broadened psychology, for (like functionalism) it fostered the study of groups that could not be studied at all through introspection, including animals, infants, and mentally disturbed persons. Behaviorism soon became the predominant American school of experimental psychology and remained so until the early 1960s.

Critics of behaviorism have often accused its proponents of denying the existence of ideas and thoughts—of believing "that human beings do not think or ponder or worry, but instead only *think* that they do" (C. Sherif, 1979). This criticism is unfair. In everyday conversation, behaviorists are as likely as anyone else to say that they think this or feel that. They realize that they themselves are conscious! But Skinner and other behaviorists parted company with nonbehaviorists in their insistence that thoughts and feelings could not *explain* behavior; they were simply behaviors to be explained. The prediction and modification of behavior depended on specifying the environmental conditions that maintained the behavior, not in describing people's thoughts or feelings. That is why behaviorists viewed discussions of the mind with suspicion.

Eventually, however, it became apparent to most psychologists that behavioral principles were not the only principles of learning. People also learn by observation, imitation, and insight; and they learn by thinking about what they see around them. One outgrowth of behaviorism, **social-learning theory** (today often called *cognitive social-learning theory*), which emerged in the 1960s, combines elements of classic behaviorism with research on thinking and consciousness. It emphasizes, for example, how people's plans, perceptions, and expectations influence their behavior. As Albert

behaviorism A psychological approach that emphasizes the study of observable behavior and the role of the environment as a determinant of behavior.

social-learning theory (or *cognitive social-learning theory*) The theory that behavior is learned and maintained through observation and imitation of others, positive consequences, and cognitive processes such as plans and expectations.

Bandura (1986), one leading proponent of this approach, has observed, "If actions were determined solely by external rewards and punishments, people would behave like weathervanes, constantly shifting direction to conform to whatever momentary influence happened to impinge on them"—but people don't (always) act like weathervanes. Today, most psychologists feel comfortable combining elements of behaviorism with approaches that incorporate the study of thoughts, values, and intentions.

What can learning approaches tell us about aggression? Behaviorists do not probe the inner lives or motives of violent people. Instead, they seek to identify the situations and payoffs that promote violence. They argue that violent behavior can be reduced or eliminated by withdrawing the rewards that maintain it and by rewarding cooperative, friendly behavior instead. Social-learning research also suggests that many children learn to hit, kick, and—in some horrifying cases—even kill by imitating what their parents, peers, and media heroes do (Bandura, 1973; Eron, 1995). It follows that a society that wishes to reduce violence should not celebrate bullies or lawless vigilantes as role models to be admired, and parents should not model violence in the home by using it against their children or each other.

Because of its many practical applications, the learning perspective has touched many lives. Behavioral techniques have helped people eliminate unreasonable fears, quit smoking, lose weight, toilet-train their toddlers, control anger, and improve their study habits. Social-learning techniques have helped raise people's self-confidence, motivation, and achievement. The behaviorists' insistence on precision and objectivity did much to advance psychology as a field, and learning research in general has given psychology some of its most reliable findings.

THE COGNITIVE PERSPECTIVE

During the 1950s and 1960s, a new emphasis in psychology on the workings of the mind gathered momentum from an unexpected source: the development of the computer, which gave scientists a method and a metaphor for studying problem solving, informational feedback, and other mental processes. The result was the rise of the cognitive perspective in psychology. (The word *cognitive* comes from the Latin for "to know.")

Cognitive psychologists emphasize people's perceptions, thought processes, and interpretations of events. They note that your reaction to a problem will depend in part on whether you interpret it as a challenge or "cry over spilt milk."

Cognitive psychologists argued that we cannot know why people do the things they do without knowing what is going on in their heads—how they think, remember, solve problems, explain experiences, and form beliefs. Cognitive researchers did not return to the structuralists' dependence on introspection; instead, they developed new ways to infer mental processes from observable behavior. For example, by examining the errors people make when they try to recall words from a list, cognitive psychologists were able to draw conclusions about whether words are stored in memory as sounds or as meanings. With the development of such techniques, the mind again became a respectable topic of scientific study.

One of the most important contributions of this perspective has been to show that our explanations and perceptions affect what we do and feel. All of us are constantly seeking to make sense of the world and of our own physical and mental states. Our ideas may not always be realistic or sensible, but they continually influence our actions and choices. For example, people who are quick to behave violently often assume that others are insulting them, even in the absence of evidence. If someone does something they dislike, they attribute the action to meanness and malice. They see provocation everywhere. In contrast, nonviolent people are able to take another person's perspective. If someone does something they dislike, they are apt to say, "He's had a bad day" instead of "He's a rotten person." They can generate alternative ways of solving disagreements. Thus, in the cognitive view, the solution to violence is to change thinking patterns.

Hardly a topic in psychology has remained unaffected by what is now called the "cognitive revolution." Cognitive researchers have studied how people explain their own behavior, understand a sentence, form opinions, use reasoning to solve problems, and remember events. With new methods, they have been able to study phenomena that were once only the stuff of speculation, such as sleeping, dreaming, hypnosis, and states of consciousness. They are designing computer programs that perform complex cognitive tasks and that predict how humans will perform such tasks, too.

Like every other approach to psychology, the cognitive perspective has its critics. They point out that although perceptions and interpretations are important, we must not overlook the impact of external events—job conditions, family situations, experiences and losses—on people's behavior. Critics also complain that often there is no way to choose among competing cognitive explanations. Yet the cognitive approach is one of the strongest forces in psychology today, and it has inspired an explosion of research on the complex workings of the mind.

THE PSYCHODYNAMIC PERSPECTIVE

So far, we have been discussing psychology only as a scientific discipline. Psychology as a method of psychotherapy was born in Vienna, Austria. There, in 1900, an obscure physician published a book titled *The Interpretation of Dreams.* The book was not exactly an overnight sensation; during the next eight years, the publisher managed to sell only 600 copies. Who could possibly have known that the author's ideas would profoundly influence the psychology, literature, and art of the twentieth century?

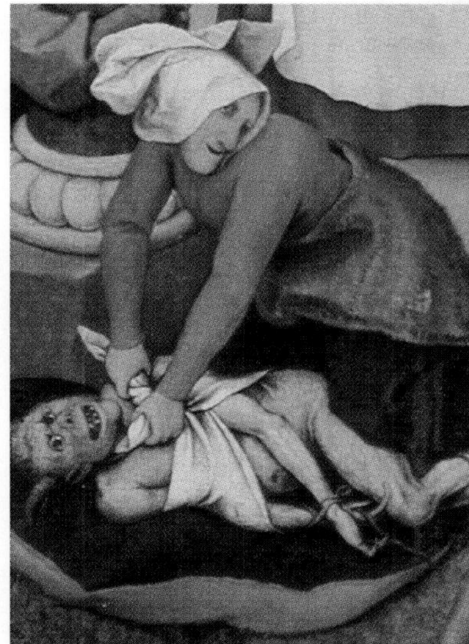

Psychodynamic psychologists explain behavior largely in terms of unconscious needs and motives. Psychoanalysts, for example, emphasize the unconscious struggle to control the instinctive "demons" of aggression and sexuality.

That author was Sigmund Freud (1856–1939), whose name today is as much a household word as Einstein's. A neurologist by training, Freud originally hoped for a career as a medical researcher, but research did not pay well, and family responsibilities forced him to go into private practice as a physician. As Freud listened to his patients' reports of depression, nervousness, and obsessive habits, he became convinced that many of their symptoms had mental, not bodily, causes. Psychological distress was due, he concluded, to conflicts, memories, and emotional traumas that went back to early childhood. Freud's ideas eventually evolved into a broad theory of personality, and both his theory and his methods of treating people with emotional problems became known as **psychoanalysis.**

Freud argued that conscious awareness is merely the tip of a mental iceberg. Beneath the visible tip, he said, lies the unconscious part of the mind, containing unrevealed wishes, passions, guilty secrets, unspeakable yearnings, and conflicts between desire and duty. We are not aware of our unconscious urges and thoughts as we go blithely about our daily business, yet they make themselves known—in dreams, slips of the tongue, apparent accidents, and even jokes. Freud (1905a) wrote, "No mortal can keep a secret. If the lips are silent, he chatters with his fingertips; betrayal oozes out of him at every pore." In the Freudian view, unconscious forces have more power over behavior than consciousness does. Whereas a behaviorist is concerned with observable acts, a psychoanalyst tries to dig below the surface of a person's behavior to get to the roots of personality. Psychoanalysts think of themselves as archeologists of the mind.

Freud addressed the issue of violence by arguing that aggression (along with sexuality) is an instinct that is lodged in the unconscious. The duty of society, he said, is to help people channel their aggressive energy into productive, socially useful activities. A Freudian might say that a football player, a rap singer, and a surgeon are all channeling their aggressive energy in constructive directions. Aggressive energy that is not channeled in this way will inevitably be released in violent actions such as murder and war.

psychoanalysis A theory of personality and a method of psychotherapy, originally formulated by Sigmund Freud, which emphasizes unconscious motives and conflicts.

Psychoanalysis continues today as a school of therapy and an approach to explaining human nature. It has been a major influence on modern **psychodynamic** theories of personality, which emphasize unconscious dynamics within the individual, such as inner forces, conflicts, or instinctual energy. Freud borrowed the idea of the conservation of energy from nineteenth-century physics: Within any system, he thought, energy can be shifted or transformed, but the total amount remains the same. Psychological energy—the energy it takes to carry out mental and emotional processes such as thinking and dreaming—was, to Freud, a form of physical energy. Although modern psychodynamic theories differ from classical psychoanalysis, they share Freud's **intrapsychic** view of the individual, emphasizing the internal mechanisms of the *psyche* or mind.

Psychodynamic psychology is the thumb on the hand of psychology—connected to the other fingers, but also set apart from them because it differs radically from the others in its language, methods, and standards of acceptable evidence. Many research psychologists working from other perspectives don't think that psychodynamic approaches belong in academic psychology at all. They point out that many psychodynamic assumptions are impossible to verify. Whereas the other perspectives originated in scientific research, they argue, the psychodynamic perspective originated in psychoanalysis and therefore belongs with philosophy and literature rather than social science.

Nevertheless, the psychodynamic perspective has had an influence on mainstream psychology. Some researchers are studying unconscious processes such as denial, rationalization, and self-delusion—which, according to Freud, the conscious mind uses to protect itself from threatening information. Research has verified that prolonged emotional conflict may indeed play itself out in physical symptoms and self-defeating actions. The psychodynamic perspective continues to be important, too, because it tackles the great existential dilemmas, such as alienation in a lonely world and the fear of death.

THE SOCIOCULTURAL PERSPECTIVE

For the most part, the study of psychology has been the study of the individual—that is, the behavioral, psychodynamic, cognitive, and biological forces that affect an individual's behavior. During the 1930s and 1940s, some researchers began to question this focus. They wanted to know how dictators such as Adolf Hitler could persuade people to commit the atrocities that led to the deaths of Anne Frank and millions of others. They wondered why apparently nice people often hold hateful prejudices and whether such attitudes could be changed. They asked how cultural values and political systems affect everyday experience. The view that emerged from these questions is the sociocultural perspective.

Researchers working from this perspective have shown that social contexts shape every aspect of human behavior, from how (and whether!) we kiss to what and where we eat. Yet most of us underestimate the influence of the historical and social context in which we happen to find ourselves. We are like fish that are unaware they live in water, so obvious is water in their lives. Sociocultural psychologists study the water and ask how it affects everything that swims in it.

Psychologists who emphasize the social side of the sociocultural perspective might study how standards of masculinity and femininity influence the expression of emotion, how job opportunities affect a person's goals and ambitions, or how being in a group affects attitudes and the desire to conform. They study how each of us is affected by other people—spouses, lovers, friends, bosses, parents, and strangers.

psychodynamic Refers to psychological approaches that emphasize unconscious dynamics within the individual, such as inner forces, conflicts, or the movement of instinctual energy.

intrapsychic Within the mind (psyche) or self.

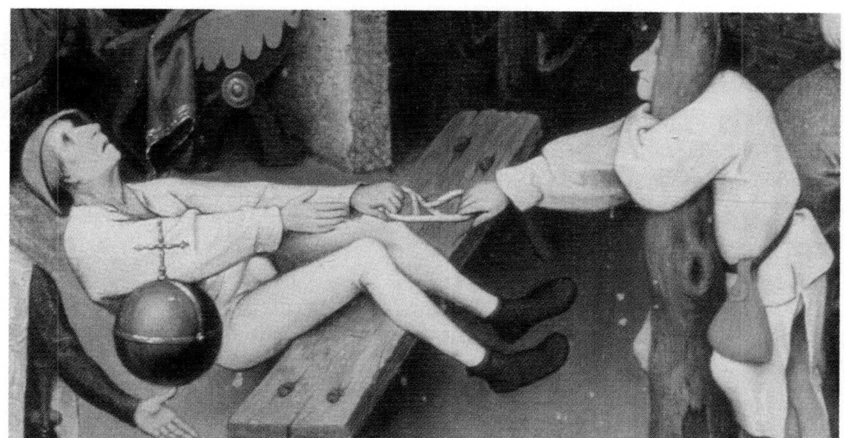

Psychologists who take a sociocultural perspective focus on the many outside influences on behavior, ranging from the immediate situation to the larger culture. They might ask why relationships in some societies are a tug-of-war, whereas those in other societies are more cooperative.

They study how we emulate our heroes, conform to peer groups, obey authorities, and blossom or wilt in relationships.

Psychologists who emphasize the cultural side of this perspective study how cultural rules affect behavior. Sometimes the rules are explicit: "Every adult woman must cover her face and hair in public." Sometimes they are implicit and unspoken: "The correct nose-to-nose distance for talking to a friend is about 20 inches." Cultural psychologists might look at how a society's emphasis on individualism or group loyalty affects people's behavior at work; how cultural expectations about children's family responsibilities affect moral development; or how cultural rules and attitudes about sex affect people's experiences, pleasure, and responsiveness.

In the sociocultural view, the reasons for violence do not reside in instincts, brain circuits, or personality traits, but in economic and political arrangements and in social and cultural rules about when to aggress and against whom. When societies are small and close-knit, and when individuals must cooperate to survive, people tend to fear and avoid aggression. The Inuit (Eskimos), for example, often regard the mildest protest, the slightest raised tone, the merest hint of a frown as a serious threat. The Inuit consider anger to be dangerous and intolerable, appropriate only for babies, the insane, the sick—and *kaplunas,* white people (Briggs, 1970). Sociocultural researchers have identified some of the situational, economic, and cultural factors that encourage anger and aggression, both within the society and against outsiders. The reduction of violence, therefore, requires not just individual change but also social and cultural change.

Critics of the sociocultural perspective worry that it can lead to glib generalizations and stereotypes about ethnic groups, nations, and cultures. But because human beings are social animals who have much in common and who also are profoundly affected by their different cultural worlds, this perspective has made psychology a more representative and scientific discipline.

TWO INFLUENTIAL MOVEMENTS IN PSYCHOLOGY

You will be encountering the theories, findings, and methods of four of the five perspectives throughout this book. (The psychodynamic approach has had its greatest influence on personality theories and clinical practice and is discussed primarily in sections on those topics.) Not all schools of psychology, however, fall neatly into one of these perspectives.

In the 1960s, for example, Abraham Maslow, Rollo May, and Carl Rogers rejected the psychoanalytic emphasis on unconscious conflict as being too pessimistic a view of human nature, and they rejected the behavioral approach as being too mechanistic and "mindless" a view of human nature. Human behavior, they argued, is not completely determined by either unconscious dynamics or the environment. People are capable of free will and therefore have the ability to make more of themselves than psychoanalysts or behaviorists would predict. It was time, said Maslow, May, and Rogers, for a new direction in psychology, which they called **humanist psychology** (or *humanism*). Its goal would be to help people express themselves creatively and achieve their full potential. As Maslow (1971) wrote, "When you select out for careful study very fine and healthy people, strong people, creative people, saintly people, sagacious people . . . then you get a very different view of mankind. You are asking how tall can people grow, what can a human being become?"

Although humanism is no longer a dominant school in psychology, it has had considerable influence both inside and outside the field. Many psychologists across all perspectives embrace some humanist ideas, although most regard humanism as a philosophy of life rather than a systematic approach to psychology. Further, many topics raised by the humanists, such as creativity and altruism (unselfish helpfulness to others), have been studied by scientific psychologists in other perspectives. But humanism has probably had its greatest influence in psychotherapy, as well as in the "human potential" and self-help movements.

Another movement that emerged in the 1970s was **feminist psychology.** As women began to enter psychology in greater numbers, they documented evidence of a pervasive bias in the research methods and in the very questions that researchers had been asking (Bem, 1993; Crawford & Marecek, 1989; Hare-Mustin & Marecek, 1990). They noted the large number of studies that used only men as subjects—and usually only young, white, middle-class men, at that—and showed why it was often inappropriate to generalize to everyone else from such a narrow research base.

Today, women and men who call themselves feminist psychologists may identify with any of the five major perspectives, or they may draw on research from several approaches in analyzing gender relations and the reasons for the behavior of the two sexes. Feminist psychologists have spurred the growth of research on topics traditionally ignored in psychology, such as menstruation, motherhood, the dynamics of power in close relationships, women's life-span issues, and reasons for the changing definitions of masculinity and femininity. They have critically examined the male bias in psychotherapy, starting with Freud's own case studies (Hare-Mustin, 1991). And they have analyzed the social consequences of psychological findings, showing how research has often been used to justify the lower status of women and other disadvantaged groups.

Critics, both outside and within this movement, are concerned that some feminist psychologists are replacing a male bias in research with a female bias—for example, by doing studies of women only and then drawing conclusions about gender differences, or by replacing the "women are inferior to men" stereotype with a "women are superior to men" stereotype (Tavris, 1992; Yoder & Kahn, 1993). They also note that the overriding goal of feminist psychologists—promoting gender equality—sometimes leads them to embrace conclusions that are intuitively appealing but that lack solid empirical support (Mednick, 1989; Peplau & Conrad, 1989; Stimpson, 1996). Feminist psychologists, however, remind us that research and psychotherapy are social processes, affected by all the attitudes and values that people bring to any enterprise. To improve psychology and make it more socially useful, they say, we must become aware of our biases and attempt to correct them. This argument has inspired other movements that are striving to eliminate bias in studies of cultural groups, gay men and lesbians, old people, disabled people, and the poor.

humanist psychology A psychological approach that emphasizes personal growth and the achievement of human potential, rather than the scientific understanding and assessment of behavior.

feminist psychology A psychological approach that analyzes the influence of social inequities on gender relations and on the behavior of the two sexes.

A NOTE ON PSYCHOLOGY'S MULTIPLE PERSONALITIES

The differences among the perspectives of psychology are very real; they have produced passionate arguments and sometimes stony silences among their defenders. But not all psychologists feel they must swear allegiance to one approach or another. Many, if not most, are *eclectic*, using what they believe to be the best features of diverse schools of thought. Further, most psychological scientists agree on basic guidelines about what is and what is not acceptable in their discipline. Most believe in the importance of gathering empirical evidence and not relying on hunches. Nearly all reject supernatural explanations of events—evil spirits, psychic forces, miracles, and so forth. This insistence on rigorous standards of proof sets psychology apart from nonscientific explanations of human experience (see "Puzzles of Psychology" on pp. 22–23).

Some psychologists seek a unifying *paradigm*—a guiding model or theory—that will bring all of psychology's approaches together under one intellectual tent (Gibson, 1994). Gregory Kimble (1994, 1996) argues that "there are patterns—something like the laws that Newton showed us—that are general enough to bring intellectual togetherness to psychology." For Kimble, a behaviorist, the laws of behavior provide that "togetherness." But evolutionary psychologists think that *their* paradigm is the one to unite psychology. And psychodynamic psychologists think that theirs is.

Other psychologists believe that "intellectual togetherness" is a pipe dream. The diverse strands of psychological research can never be woven together into a coherent science, they maintain. Sigmund Koch (1992), for example, suggests that we stop speaking of "the study of psychology" as if psychology were a single thing, and instead speak of "the psychological studies." As we saw in the case of aggression, some explanations of behavior are to be found in biology; some in learning and cognitive processes; some in unconscious dynamics; and some in the effects of social pathology—poverty, unemployment, prejudice, and urban stresses. Today the field of psychology is like a giant mosaic made up of many fragments. Put all the pieces together, though, and the result is a rich, multicolored, absorbing portrait of humanity.

Quick Quiz

A. Anxiety is a common problem. To find out whether you fully understand the five major perspectives in psychology, match each possible explanation of anxiety on the left with a perspective on the right.

1. Anxious people often think about the future in distorted ways.
2. Anxiety is due to forbidden, unconscious desires.
3. Anxiety symptoms often bring hidden rewards, such as being excused from exams.
4. Excessive anxiety can be caused by a chemical imbalance.
5. A national emphasis on competition and success promotes anxiety about failure.

a. behavioral
b. psychodynamic
c. sociocultural
d. biological
e. cognitive

B. Different assumptions about human behavior can lead to different conclusions. What assumption distinguishes cognitive psychology from behaviorism? What assumption distinguishes the psychodynamic perspective from the sociocultural perspective?

Answers:

A. 1. e 2. b 3. a 4. d 5. c B. Cognitive psychologists assume that thoughts and feelings can explain behavior; behaviorists assume that thoughts and feelings are behaviors to be explained. Psychodynamic psychologists assume that behavior is driven largely by internal (intrapsychic) factors, such as unconscious urges and personality traits; the sociocultural perspective assumes that behavior is determined largely by social and cultural contexts.

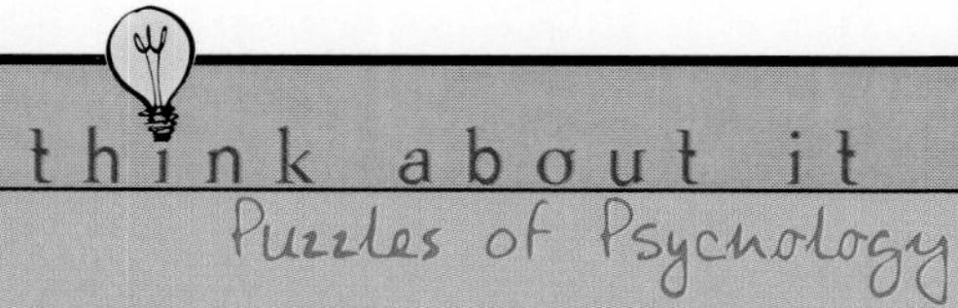

Psychics, Psychology, and Storytelling

You have probably heard that human beings differ from other animals because we have language, use tools, or can think. But to communications psychologist George Gerbner (1988), we are unique because we tell stories—and live by the stories we tell. All of us need to explain ourselves and the world around us. We are constantly constructing stories that will make sense of confusing, surprising, or unfair events. Which of these stories are right?

Psychology and other sciences offer certain stories about human behavior; they are called "theories." But psychology has plenty of nonscientific competitors: palm readers, graphologists, "channelers," fortunetellers, numerologists, and the most popular—astrologers. Are you having romantic problems? An astrologer may advise you to choose an Aries instead of an Aquarius as your next love. Are you fighting the battle of the bulge? An expert in "past-lives regression" will explain that the problem is not in your unhappy childhood but in your unhappy previous life; perhaps in the fourteenth century, you were a starving serf. Many of these self-defined healers operate in effect as unlicensed psychological counselors. You hear about their famous clients all the time—movie stars, rock singers, Wall Street brokers, even politicians.

Many stories told by psychology's competitors help people feel better, reassure people that they are normal, or simplify a complicated world. But in the scientific view, for a story or theory to be *true*, or valid, it must predict behavior or events more reliably and accurately than could be done by mere guessing. Further, you have to make predictions in advance of, not after, the fact. You don't get to survive an earthquake and *then* argue that the planets predicted it.

At the start of every year, self-proclaimed psychics make their forecasts. But whenever anyone has actually checked up on those predictions, most of them have turned out to be dead wrong. For example, 1994 was supposed to be the year that Charles Manson got a sex-change operation and was freed from prison (*Weekly World News*); that Madonna married a Middle Eastern sheik and became a "totally traditional wife" (*Globe*); and that Whoopi Goldberg gave up acting to join a convent (*National Enquirer*). (Have you ever wondered why so many of these psychics are far from affluent? If they can foretell the future, why haven't they made fortunes in the stock market or the lottery?)

Moreover, no psychic has ever found a missing child, identified a serial killer, or helped police solve any other crime solely by using "psychic powers"—in spite of frequent reports in the mass media that psychics do this all the time (Rowe, 1993). The terrible batting average of psychics, however, did not stop the U.S. Department of Defense from wasting $20 million over a period of two decades on so-called psychics who were hired

WHAT PSYCHOLOGISTS DO

Now you know the main viewpoints that guide psychologists in their work. But what do psychologists actually do with their time between breakfast and dinner?

When most people hear the word *psychologist*, they imagine a therapist listening intently while a client, perhaps stretched out on a couch, pours forth his or her troubles. Many psychologists do in fact fit this image, though chairs are more common than couches these days. Many others, however, do not (see Table 1.1, p. 24). The professional activities of psychologists generally fall into three categories: (1) teaching and doing research in colleges and universities; (2) providing health or mental-health services, often referred to as *psychological practice;* and (3) conducting research or applying its findings in nonacademic settings such as business, sports, government, law, and the military. Many psychologists wear more than one professional hat. A teacher at a university might spend half the day doing laboratory research and the other half teaching psychology courses, besides occasionally serving as a professional consultant in legal cases or for government policy makers. A scientist–practitioner might see patients in a mental-health clinic three days a week and do research in a hospital on the causes of depression the other two.

to provide specific military information, such as the location of Libyan dictator Moammar Kadafi in 1986. One psychic said, "I see sand. I see water. I see a mosque. . . ." Very helpful.

Astrologers do no better than psychics. In a review of many studies of predictions made by astrologers, Geoffrey Dean (1986/1987, 1987) found that their predictions had only chance-level accuracy. The occasional on-target predictions of astrologers are the result of shrewd guesses, vagueness ("A tragedy will strike the country this spring"), or inside information ("Movie star A will marry director B"). After studying the appeal of astrology in the face of its continued failure to confirm any of its premises or predictions, Dean concluded that astrology is "psychological chewing gum, satisfying but ultimately without real substance." The study of psychology, we believe, provides substance.

In this book, you will learn that psychology tells more than one story. A psychoanalyst's explanation of your personality will not be the same as a cognitive psychologist's, and neither account will be the same as a behaviorist's. The task of the scientist is to separate belief from evidence and to consider all available information, including any counterevidence. In later chapters, we will be offering you ways to think critically about competing psychological approaches, as well as about those of psychology's nonscientific rivals—to determine which theories actually predict human behavior best. In the meantime, ask yourself what else you need to know to evaluate a theory besides the fact that it is coherent and appealing, and you want it to be true. What is the harm in accepting an explanation of behavior that has no evidence to support it? Does it matter whether we attribute our fates to the alignment of heavenly bodies, past lives, spirit guides, psychic energy, or our own decisions and actions? Think about it.

I see you being less gullible in the future.

PSYCHOLOGICAL RESEARCH

Most psychologists who do research have doctoral degrees (Ph.D.s or Ed.D.s, doctorates in education). Psychological researchers work for universities and colleges, the government, the military, private research institutes, and business. Some, seeking knowledge for its own sake, work in **basic psychology,** doing "pure" research. Others, concerned with the practical uses of knowledge, work in **applied psychology.** A psychologist doing basic research might ask, "How do children, adolescents, and adults differ in their approach to moral issues such as honesty?" An applied psychologist might ask, "How can knowledge about moral development be used to prevent teenage violence?" A psychologist in basic science might ask, "Can a chimpanzee or a gorilla learn to use sign language?" An applied psychologist might ask, "Can techniques used to teach sign language to a chimpanzee be used to help mentally impaired or disturbed children who do not speak?"

basic psychology The study of psychological issues in order to seek knowledge for its own sake rather than for its practical application.

applied psychology The study of psychological issues that have direct practical significance and the application of psychological findings.

Applied psychologists have made important contributions in areas as diverse as education, health, marketing, management, consumer behavior, industrial design, worker productivity and satisfaction, and urban planning. Although basic psychology can sometimes lead to useful discoveries by accident, such accidents cannot be

TABLE 1.1 What Is a Psychologist?

A psychologist has an advanced degree; many psychologists are psychotherapists (clinicians), but others do research, teach, work in business, or consult.

Academic/Research Psychologists	Clinical Psychologists	Psychologists in Industry, Law, or Other Settings
Specialize in areas of pure or applied research, such as:	*May work in any of these settings, or in some combination:*	*Do research or serve as consultants to institutions on, for example:*
Human development	Private practice	Sports
Psychometrics (testing)	Mental health clinics or services	Consumer issues
Health	Hospitals	Advertising
Education	Research	Organizational problems
Industrial/organizational psychology	Teaching	Environmental issues
Consumer psychology		Public policy
Physiological psychology		Survey research and opinion polls
Perception and sensation		

depended on. On the other hand, insisting that psychological research always be relevant is like trying to grow flowers by concentrating only on the blossoms and ignoring the roots (Walker, 1970). Basic research is root research. Without it, there would be little scientific knowledge to apply.

Psychologists' findings, both basic and applied, fill this book, so you can get a good idea of *what* psychologists study and teach by scanning the table of contents on pages vi to xv. Here are a few of the major nonclinical specialties in psychology:

- *Experimental psychologists* conduct laboratory studies of learning, motivation, emotion, sensation and perception, physiology, and cognition. Don't be misled by the term *experimental,* though; other researchers also do experiments.
- *Educational psychologists* study psychological principles that explain learning and search for ways to improve educational systems. Their interests range from the application of findings on memory and thinking to the use of rewards to encourage achievement.
- *Developmental psychologists* study how people change and grow over time, physically, mentally, and socially. In the past, their focus was mainly on childhood, but many now study adolescence, young adulthood, the middle years, or old age.
- *Industrial/organizational psychologists* study behavior in the workplace. They are concerned with group decision making, employee morale, work motivation, productivity, job stress, personnel selection, marketing strategies, equipment design, and many other issues.
- *Psychometric psychologists* design and evaluate tests of mental abilities, aptitudes, interests, and personality. Nearly all of us have had firsthand experience with one or more of these tests in school, at work, or in the military.

THE PRACTICE OF PSYCHOLOGY

Psychological practitioners, whose goal is to understand and improve physical and mental health, work in mental hospitals, general hospitals, clinics, schools, counseling centers, and private practice. During the past two decades, the proportion of psychologists who are practitioners has greatly increased; today, practitioners account for well over two-thirds of new psychology doctorates and members of the American Psychological Association (APA), psychology's largest professional organization (Shapiro & Wiggins, 1994). Some practitioners are *counseling psychologists,* who generally help people deal with problems of everyday life, such as test anxiety, family conflicts, or low job motivation. Others are *school psychologists,* who work with parents, teachers, and students to enhance students' performance and resolve emotional difficulties. The majority, however, are *clinical psychologists,* who diagnose, treat, and study mental or emotional problems. Clinical psychologists are trained to do psychotherapy with highly disturbed people, as well as with those who are simply troubled or unhappy or who want to learn to handle their problems better. (As we will see in Chapter 16, there are many kinds of psychotherapy.)

In almost all states, a license to practice clinical psychology requires a doctorate. Most clinical psychologists have a Ph.D., some have an Ed.D., and a smaller but growing number have a Psy.D. (doctorate in psychology, pronounced "sy-dee"). Clinical psychologists typically do four or five years of graduate work in psychology, plus at least a year's internship under the direction of a practicing psychologist. Clinical programs leading to a Ph.D. or Ed.D. are usually designed to prepare a person both as a scientist and as a clinical practitioner; they require completion of a dissertation, a major scholarly project (usually involving research) that contributes to knowledge in the field. Programs leading to a Psy.D. focus on professional practice and do not usually require a dissertation. However, they do require the student to complete a research study, theoretical paper, literature review, or some other scholarly project.

People often confuse the terms *psychotherapist, psychoanalyst, clinical psychologist,* and *psychiatrist,* but these terms do not mean the same thing. Anyone who does any kind of psychotherapy is a psychotherapist. In fact, in most states anyone can say

Some psychologists are researchers, others are practitioners, and some are both. On the left, Patricia Goldman-Rakic and her colleagues use technology to study the brain mechanisms underlying mental processes. On the right, a clinical psychologist helps a couple in therapy.

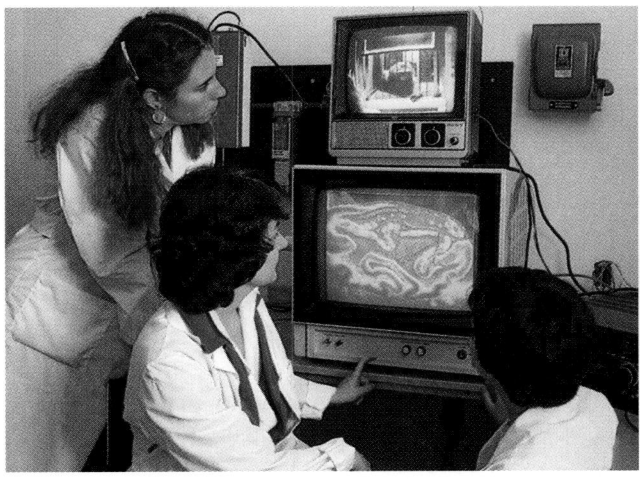

that he or she is a "therapist" of one sort or another without having any training at all. A *psychoanalyst* is a person who practices one particular form of therapy, psychoanalysis. To call yourself a psychoanalyst, you must have an advanced degree (usually an M.D. or a Ph.D.), get specialized training at a psychoanalytic institute, and undergo extensive psychoanalysis yourself. **Psychiatry** is the medical specialty concerned with mental disorders, maladjustment, and abnormal behavior. Psychiatrists are medical doctors (M.D.s) who have had three or four years of general medical training, a yearlong internship in general medicine, and a three-year residency in psychiatry. During the residency period, a psychiatrist learns to diagnose and treat psychiatric patients under the supervision of more experienced physicians. Some psychiatrists go on to do research on mental problems, such as depression or schizophrenia, rather than work with patients.

Psychiatrists and clinical psychologists do similar work, but they differ in important ways. Psychiatrists are more likely to treat severe mental disorders. They tend to be more medically oriented because they have been trained to diagnose physical problems that can cause mental ones. In addition, psychiatrists can write prescriptions and clinical psychologists cannot (at least not yet; many psychologists are pressing for prescription-writing privileges). Psychiatrists, however, are often untrained in psychological theories and methods. These differences can affect approaches to diagnosis and treatment (see Chapter 16). For example, if a patient is depressed, a psychiatrist will tend to look for organic causes. A clinical psychologist is more likely to look for the psychological and social origins of the depression.

Social workers, school counselors, and marriage, family, and child counselors also do mental-health work. These professionals ordinarily treat general problems in adjustment rather than mental disturbance, but their work may bring them into contact with people who have serious problems and would not otherwise seek professional help—violent delinquents, sex offenders, individuals involved in domestic and child abuse. Licensing requirements vary from state to state but usually include a master's degree in psychology or social work and one or two years of supervised experience. (For a summary of the types of psychotherapists and the training they receive, see Table 1.2.)

Many research psychologists are worried about an increase in poorly trained psychotherapists across America (Dawes, 1994; Poole et al., 1995). Many of these therapists are unschooled in research methods and the empirical findings of psychology, and they use therapy techniques that have not been tested and validated (we will return to this issue in Chapter 16). Some practitioners, too, are concerned about the

psychiatry The medical specialty concerned with mental disorders, maladjustment, and abnormal behavior.

TABLE 1.2 ***Types of Psychotherapists***

Psychotherapist	A person who does psychotherapy: may have anything from no degree to an advanced professional degree; the term is unregulated
Clinical psychologist	Has a Ph.D., Ed.D., or Psy.D.
Psychoanalyst	Has specific training in psychoanalysis after an advanced degree (M.D. or Ph.D.)
Psychiatrist	A medical doctor (M.D.) with a specialty in psychiatry
Licensed social worker (LSW); school psychologist; marriage, family, and child counselor (MFCC)	Licensing requirements vary; generally has at least an M.A. in psychology or social work

lack of a uniform, national standard of professional education (Fox, 1994). Some years ago, such concerns contributed to the formation of the American Psychological Society, an organization devoted to the needs and interests of psychology as a science. Many practitioners, on the other hand, accuse psychological scientists of living in an ivory tower and of showing too little concern for helping people to solve problems in the real world.

Partly because of these tensions, and partly because the media and the public persist in equating "psychologist" with "psychotherapist," some psychological scientists think it is time to use other labels to describe what they do and to yield the word *psychologist* to its popular meaning. Research psychologists, they say, should call themselves "cognitive scientists," "behavioral scientists," "neuroscientists," and so forth, depending on their area of study. This change in language is already underway and gathering steam. At present, however, the word *psychologist* still embraces all the cousins in psychology's sprawling family.

PSYCHOLOGY IN THE COMMUNITY

In recent decades, psychology has expanded rapidly in terms of scholars, publications, and specialties. The American Psychological Association now has 49 divisions. Some of these divisions represent the major fields described in this chapter, such as developmental psychology and physiological psychology. Others represent specific research or professional interests, such as the psychology of women, ethnic minority issues, sports, the arts, environmental concerns, gay and lesbian issues, peace, psychology and the law, and health.

As psychology has expanded, many psychologists have found ways to contribute to their communities, in about as many fields as you can think of. They consult with companies to improve worker satisfaction and productivity. They establish programs to improve race relations and reduce tensions between ethnic communities. They advise commissions on how pollution and noise affect mental health. They do research for the military. They do rehabilitation training for people who are physically or mentally disabled. They educate judges and juries about the reliability of eyewitness testimony. They assist the police in emergencies involving hostages or disturbed persons. They conduct public-opinion surveys. They run suicide-prevention hot lines. They advise zoos on the care and training of animals. They help coaches improve the athletic performance of their teams. And on and on.

Psychologists work in all sorts of settings, from classrooms to courtrooms. On the left, prison psychologist Patricia Frisch counsels a San Quentin inmate. On the right, Louis Herman studies a dolphin's ability to understand an artificial language comprised of hand signals. In response to the gestural sequence "person" and "over," the dolphin will leap over the person in the pool.

GET INVOLVED

To get an idea of just how broad a discipline psychology is, take any newspaper and circle the headlines of those stories about which psychology might be able to offer insights. Don't skip the sports, business, and "people" sections! How many headlines did you mark? What kinds of psychologists would study the topics you circled?

Is it any wonder that people are a little fuzzy about what a psychologist is? Cognitive psychologist George Miller has related what happens when he tells people his profession: "Some people say: 'So you're a psychologist. I think my wife's calling,' and off they go. Then there's the opposite reaction: 'So you're a psychologist. Well I'm something of a psychologist myself,' and they describe how they trained their dog to bring in the newspaper. Other people ask about their children's test scores, and still others want me to interpret their dreams. All I can say is: 'I'm not that kind of psychologist!' " (in J. Miller, 1983).

Quick Quiz

A. Let's see if you're clear about what psychologists do. Which kinds of psychologists are most likely to have the following job descriptions?

1. Studies emotional development during childhood
2. Does laboratory studies of visual perception in animals
3. Treats eating disorders of patients in a mental-health clinic
4. Consults with industry on marketing strategies

B. A psychotherapist who has an M.D. and tends to take a medical approach to emotional problems is likely to be a ___________, whereas a therapist who has a Ph.D., Psy.D., or Ed.D. and addresses the psychological origins of emotional problems is likely to be a ___________.

Answers:

A. 1. developmental 2. experimental 3. clinical 4. industrial/organizational B. psychiatrist, clinical psychologist

THINKING CRITICALLY AND CREATIVELY ABOUT PSYCHOLOGY

One of the greatest benefits of studying psychology is that you learn not only how the brain works in general but also how to use yours in particular—by thinking critically. **Critical thinking** is the ability and willingness to assess claims and make objective judgments on the basis of well-supported reasons. It is the ability to look for flaws in arguments and to resist claims that have no supporting evidence. Critical thinking, however, is not merely negative thinking. It also fosters the ability to be *creative and constructive*—to come up with possible explanations for events, think of implications of research findings, and apply new knowledge to social and personal problems. You can't separate critical thinking from creative thinking, for it is only when you question *what is* that you can begin to imagine *what can be.*

critical thinking The ability and willingness to assess claims and to make objective judgments on the basis of well-supported reasons.

These days, most people know that you have to exercise the body to keep it in shape, but they may not realize that clear thinking also requires effort and practice—that unlike breathing, it's not automatic. All around us, we can see examples of flabby thinking, lazy thinking, emotional thinking, and nonthinking. Sometimes

...BUT THERE'S NO PROOF THAT THEY DIDN'T DANCE EITHER!

It's not enough to say that something "could" be true; critical thinkers demand that claims be supported by evidence.

people justify their mental laziness by proudly telling you they are open-minded. "It's good to be open-minded," philosopher Jacob Needleman once replied, "but not so open that your brains fall out."

One prevalent misreading of what it means to be open-minded is the idea that all opinions are created equal and that everybody's beliefs are as good as everybody else's. On matters of religious faith or personal preferences, that's true; if you prefer the look of a Ford Escort to the look of a Honda Civic, no one can argue with you. But if you say, "The Ford is a better car than a Honda," you have gone beyond mere opinion. Now you have to support your belief with evidence of the car's reliability, track record, safety, and the like (Ruggiero, 1991). And if you say, "Fords are the best in the world and Hondas do not exist; they are a conspiracy of the Japanese government," you forfeit the right to have your opinion taken seriously. Your opinion, if it ignores reality, is *not* equal to any other.

In the United States, the idea that every issue has two sides has added to the confusion between beliefs based on matters of taste, preference, and wishful thinking and beliefs based on good reasoning and solid evidence. For example, some college newspaper editors have used the "two sides" idea to justify their acceptance of advertisements for revisionist books claiming that the Holocaust never took place. But as Deborah Lipstadt, author of *Denying the Holocaust* (1993), observes, the question of whether the Holocaust occurred does not have two sides; debating this is like debating whether the Roman Empire existed or whether there really was a French Revolution. The First Amendment states that Congress shall make no law abridging freedom of speech, notes Lipstadt (1994), but "It says nothing about a paper's obligation to publish every absurd claim that comes its way," nor does it require that every opinion, no matter how half-baked, be given the same standing.

Critical thinking involves a set of skills that will help you distinguish arguments based on solidly grounded evidence from those that float along on delusion or wishful dreams. Patricia King and Karen Kitchener, who have studied what they call *reflective judgment* and we call critical thinking, find that people don't usually use such skills until their mid-20s or until they have had many years of higher education—if then (Kitchener & King, 1990; King & Kitchener, 1994). (We will be discussing this research further in Chapter 8.) That does not mean that people *can't* think critically. Even young children may do so, though they may not get much credit for it. We know one fourth-grader who, when told that ancient Greece was the "cradle of democracy," replied, "But what about women and slaves, who couldn't vote and had no rights? Was Greece a democracy for them?" That's critical thinking. And it is also creative thinking, for once you question the assumption that Greece was a democracy for everyone, you can begin to imagine other interpretations of ancient Greek civilization.

Many educators, philosophers, and psychologists believe that contemporary education shortchanges students by not encouraging them to think critically and creatively. Too often, say these critics, both teachers and students view the mind as a bin for storing the right answers or a sponge for soaking up knowledge. The mind is neither a bin nor a sponge. Remembering, thinking, and understanding are all active processes. They require judgment, choice, and the weighing of evidence. Unfortunately, children who challenge prevailing opinion at home or in school are often called "rebellious" rather than "involved." As a result, say the critics, many high school and college graduates cannot formulate a rational argument or see through misleading advertisements and propaganda that play on emotions. They do not know how to go about deciding whether to have children, make an investment, or support a political proposal. They do not know how to come up with imaginative solutions to their problems.

You can apply critical thinking to any subject you study or problem you encounter, but it is particularly relevant to psychology, for three reasons. First, the field itself includes the study of thinking, problem solving, creativity, and curiosity, and so by its very nature fosters critical and creative thinking. Second, psychology also includes the study of *barriers* to clear thinking, such as the human propensity for rationalization, self-deception, and biases in perception. Third, the field of psychology generates many competing findings on topics of personal and social relevance, and people need to be able to evaluate these findings and their implications. Critical thinking can help you separate true psychology from the psychobabble that clutters the airwaves and bookstores.

In part, learning to think critically means following the rules of logic. But there are also other guidelines involved (Ennis, 1985; Halpern, 1995; Paul, 1984; Ruggiero, 1991). Here are eight of the essential ones, which we emphasize throughout this book.

ASK QUESTIONS; BE WILLING TO WONDER What is the one kind of question that most exasperates parents of young children? "Why is the sky blue, Mommy?" "Why doesn't the plane fall?" "Why don't pigs have wings?" Unfortunately, as children grow up, they tend to stop asking "why" questions. (Why do you think this is?) Psychologist Bob Perloff (1992) has reflected on a few questions he would like to have answered: "Why are moths attracted to wool but indifferent to cotton?" he asks. "How is it that there exist minuscule organisms so small that they cannot be seen by the naked eye? . . . Why is dust? Why is a rainbow arched? I used to feel foolish, even dumb, because I didn't know why or how the sun shines until I learned very recently that the astrophysicists themselves are in a quandary about this."

"The trigger mechanism for creative thinking is the disposition to be curious, to wonder, to inquire," observed Vincent Ruggiero (1988). "Asking 'What's wrong here?' and/or 'Why is this the way it is, and how did it come to be that way?' leads to the identification of problems and challenges." Some occupations actually teach their trainees to think this way. Industrial engineers are taught to walk through a company and question everything, even procedures that have been used for years. But other occupations teach trainees to accept the existing system as "received wisdom" and they discourage criticism.

We hope that you will not approach psychology as received wisdom but will ask many questions about the theories and findings we present in this book. Be on the lookout, too, for questions about human behavior that are *not* answered in the chapters that follow. If you do that, you will not only be learning psychology, you will also be learning to think the way psychologists do.

DEFINE YOUR TERMS Once you've raised a question, the next step is to identify the issues in clear and concrete terms. "What makes people happy?" is a fine question for midnight reveries, but it will not lead to answers unless you have specified what you mean by "happy." Does happiness require being in a constant state of euphoria? Does it simply mean feeling a pleasant contentment with life? Does it mean the absence of serious problems or pain?

Vague or inadequate terms in a question can lead to misleading or incomplete answers. For example, asking, "Can animals learn language?" assumes that language is an all-or-none ability, and the question allows for only two possible answers, yes or no. But putting the question another way—"Which aspects of language might certain animals be able to acquire?"—takes into account the fact that language requires many different abilities. It also acknowledges that there are differences among species and opens up a range of possible answers, as we will see in Chapter 8.

EXAMINE THE EVIDENCE Have you ever heard someone in the heat of argument exclaim, "I just know it's true, no matter what you say" or "That's my opinion; nothing's going to change it" or "If you don't understand my position, I can't explain it"? Have you ever made such statements yourself? Accepting a conclusion without evidence, or expecting others to do so, is a sure sign of uncritical thinking. A critical thinker asks, *What evidence supports or refutes this argument and its opposition? How reliable is the evidence?* If it is not possible to check the reliability of the evidence directly, the critical thinker considers whether it came from a reliable source.

Some pop-psych claims have been widely accepted on the basis of poor evidence or even no evidence at all. For example, many people believe that it is psychologically and physically healthy to ventilate their anger at the first person, pet, or piece of furniture that gets in their way. Actually, studies across many fields suggest that sometimes expressing anger is beneficial, but more often it is not. Often it makes the angry person angrier, makes the target of the anger angry back, lowers everybody's self-esteem, and fosters hostility and aggression (see Chapter 10). Yet the belief that expressing anger is always healthy persists, despite the evidence to the contrary. Can you think of some reasons why this might be so?

ANALYZE ASSUMPTIONS AND BIASES Critical thinkers evaluate the assumptions and biases that lie behind arguments. They ask how these assumptions and biases influence claims and conclusions in the books they read, the political speeches they hear, the news programs they watch, and the ads that bombard them every day. Critical thinkers also are aware of their own assumptions and are willing to question them. For example, many people automatically adopt their parents' ways of doing things. When faced with difficult problems, they will reach for familiar solutions, saying, "If my dad voted Republican (or Democratic), then I should," or "I was brought up to believe that the best way to discipline children is to spank them." But critical thinking requires us to examine our biases when the evidence contradicts them. Everyone, of course, carries around a headful of assumptions about how the world works: Do people have free will, or are they constrained by biology and upbringing? Are government programs the solution to poverty, or would private programs do better? If we don't make our assumptions explicit, our ability to interpret evidence objectively can be seriously impaired.

AVOID EMOTIONAL REASONING Emotion has a place in critical thinking. Passionate commitment to a view can motivate a person to think boldly without fear of what others will say, to defend an unpopular idea, and to seek evidence for creative new theories. Moreover, in the absence of compassion and pity, logic and reason can lead to misguided or even destructive decisions and actions. Indeed, some of the most sadistic killers and military strategists in history have been bright, even brilliant, thinkers. But when gut feelings replace clear thinking, the results are equally dangerous. "Persecutions and wars and lynchings," observed Edward de Bono (1985), "are all a result of gut feeling."

Because our feelings seem so right, it is hard to understand that people with opposing views feel just as strongly as we do. But they usually do, which means that feelings alone are not a reliable guide to the best position. You probably already hold strong beliefs about child rearing, drugs, astrology, the causes of crime, racism, the origins of intelligence, gender differences, homosexuality, and many other issues. As you read this book, you may find yourself quarreling with findings that you dislike. Disagreement is fine; it means you are reading actively. All we ask is that you think about *why* you are disagreeing: Is it because the results conflict with an assumption you hold dear, or because the evidence is unpersuasive? Keep in mind the words of the English poet and essayist Alexander Pope: "What reason weaves, by passion is undone."

Thinking Critically and Creatively About Psychological Issues

Ask questions; be willing to wonder

A Chinese man standing alone against awesome military might inspired millions during the 1989 rebellion in Tiananmen Square. Why do some people have the courage to risk their lives for their beliefs? Why do so many others go along with the crowd or mindlessly obey authority? Social psychologists probe these questions in depth, as we will see in Chapter 17.

Define your terms

People refer to intelligence all the time, but what is it exactly? Does the musical genius of a world-class violinist like Anne-Sophie Mutter count as intelligence? Is intellectual ability captured by an IQ score, or does it also include wisdom and practical "smarts"? We will consider some answers in Chapter 8.

DON'T OVERSIMPLIFY A critical thinker looks beyond the obvious, resists easy generalizations, and rejects either–or thinking. For example, is it better to feel you have control over what happens to you or to accept with tranquility whatever life serves up? Either answer oversimplifies. As we will see in Chapter 14, control has many important benefits, but sometimes it's best to "go with the flow."

Often, in a disagreement, you will hear someone *arguing by anecdote*—generalizing from a personal experience or a few examples to everyone. One crime committed by a paroled ex-convict means parole should be abolished; one friend who hates his or her school means that everybody who goes there hates it. Anecdotes are often the source of stereotyping as well: One dishonest welfare mother means they are all dishonest; one encounter with an unconventional Californian means they are all flaky. And many people make themselves miserable by generalizing from a single unfortunate event to a whole pattern of defeat: "I did poorly on this test, and now I'll never get through college or have a job or kids or anything." Critical thinkers want more evidence than one or two stories before drawing such global conclusions.

CONSIDER OTHER INTERPRETATIONS A critical thinker creatively formulates hypotheses that offer reasonable explanations of the topic at hand. The goal is to find an explanation that accounts for the most evidence with the fewest assumptions. This is called the *principle of Occam's razor,* after the fourteenth-century

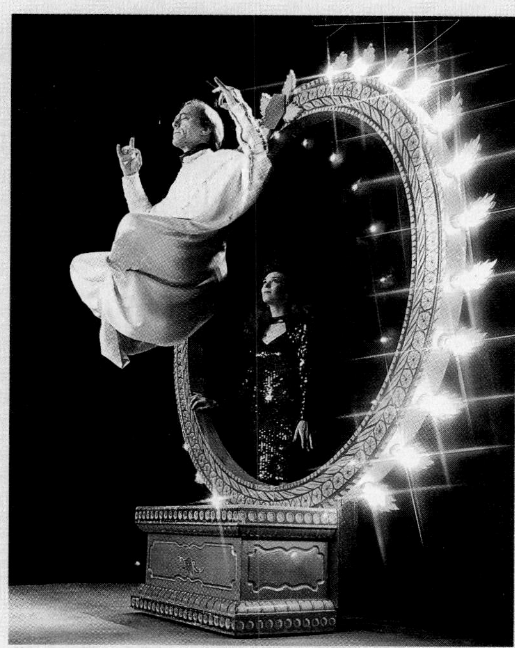

Examine the evidence

When demonstrating "levitation," illusionists such as André Kole take advantage of the fact that people will trust the evidence of their own eyes even when such evidence is misleading, as discussed in Chapter 6.

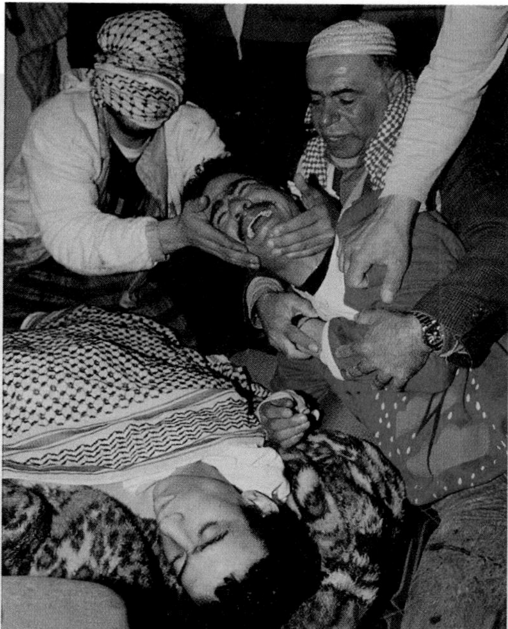

Analyze assumptions and biases

Many North Americans assume that men are "naturally" less expressive emotionally than women. But this Palestinian man, grieving over his dead son, does not fit Western stereotypes. As we will see in Chapters 10 and 18, cultural rules have a powerful influence on when, how, and to whom we express our feelings.

philosopher William of Occam, who proposed it. For example, suppose a fortune-teller offers to read your palm and predict your future. One of two things must be true (Steiner, 1989):

- The fortune-teller can actually sort out the infinite number of interactions among people, animals, events, objects, and circumstances that could affect your life, and know for sure the outcome. Moreover, this particular fortune-teller is able to alter all the known laws of physics and defy the hundreds of studies showing that no one, under proper procedures for validating psychic predictions, has been able to read the future.

OR

- The fortune-teller is faking it.

According to the maxim of Occam's razor, the second alternative is preferable because it requires the fewest assumptions.

On the other hand, critical thinkers are also careful not to shut out alternative explanations too soon. They generate as many interpretations of the evidence as possible before settling on the most likely one. For example, suppose a news bulletin reports that people who are severely depressed are more likely than nondepressed people to develop cancer. Before you can conclude that depression causes cancer, what other explanations might be possible? Perhaps the depressed people who were studied were more likely to smoke and drink too much, and those unhealthful habits caused the cancer. Perhaps an early, undetected cancer was responsible for the feelings of depression.

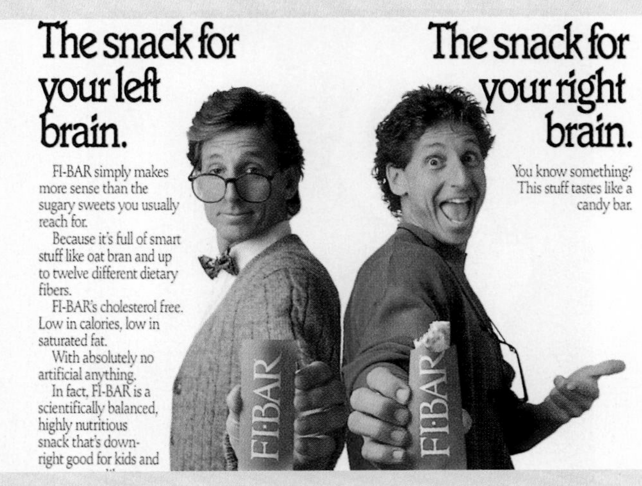
The snack for your left brain.
FI-BAR simply makes more sense than the sugary sweets you usually reach for.
Because it's full of smart stuff like oat bran and up to twelve different dietary fibers.
FI-BAR's cholesterol free. Low in calories, low in saturated fat.
With absolutely no artificial anything.
In fact, FI-BAR is a scientifically balanced, highly nutritious snack that's down-right good for kids and
The snack for your right brain.
You know something? This stuff tastes like a candy bar.
FI-BAR
FI-BAR

Don't oversimplify

Is the left side of the brain entirely analytic, rational, and sensible and the right side always intuitive, emotional, and spontaneous? The two hemispheres of the brain do have some specialized talents, but it's easy to exaggerate the differences, as we will see in Chapter 4.

KEEP ABORTION LEGAL
KEEP ABORTION LEGAL
KEEP ABORTION LEGAL
KEEP ABORTION LEGAL

Avoid emotional reasoning

Passionate feelings about controversial issues can keep us from considering other viewpoints. The resolution of differences requires that we move beyond emotional reasoning and instead weigh point and counterpoint, as discussed in Chapter 8.

TOLERATE UNCERTAINTY Ultimately, learning to think critically teaches us one of the hardest lessons of life: how to live with uncertainty. It is important to examine the evidence before drawing conclusions, but sometimes there is little or no evidence available. Sometimes the evidence merely allows us to draw tentative conclusions. And sometimes the evidence seems good enough to permit strong conclusions . . . until, exasperatingly, new evidence throws our beliefs into disarray. Critical thinkers are willing to accept this state of uncertainty. They are not afraid to say, "I don't know" or "I'm not sure."

The desire for certainty often makes people uncomfortable when experts cannot give them the answers they want. Patients may demand of their doctors, "What do you mean you don't know what's wrong with me? Find out, and fix it!" Students may demand of their professors, "What do you mean it's a controversial issue? Just tell me the answer!" Critical thinkers, however, know that the more important the question, the less likely it is to have a single obvious answer.

The need to accept a certain amount of uncertainty does not mean that we must abandon all beliefs and convictions. That would be impossible, in any case: We all need values and principles to guide our actions. As Vincent Ruggiero (1988) writes, "It is not the embracing of an idea that causes problems—it is the refusal to relax that embrace when good sense dictates doing so."

Like the man who was delighted to learn he had been speaking prose all his life, many people are pleased to find that they already know some of these guidelines of critical and creative thinking. They do it, we might say, without thinking about it. Still, all of us could benefit from shaping up our mental muscles. In this book, you

Consider other interpretations

The Rastafarian church regards ganja *(marijuana) as a "wisdom weed." Will these young Jamaican members react to the drug in the same way as someone who buys it on the street and smokes it alone or at a party? Although people commonly attribute the effects of psychoactive substances solely to the drugs, an alternative explanation emphasizes the impact of setting, motives, and cultural practices, as we will see in Chapters 5 and 15.*

Tolerate uncertainty

Many questions have no easy answers. For example, a number of theories have been offered to explain sexual orientation, but no single explanation can account for the many variations of homosexuality or of heterosexuality, as we will see in Chapter 11.

will have many opportunities to apply critical thinking to psychological theories and to everyday life. From time to time, questions in the margin, accompanied by a glowing light bulb like the one next to the paragraphs above, will draw your attention to discussions in which critical thinking is particularly important. (Feel free to find others!) The light bulb will also appear from time to time in Quick Quizzes, to signal a question that gives you practice in critical thinking skills, and in boxes in every chapter called "Think About It." One kind of Think About It, "Puzzles of Psychology," explores issues that have no easy answers; another, "Issues in Popular Culture," will help you critically evaluate pop-psych claims that make the headlines and the talk shows.

Keep in mind, though, that critical thinking is a process, not a once-and-for-all accomplishment. No one ever becomes a perfect critical thinker, entirely unaffected by emotional reasoning and wishful thinking. Moreover, critical thinking is as much an attitude as it is a set of skills. Sharp debaters can learn to poke holes in the arguments of others, while twisting facts or conveniently ignoring arguments that might contradict their own position. True critical thinking, in the words of philosopher Richard W. Paul (1984), is "fair-mindedness brought into the heart of everyday life."

Perhaps, then, the best way to think about critical thinking is that it is a tool to guide us on a lifelong quest for understanding—a tool that we must keep sharpening. As knowledge grows, so does ignorance, for the more we know, the more questions we think to ask (Kuhn, 1981). As findings accumulate, existing theories become strained. Eventually, they cannot explain all the evidence, no matter how they are stretched. It is like trying to fit a queen-sized sheet onto a king-sized bed. When you tuck the sheet in at the head of the bed, it is too short at the bottom; when you tuck it in at the bottom, it is too short at the top. Eventually you have to get a new sheet or a new bed. Similarly, the scientist eventually is forced either to show that the new findings are wrong or to go out and get a new theory.

Does that mean that there is no such thing as intellectual progress? Not at all. After a theory falls apart, a new and better one may arise from its ashes, explaining more facts, solving more puzzles. This can be frustrating for people who want psychology and other sciences to hand them absolute truths. But it is exciting for those who love the pursuit of understanding as much as the collection of facts. As neuroscientist John C. Eccles (1981) recalled, his training taught him to "rejoice in the refutation of a cherished hypothesis, because that, too, is a scientific achievement and because much has been learned by the refutation."

If you are ready to share in the excitement of studying psychology—if you, like Eccles, love a mystery—then you are ready to read on.

Taking Psychology with You

What Psychology Can Do for You—and What It Can't

If you intend to become a psychologist or a mental-health professional, you have an obvious reason for taking a course in psychology. But psychology can contribute to your life in many ways, whether you plan to work in the field or not. Here are a few things psychology can do for you:

- *Make you a more informed person.* One purpose of education is to acquaint people with their cultural heritage and with humankind's achievements in literature, the humanities, and science. Because psychology plays a large role in contemporary society, being a well-informed person requires knowing something about psychological methods and findings.

- *Satisfy your curiosity about human nature.* When the Greek philosopher Socrates admonished his students to "know thyself," he was only telling them to do what they wanted to do anyway. Throughout history, the topic that has puzzled and fascinated human beings most has been . . . human beings. Psychology, along with the other social sciences, literature, history, and philosophy, can contribute to a better understanding of yourself and others.

• *Help you increase control over your life.* Throughout this book, we will be suggesting ways in which you can apply the findings of psychology to your own life. Psychology cannot solve all your problems, but it does offer techniques that may help you handle your emotions, improve your memory, and eliminate unwanted habits. It can also foster an attitude of objectivity that is useful for analyzing your behavior and your relationships with others.

• *Help you on the job.* A bachelor's degree in psychology is useful for getting a job in a helping profession, for example, as a welfare caseworker or a rehabilitation counselor. But the study of psychology is helpful in all jobs in which psychological insights are useful. Anyone who works as a nurse, doctor, member of the clergy, police officer, or teacher can put psychology to work on the job. So can waiters, flight attendants, bank tellers, salespeople, receptionists, and others whose jobs involve customer service. Finally, psychology can be useful to those whose jobs require them to predict people's behavior—for example, labor negotiators, politicians, advertising copywriters, managers, product designers, buyers, market researchers, magicians. . . .

• *Give you insights into political and social issues.* Crime, drug abuse, discrimination, and war are not only social issues but also psychological ones. Psychological knowledge alone cannot solve the complex political, social, and ethical problems that plague every society, but it can help you make informed judgments about them. For example, if you know that involuntary crowding often leads to stress, hostility, and difficulty concentrating, this knowledge may affect your views on which programs to support for schools and prisons. If you know how cultural practices affect rates of drug use and abuse, this knowledge may affect your views about the war on drugs.

We are optimistic about psychology's role in the world, but we want to caution you that sometimes people expect things from psychology that it cannot deliver. For example:

• *It can't tell you the meaning of life.* Some people follow individual psychologists the way others follow religious leaders and gurus, hoping for enlightenment. Be wary, though, of anyone who promises instant wisdom. A philosophy about the purpose of life requires not only the acquisition of knowledge but also reflection and a willingness to learn from life's experiences.

• *It won't relieve you of responsibility for your actions.* It is one thing to understand the origins of offensive or antisocial behavior and another thing to excuse it. Knowing that your short temper is a result, in part, of your unhappy childhood doesn't give you a green light to yell at your family. Nor does scientific neutrality mean that *society* must be legally or morally neutral. A better understanding of the origins of child beating may help us to reduce child abuse and treat offenders, but we can still hold child beaters accountable for their behavior.

• *It doesn't provide simple answers to complex questions.* You have already learned that psychologists, like other scientists, often disagree among themselves. This disagreement is a normal result of their differing perspectives and methods, and it reflects the fact that most human phenomena—from violence to love—do not lend themselves to one-note explanations. Therefore, rather than becoming attached to any one approach ("Medication will one day cure all mental illnesses"; "With the right environment, any child can become a Mozart"), the critical thinker will try to integrate the best contributions of each. In the epilogue to this book, we suggest how such an integration might apply to problems in love and work.

Three decades ago, in a presidential address to the APA, George Miller (1969) called on his colleagues to "give psychology away." It was time, he said, for them to emerge from their laboratories and to make an impact on the world. "Psychological facts," he said, "should be passed out freely to all who need and can use them."

Ever since, critics have complained that psychologists don't know enough to "give it away." We don't agree. Human behavior is complicated, but that doesn't mean it is beyond understanding; even love is yielding its secrets. At the end of each chapter, starting with the next one, you will have the opportunity to decide whether psychology does, in fact, have something to give away. The "Taking Psychology with You" section will suggest ways to apply psychological findings to your own life—at school, on the job, or in your relationships.

SUMMARY

A MATTER OF DEFINITION

1) *Psychology* is the study of behavior and mental processes and how they are affected by an organism's external and internal environment. In its methods and its reliance on evidence, it differs from pseudoscience and "psychobabble."

2) Psychological findings sometimes confirm, but often contradict, common sense. When psychological results do seem obvious, it is often because people overestimate the ability they might have had to predict the outcome of a study in advance. In any case, a result does not have to be surprising to be scientifically important.

PSYCHOLOGY'S PAST: FROM THE ARMCHAIR TO THE LABORATORY

3) Until the late 1800s, psychology was not a science. A lack of *empirical* evidence often led to serious errors in the description and explanation of behavior. But psychology's forerunners also made valid observations and had useful insights.

4) The official founder of scientific psychology was Wilhelm Wundt, whose work led to *structuralism*, the first of many approaches to the field. Structuralism emphasized the analysis of immediate experience into basic elements. It was soon abandoned because of its reliance on introspection. Another early approach, *functionalism*, emphasized the purpose of behavior. It, too, did not last long as a distinct school of psychology, but it greatly affected the course of psychological science.

PSYCHOLOGY'S PRESENT: BEHAVIOR, BODY, MIND, AND CULTURE

5) Five points of view predominate today in psychology. The *biological perspective* emphasizes bodily events associated with actions, thoughts, and feelings. The *learning perspective* emphasizes the study of observable behavior and rejects mentalistic explanations (*behaviorism*) or combines elements of behaviorism with the study of thoughts, values, and intentions (*social-learning theory*). The *cognitive perspective* emphasizes mental processes in perception, problem solving, belief formation, and other human activities. The *psychodynamic perspective*, which originated with Freud's theory of *psychoanalysis*, emphasizes *intrapsychic*, unconscious motives, conflicts, and desires. The *sociocultural perspective* emphasizes how social and cultural rules, values, and expectations affect individual beliefs and behavior. Each of these approaches has made an important contribution to psychology, and each also has its critics.

6) Not all approaches to psychology fit neatly into one of the five major perspectives. Two important social movements, *humanist psychology* and *feminist psychology*, have influenced the questions researchers ask, the methods they use, and their awareness of biases in the field.

7) Many, if not most, psychologists are eclectic, drawing on more than one school of psychology. However, they disagree about whether it will ever be possible to unite psychology under a single unifying paradigm or whether the discipline will continue to be a mosaic of smaller theories and findings.

WHAT PSYCHOLOGISTS DO

8) Psychologists teach, do research, and provide mental-health services (psychological practice). *Applied psychologists* are concerned with the practical uses of psychological knowledge. *Basic psychologists* are concerned with knowledge for its own sake. Psychological specialties include, among many others, experimental, educational, developmental, industrial/organizational, psychometric, counseling, school, and clinical psychology.

9) *Psychotherapist* is an unregulated word for anyone who does therapy, including even persons who have no credentials or training at all. Licensed therapists differ according to their training and approach: *Clinical psychologists* have a Ph.D., Ed.D., or Psy.D.; *psychiatrists* have an M.D.; *psychoanalysts* are trained in special psychoanalytic institutes; and social workers, school counselors, and marriage, family, and child counselors usually have a master's degree in psychology or social work.

THINKING CRITICALLY AND CREATIVELY ABOUT PSYCHOLOGY

10) One of the greatest benefits of studying psychology is the development of *critical-thinking* skills and attitudes. The critical thinker asks questions, defines terms and issues clearly and accurately, examines the evidence, analyzes assumptions and biases, avoids emotional reasoning, avoids oversimplification, considers alternative interpretations, and tolerates uncertainty. Critical thinking is not for those who want psychology to give final answers and simple solutions, but it can open up many exciting paths in the pursuit of understanding.

KEY TERMS

Use this list to check your understanding of terms and people in this chapter. If you have trouble with a term, you can find it on the page listed.

Possible answers for the "Get Involved" exercise on p. 7: "Opposites attract"; "He who hesitates is lost"; "The pen is mightier than the sword"; "Winning isn't everything, it's the only thing" (often attributed to Vince Lombardi); "You're never too old to learn."

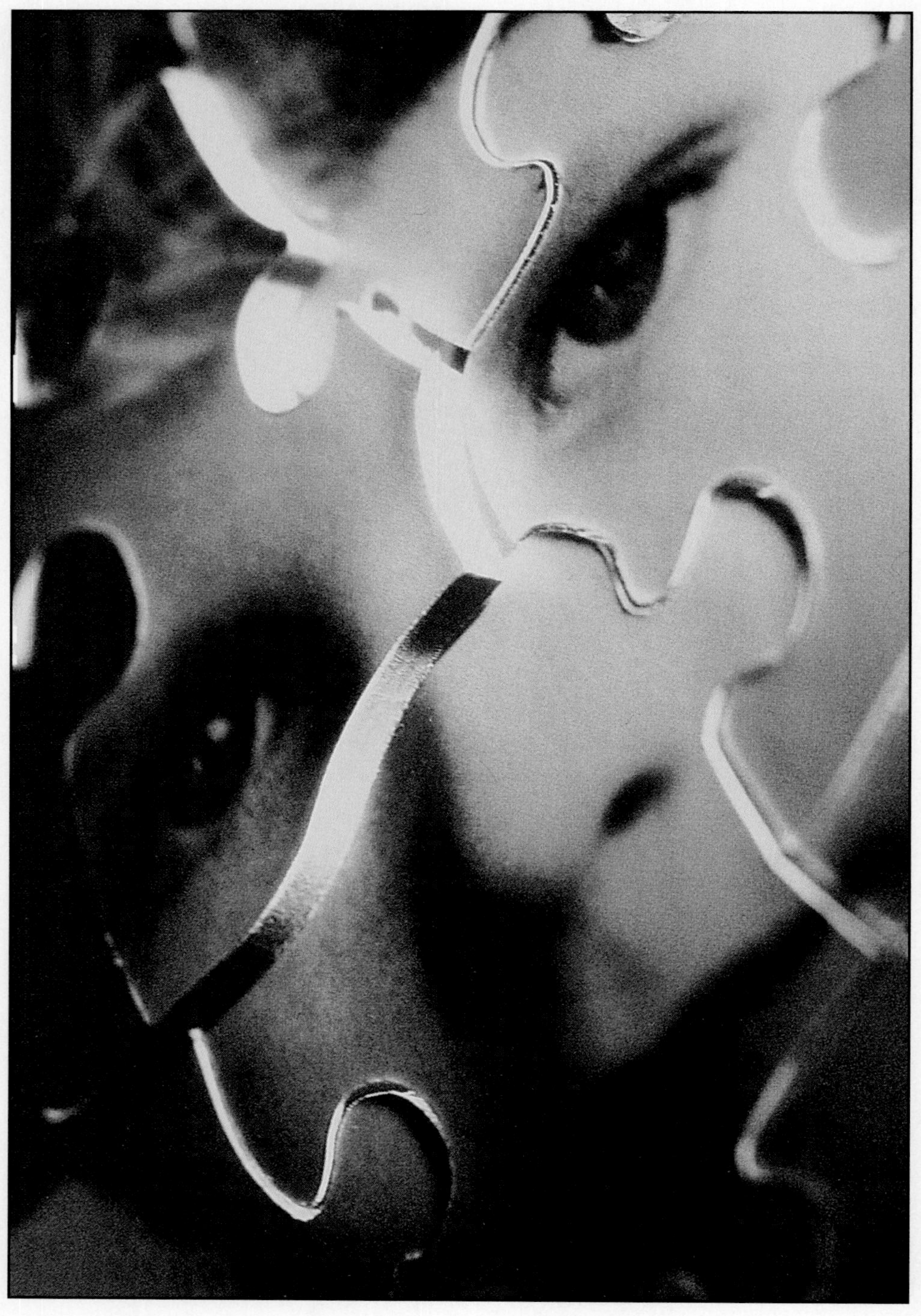

[The essence of science is] to sit down before the fact as a little child,
be prepared to give up every preconceived notion,
follow humbly wherever and to whatever abyss nature leads,
or you shall learn nothing.

Thomas Huxley

CHAPTER TWO

How Psychologists Know What They Know

SUPPOSE THAT YOU ARE THE PARENT of a 9-year-old boy who has been diagnosed as autistic. Your child lives in a silent world of his own, cut off from normal social interaction. He rarely looks you in the eyes. He rocks back and forth for hours, staring aimlessly. Sometimes he does self-destructive things, such as biting through the skin on his fingers or poking pencils in his ears. He does not speak, and he cannot function in a public classroom. You are determined to do something to help him.

"Facilitated communication" is thought by some to be a breakthrough for autistic people. But what does controlled research show?

Imagine your excitement, then, when you hear glowing reports on TV about a new technique, devised by an Australian teacher and now used by several American clinics, that seems to offer your child a way out of his mental prison. According to proponents of this technique, when children who are autistic or mentally impaired are placed in front of a keyboard and an adult gently places a hand over the child's hand or forearm, children who have never used words before are able to peck out complete sentences. One child reportedly typed, "I amn not a utistivc on thje typ" (I am not autistic on the typewriter). You find a clinic that will try such "facilitated communication" with your son. The fee is steep, but you are desperate.

The situation we have described is not hypothetical. In the past few years, thousands of hopeful parents have been drawn to the promise of facilitated communication. Suddenly, after years of profound impairment, their children appear able to answer questions, convey their needs, and divulge their thoughts. Reportedly, some children, through their facilitators, have even mastered high-school-level math and reading; some have written poetry of astonishing beauty, and some have typed out secrets, such as sexual molestation by their fathers and mothers. Facilitated communication, say its boosters, is a miracle.

Or is it?

Psychological scientists have not been content with claims about the effectiveness of this method or persuaded by testimonials. Instead, they have put those claims and testimonials to the test in controlled experiments involving hundreds of autistic children and adults and their facilitators (Jacobson & Mulick, 1994; Mulick, 1994). In one study, researchers arranged things so that the facilitator, although guiding the child's hand, could not see a series of pictures being presented to the child or hear the questions the child was being asked about the pictures. Under these conditions, autistic children did not show any unexpected linguistic abilities (Eberlin et al., 1993). In another study, autistic adults sometimes saw the same picture as the facilitators and sometimes a different one; the only correct descriptions produced by the autistic individuals were for the pictures shown to the facilitator—whether the autistic person saw the pictures or not (Wheeler et al., 1993).

What happens in facilitated communication, this research shows, is exactly what happens when a medium guides a person's hand over a Ouija board to help the person receive "messages" from a "spirit": The person doing the "facilitating" is unconsciously nudging the other person's hand in the desired direction. Facilitated communication, on closer inspection, turns out to be *facilitator* communication. This finding is vitally important, because if parents waste their time and money on a treatment that doesn't work, they may never get genuine help for their children, and they may suffer terribly when their false hopes are finally demolished by reality.

You can see, then, why research methods are so important to psychologists. These methods, which are the tools of the psychologist's trade, allow researchers to distinguish the truth from unfounded belief. They offer a way to sort out conflicting views and to correct false ideas that may otherwise cause people enormous harm. They tell psychologists when to replace simplistic questions with more sophisticated and valuable ones. As we will see in this book, an innovative or clever research method can even reveal answers to questions that once seemed impossible to study.

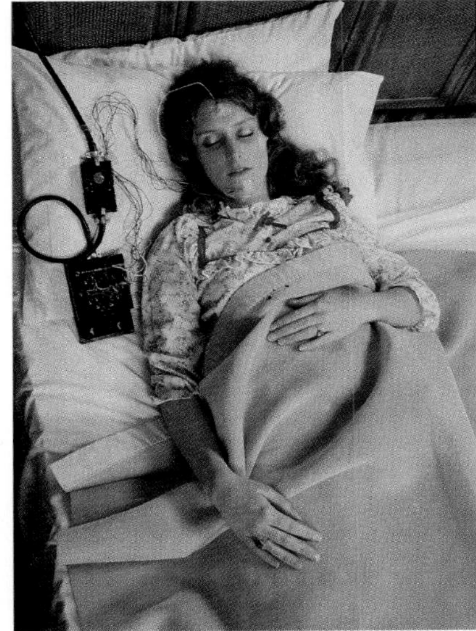

Innovative methods have enabled psychologists to study many questions that once seemed unanswerable. Here, a volunteer in a sleep experiment slumbers peacefully while researchers measure her brain and muscle activity. If awakened during periods of rapid eye movement (REM), she is likely to report that she has been dreaming.

SCIENCE VERSUS PSEUDOSCIENCE

Perhaps you are saying to yourself, "Okay, psychologists need to know about research methods, but why do *I* have to? Why not cut right to the findings?" In this section, we will answer that question and then look at some basic scientific principles that you will need to understand if you are to distinguish good science from bad.

WHY STUDY METHODOLOGY?

One reason to study methodology is that it can help you identify fallacies in your own or other people's thinking. For instance, we are all vulnerable to the *confirmation bias,* the tendency to look for evidence that supports our ideas and ignore evidence that does not (see Chapter 8). Sometimes this bias can have profound personal consequences. Some adults who were physically abused early in life are afraid to have children of their own because they think their experience has ruined them as potential parents. Social workers, judges, and other professionals sometimes make the same assumption: One judge denied a woman custody of her children solely because the woman had been abused as a child, even though she had never harmed her own children. Judgments such as these stem from the notion that abuse inevitably breeds abuse—an inference based mainly on the confirming cases of abused children who later became abusive adults. What about children who suffer abuse but do not grow up to mistreat their children? A person knowledgeable about scientific methods would want to know about both groups, and also about people who were not abused as children and then grew up to be—or not to be—abusive parents (see Table 2.1). When you take *all* the existing data into account, you find that although being abused as a child is certainly a risk factor for becoming an abusive parent, and for other destructive behaviors as well, fully 70 percent of abused children do not later repeat their parents' cruelties (Kaufman & Zigler, 1987; Widom, 1989).

EXAMINE THE EVIDENCE

A psychotherapist has published a paper in which she describes the many abusive parents she has treated who were themselves mistreated as children. Does this mean that most children who are abused will grow up to become abusive parents? What other evidence should be considered?

A second, related reason for studying methodology is to become a more critical and sophisticated consumer of psychological findings reported in books, magazines, newspapers, and on TV. You are constantly being subjected to conflicting claims

TABLE 2.1 *Examining the Evidence*

Is an abused child likely to become an abusive parent? People often base their answers solely on confirming cases, represented by the upper left-hand cell of this table. Psychological researchers consider all four types of evidence in the table.

		Abused as a child?	
		Yes	**No**
Abusive parent?	**Yes**	Abused children who become abusive parents	Nonabused children who become abusive parents
	No	Abused children who do not become abusive parents	Nonabused children who do not become abusive parents

about matters that can affect your life—claims, for example, about how you should break bad habits, manage your emotions, dress for success, settle disputes, overcome shyness, improve your love life, or reduce stress. Not all studies on such matters are good ones, and some advice from self-styled experts is based on no evidence at all.

Because of the dramatic human consequences of misguided psychological advice and the usefulness of well-supported findings, consumers of psychology need to know how to distinguish good research from bad. We hope that when you hear and read about psychological issues, you will consider not only what the findings say, but also how the information was obtained and how the results were interpreted, using guidelines presented in this chapter.

WHAT MAKES RESEARCH SCIENTIFIC?

When we refer to psychologists as scientists, we do not mean that they work with complicated gadgets and machines or wear white lab coats (although some do). The scientific enterprise has more to do with attitudes and procedures than with apparatus and apparel. Philosophers and scientists have written many fat books on the features that distinguish science from other ways of knowing. Here are a few key characteristics of the ideal scientist:

1. *Precision.* Scientists sometimes launch an investigation because they have a hunch about some behavior, based on previous findings or casual observations. Often, however, they start out with a general **theory,** an organized system of assumptions and principles that purports to explain certain phenomena and how they are related. A scientific theory is not just someone's personal opinion, as people imply when they say "It's only a theory." Theories that come to be accepted within the scientific community are consistent with many observations and empirical findings and are inconsistent with only a few or none (Stanovich, 1996).

From a hunch or theory, the scientist derives a **hypothesis,** a statement that attempts to describe or explain a given behavior. Initially, the hypothesis may be stated quite generally, as in "Misery loves company." But before any research can be done, it must be made more specific. For example, "Misery loves company" might be rephrased as "People who are anxious about a threatening situation tend to seek out others who face the same threat."

A hypothesis, in turn, leads to explicit predictions about what will happen in a particular situation. In a prediction, terms such as *anxiety* or *threatening situation* are

theory An organized system of assumptions and principles that purports to explain a specified set of phenomena and their interrelationships.

hypothesis A statement that attempts to describe or explain a given behavior or set of events.

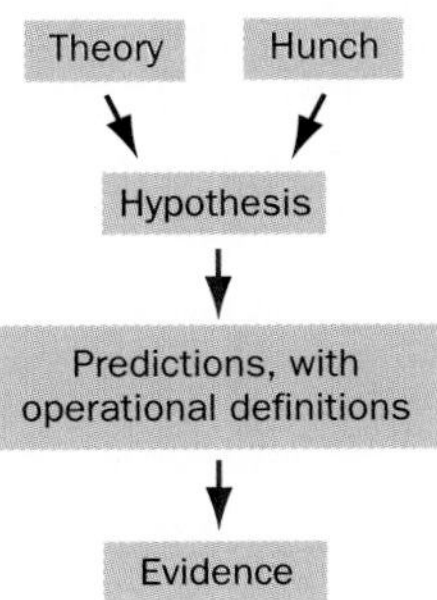

given **operational definitions,** specifications about how the phenomena in question are to be observed and measured. *Anxiety* might be defined operationally as a score on an anxiety questionnaire, and *threatening situation* might be defined as the threat of an electrical shock. The prediction might be, "If you raise people's anxiety scores by telling them they are going to receive electrical shocks, and then you give them the choice of waiting alone or with others in the same situation, they will be more likely to choose to wait with others than they would be if they were not anxious." The prediction is then tested, using careful, systematic procedures. (In contrast, as we saw in Chapter 1, pseudoscientists often hide behind vague, empty terms and make predictions that are nearly meaningless.)

2. *Skepticism.* Scientists do not accept ideas on faith or authority; their motto is "Show me!" Some of the greatest scientific advances have been made by those who dared to doubt what everyone else assumed to be true: that the sun revolves around the earth, that illness can be cured by applying leeches to the skin, that madness is a sign of demonic possession. "Ask an impertinent question," wrote British scientist Jacob Bronowski (1973), "and you are on the way to a pertinent answer." In the world of the researcher, skepticism means exercising caution in accepting conclusions, both new and old. Caution, however, must be balanced by an openness to new ideas and evidence. Otherwise, the scientist may wind up as shortsighted as the famous physicist Lord Kelvin, who at the end of the nineteenth century reputedly declared with great confidence that radio had no future, X rays were a hoax, and "heavier-than-air flying machines" were impossible.

3. *Reliance on empirical evidence.* Unlike plays and poems, scientific theories and hypotheses are not judged by how pleasing or entertaining they are. An idea may initially generate excitement because it is plausible, imaginative, or appealing. But no matter how true or right it may seem, eventually it must be backed by evidence if it is to be taken seriously. As Nobel Prize–winning scientist Peter Medawar (1979) wrote, "The intensity of the conviction that a hypothesis is true has no bearing on whether it is true or not." Further, as we noted in Chapter 1, the evidence for a scientific idea must be empirical—that is, based on careful and systematic observation. A collection of anecdotes or an appeal to authority will not do.

Consider again the problem of childhood autism. At one time, many clinicians thought that this disorder was caused by a rejecting, cold "refrigerator mother." They were influenced in this belief by the writings of the eminent psychoanalyst Bruno Bettelheim, especially his book *The Empty Fortress* (1967). Bettelheim's only evidence consisted of case studies of 3 autistic children whose mothers had a history of psychological problems. He also alluded to 37 other cases he had treated, but he published no facts about them, and he seems to have exaggerated the number of children he cured (Pollak, 1997). Yet Bettelheim's authority was so great that many people accepted his claims in spite of his meager data. Then some researchers began to have doubts about Bettelheim's ideas. Instead of relying on subjective impressions, as Bettelheim had done, they compared the parents of autistic children with parents who did not have an autistic child, using standardized tests of psychological adjustment and analyzing their data statistically. The results were clear: The two groups of parents did not differ in terms of personality traits, marital adjustment, or family life (DeMyer, 1975; Koegel et al., 1983). Bruno Bettelheim had been wrong, and because of his advice, thousands of parents had mistakenly believed that they were responsible for their children's disorder, suffering needless guilt and remorse. Today, scientists generally agree that autism stems from a neurological problem rather than from any psychological problems of the parents.

4. *Willingness to make "risky predictions."* A scientist must state an idea in such a way that it can be *refuted,* or disproved by counterevidence. This principle, known as

operational definition A precise definition of a term in a hypothesis, which specifies the operations for observing and measuring the process or phenomenon being defined.

∴ can something be falsified

the **principle of falsifiability,** does not mean that the idea *will* be disproved, only that it *could* be if contrary evidence were to be discovered. Another way of saying this is that a scientist must risk disconfirmation by predicting not only what will happen, but also what will *not* happen. In the "misery loves company" study, the hypothesis would be refuted if most anxious people went off alone to sulk and worry, or if anxiety had no effect on their behavior. A willingness to make "risky" predictions forces the scientist to take such negative evidence seriously. Any researcher who refuses to go out on a limb and risk disconfirmation is not a true scientist; and any theory that purports to explain everything that could conceivably happen is unscientific.

The principle of falsifiability is violated all the time by people claiming to have psychic powers. For example, some people think they can find subterranean water by holding a "dowsing rod" out in front of them and walking around until the rod bends down toward water hidden below. Some dowsers use special steel rods; others prefer such mundane objects as a straightened coat hanger or a forked branch. Dowsers believe that they have special psychic powers that account for the rod's behavior; actually the rod bends because of the involuntary movements of their own hands. (Unconscious hand movements again!) Illusionist and professional debunker James Randi (1982) has been challenging dowsers' claims for years by conducting controlled tests using scientific procedures to which the dowsers themselves agree. He predicts that the dowsers will do no better than chance, and he offers a reward of thousands of dollars to any dowser who proves him wrong. Randi has never lost a cent; invariably the dowsers perform at chance levels. Yet despite these failures, they rarely lose faith in their abilities. Ignoring the principle of falsifiability, they blame the negative results on the alignment of the planets, or sunspots, or bad vibes from spectators. To a dowser, it really doesn't matter how the dowsing demonstration turns out because the dowser has all the bases covered in advance (see Figure 2.1).

If you keep your eyes open, you will find other violations of the principle of falsifiability. For example, research psychologists, the FBI, and police investigators have been unable to substantiate the supposedly murderous activities of satanic cults (Goodman et al., 1995; Hicks, 1991). But that doesn't keep some police officers and therapists from believing that such cults and their crimes are widespread. Believers say they are not surprised by the lack of evidence because satanic cults cover up their activities by eating bodies or burying them. The FBI's failure to find the evidence is "proof," they say, that the FBI is part of a conspiracy to support the satanists. To believers, then, the lack of evidence of satanic cults is actually a sign of the cults' success. But think about that claim. If a lack of evidence can count as evidence, then what could possibly count as *counter*evidence?

5. *Openness.* Scientists must be willing to tell others where they got their ideas, how they tested them, and what the results were. They must do this clearly and in detail so that other scientists can repeat, or *replicate,* their studies and verify the findings.

Replication is an important part of the scientific process because sometimes what seems to be a fabulous phenomenon turns out to be only a fluke. For example, many years ago, a team of researchers trained flatworms to cringe in response to a flashing light, and then they killed the worms, ground them into a mash, and fed the mash to a second set of worms. This cannibalistic diet, the researchers reported, sped up acquisition of the cringe response in the second group of worms (McConnell, 1962). As you can imagine, this finding caused tremendous excitement. If worms could learn faster by ingesting the "memory molecules" of their fellow worms, could memory pills be far behind? Students joked about grinding up professors; professors joked about doing brain transplants in students. But alas, the results could not be replicated, and talk of memory pills eventually faded away.

principle of falsifiability The principle that a scientific theory must make predictions that are specific enough to expose the theory to the possibility of disconfirmation; that is, the theory must predict not only what will happen, but also what will not happen.

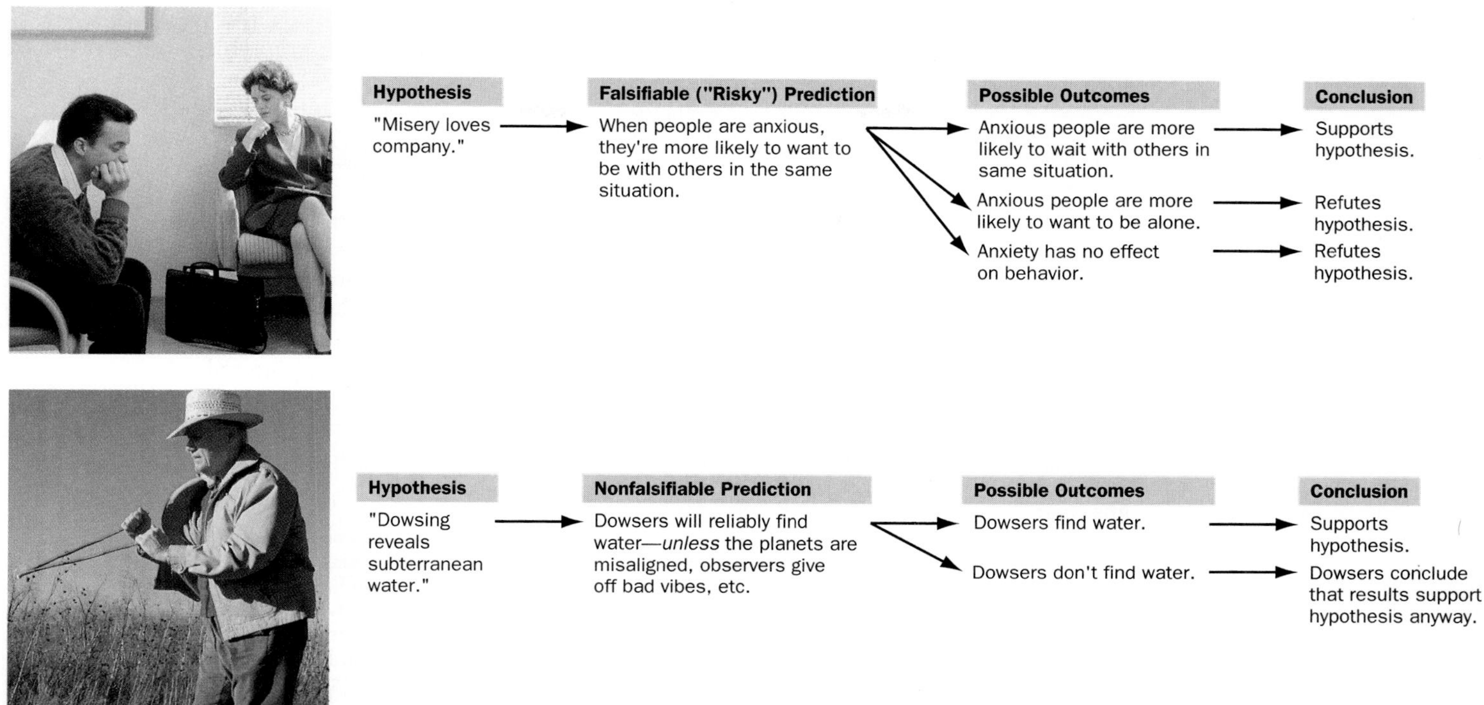

Figure 2.1
The Principle of Falsifiability

The scientific method requires researchers to expose their ideas to possible counterevidence. In contrast, pseudoscientists and people claiming psychic powers typically interpret *all* possible outcomes as support for their assertions, and so their claims are untestable.

Do psychologists and other scientists always live up to the lofty standards expected of them? Of course not. Being human, they may put too much trust in their personal experiences. They may deceive themselves. They may permit ambition to interfere with openness. They may fail to put their theories fully to the test: It is always easier to be skeptical about someone else's ideas than about your own pet theory.

Commitment to one's theories is not in itself a bad thing. Passion is the fuel of progress. It motivates researchers to think boldly, defend unpopular ideas, and do the extensive testing that is often required to support an idea. But passion can also cloud perceptions and in some sad cases has even led to deception and fraud. That is why science must be a *communal* activity. Scientists are expected to share their evidence and procedures with others. They are expected to submit their results to professional journals, which send the findings to experts in the field for comment before publishing them. Through this process, called *peer review,* scientists demonstrate that their position is well supported. The scientific community—in our case, the psychological community—acts as a jury, scrutinizing and sifting the evidence, approving some viewpoints and relegating others to the scientific scrap heap. This public process is not perfect, but it does give science a built-in system of checks and balances. Individuals are not necessarily objective, honest, or even rational, but science forces them to justify their claims.

Quick Quiz

Test your understanding of science by identifying which of its rules was violated in each of the following cases.

1. For years, writer Norman Cousins told how he had cured himself of a rare, life-threatening disease through a combination of humor and vitamins. In a best-selling book about his experience, he recommended the same approach to others.
2. Alfred Russel Wallace, an eminent nineteenth-century British naturalist, became fascinated by attempts to communicate with the dead. To prove that such communication was possible, he had mediums conduct séances. He trusted these mediums and was persuaded by their demonstrations.
3. Benjamin Rush, a physician and signer of the Declaration of Independence, believed that illnesses accompanied by fever should be treated by bloodletting. During an outbreak of yellow fever, many patients whom he treated in this manner died. Yet Rush did not lose faith in his approach; he attributed each case of improvement to his treatment and each death to the severity of the disease (Stanovich, 1996).

Answers:

1. Cousins offered only a personal account and did not gather empirical evidence from controlled studies or consider cases of sick people who were not helped by humor and vitamins. 2. Wallace was gullible rather than skeptical. 3. Rush violated the principle of falsifiability: He interpreted a patient's survival as support for his treatment and explained a death by saying that the person had been too ill for the treatment to work. Thus there was no possible counterevidence that could refute the theory (which, by the way, was dead wrong—the "treatment" was actually as dangerous as the disease).

FERRETING OUT THE FACTS: DESCRIPTIVE STUDIES

Psychologists use several different methods in their research, depending on the kinds of questions they want to answer. These methods are not mutually exclusive. Just as a police detective may use a magnifying glass *and* a fingerprint duster *and* interviews of suspects to figure out "who done it," psychological sleuths often draw on different techniques at different stages of an ongoing investigation.

Many psychological methods are descriptive in nature. **Descriptive methods** allow a researcher to describe and predict behavior but not necessarily to choose one explanation over other, competing ones. Some of these methods are used primarily by clinicians to describe and understand the behavior of individuals. Others are used primarily by researchers to compare groups of people and arrive at generalizations about behavior. And some methods can be used in either way. In this section, we will discuss the most common descriptive methods. As you read, you might want to list each method's advantages and disadvantages on a piece of paper. When you finish this and the next two sections, check your list against the one in Table 2.2 on page 64.

CASE STUDIES

A **case study** (or *case history*) is a detailed description of a particular individual. It may be based on careful observation or on formal psychological testing. It may include information about the person's childhood, dreams, fantasies, experiences, relationships, and hopes—anything that will provide insight into the person's behavior. Case studies are most commonly used by clinicians, but they are sometimes used by academic researchers as well. They are especially valuable in the investigation of a new topic. Many language researchers, for example, have started out by keeping detailed diaries on the language development of their own children. A case study can be a rich source of hypotheses for future research.

descriptive methods Methods that yield descriptions of behavior but not necessarily causal explanations.

case study A detailed description of a particular individual being studied or treated.

Case studies illustrate psychological principles in a way that abstract generalizations and cold statistics never can. They also produce a more detailed picture of an individual than other methods do. Often, however, case studies depend on people's memories of the past, and such memories may be both selective and inaccurate. Also, it is often hard to choose one interpretation of a case over another. Most important, the case-study method has limited usefulness for psychologists who want to generalize about human behavior, because a person who is the subject of a case study may be unlike most other people about whom the researcher would like to draw conclusions. (Recall that one of Bruno Bettelheim's errors was to assume that the mothers he studied were representative of all parents of autistic children.)

Still, case studies can be enlightening when practical or ethical considerations prevent information from being gathered in other ways, or when unusual circumstances shed light on an issue. Here's an example. Many psychologists believe that a critical period for normal language development occurs between age 1 and age 5 or 6, with the likelihood of mastering a first language declining steadily after that and falling off drastically at puberty (Curtiss, 1977; Pinker, 1994b; Tartter, 1986). During these years, children need to hear speech (or if they are deaf, to see signs) and to enjoy close relationships with people who give them an opportunity to practice the arts and skills of conversation. If children lack these early experiences, they will be unable to catch up completely later on, no matter how much tutoring they are given. How can psychologists test this hypothesis? Obviously, they cannot put children in solitary confinement until adolescence! However, they can study the tragic cases of children who were abandoned, abused, and isolated by their parents and were therefore prevented from acquiring language until they were rescued, sometimes after many years of solitude. Such cases often leave important questions unanswered: How long was the child alone? At what age was the child isolated or abandoned? Was the child born mentally impaired? Did the child have a chance to learn any language before the ordeal began? Nonetheless, these cases can still provide valuable information.

One such case involved a 13-year-old girl whose parents had locked her up in one small room since she was $1\frac{1}{2}$ years old. During the day, they usually kept her strapped in a child's potty seat. At night, they confined her to a straitjacket-like sleeping bag. The mother, a battered wife who lived in terror of her severely disturbed husband, barely cared for her daughter. Although the child may have been able to hear some speech through the walls of her room, there was no television or radio in the home, and no one spoke a word to her. If she made the slightest sound, her father beat her with a large piece of wood.

Genie, as researchers later called her, hardly seemed human when she was finally set free. She did not know how to chew or to stand erect, and she was not toilet trained. She slobbered uncontrollably, masturbated in public, and spat on anything that was handy, including herself and other people. When she was first observed by psychologists, her only sounds were high-pitched whimpers. She understood only a few words, most of them probably learned shortly after her release. Yet Genie was alert and curious. Placed in a hospital rehabilitation center and then a foster home, she developed physically, learned some basic rules of social conduct, and established relationships with others. Gradually she began to use words and understand short sentences. Eventually she was able to use language to convey her needs, describe her moods, and even tell lies. Her grammar and pronunciation of words, however, remained abnormal, even after several years. She could not use pronouns correctly, ask questions, produce proper negative sentences, or use the little word endings that communicate tense, conjunction, number, and possession (Curtiss, 1977, 1982;

This picture was drawn by Genie, a young girl who endured years of isolation and mistreatment. It shows one of her favorite pastimes: listening to researcher Susan Curtiss play the piano. Genie's drawings were used along with other case material to study her mental and social development.

Rymer, 1993). Such sad evidence, and other similar cases, support the hypothesis that a critical period exists for language acquisition.

Ironically, then, unusual cases can sometimes shed light on a general question about human functioning. Most case studies, however, are sources, rather than tests, of hypotheses. You should be extremely cautious about pop-psych books and TV programs that present only testimonials and vivid case histories as evidence.

OBSERVATIONAL STUDIES

The man asking for a handout is in reality a psychologist doing an observational study to find out how people react to panhandlers. A tape recorder hidden beneath his shirt records their responses.

In **observational studies,** the researcher systematically observes and records behavior without interfering in any way with the people (or animals) being observed. Unlike case studies, observational studies usually involve many subjects (participants). Often an observational study is the first step in a program of research; it is helpful to have a good description of behavior before you try to explain it.

The primary purpose of *naturalistic observation* is to describe behavior as it occurs in the natural environment. Ethologists such as Jane Goodall and the late Dian Fossey used this method to study apes and other animals in the wild. Psychologists use naturalistic observation wherever people happen to be—at home, on playgrounds or streets, in schoolrooms, or in offices. In one study using naturalistic observation, a social psychologist and his students ventured into a common human habitat: bars. They wanted to know whether people in bars drink more when they are in groups than when they are alone. They visited all 32 pubs in a midsized city, ordered beers, and recorded on napkins and pieces of newspaper how much the other patrons imbibed. They found that drinkers in groups consumed more than individuals who were alone. Those in groups didn't drink any faster; they just lingered in the bar longer (Sommer, 1977).

Note that the student researchers in this study did not rely on their impressions or memories of how much people drank. In observational studies, it is important to *count, rate,* or *measure* behavior in a systematic way. These procedures help to minimize the tendency of most observers to notice only what they expect or want to see. Careful record keeping ensures accuracy and allows different observers to cross-check their observations for consistency. Note, too, that the researchers who studied drinking habits took pains to avoid being obvious about what they were doing. If they had marched in with video cameras and announced that they were psychology students, the bar patrons might not have behaved naturally. In many studies, researchers have concealed themselves entirely. When such precautions are taken, naturalistic observation gives us a glimpse of people as they really are, in their normal social contexts. However, it does not tell us what *causes* their behavior. For example, the barroom results do not necessarily mean that being in a group makes people drink a lot. People may join a group because they are already interested in drinking and find it more comfortable to hang around the bar if they are with others.

observational study A study in which the researcher carefully and systematically observes and records behavior without interfering with the behavior; it may involve either naturalistic or laboratory observation.

GET INVOLVED

Try a little naturalistic observation of your own. Go to a public place where people voluntarily seat themselves near others, such as a movie theater or a cafeteria with large tables. If you choose a setting where many people enter at once, you might recruit some friends to help you; you can divide the area into sections and assign each observer one section to observe. As individuals and groups sit down, note how many seats they leave between themselves and the next person. On the average, how far do people tend to sit from strangers? Once you have your results, see how many possible explanations you can come up with.

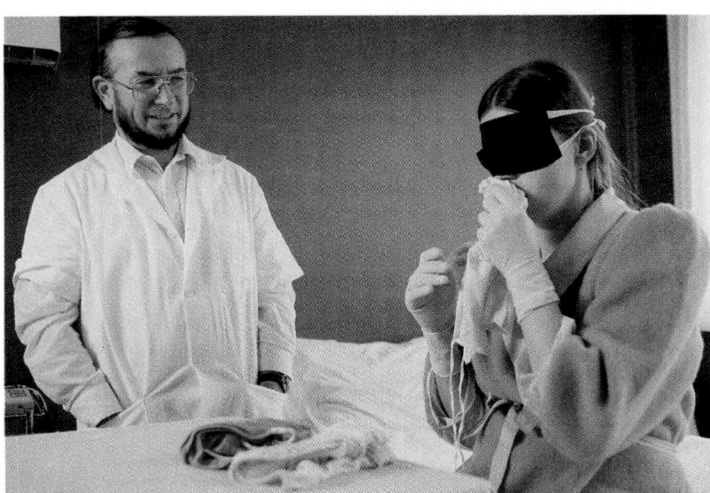

In the natural environment, with its many distractions and scents, it might be hard to tell whether mothers and infants can recognize one another's odors. But using laboratory methods, French ethologist Hubert Montagner (1985) found that mothers can actually distinguish their own baby's shirt from the shirts of other newborns on the basis of smell alone.

Sometimes it is preferable or necessary to make observations in the laboratory rather than in real-world settings. In *laboratory observation,* the psychologist has more control. He or she can use sophisticated equipment, determine how many people will be observed at once, maintain a clear line of vision while observing, and so forth. Suppose, for example, that you wanted to know how infants of different ages respond when left in the company of a stranger. You could observe children at a nursery school, but most would probably already be toddlers and would know the nursery-school teachers. You could visit private homes, but that might be slow and inconvenient. A solution would be to have parents and their infants come to your laboratory, observe them playing together for a while through a one-way window, then have a stranger enter the room and, a few minutes later, have the parent leave. You could record signs of distress, interactions with the stranger, and other behavior. If you did this, you would find that very young infants carry on cheerfully with whatever they are doing when the parent leaves. However, by the age of about 8 months, children often burst into tears or show other signs of what child psychologists call "separation anxiety" (Ainsworth, 1979).

One shortcoming of laboratory observation is that the presence of researchers and special equipment may cause subjects to behave differently than they would in their usual surroundings. Another is that laboratory observations, like naturalistic observations, are more useful for describing behavior than for explaining it. If we observe infants protesting whenever a parent leaves the room, we cannot be sure *why* they are protesting. Is it because they have become attached to their parents and want them nearby, or have they learned from experience that crying brings attention and affection? It is hard to know on the basis of observational studies alone.

TESTS

Psychological tests, sometimes called *assessment instruments,* are procedures used for measuring and evaluating personality traits, emotional states, aptitudes, interests, abilities, and values. Typically, such tests require people to answer a series of written or oral questions. The answers may then be totaled to yield a single numerical score (or a set of scores) that reveals something about the person. *Objective tests,* also called "inventories," measure beliefs, feelings, or behaviors of which an individual is aware; *projective tests* are designed to tap unconscious feelings or motives (see Chapter 12).

psychological tests Procedures used to measure and evaluate personality traits, emotional states, aptitudes, interests, abilities, and values.

At one time or another, most people have probably taken a psychological test, such as an intelligence test, achievement test, or vocational-aptitude test. You may have taken other kinds of tests when applying for a job, joining the military, or starting psychotherapy. Hundreds of psychological tests are used in industry, education, research, and the helping professions. Some are given to individuals, others to large groups. These measures help clarify differences among individuals, as well as differences in the reactions of the same individual on different occasions or at different stages of life. They may be used to promote self-understanding, to evaluate treatments and programs, or, in scientific research, to draw generalizations about human behavior. Well-constructed psychological tests are a great improvement over simple self-evaluation because many people have a distorted view of their own abilities and traits.

One test of a good test is whether it is **standardized**—that is, whether there are uniform procedures for giving and scoring it. It would hardly be fair to give some people detailed instructions and plenty of time and others only vague instructions and limited time. Those who administer the test must know exactly how to explain the tasks involved, how much time to allow, and what materials to use. Scoring is usually done by referring to **norms,** or established standards of performance. The usual procedure for developing norms is to give the test to a large group of people who resemble those for whom the test is intended. Norms tell users of the test which scores can be considered high, low, or average.

Test construction, administration, and interpretation present many challenges. For one thing, the test must be **reliable**—that is, it must produce the same results from one time and place to the next. A vocational-interest test is not reliable if it tells Tom that he would make a wonderful engineer but a poor journalist, but then gives different results when Tom retakes the test a week later.

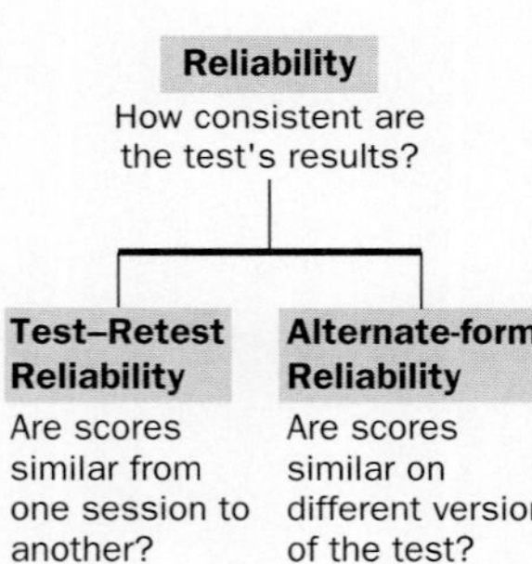
Reliability
How consistent are the test's results?
Test–Retest Reliability
Are scores similar from one session to another?
Alternate-forms Reliability
Are scores similar on different versions of the test?

Psychologists evaluate a test's reliability in several ways. One common way is to measure *test–retest reliability* by giving the test twice to the same group of people, then comparing the two sets of scores statistically. If the test is reliable, individuals' scores will be similar from one session to another. This method has a drawback, however: People tend to do better the second time they take a test, after they have become familiar with the strategies required and the test items used. A solution is to compute *alternate-forms reliability,* by giving different versions of the same test to the same group on two separate occasions. The items on the two forms are similar in format but are not identical in content. With this method, performance cannot improve because of familiarity with the items, although people may still do somewhat better the second time around because they have learned the general strategies and procedures expected of them.

In order to be useful, a test must also be **valid;** that is, it must measure what it sets out to measure. A creativity test is not valid if what it actually measures is verbal sophistication. If the items broadly represent the trait in question, the test is said to have *content validity.* Suppose you constructed a test to measure employees' job satisfaction. If your test tapped a broad sampling of relevant beliefs and behaviors (e.g., "Do you feel you have reached a dead end at work?" "Are you bored with your assignments?"), it would have content validity. If the test asked only how workers felt about their salary level, it would lack content validity and would be of little use; after all, workers who are satisfied with their pay do not necessarily enjoy their work, and workers can enjoy their work without necessarily feeling that they are paid well.

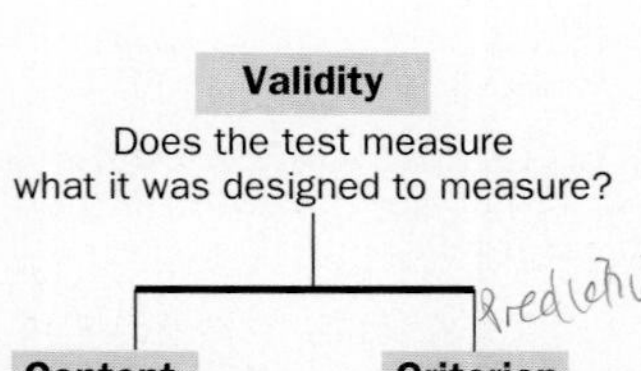
Validity
Does the test measure what it was designed to measure?
Content Validity
Do items broadly represent the trait in question?
Criterion Validity
Do the test results predict other measures of the trait?

Most tests are also judged on *criterion validity,* the ability to predict other, independent measures, or criteria, of the trait in question. The criterion for a scholastic aptitude test might be college grades; the criterion for a test of shyness might be behavior in social situations. To find out whether your job-satisfaction test had criterion validity, you might return a year later to see whether it correctly predicted absenteeism, resignations, or requests for job transfers.

Unfortunately, teachers, parents, and employers do not always stop to question a test's validity, especially when results are summarized in a single number such as an IQ score or a job applicant's ranking. Instead, they simply assume that the test measures what it claims to measure. Robert Sternberg (1988) has noted that this assumption is especially common with mental tests, even though, he argues, such tests tap only a limited set of abilities important for intelligent behavior. "There is an allure to exact-sounding numbers," says Sternberg. "An IQ of 119, an SAT score of 580, a mental abilities score in the 74th percentile—all sound very precise. . . . But the appearance of precision is no substitute for the fact of validity."

Among psychologists and educators, the validity of even some widely used tests is controversial. For example, "integrity tests," which probe for such personality traits as hostility to authority, conscientiousness, and "wayward impulses," are given to millions of job applicants each year in an effort to predict dishonesty and drug use in the workplace. Such tests may be more reliable and valid than interviews and other methods, but they generally fail to meet the standards of experts in assessment. Experts disagree about what these tests are actually measuring, and some are extremely worried that many people who fail such tests are not actually dishonest (Camera & Schneider, 1994; Sackett, 1994; Saxe, 1994).

The Scholastic Assessment Test (SAT)—formerly called the Scholastic Aptitude Test—has also come under fire. Stuart Katz and his colleagues studied the reading-comprehension section of this test, which requires students to read a passage and then answer multiple-choice questions about it (Katz, Blackburn, & Lautenschlager, 1991; Katz & Lautenschlager, 1994). Undergraduates, they found, can do well on most questions *even without reading the passages,* although not as well as when they do read them. Katz and his colleagues concluded that SAT reading-comprehension items do not measure pure reading comprehension, as they are purported to do; these items also tap general knowledge and test-taking skills.

Criticisms and reevaluations of psychological tests keep psychological assessment honest and scientifically rigorous. In contrast, the pseudoscientific psychological tests frequently found in magazines and newspapers usually have not been evaluated for validity or reliability. These questionnaires often have inviting headlines such as "How's Your Power Motivation?" or "Are You Self-destructive?" or "The Seven Types of Lover," but they are only lists of questions that someone thought sounded good.

SURVEYS

Psychological tests usually generate information about people indirectly. In contrast, **surveys** are questionnaires and interviews that gather information about people by asking them *directly* about their experiences, attitudes, or opinions. Most people are familiar with surveys in the form of national opinion polls, such as the Gallup and Roper polls. Surveys have been done on many topics, from consumer preferences to sexual preferences—and sometimes they not only reflect people's attitudes and behavior but also influence them (see "Puzzles of Psychology").

Surveys produce bushels of data, but they are not easy to do well. The biggest hurdle is getting a **representative sample,** a group of subjects that represents the larger population that the researcher wishes to describe. Suppose you want to know about drug use among college sophomores. It would not be practical to question every college sophomore in the country; instead, you must choose a sample. Special selection procedures can be used to ensure that this sample will contain the same proportion of women, men, blacks, whites, poor people, rich people, Catholics, Jews, and so on as in the general population of college sophomores.

standardize In test construction, to develop uniform procedures for giving and scoring a test.

norms In test construction, established standards of performance.

reliability In test construction, the consistency, from one time and place to another, of scores derived from a test.

validity The ability of a test to measure what it was designed to measure.

surveys Questionnaires and interviews that ask people directly about their experiences, attitudes, or opinions.

representative sample A sample that matches the population in question on important characteristics, such as age and sex.

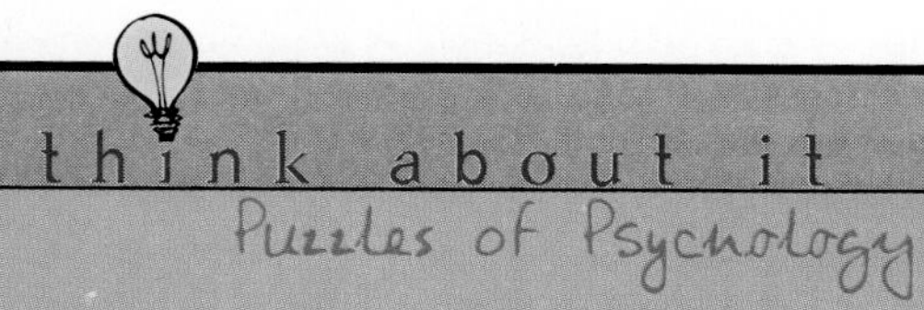

Surveys, Public Opinion, and You

According to a nationwide survey, 67 percent of all students have had sexual intercourse by age 16.

According to a nationwide survey, 27 percent of all students have had sexual intercourse by age 16.

Do you find yourself wanting to believe one of these results rather than the other because it matches your own sexual history? Would one figure make you feel normal and the other make you feel odd? Might either finding influence you to change your own behavior? If so, you are not alone. Opinion polls and surveys not only reflect but can also *affect* people's feelings and behavior.

Many people form their views by studying a sample of one: themselves. Or perhaps they expand the sample a bit to include their sister, their best friend, and the neighborhood grocer. They assume that their own beliefs and actions, or those of people they know, are typical of "most people." Gary Marks and Norman Miller (1987) called this tendency the *false-consensus effect.* By overestimating the degree of agreement between themselves and others, said Marks and Miller, people maintain their self-esteem and reduce the discomfort of feeling different or weird. But the false-consensus effect can also keep people from recognizing other points of view and can make them discount information that challenges their own ways.

In addition to thinking that everyone is like them, people tend to think that they themselves *ought* to be like everyone else. As a consequence, when they find themselves in the minority, they may become apathetic, concluding that "there's no point trying to do anything." Or they may do things they consider wrong, or alter their beliefs, because "everybody" (according to the surveys) is doing something or feels a certain way, and they don't want to be different. This tendency to unconsciously tailor opinions to fit prevailing trends makes public opinion a potent form of social control. Sociologist Elisabeth Noelle-Neumann (1984) described a German election in which two parties were neck and neck until polls gave one party a slight edge. "And then, right at the end, people jumped on the bandwagon," she wrote. "As if caught in a current, 3–4 percent of the votes were swept in the direction of the general expectation of who was going to win."

How can people resist the false-consensus effect? What can be done to limit the influence of political polls during elections? How will you react if you come across findings in this book that show your opinions or habits to be in the minority? Think about it.

Every time I think I'm part of a normal relationship...
Someone publishes a new survey.

ANALYZE ASSUMPTIONS AND BIASES

A magazine has just published a survey of its female readers, called "The Sex Life of the American Wife." The survey reports that "Eighty-seven percent of all wives like to make love in rubber boots." The assumption is that this sample is representative of married American women. Is this assumption justified? What would be a more accurate title for the survey?

A sample's size is less critical than its representativeness; a small but representative sample may yield extremely accurate results, whereas a survey or poll that fails to use proper sampling methods may yield questionable results, no matter how large the sample. A radio station that asks its listeners to vote yes or no by telephone on a controversial question is hardly conducting a scientific poll. Only those who feel quite strongly about the issue *and* who happen to be listening to that particular station are likely to call in, and those who feel strongly may be likely to take a particular side. A psychologist or statistician would say that the poll suffers from a **volunteer bias:** Those who volunteer probably differ from those who stay silent.

Many magazines—*Redbook, Cosmopolitan, Playboy, The Ladies' Home Journal*—have done highly publicized surveys on the sexual habits and attitudes of their readers, but these surveys, too, are vulnerable to the volunteer bias. Readers motivated to respond to such surveys may be more (or possibly less) sexually active, on the average, than those who do not respond. In addition, people who read magazines regularly tend to be younger, more educated, and more affluent than the population as a whole, and these characteristics may affect the results. When you read about a survey (or any other kind of study), always ask what sorts of people participated. A biased, nonrepresentative sample does not necessarily mean that a survey is worthless or uninteresting, but it does mean that the results may not hold for other groups.

Another problem with surveys is that people sometimes lie. This is especially likely when the survey is about a touchy topic ("What? Me do that disgusting/dishonest/fattening thing? Never!"). The likelihood of lying is reduced when respondents are guaranteed anonymity. Also, there are ways to check for lying—for example, by asking a question several times with different wording. But not all surveys use these techniques, and even when people are trying to be truthful, they may misinterpret the survey questions or misremember the past (Tanur, 1992).

When considering the results of a survey or opinion poll, it is also important to notice how the questions were phrased. Political pollsters often design questions to produce the results they want. A Republican might ask people whether they support "increasing the amount spent on Medicare at a slower rate," whereas a Democrat might ask whether people favor "cuts in the projected growth of Medicare." The two phrases mean the same thing, but respondents are likely to react more negatively when the word "cuts" is used (Kolbert, 1995).

As you can see, although surveys can be extremely informative, they must be conducted and interpreted carefully.

volunteer bias A shortcoming of findings derived from a sample of volunteers instead of a representative sample.

Quick Quiz

A. Which descriptive method would be most appropriate for studying each of the following topics? (All of these topics, by the way, have been the focus of study by psychologists.)

1. Ways in which the games of boys differ from those of girls
2. Changes in attitudes toward nuclear disarmament after a television movie about nuclear holocaust
3. The math skills of children in the United States versus Japan
4. Physiological changes that occur when people watch violent movies
5. The development of a male infant who was reared as a female after his penis was accidentally burned off during surgery on the foreskin

a. case study
b. naturalistic observation
c. laboratory observation
d. survey
e. test

B. Professor Flummox gives his new test of aptitude for studying psychology to his psychology students at the start of the year. At the end of the year, he finds that those who did well on the test averaged only a C in the course. The test lacks ________.

C. Over a period of 55 years, an 80-year-old British woman sniffed large amounts of cocaine, which she obtained legally under British regulations for the treatment of addicts. Yet the woman appeared to show no negative effects, other than drug dependence (Brown & Middlefell, 1989). What does this case tell us about the dangers or safety of cocaine?

Answers:

A. 1. b 2. d 3. e 4. c 5. a B. validity (more specifically, criterion validity) C. Not much. Snorting cocaine may be relatively harmless for some people, such as this woman, but extremely harmful for others. Also, the cocaine she received may have been less potent than cocaine purchased on the street. Critical thinking requires that we resist generalizing from a single case.

LOOKING FOR RELATIONSHIPS: CORRELATIONAL STUDIES

In descriptive research, psychologists often want to know whether two or more phenomena are related, and if so, how strongly. To obtain this information, they do **correlational studies.** If a researcher surveys college students to find out how many hours a week they spend watching television, the study is not correlational. However, if the researcher looks for a relationship between hours in front of the television set and grade-point average, then it is.

The word **correlation** is often used as a synonym for relationship. Technically, however, a correlation is a numerical measure of the *strength* of the relationship between two things. The "things" may be events, scores, or anything else that can be recorded and tallied. In psychological studies, such things are called **variables** because they can vary in quantifiable ways. Height, weight, age, income, IQ scores, number of items recalled on a memory test, number of smiles in a given time period—anything that can be measured, rated, or scored can serve as a variable.

Correlations always occur between *sets* of observations. Sometimes the sets come from one individual. Suppose you wanted to know whether fluctuations in a particular person's temperature were related to that person's alertness. Body temperature varies about a degree over a 24-hour period, and this variation can be gauged with a special thermometer. To check for a relationship between temperature and alertness, you would need to obtain several measurements for each variable, over the course of the day. Of course, your results would hold only for that individual. In psychological research, sets of correlated observations usually come from many individuals or are used to compare groups of people. For example, in research on the origins of intelligence, psychologists look for a relationship between the IQ scores of parents and children. To do this, the researchers must gather scores from a set of parents and from the children of these parents. You cannot compute a correlation if you know the IQs of only one particular parent–child pair. To say that a relationship exists, you need more than one pair of values to compare.

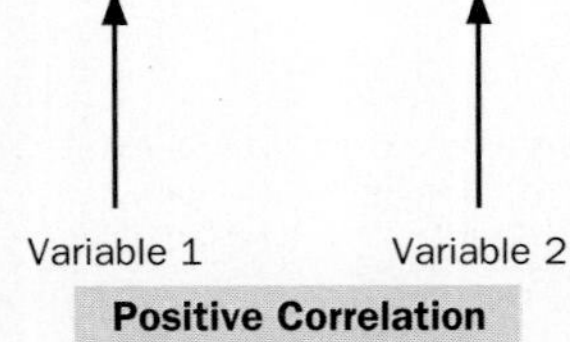

A **positive correlation** means that high values of one variable are associated with high values of the other, and that low values of one variable are associated with low values of the other. Height and weight are positively correlated, for example; so are IQ scores and school grades. Rarely is a correlation perfect, however. Some tall people weigh less than some short ones; some people with average IQs are superstars in the classroom, and some with high IQs get poor grades. Figure 2.2a shows a positive correlation obtained in one study between men's educational levels and their annual incomes. Each dot represents a man; you can find each man's educational level by drawing a horizontal line from his dot to the vertical axis. You can find his income by drawing a vertical line from his dot to the horizontal axis.

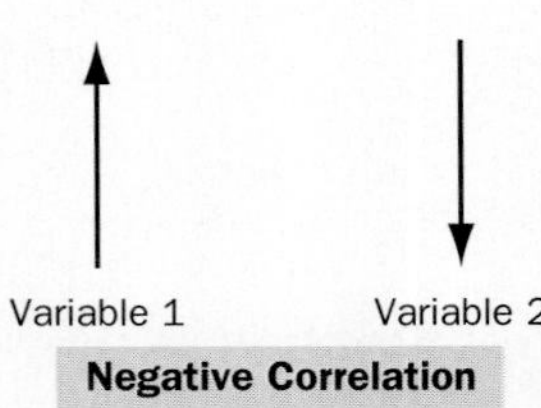

A **negative correlation** means that high values of one variable are associated with *low* values of the other. Figure 2.2b shows a negative correlation between average income and the incidence of dental disease for groups of 100 families. Each dot represents a group. In general, as you can see, the higher the income, the fewer the dental problems. In the automobile business, the older the car, the lower the price, except for antiques and models favored by collectors. As for human beings, in general, the older adults are, the fewer miles they can run, the fewer crimes they are likely to commit, and the fewer hairs they have on their heads. See whether you can think of other variables that are negatively correlated. Remember, though, a negative correlation means that a certain kind of relationship exists. If there is no relationship between two variables, we say that they are *uncorrelated.* Shoe size and IQ scores are uncorrelated.

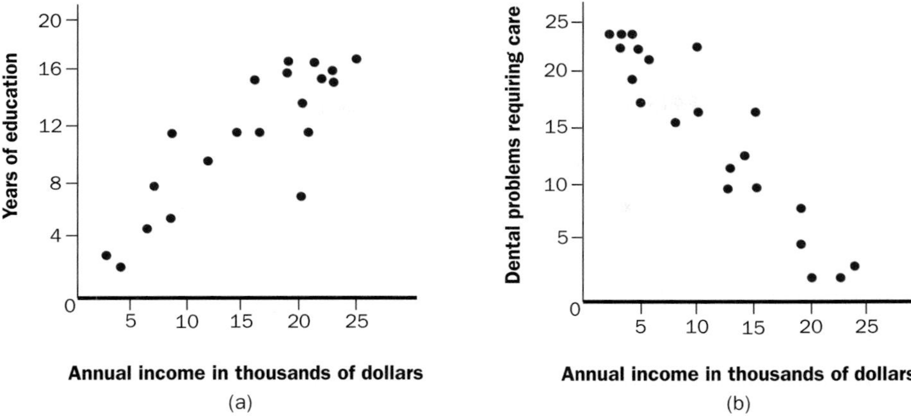

Figure 2.2
Correlations

Graph (a) shows a positive correlation; in general, the higher the education the higher the income. Graph (b) shows a negative correlation; in general, the higher income, the fewer the dental problems. (From Wright, 1976.)

The statistic used to express a correlation is called the **coefficient of correlation.** This number conveys both the size of the correlation and its direction. A perfect positive correlation has a coefficient of +1.00, and a perfect negative correlation has a coefficient of –1.00. Suppose you weighed ten people and listed them in order, from lightest to heaviest. Then suppose you measured their heights and listed them in order, from shortest to tallest. If the names on the two lists were in exactly the same order, the correlation between weight and height would be +1.00. If you hear that the correlation between two variables is +.80, it means that the two are very strongly related. If you hear that the correlation is –.80, the relationship is just as strong, but it is negative. When there is no association between two variables, the coefficient is zero or close to zero.

Correlations allow researchers, using statistical techniques, to make general predictions about a variable if they know how it is related to another one. But because correlations are rarely perfect, predictions about a particular individual may be inaccurate. If you know that a person is well educated, you might predict, in the absence of any other information, that the person is fairly well off because education and income are positively correlated. You would not be able to say exactly how much the person earned, but you would probably guess that the person's income was relatively high. You could be wrong, though, because the correlation is far from perfect. Some people with doctorates earn low salaries, and some people with only a grade-school education make fortunes.

Correlational studies in the social sciences are common and are often reported in the news. But beware; correlations can be misleading. The important thing to remember is that *a correlation does not show causation.* It is easy to assume that if A predicts B, A must be causing B—that is, making B happen—but that is not necessarily so. The number of storks nesting in some European villages is reportedly correlated (positively) with the number of human births in those villages. Therefore, knowing when the storks nest allows you to predict when more births than usual will occur. But clearly that doesn't mean that storks bring babies or that babies attract storks! Human births seem to be somewhat more frequent at certain times of the year (you might want to speculate on the reasons), and the peaks just happen to coincide with the storks' nesting periods.

correlational study A descriptive study that looks for a consistent relationship between two phenomena.

correlation A measure of how strongly two variables are related to one another.

variables Characteristics of behavior or experience that can be measured or described by a numeric scale; variables are manipulated and assessed in scientific studies.

positive correlation An association between increases in one variable and increases in another.

negative correlation An association between increases in one variable and decreases in another.

coefficient of correlation A measure of correlation that ranges in value from –1.00 to +1.00.

GET INVOLVED

Try your hand at gathering and plotting some correlational data. If your classes vary in size, in each one, count the number of times students speak up to comment or ask a question. Every time a student has the floor, tally one act of participation; if the same student participates three times, that would be three acts. If students at your school tend to be quiet and reserved in class, you may have to repeat this procedure over several days. Also count (or estimate) the total number of students in the class. Then plot the results, using a graph such as the one on the right. For example, if students in a class of 75 speak 9 times, you would put a dot at the point where a line going across from the 9 and a line going up from midway between 60 and 90 intersect on the graph.

Is there a relationship between class size and amount of participation by students? If so, is the correlation positive or negative? If no relationship is apparent, try recomputing your participation figures as the proportion of the class that participates. For example, if 5 people participate and the class size is 50, the score for that class will be 1/10, or .10. If 7 participate, the score will be .14. Now is there a relationship?

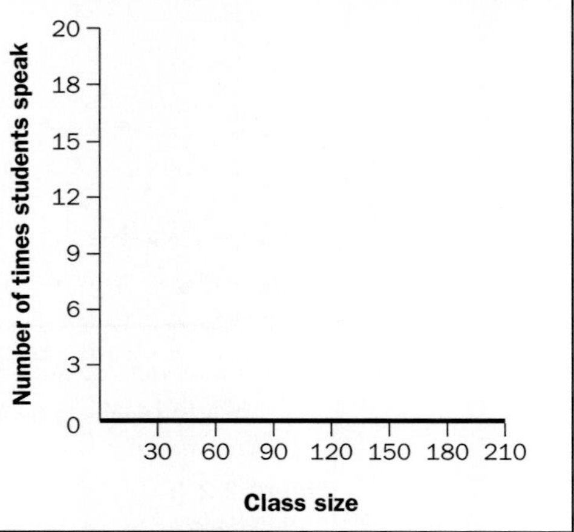

The coincidental nature of the correlation between nesting storks and human births may seem obvious, but in other cases, unwarranted conclusions about causation are more tempting. For example, television watching is positively correlated with children's aggressiveness. Therefore, many people assume that watching television (A), with its violent programs, causes aggressiveness (B):

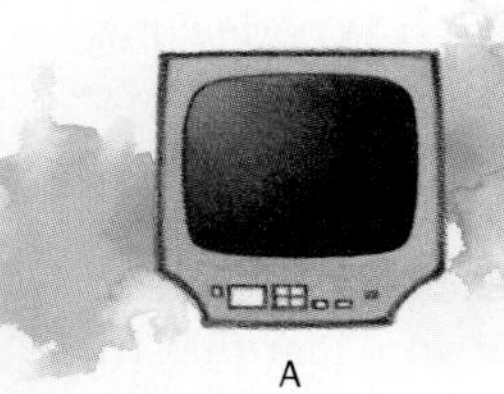

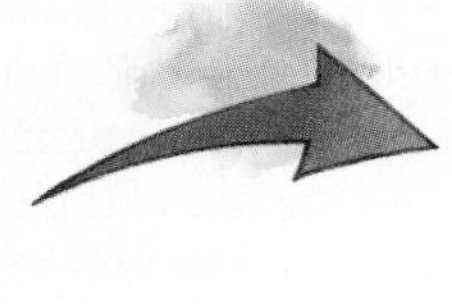
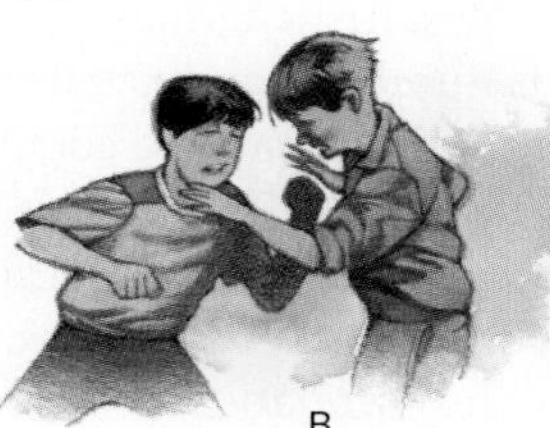

But it is also possible that being highly aggressive (B) causes children to watch more television (A):

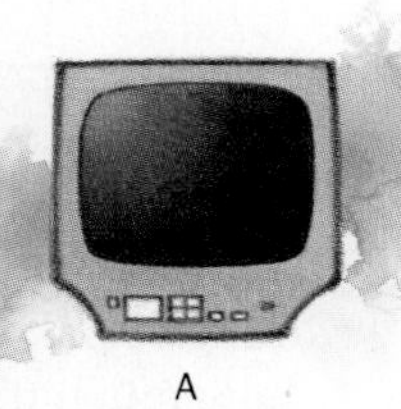

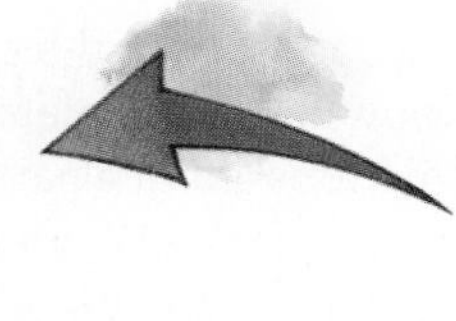
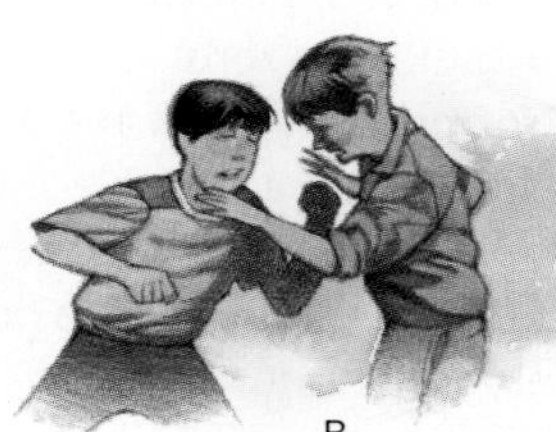

And there is yet another possibility: Growing up in a violent household (C) could cause children to be both aggressive *and* to watch television:

Psychologists are still debating which of these relationships is the strongest; actually, there is evidence for all three (APA Commission on Violence and Youth, 1993; Eron, 1982, 1995; Eron & Huesmann, 1987; Oskamp, 1988).

The moral of the story: When two variables are associated, one variable may or may not be causing the other.

Quick Quiz

A. Are you clear about correlations? Find out by indicating whether each of the following findings is a positive correlation or a negative correlation.

1. The higher a child's score on an intelligence test, the less physical force her mother is likely to use in disciplining her.
2. The higher a male monkey's level of the hormone testosterone, the more aggressive he is likely to be.
3. The older people are, the less frequently they tend to have sexual intercourse.
4. The hotter the weather, the more crimes against persons (such as muggings) tend to occur.

B. Now see whether you can generate two or three alternative explanations for each of the preceding findings.

Answers:

A. 1. negative correlation 2. positive correlation 3. negative correlation 4. positive correlation B. 1. Physical force may impair a child's intellectual growth; brighter children may elicit less physical discipline from their parents; or brighter mothers may tend to have brighter children and may also tend to use less physical force. 2. The hormone may cause aggressiveness, or acting aggressively may stimulate hormone production. 3. Older people may have less interest in sex than younger people, may have less energy, or may think they are supposed to have less interest in sex and behave accordingly; older people may also have trouble finding sexual partners. 4. Hot temperatures may make people edgy and cause them to commit crimes; potential victims may be more plentiful in warm weather because more people stroll outside and go out at night; criminals may find it more comfortable to be out committing their crimes in warm weather than in cold. (Our explanations for these correlations are not the only ones possible.)

HUNTING FOR CAUSES: THE EXPERIMENT

Researchers often propose explanations of behavior on the basis of descriptive studies, but to actually track down the causes of behavior, they rely heavily on the experimental method. An **experiment** allows the researcher to *control* the situation being studied. Instead of being a passive recorder of what is going on, the researcher actively does something that he or she thinks will affect the subjects' behavior and then observes what happens. These procedures allow the experimenter to draw conclusions about cause and effect.

EXPERIMENTAL VARIABLES

Suppose you are a psychologist and you come across reports that cigarette smoking improves performance on simple reaction-time

Everyone knows that alcohol and the operation of heavy machinery don't mix—but what about the effects of nicotine on such work? How might an experiment answer this question?

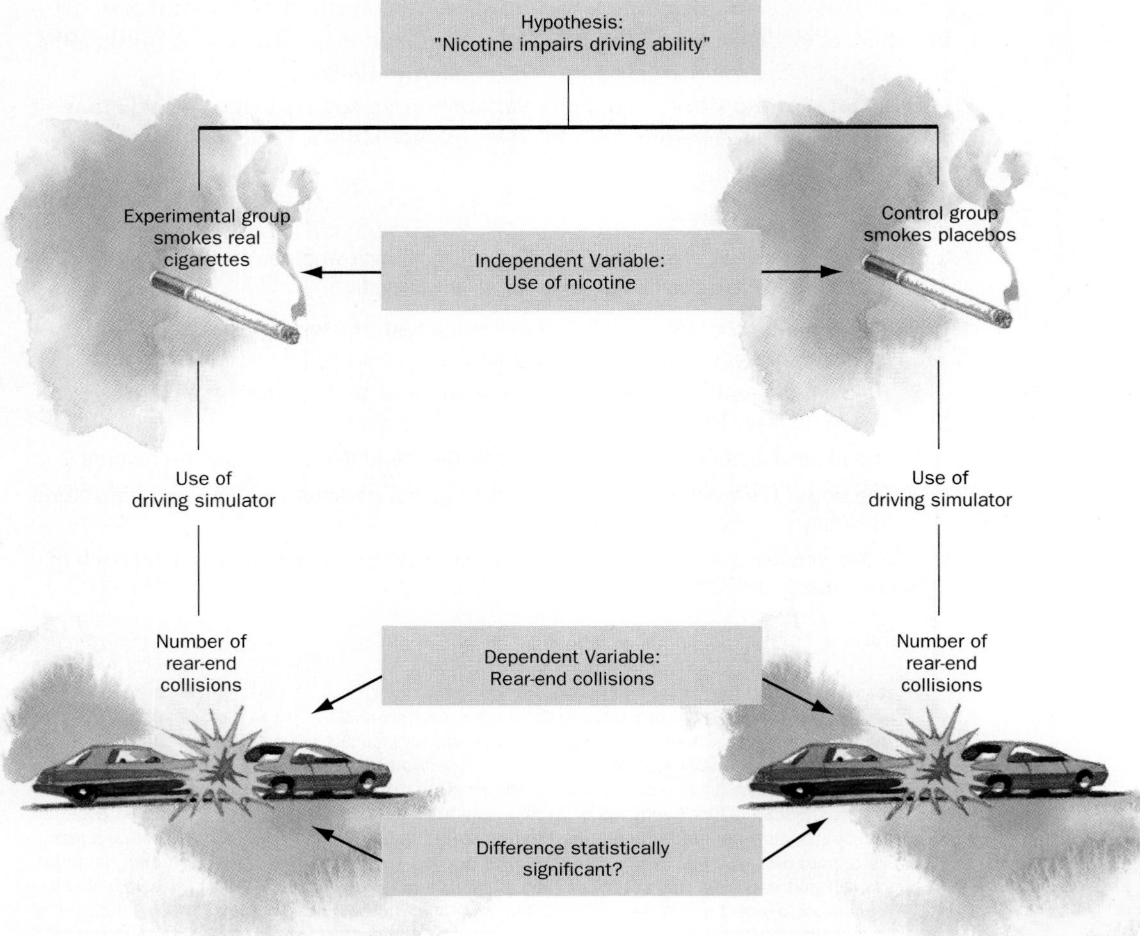

Figure 2.3
Do Smoking and Driving Mix?

The text describes this experimental design to test the hypothesis that nicotine in cigarettes impairs driving skills.

tasks. You do not question these findings, but you have a hunch that nicotine may have the opposite effect on more complex or demanding kinds of behavior, such as driving. You know that on the average, smokers have more car accidents than nonsmokers, even when differences in alcohol consumption, age, and other factors are taken into account (DiFranza et al., 1986). But this relationship doesn't prove that smoking *causes* accidents. Smokers may be greater risk-takers than nonsmokers, whether the risk is lung cancer or trying to beat a red light. Or perhaps the distraction of falling cigarette ashes or of fumbling for the lighter explains the relationship, rather than smoking itself. So you decide to do an experiment. In a laboratory, you ask smokers to "drive" using a computerized driving simulator equipped with a stick shift and a gas pedal. The object, you tell them, is to maximize distance by driving as fast as possible on a winding road while avoiding rear-end collisions. At your request, some of the subjects smoke a cigarette immediately before climbing into the driver's seat. Others do not. You are interested in comparing how many collisions the two groups have. The basic design of this experiment is illustrated in Figure 2.3, which you may want to refer back to as you read the next few pages.

experiment A controlled test of a hypothesis in which the researcher manipulates one variable to discover its effect on another.

The aspect of an experimental situation manipulated or varied by the researcher is known as the **independent variable.** The reaction of the subjects—the behavior that the researcher tries to predict—is the **dependent variable.** Every experiment has at least one independent and one dependent variable. In our example, the independent variable is nicotine use: one cigarette versus none. The dependent variable is the number of rear-end collisions.

Ideally, everything about the experimental situation *except* the independent variable is held constant—that is, kept the same for all subjects. You would not have some people use a stick shift and others an automatic, unless shift type were an independent variable. Similarly, you would not have some people go through the experiment alone and others perform in front of an audience. Holding everything but the independent variable constant ensures that whatever happens is due to the researcher's manipulation and nothing else. It allows you to rule out other interpretations.

Understandably, students often have trouble keeping independent and dependent variables straight. You might think of it this way: The dependent variable—the outcome of the study—*depends* on the independent variable. When psychologists set up an experiment, they think, "If I do (such and such), the subjects in my study will do (such and such)." The first "such and such" represents the independent variable; the second represents the dependent variable:

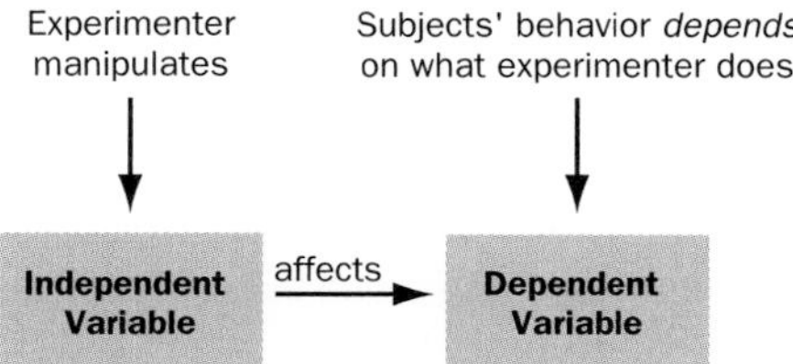

Most variables may be either independent or dependent, depending on what the experimenter is manipulating and trying to predict. If you want to know whether eating chocolate makes people nervous, then the amount of chocolate eaten is the independent variable. If you want to know whether feeling nervous makes people eat chocolate, then the amount of chocolate eaten is the dependent variable.

independent variable A variable that an experimenter manipulates.

dependent variable A variable that an experimenter predicts will be affected by manipulations of the independent variable.

Quick Quiz

Name the independent and dependent variables in studies designed to answer the following questions:

1. Whether sleeping after learning a poem improves memory for the poem
2. Whether the presence of other people affects a person's willingness to help someone in distress
3. Whether people get agitated from listening to heavy-metal music
4. Whether drinking caffeinated coffee makes people more talkative

Answers:

1. Opportunity to sleep after learning is the independent variable; memory for the poem is the dependent variable. 2. The presence of other people is the independent variable; willingness to help others is the dependent variable. 3. Exposure to heavy-metal music is the independent variable; agitation is the dependent variable. 4. Coffee drinking (caffeinated vs. decaffeinated) is the independent variable; talkativeness is the dependent variable. (Now, can you think up some ways to do experiments that might answer these questions?)

EXPERIMENTAL AND CONTROL CONDITIONS

Experiments usually require both an experimental condition and a comparison, or **control condition**. In the control condition, subjects are treated exactly like those in the experimental condition, except that they are not exposed to the same treatment, or manipulation of the independent variable. Without a control condition, you can't be sure that the behavior you are interested in would not have occurred anyway, even without your manipulation. In some studies, the same subjects can be used in both the control and the experimental conditions; they are said to serve as their own controls. In other studies, subjects are assigned to either an *experimental group* or a *control group*.

CONSIDER OTHER INTERPRETATIONS

You've developed a new form of therapy that you believe cures anxiety: Sixty-three percent of the people who go through your program improve. What else, besides your therapy, could account for this result? Why shouldn't you rush out to open an anxiety clinic?

In the nicotine experiment, the people who smoke before driving make up the experimental group, and those who refrain from smoking make up the control group. We want these two groups to be roughly the same in terms of average driving skill. It wouldn't do to start out with a bunch of reckless roadrunners in the experimental group and a bunch of tired tortoises in the control group. We probably also want the two groups to be similar in average intelligence, education, smoking history, and other characteristics so that none of these variables will affect our results. To accomplish this, we can use **random assignment** to place people in the groups. We might randomly give each person a number, then put all those with even numbers in the experimental group and all those with odd numbers in the control group. At the beginning of the study, each subject will have the same probability as any other subject of being assigned to a given group. If we have enough participants in our study, individual differences among them are likely to be roughly balanced in the two groups. However, for some characteristics, such as whether subjects are male or female, we may decide not to depend on random assignment. Instead, we may deliberately assign an equal number of people from each category to each group.

Sometimes, researchers use several experimental or control groups. For example, in our nicotine study, we might want to examine the effects of different levels of nicotine by having people smoke one, two, or three cigarettes before "driving," and then comparing each of these experimental groups to each other and to a control group of nonsmokers as well. For now, however, let's focus just on experimental subjects who smoked one cigarette.

We now have two groups. We also have a problem. In order to smoke, the experimental subjects must light up and inhale. These acts might set off certain expectations—of feeling relaxed, getting nervous, feeling confident, or whatever. These expectations, in turn, might affect driving performance. It would be better to have the control group do everything the experimental group does *except* use nicotine. Therefore, let's change the experimental design a bit. Instead of having the control subjects refrain from smoking, we will give them a **placebo,** a fake treatment. Placebos, which are used frequently in drug research, often take the form of pills or injections containing no active ingredients. Assume that it's possible in the nicotine study to use phony cigarettes that taste and smell like the real thing but that contain no active ingredients. Our control subjects will not know their cigarettes are fake and will have no way of distinguishing them from real ones. Now if they have substantially fewer collisions than the experimental group, we will feel safe in concluding that nicotine increases the probability of an auto accident. (Placebos, by the way, sometimes produce effects that are as strong or nearly as strong as those of a real treatment. Thus, phony injections are often surprisingly effective in eliminating pain. Such placebo effects are a puzzle awaiting scientific solution.)

control condition In an experiment, a comparison condition in which subjects are not exposed to the same treatment as in the experimental condition.

random assignment A procedure for assigning people to experimental and control groups, in which each individual has the same probability as any other of being assigned to a given group.

placebo An inactive substance or fake treatment used as a control in an experiment or given by a medical practitioner to a patient.

EXPERIMENTER EFFECTS

Because expectations can influence the results of a study, subjects should not know whether they are in an experimental or a control group. When this is so (as it usually is), the experiment is said to be a **single-blind study.** But subjects are not the only ones who bring expectations to the laboratory; so do researchers. Their expectations and hopes for a particular result may cause them to inadvertently influence the participants' responses through facial expressions, posture, tone of voice, or some other cue.

Many years ago, Robert Rosenthal (1966) demonstrated how powerful such **experimenter effects** can be. He had students teach rats to run a maze. Half the students were told that their rats had been bred to be "maze bright," and half were told that their rats had been bred to be "maze dull." In reality, there were no genetic differences between the two groups of rats, yet during the experiment, the supposedly brainy rats actually did learn the maze more quickly, apparently because of the way the students treated them. If an experimenter's expectations can affect a rodent's behavior, reasoned Rosenthal, surely they can affect a human being's.

Rosenthal (1994) went on to demonstrate this point in many other studies. In one, he learned that the cues an experimenter may give subjects can be as subtle as the smile on the Mona Lisa; in fact, the cue may *be* a smile. Rosenthal found that male researchers were far more likely to smile at female subjects than at males. Because one smile tends to invite another, such behavior on the part of the experimenter could easily ruin a study of gender differences in friendliness or cooperation. "It may be a heartening finding to know that chivalry is not dead," noted Rosenthal wryly, "but as far as methodology is concerned it is a disconcerting finding."

One solution to the problem of experimenter effects is to do a **double-blind study.** In such a study, the person running the experiment, the one having actual contact with the subjects, does not know which subjects are in which groups until the data have been gathered. Double-blind procedures are standard in drug research. Different doses of a drug are coded in some way, and the person administering the drug is kept in the dark about the code's meaning until after the experiment. To run our nicotine study in a double-blind fashion, we would keep the person dispensing the cigarettes from knowing which ones were real and which were placebos. In psychological research, double-blind studies are often more difficult to design than those that are single-blind. The goal, however, is always to control everything possible in an experiment.

Because experiments allow conclusions about cause and effect, they have long been the method of choice in psychology. However, like all methods, the experiment has its limitations. The laboratory encourages a certain kind of relationship between

single-blind study An experiment in which subjects do not know whether they are in an experimental or a control group.

experimenter effects Unintended changes in subjects' behavior due to cues inadvertently given by the experimenter.

double-blind study An experiment in which neither the subjects nor the individuals running the study know which subjects are in the control group and which are in the experimental group until after the results are tallied.

GET INVOLVED

Prove to yourself how easy it is for experimenters to affect the behavior of a study's participants by giving off nonverbal cues. As you walk around campus, quickly glance at individuals approaching you and either smile or maintain a neutral expression. Try to keep the duration of your glance the same whether you smile or not. You might record the results on a piece of paper or speak them into a tape recorder as you collect them instead of relying on your memory. Chances are that people to whom you smile will smile back at you, whereas those whom you approach with a neutral expression will wear a neutral expression themselves. What does this fact tell you about the importance of doing double-blind studies in psychology?

researchers and their subjects, one in which the researcher determines what the questions are and which behaviors will be recorded, and the participants try to do as they are told. In their desire to cooperate, advance scientific knowledge, or present themselves in a positive light, participants may act in ways that they ordinarily would not (Kihlstrom, 1995). Thus, research psychologists confront a dilemma: The more control they exercise over the situation, the more unlike real life it may be. For this reason, many psychologists are calling for more *field research*, the careful study of behavior in natural contexts, as well as careful evaluation of how participants in experiments perceive their situation and the role they are to play in it.

Now that we have come to the end of our discussion of research methods, how did you do on your list of their advantages and disadvantages? You can find out by comparing your list with the one in Table 2.2.

TABLE 2.2 ***Research Methods in Psychology: Their Advantages and Disadvantages***

Method	Advantages	Disadvantages
Case study	Good source of hypotheses Provides in-depth information on individuals Unusual cases can shed light on situations or problems that are unethical or impractical to study in other ways	Individual may not be representative or typical Difficult to know which subjective interpretation is best
Naturalistic observation	Allows description of behavior as it occurs in the natural environment Often useful in first stages of a research program	Allows researcher little or no control of the situation Observations may be biased Does not allow firm conclusions on cause and effect
Laboratory observation	Allows more control than naturalistic observation Allows use of sophisticated equipment	Allows researcher only limited control of the situation Observations may be biased Does not allow firm conclusions on cause and effect Behavior in the laboratory may differ from behavior in the natural environment
Test	Yields information on personality traits, emotional states, aptitudes, abilities	Difficult to construct tests that are valid and reliable
Survey	Provides large amount of information on large numbers of people	If sample is nonrepresentative or biased, it may be impossible to generalize from the results Responses may be inaccurate or untrue
Correlational study	Shows whether two or more variables are related Allows general predictions	Does not permit identification of cause and effect
Experiment	Allows researcher to control situation Permits researcher to identify cause and effect	Situation is artificial, and results may not generalize well to the real world Sometimes difficult to avoid experimenter effects

Quick Quiz

A. What's wrong with these two studies?

1. A kidney specialist and a psychiatrist treated mentally disordered patients by filtering their blood through a dialysis machine, normally used with kidney patients. They reported several cases of dramatic improvement, which they attributed to the removal of an unknown toxin (Wagemaker & Cade, 1978).
2. A sex researcher surveyed women on their feelings about men and love. She sent out 100,000 lengthy questionnaires to women's groups and got back 4,500 replies (a 4.5 percent return rate). On the basis of these replies, she reported that 84 percent of women are dissatisfied with their relationships, 98 percent want more communication, and 70 percent of those married five years or more have had extramarital affairs (Hite, 1987).

B. On a talk show, Dr. Blitznik announces a fabulous program: Chocolate Immersion Therapy. "People who spend one day a week doing nothing but eating chocolate are soon cured of eating disorders, depression, drug abuse, and poor study habits," says Dr. Blitznik. What should you find out about "C.I.T." before signing up?

Answers:

A. 1. The dialysis study had no control group and was not double-blind. Patients' expectations that the "blood-cleansing" equipment would wash their madness out of them might have influenced the results, and so might the researchers' expectations. In later studies, using double-blind procedures, control subjects had their blood circulated through the machine, but the blood was not actually filtered. Little improvement occurred in either the experimental or the control condition, and the real treatment was no better than the fake treatment (Carpenter et al., 1983). 2. Because of the way the sample was recruited and the low return rate, the findings may be flawed by a volunteer bias. Although this research produced information on the feelings of many women, figures and percentages from the study are not necessarily valid for the general population. B. *Some questions to ask:* Is there research showing that people who go through C.I.T. did better than those in a control group who did not have the therapy, or who had a different therapy—say, Broccoli Immersion Therapy? If so, how many people were studied? How were they selected, and how were they assigned to the therapy and no-therapy groups? Did the person running the experiment know who was getting C.I.T. and who wasn't? How long did the "cures" last? Has the research been replicated by others?

EVALUATING THE FINDINGS: WHY PSYCHOLOGISTS USE STATISTICS

If you are a psychologist who has just done an observational study, a survey, or an experiment, your work has only just begun. Once you have some results in hand, you must do three things with them: (1) describe them, (2) assess how reliable and meaningful they are, and (3) figure out how to explain them.

DESCRIPTIVE STATISTICS: FINDING OUT WHAT'S SO

Let's say that 30 people in the nicotine experiment smoked real cigarettes, and 30 smoked placebos. We have recorded the number of collisions for each person on the driving simulator. Now we have 60 numbers. What can we do with them?

The first step is to summarize the data. The world does not want to hear how many collisions each person had. It wants to know what happened in the nicotine group as a whole, compared to what happened in the control group. To provide this information, we need numbers that sum up our data. Such numbers, known as **descriptive statistics,** are often depicted in graphs and charts.

descriptive statistics Statistics that organize and summarize research data.

Averages can be misleading if you don't know how much events deviated from the statistical mean and how they were distributed.

A good way to summarize the data is to compute group averages. The most commonly used type of average is the **arithmetic mean.** (For two other types, see the Appendix.) It is calculated by adding up all the individual scores and dividing the result by the number of scores. We can compute a mean for the nicotine group by adding up the 30 collision scores and dividing the sum by 30. Then we can do the same for the control group. Now our 60 numbers have been boiled down to 2. For the sake of our example, let's assume that the nicotine group had an average of 10 collisions, whereas the control group's average was only 7.

We must be careful, however, about how we interpret these averages. An arithmetic mean does *not* necessarily tell us what is typical; it merely summarizes a mass of data. It is possible that no one in our nicotine group actually had 10 collisions. Perhaps half the people in the group were motoring maniacs and had 15 collisions, whereas the others were more cautious and had only 5. Perhaps almost all the subjects had 9, 10, or 11 collisions. Perhaps accidents were evenly distributed between 0 and 15.

arithmetic mean An average that is calculated by adding up a set of quantities and dividing the sum by the total number of quantities in the set.

range A measure of the spread of scores, calculated by subtracting the lowest score from the highest score.

variance A measure of the dispersion of scores around the mean.

The mean does not tell you about such variation in subjects' responses. For that, there are other statistics. One, the **range,** gives the difference between the lowest and the highest score in a distribution of scores. If the lowest number of collisions in the nicotine group was 5 and the highest was 15, the range would be 10. Another, the **variance,** is more informative; it tells you how clustered or spread out the individual scores are around the mean (see Figure 2.4). The more spread out they are, the less

Figure 2.4
Same Mean, Different Variances

In both distributions of scores the mean is 5, but in (a) the scores are clustered around the mean, whereas in (b) they are widely dispersed.

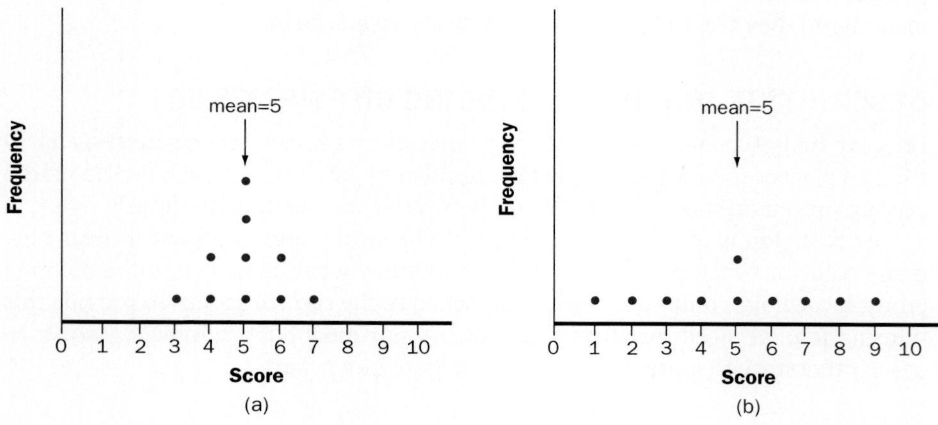

"typical" the mean is. But unfortunately, when research is reported in newspapers or on the nightly news, you usually hear only about the mean. There are other kinds of descriptive statistics as well, including the coefficient of correlation, which we covered earlier. Descriptive statistics are discussed in greater detail in the Appendix.

INFERENTIAL STATISTICS: ASKING "SO WHAT?"

At this point in our nicotine study, we have one group with an average of 10 collisions and another with an average of 7. Should we break out the champagne? Try to get on TV? Call our mothers?

Better hold off. Descriptive statistics do not tell us whether the outcome is anything to write home about. Perhaps if one group had an average of 15 collisions and the other an average of 1, we could get excited. But rarely does a psychological study hit you between the eyes with a sensationally clear result. In most cases, there is some possibility that the difference between the two groups was due simply to chance. Perhaps the people in the nicotine group just happened to be a little more accident-prone, and their behavior had nothing to do with the nicotine.

To find out how significant the data are, the psychologist uses **inferential statistics** These statistics do not merely describe or summarize the data. They permit a researcher to draw *inferences* (conclusions based on evidence) about how impressive the findings are. There are many inferential statistics to choose from, depending on the kind of study and what the researcher wants to know. Like descriptive statistics, inferential statistics involve the application of mathematical formulas to the data (see Appendix).

The most commonly used procedure for drawing inferences in psychology has been the *significance test.* This test tells the researcher how likely it is that the result of the study occurred by chance. More precisely, it reveals the probability of obtaining an effect as large as (or larger than) the one observed if manipulating the independent variable actually has no reliable effect on the behavior in question. In our nicotine study, a significance test will tell us how likely it is that the difference between the nicotine group and the placebo group occurred by chance. It is impossible to rule out chance entirely. However, if the likelihood that the result occurred by chance is extremely low, we say that the result is **statistically significant.** This means that the probability that the difference is "real" is overwhelming—not certain, mind you, but overwhelming. By convention, psychologists consider a result to be significant if it would be expected to occur by chance 5 or fewer times in 100 repetitions of the study. Another way of saying this is that the result is significant at the .05—"point oh five"—level. If the difference could be expected to occur by chance in 6 out of 100 studies, we would have to say that the results failed to support the hypothesis—that the difference we obtained might well have occurred merely by chance—although we might still want to do further research to be sure. You can see that psychologists refuse to be impressed by just any old result.

Inferential statistics are necessary because a result that seems unlikely may not really be so unlikely at all. For example, how probable do you think it is that in a room of 25 people, at least 2 will have the same birthday? The odds may seem remote, but in fact they are better than even. If there are only 10 people in the room, the chances are still 1 in 9. Among U.S. presidents, two had the same birthday (Warren Harding and James Polk), and three died on the fourth of July (John Adams, the second president; Thomas Jefferson, the third; and James Monroe, the fifth). Surprising? No. Such coincidences are not statistically striking at all.

inferential statistics Statistical tests that allow researchers to assess how likely it is that their results occurred merely by chance.

statistically significant A term used to refer to a result that is extremely unlikely to have occurred by chance.

GET INVOLVED

Here's a way to help yourself understand statistical significance. Toss a coin ten times, and record the number of heads and tails. Repeat this procedure 10 times. If the coin is fair, about half the tosses should produce heads and half should produce tails. But for any particular block of ten tosses, the results may vary from what chance would predict; you might get 6 tails and 4 heads, say, or 3 tails and 7 heads—purely by chance. The likelihood of getting 9 or 10 tails (or heads), however, is very low. If you flipped the coin just 10 times and got such a result, you might conclude that something other than chance was operating (perhaps the coin is worn down more on one edge). Similarly, researchers must decide whether their results are fairly likely to have occurred by chance (as in 6 tails and 4 heads) or are highly unlikely (as in 10 tails and no heads). In the latter case, the result is considered statistically significant.

Statistically significant results allow psychologists to make many general predictions about human behavior. These predictions are usually stated as probabilities ("On average, we can expect 60 percent of all students to do X, Y, or Z"). However, they do not usually tell us with any certainty what a particular individual will do in a situation. Probabilistic results are typical of all the sciences. Medical research, for example, can tell us that the odds are high that someone who smokes will get lung cancer, but because many variables interact to produce any particular case of cancer, research can't tell us for sure whether Aunt Bessie, a two-pack-a-day smoker, will come down with the disease.

By the way, a nicotine study similar to our hypothetical example, but with somewhat more complicated procedures, has actually been done (Spilich, June, & Renner, 1992). Smokers who lit up before driving got a little farther on the simulated road, but they also had significantly more rear-end collisions on average (10.7) than did temporarily abstaining smokers (5.2) or nonsmokers (3.1). After hearing about this research, the head of Federal Express banned smoking on the job among all of the company's 12,000 drivers (George Spilich, personal communication).

Quick Quiz

Check your understanding of the descriptive–inferential distinction by placing a check in the appropriate column for each phrase:

	Descriptive statistics	**Inferential statistics**
Summarize the data	_______	_______
Give likelihood of data occurring by chance	_______	_______
Include the mean	_______	_______
Give measure of statistical significance	_______	_______
Tell you whether to call your mother	_______	_______

Answers:

1. descriptive 2. inferential 3. descriptive 4. inferential 5. inferential

FROM THE LABORATORY TO THE REAL WORLD: INTERPRETING THE FINDINGS

The last step in any study is to figure out what the findings mean. Trying to understand behavior from uninterpreted findings is like trying to become fluent in Portuguese by reading a Portuguese–English dictionary. Just as you need the grammar of Portuguese to tell you how the words fit together, the psychologist needs hypotheses and theories to explain how the facts that emerge from research fit together.

CHOOSING THE BEST EXPLANATION Sometimes it is hard to choose between competing explanations. Does nicotine disrupt driving by impairing coordination, by increasing a driver's vulnerability to distraction, by interfering with the processing of information, or by distorting the perception of danger? In general, the best explanation is the one that accounts for the greatest number of existing findings and makes the most accurate predictions about new ones.

Often the explanation for a finding will need to take into account many factors. We saw earlier, for example, that being abused as a child does not inevitably turn a person into an abusive parent. Many influences, including life stresses, exposure to violence on television, and the nature of the abuse, interact in complicated ways to determine the kind of parent a person becomes (Widom, 1989). Fortunately, with special statistical procedures, psychologists can often analyze how much each variable contributes to a result and how the variables interact.

In interpreting any particular study, we must also not go too far beyond the facts. There may be several explanations that fit those facts equally well, which means that more research will be needed to determine the best explanation. Rarely does one study prove anything, in psychology or any other field. That is why you should be suspicious of headlines that announce a major scientific breakthrough. Scientific progress usually occurs gradually, not in one fell swoop.

Sometimes the best interpretation of a finding does not emerge until a hypothesis has been tested in different ways. Although the methods we have described tend to be appropriate for different questions (see Table 2.3), different methods can also complement each other. That is, one method can be used to confirm, disconfirm, or extend the results obtained with another. If the findings of studies using various methods converge, there is greater reason to be confident about them. On the other hand, if they conflict, researchers will know they must modify their hypotheses or do more research.

As an example, when psychologists compare the mental-test scores of young people and old people, they usually find that younger people outscore older ones. This type of research, in which groups are compared at a given time, is called **cross-sectional:**

Cross-sectional Study

Different groups compared at one time:

Group A (20-year-olds)
Group B (50-year-olds) — compared
Group C (80-year-olds)

Other researchers, however, have used **longitudinal studies** to investigate mental abilities across the life span. In a longitudinal study, the same people are followed over a period of time and are reassessed at regular intervals:

cross-sectional study A study in which subjects of different ages are compared at a given time.

longitudinal study A study in which subjects are followed and periodically reassessed over a period of time.

Longitudinal Study

Same group compared at different times:

Group A at age 20 → Group A at age 50 → Group A at age 80

In contrast to cross-sectional studies, longitudinal studies find that as people age, they often continue to perform as well as they ever did on many types of mental tests. A general decline in ability does not usually occur until the seventh or eighth decade of life (Baltes & Graf, 1996; Schaie, 1993). Why do results from the two types of studies conflict? Apparently, cross-sectional studies measure generational differences; younger generations tend to outperform older ones on many tests, perhaps because they are better educated or more familiar with the types of items used on the tests. Without longitudinal studies, we might falsely conclude that mental ability inevitably declines sharply with age.

TABLE 2.3 *Psychological Research Methods Contrasted*

Psychologists may use different methods to answer different questions about a topic. To illustrate, this table shows some ways in which the methods described in this chapter can be used to study different questions about aggression. The methods listed are not necessarily mutually exclusive. That is, sometimes two or more methods can be used to investigate the same question. As discussed in the text, findings based on one method may extend, support, or disconfirm findings based on another.

Method	Purpose	Example
Case study	To understand the development of aggressive behavior in a particular individual; to formulate research hypotheses about the origins of aggressiveness	Developmental history of a serial killer
Naturalistic observation	To describe the nature of aggressive acts in early childhood	Observation, tallying, and description of hitting, kicking, etc., during free-play periods in a preschool
Laboratory observation	To find out whether aggressiveness in pairs of same-sex and different-sex children differs in frequency or intensity	Observation through a one-way window of same-sex and different-sex pairs of preschoolers; pairs must negotiate who gets to play with an attractive toy that has been promised to each child
Test	To compare the personality traits of aggressive and nonaggressive persons	Administration of personality tests to violent and nonviolent prisoners
Survey	To find out how common domestic violence is in the United States	Questionnaire asking anonymous respondents (in a sample representative of the U.S. population) about the occurrence of slapping, hitting, etc. in their homes
Correlational study	To examine the relationship between aggressiveness and television viewing	Administration to college students of a paper-and-pencil test of aggressiveness and a questionnaire on number of hours spent watching TV weekly; computation of correlation coefficient
Experiment	To find out whether high air temperatures elicit aggressive behavior	Arrangement for individuals to "shock" a "learner" (actually a confederate of the experimenter) while seated in a room heated to either 72°F or 85°F

JUDGING THE RESULT'S IMPORTANCE Sometimes psychologists agree on the reliability and meaning of a finding, but not on its ultimate relevance for theory or practice. Statistical significance alone does not provide the answer. A result may be statistically significant at the "point oh five level" but at the same time be small and of minor consequence in everyday life. On the other hand, a result may not quite reach statistical significance yet be worth following up on. Other serious criticisms, beyond the scope of this book, have also been leveled against traditional tests of significance (Falk & Greenbaum, 1995; Hunter, 1997; G. Loftus, 1993). Because of these criticisms, a hot dispute is raging about the value of significance tests, and many psychologists now prefer other statistical procedures (Shea, 1996). Some of these procedures permit the researcher to estimate how much of the variance among the scores in a study was accounted for by the independent variable. Sometimes this *effect size* turns out to be small, even when the results were statistically significant.

One increasingly popular statistical technique, called **meta-analysis,** combines and analyzes data from many studies, instead of assessing each study's results separately. Meta-analysis tells the researcher how much of the variation in scores across *all* the studies examined can be explained by a particular variable. For example, one recent meta-analysis of nearly 50 years of research on gender differences found that differences on some spatial–visual tasks are substantial, with males doing better on the average (Voyer, Voyer, & Bryden, 1995). In other words, gender accounts for a good deal of the variance in performance on such tasks. In contrast, other meta-analyses have shown that some stereotypical gender differences—notably in verbal ability, math ability, and aggressiveness—are reliable but surprisingly small, with gender accounting for only 1 to 5 percent of the variance in scores (Eagly & Carli, 1981; Feingold, 1988; Hyde, 1981, 1984b; Hyde, Fennema, & Lamon, 1990; Hyde & Linn, 1988). When scores for males and females are plotted on a graph, they greatly overlap (see Figure 2.5).

Critics of meta-analysis argue that this method is like combining apples and oranges; the blend is interesting, but it is bland—and it obliterates the distinctive flavors of the original ingredients. For example, research on verbal abilities has often

meta-analysis A procedure for combining and analyzing data from many studies; it determines how much of the variance in scores across all studies can be explained by a particular variable.

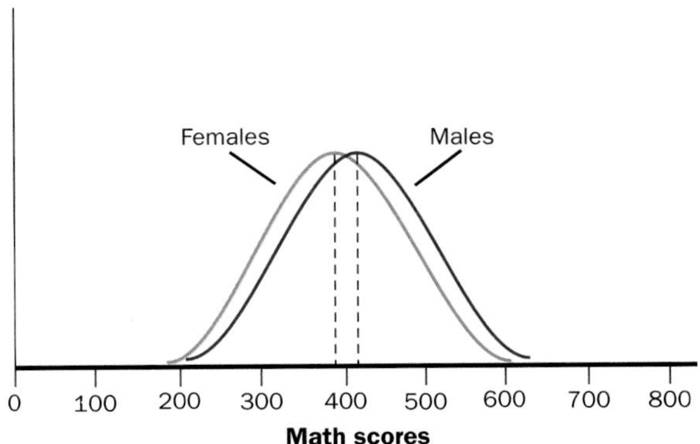

Figure 2.5
Is This a Meaningful Difference?

On average, seventh-grade boys do better than seventh-grade girls on the mathematics section of the SAT. But although the difference is statistically reliable, it is small; as you can see, the scores greatly overlap. (From Sapolsky, 1987, based on data from Benbow & Stanley, 1983.)

relied on studies of high-school students. But students who don't read well are more likely to drop out of high school, and these dropouts are more likely to be male than female. Thus a meta-analysis may fail to identify an overall female advantage on verbal tests (Halpern, 1989). Similarly, a meta-analysis that combines studies of all math skills will miss a male advantage on problems of spatial visualization (McGuinness, 1993). Meta-analyses that turn up no overall sex differences in cognitive abilities are appealing to many people but ultimately unhelpful, critics believe, because such analyses gloss over differences that educators should know about if they want *all* children to do well. Nevertheless, on topics that have generated dozens and even hundreds of studies, meta-analysis has been the most promising way of finding patterns in results, as long as its limitations are taken into account.

EVALUATING RESEARCH METHODS: SCIENCE UNDER SCRUTINY

Rigorous research methods are the very heart of science, so it is not surprising that psychologists spend considerable time discussing and debating their procedures for collecting, evaluating, and presenting data. In recent years, such debates have gone far beyond such matters as when to use questionnaires versus interviews or how best to analyze the results.

KEEPING THE ENTERPRISE ETHICAL

One set of issues has to do with the ethics of research. The American Psychological Association (APA) recognizes the need for ethical guidelines and has a formal code that all members must follow, both in clinical practice and in psychological research. The APA code calls on psychological scientists to respect the dignity and welfare of their subjects. It states that human subjects must voluntarily consent to participate in a study and must know enough about it to make an intelligent decision, a doctrine known as *informed consent.* Investigators must protect participants from physical and mental discomfort or harm, and if any risk exists, subjects must be warned in advance and given an opportunity to decline to take part. Once a study begins, a subject must be free to withdraw from it at any time. Federal regulations also govern scientific research, and in most colleges and universities, an ethics committee must approve all proposed studies.

One ethical issue has provoked continuing debate: the use and treatment of animals in research. As of the mid-1980s, animals were being used in only about 7 or 8 percent of psychological studies, and 95 percent of the animals were rodents (American Psychological Association, 1984); and in recent years, the use of animals appears to have declined (Dewsbury, 1996). Nonetheless, in certain areas of psychological research, animals still play a crucial role. Psychologists are especially partial to the

Animals are used in psychological research to study learning, memory, emotion, motivation, and many other topics. Here a rat learns to find food in a radial maze.

Norwegian white rat, which is bred specifically for research purposes, but they also occasionally use pigeons, cats, monkeys, apes, and other species. Most studies do not involve harm or discomfort to the animals (e.g., research on mating in hamsters), but some do (e.g., studies in which infant monkeys are reared apart from their mothers and as a consequence develop abnormal behaviors). Some studies even require the animal's death, as when rats brought up in deprived or enriched environments are sacrificed so that their brains can be examined for specific effects.

Psychologists who study animals are sometimes interested in comparing species, or they hope to learn more about a particular species. Their work generally falls into the area of basic science, but it often produces practical benefits. For example, using behavioral principles, farmers have been able to reduce crop destruction by birds and deer without resorting to their traditional method—shooting the animals. Other psychologists are primarily interested in principles that apply to both animals and people. Because many animals have biological systems or behavioral patterns similar to those of human beings, using animals often allows more control over variables than would otherwise be possible. In some cases, practical or ethical considerations prevent the use of human beings as subjects. And studying animals can clarify important theoretical issues. For example, we might not attribute the greater life expectancy of women solely to "lifestyle" factors and health practices if we find that a male–female difference exists in other mammals as well.

Animal studies have led to numerous improvements in human health and well-being. Findings from these studies have helped psychologists and other researchers develop methods for treating bed-wetting; teach retarded children to communicate; devise therapies for substance abuse; combat life-threatening malnutrition caused by chronic vomiting in infants; rehabilitate patients with neurological disorders and sensory impairment; teach people to control high blood pressure and headaches; treat suicidal depression; develop better ways to reduce chronic pain; train animal companions for the disabled; and understand the mechanisms underlying memory loss and senility—to name only a few benefits (Feeney, 1987; Greenough, 1991; N. Miller, 1985).

In recent years, however, animal research has provoked angry disputes over the welfare of animals and even over whether to do any animal research at all. Some people on both sides have taken extreme positions. In one survey, 85 percent of committed animal-rights activists (versus 17 percent of a more representative group of respondents) endorsed the statement, "If it were up to me, I would eliminate all research using animals" (Plous, 1991). For their part, some psychologists have refused to acknowledge that confinement in laboratories can be psychologically and physically harmful for some species.

On the positive side, this conflict has motivated many psychologists to find ways to improve the treatment of animals that are needed in research. The APA's ethical code has always contained provisions covering the humane treatment of animals, and in the past decade, more comprehensive guidelines have been formulated. Federal laws have also been passed to strengthen regulations governing the housing and care of research animals. Every experiment involving vertebrates must now be reviewed by a committee that includes representatives from the research institution and the community.

Most psychologists, however, oppose proposals to ban or greatly reduce animal research (Plous, 1996). The APA and other scientific organizations believe that legislation to protect animals is desirable but must not jeopardize research that increases scientific understanding and improves human welfare. The difficult task—one that promises to be with us for many years—is to balance the many benefits of animal research with an acknowledgment of past abuses and a compassionate attitude toward species other than our own.

THE MEANING OF KNOWLEDGE

The continuing arguments over ethical issues show that research methods in psychology can provoke as much disagreement as the findings do. Conflict exists not only about how to do research, but also about what research in general can and cannot reveal. Indeed, heated exchanges are raging in all the sciences and humanities about the very meaning of knowledge itself.

For the past three centuries, the answer seemed clear enough. Knowledge was the discovery of some reality "out there," and the way to find it was to be objective, value free, and detached. The purpose of a theory was to map or reflect this reality. A clear line was assumed to exist between the knower, on one side, and the phenomenon under study, on the other—and the knower wasn't supposed to cross that line.

Today, many scholars are questioning these fundamental assumptions. Adherents of *postmodernism* argue that detached objectivity, long considered the cornerstone of Western science, is a myth. In the postmodern view, the observer's values, judgments, and status in society inevitably affect how events are studied, how they are explained, and even how they take place. Scholars and researchers, in this view, are not exempt from subjectivity. Because they do their work at a particular time and in a particular culture, they bring with them shared assumptions and worldviews that influence what they count as an important fact, what parts of reality they notice, and how they determine standards of excellence. If you have encountered arguments about which books should be counted as classics—the familiar greats of Western literature alone, or modern works by women and non-European writers as well—you have already observed a postmodern conflict.

social constructionism The view that there are no universal truths about human nature because people construct reality differently, depending on their culture, the historical moment, and the power arrangements within their society.

In the social sciences, a postmodern theory called **social constructionism** holds that knowledge isn't so much discovered as it is created or invented (Gergen, 1985; Guba, 1990; Hare-Mustin & Marecek, 1990; Rosaldo, 1989). Our understanding of things does not merely mirror what's "out there"; it organizes and orders it. Consider the concept of race. Many people speak of "blacks" or "Asians" or "whites" as if the boundaries between these groups were self-evident based on physical differences.

What race do these Brazilian children belong to? The fact that societies define racial categories differently shows that people have varying ways of perceiving and organizing "reality." This can pose problems for psychologists and other scientists who want to define and explain some phenomenon—such as "racial differences."

But there are many ways to define race. Some societies base their definitions on ancestry, not on any obvious physical attribute such as skin color; a person can look white but be considered black if he or she has a single black ancestor. Indeed, as recently as 1970, Louisiana laws held that anyone with as little as $\frac{1}{32}$ "Negro blood" was black (Jones, 1991). South Africa has used ancestry to differentiate blacks from "coloreds" (people of mixed ancestry) for political and legal purposes. But in South America, where people come in all shades and many combinations of European, Native American, and African ancestry, this kind of classification does not exist. Besides, why should skin color or hair type be the primary physical basis for distinguishing races? As physiologist Jared Diamond (1994) observes, "There are many different, equally valid procedures for defining races, and those different procedures yield very different classifications." You could, for example, make distinctions based on gene frequencies for sickle-cell anemia, on types of fingerprints, on amount of body hair, on shape of buttocks, or on body shape. One classification would group Italians, Greeks, and most African blacks into one race and the Xhosas of South Africa and Swedes into another. Another would put Swedes and Italians into the same racial category as New Guineans and American Indians.

In psychology, as in science in general, there are no agreed-on definitions of race, and some researchers think the concept is too vague and misleading to be useful (Yee et al., 1993; Zuckerman, 1990). Because the concept of race falsely implies the existence of physically unique and separate groups and is problematic from a scientific point of view, in this book, we will avoid the term *race* whenever possible. Instead, we will use the term *ethnic group* to refer to people who share a common culture, religion, or language.

In psychology, social-constructionist debates about science are especially challenging. Psychologists have always sought to understand human behavior and mental processes. Now they are being asked to analyze their own behavior as psychologists and to examine how their own assumptions, values, gender, place in society, and cultural experiences affect their conclusions. Some welcome this development, but others react to postmodern views with alarm. They fear that postmodern criticisms mean we can never know the truth about anything and so we might as well give up on science, uniform standards of criticism, and the effort to apply objective methods. They fear that a legitimate critique of the limitations of research is turning into an attack on all traditional methods of research, which in effect is throwing out the baby (rigorous standards and useful findings) with the bath water (bias and narrow-mindedness) (Gross & Levitt, 1994; Peplau & Conrad, 1989; Smith, 1994).

This is a serious and interesting debate that is not going to be resolved soon, which is why we have raised it here. Our own position, which guides our approach in this book, falls somewhere between traditionalism and postmodernism. We think that understanding how knowledge is constructed by scholars and researchers is essential to the study of psychology. New ways of looking at knowledge and of doing research have the potential to expand and enrich our understanding of behavior (Gergen, 1994). But for us, as for all scientific psychologists, some things will remain the same: an insistence on standards of evidence, a reliance on verifiable results, and an emphasis on critical thinking. That is why we hope that as you read the following chapters, you will resist the temptation to skip descriptions of how studies were done. If the assumptions and methods of a study are faulty, so are the results and the conclusions based on them. Ultimately, what we know about human behavior is inseparable from how we know it.

Taking Psychology with You

"Intuitive Statistics": Avoiding the Pitfalls

Everyone uses intuition and hunches to generate hypotheses about human behavior. Scientists are required to confirm their hypotheses through careful research and rigorous statistical analysis. In daily life, though, people usually test their ideas through casual observation and the use of "intuitive statistics," notions about probabilities that may or may not be correct. These unscientific methods often work well but can sometimes lead to errors. You can take Chapter 2 with you by watching out for common statistical mistakes in your own thinking.

For example, you have learned how misleading it can be to "accentuate the positive and eliminate the negative" by ignoring nonoccurrences of a phenomenon (see p. 43). Sherlock Holmes, the legendary detective, was aware of the value of nonoccurrences. In one adventure he invited a police inspector to consider "the curious incident of the dog in the nighttime." The inspector protested that the dog did nothing in the nighttime. Holmes replied that *that* was the curious incident: The dog's silence proved that the intruder in the mystery was someone well known to the dog (Ross, 1977). Like Sherlock Holmes, we all need to be aware of what nonoccurrences can tell us.

Other intuitive statistics can trap us in false conclusions. For example, how would you answer the following questions?

1. If black has come up three times in a row on the roulette wheel, would you be inclined to bet next on red or on black?

2. Where are you more worried about safety, in a car or in an airplane?

3. If your psychology instructor has a friend who is a professor, and if that person is socially rather shy, is slight of stature, and likes to write poetry, is the friend's field more likely to be in Chinese studies or psychology?

When presented with the first question, many people say that it is red's "turn" to win. Yet black and red are equally likely to win on the fourth play, just as they were on the first three (assuming that the wheel is fair). How could the probabilities change from one play to the other? A roulette wheel has no memory! The same is true for tossing coins. If you get three heads, the chance of a head on the fourth toss is still .50; the probability of a head or a tail does not change from toss to toss. But it is perfectly normal to get a run of either heads or tails, even though over the long run (if the coin is fair), there will be a balance of heads and tails. Because many people don't understand these facts of probability, they often succumb to the *gambler's fallacy,* the belief that a run of one event alters the chances of that event occurring again. The gambler's fallacy is common outside the casino as well. Many people think that parents with three girls are due for a boy, but the odds are the same as they always were: 50 percent for most people; more or less than 50 percent when the man produces an above-average supply of male-producing or female-producing sperm.

What about the second question? You may already know that airplanes are far safer than cars, even controlling for number of passenger miles traveled. Yet most of us still feel safer in cars because we overestimate the probability of an event when examples are readily available in memory (Tversky & Kahneman, 1973). We can all recall specific airplane disasters; they make headlines because so many people die at once. A single vivid plane crash lingers longer in memory than the many auto accidents regularly reported in the local newspaper. Thus airplane fatalities *seem* more likely. On the other hand, we don't want to simplify; driving may not be riskier for everyone. Your age, driving habits, and seat-belt use, as well as the type of car you drive, all affect your risk of dying in a traffic accident.

Finally, on the third question, many people predict that the instructor's friend is a professor of Chinese studies (Ross, 1977). But this is unlikely because there are very few professors of Chinese studies in the United States, and there are thousands of professors of psychology. Also, a psychology instructor is likely to have more friends in psychology than in Chinese studies. People go astray on this question because they are influenced by their stereotypes about people, and they ignore statistical probabilities.

This little exercise shows you how intuitions can be clouded by biases and fallacies despite people's best efforts to be rational. The scientific approach is the psychologist's way of avoiding such pitfalls.

SUMMARY

SCIENCE VERSUS PSEUDOSCIENCE

1) Research methods provide a way for psychologists to separate well-supported conclusions from unfounded belief. An understanding of these methods can also help people think critically about psychological issues and become astute consumers of psychological and other scientific findings.

2) The ideal scientist states hypotheses and predictions precisely; is skeptical of claims that rest solely on faith or authority; relies on empirical evidence; is willing to comply with the principle of falsifiability; and is open about describing methods and results so that findings can be replicated. In contrast, pseudoscientists ignore these requirements. The public nature of science gives it a built-in system of checks and balances.

FERRETING OUT THE FACTS: DESCRIPTIVE STUDIES

3) *Descriptive methods* allow a researcher to describe and predict behavior but not necessarily to choose one explanation over others. Such methods include case studies, observational studies, psychological tests, surveys, and correlational methods. Some descriptive methods are used both by clinicians and by researchers.

4) *Case studies* are detailed descriptions of individuals. They are often used by clinicians. In research, they can be valuable in exploring new topics and addressing questions that would otherwise be difficult or impossible to study. But because the person under study may not be representative of people in general, case studies are typically sources rather than tests of hypotheses.

5) In *observational studies,* the researcher systematically observes and records behavior without interfering in any way with the behavior. *Naturalistic observation* is used to obtain descriptions of how subjects behave in their natural environments. *Laboratory observation* allows more control and the use of special equipment; behavior in the laboratory, however, may differ in certain ways from behavior in natural contexts.

6) *Psychological tests* are used to measure and evaluate personality traits, emotional states, aptitudes, interests, abilities, and values. A good test is one that has been *standardized* and is both *valid* and *reliable.* Teachers, parents, and employers do not always stop to question a test's validity, especially when results are summarized in a single number. Some widely used tests have inadequate reliability and validity.

7) *Surveys* are questionnaires or interviews that ask people directly about their experiences, attitudes, and opinions. Precautions must be taken to obtain a sample that is *representative* of the larger population that the researcher wishes to describe and that yields results that are not skewed by a *volunteer bias.* Findings can be affected by the fact that respondents sometimes lie, misremember, or misinterpret the questions.

LOOKING FOR RELATIONSHIPS: CORRELATIONAL STUDIES

8) In descriptive research, studies that look for relationships between phenomena are known as *correlational.* A *correlation* is a measure of the strength of a positive or negative relationship between two variables. A correlation does *not* show a causal relationship between the variables.

HUNTING FOR CAUSES: THE EXPERIMENT

9) *Experiments* allow researchers to control the situation being studied, manipulate an *independent variable,* and assess the effects of the manipulation on a *dependent variable.* Experimental studies usually require a comparison or *control* condition. *Single-blind* and *double-blind* procedures can be used to prevent the expectations of the subjects or the experimenter from affecting the results. Because experiments allow conclusions about cause and effect, they have long been the method of choice in psychology. However, like laboratory observations, experiments create a special situation that may call forth behavior not typical in other environments.

EVALUATING THE FINDINGS: WHY PSYCHOLOGISTS USE STATISTICS

10) Psychologists use *descriptive statistics*, such as the mean, range, and variance, to summarize data. They use *inferential statistics* to find out how likely it is that the results of a study occurred merely by chance. The results are said to be *statistically significant* if this likelihood is very low. Statistically significant results allow psychologists to make predictions about human behavior, but, as in all sciences, probabilistic results do not tell us with any certainty what a particular individual will do in a situation.

11) Choosing among competing interpretations of a finding can be difficult. Often, explanations must take into account many factors, and care must be taken to avoid going beyond the facts. Sometimes the best interpretation does not emerge until a hypothesis has been tested in more than one way—for example, by using both *cross-sectional* and *longitudinal* methods.

12) Statistical signficance does not always imply real-world importance because the proportion of the variance among scores accounted for by a particular variable may be small. Conversely, a result that does not quite reach significance may be potentially useful. Therefore, many psychologists are turning to other statistical measures. The technique of *meta-analysis*, for example, reveals how much of the variation in scores across many different studies can be explained by a particular variable. Meta-analysis is useful for finding patterns in results, so long as some limitations of this method are kept in mind.

EVALUATING RESEARCH METHODS: SCIENCE UNDER SCRUTINY

13) A continuing ethical issue in psychological research concerns the use and treatment of animals. Debate on this issue has led to more comprehensive guidelines in the APA ethical code and new federal laws. But most psychologists oppose banning or drastically reducing animal research.

14) Adherents of *postmodernism* argue than an observer's values, judgments, and status in society inevitably affect which events are studied, how they are studied, and how they are explained. One postmodern theory, *social constructionism*, holds that knowledge is not so much discovered as it is created or invented. Some scholars are alarmed by postmodernism, fearing that a legitimate critique of the limitations of research is turning into an attack on all traditional methods. However, these new ideas have the potential for expanding and enriching our understanding of human behavior, if combined with a traditional insistence on critical thinking and standards of evidence.

KEY TERMS

confirmation bias 43
theory 44
hypothesis 44
operational definition 45
principle of falsifiability 46
replicate 46
descriptive methods 48
case study 48
observational studies 50
naturalistic observation 50
laboratory observation 51
psychological tests 51
standardize 52
norms (in testing) 52
reliability 52
  test–retest reliability 52
  alternate-forms reliability 52
validity 52
  content validity 52
  criterion validity 52
surveys 53
sample 53
representative sample 53
volunteer bias 54
correlational study 56
correlation 56
variables 56
positive correlation 56
negative correlation 56
coefficient of correlation 57
experiment 59
independent variable 61
dependent variable 61
control condition 62
experimental/control groups 62
random assignment 62
placebo 62
single-blind study 63
experimenter effects 63
double-blind study 63
descriptive statistics 65
arithmetic mean 66
range 66
variance 66
inferential statistics 67
statistically significant 67
cross-sectional study 69
longitudinal study 69
meta-analysis 71
postmodernism 74
social constructionism 74

No two plants are exactly alike.
They're all different, and as a consequence,
you have to know that difference.
I start with the seedling, and . . . I don't feel I really know the story
if I don't watch the plant all the way along.

Barbara McClintock

CHAPTER THREE
Evolution, Genes, and Behavior

The long and short of it: Human beings are similar and *different.*

THINK OF ALL THE WAYS that human beings are alike. Everywhere, no matter what their backgrounds or where they live, people love, work, argue, dance, sing, complain, and gossip. They rear families, celebrate marriages, and mourn losses. They reminisce about the past and plan for the future. They help their friends and fight with their enemies. They smile with amusement, frown with displeasure, and glare in anger. Where do all these commonalities come from?

Think of all the ways that human beings differ. Some are extroverts, always ready to throw a party, make a new friend, or speak up in a crowd; others are shy and introverted, preferring the safe and familiar. Some are trailblazers, ambitious and enterprising; others are placid, content with the way things are. Some take to book learning like a cat to catnip; others don't do so well in school but have lots of street smarts and practical know-how. Some are overwhelmed by even the most petty problems; others, faced with severe difficulties, remain calm and resilient. Where do all these differences come from?

For many years, psychologists trying to answer these questions tended to fall into two camps. On one side were the *nativists*, who emphasized genes and inborn characteristics, or nature; on the other side were the *empiricists*, who focused on learning and experience, or nurture. Edward L. Thorndike (1903), one of the leading psychologists of the early 1900s, staked out the nativist position when he claimed that "in the actual race of life . . . the chief determining factor is heredity." But his contemporary, behaviorist John B. Watson (1925), insisted that experience could write virtually any message on the blank slate of human nature: "Give me a dozen healthy infants, well-formed, and my own specified world to bring them up in and I'll guarantee to take any one at random and train him to become any type of specialist I might select—doctor, lawyer, artist, merchant-chief and yes, even beggar-man and thief, regardless of his talents, penchants, tendencies, abilities, vocations, and race of his ancestors."

In this chapter, we focus mostly on the nature side of the debate and the findings of two related fields in psychology. Researchers in **behavioral genetics** study the contribution of heredity to individual differences in personality, mental ability, and other human characteristics. Researchers in **evolutionary psychology** emphasize the evolutionary mechanisms that might help explain commonalities in language learning, perception, memory, sexual behavior, decision making, emotion, and many other aspects of human psychology (Barkow, Cosmides, & Tooby, 1992). Evolutionary psychology, which has emerged in the past few years as a growing force in psychology, overlaps with **sociobiology,** an interdisciplinary field that looks for evolutionary explanations of social behavior in animals, including human beings.

behavioral genetics An interdisciplinary field of study concerned with the genetic bases of behavior and personality.

evolutionary psychology A field of psychology emphasizing evolutionary mechanisms that may help explain human commonalities in cognition, development, emotion, social practices, and other areas of behavior.

sociobiology An interdisciplinary field of study that emphasizes evolutionary explanations of social behavior in animals, including human beings.

In the past, exchanges between the two sides of the nature–nurture issue sometimes sounded like a boxing match: "In this corner, we have Heredity, and in this corner, we have Environment. Okay, you guys, come out fighting." Today, no one argues in terms of nature *or* nurture; all scientists understand that heredity and environment interact to produce not only our psychological traits but even most of our physical ones. Children can inherit a tendency to be nearsighted, for instance, but whether nearsightedness actually develops may depend on whether a child reads a lot or sits for hours staring at a TV set or computer monitor (Curtin, 1985; Gwiazda et al., 1993). In societies that lack a written language—societies in which nobody reads— nearsightedness is extremely rare.

WHAT'S IN A GENE?

genes The functional units of heredity; they are composed of DNA and specify the structure of proteins.

chromosomes Within every body cell, rod-shaped structures that carry the genes.

Let's begin by looking at what genes are and how they operate. **Genes,** the basic units of heredity, are located on **chromosomes,** rod-shaped structures found in every cell of the body. Each sperm cell and each egg cell (ovum) possesses 23 chromosomes, so when a sperm and egg unite at conception, the fertilized egg, and all the

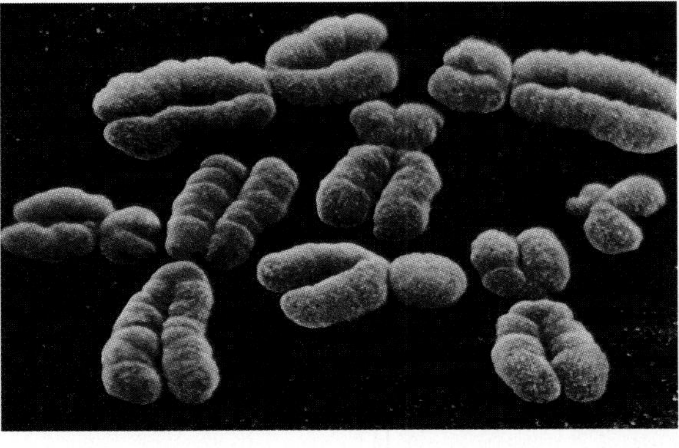

Human chromosomes, magnified almost 55,000 times.

body cells that eventually develop from it (except for sperm cells and ova), contain 46 chromosomes—23 pairs.

One of these chromosome pairs usually determines a person's anatomical sex; it consists of an "X" chromosome from the mother's egg and either an X or a "Y" chromosome from the father's sperm. Because all eggs carry only an X, whereas sperm can carry either an X or a Y, it is the father's sperm that determines the offspring's sex. If the father contributes an X, the offspring is female (XX); if the father contributes a Y, the offspring is male (XY). (The rare exceptions are children who, because of hormonal or chromosomal anomalies, are born with genitals that conflict with their chromosomes.) When Henry VIII of England blamed Anne Boleyn for bearing a daughter instead of a son, he was following a long tradition—still alive in some societies—of assuming that the mother determines a child's sex. Had he known then what we know now about genetics, his unfortunate queen might have kept her crown and her head!

Chromosomes consist of threadlike strands of **DNA (deoxyribonucleic acid)** molecules, and genes consist of small segments of this DNA. Each human chromosome contains thousands of genes, each with a fixed location; collectively, the 100,000 or so human genes are referred to as the human **genome.** Within each gene, four basic elements of DNA (called *bases*)—identified by the letters A, T, C, and G, and numbering in the thousands or even tens of thousands—are arranged in a particular order: for example, ACGTCTCTATA. . . . This sequence forms a chemical code that helps determine the synthesis of a particular protein by specifying the sequence of amino acids that form the protein. In turn, proteins directly or indirectly affect virtually all of the structural and biochemical characteristics of the organism.

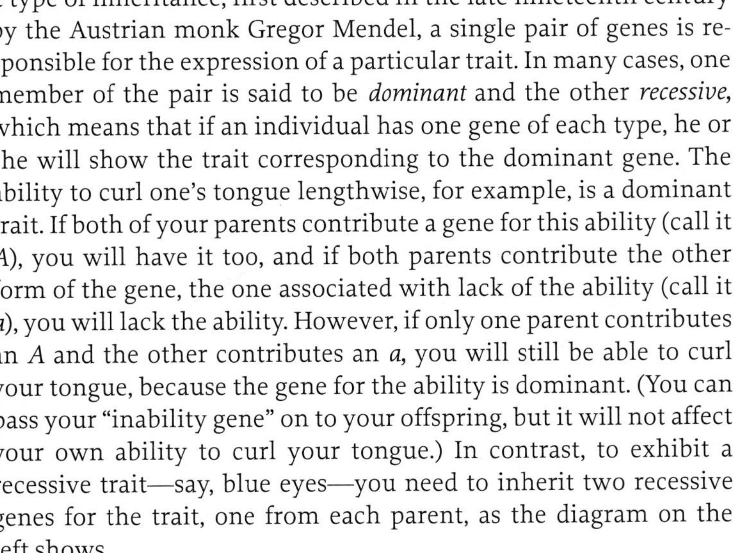

In the simplest type of inheritance, first described in the late nineteenth century by the Austrian monk Gregor Mendel, a single pair of genes is responsible for the expression of a particular trait. In many cases, one member of the pair is said to be *dominant* and the other *recessive*, which means that if an individual has one gene of each type, he or she will show the trait corresponding to the dominant gene. The ability to curl one's tongue lengthwise, for example, is a dominant trait. If both of your parents contribute a gene for this ability (call it *A*), you will have it too, and if both parents contribute the other form of the gene, the one associated with lack of the ability (call it *a*), you will lack the ability. However, if only one parent contributes an *A* and the other contributes an *a*, you will still be able to curl your tongue, because the gene for the ability is dominant. (You can pass your "inability gene" on to your offspring, but it will not affect your own ability to curl your tongue.) In contrast, to exhibit a recessive trait—say, blue eyes—you need to inherit two recessive genes for the trait, one from each parent, as the diagram on the left shows.

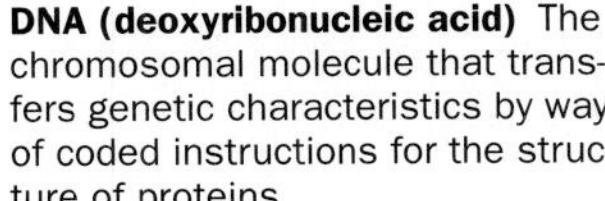

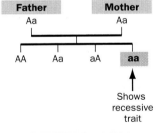

DNA (deoxyribonucleic acid) The chromosomal molecule that transfers genetic characteristics by way of coded instructions for the structure of proteins.

genome The full set of genes in each cell of an organism (with the exception of sperm and egg cells).

In albinism, a recessive trait, hair pigmentation is absent and skin color is light. If each parent carries one recessive gene for albinism, neither parent will show the trait. Each offspring, however, will have a one in four chance of inheriting both recessive genes and showing the trait, as the diagram indicates. ("A" represents the dominant gene, "a" the recessive one.) That was the case for the African-American child in this photo.

GET INVOLVED

Ask the members of your family, one person at a time, to clasp their hands together. Include aunts and uncles, grandparents, cousins—as many biological relatives as possible. Which thumb does each person put on top?

About half of all people fold the left thumb over the right and about half fold the right thumb over the left, and these responses tend to run in families. Do your own relatives show one tendency over the other? (If your family is an adoptive one, of course, there is less chance of finding a trend.) Try the same exercise with someone else's family; do you get the same results? Even for behavior as simple as thumb folding, the details of how genes exert their effect remain uncertain (Jones, 1994).

Most human traits, even such a seemingly straightforward one as height, depend on more than one gene pair, which complicates matters enormously and makes tracking down the genetic contributions to a trait extremely difficult. Identifying even a single gene is daunting; biologist Joseph Levine and geneticist David Suzuki (1993) compared the task to searching for a particular person when all you know is that the person lives somewhere on earth. There are about 3 *billion* units of DNA (all those As, Ts, Cs, and Gs) in the complete set of human chromosomes. So to locate a gene, you cannot just peer through a microscope. Instead, researchers must clone (produce copies of) several stretches of DNA on a chromosome, then use indirect methods to locate a given gene.

One method, which has been used to search for the genes associated with physical and mental conditions, involves doing **linkage studies.** These studies take advantage of the tendency of some genes lying close together on a chromosome to be inherited together across generations. The researchers start out by looking for *markers*, DNA segments that vary considerably among individuals and whose locations on the chromosomes are already known. They then look for patterns of inheritance of these markers in large families in which a particular condition is common. If a marker tends to exist in individuals who have the condition and not in those who don't, then the gene involved in the condition is apt to be located nearby on the chromosome, and the researchers have some idea where to search for it. The linkage method was used to locate the gene responsible for *Huntington's disease*, a fatal condition that usually strikes people in middle age, causing involuntary spasms and twisting movements of the body, facial grimacing, memory lapses, impulsive behavior, and sometimes paranoia, depression, and other psychological symptoms (Huntington's Disease Collaborative Research Group, 1993). Although only one gene was involved, the search took a decade of painstaking work.

An international collaboration of researchers, working on the Human Genome Project, is now rushing to map the entire human genome—all 3 billion units of DNA—and some optimistic scientists expect success within only a few years. They are working not only with linkage studies but also with high-tech methods that have been devised only recently. But finding any particular gene is still a long, laborious process, and even when you find it, you don't automatically know its role in physical or psychological functioning. That is one reason why the Human Genome Project has been controversial; no one is quite sure what the ultimate payoffs will be. (One possibility is increased genetic testing, which we discuss in "Puzzles of Psychology.")

linkage studies Studies that look for patterns of inheritance of genetic markers in large families in which a particular condition is common; the markers consist of DNA segments that vary considerably among individuals and that have known locations on the chromosomes.

Scientists commonly refer to *the* human genome, but each of us, with the exception of identical twins, is a unique genetic mosaic, one that never existed before and will never exist again. Our uniqueness is due to the way inheritance operates. When the body cells that produce sperm cells and egg cells divide, one member of each original chromosome pair goes to one new cell, and the other member goes to the

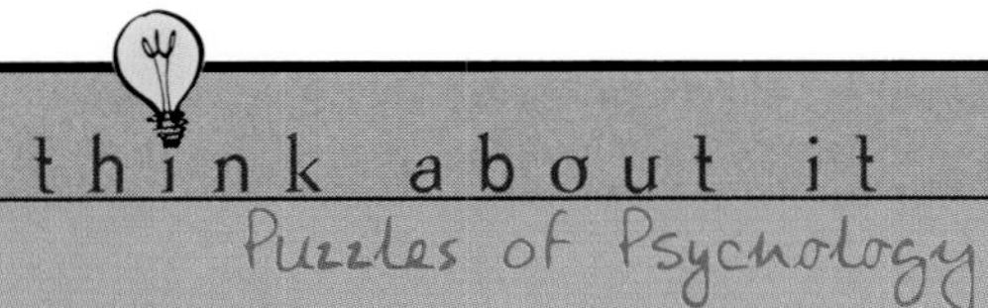

Genetic Testing: Promise or Threat?

Suppose you read in the newspaper that scientists have located a gene that increases the risk of developing Alzheimer's disease before age 60. There happen to be many cases of this condition in your family tree. Would you want to be tested to find out whether you have the gene?

This question is no longer hypothetical. In the past few years, scientists have located genes known or thought to be involved in a number of disorders, including heart disease, some kinds of colon cancer, cystic fibrosis, Huntington's disease, and certain types of Alzheimer's disease and inherited breast cancer. Supporters of genetic research are exhilarated by these findings. Such discoveries, they hope, will lead to new ways of testing for genetic mutations involved in diseases and to new treatments, including the insertion of normal genes directly into patients' tissues. In one widely reported case, a little girl benefited from an experimental genetic treatment for cystic fibrosis. It is impossible not to feel thrilled at the possibility that science will prolong her life and allow her to play like other children. You can see why scientists are excited.

But genetic breakthroughs also raise many disturbing questions about how the new information will be used. One possibility, for example, is that insurance companies will refuse coverage to adults and children who are currently healthy but who, because of their DNA, have some genetic predisposition for developing a disease or disorder later in life. Employers who pay insurance premiums for their workers may refuse to hire people whose DNA is not up to company standards. And even if the information can be kept private, people might become needlessly depressed and anxious if they know that *someday* they may die of a specific disease that currently has no cure.

Of course, it is natural, if you are going to be a parent, to want to avoid having a child who will suffer the agonies of a fatal or painful disease. But what if prenatal genetic testing reveals that your child may have a mild or treatable disease, or a disease that will not strike until old age? As one writer asks, "Many parents now abort fetuses with genes for Huntington's and cystic fibrosis, but what do you do with the knowledge that your unborn child has a sixty-five-per-cent chance of contracting breast cancer in her forties, or a ninety-per-cent chance of developing Alzheimer's in his fifties? Or that your child carries a gene for manic depression? Or a gene for obesity?" (Seabrook, 1994). What if the condition is *dyslexia*, which makes it hard but not impossible to learn to read; or homosexuality, which is not a disorder at all but which some people fear; or being very short, which in some quarters is a social disadvantage but is hardly a disability? What if the condition is femaleness? In many cultures, parents prefer sons to daughters; indeed, in China and India, the use of prenatal sonograms to determine the sex of the fetus has resulted in the abortion of millions of female fetuses. As a result, the sex ratio in these societies has become seriously skewed.

The ability to reject fetuses that are deemed not good enough could lead, in turn, to a tendency to view children as products. Will anyone want to be stuck with an imperfect model? Daniel Koshland (1988/1989), a molecular biologist and former editor in chief of *Science*, the foremost scientific journal in the United States, has asked, "If a child destined to have a permanently low IQ could be cured by replacing a gene, would anyone really argue against that?" Well, yes, some people might. For one thing, as this chapter will emphasize again and again, genes don't destine someone to have a particular IQ or any other trait. For another, variations in human abilities and traits—even those that cause individual hardship—are necessary for the adaptive functioning of complex societies, and eliminating them might have unexpected but disastrous social consequences. Further, what would the effects be on a child whose parents expected him or her to be perfect and were disappointed when, inevitably, the child was not?

Critics also worry about the social implications of genetic research. Once people learn that a gene is associated with some condition, they often ignore the economic and environmental factors that contribute to it. It is easy to make this mistake because of the language that researchers themselves sometimes use. As biologist Ruth Hubbard and writer Elijah Wald (1993) have observed, when scientists say that genes "control," "program," or "determine" behavior, or when they refer to genes "for" this or that trait, their words imply an inevitability that does not actually exist. (In this book, we have made a concerted effort to avoid this kind of deterministic language.)

For example, interest in genetic factors in intelligence may deflect attention from social and environmental influences, such as poorly equipped classrooms and toxins that cause subtle brain damage and learning problems. Likewise, the recent discovery of "obesity genes" could divert attention from the fact that high-fat foods and inactivity are the primary causes of overweight in our society. In an opinion essay in *The New York Times* (December 15, 1994), Kelly Brownell, a scientist who has studied weight and eating for many years, noted that when laboratory rats are given cheese curls, chocolate bars, marshmallows, and cookies, they ignore nutritious food and become obese. "Yet we do not fault these animals for a lack of discipline, nor need we change their biology," wrote Brownell. "Remove bad foods and the rats stay thin."

In the coming years, many of us will have to face decisions about genetic testing. Would you be tested if some of your relatives had a disease that was influenced by heredity? How would you cope if the results were unfavorable? How serious and how likely would an inherited condition have to be before you would consider aborting a fetus? Would you want your employer to have information about your DNA? Would you want to know, while you are still young, that you carry genes associated with Alzheimer's disease, Huntington's disease, or other disorders that usually don't strike until middle or old age? How might this information change your life? Think about it.

other new cell. That is why sperm cells and egg cells contain only 23 *unpaired* chromosomes.

Chance alone decides which member of each chromosome pair goes to a particular sperm or egg. When you work out the mathematics, you find that each sperm- or egg-producing cell has the potential to produce more than 8 million chromosome combinations in each new sperm or egg. But the actual diversity is far greater because genes can spontaneously change, or *mutate,* during formation of a sperm or an egg, due to an error in the copying of the original DNA sequence, and also because small segments of genetic material are apt to *cross over* (exchange places) between members of a chromosome pair before the final division.

The upshot is that each of us is the potential parent (given the time and energy) of billions of genetically different offspring. And because it takes two to make a baby, and each parent contributes one of billions of possible combinations to each child, the potential number of genetic combinations from any given set of parents is staggering. Thus siblings, who share (on average) half their genes, can be unlike each other in many ways. And children, who share (on average) half their genes with each parent, can be quite unlike their parents—in purely *genetic* terms.

Quick Quiz

1. The basic units of heredity are called (a) chromosomes, (b) Xs and Ys, (c) genes, (d) DNA molecules.
2. *True or false:* Typically, a human trait can be traced to a single gene or pair of genes.
3. Each of us is a unique genetic mosaic. What three processes during the formation of sperm and eggs explain this uniqueness?

Answers:

1. c 2. false 3. the random nature of chromosome-pair division, spontaneous genetic mutations, and crossover of genetic material between members of a chromosome pair before the final division.

Many people at first ridiculed Darwin's notion that humans share a common ancestor with other primates. In this nineteenth-century cartoon, a monkeylike Darwin shows an ape how closely he resembles people. Today, evolutionary principles, which have long guided the biological sciences, are having a growing influence on psychological science as well.

OUR HUMAN HERITAGE: THE GENETICS OF SIMILARITY

Just as genes guarantee human diversity, so they also guarantee some fundamental human similarities. These similarities can be traced to our evolutionary history. As British geneticist Steve Jones (1994) writes, "Genetics is the key to the past. Every human gene must have an ancestor. . . . Each gene is a message from our forebears and together they contain the whole story of human evolution."

Evolution is basically a change in the gene frequencies within a population over many generations. As particular genes become more or less common in the population, so do genetically influenced characteristics. Why do these frequencies change? For one thing, although parents pass on their genes to their offspring, new genetic variations keep arising as genes spontaneously mutate and recombine. According to the principle of **natural selection,** first formulated in general terms by the British naturalist Charles Darwin in *On the Origin of Species* (1859/1964), the fate of these genetic variations depends on the environment. (Darwin didn't actually know about genes, whose discovery was not yet widely known; but he did know that characteristics must somehow be transmitted from one generation to the next.) If, in a particular environment, individuals with a genetically influenced trait tend to be more successful in finding food, surviving the elements, fending off enemies, and staying alive until they can reproduce, their genes will become more and more common in

Evolutionary changes sometimes occur rapidly in response to sudden changes in the environment. The peppered moth has a light form and a dark form. Dark moths were once rare because they stood out against the light green lichen on trees and were apt to be eaten by predators before they could pass on their genes. In the nineteenth century, when pollution from coal-burning factories blackened the lichen (left), dark wings became adaptive and light ones maladaptive. By the late 1940s, 98 percent of all peppered moths were dark. Then pollution-control devices were installed and the trees lightened again (right). Since then, light-colored moths have made a comeback.

the population; over many generations, these genes may spread throughout the species. In contrast, individuals whose traits are not as adaptive in the struggle for survival will not be as reproductively fit: They will tend to die before reproducing, so their genes (and traits) will become less and less common and may eventually become extinct. Scientists debate how gradually or abruptly such changes occur and whether competition for survival is always the primary mechanism of change (Gould & Eldredge, 1977), but they agree on the basic processes of evolution, and evolutionary principles guide all the biological sciences.

Scientists who study evolution often start with some observed phenomenon (such as why the male peacock has such fabulous feathers) and then try to explain it in evolutionary terms after the fact (his preening display gets the attention of the female). But some evolutionary psychologists are taking a different tack. They begin by asking what sorts of challenges human beings might have faced in their prehistoric past—having to decide which foods were safe to eat, for example, or needing to size up a stranger's intentions quickly. They then draw inferences about the behavioral tendencies and psychological mechanisms that might have been selected because they helped our forebears solve these survival problems and enhance reproductive fitness. (No assumption is made about whether the behavior is adaptive or intelligent in the *present* environment.) Taste preferences might have evolved, for example, so that people would not eat poisonous or rancid food. Evolutionary psychologists then do research, including cross-cultural studies, to see whether their inferences are correct. Their guiding assumption is that the human mind is not a general-purpose computer but instead evolved as a collection of specialized and independent "modules" to handle specific survival problems (Buss, 1995; Cosmides, Tooby, & Barkow, 1992; Mealey, 1996). Culture and personal experience can affect which brain mechanisms actually get triggered, but everyone is born with all the "wiring" for all of the mechanisms.

evolution A change in gene frequencies within a population over many generations; a mechanism by which genetically influenced characteristics of a population change.

natural selection The evolutionary process in which individuals with genetically influenced traits that are adaptive in a particular environment tend to survive and to reproduce in greater numbers than do other individuals; as a result, their traits become more common in the population.

Critics of evolutionary psychology worry about the tendency of its advocates to assume that *every* behavior has biological, adaptive origins. They argue that the idea of mental modules is no improvement over the once popular notion in psychology that virtually every human activity and capacity, from cleanliness to cruelty, is instinctive. Evolutionary psychologists, however, contend that by drawing on different kinds of evidence they can distinguish behavior that has a biological origin from behavior that does not. As Steven Pinker (1994b) explains,

> Using biological anthropology, we can look for evidence that the problem is one that our ancestors had to solve in the environments in which they evolved—so language and face recognition are at least candidates for innate modules, but reading and driving are not. Using data from psychology and ethnography, we can test the following prediction: when children solve problems for which they have mental modules, they should look like geniuses, knowing things they have not been taught; when they solve problems that their minds are not equipped for, it should be a long hard slog. Finally, if a module for some problem is real, neuroscience should discover that the brain tissue computing the problem has some kind of physiological cohesiveness, such as constituting a circuit or subsystem.

INNATE HUMAN CHARACTERISTICS

All primates, including human beings, are innately disposed to explore the environment, manipulate objects, play, and "monkey around."

Because of our common evolutionary history, many abilities, tendencies, and characteristics are universal in human beings and either are present at birth or develop as the child matures, given certain experiences. These traits include not just the obvious ones, such as being able to stand on two legs or to grasp objects with the forefinger and thumb, but less obvious ones as well. For example, babies are born with a number of reflexes—simple, automatic responses to specific stimuli—such as sucking and grasping (see Chapter 13). An attraction to novelty also seems to be part of our evolutionary heritage, and that of many other species, as well. If a rat has had its dinner, it will prefer to explore an unfamiliar wing of a maze rather than the familiar wing where food is. Human babies, too, reveal a surprising interest in looking at and listening to unfamiliar things—which, of course, includes most of the world. A baby will even stop nursing if someone new enters his or her range of vision.

Among all birds and mammals, the desire to explore and manipulate objects is also innate. Primates especially like to "monkey" with things, taking them apart and scrutinizing the pieces, apparently for the sheer pleasure of it (Harlow, Harlow, & Meyer, 1950). And from the first, human babies explore and manipulate their small worlds. They grasp whatever is put into their tiny hands, they shake rattles, they bang pots. For human beings, the natural impulse to handle interesting objects can be overwhelming, which may be one reason why the command "don't touch" is so often ignored by children, museum-goers, and shoppers.

A related motive, in many species, including our own, is the innate impulse to play, fool around, and imitate others.

Think of kittens and lion cubs, puppies and pandas, and all young primates, who will play with and pounce on each other all day until hunger or naptime calls. Some researchers argue that play and exploration are biologically adaptive because they help members of a species find food and other necessities of life and learn to cope with their environments. Indeed, the young of many species enjoy *practice play,* behavior that will later be used for serious purposes when they are adults (Vandenberg, 1985). A kitten, for example, will stalk and attack a ball of yarn. In human beings, play is part of a child's socialization, teaching children how to get along with others and giving them a chance to practice their motor and linguistic skills (Pellegrini & Galda, 1993).

Evolutionary and other psychologists have speculated on other kinds of behavior that might be influenced by tendencies inherited because they were useful during the history of our species. For example, David Geary (1995) argues that certain arithmetic skills must be "biologically primary"—a result of evolutionary demands—because such skills appear long before infants can count verbally, are found in children around the world, and exist even in nonhuman primates. Incredibly, by the age of only *1 week,* infants show an understanding that a set of three items differs from a set of two items, indicating a rudimentary understanding of number. By 18 months, infants know that four is more than three, which is more than two, which is more than one—suggesting that the brain is designed to understand "more than" and "less than" relationships for small numbers. (In Chapter 13, we'll tell you how researchers are able to measure these skills.) But don't get too excited. The hard stuff—like long division, fractions, and geometry—does not come naturally at all for most of us; we have to work at learning it.

In later chapters, we will consider the adaptive aspects of sensory and perceptual abilities (Chapter 6), learning (Chapter 7), emotion (Chapter 10), attachment (Chapter 11), and stress reactions (Chapter 14). For now, let us look more closely at two areas that have been of great interest to evolutionary psychologists: the development of language and mating practices around the world.

Quick Quiz

How highly evolved is your understanding of evolutionary psychology?

1. Which is the *best* statement of the principle of natural selection? (a) Over time, the environment naturally selects some traits over others. (b) Particular genetic variations become more common over time if they are adaptive in a particular environment. (c) A species constantly improves as parents pass along their best traits to their offspring.
2. The guiding principle of evolutionary psychology is that the human mind evolved as (a) a collection of specialized modules to handle specific survival problems; (b) a general-purpose computer that adapts to any situation; (c) a collection of specific instincts for every human activity or capacity.
3. Which of the following is *not* part of our biological heritage? (a) a sucking reflex at birth; (b) a motive to explore and manipulate objects; (c) an avoidance of novel, unfamiliar objects; (d) a tendency to play and imitate others.

Answers:

1. b 2. a 3. c

THE CAPACITY FOR LANGUAGE

Try to read this sentence aloud:

Kamaunawezakusomamanenohayawewenimtuwamaanasana.

Can you tell where one word begins and another ends? Unless you happen to know Swahili, the syllables of this sentence probably sound like gibberish.*

Human beings appear to have an inborn facility for acquiring language, even when they can't hear speech. In North America, hearing-impaired people use American Sign Language (ASL) to express not only everyday meanings but also poetic and musical ones. Deaf children learn to sign in ASL as easily as hearing children learn to speak.

Well, to a baby learning its native tongue, *every* sentence must, at first, be gibberish. How, then, does an infant pick out discrete syllables and words from the jumble of sounds in its environment, much less figure out what those words mean? Is there something special about a baby's brain that allows the baby to tune in to language and discover how it works? Darwin thought so: Language, he wrote, "is not a true instinct, for every language has to be learned. It differs, however widely from all other arts, for man has an instinctive tendency to speak" (Darwin, 1874). Modern research is supporting Darwin's view.

To understand this issue, we must first appreciate that a **language** is not just any old communication system; it is a system for combining elements that are in themselves meaningless into utterances that convey meaning. The elements are usually sounds, but not always. In North America, many hearing-impaired people use as their primary language American Sign Language (ASL), which is based on gesture rather than sound, and in other countries, deaf people have developed other gestural languages.

Whether spoken or signed, language allows us to express and comprehend an infinite number of novel utterances, created on the spot. We seem to be the only species that does this naturally. Other primates use a variety of grunts and screeches to warn each other of danger, attract attention, and express emotions, but the sounds are not combined to produce original sentences (at least, as far as we can tell). Bongo may make a certain sound when he encounters food, but he cannot say, "The bananas in the next grove are a lot riper than the ones we ate last week and sure beat our usual diet of termites."

Except for a few fixed phrases ("How are you?" "Get a life"), most of the utterances we produce or hear over a lifetime are new. Thus you will find few, if any, sentences in this book that you have read, heard, or spoken before in exactly the same form. Yet you can understand what you are reading, and you can produce new sentences of your own. According to most *psycholinguists* (researchers who study the psychology of language), you do this by applying a large but finite set of rules that make up the grammar of your language. Rules of *syntax* tell you which strings of sounds (or gestural signs) form acceptable utterances and which ones do not. Most people cannot actually state the syntactic rules of their grammar (e.g., "Adjectives usually precede the noun they describe"), yet they are able to apply them, without even thinking about it. No native speaker of English would say, "He threw the ball big."

For adults, mastering the vocabulary and rules of a new language can be an intimidating task. But children acquire new words at an amazingly rapid rate—about 9 a day, for a total of more than 14,000 new words during the preschool years. They absorb these words as they encounter them in conversation, typically after hearing only one or two uses of a word in context (Rice, 1989). In a few short years, a child is able to string all those new words together in sentences that make sense, and, most impressive of all, produce and understand an infinite number of new word combinations.

language A system that combines meaningless elements such as sounds or gestures to form structured utterances that convey meaning.

Where do these dazzling abilities come from? Until the middle of this century, many psychologists assumed that children learned to speak by imitating adults and paying attention when adults corrected their mistakes. Then along came linguist

**Kama unaweza kusoma maneno haya, wewe ni mtu wa maana sana,* in Swahili means, "If you can read these words, you are a remarkable person."

Noam Chomsky (1957, 1980), who argued that language was far too complex to be learned bit by bit, as one might learn a list of world capitals or the rules of algebra. Chomsky observed that children not only can figure out which sounds form words but also can take the *surface structure* of a sentence—the way the sentence is actually spoken—and apply rules of syntax to infer an underlying *deep structure* that contains meaning. For example, although "Mary kissed John" and "John was kissed by Mary" have different surface structures, a 5-year-old knows that the two sentences have essentially the same deep structure, in which Mary is the actor and John the recipient of the action. The human brain, said Chomsky, must therefore contain a *language acquisition device,* a mental module that allows young children to develop language if they are exposed to an adequate sampling of speech. Just as a bird is designed to fly, human beings are designed to use language.

THE FAR SIDE/GARY LARSON
Hang him, you idiots. Hang him. String him up is a figure of speech

To "get" this cartoon, you must realize that "string him up" could have two different meanings, or "deep structures." Young children's ability to infer such deep structures suggests that the capacity for language acquisition is innate.

Chomsky and others have presented several arguments to support this position (Crain, 1991; Pinker, 1994b):

1. *Children everywhere seem to go through similar stages of linguistic development,* whether they are learning Polish, English, or Chinese (Bloom, 1970; Slobin, 1970). For example, children first form negatives simply by adding *no* or *not* at the beginning or end of a sentence ("No get dirty"); and at a later stage, they will often use double negatives ("He don't want no milk" "Nobody don't like me"), even when their language does not allow such constructions (Klima & Bellugi, 1966; McNeill, 1966). Such facts fit the theory that children are born with a sort of "universal grammar," which is another way of saying that the brain is disposed to notice the features common to all languages (nouns, verbs, phrase structures, and so forth), as well as the variations that can occur. In this view, it is the universal grammar that enables a child to hear the sentence "John likes fish," infer its deep structure, and come up with the similar sentence "Mary eats apples." And it is the same universal grammar that allows the child to know that "John likes fish" is different from "John might fish," because otherwise the child would say "John might apples" (Pinker, 1994b). (We will discuss the stages of language development further in Chapter 13.)

2. *Children combine words in ways that adults never would, so children could not simply be imitating.* They reduce a parent's sentences ("Let's go to the store!") to their own two-word version ("Go store!") and make errors an adult would not ("The alligator goed kerplunk," "Daddy taked me," "Hey, Horton heared a Who") (Ervin-Tripp, 1964; Marcus et al., 1992). Such errors are not random, however; they show that the child has grasped a grammatical rule (add the *t* or *d* sound to make a verb past tense, as in *walked* and *hugged*) and is overgeneralizing it (*taked, goed*). Helen Bee (1997) reported this charming conversation between a 6-year-old and a 3-year old, who were arguing about the relative dangers of forgetting to feed pet goldfish or feeding them too much:

6-year-old: It's worse to forget to feed them.

3-year-old: No, it's badder to feed them too much.

6-year-old: You don't say badder, you say worser.

3-year-old: But it's baddest to give them too much food.

6-year-old: No it's not. It's worsest to forget to feed them.

These children had learned a rule for comparisons (*-er* and *-est* endings) but had not yet learned all the exceptions. Such errors, which are called *overregularizations,* are really quite smart because they show that children are actively seeking regular, predictable rules of language.

GET INVOLVED

How would you complete these sentences, spoken aloud?

This morning I saw one sik. Later I saw two more ___________.

This morning I saw one wug. Later I saw two more ___________.

This morning I saw one litch. Later I saw two more ___________.

Think about the sounds you added to each nonsense word; they differed, didn't they? In English, the plural form of most nouns depends on the last sound of the singular form—and more specifically, on the part of the mouth used to make the sound, the way in which the mouth is constricted, and the presence or absence of vibration in the vocal cords. The precise rules are too complicated to describe here, yet every speaker of English has an implicit knowledge of these rules, and will correctly add an s *sound to* rat *to make* rats, *a* z *sound to* rag *to make* rags, *and an* iz *sound to* radish *to make* radishes. *(The only exceptions are people with a rare genetic disorder, as described in the text.) When 5- and 6-year-olds are asked for the plural versions of nonsense words, they easily apply the appropriate rules (Berko, 1958). Such evidence has helped to convince many psychologists that human beings have an innate tendency to infer the rules of grammar.*

3. *Adults do not consistently correct their children's syntax.* Learning explanations of language acquisition assume that children are rewarded for saying the right words and are punished for making errors. But parents don't stop to correct every error in their children's speech, so long as they can understand what the child is trying to say (Brown, Cazden, & Bellugi, 1969). Indeed, parents often *reward* children for incorrect statements! The 2-year-old who says "Want milk!" is likely to get it; most parents would not wait for a more grammatical (or polite) request. Yet by the tender age of 3, as Steven Pinker (1994b) writes, the child has become "a grammatical genius—master of most constructions, obeying rules far more often than flouting them, respecting language universals, erring in sensible, adultlike ways, and avoiding many kinds of errors altogether."

4. *Even children who are profoundly retarded acquire language.* Indeed, they typically show a facility for language that exceeds by far their abilities in other areas (Bellugi et al., 1992; Smith, Tsimpli, & Ouhalla, 1993).

Chomsky's ideas so revolutionized thinking about language and human nature that some linguists now refer to the initial publication of his ideas as The Event (Rymer, 1993). Chomsky completely changed the way researchers ask questions about language development, and even the terms they use (language "acquisition" replaced language "learning"). Since then, some scientists have returned to the learning approach, devising computer models that mimic aspects of language acquisition (e.g., finding patterns in speech) without assuming any prior mental rules of grammar (Rumelhart & McClelland, 1987). And research now shows that the speech of children learning different languages exhibits not only similarities but also dissimilarities (Slobin, 1985, 1991). However, many if not most psycholinguists accept Chomsky's argument that the human faculty for language is biologically based. Although Chomsky himself has avoided the evolutionary implications, others argue that language evolved in our species because it permitted our forebears to convey precise information about time, space, objects, and events, and to negotiate alliances that were necessary for survival (Pinker, 1994b).

The next logical step might be to identify the specific brain modules and genes that contribute to our ability to acquire language. One clue comes from a fascinating

Canadian study of a large three-generation British family with a rare genetic disorder that prevents normal language acquisition (Gopnik, 1991; Matthews, 1994). Family members who are affected with this disorder have normal intelligence and perceptual abilities, but they cannot infer specific kinds of grammatical rules, including those for changing tenses or constructing plurals—rules that normal children learn easily and unconsciously. For example, they can learn the distinction between *mice* and *mouse* but cannot learn the general rule about adding an *s*, *z*, or *iz* sound to make a noun plural, as in *bikes* (*s*), *gloves* (*z*), and *kisses* (*iz*). Instead, they must learn each plural as a separate item, and they make many errors. Yet their other grammatical abilities are unimpaired. The pattern of inheritance seen in this study and others suggests that the disorder may be due to a single dominant gene (Gopnik, 1994).

But remember: In any complex behavior, nature and nurture normally interact. Although most children have the capacity to acquire language from mere exposure to it, many parents help things along. Even though parents may not go around correcting their children's speech all day, neither do they ignore their children's errors. For example, they are more likely to repeat verbatim a child's well-formed sentence than a sentence with errors ("That's a horse, mommy!" "Yes, that's a horse"). And when the child makes a mistake or produces a clumsy sentence, parents almost invariably respond by recasting it or expanding its elements ("Monkey climbing!" "Yes, the monkey is climbing the tree") (Bohannon & Stanowicz, 1988). In turn, children are more likely to imitate adult recasts and expansions, suggesting that they are learning from them (Bohannon & Symons, 1988). They also imitate their parents' accents, inflections, and tone of voice, and they will repeat some words that the parent tries to teach ("This is a ball, Erwin." "Baw").

Language therefore depends on both biological readiness and social experience. Children who are abandoned and abused, and who are not exposed to language for years (such as Genie, whom we discussed in Chapter 2), rarely speak normally. Such sad evidence suggests a *critical period* in language development during the first few years of life or possibly the entire first decade (Curtiss, 1977; Lenneberg, 1967; Tartter, 1986). During these years, children do not need to hear *speech*—deaf children's acquisition of sign language parallels the development of spoken language—but they do need close relationships and practice in conversation.

COURTSHIP AND MATING

Most psychologists agree that the evolutionary history of our species has made certain kinds of learning either difficult or easy. Most acknowledge that simple behaviors, such as smiling or having a preference for sweet tastes, resemble *instincts*, chains of reflexes that are relatively uninfluenced by learning and that occur in all members of the species. And most agree that human beings inherit some of their cognitive, perceptual, emotional, and linguistic capacities. But social scientists disagree heartily about the biological and evolutionary origins of complex social customs, such as those surrounding mating and marriage.

AVOID OVERSIMPLIFICATION

Certain sex differences in courtship and mating are common in cultures around the world and among nonhuman mammals as well. But human sexual behavior also varies in many ways. Do genes hold culture on a tight leash, a long and flexible one, or none at all?

In psychology, and in other social sciences as well, the evolutionary viewpoint on mating practices has been strongly influenced by the writings of sociobiologists. Sociobiologists contend that evolution has bred into each of us a tendency to act in ways that maximize our chances of passing on our genes, and to help our close biological relatives, with whom we share many genes, do the same. This impulse to act in ways that ensure the survival of our personal genetic code, sociobiologists argue, is the primary motivation behind much of our social behavior, from altruism (concern for others) to xenophobia (fear of strangers) (Wilson, 1975, 1978). In the so-

This Kenyan man has 40 wives and 349 children. Although he is unusual, in societies around the world it is far more common for men to have many wives than for women to have many husbands. Sociobiologists and evolutionary psychologists attribute this difference to the evolution of different sexual and marital strategies in males and females.

ciobiological view, just as nature has selected physical characteristics that have proved adaptive, so it has selected psychological traits and social customs that aid individuals in propagating their genes. Customs that enhance the odds of such transmission survive in the form of kinship bonds, courtship rituals, dominance arrangements, taboos against female adultery, and many other aspects of social life.

Sociobiologists believe that because the males and females of most species have faced different survival and mating problems, they have evolved to differ profoundly in aggressiveness, social dominance, and sexual strategies (Symons, 1979; Trivers, 1972). In this view, it pays for males to compete with other males for access to young and fertile females, and to try to win and then inseminate as many females as possible. The more females a male mates with, the more genes he can pass along. (The world's record in this regard was achieved by a man who fathered 899 children [Daly & Wilson, 1983].) In contrast, females need to shop for the best genetic deal, as it were, because they can conceive and bear only a limited number of offspring. Having such a large biological investment in each pregnancy, they can't afford to make mistakes. Besides, mating with a lot of different men would produce no more offspring than staying with just one. So, females try to attach themselves to dominant males, who have resources and status and are likely to have "superior" genes.

According to sociobiologists, the result of these two opposite sexual strategies is that, in general, males want sex more often than females do; males are often fickle and promiscuous, whereas females are usually devoted and faithful; males are drawn to sexual novelty and even rape, whereas females want stability and security; males are relatively undiscriminating in their choice of partners, whereas females are cautious and choosy; and males are competitive and concerned about dominance, whereas females are less so.

Evolutionary psychologists agree with much of this argument. However, unlike the sociobiologists, most evolutionary psychologists do not consider human beings to be "reproductive-fitness maximizers" whose main motive is to perpetuate their genes. As evolutionary psychologist David Buss (1995) points out, if men had a conscious or unconscious motive to maximize their reproductive fitness, they would be lining up to make donations to sperm banks! Instead, say evolutionary psychologists, evolved behavioral tendencies are the *end products* of two evolutionary processes. One is *natural selection*, which, as we've seen, occurs when characteristics within a population increase in frequency because they help individuals survive.

The other is *sexual selection,* which occurs when characteristics increase in frequency because they help individuals compete for or attract sexual partners.

According to evolutionary psychologists, some of the "end products" of these processes are mating preferences and strategies similar to those described by the sociobiologists. They cite evidence from hundreds of studies, such as one massive project in which 50 scientists studied 10,000 people in 37 cultures located on six continents and five islands (Buss, 1994). Such studies have found that around the world, men are more violent than women, more socially dominant, more interested in the youth and beauty of their sexual partners (presumably because youth is associated with fertility), more sexually jealous and possessive of their partners (presumably because males can never be 100 percent sure that their children are really theirs genetically), quicker to have sex with partners they don't know well, and more inclined toward polygamy and promiscuity (presumably so that their sperm will be distributed as widely as possible). Women, in contrast, tend to emphasize the financial resources or prospects of a potential mate, his status, and his willingness to commit to a relationship (Bailey et al., 1994; Buss, 1994, 1996; Buunk et al., 1996; Daly & Wilson, 1983; Sprecher, Sullivan, & Hatfield, 1994). It is no accident, say evolutionary psychologists, that the sex differences found so often in human societies are the very ones found among other mammals. As Douglas Kenrick and Melanie Trost (1993) wryly observe, hamadryas baboons and Ugandan kob antelopes are unlikely to have been influenced by human social customs and technology, such as television, so some other explanation of the similarities between such animals and our own species is necessary. That explanation, they believe, starts with our genes.

Critics of the evolutionary approach acknowledge that sex differences exist, but they differ in how they explain those differences. It is a mistake, they say, to argue by analogy. Two species may behave in a similar fashion, but this does not necessarily mean that the *origins* of the behavior are the same in both species. For example, a male scorpion fly that coerces a female into copulation can hardly have the same motives as a human rapist, but some sociobiologists apply the word *rape* to the behavior of both the fly and the man (Thornhill, 1980). In this way, says geneticist Richard Lewontin (1993), "Human categories are laid on animals by analogy, partly as a matter of convenience of language, and then these traits are 'discovered' in animals and laid back on humans as if they had a common origin."

Moreover, animal behavior does not always conform to the stereotypes of the sexually promiscuous male and the coy and choosy female (Hrdy, 1988; Hubbard, 1990). In many species—including birds, fish, mammals, and primates—females are sexually ardent and often have many male partners. In these species, the female's sexual behavior does not seem to depend only on the goal of being fertilized by the male, because females actively solicit males when the females are not ovulating and even when they are already pregnant. And in many primate species, males do not just mate and run; they stick around, feeding the infants, carrying them on their backs, and protecting them against predators (Hrdy, 1988; Taub, 1984).

A basic sociobiological assumption is that females across species have a greater investment in child rearing than males do, but there are many exceptions. Female emperor penguins, for example, take off every winter, leaving males like this one behind to care for the kids.

These findings have sent primatologists and evolutionary theorists scurrying to figure out the evolutionary benefits of female promiscuity and male nurturance. Perhaps, in some species, females need sperm from several males in order to ensure conception by the healthiest sperm (Baker, 1996). Perhaps, in some species, females mate with numerous males precisely to make paternity uncertain; that way, male partners will be more invested in, and tolerant of, the female's infants, who could, after all, be their own (Hrdy, 1988).

But critics of evolutionary theories take exception to this entire line of reasoning. The evidence of female promiscuity in other species, they say, has no more relevance to human behavior than does evidence of female fidelity. Among human beings, sexual behavior is extremely varied and changeable. Human cultures range from those in which women have many children to those in which they have very few; from those in which men are intimately involved in child rearing to those in which they do nothing at all; from those in which women may have many lovers to those in which women may be killed if they have sex outside of marriage. Even within a given culture, sexual attitudes and practices vary tremendously (Laumann et al., 1994). Such variations, say the critics, argue against a single, genetically determined sexual strategy. In rebuttal, evolutionary theorists reply that cultural variation does not negate the importance of biology. "Evolutionary theorists do not deny that there is a great variation in the range of human social behavior," observe Kenrick and Trost (1993), but "they believe that, underneath all the variation, it is possible to discern some regularities in human behavior."

This may seem like a moderate conclusion, but debate over these matters can get quite heated, mainly because of worries that evolutionary arguments will be used to justify social and political inequalities and violent behavior. For example, such arguments could be used to conclude that rape is a biological imperative—modifiable, perhaps, but impossible to eliminate. Or they could be used to conclude that men are destined to control business and politics. Edward Wilson (1975), one of the leading proponents of sociobiology, once wrote that because of genetics, "Even with identical education and equal access to all professions [for both sexes], men are likely to continue to play a disproportionate role in political life, business, and science." This is not a message that people who hope for gender equality welcome! In 1978, demonstrators at a meeting of the American Association for the Advancement of Science dumped water on Wilson's head, chanting "Wilson, you're all wet!" The American Anthropological Association even considered censuring him until Margaret Mead, a loyal member of the "nurture" camp if ever there was one, defended him by reminding the association that censure would be equivalent to book burning (Wilson, 1994).

Ultimately, the central issue in this debate has to do with the relative power of biology and culture. In *On Human Nature* (1978), Wilson argued that genes hold culture on a leash. The big question, replied paleontologist Stephen Jay Gould (1987), is this: How long and tight is that leash? Is it only one foot long, in which case a society doesn't have much room to maneuver and change, or is it ten feet long, in which case biology merely establishes a broad range of possibilities? To most sociobiologists, the near universality of certain human customs is evidence that the leash is short and tight. To most psychologists who take a nonevolutionary approach, the enormous variation among individuals and societies is evidence that the leash is long and flexible. Most evolutionary psychologists seem to fall somewhere in the middle. They emphasize the adaptive nature of mating and courtship tendencies in the environments in which our species evolved, but they also acknowledge that some of these customs may no longer be adaptive in our current environments, and they believe that human beings have evolved to be flexible enough to change when the environment demands (Buss, 1995; Mealey, 1996).

Quick Quiz

1. Name four arguments for the existence of an innate "universal grammar."
2. According to sociobiologists, human social customs reflect a motive of individuals to act in ways that ensure the survival of (a) the species, (b) their particular ethnic or national group, (c) their personal genetic code.
3. Which of the following would an evolutionary psychologist expect to be more typical of males than of females? (a) promiscuity, (b) choosiness about sexual partners, (c) concern with dominance, (d) interest in young partners, (e) emphasis on physical attractiveness of partners.

4. A friend of yours, who has read some sociobiology, tells you that men will *always* be more sexually promiscuous than women because during evolution, the best reproductive strategy for male primates has been to inseminate lots of females. What kind of evidence would you need to evaluate this claim?

Answers:

1. Children everywhere seem to go through similar stages of linguistic development; children combine words in ways that adults never would; adults do not consistently correct their children's syntax; and even profoundly retarded children acquire language. 2. c 3. all but b 4. You would not want to look just for confirming evidence (recall the principle of falsifiability). You would want to look also for evidence of female promiscuity and male monogamy among humans and other species and changes in sexual customs in response to changing social conditions.

OUR HUMAN DIVERSITY: THE GENETICS OF DIFFERENCE

We turn now to the second great issue in the nature–nurture debate: the origins of the differences among us. We will begin with a critical discussion of what heritability means and how it can be estimated. Then, to illustrate how behavioral geneticists study differences that might be partly heritable, we will examine two (unrelated!) topics: weight and intelligence. In Chapter 12, we will discuss behavioral-genetic explanations of personality, and in Chapter 15, we will consider behavioral-genetic explanations of mental disorders.

THE HERITABILITY HUNT

Suppose you want to measure flute-playing ability in a large group of music students. You have some independent raters assign each student a score, from 1 to 20, and when you plot the scores, you see that they vary considerably. Some people are what you might call melodically disadvantaged and should forget about a career in music; others are flute geniuses, practically ready for Carnegie Hall; and the rest fall somewhere in between. What causes the variation in this group of students? Why are some so musically talented and others so inept? Are these differences primarily genetic, or are they the result of experience and motivation?

DEFINE YOUR TERMS

What does it mean to say that some trait is "highly heritable"? If you want to improve your flute playing and someone tells you that musical ability is heritable, should you stop practicing?

The methods used by behavioral geneticists to study such questions typically yield a statistical estimate of the *proportion of the total variance in a trait* that is attributable to *genetic variation within a group.* This estimate is known as the trait's **heritability.** Because the heritability of a trait is expressed as a proportion, the maximum value it can have is 1.0. Height is highly heritable; that is, within a group of equally well-nourished individuals, most of the variation among them will be accounted for by their genetic differences. In contrast, table manners have low heritability because most variation among individuals is accounted for by differences in upbringing. Our guess is that flute-playing ability falls somewhere in the middle.

heritability A statistical estimate of the proportion of the total variance in some trait within a group that is attributable to genetic differences among individuals within the group.

Many people hold completely mistaken ideas about heritability. You can't understand the nature–nurture issue without understanding this concept, and especially the following important facts:

1. *"Heritable" does not mean the same thing as "genetic."* Heritability applies only to traits that vary in a population. Many genetic traits, such as breathing, are crucial for life and therefore do not vary; if you are alive, you breathe. Such traits are 100 percent genetic, but their calculated heritability would be zero because there is no variation to explain. (Of course, a tendency to develop a breathing disorder, such as asthma, can be partly heritable.)

2. *An estimate of heritability applies only to a particular group living in a particular environment, and estimates may differ for different groups.* Suppose that all the children in Oz County are affluent, eat plenty of high-quality food, have kind and attentive parents, and go to the same top-notch schools. Because their environments are similar and are optimal for cognitive development, the intellectual differences among them will probably be due largely to their genetic differences. That is, mental ability in this group will be highly heritable. In contrast, the children in Normal County are rich, poor, and in between. Some of them have healthy diets; others live on fatty foods and cupcakes. Some attend good schools; others go to inadequate ones. Some have doting parents, and some have unloving and neglectful ones. Because these children's intellectual differences might be due largely to their environmental differences, estimates of the heritability of intelligence may be lower in this group.

3. *Heritability estimates do not apply to individuals, only to variations within a group.* As we saw earlier, each individual is a unique genetic mosaic. Each individual also has a unique history in terms of family relationships, intellectual training, and motivation. For these reasons, no one can say whether your genius at, say, flute playing is a result of inherited musical talent, living all your life in a family of devoted flute players, a private obsession that you acquired at age 6 when you saw the opera *The Magic Flute*—or a combination of all three. For one person, genes may make a tremendous difference in some aptitude or disposition; for another, the environment may be far more important.

4. *Even highly heritable traits can be modified by the environment.* Although height is highly heritable, malnourished children may not grow to be as tall as they would with sufficient food. Conversely, if children eat a supernutritious diet, they may grow to be taller than anyone thought they could. The same principle applies to psychological traits, although some writers have failed to realize this. Some biological determinists, for example, have argued that because IQ is highly heritable, IQ and school achievement cannot be boosted much. But even if the first part of the statement is true, the second part does not necessarily follow.

5. *Genes turn "on" and "off" over a lifetime.* Although some of these changes are "preprogrammed," factors such as stress and nutrition can also probably cause specific genes to be activated or deactivated (McClearn, 1993). As a result, the relative contribution of these genes to a particular behavior may wax and wane.

Scientists have no way to estimate the heritability of a trait or behavior directly, so they must *infer* it by studying people whose degree of genetic similarity is known. You might think that the simplest approach would be to compare blood relatives within families; everyone knows of families that are famous for some talent or trait. But anecdotes and isolated examples can always be answered with counterexamples. There were seven generations of musical Bachs, but Mendelssohn's father was a banker, Chopin's a bookkeeper, and Schubert's a schoolmaster, and their mothers were not known to have musical talent (Lewontin, 1982). Results from controlled studies of families are also inconclusive, for close relatives usually share environments, as well as genes. If Carlo's parents and siblings all love lasagna, that doesn't mean a taste for lasagna is heritable. The same applies if everyone in Carlo's family has a high IQ, is mentally ill, or is moody.

There are two ways out of this bind. One is to study adopted children (e.g., Loehlin, Horn, & Willerman, 1996; Plomin & DeFries, 1985). Such children share half their genes, but not their environment, with each birth parent. On the other hand, they share an environment with their adoptive parents and siblings, but not their genes. Researchers can compare correlations between the children's traits and those of their biological and adoptive relatives and can use the results to estimate heritability.

The other approach is to compare **identical (monozygotic) twins** with **fraternal (dizygotic) twins.** Identical twins are created when a fertilized egg divides into two parts that then develop into two separate embryos. Because the twins come from the same fertilized egg, they share all their genes, barring genetic mutations or other accidents. (They may be slightly different at birth, however, because of birth complications, differences in the blood supply to the two fetuses, or other chance factors.) In contrast, fraternal twins develop when a woman's ovaries release two eggs instead of one, and each egg is fertilized by a different sperm. Fraternal twins are wombmates but are no more alike genetically than any other two siblings, and they may be of different sexes. By comparing groups of same-sex fraternal twins to groups of identical twins, psychologists can try to estimate heritability. The assumption is that if identical twins are more alike than fraternal twins, the increased similarity must be genetic.

Perhaps, however, environments shared by identical twins differ from those shared by fraternal twins. People may treat identical twins, well, identically, or they may go to the other extreme by emphasizing the twins' differences (although no one has ever shown that such practices actually affect the traits of twins). To avoid this problem, investigators have studied identical twins who were separated early in life and reared apart. (Until recently, adoption policies and attitudes toward illegitimacy permitted such separations to occur.) In theory, separated identical twins share all their genes but not their environments. Any similarities between them should be primarily genetic and should permit a direct estimate of heritability.

In an important project begun in 1979, an interdisciplinary team at the University of Minnesota has tested and interviewed hundreds of identical and fraternal twins reared apart (Bouchard, 1984, 1995, 1997a; Bouchard et al., 1990, 1991; Tellegen et al., 1988). Subjects have undergone comprehensive psychological and medical monitoring and have answered thousands of written questions. Information is now available on many sets of reunited twins and also on many twins reared together.

identical (monozygotic) twins Twins that develop when a fertilized egg divides into two parts that develop into separate embryos.

fraternal (dizygotic) twins Twins that develop from two separate eggs fertilized by different sperm; they are no more alike genetically than are any other pair of siblings.

Everyone is fascinated by twins, including psychologists. Identical twins Gerald Levey (left) and Mark Newman, who were separated shortly after birth and grew up in different cities, have been studied by psychologists at the Minnesota Center for Twin and Adoption Research. When Gerald and Mark were reunited at age 31, they discovered that they shared some astounding similarities. Both are volunteer firefighters, wear mustaches, and are bachelors. They are exactly the same height and weight. Both men like to hunt, watch old John Wayne movies, and eat Chinese food after a night on the town. They drink the same brand of beer, hold the can with the little finger curled under it, and crush the can when it's empty. The challenge for researchers is to determine which of these traits and behaviors are influenced strongly by heredity, and which result mainly from environmental factors such as social class and upbringing.

Separated at birth, the Mallifert twins meet accidentally.

Behavioral-genetics research is transforming our understanding of behavior that was once explained solely in psychological terms, and nowhere is this more true than in the study of body weight and shape, as we are about to see.

Quick Quiz

1. Diane hears that basket-weaving ability is highly heritable and concludes that her own low performance must be due mostly to genes. What's wrong with her reasoning?
2. Bertram hears that some mental ability is highly heritable and concludes that schools should stop trying to improve the skills of children who seem to lack the ability. What's wrong with his reasoning?
3. Carpentry skills seem to run in Andy's family. Why shouldn't Andy conclude that his talent is genetic?

Answers:

1. Heritability applies only to differences among individuals within a group, not to particular individuals. 2. A trait may be highly heritable *and* susceptible to modification and improvement. 3. Family members share environments as well as genes.

BODY WEIGHT AND SHAPE

ASK QUESTIONS

Obesity is caused mainly by psychological problems that drive people to overeat, isn't it? When researchers began to question this obvious assumption, they were in for a surprise.

At one time, most psychologists thought that being fat was a sign of emotional disturbance. If you were overweight, it was because you hated your mother, feared intimacy, or were trying to fill an emotional hole in your psyche by loading up on rich desserts. The evidence for this belief, however, came mainly from self-reports, and many studies were seriously flawed: They lacked control groups, and they overlooked the possibility that people were saying what they thought researchers wanted to hear (Allison & Heshka, 1993). When researchers put this popular idea to the test, they found no support for it. On average, they discovered, fat people are no more and no less emotionally disturbed than average-weight people (Stunkard, 1980).

Even more surprising, studies showed that *heaviness is not always caused by overeating* (C. Bouchard et al., 1990). Many heavy people do eat large quantities of food, but so do some very thin people. Many thin people eat very little, but so do some obese people. In one study that carefully monitored everything that subjects were eating, two 260-pound women maintained their weights while consuming only 1,000 calories a day (Wooley, Wooley, & Dyrenforth, 1979). In another study, in which volunteers were required to gorge themselves for months, it was as hard for slender people to gain weight as it is for most heavy people to lose weight. The minute the study was over, the slender people lost weight as fast as dieters gain it back (Sims, 1974).

One theory that integrates such findings argues that a biological mechanism keeps a person's body weight at a genetically influenced **set point** —the weight the person stays at when not consciously trying to gain or lose (Lissner et al., 1991). According to this theory, everyone has a genetically programmed *basal metabolism rate,* the rate at which the body burns calories for energy, and a fixed number of *fat cells,* which store fat for energy. The fat cells can change in size but not in number. A complex interaction of metabolism, fat cells, and hormones keeps people at the weight their bodies are designed to be. When a heavy person diets, the body's metabolism slows down to conserve energy (and fat reserves). When a thin person overeats, metabolism speeds up, burning energy. Set-point theory, which has been supported by dozens of studies of animals and human beings, explains why most people who go on restricted diets eventually gain their weight back: They are returning to their set-point weight (Leibel, Rosenbaum, & Hirsch, 1995; Levitan & Ronan, 1988).

Is this man heavy because of his genes, his diet, or both? Does your answer affect how you feel about him—sympathetic, neutral, or contemptuous?

In twin and adoption studies, estimates of the heritability of body weight and shape vary quite a bit, ranging from 25 percent to 80 percent (Allison et al., 1994; C. Bouchard et al., 1990; Stunkard et al., 1990). But it seems clear that size and weight differences among people can be explained to some extent by their genetic differences. Consider:

- In a study of 171 Pima Indians in Arizona, researchers found that two-thirds of the women and half of the men became obese over time, and the slower their metabolisms, the greater the weight gain. After adding anywhere from 20 to 45 pounds, however, the Pimas stopped gaining weight. Now their metabolic rates rose, and their weights stabilized at the new, higher level (Ravussin et al., 1988). Many Pimas apparently have a set point for plumpness.
- In a study of 18 infants at 3 months of age, the babies of overweight mothers generated 21 percent less energy than the babies of normal-weight mothers, although the babies were all eating the same amount. By the age of 1 year, these lower-metabolism babies had become overweight (Roberts et al., 1988).
- Genes also affect whether the body will convert excess calories into fat or muscle, and what the basic body *shape* will be (pear, apple, hourglass, tree trunk, and so on). Pairs of adult identical twins who have been raised in different families are just as similar in body weight and shape as twins raised together. The early family environment has almost no effect at all on body shape, weight gain, or percentage of fat in the body (Stunkard et al., 1990). In a study of 12 pairs of adult male identical twins, Claude Bouchard and his colleagues (1990) confined the men to a dormitory for 100 days, where they were forbidden to exercise and were given a diet that contained 1,000 extra calories a day. In each pair of twins, both members gained almost exactly the same amount of weight, but the differences *between* twin pairs was astonishing. One pair of twins gained $9\frac{1}{2}$ pounds, but another pair gained almost 30—all of them on only 1,000 extra calories a day. Some pairs of twins gained weight on their hips and thighs; others gained weight around the waist.

set point The genetically influenced weight range for an individual, thought to be maintained by a biological mechanism that regulates food intake, fat reserves, and metabolism.

Body weight and shape are strongly affected by genetic factors. Set-point theory helps explain why the Pimas of the American Southwest (left) gain weight easily but lose it slowly, whereas the Bororo nomads of Nigeria (right) can eat a lot of food yet remain slender.

Enormous progress has been made in identifying the genes involved in some types of obesity. One team of researchers isolated a genetic variation that causes mice to become obese (Zhang et al., 1994). The usual form of the gene, called "obese," or *ob* for short, causes fat cells to secrete a hormonelike protein, which the researchers named *leptin* (from the Greek *leptos*, "slender"). Leptin travels through the blood to a brain area called the *hypothalamus*, which is involved in the regulation of appetite. Varying levels of this substance signal how large or small the body's fat cells are, so that the brain can regulate appetite and metabolism to maintain the animal's or person's set point. Injecting leptin into mice reduces the animals' appetites, speeds up their metabolisms, and makes them more active; as a result, the animals shed weight, even if they are not overweight to begin with (Halaas et al., 1995).

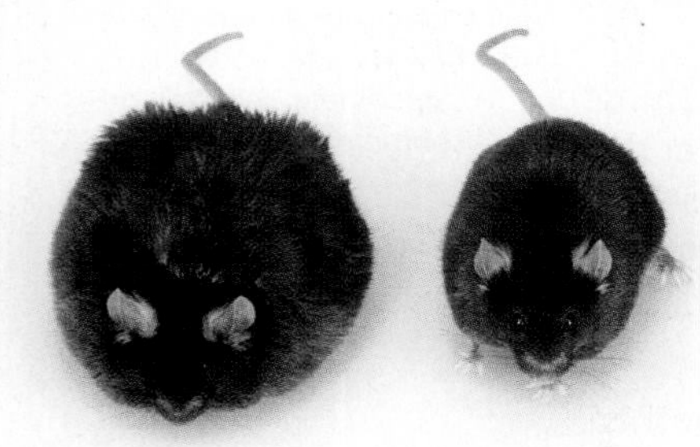

Genes contribute to some forms of obesity. Both mice shown here have a mutation in the ob gene, which normally directs the synthesis of leptin, a substance that helps regulate appetite and metabolism. The mutation usually makes mice chubby, like the one on the left. But when leptin is injected daily, the mice remain almost normal in weight, like the one on the right, because they eat less and burn more calories.

The role of leptin in human obesity, as you might expect, is more complicated. Some obese people may gain weight rapidly because they have the variant form of the *ob* gene and their leptin levels are low (Ravussin et al., 1997). Other obese people, however, have very *high* leptin levels. They produce plenty of leptin, but they are insensitive to it, probably because of a gene that prevents cells in the brain from responding normally to leptin's signals (Chua et al., 1996; Considine et al., 1996; Maffei et al., 1995). As a result, they stay hungry and continue eating even when the body has enough stored fat to meet current energy demands. Other genes and body chemicals, too, are involved in appetite and weight regulation. According to evolutionary psychologists, genes that predispose individuals to obesity probably exist in our species because, in the past, starvation was all too often a real possibility, and a tendency to store calories in the form of fat provided a definite survival advantage.

Most Americans still mistakenly blame obesity on slothfulness, gluttony, and weakness of will (Crandall, 1994). The discovery of genetic influences on body weight and shape may help to combat their prejudice toward obese individuals. But to many researchers, obesity is a legitimate matter of medical concern because it is associated with a higher risk of heart disease, hypertension, diabetes, some cancers, and other diseases. Should seriously overweight people try to fight their set points, or should they instead fight society's prejudices? Does the genetic research mean that trying to lose weight is hopeless anyway?

The behavioral-genetic research on obesity shows again the danger of either/or thinking. Genes set limits for body weight and shape, but other factors affect weight within that range. One such factor is eating habits. If you consume the high-fat junk-food diet that so many North Americans love (indeed, that human beings might be evolutionarily primed to love), and if you eat such food in the large quantities that most Europeans and Asians find excessive and alarming, you are likely to be heavier than if you eat a low-fat diet in moderate portions. It may not be only a matter of calories: a high-fat diet may actually change an individual's set point for body weight by somehow increasing the body's resistance to leptin (Frederich et al., 1995). As one physician wrote to *The New York Times*, "Perhaps the flaw lies not so much in our mutations as in McDonald's."

A second factor is exercise, which boosts the body's metabolic rate and may lower its set point. In one study of 18 obese women who were on severely restricted diets, metabolic rates dropped sharply, as set-point theory would predict. But the women who combined the diet with moderate physical activity—daily walking—lost weight, and their metabolic rates rose almost to previous levels (Wadden et al., 1990). This study suggests why changes in weight often accompany major changes in habits and activity levels. People start walking to work (or stop). They become lethargic after losing a job (and gain weight), or excited when they fall in love (and lose weight).

In turn, culture has an enormous influence on how and what people eat and how much exercise they get. During the 1950s and 1960s, surveys found that about 7 percent of American men and 14 percent of women were trying to lose weight. Over the years, the numbers rose steadily, until today about a quarter of all men and two-fifths of all women say they are dieting (Horm & Anderson, 1993; Serdula et al., 1993). Yet all this dieting has not produced a thinner population. In fact, the prevalence of obesity has jumped dramatically in the past few decades (Kuczmarski et al., 1994). The reasons no doubt have less to do with obesity genes than with the increased abundance of high-fat foods, the habit of eating high-calorie food on the run rather than leisurely meals, the rise in energy-saving (fat-conserving!) devices, the popularity of television over active hobbies, and increasingly sedentary lifestyles (Brownell & Rodin, 1994).

The research on weight contains a lesson that applies to many other areas of behavior: Within a given environment, genes and other biological factors place some limits on how much a person can change. These factors interact with environmental ones to shape—sometimes quite literally—who we are. Even if you make daily trips to the gym and eat a healthy diet, you may never look like the current cultural ideal, which is physically impossible for many people. Still, there is much you can do to maintain your healthiest personal weight, as we discuss in "Taking Psychology with You" at the end of this chapter.

Quick Quiz

Is all this information about food making you hungry for knowledge?

1. According to set-point theory, when a thin person overeats, metabolism tends to ____________, whereas when a heavy person diets, metabolism tends to ____________.
2. Twin studies indicate that genes contribute not only to differences in weight but also to differences in body ____________.
3. Bill, who is thin, reads in the newspaper that genes set the range of body weight and shape. "Oh, good," he exclaims, "now I can eat all the junk food I want; I was born to be skinny." What's wrong with Bill's conclusion?

Answers:

1. increase; slow down 2. shape 3. Bill is right to recognize that there may be limits to how heavy he can become. But he is oversimplifying and jumping to conclusions. Even people who have a set point for leanness will gain some weight on fatty foods and excess calories, especially if they don't exercise; also, rich junk food is unhealthy for reasons that have nothing to do with overweight.

ORIGINS OF INTELLIGENCE

Most people think that differences in body weight are due entirely to psychological factors, but, as we have seen, heredity is also involved. In contrast, many people think that individual differences in intelligence are due entirely to hereditary factors, but, as we will see, psychology is also very much involved. Likewise, many people think that weight is easier to change than it is—and that IQ is harder to change than it is. In this section, we consider how biology and learning affect intelligence just as they affect weight.

In heritability studies, the usual measure of intellectual functioning is an **intelligence quotient,** or **IQ** score. The term "IQ" is a holdover from the early days of psychological testing, when intelligence tests were given only to children. A child's *mental age* (MA)—the child's level of intellectual development relative to other children's—was divided by the child's chronological age (CA) and multiplied by 100 to yield an *intelligence quotient* (IQ). Thus a child of 8 who performed like the average 6-year-old would have a mental age of 6 and an IQ of 75 (6 divided by 8, times 100); and a child of 8 who scored like an average 10-year-old would have a mental age of 10 and an IQ of 125 (10 divided by 8, times 100). All average children, regardless of age, would have an IQ of 100 because MA and CA would be the same. (In actual calculations, months were used, not years, to yield a more precise figure.)

This method of figuring IQ had a serious flaw. At one age, scores might cluster tightly around the average, whereas at another age, they might be somewhat more dispersed. As a result, the IQ score necessary to be in the top 10 or 20 or 30 percent of one's age group varied, depending on one's age. Because of this problem, and because the IQ formula did not make much sense for adults, today's intelligence tests are scored differently. Usually, the average is arbitrarily set at 100, and test scores—still informally referred to as "IQs"—are computed from tables based on norms established for the tests. A score still reflects how a person compares with other people, either children of a particular age or adults in general. At all ages, the distribution of scores approximates a normal (bell-shaped) curve, with scores near the average (mean) most common and very high or very low scores rare (see Figure 3.1).

intelligence quotient (IQ) A measure of intelligence originally computed by dividing a person's mental age by his or her chronological age and multiplying the result by 100; it is now derived from norms provided for standardized intelligence tests.

IQ tests have many critics, and in fact, the entire concept of intelligence is controversial. Some psychologists believe that intelligence is a single quality that can be summed up by a single number; others cite evidence that intelligence comes in many varieties. Moreover, nearly all aspects of intelligence are affected by culture,

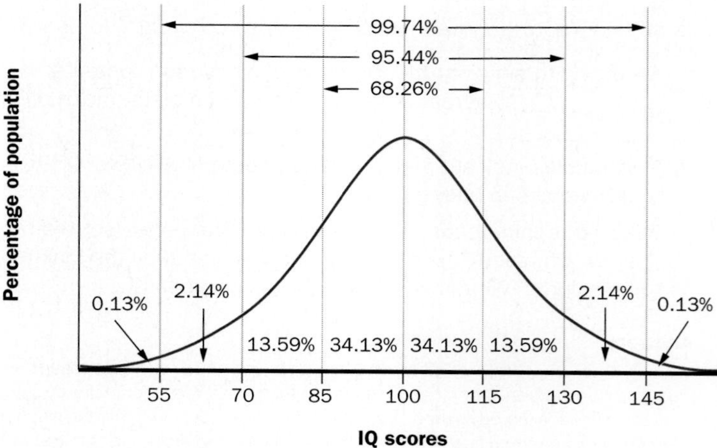

Figure 3.1
Expected Distribution of IQ Scores

In a large population, IQ scores tend to be distributed on a normal (bell-shaped) curve. On most tests, about 68 percent of all people will score between 85 and 115; about 95 percent will score between 70 and 130; and about 99.7 percent will score between 55 and 145. In any actual sample, however, the distribution will depart somewhat from the theoretical ideal. In particular, very low scores will outnumber very high ones because of mental retardation caused by neurological disorders.

and the IQ test itself has many intrinsic biases. (We will discuss kinds of intelligence and their cultural origins in Chapter 8.) Most heritability estimates are based on the intelligence-test scores of white people living in middle-class environments. Keep in mind, then, that heritability studies are estimating only the heritability of those mental skills that contribute to IQ test scores, not necessarily all aspects of mental performance, and that the tests are likely to be more valid for some groups than for others.

VARIATIONS WITHIN GROUPS Despite these important qualifications, it is clear that individual variations in IQ test scores are partly heritable. Overall, behavioral-genetic studies of children and adolescents estimate heritability to be about .50; that is, about half of the variance in IQ scores is explainable by genetic differences (Chipuer, Rovine, & Plomin, 1990; Plomin, 1989). And studies of adults tend to get higher estimates—in the .70 to .80 range (Bouchard, 1995; McGue et al., 1993). Although heritability estimates range widely across studies, depending on the methods used, from as low as .10 to almost .90, the scores of identical twins are always more highly correlated than those of fraternal twins. In fact, the scores of identical twins reared *apart* are more highly correlated than those of fraternal twins reared *together*, as you can see in Figure 3.2. In adoption studies, the scores of adopted children are more highly correlated with those of their birth parents than with those of their biologically unrelated adoptive parents. As adopted children grow into adolescence, the correlation between their IQ scores and those of their biologically unrelated family members diminishes; and in adulthood, the correlation is *zero* (Bouchard, 1997b; Scarr, 1993; Scarr & Weinberg, 1994).

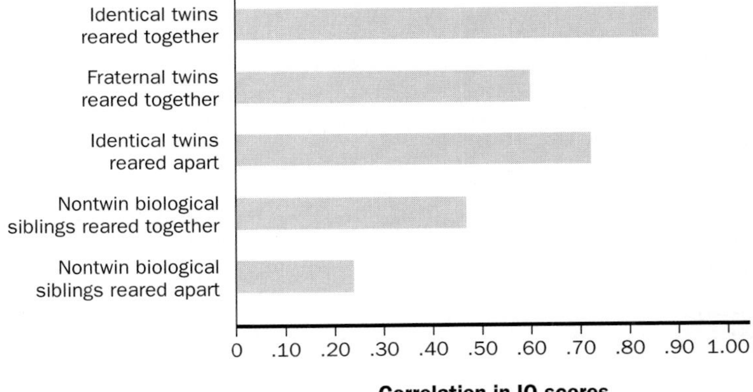

Figure 3.2
Correlations in Siblings' IQ Scores

The IQ scores of identical twins are highly correlated, even when they are reared apart. The figures represented in this graph are based on average correlations across many studies (Bouchard & McGue, 1981).

These are dramatic findings, but they do not mean that genes are the whole story. If heredity accounts for only part of why people differ in their scores on mental tests, then the environment (and random errors in measurement) must account for the rest. As Robert Plomin (1989), a leading behavioral geneticist, has observed, "The wave of acceptance of genetic influence on behavior is growing into a tidal wave that threatens to engulf the second message of this research: These same data provide the best available evidence for the importance of environmental influences."

The following environmental influences can have a negative impact on mental ability, even when heritability is fairly high. Some have been implicated in the lower IQ scores of children from poor and working-class families, as compared with those from middle-class families:

- *Poor prenatal care.* If a pregnant woman is malnourished, contracts infections, takes certain drugs, smokes, drinks excessively, or is exposed to environmental pollutants, her child is at risk of having learning disabilities and a reduced IQ.
- *Malnutrition.* The average IQ gap between severely malnourished and well-nourished children can be as high as 20 points (Stoch & Smythe, 1963; Winick, Meyer, & Harris, 1975).
- *Exposure to toxins.* Lead, for example, can damage the nervous system, producing attention problems, lower IQ scores, and poorer school achievement (Needleman et al., 1990, 1996). Nearly 9 percent of all children in the United

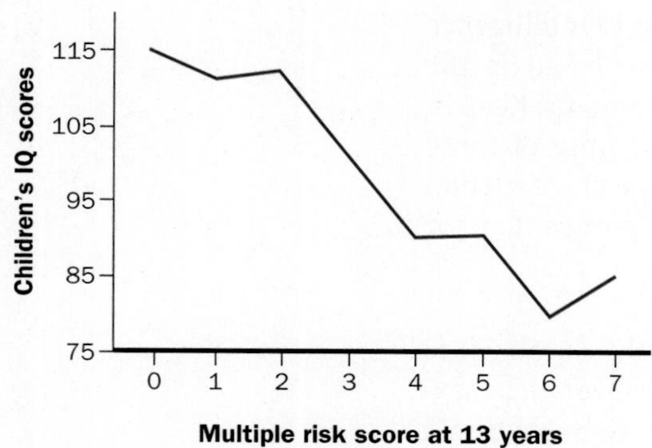

Figure 3.3
Family Risk Factors and IQ

The greater the number of stressful family circumstances, the lower a child's IQ score is likely to be (Sameroff & Seifer, 1989). An enormous gap exists between the average IQ scores of children with no stressful family circumstances and the scores of those with many, as you can see from this graph.

States ages 1 to 5 are exposed to dangerous levels of lead from lead paint and old lead pipes, and for black children ages 1 and 2 the percentage rises to 21.6 (Brody et al., 1994).

- *Large family size.* The average IQ in a family tends to decline as the number of children rises (Belmont & Marolla, 1973). Birth order also makes a difference: IQ tends to decline slightly in each successive child (Zajonc & Markus, 1975). Most researchers attribute these facts to the reduced time parents with many children can spend with each child.
- *Stressful family circumstances.* The Rochester Longitudinal Study has examined family risk factors in the development of several hundred children from birth through early adolescence (Sameroff et al., 1987; Sameroff & Seifer, 1989). Factors that predict reduced intellectual competence include a father who does not live with the family, a mother with a history of mental illness, limited parental work skills, and a history of stressful events during the child's early life. On average, each risk factor reduces a child's IQ score by 4 points. Children with no risk factors score more than *30 points higher* than those with seven risk factors (see Figure 3.3).

In contrast, a healthy and stimulating environment can raise mental performance. In a longitudinal study called the Abecedarian Project, inner-city children who got lots of mental enrichment at home and in daycare or school, starting in infancy and lasting throughout childhood, had higher IQs by age 12 than did children in a control group (Campbell & Ramey, 1994, 1995). The increases were not trivial: They averaged 15 to 30 points.

In school, individual experiences, such as having an inspiring teacher or winning a prize in a science fair, can affect a child's aptitudes and achievements (Dunn & Plomin, 1990). Children's mental abilities also improve when parents spend time with them, encourage them to think things through, read to them, provide toys and field trips, and expect them to do well (Bee et al., 1982; Bradley & Caldwell, 1984). Children also develop cognitively when parents talk to them about many topics, describe things accurately and fully, and answer their children's questions (Clarke-Stewart, VanderStoep, & Killian, 1979).

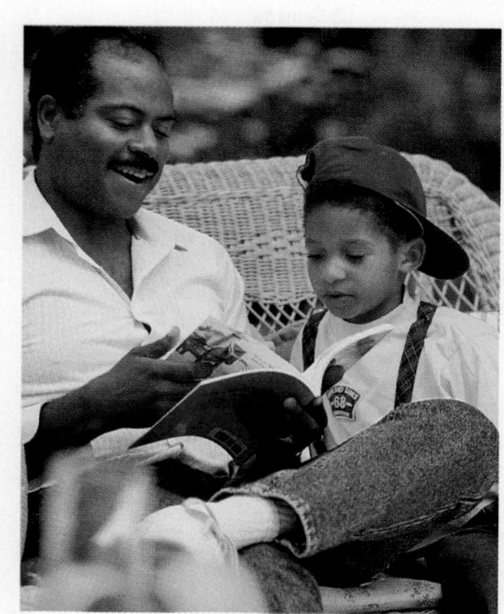

It's extremely important for parents to stimulate their children intellectually by reading to them, asking them questions, and providing books and games.

These parenting skills can be taught. In one study, 30 middle-class parents learned during two brief training sessions to ask open-ended questions when reading to their toddlers ("What is the cat doing?") instead of merely asking the children to point out objects or answer yes–no questions ("Is the cat asleep?"). The parents also learned to expand on the children's answers, provide alternative responses, correct inaccurate responses, and give plenty of praise. Parents in a control group read just as often to their children but did not get the special instruction. After only a month, the children in the experimental group were $8\frac{1}{2}$ months ahead of those in the control group in their expressive-language skills and 6 months ahead of them in vocabulary skills (Whitehurst et al., 1988). A similar study, in which parents and teachers read interactively with low-income children, also produced highly significant vocabulary enhancement (Whitehurst et al., 1994). The implications are enormous when you consider that by one estimate, the average low-income child enters first grade with only 25 hours of one-on-one picture-book reading, compared with 1,000 to 1,700 hours for middle-class children (Adams, 1990).

The children of migrant workers (left) often spend long hours in backbreaking field work and may miss out on the educational opportunities and intellectual advantages available to middle-class children (right).

Probably the best evidence for the importance of environmental influences on intelligence is the fact that IQ scores in developed countries have been climbing for at least three generations (Flynn, 1987) (see Figure 3.4). Genes in these countries can't possibly have changed enough to account for this rise in scores. The causes are still being debated, but most cognitive psychologists believe that they include improvements in education, an increasing emphasis on skills required by technology, and better nutrition (Neisser et al., 1996).

We see, then, that heredity may provide the range of a child's intellectual potential, but many other factors affect where in that range the child will fall. The same heritability studies illustrate both conclusions. For example, as we noted, the IQ

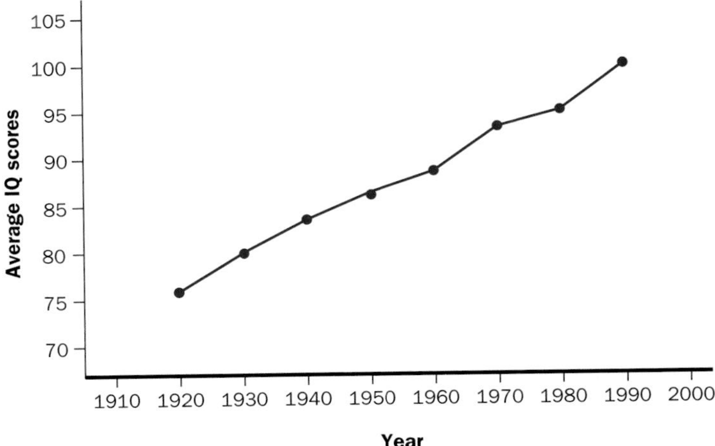

Figure 3.4
Climbing IQ Scores

Raw scores on IQ tests have been rising in developed countries for many decades, at a rate much too steep to be accounted for by genetic changes. Because test norms are periodically readjusted to set the average score at 100, most people are unaware of the increase. On this graph (adapted from Horgan, 1995), average scores are calibrated according to 1989 norms. As you can see, performance was much lower in 1918 than in 1989.

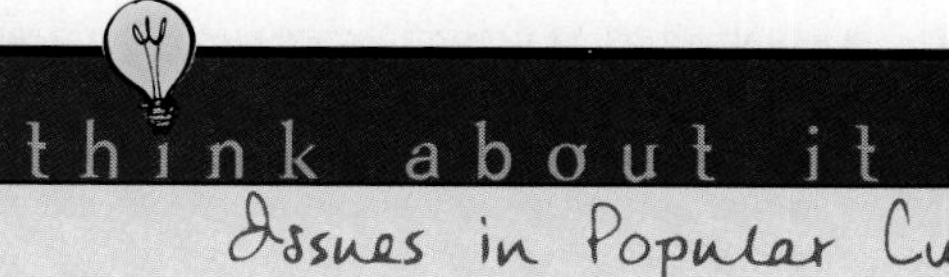

Genes, Intolerance, and IQ

A hammer can be used to build a house or to bash a head. Mental tests are tools, too, and the way they are used depends on the temper of the times, political trends in society, and scientists' own intentions and prejudices. History amply documents that scientific research about intelligence is not a neutral matter.

Consider the origins of the IQ test itself. In 1904, the French Ministry of Education asked psychologist Alfred Binet (1857–1911) to design a test that would identify slow learners. School attendance had just been made mandatory, but some children did not learn well in ordinary classrooms and needed special help. The ministry was reluctant to let teachers identify such children because the teachers might have prejudices about poor children or might assume that shy or disruptive children were retarded. What was needed was an objective test that would reveal who would benefit from remedial work, and that test is what Binet developed. But something happened to Binet's test and the French intentions to help *individual* children when the test crossed the ocean to America. In America, a revised version of the test was used to assign children to school tracks, according to their alleged natural ability—not to bring slow learners up to average. IQ scores also became a political tool, used for arguing that some ethnic groups were inherently smarter than others.

For example, as soon as he got his hands on the IQ test, Henry Goddard (1917), a leading American educator, gave it to a group of immigrants at Ellis Island. Many of the immigrants knew little or no English, and they could neither read nor write their own language. Yet no sooner did they get off the boat after a long and tiring journey than they found themselves taking an IQ test. The results: 83 percent of the Jews, 80 percent of the Hungarians, 79 percent of the Italians, and 87 percent of the Russians scored as "feeble-minded," with a mental age lower than 12 years. Goddard concluded that low intelligence and poor character were inherited and that "undesirables" should be prevented from having children. He acknowledged that deprivation might explain these results, but he did not recognize that the results themselves had no validity, given the conditions under which they were obtained.

A more ambitious study of IQ was done during World War I, when 1.5 million soldiers took the first mass-produced intelligence tests in America. The purpose was to eliminate "feeble-minded" recruits and to determine who should become an officer. To everyone's astonishment, the average mental age of white men was only 13, just a notch above the "moron" level; blacks and eastern and southern Europeans scored even lower, on average. Once again many citizens (of northern European extraction, anyway) concluded that the nation's intelligence was declining because of the influx of immigrants and their "breeding habits," ignoring the abominable conditions under which the tests were given, the confusing instructions used, and the lack of education of many of the men.

The 1920s saw a growth in eugenics movements in North America and Europe. Eugenicists argued that government should help improve humanity by discouraging births among the lower socioeconomic classes and others presumed to have genetically inferior traits. Some called for the forced sterilization of people with low IQs and for strict limits on immigration. They were inspired by *Social Darwinism*, the idea that the prevailing social order reflects the "survival of the fittest" (the phrase was coined by the English political philosopher Herbert Spencer in the 1840s). These ideas were taken to their extreme during the 1930s and 1940s by the Nazis, who used them as a rationale for exterminating 12 million people in the Holocaust. When the extent of the Nazi atrocities became known, most scholars turned away in disgust from all biological explanations of mental abilities. For three

scores of adopted children correlate more highly with their birth parents' scores than with those of their adoptive parents. That is, if Johnny scores high relative to other adopted children, his birth parents are likely to score high relative to other adults who have put their children up for adoption. This fact supports the heritability of intelligence as measured by IQ tests. However, in *absolute* terms, Johnny's IQ may differ considerably from the scores of his birth parents: Indeed, on the average, adopted children have IQs that are 10 to 20 points higher than those of their birth parents (Scarr & Weinberg, 1977). Most psychologists believe that this difference exists because adoptive families are generally smaller, wealthier, and better educated than other families—and these environmental factors are associated with higher IQs in children.

decades, the prevailing doctrine was that culture and environment were the primary if not the sole determinants of intelligence. But now behavioral-genetic research, as we report in this chapter, has called that belief into question. Few scholars dispute that differences among individuals are due in part to heredity; a Forrest Gump can never become an Einstein.

What does this research mean for individuals or social policies? In 1994, a heated debate erupted after publication of *The Bell Curve: Intelligence and Class Structure in American Life*, by the late psychologist Richard Herrnstein and conservative political theorist Charles Murray. If the book had been about the bell curve of intelligence *within* groups, it would not have generated much controversy. But, in the old American tradition, it is really about differences between groups, and some of its arguments would be familiar to any Social Darwinist.

Herrnstein and Murray argued that (a) intelligence is a single, measurable quality that is largely heritable; (b) because low-IQ people are having more children than high-IQ people, the nation's intelligence level is declining (the same argument that Goddard made years ago); (c) the United States may soon be divided into a huge low-IQ underclass and a "cognitive meritocracy" of wealthy, well-educated, high-IQ people; and (d) educational programs have done little to raise IQs. Many people, these authors concluded, will never learn enough to repay the cost of teaching them, and resources spent on such people would be better spent on the gifted. The implication of *The Bell Curve* is that the gap in IQ scores between the average white and the average black child can never be closed.

Critical reviewers of the book have attacked its scholarship, methods, assumptions, and conclusions (Gould, 1994; Holt, 1994; Lane, 1994; Steele, 1994). They point out, as we do in this chapter, that heritability estimates based on differences *within* a group cannot legitimately be used to compare differences *between* groups. They reject the notion that intelligence can be captured by a single number. They acknowledge that programs such as Head Start have failed to permanently alter preschoolers' IQs, but these remedial efforts, they argue, have been a matter of too little too late. (As noted in the text, early, intensive intervention can raise IQ scores dramatically.) Such efforts, say the critics, should be expanded, not cut back.

Supporters of hereditarian arguments reply that their opponents have their own political ax to grind, and that they have a right to do research into matters that they regard as interesting intellectual questions without being automatically branded as racists or elitists (Rushton, 1993). Flaws in the studies of environmentalists, they argue, are often overlooked or rationalized, whereas the methods of hereditarians are scrutinized and attacked. The critics, in turn, note that the political implications of "interesting intellectual questions" can't be ignored. Stephen Jay Gould (1994) observes that *The Bell Curve* appeared at a moment in American history when taxpayers were in the mood to slash social programs. At such times, people are more likely to accept uncritically the message that the beneficiaries of these programs cannot be helped anyway.

The political nature of the IQ controversy raises some hard questions about the relationship between society and science. Why have Americans been so concerned about group differences in IQ for so many decades? Can the study of such differences truly be beneficial, or, given today's political climate and the persistence of prejudice, does it promote class and racial bias? Should scientists consider the political ramifications of their research, or should they leave that problem to others? Finally, once we have research on an issue as explosive as group differences in some ability, what lesson should be drawn—to accept those differences, or try to eliminate them?

VARIATIONS BETWEEN GROUPS So far, we have considered intellectual differences only *within* a group of individuals. For many years, researchers have also wondered about the origins of differences *between* groups. Unfortunately, the history of this issue has been marred by ethnic, class, and gender prejudice (see "Issues in Popular Culture"). Too often, in the words of Stephen Jay Gould (1981/1996), interpretations of research have been bent to support the belief that some groups are destined by "the harsh dictates of nature" to be subordinate to others.

In recent years, most of the interest in group differences has focused on black–white differences in IQ. African-American children score, on average, some 10 to 15 points lower on IQ tests than do white children.

EXAMINE ASSUMPTIONS

Behavioral-genetic studies, on the average, show the heritability of intelligence to be high. A popular book argues that heredity must play a similarly large role in average IQ differences between ethnic groups. What's wrong with the assumption behind that reasoning?

Keep in mind that we are talking about averages; the distributions of scores for black children and white children overlap considerably.

A few psychologists have proposed a genetic explanation of this difference (Jensen, 1969, 1981; Rushton, 1988). As you can imagine, these theories have provoked an emotional response. Genetic explanations are music to the ears of people who consider whites to be inherently superior to blacks (but who usually ignore the fact that Asians, on the average, score higher on IQ tests than whites do). Racists often cite such theories to justify their own hatreds, and politicians have used them to argue for cuts in programs that would benefit blacks and other minorities. It is vital, therefore, that we all know how to evaluate genetic theories of group differences. What are the facts?

One fatal flaw in genetic theories of black–white differences is their use of heritability estimates based mainly on white samples to estimate the role heredity plays in group differences. This problem sounds pretty technical, but it is not really difficult to understand, so stay with us.

Consider, first, not people but tomatoes. (This "thought experiment," illustrated in Figure 3.5, is based on Lewontin, 1970.) Suppose you have a bag of tomato seeds that vary genetically; all things being equal, some will produce tomatoes that are puny and tasteless, and some will produce tomatoes that are plump and delicious. Now you take a bunch of these seeds in your left hand and another bunch from the same bag in your right hand. Though one seed differs genetically from another, there is no average difference between the seeds in your left hand and those in your right. You plant the left hand's seeds in pot A, with some soil that you have doctored with nitrogen and other nutrients, and you plant the right hand's seeds in pot B, with soil from which you have extracted nutrients. When the tomato plants grow, they will vary within each pot in terms of height, the number of

Figure 3.5
The Tomato Plant Experiment

In the hypothetical experiment described in the text, even if the differences among plants within each pot were due entirely to genetics, the average difference *between* pots could be environmental. The same general principle applies to individual and group differences among human beings.

tomatoes produced, and the size of the tomatoes, purely because of genetic differences. But there will also be an average difference between the plants in pot A and those in pot B: The plants in pot A will be healthier and bear more tomatoes. This difference *between* pots is due entirely to the different soils—even though the heritability of the *within*-pot differences is 100 percent.

The principle is the same for people as it is for tomatoes. As we have seen, intellectual differences *within* groups are at least partly genetic, but that does not mean that differences *between* groups are genetic. Blacks and whites do not grow up, on the average, in the same "pots" (environments). Because of a long legacy of racial discrimination and de facto segregation, black children (as well as Latino and other minority children) often receive far fewer nutrients—literally, in terms of food, and figuratively, in terms of education, encouragement by society, and intellectual opportunities. Moreover, ethnic groups differ in countless cultural ways that affect their performance on IQ tests (as we will discuss in detail in Chapter 8).

One sure way to settle the question of inherent racial differences would be to gather IQ information on blacks and whites who were reared in exactly the same circumstances. This task is nearly impossible at present in the United States, where racism affects the lives of even affluent, successful African-Americans (Cose, 1994; Staples, 1994). However, the handful of studies that have overcome past methodological problems fails to reveal any genetic differences between blacks and whites in whatever it is that IQ tests measure (Lewontin, 1982; Mackenzie, 1984). For example, children fathered by both black and white American soldiers in Germany after World War II and reared in similar German communities by similar families did not differ significantly in IQ (Eyferth, 1961). Moreover, degree of African ancestry (which can be roughly estimated from skin color, blood analysis, and genealogy) is not related to measured intelligence, as a genetic theory of black–white differences would predict (Scarr et al., 1977).

An intelligent reading of the research on intelligence, therefore, does not direct us to conclude that differences among cultural, ethnic, or national groups are permanent, genetically determined, or signs of any group's superiority. On the contrary, the research suggests that we should make sure that all children grow up in the best possible soil, with room for the smartest and the slowest to find a place in the sun.

Quick Quiz

Are you thinking intelligently about intelligence?

1. Estimates of the heritability of intelligence (a) put heritability at about .90, (b) show heritability to be low at all ages, (c) average about .50 for children and adolescents.
2. Name five environmental factors associated with reduced mental ability.
3. *True or false:* If a trait is highly heritable within a group, then between-group differences in the trait must also be due mainly to heredity.
4. The available evidence (does/does not) show that ethnic differences in average IQ scores are due to genetic differences.

Answers:

1. c 2. poor prenatal care, malnutrition, exposure to toxins, large family size, and stressful family circumstances 3. false 4. does not

IN PRAISE OF HUMAN VARIATION

This chapter opened with two simple questions: What makes us alike as human beings, and why do we differ? Here is the pop-psych answer to these questions:

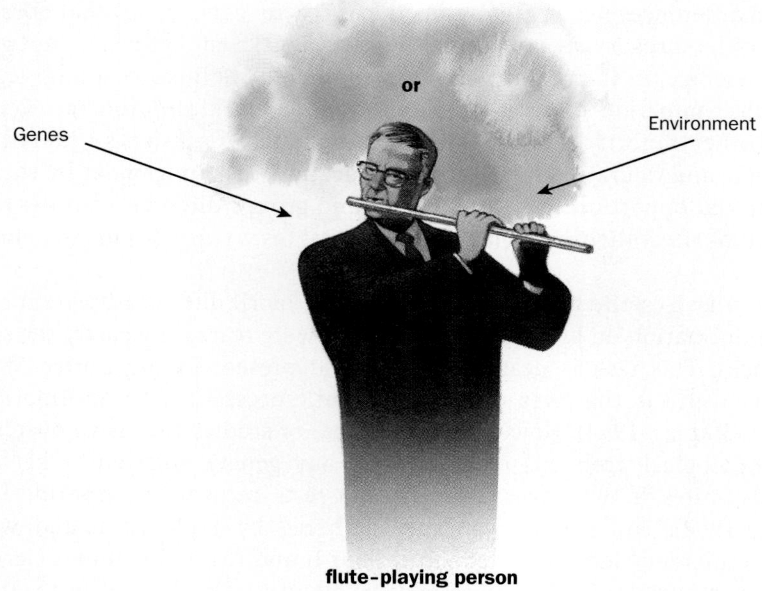

And here is the more complicated view that emerges from the study of human development:

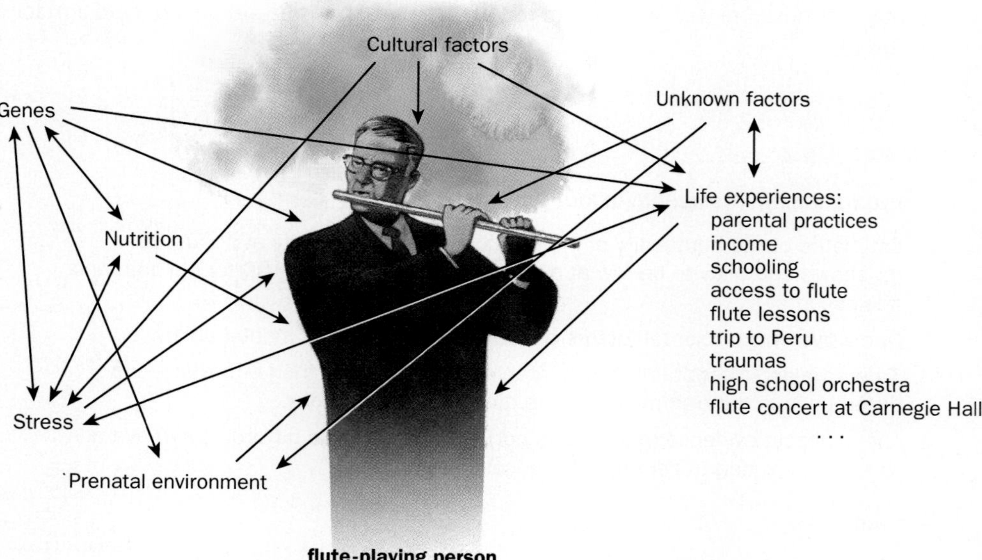

As we have seen, heredity and environment always interact to produce the unique mixture of qualities that make up a human being. Yet even this answer is much too simple, because each of us is, in a sense, *more* than the sum of the individual influences on us. Once these influences become a part of us, they blend and become indistinguishable. We can no more speak of genes, or of the environment, "causing" personality or intelligence than we can speak of butter, sugar, or flour individually causing the taste of a cake (Lewontin, Rose, & Kamin, 1984). Yet we do speak that way. Why? Perhaps out of a desire to make things clearer than they actually are, or sometimes to justify prejudices about culture, ethnicity, gender, or class.

TOLERATE UNCERTAINTY

Many people would like to specify precisely how much genes and the environment independently contribute to human qualities. But is this goal achievable? Is a human being like a jigsaw puzzle, made up of separate components, or more like a cake, with blended ingredients that interact to produce its unique taste?

Nature, however, loves diversity. Biologists agree that the fitness of any species depends on this diversity. If all members of a species had exactly the same strengths and weaknesses, the species could not survive changes in the physical or social environment. With diversity, at least some members have a good chance of survival. When we see the world as behavioral geneticists and evolutionary psychologists do, we realize that each of us has something valuable to contribute, whether it is artistic talent, academic ability, creativity, social skill, athletic prowess, a sense of humor, mechanical aptitude, practical wisdom, a social conscience, or the energy to get things done. The challenge, for any society, is to promote the potential of each of its members.

Taking Psychology with You

How to Lose Weight—and Whether You Should

The cultural ideal for body size in North America and Europe has been getting decidedly thinner. Brett Silverstein and his colleagues documented the changing female ideal in this century by computing a bust-to-waist ratio of the measurements of models in popular women's magazines (Silverstein, Peterson, & Perdue, 1986). The ideal body type became thin, as opposed to voluptuously curvy, twice during this century: in the mid-1920s and from the mid-1960s to the present. Some of today's most sought-after fashion models look like they're starving to death—and perhaps they are.

Why did these changes occur? Silverstein found that men and women associate the curvy, big-breasted female body with femininity, nurturance, and motherhood; hence big breasts are fashionable in eras that celebrate women's role as mothers. But people also, alas, associate femininity with incompetence. Thus, in every era in which women have entered traditionally male spheres of education and work, as they are doing now, women have tried to look boyishly thin in order to avoid the risk of appearing "feminine" and stupid. In recent years, a biologically impossible female ideal has appeared, possibly reflecting national ambivalence about whether women's proper role is domestic or professional: the big-breasted but narrow-hipped body shape.

Many women, therefore, face a dilemma. Evolution has programmed them for a reserve of fat necessary for the onset of menstruation, healthy childbearing, and nursing. The result of the battle between biological design and social standards is that many women today—as in the 1920s—are obsessed with weight, continually dieting, or suffering from eating disorders such as *anorexia nervosa* (self-starvation) or *bulimia* (bingeing and vomiting).

The obsession about achieving the ideal female body shape, Silverstein hypothesized, should be most likely to occur in women who value achievement, higher education, and careers, especially male-dominated careers. Being thin allows them to identify with male competence and to actively distance themselves from femininity. And that is just what research finds. College women who develop eating disorders are also more likely than other women to say that their parents believe a woman's place is in the home, their mothers are unhappy with their lives, their fathers think their mothers are unintelligent, and their fathers treat sons as being more intelligent than daughters (Silverstein & Perlick, 1995).

While many normal-weight women struggle to fit the cultural ideal, many overweight men and women struggle to fit the medical ideal. A large minority of Americans are overweight—that is, their body mass exceeds the healthy standard by 25 to 30 percent—and as we noted earlier, obesity is increasing (Kuczmarski et al., 1994). Experts disagree about the best course of action for overweight people. Many believe that dieting is unhealthy and may even contribute to medical problems and eating disorders (Garner & Wooley, 1991). Others conclude that dieting and weight loss can help reduce the health risks associated with overweight. They point to research showing that even modest weight loss has medical benefits, such as lowered blood pressure. And they note that findings on the risks of dieting are inconsistent (Brownell & Rodin, 1994). So what's an overweight person to do? Research offers some suggestions:

• *Be realistic about your need to diet.* As Kelly Brownell and Judith Rodin (1994) observe, dieting and a 10 percent reduction in weight may be of benefit to an obese older man with high blood pressure but unhealthy for a teenage girl who is not overweight.

• *Avoid fad diets* that restrict you to only a few foods or put you on starvation rations. People on these diets often become obsessed with food, get depressed and anxious when they slip off the diet, and ultimately binge, which restores the lost weight—plus some. It is far better to permanently alter your eating habits by reducing fat intake and eating more grains, fruits, and vegetables.

• *Get more exercise,* which may raise your metabolic rate and which, when combined with a low-fat diet, is associated with more weight loss than dieting alone (Foreyt et al., 1993). You do not have to become a marathon runner, but you can increase your activity level—for example, by walking instead of driving to work or school.

• *Avoid yo-yo dieting,* in which you repeatedly lose and gain weight. Yo-yo dieting is linked to a higher-than-normal risk of cardiovascular disease, hypertension, and other chronic diseases (Brownell & Rodin, 1994; Ernsberger & Nelson, 1988; Lissner et al., 1991). It is also psychologically debilitating and may cause an obese person to give up.

• *Find ways to nurture and reward yourself other than eating.* People who develop eating disorders are more self-critical than healthy eaters, and they are more likely to use food to assuage hurt feelings and low self-esteem (Lehman & Rodin, 1989).

• *Avoid amphetamines and other diet pills,* which can be far more dangerous to your health than a few pounds and can become addictive. Diet pills raise the metabolic rate only as long as you take them. When you stop taking them, the pounds return.

• *Seek treatment if you have an eating disorder.* If you are mistakenly trying to control weight by frequent vomiting and abuse of laxatives, you can break this harmful pattern by joining an eating-disorders program; school counselors and health clinics can direct you to suitable programs.

Remember that the biological disposition to gain weight varies from person to person, and that even with exercise, genetic factors limit how much you can change. Think carefully and critically about the reasons that you are dieting. Are you really overweight? Are you trying to look like a real person or a magazine model? Whose standards are you following, and why?

SUMMARY

1) From the perspective of *evolutionary psychologists* and *behavioral geneticists,* a key to understanding the qualities that unite human beings as a species and the qualities that differentiate them as individuals can be found in genes. Yet all scientists also understand that heredity and environment interact to produce not only psychological traits but also most physical ones.

WHAT'S IN A GENE?

2) *Genes*, the basic units of heredity, are located on *chromosomes*, which consist of strands of *DNA*. Within each gene, a sequence of four elements of DNA constitutes a chemical code that helps determine the synthesis of a particular protein. In turn, proteins directly or indirectly affect virtually all the structural and biochemical characteristics of the organism.

3) In the simplest type of inheritance, a single pair of genes is responsible for the expression of a trait; in many cases, one member of the pair is *dominant* and the other *recessive*. Most human traits, however, depend on more than one gene pair, which makes tracking down the genetic contributions to a trait extremely difficult. One method for doing so involves the use of *linkage studies*.

4) The way in which heredity operates ensures that each individual (with the exception of identical twins) will be a unique genetic mosaic. Each sperm- or egg-producing cell has the potential to produce millions of chromosome combinations in each new sperm or egg, and mutations and the crossover of segments of genetic material produce even greater genetic diversity. Thus, two people who are genetically related can be very different in purely genetic terms.

OUR HUMAN HERITAGE: THE GENETICS OF SIMILARITY

5) Evolutionary psychologists believe that the mind is not a general-purpose computer but instead evolved as a collection of specialized, independent mental modules to handle specific survival problems. Many fundamental human similarities can be traced to the evolutionary workings of *natural selection*—for example, inborn reflexes, an attraction to novelty, a motive to explore and manipulate objects, and a motive to play and to imitate others.

6) Human beings are the only species that uses language to express and comprehend an infinite number of novel utterances. Noam Chomsky argued that the ability to take the *surface structure* of an utterance and apply rules of *syntax* to infer its underlying *deep structure* must depend on an innate faculty for language, a universal grammar; many others have supported this view and have explored its evolutionary implications. However, parental practices, such as repeating correct sentences verbatim and recasting incorrect ones, appear to aid in language acquisition. Case studies of children deprived of exposure to language suggest that a *critical period* exists for acquiring a first language.

7) Controversy exists about the biological and evolutionary origins of mating and marriage practices. *Sociobiologists* maintain that people's tendency to act in ways that ensure the survival of their personal genetic code is the primary motivation behind most social customs, including those related to courtship and sexual behavior. In this view, males and females have developed different reproductive strategies, so that, for example, males are on the average more promiscuous than females. Most evolutionary psychologists reject the notion of a reproductive-fitness motive, but they agree that different kinds of mating and survival problems faced by the sexes in the past have resulted in gender differences in mating preferences. Cross-cultural studies support many evolutionary predictions, but critics argue that human sexual behavior is too varied and changeable to fit a single evolutionary explanation, and many take exception to the entire line of evolutionary reasoning. They also worry that evolutionary arguments will be used politically to justify inequality between the sexes.

OUR HUMAN DIVERSITY: THE GENETICS OF DIFFERENCE

8) Behavioral geneticists study differences among individuals, often by using studies of twins and adopted children to estimate the *heritability* of traits and abilities—the extent to which differences in a trait or ability within a group of individuals are accounted for by genetic differences. Heritability estimates do not apply to specific individuals or to differences between groups; they apply only to differences within a particular group living in a particular environment. Further, even a highly heritable trait may be susceptible to environmental modification.

9) Genetic research is altering our understanding of body weight and shape. According to *set-point theory*, hunger, weight, and eating are regulated by a complex set of bodily mechanisms that keep people within a certain genetically influenced weight range. Genes influence body shape, distribution of fat, and whether the body will convert excess calories into fat, and they may help account for certain types of obesity. Some obese people have low levels of, or are insensitive to, *leptin*, a hormonelike substance that enables the brain to regulate appetite and metabolism. However, weight is also influenced by culturally influenced eating habits and by exercise, which may raise metabolism and lower a person's set point.

10) Heritability estimates for intelligence (as measured by IQ tests, which have come under fire by critics) vary widely, but these estimates average about .50 for children and adolescents and .70 to .80 for adults. Individual differences in mental performance and IQ are also influenced by environmental factors. Poor prenatal care, malnutrition, exposure to toxins, large family size, and stressful family circumstances are associated with lower performance; a healthy and stimulating environment can raise performance.

11) Research on group differences in IQ has focused on average black–white differences. The history of debate on this issue has often been marred by ethnic and class prejudice, as discussed in "Issues in Popular Culture." Genetic explanations have often mistakenly used heritability estimates derived from one group to estimate the genetic contribution to group differences—an invalid procedure. The available evidence fails to support genetic explanations of these differences.

IN PRAISE OF HUMAN VARIATION

12) Neither nature nor nurture can entirely explain people's similarities or differences. Genetic and environmental influences blend and become indistinguishable in the development of any individual.

KEY TERMS

nativists versus empiricists 82
behavioral genetics 82
evolutionary psychology 82
sociobiology 82
genes 82
chromosomes 82
DNA (deoxyribonucleic acid) 83
genome 83

bases 83

dominant/recessive genes 83

linkage studies 84

mutate 86

evolution 86

natural selection 86

Charles Darwin 86

language 90

syntax 90

surface structure/deep structure 91

language acquisition device 91

universal grammar 91

overregularizations 91

critical period (for language acquisition) 93

heritability 97

identical (monozygotic) twins 99

fraternal (dizygotic) twins 99

set point 101

intelligence quotient (IQ) 104

mental age 104

Social Darwinism 108

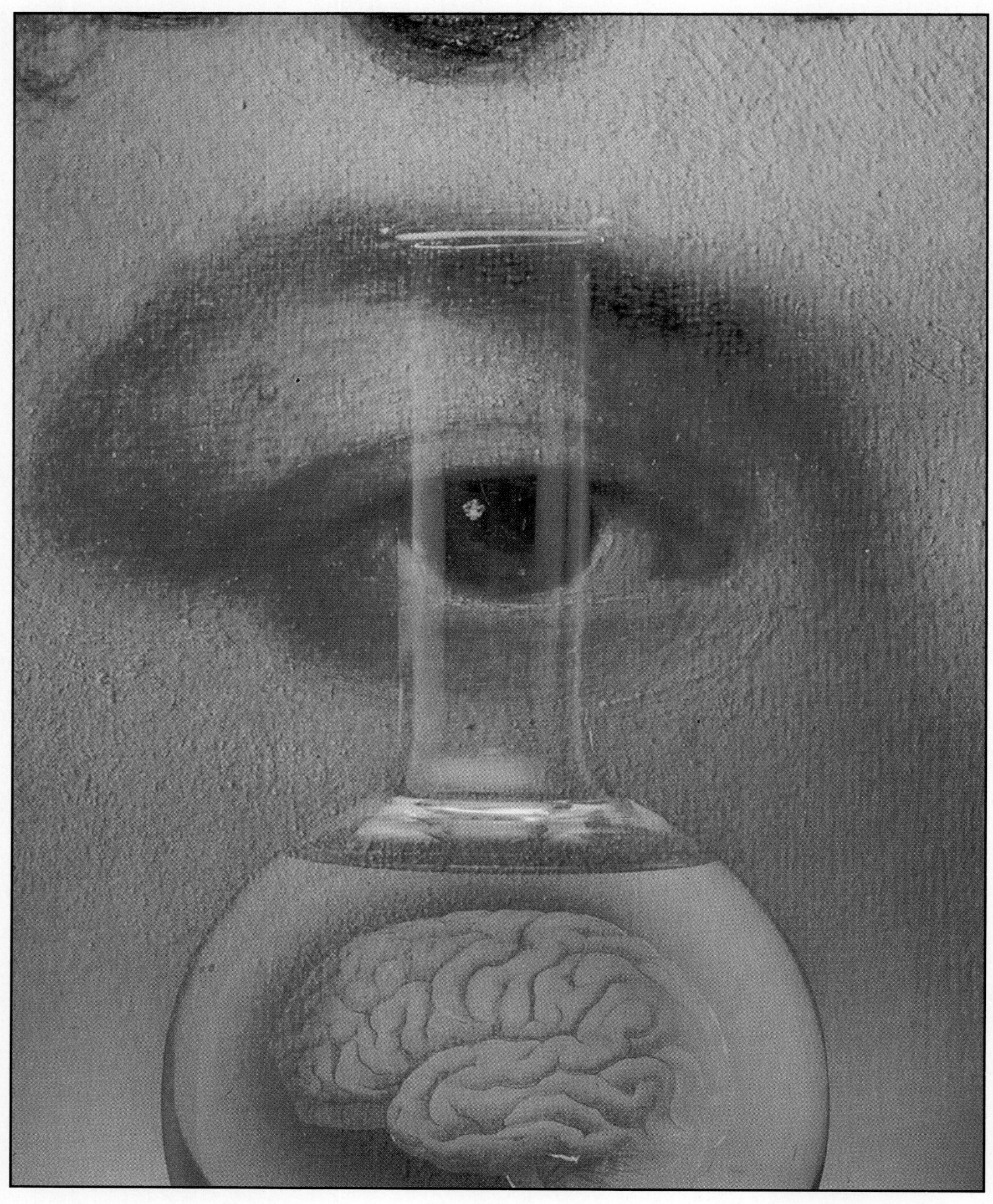

It's amazing to think that the body feeds the brain sugar and amino acids,
and what comes out is poetry and pirouettes.

Robert Collins

CHAPTER FOUR
Neurons, Hormones, and the Brain

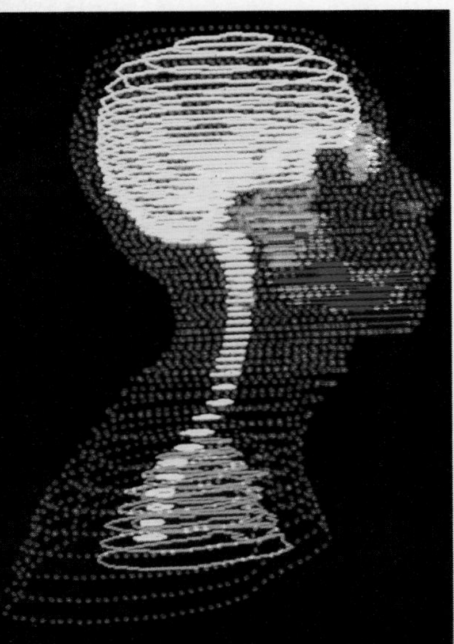

EMILY D., A FORMER ENGLISH TEACHER AND POET, had a tumor in an area on the right side of the brain that processes the expressive qualities of speech, such as rhythm, inflection, and intonation. Although Emily D. could understand words and sentences perfectly well, she could not tell whether a speaker was indignant, cheerful, or dejected unless she carefully analyzed the person's facial expressions and gestures, and unfortunately, fading vision limited her ability to do so. Emily D.'s brain damage had left her entirely deaf to the emotional nuances of speech, the variations of tone and cadence that can move a listener to laughter, tears, or outrage. But she had one skill that many people lack. Because she could not be swayed by histrionics or tone of voice, she could easily spot a liar.

Dr. P., a cultured and charming musician of great repute, suffered damage in a part of the brain that handles visualization. Although his vision remained sharp and his abstract reasoning keen, he could no longer recognize people or objects, or even dream in visual images. He would pat the heads of water hydrants and parking meters, thinking them to be children, or chat with pieces of furniture and wonder why they did not reply. He could spot a pin on the floor but did not know his own face in the mirror. Once, when looking around for his hat, he thought his wife's head was the hat and tried to lift it off. Neurologist Oliver Sacks, who studied Dr. P., came to call him "the man who mistook his wife for a hat" (Sacks, 1985).

These two fascinating cases, reported by Sacks, show us that the brain is the bedrock of behavior. **Neuropsychologists,** along with neuroscientists from other disciplines, explore that bedrock, searching for the basis of behavior in the brain and the rest of the nervous system. Among their many interests are the biological foundations of consciousness (Chapter 5), perception (Chapter 6), memory (Chapter 9), emotion (Chapter 10), stress (Chapter 14), and mental disorders (Chapter 15). In this chapter, we describe the structure of the brain and the rest of the nervous system as background for our later discussions.

At this very moment, your own brain, assisted by other parts of your nervous system, is busily taking in these words. Whether you are excited, curious, or bored, your brain is registering some sort of emotional reaction to the material. As you continue reading, your brain will (we hope) store away much of the information in this chapter for future use. Later on, your brain may enable you to smell a flower, climb the stairs, greet a friend, solve a personal problem, or chuckle at a joke. But the brain's most startling accomplishment, by far, is its knowledge that it is doing all these things. This self-awareness makes brain research different from the study of anything else in the universe. Scientists must use the cells, biochemistry, and circuitry of their own brains to understand the cells, biochemistry, and circuitry of brains in general.

Because the brain is the site of consciousness, people disagree vehemently about what language to use in describing it. One reviewer who read this chapter before publication took issue with the way we wrote the preceding paragraph. How, he wanted to know, could we talk about "your" brain doing this or that; after all, if the brain is where consciousness happens, where is the "you" who is "using" that brain? Another reviewer had exactly the opposite complaint; she objected when we wrote that the brain interprets events, stores information, or registers emotions, because she felt we were depersonalizing human beings and implying that brain mechanisms completely explain behavior. "I think people do these things," she wrote, "not brains. Brains are not actors." You can see our problem. After much discussion, we finally decided to stick with everyday constructions such as "We use our brains," but we want you to know that we are simply resorting to a convenient linguistic shorthand, without assuming the existence of an independent brain "operator" doing the using. On the other hand, we also do not want to imply that brain mechanisms are all you need to understand about behavior.

neuropsychology The field of psychology concerned with the neural and biochemical bases of behavior and mental processes.

William Shakespeare had an opinion on this matter; he once called the brain "the soul's frail dwelling house." Actually, though, the brain is more like the main room in a house filled with many alcoves and passageways—the "house" being the nervous system as a whole. Before we can understand the windows, walls, and furniture of this house, we need to become acquainted with the overall floor plan. It's a pretty technical floor plan, which means that you will be learning many new terms, but you will need to know these terms in order to understand how psychologists with a biological perspective go about explaining psychological topics.

THE NERVOUS SYSTEM: A BASIC BLUEPRINT

The function of a nervous system is to gather and process information, produce responses to stimuli, and coordinate the workings of different cells. Even the lowly jellyfish and the humble worm have the beginnings of such a system. In very simple organisms that do little more than move, eat, and eliminate wastes, the "system" may be no more than one or two nerve cells. In human beings, who do such complex things as dance, cook, and take psychology courses, the nervous system contains billions of cells. For purposes of description, scientists divide this intricate network into two main parts, the central nervous system and the peripheral (outlying) nervous system (see Figure 4.1).

central nervous system (CNS) The portion of the nervous system consisting of the brain and spinal cord.

spinal cord A collection of neurons and supportive tissue running from the base of the brain down the center of the back.

reflex An automatic response to a stimulus.

THE CENTRAL NERVOUS SYSTEM

The **central nervous system (CNS)** receives, processes, interprets, and stores incoming sensory information—information about tastes, sounds, smells, color, pressure on the skin, the state of internal organs, and so forth. It also sends out messages destined for muscles, glands, and internal organs. It is usually conceptualized as having two components: the brain, which we will consider in detail later, and the **spinal cord.** The spinal cord is actually an extension of the brain. It runs from the base of the brain down the center of the back, protected by a column of bones (the spinal column), and it acts as a bridge between the brain and the parts of the body below the neck.

The spinal cord produces some behaviors on its own, without any help from the brain. These spinal **reflexes** are automatic, requiring no conscious effort. For example, if you accidentally touch a hot iron, you will immediately pull your hand away, even before the brain has had a chance to register what has happened. Nerve impulses bring a message to the spinal cord (hot!), and the spinal cord immediately sends out a command via other nerve impulses, telling muscles in your arm to contract and to pull your hand away from the iron. (Reflexes above the neck, such as sneezing and blinking, involve the lower part of the brain rather than the spinal cord.)

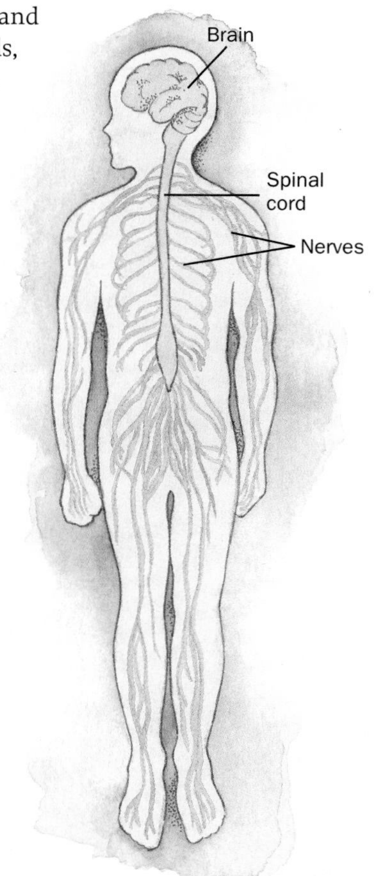

Figure 4.1
The Central and Peripheral Nervous Systems

The central nervous system, shown here in yellow, includes the brain and the spinal cord. The peripheral nervous system, shown in red, consists of 43 pairs of nerves that transmit information to and from the central nervous system. Twelve pairs of cranial nerves in the head enter the brain directly; 31 pairs of spinal nerves enter the spinal cord at the spaces between the vertebrae of the spine.

The neural circuits underlying many spinal reflexes are linked to other neural pathways that run up and down the spinal cord, to and from the brain. Because of these connections, reflexes can sometimes be influenced by thoughts and emotions. An example is erection in men, a spinal reflex that can be inhibited by anxiety or distracting thoughts, and initiated by erotic thoughts. Some reflexes can be brought under conscious control. If you concentrate, you may be able to keep your knee from jerking when it is tapped, as it normally would. Similarly, most men can learn to voluntarily delay ejaculation, another spinal reflex.

THE PERIPHERAL NERVOUS SYSTEM

The **peripheral nervous system (PNS)** handles the central nervous system's input and output. It contains all portions of the nervous system outside the brain and spinal cord, right down to nerves in the tips of the fingers and toes. If your brain could not collect information about the world by means of a peripheral nervous system, it would be like a radio without a receiver. In the peripheral nervous system, *sensory nerves* carry messages from special receptors in the skin, muscles, and other internal and external sense organs to the spinal cord, which sends them along to the brain. These nerves put us in touch with both the outside world and the activities of our own bodies. *Motor nerves* carry orders from the central nervous system to muscles, glands, and internal organs. They enable us to move our bodies, and they cause glands to contract and to secrete substances, including chemical messengers called *hormones.*

peripheral nervous system (PNS) All portions of the nervous system outside the brain and spinal cord; it includes sensory and motor nerves.

somatic nervous system The subdivision of the peripheral nervous system that connects to sensory receptors and to skeletal muscles.

autonomic nervous system The subdivision of the peripheral nervous system that regulates the internal organs and glands.

Scientists further divide the peripheral nervous system into two parts: the somatic (bodily) nervous system and the autonomic (self-governing) nervous system. The **somatic nervous system,** sometimes called the *skeletal nervous system,* consists of nerves that are connected to sensory receptors and to the skeletal muscles that permit voluntary action. When you sense the world around you, or when you turn off a light or write your name, your somatic system is active. The **autonomic nervous system** regulates the functioning of blood vessels, glands, and internal (visceral) organs such as the bladder, stomach, and heart. When you happen upon the secret object of your desire, and your heart starts to pound, your hands get sweaty, and your cheeks feel hot, you can blame your autonomic nervous system.

The autonomic nervous system works more or less automatically, without a person's conscious control. We say more or less because some people can learn to heighten or suppress their autonomic responses intentionally. In India, some yogis can slow their heartbeats and metabolisms so dramatically that they can survive in a sealed booth long after most of us would have died of suffocation. And in the 1960s and 1970s, Neal Miller and his colleagues showed that many other people can learn to control their visceral responses, by taking advantage of a technique called *biofeedback* (Miller, 1978). In biofeedback, monitoring devices track the bodily process in question and deliver a signal, such as a light or a tone, whenever a person makes the desired response. The person may either use a prearranged method to produce the desired response or simply try to increase the signal's frequency in any way that he or

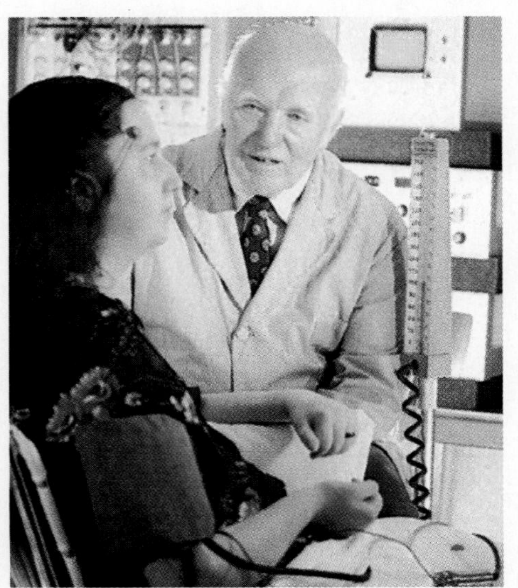

Some patients with spinal cord injuries lose consciousness when they sit upright because their blood pressure plunges. Here, Neal Miller, a pioneer in biofeedback research, trains a patient to control her blood pressure at will, using biofeedback techniques.

she chooses. Using biofeedback, some people have learned to control such autonomic responses as blood pressure, blood flow, heart rate, and skin temperature. Some clinicians are therefore using biofeedback training to treat high blood pressure, asthma, and migraine headaches, although there is controversy about success rates and about what, exactly, is being controlled—the actual autonomic responses, or responses that can be voluntarily produced, such as breathing, which then in turn affect the autonomic system.

The autonomic nervous system is itself divided into two parts: the **sympathetic nervous system** and the **parasympathetic nervous system.** These two parts work together, but in opposing ways, to adjust the body to changing circumstances (see Figure 4.2). To simplify, the sympathetic system acts like the accelerator of a car, mobilizing the body for action and an output of energy. It makes you blush, sweat, and breathe more deeply, and it pushes up your heart rate and blood pressure. When you are in a situation that requires you to fight, flee, or cope, the sympathetic nervous system whirls into action. The parasympathetic system is more like a brake: It does not stop the body, but it does tend to slow things down or keep them running smoothly. It enables the body to conserve and store energy. If you have to jump out of the way of a speeding motorcyclist, sympathetic nerves increase your heart rate. Afterward, parasympathetic nerves slow it down again and keep its rhythm regular. Both systems are involved in emotion and reactions to stress.

sympathetic nervous system The subdivision of the autonomic nervous system that mobilizes bodily resources and increases the output of energy during emotion and stress.

parasympathetic nervous system The subdivision of the autonomic nervous system that operates during relaxed states and that conserves energy.

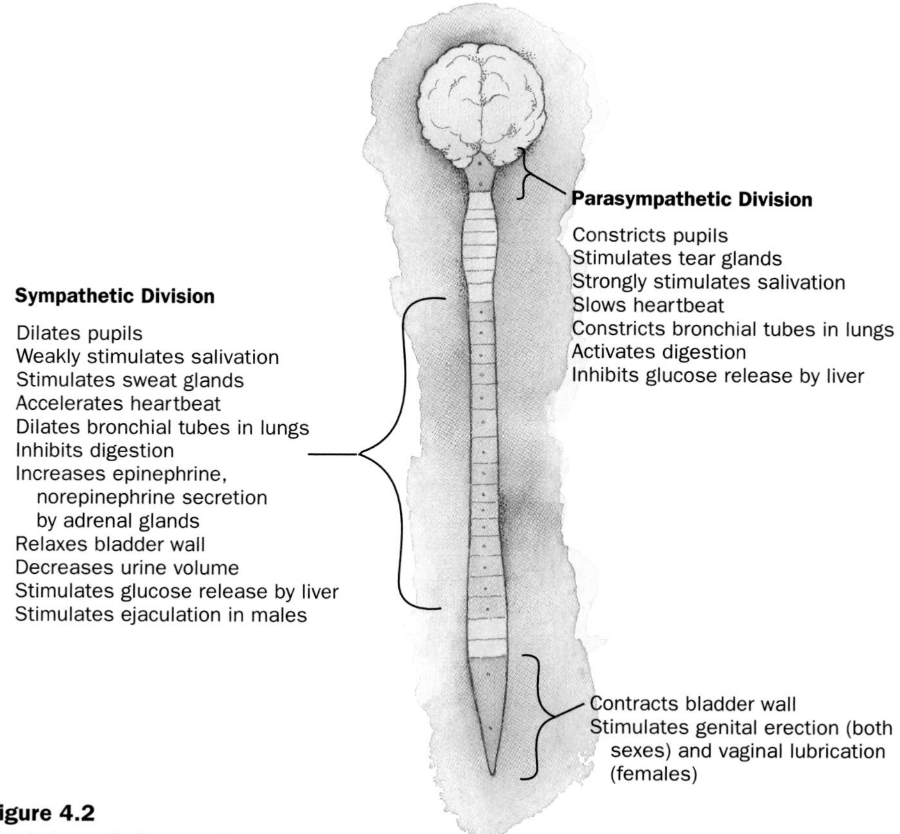

Figure 4.2
The Autonomic Nervous System

In general, the sympathetic division of the autonomic nervous system prepares the body to expend energy, and the parasympathetic division restores and conserves energy. Sympathetic nerve fibers exit from areas of the spinal cord shown in purple in this illustration; parasympathetic fibers exit from the base of the brain and from spinal cord areas shown in green.

Quick Quiz

Pause now to test your memory by mentally filling in the missing parts of the nervous system "house." Then see whether you can briefly describe what each part of the system does.

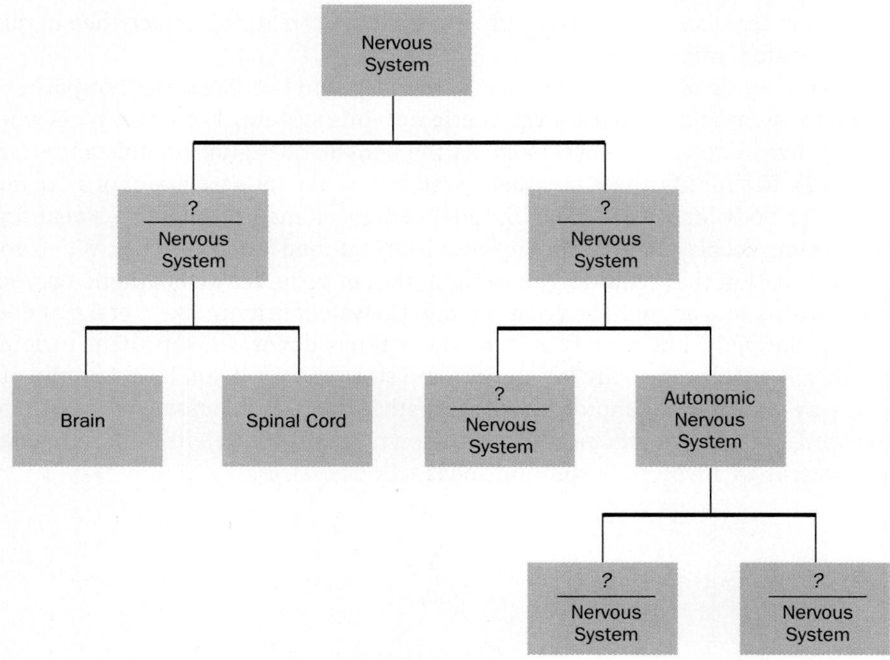

Answers:

Check your answers against Figure 4.5 on page 126. If you had difficulty, or if you could label the parts but forgot what they do, review the preceding section, and try again.

COMMUNICATION IN THE NERVOUS SYSTEM: THE NUTS AND BOLTS

The blueprint we have just described provides only a general idea of the nervous system's structure. Now let's turn to the details.

The nervous system is made up in part of **neurons,** or *nerve cells.* These neurons are held in place by **glial cells** (from the Greek for "glue"). Glial cells, which greatly outnumber neurons, also provide the neurons with nutrients, insulate the neurons, and remove cellular debris when the neurons die. Many neuroscientists suspect that glial cells carry electrical or chemical signals between parts of the nervous system, and that these signals somehow influence the activity of neighboring neurons. It is the neurons, however, that are the communication specialists, transmitting signals to, from, or within the central nervous system.

Although neurons are often called the building blocks of the nervous system, in structure they are more like snowflakes than blocks—exquisitely delicate, and differing from one another greatly in size and shape (see Figure 4.3). In the giraffe, a neuron that runs from the spinal cord down the animal's hind leg may be nine feet long! In the human brain, neurons are microscopic. No one is sure how many neurons the human brain contains, but a typical estimate is 100 billion, about the same number as there are stars in our galaxy—and some estimates go much higher.

neuron A cell that conducts electrochemical signals; the basic unit of the nervous system. Also called a *nerve cell.*

glial cells Cells that hold neurons in place, insulate neurons, and provide neurons with nutrients.

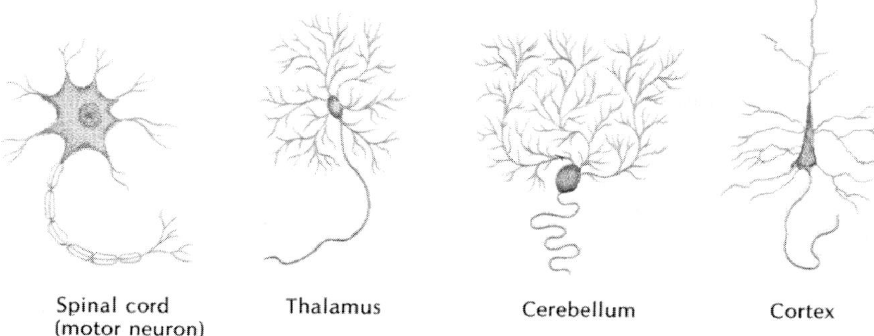

Figure 4.3
Different Kinds of Neurons

Neurons vary in size and shape, depending on their location and function. More than 200 types of neurons have been identified in mammals.

THE STRUCTURE OF THE NEURON

As you can see in Figure 4.4, a neuron has three main parts: *dendrites*, a *cell body*, and an *axon*. The **dendrites** look like the branches of a tree; indeed, the word *dendrite* means "little tree" in Greek. Dendrites act like antennas, receiving messages from as many as 10,000 other nerve cells and transmitting these messages toward the cell body. The **cell body,** which is shaped roughly like a sphere or a pyramid, contains the biochemical machinery for keeping the neuron alive. It also determines whether the neuron should "fire"—that is, transmit a message to other neurons—based on the number of inputs from other neurons. The **axon** (from the Greek for "axle") is like the tree's trunk, though more slender. It transmits messages away from the cell body to other neurons or to muscle or gland cells. Axons commonly divide at the end into branches, called *axon terminals.* In adult human beings, axons vary from only four thousandths of an inch to a few feet in length. Dendrites and axons give each neuron a double role: As one researcher put it, a neuron is first a catcher, then a batter (Gazzaniga, 1988).

Many axons, especially the larger ones, are insulated by a surrounding layer of fatty material called the **myelin sheath,** which is derived from glial cells (see Figure 4.4). This covering is divided into segments that make it look a little like a string of link sausages.

dendrites A neuron's branches that receive information from other neurons and transmit it toward the cell body.

cell body The part of the neuron that keeps it alive and determines whether it will fire.

axon A neuron's extending fiber that conducts impulses away from the cell body and transmits them to other neurons.

myelin sheath A fatty insulation that may surround the axon of a neuron.

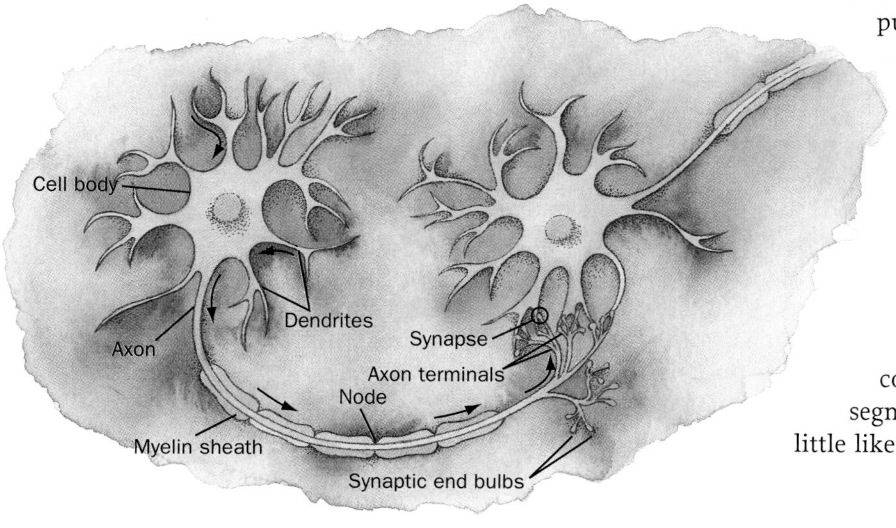

Figure 4.4
The Structure of a Neuron

Incoming neural impulses are received by the dendrites of a neuron and are transmitted to the cell body. Outgoing signals pass along the axon to terminal branches.

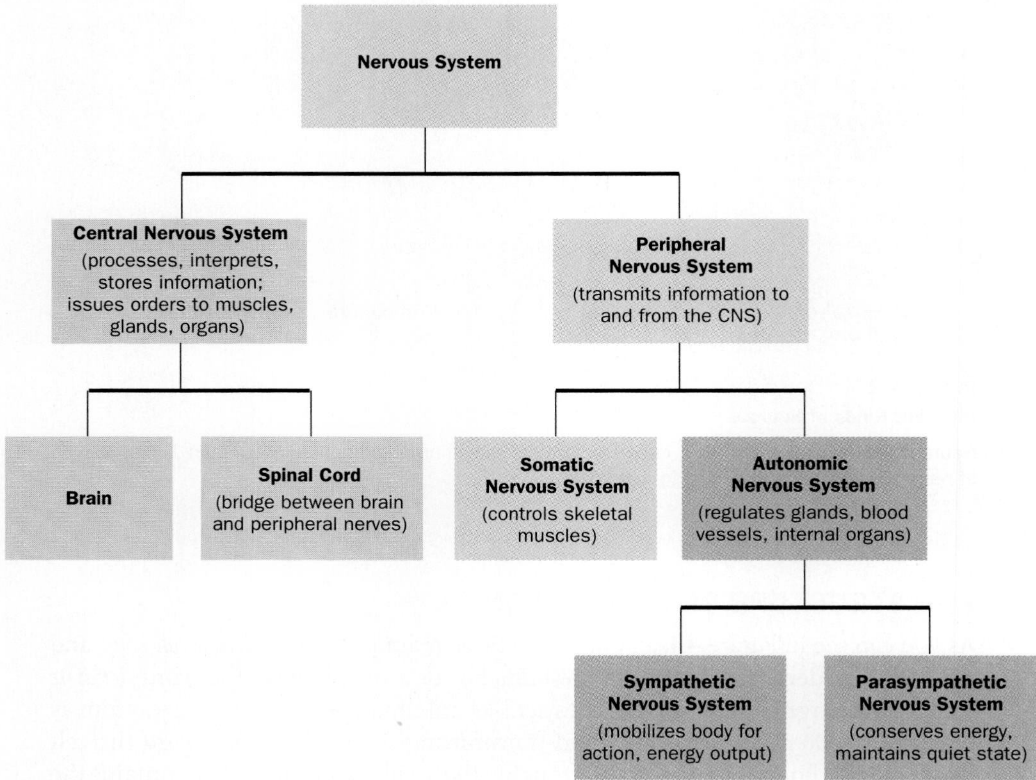

Figure 4.5
How the Nervous System is Organized
Use this diagram to check your answers to the Quick Quiz on page 124.

One of its purposes is to prevent signals in adjacent cells from interfering with each other. Another, as we will see shortly, is to speed up the conduction of neural impulses. In individuals with multiple sclerosis, loss of myelin causes erratic nerve signals, leading to loss of sensation, weakness or paralysis, lack of coordination, or vision problems.

In the peripheral nervous system, the fibers of individual neurons (axons and sometimes dendrites) are collected together in bundles called **nerves,** rather like the lines in a telephone cable. (In the central nervous system, similar bundles of neuron fibers are called *tracts.*) The human body has 43 pairs of peripheral nerves; one nerve from each pair is on the left side of the body, and the other is on the right. Most of these nerves enter or leave the spinal cord, but the 12 pairs that are in the head, the *cranial nerves,* connect directly to the brain. In Chapter 6, we will discuss three cranial nerves involved in sensory processing: the *olfactory nerve,* involved in smell; the *auditory nerve,* involved in hearing; and the *optic nerve,* involved in vision.

Until a decade ago, neuroscientists thought that neurons in the central nervous system could neither reproduce nor regenerate to any significant degree. They assumed that if these cells were injured or damaged, no one could do anything about it. But animal studies have challenged these assumptions. In one study, researchers got severed axons in the spinal cords of rats to regrow by blocking the effects of nerve-growth-inhibiting substances found in the myelin sheath (Schnell & Schwab, 1990). In another, researchers induced severed optic nerves in hamsters to regenerate by laying down a trail of transplanted nervous tissue from the animals' legs (Keirstead et al., 1989). What's more, Canadian neuroscientists have discovered that

nerve A bundle of nerve fibers (axons and sometimes dendrites) in the peripheral nervous system.

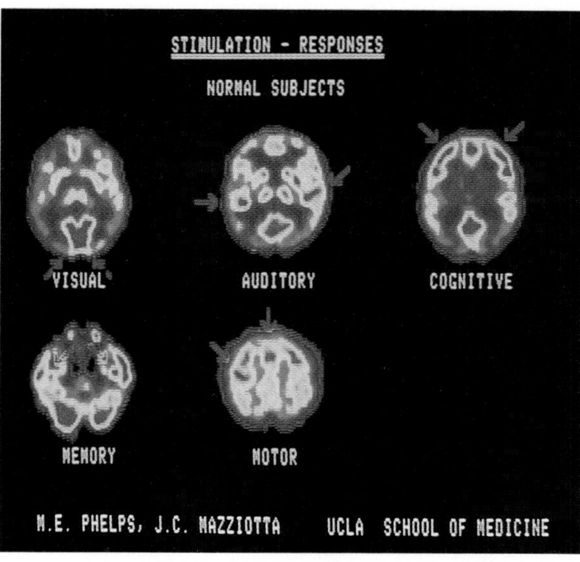

(a)

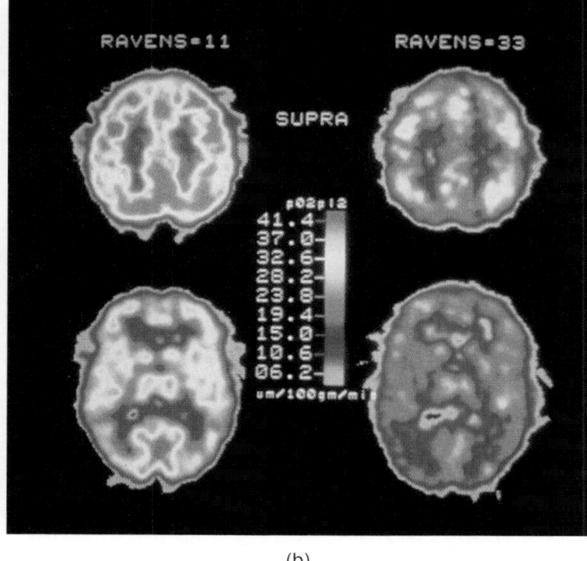

(b)

Figure 4.8
PET Scans of Metabolic Activity in the Brain

In the PET scans in photo (a), red indicates areas of highest activity and violet, areas of lowest activity. Clockwise starting from the upper left, the arrows point to regions that are most active when the person looks at a complicated visual scene, listens to a sound, performs a mental task, moves the right hand, or recalls stories heard previously. The scans in photo (b) show that during an abstract reasoning task, the brains of high scorers (right) metabolized less glucose per minute than the brains of low scorers (left)—suggesting that the brains of high scorers were working more efficiently (Haier et al., 1988).

active and are consuming glucose rapidly. The substance emits radiation, which is a telltale sign of activity, like cookie crumbs on a child's face. The radiation is detected by a scanning device, and the result is a computer-processed picture of biochemical activity on a display screen, with different colors indicating different activity levels.

PET scans, which were originally designed to diagnose abnormalities, have produced evidence that certain brain areas in people with emotional disorders are either unusually quiet or unusually active. But PET technology can also show which parts of the brain are active during ordinary activities and emotions (see Figure 4.8a). It lets researchers see which areas are busiest when a person hears a song, recalls a sad memory, works on a math problem, or shifts attention from one task to another.

PET scans are also being used to study the physiological correlates of intelligence. Most neuropsychologists doubt that intelligence has anything to do with the gross anatomy of the brain—no one, for instance, has been able to find anything remarkable about Einstein's brain. What more probably matters is the wiring of neural circuits, the amount or efficiency of neurotransmitters, or metabolism rates. PET-scan studies find, for example, that when people are working on intellectual tasks, the brains of those who score high are *less* active than those of people who do poorly (Haier et al., 1988; Parks et al., 1988) (see Figure 4.8b). A plausible explanation is that in high scorers, fewer circuits are required for the task, or perhaps fewer neurons per circuit; neurologically, in other words, their brains are operating more efficiently. Such biological differences could be genetic, but they could also develop as the result of experience. When participants in one study were given the opportunity to practice a computer game over a period of several weeks, their glucose-metabolism rates during the sessions gradually fell (Haier et al., 1992).

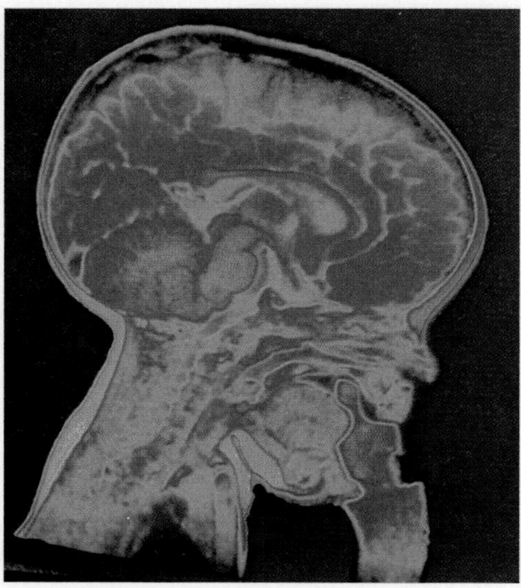

Figure 4.9
MRI at Work

This MRI shows a child's brain—and the bottle he was drinking from while the image was obtained.

Another technique, **MRI (magnetic resonance imaging),** allows the exploration of "inner space" without injecting chemicals. Powerful magnetic fields and radio frequencies are used to produce vibrations in the nuclei of atoms making up body organs, and these vibrations are then picked up as signals by special receivers. A computer analyzes the signals, taking into account their strength and duration, and converts them into a high-contrast picture (see Figure 4.9). Like the PET scan, MRI is used both for diagnosing disease and for studying normal brains. Conventional MRI is too slow to map activity over time, but recent breakthroughs in computer hardware and software have led to faster techniques that can capture brain changes during specific mental activities, such as thinking of a word or looking at a scene (Rosen et al., 1993). Fast, or "functional," MRI works indirectly; it detects blood flow by picking up magnetic signals from blood that has given up its oxygen to active brain cells. We will be reporting some of the incredible findings revealed by functional MRI research throughout this book—findings on memory, sex differences, depression, schizophrenia, and even how psychotherapy affects brain activity.

Still other techniques are becoming available with each passing year. One of the newest combines EEG and MRI technology (see Figure 4.10). The researcher or clinician first uses electrodes to record electrical signals from 128 points on the scalp. A new reading is taken every few milliseconds. A computer is then used to map ongoing, changing neuronal activity at the surface of a three-dimensional MRI image of

MRI (magnetic resonance imaging) A method for studying body and brain tissue, using magnetic fields and special radio receivers.

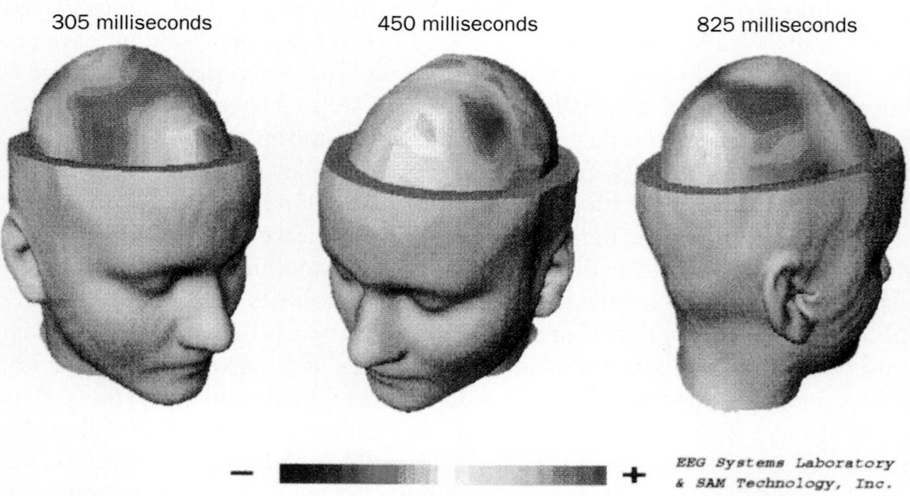

Figure 4.10
Brain Activity in 3-D

By combining a new technology, MRI, with an old one, the EEG, researchers can monitor electrical changes in brain cells from moment to moment while a person works on a task. These computer models show changes on the brain's surface during a 1-second interval as a person compares the location of a stimulus with the location of another one seen moments before.

the brain (Gevins et al., 1994). The result is something like a movie of ongoing changes in brain-cell activity.

As you can see, the brain can no longer hide from researchers behind the fortress of the skull. It is now possible to get a clear visual image of our most enigmatic organ without so much as lifting a scalpel.

A TOUR THROUGH THE BRAIN

All modern theories of how the brain functions assume that different brain parts perform different (though overlapping) tasks. This concept, known as **localization of function,** goes back at least to Joseph Gall (1758–1828), the Austrian anatomist who thought that personality traits were reflected in the development of different areas of the brain (see Chapter 1). Gall's theory of *phrenology* was completely wrong-headed (so to speak), but his general notion of specialization in the brain had merit.

To learn about what the various brain structures do, let's take an imaginary stroll through the brain. Pretend, now, that you have shrunk to a microscopic size and that you are wending your way through the "soul's frail dwelling house," starting at the lower part, just above the spine. For ease of description, we can think of that house as having three main sections: the *hindbrain,* the *midbrain,* and the *forebrain.* (These terms have fallen somewhat out of favor, but they do provide a useful way of organizing the areas of the brain.) In general, the more reflexive or automatic a behavior is, the more likely it is to involve areas in the hindbrain and midbrain, and the more complex a behavior, the more likely it is to involve the forebrain. Figure 4.11 shows the major structures of the brain; you may want to refer to it as we take our tour.

localization of function Specialization of particular brain areas for particular functions.

brain stem The part of the brain at the top of the spinal cord, consisting of the medulla and pons.

medulla A structure in the brain stem responsible for certain automatic functions, such as breathing and heart rate.

pons A structure in the brain stem involved in, among other things, sleeping, waking, and dreaming.

THE HINDBRAIN: VITAL FUNCTIONS

We begin at the base of the skull with the **brain stem,** which began to evolve some 500 million years ago in segmented worms. The brain stem looks like a stalk rising out of the spinal cord. Pathways to and from upper areas of the brain pass through its two main structures, the **medulla** and the **pons.** The pons is involved in (among other things) sleeping, waking, and dreaming. The medulla is responsible for bodily functions that do not have to be consciously willed, such as breathing and heart rate. Hanging has long been used as a method of execution because when it breaks the neck, nervous pathways from the medulla are severed, stopping respiration.

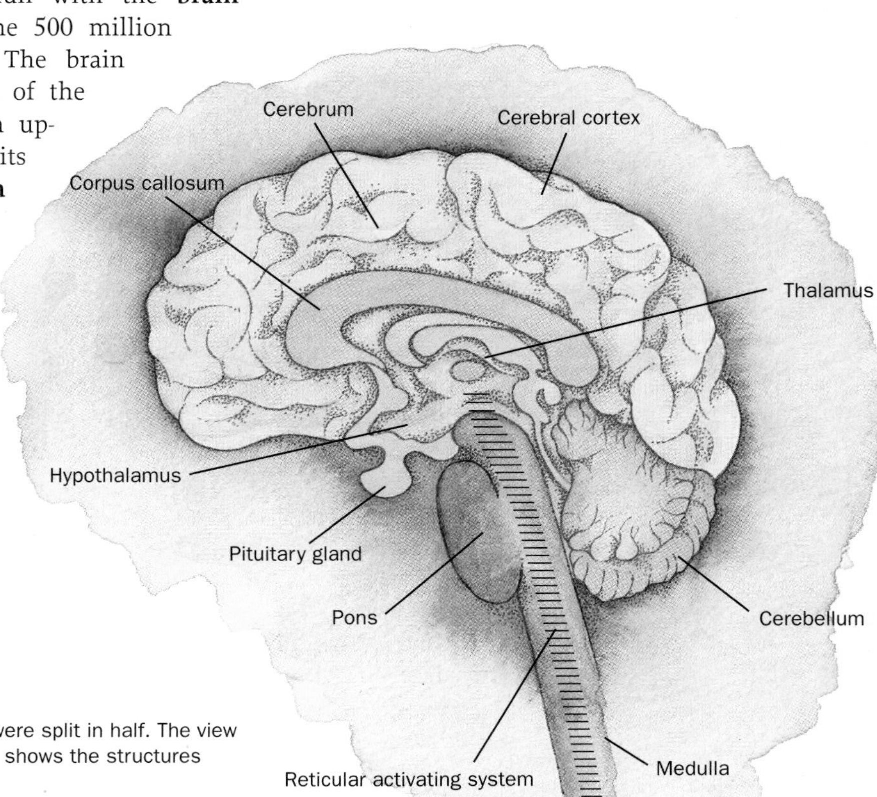

Figure 4.11
The Human Brain

This cross section depicts the brain as if it were split in half. The view is of the inside surface of the right half, and shows the structures described in the text.

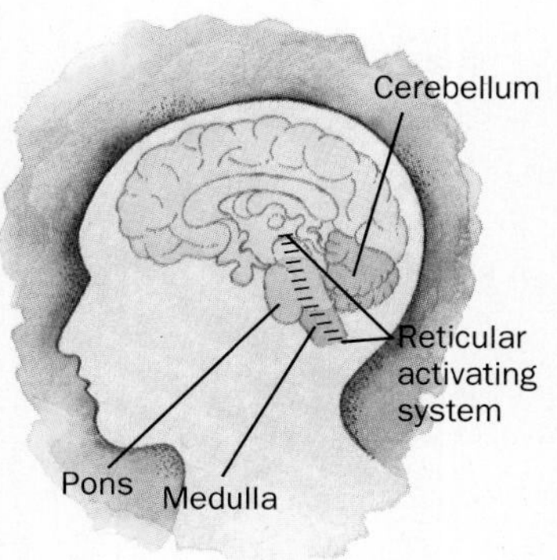

Extending upward from the core of the brain stem is the **reticular activating system (RAS).** This dense network of neurons, which has connections with many higher areas of the brain, screens incoming information and arouses the higher centers when something happens that demands their attention. Without the RAS, we could not be alert or perhaps even conscious.

Standing atop the brain stem and looking toward the back part of the brain, we see a structure about the size of a small fist. It is the **cerebellum,** or "lesser brain," which contributes to a sense of balance and coordinates the muscles so that movement is smooth and precise. If your cerebellum were damaged, you would probably become exceedingly clumsy and uncoordinated. You might have trouble using a pencil, threading a needle, or riding a bicycle. Some researchers think that the cerebellum also plays a role in analyzing sensory information and in mental tasks such as solving a puzzle or generating words (Fiez, 1996; Gao et al., 1996). In addition, this structure is involved in remembering certain kinds of simple skills, as we'll see in Chapter 9.

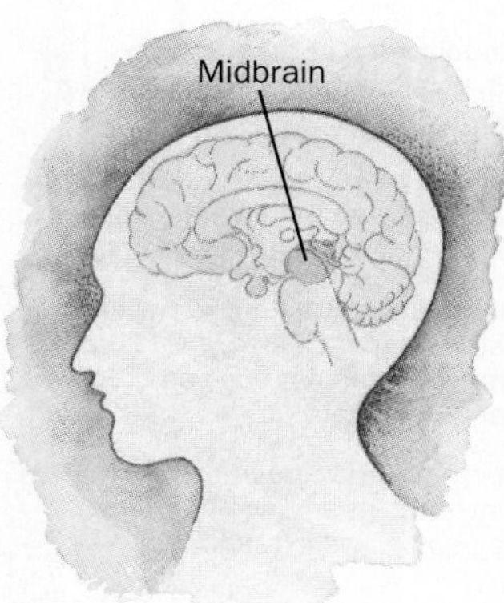

THE MIDBRAIN: IMPORTANT WAY STATIONS

Above the brain stem is the *midbrain,* which contains neural tracts that run to and from the upper and lower portions of the brain. One area of the midbrain receives information from the visual system and is involved in eye movements. Some researchers consider the midbrain to be part of the brain stem. In this book we will not be concerned with details about the midbrain's structure.

THE FOREBRAIN: EMOTIONS, MEMORY, AND THOUGHT

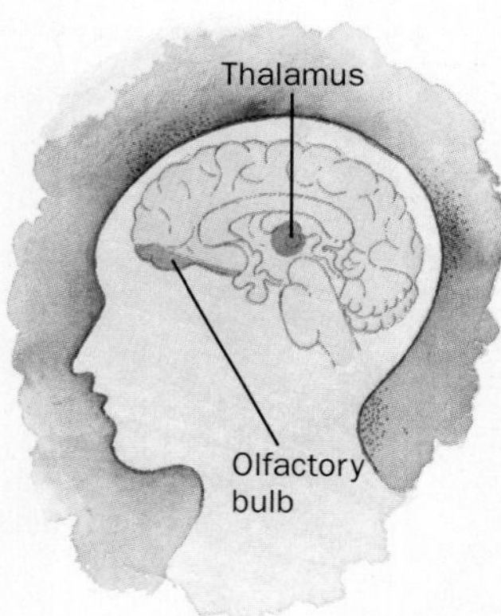

Deep in the brain's interior, we can see the **thalamus,** the busy traffic officer of the brain. As sensory messages come into the brain, the thalamus directs them to higher centers. For example, the sight of a sunset sends signals that the thalamus directs to a vision area, and the sound of an oboe sends signals that the thalamus sends on to an auditory area. The only sense that completely bypasses the thalamus is the sense of smell, which has its own private switching station, the *olfactory bulb.* The olfactory bulb lies near areas that are involved in emotion. Perhaps that is why particular odors—the smell of fresh laundry, gardenias, a steak sizzling on the grill—often rekindle memories of important personal experiences.

Beneath the thalamus sits a structure called the **hypothalamus** (*hypo* means "under"). It is involved in drives associated with the survival of both the individual and the species—hunger, thirst, emotion, sex, and reproduction. It regulates body temperature by triggering sweating or shivering, and it controls the complex operations of the autonomic nervous system. As we will see in the next chapter, it also contains a neurological clock that regulates the body's biological rhythms.

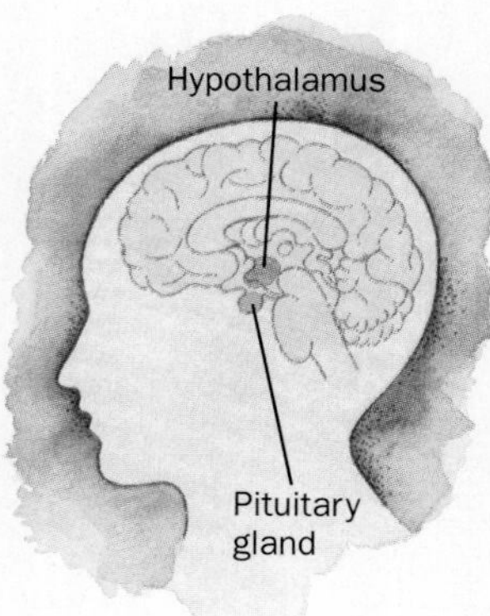

Hanging down from the hypothalamus, connected to it by a short stalk, is a cherry-sized endocrine gland called the **pituitary gland.** The pituitary is often called the body's "master gland" because the hormones it secretes affect many other endocrine glands. The master, however, is really only a supervisor. The true boss is the hypothalamus, which sends chemicals to the pituitary that tell it when to "talk" to the other endocrine glands. The pituitary, in turn, sends hormonal messages out to these glands.

The hypothalamus has many connections to a set of loosely interconnected structures that form a sort of border on the underside of the brain's "cauliflower." Together, these structures make up the **limbic system** of the brain, shown in Figure 4.12. (*Limbic* comes from the Latin word for "border.") Some anatomists include the hypothalamus and parts of the thalamus in the limbic system. Although the reality

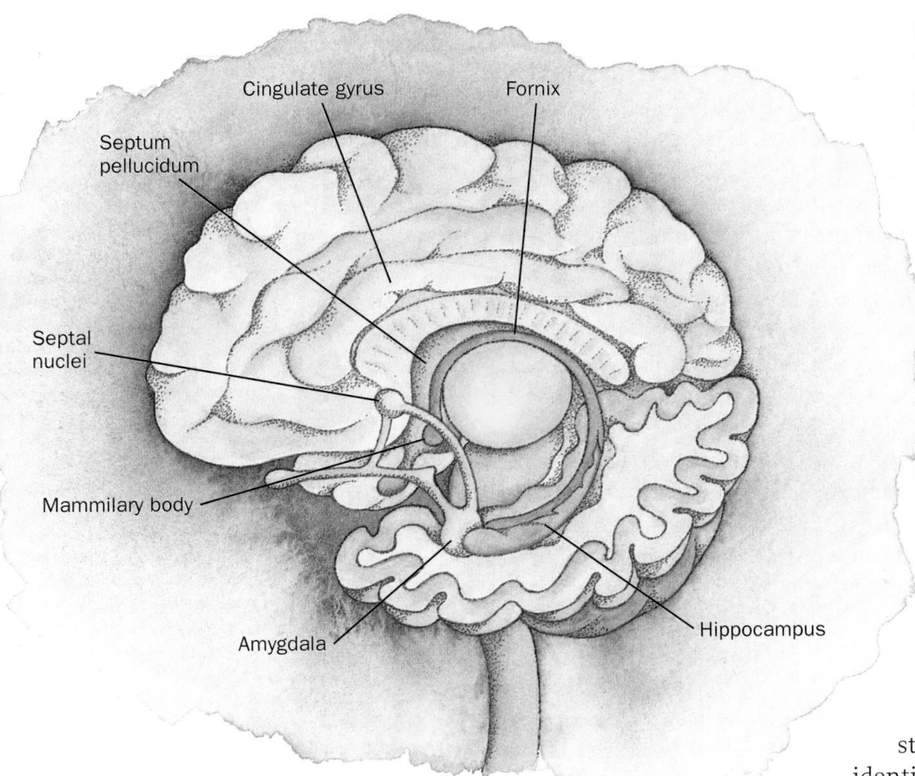

Figure 4.12
The Limbic System
Structures of the limbic system play an important role in memory and emotion.

of the limbic system as an integrated set of structures is now under dispute (LeDoux, 1996), it's clear that structures traditionally identified as limbic are heavily involved in emotions that we share with other animals (MacLean, 1993).

Many years ago, James Olds and Peter Milner hypothesized that there were "pleasure centers" in the limbic system (Olds, 1975; Olds & Milner, 1954). They trained rats to press a lever in order to get a buzz of electricity delivered through tiny electrodes to the limbic system. Some rats would press the bar thousands of times an hour, for 15 or 20 hours at a time, until they collapsed from exhaustion. When they revived, they went right back to the bar. When forced to make a choice, the little hedonists opted for electrical stimulation over such temptations as water, food, and even an attractive rat of the other sex that was making provocative gestures. (You may be either relieved or disappointed to know that human beings do not act like rats in this regard; the comparable experience merely feels "pleasant" to humans [Sem-Jacobsen, 1959].) Today, researchers believe that brain stimulation activates neural pathways rather than discrete "centers," and that changes in neurotransmitter or neuromodulator levels are involved.

One limbic structure that especially concerns psychologists is the **amygdala,** which appears to be responsible for evaluating sensory information, quickly determining its emotional importance, and contributing to the initial decision to approach or withdraw from a person or situation (see Chapter 10). The amygdala also plays an important role in mediating anxiety and depression; PET scans find that depressed and anxious patients show increased neural activity in this structure (Schulkin, 1994).

Another important limbic area is the **hippocampus,** which has a shape that must have reminded someone of a sea horse, for that is what its name means. This structure is larger in human beings than in any other species. One of its tasks seems to be to compare sensory messages with what the brain has learned to expect about the world. When expectations are met, the hippocampus tells the reticular activating system, the brain's arousal center, to "cool it." It wouldn't do to be highly aroused in

reticular activating system (RAS) A dense network of neurons found in the core of the brain stem; it arouses the cortex and screens incoming information.

cerebellum A brain structure that regulates movement and balance, and that is involved in the learning of certain kinds of simple responses.

thalamus A brain structure that relays sensory messages to the cerebral cortex.

hypothalamus A brain structure involved in emotions and drives vital to survival, such as fear, hunger, thirst, and reproduction; it regulates the autonomic nervous system.

pituitary gland A small endocrine gland at the base of the brain, which releases many hormones and regulates other endocrine glands.

limbic system A group of brain areas involved in emotional reactions and motivated behavior.

amygdala A brain structure involved in the arousal and regulation of emotion and the initial emotional response to sensory information.

hippocampus A brain structure involved in the storage of new information in memory.

response to *everything.* What if neural alarm bells went off every time a car went by, a bird chirped, or you felt your saliva trickling down the back of your throat?

The hippocampus has also been called the "gateway to memory" because, along with other brain areas, it enables us to store new information about facts and events—the kind of information you need to identify a flower, tell a story, or recall a vacation trip. The information then goes on to be stored in the cerebral cortex, which we will be discussing shortly; but without the hippocampus, the information would never get to its ultimate destination.

We know about this function of the hippocampus in part from research on brain-damaged patients with severe memory problems. The case of one man, known to researchers as H. M., is thought to be the most intensely studied in the annals of medicine, and it is still being studied today (Corkin, 1984; Milner, 1970; Ogden & Corkin, 1991). In 1953, when H. M. was 27, surgeons removed most of his hippocampus, along with part of the amygdala. The operation was a last-ditch effort to relieve H. M.'s severe and life-threatening epilepsy. People who have epilepsy, a neurological disorder that has many causes and takes many forms, often have seizures. Usually, the seizures are brief, mild, and controllable by drugs, but in H. M.'s case, they were unrelenting and uncontrollable.

The operation did achieve its goal: Afterward, the young man's seizures were milder and could be managed with medication. His memory, however, had been affected dramatically. Although H. M. continued to recall most events that had occurred before the operation, he could no longer remember new experiences for much longer than 15 minutes; they vanished like water down the drain. With sufficient practice, H. M. could acquire new manual or problem-solving skills, such as solving a puzzle or playing tennis, but he could not remember having learned these skills. He would read the same magazine over and over without realizing it. He could not recall the day of the week, the year, or even his last meal. Today, many years later, he will occasionally recall an unusually emotional event, such as the assassination of someone named Kennedy. He sometimes remembers that both his parents are dead, and he knows he has memory problems. But, according to Suzanne Corkin, who has studied H. M. extensively, these "islands of remembering" are the exceptions in a vast sea of forgetfulness. This good-natured man still does not know the scientists who have studied him for decades. Although he is now in his seventies, he thinks he is much younger, and he can no longer recognize a photograph of his own face; he is stuck in a time warp from the past. (We will meet H. M. again when we discuss memory in Chapter 9.)

At this point in our tour, the largest part of the brain still looms above us. It is the cauliflower-like **cerebrum,** where the higher forms of thinking take place. The complexity of the human brain's circuitry far exceeds that of any computer in existence, and much of its most complicated wiring is packed into this structure. Compared with many other creatures, we humans may be ungainly, feeble, and thin-skinned, but our well-developed cerebrum enables us to overcome these limitations and creatively control our environment (and, some would say, to mess it up).

The cerebrum is divided into two separate halves, or **cerebral hemispheres,** connected by a large band of fibers called the **corpus callosum.** In general, the right hemisphere is in charge of the left side of the body and the left hemisphere is in charge of the right side of the body. As we will see shortly, the two hemispheres also have somewhat different tasks and talents, a phenomenon known as **lateralization.**

Working our way right up through the top of the brain, we find that the cerebrum is covered by several thin layers of densely packed cells known collectively as the **cerebral cortex.** Cell bodies in the cortex, as in many other parts of the brain, produce a grayish tissue; hence the term *gray matter.* In other parts of the brain (and in

cerebrum [suh-REE-brum] The largest brain structure, consisting of the upper part of the forebrain; it is in charge of most sensory, motor, and cognitive processes. From the Latin for "brain."

cerebral hemispheres The two halves of the cerebrum.

corpus callosum The bundle of nerve fibers connecting the two cerebral hemispheres.

lateralization Specialization of the two cerebral hemispheres for particular psychological operations.

cerebral cortex A collection of several thin layers of cells covering the cerebrum; it is largely responsible for higher mental functions. *Cortex* is Latin for "bark" or "rind."

the rest of the nervous system), long, myelin-covered axons prevail, providing the brain's *white matter.* Although the cortex is only about 3 millimeters thick, it contains almost three-fourths of all the cells in the human brain. If these cells were stretched out end to end, they would span the distance from the earth to the moon and back again, and then back to the moon (J. Davis, 1984).

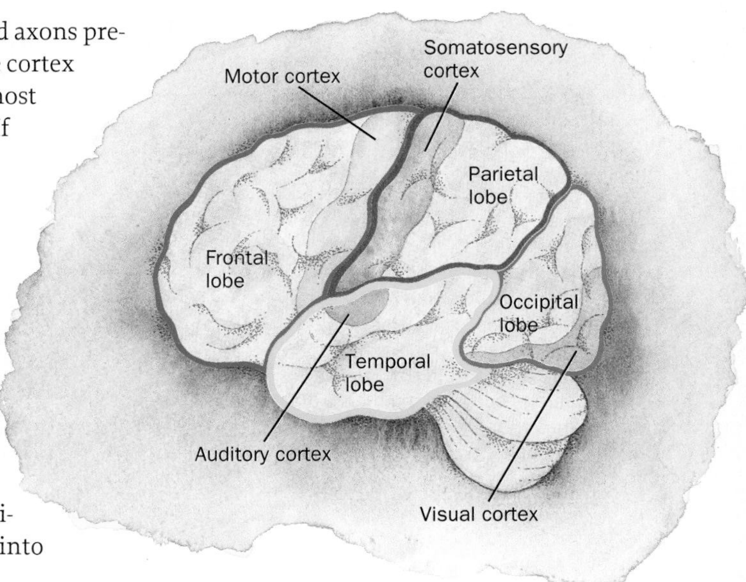

Figure 4.13
Lobes of the Cerebrum

The cortex has many deep crevasses and wrinkles. These folds and fissures in the brain's surface enable it to contain its billions of neurons without requiring us to have the heads of giants—heads that would be too big to permit us to be born. In other mammals, which have fewer neurons, the cortex is less crumpled; in rats, it is quite smooth. On each cerebral hemisphere, especially deep fissures divide the cortex into four distinct regions, or lobes (see Figure 4.13):

- The *occipital lobes* (from the Latin for "in back of the head") are at the lower back part of the brain. Among other things, they contain the *visual cortex,* where visual signals are processed. Damage to the visual cortex can cause impaired visual recognition or blindness.
- The *parietal lobes* (from the Latin for "pertaining to walls") are at the top of the brain. They contain the *somatosensory cortex,* which receives information about pressure, pain, touch, and temperature from all over the body. This sensory information tells you what the movable parts of your body are doing at every moment. The areas of the somatosensory cortex that receive signals from the hands and the face are disproportionately large because these body parts are particularly sensitive.
- The *temporal lobes* (from the Latin for "pertaining to the temples") are at the sides of the brain, just above the ears, behind the temples. They are involved in memory, perception, emotion, and language comprehension, and they contain the *auditory cortex,* which processes sounds.
- The *frontal lobes,* as their name indicates, are located toward the front of the brain, just under the skull in the area of the forehead. They contain the *motor cortex,* which issues orders to the 600 muscles of the body that produce voluntary movement. They also seem to be responsible for the ability to make plans, think creatively, and take initiative.

When a surgeon probes these four pairs of lobes with an electrode, different things tend to happen. If current is applied to the somatosensory cortex in the parietal lobes, the patient may feel tingling in the skin or a sense of being gently touched. If the visual cortex in the occipital lobes is stimulated, the person may report a flash of light or swirls of color. However, there is considerable overlap in what the lobes do. And in most areas of the cortex, nothing happens as a result of electrical stimulation. These "silent" areas, sometimes called the *association cortex,* appear to be responsible for higher mental processes.

The silent areas of the cortex are finally beginning to reveal their secrets. Psychologists are especially interested in the forwardmost part of the frontal lobes, the *prefrontal cortex.* This area barely exists in mice and rats and takes up only 3.5 per-

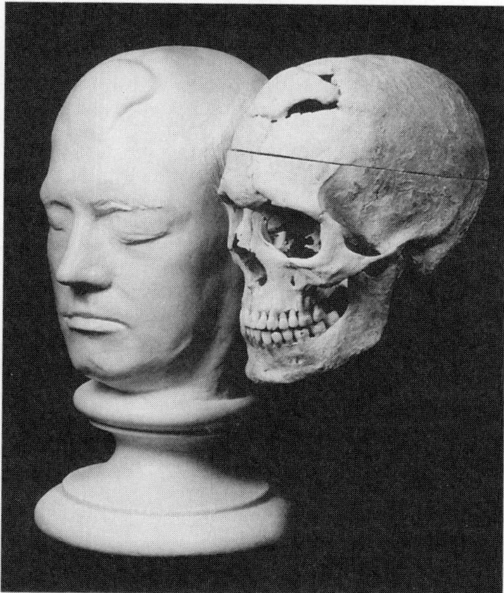

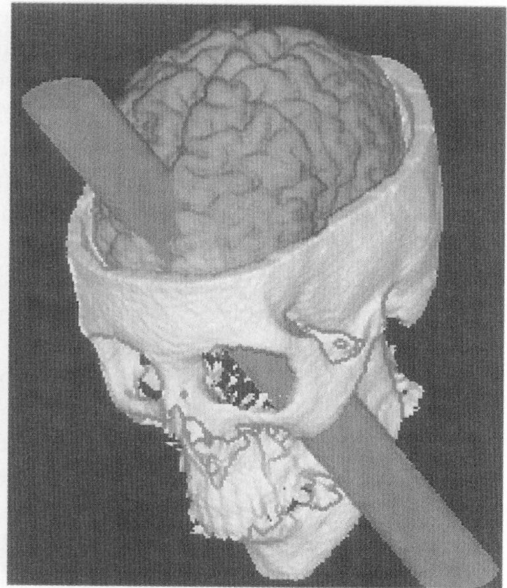

Figure 4.14
A Famous Skull

On the left is Phineas Gage's skull and a cast of his head, on display at Harvard Medical School. You can see where the tamping iron penetrated, dramatically altering his behavior and personality. The exact location of the brain damage remained controversial until Hanna and Antonio Damasio and their colleagues (1994) used measurements of Gage's skull and MRIs of normal brains to plot possible trajectories of the tamping iron. The reconstruction on the right shows that the damage occurred in an area of the prefrontal cortex thought to be involved in emotional processing and rational decision making.

cent of the cerebral cortex in cats, about 7 percent in dogs, and 17 percent in chimpanzees. In human beings, it accounts for fully 29 percent of the cortex (Pines, 1983).

Scientists have long known that the frontal lobes, and the prefrontal cortex in particular, must have something to do with personality. The first clue appeared in 1848, when a bizarre accident drove an inch-thick, $3\frac{1}{2}$-foot-long iron rod clear through the head of a young railroad worker named Phineas Gage. As you can see in Figure 4.14, the rod (which is still on display at Harvard University, along with Gage's skull) entered beneath the left eye and exited through the top of the head, destroying much of the prefrontal cortex (H. Damasio et al., 1994). Miraculously, Gage survived this trauma. What's more, he retained the ability to speak, think, and remember. But his friends complained that he was "no longer Gage." In a sort of Jekyll-and-Hyde transformation, he had changed from a mild-mannered, friendly, efficient worker into a foul-mouthed, ill-tempered, undependable lout who could not hold a steady job or stick to a plan. His employers had to let him go, and he was reduced to exhibiting himself as a circus attraction.

This sad case and other cases of frontal-lobe damage suggest that parts of the frontal lobes are involved in social judgment, rational decision making, and the ability to set goals and to make and carry through plans—or what is commonly called "will." As neurologist Antonio Damasio (1994) writes, "Gage's unintentional message was that observing social convention, behaving ethically, and, in general, making decisions advantageous to one's survival and progress, require both knowledge of rules and strategies *and* the integrity of specific brain systems." Interestingly, the mental deficits that characterize damage to these areas are accompanied by a flattening out of emotion and feeling, which suggests that normal emotions are necessary for everyday reasoning and decision making.

The frontal lobes also govern the ability to do a series of tasks in the proper sequence and to stop doing them at the proper time. The pioneering Soviet psychologist Alexander Luria (1980) studied many cases in which damage to the frontal lobes disrupted these abilities. One man observed by Luria kept trying to light a match after it was already lit. Another planed a piece of wood in the hospital carpentry shop until it was gone, and then went on to plane the workbench!

Some researchers believe that damage to the prefrontal cortex, caused by birth complications or child abuse, might help account for some cases of criminally violent behavior (Raine, Brennan, & Mednick, 1994). A PET-scan study found that accused murderers had less brain activity in this area than did control subjects who were matched for age and sex (Raine, Buchsbaum, et al., 1994). These results raise troubling legal questions: Should violent individuals who have damage in the prefrontal cortex be held responsible for their acts? And what treatment or punishment should they receive?

Quick Quiz

It's time to see how your own brain is working. Match each description on the left with a term on the right.

1. Filters out irrelevant information
2. Known as the "gateway to memory"
3. Controls the autonomic nervous system; involved in drives associated with survival
4. Consists of two hemispheres
5. Wrinkled outer covering of the brain
6. Site of the motor cortex; associated with planning, thinking creatively, and taking initiative

a. reticular activating system
b. cerebrum
c. hippocampus
d. cerebral cortex
e. frontal lobes
f. hypothalamus

Answers:

1. a 2. c 3. f 4. b 5. d 6. e

THE TWO HEMISPHERES OF THE BRAIN

We have seen that the cerebrum is divided into two hemispheres that control opposite sides of the body. Although similar in structure, these hemispheres have somewhat separate talents, or areas of specialization.

SPLIT BRAINS: A HOUSE DIVIDED

In a normal brain, the two hemispheres communicate with one another across the corpus callosum, the bundle of fibers that connects them. Whatever happens in one side of the brain is instantly flashed to the other side. What would happen, though, if the communication lines were cut?

An early clue occurred in a case study published in 1908. A mentally disturbed woman repeatedly tried to choke herself with her left hand. She would try with her right hand to pull the left hand away from her throat, but she claimed that the left hand was beyond her control. She also did other destructive things, such as throwing pillows around and tearing her sheets—but only with her left hand. A neurologist suspected that the woman's corpus callosum had been damaged and the two sides of the brain could no longer communicate. When the woman died, an autopsy showed that he was right (Geschwind, in J. Miller, 1983).

This case suggested that the two sides of the brain can feel different emotions. What would happen if they were completely out of touch? Would they think different thoughts and store different memories? In 1953, Ronald E. Myers and Roger W. Sperry took the first step toward answering this question by severing the corpus callosum in cats. They also cut parts of the nerves leading from the eyes to the brain.

Normally, each eye transmits messages to both sides of the brain. After this procedure, a cat's left eye sent information only to the left hemisphere, and its right eye sent information only to the right hemisphere.

At first, the cats did not seem to be affected much by this drastic operation. But Myers and Sperry showed that something profound had happened. They trained the cats to perform tasks with one eye blindfolded. For example, a cat might have to push a panel with a square on it to get food but ignore a panel with a circle. Then the researchers switched the blindfold to the cat's other eye and tested the animal again. Now the cats behaved as if they had never learned the trick. Apparently, one side of the brain didn't know what the other side was doing. It was as if the animals had two minds in one body. Later studies confirmed this result with other species, including monkeys (Sperry, 1964).

In all the animal studies, ordinary behavior, such as eating and walking, remained normal. Encouraged by this finding, a team of surgeons led by Joseph Bogen decided in the early 1960s to try cutting the corpus callosum in patients with debilitating, uncontrollable epilepsy. In severe forms of this disease, disorganized electrical activity spreads from an injured area to other parts of the brain. The surgeons reasoned that cutting the connection between the two halves of the brain might stop the spread of electrical activity from one side to the other. As in the case of H. M., the operation was a last resort.

The results of this *split-brain surgery* generally proved successful. Seizures were reduced and sometimes disappeared completely. As an added bonus, these patients gave scientists a chance to find out what each half of the brain can do when it is quite literally cut off from the other. It was already known that the two hemispheres are not mirror images of each other. In most people, language is largely handled by the left hemisphere: speech production in an area of the left frontal lobe known as *Broca's area*, and meaning and language comprehension in an area of the left temporal lobe known as *Wernicke's area*. (The two areas are named after the scientists who first described them.) Thus, a person who suffers brain damage because of a stroke—a blockage in or rupture of a blood vessel in the brain—is much more likely to have language problems if the damage is in the left side than if it is in the right. How would splitting the brain affect language and other abilities?

In their daily lives, split-brain patients did not seem much affected by the fact that the two sides of their brains were incommunicado. Their personalities and general intelligence remained intact; they could walk, talk, and in general lead normal lives. Apparently, connections in the undivided brain stem kept body movements normal. But in a series of ingenious studies, Sperry and his colleagues (and later other researchers) showed that perception and memory had been affected, just as they had been in earlier animal research. In 1981, Sperry won a Nobel Prize for this work.

To understand this research, you must know how nerves connect the eyes to the brain. (The human patients, unlike Myers and Sperry's cats, did not have these

GET INVOLVED

Have a right-handed friend tap on a paper with a pencil held in the right hand, for one minute. Then have the person do the same with the left hand, using a fresh sheet of paper. Finally, repeat the procedure, having the person talk at the same time as tapping. For most people, talking will decrease the rate of tapping—but more for the right hand than for the left, probably because both activities involve the same hemisphere, and there is "competition" between them. (Left-handed people vary more in terms of which hemisphere is dominant for language, so the results for them will be more variable.)

nerves cut.) If you look straight ahead, everything in the left side of the scene before you—the "visual field"—goes to the right half of your brain, and everything in the right side of the scene goes to the left half of your brain. This is true for *both* eyes (see Figure 4.15).

The procedure was to present information only to one or the other side of the subjects' brains. In one early study (Levy, Trevarthen, & Sperry, 1972), the researchers took photographs of different faces, cut them in two, and pasted different halves together. The reconstructed photographs were then presented on slides. The person was told to stare at a dot on the middle of the screen, so that half the image fell to the left of this point and half to the right. Each image was flashed so quickly that the person had no time to move his or her eyes. When the subjects were asked to say what they had seen, they named the person in the right part of the image (which would be the little boy in Figure 4.16 on p. 146). But when they were asked to *point* with their left hands to the face they had seen, they chose the person in the left side of the image. Further, they claimed they had noticed nothing unusual about the original photographs! Each side of the brain saw a different half-image and automatically filled in the missing part. Neither side knew what the other side had seen.

Why did the patients name one side of the picture but point to the other? Speech centers are in the left hemisphere. When the person responded with speech, it was the left side of the brain doing the talking. When the person pointed with the left hand, which is controlled by the right side of the brain, the right brain was giving *its* version of what the person had seen.

In another study, the researchers presented slides of ordinary objects and then suddenly flashed a slide of a nude woman. Both sides of the brain were amused, but because only the left side has speech, the two sides responded differently. When the picture was flashed to her left hemisphere, one woman laughed and identified it as a nude. When it was flashed to her right hemisphere, she said nothing but

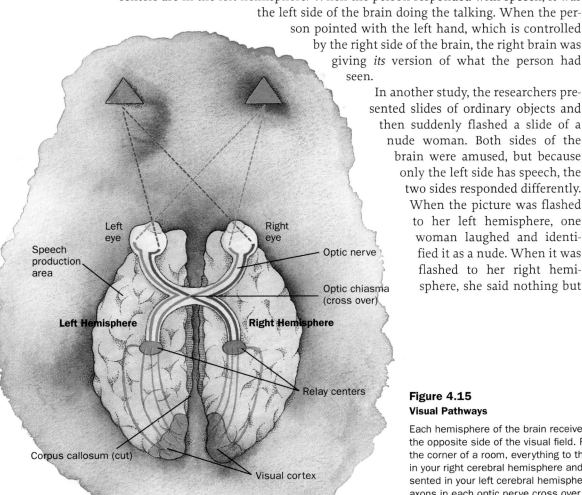

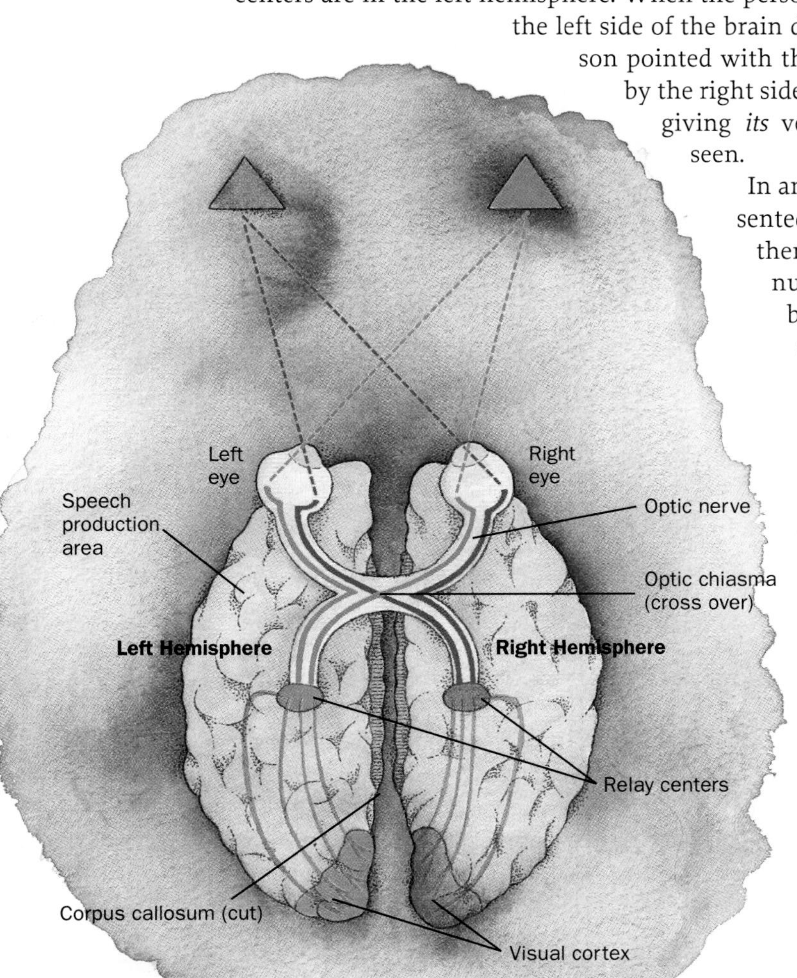

Figure 4.15
Visual Pathways

Each hemisphere of the brain receives information from the eyes about the opposite side of the visual field. For example, if you stare directly at the corner of a room, everything to the left of the juncture is represented in your right cerebral hemisphere and everything to the right is represented in your left cerebral hemisphere. This is so because half the axons in each optic nerve cross over (at the optic chiasma) to the opposite side of the brain. Normally, each hemisphere immediately shares its information with the other one, but in split-brain patients, severing the corpus callosum prevents such communication.

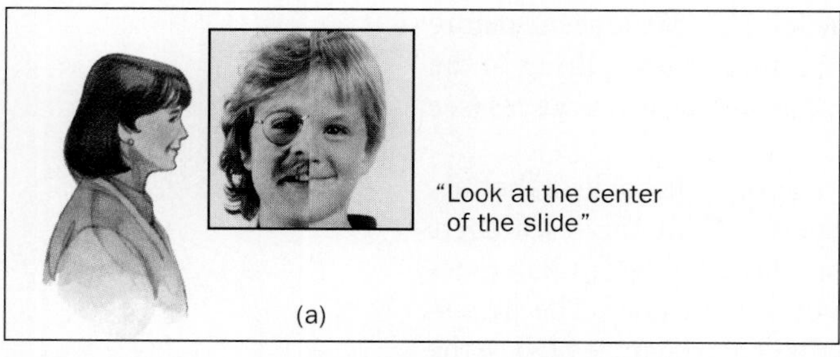

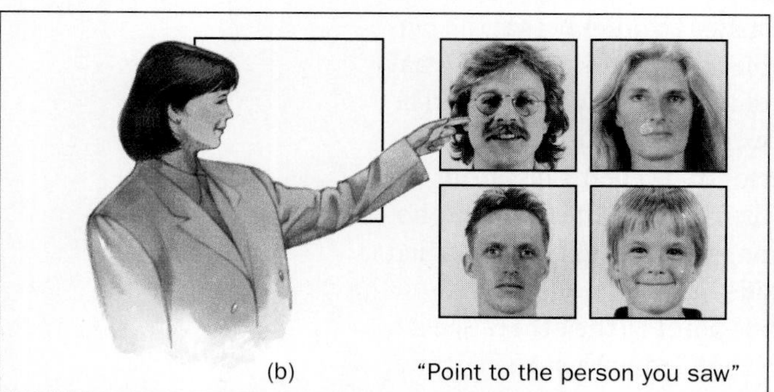

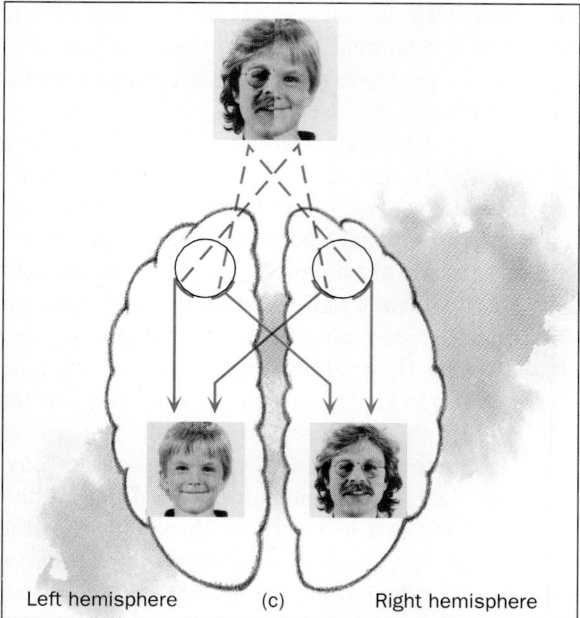

Figure 4.16
Divided Brain, Divided View

When split-brain patients were shown composite photographs (a) and were then asked to pick out the face they had seen from a series of intact photographs (b), they said they had seen the face on the right side of the composite—yet they pointed with their left hands to the face that had been on the left. Because the two hemispheres of the brain could not communicate, the verbal left hemisphere was aware of only the right half of the picture, and the relatively mute right hemisphere was aware of only the left half (c).

began to chuckle. Asked what she was laughing at, she said, "I don't know . . . nothing . . . oh—that funny machine." The right hemisphere could not describe what it had seen, but it reacted emotionally, just the same (Gazzaniga, 1967).

A QUESTION OF DOMINANCE

Several dozen people have undergone the split-brain operation since the mid-1960s, and research on left–right differences has also been done with people whose brains are intact. Electrodes and PET scans have been used to gauge activity in the left and right hemispheres while people perform different tasks. The results confirm that nearly all right-handed people and a majority of left-handers process language mainly in the left hemisphere. The left side is also more active during some logical, symbolic, and sequential tasks, such as solving math problems and understanding technical material. Because of its cognitive talents, many researchers refer to the left hemisphere as *dominant.* They believe that the left hemisphere usually exerts control over the right hemisphere. One well-known split-brain researcher, Michael Gazzaniga (1983), has argued that without help from the left side, the right side's mental skills would probably be "vastly inferior to the cognitive skills of a chimpanzee." He and others also believe that the left hemisphere is constantly trying to explain actions and emotions generated by brain parts whose workings are nonverbal and outside of awareness.

You can see in split-brain patients how the left brain concocts such explanations. In one classic example, a picture of a chicken claw was flashed to a patient's left hemisphere, a picture of a snow scene to his right. The task was to point to a related image for each picture from an array, with a chicken the correct choice for the claw and a shovel for the snow scene. The patient chose the shovel with his left hand and the chicken with his right. When asked to explain why, he responded (with his left hemisphere) that the chicken claw went with the chicken, and the shovel was for cleaning out the chicken shed. The left brain had seen the left hand's response but did not know about the snow scene, so it interpreted the response by using the information it did have (Gazzaniga, 1988). In people with intact brains, says Gazzaniga, the left brain's interpretations account for the sense of a unified, coherent identity. (For more on the brain and self-awareness, see "Puzzles of Psychology.")

Other researchers, including Sperry (1982), have rushed to the right hemisphere's defense. The right side, they point out, is no dummy. It is superior in problems requiring spatial–visual ability, the ability you use to read a map or follow a dress pattern, and it excels in facial recognition and the ability to read facial expressions. (Dr. P. and Emily D., described at the beginning of this chapter, both had damage in the right hemisphere.) It is active during the creation and appreciation of art and music. It recognizes nonverbal sounds, such as a dog's barking. The right brain also has some language ability. Typically, it can read a word briefly flashed to it and can understand an experimenter's instructions. In a few split-brain patients, language ability has been quite well developed. And the right brain actually outperforms the left at understanding familiar idioms and metaphors (such as "turning over a new leaf") (Van Lancker & Kempler, 1987).

Some researchers have credited the right hemisphere with having a cognitive style that is intuitive and holistic (in which things are seen as wholes), in contrast to the left hemisphere's more rational and analytic mode. However, many researchers are concerned about popular misinterpretations of this conclusion. Books

"Mama and I fixed a lovely dinner. I used the right side of my brain, and she used the left side of her brain."

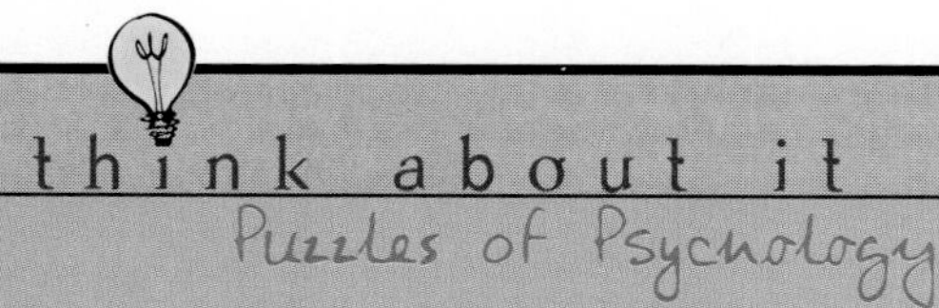

Where Is Your Self?

When we think about the remarkable blob of tissue in our heads that allows us to remember, to dream, and to think—the blob that can make our existence a hideous nightmare when it is diseased—we are led, inevitably, to the oldest question of all: Where, exactly, is the mind?

When you say, "I am feeling unhappy," your amygdala, your serotonin receptors, your endorphins, and all sorts of other brain parts and processes are active, but who, exactly, is the "I" doing the feeling? When you say, "I've decided to have a hot dog instead of a hamburger," who is the "I" doing the choosing? When you say, "My mind is playing tricks on me," who is the "me" watching your mind play those tricks, and who is it that's being tricked? How can the self observe itself? Isn't that a little like a finger pointing at its own tip?

The ancient Egyptians reportedly believed that the "self" controlling actions and thoughts was a little person, a *homunculus*, residing in the head. French philosopher René Descartes thought the soul made contact with the body in the brain's pineal gland. Western religions have resolved the problem by teaching that an immortal self or soul exists entirely apart from the mortal brain—a position known in philosophy as *dualism*. But most modern brain scientists, with some notable exceptions, consider mind to be a matter of matter—a position known as *materialism*. Although they may have personal religious convictions about a soul, most assume that "mind" or "self-awareness" can be explained in physical terms as a product of the cerebral cortex. They regard the brain as a fabulous, exceedingly complex machine that will one day be understood in terms of its parts, without reference to some invisible manager pulling the levers; in the words of British philosopher Gilbert Ryle (1949), there is no "ghost in the machine." If that is so, then it makes no sense, really, to say "I have a brain" or "We think with our brains" or "Boy, she's really using her brain"—although we all use such everyday constructions—because we *are* our brains! There's no one else in there.

"THEN IT'S AGREED—YOU CAN'T HAVE A MIND WITHOUT A BRAIN, BUT YOU CAN HAVE A BRAIN WITHOUT A MIND."

Some scientists suggest that the sense of self is merely a reflection, a kind of byproduct, of some overall control mechanism in the brain. Many others, however, think no such mechanism exists. Neurologist Richard Restak (1983, 1994) has noted that many of our actions and choices occur without direction by a conscious self. He concludes that "There is not a center in the brain involved in the exercise of will any more than there is a center in the brain of the swan responsible for the beauty and complexity of its flight. Rather, the brains of all creatures are probably organized along the lines of multiple centers and various levels."

Likewise, brain researcher Michael Gazzaniga (1985) has proposed that the brain is organized as a loose confederation of independent modules, or mental systems, all working in parallel. The sense of a unified self is an illusion, he says; it occurs because the one verbal module, an "interpreter" (usually in the left hemisphere), is constantly coming up with theories to explain the actions, moods, and thoughts of the other modules. In a similar vein, cognitive scientist Daniel Dennett (1991) suggests that the brain or mind consists of a "pandemonium of homunculi"—brain parts that deal with different aspects of thought and perception, constantly conferring with each other and revising their "drafts" of reality.

Such views come close to those of Eastern spiritual traditions. Buddhism, for example, teaches that the self is not a unified "thing" but rather a collection of thoughts, perceptions, concepts, and feelings that shift and change from moment to moment. In this view, the unity and the permanence of the self are a mirage. Such notions are contrary, of course, to what most people in the West, including psychologists, have always assumed about their "selves."

We are not about to settle here a question that has plagued philosophers for thousands of years. Inevitably, though, as we think about the brain, we must think about how the brain can think about itself. What do you think about the existence and location of your "self" . . . and who, by the way, is doing the thinking?

and programs that promise to "beef up your brain," they observe, tend to oversimplify and exaggerate hemispheric differences. The differences are relative, not absolute—a matter of degree. In most real-life activities, the two hemispheres cooperate naturally, with each making a valuable contribution (Kinsbourne, 1982; J. Levy, 1985). As Sperry (1982) himself once noted, "The left–right dichotomy . . . is an idea with which it is very easy to run wild."

The snack for your left brain.
FI-BAR simply makes more sense than the sugary sweets you usually reach for.
Because it's full of smart stuff like oat bran and up to twelve different dietary fibers.
FI-BAR's cholesterol free. Low in calories, low in saturated fat.
With absolutely no artificial anything.
In fact, FI-BAR is a scientifically balanced, highly nutritious snack that's down-right good for kids and grown-ups alike.
The snack for your right brain.
You know something? This stuff tastes like a candy bar.
FI·BAR
FI·BAR

It's easy to exaggerate the differences between the left and right brain hemispheres.

Quick Quiz

Use as many parts of your brain as necessary to answer these questions.

1. Keeping in mind that both sides of the brain are involved in most activities, see whether you can identify which of the following is *most* closely associated with the left hemisphere: (a) enjoying a musical recording; (b) wiggling the left big toe; (c) giving a speech in class; (d) balancing a checkbook; (e) recognizing a long-lost friend

2. Over the past three decades, thousands of people have taken courses and bought tapes that promise to develop the "creativity" and "intuition" of their right hemispheres. What characteristics of human thought might explain the eagerness of some people to glorify "right-brainedness" and disparage "left-brainedness" (or vice versa)?

Answers:

1. c, d 2. *One possible answer:* Human beings like to make sense of the world, and one easy way to do that is to divide humanity into opposing categories. This kind of either–or thinking can lead to the conclusion that "fixing up" one of the categories (e.g., making left-brained types more right-brained) will make individuals happier and the world a better place. If only it were that simple!

TWO STUBBORN ISSUES IN BRAIN RESEARCH

If you have mastered the definitions and descriptions in this chapter, you are prepared to read popular accounts of advances in neuropsychology intelligently. But many mysteries remain about how the brain works, and we will end this chapter with two of them.

WHERE ARE OUR THOUGHTS AND MEMORIES STORED?

One of the most persistent questions in brain research concerns the location of information in the brain: Which circuits contain information about your first date, your best friend's face, or how to use a computer?

Most neuroscientists believe that the neural changes associated with individual thoughts, memories, and perceptions must be *localized,* confined to specific areas of the brain. One reason is that brain damage can have extremely specific effects on

DON'T OVERSIMPLIFY

Is a piece of information stored in one specific area or distributed throughout the brain? Researchers have generally assumed that only one answer can be true. Could both be true?

perception and memory, depending on exactly where the damage is. In one study, for example, two female stroke patients both had problems with verbs. One woman could read or speak verbs but had trouble writing them; the other could do only the reverse. The first woman had no trouble writing down the word *crack* after hearing the sentence "There's a crack in the mirror" (in which *crack* is a noun), but she could not write the word after hearing "Don't crack the nuts in here" (in which *crack* is a verb). The other woman could write *crack* as both a noun and a verb, but she couldn't speak it as a verb (Caramazza & Hillis, 1991). In another study (Cubelli, 1991), two brain-damaged patients were unable to correctly write down the vowels in words but had no trouble writing the consonants. Some patients can recognize manufactured items, such as photographs, tools, or books, but not natural objects; others can recognize most natural objects but cannot distinguish among different animals, or fruits, or vegetables (A. Damasio, 1990).

In part because of such findings, localization remains the guiding principle of modern brain theories. However, a minority view holds that perceived, learned, or remembered information is *distributed* across large areas of the brain. One of the first to make this argument was Karl Lashley, who many decades ago set out to find where specific memories were stored in the rat's brain. His search turned out to be as frustrating as looking for a grain of sugar in a pile of sand. Lashley trained rats to run a complicated maze in order to find food, then destroyed a part of each rat's cortex (without killing the rat). Destroying any section of the cortex led to some impairment in the rat's ability to find the food, though the size of the area damaged was more important than where the damage was located. Yet even when Lashley removed over 90 percent of a rat's visual cortex, the animal could still make its way through the maze. After a quarter of a century, Lashley (1950) finally gave up searching for specific memory traces. He jokingly remarked that perhaps "learning just is not possible." More seriously, he concluded that every part of the cortex must somehow influence every other part.

How might the brain function as an integrated whole? According to one theory (John et al., 1986), when we learn that Columbus discovered America or remember that 6 times 8 equals 48, it is not because particular cells fire or because a connection among cells is formed. What matters is the *average pattern* of cell activity throughout the brain, a pattern that has a unique rhythm. The billions of cells in the brain are like the members of a gigantic orchestra. Each instrument is making noise in a more or less random way, as when an orchestra is tuning up. When a thought or memory occurs, most of the instruments in one section start to play a tune that has a definite rhythm. However, some instruments in other sections do so as well.

Another approach compares brain processes to holography (Pribram, 1971, 1982). Holography is a system of photography in which a three-dimensional image is reproduced by means of light-wave patterns that are recorded on a photographic plate or film (the hologram). Information about any point in the image is distributed throughout the hologram. Thus any given area of the hologram contains the information necessary for producing the entire image. Similarly, some forms of knowledge may be dispersed throughout the brain, just as Karl Lashley thought.

Holistic theories have the virtue of being able to explain the remarkable *plasticity*, or flexibility, of the brain. In people with brain damage, this plasticity sometimes produces dramatic recoveries. Individuals who cannot recall simple words after a stroke may be speaking normally within a matter of months. Patients who cannot move an arm after a head injury may regain full use of it after physical therapy. A

fect the way brains are organized and how they function. Second, brain organization—the proportion of brain cells found in any part of the brain—varies considerably from person to person. As Roger Sperry (1982) noted, "The individuality inherent in our brain networks makes that of fingerprints or facial features gross and simple by comparison." Therefore, any sweeping generalizations about the brain, whether they are about the left and right hemispheres, localization of function, or sex differences, are bound to be oversimplifications.

As we have seen, the more we know about our physical selves, the better we will understand our psychological selves. In evaluating biological research, however, we must be wary of media hype, avoid unwarranted conclusions, and resist the temptation to "overbiologize." The human brain is a miraculous organ, but analyzing human behavior in terms of physiology alone is like analyzing the Taj Mahal solely in terms of the materials that were used to build it. Even if we could monitor every cell and circuit of the brain, we would still want to understand the circumstances, thoughts, and social rules that affect whether we are gripped by hatred, consumed by grief, lifted by love, or transported by joy.

Food for Thought: Diet and Neurotransmitters

"Vitamin improves sex!"

"Mineral boosts brainpower!"

"Chocolate chases the blues!"

Claims such as these have long given nutritional theories of behavior a bad reputation. In the late 1960s, when Nobel laureate Linus Pauling proposed that some mental disorders be treated with massive doses of vitamins, few researchers listened. Mainstream medical authorities classified Pauling's vitamin therapy with such infamous cure-alls as snake oil and leeches.

Today, most mental-health professionals remain skeptical of nutritional treatments for mental illness. But they may have to eat at least some of their words, as respect grows for the role that nutrients might play in mood and performance. The underlying premise of these treatments, that diet affects the brain and therefore behavior, is getting a second look. Claims that sugar or common food additives lead to undesirable behavior in otherwise normal people remain controversial. However, in some cases of disturbance, diet may make a difference. In one double-blind study, researchers asked depressed patients to abstain from refined sugar and caffeine. Over a three-month period, these patients showed significantly more improvement in their symptoms than did another group of patients who refrained from red meat and artificial sweeteners instead (Christensen & Burrows, 1990).

Some of the most exciting work on diet and behavior has looked at the role that nutrients play in the synthesis of neurotransmitters, the brain's chemical messengers. *Tryptophan,* an amino acid found in protein-rich foods (dairy products, meat, fish, and poultry), is a precursor (building block) of the neurotransmitter serotonin. *Tyrosine,* another amino acid found in proteins, is a precursor of norepinephrine, epinephrine, and dopamine. *Choline,* a component of the lecithin found in egg yolks, soy products, and liver, is a precursor of acetylcholine.

In the case of tryptophan, the path between the dinner plate and the brain is indirect. Tryptophan leads to the production of serotonin, which appears to reduce alertness, promote relaxation, and hasten sleep. Because tryptophan is found in protein, you might think that a high-protein meal would make you drowsy and that carbohydrates (sweets, bread, pasta, potatoes) would leave you relatively alert. Actually, the opposite is true. High-protein foods contain several amino acids, not just tryptophan, and they all compete for a ride on carrier molecules headed for brain cells. Because tryptophan occurs in foods in small quantities, it doesn't stand much of a chance *if* all you eat is protein. It is in the position of a tiny child trying to push aside a crowd of adults for a seat on the subway. Carbohydrates, however, stimulate the production of the hormone insulin, and insulin causes all the other amino acids to be drawn out of the bloodstream while having little effect on tryptophan. So carbohydrates increase the odds that tryptophan will make it to the brain (Wurtman, 1982). Paradoxically, then, a high-carbohydrate, no-protein meal is likely to make you relatively calm or lethargic and a high-protein one is likely to promote alertness, all else being equal. Studies with human beings support this conclusion (Spring, Chiodo, & Bowen, 1987; Wurtman & Lieberman, 1982–1983).

How else might nutrition affect mental and physical performance? In a report commissioned by the U.S. Army, the National Academy of Sciences reviewed existing animal and human studies on this question (Marriott, 1994). These studies suggest that (1) tyrosine can reduce symptoms that occur in extreme cold and at high altitudes, such as fuzzy thinking, headache, and nausea; (2) carbohydrates can prolong endurance under stressful conditions, increase fine-motor coordination, improve mood, and help people sleep; (3) choline can enhance memory and strengthen muscles and the immune system; and (4) caffeine improves alertness and mental performance (although in high doses it can cause anxiety and insomnia).

Keep in mind, though, that research in this area is just beginning. Individuals differ in how they respond to different nutrients, and of course many other factors also influence mood and behavior. The effects of nutrients are subtle, and some of these effects depend on a person's age, the circumstances, and the time of day when a meal is eaten. Nutrients can and do affect the brain and behavior, but these nutrients interact with each other in complex ways. If you don't eat protein, you won't get enough tryptophan, but if you go without carbohydrates, the tryptophan found in protein will be useless. And trying to rev yourself up with too many nutritional supplements can actually be dangerous. The moral of the story: If you're looking for brain food, you are most likely to find it in a well-balanced diet.

SUMMARY

1) The brain is the origin of consciousness, perception, memory, emotion, and reasoning. People debate what language to use in describing the brain, and where the "you" is that is "using" your brain.

THE NERVOUS SYSTEM: A BASIC BLUEPRINT

2) The function of the nervous system is to gather and process information, produce responses to stimuli, and coordinate the workings of different cells. Scientists divide it into the *central nervous system (CNS)* and the *peripheral nervous system (PNS).* The CNS, which includes the brain and spinal cord, receives, processes, interprets, and stores information and sends messages destined for muscles, glands, and organs. The PNS transmits information to and from the CNS by way of sensory and motor nerves.

3) The peripheral nervous system is made up of the *somatic nervous system,* which permits sensation and voluntary actions, and the *autonomic nervous system,* which regulates blood vessels, glands, and internal (visceral) organs. The autonomic system usually functions without conscious control. Although some people can learn to heighten or suppress autonomic responses, using *biofeedback* techniques, it is unclear whether this control is direct or indirect.

4) The autonomic nervous system is divided into the *sympathetic nervous system,* which mobilizes the body for action, and the *parasympathetic nervous system,* which conserves energy.

COMMUNICATION IN THE NERVOUS SYSTEM: THE NUTS AND BOLTS

5) *Neurons,* supported by *glial cells,* are the basic units of the nervous system. Each neuron consists of *dendrites,* a *cell body,* and an *axon.* In the peripheral nervous system, axons (and sometimes dendrites) are collected together in bundles called *nerves.* Many axons are insulated by a *myelin sheath* that speeds up the conduction of neural impulses and prevents signals in adjacent cells from interfering with one another. Recent research has challenged the old assumption that neurons in the human central nervous system cannot be induced to regenerate or multiply.

6) Communication between two neurons occurs at the *synapse.* Many synapses have not yet formed at birth. During development, axons and dendrites continue to grow as a result of both physical maturation and experience with the world, and throughout life, new learning results in new synaptic connections in the brain. Thus, the brain's circuits are not fixed and immutable but are continually changing in response to information, challenges, and changes in the environment.

7) When a wave of electrical voltage (*action potential*) reaches the end of a transmitting axon, *neurotransmitter* molecules are released into the *synaptic cleft.* When these molecules bind to receptor sites on the receiving neuron, that neuron becomes either more or less likely to fire. The message that reaches a final destination depends on how frequently particular neurons are firing, how many are firing, what types are firing, and where they are located.

8) Through their effects on nerve circuits, neurotransmitters play a critical role in mood, memory, and psychological well-being. Abnormal levels of neurotransmitters have been implicated in several disorders, including depression, childhood autism, and Parkinson's disease.

9) *Endorphins,* which act primarily as *neuromodulators* that affect the action of neurotransmitters, reduce pain and promote pleasure. Endorphin levels seem to shoot up when an animal or person is afraid or is under stress. Endorphins may also be linked to the pleasures of social contact.

10) *Hormone* levels affect, and are affected by, the nervous system. Psychologists are especially interested in *melatonin,* which appears to regulate daily biological rhythms; the *adrenal hormones,* which are involved in emotions and stress; and the *sex hormones,* which are involved in the physical changes of puberty, the menstrual cycle (estrogen), and sexual arousal (testosterone).

EAVESDROPPING ON THE BRAIN

11) Researchers study the brain by observing patients with brain damage; by using the *lesion method* with animals; and by using such techniques as electroencephalograms (*EEGs*), positron emission tomography (*PET scans*), and magnetic resonance imaging (*MRI*).

A TOUR THROUGH THE BRAIN

12) All modern brain theories assume *localization of function.* In the *hindbrain,* the *brain stem* controls automatic functions such as heartbeat and breathing. The *reticular activating system (RAS)* screens incoming information and is responsible for alertness. The *cerebellum* contributes to balance and muscle coordination and may also play a role in some higher mental operations.

13) In the *forebrain,* the *thalamus* directs sensory messages to appropriate higher centers. The *hypothalamus* is involved in emotion and in drives associated with survival, controls the operations of the autonomic nervous system, and sends out chemicals that tell the *pituitary gland* when to "talk" to other endocrine glands.

14) The *limbic system* is involved in emotions that we share with other animals, and it contains pathways involved in pleasure. Within this system, the *amygdala* is responsible for evaluating sensory information and quickly determining its emotional importance, and for the initial decision to approach or withdraw from a person or situation. The *hippocampus* has been called the "gateway to memory" because it plays a critical role in the formation of long-term memories for facts and events.

15) Much of the brain's circuitry is packed into the *cerebrum,* which is divided into two hemispheres and is covered by thin layers of cells known collectively as the *cerebral cortex.* The *occipital, parietal, temporal,* and *frontal lobes* of the cortex have specialized (but partially overlapping) functions. The *association cortex* appears to be responsible for higher mental processes. The frontal lobes, particularly areas in the *prefrontal cortex,* are involved in social judgment, the making and carrying out of plans, and decision making.

THE TWO HEMISPHERES OF THE BRAIN

16) Studies of split-brain patients, who have had the *corpus callosum* cut, show that the two cerebral hemispheres have somewhat different talents. In most people, language is processed mainly in the left hemisphere, which generally is specialized for logical, symbolic, and sequential tasks. The right hemisphere is associated with spatial–visual tasks, facial recognition, and the creation and appreciation of art and music. However, in most mental activities, the two hemispheres cooperate as partners, with each making a valuable contribution.

TWO STUBBORN ISSUES IN BRAIN RESEARCH

17) Most scientists believe that the neural changes associated with specific thoughts, memories, and perceptions are *localized,* but another view holds that information is *distributed* across large areas of the cerebral cortex and that the brain functions as an integrated whole. These two views can be reconciled by recognizing that the typical thought or memory consists of many pieces of information, which may be stored at separate sites, with all the sites participating in the representation of an object or event.

18) Sex differences have been observed in anatomical studies of animal brains. Sex differences in human brains, however, have been more elusive, and there is controversy about their existence and their meaning. It is unclear how and even whether reported brain differences are related to actual behavior or talents.

19) In evaluating research on the brain and behavior, it is important to remember that individual brains vary considerably in their organization, and also that experiences and environments affect brain development. Findings about the brain are most illuminating when they are integrated with psychological and cultural ones.

KEY TERMS

neuropsychology 120
central nervous system 121
spinal cord 121
reflex 121
peripheral nervous system 122
sensory nerves 122
motor nerves 122
somatic nervous system 122
autonomic nervous system 122
biofeedback 122
sympathetic nervous system 123
parasympathetic nervous system 123
neuron 124
glial cells 124
dendrites 125
cell body 125
axon 125
axon terminals 125
myelin sheath 125
nerve 126

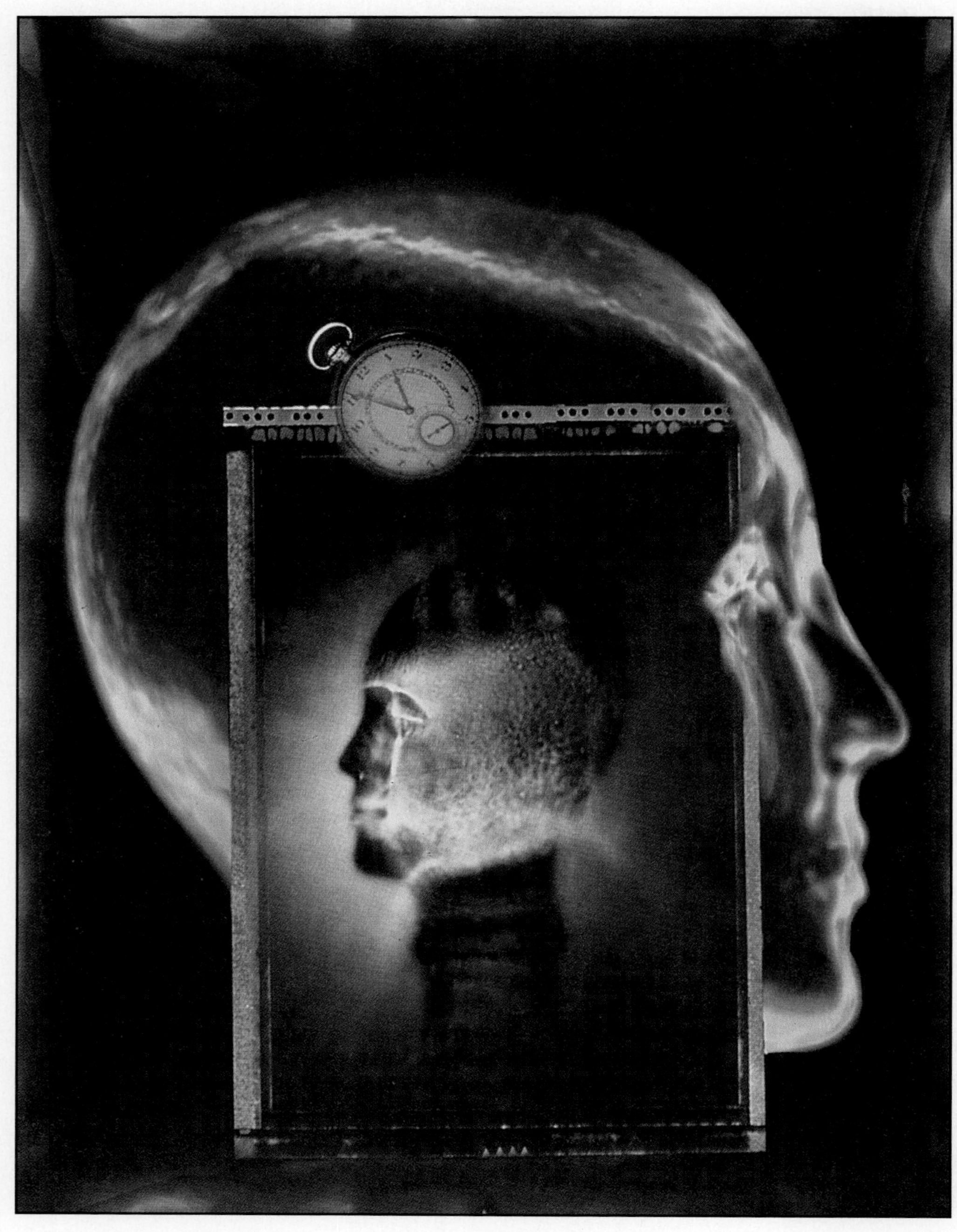

Among the millions of nerve cells that clothe
parts of the brain there runs a thread.
It is the thread of time, the thread that has run through
each succeeding wakeful hour of the individual's past life.

Wilder G. Penfield

CHAPTER FIVE

Body Rhythms and Mental States

IN LEWIS CARROLL'S IMMORTAL STORY *Alice's Adventures in Wonderland,* the ordinary rules of everyday life keep dissolving in a sea of logical contradictions. First Alice shrinks to within only a few inches of the ground, then she shoots up taller than the treetops. The crazy antics of Wonderland's inhabitants make her smile one moment and shed a pool of tears the next. "Dear dear!" muses the harried heroine. "How queer everything is today! And yesterday things went on just as usual. I wonder if I've been changed in the night? Let me think: *was* I the same when I got up this morning? I almost think I can remember feeling a little different. But if I'm not the same, the *next* question is, 'Who in the world am I?' Ah, *that's* the great puzzle!"

In a way, we all live in a sort of Wonderland. For a third of our lives, we reside in a realm where the ordinary rules of logic and experience are suspended: the dream world of sleep. Throughout the day, mood, alertness, efficiency, and **consciousness** itself—the awareness of ourselves and the environment—are in perpetual flux, sometimes shifting as dramatically as Alice's height.

Starting from the assumption that mental and physical states are as intertwined as sunshine and shadow, psychologists, along with other scientists, are exploring the links between these fluctuations in subjective experience and predictable changes in brain activity, hormone levels, and the actions of neurotransmitters. They have come to view changing **states of consciousness** as part of an ebb and flow of experience over time, associated with predictable bodily events. For example, dreaming, traditionally classified as a state of consciousness, is also part of a 90-minute cycle of brain activity. Alternating periods of dreaming and nondreaming during the night occur in a regular pattern, or **biological rhythm.**

Examining a person's subjective experience in terms of ongoing rhythms is a little like watching a motion picture of consciousness. Studying subjective experience in terms of distinct states is more like looking at separate snapshots of consciousness. In this chapter, we will first run the motion picture, to see how functioning and consciousness vary predictably over time. Then we will zoom in on one specific "snapshot" of the world of dreams and examine it in some detail. Finally, we will turn to some ways in which people try to "retouch the film" by deliberately altering consciousness.

BIOLOGICAL RHYTHMS: THE TIDES OF EXPERIENCE

Have you ever seen an advertisement for "biorhythm charts" that supposedly predict, solely on the basis of the time and date of your birth, how your mood, alertness, and physical performance will fluctuate over your lifetime? People who sell these charts claim they can tell you when you'll have good days and when you'll be susceptible to accidents, errors, and illness. Whenever researchers have taken the trouble to test such claims scientifically—for example, by examining occupational accidents or the performance of sports stars in light of the charts' predictions—they have failed to find any support whatsoever for them (e.g., Wheeler, 1990). Yet biorhythm charts continue to be marketed; apparently, one human characteristic that does not fluctuate much is gullibility!

It *is* true, however, that the human body does not operate in an unvarying way 24 hours a day, 7 days a week, 52 weeks a year. We've got rhythm; in fact, we experience dozens of periodic, more or less regular ups and downs in physiological functioning. A biological clock in our brains governs the waxing and waning of hormone levels, urine volume, blood pressure, and even the responsiveness of brain cells to stimulation. Such physiological fluctuations are what scientists mean by "biological rhythms."

consciousness Awareness of the environment and of one's own existence, sensations, and thoughts.

states of consciousness Distinctive and discrete patterns in the functioning of consciousness, characterized by particular modes of perception, thought, memory, or feeling.

biological rhythm A periodic, more or less regular fluctuation in a biological system; may or may not have psychological implications.

The body's rhythms are typically synchronized with external events, such as changes in clock time and daylight—a process called **entrainment.** But many rhythms will continue to occur even in the absence of all external time cues; they are *endogenous,* or generated from within. These rhythms fall into three categories:

1. **Circadian rhythms** occur approximately every 24 hours. The best-known circadian rhythm is the sleep–wake cycle, but there are hundreds of others that affect physiology and performance. For example, body temperature fluctuates about 1 degree centigrade each day, peaking, on average, in the late afternoon and hitting a low point, or trough, in the wee hours of the morning.

2. **Infradian rhythms** occur less often than once a day—for example, once a month, or once a season. In the animal world, infradian rhythms are common: Birds migrate south in the fall, bears hibernate in the winter, and marine animals become active or inactive, depending on bimonthly changes in the tides. In human beings, the female menstrual cycle, which occurs every 28 days on the average, is an example of an infradian rhythm.

3. **Ultradian rhythms** occur more often than once a day, frequently on roughly a 90-minute schedule. The best-studied ultradian rhythm, as we will see, occurs during sleep, but many other physiological changes and behaviors may also follow an ultradian pattern when social customs do not intervene. They include stomach contractions, hormone levels, susceptibility to visual illusions, performance on verbal and spatial tasks, brain-wave responses during specific cognitive tasks, alertness, and daydreaming (Escera, Cilveti, & Grau, 1992; Klein & Armitage, 1979; Kripke, 1974; Lavie, 1976).

Biological rhythms

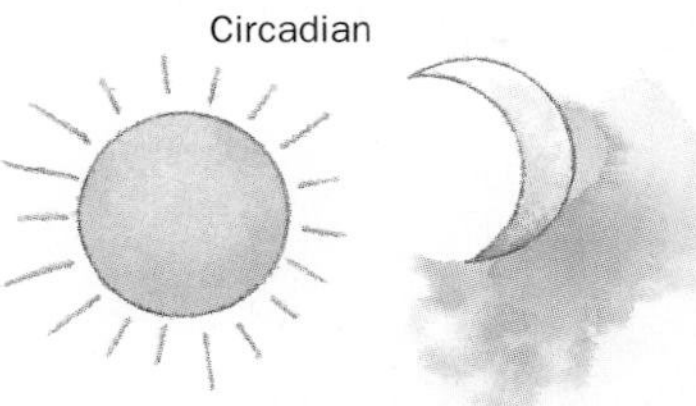

Ultradian

Psychologists and other researchers are just beginning to recognize the potential impact of biological rhythms on their own work. A review of research done with rats, mice, and hamsters found that most studies have been conducted during the day, with the lights on, even though these rodents are normally active at night and sleep during the day. The authors noted that "The field of psychology has been frequently criticized for being extensively based on studies of white male rats.... Perhaps that indictment should be revised to read '*sleepy* white male rats'!" (Brodie-Scott & Hobbs, 1992).

Human beings, too, can be influenced by the time of day when the research was conducted. In one study, most young adults said they preferred the evening for doing mental work, whereas most elderly adults expressed a preference for the morning. On a memory test given in the late afternoon, the younger subjects performed much better than the older ones, but when the test took place in the early morning, the younger people's scores fell, the older people's scores rose, and the performance of the two groups no longer differed significantly. Studies of aging and mental function that are done in the afternoon, therefore, may give a false picture of age differences in memory (May, Hasher, & Stoltzfus, 1993).

With better understanding of our internal tempos, we may be able to design our days to take the best advantage of our bodies' natural rhythms. Let's look more closely at how these cycles operate.

CIRCADIAN RHYTHMS

Circadian rhythms exist in plants, animals, insects, and human beings. They reflect the adaptation of organisms to the many changes associated with the rotation of the earth on its axis, such as changes in light, air pressure, temperature, and wind.

During everyday life our bodies adapt to a strict 24-hour schedule. External time cues, both artificial and natural, abound, and our biological rhythms become entrained to them. To identify endogenous circadian rhythms, therefore, scientists

entrainment The synchronization of biological rhythms with external cues, such as fluctuations in daylight.

circadian [sur-CAY-dee-un] rhythm A biological rhythm with a period (from peak to peak or trough to trough) of about 24 hours; from the Latin *circa,* "about," and *dies,* "a day."

infradian [in-FRAY-dee-un] rhythm A biological rhythm that occurs less frequently than once a day; from the Latin for "below a day."

ultradian [ul-TRAY-dee-un] rhythm A biological rhythm that occurs more frequently than once a day; from the Latin for "beyond a day."

Stefania Follini (left) spent 4 months in a New Mexico cave (above), 30 feet below ground, as part of an Italian study on biological rhythms. Her only companions were an impersonal computer and two friendly mice. In the absence of clocks, natural light, or variations in temperature, she tended to stay awake for 20 to 25 hours and then sleep for 10. Because her days were longer than usual, when she emerged she thought she had been in the cave for only 2 months.

must isolate volunteers from sunlight, clocks, environmental sounds, and all other cues to time. Artificial light is kept constant, varied by the researcher, or turned on and off by the volunteers when they retire or awaken. Some hardy souls have spent weeks or even months alone in caves and salt mines, linked to the outside world only by a one-way phone line and a cable transmitting physiological measurements to the surface. More often, volunteers live in specially designed bunkers or rooms equipped with stereo systems, comfortable furniture, and temperature controls.

In a typical study, a person sleeps, eats, and works whenever he or she wishes, free of the tyranny of the timepiece. Living without time cues is called *free-running.* In the absence of such cues, a few people live a "day" that is much shorter or longer than 24 hours—18 hours, say, or 36. If they are allowed to take daytime naps, however, most people soon settle into a day that averages about 24.3 hours (Timothy Monk, personal communication; Moore, 1997). Temperature, blood pressure, and hormone cycles usually follow suit.

Circadian rhythms are controlled by a biological "clock," or overall coordinator, located in a tiny teardrop-shaped cluster of cells in the hypothalamus called the *suprachiasmatic nucleus (SCN).* Neural pathways from the back of the eye to the SCN allow the SCN to respond to changes in light and dark. Normally, the rhythms governed by the nerve cells in this clock are synchronized, just as wristwatches can be synchronized. Their peaks may occur at different times, but they occur in phase with one another; if you know when one rhythm peaks, you can predict when another will.

Fluctuating levels of hormones and neurotransmitters, regulated by the SCN, in turn provide feedback that affects the functioning of the SCN. For example, one hormone, **melatonin,** which is secreted during the dark hours by the pineal gland, deep within the brain, appears to help keep the biological clock in phase with the light–dark cycle (Haimov & Lavie, 1996; Lewy et al., 1992). It may also directly promote sleep. The pineal gland responds to light and dark via complex connections that originate in the back of the eye. Interestingly, in many (though not all) blind

melatonin A hormone secreted by the pineal gland; it is involved in the regulation of circadian rhythms.

people who lack light perception, the normal melatonin cycle is absent; as a result, circadian rhythms are disrupted, and insomnia and other sleep problems occur (Czeisler et al., 1995). Melatonin treatments have been used to synchronize the disturbed sleep–wake cycles of such people (Tzischinsky et al., 1992).

Melatonin supplements can also help some sighted people who suffer from chronic insomnia, especially older people, who often show a decline in the hormone (Garfinkel et al., 1995; Haimov & Lavie, 1996). These supplements should be used with caution, however. Because they are classified as a dietary supplement rather than a drug, there are no federal standards for quality, dosage, and timing. Also, the long-term safety of such treatments is not known.

When a person's normal routine changes, circadian rhythms may be thrown out of phase with one another. Such *internal desynchronization* often occurs when people take airplane flights across several time zones. Sleep and wake patterns usually adjust quickly, but temperature and hormone cycles can take several days to return to normal. The resulting "jet lag" affects energy level, mental skills, and motor coordination. A miniversion of jet lag occurs in some people when they have to "spring forward" into daylight savings time, losing an hour from the 24-hour day. They may sleep less well than usual and feel a little out of sorts during the week following the time change. In contrast, "falling back" into standard time, which produces a 25-hour day and time for extra sleep, does not seem to be a strain (Monk & Aplin, 1980).

Internal desynchronization also occurs when workers must adjust to a new shift. Efficiency drops, the person feels tired and irritable, accidents become more likely, and sleep disturbances and digestive disorders may occur. For people such as police officers, emergency-room personnel, airline pilots, truck drivers, and nuclear-power-plant operators, the consequences can be serious, and even a matter of life and death. A National Commission on Sleep Disorders concluded that lack of alertness in night-shift equipment operators may have contributed to the 1989 Exxon *Valdez* oil spill off the coast of Alaska and the disastrous accidents at the Three Mile Island and Chernobyl nuclear power plants. And in 1995 the National Transportation Safety Board reported that truck drivers who fall asleep at the wheel are responsible for up to 1,500 road deaths a year; driver fatigue is a greater safety problem than alcohol or other drugs.

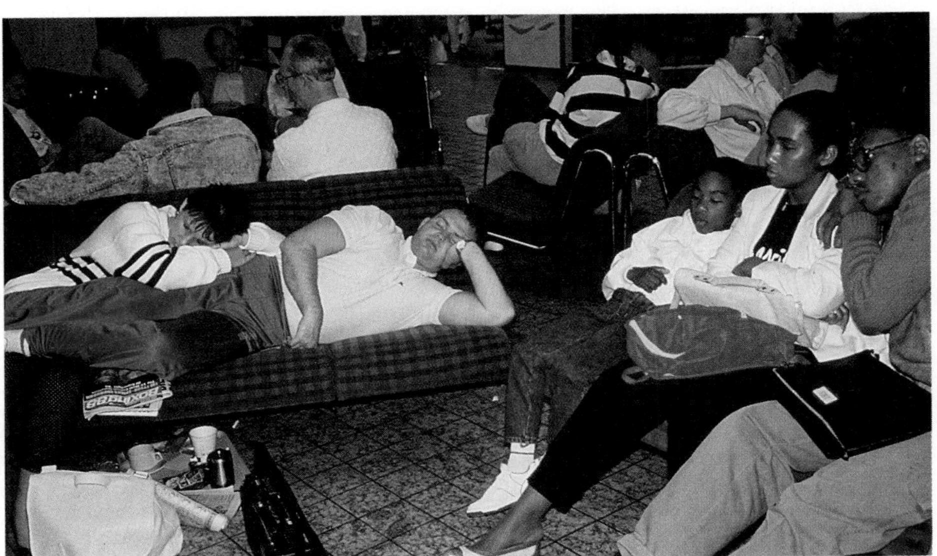

Travel can be exhausting, and jet lag makes it worse. Because most people, when freed from the clock, have a natural day that is slightly longer than 24 hours, jet lag tends to be more noticeable and long-lasting after eastbound travel (which shortens the day) than after westbound travel (which lengthens it).

GET INVOLVED

For at least two days, except when you are sleeping, keep an hourly record of your mental alertness level, using this five-point scale: 1 = extremely drowsy or mentally lethargic; 2 = somewhat drowsy or mentally lethargic; 3 = moderately alert; 4 = alert and efficient; 5 = extremely alert and efficient. Does your alertness level appear to follow an ultradian or circadian rhythm? If so, when does it tend to peak and plummet? Is this cycle the same on weekends as during the week? Most important, how well does your schedule mesh with your natural fluctuations in alertness?

Night work itself is not necessarily the problem: With a schedule that always stays the same (even on weekends), people can often adapt. However, many swing- and night-shift assignments are made on a rotating basis, so circadian rhythms never have a chance to resynchronize. Ideally, a rotating work schedule should follow circadian principles by switching workers as infrequently as possible and by always moving them forward to a later schedule rather than backward to an earlier one. For example, if you've been working from midnight to 8:00 A.M., your next shift should be 8:00 A.M. to 4:00 P.M.

Researchers are now working on ways to hasten recovery from jet lag and ease people's adjustment to new work shifts. One approach is to use bright lights to "reset" the clock in the SCN, just as you would reset a mechanical or electronic clock forward or backward (Dawson, Lack, & Morris, 1993; Eastman et al., 1994). In the laboratory, even relatively dim light can reset the circadian pacemaker (Boivin et al., 1996). Another approach is to give small amounts of melatonin on a controlled schedule, or to combine melatonin with light treatments (Lewy, Ahmed, & Sack, 1995; Samel et al., 1991). However, procedures that seem promising in the laboratory do not always work out so well in the real world, where people are exposed to many natural and artificial time cues. In one study, adults went to bed two hours later on each of five nights and were also exposed to bright lights, which in the laboratory can shift the rhythm of the body's temperature. Under the more natural conditions of this study, the subjects' temperature rhythms stubbornly refused to conform to their new sleep schedule (Gallo & Eastman, 1993).

We want to emphasize that circadian rhythms are not perfectly regular and can be affected by illness, stress, fatigue, excitement, drugs, and even ordinary daily experiences. Even the timing of exercise can influence circadian rhythms and may help determine, along with genetic influences, whether a person is a "night owl" or an "early bird" (Mistlberger, 1991). Further, circadian rhythms differ greatly from individual to individual: Some people are feeling their oats by 7 in the morning; others aren't ready for action until noon. You may be able to learn about your own personal pulses through careful self-observation, and you may want to try putting that information to use when planning your daily schedule.

MOOD AND LONG-TERM RHYTHMS

According to Ecclesiastes, "To every thing there is a season, and a time for every purpose under heaven." Modern science agrees: Long-term (infradian) cycles have been observed in everything from the threshold for tooth pain to conception rates. Folklore holds that our moods follow infradian cycles, too—particularly in response to seasonal changes and, in women, menstrual changes. But do they?

DOES THE SEASON AFFECT MOODS? Clinicians report that some people become depressed every winter, when periods of daylight are short, and improve each spring, as daylight increases—a pattern that has come to be known as *seasonal affective disorder (SAD).* One theory holds that the winter doldrums are related to abnormal fluctuations in melatonin, which usually peaks during the night and falls with the approach of day (Lewy et al., 1987). Some physicians and therapists have therefore been treating "SAD" patients with phototherapy, having them sit in front of fluorescent lights at specific times of the day. But a British study found no differences at all in the melatonin rhythms of "SAD" patients and controls (Checkley et al., 1993), and even the researchers who originally proposed the theory no longer argue that melatonin abnormalities play a direct role.

Further, although a recent meta-analysis by two Hong Kong researchers (Lee & Chan, 1996) found that phototherapy produces a better outcome than no light treatment, studies of phototherapy have had many methodological problems, and it has been difficult to rule out placebo effects when "SAD" patients cheer up. Most important, although many clinicians assume that "SAD" must have a biological basis, no one has yet found one, or has proven that long-term cycles in depression are actually endogenous. The winter blues could be caused by the mental association of short days with cold weather, inactivity, social isolation (because people don't go out as much), or even the holidays, which some people find depressing.

DOES THE MENSTRUAL CYCLE AFFECT MOODS? One infradian rhythm that clearly is endogenous is the menstrual cycle, which is characterized by the ebb and flow of the hormones estrogen and progesterone over a period of roughly 28 days. During the first half of the cycle, an increase in estrogen causes the lining of the uterus to thicken in preparation for a possible pregnancy. At midcycle, the ovaries release a mature egg, or ovum. After ovulation, the ovarian sac that contained the egg begins to produce progesterone, which helps prepare the uterine lining to receive the egg. Then, if conception does not occur, estrogen and progesterone levels fall, the uterine lining sloughs off as the menstrual flow, and the cycle begins again.

For psychologists, the interesting question is whether these physical changes are correlated with emotional or intellectual changes—as folklore and tradition would have us believe. Since the 1970s, a vague cluster of symptoms associated with the days preceding menstruation—including fatigue, headache, irritability, and depression—has come to be thought of as an illness and has been given a label: "premenstrual syndrome (PMS)." Some books refer to "millions" of sufferers or assert that most women have "PMS," although no statistics back up such claims. Proposed explanations include progesterone deficiency, estrogen/progesterone imbalance, neurotransmitter imbalances, water retention, high sodium levels, and a fall in the level of endorphins, the brain's natural opiates. Yet biomedical research provides no consistent support for any of these theories, and it provides evidence against some of them. For example, in one study, researchers gave "PMS" patients a drug that blocks the hormonal changes that normally occur premenstrually; yet the women still reported symptoms, indicating that hormone changes could not be responsible (Schmidt et al., 1991).

Further, despite many anecdotes and testimonials, most treatments—including progesterone, the most commonly prescribed remedy—do not work any better than a placebo (Freeman et al., 1990). Some controlled studies do report success with antidepressants such as Prozac, but in these cases it's hard to know what, exactly, is being treated: true "PMS," or chronic depression that worsens before menstruation.

We do not put "PMS" in quotes because we deny the reality of the physical symptoms of menstruation. Of course physical symptoms occur, including cramps, breast tenderness, and water retention (although women vary tremendously, with some having no symptoms and others

EXAMINE THE EVIDENCE

Many women say they become more irritable or depressed premenstrually. Does the evidence support their self-reports? How might attitudes and expectations be affecting these accounts? What happens when people of both sexes report their daily moods and feelings without knowing that menstruation is being studied?

many). And of course these physical symptoms can make some women feel grumpy, just as back pain or a pulled Achilles tendon can make a person feel grumpy. We put "PMS" in quotes because it is an undefined hodgepodge of physical and *emotional* symptoms and because the belief that emotional symptoms are *reliably and universally* tied to the menstrual cycle has not been supported.

It's true that many women do say they have emotional changes, but self-reports can be a poor guide to reality, no matter how valid they feel to the person doing the reporting. A woman might easily attribute a blue mood to her impending period, although at other times of the month she would blame a stressful day or a poor grade on an English paper. She might notice that she feels depressed or irritable when these moods happen to occur premenstrually but overlook times when such moods are *absent* premenstrually.

A woman's perceptions of her own emotional ups and downs can also be influenced by cultural attitudes and myths about menstruation. Although women all over the world report having menstrual cramps, the concept of a special *pre*menstrual package of symptoms is uniquely Western, popular mainly among the British and North Americans. Even the name of the questionnaire used in a study can reflect cultural biases, and can thereby affect a woman's self-report. The "Menstrual Distress Questionnaire," which asks primarily about negative symptoms, elicits more negative responses when it is given alone than when it is preceded by a "Menstrual Joy Questionnaire" that asks about positive changes such as "high spirits" and "vibrant activity" (Chrisler et al., 1994).

To get around these problems, some psychologists have polled women about their psychological and physical well-being *without revealing the true purpose of the study* (e.g., Alagna & Hamilton, 1986; AuBuchon & Calhoun, 1985; Burke, Burnett, & Levenstein, 1978; Englander-Golden, Whitmore, & Dienstbier, 1978; Gallant et al., 1991; Parlee, 1982; Rapkin, Chang, & Reading, 1988; Slade, 1984; Vila & Beech, 1980). Using a double-blind procedure, these researchers have had women report symptoms for a single day and have then gone back to see what phase of the menstrual cycle the women were in; or they have had women keep daily records over an extended period of time. Some of these studies have included a control group that is usually excluded from research on hormones and moods: men! Here are some of the major findings:

- Overall, women and men do not differ significantly in the emotional symptoms they report or the number of mood swings they experience in the course of a month, as you can see in Figure 5.1 (McFarlane, Martin, & Williams, 1988).
- A few women do become irritable or depressed before menstruation; others become happier or more energetic. But for most women, the relationship between cycle stage and symptoms is weak or nonexistent; they typically do *not* follow the "PMS" pattern even when they think they do (McFarlane & Williams, 1994). They may recall their moods as having been more unpleasant before or during menstruation, but, as you can also see in Figure 5.1, their own daily reports fail to bear them out.
- Most women and men show some cyclicity in their moods, but their cycles are entirely idiosyncratic. Some people feel best on the weekends, for example (McFarlane & Williams, 1994).
- Even when women know that menstruation is being studied, most do not *consistently* report negative (or positive) psychological changes from one cycle to the next. Their moods and emotional symptoms vary far more in degree and direction than we would expect if predictable hormone fluctuations were the main reason for these changes (Walker, 1994). In fact, only about 5 percent of

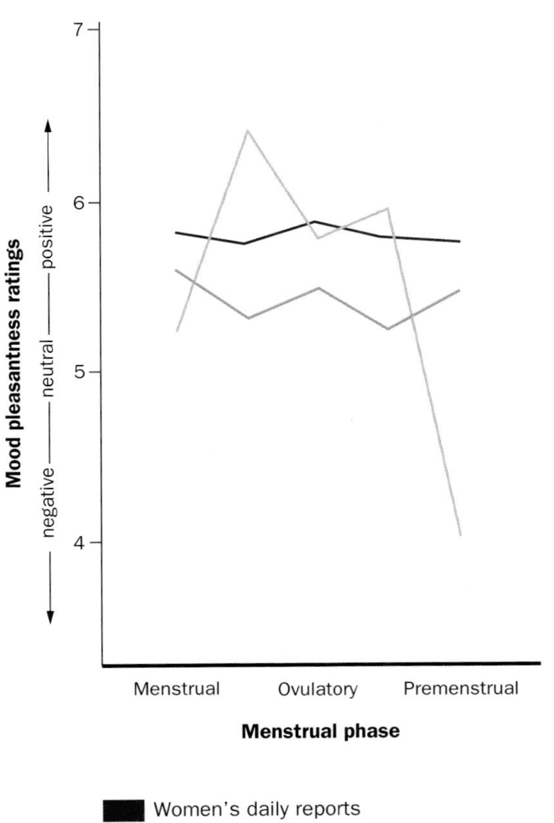

Figure 5.1
Mood Changes in Men and Women

In a study that challenged popular stereotypes about "PMS," college women and men recorded their moods daily for 70 days without knowing the purpose of the study. As this graph shows, when women were asked to recall their moods, they said their moods had been more negative premenstrually (blue line)—but their daily diaries did not bear this out (purple line). Both sexes experienced only moderate mood changes, and there were no significant differences between women and men at any time of the month (McFarlane, Martin, & Williams, 1988).

women who think they have "PMS" show the PMS pattern of symptoms over two consecutive cycles (Kessler et al., in press).

- No reliable relationship exists between cycle stage and work efficiency, problem solving, motor performance, memory, college exam scores, creativity, or any other behavior that matters in real life (Golub, 1992; Richardson, 1992).

Do these findings surprise you? These results, reported many times since the late 1970s, are unknown to most people and are widely ignored by doctors, therapists, and the media. (So entrenched is the belief that "most women suffer from PMS" that we have occasionally been accused of "bias" for reporting the psychological studies that call this belief into question.) Premenstrual symptoms have come to be defined almost solely in medical and psychiatric terms, for reasons we discuss in "Issues in Popular Culture."

GET INVOLVED

Go to your local drugstore and find the over-the-counter medications for menstrual symptoms. How many different brands are there? Do the containers mention only physical symptoms, such as water retention and cramps, or do they also mention emotional symptoms? Do they refer to "PMS" or "premenstrual tension" as an illness? Are the active ingredients in these products unique to them, or are they generic painkillers such as ibuprofen? What kinds of claims are made for these remedies, and how would you evaluate those claims based on the information in this chapter?

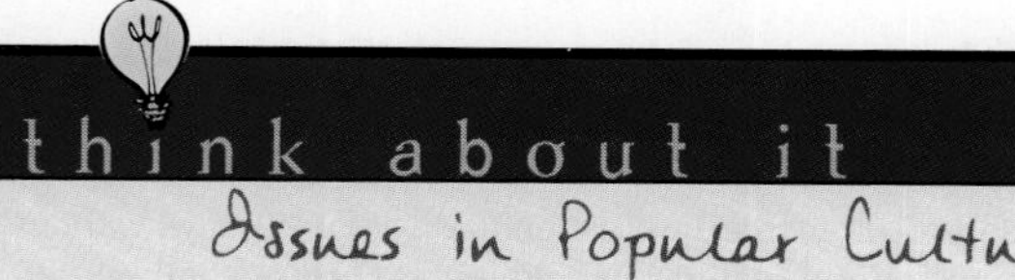

Thinking Calmly About Raging Hormones

Imagine this cartoon: Joan of Arc, in a full coat of armor, with sword resting in her hand, sits forlornly on a grassy hill, weeping her heart out and vowing to "raise such a battle-cry that you will remember it forever!" The cartoon's caption reads, "PMS Attacks in History." Cartoons like this one have been making the rounds in recent years. Popular magazines, too, have promoted the view that women's hormones drive them a bit bonkers, with article titles such as "Dr. Jekyll and Ms. Hyde" and "The Taming of the Shrew Inside of You" (Chrisler et al., 1994).

As we discuss in this chapter, medical and psychological research shows that serious distress due specifically to menstruation is rare. So what is going on here? Why, despite all the counterevidence, are people so ready to accept the notion that women are emotionally unstable because of their hormones? And why is the hormonal excuse for the goose ("Of course she's angry, she's having her period") not the same for the gander ("Of course he's angry, he has all those male hormones")? Why has so much attention and funding been devoted to "PMS" and not to, say, "HTS"—HyperTestosterone Syndrome?

To answer these questions, we must consider cultural attitudes toward women's bodies, and also how social, economic, and political forces shape research and the public's reaction to research findings. As Emily Martin (1987) has shown, a negative attitude toward female reproductive processes pervades many cultures. This bias turns up subtly in supposedly objective anatomy textbooks, which describe the process of menstruation only in terms of deprivation, deficiency, loss, and shedding of the lining of the uterus. The lining of the stomach is shed and replaced regularly too, Martin observes, but textbooks do not describe this process as one of "degenerating" or shedding of the stomach lining. Instead, Martin found, they emphasize "the periodic *renewal* of the lining of the stomach." Stomachs, which both sexes have, are described positively; uteruses, which only women have, are described negatively. And although a large proportion of the male ejaculate is composed of waste material, adds Martin, "The texts make no mention of a shedding process let alone processes of deterioration and repair in the male reproductive tract."

Other factors also have helped to make "PMS" a part of the popular culture. First is the reaction of women themselves. When the term was first proposed in the 1970s, many women welcomed it as a validation of the normal physical changes of the menstrual cycle, a sign that women's health concerns were finally being taken seriously after years of neglect, or as a welcome explanation for uncomfortable feelings of anger or sadness.

Second, the label "PMS" became an official medical and psychiatric diagnosis, one that insurance companies recognized for purposes of compensation for treatment. Mary Parlee (1994), who has been studying the psychology of menstruation for two decades, notes that as the medical view gained ascendancy, psychological research lost out. Today, investigators who propose to do clinical medical studies of "PMS" are far more likely to get funding than those who propose psychological studies, even though "PMS" has never been shown to be a physiologically caused condition. In 1994, over the objections of many psychologists, the American Psychiatric Association included "premenstrual phase dysphoric disorder" (PMDD) in the *Diagnostic and Statistical Manual of Mental Disorders*, the official bible of psychiatric diagnosis. "PMDD" is supposed to describe only the very small percentage of women who are severely affected by premenstrual mood changes, but its characteristics do not differ from those of "PMS."

A third factor in the rising popularity of "PMS" is that it confirms the old superstition that hormones make women (but not men) unstable. Critics point out that in such a cultural context, the PMS label is often used to stigmatize women or to dismiss their legitimate grievances as all a matter of hormones (Caplan, 1995; Gise, 1988; Koeske, 1987). As one of our students said, "I like being able to use PMS as the reason for losing my temper with my boyfriend, but I really *hate* it when I'm trying to tell him something that bothers me and he says, 'Oh, you must just have PMS.'"

It seems, then, that in reflecting on the popular culture's fondness for PMS jokes—and on the attitudes toward female physiology that underlie them—critical thinkers might do well to ask who is having the last laugh.

The focus on women's moods and symptoms obscures the fact that men also have emotional ups and downs. Could these changes be linked to hormones? Testosterone, an important androgen (masculinizing hormone), fluctuates daily in all men, usually reaching a peak in the morning. It also follows a longer, infradian cycle in some men, the length of the cycle varying from one individual to another (Doering et al., 1974). So far, efforts to relate testosterone levels to psychological state have been sparse and their results conflicting and hard to interpret. For example, in one study, testosterone rose in men who were feeling elated after winning a $100 prize in a tennis match (Mazur & Lamb, 1980). But in another, teenagers with characteristically high testosterone levels had a tendency to feel sad, not elated (Susman et al., 1987). In a study of 4,462 men, James Dabbs and Robin Morris (1990) found that high testosterone levels were associated with delinquency, drug use, having many sex partners, abusiveness, and violence—and were not associated with any positive behaviors. But these results do not mean that men are victims of their hormones or that high testosterone levels constitute a syndrome. The reasons for antisocial behavior are far more complicated than testosterone levels, and besides, the findings were only correlational.

In actuality, few people of either sex are likely to undergo personality shifts because of their hormones. To be sure, hormonal conditions may produce psychological symptoms, just as a brain tumor or thyroid problem might, and chronic pain or discomfort can make anyone depressed. But the body only provides the clay for our symptoms; learning and culture mold that clay, by teaching us which symptoms are important or worrisome and which are not. The impact of any bodily change—whether it is circadian, ultradian, or infradian—depends on how we interpret it and how we respond to it.

Quick Quiz

There are no hormonal excuses for avoiding this quiz!

1. The functioning of the biological clock governing circadian rhythms is affected by the hormone ___________.
2. Jet lag occurs because of internal ___________.
3. Which term describes the menstrual cycle? (a) circadian, (b) infradian, (c) ultradian
4. For most women, the days before menstruation are reliably associated with (a) depression, (b) irritability, (c) elation, (d) creativity, (e) none of these, (f) a and b.
5. A researcher tells her male subjects that testosterone usually peaks in the morning and that it probably causes hostility. She then asks them to fill out a "Hyper-Testosterone Syndrome (HTS) Survey" in the morning and again at night. Based on menstrual-cycle findings, what results might she get? How could she improve her study?

Answers:

1. melatonin 2. desynchronization 3. b 4. e 5. Because of the expectations that the men now have about testosterone, they may be biased to report more hostility in the morning. It would be better to keep them in the dark about the hypothesis, use a neutral title on the questionnaire (say, "Health and Mood Checklist"), and measure their actual hormone levels at different points in the day (because individuals vary in their biological rhythms). Also, a control group of women could be added, to see whether their hostility levels vary in the same way that men's do.

THE RHYTHMS OF SLEEP

Perhaps the most perplexing of all our biological rhythms is the one governing sleep and wakefulness. Human beings and most other animals curl up and go to sleep at least once every 24 hours, but the reason remains something of a puzzle. After all, sleeping puts an organism at risk: Muscles that are usually ready to respond to danger relax, and senses grow dull. As the late British psychologist Christopher Evans (1984) once noted, "The behavior patterns involved in sleep are glaringly, almost insanely, at odds with common sense." Then why is sleep such a profound necessity?

WHY WE SLEEP One likely function of sleep is to provide a "time-out" period, so that the body can restore depleted reserves of energy, eliminate waste products

During the Great Depression of the 1930s, marathon dancers competed for prize money by trying to dance longer than other contestants—and suffered many of the effects of sleep deprivation.

from muscles, repair cells, strengthen the immune system, or recover physical abilities lost during the day. The idea that sleep is for physical recuperation accords with the undeniable fact that at the end of the day we feel tired and crave sleep. Though most people can function fairly normally after a day or two of sleeplessness, especially when doing interesting tasks, sleep deprivation that lasts for four days or longer is quite uncomfortable. In animals, forced sleeplessness leads to infections and eventually death (Rechtschaffen et al., 1983), and the same may be true for people. There is a case on record of a man who, at age 51, abruptly began to lose sleep. After sinking deeper and deeper into an exhausted stupor, he developed a lung infection and died. An autopsy showed that he had lost almost all the large neurons in two areas of the thalamus that have been linked to sleep and hormonal circadian rhythms (Lugaresi et al., 1986).

Nonetheless, when people go many days without any sleep, they do not then require an equal period of time to catch up; one night's rest usually eliminates all symptoms of fatigue (Dement, 1978). Moreover, the amount of time we sleep does not necessarily correspond to how active we have been; even after a relaxing day on the beach, we usually go to sleep at night as quickly as usual. For these reasons, simple rest or energy restoration cannot be the sole purpose of sleep.

Although most people still function pretty well after losing a single night's sleep, mental flexibility, attention, and creativity may suffer (Dement, 1992; Horne, 1988). So sleep must have as much to do with brain function as with bodily restoration. Laboratory studies and observations of people participating in "wake-athons" have shown that after several days of sleep loss, people become irritable and begin to have hallucinations and delusions (Dement, 1978; Luce & Segal, 1966). Even a brief increase or decrease in sleep time may affect performance: In April, on the Monday after the change to daylight savings time and the loss of an hour's sleep, traffic accidents increase by several percentage points; then, in October, on the Monday after clocks "fall back" to standard time and people gain an hour of sleep, accidents decrease (Coren, 1996).

As we will discuss in our section on dreaming, sleep may also play a role in learning and memory. It seems to provide a time for "mental housekeeping," when unnecessary neural connections can be jettisoned and important ones can be strengthened

Whatever your age, sometimes the urge to sleep is irresistible. Yet the psychological and physical functions of sleep are still not fully understood.

GET INVOLVED

Get an idea of the variation in people's sleep patterns by asking some friends and relatives what time they typically go to sleep and what time they get up, and whether they routinely take daytime naps. Ask them, too, whether this pattern is their natural one or is simply required by their schedule (e.g., having to be at school or the office by 9:00 A.M.). Do people sleep longer on weekends, and if so, what does this fact suggest about the adequacy of their sleep during the week?

and made permanent. It is clear that during sleep, the brain is not just resting. On the contrary, most of the brain remains quite active, as we are about to see.

THE REALMS OF SLEEP Until the early 1950s, little was known about sleep. Then a breakthrough occurred in the laboratory of physiologist Nathaniel Kleitman, who at the time was the only person in the world who had spent an entire career studying sleep. Kleitman had given one of his graduate students, Eugene Aserinsky, the tedious task of finding out whether the slow, rolling eye movements that characterize the onset of sleep continue throughout the night. To both men's surprise, eye movements did indeed occur, but they were rapid, not slow (Aserinsky & Kleitman, 1955). Using the electroencephalograph to measure the brain's electrical activity (see Chapter 4), these researchers, along with another of Kleitman's students, William Dement, were able to correlate these rapid eye movements with changes in sleepers' brain-wave patterns (Dement, 1992). Volunteers were soon spending their nights sleeping in laboratories while scientists observed them and measured changes in their brain activity, muscle tension, breathing, and other physiological responses.

As a result of this research, today we know that sleep is not an unbroken state of rest. In adults, periods of **rapid eye movement (REM)** alternate with periods of fewer eye movements, or *non-REM* (NREM), in an ultradian cycle that recurs, on the average, every 90 minutes or so. The REM periods last from a few minutes to as long as an hour, averaging about 20 minutes in length. Whenever they begin, the pattern of electrical activity from the sleeper's brain changes to resemble that of alert wakefulness. Non-REM periods are themselves divided into shorter, distinct stages, each associated with a particular brain-wave pattern (see Figure 5.2).

When you first climb into bed, close your eyes, and relax, your brain emits bursts of **alpha waves.** On an EEG recording, alpha waves have a regular rhythm, high amplitude (height), and a low frequency of 8 to 12 cycles per second. Alpha activity is associated with relaxing or not concentrating on anything in particular. Gradually, these waves slow down even further, and you drift into the Land of Nod, passing through four stages, each deeper than the previous one:

Stage 1. Your brain waves become small and irregular, indicating activity with low voltage and mixed frequencies. You feel yourself drifting on the edge of consciousness, in a state of light sleep. If awakened, you may recall fantasies or a few visual images.

Stage 2. Your brain emits occasional short bursts of rapid, high-peaking waves called *sleep spindles.* Minor noises probably won't disturb you.

Stage 3. In addition to the waves characteristic of Stage 2, your brain occasionally emits very slow waves of about 1 to 3 cycles per second, with very high peaks. These **delta waves** are a sure sign that you will be hard to arouse. Your breathing and pulse have slowed down and your muscles are relaxed.

rapid eye movement (REM) sleep Sleep periods characterized by eye movement, loss of muscle tone, and dreaming.

alpha waves Relatively large, slow brain waves characteristic of relaxed wakefulness.

delta waves Slow, regular brain waves characteristic of Stage 3 and Stage 4 sleep.

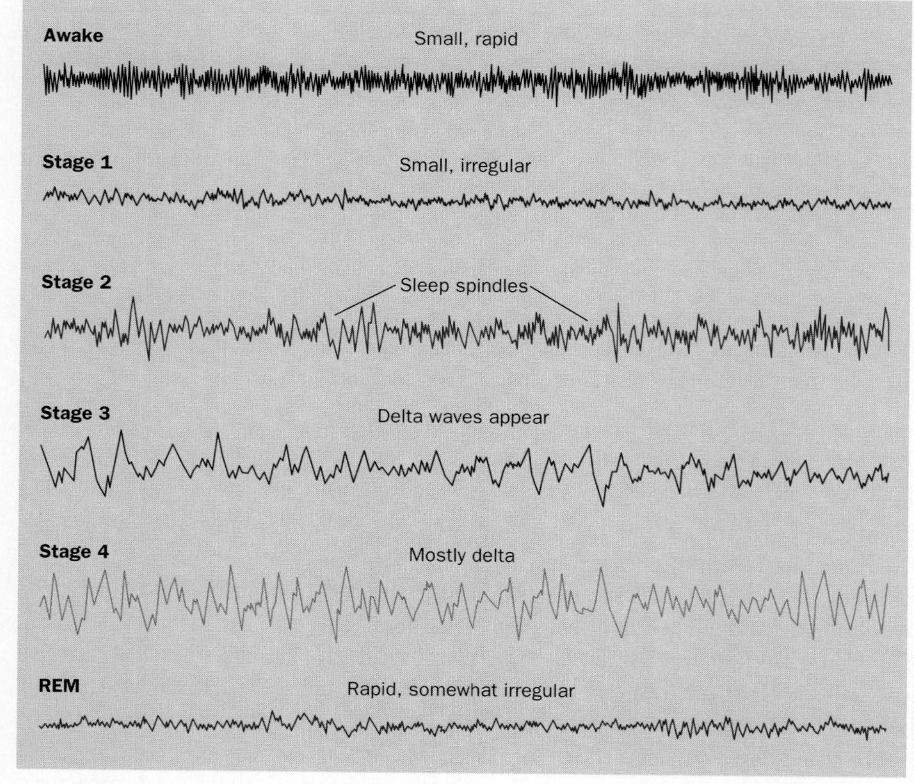

Figure 5.2
Brain-Wave Patterns During Wakefulness and Sleep

Most types of brain waves are present throughout sleep, but different ones predominate at different stages.

Stage 4. Delta waves have now largely taken over, and you are in deep sleep. It will probably take vigorous shaking or a loud noise to awaken you, and you won't be very happy about it. Oddly enough, though, if you talk or walk in your sleep, this is when you are likely to do so. (The causes of sleepwalking are unknown; it occurs mostly in children.)

This sequence of stages takes about 30 to 45 minutes. Then it reverses, and you move back up the ladder from Stage 4 to 3 to 2 to 1. At that point, about 70 to 90 minutes after the onset of sleep, something peculiar happens. Stage 1 does not turn into drowsy wakefulness, as one might expect. Instead, your brain begins to emit long bursts of very rapid, somewhat irregular waves, similar to those produced during Stage 1. Your heart rate increases, your blood pressure rises, and your breathing becomes faster and more irregular. Small twitches in your face and fingers may occur. In men, the penis becomes somewhat erect as vascular tissue relaxes and blood fills the genital area faster than it exits. In women, the clitoris enlarges and vaginal lubrication increases. At the same time, most of your skeletal muscles go as limp as a rag doll, preventing your aroused brain from producing physical movement. You have entered the realm of REM.

Because the brain is extremely active while the body is almost devoid of muscle tone, REM sleep has also been called "paradoxical sleep." It is during these periods that you are most likely to dream (Aserinsky & Kleitman, 1955). Even people who claim they never dream at all will report dreams if awakened in a sleep laboratory during REM sleep. Dreaming is also sometimes reported during non-REM sleep, but less often, and the images are less vivid and more realistic than those reported during REM sleep.

The study of REM has opened a window on the world of dreams. We now know, for example, that dreams do not take place in an instant, as people used to think, but in "real time." When volunteers are awakened 5 minutes after REM starts, they report shorter dreams than when they are awakened after 15 minutes (Dement & Kleitman, 1957). If you dream that you are singing all the verses to "A Hundred Bottles of Beer on the Wall," your dream will probably last as long as it would take you to sing the song. Most dreams take several minutes, and some last much longer.

REM and non-REM sleep continue to alternate throughout the night, with the REM periods tending to get longer and closer together as the hours pass (see Figure 5.3). An early REM period may last only a few minutes, whereas a later one may go on for 20 or 30 minutes and sometimes as long as an hour—which is why people are likely to be dreaming when the alarm clock goes off in the morning. In the later part of sleep, Stages 3 and 4 become very short or disappear. But the cycles are far from regular. An individual may bounce directly from Stage 4 back to Stage 2, or go from REM to Stage 2 and then back to REM. Also, the time between REM and non-REM is highly variable, differing from person to person and also within any given individual.

The purpose of REM sleep is still a matter of debate, but clearly it does have a purpose. If you wake people every time they lapse into REM sleep, nothing dramatic will happen. When finally allowed to sleep normally, however, they will spend a much longer time than usual in the REM phase, and it will be hard to rouse them. Electrical brain activity associated with REM may burst through into quiet sleep and even into wakefulness. The subjects will seem to be making up for something they were deprived of. Many people think that in adults, at least, this "something" has to do with dreaming, to which we now turn.

Because cats sleep so much—up to 80 percent of the time!—it's easy to catch them in the various stages of slumber. A cat in non-REM sleep (top) remains upright, but during the REM phase (bottom), its muscles go limp and it flops onto its side.

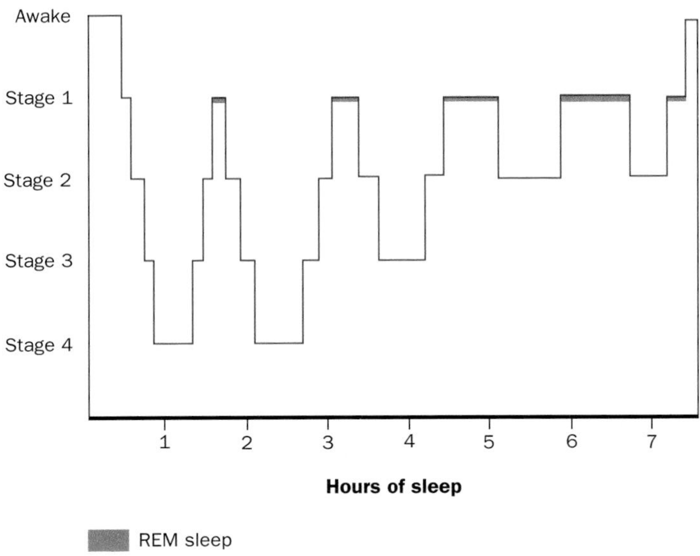

Figure 5.3
A Typical Night's Sleep for a Young Adult

In this graph, the horizontal colored bars represent time spent in REM sleep. REM periods tend to lengthen as the night wears on; but Stages 3 and 4, which dominate non-REM sleep early in the night, may disappear as morning approaches. (From Kelly, 1981.)

Quick Quiz

Match each term with the appropriate phrase.

1. REM periods	a. delta waves and talking in one's sleep
2. alpha	b. irregular brain waves and light sleep
3. Stage 4 sleep	c. relaxed but awake
4. Stage 1 sleep	d. active brain but inactive muscles

Answers:

1.d 2.c 3.a 4.b

EXPLORING THE DREAM WORLD

Every culture has its theories about dreams. In some cultures, dreams are thought to occur when the spirit leaves the body to wander the world or speak to the gods. In others, dreams are thought to reveal the future; in the Bible, it was while Joseph was dreaming that he learned that Egypt would suffer a famine. A Chinese Taoist of the third century B.C. pondered the possible reality of the dream world. He told of dreaming that he was a butterfly flitting about. "Suddenly I woke up and I was indeed Chuang Tzu. Did Chuang Tzu dream he was a butterfly, or did the butterfly dream he was Chuang Tzu?"

In dreaming, the focus of attention is inward, though sometimes an external event such as the sound of a siren can influence the dream. While a dream is in progress, it may be vivid or vague, terrifying or peaceful, colorful or bland. It may also seem to make perfect sense—until you wake up. Then it is often recalled as illogical and bizarre. The flow of a dream is usually not as smooth as the flow of waking consciousness; events occur without transitions. REM dreams, which as we noted are usually more vivid than non-REM dreams, are often reported as adventures or stories. Non-REM dreams tend to be described as vague, fragmentary, unemotional, and commonplace.

Ordinarily, during dreaming, you have no background awareness of where you are or of your own body. Some people, however, report **lucid dreams,** in which they know they are dreaming and they feel as though they are conscious. Some can even produce lucid dreams at will or in response to a light cue from a biofeedback device, and can control the action in these dreams, much as a scriptwriter decides what will happen in a movie (LaBerge, 1986; LaBerge & Levitan, 1995). In the sleep laboratory, they may even be able to signal that they are having a lucid dream by moving their eyes in a prearranged way. In one case, a young woman was taught to use lucid dreaming to modify her frequent nightmares and make them less frightening (Abramovitch, 1995).

Studies of lucid dreamers raise an issue that has been bothering sleep researchers for years: Do the eye movements of REM sleep correspond to events in a dream? Some researchers think that eye movements are no more related to dream content than are inner-ear muscle contractions, which also occur during REM sleep. Every mammal studied except the spiny anteater, the bottlenose dolphin, and the porpoise exhibits REM sleep, as do human fetuses—but we might not want to credit mice, opossums, or human fetuses with what we ordinarily call dreams. Even moles, which can hardly move their eyes, show EEG patterns that denote REM sleep. Further, although children's eyes move during REM sleep, the imagery in children's dreams tends to be fairly static until age 6 or so, and their cognitive limitations may keep them from creating true narratives in dreams until age 7 or 8 (Foulkes et al.,

lucid dream A dream in which the dreamer is aware of dreaming.

1990). On the other hand, in adult dreamers, eye movements resemble those of waking life, when the eyes and head move in synchrony as the person moves about and changes the direction of his or her gaze—even though during dreaming the head and body stay still (J. H. Herman, 1992). In skilled lucid dreamers, eye movements correspond to actions in their dreams, suggesting that in adults, at least, the eyes may indeed track dream images, actions, and events (Schatzman, Worsley, & Fenwick, 1988).

Why do these dream images arise at all? Why doesn't the brain just rest, switching off all thoughts and images and launching us into a coma? Why, instead, do we spend our nights flying through the air, battling monsters, or flirting with an old flame in the fantasy world of our dreams?

DREAMS AS UNCONSCIOUS WISHES

Throughout history and across many cultures, people have believed that dreams express hidden wishes and desires and have developed rituals for analyzing the meanings of dreams (Krippner & Hillman, 1990). In psychology, one of the first theorists to take dreams seriously was Sigmund Freud, the founder of psychoanalysis; he, too, emphasized hidden messages from the mind. After analyzing many of his patients' dreams and some of his own, Freud concluded that our nighttime fantasies provide a "royal road to the unconscious." In dreams, said Freud, we are able to gratify forbidden or unrealistic wishes and desires, often sexual, that have been forced into the unconscious part of the mind. If we did not dream, energy invested in these wishes and desires would build up to intolerable levels, threatening our very sanity.

According to Freud, every dream is meaningful, no matter how absurd it might seem. But if a dream's message arouses anxiety, the rational part of the mind must disguise and distort it. Otherwise, the dream would intrude into consciousness and waken the dreamer. In dreams, therefore, one person may be represented by another—for example, a father by a brother—or even by several different characters. Similarly, thoughts and objects are translated into symbolic images. A penis may be disguised as a snake, umbrella, or dagger; a vagina, as a tunnel or cave; and the human body, as a house.

To understand a dream, Freud said, we must distinguish its *manifest content*, the aspects of it that we consciously experience during sleep and may remember upon wakening, from its *latent* (hidden) *content*, the unconscious wishes and thoughts being expressed symbolically. Freud warned against the simpleminded translation of symbols, however. Each dream had to be analyzed in the context of the dreamer's waking life, as well as the person's associations to the dream's contents. Not everything in a dream is symbolic. Sometimes, Freud cautioned, "A cigar is only a cigar."

Most psychologists today accept Freud's notion that dreams are more than incoherent ramblings of the mind, but many quarrel with his interpretations, which they find far-fetched. They point out that there are no reliable rules for interpreting the latent content of dreams, and no objective way to know whether a particular interpretation is correct. Popular books that try to tell you what your dreams mean may be fun to read, but they are only the writer's personal hunches.

DREAMS AS PROBLEM SOLVING

Another explanation holds that dreams reflect not deep-seated or infantile wishes but rather the ongoing emotional preoccupations of waking life—relationships, work, sex, or health (Webb & Cartwright, 1978). In this view, the symbols and metaphors in dreams convey the dream's true meaning, rather than disguising it. One psychologist, Gayle Delaney, told of a woman who dreamed she was swimming

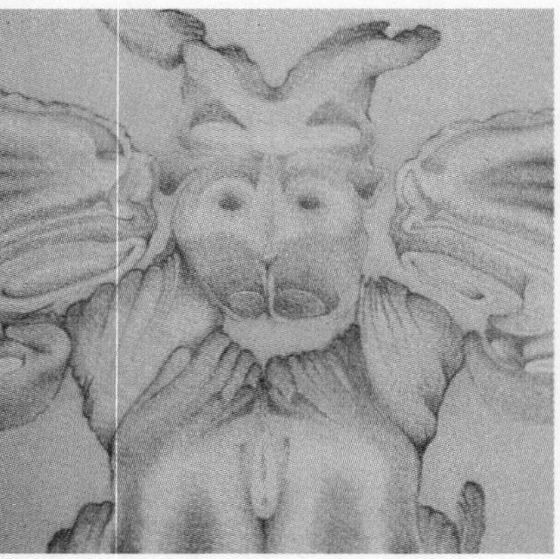

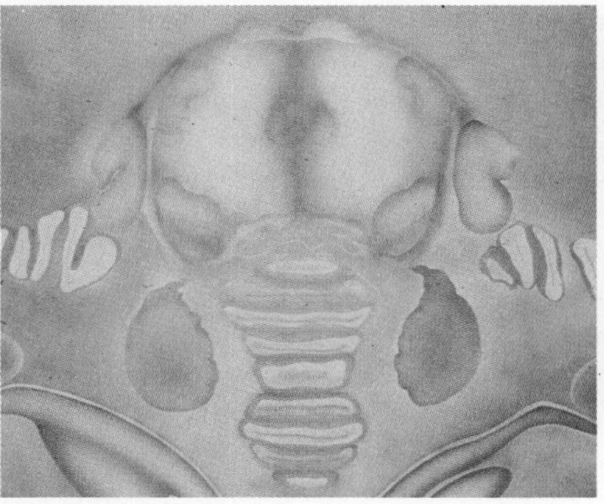

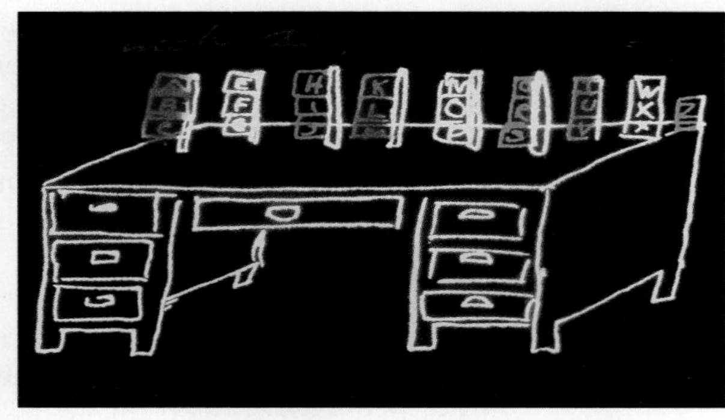

These drawings from dream journals show that the images in dreams can be either abstract or literal. The two fanciful paintings on the left represent the dreams of a person who worked all day long with brain tissue, which the drawings rather resemble. The desk on the right was sketched in 1939 by a scientist to illustrate his dream about a mechanical device for instantly retrieving quotations—a sort of early desktop computer.

underwater. The woman's 8-year-old son was on her back, his head above the water. Her husband was supposed to take a picture of them, but for some reason he wasn't doing it, and she was starting to feel as if she were going to drown. To Delaney, the message was obvious: The woman was "drowning" under the responsibilities of child care, and her husband wasn't "getting the picture" (in Dolnick, 1990). Another psychologist, Alan Siegel (1991), reported the case of a father-to-be who dreamed of swimming downhill, with instructions from his wife's labor coach, and emerging in the locker room wrapped in a towel. When asked for his interpretation, the man said the dream meant he should swim more at the gym! To Siegel, however, the dream was about the man's anxiety over the impending childbirth and parenthood.

Dreams may also give us an opportunity to deal with emotional issues, even if we forget the dreams later. When we are relatively free of problems, we may use dreams simply to exercise our creativity. But during a crisis, our dream machinery goes into high gear, and emotional concerns activate images in memory (Cartwright & Lloyd, 1994). Rosalind Cartwright finds that in depressed people going through a divorce, the first dream of the night often comes sooner than it ordinarily would, the dream lasts longer, and it is more emotional and storylike—and this pattern, she reports, relates to recovery. The content of these people's dreams suggests that they are working on issues of loss and new responsibilities. Cartwright (1990) concludes that getting through a divorce (and by implication, other crises) takes "time, good friends, good genes, good luck, and a good dream system."

DREAMS AS A BY-PRODUCT OF MENTAL HOUSEKEEPING

A third approach views dreams as a by-product of the mental housekeeping mentioned earlier. Christopher Evans (1984) argued that the brain must periodically shut out sensory input so that it can process and assimilate new data and update what has already been stored. It divides new information into "wanted" and "unwanted" categories, makes new associations, and revises old "programs"—to use a computer analogy—in light of the day's experiences. The data on which the brain works include not only recent events, but also ideas, obsessions, worries, wishes, and thoughts about the past. What we recall as dreams are really only brief snippets from an ongoing process of sorting, scanning, and sifting that occurs most intensely during REM

TABLE 5.1 ***Some Psychoactive Drugs and Their Effects***

	Type of Drug	Common Effects	Results of Abuse/Addiction
Amphetamines	Stimulant	Wakefulness, alertness, raised metabolism, elevated mood	Nervousness, headaches, loss of appetite, high blood pressure, delusions, psychosis, heart damage, convulsions, death
Cocaine	Stimulant	Euphoria, excitation, boost of energy, suppressed appetite	Excitability, sleeplessness, sweating, paranoia, anxiety, panic, depression, heart damage, heart failure, injury to nose if sniffed
Tobacco (nicotine)	Stimulant	Varies, from alertness to calmness, depending on mental set, setting, and prior arousal; decreases appetite for carbohydrates	*Nicotine:* heart disease, high blood pressure, impaired circulation *Tar:* lung cancer, emphysema, mouth and throat cancer, many other health risks
Caffeine	Stimulant	Wakefulness, alertness, shortened reaction time	Restlessness, insomnia, muscle tension, heartbeat irregularities, high blood pressure
Alcohol (1–2 drinks)	Depressant	Depends on setting, mental set; tends to act like a stimulant because it reduces inhibitions, anxiety	
Alcohol (several/ many drinks)	Depressant	Slowed reaction time, tension, depression, reduced ability to store new memories or to retrieve old ones, poor coordination	Blackouts, cirrhosis, organic damage, mental and neurological impairment, psychosis, possibly death
Tranquilizers (e.g., Valium); barbiturates (e.g., phenobarbital)	Depressant	Reduced anxiety and tension, sedation	Increased dosage needed for effects; impaired motor and sensory functions, impaired permanent storage of new information, withdrawal symptoms; possibly convulsions, coma, death (especially when taken with other drugs)
Opium, heroin, morphine	Opiate	Euphoria, relief of pain	Loss of appetite, nausea, constipation, withdrawal symptoms, convulsions, coma, possibly death
LSD, psilocybin, mescaline	Psychedelic	Exhilaration, visions and hallucinations, insightful experiences	Psychosis, paranoia, panic reactions
Marijuana	Mild psychedelic (classification controversial)	Relaxation, euphoria, increased appetite, reduced ability to store new memories, other effects depending on mental set and setting	Throat and lung irritation, lung damage (if smoked), impaired immunity; long-term effects not well established

1. **Stimulants,** such as cocaine, amphetamines ("uppers"), nicotine, and caffeine, speed up activity in the central nervous system. In moderate amounts, they tend to produce feelings of excitement, confidence, and well-being or euphoria. In large amounts, they make a person anxious, jittery, and hyperalert. In very large doses, they may cause convulsions, heart failure, and death.

Amphetamines are synthetic drugs usually taken in pill form. Cocaine ("coke") is a natural drug, derived from the leaves of the coca plant. Rural workers in Bolivia and Peru chew coca leaf every day, without apparent ill effects. In North America, the drug is usually inhaled ("snorted"), injected, or smoked in the highly refined form known as "crack." These methods give the drug a more immediate, powerful, and dangerous effect than when coca leaf is chewed. Amphetamines and cocaine make users feel peppy but do not actually increase energy reserves. Fatigue, irritability, and depression may occur when the effects of these drugs wear off.

stimulants Drugs that speed up activity in the central nervous system.

2. Depressants, such as alcohol, tranquilizers, and barbiturates, slow down activity in the central nervous system. Also known as *sedatives,* they usually make a person feel calm or drowsy, and they may reduce anxiety, guilt, tension, and inhibitions. In large amounts, they may produce insensitivity to pain and other sensations. Like stimulants, in very large doses they can cause convulsions and death.

People are often surprised to learn that alcohol is a central nervous system depressant. Paradoxically, in small amounts, alcohol has some of the effects of a stimulant, not because it is a stimulant but because it suppresses activity in parts of the brain that normally inhibit such behaviors as loud laughter and clowning around. Like barbiturates and opiates, alcohol can be used as an anesthetic; if you drink enough, you will eventually pass out. Extremely large amounts of alcohol can kill, by inhibiting the nerve cells in the brain areas that control breathing and heartbeat. But *moderate* social drinking—a drink or two of wine or liquor a day—is associated with a variety of health benefits, especially for men, including a reduction in the risk of heart attacks and increased longevity (Gaziano & Hennekens, 1995; Gronbaek et al., 1995; Klatsky, 1994).

3. Opiates include opium, derived from the opium poppy; morphine, a derivative of opium; heroin, a derivative of morphine; and synthetic drugs such as methadone. All of these drugs relieve pain, mimicking the action of endorphins, and most have a powerful effect on the emotions. When injected, they may produce a sudden feeling of euphoria, called a "rush." They may also decrease anxiety and motivation, although the effects vary.

4. Psychedelic drugs alter consciousness by disrupting the normal perception of time and space, as well as normal thought processes. Sometimes, psychedelics produce hallucinations, especially visual ones. Some psychedelics, such as lysergic acid diethylamide (LSD), are made in the laboratory. Others, such as mescaline (from the peyote cactus) and psilocybin (from certain species of mushrooms), are natural substances. Emotional reactions to psychedelics vary from person to person, and from one time to another for any individual. A "trip" may be mildly pleasant or unpleasant, a mystical revelation or a nightmare.

Two commonly used drugs, anabolic steroids and marijuana, fall outside these four classifications. Anabolic steroids, which have legitimate medical uses, are synthetic derivatives of testosterone that are taken in pill form or by injection. Because they are thought to increase muscle mass and strength when they are combined with weight-bearing exercise, athletes and bodybuilders often use them illegally. As reports of use by high school and even junior high school athletes have increased, concern about these drugs has grown. Numerous negative physical effects have been reported, including heart and liver disease, decreased testicular size, and penile erection problems (Pope & Katz, 1992). Whether anabolic steroids are psychoactive, however, is still an open question. Anecdotal and clinical reports cite both positive psychological effects (e.g., increased sex drive, increased confidence, and reduced fatigue during training) and negative ones (e.g., increased aggression, irritability, anxiety, and even psychosis). However, most studies of anabolic steroids have used questionable sampling strategies or have relied on unverified self-reports. Therefore, no firm conclusions can yet be drawn about the psychological effects of these drugs.

Marijuana ("pot," "grass," "weed"), which is smoked or, less commonly, eaten in foods such as brownies, is probably the most widely used illicit drug in North America and Europe. Some researchers classify it as a mild psychedelic, but others feel that its chemical makeup and its psychological effects place it outside the major classifications. The active ingredient in marijuana is tetrahydrocannabinol (THC), derived from the hemp plant, *Cannabis sativa.* In some respects, THC appears to be a

depressants Drugs that slow down activity in the central nervous system.

opiates Drugs, derived from the opium poppy, that relieve pain and commonly produce euphoria.

psychedelic drugs Consciousness-altering drugs that produce hallucinations, change thought processes, or disrupt the normal perception of time and space.

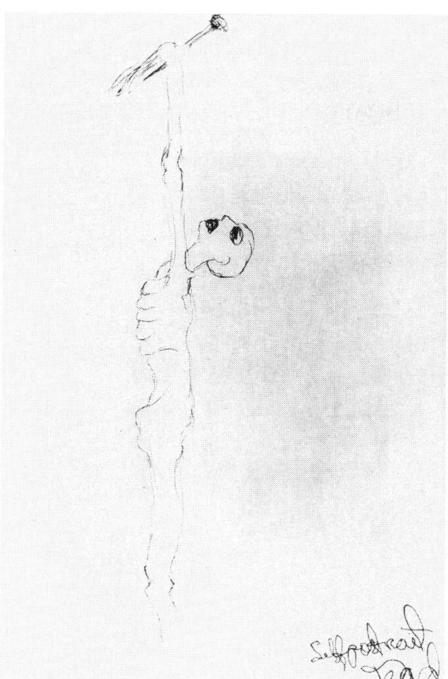

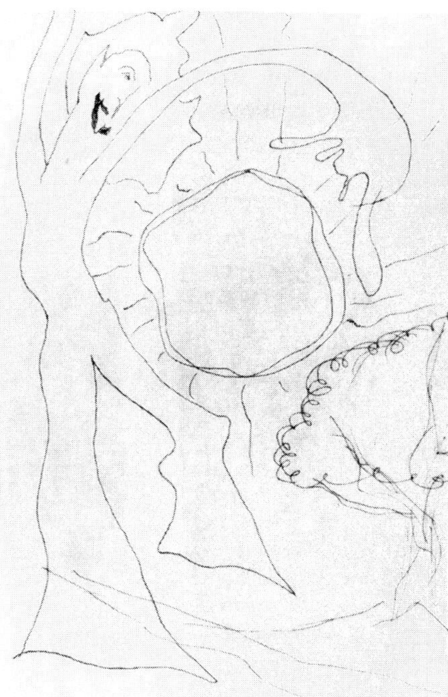

An LSD "trip" may be a ticket to agony or ecstasy. Both of these drawings were done under the influence of the drug.

mild stimulant, increasing heart rate and making tastes, sounds, and colors seem more intense. But users often report reactions ranging from mild euphoria to relaxation, or even sleepiness. Time often seems to go by slowly. In moderate doses, marijuana can interfere with the transfer of information to long-term memory, a characteristic it shares with alcohol. In large doses, it can cause hallucinations and a sense of unreality. Sometimes the drug impairs coordination, concentration, visual perception, and reaction times, though it is not clear how long these effects last.

THE PHYSIOLOGY OF DRUG EFFECTS

Psychoactive drugs produce their effects primarily by acting on brain neurotransmitters, the substances that carry messages from one nerve cell to another. They may increase or decrease the release of neurotransmitters at the synapse; prevent the reabsorption ("reuptake") of a neurotransmitter after its release; block the effects of a neurotransmitter on a receiving nerve cell; or bind to receptors that would ordinarily be triggered by a neurotransmitter or a neuromodulator. Figure 5.4 shows how one drug, cocaine, increases the amount of norepinephrine and dopamine in the brain by blocking the reabsorption of these substances.

Such biochemical changes in the brain can have cognitive and emotional effects. For example, because of alcohol's effect on parts of the brain involved in judgment, drinkers often are unable to gauge their own competence. Even moderate amounts of alcohol can affect perception, response time, coordination, and balance, despite the drinker's own impression of unchanged or even improved performance. Liquor also affects memory, possibly by interfering with the work of the neurotransmitter serotonin. Information stored before a drinking session remains intact during the session but is retrieved more slowly (Stempel, Beckwith, & Petros, 1986). The ability to store new memories for later use also suffers, even after just two or three drinks (Parker, Birnbaum, & Noble, 1976). Consuming small amounts does not seem to af-

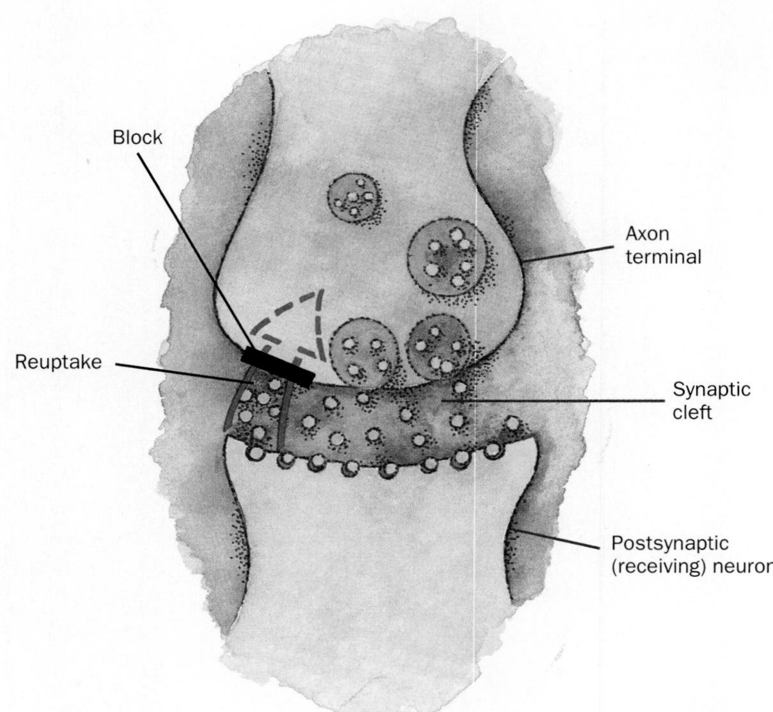

Figure 5.4
Cocaine's Effect on the Brain

Cocaine blocks the brain's reabsorption ("reuptake") of the neurotransmitters dopamine and norepinephrine, so levels of these substances rise. The result is overstimulation of certain brain circuits and a brief euphoric high. Then, when the drug wears off, a depletion of dopamine may cause the user to "crash," and become sleepy and depressed.

fect *sober* mental performance, but even occasional heavy drinking impairs later abstract thought. In other words, a Saturday night binge is potentially more dangerous than a daily drink.

Animal studies suggest that repeated use of certain drugs, including *designer drugs* (easily synthesized variations of other drugs), can cause permanent brain damage. For example, the drug "Ecstasy" (MDMA) may permanently damage cells that produce serotonin (Ricaurte et al., 1988). The dosages given to animals, however, have been enormous, and the generalizability of such findings to human beings remains highly controversial. Some researchers have concluded that there is no evidence that *light or moderate* use of recreational drugs can damage the human brain enough to affect cognitive functioning, although all agree that heavy or frequent use of any drug is another matter (see Chapter 15).

The use of some psychoactive drugs, such as heroin and tranquilizers, can lead to **tolerance:** As time goes by, more and more of the drug is needed to get the same effect. When habitual heavy users stop taking a drug (whether it causes tolerance or not), they may suffer severe **withdrawal symptoms,** such as nausea, abdominal cramps, muscle spasms, depression, and sleep problems, depending on the drug. Tolerance and withdrawal are often assumed to be purely physiological matters, but in Chapter 7, we will see that learning also plays a role.

CONSIDER OTHER INTERPRETATIONS

One person takes a drink and flies into a rage. Another has a drink and "mellows out." What qualities of the user rather than the drug might account for this difference?

THE PSYCHOLOGY OF DRUG EFFECTS

People often talk as if the effects of a drug were automatic, the inevitable result of the drug's chemistry ("I couldn't help what I said; the booze made me do it"). But reactions to a psychoactive drug involve more than the drug's chemical properties. When people take an opiate such as heroin or morphine recreationally, for example, they usually get high. Yet when people take opiates to relieve chronic and incapacitating pain, the narcotics do *not* make them high or addicted; they just remove the pain (Portenoy, 1994). So if we want to understand drugs, we must know more than their biochemistry. Drug responses also depend on a person's physical condition, experience with the drug, environmental setting, and mental set:

1. *Physical condition* includes body weight, metabolism, initial state of emotional arousal, and individual tolerance for the drug, which may be affected by the person's sex and by genetic factors (Cloninger, 1990). A drug may have one effect after a tiring day and a different one after a rousing quarrel. The effect may also vary with the time of day because of the body's circadian rhythms.

2. *Experience with the drug* refers to the number of times the drug has been used and the levels of past usage. Trying a drug—a cigarette, an alcoholic drink, a stimulant—for the first time is often a neutral or unpleasant experience. But reactions may change once a person has become familiar with the drug's effects.

3. *Environmental setting* greatly affects an individual's response to a drug. Setting is the reason that a person can have one glass of wine at home alone and feel sleepy but have three glasses of wine at a party and feel full of pep. It is the reason that a person might feel happy and high drinking with good friends but fearful and nervous drinking with strangers. In one study of reactions to alcohol, researchers found that most of the drinkers became depressed, angry, confused, and unfriendly. Then it dawned on them that anyone might become depressed, angry, confused, and unfriendly if asked to drink bourbon at 9:00 A.M. in a bleak hospital room, which was the setting for the experiment (Warren & Raynes, 1972).

4. *Mental set* refers to expectations about the drug's effects, the reasons for taking the drug, and whether a person wants to justify some behavior by being "under the influence." Some people drink to become more sociable, friendly, or seductive; some drink to try to reduce feelings of anxiety or depression; and some drink in order to have an excuse for abusiveness or violence. Addicts use drugs to escape from the real world; people living with chronic pain use the same drugs in order to function in the real world.

During the 1980s, researchers compared people who were drinking liquor (vodka and tonic) with those who *thought* they were drinking liquor but were actually getting only tonic and lime juice. (Vodka has a subtle taste, and most people cannot tell the real and phony drinks apart.) The experimenters found a *"think-drink" effect:* Men

tolerance Increased resistance to a drug's effects accompanying continued use; as tolerance develops, larger doses are required to produce effects once brought about by smaller ones.

withdrawal symptoms Physical and psychological symptoms that occur when someone addicted to a drug stops taking it.

The motives for using a drug, expectations about its effects, and the setting in which it is used all contribute to a person's reactions to the drug.

This cartoon, which pokes fun at the things people do to alter consciousness and make themselves feel better, reminds us that many stimulants and depressants are neither chemical nor illegal.

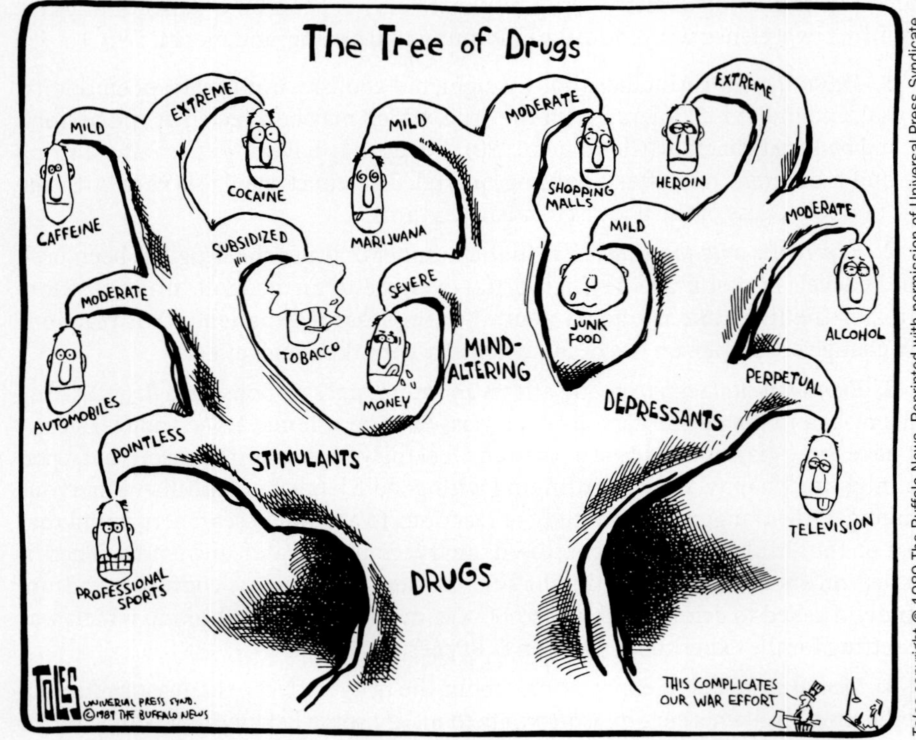

behaved more belligerently when they thought they were drinking vodka than when they thought they were drinking plain tonic water, regardless of the actual content of the drinks. Both sexes reported feeling sexually aroused when they thought they were drinking vodka, whether they actually got vodka or not (Abrams & Wilson, 1983; Marlatt & Rohsenow, 1980).

Because so many crimes of violence are committed when the participants have been drinking and because so many marital quarrels accompany drinking, alcohol is often assumed to "release" anger and aggression. Alcohol does in fact increase the likelihood of aggressive behavior, but not on its own: People must be aware that they are consuming liquor (Bushman, 1993). According to cognitive researchers, therefore, the real source of aggression is not in the alcohol but in the mind of the drinker. About half of all men arrested for assaulting their wives claim to have been drinking at the time. Yet most of these men do not have enough alcohol in their bloodstreams to qualify as legally intoxicated, and many have not been drinking immediately prior to being violent (Gelles & Straus, 1988). This finding suggests that alcohol did not make the men violent, but rather that *their use of alcohol provided an excuse to behave violently.* Indeed, the link between alcohol and aggression weakens when people believe they will be held responsible for their actions while drunk (Critchlow, 1983).

None of this means that alcohol and other drugs are merely placebos; drugs do have physiological effects, many of them quite powerful. Smoking cigarettes, for example, is seriously hazardous to your health, no matter how cool you think they are or what you expect them to do for you. However, people's expectations and beliefs play a role in all physiological drug reactions. These expectations and beliefs, in turn, are shaped by the culture in which a person lives. Many people start their day

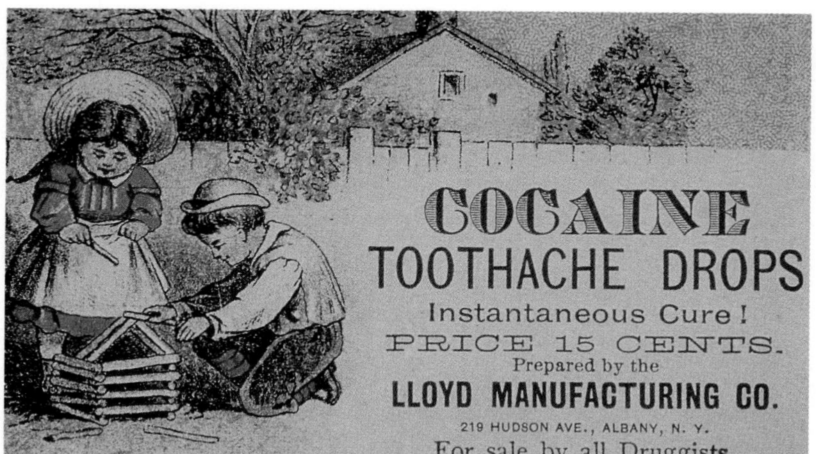

Before it was banned in the United States in the 1920s, cocaine was widely touted as a cure for everything from toothaches to timidity. It was used in teas, tonics, throat lozenges, and even soft drinks (including, briefly, Coca-Cola, which derived its name from the coca plant). Ingesting it had a less powerful effect than sniffing, injecting, or smoking it, as is done today. However, as cocaine use became associated in the popular mind with criminality and as concern about abuse grew, public opinion turned against it.

with a cup of coffee because it increases alertness. But when coffee was first introduced in Europe, people protested against it. Women said it suppressed their husbands' sexual performance and made men inconsiderate, and maybe it did! In the nineteenth century, Americans regarded marijuana as a mild sedative with no "mind-altering" properties. They didn't expect it to give them a high, and it didn't; it merely put them to sleep (Weil, 1972/1986). Today's marijuana is more potent, but motives for using it have also changed, and these changes have no doubt affected how people respond to the drug's physiological effects.

Because the consequences of drug *abuse* are so devastating to individuals and to society, it is often difficult for people to think critically about drug *use.* (Drug abuse and addiction are discussed further in Chapter 15.) In "Puzzles of Psychology," we discuss the implications of research on drugs for social policy and personal choice.

Quick Quiz

A. See whether you can name the following:

1. An illegal stimulant
2. Two drugs that interfere with the formation of new long-term memories
3. Three types of depressant drugs
4. A legal "recreational" drug that acts as a depressant on the central nervous system
5. Four factors that influence a person's psychological reactions to a drug

B. A bodybuilder who has been illegally taking anabolic steroids says the drugs make him more aggressive. What are some other possible interpretations?

Answers:

A. 1. cocaine; also some amphetamines 2. marijuana and alcohol 3. barbiturates, tranquilizers, and alcohol 4. alcohol 5. the person's physical condition, prior experience with the drug, mental set, and the environmental setting B. The bodybuilder's increased aggressiveness may be due to his expectations (a placebo effect); bodybuilding itself may increase aggressiveness; the culture of the bodybuilding gym may encourage aggressiveness; other influences in his life or other drugs he is taking may be making him more aggressive; or he may only think he is more aggressive, and his behavior may contradict his self-perceptions.

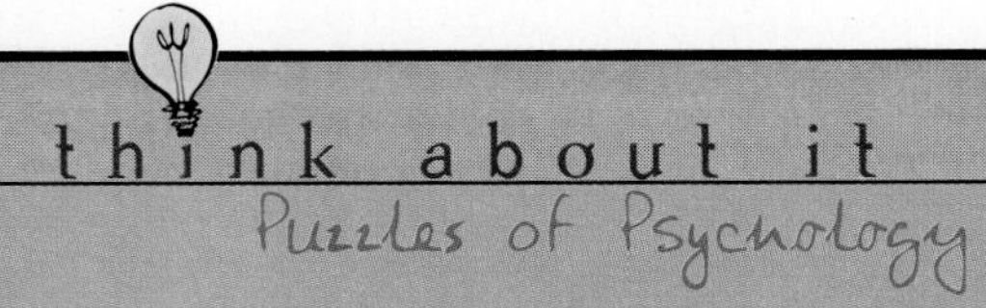

What Should We Do About Drugs?

Debates about drug policy are typically framed by two extreme positions. At one extreme, some people cannot accept evidence that their favorite drug—be it coffee, tobacco, alcohol, or marijuana—might have harmful effects. At the other extreme, some people cannot accept the evidence that their most hated drug—whether it is alcohol, morphine, or the coca leaf—might not be dangerous in all forms or amounts, and might even have some beneficial effects. Both sides often confuse extremely potent drugs with others that have only subtle effects or are safe in moderate amounts, and fail to distinguish light or moderate use of a drug from heavy or excessive use.

All societies draw a line between legal drugs that are considered "good" and illegal drugs that are considered "bad," but this distinction is usually made without any medical or biological basis (Gould, 1990; Weil, 1972/1986). As a result, some odd situations have occurred. For example, in the United States, methadone is a legal controlled substitute for heroin, yet both drugs are opiates. As Stephen Jay Gould (1990) has observed, to say that methadone blocks the craving for heroin is like saying that a Coke blocks the craving for a Pepsi. Nicotine, which of course is legal, is as addictive as heroin and cocaine, which are illegal; and tobacco use contributes to more than 400,000 deaths in the United States every year, about 20 times the number of deaths from all other forms of drug use combined (McGinnis & Foege, 1993). Narcotics, which can devastate the lives of addicts, permit people with chronic pain to live productive, pain-free lives (Portenoy, 1994); but because narcotics are illegal, the people who most need them are often deprived of them or are treated as addicts if they do use them.

The line between legal and illegal drugs is therefore an arbitrary one, drawn for social, economic, and cultural reasons. But once drawn, the line comes to be regarded as inevitable. When former Surgeon General Jocelyn Elders suggested, in 1993, that perhaps it would be worth studying the possibility of legalizing the drugs that many addicts commit theft or murder to get, her suggestion was met with waves of outrage. Once a drug is declared illegal, it seems, many people assume it is deadly, even though some legal drugs are more dangerous than illegal ones.

Consider reactions to studies of marijuana. In the 1970s, a research team studied a group of working-class Costa Rican men who had smoked an average of almost 10 marijuana cigarettes ("joints") daily for 17 years. The researchers found no significant physical or psychological differences between these men and a matched group of nonusers. Years later, another team restudied some of the same men. On tests that had been used earlier, the marijuana users showed no evidence of deterioration, although they had now been smoking for 30 years. On three *new* tests of sustained attention, organizing skills, and short-term memory, the users did do worse than the controls, but the differences were subtle (Page, Fletcher, & True, 1988).

Are you more impressed by these men's normal performance on the old tests or by their somewhat inferior performance on the new tests? Those who are worried about marijuana's effects emphasize the latter. In North America, they point out, even slight impairment of performance might be troublesome because many people hold jobs requiring mental exertion and alertness. Others, however, note that very few Americans or Canadians smoke 10 joints a

THE RIDDLE OF HYPNOSIS

In England not long ago, a wave of panic followed the success of a stage magician who could allegedly induce people through hypnosis to do dangerous things, such as jump off the stage and hurt themselves. Across North America, stage hypnotists, "past-lives channelers," and some psychotherapists have reported dramatic performances by hypnotized people who have been "age-regressed" to earlier years or even earlier centuries. And a few therapists claim that hypnosis has helped their patients recall alleged abductions by extraterrestrials (Fiore, 1989). What are we to make of such claims?

hypnosis A procedure in which the practitioner suggests changes in the sensations, perceptions, thoughts, feelings, or behavior of the subject.

The Division of Psychological Hypnosis of the APA defines **hypnosis** as a procedure in which the practitioner suggests changes in the sensations, perceptions, thoughts, feelings, or behavior of the subject (Kirsch & Lynn, 1995). Because hypnosis has been used for everything from parlor tricks and stage shows to medical and psychological treatments, it is important to understand just what this procedure can day for 30 years. Moreover, the slight deficits that were observed in Costa Rica could have been due to the temporary effects of recent smoking and not to any permanent effects of long-term use. The subjects were asked to abstain from smoking for two days before being tested, but it can take days or even weeks for the body to rid itself of THC.

Heavy, prolonged use of marijuana does pose some physical dangers, including lung damage when the drug is smoked (Wu et al., 1988). However, when used occasionally and in moderation, marijuana is less harmful than cigarettes or alcohol—unless, of course, it is mixed with other, more hazardous drugs. Some people believe that much of the marijuana now available on the street has greater concentrations of THC than the marijuana used a generation ago. But that may not be true. In any case, advocates point out that users can adjust to stronger marijuana by smoking less of the drug—just as a person might choose to drink one potent martini instead of two less potent vodka tonics (Danish, 1994).

In their book *Marihuana, the Forbidden Medicine,* Lester Grinspoon and James Bakalar (1993) reviewed the evidence of marijuana's medical benefits: It reduces the nausea and vomiting that often accompany chemotherapy treatment for cancer and AIDS; it reduces the physical tremors, loss of appetite, and other symptoms caused by multiple sclerosis; it helps reduce the frequency of seizures in some epileptic patients; and it alleviates the retinal swelling caused by glaucoma. Critics reply that most of these claims have not been validated with controlled studies, but apparently the medical benefits of marijuana are accepted by many physicians. In a survey of 1,035 cancer specialists, half said they would prescribe marijuana if it were legal, and 44 percent had already recommended its illegal use to their patients (Doblin & Kleiman, 1991). (In 1996, Californians and Arizonans voted to legalize the medical use of marijuana—but the federal government immediately vowed to continue its opposition to all marijuana use, including medical.

Some people are committed to the eradication of all illegal drugs, and some think that all drugs should be decriminalized. Others are more selective: For example, they would legalize narcotics for people who are in chronic pain and marijuana for recreational and medicinal use, but they would ban tobacco. Still others think that people who use drugs should not be punished, but that social policies should regulate where drugs are used (never at work, for example); that addicts should be treated in clinics rather than imprisoned; and that educational policy should encourage people to avoid drugs for their health—in short, the current approach to cigarette smoking. Andrew Weil, a physician who has been an outspoken critic of the war on drugs, nevertheless strongly advises people to satisfy their psychological needs without using drugs at all.

Where, given the research findings, do you stand in the drug debate? Given the near universality of drug use, is total prohibition of all drugs the answer? Which psychoactive drugs, if any, should be prohibited? How might we create mental sets and environmental settings that promote safe recreational use of some drugs, minimize the likelihood of drug abuse, and permit the medicinal use of beneficial drugs? What do you think?

do and what it cannot do. We will begin with a general look at what hypnosis is and will then consider two conflicting approaches that attempt to account for it.

THE NATURE OF HYPNOSIS

During hypnosis, the hypnotist typically suggests that the person being hypnotized feels relaxed, is getting sleepy, and feels the eyelids getting heavier and heavier. In a singsong or monotonous voice, the hypnotist assures the subject that he or she is sinking "deeper and deeper" but is not actually falling asleep. Sometimes the hypnotist has the person concentrate on a color or a small object, or on certain bodily sensations. People who have been hypnotized report that the focus of attention turns outward, toward the hypnotist's voice. The experience is sometimes likened to total absorption in a good book, a play, or a favorite piece of music.

Researchers agree on the following general points about hypnosis (Kirsch & Lynn, 1995; Nash & Nadon, 1997):

1. *The hypnotic state is not sleep.* A hypnotized person's brain waves are similar to those of ordinary wakefulness. The person almost always remains fully aware of what is going on and remembers the experience later, unless explicitly instructed to forget it. Even then, the memory can be restored by a prearranged signal.

2. *Hypnotic responsiveness depends more on the efforts and qualities of the person being hypnotized than on the skill of the hypnotist.* People who can easily become absorbed in their activities, and who can suspend ordinary reality and become involved in the world of imagination, make good hypnotic subjects (J. R. Hilgard, 1979; Nadon et al., 1991). Children as young as 4 years old can be hypnotized, but a child's ability to respond usually increases with time, stabilizing in adolescence (Morgan, Johnson, & Hilgard, 1974). Individuals differ in their hypnotizability, but even those who are low in the ability can be trained to be more hypnotizable (Spanos, DuBreuil, & Gabora, 1991).

3. *Hypnotized people cannot be forced to do things they do not want to do.* An individual must choose to turn initiative over to the hypnotist and to cooperate with the hypnotist's suggestions (Lynn, Rhue, & Weekes, 1990). Like psychoactive drugs, hypnosis can be used to justify letting go of inhibitions ("I know this looks silly, but after all, I'm hypnotized"). And it's true that hypnotized individuals may comply with a suggestion to take off an article of clothing or do something that looks dangerous (such as putting a hand in what seems to be fuming acid). However, there is no evidence that hypnotized people will do anything that actually goes against their morals or that constitutes a real threat (Laurence & Perry, 1988). (In the case of the British hypnotist that opened this section, worry over his "magic powers" eventually evaporated, as did complaints of injury.)

4. *Hypnotic inductions increase a person's suggestibility but only to a modest degree; people will accept suggestions with and without hypnosis.* All of the apparently astounding things that people do while hypnotized can also be done in the waking state, *if* people are sufficiently motivated and *if* they believe they can succeed. For example, when a stage hypnotist has a hypnotized person stretch out rigid as a plank between two chairs, with the head on the back of one chair and ankles on the back of another, nothing special is actually occurring. Most unhypnotized people can do the same thing; they only think they can't. Although hypnotic suggestions sometimes lead to feats of great strength, pain reduction, hallucinations, and even the disappearance of warts, suggestion alone, without the special procedures of hypnosis, can produce exactly the same results, so long as people are encouraged to relax, concentrate, and do their best (e.g., Chaves, 1989; Spanos, Stenstrom, & Johnson, 1988).

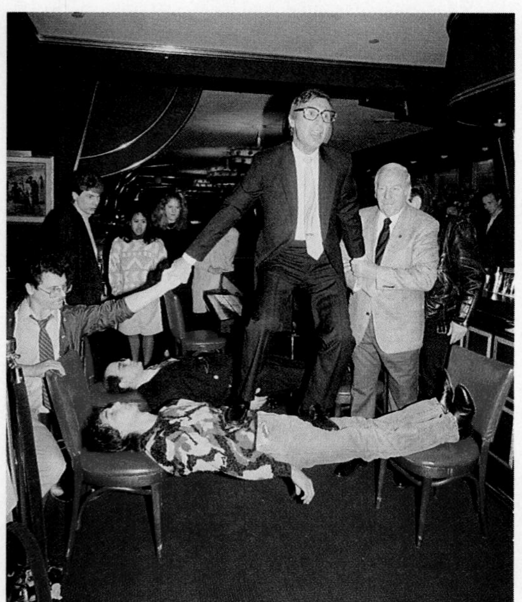

Amazing, right? Or maybe not. This stage hypnotist's audience believes that the man he's standing on can support his weight without flinching because he's hypnotized, but most unhypnotized people can do the same thing. The only way to find out if hypnosis produces unique results is to do research with control groups.

5. *Hypnosis does not increase the accuracy of memory.* Many people assume that hypnosis can help people accurately recall forgotten experiences. Sometimes hypnosis *can* be used successfully to jog the memories of crime victims. After the 1976 kidnapping of a busload of schoolchildren in Chowchilla, California, the bus driver was able under hypnosis to recall all but one of the license-plate numbers on the kidnappers' car. That clue provided a breakthrough in the investigation. But in other cases, hypnotized witnesses, despite feeling confident about their memories, have been completely mistaken. Although hypnosis does sometimes boost the amount of information recalled, it also increases *errors*, perhaps because hypnotized people are more willing than others to guess, or because they mistake vividly imagined possibilities for actual memories (Dinges et al., 1992; Kihlstrom, 1994; Nash & Nadon, 1997). Because pseudomemories and errors are so common in hypnotically induced recall, the American Psychological Association and the American Medical Association oppose the use of "hypnotically refreshed" testimony in courts of law.

6. *Hypnosis does not produce a literal reexperiencing of long-ago events.* When Michael Yapko (1994), a clinical psychologist who uses hypnosis in his own practice, surveyed 869 members of the American Association of Marriage and Family Therapists, he discovered that more than half believed that "hypnosis can be used to recover memories from as far back as birth." This belief is dead wrong.

EXAMINE THE EVIDENCE

Under hypnosis, Jim cheerfully describes the chocolate cake at his fourth birthday and Joan remembers a former life as a twelfth-century French peasant. But lemon cake was served at Jim's party and Joan can't speak twelfth-century French. How can we account for these vivid but incorrect memories? What is really going on during hypnosis?

Michael Nash (1987), who reviewed six decades of scientific research on hypnotic age regression, found that when people are regressed to an earlier age, their mental and moral performance remains "essentially adult in nature." Their brain-wave patterns and reflexes do not become childish; they do not show any signs of outgrown emotional disorders; they do not reason as children do or show child-sized IQs. It is true that they may use baby talk or report that they feel 4 years old again. But the reason is not that they *are* 4; they are just willing to play the role. They will do the same when they are hypnotically *progressed* ahead—say, to age 70 or 80—or regressed to "past lives." Their belief that they are 7 or 70 or 7,000 years old may be sincere and convincing, but it is based on elaborate fantasy and role playing.

In a fascinating program of research that dramatically demonstrated how fantasy and role playing can lead to false memories under hypnosis, Nicholas Spanos and his colleagues (Spanos, Menary, et al., 1991) directed hypnotized Canadian university students to regress past their own births to previous lives. About a third of the students reported they could do so. But when they were asked, while supposedly "reliving" a past life, to name the leader of their country, say whether the country was at peace or at war, or describe the money used in their community, the students could not do it. One young man, who thought he was Julius Caesar, said the year was 50 A.D. and he was emperor of Rome—but Caesar died in 44 B.C. and was never crowned emperor, and besides, dating years as A.D. or B.C. did not begin until several centuries later.

7. *Hypnotic suggestions are not just placebos; they have been used effectively for many medical and psychological purposes.* For example, hypnotic suggestions have been used to get rid of headaches; anesthetize people undergoing dental work, surgery, or childbirth; eliminate unwanted habits such as smoking or nail biting; improve study skills; reduce nausea in cancer patients undergoing chemotherapy; pump up the confidence of athletes; and reduce severe pain (Kirsch, Montgomery, & Saperstein, 1995; Stam, 1989).

THEORIES OF HYPNOSIS

For many years, the leading explanation for hypnosis was that it produces a true altered state, different subjectively and objectively from normal wakefulness. However, no identifiable markers, either physiological or in subjective self-report, have ever been found to characterize such a state (Kirsch & Lynn, 1995). Hypnotic inductions do not produce predictable changes in brain waves, eye movements, skin resistance, or any other measurable response.

Ernest Hilgard, who studied hypnosis for many years, has argued that such responses are not critical for concluding that hypnosis differs from ordinary waking consciousness. After all, he notes, scientists readily accepted the reality of dreams and the existence of sleep as a separate state before anyone knew about REM stages or EEG patterns. Hilgard's own belief is that hypnosis, like lucid dreams and even simple distraction, involves *dissociation*, a split in consciousness in which one part of the mind operates independently of another (Hilgard, 1977, 1986). In many hypnotized persons, says Hilgard, only one of the parts goes along with the hypnotic suggestion. The other part is like a *hidden observer*, watching but not participating. Unless given special instructions, the hypnotized person remains unaware of the observer.

Hilgard attempted to question the hidden observer directly. For example, he and his colleagues had their hypnotized subjects submerge an arm in ice water for several seconds, an experience that is normally excruciating. They told the subjects that they would feel no pain, but that the nonsubmerged hand would be able to signal the level of any hidden pain by pressing a key. In this situation, many people said they felt little or no pain while their free hand was busily pressing one of the keys. After coming "out" of hypnosis, these people continued to insist that they were pain-free—unless the hypnotist asked the hidden observer to issue a separate report.

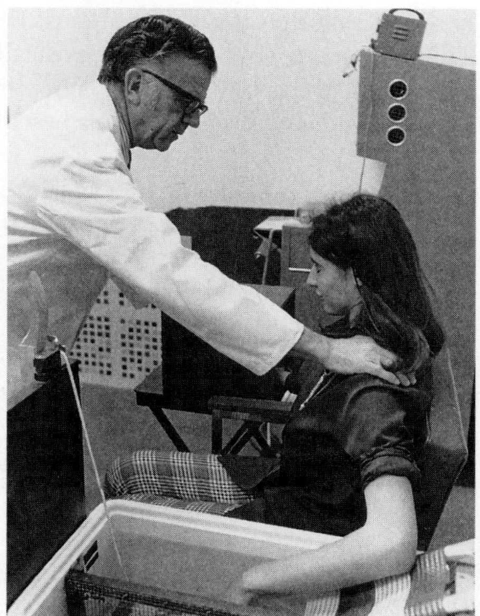

A person whose arm is immersed in ice water ordinarily feels intense pain. But Ernest Hilgard, a pioneer in hypnosis research, found that when hypnotized people are told the pain will be minimal, they report little or no discomfort. Like the young woman shown here in one of Hilgard's studies, they seem unperturbed.

One appealing aspect of explanations based on dissociation is that they fit in well with recent research on nonconscious mental processing (see Chapters 6 and 8). They are also consistent with recent brain theories, which propose that one part of the brain operates as an interpreter and reporter of activities carried out unconsciously by other brain parts (see Chapter 4).

Nevertheless, many psychologists believe that there is less to the hypnotic state than meets the eye. Some flat-out reject the idea that hypnosis produces a special state at all, noting that no objective method exists to verify that the hypnotized person is in such a state. If a hypnotist suggests that a person hold an arm out rigidly and the person does so, all that really tells us is that the person is suggestible (Barber, 1979; Weitzenhoffer, 1995). In fact, the very notion of a hypnotic state is circular: How do we know that a person is hypnotized? Because he or she obeys the hypnotist's suggestions. And why does the person obey those suggestions? Because the person is hypnotized!

Some researchers hold *sociocognitive explanations* of what happens under hypnosis, regarding the behavior of the hypnotized person as falling along a continuum of normal social and cognitive processes (Spanos, 1991). In this view, the effects of hypnosis result from an interaction between the personal abilities and beliefs of the subject and the social influence of the hypnotist. The hypnotized person is basically playing the part of a hypnotized person, a part that has analogies in ordinary life, where we willingly submit to the suggestions of parents, teachers, doctors, therapists, and television commercials (Sarbin, 1991; Sarbin & Coe, 1972). The person is not merely faking or playacting, however; the role of hypnotized person, like many other social roles, is so engrossing and involving that actions required by the role may occur without conscious intent. Thus a person who has been instructed to fake a hypnotic state to fool an observer will tend to overplay the role and will stop playing it as soon as the observer leaves the room, whereas hypnotized subjects will continue to follow the hypnotic suggestions even when they think they are not being watched (Kirsch et al., 1989; Spanos et al., 1993).

Sociocognitive views, which emphasize the importance of the qualities of the individual interacting with the suggestions of the hypnotist, explain why some people under hypnosis report spirit possession or "memories" of alien abductions (Baker, 1992; Spanos, 1996). Such persons may have a need to "escape the self" by turning control over to someone else (Newman & Baumeister, 1994). Often, the hypnotist readily assumes such control, shaping the person's story by giving subtle and not-so-subtle hints about what the person should say. Here is an exchange between one therapist who believes in UFO abductions and a supposed abductee who has been hypnotized (from Fiore, 1989, quoted in Newman & Baumeister, 1994):

Dr. Fiore: Now I'm going to ask you a few questions at this point. You will remember everything because you want to remember. When you were being poked everywhere, did they do any kind of vaginal examination?

Sandi: I don't think they did.

Dr. Fiore: Now you're going to let yourself know if they put a needle in any part of your body, other than the rectum.

Sandi: No. They were carrying needles around, big ones, and I was scared for a while they were going to put one in me, but they didn't. [*Body tenses.*]

Dr. Fiore: Now just let yourself relax. At the count of three you're going to remember whether they did put one of those big needles in you. If they did, know that you're safe, and it's all over, isn't it? And if they didn't, you're going to remember that too, at the count of three. One . . . two . . . three.

Sandi: They did.

Similarly, in the studies of past-life regression mentioned earlier, the students who believed they were reliving a past life fulfilled the requirements of the role—by weaving events, places, and persons from their present lives into their accounts. Their descriptions and their acceptance of their regression experiences as real were also influenced by what the hypnotist told them. The researchers concluded that the act of "remembering" another "self" involves the construction of a fantasy that accords not only with the rememberer's own beliefs but also with the beliefs of others—in this case, the authoritative hypnotist (Spanos, Menary, et al., 1991).

Theorists who think of hypnosis as a state of consciousness or a special process and those who emphasize sociocognitive explanations agree on many issues. They agree, for example, that hypnosis does *not* create a *unique* altered state in which people can do extraordinary things, memories become sharper, or early experiences can be replayed with perfect accuracy. Irving Kirsch and Steven Jay Lynn (1995), in reviewing the spirited debate that infuses the study of hypnosis today, note that most researchers also attribute the impressive effects of hypnosis to a combination of social influences and the personal abilities and efforts of the hypnotized person, and not to a mysterious "trance." Whatever hypnosis is, by studying it, psychologists are learning much about human suggestibility, the power of imagination, and the way we perceive the present and remember the past.

"THE WITNESS HAS BARKED, MEOWED AND GIVEN US FIVE MINUTES OF BABY TALK. I'D SAY HYPNOSIS IS NOT THE ANSWER."

Quick Quiz

A. True or false:

1. A hypnotized person is usually aware of what is going on and remembers the experience later.
2. Hypnosis gives us special powers that we do not ordinarily have.
3. Hypnosis reduces errors in memory.
4. Hypnotized people play no active part in their behavior and thoughts.
5. According to Hilgard, hypnosis is a state of consciousness involving a "hidden observer."
6. Sociocognitive theorists view hypnosis as mere faking or conscious playacting.

B. Some people believe that hypnotic suggestions can bolster the immune system and even help cure cancer. However, findings on this issue, mostly case reports, are contradictory, and positive results have been hard to replicate (Stam, 1989). One therapist dismissed this problem by saying that a negative result just means that the hypnotist lacks skill or the right personality. As a critical thinker, can you spot what's wrong with his reasoning? (Think back to the qualities of the ideal scientist discussed in Chapter 2.)

Answers:

A. 1. true 2. false 3. false 4. false 5. true 6. false B. The therapist's argument violates the principle of falsifiability. If a result is positive, he counts it as evidence. But if a result is negative, he refuses to count it as counterevidence ("Maybe the hypnotist just wasn't good enough"). With this kind of reasoning, there is no way to tell whether the hypothesis is right or wrong.

As we have seen in this chapter, fluctuations and changes in consciousness, though interesting in and of themselves, also show us how people's expectations and explanations of their own mental and physical states affect what they do and how they feel. Under scientific scrutiny, biological rhythms, dreams, drug-induced states, and hypnosis—phenomena once thought beyond the pale of science—can deepen our understanding of the intimate relationship between body and mind.

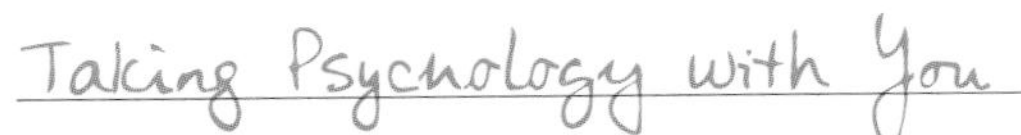

How to Get a Good Night's Sleep

You hop into bed, turn out the lights, close your eyes, and wait for slumber. An hour later, you're still waiting. Finally you drop off, but at 3:00 A.M., to your chagrin, you're awake again. By the time the rooster crows, you have put in a hard day's night.

Insomnia affects most people at one time or another—and many people most of the time. In search of relief, Americans spend hundreds of millions of dollars each year on sleeping aids. Usually, their money is not well spent. Most over-the-counter pills are almost worthless for inducing sleep, and some prescription drugs can actually make matters worse. Barbiturates greatly suppress REM sleep, a result that eventually causes wakefulness, and they also suppress Stages 3 and 4, the deeper stages of sleep. Other medications, known as benzodiazepines, lead to tolerance more slowly, but they produce a breakdown product that stays in the body during the day and causes diminished alertness and hand–eye coordination problems (Kelly, 1981). Melatonin supplements may help some people, but no one knows what dosages are safe and effective. Most physicians prescribe sleeping remedies for only very short periods of time. Said one well-known sleep researcher, "Let me put a person on sleeping pills for a month, and I'll guarantee broken sleep" (Webb, quoted in Goleman, 1982). Sleep research suggests better alternatives:

- *Be sure you actually have a sleep problem.* Many people only *think* they don't sleep well. People complaining of insomnia often greatly overestimate how long it takes them to nod off and underestimate how much sleep they actually get (Bonnet, 1990). In one study, 55 people reporting for help at a sleep clinic were observed for several nights in the laboratory. Most of them took less than 30 minutes to fall asleep. Only 30 got less than $6\frac{1}{2}$ hours of sleep per night, and only 26 were awake for a total of more than 30 minutes during the night (Carskadon, Mitler, & Dement, 1974).

The amount of time spent sleeping is not a good criterion of insomnia in any case. Many people need more than the standard eight hours of sleep, and some research suggests that most of us would be more alert during the day if we could sleep longer at night (Dement, 1992). On the other hand, some people get by on as little as three or four hours. As people age, they typically sleep more lightly, and they often break up sleep into nighttime slumber and an afternoon nap. Young people, too, can benefit from napping, which many researchers feel is biologically beneficial. The real test for diagnosing a sleep deficit is how you feel during the day. Do you doze off without intending to? Do you feel drowsy at meetings or in class? If you function well with less sleep than most people get, you probably shouldn't worry, since worrying itself can cause insomnia.

• *Get a correct diagnosis of the sleep problem.* Once you know you have a problem, you need to identify the cause. Disruption of sleep can result from psychological disturbances, such as depression, and from physical disorders. In *sleep apnea,* breathing periodically stops for a few moments, causing the person to choke and gasp. Breathing may stop hundreds of times a night, often without the person knowing it, and chronic apnea may lead to high blood pressure or irregular heartbeat. Sleep apnea has several causes, from blockage of air passages to failure of the brain to control respiration correctly. In *narcolepsy,* another serious disorder, an individual is subject to irresistible and unpredictable daytime attacks of sleepiness lasting from 5 to 30 minutes. For reasons not yet clear, narcoleptics often lapse immediately into REM sleep, even during the briefest naps. A quarter of a million people in the United States alone suffer from this condition, many without knowing it.

• *Avoid excessive use of alcohol or other drugs.* Many drugs interfere with sleep. For instance, coffee, tea, cola, and chocolate all contain caffeine, which is a stimulant; alcohol suppresses REM sleep; and tranquilizers such as Valium and Librium reduce Stage 4 sleep.

• *Don't associate the bedroom with wakefulness.* When environmental cues are repeatedly associated with some behavior, they can come to trigger the behavior (Bootzin, Epstein, & Wood, 1991). If you don't want your bedroom to trigger wakefulness, avoid reading, studying, and watching TV there. Also avoid lying awake for hours waiting for sleep because your frustration will cause arousal that can be associated with the bedroom. If you can't sleep, get up and do something else, preferably something dull and relaxing, in another room. When you feel drowsy, try sleeping again.

• *Take care of your health.* As your grandmother probably told you, good health habits are important for good sleep. Nutrition is one area to watch. The amino acid tryptophan promotes the onset of sleep, and other dietary elements may also influence alertness and relaxation. Exercise during the day also enhances sleep, but it should be avoided right before bedtime because in the short term it heightens alertness.

Finally, because much if not most insomnia is related to anxiety and worry, it makes sense to get to the source of your problems. You can't expect to sleep well with stress hormones pouring through your bloodstream and worries crowding your mind. In an evolutionary sense, sleeplessness is an adaptive response to danger and threat. As Woody Allen once said, "The lamb and the lion shall lie down together, but the lamb will not be very sleepy." When your anxieties decrease, so may your sleepless nights.

SUMMARY

BIOLOGICAL RHYTHMS: THE TIDES OF EXPERIENCE

1) *Consciousness* is the awareness of oneself and the environment. *States of consciousness,* which are distinct patterns of consciousness, are often associated with *biological rhythms*—periodic fluctuations in physiological functioning. These rhythms are typically *entrained* (synchronized) to external cues, but many are also *endogenous,* generated from within. *Circadian* fluctuations occur about once a day; *infradian* rhythms are longer; and *ultradian* rhythms are shorter, often occurring on about a 90-minute cycle.

2) When people are allowed to "free-run," living in isolation from all time cues, they tend to live a day that is slightly longer than 24 hours. Circadian rhythms are governed by a biological "clock" in the *suprachiasmatic nucleus (SCN)* of the hypothalamus. The SCN is affected by the hormone *melatonin,* which is responsive to changes in light and dark, and increases during the dark hours. When a person's normal routine changes, the person may experience *internal desynchronization,* in which the usual circadian rhythms are thrown out of phase with one another.

3) Folklore holds that moods follow infradian cycles. Some people do show a recurrence of depression every winter, in a pattern that has been labeled *seasonal affective disorder* (SAD). However, this pattern may or may not be endogenous. No biological cause has been identified, and it has been difficult to rule out placebo effects in the most common treatment, phototherapy.

4) One infradian rhythm that is endogenous is the menstrual cycle, during which various hormones rise and fall predictably. Physical symptoms associated with the cycle usually have a biological cause, but well-controlled (double-blind) studies on "PMS" do not support claims that emotional symptoms are reliably and universally tied to the menstrual cycle. Overall, women and men do not differ in the emotional symptoms they report or in the number of mood swings they experience over the course of a month. Expectations and learning affect how we interpret bodily and emotional changes. Few people of either sex are likely to undergo dramatic monthly mood swings or personality changes because of hormones.

5) Sleep, which recurs on a circadian rhythm, seems to be necessary not only for bodily restoration but also for normal brain function. During sleep, periods of *rapid eye movement,* or *REM,* alternate with non-REM sleep in an ultradian rhythm. Non-REM sleep is divided into four stages on the basis of characteristic brain-wave patterns. During REM sleep, the brain is active, and there are other signs of arousal, yet most of the skeletal muscles are limp; dreams are reported most often during REM sleep.

EXPLORING THE DREAM WORLD

6) The psychoanalytic explanation of dreams is that they allow us to gratify forbidden or unrealistic wishes and desires that have been forced into the unconscious part of the mind. In dreams, according to Freud, thoughts and objects are disguised as symbolic images. Most psychologists today accept the notion that dreams are more than incoherent ramblings of the mind, but many psychologists quarrel with specific psychoanalytic interpretations.

7) The problem-solving explanation of dreams emphasizes the opportunity that dreams provide for working through emotional issues, especially during times of crisis. Findings on the dreams of divorced people provide support for this explanation.

8) Another view holds that dreams are the by-product of mental housekeeping. According to this information-processing approach, dreams are merely random snippets from an ongoing process that is otherwise inaccessible to consciousness. During sleep, the brain may scan and sort through new data, or unneeded synaptic associations in the brain may be weakened. REM sleep has also been associated with the consolidation of memories, during which the synaptic changes associated with a recently stored memory become durable and stable.

9) The *activation–synthesis theory* of dreaming holds that dreams occur when the cortex tries to make sense of spontaneous neural firing initiated in the pons. The resulting interpretation, or synthesis of the signals with existing knowledge and memories, is the dream. In this view, which has been supported by physiological evidence, dreams do not disguise unconscious wishes, but they can reveal a person's perceptions, conflicts, and concerns.

CONSCIOUSNESS-ALTERING DRUGS

10) In all cultures, people have found ways to produce *altered states of consciousness.* For example, *psychoactive drugs* alter cognition and emotion by acting on neurotransmitters in the brain. Most psychoactive drugs are classified as *stimulants, depressants, opiates,* or *psychedelics,* depending on their central nervous system effects and their impact on behavior and mood. However, two common drugs, anabolic steroids and marijuana, fall outside these categories. The use of some psychoactive drugs leads to *tolerance,* in which increasing dosages are needed for the same effect, and *withdrawal symptoms* if an addict tries to quit.

11) The effects of a psychoactive drug cannot be explained solely in terms of its chemical properties. Reactions to a drug are also influenced by the user's physical condition, prior experience with the drug, environmental setting, and *mental set*—the person's expectations and motives for taking the drug. Expectations and beliefs about drugs are affected by a person's culture. People often find it difficult to distinguish abuse from use and to think critically about research findings on drug effects.

THE RIDDLE OF HYPNOSIS

12) *Hypnosis* is a procedure in which the practitioner suggests changes in the sensations, perceptions, thoughts, feelings, or behavior of the subject. Hypnotic responsiveness depends more on the efforts and qualities of the person being hypnotized than on the skill of the hypnotist. Although hypnosis has been used successfully for many medical and psychological purposes, it does not produce special abilities. Although hypnosis can sometimes improve memory for facts about real events, it also results in confusion between fact and vividly imagined possibilities. Therefore, "hypnotically refreshed" accounts are often full of errors and pseudomemories.

13) Some researchers believe that hypnosis involves a split in consciousness. Others regard it as a product of normal social and cognitive processes, a form of role playing in which the hypnotized person uses active cognitive strategies, including imagination, to comply with the hypnotist's suggestions. The role is so engrossing that the person interprets it as real.

14) Sociocognitive processes can account for hypnotized subjects' apparent age and past-life "regressions," and their reports of alien abductions; they are simply playing a role based on fantasy, imagination, and suggestion.

KEY TERMS

consciousness 162
states of consciousness 162
biological rhythm 162
entrainment 163
endogenous 163
circadian rhythm 163
infradian rhythm 163
ultradian rhythm 163
free-running 164
suprachiasmatic nucleus (SCN) 164
melatonin 164
internal desynchronization 165
menstrual cycle 167
"premenstrual syndrome (PMS)" 167
rapid eye movement (REM) sleep 173
non-REM sleep 173
alpha waves 173
delta waves 173
lucid dream 176
psychoanalytic theory of dreams 177
manifest versus latent content of dreams 177

problem-solving approach to dreams 177

mental-housekeeping approach to dreams 178

activation–synthesis theory of dreams 179

altered states of consciousness 182

psychoactive drug 182

stimulants 183

depressants 184

opiates 184

psychedelic drugs 184

anabolic steroids 184

marijuana 184

tolerance 186

withdrawal symptoms 186

"think-drink" effect 187

hypnosis 190

hidden observer 194

sociocognitive theories of hypnosis 195

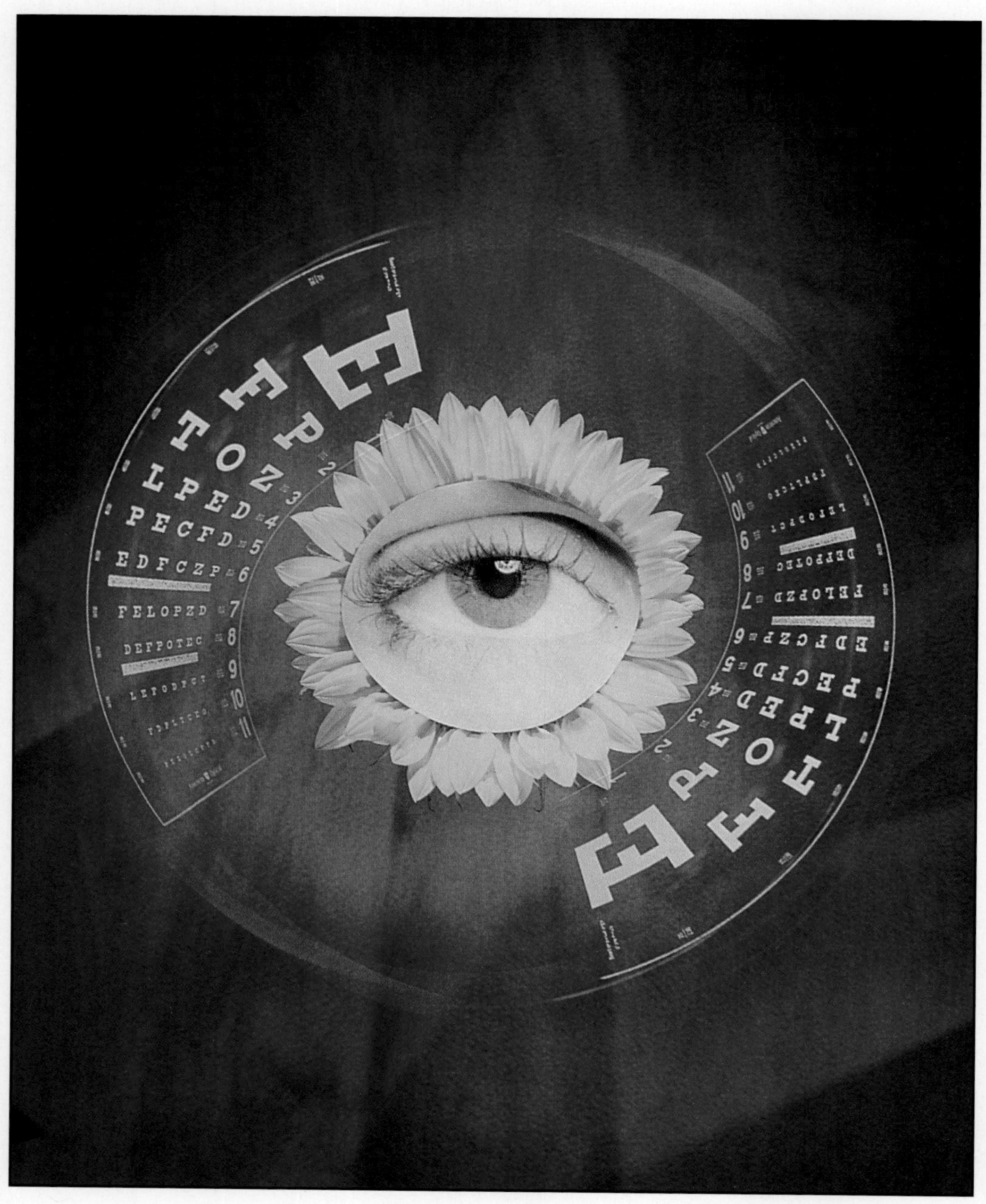

Nothing we use or hear or touch can be expressed
in words that equal what is given by the senses.

—Hannah Arendt

CHAPTER SIX

Sensation and Perception

WHEN HE WAS ONLY 10 MONTHS OLD, S. B. went blind. An infection damaged his corneas, the transparent membranes on the front surfaces of the eyes, leaving him sightless. As he grew into adulthood, S. B. adjusted well to his disability; a cheerful and independent man, he married, supported himself, and led an active life. But through the years, he continued to dream of regaining his sight.

At last, when S. B. was 52, a doctor successfully performed corneal transplant surgery. Almost as soon as the bandages were removed, S. B. was able to identify common objects and letters of the alphabet. Within days, he could make his way down corridors without touching the walls and could even tell time from a large wall clock. But strange gaps existed in his visual world. Although S. B.'s eyes now functioned well, he seemed blind to objects or parts of objects that he had never touched. He could not read facial expressions well or recognize pictures of scenery. Gradually, his visual abilities improved, yet months after surgery his perception of the world remained limited and distorted by his previous sensory experiences. When asked to draw a bus, he produced the sketch in the margin—leaving out the front end, which he had never felt with his hands. In many ways, S. B. continued to lead the life of a blind man until his death three years after the operation (Gregory & Wallace, 1963).

S. B.'s story is unusual, but it contains some important lessons for us all. Like S. B., we all depend on our senses for our everyday understanding of physical reality. Also like S. B., we have only a partial perception of that reality. Even with normal eyesight and hearing, we are blind to most of the electromagnetic energy waves around us and deaf to most of the pressure waves that fill the air. And because of expectations shaped by our previous experiences, even with normal sensory abilities, we may look but not see, listen but not hear.

Yet despite these limitations, our sensory and perceptual capacities are astonishingly complex and sensitive. In this chapter, you will learn how your sense organs take in information from the environment and how your brain interprets and organizes that information to construct a model of the world. The boundary between these two processes is not always easy to draw because they occur so quickly and because some organization occurs even before incoming signals reach the brain. However, as a way of conceptualizing what is going on, psychologists have traditionally called the first process *sensation* and the second *perception.*

Sensation is the detection of physical energy emitted or reflected by physical objects. The cells that do the detecting, called **sense receptors,** are located in the *sense organs*—the eyes, ears, tongue, nose, skin, and internal body tissues. The receptors for smell, pressure, pain, and temperature are structural extensions (dendrites) of sensory neurons. The receptors for vision, hearing, and taste are distinct cells separated from sensory neurons by synapses. Sensory processes produce an immediate awareness of sound, color, form, and other building blocks of consciousness. They tell us what is happening, both inside our bodies and in the world beyond our own skins.

Without sensation, we would lose touch—literally—with reality. Yet sensation alone is not sufficient for making sense of the world impinging on our senses; for that, we also need **perception,** the set of processes that organize and interpret sensory impulses. Perception tells us where one object begins and another ends, and it assembles the features of sensory experience into meaningful patterns. Our sense of vision produces a two-dimensional image on the back of the eye, but we *perceive* the world in three dimensions. Our sense of hearing brings us the sound of a C, an E, and a G played simultaneously on the piano, but we *perceive* a C-major chord.

sensation The detection of physical energy emitted or reflected by physical objects; it occurs when energy in the external environment or the body stimulates receptors in the sense organs.

sense receptors Specialized cells that convert physical energy in the environment or the body to electrical energy that can be transmitted as nerve impulses to the brain.

perception The process by which the brain organizes and interprets sensory information.

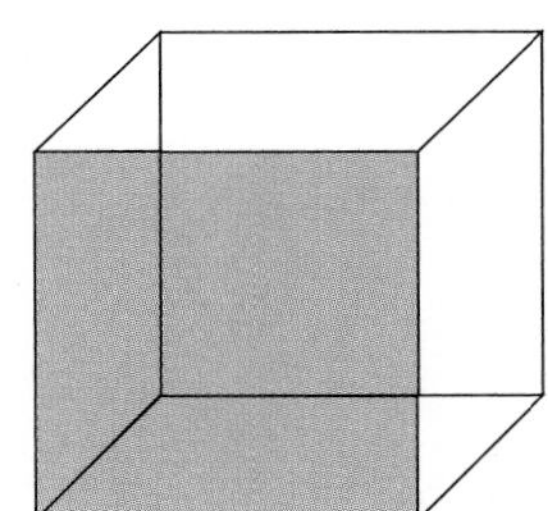

Look at the drawing of the cube in the margin. If you stare at the cube, it will flip-flop in front of your eyes. The surface on the outside and front will suddenly be on the inside and back, or vice versa. Sensory receptors at the back of your eyes detect black lines on a field of white, but because your brain can interpret the sensory image in alternative ways, you *perceive* two different cubes. The ambiguity is not only in the picture but also in the eye (actually, the brain) of the beholder. Something similar happens when you repeat certain speech sounds. Say the word "say" over and over again. "Say" will soon become "ace," and then "ace" will shift back to "say." The sound signal does not change, only your perception of it.

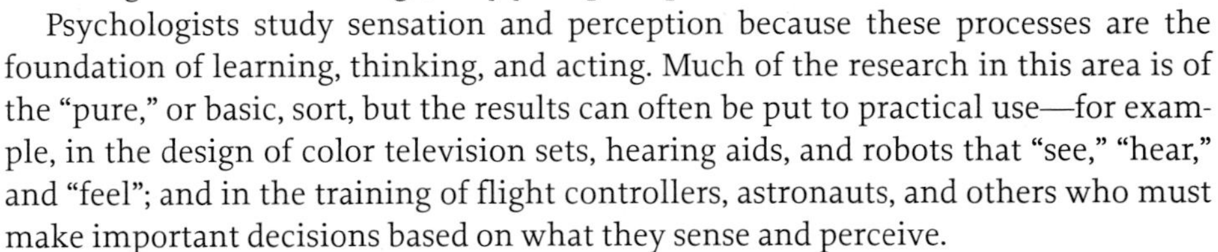

Psychologists study sensation and perception because these processes are the foundation of learning, thinking, and acting. Much of the research in this area is of the "pure," or basic, sort, but the results can often be put to practical use—for example, in the design of color television sets, hearing aids, and robots that "see," "hear," and "feel"; and in the training of flight controllers, astronauts, and others who must make important decisions based on what they sense and perceive.

OUR SENSATIONAL SENSES

At some point you probably learned that there are five senses, corresponding to five sense organs: vision (eyes), hearing (ears), taste (tongue), touch (skin), and smell (nose). The senses have been categorized in this way at least since Aristotle's time. Actually, however, there are more than five senses, though scientists disagree about the exact number. The skin, which is the organ of touch or pressure, also senses heat, cold, and pain, not to mention itching and tickling. The ear, which is the organ of hearing, also contains receptors that account for a sense of balance. The skeletal muscles contain receptors responsible for a sense of bodily movement.

All of our senses evolved to help us survive. Even pain, which causes so much human misery, is an indispensable part of our evolutionary heritage, for it alerts us to illness and injury. In rare cases, people have been born without a sense of pain. Although free of the hurts and aches that plague the rest of us, they lead difficult lives. Because they feel none of pain's warnings, they burn, bruise, and cut themselves more than other people do. One young woman developed inflamed joints because she failed to turn over in her sleep or to shift her weight while standing, acts that people with normal pain sensation perform automatically. At the age of only 29, she died from massive infections, due in part to skin and bone injuries (Melzack, 1973).

Sensory experiences contribute immeasurably to the quality of life, even when they are not directly helping us survive. They entertain us, amuse us, soothe us, inspire us. If we really pay attention to our senses, said poet William Wordsworth, we can "see into the life of things" and hear "the still, sad music of humanity."

THE RIDDLE OF SEPARATE SENSATIONS

Sensation begins with the sense receptors. When these receptors detect an appropriate stimulus—light, mechanical pressure, or chemical molecules—they convert the energy of the stimulus into electrical impulses that travel along nerves to the brain. This conversion of one form of energy into another is known as **transduction.** Sense receptors are biological transducers. Radio receivers, which convert radio waves into sound waves, are mechanical transducers, as are Geiger counters, television sets, and electronic eyes.

transduction The conversion of one form of energy to another; sensory receptors are biological transducers.

Sense receptors are like military scouts who scan the terrain for signs of activity and relay a message when they detect something. These scouts cannot make many decisions on their own. They must transmit what they learn to field officers—sensory neurons in the peripheral nervous system. The field officers in turn must report to generals at a command center—the cells of the brain. The generals are responsible for analyzing the reports, combining information brought in by different scouts, and deciding what it all means.

The "field officers" in the sensory system all use exactly the same form of communication, a neural impulse. It is as if they must all send their messages on a bongo drum and can only go "boom." How, then, are we able to experience so many different kinds of sensations? The answer is that the nervous system *encodes* the messages, using two basic kinds of code. One kind, which is *anatomical,* was first described as far back as 150 A.D. by the Greek physician Galen, and in 1826 the German physiologist Johannes Müller elaborated on it in his *doctrine of specific nerve energies.* According to this doctrine, different sensory modalities exist because signals received by the sense organs stimulate different nerve pathways, which terminate in different areas of the brain. Signals from the eye cause impulses to travel along the optic nerve to the visual cortex. Signals from the ear cause impulses to travel along the auditory nerve to the auditory cortex. Light and sound waves produce different sensations because of these anatomical differences.

Although some of the physiological details proposed by Müller have since been shown to be wrong, his fundamental concept is generally correct. The doctrine of specific nerve energies implies that what we know about the world ultimately reduces to what we know about the state of our own nervous system. Therefore, if sound waves could stimulate nerves that end in the visual part of the brain, we would "see" sound. In fact, a similar sort of crossover does occur when you close your right eye, press lightly on the right side of the lid, and "see" a flash of light seemingly coming from the left. The pressure produces an impulse that travels up the optic nerve to the visual area in the right side of the brain, where it is interpreted as coming from the left side of the visual field.

Anatomical encoding, however, does not completely solve the riddle of separate sensations. It accounts well for our ability to distinguish visual from auditory signals, but linking the different skin senses to distinct nerve pathways has proven difficult. The doctrine of specific nerve energies also fails to explain variations of experience within a particular sense—the sight of pink versus red, the sound of a piccolo versus the sound of a tuba, or the feel of a pinprick versus the feel of a kiss. An additional kind of code is therefore necessary.

This second kind of code has been called *functional* (Schneider & Tarshis, 1986). Functional codes rely on the fact that particular receptors and neurons fire, or are inhibited from firing, only in the presence of specific sorts of stimuli. At any particular time, then, some cells in the nervous system are firing, and some are not. Information about *which* cells are firing, *how many* cells are firing, the *rate* at which cells are firing, and the *patterning* of each cell's firing constitutes a functional code. You might think of such a code as the neurological equivalent of the Morse code. Functional encoding may occur all along a sensory route, starting in the sense organs and ending in the brain. As we will see, much remains to be learned about how functional encoding allows us to form an overall perception of an object.

MEASURING THE SENSES

Just how sensitive are our senses? The answer comes from the field of **psychophysics,** which is concerned with how the physical properties of stimuli are related to our psychological experience of them. Drawing on principles from both physics and psychology, psychophysicists have studied how the strength or intensity of a stimulus affects the strength of sensation in an observer.

psychophysics The area of psychology concerned with the relationship between physical properties of stimuli and sensory experience.

ABSOLUTE THRESHOLDS One way to find out how sensitive the senses are is to present people with a series of signals that vary in intensity and ask them to say which signals they can detect. The smallest amount of energy that a person can detect reliably is known as the **absolute threshold.** The word *absolute* is a bit misleading because people detect borderline signals on some occasions and miss them on others. "Reliable" detection is said to occur when a person can detect a signal 50 percent of the time.

If you were having your absolute threshold for brightness measured, you might be asked to sit in a dark room and look at a wall or screen. You would then be shown flashes of light varying in brightness, one flash at a time. Your task would be to say whether you noticed a flash. Some flashes you would never see. Some you would always see. And sometimes you would miss seeing a flash, even though you had noticed one of equal brightness on other trials. Such errors seem to occur in part because of random firing of cells in the nervous system, which produces fluctuating background noise, something like the background noise in a stereo system.

By studying absolute thresholds, psychologists have found that our senses are very sharp indeed. If you have normal sensory abilities, you can see a candle flame on a clear, dark night from 30 miles away. You can hear a ticking watch in a perfectly quiet room from 20 feet away. You can taste a teaspoon of sugar diluted in two gallons of water, smell a drop of perfume diffused through a three-room apartment, and feel the wing of a bee falling on your cheek from a height of 1 centimeter (Galanter, 1962).

Yet, despite these impressive sensory skills, our senses are tuned in to only a narrow band of physical energies. For example, as mentioned earlier, we are sensitive visually to only a tiny fraction of all electromagnetic energy (see Figure 6.1). Other species can pick up signals that we cannot. Dogs can detect high-frequency sound waves that are beyond our range, as you know if you have ever called your pooch with a "silent" doggie whistle. Bats and porpoises can hear sounds two octaves beyond our range. As we discuss in "Puzzles of Psychology," sensory differences among species raise some intriguing questions about the nature of reality.

absolute threshold The smallest quantity of physical energy that can be reliably detected by an observer.

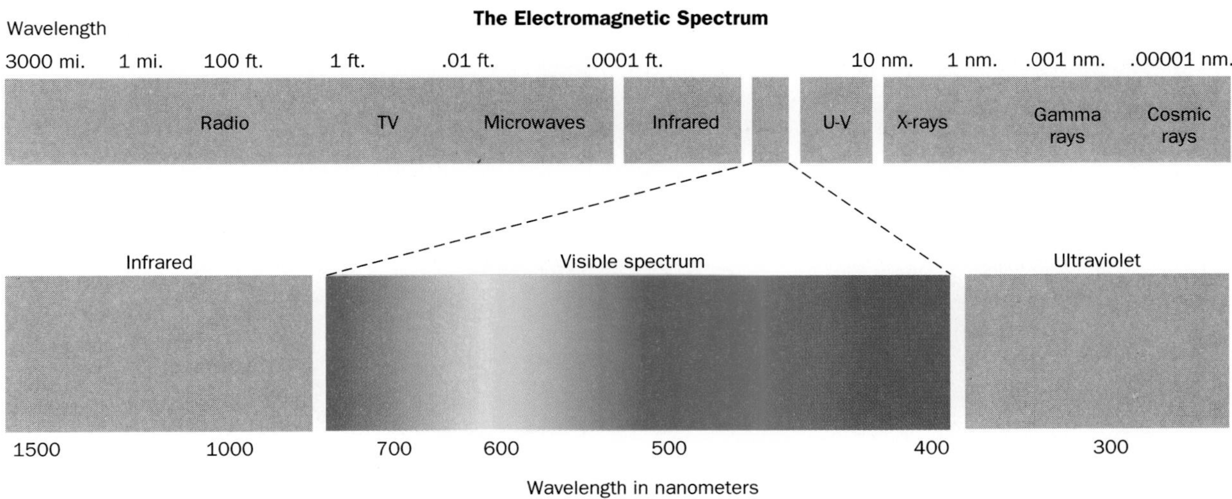

Figure 6.1
The Visible Spectrum of Electromagnetic Energy
Our visual system detects only a small fraction of the electromagnetic energy around us.

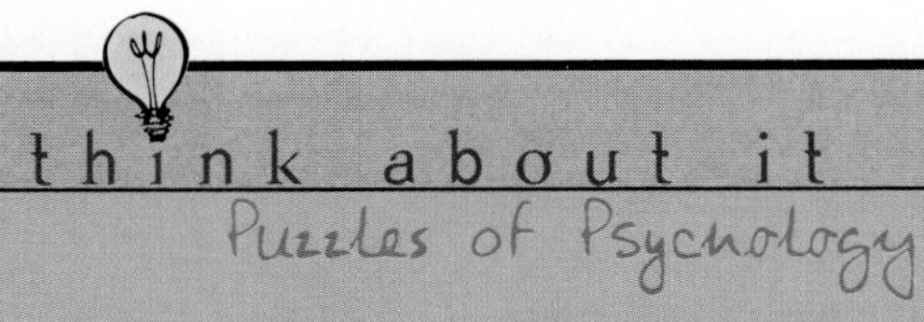

In Search of the Real World

Three baseball umpires were arguing about how to tell balls from strikes. The first said, "I calls 'em as I sees 'em." The second said, "I calls 'em as they is." The third said, "They ain't nothin' until I calls 'em!"

This old story raises an issue pondered by philosophers through the ages: Is reality "out there" in the environment or "in here" in a person's mind? Suppose a tree falls in the forest and there is no one around to hear the crash. Is there a noise? *Objectivists* say yes. They believe in the objective reality of a material world that exists completely apart from the perceiver. *Solipsists* (from the Latin words for "alone" and "self") say no. They argue that reality exists solely in the mind of the perceiver. For a solipsist, even the tree has no independent reality; it "ain't nothin' " until you perceive it. Psychologists usually take the middle ground in this debate. They accept that there is a physical reality: A falling tree disturbs air molecules and produces pressure waves. But they also recognize that hearing, like all sensations, is a subjective experience, and so *noise* cannot be said to occur unless someone experiences it.

Because sensation is a subjective experience, our ideas about reality must be affected by our sensory abilities and limitations. That is, things appear to us as they do not only because of *their* nature but also because of *ours*. If the entire human race were totally deaf, we might still talk about pressure waves, but we would have no concept of sound. Similarly, if we were all completely color-blind, we might still talk about the wavelengths of light, but we would have no concept of color.

The human way of sensing and perceiving the world is certainly not the only way. Because different species have different needs, their bodies are attuned to different aspects of physical reality than ours are. Bees are blind to red, but they can see ultraviolet light, which merely gives human beings a sunburn. Flowers that appear to us to be a single color must look patterned to a bee, because different parts of flowers reflect ultraviolet light to a different extent. The ultraviolet light gives fresher, nectar-laden flowers a different appearance than older flowers—useful information for a bee. Neither our perception nor the bee's is more "correct"; each system has evolved to meet the needs of the organism.

Some animal sensory systems seem to have no equivalent at all in human beings. Some fish apparently sense distortions of electrical fields through special receptors on the surface of their bodies (Kalmijn, 1982). Some snakes have an organ, in a pit on the head, that detects infrared rays. This organ permits them to sense heat given off by the bodies of their prey. The slightest change in temperature sends a message racing to the snake's brain. There the message is combined with information from the eyes, so that the snake actually sees an infrared pattern—and locates its prey with deadly accuracy, even in the dark (Newman & Hartline, 1982).

Our sensory windows on the world, then, are partly shuttered. But we can use reason, ingenuity, and technology to pry open those shutters. Ordinary perception tells us that the sun circles the earth, but the great astronomer Copernicus was able to figure out nearly five centuries ago that the opposite is true. Ordinary perception will never let us see ultraviolet and infrared rays directly (unless evolution or genetic engineering drastically changes the kind of organism we are), but we know they are there, and we can measure them.

If science can enable us to overturn the everyday evidence of our senses, who knows what surprises about "reality" are still in store for us? Think about it.

The flower on the left was photographed in normal light. The one on the right, photographed under ultraviolet light, is what a butterfly, equipped with ultraviolet receptors, might see. The hundreds of tiny bright spots are nectar sources.

DIFFERENCE THRESHOLDS Psychologists also study sensory sensitivity by having people compare two stimuli and judge whether they are the same or different. A subject might be asked to compare the weight of two blocks, the brightness of two lights, or the saltiness of two liquids. The smallest difference in stimulation that a person can detect reliably (again, half of the time) is called the **difference threshold,** or *just noticeable difference* (jnd). When you compare two stimuli, A and B, the difference threshold will depend on the intensity or size of A. The larger or more intense A is, the greater the change must be before you can detect a difference. If you are comparing the weights of two pebbles, you might be able to detect a difference of only a fraction of an ounce, but you would not be able to detect such a subtle difference if you were comparing two massive boulders.

According to **Weber's law** (named for Ernst Weber, who proposed it in the early 1800s), when a person compares two stimuli, the size of the change necessary to produce a jnd is a *constant proportion* of the original stimulus, as long as the stimuli are not too extreme. The value of the proportion, however, depends on which dimension is being measured. For example, if you are like most people, you will start to detect a change in loudness when the change is equal to one-tenth of the original stimulus—when the second stimulus is 10 percent louder or quieter than the first one. In contrast, you will detect a change in the brightness of light when the change is equivalent to only one-sixtieth of the original stimulus.

In everyday life, we may sometimes think we can detect a difference between stimuli when we can't. For example, many people say they prefer one of the two leading colas to the other, and ads often capitalize on that claim. Years ago, as a class project, undergraduate students at Williams College put cola preference claims to the test. They presented tasters with three glasses of cola, two of one leading brand and one of the other (or vice versa), and asked them which drink they liked most and least. Each taster was given three trials. Most of the tasters were inconsistent in their preferences, indicating that they had trouble telling the two brands apart (Solomon, 1979). Apparently, the difference between the two tastes exceeded the students' difference thresholds.

SIGNAL-DETECTION THEORY Despite their usefulness, the procedures we have described for measuring sensory thresholds have a serious limitation. Measurements for any given individual may be affected by the person's general tendency, when uncertain, to respond, "Yes, I noticed a signal (or a difference)" or "No, I didn't notice anything." Some people are habitual yea-sayers, willing to gamble that the signal was really there. Others are habitual naysayers, cautious and conservative. In addition, alertness, motives, and expectations can influence how a person responds on any given occasion. If you are in the shower and you're expecting an important call, you may think you heard the telephone ring when it didn't. In laboratory studies, when observers want to impress the experimenter, they may lean toward a positive response.

Fortunately, these problems of *response bias* are not insurmountable. According to **signal-detection theory,** an observer's response in a detection task can be divided into a *sensory process*, which depends on the intensity of the stimulus, and a *decision process*, which is influenced by the observer's response bias. Methods are available for separating these two components. For example, the researcher can include some trials ("catch trials") in which no stimulus is presented and others in which a weak stimulus is presented. Yea-sayers will have more "hits" than naysayers when a weak stimulus is presented, but they will also have more "false alarms" when no stimulus is presented. As the number of catch trials increases, people in general will become more likely to say "nay." All this information can be fed into a mathematical formula

difference threshold The smallest difference in stimulation that can be reliably detected by an observer when two stimuli are compared; also called *just noticeable difference (jnd).*

Weber's law A law of psychophysics stating that the change necessary to produce a just noticeable difference is a constant proportion of the original stimulus.

signal-detection theory A psychophysical theory that divides the detection of a sensory signal into a sensory process and a decision process.

that yields separate estimates of a person's response bias and sensory capacity. The individual's true sensitivity to a signal of any particular intensity can then be predicted.

The old method of measuring thresholds assumed that a person's ability to detect a stimulus depended solely on the stimulus. Signal-detection theory assumes that at any given moment, a person's sensitivity to a stimulus depends on a decision that he or she actively makes—that there is no single "threshold." Signal-detection methods have many real-world applications, from screening applicants for jobs requiring keen hearing to training air-traffic controllers, whose decisions about the presence or absence of a blip on a radar screen may mean the difference between life and death.

SENSORY ADAPTATION

Variety, they say, is the spice of life. It is also the essence of sensation, for our senses are designed to respond to change and contrast in the environment (see Figure 6.2). When a stimulus is unchanging or repetitious, sensation often fades or disappears. Receptors or nerve cells higher up in the sensory system get "tired" and fire less frequently. The resulting decline in sensory responsiveness is called **sensory adaptation.** Such adaptation is usually useful because it spares us from having to respond to unimportant information; for example, most of the time you have no need to feel your watch sitting on your wrist. Sometimes, however, adaptation can be hazardous, as when you no longer smell a gas leak that you noticed when you first entered the kitchen.

We never completely adapt to extremely intense stimuli—a terrible toothache, the odor of ammonia, the heat of the desert sun. And we rarely adapt completely to visual stimuli, whether they are weak or intense. Eye movements, voluntary and involuntary, cause the location of an object's image on the back of the eye to keep changing, so that visual receptors don't have a chance to "fatigue." But in the laboratory, researchers can stabilize the image of a simple pattern, such as a line, at a particular point on the back of a person's eye. They use an ingenious device consisting of a tiny projector mounted on a contact lens. Although the eyeball moves, the image of the object stays focused on the same receptors. In minutes, the image begins to disappear.

sensory adaptation The reduction or disappearance of sensory responsiveness that occurs when stimulation is unchanging or repetitious.

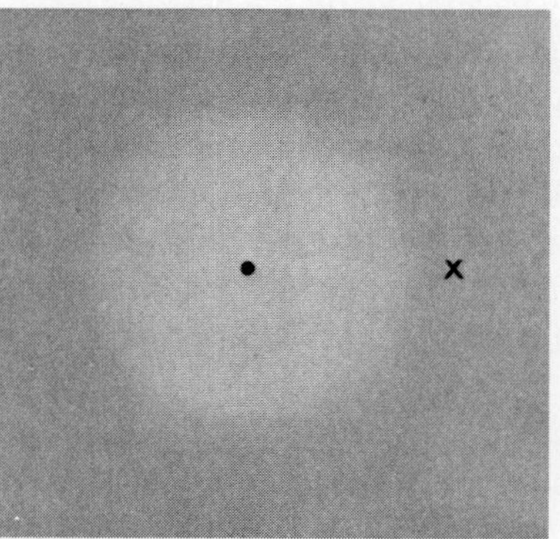

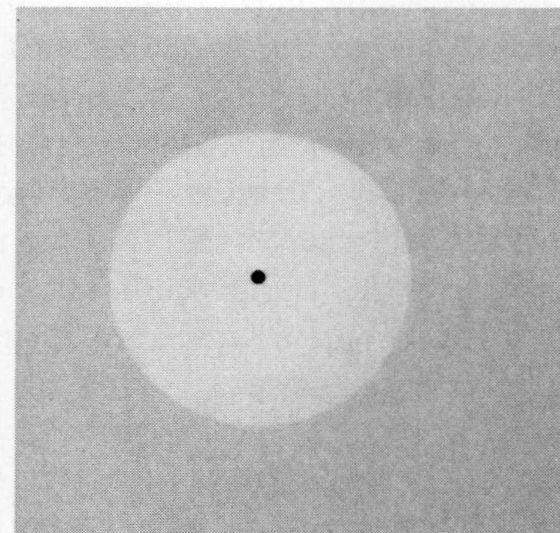

Figure 6.2
Now You See It, Now You Don't

Sensation depends on change and contrast in the environment. Hold your hand over one eye and stare steadily at the dot in the middle of the circle on the right. You should have no trouble maintaining an image of the circle. However, if you do the same with the circle on the left, the image will fade. The gradual change from light to dark does not provide enough contrast to keep the visual receptors in your eye firing at a steady rate. The circle reappears only if you close and reopen your eye or you shift your gaze to the X.

What would happen if our senses adapted to *most* incoming stimuli? Would we sense nothing, or would the brain substitute its own images for the sensory experiences no longer available by way of the sense organs? In early studies of **sensory deprivation,** researchers studied this question by isolating male volunteers from all patterned sight and sound. Vision was restricted by a translucent visor; hearing by a U-shaped pillow and by noise from an air conditioner and fan; and touch by cotton gloves and cardboard cuffs. The volunteers took brief breaks to eat and use the bathroom, but otherwise, they lay in bed, doing nothing. The results were dramatic. Within a few hours, many of the men felt edgy. Some were so disoriented that they quit the study the first day. Those who stayed longer became confused, restless, and grouchy. Many reported hallucinations—at first simple images, then more bizarre visions, such as a squadron of marching squirrels, or a procession of marching eyeglasses. Few men were willing to remain in the study for more than two or three days (Heron, 1957).

These findings made headlines, of course. But the notion that sensory deprivation is unpleasant or even dangerous turned out to be an oversimplification (Suedfeld, 1975). In many of the studies, the experimental procedures themselves probably aroused anxiety: Participants were told about "panic buttons" and were asked to sign "release from legal liability" forms. Later research, using better methods, showed that hallucinations are less dramatic and less disorienting than at first thought. In fact, many people enjoy time-limited periods of deprivation, and some perceptual and intellectual abilities actually improve. The response to sensory deprivation is affected by a person's expectations and interpretations of what is happening. Reduced sensation can be scary if you are locked in a room for an indefinite period but relaxing if you have retreated to that room voluntarily for a little time out—or if you are paying cash money for a session in a "relaxation chamber."

DON'T OVERSIMPLIFY

You're in a dark room, isolated from sight, sound, smell, and taste. Will you hallucinate and beg to be released, or will you find the experience restful and soothing? What might affect your reaction?

Still, it is clear that the human brain requires a minimum amount of sensory stimulation in order to function normally. This need may help explain why people

sensory deprivation The absence of normal levels of sensory stimulation.

The effects of sensory deprivation depend on the circumstances. Choosing to relax for an hour in a solitary flotation tank is one thing; being imprisoned in a dark cell, alone and against your will, is another.

who live alone often keep the radio or television set running continuously and why prolonged solitary confinement is experienced as a form of torture.

SENSORY OVERLOAD

If too little stimulation can be bad for you, so can too much. Excessive stimulation can lead to fatigue and mental confusion. If you have ever felt exhausted, nervous, and headachy after a day crammed with hectic activities—feeling you have too much to do with too little time to do it—then you know firsthand about sensory overload.

What would stock and commodity traders, who operate amid constant pandemonium, do without selective attention?

When people find themselves in a state of overload, they often cope by blocking out unimportant sights and sounds and focusing only on those they find interesting or useful. Psychologists have dubbed this the "cocktail party phenomenon" because at a cocktail party, a person typically focuses on just one conversation, ignoring other voices, the clink of ice cubes, music, and bursts of laughter across the room. The competing sounds all enter the nervous system, enabling the person to pick up anything important—even the person's own name, spoken by someone several yards away. Unimportant sounds, though, are not fully processed by the brain.

The capacity for **selective attention** protects us in daily life from being overwhelmed by all the sensory signals impinging on our receptors. The brain is not forced to respond to everything the sense receptors send its way. The "generals" in the brain can choose which "field officers" get past the command center's gates. Those that don't seem to have anything important to say are turned back.

Quick Quiz

If you're not overloaded, try answering these questions.

1. Even on the clearest night, some stars cannot be seen by the naked eye because they are below the viewer's ___________ threshold.
2. If you jump into a cold lake, but moments later the water no longer seems so cold, sensory ___________ has occurred.
3. If you are immobilized in a hospital bed, with no roommate and no TV or radio, and you feel edgy and disoriented, you may be suffering the effects of ___________.
4. During a break from your job as a waiter, you decide to read. For 20 minutes, you are so engrossed that you fail to notice the clattering of dishes or orders being called out to the cook. This is an example of ___________.
5. In real-life detection tasks, is it better to be a "naysayer" or a "yea-sayer"?

Answers:

1. absolute 2. adaptation 3. sensory deprivation 4. selective attention 5. Neither; it depends on the consequences of a "miss" or "false alarm" and the probability of an event occurring. You might want to be a "yea-sayer" if you're just out the door, you think you hear the phone ringing, and you're expecting a call about a job interview. You might want to be a "naysayer" if you're just out the door, you think you hear the phone, and you're on your way to a job interview and don't want to be late.

VISION

selective attention The focusing of attention on selected aspects of the environment and the blocking out of others.

Vision is the most frequently studied of all the senses, and with good reason. More information about the external world comes to us through our eyes than through any other sense organ. Because we are most active in the daytime, we are "wired" to take advantage of the sun's illumination. Animals that are active at night tend to rely more heavily on hearing.

WHAT WE SEE

The stimulus for vision is light; even cats, raccoons, and other creatures famous for their ability to get around in the dark need *some* light to see. Visible light comes from the sun and other stars and from lightbulbs, and is also reflected off objects. Light travels in the form of waves, and the way we see the world—our sensory experience—is affected by the characteristics of these waves:

1. **Hue,** the dimension of visual experience specified by color names, is related to the wavelength of light—that is, to the distance between the crests of a light wave. Shorter waves tend to be seen as violet and blue, and longer ones as orange and red. (We say "tend to" because other factors also affect color perception, as we will see later.) The sun produces white light, a mixture of all the visible wavelengths. Sometimes, drops of moisture in the air act like a prism: They separate the sun's white light into the colors of the visible spectrum, and we are treated to a rainbow.

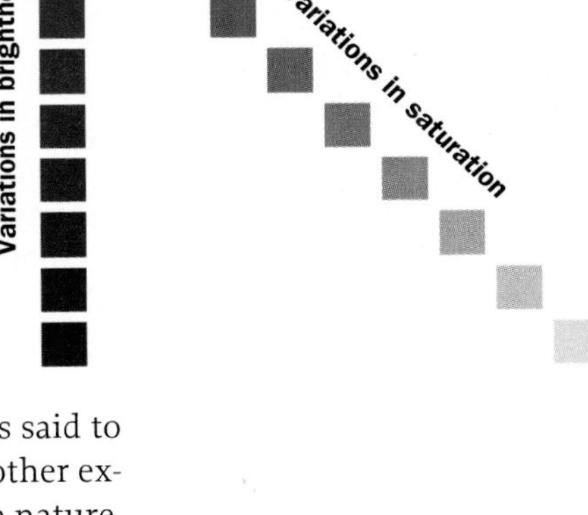

2. **Brightness** is the dimension of visual experience related to the amount, or intensity, of the light an object emits or reflects. Intensity corresponds to the amplitude (maximum height) of the wave. Generally speaking, the more light an object reflects, the brighter it appears. However, brightness is also affected by wavelength: Yellows appear brighter than reds and blues when physical intensities are actually equal. (For this reason, some fire departments have switched from red engines to yellow ones.)

3. **Saturation** (colorfulness) is the dimension of visual experience related to the **complexity of light**—that is, to how wide or narrow the range of wavelengths is. When light contains only a single wavelength, it is said to be "pure," and the resulting color is said to be completely saturated. At the other extreme is white light, which lacks any color and is completely unsaturated. In nature, pure light is extremely rare. Usually we sense a mixture of wavelengths, and we see colors that are duller and paler than completely saturated ones.

Note that hue, brightness, and saturation are all *psychological* dimensions of visual experience, whereas wavelength, intensity, and complexity are all *physical* properties of the visual stimulus, light.

AN EYE ON THE WORLD

Light enters the visual system through the eye, a wonderfully complex and delicate structure that is often compared, rather loosely, to a camera. As you read this section, examine Figure 6.3. Notice that the front part of the eye is covered by the transparent *cornea.* The cornea protects the eye and bends incoming light rays toward a *lens* located behind it. A camera lens focuses incoming light by moving closer to or farther from the shutter opening. However, the lens of the eye works by subtly changing its shape, becoming more or less curved to focus light from objects that are close by or far away. The amount of light that gets into the eye is controlled by muscles in the *iris,* the part of the eye that gives it color. The iris surrounds the round opening, or *pupil,* of the eye. When you enter a dim room, the pupil widens, or dilates, to let more light in. When you emerge into bright sunlight, the pupil gets smaller, contracting to allow

hue The dimension of visual experience specified by color names and related to the wavelength of light.

brightness Lightness or luminance; the dimension of visual experience related to the amount of light emitted from or reflected by an object.

saturation Vividness or purity of color; the dimension of visual experience related to the complexity of light waves.

complexity of light Refers to the number of different wavelengths contained in light from a particular source.

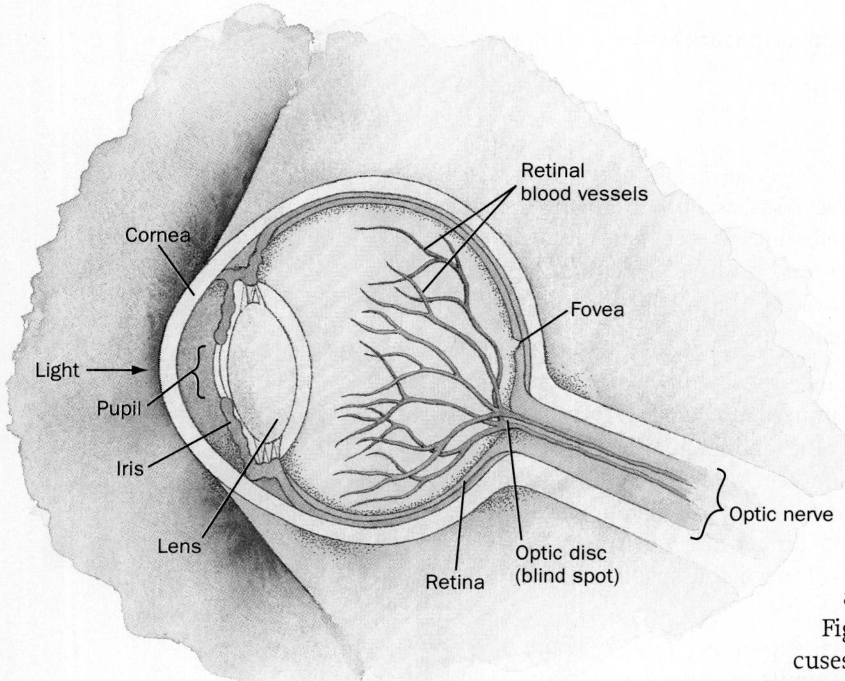

Figure 6.3
Major Structures of the Eye

Light passes through the pupil and lens and is focused on the retina at the back of the eye. The point of sharpest vision is at the fovea.

in less light. You can see these changes by watching your eyes in a mirror as you change the lighting.

The visual receptors are located in the back of the eye, or **retina.** In a developing embryo, the retina forms from tissue that projects out from the brain, not from tissue destined to form other parts of the eye; thus the retina is actually an extension of the brain. As Figure 6.4 shows, when the lens of the eye focuses light on the retina, the result is an upside-down image (which can actually be seen with an instrument used by eye specialists). Light from the top of the visual field stimulates light-sensitive receptor cells in the bottom part of the retina, and vice versa. The brain interprets this upside-down pattern of stimulation as something that is right side up.

About 120 to 125 million receptors in the retina are long and narrow and are called **rods.** Another 7 or 8 million receptors are cone-shaped and are called, appropriately enough, **cones.** The center of the retina, or *fovea,* where vision is sharpest, contains only cones, clustered densely together. From the center to the periphery, the ratio of rods to cones increases, and the outer edges contain virtually no cones.

Rods are more sensitive to light than cones are. They enable us to see in dim light and at night. (Cats see well in dim light in part because they have a high proportion of rods.) Because rods occupy the outer edges of the retina, they also handle peripheral (side) vision. That is why you can sometimes see a star from the corner of your eye even though it is invisible when you gaze straight at it. But rods cannot distin-

retina Neural tissue lining the back of the eyeball's interior, which contains the receptors for vision.

rods Visual receptors that respond to dim light but are not involved in color vision.

cones Visual receptors involved in color vision.

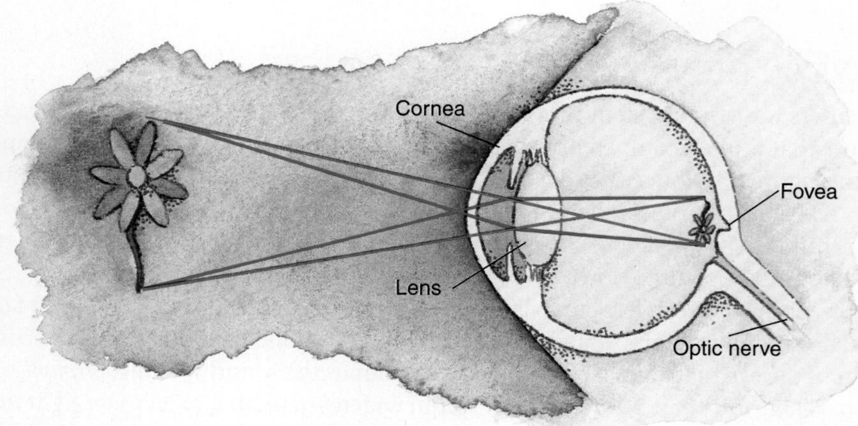

Figure 6.4
The Retinal Image

When we look at an object, the light pattern on the retina is upside down. René Descartes was probably the first person to demonstrate this fact. He cut a piece from the back of an ox's eye and replaced the piece with paper. When he held the eye up to the light, he saw an upside-down image of the room on the paper!

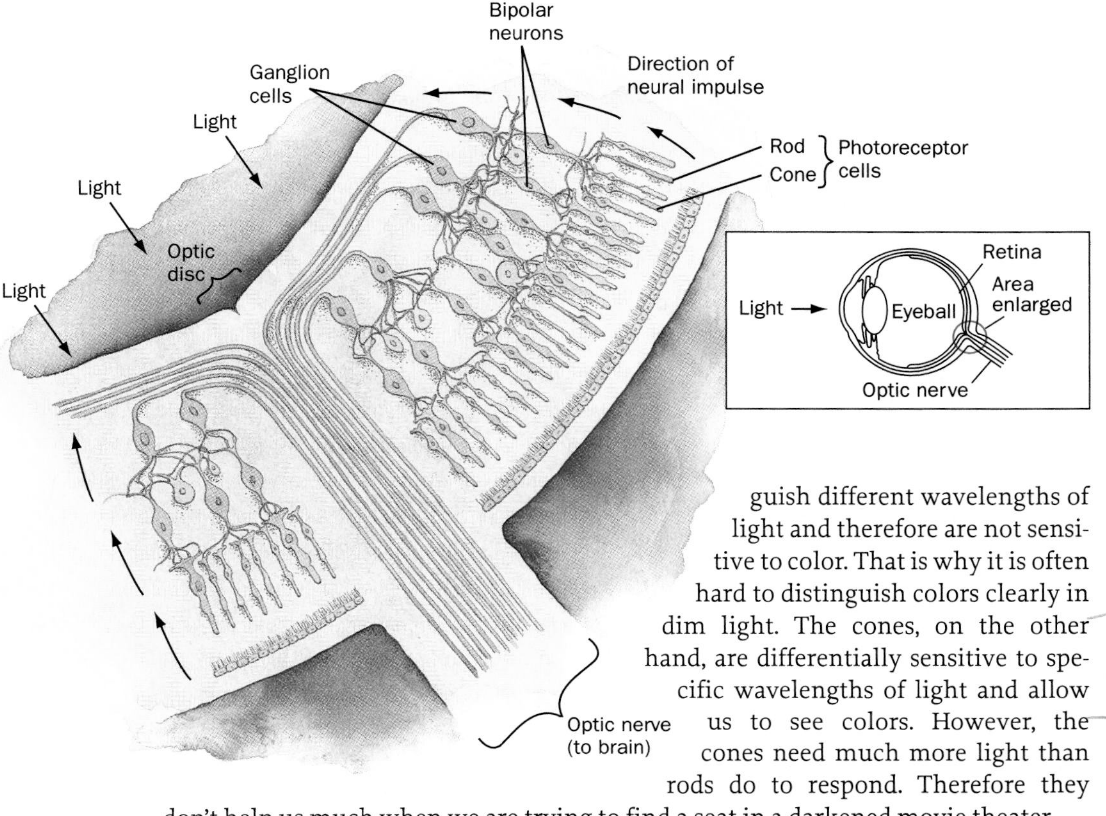

Figure 6.5
The Structures of the Retina

For clarity, all cells in this drawing are greatly exaggerated in size. In order to reach the receptors for vision (the rods and cones), light must pass through the ganglion cells and bipolar neurons as well as the blood vessels that nourish them (not shown). Normally we do not see the shadow cast by this network of cells and blood vessels because the shadow always falls on the same place on the retina, and such stabilized images are not sensed. But when an eye doctor shines a moving light into your eye, the treelike shadow of the blood vessels falls on different regions of the retina and you may see it—a rather eerie experience.

guish different wavelengths of light and therefore are not sensitive to color. That is why it is often hard to distinguish colors clearly in dim light. The cones, on the other hand, are differentially sensitive to specific wavelengths of light and allow us to see colors. However, the cones need much more light than rods do to respond. Therefore they don't help us much when we are trying to find a seat in a darkened movie theater.

We have all noticed that it takes some time for our eyes to adjust fully to dim illumination. This process of **dark adaptation**, which involves chemical changes in the rods and cones, occurs in two phases. The cones adapt quickly, within 10 minutes or so, but never become very sensitive to the dim illumination. The rods adapt more slowly, taking 20 minutes or longer, but are ultimately much more sensitive. After the first phase of adaptation, you can see better but not well; after the second phase, your vision is as good as it will get.

Rods and cones are connected by synapses to *bipolar neurons*, which in turn communicate with neurons called **ganglion cells** (see Figure 6.5). Usually, a single cone communicates (via a bipolar neuron) with a single ganglion cell; it has a "private line." Rods, in contrast, must communicate via a "party line." That is, whole groups of rods, covering a particular area of the retina, send their messages to a single ganglion cell.

The axons of the ganglion cells converge to form the *optic nerve*, which carries information out through the back of the eye and on to the brain. Where the optic nerve leaves the eye, at the *optic disc*, there are no rods or cones. The absence of receptors produces a blind spot in the field of vision. Normally we are unaware of the blind spot because (1) the image projected on the spot is hitting a different, "nonblind" spot in the other eye; (2) our eyes move so fast that we can pick up the complete image; and (3) the brain tends to fill in the gap. You can find your blind spot by following the instructions in the Get Involved exercise on the following page.

dark adaptation A process by which visual receptors become maximally sensitive to dim light.

ganglion cells Neurons in the retina of the eye that gather information from receptor cells (by way of intermediate bipolar cells); their axons make up the optic nerve.

WHY THE VISUAL SYSTEM IS NOT A CAMERA

Because the eye is often compared with a camera, it is easy to assume that the visual world is made up of a mosaic of dots, as in a photograph. But unlike a camera, the vi-

GET INVOLVED

A blind spot exists where the optic nerve leaves the back of your eye. Find the blind spot in your left eye by closing your right eye and looking at the magician. Then slowly move the book toward and away from yourself. The rabbit should disappear when the book is between 9 and 12 inches from your eye.

sual system is not a passive recorder of the external world. Instead of simply registering spots of light and dark, neurons in the system build up a picture of the world by detecting its meaningful features.

Ganglion cells and cells in the thalamus of the brain code simple features in the environment, such as spots of light and dark. In mammals, special **feature-detector** cells in the visual cortex code more complex features. This fact was first demonstrated by David Hubel and Torsten Wiesel (1962, 1968), who painstakingly recorded impulses from individual cells in the brains of cats and monkeys. (In 1981, they received a Nobel Prize for their work.) Hubel and Wiesel found that different neurons were sensitive to different patterns projected on a screen in front of the animals' eyes. Most cells responded maximally to moving or stationary lines that were oriented in a particular direction and located in a particular part of the visual field. One type of cell might fire most rapidly in response to a horizontal line in the lower right part of the visual field, another to a diagonal line at an angle in the upper left part of the visual field. In the real world, such features make up the boundaries and edges of objects.

Since this pioneering work was done, scientists have found that other cells in the visual system have more complex kinds of specialties. For example, in primates, the visual cortex contains cells that respond maximally to bull's-eyes, spiral patterns, or concentric circles (Gallant, Braun, & Van Essen, 1993), and the temporal lobe contains visual cells that "prefer" a starlike shape (Sáry, Vogels, & Orban, 1993). Even more intriguing, some cells in the temporal lobe respond maximally to *faces* (Desimone, 1991; Young & Yamane, 1992). But no one is sure whether cells that respond to such complex forms are responding to the overall form or to some specific component of it. And to complicate matters further, it is not only the frequency of a cell's firing that contains information but also the *pattern* or *rhythm* with which it fires (Richmond & Optican, 1990).

The brain's job is to take fragmentary information about lines, angles, shapes, motion, brightness, texture, and other features of what we see, and come up with a unified view of the world. How on earth does it do this? We saw in Chapter 4 that as neurons converge at a synapse, their overall pattern of firing determines whether the neuron on the other side of the synapse is excited or inhibited. The firing (or inhibition) of that neuron, then, actually conveys information to the *next* neuron along the sensory route about what was happening in many other cells. Eventually, a single

feature detectors Cells in the visual cortex that are sensitive to specific features of the environment.

"hypercomplex" cell in the cortex of the brain may receive information that was originally contained in the firing of thousands of different visual receptors. But most researchers believe that the perception of a visual stimulus ultimately depends not just on the firing of a single hypercomplex cell but also on the simultaneous activation of many cells in different parts of the brain, and the overall pattern of firing of these groups of cells. Researchers are now using computer models to try to figure out how this intricate process might take place.

HOW WE SEE COLORS

For 300 years, scientists have been trying to figure out why we see the world in living color. One approach, the **trichromatic theory** (also known as the *Young–Helmholtz theory*), assumed that three mechanisms in the visual system, each especially sensitive to a range of wavelengths, interacted in some way to produce all the different color sensations. Another approach, the **opponent-process theory,** assumed that the visual system treated particular pairs of colors—blue/yellow and red/green—as opposing or antagonistic, which would explain why we can describe a color as bluish green but not as reddish green. Both views, it turns out, are valid; each explains a different level of processing.

The trichromatic theory applies to the first level of processing, which occurs in the retina. The retina contains three types of cones. One type responds maximally to blue (or more precisely, to a range of wavelengths near the short end of the spectrum, which give rise to the experience of blue), another to green, and a third to red. The hundreds of colors we see result from the combined activity of these three types of cones.

Total color blindness is usually due to a genetic variation that causes cones of the retina to be absent or malfunctional. The visual world then consists of black, white, and shades of gray. Many animal species are totally color-blind, but the condition is extremely rare in human beings. Most "color-blind" people are actually *color deficient.* Usually, the person is unable to distinguish red and green; the world is painted in shades of blue, yellow, brown, and gray. In rarer instances, a person may be blind to blue and yellow and may see only reds, greens, and grays. Color deficiency is found in about 8 percent of white men, 5 percent of Asian men, and 3 percent of black men and Native American men (Sekuler & Blake, 1994). Because of the way the condition is inherited, it is very rare in women. One story has it that John Dalton, a respectable eighteenth-century Quaker physician who published the first study of color deficiency and was color deficient himself, once startled his colleagues by wearing red hose—which he saw as brown. But fortunately for people who are color deficient, this condition does not usually interfere with daily living. A person who is blind to red and green can respond correctly to traffic lights, for instance, because the lights differ in position and brightness, as well as in hue.

The opponent-process theory applies to the second stage of color processing, which occurs in ganglion cells in the retina and in neurons in the thalamus of the brain. These cells, known as *opponent-process cells,* either respond to short wavelengths but are inhibited from firing by long wavelengths, or vice versa (DeValois & DeValois, 1975). Some opponent-process cells respond in opposite fashion to red and green; they fire in response to one and turn off in response to the other. Others respond in opposite fashion to blue and yellow. (A third system responds in opposite fashion to white and black and thus yields information about brightness.) The net result is a color code that is passed along to the higher visual centers. Opposing colors cannot be coded at the same time, which is why we never see a reddish green or a bluish yellow.

trichromatic theory A theory of color perception that proposes three mechanisms in the visual system, each sensitive to a certain range of wavelengths; their interaction is assumed to produce all the different experiences of hue.

opponent-process theory A theory of color perception that assumes that the visual system treats pairs of colors as opposing or antagonistic.

GET INVOLVED

Opponent-process cells that switch on or off in response to green send an opposite message—"red"—when the green is removed, producing a negative afterimage. Stare at the black dot in the middle of this heart for at least 20 seconds. Then shift your gaze to a white piece of paper or a white wall. Do you get a "change of heart"? You should see an image of a red heart with a blue border.

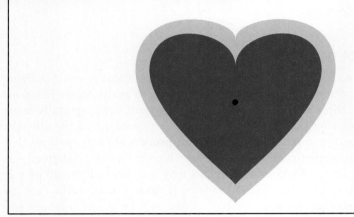

Figure 6.6
Color in Context

The way you perceive a color depends on the colors around it. In this work by Joseph Albers, the adjacent Xs in each pair are actually the same color, but against different backgrounds they look different.

Opponent-process cells that are *inhibited* by a particular color seem to produce a burst of firing when the color is removed, just as they would if the opposing color were present. Similarly, cells that *fire* in response to a color stop firing when the color is removed, just as they would if the opposing color were present. These facts seem to explain why we are susceptible to *negative afterimages* when we stare at a particular hue—why we see, for instance, red after staring at green (see the Get Involved exercise on this page). A sort of neural rebound effect occurs: The cells that switch on or off to signal the presence of "green" send the opposite signal ("red") when the green is removed—and vice versa.

Unfortunately, two-stage theories do not yet provide a complete explanation of color vision. The wavelengths reflected by an object do not by themselves account for whether we see the object as mauve or magenta, purple or puce. The perceived color of an object also depends on the wavelengths reflected by *everything around it*—a fact well-known to artists and interior designers. (See Figure 6.6.) Thus you never see a good, strong red unless other objects in the surroundings reflect the green and blue part of the spectrum. Edwin Land (1959), inventor of the Polaroid camera, worked out precise rules that predict exactly how an object will appear, given the wavelengths reflected by all the objects in a scene. Researchers are now working to understand how the brain uses such information (Brainard, Wandell, & Chichilnisky, 1993).

CONSTRUCTING THE VISUAL WORLD

We do not see a retinal image; that image is merely grist for the mill of the mind, which actively interprets the image and constructs the world from the often fragmentary data of the senses (see Figure 6.7). In the brain, sensory signals that give rise to vision, hearing, taste, smell, and touch are combined from moment to moment to produce a unified model of the world. This is the process of perception.

Figure 6.7
Perception Is Meaningful

Perceptual processes organize and interpret data from our senses. For example, chances are that you see more than a random collection of light and dark splotches in this picture. If not, try holding the picture a little farther away from you.

FORM PERCEPTION To make sense of the world, we must know where one thing ends and another begins, and we must do this in all our sensory modalities. In vision, we must separate the teacher from the lectern; in hearing, we must separate the piano solo from the orchestral accompaniment; and in taste, we must separate the marshmallow from the hot chocolate. This process of dividing up the world occurs so rapidly and effortlessly that we take it completely for granted—until we must make out objects in a heavy fog or words in the rapid-fire conversation of someone speaking a foreign language.

The Gestalt psychologists, whom we introduced in Chapter 1, were among the first to study how people organize the world visually into meaningful units and patterns. In German, *gestalt* means "pattern" or "configuration." The Gestalt psychologists' motto was "The whole is more than the sum of its parts." They observed that when we perceive something, properties emerge from the whole configuration that are not found in any particular component. When you watch a movie, for example, the motion you "see" is nowhere in the film, which consists of separate static frames projected at 24 frames per second.

Although the Gestalt psychologists had ideas about the physiology of visual perception that are no longer accepted, many of their observations remain useful. For instance, they noted that we always organize the visual field into *figure* and *ground.* The figure stands out from the rest of the environment, which provides a formless background (see Figure 6.8). Some things stand out as figure by virtue of their intensity or size; it is hard to ignore the blinding flash of a camera or a tidal wave ap-

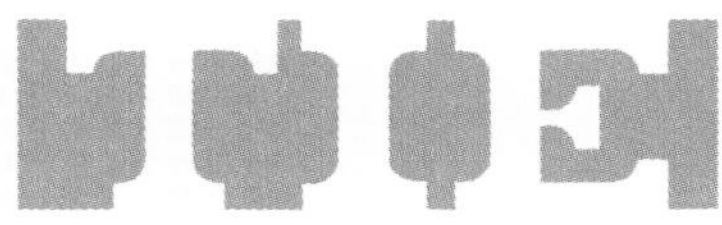

Figure 6.8
Figure and Ground

Both the woodcut *Heaven and Hell* by M. C. Escher and the blue and white drawing have two possible interpretations, which keep alternating depending on which part is seen as figure and which as ground. Do you see the goblins and angels in the woodcut and the word in the drawing?

proaching your piece of beach. Unique objects also stand out, such as a banana in a bowl of oranges. Moving objects in an otherwise still environment, such as a shooting star, will usually be seen as figure. Indeed, it is hard to ignore a sudden change of any kind in the environment because our brains are geared to respond to change and contrast. However, selective attention, the ability to concentrate on some stimuli and to filter out others, gives us some control over what we perceive as figure and ground.

Here are some other Gestalt strategies that the visual system uses to group sensory building blocks into perceptual units:

1. *Proximity.* Things that are near each other tend to be grouped together. Thus you perceive the dots on the left as three groups of dots, not as 12 separate, unrelated ones. Similarly, you perceive the pattern on the right as vertical columns of dots, not as horizontal rows:

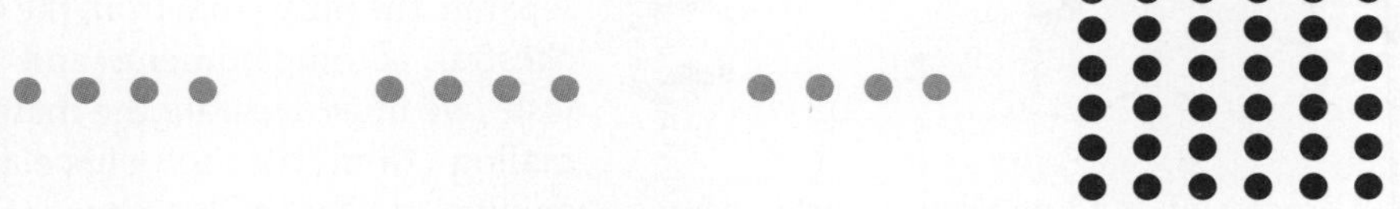

2. *Closure.* The brain tends to fill in gaps in order to perceive complete forms. This is fortunate because we often need to decipher less than perfect images. The following figures are easily perceived as a triangle, a face, and the letter *e*, even though none of the figures is complete:

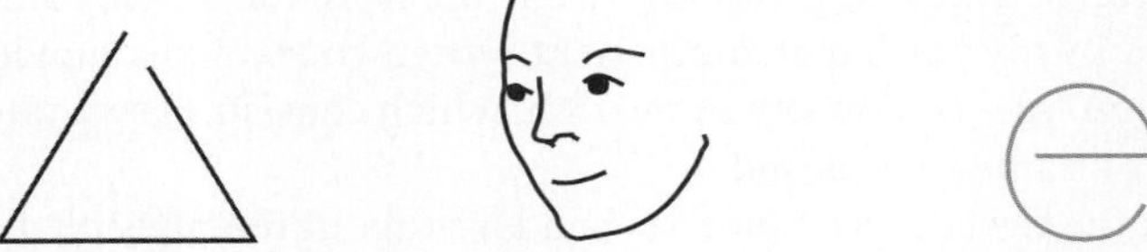

3. *Similarity.* Things that are alike in some way (for example, in color, shape, or size) tend to be perceived as belonging together. In the figure on the left, you see the circles as forming an *x*. In the one on the right, you see horizontal bars rather than vertical columns because the horizontally aligned stars share the same color:

4. *Continuity.* Lines and patterns tend to be perceived as continuing in time or space. You perceive the figure on the left as a single line partially covered by an oval rather than as two separate lines touching an oval. In the figure on the right, you see two lines, one curved and one straight, instead of two curved and two straight lines, touching at one focal point:

One psychologist has estimated that adults must readily discriminate among 30,000 different familiar objects in the environment (Biederman, 1987). Gestalt and other perceptual principles help explain why we have trouble discriminating some of these visual forms. Objects manufactured by human beings may be designed with little thought for how the mind works, which is why it can be a major challenge to figure out how to use a new microwave, camera, or VCR (Norman, 1988). Good design requires, among other things, that crucial distinctions be visually obvious. For instance, knobs and switches with different functions should differ in color, texture, or shape, and they should stand out as "figure." But on many VCRs, it is hard to tell the rewind button from the fast-forward button.

With a little ingenuity and a knowledge of perceptual principles, people can often correct such flaws in the design of machines and products. Control-room operators in one nuclear power plant cleverly solved the problem of similar knobs on adjacent switches: They placed distinctively shaped beer-keg handles over them, one labeled Heineken's, the other Michelob (Norman, 1988). Can you think of some ways to overcome problems of poor design in your own environment?

DEPTH AND DISTANCE PERCEPTION Ordinarily we need to know not only what something is, but also where it is. Touch gives us this information directly, but vision does not, so we must use certain cues to *infer* an object's location by estimating its distance or depth. To perform this remarkable feat, we rely in part on **binocular cues** —cues that require the use of two eyes. The eyes are about $2\frac{1}{2}$ inches apart on the face. As they converge on objects close by or far away, the angle of convergence changes, providing information about distance. The two eyes also receive slightly different retinal images of the same object. You can easily prove this by holding a finger about 12 inches in front of your face and looking at it with only one eye at a time. Its position will appear to shift when you change eyes. Now hold up two fingers, one closer to your nose than the other. Notice that the amount of space between the two fingers appears to change when you switch eyes. The slight difference in lateral (sideways) separation between two objects, as seen by the left eye and the right eye, is called **retinal disparity.** Because retinal disparity increases as the distance between two objects increases, the brain can use this disparity to infer depth and calculate distance. Retinal disparity is mimicked by 3-D movies and slide viewers (stereoscopes), which project two images, one as seen by the left eye and one as seen by the right, to create the illusion of depth.

Binocular cues only help us estimate distances up to about 50 feet. For objects farther away, we must rely on **monocular cues,** cues that do not depend on using both eyes. One such cue is *interposition:* When an object is interposed between the viewer and a second object, partly blocking the view of the second object, the first object is perceived as being closer. Another monocular cue is *linear perspective:* When two lines known to be parallel appear to be coming together or converging, they imply the existence of depth. For example, if you are standing between railroad tracks, they appear to converge in the distance. A third monocular cue is *relative size:* The smaller the retinal image of an object, the farther away the object appears to be. These and other monocular cues are illustrated in Figure 6.9.

VISUAL CONSTANCIES: WHEN SEEING IS BELIEVING You might be able to see what things are and where they are, but your perceptual world would be a confusing place without another important perceptual skill. Lighting conditions, viewing angles, and the distances of stationary objects are all continually changing as we move about, yet we rarely confuse these changes with changes in the objects themselves. This ability to perceive objects as stable or unchanging even though the sen-

binocular cues Visual cues to depth or distance requiring two eyes.

retinal disparity The slight difference in lateral separation between two objects as seen by the left eye and the right eye.

monocular cues Visual cues to depth or distance that can be used by one eye alone.

(a) (b) (c) (d) (e) (f) (g)

Figure 6.9
Monocular Cues to Depth

Most cues to depth do not depend on having two eyes. Some monocular (one-eyed) cues are: (a) **Interposition** (partial overlap). An object that partly blocks or obscures another one must be in front of the other one and is therefore seen as closer. (b) **Motion parallax.** When an observer is moving, objects appear to move at different speeds and in different directions. The closer an object, the faster it seems to move; and close objects appear to move backward, whereas distant ones seem to move forward. (c) **Light and shadow.** Both attributes give objects the appearance of three dimensions. (d) **Relative size.** The smaller an object's image on the retina, the farther away the object appears. (e) **Relative clarity.** Because of particles in the air—from dust, fog, or smog—distant objects tend to look hazier, duller, or less detailed. (f) **Texture gradients.** Distant parts of a uniform surface appear denser; that is, its elements seem spaced more closely together. (g) **Linear perspective.** Parallel lines will appear to be converging in the distance; the greater the apparent convergence, the greater the perceived distance. This cue is often exaggerated by artists to convey an impression of depth.

sory patterns they produce are constantly shifting is called **perceptual constancy.** The best-studied constancies are visual. They include the following:

perceptual constancy The accurate perception of objects as stable or unchanged despite changes in the sensory patterns they produce.

1. *Shape constancy.* We continue to perceive objects as having a constant shape, even though the shape of the retinal image changes when our point of view changes. If you hold a Frisbee directly in front of your face, its image on the retina will be

round. When you set the Frisbee on a table, its image becomes elliptical, yet you continue to identify the Frisbee as round.

2. *Location constancy.* We perceive stationary objects as remaining in the same place, even though the retinal image moves about as we move our eyes, heads, and bodies. As you drive along the highway, telephone poles and trees fly by—on your retina. But you know that objects such as telephone poles and trees move by themselves only in cartoons, and you also know that your body is moving, so you perceive the poles and trees as staying put.

3. *Brightness constancy.* We continue to see objects as having a relatively constant brightness, even though the amount of light they reflect changes as the overall level of illumination changes. Snow remains white even on a cloudy day. In fact, it is possible for a black object in strong sunlight to reflect more light than a white object in the shade. We are not fooled, though, because the brain registers the total illumination in the scene, and we automatically take this information into account in the perception of any particular object's brightness.

4. *Color constancy.* We see an object as maintaining its hue despite the fact that the wavelength of light reaching our eyes may change somewhat. For example, outdoor light is "bluer" than indoor light, and objects outdoors therefore reflect more "blue" light than those indoors. Conversely, indoor light from a lamp is rich in long wavelengths and is therefore "yellower." Yet objects usually look the same color in both places. The explanation involves sensory adaptation, which we discussed earlier. Outdoors, we quickly adapt to short-wavelength (bluish) light, and indoors, we adapt to long-wavelength light. As a result, our visual responses are similar in the two situations. Also, as we saw earlier, the brain takes into account all the wavelengths in the visual field when computing the color of a particular object. If a lemon is bathed in bluish light, so, usually, is everything else around it. The increase in blue light reflected by the lemon is "canceled" in the visual cortex by the increase in blue light reflected by the lemon's surroundings, and so the lemon continues to look yellow.

By DAN PIRARO

When size constancy fails.

5. *Size constancy.* We continue to see an object as having a constant size even when its retinal image becomes smaller or larger. A friend approaching on the street does not seem to be growing; a car pulling away from the curb does not seem to be shrinking. Size constancy depends in part on familiarity with objects. You *know* people and cars don't change size just like that. It also depends on the apparent distance of an object. When you move your hand toward your face, your brain registers the fact that the hand is getting closer, and you correctly perceive its unchanging size. There is, then, an intimate relationship between perceived size and perceived distance.

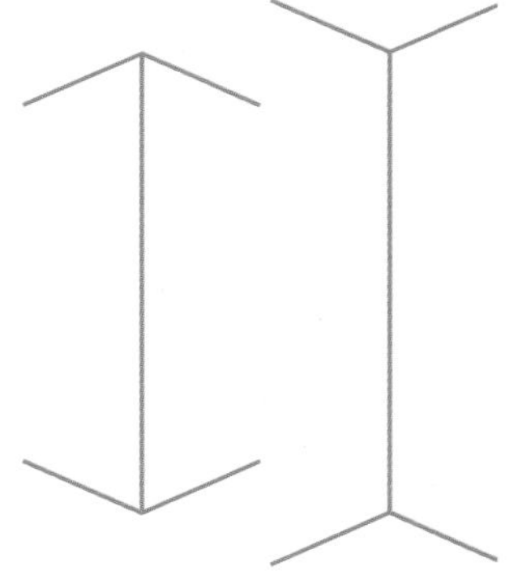

VISUAL ILLUSIONS: WHEN SEEING IS MISLEADING Perceptual constancies allow us to make sense of the world. Occasionally, however, we can be fooled, and the result is a **perceptual illusion.** For psychologists, illusions are valuable because they are *systematic* errors that provide us with hints about the perceptual strategies of the mind.

Although illusions can occur in any sensory modality, visual illusions have been studied more than other kinds. Visual illusions sometimes occur when the strategies that normally lead to accurate perception are overextended to situations where they don't apply. Compare the two lines in the margin. If you are like most people, you perceive the line on the right as slightly longer than the one on the left. Yet if you measure

perceptual illusion An erroneous or misleading perception of reality.

the lines, you will find that they are exactly the same length. This is the Müller–Lyer illusion, named after the German sociologist who first described it in 1889.

One explanation for the Müller–Lyer illusion is that the figures contain perspective cues that normally suggest depth (Gregory, 1963). The line on the left is like the near edge of a building; the one on the right is like the far corner of a room:

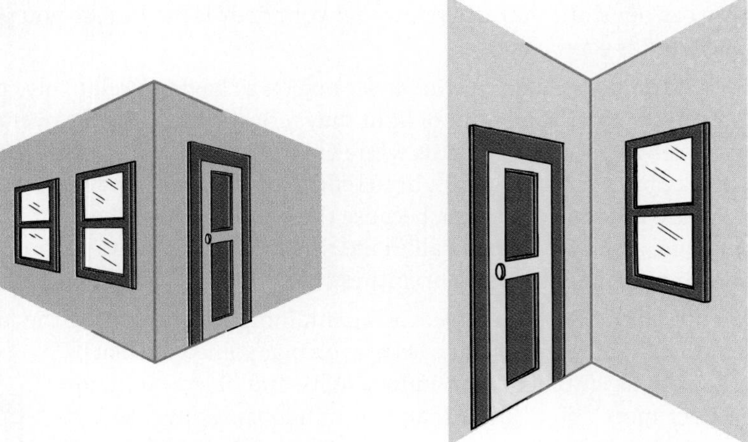

Although the two lines produce the same-sized retinal image, the one with the outward-facing branches suggests greater distance. We are fooled into perceiving it as longer because we automatically apply a rule about the relationship between size and distance that is normally very useful. The rule is that when two objects produce the same-sized retinal image and one is farther away, the farther one is larger. The problem, in this case, is that there is no actual difference in the distance of the two lines, so the rule is inappropriate.

Just as there are size, shape, location, brightness, and color constancies, so there are size, shape, location, brightness, and color illusions. Some illusions are simply a matter of physics. Thus a chopstick in a half-filled glass of water looks bent because water and air refract light differently. Other illusions occur due to misleading messages from the sense organs, as in sensory adaptation. Still others, like the Müller–Lyer illusion, seem to occur because the brain misinterprets sensory information. Figure 6.10 shows other startling illusions.

In everyday life, most illusions are harmless, or even useful. For example, when lights flash on and off in patterns on electric signs, images occur successively across the retina, much as they do when actual objects move, and so we perceive the images in the sign as moving. The result of this apparent motion may be dancers kicking up their heels on a Las Vegas billboard or news headlines scrolling across a building in New York's Times Square. Occasionally, however, an illusion interferes with the normal performance of some skill. In baseball, two types of pitches that drive batters batty are the rising fastball, in which the ball seems to jump a few inches when it reaches home plate, and the breaking curveball, in which the ball seems to loop toward the batter and then plummet at the last moment. Both of these pitches are physical impossibilities; according to one explanation, they are illusions that occur when batters misestimate a ball's speed and momentarily shift their gaze to where they think it will cross home plate (Bahill & Karnavas, 1993). Illusions may also lead to accidents. For example, because large objects often appear to move more slowly than small ones, drivers sometimes underestimate the speed of onrushing trains at railroad crossings and think they can "beat" the train, with tragic results.

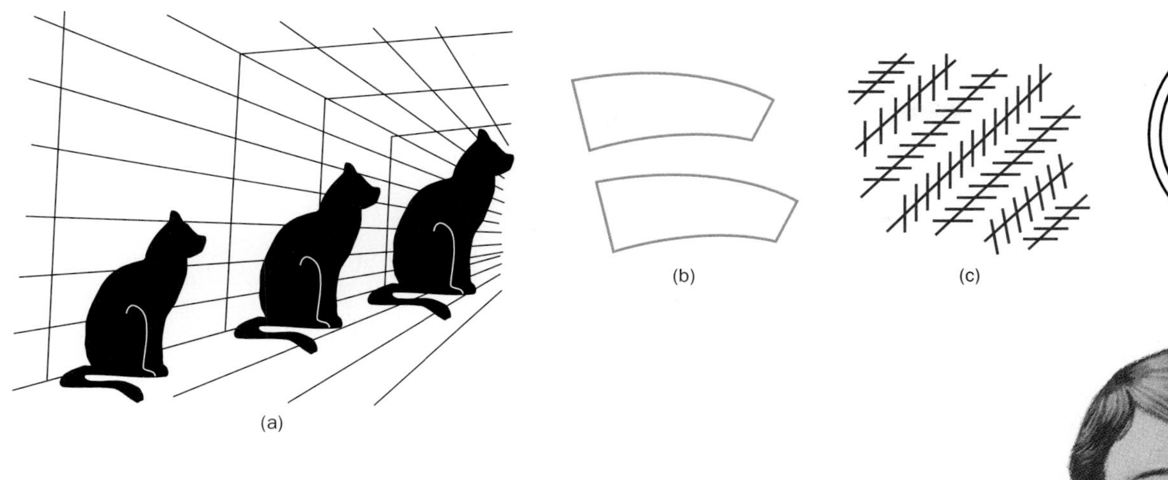

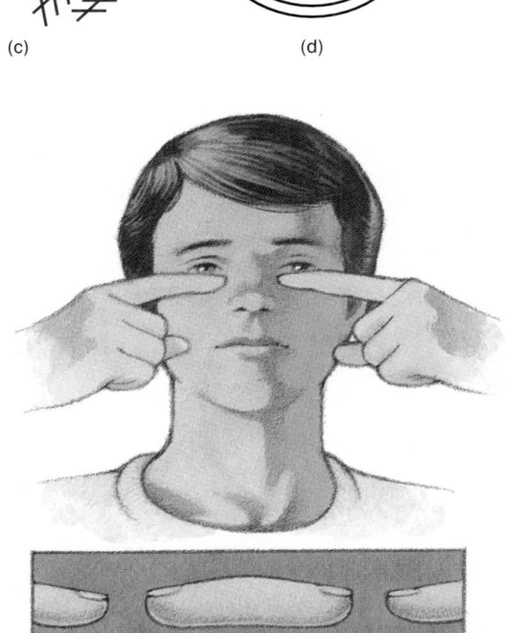

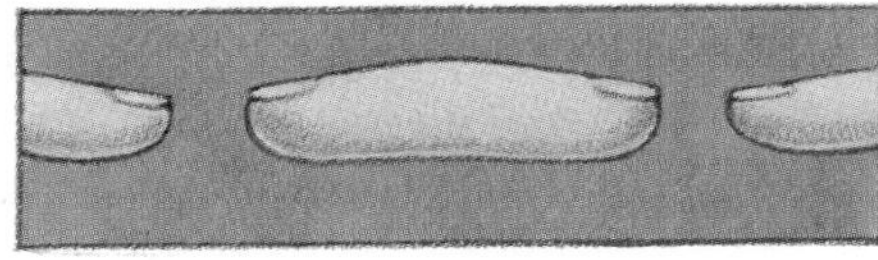

Figure 6.10
Some Visual Illusions

Although perception is usually accurate, we can be fooled. In (a) the cats as drawn are all the same size; in (b) the two figures are the same size; in (c) the diagonal lines are all parallel; and in (d) the sides of the square are all straight. To see the illusion depicted in (e), hold your index fingers 5 to 10 inches in front of your eyes as shown, then focus straight ahead. Do you see a floating "fingertip frankfurter"? Can you make it shrink or expand? Why does this illusion occur?

Quick Quiz

Can you accurately perceive these questions?

1. How can two Gestalt principles help explain why you can make out the Big Dipper on a starry night?
2. *True or false:* Binocular cues help us locate objects that are very far away.
3. Hold one hand about 12 inches from your face and the other one about 6 inches away. (a) Which hand will cast the smaller retinal image? (b) Why don't you perceive that hand as smaller?

Answers:

1. Proximity of certain stars encourages you to see them as clustered together to form a pattern; closure allows you to "fill in the gaps" and see the contours of a "dipper." 2. false 3. a. The hand that is 12 inches away will cast a smaller retinal image. b. Your brain takes the differences in distance into account in estimating size; also, you know how large your hands are.

HEARING

Like vision, the sense of hearing, or *audition*, provides a vital link with the world around us. When damage to the auditory system causes hearing loss, the consequences go beyond the obvious loss of auditory information. Because we use hearing to monitor our own speech, when deafness is present at birth or occurs early in life, speech development is hindered. When people lose their hearing, they sometimes come to feel socially isolated because social relationships rely so heavily on hearing others. That is why many deaf people feel strongly about teaching deaf children American Sign Language (ASL), which allows them to communicate normally with and forge close relationships with other signers.

WHAT WE HEAR

The stimulus for sound is a wave of pressure created when an object vibrates (or, sometimes, when compressed air is released, as in a pipe organ). The vibration (or release of air) causes molecules in a transmitting substance to move together and apart. This movement produces variations in pressure that radiate in all directions. The transmitting substance is usually air, but sound waves can also travel through water and solids. That is why, in old movie Westerns, Indian scouts would sometimes put an ear to the ground to find out whether anyone was approaching.

As with vision, psychological aspects of our auditory experience are related in a predictable way to physical characteristics of the stimulus—in this case, a sound wave:

1. **Loudness** is the dimension of auditory experience related to the intensity of a wave's pressure. Intensity corresponds to the amplitude, or maximum height, of the wave. The more energy contained in the wave, the higher it is at its peak. Perceived loudness is also affected by pitch—how high or low a sound is. If low and high sounds produce waves with equal amplitudes, the low sound may seem quieter.

Sound intensity is measured in units called *decibels* (dB). A decibel is one-tenth of a *bel*, a unit named for Alexander Graham Bell, the inventor of the telephone. The average absolute threshold of hearing in human beings is zero decibels. Decibels are not equally distant, as inches on a ruler are. A sound of 60 decibels (such as that of a sewing machine) is not one-fifth louder than one at 50 decibels (such as that of a refrigerator); it is ten times louder. Table 6.1 shows the intensity in decibels of some common sounds.

2. **Pitch** is the dimension of auditory experience related to the frequency of the sound wave and, to some extent, its intensity. **Frequency** refers to how rapidly the air (or other medium) vibrates—that is, the number of times per second the wave cycles through a peak and a low point. One cycle per second is known as 1 *hertz* (Hz). The healthy ear of a young person normally detects frequencies in the range of 16 Hz (the lowest note on a pipe organ) to 20,000 Hz (the scraping of a grasshopper's legs).

3. **Timbre** is the distinguishing quality of a sound. It is the dimension of auditory experience related to the complexity of the sound wave—to the relative breadth of the range of frequencies that make up the wave. A pure tone consists of only one frequency, but in nature, pure tones are extremely rare. Usually what we hear is a complex wave consisting of several subwaves with different frequencies. A particular combination of frequencies results in a particular timbre. Timbre is what makes a note played on a flute, which produces relatively pure tones, sound different from the same note played on an oboe, which produces very complex sounds.

When many frequencies are present but are not in harmony, we hear noise. When all the frequencies of the sound spectrum occur, they produce a hissing sound called *white noise.* White noise is named by analogy to white light. Just as white light includes all wavelengths of the visible light spectrum, so white noise includes all frequencies of the sound spectrum.

loudness The dimension of auditory experience related to the intensity of a pressure wave.

pitch The dimension of auditory experience related to the frequency of a pressure wave; height or depth of a tone.

frequency (of a sound wave) The number of times per second that a sound wave cycles through a peak and low point.

timbre The distinguishing quality of a sound; the dimension of auditory experience related to the complexity of the pressure wave.

TABLE 6.1 *Sound Intensity Levels in the Environment*

The following decibel levels apply at typical working distances. Each ten-point increase on the decibel scale represents a tenfold increase in sound intensity over the previous level. Even some everyday noises can be hazardous to hearing if exposure goes on for too long a time.

Typical Level (Decibels)	Example	Dangerous Time Exposure
0	Lowest sound audible to human ear	—
30	Quiet library, soft whisper	—
40	Quiet office, living room, bedroom away from traffic	—
50	Light traffic at a distance, refrigerator, gentle breeze	—
60	Air conditioner at 20 feet, conversation, sewing machine	—
70	Busy traffic, noisy restaurant (constant exposure)	Critical level begins
80	Subway, heavy city traffic, alarm clock at 2 feet, factory noise	More than 8 hours
90	Truck traffic, noisy home appliances, shop tools, lawn mower	Less than 8 hours
100	Chain saw, boiler shop, pneumatic drill	Less than 2 hours
120	Rock concert in front of speakers, sandblasting, thunderclap	Immediate danger
140	Gunshot blast, jet plane at 50 feet	Any length of exposure time is dangerous
180	Rocket launching pad	Hearing loss inevitable

Source: Reprinted with permission from the American Academy of Otolaryngology—Head and Neck Surgery, Washington, D.C.

AN EAR ON THE WORLD

As Figure 6.11 shows, the ear has an outer, a middle, and an inner section. The soft, funnel-shaped outer ear is well designed to collect sound waves, but hearing would still be quite good without it. The essential parts of the ear are hidden from view, inside the head.

A sound wave passes into the outer ear and through an inch-long canal to strike an oval-shaped membrane called the *eardrum.* The eardrum is so sensitive that it can respond to the movement of a single molecule! A sound wave causes it to vibrate with the same frequency and amplitude as the wave itself. This vibration is passed along to three tiny bones in the middle ear, the smallest bones in the human body. These bones, known informally as the "hammer," the "anvil," and the "stirrups," move one after the other, which has the effect of intensifying the force of the vibration. The innermost bone, the stirrup, pushes on a membrane that opens into the inner ear.

The actual organ of hearing, the *organ of Corti,* is a chamber inside the **cochlea,** a snail-shaped structure within the inner ear. The organ of Corti plays the same role in hearing that the retina plays in vision. It contains the all-important receptor cells,

cochlea [KOCK-lee-uh] A snail-shaped, fluid-filled organ in the inner ear, containing the receptors for hearing.

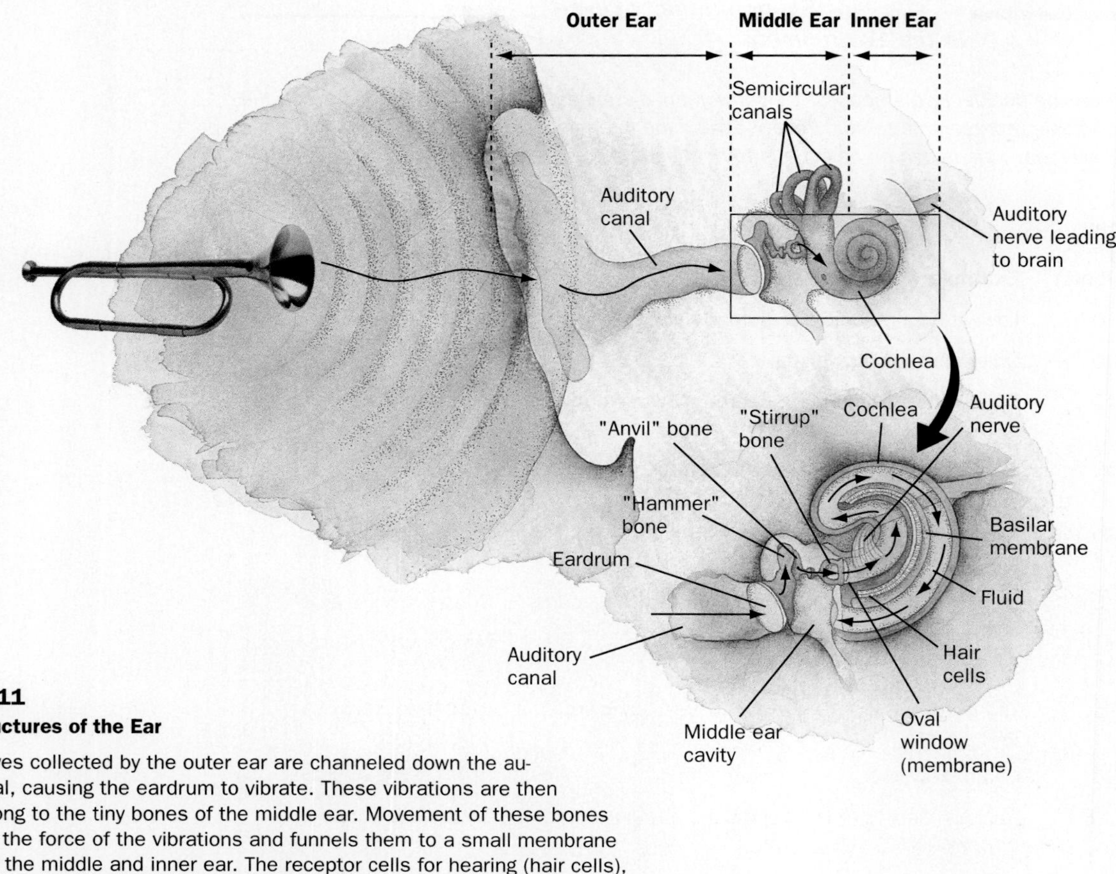

Figure 6.11
Major Structures of the Ear

Sound waves collected by the outer ear are channeled down the auditory canal, causing the eardrum to vibrate. These vibrations are then passed along to the tiny bones of the middle ear. Movement of these bones intensifies the force of the vibrations and funnels them to a small membrane separating the middle and inner ear. The receptor cells for hearing (hair cells), located in a small organ within the snail-shaped cochlea, initiate nerve impulses that travel along the auditory nerve to the brain.

which in this case look like bristles and are called *hair cells*, or *cilia*. Exposure to extremely loud noise for a brief period, or more moderate levels of noise for a sustained period, can damage these fragile cells. They flop over, like broken blades of grass, and if the damage reaches a critical point, hearing loss occurs.

In our society, with its ubiquitous office machines, automobiles, power saws, leaf blowers, jackhammers, and stereos (often played at full blast and listened to through headphones), such impairment is common. Many college students already have impaired hearing because of damage to the cilia. Our noisy environment also helps explain why so many older people cannot hear as well as they once did (especially the higher frequencies), although some receptor cells in the ear are also lost normally with age. Research suggests that hair cells might be able to regenerate after damage if they are stimulated by a substance that promotes nerve growth (Defebvre et al., 1993). Someday this research may lead to techniques that restore hearing, but you shouldn't count on it; try to avoid the loud noises that damage these fragile cells.

The hair cells of the cochlea are embedded in the rubbery *basilar membrane*, which stretches across the interior of the cochlea. When pressure reaches the cochlea, it causes wavelike motions in fluid within the cochlea's interior. These motions push on the basilar membrane, causing it to move in a wavelike motion too. Just above the hair cells is yet another membrane. As the hair cells rise and fall, their tips brush against it, and they bend. This causes the hair cells to initiate a signal that is passed along to the *auditory nerve,* which then carries the message to the brain. The particular pattern of hair-cell movement is affected by the manner in which the basilar membrane moves. This pattern determines which neurons fire and how rapidly they fire, and the resulting code in turn determines the sort of sound we hear. For example, we discriminate high-pitched sounds largely on the basis of where activity occurs along the basilar membrane; activity at different sites leads to different neural codes. We discriminate low-pitched sounds largely on the basis of the frequency of the basilar membrane's vibration; again, different frequencies lead to different neural codes.

Could anyone ever imagine such a complex and odd arrangement of bristles, fluids, and snail shells if it didn't already exist?

The spiraled interior of a guinea pig's cochlea, shown here, is almost identical to that of a human cochlea.

CONSTRUCTING THE AUDITORY WORLD

Just as we do not see a retinal image, so we do not hear a chorus of brushlike tufts bending and swaying in the dark recesses of the cochlea. Just as we do not see a jumbled collection of lines and colors, so we do not hear a disconnected cacophony of pitches and timbres. Instead, we use our perceptual powers to organize patterns of sound and to construct a meaningful auditory world.

For example, in class, your psychology instructor hopes you will perceive his or her voice as *figure* and the hum of a passing airplane, cheers from the athletic field, or distant sounds of a construction crew as *ground.* Whether these hopes are realized will depend, of course, on where you choose to direct your attention. Other Gestalt principles also seem to apply to hearing. The *proximity* of notes in a melody tells you which notes go together to form phrases; *continuity* helps you follow a melody on one violin when another violin is playing a different melody; *similarity* in timbre and pitch helps you pick out the soprano voices in a chorus and hear them as a unit; *closure* helps you understand a radio announcer's words even when static makes some of the individual sounds unintelligible.

Besides our need to organize sounds, we also need to know where they are coming from. We can estimate the *distance* of a sound's source by using loudness as a cue. For example, we know that a train sounds louder when it is 20 yards away than when it is a mile off. To locate the *direction* a sound is coming from, we depend in part on the fact that we have two ears. A sound arriving from the right reaches the right ear a fraction of a second sooner than it reaches the left ear, and vice versa. The sound may also provide a bit more energy to the right ear (depending on its frequency) because it has to get around the head to reach the left ear. Localizing sounds that are coming from directly in back of you or from directly above your head is hard because such sounds reach both ears at the same time. When you turn or cock your head, you are actively trying to overcome this problem. Many animals don't have to do this; they can move their ears independently of the head.

Research with animals is clarifying the physiology of sound location. As we saw, in the visual system, many cells are "tuned" to a specific part of the visual field. Similarly, in areas of the brain that process sounds before they reach the auditory cortex, cells are "tuned" to specific parts of the auditory field; they respond either to disparities in the arrival time of a sound at the two ears or to differences in a sound's intensity at the two ears (Konishi, 1993). In the auditory cortex itself, any given cell can respond to any location, but sounds at different locations produce different *patterns* of firing over time (Middlebrooks et al., 1994). One pattern might mean "in back of me" and another "off to the right side." The combined activity of many such neurons helps to convey the precise location of the sound. Nonetheless, even people with normal hearing find it difficult to locate objects through sound alone, as you know if you have ever played blindfold games such as Marco Polo. Our eyes provide fuller information on distance than our ears do because they provide direct perception of a three-dimensional world.

Quick Quiz

How well can you detect the answers to these questions on hearing?

1. Which psychological dimensions of hearing correspond to the intensity, frequency, and complexity of the sound wave?
2. Willie Nelson has a nasal voice, and Ray Charles has a gravelly voice. Which psychological dimension of hearing describes the difference?
3. An extremely loud or sustained noise can permanently damage the ___________ of the ear.
4. During a lecture, a classmate draws your attention to a buzzing fluorescent light that you had not previously noticed. What will happen to your perception of figure and ground?

Answers:

1. loudness, pitch, timbre 2. timbre 3. hair cells (cilia) 4. The buzzing sound will become figure and the lecturer's voice will become ground, at least momentarily.

OTHER SENSES

Psychologists have been particularly interested in vision and audition because of the importance of these senses to human survival. However, research on the other senses is growing dramatically, as awareness of how they contribute to our lives increases and new ways are found to study them.

TASTE: SAVORY SENSATIONS

papillae [pa-PILL-ee] Knoblike elevations on the tongue, containing the taste buds. (Singular: *papilla.*)

taste buds Nests of taste-receptor cells.

Taste, or *gustation*, occurs because chemicals stimulate thousands of receptors in the mouth. These receptors are located primarily on the tongue, but some are also found in the throat, inside the cheeks, and on the roof of the mouth. If you look at your tongue in a mirror, you will notice many tiny bumps; they are called **papillae** (from the Latin for "pimple"), and they come in several forms. In all but one form, **taste buds** line the sides of each papilla (see Figure 6.12). The buds, which up close look a little like a segmented orange, are commonly referred to, mistakenly, as the receptors for taste. The actual receptor cells are *inside* the buds, 15 to 50 to a bud. These cells send tiny fibers out through an opening in the bud; the receptor sites are on these fibers. The receptor

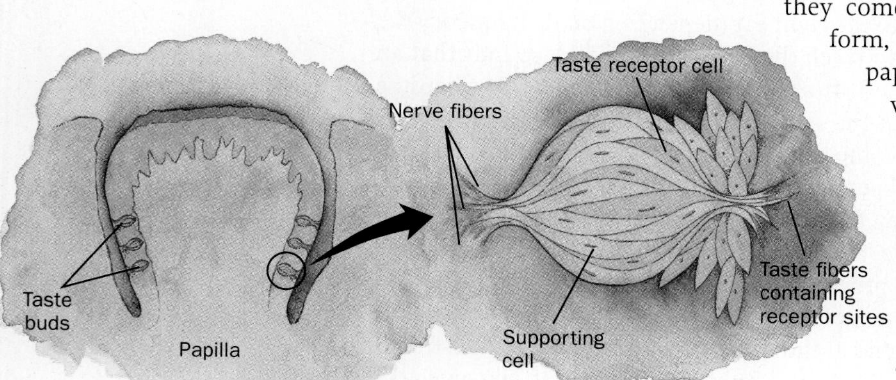

Figure 6.12
Taste Receptors

The illustration on the left shows taste buds lining the sides of a papilla on the tongue's surface. The illustration on the right shows an enlarged view of a single taste bud.

cells are replaced by new cells about every 10 days. However, after age 40 or so, the total number of taste buds (and therefore receptors) declines, which is probably why older people can often enjoy strong tastes that children may detest.

There appear to be four basic tastes: *salty, sour, bitter,* and *sweet,* each produced by a different type of chemical. Until recently, most textbooks included a "tongue map," showing areas supposedly most sensitive to these tastes. But then physiological psychologist Linda Bartoshuk (1993) found that the map was based on a misleading graph published in 1942—and it was simply wrong. The four basic tastes can be perceived at any spot on the tongue that has receptors, and differences among the areas are small. Interestingly, the center of the tongue contains no taste buds, and so it cannot produce *any* sort of taste sensation. But, as in the case of the eye's blind spot, you will not usually notice the lack of sensation because the brain fills in the gap.

When you bite into an egg or a piece of bread or an orange, its unique flavor is composed of some combination of the four basic taste types. The physiological details, however, are still not well understood. For example, it is not clear whether the four tastes are really points on a continuum, as colors are, or are distinct and are associated with different types of nerve fibers.

Human beings are born with a sweet tooth (Bartoshuk & Beauchamp, 1994). Just a few drops of sugar water will calm a crying newborn and raise an infant's pain threshold, perhaps because the sugar somehow activates endorphins, the body's natural opiates (Smith, Fillion, & Blass, 1990). Our species also seems to have a natural dislike for bitter substances, probably because many poisonous substances are bitter. A baby will wrinkle up its nose if you try to feed it something bitter. But taste is also a matter of culture. For example, many North Americans who enjoy raw oysters, raw smoked salmon, and raw herring are nevertheless put off by other forms of raw seafood that are popular in Japan, such as sea urchin and octopus.

Individual tastes also vary. The French have a saying, *Chacun à son goût* ("each to his own taste"). Why do some people within a culture gobble up a dish that makes others turn green? Experience undoubtedly plays a role; as we will see in Chapter 7, a taste or distaste for a particular food can be learned. Individual differences in taste sensitivity are also related to the density of taste buds; human tongues can have as few as 500 or as many as 10,000 taste buds (Miller & Reedy, 1990). Genetic differences, too, make people more or less sensitive to the chemicals in particular foods (Bartoshuk, 1993). For example, some people experience a bitter taste from saccharin, caffeine, and other substances, but others do not. People who are "supertasters" for bitter substances have more taste buds on their tongues than do "nontasters," who are less sensitive to such substances. Further, as Figure 6.13 shows, in supertasters, papillae of a certain type are smaller, are more densely packed, and look different than those in nontasters (Anliker et al., 1991; Reedy et al., 1993).

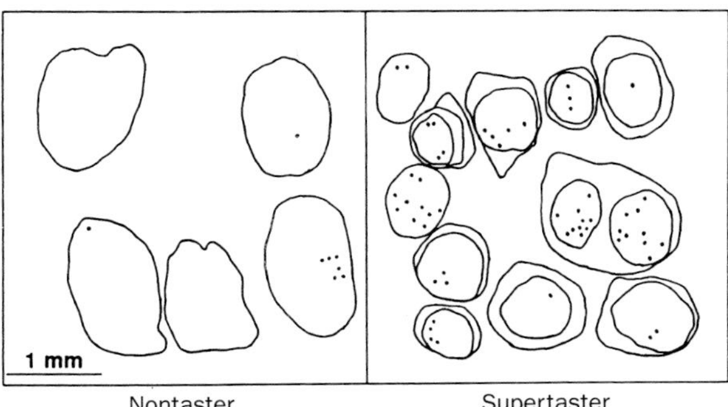

Figure 6.13
On the Tip of the Tongue

In these tracings, taken from videotapes of two tongues, the dots indicate openings to taste buds. "Supertasters" for certain bitter compounds have more taste buds and more fungiform (mushroom-shaped) papillae on the tip and sides of the tongue (right) than do "nontasters" (left). Their papillae are also surrounded by rings of tissue not seen in a nontaster. These differences help explain why one person's bitter pill isn't always so bitter to another. (From Reedy et al., 1993.)

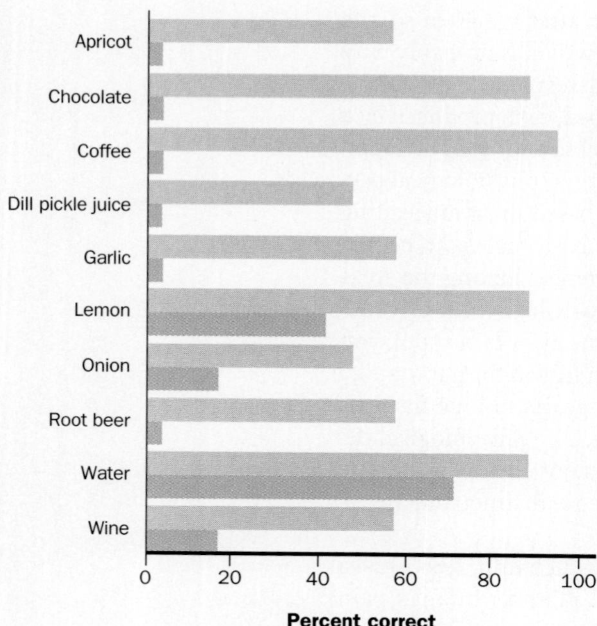

Figure 6.14
Taste Test

The yellow bars show the percentages of people who could identify a substance dropped on the tongue when they were able to smell it. The blue bars show the percentages who could identify a substance when they were prevented from smelling it. (From Mozell et al., 1969.)

The attractiveness of a food can be affected by its temperature and texture. As Goldilocks found out, a bowl of cold porridge isn't nearly as delicious as one that is properly heated. And any peanut-butter fan will tell you that chunky and smooth peanut butters just don't taste the same. Even more important for taste is a food's odor. Subtle flavors such as chocolate and vanilla would have little taste if we could not smell them (see Figure 6.14). The dependence of taste on smell explains why you have trouble tasting your food when you have a stuffy nose. Most people who chronically have trouble tasting things probably have a problem with smell, not taste per se. The total loss of taste is extremely rare; Linda Bartoshuk (1990) reported that in a decade of evaluating disorders of smell and taste, she met only two people who could not taste a thing.

SMELL: THE SENSE OF SCENTS

The great author and educator Helen Keller, who was blind and deaf from infancy, once called smell "the fallen angel of the senses." Yet our sense of smell, or *olfaction*, although seemingly crude when compared to a bloodhound's, is actually quite good—and more useful than most people realize. People can detect thousands of odors. And they can smell some substances before odor-sensitive machines detect them, which is why human beings are often hired to detect odors in chemical plants and laboratories and to detect the freshness of fish at fish markets.

The receptors for smell are specialized neurons embedded in a tiny patch of mucous membrane in the upper part of the nasal passage, just beneath the eyes (see Figure 6.15). These receptors, about 5 million of them in each nasal cavity, respond to chemical molecules in the air. When you inhale, you pull these molecules into the nasal cavity, but they can also enter from the mouth, wafting up the throat like smoke up a chimney. Somehow, these molecules trigger responses in the receptors that combine to yield the yeasty smell of freshly baked bread or the spicy fragrance of a eucalyptus tree. But the neural code for smell, like that for taste, is still poorly understood. Mysteriously, molecules with different shapes can give rise to similar smells, and molecules with similar shapes can give rise to different smells.

GET INVOLVED

Demonstrate for yourself that smell enhances the sense of taste. Take a bite of a slice of apple, holding your nose, and then do the same with a slice of potato. You may find that you can't taste much difference! If you think you do taste a difference, maybe your expectations are influencing your response. Try the same thing, but close your eyes and have someone else feed you the slices. Can you still tell them apart?

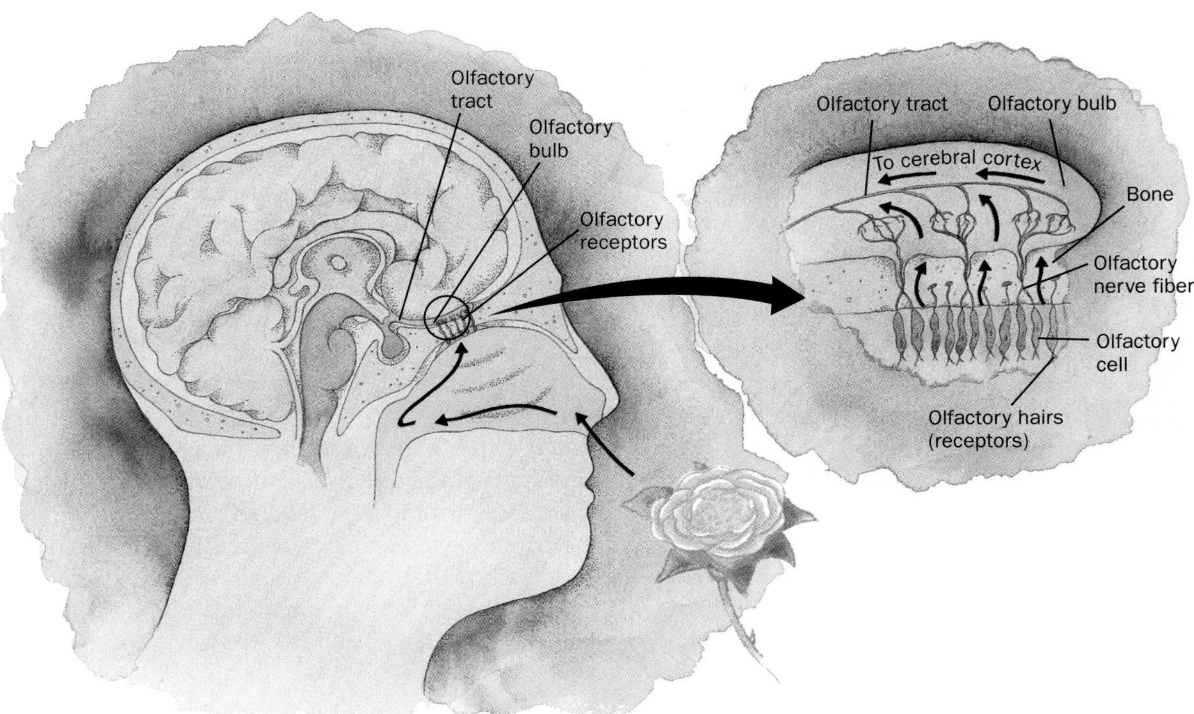

Figure 6.15
Receptors for Smell

Airborne chemical molecules (vapors) enter the nose and circulate through the nasal cavity, where the smell receptors are located. The receptors' axons make up the olfactory nerve, which carries signals to the brain. Sniffing draws more vapors into the nose and speeds their circulation. Vapors can also reach the nasal cavity through the mouth by way of a passageway from the throat.

One complicating factor in the study of olfaction is that so many words exist for describing smells (rotten, burned, musky, fruity, spicy, flowery, resinous, putrid, etc.), and researchers do not agree on which smells, if any, are basic. Also, as many as a *thousand* receptor types may exist (Buck & Axel, 1991). This kind of system is quite unlike the one involved in vision, where only three basic receptor-cell types are involved, or the one involved in taste, where there seem to be four basic types.

Signals from the receptors are carried to the brain's olfactory bulb by the olfactory nerve, which is made up of the receptors' axons. However, the discovery of so many different receptor types means that a great deal of the processing necessary for odor discrimination may also occur within the nose itself. Such a system may have originally evolved because most animals were heavily dependent on smell for finding food or detecting predators. With their small brains, they needed a lot of specialized receptor cells to do the actual work of olfaction. Although smell is less vital for human survival than for the survival of other animals, it is still important. We sniff out danger by smelling smoke, food spoilage, or poison gases. Thus a deficit in the sense of smell is nothing to turn up your nose at. Such a loss can come about because of infection or disease, or because of cigarette or pipe smoking. In one study in which people took a whiff of 40 common odors, such as pizza, motor oil, and banana, smokers were nearly twice as likely as nonsmokers to show impaired ability. The researchers also found that a person who has smoked two packs a day for 10 years must abstain from cigarettes for 10 more years before odor detection will return to normal (Frye, Schwartz, & Doty, 1990).

Smell has not only evolutionary but also cultural significance. These pilgrims in Japan are purifying themselves with holy incense for good luck and health. Incense has always been an important commodity; in the New Testament, the gifts of the Magi included frankincense and myrrh.

Folklore tells us that smells not only aid survival but also contribute to the sexual "chemistry" that seems to occur between some people. Interest has centered on *pheromones,* odorous chemical substances released by one member of a species that affect the physiology or behavior of other members. In many species, pheromones play a role in sexual behavior. A female cat in heat will attract, through scent, all the unneutered tomcats in the neighborhood. A female moth emits pheromones to entice male suitors who are miles away. Human beings, too, may produce pheromones, a fact that has inspired one American perfume company to bring out a pheromone-based scent that it promises will "trigger an intense magnetic reaction" in persons of the other sex. But before you head for the perfume counter, we should tell you that there is no evidence that eau de pheromone can influence, let alone *compel,* human sexual behavior, or that it can increase sexual allure. Natural or learned reactions to smells may well play a role in sexual attraction, but in sexual matters, human beings are generally more affected by what the brain learns and the eyes see than what the nose knows.

Human odor preferences, like taste preferences, vary. In some societies, people use rancid fat as a hair pomade, but anyone in North America who did so would quickly have a social problem. Within a particular culture, context and experience are all-important. The very same chemicals that contribute to unpleasant body odors and bad breath also contribute to the pleasant bouquet and flavor of cheese.

SENSES OF THE SKIN

The skin's usefulness is more than just skin deep. Besides protecting our innards, our 2 square yards of skin help us identify objects and establish intimacy with others. By providing a boundary between ourselves and everything else, the skin also gives us a sense of ourselves as distinct from the environment.

The skin senses include *touch* (or pressure), *warmth, cold,* and *pain.* At one time, it was thought that these four senses were associated with four distinct kinds of receptors, or "end organs," but this view is now in doubt. The skin does contain spots that are particularly sensitive to cold, warmth, pressure, and pain. But except in the case of pressure, no simple correspondence exists between the sensation a person feels at a given spot and the type of receptor found there. Recent research has therefore concentrated more on the neural codes involved in the skin senses than on the receptors themselves.

Pain, which is both a skin sense and an internal sense, has come under special scrutiny. Pain differs from other senses in an important way: When the stimulus producing pain is removed, the sensation may continue—sometimes for years. Chronic pain disrupts lives, puts stress on the body, keeps people from their jobs, and causes depression and despair. (For ways of coping with pain, see "Taking Psychology with You.")

gate-control theory The theory that the experience of pain depends in part on whether pain impulses get past a neurological "gate" in the spinal cord and thus reach the brain.

According to the **gate-control theory** of pain, the experience of pain depends partly on whether pain impulses get past a "gate" in the spinal cord and thus reach the brain (Melzack & Wall, 1965). The gate is made up of neurons that can either transmit or block pain messages from the skin, muscles, and internal organs. Pain fibers (like other kinds of fibers in the nervous system) are always active. When in-

Quick Quiz

Can you make some sense out of the following sensory problems?

1. April always has trouble tasting foods, especially those with subtle flavors. What's the most likely explanation of her difficulty?
2. May has chronic shoulder pain. How might the gate-control theory explain it?
3. June, a rock musician, discovers she can't hear as well as she used to. What's a likely explanation?

Answers:

1. An impaired sense of smell, possibly due to disease, illness, or cigarette smoking. 2. Nerve fibers that normally close the pain "gate" may have been damaged. Or it may be that pain-producing activity in the brain is, for some reason, continuing even without pain impulses from the spinal cord. 3. Hearing impairment has many causes, but in June's case, we might suspect that prolonged exposure to loud music has damaged the hair cells of her cochlea.

PERCEPTUAL POWERS: ORIGINS AND INFLUENCES

What happens when babies first open their eyes? Do they see the world the way adults do? Do they hear the same sounds, smell the same smells, taste the same tastes? Are their strategies for organizing the world wired into their brains from the beginning? Or is an infant's world, as William James once suggested, only a "blooming, buzzing confusion," waiting to be organized by experience and learning? Modern research suggests that the truth lies somewhere between these two extremes.

INBORN ABILITIES AND PERCEPTUAL LESSONS

One way to study the origins of perceptual abilities is to see what happens when the usual perceptual experiences of early life fail to occur. To do so, researchers study animals whose sensory and perceptual systems are similar to our own, such as cats. What they find is that without certain experiences during critical periods of development, perception develops abnormally.

Researchers studying vision, for example, have discovered that when newborn animals are reared in total darkness for weeks or months, or are fitted with translucent goggles that permit only diffuse light to get through, or are allowed to see only one visual pattern and no others, visual development is impaired. In one famous study, kittens were exposed to vertical stripes but not horizontal ones, or vice versa. Special collars kept them from seeing anything else, even their own bodies. After several months, the kittens exposed only to vertical stripes seemed blind to all horizontal contours; they bumped into horizontal obstacles and ran to play with a bar that an experimenter held vertically but not a to bar held horizontally. In contrast, those exposed only to horizontal stripes bumped into vertical obstacles and ran to play with horizontal bars but not vertical ones (Blakemore & Cooper, 1970).

How would you interpret these results? One answer that might occur to you is that cats need to learn to see horizontal and vertical lines in order to develop normal vision. But there is another possibility: Normal experience may merely ensure the survival of skills *already present* at birth in rudimentary form. Physiological studies suggest that this second interpretation is the correct one, at least in the case of line perception. The brains of newborn kittens are equipped with exactly the same kinds of feature-detector cells that adult cats have. When kittens are kept from seeing lines of a particular orientation, such as horizontal or vertical ones, cells sensitive to those

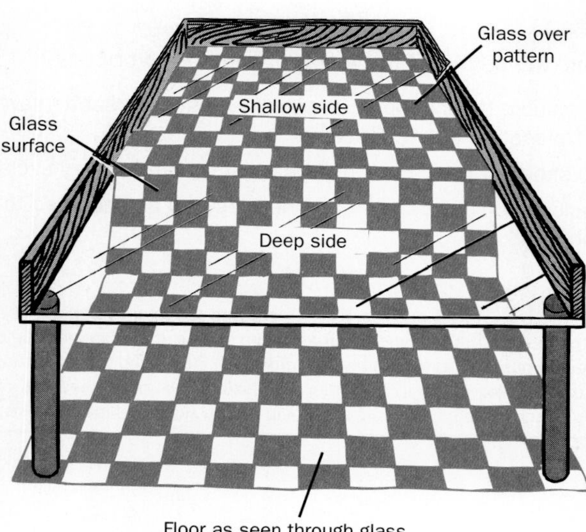

Figure 6.16
A Cliff-hanger

Infants as young as 6 months usually hesitate to crawl past the apparent edge of a visual cliff, which suggests that they are able to perceive depth.

orientations deteriorate or change, and perception suffers (Hirsch & Spinelli, 1970; Mitchell, 1980). Moreover, there seems to be a critical period in cats, during the first three months after birth, when exposure to verticality and horizontality is crucial. If a kitten doesn't get this exposure, its vision will continue to be abnormal even after many years of living in a normal environment.

From findings such as these, psychologists have concluded that human infants are probably born with an ability to detect and discriminate the edges and angles of objects. Direct observations of infants and their reactions to sensory stimuli show that they have other visual talents, as well. They can discriminate sizes and colors very early, possibly at birth. They can distinguish contrasts, shadows, and complex patterns after only a few weeks. Even depth perception occurs early and may be present from the beginning.

Testing an infant's perception of depth requires considerable ingenuity. One clever procedure that was used for decades was to place infants on a device called a *visual cliff* (Gibson & Walk, 1960). The "cliff" is a pane of glass covering a shallow surface and a deep one (see Figure 6.16). Both surfaces are covered by a checkerboard pattern. The infant is placed on a board in the middle, and the child's mother tries to lure the baby across either the shallow or the deep side. Babies as young as 6 months of age will crawl to their mothers across the shallow side but will refuse to crawl out over the "cliff." Their hesitation shows that they have depth perception.

Of course, by 6 months of age, a baby has had quite a bit of experience with the world. But infants younger than 6 months, even though they are unable to crawl, can also be tested on the visual cliff. At only 2 months of age, babies show a drop in heart rate when placed on the deep side of the cliff, but no change when they are placed on the shallow side. A slowed heart rate is usually a sign of increased attention. Thus, although these infants may not be frightened the way an older infant would be, it seems they can notice the difference in depth (Banks & Salapatek, 1984). By age 5 months, infants can even coordinate visual information with auditory cues to judge distance. Thus they are more likely to look at a video of an advancing or a retreating train when increasing or fading engine noises "match" what they are seeing than when there is a conflict (Pickens, 1994).

Another line of evidence also supports the notion that some visual abilities are prewired: case histories of people who have gained sight after a lifetime of blindness. Like S. B., whose case we described at the start of this chapter, these individuals may have many visual limitations. On the other hand, even though they have never seen before, when their bandages are removed, they can distinguish figure from ground, scan objects, and follow moving objects with their eyes. Thus these abilities, at least, seem to be inborn.

We have been talking only about vision, but clearly other sensory abilities are also inborn or develop very early. For example, we saw earlier that infants have a distinct preference for sweet tastes and dislike bitter ones. They can also distinguish salty from sweet. They react strongly to certain smells, such as garlic and vinegar, but less strongly to others, such as licorice and alcohol, showing that they can discriminate among odors. They can distinguish a person's voice from other kinds of sounds. And they will startle to a loud noise and turn their heads toward its source, showing that they perceive sound as being localized in space.

An infant's world, then, is far from the blooming, buzzing confusion that William James took it to be. A young child's perceptual world is not identical to an adult's; neurological connections are not completely formed, so an infant's senses are less acute. But if learning to perceive is compared to going to school, nature has allowed us to skip kindergarten and possibly even the first grade.

PSYCHOLOGICAL AND CULTURAL INFLUENCES ON PERCEPTION

The fact that some perceptual processes appear to be innate does not mean that all people perceive the world in the same way. A camera doesn't care what it "sees." A tape recorder doesn't ponder what it "hears." A robot arm on a factory assembly line holds no opinion about what it "touches." But because we human beings care about what we see, hear, taste, smell, and feel, psychological factors can influence what we perceive and how we perceive it:

1. *Needs.* When we need something, have an interest in it, or want it, we are especially likely to perceive it. For example, hungry individuals are faster than others at seeing words related to hunger when the words are flashed briefly on a screen (Wispé & Drambarean, 1953).

Many years ago, two researchers discovered that the desire of sports fans to have their team win can affect what they see during a game. Sports fans, of course, tend to regard their own team as the good guys and the opposing team as the dirty rats. In the study, Princeton and Dartmouth students were shown a movie of a football game between their two teams. The game, which Dartmouth won, was a rough one. Several players were injured, including Princeton's star quarterback. Princeton students viewing the film saw Dartmouth players commit an average of 9.8 rule infractions. They considered the game "rough and dirty." Dartmouth students, on the other hand, noticed only half as many infractions by their team. They considered the game rough but fair (Hastorf & Cantril, 1954).

2. *Beliefs.* What a person holds to be true about the world can affect the interpretation of ambiguous sensory signals. Suppose you spot a round object hovering high in the sky. If you believe that extraterrestrials occasionally visit the earth, you may "see" the object as a spaceship. But if you think such beliefs are hogwash, you are more likely to see a weather balloon. An image of a crucified Jesus on a garage door in Santa Fe Springs, California, caused great excitement among people who were ready to believe that divine messages may be found on everyday objects. The image

People often see what they want to see. A man in Nashville bought a cinnamon bun at a coffee shop and thought he saw a likeness of Mother Teresa in it. The bun was shellacked and is now enshrined at the coffee shop, where hundreds have come to see it.

was actually caused by two streetlights that merged the shadows of a bush and a "For Sale" sign in the yard.

3. *Emotions.* Emotions can also influence our interpretation of sensory information. A small child afraid of the dark may see a ghost instead of a robe hanging on the door, or a monster instead of a beloved doll. Pain, in particular, is affected by emotion. Soldiers who are seriously wounded often deny being in much pain, even though they are alert and are not in shock. Their relief at being alive may offset the anxiety and fear that contribute so much to pain (although other explanations are also possible). Conversely, negative emotions such as anger, fear, sadness, or depression can prolong and intensify a person's pain (Fernandez & Turk, 1992; Fields, 1991).

4. *Expectations.* Previous experiences often affect how we perceive the world. The tendency to perceive what you expect is called a **perceptual set.** Perceptual sets can come in handy; they help us fill in words in sentences, for example, when we haven't really heard every one. But perceptaul sets can also cause misperceptions. In Center Harbor, Maine, local legend has it that veteran newscaster Walter Cronkite was sailing into port one day when he heard a small crowd on shore shouting "Hello, Walter . . . Hello, Walter." Pleased, he waved and took a bow. Only when he ran aground did he realize what they had really been shouting: "Low water . . . low water."

By the way, there is a misspelled word in the previous paragraph. Did you notice it? If not, probably it was because you expected all the words in this book to be spelled correctly. When we read, expectations can cause us to add an element that's missing (*univerity* becomes *university*); delete an element (*hosppital* becomes *hospital*); modify an element (*unconscicus* becomes *unconscious*); or transpose elements (*nervuos* becomes *nervous*) (Lachman, 1996).

Our needs, beliefs, emotions, and expectations are all affected, in turn, by the culture we live in. Different cultures give people practice with different environments. In a classic study done in the 1960s, researchers found that members of some African tribes were much less likely to be fooled by the Müller–Lyer illusion and other geometric illusions than were Westerners. In the West, the researchers observed, people live in a "carpentered" world, full of rectangular structures built with the aid of saws, planes, straight edges, and carpenter's squares. Westerners are also used to interpreting two-dimensional photographs and perspective drawings as representations of a three-dimensional world. Therefore, they interpret the kinds of angles used in the Müller–Lyer illusion as right angles extended in space—just the sort of habit that would increase susceptibility to the illusion. The rural Africans in the study, living

perceptual set A habitual way of perceiving, based on expectations.

GET INVOLVED

Can you draw a chair this well? If not, perhaps your perceptual expectations about chairs are getting in the way. Art educator Betty Edwards (1986) has used several techniques to help people see and draw what is really "out there." In one assignment, her students draw the empty spaces between the lines or shapes of an object, instead of the object itself; that technique produced the drawing shown here. Why not try it yourself with some simple object, such as a chair, a cup, or your own hand with your index finger touching your thumb? You may find yourself perceiving the world around you in a fresh new way.

in a less carpentered environment and in round huts, seemed more likely to take the lines in the figures literally, as two-dimensional, which could explain why they were less susceptible to the illusion (Segall, Campbell, & Herskovits, 1966).

This research was followed by a flurry of replications in the 1970s, showing that it was indeed culture that produced the differences between groups (Segall, 1994; Segall et al., 1990). Since then, there has been little further work on the fascinating intersection of culture and visual illusions. However, as we will be seeing throughout this book, culture affects perception in many other ways: by shaping our stereotypes, directing our attention, and telling us what is important to notice and what is not.

PUZZLES OF PERCEPTION

We come, finally, to two intriguing questions about perception that have captured the public's imagination for years. First, can we perceive, through our usual sensory channels, what is happening in the world, even though we have no conscious awareness of doing so? Second, can we pick up signals from the world or from other people without using our usual sensory channels at all?

CONSCIOUS AND NONCONSCIOUS PERCEPTION

Certainly many aspects of perception occur outside of awareness. As we have seen, before we can recognize or identify something, we must analyze its basic features. In the case of vision, we must make out edges, colors, textures, and differences in the reflectance of light. We must separate figure from ground, calculate distance or depth, and adjust for changing patterns of stimulation on the retina. All this we do without any conscious intention or awareness.

Persons who are blind to half of the visual field because of damage in the visual cortex provide striking evidence for the nonconscious nature of basic perceptual processes. When these people are presented with a brief flash of light in the part of the visual field affected, they deny seeing it. But when they are asked to *guess* where the light is by pointing to it or by directing their eyes toward it, some do much better than chance, although they continue to deny seeing anything—a phenomenon known as "blindsight." A patient may even be able to distinguish a vertical line from a horizontal one, or an *X* from an *O*, with better than chance accuracy. Most researchers believe that blindsight occurs because messages from the eyes reach parts of the brain other than the visual cortex, areas that handle elementary kinds of visual information without a person's conscious awareness (Braddock et al., 1992; Ptito et al., 1991; Stoerig, 1993; Weiskrantz, 1992). They point out that blindsight has been observed in monkeys that have had both halves of the visual cortex removed and in children who have had an entire hemisphere removed.

What about more complicated perceptual tasks, such as registering and deciphering speech? As we saw earlier in our discussion of selective attention and the "cocktail party phenomenon," even when people are oblivious to unattended speech sounds, they are processing and recognizing those sounds at some level. Other tantalizing evidence of nonconscious perception comes from studies of people anesthetized and apparently unconscious during surgery, who have later shown signs of having heard remarks made by doctors (or researchers) during the operation (Bennett, 1988; Kihlstrom et al., 1990; Millar & Watkinson, 1983; Sebel, Bonke, & Winograd, 1993). However, it is not always clear in this research just how deeply anesthetized the patients really were.

EXAMINE THE EVIDENCE

For only $29.95, a "subliminal tape" promises to tune up your sluggish motivation. It's true that many perceptual processes occur outside of awareness, but does that mean that "subliminal" tapes can change your behavior or improve your life?

The sorts of nonconscious processes we have been discussing all involve stimuli that would be *above* the absolute threshold—loud enough or bright enough to be perceived—if a person were consciously attending to them. Is it also possible to perceive and respond to messages that are *below* the threshold—too quiet to be consciously heard (in the case of hearing) or too brief or dim to be consciously seen (in the case of vision), even when you are trying your best to hear or see them? Perhaps you have seen ads for products that will allow you to take advantage of such "subliminal perception." Or perhaps you have heard that subliminal perception doesn't really exist. What are the facts?

First, considerable evidence exists that a simple visual stimulus *can* affect a person's responses to a task even when the person has no awareness of seeing the stimulus. For example, in one study, people subliminally exposed to a face tended to prefer the face over one they did not "see" in this way (Bornstein, Leone, & Galley, 1987). In another study, words were briefly flashed on a screen and were then immediately masked by a pattern of *X*'s and *O*'s. Subjects said they could not read the words or even tell whether a word had appeared at all. But when an "invisible" word (e.g., *bread*) was followed by a second, visible word that was either related in meaning (e.g., *butter*) or unrelated (e.g., *bubble*), the subjects were able to read the related word more quickly (Dagenbach, Carr, & Wilhelmsen, 1989).

Findings such as these have convinced many psychologists that people often know more than they know they know (Greenwald, 1992; Moore, 1992). In fact, nonconscious processing appears to occur not only in perception, but also in memory, thinking, and decision making, as we will see in Chapters 8 and 9. However, the real-world implications of subliminal perception are not as dramatic as you might think. Even in the laboratory, where researchers have considerable control, the phenomenon is hard to demonstrate. The strongest evidence comes from studies using simple stimuli (faces or single words, such as *bread*), rather than complex stimuli such as sentences ("Eat whole-wheat bread, not white bread"). Even with single words, the influence of the subliminal stimulus is short-lived—in one recent study, only 100 milliseconds (Greenwald, Draine, & Abrams, 1996). Some psychoanalytic researchers have reported that the sentence "Mommy and I are one," presented subliminally, can make anxious, depressed, or disturbed patients feel better (Silverman & Weinberger, 1985). However, serious questions exist about the methods used by these researchers, and most psychologists remain skeptical about these claims.

Timothy Moore, one such skeptic, told us he will be convinced when the "Mommy" stimulus gets positive results in comparison to a control stimulus that merely changes two letters: "Tommy and I ate one."

Moreover, while visual subliminal perception may occur under certain conditions, subliminal *persuasion,* the subject of many popular books and magazine articles, is quite another matter. Empirical research has uncovered no basis whatsoever for believing that Madison Avenue can seduce us into buying soft drinks or voting for political candidates by flashing subliminal slogans on television, or by slipping subliminal images into magazine ads or supermarket music—as we discuss further in "Issues in Popular Culture."

Quick Quiz

Suppose you hear about a study that appeared to find evidence of "sleep learning"—the ability to perceive and retain material played on an audiotape while a person sleeps. What would you want to know about this research before deciding to tape this chapter and play it by your bedside all night instead of studying it in the usual way?

Answer:

You might ask about the kinds of stimuli used (in studies of other kinds of nonconscious perception, positive results have been obtained with very simple stimuli, not running text); whether the results were large enough to have practical consequences; and most important, how it was determined that the subjects were really asleep while the tape was playing. (When EEG measurements are used to verify that subjects are actually sleeping, no "sleep learning" takes place. So if you want to learn the material in this chapter, you'll have to stay awake!)

EXTRASENSORY PERCEPTION: REALITY OR ILLUSION?

Eyes, ears, mouth, nose, skin—we rely on these organs for our experience of the external world. Some people, however, claim they can send and receive messages about the world without relying on the usual sensory channels, by using *extrasensory perception (ESP).*

Reported ESP experiences (also known as *Psi,* a shortening of "psychic phenomena") fall into four general categories: (1) *Telepathy* is direct communication from one mind to another without the usual visual, auditory, and other sensory signals. If you try to guess what number someone is thinking or what card a person is holding, you are attempting telepathy. (2) *Clairvoyance* is the perception of an event or fact without normal sensory input. If a man suddenly "knows" that his wife has just died, yet no one has informed him of the death, he might be called clairvoyant. (3) *Precognition* is the perception of an event that has not yet happened. Fortune-tellers make their livings by claiming to read the future in tea leaves or in a person's palm. (4) *Out-of-body experiences* involve the perception of one's own body from "outside," as an observer might see it. The person feels that he or she has left the physical body entirely. Such experiences are often reported by persons who have been near death, but some people say they can bring them on at will.

Some types of ESP are more plausible than others, given what we know about the physical world. Normal perception depends on the ability to detect changes in energy. Conceivably, telepathy could involve something similar: the sending and receiving of changes in energy through channels that have not yet been identified. Other forms of ESP, however, challenge everything we suppose to be true about the way the world and the universe

THE FAR SIDE By GARY LARSON

For the most part, the meeting was quite successful. Only a slight tension filled the air, stemming from the unforeseen faux pas of everyone wearing the same dress.

think about it

Issues in Popular Culture

Subliminal Persuasion

In 1957, a public-relations executive issued a press release describing a brave new tactic in advertising. Movie audiences in New Jersey, the executive said, had been unwittingly persuaded to "drink Coca-Cola" and "eat popcorn" when these messages were superimposed on the film they were watching. The messages were flashed on the screen so quickly that no one could tell they were there, yet people had supposedly flocked to the refreshment counter with cravings for Coke and a bad case of the munchies. Although the marketing firm responsible for this gimmick offered no proof of these results, the report caused considerable public panic. If consumers could be induced by subliminal messages to buy snacks, what was to prevent unscrupulous politicians from using the same techniques for more sinister purposes? What was to prevent the media from using them for their own sneaky goals, as a Seattle radio station tried to do by broadcasting the "subaudible" message, "TV's a bore" (Moore, 1982)?

Later, the whole thing turned out to be a hoax, and hysteria over the threat of subliminal manipulation faded. But claims about subliminal techniques refused to die. In the 1970s, a best-selling book titled *Subliminal Seduction* warned that pictures cleverly hidden in magazine advertisements were inducing consumers to buy products they didn't really want. Finding these supposed pictures became a sort of parlor game—the 1970s version of "Where's Waldo?"

In the mid-1980s, subliminal persuasion was reborn in still another form: Parents worried that "subliminal" messages recorded on music albums were influencing young people to commit immoral or dangerous acts. In 1990, the parents of two young men who had tried to commit suicide (one succeeded, one survived but was seriously injured) brought suit against the rock group Judas Priest. A subliminal message ("DO IT") on one of the band's albums, claimed the parents, had provoked the boys' suicidal impulses. Psychologists brought in to testify for the defense demonstrated that there is no evidence that such messages can affect behavior: Carefully controlled research shows that they aren't processed as meaningful speech and can't possibly affect either actions or attitudes (Begg, Needham, & Bookbinder, 1993; Vokey & Read, 1985). The defense also pointed out that millions of other people had listened to the album without killing themselves, and that other factors were more likely to have led to the suicides. These young men, for example, had had a history of emotional disturbance, delinquency, drug abuse, and family violence (Moore, 1996). The parents lost their suit.

Today, the belief in subliminal persuasion lives on, except that now these techniques are said to be beneficial rather than harmful. Countless subliminal tapes promise, among other things, to help you slim down, stop smoking, relieve stress, read faster, lower your cholesterol, stop biting your nails, overcome jet lag, stop taking drugs, stop swearing, and enlarge your bust. (Our favorite title is "Housekeeping with Love.") One company even markets a tape

operate. Precognition, for instance, contradicts our usual assumptions about time and space. If it exists, then tomorrow is as real as today, and future events can be known, even though they cannot have caused physical changes in the environment.

EXAMINE THE EVIDENCE

It might be fun to have ESP, especially before a tough exam or a blind date. However, it's one thing to wish ESP existed and another to conclude that it does. What kind of evidence would convince you that ESP is real, and what kind is only wishful thinking?

EVIDENCE—OR COINCIDENCE? Much of the "evidence" for extrasensory perception comes from anecdotal accounts. Unfortunately, people are not always reliable reporters. They often embellish and exaggerate, or recall only parts of an experience. They also tend to forget incidents that don't fit their beliefs, such as "premonitions" of events that fail to occur. Many ESP experiences could merely be unusual coincidences that are memorable because they are dramatic. What passes for telepathy, clairvoyance, or precognition could also be based on what a person knows or deduces through ordinary means. If Joanne's father has had two heart attacks, her premonition that her father will die shortly (followed, in fact, by her father's death) may not really be so impressive.

The scientific way to establish a phenomenon is to produce it under controlled conditions. Extrasensory perception has been studied extensively by researchers in "just for newborns." These tapes earn $50 million a year, and most laypeople assume they work. What can psychological research tell us about their effectiveness?

The answer is clear as a bell: A substantial body of research shows that the manufacturers' claims have no support because people cannot discriminate a tape with a supposedly subliminal message from a "placebo" tape—one that they think has a message but doesn't (Eich & Hyman, 1992; Merikle & Skanes, 1992; Moore, 1995). In one typical study, some 200 college students and other adults listened every day to commercially available tapes that claimed to improve memory or boost self-esteem. Some people thought they were using memory tapes but were actually using self-esteem tapes, or vice versa. Others listened to correctly labeled tapes. These people had all volunteered, and they wanted the tapes to work. At the end of a month, about half thought they had improved in the area corresponding to the label they had received, *whether the label was correct or not.* In reality, there were no actual improvements beyond a general placebo effect (Greenwald et al., 1991).

In another study, female university students and staff members listened to weight-loss tapes (Merikle & Skanes, 1992). All of the women were overweight, and all believed the tapes could help them shed extra pounds. One group of women listened to tapes purchased from the manufacturer, another group listened to a placebo tape with no message on it, and a third group didn't listen to any tape at all. Each woman was weighed once a week for five weeks. By the end of the study, all of the women had lost weight, and the amount lost was about the same for all three groups. The researchers suggested that regular use of subliminal weight-loss tapes may simply make people more aware of weight and dieting.

As we discuss in the text, subliminal *perception*—detection of a signal at better than chance levels even when you think you didn't see or hear it—appears to be a real phenomenon. But the carefully controlled conditions in which it occurs in the laboratory rarely occur out in the real world. Timothy Moore (1995), who has studied subliminal perception for years, says that although future research could reveal some as-yet-undiscovered therapeutic use of sublimation stimulation, "given our current understanding of unconscious cognition the possibility seems very remote." As for subliminal tapes, Moore (1992) concludes that they are sheer quackery, part of a long tradition of selling useless products to vulnerable customers who want quick cures. (The tape companies are not pleased; one manufacturer called Moore an "intellectual terrorist," and other scientists who have criticized the tapes have also been subjected to personal attacks by some industry defenders.)

If advertisers want you to buy something, therefore, they would do better to spend their money on *above*-threshold messages that you can consciously evaluate. And if you want to improve yourself or your life, we encourage you to do so—but you'll probably have to do it the old-fashioned way: by working at it.

the field of **parapsychology.** In a typical study, a person might be asked to guess which of five symbols will appear on a card presented at random. A "sender" who has already seen the card tries to transmit a mental image of the symbol to the person. Although most people do no better than chance at guessing the symbols, in some studies, a few people have consistently done somewhat better than chance. But ESP studies have often been sloppily designed, with inadequate precautions against fraud and improper statistical analysis. When skeptical researchers try to repeat the studies, they get negative results. After an exhaustive review, the National Research Council concluded that there was "no scientific justification . . . for the existence of parapsychological phenomena" (Druckman & Swets, 1988).

The issue has not gone away, however. A few years ago, a well-known social psychologist, Daryl Bem, made waves in the psychological community when he reported a series of ESP studies carried out with the late Charles Honorton, a British parapsychologist. Bem and Honorton (1994) studied telepathy (they called it the "anomalous process of information transfer") by using a variation of a method known as the *ganzfeld* ("total field") procedure. A sender sits in a soundproof room and concentrates on a picture or video clip selected at random by a computer. A receiver sits in another soundproof room; at the end of the transmission period, the

parapsychology The study of purported psychic phenomena such as ESP and mental telepathy.

receiver is shown four pictures or video clips and is asked to pick out the one that most closely matched his or her mental imagery during the transmission period. If the receiver selects the stimulus that was "sent," that trial is counted as a "hit." Bem and Honorton reported an overall hit rate of about 33 percent, whereas chance would predict only 25 percent.

The methods used by Bem and Honorton were far superior to those of previous researchers, but of course, their methods and findings have been subjected to much critical interpretation. Ray Hyman (1994), a leading critic of parapsychology, has pointed out possible flaws in the way the target stimuli were randomized and selected. Everyone agrees that the findings need to be replicated in other laboratories. It will be interesting to see what happens, although we think it is safe to say that caution is warranted. The history of research on psychic phenomena has been one of initial enthusiasm followed by disappointment when results cannot be replicated, and the thousands of studies done over the past 50 years have failed to make a convincing case for ESP.

LESSONS FROM A MAGICIAN Despite the lack of evidence for ESP, about half of all Americans say they believe in it. Perhaps you yourself have had an experience that seemed to involve ESP or have seen a convincing demonstration by someone else. Surely you can trust the evidence of your own eyes—or can you? We will answer with a true story that contains an important lesson, not only about ESP but also about ordinary perception as well.

During the 1970s, physician Andrew Weil (whose writings on drug use we discussed in Chapter 5) set out to investigate the claims of a self-proclaimed psychic named Uri Geller (Weil, 1974a, 1974b). Geller seemed able to bend keys without touching them, start broken watches, and guess the nature of simple drawings hidden in sealed envelopes. Although he had performed as a stage magician in Israel, his native country, he denied using trickery. His powers, he said, came from energy from another universe.

Weil, who believed in telepathy, felt that ESP might be explained by principles of modern physics and was receptive to Geller's claims. When he met Geller at a private

"Seeing is believing," goes the saying, but is it? The engraving on the left shows a "living half-woman," seemingly swinging in mid-air. The sketch on the right shows how the illusion is produced. The woman reclines on an artificial bust, her body supported by another swing and hidden by black curtains. Due to a trick of lighting, the viewer sees only the swing, the face, the necklace, and the sword beneath the swing. The moral: Be skeptical about paranormal claims, even if you "saw it with your own eyes."

gathering, he was not disappointed. Geller correctly identified a cross and a Star of David sealed inside separate envelopes. He made a stopped watch start running and a ring sag into an oval shape, apparently without touching them. He made keys change shape in front of Weil's very eyes. Weil came away a convert. What he had seen with his own eyes seemed impossible to deny . . . until he met The Amazing Randi.

James Randi, whom we met in Chapter 2, is a well-known magician who is dedicated to educating the public about psychic deception. To Weil's astonishment, Randi was able to duplicate much of what Geller had done. He, too, could bend keys and guess the contents of sealed envelopes. But Randi's feats were only tricks, and he was willing to show Weil exactly how they were done. Weil suddenly experienced "a sense of how strongly the mind can impose its own interpretations on perceptions; how it can see what it expects to see, but not see the unexpected."

Weil was dis-illusioned—literally. He was forced to admit that the evidence of one's own eyes is not always reliable. Even when he knew what to look for in a trick, he could not catch The Amazing Randi doing it. Weil learned that our sense impressions of reality are not the same as reality. Our eyes, our ears, and especially our brains can play tricks on us.

The great Greek philosopher Plato once said that "knowledge is nothing but perception," but in fact, simple perception is *not* always the best path to knowledge. The truth about human behavior is most likely to emerge if we are aware of how our beliefs and assumptions shape and alter our perceptions. As we have seen throughout this chapter, we do not passively register the world "out there." We mentally construct it.

Taking Psychology with You

Living with Pain

Temporary pain is an unpleasant but necessary part of life, a warning of disease or injury. Chronic pain, which is ongoing or recurring, is another matter, a serious problem in itself. Back injuries, arthritis, migraine headaches, serious illnesses such as cancer—all can cause unrelieved misery to pain sufferers and their families. Chronic pain can also impair the immune system (Page et al., 1993), and such impairment can put patients at risk of further complications from their illnesses.

At one time, the only way to combat pain was with drugs or surgery, which were not always effective. Today, we know that the experience of pain is affected by attitudes, actions, emotions, and circumstances, and that treatment must take into account psychology as well as biology. Even social roles can influence a person's response to pain. For example, although women tend to report greater pain than men do, a real-world study of people who were in pain for more than six months found that men suffered more severe psychological distress than women, possibly because the male role made it hard for them to admit their pain (Snow et al., 1986).

Many pain-treatment programs encourage patients to manage their pain themselves instead of relying entirely on health-care professionals. Usually, these programs combine several strategies:

- *Painkilling medication.* Doctors often worry that patients will become addicted to painkillers or will develop a tolerance to the drugs. The physicians will therefore give a minimal dose, then wait until the effects wear off and the patient is once again in agony before giving more. This approach is ineffective and ignores the fact that addiction depends in part on the motives for which a drug is taken and the circumstances under which it is used (see Chapters 5 and 15). The method now recommended by experts (although doctors and hospitals do not always follow the advice) is to give pain sufferers a continuous dose of painkiller in whatever amount is necessary to keep them pain-free, and to allow them to do this for themselves when they leave the hospital. This strategy leads to *reduced* dosages rather than larger ones and does not lead to drug dependence (Hill et al., 1990; Portenoy, 1994).

- *Spouse or family involvement.* When a person is in pain, friends and relatives understandably tend to sympathize and to excuse the sufferer from regular responsibilities. The sufferer takes to bed, avoids physical activity, and focuses on the pain. As we will see in Chapter 7, attention from others is a powerful reinforcer of whatever behavior produces the attention. Also, focusing on pain tends to increase it, and inactivity can lead to shortened muscles, muscle spasms, and fatigue. So sympathy and attention can sometimes backfire and may actually prolong the agony (Flor, Kerns, & Turk, 1987). For this reason, many pain experts now encourage family members to resist rewarding or reinforcing the pain and to reward activity, exercise, and wellness instead. This approach, however, must be used carefully, preferably under the direction of a professional, because a patient's complaints about pain are an important diagnostic tool for the physician (Rodgers, 1988).

• *Self-management.* When patients learn to identify how, when, and where their pain occurs, this knowledge helps them determine whether the pain is being maintained by external events. Just having a sense of control over pain can have a powerful pain-reducing effect. In one study, students who monitored their pain while their hand was submerged in freezing water showed more rapid recovery from the pain than did students who had tried to suppress their awareness of pain sensations or distract themselves, apparently because the monitoring students had a sense of control (Cioffi & Holloway, 1993). Patients also need muscle "reeducation"; instead of tensing muscles in response to pain, which only makes the pain worse, patients can learn to relax them (Keefe & Gil, 1986).

• *Biofeedback, hypnosis, and progressive relaxation.* These techniques have all been successful with some patients. (We discussed biofeedback in Chapter 4, hypnosis in Chapter 5.) It is unclear, however, whether biofeedback and progressive relaxation are applicable to all types of chronic pain.

• *Cognitive-behavioral therapy.* Cognitive-behavioral strategies teach people to recognize the connections among thoughts, feelings, and pain; substitute adaptive thoughts for negative ones; and use coping strategies such as distraction, relabeling of sensations, and imagery to alleviate suffering (see Chapter 16). All these techniques increase feelings of control and reduce feelings of inadequacy.

For further information about help for pain, you can contact pain clinics or services in teaching hospitals and medical schools. There are many reputable clinics around the country, some specializing in specific disorders. But take care: There are also many untested therapies and quack practitioners who only prey on people's pain.

SUMMARY

1) *Sensation* is the detection and direct experience of physical energy as a result of environmental or internal events. *Perception* is the process by which sensory impulses are organized and interpreted.

OUR SENSATIONAL SENSES

2) Sensation begins with the sense receptors, which convert the energy of a stimulus into electrical impulses that travel along nerves to the brain, a conversion of energy called *transduction.* Separate sensations can be accounted for by *anatomical codes* (the *doctrine of specific nerve energies*) and *functional codes* in the nervous system. Controversy still exists about how functional encoding yields an overall perception of a stimulus.

3) Psychologists in the area of *psychophysics* have studied sensory sensitivity by measuring *absolute* and *difference thresholds. Signal-detection theory,* however, denies the existence of an absolute threshold; it holds that an observer's response in a detection task consists of both a sensory process and a decision process, and will vary with the person's motivation, alertness, and expectations. This theory has led to improved methods for estimating individual sensitivity to stimuli.

4) Our senses are designed to respond to change and contrast in the environment. When stimulation is unchanging, *sensory adaptation* occurs. Too little stimulation can cause *sensory deprivation,* and too much stimulation can cause *sensory overload,* which is why we exercise *selective attention.*

VISION

5) Vision is affected by the wavelength, frequency, and complexity of light, which produce the psychological dimensions of visual experience—*hue, brightness,* and *saturation.* The visual receptors, *rods* and *cones,* are located in the *retina* of the eye. Rods are responsible for vision in dim light; cones are responsible for color vision. The visual world is not a mosaic of light and dark spots but a collection of lines and angles detected and integrated by special *feature-detector cells* in the visual areas of the brain. The eye is not a camera; the brain takes in fragmentary information about lines, angles, shapes, motion, brightness, texture, and other features of what we see, and comes up with a unified view of the world.

6) The *trichromatic* and *opponent-process* theories of color vision apply to different stages of processing. In the first stage, three types of cones in the retina respond selectively to different wavelengths of light. In the second, *opponent-process cells* in the retina and the thalamus respond in opposite fashion to short and long wavelengths of light.

7) Perception involves the active construction of a model of the world from moment to moment. The *Gestalt principles* (e.g., *figure and ground, proximity, closure, similarity,* and *continuity*) describe visual strategies used in form perception. Gestalt and other perceptual principles can be used to improve the design of everyday objects.

8) We localize objects in visual space by using both *binocular* and *monocular* cues. Monocular cues to depth include interposition, linear perspective, and relative size. *Perceptual constancies* of shape, location, brightness, color, and size allow us to perceive objects as stable despite changes in the sensory patterns they produce. *Perceptual illusions* occur when sensory cues are misleading or when we misinterpret cues; illusions provide useful hints about perceptual processing.

HEARING

9) Hearing (*audition*) is affected by the intensity, frequency, and complexity of pressure waves in the air or other transmitting substance, corresponding to the experience of loudness, pitch, and timbre of the sound. The receptors for hearing are hair cells (cilia) embedded in the *basilar membrane,* in the interior of the *cochlea.* The sounds we hear are determined by patterns of hair-cell movement, which produce different neural codes. Gestalt principles apply to auditory as well as visual perception. When we localize sounds, we use as cues subtle differences in how pressure waves reach our ears.

OTHER SENSES

10) Taste (*gustation*) is a chemical sense. Elevations on the tongue, called *papillae,* contain many *taste buds.* There are four basic tastes—salty, sour, bitter, and sweet. Responses to a particular taste depend on culture, genetic differences among individuals ("supertasters" can taste a bitter compound that nontasters cannot), the texture and temperature of the food, and above all, the food's smell.

11) Smell (*olfaction*) is also a chemical sense. No basic odors have been identified, and the neural code for smell remains to be worked out. There may be as many as a thousand different receptor types for smell, and much of the processing for smell may occur within the nose itself. Cultural and individual differences affect people's responses to particular odors. *Pheromones* have not yet been shown to play a role in human sexual response.

12) The skin senses include touch (pressure), warmth, cold, and pain. Except in the case of pressure, no simple correspondence seems to exist between these four senses and different types of receptors. Pain is both a skin sense and an internal sense. According to the *gate-control theory,* the experience of pain depends on whether neural impulses get past a "gate" in the spinal cord and reach the brain. This theory, although it does not completely explain pain, has led to important advances in pain treatment.

13) *Kinesthesis* tells us where our body parts are located, and *equilibrium* tells us the orientation of the body as a whole. Together, these two senses provide us with a feeling of physical embodiment.

PERCEPTUAL POWERS: ORIGINS AND INFLUENCES

14) Studies of animals, human infants, and blind people who have recovered their sight suggest that many fundamental perceptual skills are inborn or acquired shortly after birth. By using the *visual cliff,* for example, psychologists have learned that babies have depth perception by the age of 6 months and possibly even earlier. However, without certain experiences early in life, cells in the nervous system deteriorate, change, or fail to form appropriate neural pathways, and perception is impaired.

15) Psychological influences on perception include needs, beliefs, emotions, and expectations. These influences are affected by culture, which gives people practice with certain kinds of experiences. Because psychological factors affect the way we construct the perceptual world, the evidence of our senses is not always reliable.

PUZZLES OF PERCEPTION

16) Many perceptual processes occur outside of awareness and without conscious intention. In the laboratory, simple visual subliminal messages can influence behavior, at least briefly. However, there is no evidence that complex behaviors (such as losing weight or raising self-esteem) can be manipulated by "subliminal-perception" tapes, as discussed in "Issues in Popular Culture."

17) *Extrasensory perception (ESP)* refers to paranormal abilities such as telepathy, clairvoyance, precognition, and out-of-body experiences. Believers in ESP tend to overlook disconfirming evidence—for example, times when they "knew" something bad was going to happen and it didn't. There is to date no replicated and convincing evidence for ESP. Many so-called psychics take advantage of people's desire to believe in ESP, but what they do is no different from the tricks of any good magician. The story of ESP supports the most important fact about human perception: that it does not merely capture objective reality, but also reflects our needs, biases, and beliefs.

KEY TERMS

sensation 204
sense receptors 204
perception 204
transduction 205
anatomical codes 206
doctrine of specific nerve energies 206
functional codes 206
psychophysics 206
absolute threshold 207
difference threshold and jnd 209
Weber's law 209
signal-detection theory 209
sensory adaptation 210
sensory deprivation 211
selective attention 212
hue 213
brightness 213
saturation 213
complexity of light 213
retina 214

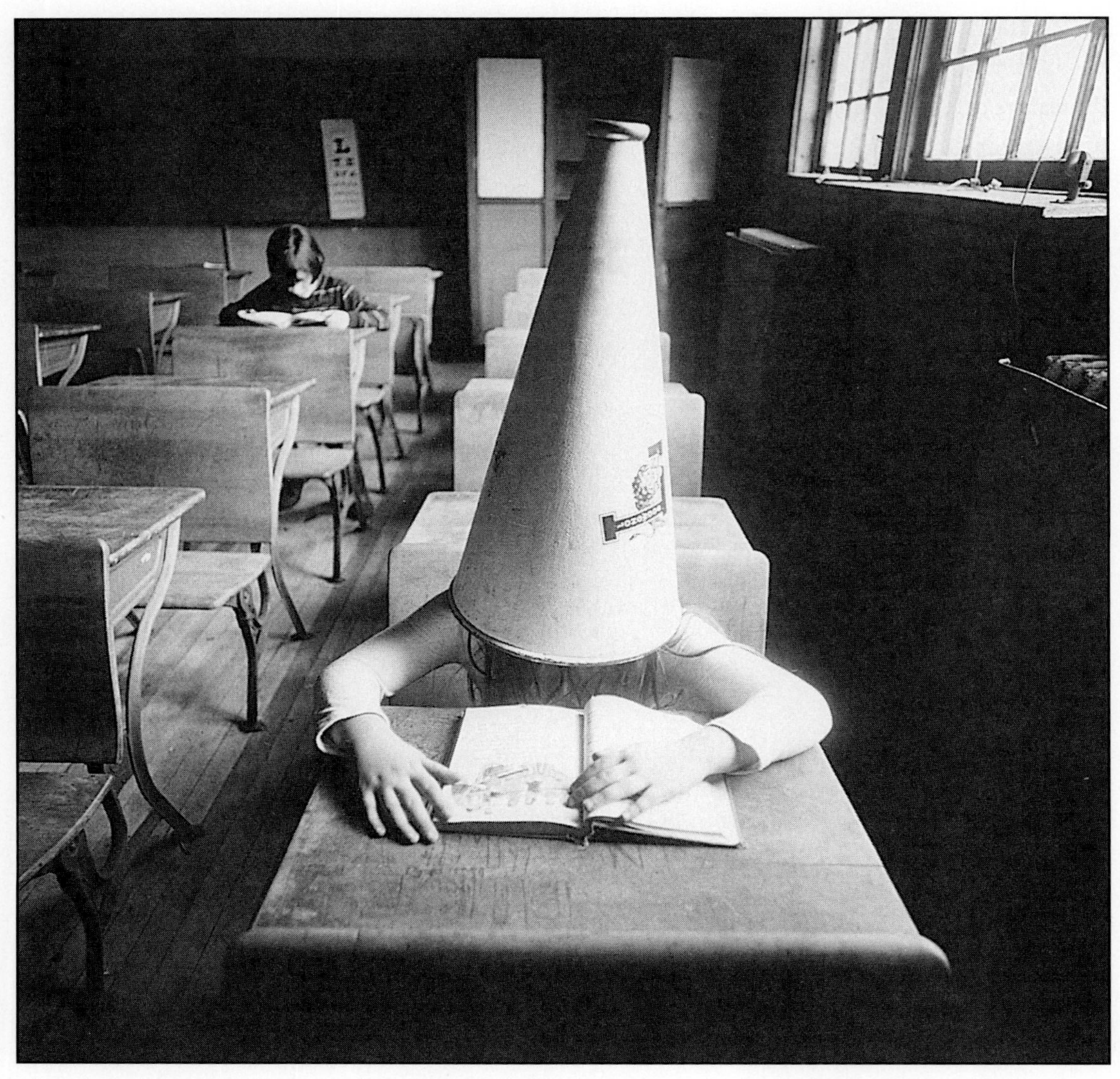

[R]eward and punishment . . . these are the spur and reins
whereby all mankind are set on work, and guided.

—John Locke

CHAPTER SEVEN

Learning

IT'S JANUARY 1, A BRAND-NEW YEAR. The sins and lapses of the old year are behind you; you're ready for a fresh start. Optimistically, you sit down to record your New Year's resolutions:

1. Eat healthfully; no more extra-rich ice cream.
2. Raise grades; spend more time studying.
3. Be easier to get along with; control temper.
4. Get more exercise; take up jogging.
5. Control spending; pay off credit card.
6. (You fill in the blank.)

How likely are you to achieve these goals? Some people do fulfill most of their resolutions, but for others, the road to frustration is paved with good intentions. Within weeks, days, or even hours, they find themselves backsliding ("Well, maybe just one *small* dish of ice cream"). They may end up feeling like the proverbial old dog, unable to learn new tricks. In fact, however, all of us can learn new tricks: By studying the laws of learning, we can improve our ability to change behavior in desirable ways—as we will see in this chapter.

In ordinary speech, the word *learning* often refers to classroom activities, such as memorizing the facts of geography, or to the acquisition of practical skills, such as carpentry or sewing. But to psychologists, **learning** is *any* relatively permanent change in behavior that occurs because of experience (excluding changes due to fatigue, injury, or disease). Experience is the great teacher, providing the essential link between the past and the future and enabling an organism to adapt to changing circumstances in order to survive and thrive. Our species is more dependent on learning than is any other, but learning is a fundamental process in all animals, from the lowliest backyard bug to the most eminent human scholar.

Research on learning has been heavily influenced by **behaviorism,** the school of psychology that accounts for behavior in terms of observable events, without reference to such hypothetical mental entities as "mind" or "will." Behaviorists have focused on a basic kind of learning called **conditioning,** which involves associations between environmental stimuli and responses. They have shown that two types of conditioning, *classical conditioning* and *operant conditioning,* can explain much of human behavior. But as we will see, other approaches, collectively known as *social-learning theories,* hold that omitting mental processes from explanations of human learning is like omitting passion from descriptions of sex: You may explain the form, but you miss the substance. To social-learning theorists (and cognitive theorists, as well), learning is not so much a change in behavior as a change in *knowledge* that has the *potential* for affecting behavior.

CLASSICAL CONDITIONING: NEW REFLEXES FROM OLD

At the turn of the century, the great Russian physiologist Ivan Pavlov (1849–1936) was studying salivation in dogs, as part of a research program on digestion. His work would shortly win him the Nobel Prize in physiology and medicine. One of Pavlov's procedures was to make a surgical opening in a dog's cheek and insert a tube that conducted saliva away from the animal's salivary gland so that the saliva could be measured. To stimulate the reflexive flow of saliva, Pavlov placed meat powder or other food in the dog's mouth. This procedure was later refined by others (see Figure 7.1).

learning A relatively permanent change in behavior (or behavioral potential) due to experience.

behaviorism An approach to psychology that emphasizes the study of observable behavior and the role of the environment as a determinant of behavior.

conditioning A basic kind of learning that involves associations between environmental stimuli and the organism's responses.

Ivan Pavlov is in the center, flanked by his students and a canine subject.

Pavlov was a truly dedicated scientific observer. Many years later, as he lay dying, he even dictated his sensations for posterity! During his salivation studies, Pavlov noticed something that most people would have overlooked or dismissed as trivial. After a dog had been brought to the laboratory a number of times, it would start to salivate *before* the food was placed in its mouth. The sight or smell of the food, the dish in which the food was kept, even the sight of the person who delivered the food or the sound of the person's footsteps were enough to start the dog's mouth watering. This new salivary response clearly was not inborn but was acquired through experience.

At first, Pavlov treated the dog's drooling as an annoying "psychic secretion." But after reviewing the literature on reflexes, he realized that he had stumbled onto an important phenomenon, one that he came to believe was the basis of all learning in human beings and other animals. He called that phenomenon a "conditional" reflex—conditional because it depended on environmental conditions. Later, an error in the translation of his writings transformed "conditional" into "conditioned," the word most commonly used today.

Figure 7.1
A Modification of Pavlov's Method

In this apparatus, which was based on Pavlov's techniques, saliva from a dog's cheek flowed down a tube and was measured by the movement of a needle on a revolving drum.

Pavlov soon dropped what he had been doing and turned to the study of conditioned reflexes, to which he devoted the last three decades of his life. Why were his dogs salivating to aspects of the environment other than food? Pavlov decided that it was pointless to speculate about his dogs' thoughts, wishes, or memories. Instead, he analyzed the environment in which the conditioned reflex arose. The original salivary reflex, according to Pavlov, consisted of an **unconditioned stimulus (US),** food, and an **unconditioned response (UR),** salivation. By an *unconditioned stimulus,* Pavlov meant an event or thing that elicits a response automatically or reflexively. By an *unconditioned response,* he meant the response that is automatically produced:

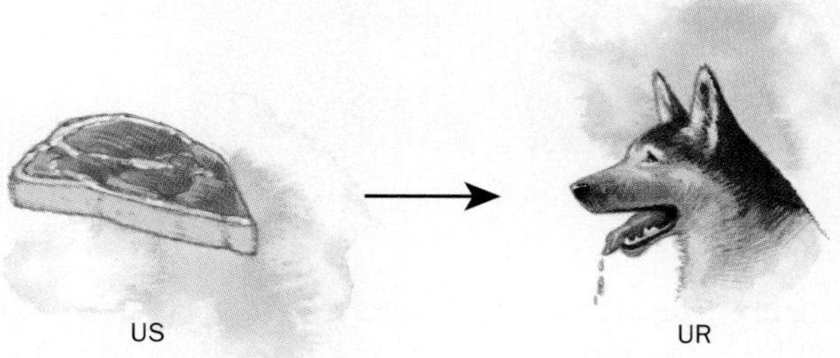

Learning occurs, Pavlov said, when some neutral stimulus is regularly paired with an unconditioned stimulus. The neutral stimulus then becomes a **conditioned stimulus (CS),** which elicits a learned or **conditioned response (CR)** that is usually similar to the original, unlearned one. In Pavlov's laboratory, the sight of the food dish, which had not previously elicited salivation, became a CS for salivation:

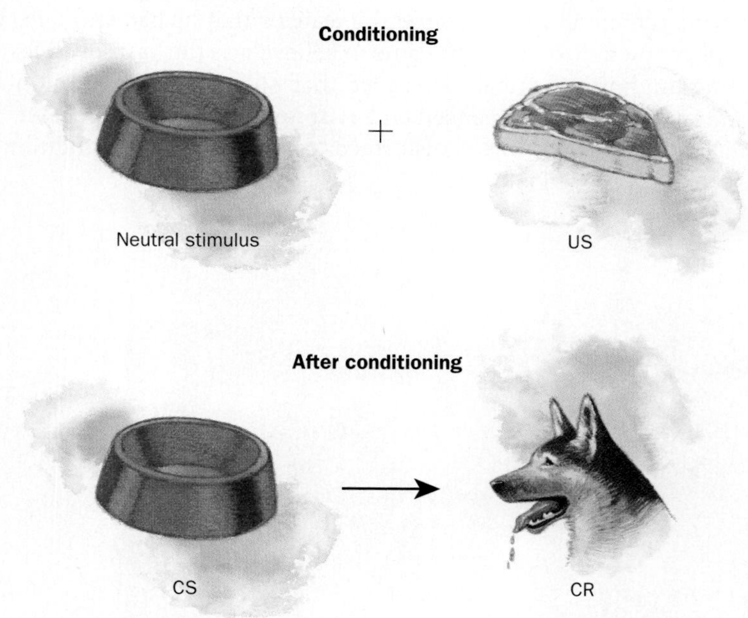

unconditioned stimulus (US) The classical-conditioning term for a stimulus that elicits a reflexive response in the absence of learning.

unconditioned response (UR) The classical-conditioning term for a reflexive response elicited by a stimulus in the absence of learning.

conditioned stimulus (CS) The classical-conditioning term for an initially neutral stimulus that comes to elicit a conditioned response after being associated with an unconditioned stimulus.

conditioned response (CR) The classical-conditioning term for a response that is elicited by a conditioned stimulus; occurs after the conditioned stimulus is associated with an unconditioned stimulus.

In a series of experiments, Pavlov showed that a wide variety of stimuli can become a conditioned stimulus for salivation—the ticking of a metronome, the musical tone of a tuning fork, the vibrating sound of a buzzer, a triangle drawn on a large card, even a pinprick or an electric shock. None of these stimuli naturally elicits salivation, but if paired with food, all of them will (although some associations are easier to establish than others). The optimal interval between the presentation of the neutral stimulus and the presentation of the US depends on the kind of response being conditioned; in the laboratory, the interval is often less than a second.

The procedure by which a neutral stimulus becomes a conditioned stimulus became known as **classical conditioning** and is also sometimes called *Pavlovian* or *respondent conditioning.* Because the terminology of classical conditioning can be hard to learn, let's pause for a Quick Quiz before going on.

Quick Quiz

See whether you can name the four components of classical conditioning in these two situations.

1. Five-year-old Samantha is watching a storm from her window. A huge bolt of lightning is followed by a tremendous thunderclap, and Samantha jumps at the noise. This happens several more times. There is a brief lull and then another lightning bolt. Samantha jumps in response to the bolt.
2. Gregory's mouth waters whenever he eats anything with lemon in it. One day, while reading an ad that shows a big glass of lemonade, Gregory notices his mouth watering.

Answers:

1. US = the thunderclap; UR = jumping elicited by the noise; CS = the sight of the lightning; CR = jumping elicited by the lightning. 2. US = the taste of lemon; UR = salivation elicited by the taste of lemon; CS = the picture of a glass of lemonade; CR = salivation elicited by the picture.

Since Pavlov's day, researchers have established that nearly any automatic, involuntary response can become a conditioned response—for example, heartbeat, stomach secretions, blood pressure, reflexive movements, blinking, or muscle contractions. For optimal conditioning, the stimulus to be conditioned should *precede* the unconditioned stimulus rather than follow it or occur simultaneously with it. This makes sense, because in classical conditioning, the conditioned stimulus becomes a kind of signal for the unconditioned stimulus. It enables the organism to *prepare* for an event that is about to happen. In Pavlov's studies, for instance, a bell or buzzer was a signal that meat was coming, and the dog's salivation was preparation for digesting food.

Indeed, today, many psychologists contend that what an animal or person actually learns in classical conditioning is not merely an association between two paired stimuli that occur close together in time, but rather *information* conveyed by one stimulus about another. In this view, the mere pairing of an unconditioned stimulus and a neutral stimulus is not sufficient to produce learning; to become a conditioned stimulus, the neutral stimulus must reliably *signal,* or *predict,* the unconditioned stimulus (Rescorla, 1968, 1988; Rescorla & Wagner, 1972).

Suppose you are a budding behaviorist and you want to teach a rat to fear a tone. Following the usual procedure, you repeatedly sound the tone before an unconditioned stimulus for fear, such as a mild electric shock: tone, shock, tone, shock, tone, shock. . . . After 20 such pairings, the rat shows signs of fear upon hearing the tone. Now suppose you do this experiment again—on 20 trials the tone precedes the shock—but this time you randomly intersperse an additional 20 trials in which the shock occurs *without* the tone. With this method, the tone is paired with the shock just as often as in the standard procedure, but it signals shock only half of the time. In other words, the shock is equally likely to occur when the tone is absent as when

classical conditioning The process by which a previously neutral stimulus acquires the capacity to elicit a response through association with a stimulus that already elicits a similar or related response.

GET INVOLVED

Try out your behavioral skills by conditioning an eye-blink response in a friend, using classical conditioning procedures. You'll need a drinking straw and something to make a ringing sound—a spoon tapped on a water glass works well. Tell your friend that you're going to blow in his or her eye through the straw, but don't say why. Immediately before each puff of air, make the ringing sound. Repeat this procedure ten times. Then make the ringing sound but don't *puff. Your friend will probably blink anyway and may continue to do so for one or two more repetitions of the sound before the response fades. Can you identify the US, the UR, the CS, and the CR in this exercise?*

it is present. Under these conditions, the tone does not provide any information about the shock, and hardly any conditioning occurs.

From this and similar findings, Robert Rescorla (1988) has concluded that "Pavlovian conditioning is not a stupid process by which the organism willy-nilly forms associations between any two stimuli that happen to co-occur. Rather, the organism is better seen as an information seeker using logical and perceptual relations among events, along with its own preconceptions, to form a sophisticated representation of its world." Not all learning theorists agree with this conclusion or with the findings on which it is based; an orthodox behaviorist would say that it's silly to talk about the preconceptions of a rat. The important point, however, is that for some researchers, concepts such as "information seeking," "preconceptions," and "representations of the world" have opened the door to a more cognitive view of classical conditioning.

PRINCIPLES OF CLASSICAL CONDITIONING

The processes involved in classical conditioning are common to all species, from worms to *Homo sapiens.* Among the most important are extinction, higher-order conditioning, and stimulus generalization and discrimination.

EXTINCTION Conditioned responses do not necessarily last forever. If, after conditioning, the conditioned stimulus is repeatedly presented without the unconditioned stimulus, the conditioned response eventually disappears, and **extinction** is said to have occurred (see Figure 7.2). Suppose that you train a dog to salivate to the sound of a bell, but then you ring the bell every five minutes and do *not* follow it

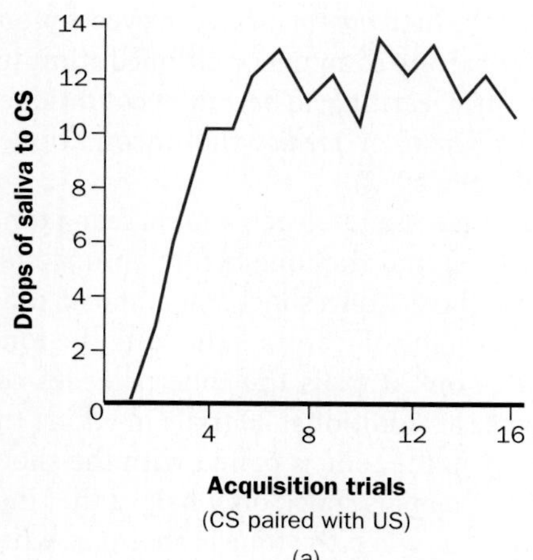

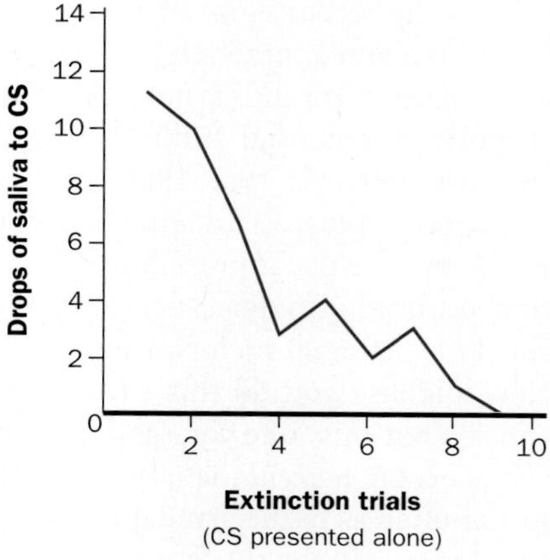

Figure 7.2
Acquisition and Extinction of a Salivary Response

When a neutral stimulus is consistently followed by an unconditioned stimulus for salivation, the neutral stimulus also comes to elicit salivation (a); that is, it becomes a conditioned stimulus. When the conditioned stimulus is repeatedly presented without the unconditioned stimulus, the conditioned salivary response weakens and eventually disappears (b); it has been extinguished.

with food. The dog will salivate less and less to the bell and will soon stop salivating altogether; salivation has been extinguished. However, if you come back the next day and ring the bell, the dog may salivate again for a few trials. The reappearance of the response, which is called **spontaneous recovery,** explains why completely eliminating a conditioned response usually requires more than one extinction session.

HIGHER-ORDER CONDITIONING Sometimes a neutral stimulus can become a conditioned stimulus by being paired with an already established CS, a procedure known as **higher-order conditioning.** Say a dog has learned to salivate to the ringing of a bell. Now you present a flash of light before ringing the bell. With repeated pairings of the light and the bell, the dog may learn to salivate to the light, although the light will probably elicit less salivation than the bell does. The procedure looks like this:

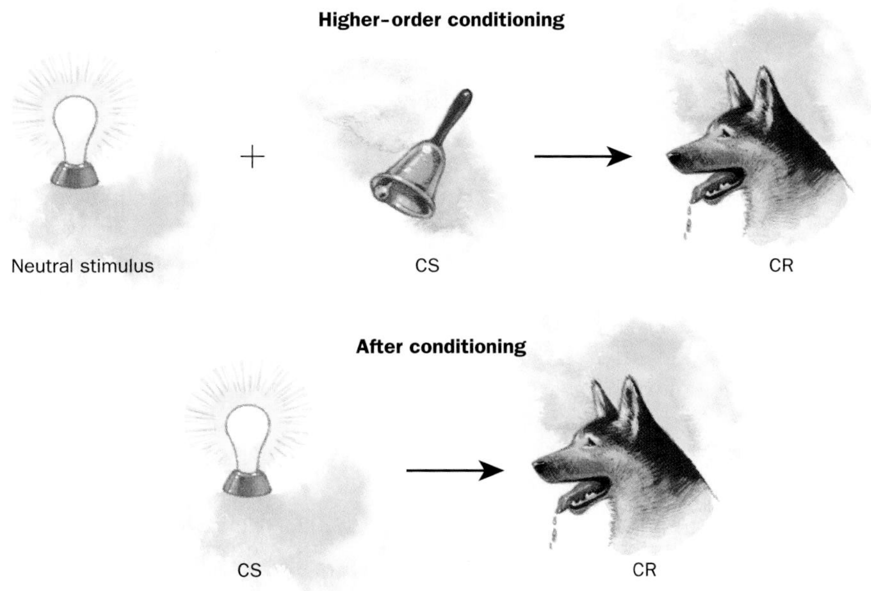

It may be that words acquire their emotional meanings through a process of higher-order conditioning. When they are paired with objects or other words that already elicit some emotional response, they, too, may come to elicit that response (Chance, 1994; Staats & Staats, 1957). For example, a child may learn a positive response to the word *birthday* because of its association with gifts and attention. Conversely, the child may learn a negative response to ethnic or national labels, such as *Swede, Turk,* or *Jew,* if those words are paired with already disagreeable words, such as *dumb* or *dirty.* Higher-order conditioning, in other words, may contribute to the formation of prejudices.

STIMULUS GENERALIZATION AND DISCRIMINATION After a stimulus becomes a conditioned stimulus for some response, other, similar stimuli may produce a similar reaction—a phenomenon known as **stimulus generalization.** For example, a dog conditioned to salivate to middle C on the piano may also salivate to D, which is one tone above C, even though D was not paired with food. Stimulus generalization is described nicely by an old English proverb: "He who hath been bitten by a snake fears a rope."

The mirror image of stimulus generalization is **stimulus discrimination,** in which *different* responses are made to stimuli that resemble the conditioned stimu-

extinction The weakening and eventual disappearance of a learned response; in classical conditioning, it occurs when the conditioned stimulus is no longer paired with the unconditioned stimulus.

spontaneous recovery The reappearance of a learned response after its apparent extinction.

higher-order conditioning In classical conditioning, a procedure in which a neutral stimulus becomes a conditioned stimulus through association with an already established conditioned stimulus.

stimulus generalization After conditioning, the tendency to respond to a stimulus that resembles one involved in the original conditioning; in classical conditioning, it occurs when a stimulus that resembles the conditioned stimulus elicits the conditioned response.

stimulus discrimination The tendency to respond differently to two or more similar stimuli; in classical conditioning, it occurs when a stimulus similar to the CS fails to evoke the CR.

lus in some way. Suppose that you condition your poodle to salivate to middle C on the piano by repeatedly pairing the sound with food. Now you play middle C on a guitar, *without* following it by food (but you continue to follow C on the piano by food). Eventually, the dog will learn to salivate to a C on the piano and not to salivate to the same note on the guitar; that is, the animal will discriminate between the two sounds.

CLASSICAL CONDITIONING IN REAL LIFE

If a dog can learn to salivate to the ringing of a bell, so can you. In fact, you probably have learned to salivate to the sound of a lunch bell, not to mention the sight of the refrigerator, the phrase *hot fudge sundae*, "mouth-watering" pictures of food in magazines, the sight of a waiter in a restaurant, and a voice calling out "Dinner's ready!" But the role of classical conditioning goes far beyond the learning of simple reflexive responses; conditioning affects us every day in many ways.

ACCOUNTING FOR TASTE We probably learn to like and dislike many things, including particular foods, through a process of classical conditioning. In the laboratory, researchers have taught animals to dislike foods or odors by pairing them with drugs that cause nausea or other unpleasant symptoms. One researcher trained slugs to associate the smell of carrots, which slugs normally like, with a bitter-tasting chemical that they detest. Soon the slugs were avoiding the smell of carrots. The researcher then demonstrated higher-order conditioning by pairing the smell of carrots with the smell of potato. Sure enough, the slugs began to avoid the smell of potato as well (Sahley, Rudy, & Gelperin, 1981).

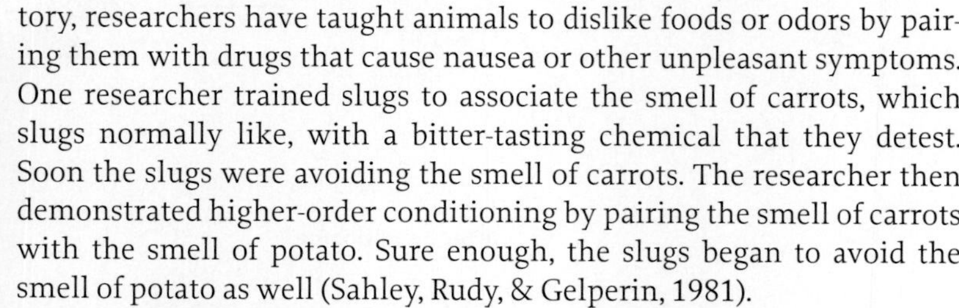

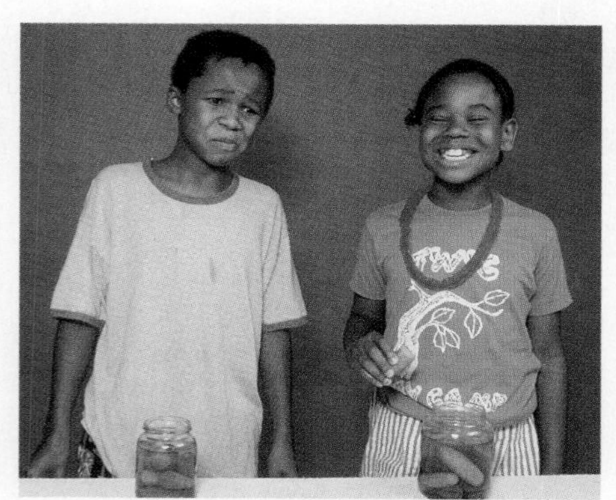

Whether we say "yum" or "yuck" to certain foods may depend on a past experience involving classical conditioning.

Martin Seligman, who has studied learned behavior in the laboratory for many years, has told how he himself was conditioned to hate béarnaise sauce. One night, shortly after he and his wife ate a delicious filet mignon with béarnaise sauce, he came down with the flu. Naturally, he felt wretched. His misery had nothing to do with the béarnaise sauce, of course, yet the next time he tried it, he found he disliked the taste (Seligman & Hager, 1972).

Sometimes we like a food, but our bodies refuse to tolerate it. This happens with allergies: You adore chocolate, say, but your skin breaks out in hives whenever you eat it. Some allergic reactions may be classically conditioned. In a study with guinea pigs, researchers paired the smell of either fish or sulphur with injection of a substance to which the animals were already allergic. After only ten pairings, the animals became allergic to the odor alone. Their blood histamine levels rose, just as they would have done after exposure to a true allergen (Russell et al., 1984). People, too, can learn to be allergic to substances that have been associated with substances to which they are already sensitive. A century ago, a physician reported using an artificial rose to provoke asthmatic symptoms in an allergic patient; since then several studies have confirmed that nonallergenic objects that have been associated with allergens can induce allergic and asthmatic symptoms in some people (Ader & Cohen, 1993; Gauci et al., 1994).

LEARNING TO LOVE—AND TO LIKE Classical conditioning involves involuntary bodily responses, and many such responses are part and parcel of human emotions. It follows that this type of learning may explain how we acquire emotional responses to objects, events, and places.

One of the first psychologists to recognize this implication of Pavlovian theory was John B. Watson, who founded American behaviorism and was an enthusiastic promoter of Pavlov's ideas. Watson believed that emotions were no more than collections of gut-level muscular and glandular responses, a view later detractors derided as "muscle-twitch psychology" (Hunt, 1993). A few such responses, said Watson, are inborn. For the sake of convenience, he called these responses fear, rage, and love, but he was really referring to patterns of movement and changes in breathing, circulation, and digestion, and not to subjective feelings. In Watson's analysis, "love" included the smiling and burbling that babies are apt to do when they are stroked and cuddled. The stroking and cuddling are unconditioned stimuli; the smiling and burbling are unconditioned responses. According to Watson, an infant learns to love other things when those things are paired with stroking and cuddling. The thing most likely to be paired with stroking and cuddling is, of course, a parent. Learning to love a parent (or anyone else, for that matter) is really no different from learning to salivate to the sound of a bell—at least in Watson's view.

Classical conditioning can also help account for other positive emotional responses. For example, many of Madison Avenue's techniques for getting us to like certain products are based on the principles first demonstrated by Pavlov, whether advertising executives realize it or not. In one study, college students looked at slides of either a beige pen or a blue pen. During the presentation, half the students heard a song from a recent musical film, and half heard a selection of traditional music from India. (The experimenter made the reasonable assumption that the show tune would be more appealing to most young Americans.) Later the students were allowed to choose one of the pens. Almost three-fourths of those who heard the popular music chose a pen that was the same color as the one they had seen in the slides. An equal number of those who heard the Indian music chose a pen that *differed* in color from the one they had seen (Gorn, 1982). In classical-conditioning terms, the music was an unconditioned stimulus for internal responses associated with pleasure or displeasure, and the pens became conditioned stimuli for similar responses. You can see why television commercials often pair their products with music, attractive people, or other appealing sounds and images.

CONDITIONED FEARS Dislikes and negative emotions such as fear, as we saw in our discussion of higher-order conditioning, can also be classically conditioned. According to behaviorists, many fears are conditioned responses to stimuli that were originally neutral. Cancer patients, for example, sometimes develop a classically conditioned fear of places and objects that have been associated with their chemotherapy treatments—the sound of a nurse's voice, the smell of rubbing alcohol, the waiting room of the clinic. In one study (Jacobsen et al., 1995), patients who drank lemon-lime Kool-Aid before their chemotherapy sessions developed an anxiety response to the drink, and they continued to feel anxious even when the drink was offered in their homes rather than at the clinic.

When a fear of an object or situation is irrational and interferes with normal activities, it qualifies as a *phobia.* To demonstrate how a phobia might be acquired, John Watson and Rosalie Rayner (1920) deliberately established a rat phobia in an 11-month-old boy named Albert. The ethics, procedures, and findings of their study have since been questioned, and no researcher today would perform such a demonstration. Nevertheless, the study remains a classic, and its main conclusion, that fears can be conditioned, is still well accepted.

"Little Albert" was a rather placid tyke who rarely cried. When Watson and Rayner gave him a furry white rat to play with (a live one, not a toy), Albert showed no fear; in fact, he was delighted. However, like most children, Albert was afraid of loud noises. Whenever a steel bar behind his head was struck with a hammer, he would jump and fall sideways onto the mattress he was sitting on. The noise was an unconditioned stimulus for the unconditioned response of fear.

Having established that Albert liked rats, Watson and Rayner set about teaching him to fear them. Again they offered him a rat, but this time, as Albert reached for it, one of the researchers struck the steel bar. Startled, Albert fell onto the mattress. The researchers repeated this procedure several times. Albert began to whimper and tremble. Finally, the rat was offered alone, without the noise. Albert fell over, cried, and crawled away as fast as he could; the rat had become a conditioned stimulus for fear:

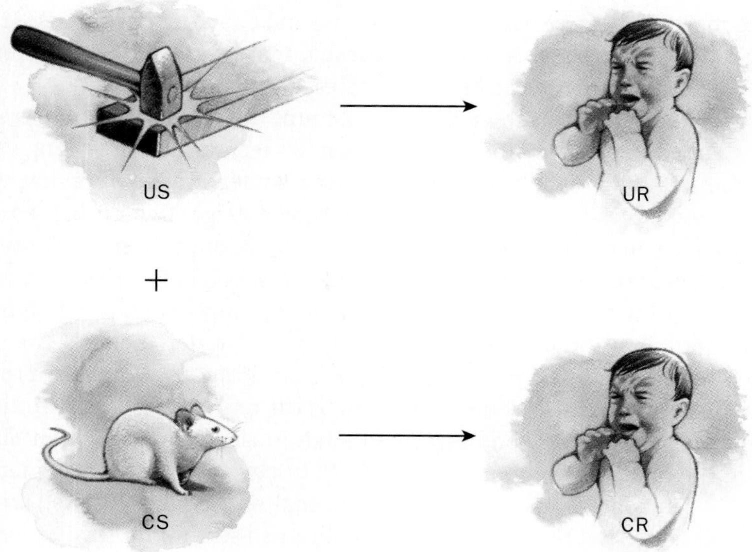

Further tests showed that Albert's fear had generalized to other hairy or furry objects, including white rabbits, cotton wool, a Santa Claus mask, and even John Watson's hair.

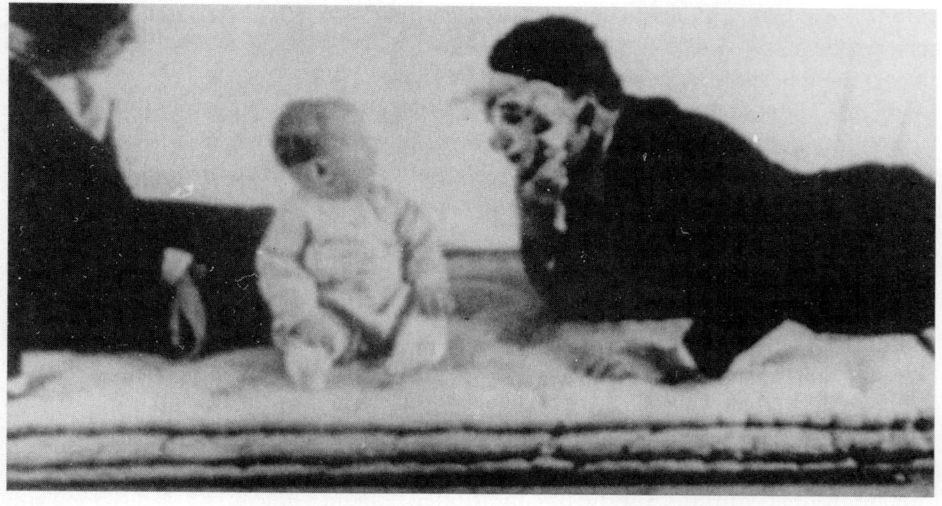

This photograph, made from a 1919 film, shows Rosalie Raynor and John Watson, in a mask, testing Little Albert for stimulus generalization. (Photo courtesy of Prof. Benjamin Harris.)

OPERANT CONDITIONING: THE CARROT AND THE STICK

At the end of the nineteenth century, in the first known scientific effort to study anger, G. Stanley Hall (1899) asked people to describe angry episodes they had experienced or observed. One informant told of a 3-year-old girl who broke out in furious, seemingly uncontrollable sobs when she was punished by being kept home from a ride. In the middle of her tantrum, the child suddenly stopped crying and asked in a perfectly calm voice if her father was in. Told no, she immediately resumed her sobbing.

An instantaneous learning experience.

Children, of course, cry for many valid reasons—pain, discomfort, fear, illness, fatigue—and these cries deserve an adult's sympathy and attention. However, even infants only a few weeks old will also learn to cry when they are *not* in physical distress if adults respond to such cries (Gewirtz, 1991). The child in Hall's study had learned, from prior experience, that an outburst of sobbing would bring her attention and possibly the ride she wanted—that her tears stood a reasonable chance of working. Her behavior, which some might label "naughty," was perfectly understandable, because it followed one of the most basic laws of learning: *Behavior becomes more or less likely depending on its consequences.*

An emphasis on environmental consequences is at the heart of **operant conditioning** (also called *instrumental conditioning*), the second type of conditioning studied by behaviorists. In classical conditioning, the animal's or person's behavior does not have such consequences; in Pavlov's procedure, the dog got food, whether it salivated or not. But in operant conditioning, the organism's response (the little girl's sobbing, for example) *operates* (produces effects) on the environment. These effects, in turn, influence whether the response will occur again. Classical and operant conditioning also tend to differ in the types of responses they involve. In classical conditioning, the response is reflexive, an automatic reaction to something happening in the environment, such as the sight of food or the sound of a bell. Generally, responses in operant conditioning are complex and are not reflexive, and they involve the entire organism—for instance, riding a bicycle, writing a letter, climbing a mountain, . . . or throwing a tantrum.

Operant conditioning has been studied since the turn of the century, although it wasn't called "operant" until later. Edward Thorndike (1898), then a young doctoral candidate, set the stage by observing cats as they tried to escape from a "puzzle box" to reach a scrap of fish that was just outside the box. At first, the cat would engage in trial and error, scratching, biting, or swatting at parts of the cage in an unorganized way. Then, after a few minutes, the cat would chance on the successful response (loosening a bolt, pulling a string, or hitting a button) and rush out to get the reward. Placed in the box again, the cat now took a little less time to escape, and after several trials, the animal immediately made the correct response. According to Thorndike's *law of effect*, the correct response had been "stamped in" by its satisfying effects (getting the food). In contrast, annoying or unsatisfying effects "stamped out" behavior. Behavior, said Thorndike, is controlled by its consequences.

This general principle was elaborated and extended to more complex forms of behavior by B. F. (Burrhus Frederic) Skinner (1904–1990). Calling his approach "radical behaviorism" to distinguish it from the behaviorism of John Watson, Skinner argued that to understand behavior we should focus on the external causes of an action and the action's consequences. Skinner was careful to avoid such terms as "satisfying"

operant conditioning The process by which a response becomes more likely to occur or less so, depending on its consequences.

and "annoying," which reflect assumptions about what an organism feels and wants. For Skinner, the explanation of behavior was to be found by looking outside the individual rather than within.

Skinner has often been called the greatest of American psychologists, and certainly he is one of the best known. Yet despite his fame, or perhaps because of it, his position is often distorted by the general public, psychology students, and even some psychologists. For example, many people think Skinner denied the existence of human consciousness and the value of studying it. It is true that Skinner's predecessor John Watson thought that psychologists should study only public (external) events, not private (internal) ones. But Skinner maintained that we can study private events, by observing our own sensory responses, the verbal reports of others, and the conditions under which such events occur. For Skinner, the private events we "see" when we examine our own "consciousness" are simply the early stages of behavior, before the behavior begins to act on the environment. These private events are as real or physical as public ones, Skinner said, although they are less accessible and harder to describe (Skinner, 1972, 1990).

Because Skinner thought the environment could and should be manipulated to alter behavior, some critics have portrayed him as cold-blooded or even sinister. But Skinner, who was a humane and mild-mannered man, felt that it would be unethical *not* to try to improve human behavior by applying behavioral principles. In recognition of his efforts, the American Humanist Association honored him with its Humanist of the Year Award.

One famous controversy regarding Skinner occurred when he invented an enclosed "living space," the Air-Crib, for his younger daughter Deborah when she was an infant. This "baby box," as it came to be known, was set up to eliminate the usual discomforts suffered by babies, including heat, cold, wetness, and confinement by blankets and clothing. It had temperature and humidity controls, so Deborah could wear just a diaper and move around freely. People imagined, incorrectly, that the Skinners were leaving their child in the baby box all the time, without giving her the cuddling that is essential to healthy development, and for years rumors circulated that Deborah had gone insane or killed herself. Actually, both of Skinner's daughters turned out to be perfectly normal. Deborah became a successful artist and writer. The other daughter, Julie, became a behaviorist and raised her own two daughters in an Air-Crib.

Whereas some psychologists, notably the humanists, have argued for the existence of free will, Skinner regarded free will as an illusion and steadfastly supported the *determinist* view that we are shaped by our environments and our genetic heritage. Skinner refused to credit personal traits, such as curiosity, or mental events, such as goals and motives, for his own or anyone else's accomplishments. Indeed, he regarded himself not as a "self" but as a "repertoire of behaviors" resulting from an envi-

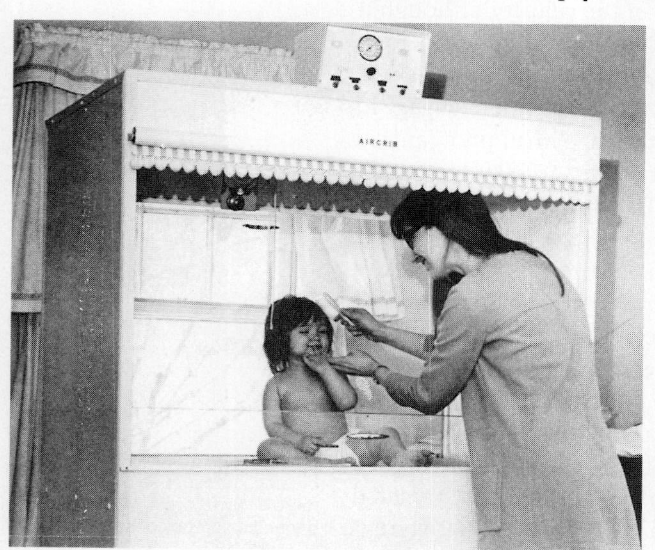

Skinner's invention of the Air-Crib reflected his belief that if you want to change someone's behavior—for example, a baby's cries of distress or discomfort—you must change the environment. The baby in this Air-Crib is Skinner's granddaughter Lisa, with her mother Julie.

ronment that encouraged looking, searching, and investigating (Bjork, 1993). "So far as I know," he wrote in the third volume of his autobiography (Skinner, 1983), "my behavior at any given moment has been nothing more than the product of my genetic endowment, my personal history, and the current setting."

REINFORCERS AND PUNISHERS: A MATTER OF CONSEQUENCE

In Skinner's analysis, which has inspired an immense body of research, a response ("operant") can lead to one of three types of consequences. The first type is neutral as far as future behavior is concerned: It neither increases nor decreases the probability that the behavior will recur. If a door handle squeaks each time you turn it, and the sound does not affect whether you turn the door handle in the future, the squeak is a neutral consequence.

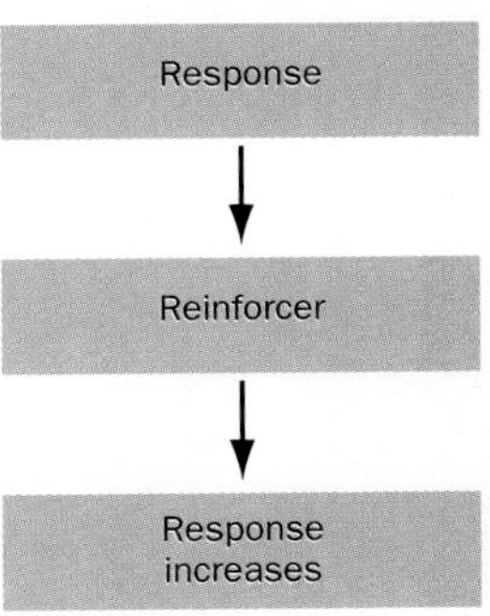

A second type of consequence involves **reinforcement** (see Figure 7.3). In reinforcement, a reinforcing stimulus, or *reinforcer,* strengthens or increases the probability of the response that it follows. When you are training your dog to sit on command, and you praise her or pat her on the head when she obeys, you are trying to reinforce the good behavior. Reinforcers are roughly equivalent to rewards, and many psychologists have no objection to the use of the words *reward* and *reinforcer* as approximate synonyms. However, strict behaviorists avoid *reward* because it is the organism, not the response, that is rewarded; the response is *strengthened.* Also, in common usage, a reward is something earned that results in happiness or satisfaction. But technically, any stimulus is a reinforcer if it strengthens the preceding behavior, whether or not the organism experiences pleasure or any other positive state. And conversely, no matter how pleasurable a stimulus is, it is not a reinforcer if it does not increase the likelihood of a response. It's pleasurable to get a paycheck, but if you get paid regardless of the effort you put into your work, the money will not reinforce "hard-work behavior."

reinforcement The process by which a stimulus or event strengthens or increases the probability of the response that it follows.

Figure 7.3
Reinforcement in Action

If the command "sit" (a) results in the desired response and the response is followed by a reinforcer (b), the response will be strengthened.

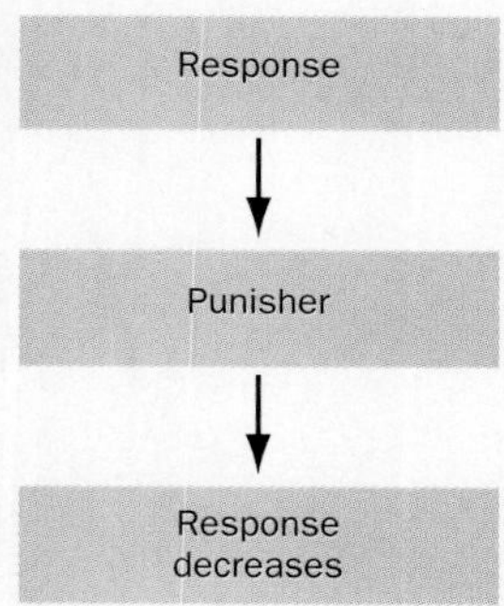

The third type of consequence involves **punishment,** which occurs when the stimulus or event that follows a response weakens it or makes it less likely to recur. Any aversive (unpleasant) stimulus or event can be a *punisher.* A dog that runs into the street and is nearly hit by a passing car will be less likely to run into the street in the future when cars are around. Later, we will see that deliberate punishment as a way of controlling behavior has many drawbacks.

As in classical conditioning, what an animal can learn through operant conditioning depends first and foremost on its physical characteristics; a fish cannot be trained to climb a ladder. And operant-conditioning procedures, like classical ones, work best when they capitalize on inborn tendencies. Years ago, Keller and Marian Breland (1961), psychologists who became animal trainers, described what happens when biological constraints are ignored. The Brelands found that animals often had trouble learning tasks that should have been easy. For example, a pig was supposed to drop large wooden coins in a box. Instead, the pig would drop the coin, push at it with its snout, throw it in the air, and push at it some more. This odd behavior actually delayed delivery of the reinforcer, so it was hard to explain in terms of operant principles. Apparently the pig's rooting instinct—its tendency to use its snout to uncover edible roots—was keeping it from learning the task. The Brelands called such a reversion to instinctive behavior **instinctive drift.**

Operant-conditioning procedures work best when they capitalize on an animal's natural responses. For example, it's easy to train pigs to hunt for truffles, a fungus that grows underground, because pigs have a natural rooting instinct.

POSITIVE AND NEGATIVE REINFORCERS AND PUNISHERS

Reinforcement and punishment may seem to be the proverbial carrot and stick, but they are not quite so simple as they seem. In our example of reinforcement, something pleasant (a doggie biscuit or a pat on the dog's head) followed the dog's response (heeling). This type of procedure is known as **positive reinforcement.** But there is another brand of reinforcement, **negative reinforcement,** which involves the *removal* of something *unpleasant.* If you politely ask your roommate to turn off some music you can't stand, and your roommate immediately complies, the likelihood of your being polite when making similar requests will probably increase. Your politeness has been strengthened (negatively reinforced) by the removal of the unpleasant music. As Table 7.1 shows, the positive–negative distinction can also be applied to punishment: Something unpleasant may occur (positive punishment), or something *pleasant* may be *removed* (negative punishment).

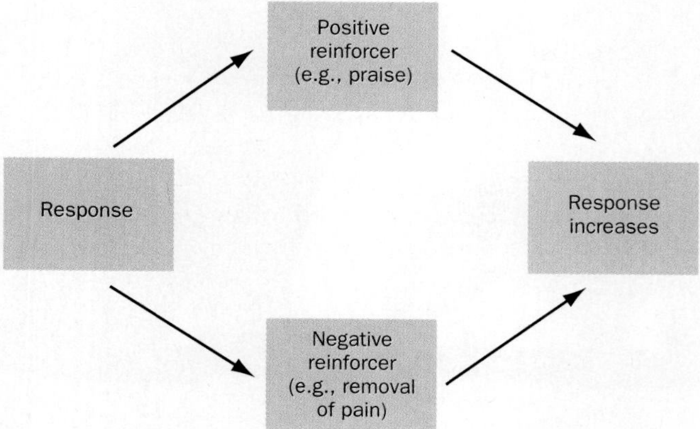

The distinction between positive and negative reinforcement has been a source of confusion and frustration for generations of students and has been known to turn strong and confident people into quivering heaps. We can assure you that if we had

TABLE 7.1 *Types of Reinforcement and Punishment*

In operant conditioning, a response increases or decreases in likelihood, depending on its consequences. The occurrence of a pleasant stimulus or the removal of an unpleasant one reinforces the response. The occurrence of an unpleasant stimulus or the removal of a pleasant one constitutes punishment, which weakens the response.

What happens to the response?	**What event follows the response?** Stimulus presented	Stimulus removed
Response increases	**Positive reinforcement** For example, completion of homework assignments increases when followed by praise.	**Negative reinforcement** For example, use of aspirin increases when followed by reduction of headache pain.
Response decreases	**Positive punishment** For example, nail biting decreases when followed by the taste of a bitter substance painted on the nails.	**Negative punishment** For example, parking in a "no parking" zone decreases when followed by loss of money (a fine).

been around when these terms were first coined, we would have complained loudly. One eminent behaviorist, Gregory Kimble (1993), has argued that it's still not too late to change their meanings so that they conform better to ordinary usage. But we doubt that changing the definitions at this point would help much because students who went on in psychology would still have to read articles and books using the old definitions. And in introductory courses, some books would be teaching one set of definitions and others a different set. That is why as textbook authors we've resigned ourselves to the traditional terms, irksome though they are.

You will master these terms more quickly if you understand that in reinforcement, "positive" and "negative" have nothing to do with "good" or "bad." They refer to *procedures*—giving something or taking something away. *With either positive or negative reinforcement, a response becomes more likely.* If you praise Ludwig for doing his homework and he starts studying more, that is positive reinforcement (of studying). If you have been nagging Ludwig to study more, and you stop the nagging when he starts his homework, that is negative reinforcement (of studying). In both cases, his studying has been reinforced. With positive reinforcement, he gets praise; with negative reinforcement, he stops getting nagged at. Think of a positive reinforcer as something that is added or obtained, and a negative reinforcer as avoidance of or escape from something unpleasant.

Recall again what happened with Little Albert. Albert learned to fear rats through a process of classical conditioning. Then, after he acquired this fear, crawling away (an operant behavior) was negatively reinforced by escape from the now-fearsome rodent. The negative reinforcement that results from escaping or avoiding something unpleasant explains why so many fears are long-lasting. When you evade a feared object or situation, you also cut off all opportunities for extinguishing your fear.

punishment The process by which a stimulus or event weakens or reduces the probability of the response that it follows.

instinctive drift The tendency of an organism to revert to an instinctive behavior over time; it can interfere with learning.

positive reinforcement A reinforcement procedure in which a response is followed by the presentation of, or increase in intensity of, a reinforcing stimulus; as a result, the response becomes stronger or more likely to occur.

negative reinforcement A reinforcement procedure in which a response is followed by the removal, delay, or decrease in intensity of an unpleasant stimulus; as a result, the response becomes stronger or more likely to occur.

Understandably, people often confuse negative reinforcement with positive punishment, because both involve an unpleasant stimulus. To keep the two straight, remember that punishment—positive or negative—*decreases* the likelihood of a response. Reinforcement—positive or negative—*increases* it. In real life, punishment and negative reinforcement often go hand in hand. If you use a choke collar on your dog to teach it to heel, a yank on the collar punishes the act of walking, but release of the collar negatively reinforces the act of standing still by your side.

PRIMARY AND SECONDARY REINFORCERS AND PUNISHERS

Food, water, light stroking of the skin, and a comfortable air temperature are naturally reinforcing because they satisfy biological needs. They are therefore known as **primary reinforcers.** Similarly, pain and extreme heat or cold are inherently punishing and are therefore known as **primary punishers.** Primary reinforcers and punishers are very effective for controlling behavior, but they also have their drawbacks. For one thing, the organism may have to be in a deprived state for a stimulus to act as a primary reinforcer; a glass of water isn't much of a reward to someone who just drank three glasses. Also, there are ethical problems with using primary punishers or taking away primary reinforcers.

Fortunately, behavior can be controlled just as effectively by **secondary reinforcers** and **secondary punishers,** which are learned. Money, praise, applause, good grades, awards, and gold stars are common secondary reinforcers. Criticism, demerits, catcalls, scoldings, fines, and bad grades are common secondary punishers. Most behaviorists believe that secondary reinforcers and punishers acquire their ability to influence behavior by being paired with primary reinforcers and punishers. If that reminds you of classical conditioning, reinforce your excellent thinking with a pat on the back! Indeed, secondary reinforcers and punishers are often called *conditioned* reinforcers and punishers.

primary reinforcer A stimulus that is inherently reinforcing, typically satisfying a physiological need; an example is food.

primary punisher A stimulus that is inherently punishing; an example is electric shock.

secondary reinforcer A stimulus that has acquired reinforcing properties through association with other reinforcers.

secondary punisher A stimulus that has acquired punishing properties through association with other punishers.

Just because a reinforcer (or punisher) is a secondary one doesn't mean it is any less potent than a primary one. Money has considerable power over most people's behavior; not only can it be exchanged for primary reinforcers such as food and shelter, but it also brings with it other secondary reinforcers, such as praise and respect. Still, like any conditioned stimulus, a secondary reinforcer such as money will eventually lose its ability to affect behavior if it cannot be paired at least occasionally with one of the stimuli originally associated with it. In 1930, a child who found a penny would be thrilled at the goodies it could buy. Today, U.S. pennies are so worthless that billions of them go out of circulation each year because people throw them away or leave them on the ground when they drop.

Quick Quiz

A. Which kind of consequence is illustrated by each of the following? (You may want to refer to the table on page 269 if you have difficulty with these items.)

1. A child nags her father for a cookie; he keeps refusing, but she keeps pleading. Finally, unable to stand the "aversive stimulation" any longer, he hands over the cookie. For him, the ending of the child's pleas is a __________. For the child, the cookie is a __________.
2. A woman wants her husband to take more responsibility for household chores. One night, he clears the dishes. She touches him affectionately on the arm. The next night, he again clears the dishes. Her touch was probably a __________.
3. A hungry toddler gleefully eats his oatmeal with his hands after being told not to. His mother promptly removes the cereal and takes the messy offender out of the high chair. The removal of the cereal is a __________.

B. Which of the following are secondary (conditioned) reinforcers: quarters spilling from a slot machine, a winner's blue ribbon, a piece of candy, an A on an exam, "frequent-flyer" points?

C. During "happy hours" in bars and restaurants, typically held in the late afternoon, drinks are sold at a reduced price, and appetizers are often free. What undesirable behavior may be rewarded by this practice?

Answers:

A. 1. negative reinforcer; positive reinforcer 2. positive reinforcer 3. punisher—or more precisely, a negative punisher—because playing with the oatmeal is likely to decrease after the behavior is punished by removal of the food (assuming the child wants the oatmeal). B. All but the candy are secondary reinforcers. C. One possible answer: The reduced prices, free appetizers, and convivial atmosphere all reinforce heavy alcohol consumption just before the commuter rush hour, thus possibly contributing to drunk driving (see Geller & Lehman, 1988).

PRINCIPLES OF OPERANT CONDITIONING

Thousands of studies have been done on operant conditioning, many using animals. A favorite experimental tool is the *Skinner box*, a cage equipped with a device that delivers food into a dish when an animal makes a desired response (see Figure 7.4). A *cumulative recorder* connected to the cage automatically records each response and produces a graph showing the cumulative number of responses across time.

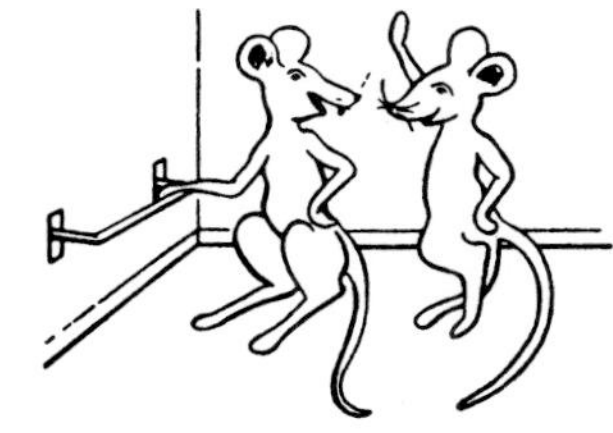

"Boy, do we have this guy conditioned. Every time I press the bar down he drops a pellet in."

Early in his career, Skinner (1938) used the Skinner box for a classic demonstration of operant conditioning. A rat that had previously learned to eat from the pellet-releasing device was placed in the box. Because no food was present, the animal proceeded to do typically ratlike things, scurrying about the box, sniffing here and there, and randomly touching parts of the floor and walls. Quite by accident, it happened to press a lever mounted on one wall, and immediately, a pellet of tasty rat food fell into the food dish. The rat continued its movements and again happened to press the bar, causing another pellet to fall into the tray. With additional repetitions of bar pressing followed by food, the animal began to behave less randomly and to press the bar more consistently. Eventually, Skinner had the rat pressing the bar as fast as it could.

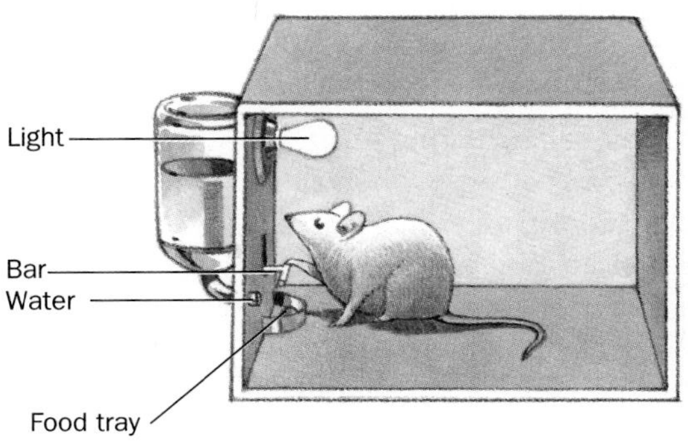

Figure 7.4
The Skinner Box

When a rat in a Skinner box presses a bar, a food pellet or drop of water is automatically released. The photo shows Skinner at work on one of the boxes.

Skinner's favorite experimental animals were pigeons, which usually are trained to peck at a disk or a key, but most behaviorists have worked with rats. By using the Skinner box and similar devices, behavioral researchers have discovered many techniques and applications of operant conditioning.

EXTINCTION In operant conditioning, as in classical, **extinction** is a procedure that causes a previously learned response to stop. In operant conditioning, extinction takes place when the reinforcer that maintained the response is removed or is no longer available. At first, there may be a spurt of responding, but then the responses gradually taper off and eventually cease. Suppose you put a coin in a vending machine and get nothing back. You may throw in another coin, or perhaps even two, but then you will probably stop trying. The next day, you may put in yet another coin, an example of *spontaneous recovery.* Eventually, however, you will give up on that machine. Your response will have been extinguished.

IMMEDIATE VERSUS DELAYED CONSEQUENCES In general, the sooner a reinforcer or punisher follows a response, the greater its effect. This principle applies especially to animals and children, but human adults also respond more reliably when they don't have to wait too long for a paycheck, a smile, or a grade. When there is delay, other responses occur in the interval, and the connection between the desired or undesired response and the consequence may not be made.

STIMULUS GENERALIZATION AND DISCRIMINATION In operant conditioning, as in classical, **stimulus generalization** may occur. That is, responses may generalize to stimuli that were not present during the original learning situation, but which resemble the original stimuli. For example, a pigeon that has been trained to peck at a picture of a circle may also peck at a slightly oval figure. But if you wanted to train the bird to discriminate between the two shapes, you would present both the circle and the oval, giving reinforcers whenever the bird pecked at the circle and withholding reinforcers when it pecked at the oval. Eventually, **stimulus discrimination** would occur.

Sometimes an animal or human being learns to respond to a stimulus only when some other stimulus, called a **discriminative stimulus,** is present. The discriminative stimulus signals whether a response, if made, will "pay off." In a Skinner box containing a pigeon, a light may serve as a discriminative stimulus for pecking at a circle. When the light is on, pecking brings a reward; when it is off, pecking is futile. The light is said to exert **stimulus control** over the pecking by setting the occasion for reinforcement to occur if the response is made. However, the response is not *compelled,* as salivation was compelled by the ringing of the bell in Pavlov's classical-conditioning studies. It merely becomes more probable (or occurs at a greater rate) in the presence of the discriminative stimulus.

Human behavior is controlled by many discriminative stimuli, both verbal ("Store hours are 9 to 5") and nonverbal (traffic lights, doorbells, the ring of a telephone, the facial expressions of others). Learning to respond correctly when such stimuli are present is an essential part of a person's socialization. In a public place, if you have to go to the bathroom, the words *Women* and *Men* are discriminative stimuli for entering one door or the other. One word tells you the response will be rewarded by the opportunity to empty a full bladder, the other that it will be punished by the jeers or protests of others.

LEARNING ON SCHEDULE Reinforcers can be delivered according to different schedules, or patterns over time. When a response is first acquired, learning is usually most rapid if the response is reinforced each time it occurs; this procedure is

extinction The weakening and eventual disappearance of a learned response; in operant conditioning, it occurs when a response is no longer followed by a reinforcer.

stimulus generalization In operant conditioning, the tendency for a response that has been reinforced (or punished) in the presence of one stimulus to occur (or be suppressed) in the presence of other, similar stimuli.

stimulus discrimination In operant conditioning, the tendency of a response to occur in the presence of one stimulus but not in the presence of other, similar stimuli that differ from it on some dimension.

discriminative stimulus A stimulus that signals when a particular response is likely to be followed by a certain type of consequence.

stimulus control Control over the occurrence of a response by a discriminative stimulus.

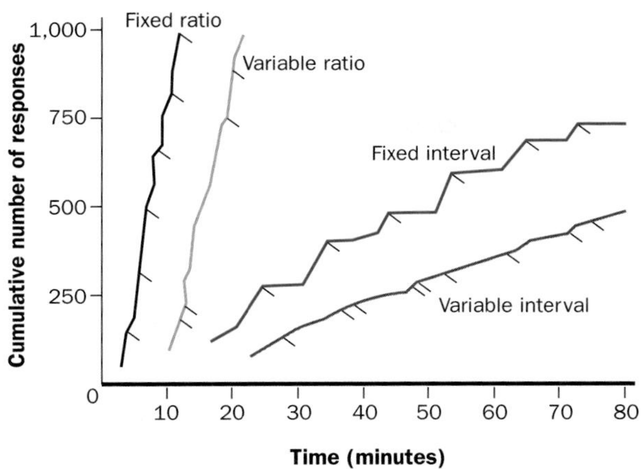

Figure 7.5
Reinforcement Schedules and Behavior
In this figure, each crosshatch indicates the delivery of a reinforcer. As you can see, different schedules of reinforcement produce different learning curves, or patterns of responding over time. For example, a fixed-ratio schedule produces a very fast rate of responding; and when a fixed-interval schedule is used, responses drop off immediately after reinforcement, resulting in a scalloped curve. (Adapted from Skinner, 1961.)

called **continuous reinforcement.** However, once a response has become reliable, it will be more resistant to extinction if it is rewarded on a **partial** or **intermittent schedule of reinforcement,** which involves reinforcing only some responses, not all of them. Skinner (1956) reported that he first happened on this property of partial reinforcement when he ran short of food pellets for his rats and was forced to deliver reinforcers less often. (Not all scientific discoveries are planned!) Years later, when he was asked how he could tolerate being misunderstood so often, he replied that he only needed to be understood three or four times a year—his own intermittent schedule of reinforcement.

Many kinds of intermittent schedules have been studied. *Ratio schedules* deliver a reinforcer after a certain number of responses have occurred. *Interval schedules* deliver a reinforcer if a response is made after the passage of a certain amount of time since the last reinforcer. The number of responses that must occur or the amount of time that must pass before the payoff may be *fixed* (constant) or *variable.* Combining the ratio and interval patterns with the fixed and variable patterns yields four types of intermittent schedules (see Figure 7.5). These variations in how the reinforcers are delivered have characteristic effects on the rate, form, and timing of behavior—effects that most people are not aware of.

1. Fixed-ratio (FR) schedules. On this type of schedule, reinforcement occurs after a fixed number of responses. An FR-2 schedule delivers a reinforcer after every other response, an FR-3 schedule after every third response, and so forth. Fixed-ratio schedules produce very high rates of responding. In the laboratory, a rat may rapidly press a bar several hundred times to get a single reward. Outside the laboratory, fixed-ratio schedules are often used by employers to increase productivity. A salesperson who must sell a specific number of items before getting a commission or a factory worker who must produce a specific number of products before earning a given wage (a system known as "piecework") are on fixed-ratio schedules. An interesting feature of fixed-ratio schedules is that performance sometimes drops off just after reinforcement. If a writer must complete four chapters before getting a check, interest and motivation will sag right after the check is received.

2. Variable-ratio (VR) schedules. On these schedules, reinforcement occurs after some average number of responses, but the number varies from reinforcement to reinforcement. A VR-5 schedule would deliver a reinforcer *on the average* after every fifth response, but sometimes after one, two, six, or seven responses, or any other number, as long as the average was five. Variable-ratio schedules produce extremely

continuous reinforcement A reinforcement schedule in which a particular response is always reinforced.

intermittent (partial) schedule of reinforcement A reinforcement schedule in which a particular response is sometimes but not always reinforced.

fixed-ratio (FR) schedule An intermittent schedule of reinforcement in which reinforcement occurs only after a fixed number of responses.

variable-ratio (VR) schedule An intermittent schedule of reinforcement in which reinforcement occurs after a variable number of responses.

high, steady rates of responding. The responses are more resistant to extinction than when a fixed-ratio schedule is used. The prime example of a variable-ratio schedule is delivery of payoffs by a slot machine. The player knows that the average number of responses necessary to win is set at a level that makes money for the house. Hope springs eternal, though. The gambler takes a chance on being in front of the machine during one of those lucky moments when fewer responses bring a payoff.

3. Fixed-interval (FI) schedules. On this type of schedule, reinforcement of a response occurs only if a fixed amount of time has passed since the previous reinforcer. A rat on an FI-10-second schedule gets a food pellet the first time it presses the bar after the passage of a 10-second interval. Pressing the bar earlier does not hasten the reward. Animals on fixed-interval schedules seem to develop a sharp sense of time. After a reinforcer is delivered, they often stop responding altogether. Then as the end of the interval approaches, responding again picks up, reaching a maximum rate right before reinforcement. Outside the laboratory, fixed-interval schedules are not common, but some behavior patterns do resemble those seen on such schedules. Suppose your sweetheart, who is away for a month, writes you a love note by E-mail every day at dinnertime. You'll probably start checking for messages around 5 P.M., and keep checking until the message arrives. Once you get it, you won't look again until the next day.

4. Variable-interval (VI) schedules. On these schedules, reinforcement of a response occurs only if a variable amount of time has passed since the previous reinforcer. A VI-10-second schedule means that the interval will average 10 seconds but will vary from reinforcement to reinforcement. Because the animal or person cannot predict when a reward will come, responding is relatively low but steady. If your sweetheart sends you 10 E-mail messages every morning, playfully spacing them at unpredictable intervals, you may check your E-mail steadily every half hour.

A basic principle of operant conditioning is that if you want a response to persist after it has been learned, you should reinforce it intermittently, not continuously. If an animal has been receiving continuous reinforcement for some response and then the reinforcement suddenly stops, the animal will soon stop responding. Because the change in reinforcement is large, from continuous to none at all, the animal will easily discern the change. But if reinforcement has been intermittent, the change will not be so dramatic, and the animal will keep responding for some period of time. Pigeons, rats, and people on intermittent schedules of reinforcement have responded in the laboratory thousands of times without reinforcement before throwing in the towel, especially on variable schedules. Animals will sometimes work so hard for an unpredictable, infrequent bit of food that the energy they expend is greater than that gained from the reward; theoretically, the animal could actually work itself to death.

It follows that if you want to get rid of a response, you should be careful not to reinforce it intermittently. If you are going to extinguish undesirable behavior by ignoring it—a child's tantrums, a friend's midnight phone calls, a parent's unasked-for advice—you must be *absolutely consistent* in withholding reinforcement (your attention). Otherwise, you will probably only make matters worse. The other person will learn that if he or she keeps up the screaming, calling, or advice giving long enough, it will eventually be rewarded. One of the most common errors people make, from a behavioral point of view, is to reward intermittently the responses they would like to eliminate.

fixed-interval (FI) schedule An intermittent schedule of reinforcement in which a reinforcer is delivered for the first response made after a fixed period of time has elapsed since the last reinforcer.

variable-interval (VI) schedule An intermittent schedule of reinforcement in which a reinforcer is delivered for a response made after a variable period of time has elapsed since the last reinforcer.

shaping An operant-conditioning procedure in which successive approximations of a desired response are reinforced; used when the desired response has a low probability of occurring spontaneously.

SHAPING For a response to be reinforced, it must first occur. But suppose you want to train a rat to pick up a marble, or a dog to stand on its hind legs and turn

GET INVOLVED

If you have a pet, you can apply the principles of operant conditioning by teaching your animal a desired behavior. Choose something simple. (Shaping complex behavior can be difficult unless you have special training.) One student we know taught her cat to willingly enter the garage for the night by feeding the animal a special treat there each evening at the same time. Soon the cat was "asking" to get into the garage at bedtime! Another student taught her pastured horse to come to her and submit willingly to the halter by rewarding the animal's occasional approach with a carrot. Soon the horse was approaching regularly and could be put on an intermittent schedule of reinforcement. Be creative, and see whether you can't make your pet better behaved or more cooperative in some way.

around, or a child to use a knife and fork properly, or a friend to play terrific tennis. Such behaviors, and most others in everyday life, have almost no probability of appearing spontaneously. You could grow old and gray waiting for them to occur so that you could reinforce them. The operant solution to this dilemma is a procedure called **shaping.**

In shaping, you start by reinforcing a tendency in the right direction, then you gradually require responses that are more and more similar to the final, desired response. The responses that you reinforce on the way to the final one are called *successive approximations.* In the case of the rat and the marble, you might deliver a food pellet if the rat merely turned toward the marble. Once this response was well established, you might then reward the rat for taking a step toward the marble. After that, you could reward it for approaching the marble, then for touching the marble, then for putting both paws on the marble, and finally for holding it. With the achievement of each approximation, the next one would become more likely, making it available for reinforcement.

Animals can learn to do some surprising things, with a little help from their human friends and the application of operant-conditioning techniques.

Using shaping and other techniques, Skinner was able to train pigeons to play Ping-Pong with their beaks and to "bowl" in a miniature alley, complete with a wooden ball and tiny bowling pins. Rats have learned equally impressive behaviors (see Figure 7.6). Animal trainers routinely use shaping to teach dogs to act as the "eyes" of the blind and to act as the "limbs" of people with spinal-cord injuries by turning on light switches, opening refrigerator doors, and reaching for boxes on supermarket shelves. Shaping works with people, too. According to one story (probably apocryphal), some university students once used eye contact as a reinforcer to shape the behavior of a famous professor who was an expert on operant conditioning. They decided to get him to deliver his lecture from a corner of the room. Each time he moved in that direction, they looked at him; otherwise, they averted their gazes. Eventually, the professor was backed into the corner, never suspecting that his behavior had been shaped.

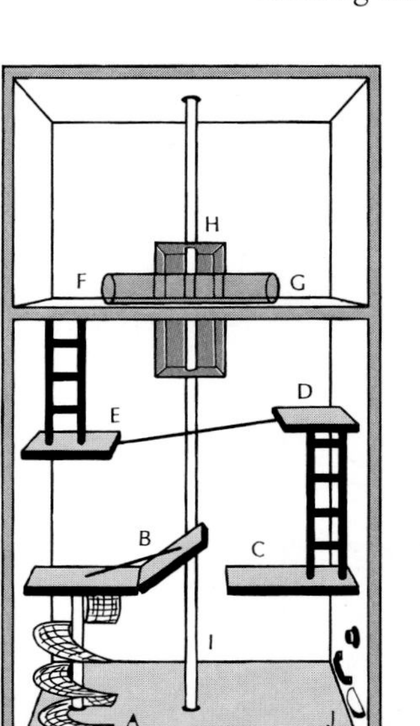

Figure 7.6
A Rat's Route

To demonstrate shaping and other operant procedures, a researcher trained a rat to perform a long sequence of activities in an apparatus resembling this one. Starting at point A, the rat climbs a ramp to B, crosses a drawbridge to C, climbs a ladder to D, crosses a tightrope to E, climbs another ladder to F, crawls through a tunnel to G, runs to H and enters an elevator, descends to I, and runs out of the elevator to J, where it presses a lever and finally receives some well-deserved food. (After Cheney, in Chance, 1994.)

CONSIDER OTHER INTERPRETATIONS

People cling to their superstitions because they seem to work. But do superstitious habits really bring good luck or ward off bad luck? Could their "effectiveness" be an illusion, explainable in terms of operant principles?

SUPERSTITION Do you cross your fingers when you're waiting for good news? Have you ever avoided walking under a ladder because doing so brings bad luck? Do you have a lucky charm in your car to protect you against accidents? Why do people hold such superstitions?

The answer, say behaviorists, has to do partly with the nature of reinforcement—which can be effective even when it is entirely coincidental. Skinner (1948) first demonstrated this fact by putting eight pigeons in boxes and rigging the boxes so that food was delivered every 15 seconds, even if the bird didn't lift a feather. Pigeons, like rats, are often in motion, so when the food came, each animal was likely to be doing *something*. That something was then reinforced by delivery of the food. The behavior, of course, was reinforced entirely by chance, but it still became more likely to occur, and thus to be reinforced again. Within a short time, six of the pigeons were practicing some sort of consistent ritual—turning in counterclockwise circles, bobbing the head up and down, swinging the head to and fro, or making brushing movements toward the floor. None of these activities had the least effect on the delivery of the reinforcer; the birds were behaving "superstitiously." It was as if they thought their movements were responsible for bringing the food.

You can see how coincidental reinforcement might account for some human superstitions. A baseball pitcher happens to scratch his left ear, then strikes out a star batter on the other team; ever after, he scratches his left ear before pitching. A student uses a purple pen on the first exam of the semester, gets an A, and from then on uses only purple pens for taking tests. Why, though, don't such superstitions extinguish? After all, the pitcher isn't going to strike out every batter, nor is the student always going to be brilliant. One answer: Intermittent reinforcement may make the response particularly resistant to extinction. If coincidental reinforcement occurs occasionally, the superstitious behavior may continue indefinitely (Schwartz & Reilly, 1985). Ironically, the fact that our little rituals only "work" some of the time ensures that we will keep using them.

Of course, superstitions persist for other reasons as well. Many superstitions are cultural and are reinforced by the agreement, approval, or attention of others. You don't have to have an accident after walking beneath a ladder, spilling the salt, or breaking a mirror to believe that these actions bring bad luck. Some superstitions are reinforced by the feeling of control over events that they provide. And people often look for evidence to justify their superstitions but ignore contrary evidence. As long as nothing awful happens when you are carrying a good-luck charm, you can credit it with protective powers; but if something bad does occur, you can always say that the charm has lost its powers (a violation of the principle of falsifiability!). Yet

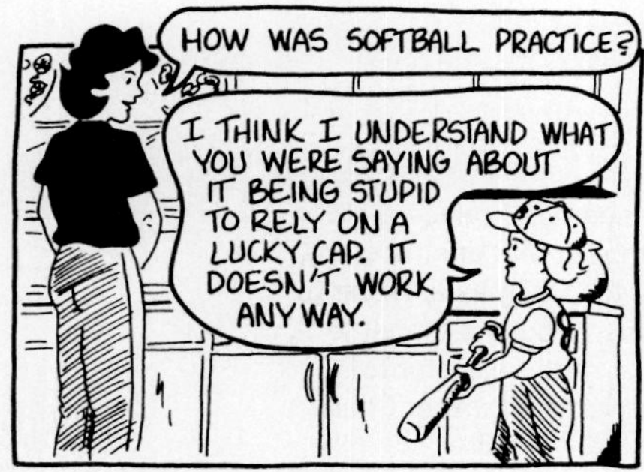

Reprinted with special permission of King Features Syndicate.

even when we know the reasons for our superstitions, they can be hard to shake. As psychologist Paul Chance (1988) wrote, "A black cat means nothing to me now, nor does a broken mirror. There are no little plastic icons on the dashboard of my car, and I carry no rabbit's foot. I am free of all such nonsense, and I am happy to report no ill effects—knock wood."

Quick Quiz

Can you apply the principles of operant conditioning? In each of the following situations, choose the best alternative, and give your reason for choosing it.

1. You want your 2-year-old to ask for water with a word instead of a grunt. Should you give him water when he says "wa-wa" or wait until his pronunciation improves?
2. Your roommate keeps interrupting you while you are studying, even though you have asked her to stop. Should you ignore her completely or occasionally respond for the sake of good manners?
3. Your father, who rarely writes to you, has finally sent a letter. Should you reply quickly or wait a while so he will know how it feels to be ignored?

Answers:

1. You should reinforce "wa-wa," an approximation of water, because complex behaviors need to be shaped. 2. From a behavioral view, you should ignore her completely because intermittent reinforcement (attention) could cause her interruptions to persist. 3. You should reply quickly if you want to encourage letter writing, because immediate reinforcement is more effective than delayed reinforcement.

OPERANT CONDITIONING IN REAL LIFE

Operant principles can clear up many mysteries about why people behave as they do. We could give you thousands of examples, but here's just one. Medical research finds that 90 percent of whiplash injuries—back and neck pain and headaches—heal on their own within days or a few weeks (Spitzer et al., 1995). Yet in some countries, notably the United States and Norway, many victims of "fender-bender" automobile accidents complain of whiplash symptoms that last for months or even years. In these countries, whiplash is so common and so taken for granted that few people have thought to question its validity. But when a Norwegian research team, concerned about the epidemic of whiplash lawsuits in Norway, conducted a study in Lithuania, they found that whiplash is virtually unknown there! Lithuanian victims of car accidents are no more likely to report chronic neck pain and headaches than people who have not been in accidents (Schrader et al., 1996). The reason? In Lithuania, no one has personal-injury insurance, and the government pays most medical bills. In other words, when there are no reinforcers for reporting whiplash, the "syndrome" disappears!

QUESTION ASSUMPTIONS

People who have been in minor car accidents often angrily sue the other party, claiming chronic pain from whiplash. Everyone assumes that whiplash is a common and serious phenomenon. But when researchers tested that assumption, they came up with some surprises.

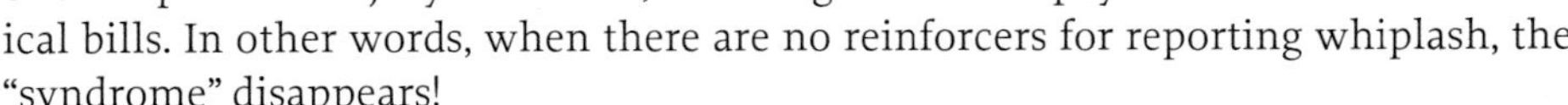

Operant principles also help us understand why people don't always behave as they would like. In this age of self-improvement, for example, personal-growth and motivational workshops provide participants with lots of reinforcement for emotional expressiveness and self-disclosure. Participants often feel that their way of interacting with others has been transformed. But when they return home and to work, where the environment is full of the same old reinforcers, punishers, and discriminative stimuli, they are often disappointed to find that their new responses have failed to generalize. A grumpy boss or a cranky spouse may still be able to "push their buttons"—a relapse that is predictable from behavioral principles.

If we could understand the environmental circumstances that control our behavior, say behaviorists, we could design a world more to our liking. Over the years, behaviorists have carried operant principles out of the narrow world of the Skinner box and into the wider world of the classroom, athletic field, prison, mental hospital, nursing home, rehabilitation ward, child-care center, factory, and office. The use of operant techniques (and classical ones) in such real-world settings is called **behavior modification.**

Behavioral principles have many practical applications. This capuchin monkey has been trained to assist her paralyzed owner by picking up objects, opening doors, helping with feeding, and performing other everyday tasks.

Many behavior-modification programs rely on a technique called the **token economy.** *Tokens* are secondary reinforcers, such as points or scrip money, that have no real value in themselves but that are exchangeable for primary reinforcers or other secondary reinforcers. They provide an easy way to reinforce behavior on a continuous schedule. Once a particular behavior is established, tokens can be phased out and replaced by more natural intermittent reinforcers, such as praise.

Behavior modification has had some enormous successes. Behaviorists have taught parents how to toilet-train their children in only a few sessions (Azrin & Foxx, 1974). They have taught autistic children who have never before spoken to use a vocabulary of several hundred words (Lovaas, 1977). They have trained disturbed and mentally retarded adults to communicate, dress themselves, mingle socially with others, and earn a living (Lent, 1968; McLeod, 1985). They have taught brain-damaged patients to control inappropriate behavior, focus their attention, and improve their language abilities (McGlynn, 1990). And they have helped ordinary folk eliminate unwanted habits, such as smoking and nail biting, or acquire wanted ones, such as practicing the piano or studying.

Yet when people try to apply the principles of conditioning to commonplace problems, their efforts sometimes fail or backfire. Both punishment and reinforcement have their pitfalls, as we are about to see.

THE PROBLEM WITH PUNISHMENT

In his novel *Walden Two* (1948/1976), Skinner imagined a utopia in which reinforcers were used so wisely that undesirable behavior was rare. Unfortunately, we do not live in a utopia; bloopers, bad habits, and antisocial acts abound, and we are faced with how to get rid of all those bad habits and behaviors.

An obvious approach might seem to be punishment. Most Western countries have banned corporal (physical) punishment of schoolchildren by principals and teachers, but in the United States, the physical punishment of children has roots in the religious belief that you must beat children or their innate wickedness will land them in hell (Greven, 1991). Thus 24 states still permit corporal punishment (I. Hyman, 1994), and other states are considering restoring this penalty for disruptive behavior, graffiti vandalism, and other problems that plague many schools. Boys, minority children, and poor white children are the most likely to be hit.

The American penal system, too, has become more severe in the punishments it metes out for crime; the United States has a higher proportion of its citizens in jail for nonviolent crimes (such as drug use) than any other developed country. And of course in daily life, people punish one another constantly, by yelling, scolding, fining, and sulking. Many people feel rewarded by a temporary feeling of control and power when they punish others in these ways. But does all this punishment work?

behavior modification The application of conditioning techniques to teach new responses or to reduce or eliminate maladaptive or problematic behavior.

token economy A behavior-modification technique in which secondary reinforcers called *tokens,* which can be collected and exchanged for primary or other secondary reinforcers, are used to shape behavior.

Sometimes punishment is unquestionably effective. Some highly disturbed children have been known to chew their own fingers to the bone, stick objects in their eyes, or tear out their hair. You can't ignore such behavior because the children are seriously injuring themselves. You can't respond with concern and affection because you may unwittingly reward the behavior. In this case, punishment works: Immediately punishing the self-destructive behavior eliminates it (Lovaas, 1977; Lovaas, Schreibman, & Koegel, 1974). Mild punishers, such as a spray of water in the face, are often just as effective as strong ones, such as electric shock; sometimes they are even more effective. A firm "No!" can also be established as a conditioned punisher.

EXAMINE THE EVIDENCE

In the United States, the answer to wrongdoing is often punishment. People assume that fines, imprisonment, yelling, and spanking are good ways to get rid of undesirable behavior. But what does the evidence show?

The effects of punishment, however, are far less predictable than many people realize, as we can see in responses to domestic violence. In a widely publicized real-life experimental intervention, men who were arrested for assaulting their wives or girlfriends were less likely to repeat the offense within six months than men who were merely talked to by the police or ordered to stay away from the victim for a few hours (Sherman & Berk, 1984). On the basis of these results, police departments across the United States adopted mandatory arrest policies in cases of domestic assault. Then more research came along showing that the conclusions had been premature: Although arrests do temporarily prevent a repeat attack, they do not usually deter domestic violence *in the long run* (Dunford, Huizinga, & Elliott, 1990; Hirschel et al., 1990; Sherman, 1992).

Further, Lawrence Sherman and his colleagues have noted that if arrest is the aspirin of criminal justice, the pill has different effects on different people at different doses (Sherman, 1992; Sherman et al., 1991). They found that brief arrests of two or three hours were generally most effective in initially reducing the chances of renewed domestic violence (when compared with a warning), although this effect disappeared within a few weeks. However, for unemployed men in the inner city, being arrested actually *increased* the long-term chances of a repeat attack. The researchers speculated that for these men, the initial fear of being arrested again wore off quickly and was replaced by anger at the woman who "caused" the arrest or at women in general. The policy of arresting violent men, therefore, poses a dilemma: On the one hand is the need to rescue the victim right after the violent episode and the moral appropriateness of punishing her attacker; on the other is the long-term need to reduce the risk of further harm to her.

Because of such complexities, simplistic efforts to "crack down" on wrongdoers often fail. Laboratory and field studies show that punishment also has other disadvantages as a method of behavioral control:

1. *People often administer punishment inappropriately or when they are so enraged that they are unable to think through what they are doing and how they are doing it.* They swing blindly or yell wildly, applying punishment so broadly that it covers all sorts of irrelevant behaviors. Even when people are not carried away by anger, they often misunderstand the proper application of punishment. One student told us his parents used to punish their children before leaving them alone for the evening because of all the naughty things they were *going* to do. Naturally, the children didn't bother to behave like angels.

2. *The recipient of punishment often responds with anxiety, fear, or rage.* Through a process of classical conditioning, these emotional side effects may then generalize to the entire situation in which the punishment occurs—the place, the person delivering the punishment, and the circumstances. Negative emotional reactions tend to create more problems than the punishment solves. For example, instead of becoming obedient or respectful, a teenager who has been severely punished may strike back or run away. As we saw in the case of domestic violence, emotional reactions to punishment may even lead to an increase in the undesirable behavior that the punishment was intended to eliminate. That may be why the physical punishment of

Harried parents often resort to physical punishment without being aware of the many negative consequences for themselves and their children. Based on your reading of this chapter, what alternatives does this mother have?

children is correlated with high rates of violence in children; violence breeds violence (I. Hyman, 1994; McCord, 1991; Straus, 1991; Weiss et al., 1992).

3. *The effects of punishment are sometimes temporary, depending heavily on the presence of the punishing person or circumstances.* All of us can probably remember some transgressions of childhood that we never dared commit when our parents were around but that we promptly resumed as soon as they were gone. All that we learned was not to get caught.

4. *Most misbehavior is hard to punish immediately.* Recall that punishment, like reward, works best if it quickly follows a response, especially with animals and children. Outside the laboratory, immediate punishment is often hard to achieve.

5. *Punishment conveys little information.* If it immediately follows the misbehavior, it may tell the recipient what *not* to do. But it doesn't communicate what the person *should* do. For example, spanking a toddler for messing in her pants will not teach her to use the potty chair. As Skinner (1968) wrote, "We do not teach [a student] to learn quickly by punishing him when he learns slowly, or to recall what he has learned by punishing him when he forgets, or to think logically by punishing him when he is illogical."

6. *An action intended to punish may instead be reinforcing because it brings attention.* Indeed, angry attention may be just what the offender is after. If a mother yells at a child who is throwing a tantrum, the very act of yelling may give him what he wants—a reaction from her. In the schoolroom, teachers who scold children in front of other students, thus putting them in the limelight, often unwittingly reward the very misbehavior they are trying to eliminate.

Why do so many people ignore warnings and threats of punishment?

Because of these drawbacks, most psychologists believe that punishment, especially severe punishment, is a poor way to eliminate unwanted behavior and should be regarded only as a last resort. When punishment is used, it should not involve physical abuse, it should be accompanied by information about what kind of behavior would be appropriate, and it should be followed, whenever possible, by the reinforcement of desirable behavior.

Fortunately, a good alternative to punishment exists: extinction of the responses you want to discourage. Of course, extinction is sometimes difficult to achieve. It is hard to ignore the child nagging for a cookie before dinner, the roommate interrupting your concentration, or the dog barking its lungs out. Moreover, the simplest form of extinction—ignoring the behavior—is not always appropriate. A teacher cannot ignore a child who is hitting a playmate. The dog owner who ignores Fido's backyard barking may soon hear "barking" of another sort—from the neighbors. A parent whose child is a TV addict can't ignore the behavior because television is rewarding to the child. One solution: Combine extinction of undesirable acts with reinforcement of alternative ones. If a child is addicted to TV, the parent might ignore the child's pleas for "just one more program" and at the same time encourage behavior that is incompatible with television watching, such as playing outdoors or building a model airplane.

It is also important to understand the reasons for a person's misbehavior before deciding how to respond to it. For example, when autistic and other disturbed children throw tantrums, attack their teachers, or do self-destructive things such as punching or poking themselves, it is often because difficult demands are being placed on them or because they are bored and frustrated. Their bizarre behavior is a way of saying, "Hey, let me out of here!" And because the behavior often works, or is reinforced by attention from adults, it tends to persist. When these children are taught to use words to ask for praise or help ("Am I doing good work?" "I don't understand"), their problem behavior decreases and often even disappears (Carr & Durand, 1985). Similarly, a child screaming in a supermarket may be saying, "I'm going out of my head with boredom. Help!" A lover who sulks may be saying, "I'm not sure you really care about me; I'm frightened." Once we understand the purpose or meaning of behavior we dislike, we may be more effective in dealing with it.

THE PROBLEM WITH REWARD

Researchers have conditioned rats thousands of times, and as far as we know, none of the rats ever refused to cooperate or felt that they were being manipulated. Human beings are different. A little girl we know came home from school one day in a huff after her teacher announced that good performance would be rewarded with play money that could later be exchanged for privileges. "Doesn't she think I can learn without being bribed?" the child asked her mother indignantly.

This child's reaction illustrates a complication in the use of reinforcers. So far, most of our examples of operant conditioning have involved **extrinsic reinforcers,** which come from an outside source and are not inherently related to the activity being reinforced. Money, praise, gold stars, applause, hugs, and thumbs-up signs are all extrinsic reinforcers. But people (and probably some other animals, too) also work for **intrinsic reinforcers,** such as enjoyment of the task and the satisfaction of accomplishment. As psychologists have applied operant conditioning in real-world settings, they have sometimes found that extrinsic reinforcement, if you focus on it exclusively, can become too much of a good thing, because in some circumstances it can kill the pleasure of doing something for its own sake.

Consider what happened when psychologists gave nursery-school children the chance to draw with felt-tipped pens (Lepper, Greene, & Nisbett, 1973). The children already liked this activity and readily took it up during free play. First, the researchers recorded how long each child spontaneously played with the pens. Then they told some of the children that if they would draw with felt-tipped pens for a man who had come "to see what kinds of pictures boys and girls like to draw with Magic Markers," they would get a prize, a "Good Player Award" complete with gold seal and red ribbon. After drawing for six minutes, each child got the award, as promised. Other children did not expect a reward and were not given one. A week later, the researchers again observed the children's free play. Those children who had expected and received a reward were spending much less time with the pens than they had before the start of the experiment. In contrast, children who were not given an award continued to show as much interest in the activity as they had shown initially, as you can see in Figure 7.7. Similar results occurred when older children were or were not rewarded for working on academic tasks.

extrinsic reinforcers Reinforcers that are not inherently related to the activity being reinforced, such as money, prizes, and praise.

intrinsic reinforcers Reinforcers that are inherently related to the activity being reinforced, such as enjoyment of the task and the satisfaction of accomplishment.

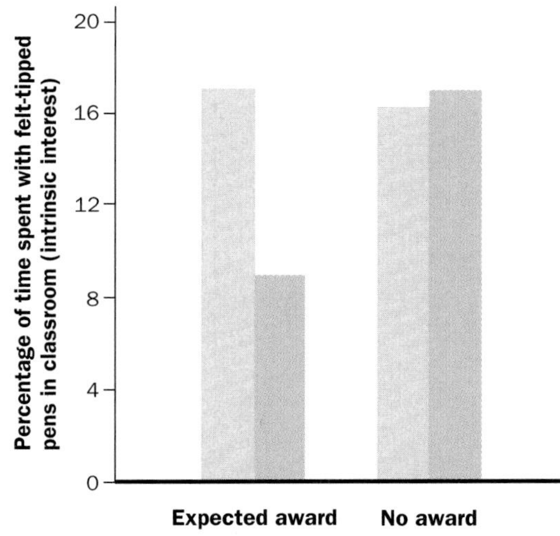

Figure 7.7
Turning Play into Work

When preschoolers were promised a prize for drawing with felt-tipped pens, the behavior temporarily increased, but after receiving the prize, the children spent less time with the pens than they had before the study began. Such results suggest that extrinsic rewards can sometimes reduce intrinsic motivation.

Because promised rewards (otherwise known as bribes) can be effective in the short term, some educators advocate using more of them. When eighth-graders were offered a dollar for every correct answer on a national math exam, they produced scores that were 13 percent higher than those of students who were simply urged to do their best, apparently because they tried harder (O'Neil, Sugrue, & Baker, 1995/1996). Should we therefore pay schoolchildren to perform well? Not necessarily; being motivated to do well on a test is not the same thing as being motivated to learn. In another study, researchers divided 9-year-old children into two groups, one in which mothers encouraged the children to learn for the intrinsic pleasure of it and another in which mothers rewarded high grades and punished low ones. By the time they were 10 years old, the children in the first group had higher motivation and better school performance. Extrinsic rewards and punishments actually seemed to impede the children's academic achievement (Gottfried, Fleming, & Gottfried, 1994). (In "Puzzles of Psychology," we discuss how high grades and praise affect students' self-esteem.)

"That is the correct answer, Billy, but I'm afraid you don't win anything for it."

Why should extrinsic rewards undermine intrinsic motivation? One possibility is that when we are paid for an activity, we interpret it as work. It is as if we say to ourselves, "I'm doing this because I'm being paid for it. Since I'm being paid, it must be something I wouldn't do if I didn't have to." When the reward is withdrawn, we refuse to "work" any longer. Another possibility is that extrinsic rewards are seen as controlling, and therefore they reduce a person's sense of autonomy and choice ("I guess I should just do what I'm told to do—and *only* what I'm told to do") (Deci & Ryan, 1987). A third, more behavioral explanation is that extrinsic reinforcement sometimes raises the rate of responding above some optimal, enjoyable level. Then the activity really does become work.

There is a trade-off, then, between the short-term effectiveness of extrinsic rewards and the long-term effectiveness of intrinsic ones. Extrinsic rewards work: How many people would trudge off to work every morning if they never got paid? In the classroom, a teacher who offers incentives to an unmotivated student may be taking

GET INVOLVED

Which of your actions are controlled primarily by extrinsic reinforcers and which by intrinsic ones? Fill in this checklist:

Activity	**Reinforcers mostly extrinsic**	**Reinforcers mostly intrinsic**	**Reinforcers about equally extrinsic and intrinsic**
Studying	_____	_____	_____
Housework	_____	_____	_____
Worship	_____	_____	_____
Personal grooming	_____	_____	_____
Job	_____	_____	_____
Dating	_____	_____	_____
Attending class	_____	_____	_____
Reading that isn't school-related	_____	_____	_____
Sports	_____	_____	_____
Cooking	_____	_____	_____

Is there an area of your life in which you'd like intrinsic reinforcement to play a larger role? What can you do to make that happen?

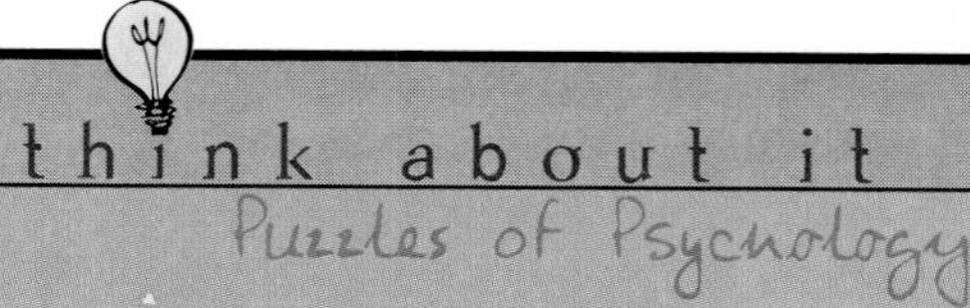

Do High Grades and Praise Raise Self-esteem?

It is popular today to blame every problem of youth, from poor academic test scores to juvenile crime, on low self-esteem. Raise self-esteem, the argument goes, and the problems will disappear. In California, a Task Force on the Social Importance of Self-esteem was convened to confirm the allegedly beneficial effects of raising self-esteem (Smelser, Vasconcellos, & Mecca, 1989). Teachers everywhere are taking this goal to heart, handing out lavish praise and high grades in hopes that students' academic performance will improve as they learn to "feel good about themselves."

One obvious result is grade inflation. In one middle school, when teachers tried to use a cutoff of a 3.5 grade point average for membership in a new academic honor society, they found that *two-thirds* of the school's 600 students were eligible, although clearly not all were doing "A" work (Celis, 1993). The teachers apparently felt obligated to give out high grades, whether the students deserved them or not. Grade inflation has infiltrated higher education, as well. In some colleges and universities, Cs, which once meant "average" or "satisfactory," are nearly extinct. (We heard about one student who was complaining about strict course requirements and said, oblivious to the irony, "Gosh, it's impossible for an average student to get an A in this class.") Pressured by parents and administrators, and worried about how students will evaluate them, many teachers go along with the trend despite their misgivings.

The problem, from a learning-theory point of view, is that to be effective, rewards must be tied to the behavior you are trying to increase. When rewards are dispensed indiscriminately, they become meaningless; they are no longer reinforcing. And when teachers praise mediocre work, that is what they are likely to get. Moreover, if a teacher gushes over work on a task that was actually easy, the hidden message may be that the child isn't very smart ("Gee, Minnie, you did a fantastic job . . . of adding two and two"). Even when the task is a challenging one, praise, if delivered too dramatically, may carry an unintended message—that the student's good work was a surprise ("Gee, Robert, you *really* did well on that paper [and who would have ever thought you could do it?]"). The result is likely to be lower, not higher, self-esteem, and reduced expectations of doing well (Kohn, 1993).

Although many people assume that self-esteem is the main ingredient of success and achievement, and its absence a major reason that children fail, there is actually no evidence to support this assumption, in spite of concerted efforts to find some (Dawes, 1994). The California task force, after reviewing virtually every study done on the relationship of self-esteem to anything (and there are thousands of them), found *no support* for any of its "intuitively correct" ideas about self-esteem (Smelser, Vasconcellos, & Mecca, 1989). Lilian Katz (1993), a professor of early childhood education, argues that "feel good about yourself" programs in schools tend to confuse self-esteem with self-involvement. Children are taught to turn their attention inward and to focus on self-gratification and self-celebration. Program after program asks children to write about such superficial things as physical attributes and consumer preferences ("What I like to watch on TV" or "What I like to eat"). In one typical curriculum she examined, Katz says, "Not once was the child asked to assume the role of producer, investigator, initiator, explorer, experimenter, wonderer, or problem-solver." Real self-esteem, Katz argues, does not come from "cheap success in a succession of trivial tasks," from phony flattery by a teacher, or from gold stars and happy faces. It emerges from effort, persistence, and the gradual acquisition of skills, and is nurtured by a teacher's genuine appreciation of the *content* of the child's work.

In recent years, studies have revealed an appalling level of illiteracy in the United States. Some high school graduates cannot read well enough to decipher a bus schedule or a warning on a nonprescription medication. Millions of people have such poor arithmetic skills that they cannot balance a checkbook or verify the change they get at the supermarket. Many students are unaware that their writing and math skills are deficient; how could they know, since they have always received high grades? The time seems right to rethink the way children are taught and schools are organized. After reading this chapter, how would you design a school system that fosters achievement, competence, and an intrinsic love of learning? What role, if any, would grades and other extrinsic reinforcers play? How would you let students know about poor performance without making them feel like failures? Think about it.

the only course of action open. If a behavior is to last when the teacher isn't around, however, extrinsic reinforcers eventually must be phased out. As one mother wrote in a *Newsweek* essay, "The winners [of prizes for schoolwork] will . . . suffer if they don't discover for themselves that they can gain the pleasure of health and strength from exercise, the joy of music from songs, the power of mathematics from counting and all of human wisdom from reading" (Skreslet, 1987). The fact that our school system relies heavily on grades and other extrinsic incentives may help explain why the average college graduate reads few books. Like all extrinsic rewards, grades induce temporary compliance but not necessarily a lifelong disposition to learn. Indeed, as children get older, they tend to become more and more dependent on grades and the teacher's approval and less and less concerned with satisfying their own curiosity (Harter & Jackson, 1992).

We do not want to leave the impression, however, that extrinsic reinforcers always diminish the pleasure of an activity. If you get money, a high grade, or a trophy for doing a task *well,* rather than for just doing it, your intrinsic motivation won't decrease (Dickinson, 1989; Eisenberger & Cameron, 1996). And if you have always loved to read or play the piano, you're likely to keep doing it even when your teacher no longer grades you or gives you gold stars (Mawhinney, 1990). Many educators and employers now avoid the trap of either–or thinking, by recognizing that most people do their best work when they get tangible rewards *and* when they have interesting, challenging, and varied kinds of work to do. (We will be discussing work motivation further in Chapter 11.)

Effective behavior modification, as you can see, is not only a science but an art. In "Taking Psychology with You," we offer some guidelines for mastering that art.

Quick Quiz

A. According to behavioral principles, what is happening here?

1. An adolescent whose parents have hit him for minor transgressions since he was small runs away from home.
2. A young woman whose parents paid her to clean her room while she was growing up is a slob when she moves to her own apartment.
3. Two parents scold their young daughter every time they catch her sucking her thumb. The thumb sucking continues anyway.

B. In a fee-for-service system of health care, doctors are paid for each visit by a patient or for each service performed, and the longer the visit, the higher the fee. In contrast, some health maintenance organizations (HMOs) pay their doctors a fixed amount per patient for the entire year. If the amount actually expended is less, the physician gets a bonus, and in some systems, if the amount expended is more, the physician is financially penalized. Given what you know about operant conditioning, what are the potential advantages and disadvantages of each system?

Answers:

A. 1. The physical punishment was painful, and through a process of classical conditioning, the situation in which it occurred also became unpleasant. Because escape from an unpleasant stimulus is negatively reinforcing, the boy ran away. 2. Extrinsic reinforcers are no longer available, and room-cleaning behavior has been extinguished. Also, extrinsic rewards may have displaced the intrinsic satisfaction of having a tidy room. 3. Punishment has failed, possibly because it rewards thumb sucking with attention or because thumb sucking still brings the child pleasure whenever the parents aren't around. B. In a fee-for-service system, the doctor is likely to provide the attention and tests that ill patients need. However, this system also rewards doctors for unnecessary tests and patient visits, contributing to the explosion in health-care costs. The policies of the HMOs will help contain these costs, but because doctors are rewarded for reducing costs and in some cases are penalized for running up charges, some patients may not get the attention or services they need.

SOCIAL-LEARNING THEORIES

For half a century, most American learning theories held that learning could be explained by specifying the behavioral "ABCs"— *antecedents* (events preceding behavior), *behaviors,* and *consequences.* Yet even during the early glory years of behaviorism, a few behaviorists were rebelling against explanations of behavior that relied solely on conditioning principles. In the 1940s, two social scientists proposed a modification they called *social-learning theory* (Dollard & Miller, 1950). In human beings, they argued, most learning is social—that is, acquired by observing other people in a social context, rather than through standard conditioning procedures. By the 1960s and 1970s, social-learning theory was in full bloom, and a new element had been added: the human capacity for higher-level cognitive processes. Its proponents agreed with behaviorists that human beings, along with the rat and the rabbit, are subject to the laws of operant and classical conditioning. But they added that human beings, unlike the rat and the rabbit, are full of attitudes, beliefs, and expectations that affect the way they acquire information, make decisions, reason, and solve problems. All these mental processes affect what individuals will do at any given moment and also, more generally, the kinds of people they become.

Orthodox behaviorists regard environmental factors and behavior as a two-way street, like this:

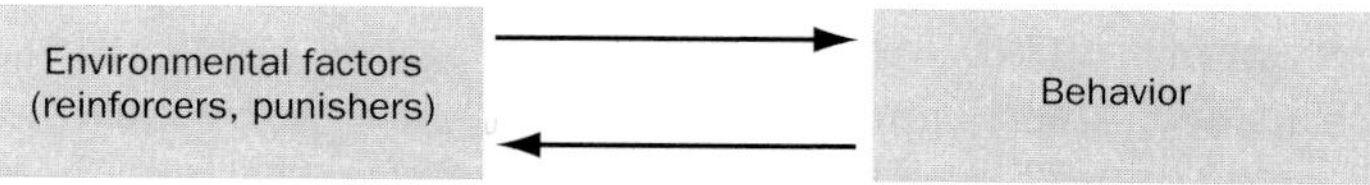

But social-learning theorists regard the environment, behavior, and a person's internalized cognitions as a circle in which all elements mutually affect each other, as in the diagram to the right.

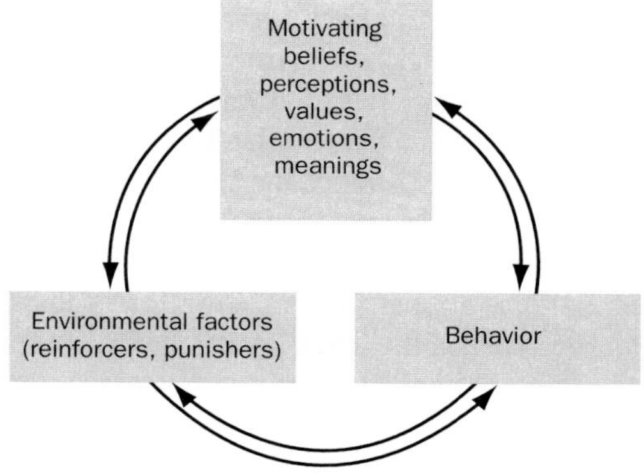

We speak of **social-learning theories** in the plural because they do not represent a single unified approach to behavior in the way that traditional behaviorism does; they differ in how much emphasis they place on cognitive processes and in how much they distance themselves from behaviorism. Some researchers continue to call themselves social-learning theorists, but the two leading advocates of this approach, Walter Mischel and Albert Bandura, call their theories *cognitive social learning* (Mischel, 1973) and *social cognitive theory* (Bandura, 1986, 1994). In general, however, social-learning theories emphasize two topics of research that distinguish them from traditional behaviorism: observational learning and the role of models, and cognitive processes such as perceptions and interpretations of events.

OBSERVATIONAL LEARNING: THE COPYCAT SYNDROME

Late one night, a friend who lives in a rural area was awakened by a loud clattering and banging. Her whole family raced outside to find the source of the commotion. A raccoon had knocked over a "raccoon-proof" garbage can and seemed to be demonstrating to an assembly of other raccoons how to open it: If you jump up and down on the can's side, the lid will pop off.

According to our friend, the observing raccoons learned from this episode how to open stubborn garbage cans, and the observing humans learned how smart raccoons can be. In short, they all benefited from **observational learning** (which behaviorists call *vicarious conditioning*): learning by watching what others do and what happens to them for doing it. Social-learning theorists emphasize that operant conditioning can and often does occur vicariously, when an animal or person observes a model (another animal or person) behaving in certain ways and experiencing the consequences (Bandura, 1977). Sometimes the learner imitates the responses shortly after

social-learning theories Theories that emphasize how behavior is learned and maintained through observation and imitation of others, positive consequences, and cognitive processes such as plans, expectations, and motivating beliefs.

observational learning A process in which an individual learns new responses by observing the behavior of another (a model) rather than through direct experience.

Like father, like daughter. Parents can be powerful role models.

observing them. At other times the learning remains latent until circumstances allow or require it to be expressed in performance. A little boy may observe a parent setting the table, threading a needle, or tightening a screw, but he may not act on this learning for years. Then the child finds he knows how to do these things, even though he has never before done them. He did not learn by doing, but by watching.

None of us would last long without observational learning. We would have to learn to avoid oncoming cars by walking into traffic and suffering the consequences or learn to swim by jumping into a deep pool and flailing around. Learning would be not only dangerous but also inefficient. Parents and teachers would be busy 24 hours a day shaping children's behavior. Bosses would have to stand over their employees' desks, rewarding every little link in the complex behavioral chains we call typing, report writing, and accounting. Observational learning also explains why parents who hit their children tend to rear hitters, and why yellers ("Be quiet!") tend to rear yellers. The children do as their parents do, not as their parents say (Grusec, Saas-Kortsaak, & Simutis, 1978).

Many years ago, Albert Bandura and his colleagues showed just how important observational learning is, especially for children who are learning the rules of social behavior (Bandura, Ross, & Ross, 1963). The researchers had nursery-school children watch a short film of two men, Rocky and Johnny, playing with toys. (Apparently, the children did not think this behavior was odd.) In the film, Johnny refuses to share his toys, and Rocky responds by clobbering him. Rocky's actions are rewarded because he winds up with all the toys. Poor Johnny sits dejectedly in the corner, while Rocky marches off with a sack full of his loot and a hobbyhorse under his arm. After viewing the film, each child was left alone for 20 minutes in a playroom full of toys, including some of the items shown in the film. Watching through a one-way mirror, the researchers found that the children were much more aggressive in their play than a control group that had not seen the film. Sometimes the children's behavior was almost a direct imitation of Rocky's. At the end of the session, one little girl even asked the experimenter for a sack!

Of course, children imitate positive activities too. Matt Groening, the creator of the cartoon *The Simpsons*, decided it would be funny if the Simpsons' 8-year-old daughter Lisa played the baritone sax. Sure enough, across the country little girls began imitating her. Cynthia Sikes, a saxophone teacher in New York, told *The New York Times* (January 14, 1996) that "When the show started, I got an influx of girls coming up to me saying, 'I want to play the saxophone because Lisa Simpson plays the saxophone.' " And Groening says his mail regularly includes photos of girls holding up their saxophones.

Behaviorists have always acknowledged the importance of observational learning; they just think it can be explained in stimulus–response terms. But social-learning theorists believe that in human beings, observational learning cannot be fully understood without taking into account the thought processes of the learner (Meltzoff & Gopnik, 1993).

COGNITIVE PROCESSES: PEERING INTO THE "BLACK BOX"

Early behaviorists liked to compare the mind to an engineer's hypothetical "black box," a device whose workings must be inferred because they can't be observed directly. To them, the box contained irrelevant wiring; it was enough to know that pushing a button on the box would produce a predictable response.

But even as early as the 1930s, a few behaviorists could not resist peeking into that black box. Edward Tolman (1938) committed virtual heresy at the time by noting that his rats, when pausing at turning points in a maze, seemed to be *deciding* which way to go. In his studies, Tolman found that sometimes the animals didn't behave as conditioning principles would predict. Sometimes the animals were clearly learning without any obvious behavioral change. What, he wondered, was going on in their little rat brains that might account for this puzzle?

In a classic experiment, Tolman and his colleague Chase Honzik (1930) placed three groups of rats in mazes and observed the rats' behavior each day for more than two weeks. The rats in Group 1 always found food at the end of the maze. Group 2 never found food. Group 3 found no food for ten days but then received food on the eleventh. The Group 1 rats, whose behavior had been reinforced with food, quickly learned to head straight for the end of the maze without going down blind alleys, whereas Group 2 rats did not learn to go to the end. But the Group 3 rats were different. For ten days, they appeared to follow no particular route. Then, on the eleventh day, when food was introduced, they quickly learned to run to the end of the maze. As Figure 7.8 shows, by the next day, they were doing as well as Group 1.

Group 3 had demonstrated **latent learning,** learning that is not immediately expressed. A great deal of human learning also remains latent until circumstances allow or require it to be expressed, as we saw in our discussion of observational learning. But latent learning poses problems for behavioral theories. Not only does it occur in the absence of any obvious reinforcer, but it also raises questions about what, exactly, is learned during learning. The rats that were not given food until the eleventh day had no reason to run toward the end during their first ten days in the maze. Yet clearly they had learned *something.*

Tolman (1948) argued that this "something" was a **cognitive map,** a mental representation of the spatial layout of the environment. You have a cognitive map of your neighborhood, which is what allows you to find your way to Fourth and Kumquat Streets even if you have never done so before; and you have a cognitive map of the city you live in, which enables you to take three different unfamiliar routes across town to the movies and still get there. More generally, according to social-learning theories, what the learner learns in observational and latent learning is not a specific

latent learning A form of learning that is not immediately expressed in an overt response; it occurs without obvious reinforcement.

cognitive map A mental representation of the environment.

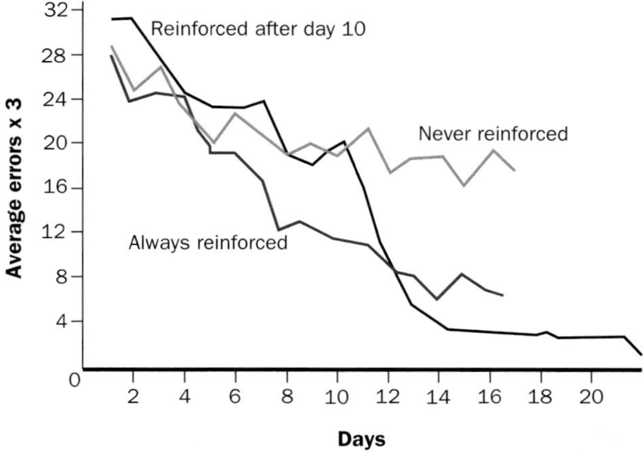

Figure 7.8
Latent Learning

In a classic experiment, rats that always found food in a complex maze made fewer and fewer errors in reaching the food, as shown by the blue curve on this graph. Rats that never found food showed little improvement, as shown by the red curve. Rats in a third group found no food for ten days, and then were given food on the eleventh. As the black curve shows, these animals showed rapid improvement from then on, quickly equaling the performance of the rats that had received food from the start. This result suggests that learning involves cognitive changes that can occur in the absence of reinforcement and that may not be acted on until a reinforcer becomes available (Tolman & Honzik, 1930).

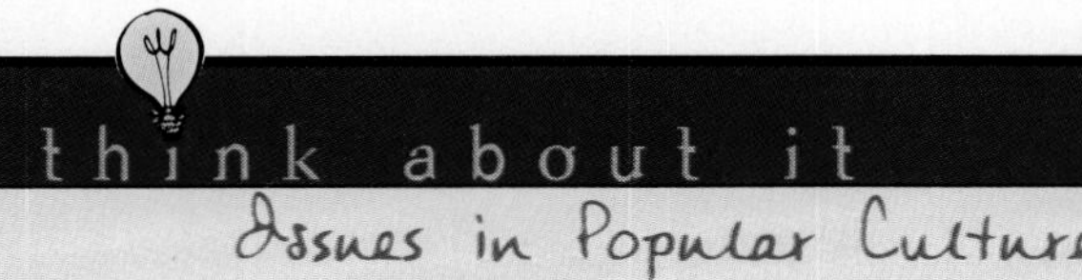

Media Violence: Getting Away with Murder

In a Connecticut town, a group of teenage boys looking for excitement telephoned an order for Chinese food so that they could rob the delivery man. When he refused to hand over the food, one of the teenagers impulsively shot him to death. Later, the boys calmly ate the food. In California, a 12-year-old girl tried to poison her teacher, and a 6-year-old boy tried to kill a neighbor's infant son.

Many psychologists and social critics blame such callous attitudes and violent behavior in part on television and movies. Children in the United States and other countries view endless killings and maimings that leave out all negative consequences. Victims are merely "blown away." Death doesn't mean grief, mourning, or pain; it means disappearing from the screen.

No one disputes that movies and television programs help shape values, attitudes, and reactions to events, including violent events. Some children do, unquestionably, imitate the aggression they observe on television and in movies (Comstock et al., 1978; Eron, 1980, 1995; Geen, 1978; Singer & Singer, 1988). A task force assembled by the American Psychological Association to study this issue concluded that "There is absolutely no doubt that higher levels of viewing violence on television are correlated with increased acceptance of aggressive attitudes and increased aggressive behavior" (APA Commission on Violence and Youth, 1993).

Leonard Eron (1995), who has been conducting longitudinal research on this issue for many years, has found support for this conclusion in studies of girls as well as boys and in countries as diverse as Australia, Finland, Israel, and Poland. Eron thinks that the reason for the link between heavy childhood viewing of TV violence and later aggressive habits is that TV violence teaches children aggressive attitudes, norms of behavior, and ways of solving problems—yelling, hitting, obliterating the enemy. TV violence, he argues, is different from violence in Shakespeare, the movies, or fairy tales. In contrast to these forms of entertainment, which are clearly absorbed as "fantasy," TV images are pervasive, repetitive, and incessant, because in most homes the TV is nearly always on.

Of course, not everyone who watches violent shows and films becomes violent (Freedman, 1988; Milavsky, 1988). Cognitive social-learning theory helps explain why. Children watch many kinds of programs and movies, and they have many models to observe besides those they see in the media; their parents and peers are also influential. Further, not everyone draws the same lessons from the violence they perceive. One person who watches Arnold Schwarzenegger destroy the bad guys might regard Arnold as the greatest hero of all times, while another sees him as an overpaid weight lifter who should take acting lessons. One person may learn from seeing people being killed in a film that violence is cool and masculine; another may conclude that violence is ugly, stupid, and self-defeating.

Moreover, the relationship between media violence and real violence works in both directions. Individuals who are habitually aggressive seek out violent media—and are more affected by violent media—than nonaggressive people. Given a choice of films to see, they prefer the violent ones; when they actually watch violent films, they feel angrier afterward than nonaggressive people do; and if given the chance to behave aggressively toward others after watching a violent film, they are more likely to do so than nonaggressive people are (Bushman, 1995). Perhaps people should be prevented from seeing a violent movie not on the basis of their age, but their scores on an aggression test!

Eron responds to these findings by noting that "The size of the relation [between television violence and aggression] is about the same as that between smoking and lung cancer. Not everyone who smokes gets lung

response but *knowledge* about responses and their consequences. We learn how the world is organized, which paths lead to which places, and which actions can produce which payoffs. This knowledge permits us to be creative and flexible in reaching our goals.

Social-learning theories also emphasize the importance of people's *perceptions* in what they learn: perceptions of the models they observe and also perceptions of themselves. Two people may observe the same event and come away with entirely different interpretations of it; they have learned, we might say, two different lessons from it. Individuals also bring different knowledge and assumptions to an event, and they notice and pay attention to different aspects of a situation. Imagine two people trying to learn how to do a perfect "tush push" in country-western line dancing: One is paying careful attention to the instructor who is modeling the complex steps, but cancer and not everybody who has lung cancer ever smoked. But no one outside the tobacco industry would deny that smoking causes cancer. Similarly, not everyone who watches violent TV becomes aggressive and not everyone who is aggressive watched television. But that doesn't mean television violence is not a cause of aggression."

Other critics of media violence point out that most research on the issue was done during the 1970s. Since then, depictions have become far more graphic, especially in action and slasher films, which are routinely shown on local and cable TV stations and which feature, with monotonous regularity, people being sawed in half by chain saws, impaled, or blown to bits. To many young people, these films are a joke and fun; the rush of adrenaline the movies produce is enjoyable. To many psychologists, graphic violence is no joke. They believe that with repeated exposure to mindless murder, viewers' responses of horror or disgust tend to extinguish, people become numb to the consequences of brutality, and increasingly gruesome depictions are needed to produce an emotional effect. Support comes from studies of slasher films, which often link erotic scenes with grisly violence. In the laboratory, viewers of such films tend to become more callous in their attitudes toward women and toward real-life rape victims (Linz, Donnerstein, & Penrod, 1988).

Violence has always been a part of storytelling, in fairy tales, myths, novels, and plays. Modern media violence, however, whether bloodless or gory, is often notable not only for what it shows but also for what it leaves out: the human face and personality of the victim, the sorrow of those the victim leaves behind (even bad guys usually have friends and families), and perhaps most important, alternative ways of resolving conflicts. People can identify with victims and survivors when violence has meaning; they will cry even for Bambi, a cartoon deer. But it is hard to feel empathy when killing is just a matter of awesome special effects.

In contrast to the glamorizing of fictional violence, news reports of *actual* violence are often sanitized. Since World War II, government censors have been concerned about media efforts to portray the realities of war: rape, disease, and bodies torn apart in battle (Fussell, 1989). Since the first "TV war," in Vietnam, battlefields and body bags have been off-limits to cameras, presumably because seeing the real carnage of war might affect public support for it. During the 1991 Persian Gulf war, television viewers saw only sleek aircraft taking off and "smart bombs" "surgically" destroying buildings. They did not get to witness the chaos and fear of battle; enemy deaths were called "collateral damage." What are the effects on viewers of *not* seeing this kind of real violence?

Should fictional violence in the media also be censored? This question raises the problem of how to decide which violent images should be censored and who should do the censoring. Some people want the government to be the censor, but that solution poses constitutional problems. Some want TV networks and producers to censor themselves—but would they? Some want to leave the matter in the hands of viewers; the "V-chip," for example, allows parents to block some violent television shows so their children can't see them. In the midst of this debate, understanding the principles of learning can be helpful. Learning theory suggests that violent films continue to be made because they make barrels of money for their producers—a powerful reinforcer! It follows that viewers can extinguish violent-film-making behavior by refusing to buy tickets to slasher and other violent action films or by turning to another station when such films are shown on television. The question is whether they would be willing to do so, or whether their own viewing behavior is being controlled by reinforcers that they have never stopped to analyze.

the other is distracted by an appealing tush-pusher down the line. And of course the two novices may differ in how much they want to learn the new dance. People make thousands of observations every day and theoretically could learn something from all of them; but if they don't *want* to learn what is being modeled, they could watch a hundred teachers and not get anywhere at all (Bandura, 1986, 1994).

Individual differences in perceptions and interpretations, then, help explain why observational learning does not produce the same results in all observers. In "Issues in Popular Culture," we discuss the implications of this fact in debates about the effects of media violence on children and adults.

Behaviorists would say that the thing we call "personality" is a set of habits and beliefs that have been rewarded over a person's lifetime. Social-learning theorists, however, maintain that these learned habits and beliefs eventually acquire a life of their own, coming to exert their own effects on behavior. In fact, they may even supersede the power of external rewards and punishers. For example, to understand why some people work hard and persist even after failing many times, such theorists argue, we need to understand cognitive factors, such as the sense of control people have about their lives and whether they are confident in their own abilities. We will be discussing the influence of motivating beliefs and internalized goals further in Chapters 11 and 12.

Quick Quiz

How latent is your learning?

1. After watching her teenage sister put on some lipstick, a little girl takes a lipstick and applies it to her own lips. She has acquired this behavior through a process of ___________.
2. Your friend asks you to meet her at a new restaurant across town; you've never been to this specific address, but you find your way there anyway because you have a good ___________ of your town.
3. To a social-learning theorist, the phenomenon of latent learning shows that we learn not specific responses but rather ___________.

Answers:

1. observational learning 2. cognitive map 3. knowledge about responses and their consequences

COGNITIONS VERSUS CONNECTIONS: WHY DOES LEARNING OCCUR?

Today, most psychologists allow for cognitions in their theories and explanations of behavior. However, to the true behaviorist, mental explanations are misleading fictions, and nothing is to be gained by using them. As behaviorist William Baum (1994) writes, "I no more have a mind than I have a fairy godmother. I can talk to you about my mind or about my fairy godmother; that cannot make either of them less fictional. No one has ever seen either one . . . such talk is no help in a science."

The tension between behaviorism and cognitive approaches to psychology can be seen in how the two approaches treat the interesting problem of insight. **Insight** is learning that appears to occur in a flash: You suddenly "see" how to solve an equation, assemble a cabinet that came with unintelligible instructions, or finish a puzzle. The human species is not the only one capable of insight. In the 1920s, Wolfgang Köhler (1925) put chimpanzees in situations in which some tempting bananas were just out of reach, then watched to see what the apes would do. Most did nothing, but a few turned out to be very clever. If the bananas were outside the cage, the animal might pull them in with a stick. If the bananas were hung overhead, and there were boxes in the cage, the chimpanzee might pile up the boxes and climb on top of them to reach the fruit. Often, the solution came after the animal had been sitting quietly for a while without actively trying to reach the bananas. It appeared as though the animal had been thinking about the problem and suddenly saw the answer.

insight A form of problem solving that appears to involve the (often sudden) understanding of how elements of a situation are related or can be reorganized to achieve a solution.

To most people, insight seems to be an entirely cognitive phenomenon—a new way of perceiving logical and cause-and-effect relationships, in which a person or animal does not simply respond to a stimulus but instead solves a problem. But behaviorists argue that insight can be explained in terms of an organism's reinforcement history, without resorting to mentalistic concepts (Windholz & Lamal, 1985).

(a)

(b)

(c)

Figure 7.9
Smart Bird

"Now, let's see. . . ." A pigeon looks at a cluster of toy bananas strung overhead (a), pushes a small box beneath the bananas (b), and then climbs on the box to peck at them (c). The bird had previously learned separate components of this sequence through a process of operant conditioning. Behaviorists view this accomplishment as evidence against the cognitive view of insight. What do you think?

Insight, they say, is just a label for the combination of previously learned patterns; it does not *explain* the behavior.

Behaviorists point out that even animals not usually credited with higher mental processes seem capable of what looks suspiciously like "insight," under some conditions. In one ingenious study, Robert Epstein and his colleagues (1984) taught four pigeons three separate behaviors, during different training sessions: to push boxes in a particular direction, to climb onto a box, and to peck at a toy banana in order to obtain grain. The birds were also taught not to fly or jump at the banana; those behaviors were extinguished. Then the pigeons were left alone with the banana suspended just out of reach overhead and the box at the edge of the cage.

"At first," the researchers observed, "each pigeon appeared to be 'confused'; it stretched and turned beneath the banana, looked back and forth from banana to box, and so on. Then each subject began rather suddenly to push the box in what was clearly the direction of the banana" (Epstein et al., 1984). Just as Köhler's chimps had done, the birds quickly solved their feeding problem by pushing the box beneath the banana and climbing onto it (see Figure 7.9). Yet few people would want to credit pigeons with complex thought processes. Epstein (1990) later devised a computer model that is amazingly accurate in predicting the pigeons' behavior in the banana-and-box situation, using only behavioral concepts. Cognitive researchers, however, are not convinced; just because the behavior of a pigeon looks something like that of a human being, they say, does not mean that its origins are the same. Cognitive studies, they maintain, show that in human beings (and possibly chimpanzees), insight requires *mentally* combining previously learned responses in new ways.

The debates between behaviorists and their critics over insight and many other kinds of learning promise to continue. In practice, behavioral and cognitive approaches are sometimes treated as different levels of analysis, rather than as conflicting approaches; many therapists, for example, combine behavioral principles with cognitive ones to treat people in psychotherapy (see Chapter 16). Nonetheless, as we will see in the next two chapters, cognitive psychologists have staked out many areas that behaviorists have traditionally regarded as foreign territory—areas in the vast country of the mind.

Taking Psychology with You

Shape Up!

Operant conditioning can seem deceptively simple. In the early 1980s, a tiny but expensive book titled *The One Minute Manager* became an enormous best-seller merely by advising managers to use praise and constructive criticism. In practice, though, behavior modification can be full of unwanted surprises, even in the hands of experts. Here are a few things to keep in mind if you want to modify someone's behavior.

• *Accentuate the positive.* Most people notice bad behavior more than good and therefore miss opportunities to use reinforcers. Parents, for example, often scold a child for bed-wetting but fail to give praise for dry sheets in the morning; or they punish a child for poor grades but fail to reward studying.

• *Reinforce small improvements.* A common error is to withhold reinforcement until behavior is perfect. Has your child's grade in math improved from a D to a C? Has your favorite date, who is usually an awful cook, managed to serve up a half-decent omelette? Has your messy roommate left some dirty dishes in the sink but vacuumed the rug? It's probably time for a reinforcer. On the other hand, you don't want to overdo praise or give it insincerely. Gushing about every tiny step in the right direction will cause your praise to lose its value, and soon nothing less than a standing ovation will do.

• *Find the right reinforcers.* You may have to experiment a bit to find which reinforcers a person (or animal) actually wants. In general, it is good to use a variety of reinforcers because the same one used again and again can get boring. Reinforcers, by the way, do not have to be *things.* You can also use valued activities, such as going out to dinner, to reinforce other behavior.

• *Always examine what you are reinforcing.* It is easy to reinforce undesirable behavior by responding to it. Suppose someone is always yelling at you at the slightest provocation, and you want it to stop. If you respond to it at all, whether by crying, apologizing, or yelling back, you are likely to reinforce it. An alternative might be to explain in a calm voice that you will henceforth not respond to complaints unless they are communicated without yelling—and then, if the yelling continues, leave. When the person does speak civilly, you can reward this behavior with your attention and goodwill.

Because you are with yourself more than with anyone else, it may be easier to modify your own behavior than someone else's. You may wish to reduce your nibbling, eliminate a smoking habit, or become more outgoing. Let's assume for the sake of discussion that you aren't studying enough. How can you increase the time you spend with your books? Some hints:

• *Analyze the situation.* Are there circumstances that keep you from studying, such as a friend who is always pressuring you to go out or a rock band that practices next door? If so, you need to change the discriminative stimuli in your environment during study periods. Try to find a comfortable, cheerful, quiet, well-lit place. Not only will you concentrate better, but you may also have positive emotional responses to the environment that may generalize to the activity of studying.

• *Set realistic goals.* Goals should be demanding but achievable. If a goal is too vague, as in "I'm going to work harder," you don't know what action to take to reach it or how to know when you get there (what does "harder" mean?). If your goal is focused, as in "I am going to study two hours every evening instead of one, and read 25 pages instead of 15," you have specified both a course of action and a goal you can achieve (and reward!).

• *Reinforce getting started.* The hardest part of studying can be getting started. (This is true of many other activities, too, as writers, joggers, and people who prepare their own income-tax returns can tell you.) You might give yourself a small bit of candy or some other reward just for sitting down at your desk or, if you study at the library, reward yourself for getting there early.

• *Keep records.* Chart your progress in some way, perhaps by making a graph. This will keep you honest, and the progress you see on the graph will serve as a secondary reinforcer.

• *Don't punish yourself.* If you didn't study enough last week, don't brood about it or berate yourself with self-defeating thoughts, such as "I'll never be a good student" or "I'm a failure." Think about the coming week instead.

Above all, be patient. Shaping behavior is a creative skill that takes time to learn. Like Rome, new habits cannot be built in a day.

SUMMARY

1) Research on learning has been heavily influenced by *behaviorism,* which accounts for behavior in terms of observable events, without reference to such hypothetical mental entities as "mind" or "will." Behaviorists have focused on two types of *conditioning:* classical conditioning and operant conditioning.

CLASSICAL CONDITIONING: NEW REFLEXES FROM OLD

2) *Classical conditioning* was first studied by Russian physiologist Ivan Pavlov. In this type of learning, when a neutral stimulus is paired with an *unconditioned stimulus (US)* that elicits some reflexive *unconditioned response (UR)*, the neutral stimulus comes to elicit a similar or related response. The neutral stimulus is then called a *conditioned stimulus (CS)*, and the response it elicits is a *conditioned response (CR)*. Nearly any kind of involuntary response can become a CR.

3) Many theorists believe that what an animal or person learns in classical conditioning is not just an association between the unconditioned and the conditioned stimulus, but information conveyed by one stimulus about another. They cite evidence that the neutral stimulus does not become a CS unless it reliably signals or predicts the US.

4) In *extinction*, the conditioned stimulus is repeatedly presented without the unconditioned stimulus, and the conditioned response eventually disappears. In *higher-order conditioning*, a neutral stimulus becomes a conditioned stimulus by being paired with an already established conditioned stimulus. In *stimulus generalization*, after a stimulus becomes a conditioned stimulus for some response, other, similar stimuli may produce the same reaction. And in *stimulus discrimination*, different responses are made to stimuli that resemble the conditioned stimulus in some way.

5) Classical conditioning may account for the acquisition of likes and dislikes, emotional responses to particular objects and events, and fears and phobias. John Watson showed how fears may be learned and then unlearned through a process of *counterconditioning*. Classical conditioning may also be involved in such aspects of drug addiction as tolerance and withdrawal.

OPERANT CONDITIONING: THE CARROT AND THE STICK

6) The basic principle of *operant conditioning* is that behavior becomes more likely to occur or less so, depending on its consequences. Responses in operant conditioning are generally not reflexive and are more complex than in classical conditioning. Research in this area is closely associated with B. F. Skinner, who called his approach "radical behaviorism."

7) In the Skinnerian analysis, a response ("operant") can lead to one of three consequences: neutral, reinforcing, or punishing. *Reinforcement* strengthens or increases the probability of a response. *Punishment* weakens or decreases the probability of a response. Reinforcement (and punishment) may be positive or negative. *Positive reinforcement* occurs when something pleasant follows a response. *Negative reinforcement* occurs when something *un*pleasant is removed. Reinforcement is called *primary* when the reinforcer is naturally reinforcing (e.g., because it satisfies a biological need) and *secondary* when the reinforcer has acquired its ability to strengthen a response through association with other reinforcers. A similar distinction is made for punishers.

8) By using the Skinner box and similar devices, behaviorists have shown that extinction, stimulus generalization, and stimulus discrimination occur in operant, as well as in classical, conditioning. They also find that immediate consequences usually have a greater effect on a response than do delayed consequences.

9) The pattern of responding in operant conditioning depends in part on the *schedule of reinforcement*. *Continuous reinforcement* leads to the most rapid learning, but *intermittent*, or *partial*, reinforcement makes a response more resistant to extinction. Intermittent schedules deliver a reinforcer after a given amount of time has passed since the last reinforcer (*interval schedules*) or after a given number of responses are made (*ratio schedules*). Such schedules may be *fixed* or *variable.* One of the most common errors people make, from a behavioral point of view, is to reward intermittently the responses they would like to eliminate.

10) *Shaping* is used to train behaviors with a low probability of occurring spontaneously. Reinforcers are given for *successive approximations* to the desired response, until the desired response is achieved.

11) Accidental or coincidental reinforcement can effectively strengthen behavior and can help account for the learning and the persistence of superstitions, although other factors are also involved.

OPERANT CONDITIONING IN REAL LIFE

12) *Behavior modification,* the application of conditioning principles, has been used successfully in many settings, often by applying a *token economy.* But reinforcement and punishment both have their pitfalls.

13) Punishment can sometimes be effective in eliminating undesirable behavior, but it has many drawbacks and may have unintended consequences. It is often administered inappropriately because of the emotion of the moment; it may produce rage and fear; its effects are often only temporary; it is hard to administer immediately; it conveys little information about what kind of behavior is desired; and an action intended to punish may instead be reinforcing because of the attention it brings. Extinction of undesirable behavior, combined with reinforcement of desired behavior, is generally preferable to the use of punishment. It is also important to understand the reasons for a person's misbehavior instead of simply trying to get rid of it without knowing why it occurs.

14) An exclusive reliance on *extrinsic reinforcement* can sometimes undermine the power of *intrinsic reinforcement.* But money and praise do not usually interfere with intrinsic pleasure when a person is rewarded for succeeding or making progress rather than for merely participating in an activity, or when a person is already extremely interested in the activity.

SOCIAL-LEARNING THEORIES

15) The 1960s and 1970s saw the increased influence of *social-learning theories,* whose proponents study the ways in which the environment, behavior, and a person's internalized motives and cognitions interact. Social-learning theorists emphasize *observational learning,* in which the learner imitates the behavior of a model; performance may be either immediate or delayed (*latent learning*). These theorists also emphasize the role of people's perceptions and motivating beliefs in explaining behavior.

COGNITIONS VERSUS CONNECTIONS: WHY DOES LEARNING OCCUR?

16) The tension between behaviorism and cognitive approaches to psychology can be seen in how the two approaches treat *insight,* learning that seems to occur suddenly and that involves the solving of a problem. Behaviorists believe insight can be understood in terms of the conditioning history of the organism. Cognitive psychologists believe that what is learned is knowledge rather than behavior. The behavioral and cognitive approaches are quite different, but many psychologists treat them as different levels of analysis and use concepts and techniques from both.

KEY TERMS

learning 254
behaviorism 254
conditioning 254
unconditioned stimulus (US) 256
unconditioned response (UR) 256
conditioned stimulus (CS) 256
conditioned response (CR) 256
classical conditioning 257
extinction (in classical conditioning) 258
spontaneous recovery 259
higher-order conditioning 259
stimulus generalization (in classical conditioning) 259
stimulus discrimination (in classical conditioning) 259
phobia 261
counterconditioning 263
operant conditioning 265
law of effect 265
free will versus determinism 266
reinforcement and reinforcers 267
punishment and punishers 268
instinctive drift 268
positive and negative reinforcement and punishment 268
primary reinforcers and punishers 270
secondary (conditioned) reinforcers and punishers 270
Skinner box 271
extinction (in operant conditioning) 272
stimulus generalization (in operant conditioning) 272
stimulus discrimination (in operant conditioning) 272
discriminative stimulus 272
stimulus control 272
continuous reinforcement 273
intermittent (partial) reinforcement 273
fixed-ratio (FR) schedule 273
variable-ratio (VR) schedule 273
fixed-interval (FI) schedule 274
variable-interval (VI) schedule 274
shaping 275
successive approximations 275
behavior modification 278
token economy 278
extrinsic versus intrinsic reinforcers 281
behavioral "ABCs" 284
social-learning theories 285
observational (vicarious) learning 285
latent learning 287
cognitive map 287
insight 290

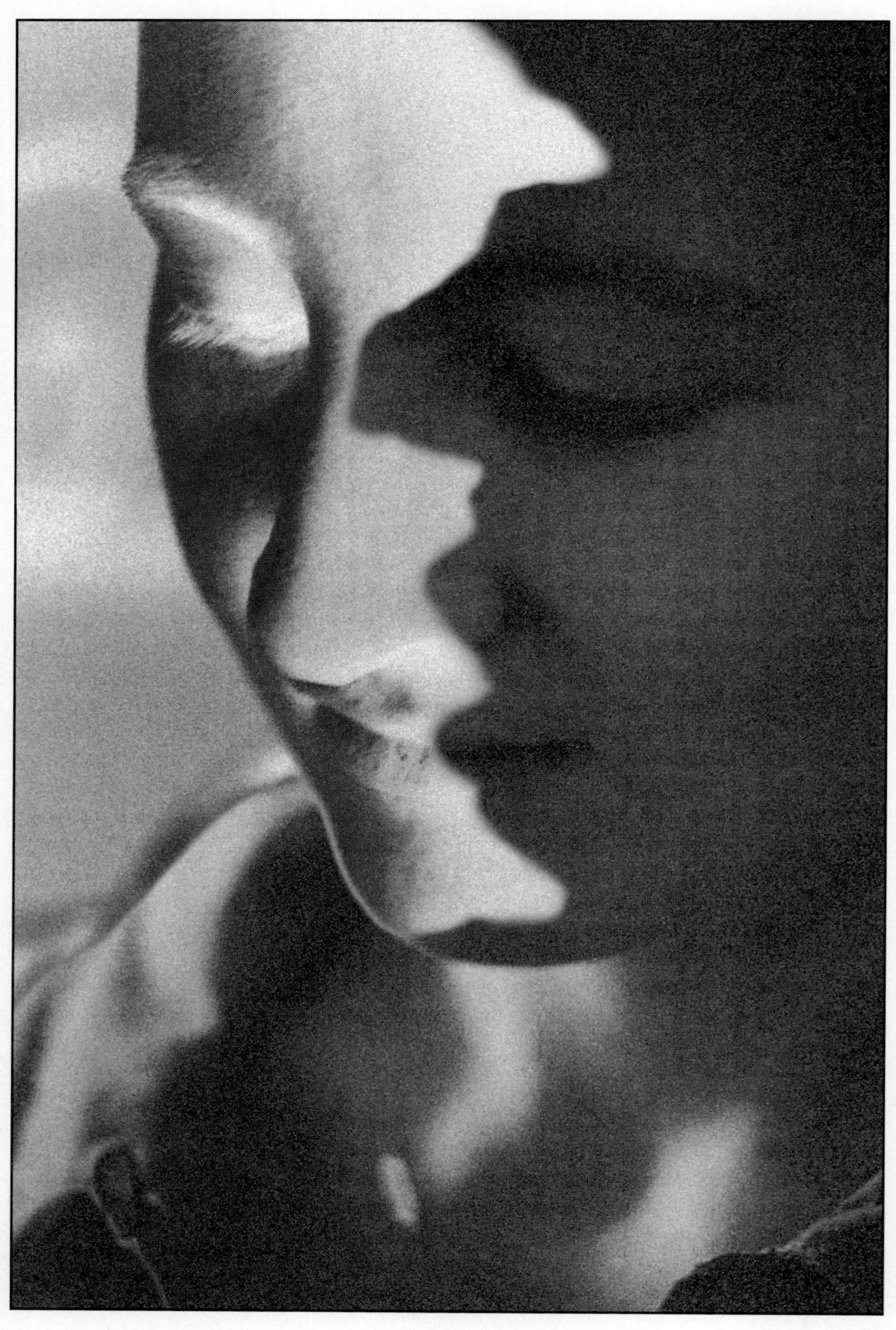

The voice of the intellect is a soft one,
but it does not rest until it has gained a hearing.

Sigmund Freud

CHAPTER EIGHT

Thinking and Intelligence

He's thinking—but how well is he thinking?

EACH DAY, IN THE COURSE OF ORDINARY LIVING, we make plans, draw inferences, concoct explanations, analyze relationships, and organize and reorganize the flotsam and jetsam of our mental world. Descartes' famous declaration, "I think, therefore I am," could just as well have been reversed: "I am, therefore I think." Our powers of thought and intelligence inspired our forebears to give our species the immodest name *Homo sapiens*, Latin for wise or rational man. But just how "sapiens" are we, really? Consider:

- As children, we all learn how clocks arbitrarily divide time into hours, minutes, and seconds. Yet every spring, when daylight savings time begins, some people fret about tampering with "God's time." One woman in Colorado even complained to a local newspaper that the "extra hour of sunlight" was burning up her front lawn!
- After the novel *Bridges of Madison County* became a best-seller, *National Geographic*, which employed the story's hero as a photographer, was besieged by callers wanting to buy the issue "with his photos in it." Similarly, after *Forrest Gump* became a hit movie, people began showing up at Gump's supposed alma mater, the University of Alabama, demanding to see his football trophies.
- A few years ago, the pilots of an Air Florida flight were going over a pretakeoff checklist. When the de-icer was mentioned, a crew member automatically responded "off," without giving it much thought. After all, it's always warm in Florida, isn't it? Unfortunately, on this occasion the weather was icy, and the plane crashed, killing 74 people.

The human mind, which has managed to come up with poetry, penicillin, and panty hose, is a miraculous thing. But the human mind has also managed to come up with traffic jams, junk mail, and war. To better understand why the same species that figured out how to get to the moon is also capable of breathtaking bumbling here on earth, in this chapter we will examine how we reason, solve problems, and grow in intelligence, as well as some sources of our mental shortcomings.

THOUGHT: USING WHAT WE KNOW

Think about what thinking does for us. It frees us from the confines of the immediate present: We can think about a trip taken three years ago, a party planned for next Saturday, or the War of 1812. It carries us beyond the boundaries of reality: We can imagine unicorns and utopias, Martians and magic. Because we think, we do not need to grope our way blindly through our problems but, with some effort and knowledge, can solve them intelligently and creatively.

To explain such abilities, many cognitive psychologists liken the human mind to an information processor, somewhat analogous to a computer but far more complex. Information-processing approaches have been useful because they capture the fact that the brain does not passively record information but actively alters and organizes it. When we take action, we physically manipulate the environment; when we think, we *mentally* manipulate internal representations of objects, activities, and situations. However, we do not manipulate all the information potentially available to us; if we did, making the simplest decision or solving the most trivial problem would be time-consuming and perhaps impossible. Imagine trying to decide whether to go out for a hamburger if that meant thinking about every hamburger you ever ate, saw a commercial for, or watched someone eat. Thinking is possible because our internal representations simplify and summarize information that reaches us from the environment.

THE ELEMENTS OF COGNITION

One type of mental representation, or unit of thought, is the **concept.** Essentially, a concept is a mental category that groups objects, relations, activities, abstractions, or qualities having common properties. The instances of a concept are seen as roughly similar. For example, *golden retriever, cocker spaniel,* and *Weimaraner* are instances of the concept *dog;* and *anger, joy,* and *sadness* are instances of the concept *emotion.* Because concepts simplify the world, we do not have to learn a new name for each thing, relation, activity, abstract state, or quality we encounter, nor do we need to treat each instance as though it were unique. You may never have seen a *basenji* or eaten *escargots,* but if you know that the first is an instance of *dog* and the second an instance of *food,* you will know, roughly, how to respond (unless you do not like to eat snails, which is what escargots are).

We form concepts through direct contact with objects and situations and also by contact with *symbols,* things that represent or stand for something else. Symbolic representations include words, mathematical formulas, maps, graphs, pictures, and even gestures. Symbols stand not only for objects but also for operations (e.g., the symbols + and ÷), relationships (e.g., = and <), and qualities (e.g., the dot in musical notation that symbolizes an abrupt or staccato quality).

What is this?

Basic concepts have a moderate number of instances and are easier to acquire than those that have either few or many instances (Rosch, 1973). What is the object pictured in the margin? You will probably call it an apple. The concept *apple* is more basic than *fruit,* which includes many more instances and is more abstract. It is also more basic than *McIntosh apple,* which is specific. Similarly, *book* is more basic than either *printed matter* or *novel.* Children seem to learn basic-level concepts earlier than others, and adults use them more often than others, because basic concepts convey an optimal amount of information in most situations.

All the qualities associated with a concept do not necessarily apply to every instance: Some apples are not red; some dogs do not bark; some birds do not fly or perch on trees. But all the instances of a concept do share a "family resemblance." When we need to decide whether something belongs to a concept, we are likely to compare it to a **prototype,** a representative example of the concept (Rosch, 1973). For instance, which dog is doggier—a golden retriever or a chihuahua? Which fruit is more fruitlike—an apple or a pineapple? Which activity is more representative of sports—football or weight lifting? Most people within a culture can easily tell you which instances are most representative, or *prototypical,* of the concept.

Concepts are the building blocks of thought, but they would be of limited use if we merely stacked them up mentally. We must also represent their relationships to one another. One way we accomplish this may be by storing and using **propositions,** units of meaning that are made up of concepts and that express a unitary idea. A proposition can express nearly any sort of knowledge (*Hortense raises basenjis*) or belief (*Basenjis are beautiful*). Propositions, in turn, are linked together in complicated networks of knowledge, associations, beliefs, and expectations. These networks, which psychologists call **cognitive schemas,** serve as mental models of aspects of the world. For example, gender schemas represent a person's beliefs and expectations about what it means to be male or female. People also have schemas about cultures, occupations, animals, geographical locations, and many other features of the social and natural environment.

Most cognitive psychologists believe that **mental images** are also important in thinking and in the construction of cognitive schemas—especially *visual images,* pictures in the mind's eye. Although no one can directly "see" another person's visual images, psychologists are able to study them indirectly. One method is to measure

concept A mental category that groups objects, relations, activities, abstractions, or qualities having common properties.

basic concepts Concepts that have a moderate number of instances and that are easier to acquire than those having few or many instances.

prototype An especially representative example of a concept.

proposition A unit of meaning that is made up of concepts and expresses a single idea.

cognitive schema An integrated mental network of knowledge, beliefs, and expectations concerning a particular topic or aspect of the world.

mental image A mental representation that mirrors or resembles the thing it represents; mental images can occur in many and perhaps all sensory modalities.

Some instances of a concept are more representative, or prototypical, than others. For example, actor Charlie Sheen clearly qualifies as a "bachelor," an unmarried man (at least, as of 1997). But is the pope a bachelor? What about Robert Redford, who is divorced and hasn't remarried?

how long it takes people to rotate an image, scan from one point to another in an image, or read off some detail from an image. The results suggest that visual images are much like images on a television screen: We can manipulate them, they occur in a mental "space" of a fixed size, and small ones contain less detail than larger ones (Kosslyn, 1980; Shepard & Metzler, 1971).

In addition to visual images, most people also report auditory images (for instance, a song, slogan, or poem you can hear in your "mind's ear"), and many report images in other sensory modalities—touch, taste, smell, or pain. Some even report kinesthetic images, feelings in the muscles and joints. Some people have learned to use mental images to visualize the possible outcomes of a decision, understand or formulate verbal descriptions, boost motivation, or improve mood (Kosslyn et al., 1990b). Imagining yourself performing an athletic skill, such as diving or sprinting, may even improve your actual performance (Druckman & Swets, 1988). Brain scans show that this mental practice activates most of the brain circuits involved in the activity itself (Stephan et al., 1995).

Albert Einstein relied heavily on visual and kinesthetic imagery for formulating ideas. The happiest thought of his life, he once recalled, occurred in 1907, when he suddenly imagined a man falling freely from the roof of a house and realized that the man would not experience a gravitational field in his immediate vicinity. This insight led eventually to Einstein's formulation of the principle of relativity, and physics was never again the same.

HOW CONSCIOUS IS THOUGHT?

When we think about thinking, most of us have in mind those mental activities, such as solving problems or making decisions, that are carried out in a deliberate way with a conscious goal in mind. However, not all mental processing is conscious.

subconscious processes Mental processes occurring outside of conscious awareness but accessible to consciousness when necessary.

Subconscious processes lie outside of awareness but can be brought into consciousness when necessary. These processes allow us to handle more information and to perform more complex tasks than if we depended entirely on conscious

Fortunately for this father, some well-learned tasks, such as holding a baby, do not require much conscious thought, so he can do other things at the same time.

thought, and they enable us to perform more than one task simultaneously (Kahneman & Treisman, 1984). Consider all the automatic routines performed "without thinking," though they might once have required careful, conscious attention: knitting, typing, driving a car, decoding the letters in a word in order to read it. Because of the capacity for automatic processing, with proper training people can even learn to perform simultaneously such complex tasks as reading and taking dictation (Hirst, Neisser, & Spelke, 1978).

Nonconscious processes remain outside of awareness but nonetheless affect behavior. For example, most of us have had the odd experience of having a solution to a problem "pop into mind" after we have given up trying to find one. Similarly, people will often say they rely on intuition rather than conscious reasoning to solve a problem. Intuition may actually be an orderly process involving two stages (Bowers et al., 1990). In the first stage, clues in the problem automatically activate certain memories or knowledge, and you begin to see a pattern or structure in the problem, although you can't yet say what it is. This nonconscious process guides you toward a hunch or a hypothesis. Then, in the second stage, your thinking becomes conscious, and you become aware of a possible solution. This stage may feel like a sudden revelation ("Aha, I've got it!"), but considerable mental work has already occurred, even though you are not aware of it.

Usually, of course, much of our thinking is conscious—but we may not be thinking very *hard.* Like the pilots who left the de-icer off, we may act, speak, and make decisions out of habit, without stopping to analyze what we are doing or why we are doing it. Ellen Langer (1989) has called this mental inertia *mindlessness.* She notes that mindless processing keeps people from recognizing when a change in context requires a change in behavior. In one study by Langer and her associates, a researcher approached people as they were about to use a photocopier and made one of three requests: "Excuse me, may I use the Xerox machine?" "Excuse me, may I use the Xerox machine, because I have to make copies?" or "Excuse me, may I use the Xerox machine, because I'm in a rush?" Normally, people will let someone go before them only if the person has a legitimate reason, as in the third request. In this study, however, people also complied when the reason sounded like an authentic explanation but was actually meaningless ("because I have to make copies"). They heard the form of the request, but not its content, and they mindlessly stepped aside (Langer, Blank, & Chanowitz, 1978).

"This CD player costs less than players selling for twice as much."

Mindlessness is a common source of irrationality.

The mindless processing of information has benefits: If we stopped to think twice about everything we did, we would get nothing done ("Okay, now I'm reaching for my toothbrush; now I'm putting a quarter-inch of toothpaste on it; now I'm brushing my upper-right molars"). But mindlessness can also lead to errors and mishaps, ranging from the trivial (putting the butter in the dishwasher or locking yourself out of the car) to the serious (driving carelessly while on "automatic pilot").

nonconscious processes Mental processes occurring outside of and not available to conscious awareness.

Jerome Kagan (1989) argues that fully conscious awareness is needed only when we must make a deliberate choice, when events happen that can't be handled automatically, and when unexpected moods and feelings arise. "Consciousness," he says, "can be likened to the staff of a fire department. Most of the time, it is quietly playing pinochle in the back room; it performs [only] when the alarm sounds." That may be so, but most of us would probably benefit if our mental firefighters paid a little more attention to their jobs. Cognitive psychologists have, therefore, devoted a great deal of study to mindful, conscious thought and the capacity to reason.

Quick Quiz

1. Stuffing your mouth with cotton candy, licking a lollipop, and chewing on a piece of beef jerky are all instances of the ___________ *eating.*
2. Which concept is most basic: *furniture, chair,* or *high chair?*
3. Which example of the concept *chair* is most prototypical: *high chair, rocking chair, dining-room chair?*
4. In addition to concepts and images, ___________, which express a unitary idea, have been proposed as a basic form of mental representation.
5. Peter's mental representation of *Thanksgiving* includes associations (e.g., to turkeys), attitudes ("It's a time to be with relatives"), and expectations ("I'm going to gain weight from all that food"). They are all part of his ___________ for the holiday.
6. Zelda discovers that she has dialed her boyfriend's number instead of her mother's, as she intended. Her error can be attributed to ___________.

Answers:

1. concept 2. chair 3. a plain, straight-backed dining-room chair will be prototypical for most people 4. propositions 5. cognitive schema 6. mindlessness

REASONING RATIONALLY

Reasoning is purposeful mental activity that involves operating on information in order to reach conclusions. Unlike impulsive or nonconscious responding, reasoning requires us to draw specific inferences from observations, facts, or assumptions.

Sometimes a reasoned decision or choice is clearly the best one, and there is a known method for arriving at it. To solve a problem in long division, for example, you need only apply an **algorithm,** a set of procedures guaranteed to produce a solution even if you don't really know how it works. To make a cake, you need only apply an algorithm called a *recipe.* But more often than not, people must make judgments and decisions under conditions of uncertainty. For these problems, no algorithms exist, or they are too complicated to apply. In these cases, people rely on **heuristics**—rules of thumb that suggest a course of action without guaranteeing an optimal solution. An investor trying to predict the stock market, a renter trying to decide whether to lease an apartment, a doctor trying to determine the best treatment for a patient, a marriage counselor advising a troubled couple, a factory owner trying to boost production: All are faced with incomplete information on which to base a decision and must therefore rely on heuristics.

How people make decisions, and whether they can use algorithms or must turn to heuristics, depends on the nature of the problem at hand. In the next two sections, we will consider several kinds of reasoning and some of the barriers to reasoning well.

reasoning The drawing of conclusions or inferences from observations, facts, or assumptions.

algorithm A problem-solving strategy guaranteed to produce a solution even if the user does not know how it works.

heuristic A rule of thumb that suggests a course of action or guides problem solving but does not guarantee an optimal solution.

DEDUCTIVE AND INDUCTIVE REASONING

Two of the most basic types of reasoning are deductive reasoning and inductive reasoning, which both involve drawing conclusions from a series of observations or propositions (*premises*).

Deductive reasoning

Premises true → Conclusion must be true

In **deductive reasoning,** if the premises are true, then the conclusion *must* be true. Deductive reasoning often takes the form of a syllogism, a simple argument consisting of two premises and a conclusion:

premise All human beings are mortal.
premise I am a human being.
conclusion Therefore I am mortal.

We all think in syllogisms, although many of our premises are implicit rather than explicitly spelled out: "I never have to work on Saturday. Today is Saturday. Therefore, I don't have to work today." However, applying deductive reasoning to abstract problems that are divorced from everyday life does not seem to come so naturally; it depends on experience and schooling. Years ago, in a study of the Kpelle tribe in Africa (Scribner, 1977), researchers gave an unschooled farmer this problem, which involves a standard Western syllogism: "All Kpelle men are rice farmers. Mr. Smith is not a rice farmer. Is he a Kpelle man?" The farmer insisted that the information did not allow a conclusion:

Kpelle man: I don't know the man in person. I have not laid eyes on the man himself.
Researcher: Just think about the statement.
Kpelle man: If I know him in person, I can answer that question, but since I do not know him in person, I cannot answer that question.

The interviewer concluded that because the Kpelle farmer was accustomed to drawing on personal knowledge alone to reach conclusions, he could not approach the task analytically. Yet in the exchange with the researcher, the man showed that he *could* reason deductively:

premise If I do not know a person, I cannot draw any conclusions about that person.
premise I do not know Mr. Smith.
conclusion Therefore I cannot draw any conclusions about Mr. Smith.

The answer that the Kpelle farmer gave was perfectly smart in his own culture's terms; it just was not what his interviewer expected. Most people everywhere can learn to reason deductively, but the areas in which they apply such reasoning will depend on their cultural experiences and needs (Serpell, 1994).

In **inductive reasoning,** the premises provide support for the conclusion, but the conclusion *could* still be false; that is, the conclusion does not follow necessarily from the premises, as it does in deductive reasoning.

Inductive reasoning

Premises true → Conclusion probably true

Often, people think of inductive reasoning as the drawing of general conclusions from specific observations, as when you generalize from past experience: "I had three good meals at that restaurant; they sure have great food." But an inductive argu-

deductive reasoning A form of reasoning in which a conclusion follows necessarily from certain premises; if the premises are true, the conclusion must be true.

inductive reasoning A form of reasoning in which the premises provide support for a conclusion, but it is still possible for the conclusion to be false.

ment can also have general premises. Two logicians (Copi & Burgess-Jackson, 1992) give this example:

premise	All cows are mammals and have lungs.
premise	All whales are mammals and have lungs.
premise	All humans are mammals and have lungs.
conclusion	Therefore probably all mammals have lungs.

Conversely, inductive arguments can have specific conclusions:

premise	Most people with season tickets to the concert love music.
premise	Jeannine has season tickets to the concert.
conclusion	Therefore Jeannine probably loves music.

Science depends heavily on inductive reasoning. In their studies, scientists make many careful observations and then draw some conclusions that they think are probably true. But in inductive reasoning, no matter how much supporting evidence you gather, it is always possible that new information will turn up to show you are wrong. For example, you might discover that the three good meals you ate at that restaurant were not at all typical—that, in fact, all the other dishes on the menu are awful. Or you might learn that Jeannine bought season tickets to the concert not because she loves music but because she wanted to impress a friend. Similarly, new scientific information may show that previous conclusions were faulty and must therefore be revised.

Almost everyone has trouble thinking logically in some situations. For example, some people may say that the following syllogism is valid, although it is not:

premise	All rich people live in big fancy houses.
premise	That person lives in a big fancy house.
conclusion	Therefore that person is rich.

"That person" may well be rich, but the conclusion does not follow from the premises. (After all, the person could live in a big, fancy house for any number of reasons—perhaps he or she inherited it or bought it when it was inexpensive.) Errors of this type occur because people mentally reverse a premise. In this case, they convert "All rich people live in big fancy houses" to "All people who live in big fancy houses are rich." The reversed premise may seem plausible, but it is not the one that was given.

DIALECTICAL REASONING AND REFLECTIVE JUDGMENT

Logic is a crucial weapon to have in your cognitive arsenal, but logic alone is often inadequate for solving psychological difficulties and social problems. One reason is that different individuals may reach different conclusions even when their logic is impeccable, if they start out with different premises. Logic only tells us that *if* the premises are true, a certain conclusion must follow (in deductive reasoning) or is probably true (in inductive reasoning). Logic does not tell us whether the premises are, in fact, true. Controversial issues tend to be those in which premises cannot be proven true or false to everyone's satisfaction. For example, your position on abortion rights will depend on your premises about when meaningful human life begins, what rights an embryo has, and what rights a woman has. People on opposing sides of this issue even disagree on how the premises should be phrased, because they have different emotional reactions to terms such as "rights," "meaningful life," and "control over one's body."

Even when we feel fairly confident about our premises, a problem may have no clearly correct solution (Galotti, 1989). In *formal* reasoning problems—the kind you might find, say, on an intelligence test or a college entrance exam—the information you need for drawing a conclusion is specified clearly, and there is a single right answer. Deductive and inductive reasoning are useful for these kinds of problems. But in *informal* reasoning problems, information may be incomplete; many approaches and viewpoints may compete, and you may have to decide which one is most reasonable, based on what you know, even though there is no clear-cut solution (see Table 8.1). Philosophers call such problems "ill structured." For example, should the government raise taxes or lower them? What is the best way to improve public education? Is this a good time to buy a car?

To think rationally about such issues, you need more than inductive and deductive logic. You also need to think dialectically. **Dialectical reasoning** is the ability to evaluate opposing points of view. Philosopher Richard Paul (1984) has described it as a process of moving "up and back between contradictory lines of reasoning, using each to critically cross-examine the other." This is what juries are supposed to do to arrive at a verdict: consider arguments for and against the defendant's guilt, point and counterpoint.

Many people have trouble with dialectical reasoning because their self-esteem depends on being right and having their beliefs accepted by others. We all have our convictions, of course, but the inability to listen with an open mind to competing views is a major obstacle to critical thinking. Some social commentators believe that the replacement of reading by television watching has also contributed to the growing inability of people to think dialectically. Television news often gives us sound bites instead of fully developed arguments, encouraging us to form quick, impulsive opinions instead of carefully considered ones. The medium through which we get

Dialectal reasoning

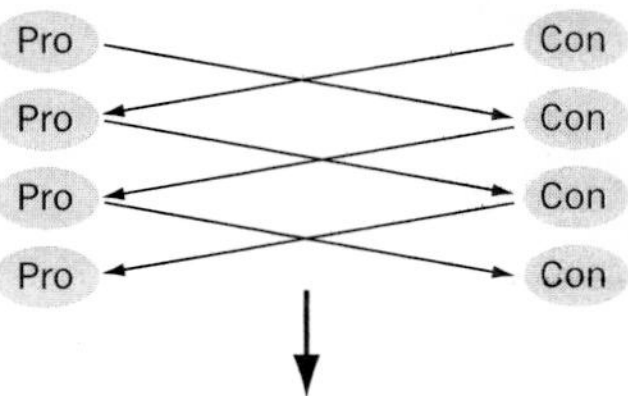

dialectical reasoning A process in which opposing facts or ideas are weighed and compared, with a view to determining the best solution or to resolving differences.

TABLE 8.1 *Two Kinds of Reasoning*

In formal reasoning, we apply rules of logic to solve well-specified problems. In informal, everyday reasoning, we must solve problems that are less clearly defined. Here are some differences between the two modes of thought:

Formal	**Informal**
All premises are supplied.	Some premises are implicit, and some are not supplied at all.
There is typically one correct answer.	There are typically several possible answers that vary in quality.
Established methods often exist for solving the problem.	Established procedures of inference that apply to the problem rarely exist.
You usually know when the problem is solved.	It is often unclear whether the current solution is good enough.
The problem is often of limited real-world interest.	The problem typically has personal relevance.
Problems are solved for their own sake.	Problems are often solved as a means of achieving other goals.

Source: Adapted from Galotti, 1989.

Deductive and inductive reasoning alone will not enable the members of this jury to reach a conclusion. They will also need to reason dialectically, weighing the evidence for and against guilt or innocence and the reasonableness of the arguments made by the attorneys.

our information may affect our ability to evaluate the message, as we discuss further in "Puzzles of Psychology."

In any case, many adults clearly have trouble thinking dialectically. Evidence comes from the research of Karen Kitchener and Patricia King, who for many years have been asking adolescents and adults of all ages and occupations where they stand on such issues as nuclear power, the safety of food additives, and the objectivity of the news media. Kitchener and King are not interested in how much people know about these issues, or even how they feel about them, but rather in how they think. More specifically, these researchers want to know whether people use *reflective judgment* in thinking about everyday problems (King & Kitchener, 1994; Kitchener & King, 1990). Reflective judgment is basically what we have called critical thinking: the ability to evaluate and integrate evidence, relate that evidence to a theory or opinion, and reach a conclusion that can be defended as reasonable or plausible. To think reflectively, you must question assumptions, consider alternative interpretations, and stand ready to reassess your conclusions in the face of new information.

King and Kitchener and their colleagues have interviewed more than 1,700 adolescents and adults, ranging in age from 14 to 65. (Some of this research has followed the same individuals for up to a decade.) First the researchers provide the interviewee with statements that describe opposing viewpoints on various topics. Then the interviewer asks: What do you think about these statements? How did you come to hold that point of view? On what do your base your position? Can you ever know for sure that your position is correct? Why do you suppose disagreement exists about this issue?

King and Kitchener have identified seven cognitive stages on the road to reflective thought, some occurring in childhood and others unfolding throughout adolescence and adulthood. At each stage, people make certain kinds of assumptions about how things are known and use certain ways of justifying or defending their beliefs. Each stage builds on the skills of the prior one and lays a foundation for successive ones.

GET INVOLVED

Here's some practice in dialectical reasoning. Choose a controversial topic, such as whether marijuana should be legalized or whether the right to abortion should be revoked. First, list all the arguments you can think of that support your own position. Then list all the arguments you can think of on the other side *of the issue. You do not have to agree with these arguments; just list them. Do you feel a mental block or emotional discomfort while doing this? Can you imagine how opponents of your position would answer your arguments? Having strong opinions is fine; you should have an (informed) opinion on matters of public interest. But does that opinion get in the way of even imagining a contrary point of view, or of altering your view if the evidence warrants?*

We will not be concerned here with the details of these stages, but only with their broad outlines. In general, people in the two early, *prereflective* stages assume that a correct answer always exists and that it can be obtained directly through the senses ("I

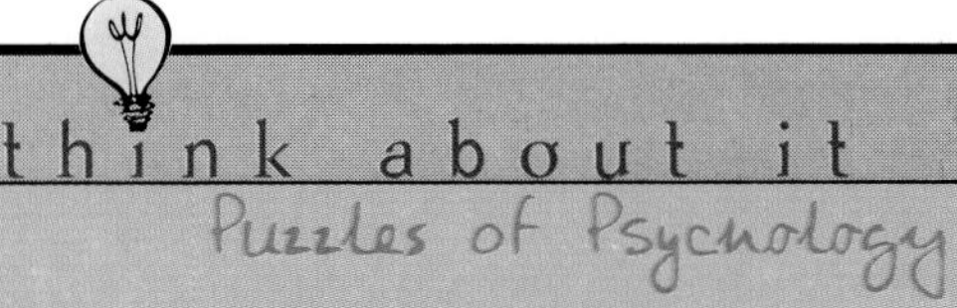

Has Television Killed Off Reading—and If So, So What?

TELEVISION IS VERY USEFUL IN OCCUPYING TIME THAT MIGHT OTHERWISE BE USED FOR THINKING!

You find yourself with a free evening, and you decide to spend it at home. A novel beckons from the bookshelf. The TV listings tempt you with a new sitcom. Which do you pick—the book or the tube? A growing number of academics, writers, and social commentators think you'll make the wrong choice.

Reading, the critics say, appears to be going out of fashion. More books are being published than ever before, but many are sold as gifts and are not necessarily read or even skimmed. More and more people are reading no books at all, and fewer and fewer people read a newspaper. Writer Katha Pollitt (1991) has observed that debates on college campuses about which books students should be required to read miss the point: If students don't read *on their own,* they won't like reading and will forget the books on the required reading list the minute they finish them, no matter what the books are. "While we have been arguing so fiercely about which books make the best medicine," Pollitt writes, "the patient has been slipping deeper and deeper into a coma."

One reason that people are reading less these days is that they are watching TV, typically for 20 to 30 hours a week. The problem, say critics, is not just television's content, which is often mindless, but the medium itself, which creates mindlessness. We watch TV primarily to amuse ourselves, but in fact television has a negative impact on both mood and alertness. Although television relaxes people while they are watching, afterward viewers are likely to feel more tense, bored, irritable, and lonely than they did before, as well as less able to concentrate. In contrast, reading tends to leave people more relaxed, in a better mood, and with improved ability to concentrate (Kubey & Csikszentmihalyi, 1990).

Because television supplies the viewer with readymade visual images, it may also discourage the development of imagination and novel ideas (Valkenburg & van der Voort, 1994). In one experiment, children *remembered* more of a story when they saw it on TV than when they heard it on radio (because visual images are memorable), but their thinking became more *imaginative* when they heard the story on the radio (because they had to imagine what the characters looked like and what they were doing). The researchers concluded that children who are raised on a mental diet limited to television "may have more information but be less imaginative, less verbally precise, and less mentally active" than earlier generations who grew up listening to the radio (Greenfield & Beagles-Roos, 1988).

The replacement of reading by television watching may be contributing to a growing inability of young people to use dialectical reasoning and reflective judgment, and an unwillingness to spend time searching for answers to intellectual problems (Suedfeld et al., 1986). Because television lumps serious issues with silly ones, sells politicians the way it sells cereal, and relies on a format of quick cuts and hot music, its critics fear that it discourages sustained, serious thought (Postman, 1985). In contrast, reading requires us to sit still and follow extended arguments. It encourages us to think in terms of abstract principles and not just personal experience. It gives us the opportunity to examine connections among statements and to spot contradictions. As writer Mitchell Stephens (1991) put it, "All television demands is our gaze."

Defenders of television believe that these criticisms are unfair. Reading has declined for many reasons, they say: the pressures of modern life, the popularity of outdoor sports, the need to juggle work and family obligations. Television not only entertains, but it also supplies information and intellectual enrichment, especially through public television programming. It gives families something to do together. It provides a diverse population with a common culture. *Mindful* television viewing, in which you analyze and discuss what you're seeing, can be mentally stimulating (Langer & Piper, 1988). And perhaps television will eventually be put to use in ways that haven't yet been thought of; after all, it took a century and a half after the printing press was invented for someone to think of producing novels and newspapers. Interactive television and CD-ROM are already changing the way people use the tube.

What do you think of these arguments? Are there books you can't wait to read, or has reading become a chore—and if so, why? Would you read more books if you watched less television? Do you know as much about world events after watching the nightly news as you do after reading a newspaper? Is disapproval of television just a reactionary response to a successful new technology? If not, what can be done to see that people control the TV instead of allowing it to control them? Think about it.

know what I've seen") or from authorities ("They said so on the news"; "That's what I was brought up to believe"). If authorities don't yet have the truth, prereflective thinkers tend to reach conclusions on the basis of what "feels right" at the moment. They do not distinguish between knowledge and belief, or between belief and evidence, and they don't see any reason for justifying a belief (King & Kitchener, 1994):

Interviewer: Can you ever know for sure that your position [on evolution] is correct?

Respondent: Well, some people believe that we evolved from apes and that's the way they want to believe. But I would never believe that way and nobody could talk me out of the way I believe because I believe the way that it's told in the Bible.

During the three *quasi-reflective* stages, people recognize that some things cannot be known with absolute certainty, but they are not sure how to deal with these situations. They realize that judgments should be supported by reasons, but they pay attention only to evidence that fits what they already believe. They know that there are alternative viewpoints, but they seem to think that because knowledge is uncertain, any judgment about the evidence is purely subjective. Quasi-reflective thinkers will defend a position by saying that "We all have a right to our own opinion," as if all opinions are created equal. Here is the response of a college student who uses quasi-reflective reasoning:

Interviewer: Can you say you will ever know for sure that chemicals [in foods] are safe?

Student: No, I don't think so.

Interviewer: Can you tell me why you'll never know for sure?

Student: Because they test them in little animals, and they haven't really tested them in humans, as far as I know. And I don't think anything is for sure.

Interviewer: When people differ about matters such as this, is it the case that one opinion is right and one is wrong?

Student: No. I think it just depends on how you feel personally because people make their decisions based upon how they feel and what research they've seen. So what one person thinks is right, another person might think is wrong. . . . If I feel that chemicals cause cancer and you feel that food is unsafe without it, your opinion might be right to you and my opinion is right to me.

In the last two stages, a person becomes capable of reflective judgment. He or she understands that although some things can never be known with certainty, some judgments are more valid than others because of their coherence, their fit with the evidence, their usefulness, and so on. People at these stages are willing to consider evidence from a variety of sources and to reason dialectically. At the very highest stage, they are able to defend their conclusions as representing the most complete, plausible, or compelling understanding of an issue, based on currently available evidence. This interview with a graduate student illustrates reflective thinking:

Interviewer: Can you ever say you know for sure that your point of view on chemical additives is correct?

Student: No, I don't think so. . . . [but] I think that we can usually be reasonably certain, given the information we have now, and considering our methodologies.

Interviewer:	Is there anything else that contributes to not being able to be sure?
Student:	Yes. . . . it might be that the research wasn't conducted rigorously enough. In other words, we might have flaws in our data or sample, things like that.
Interviewer:	How then would you identify the "better opinion"?
Student:	One that takes as many factors as possible into consideration. I mean one that uses the higher percentage of the data that we have, and perhaps that uses the methodology that has been most reliable.
Interviewer:	And how do you come to a conclusion about what the evidence suggests?
Student:	I think you have to take a look at the different opinions and studies that are offered by different groups. Maybe some studies offered by the chemical industry, some studies by the government, some private studies. . . . You wouldn't trust, for instance, a study funded by the tobacco industry that proved that cigarette smoking is not harmful . . . you have to try to interpret people's motives and that makes it a more complex soup to try to strain out.

Most people do not show evidence of reflective judgment until their middle or late twenties—if at all. That doesn't mean they're incapable of it; most studies have measured people's typical performance, not their *optimal* performance. When students get support for thinking reflectively and opportunities for practice, their thinking tends to become more complex, sophisticated, and well-grounded (Kitchener et al., 1993). This may be one reason that higher education seems to move people gradually closer to reflective judgment. Most undergraduates, whatever their age, tend to score at Stage 3 during their first year of college, and at Stage 4 as seniors; most graduate students score at Stage 4 or 5; and many advanced doctoral students perform consistently at Stage 6 (King & Kitchener, 1994). Longitudinal studies show that these differences do not occur only because lower-level thinkers are more likely to drop out along the way.

The gradual development of thinking skills among undergraduates, said Barry Kroll (1992), represents an abandonment of "ignorant certainty" in favor of "intelligent confusion." It may not seem so, but this is a big step forward! You can see why, in this book, we emphasize thinking about and evaluating psychological findings, and not just memorizing them.

Quick Quiz

Put on your thinking cap to answer these questions.

1. Most of the items Mervin bought as holiday gifts this year cost more than they did last year, so he concludes that inflation is increasing. Is he using inductive, deductive, or dialectical reasoning?
2. Yvonne is arguing with Henrietta about whether real estate is a better investment than stocks. "You can't convince me," says Yvonne. "I just know I'm right." Yvonne needs training in ____________ reasoning.
3. Seymour thinks the media have a liberal political bias, and Sophie thinks they're too conservative. "Well," says Seymour, "I have my truth and you have yours. It's purely subjective." Which of King and Kitchener's levels of thinking is Seymour at?

4. What kind of evidence might resolve the issue that Seymour and Sophie are arguing about?

Answers:

1. inductive 2. dialectical 3. quasi-reflective 4. Researchers might have raters watch a random sample of TV news shows and measure the amount of time devoted to conservative and liberal politicians or viewpoints. Or raters could read a random sample of newspaper editorials from all over the country and evaluate the editorials as liberal or conservative in outlook. You can probably think of other strategies as well. However, having people judge whether entire TV programs or newspapers are slanted in one direction or the other, based solely on their own subjective impressions, might not be informative because often people perceive only what they want or expect to perceive.

BARRIERS TO REASONING RATIONALLY

If all human beings are capable of reasoning logically, how come so many of us don't do it more? Why do we so often resist information or ideas that would be helpful? We rarely hear someone say, "Oh, thank you for explaining to me why my lifelong philosophy of child raising is wrong. I'm so grateful for the facts!" The person usually says, "Oh, buzz off, and take your cockamamie ideas with you." Why?

One answer is that normal human thought processes are subject to predictable biases that affect personal, economic, and political decision making (Simon, 1973; Tversky & Kahneman, 1986). Dozens of such biases influence the way people think and make decisions; here we report a few of them.

EXAGGERATING THE IMPROBABLE

One bias is the inclination to exaggerate the probability of very rare events—a bias that helps explain why so many people enter lotteries and why they buy airline disaster insurance.

As we saw in Chapter 2, people are especially likely to exaggerate the likelihood of a rare event if its consequences are catastrophic. One reason is the **availability heuristic,** the tendency to judge the probability of an event by how easy it is to think of examples or instances. Catastrophes stand out in our minds and are therefore more "available" than other kinds of negative events. For example, in one study, people overestimated the frequency of deaths from tornadoes and underestimated the frequency of deaths from asthma, which occur 20 times as often but do not make headlines. And these same people estimated deaths from accidents and disease to be equally frequent, even though 16 times as many people die each year from disease as from accidents (Lichtenstein et al., 1978).

People will sometimes work themselves into a froth about unlikely events, such as dying in an airplane crash, yet they will irrationally ignore dangers to human life that are harder to visualize, such as a growth in skin cancer rates due to depletion of the ozone layer in the earth's atmosphere. Similarly, parents are often more frightened about real but unlikely threats to their children, such as being kidnapped by a stranger or dying from a routine immunization shot (both horrible but extremely rare), than they are about problems more common in children, such as depression, delinquency, and poor grades (Stickler et al., 1991).

AVOIDING LOSS

In general, people making decisions try to avoid or minimize risks and losses. So when a choice is framed in terms of risk, they will respond more cautiously than when the *same* choice is framed in terms of gain: They will, for example, choose a ticket that has a 10 percent chance of winning a raffle to one that has a 90 percent chance of losing!

availability heuristic The tendency to judge the probability of a type of event by how easy it is to think of examples or instances.

Suppose you have to choose between two health programs to combat a disease expected to kill 600 people. Which would you prefer, a program that will definitely

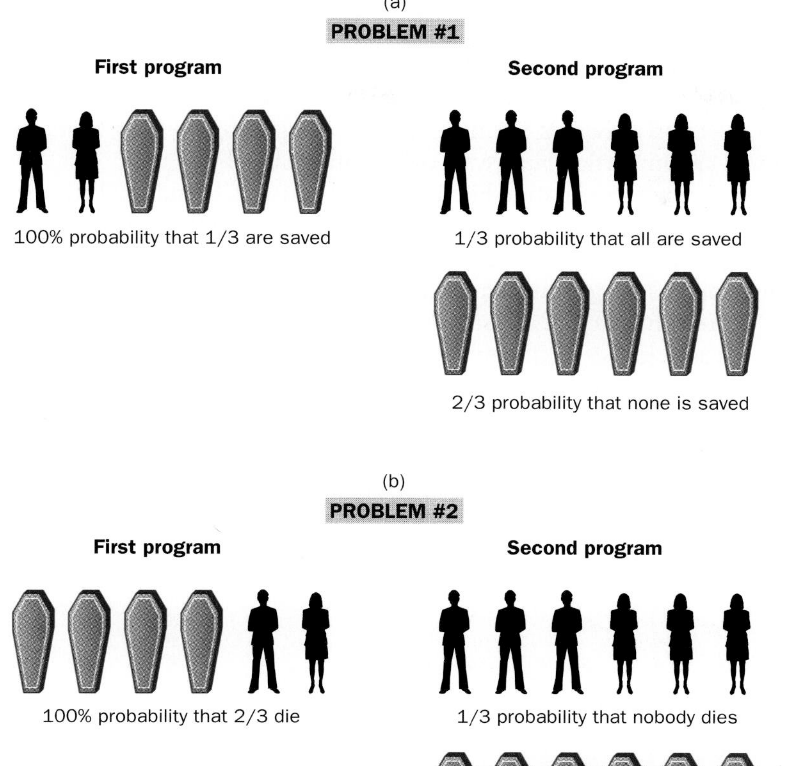

Figure 8.1
A Matter of Wording

People's decisions depend on how the alternatives are framed. When asked to choose between the programs in (a), which are described in terms of lives saved, most people choose the first program. When asked to choose between the programs in (b), which are described in terms of lives lost, most people choose the second program. Yet the alternatives in (a) are actually identical to those in (b).

save 200 people, or one with a one-third probability of saving all 600 people and a two-thirds probability of saving none? (Figure 8.1a illustrates this choice.) When subjects, including physicians, were asked this question, most said they preferred the first program. In other words, they rejected the riskier though potentially more rewarding solution in favor of a sure gain. However, people *will* take a risk if they see it as a way to *avoid loss.* Suppose now that you have to choose between a program in which 400 people will definitely die and a program in which there is a one-third probability of nobody dying and a two-thirds probability that all 600 will die. If you think about it, you will see that the alternatives are exactly the same as in the first problem; they are merely worded differently (see Figure 8.1b). Yet this time, most people choose the second solution. They reject risk when they think of the outcome in terms of lives saved, but they accept risk when they think of the outcome in terms of lives lost (Tversky & Kahneman, 1981).

Few of us will have to face a decision involving hundreds of lives, but we may have to choose between different medical treatments for ourselves or a relative. Our decision may be affected by whether the doctor frames the choice in terms of chances of surviving or chances of dying.

THE CONFIRMATION BIAS

When our primary objective is to make an accurate judgment, we usually try to think carefully and thoroughly about all relevant information. But when our main motive is to reach a conclusion about ourselves, other people, or circumstances, we tend to give in to the **confirmation bias:** We pay attention only to evidence that confirms what we want to believe. The flip side of this tendency is the *disconfirmation bias,* the tendency to ignore or find fault with evidence or arguments that point in a different direction (Edwards & Smith, 1996; Kunda, 1990). We may think we are being rational and impartial, but we are only fooling ourselves.

You can see the confirmation bias at work in yourself, friends, politicians, and editorial writers—whenever people are defending their beliefs and seeking to confirm them. Politicians, for example, are likely to accept economic news that confirms their philosophies and dismiss counterevidence as biased or unimportant. Police officers who are convinced of a suspect's guilt are likely to take anything the suspect says or does as evidence that confirms it. Unfortunately, the confirmation bias also affects many jury members. In one study, people listened to an audiotaped reenactment of an actual murder trial and then said how they would have voted and why. Instead of considering and weighing possible verdicts against the evidence, many people quickly constructed a story about what had happened and then considered only the evidence that supported their version of events. These same people were the most confident in their decision and were most likely to vote for an extreme verdict (Kuhn, Weinstock, & Flaton, 1994).

confirmation bias The tendency to look for or pay attention only to information that confirms one's own belief.

GET INVOLVED

Suppose someone deals out four cards, each with a letter on one side and a number on the other. You can only see one side of each card:

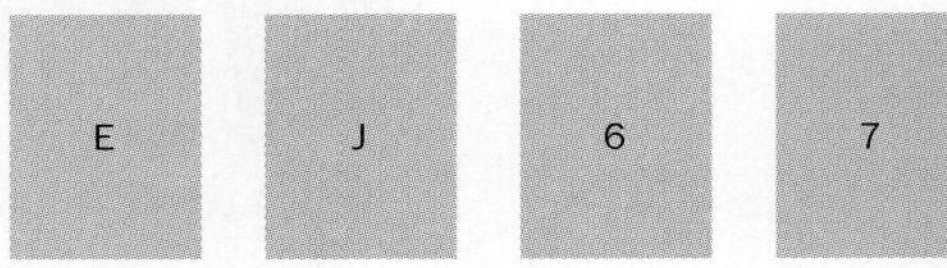

Your job is to find out whether the following rule is true: "If a card has a vowel on one side, then it has an even number on the other side." Which two cards would you need to turn over to find out?

The vast majority of people say they would turn over the E and the 6, but they are wrong. You do need to turn over the E (a vowel), because if the number on the other side is even, it confirms the rule, and if it's odd, the rule is false. However, the card with the 6 tells you nothing. The rule doesn't say that a card with an even number must always have a vowel on the other side. So it doesn't matter whether the 6 has a vowel or a consonant on the other side. The card you do need to turn over is the 7, because if it has a vowel on the other side, that disconfirms the rule.

People do poorly on this problem because they are biased to look for confirming evidence and because they ignore the possibility of disconfirming evidence. Don't feel too bad if you missed it. Most judges, lawyers, and people with doctorates do, too. On the other hand, everyone does better when the problem is more realistic. Try this one (from Griggs & Cox, 1982):

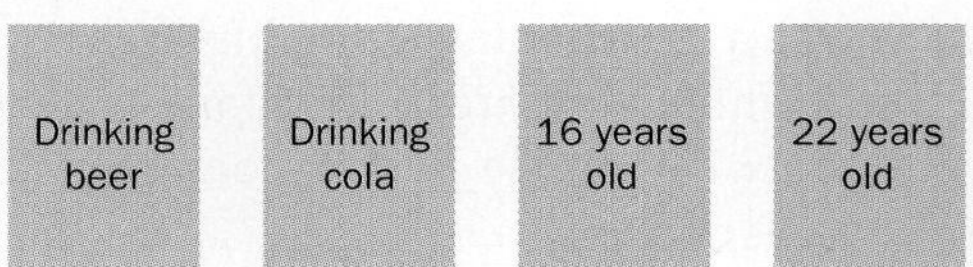

Rule: If a person is drinking beer, then the person is over 19 years of age.

Which two cards must you turn over? *The correct answer is on page 336.*

The confirmation bias can also affect how students react to what they learn. When students read about scientific findings that dispute one of their own cherished beliefs or that challenge the wisdom of their own actions, they tend to acknowledge but minimize the strengths of the research. In contrast, when a study supports their view, they will acknowledge any flaws (such as a small sample or a reliance on self-reports) but will give these flaws less weight than they would otherwise (Sherman & Kunda, 1989). In thinking critically, people apply a double standard: They think most critically about results they don't like. Even psychologists do this on occasion!

BIASES DUE TO "MIND-SETS"

Another roadblock on the way to rational decision making and problem solving is mental rigidity. When we need to solve a new problem, we may get sidetracked because of a **mental set,** a tendency to try to solve new problems by using the same heuristics, strategies, and rules that worked in the past on similar problems. Mental sets make human learning and problem solving efficient; because of them, we do not have to keep reinventing the wheel. But mental sets are not helpful when a problem calls for fresh insights and methods. They cause us to cling rigidly to the same old assumptions, hypotheses, and strategies, blinding us to better or more rapid solutions. (The "Get Involved" exercise on this page illustrates this point.)

One common "mind-set" is the tendency to find patterns in events. The quest for meaningful patterns is adaptive because it helps us understand and exert some control over life's events. But it also leads us to see meaningful patterns even when they don't exist. For example, every day the news media analyze the supposed reasons for yesterday's rise or drop in stock prices, but in actual fact, much of the fluctuation in the stock market is completely random. Similarly, many people with arthritis think that their symptoms follow a pattern, worsening with changes in the weather. They suffer more, they say, when the barometric pressure changes, or when it's damp or humid out. But when Donald Redelmeier and Amos Tversky (1996) followed 18 arthritis patients for 15 months, they found *no* association between weather conditions and the patients' self-reported pain levels, their ability to function in daily life, or a doctor's evaluation of their joint tenderness. (The patients, by the way, refused to believe these results.)

mental set A tendency to solve problems using procedures that worked before on similar problems.

GET INVOLVED

Copy the following figure, and see whether you can connect the dots by using no more than four straight lines, without lifting your pencil or pen. A line must pass through each point. Can you do it?

• • •

• • •

• • •

Most people have difficulty with this problem because they have a mental set to interpret the arrangement of dots as a square. Once having done so, they then assume that they can't extend a line beyond the "boundaries" of the square. Now that you know this, you might try again if you haven't yet solved the puzzle. *Some possible solutions are given on page 337.*

THE HINDSIGHT BIAS

Would you have been able to predict, beforehand, that Prince Charles and Princess Diana of England would divorce, or that Michael Jackson would become a father? People who learn the outcome of an event or the answer to a question tend to be sure that they "knew it all along." Armed with the wisdom of hindsight, they see the outcome that actually occurred as inevitable, and they overestimate the probability that they could have predicted what happened. Compared with judgments made *before* an event takes place, their judgments about their own ability to have predicted the event are inflated (Fischhoff, 1975; Hawkins & Hastie, 1990).

This **hindsight bias** shows up in all kinds of opinions, including political judgments ("I always knew my candidate would win"), medical judgments ("I could have told you that mole was cancerous"), and evaluations of other people's job performance ("The officers in charge of Pearl Harbor in 1941 should have known it would be attacked"). In 1991, when a blinding dust storm along a stretch of highway in California caused the worst multicar crash in U.S. history, many people angrily concluded that the highway patrol should have recognized the danger and closed the road. But from the highway patrol's standpoint, the situation was ambiguous: People had gotten through plenty of other dust storms perfectly well by slowing down or pulling off the road. Hindsight no doubt made the situation seem more straightforward in retrospect than it was at the time.

Hindsight biases may be a side effect of adaptive learning. When we try to predict the future, we consider many possible scenarios. But when we try to make sense of the past, we focus on explaining just one outcome—the one that actually occurred. This is efficient: Explaining outcomes that didn't occur can be a waste of time. As Scott Hawkins and Reid Hastie (1990) wrote, "Hindsight biases represent the dark side of successful learning and judgment." They are the dark side because when we are sure we knew something "all along," we are less willing to find out what we need to know in order to make accurate predictions in the future. In medical conferences, for example, when doctors are told what the postmortem findings were for a patient who died, they tend to think the case was easier than it actually was ("I would have known it was a brain tumor"), and so they learn less from the case than they should (Dawson et al., 1988).

COGNITIVE-DISSONANCE REDUCTION

In 1994, Americans were stunned when football legend O. J. Simpson was charged with murdering his former wife Nicole Brown and her friend Ron Goldman. Glued to their television sets, viewers watched in shock as Simpson, who had always seemed the quintessential nice guy, was pursued by a caravan of police on a Los Angeles freeway, then arrested at his home and led away in handcuffs. Some reacted by quickly revising their opinion of their fallen hero. Others, however, groped to make sense of the unimaginable. Perhaps Simpson had run from the police because he was suicidal with grief over his ex-wife's death. Perhaps one of the police investigators had planted incriminating evidence (an argument later used successfully by the defense attorneys). Perhaps the media were exploiting the case by exaggerating the evidence against Simpson. Perhaps he did kill Nicole, but only after she provoked the attack by taunting him.

To psychologists, such strategies for coming to terms with information that conflicts with existing ideas are predictable. They can be explained, said Leon Festinger (1957), by the theory of **cognitive dissonance.** "Dissonance," the opposite of consistency ("consonance"), is a state of tension that occurs when a person simultaneously holds either two cognitions (beliefs, thoughts, attitudes) that are psychologically in-

hindsight bias The tendency to overestimate one's ability to have predicted an event once the outcome is known; the "I knew it all along" phenomenon.

cognitive dissonance A state of tension that occurs when a person simultaneously holds two cognitions that are psychologically inconsistent, or when a person's belief is incongruent with his or her behavior.

This police photo of O. J. Simpson, taken after his arrest for murder, put millions of his fans into a state of cognitive dissonance, forcing them to grope for ways to resolve conflicting feelings.

consistent or a belief that is incongruent with the person's behavior. This tension is uncomfortable, and someone in a state of dissonance will therefore be motivated to reduce it—by rejecting or changing a belief, by changing a behavior, by adding new beliefs, or by rationalizing (Harmon-Jones et al., 1996).

For example, cigarette smoking is dissonant with the awareness that smoking causes illness. To reduce the dissonance, the smoker might change the behavior and try to quit; reject the evidence that smoking is bad; persuade herself that she will quit later on ("after these exams"); emphasize the benefits of smoking ("A cigarette helps me relax"); or decide that she doesn't want a long life, anyhow ("It will be shorter, but sweeter"). In a study of people who went to a clinic to quit smoking, those who later relapsed had to reduce the dissonance between "I tried to quit smoking because it's bad for me" and "I couldn't do it." Can you predict what they did? In contrast to the successful quitters, most of them lowered their perceptions of the health risks of smoking ("It's not really so dangerous") (Gibbons, McGovern, & Lando, 1991). Cigarette manufacturers are equally talented at reducing dissonance by rationalizing. When the president of one tobacco company was told that smoking during pregnancy increases the chances of having a low-birthweight baby, he replied, "Some women would prefer having smaller babies" (quoted in Kluger, 1996).

ASK QUESTIONS

Time and again, doomsday predictions fail. Have you ever wondered why people who wrongly predict a devastating earthquake or the end of the world don't feel embarrassed when their forecasts flop?

You can also see cognitive-dissonance reduction at work among members of sects who believe that doomsday is at hand. Do you ever wonder what happens to true believers when a doomsday prophecy fails? Do they ever say, "Boy, what a jerk I was"? What would dissonance theory predict?

Many years ago, Festinger and two associates explored people's reactions to failed prophecies by infiltrating a group of people who thought the world would end on December 21 (Festinger, Riecken, & Schachter, 1956). The group's leader, whom the researchers called Marian Keech, promised that the faithful would be picked up by a flying saucer and whisked to safety at midnight on December 20. Many of her followers quit their jobs and spent all their savings, waiting for the end. What would they do or say, Festinger and his colleagues wondered, to reduce the dissonance between "The world is still muddling along on the 21st" and "I predicted the end of the world and sold all my worldly possessions"?

The researchers predicted that believers who had made no public commitment to the prophecy, who awaited the end of the world by themselves at home, would simply lose their faith. But those who had acted on their conviction, waiting with Keech for the spaceship, would be in a state of dissonance. They would, said the researchers, have to *increase* their religious belief to avoid the intolerable realization that they had behaved foolishly. That is just what happened. At 4:45 A.M., long past the appointed hour of the saucer's arrival, the leader had a new vision. The world had been spared, she said, because of the impressive faith of her little band.

Cognitive-dissonance theory thus predicts how people will process information that conflicts with their existing ideas. They don't always do so rationally, by accepting new facts that are well documented; instead, they resist or rationalize the information. Here are some of the conditions under which you are particularly likely to try to reduce dissonance (Aronson, Wilson, & Akert, 1997; Taylor, Peplau, & Sears, 1997):

1. *When you feel that you have freely made a decision.* If you think you freely chose to join a group, sell your possessions, or smoke a cigarette, you will feel dissonance if these actions prove misguided. There is no dissonance, however, between "The Army drafted me; I had no choice about being here" and "I hate basic training."

2. *When you feel the decision is important and irrevocable.* If you know you cannot change your mind about a decision, or if you are strongly committed to it, you will feel dissonance if the decision proves foolhardy. There is no dissonance, however, between "I just spent a fortune on ski equipment" and "I hate skiing" if you know you can return your ski gear and get your money back.

3. *When you feel personally responsible for the negative consequences of your decisions.* If you choose a course of action that leads to disastrous but unforeseen results, you will feel dissonance if you feel responsible for the consequences. But there is no dissonance between "I took my vacation in Hawaii" and "It rained the whole week I was there," because you don't feel personally responsible for causing bad weather.

4. *When what you do violates your self-concept.* If you are in a political discussion at a party and you pretend to agree with the majority's position for the sake of harmony, you will experience dissonance only if you have a concept of yourself as honest and true to your convictions. If you are a frequent liar and you know it (and don't care), you won't feel dissonance, even if your words contradict your beliefs (Thibodeau & Aronson, 1992).

5. *When you put a lot of effort into a decision, only to find the results less than you hoped for.* The harder you work to reach a goal, or the more you suffer for it, the more you will try to convince yourself that you value the goal, even if the goal itself isn't so great after all (Aronson & Mills, 1959). This explains why hazing, whether in social clubs or in the military, turns new recruits into loyal members. The cognition "I went through a lot of awful stuff to join this group" is dissonant with the cognition ". . . only to find I hate the group." Therefore people must decide either that the hazing wasn't so bad or that they really like the group. This mental reevaluation is called the *justification of effort,* and it is one of the most popular methods of reducing dissonance.

Cognitive-dissonance theory has its limitations. It can be hard to know when two cognitions are inconsistent: What is dissonant to you may be neutral or pleasingly paradoxical to another. Moreover, some people reduce dissonance by admitting their mistakes instead of rationalizing them. Still, there is vast evidence of a motive for cognitive consistency under certain conditions, and this motive can lead to irrational decisions and actions.

Cognitive-dissonance theory predicts the "justification of effort." The more you must endure to reach a goal, the more you will value it—which may be one reason fraternities often subject pledges to disgusting, frightening, or even dangerous hazing. These initiates, blindfolded and forced to wear vomit-drenched T-shirts, were also covered with molasses and were urinated on by their new fraternity brothers. They probably became extremely devoted members.

As you can see, the decisions and judgments that people make, and the feelings of regret or pleasure that follow, are not always logical. This fact has enormous implications for decision makers in the legal system, business, medicine, government—in fact, in all areas. But before you despair about the human ability to think clearly and rationally, we should tell you that the situation is not hopeless. People are not equally irrational in all situations. When they are doing things they have some expertise in, or making decisions that have serious consequences, cognitive biases often diminish. Accountants who audit companies' books, for example, are less subject to the confirmation bias than are undergraduates in psychology experiments, perhaps because auditors can be sued if they overestimate a firm's profitability or economic health (Smith & Kida, 1991).

Further, once we understand a bias, we may be able to reduce or eliminate it. For example, we have seen that doctors are vulnerable to the hindsight bias if they already know what caused a patient's death. But Hal Arkes and his colleagues (1988) were able to reduce a similar bias in neuropsychologists. The psychologists were given a case study and asked to state one reason why each of three possible diagnoses—alcohol withdrawal, Alzheimer's disease, and brain damage—might have been applicable. This procedure forced the psychologists to consider all the evidence, not just evidence that supported the correct diagnosis. The hindsight bias evaporated, presumably because the psychologists realized that the correct diagnosis had not been so obvious at the time the patient was being treated.

Some people, of course, seem to think more clearly than others habitually; we call them "intelligent." But just what is intelligence, and how can we measure and refine it? We take up that question next.

Quick Quiz

Think rationally to answer these questions.

1. Stu takes a study break and meets a young woman at the student cafeteria. They hit it off, start to see each other regularly, and eventually get married. Says Stu, "I knew that day, when I headed for the cafeteria, that something special was about to happen." What cognitive bias is affecting Stu's thinking?
2. In a classic study of cognitive dissonance (Festinger & Carlsmith, 1959), students did some boring, repetitive tasks and then had to tell another student, who was waiting to participate in the study, that the work was interesting and fun. Half the students were offered $20 for telling this lie and the others only $1. Which students who lied decided later on that the tasks had been fun after all?

Answers:

1. the hindsight bias 2. The students who got only $1. They were in a state of dissonance, because "the task was as dull as dishwater" is dissonant with "I said I enjoyed it—and for a mere dollar, at that." Those who got $20 could rationalize that the large sum (which was really large in 1956) justified the lie.

INTELLIGENCE

The educator Sylvia Ashton-Warner once called intelligence "the tool to find the truth—a tool that must be kept sharpened." Yet much as we all desire this trait, it is hard to agree on what it is. Some psychologists equate it with the ability to reason abstractly, others with the ability to learn and profit from experience in daily life. Some emphasize the ability to think rationally, others the ability to act purposefully. These qualities are all probably part of what most people mean by **intelligence,** but theorists weigh them differently.

intelligence An inferred characteristic of an individual, usually defined as the ability to profit from experience, acquire knowledge, think abstractly, act purposefully, or adapt to changes in the environment.

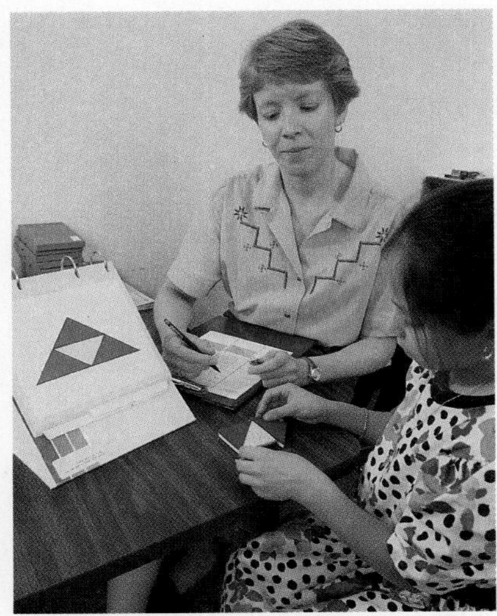
A school psychologist gives an elementary school student an intelligence test.

One of the longest-running debates in psychology is whether a global quality called "intelligence" even exists. A typical intelligence test asks you to do several things: provide a specific bit of information, notice similarities between objects, solve arithmetic problems, define words, fill in the missing parts of incomplete pictures, arrange pictures in a logical order, arrange blocks to resemble a design, assemble puzzles, use a coding scheme, or judge what behavior would be appropriate in a particular situation. Researchers use a statistical method called **factor analysis** to try to identify which basic abilities underlie performance on the various items. This procedure identifies clusters of correlated items that seem to be measuring some common ability, or factor. Some scientists believe that a general ability, or **g factor,** underlies specific abilities and talents (Herrnstein & Murray, 1994; Spearman, 1927; Wechsler, 1955). Others dispute the existence of a g factor, arguing that a person can excel in some tasks yet do poorly in others (Gould, 1994; Guilford, 1988). Disagreements over how to define intelligence have led some writers to suggest, only half-jokingly, that intelligence is "whatever intelligence tests measure."

MEASURING INTELLIGENCE: THE PSYCHOMETRIC APPROACH

The traditional approach to intelligence, the **psychometric** approach, focuses on how well people perform on standardized mental tests. The tests you take in your courses are called *achievement tests,* because they are designed to measure skills and knowledge that have been explicitly taught. *Aptitude tests,* in contrast, are designed to measure the ability to acquire skills or knowledge in the future. For example, vocational aptitude tests can help you decide whether you will do better as a mechanic or a musician, and IQ tests do a pretty good job of predicting school performance. But all mental tests are in some sense achievement tests because they assume past learning or experience with particular objects, words, or situations. The difference between achievement and aptitude tests is one of degree and intended use.

factor analysis A statistical method for analyzing the intercorrelations among various measures or test scores; clusters of measures or scores that are highly correlated are assumed to measure the same underlying trait, ability, or aptitude (factor).

g factor A general intellectual ability assumed by some theorists to underlie specific mental abilities and talents.

psychometrics The measurement of mental abilities, traits, and processes.

mental age (MA) A measure of mental development expressed in terms of the average mental ability at a given age. A child with a mental age of 8 performs on a test of mental ability at the level of the average 8-year-old.

intelligence quotient (IQ) A measure of intelligence originally computed by dividing a person's mental age by his or her chronological age and multiplying by 100; now derived from norms provided for standardized intelligence tests.

BINET'S BRAINSTORM

As we saw in Chapter 3, the first intelligence test was devised at the beginning of the twentieth century by Alfred Binet (1857–1911), when the French Ministry of Education asked Binet to design an objective test that would identify children who were slow learners and who therefore would benefit from remedial work. Wrestling with the problem, Binet had a great insight: In the classroom, the responses of "dull" children resembled those of ordinary children of younger ages. Bright children, on the other hand, responded like children of older ages. The thing to measure, then, was a child's **mental age (MA),** or level of intellectual development relative to other children's. Then instruction could be tailored to the child's capabilities.

The test devised by Binet and his colleague, Theophile Simon, measured memory, vocabulary, and perceptual discrimination. Items ranged from those that most young children could do easily to those that only older children could handle, as determined by the testing of large numbers of children. A scoring system developed later by others used a formula in which the child's mental age was divided by the child's chronological age to yield an **intelligence quotient,** or **IQ.** Still later, the modern system of scoring was devised: The average is set arbitrarily at 100, and tests are constructed so that the *standard deviation*—a measure of how much the scores are spread out around the mean—is always 15 or 16, depending on the test; individual test scores are then computed from tables (see Chapter 3).

Binet recognized that all children taking his test in France had similar cultural backgrounds, but that this might not be true elsewhere. He also emphasized that the test merely *sampled* intelligence and did not measure everything covered by that term. A test score, he said, could be useful, along with other information, for predicting school performance under ordinary conditions, but it should not be confused with intelligence itself. The purpose of testing was to identify children with learning problems, not to rank normal children.

In America, Stanford psychologist Lewis Terman revised Binet's test and established norms for American children. His version, the Stanford–Binet Intelligence Scale, was first published in 1916 and has been updated several times since. (For some sample items, see Table 8.2.) Two decades later, David Wechsler, chief psychologist at Bellevue Hospital in New York City, designed another test, expressly for adults, which became the Wechsler Adult Intelligence Scale (WAIS). It was followed by the Wechsler Intelligence Scale for Children (WISC). Although the Wechsler tests produce a general IQ score, they also provide specific scores for different kinds of ability, both verbal and nonverbal ("performance"). These tests, too, have since been revised. (For some sample items, see Figure 8.2 and Table 8.3.)

However, as we saw in Chapter 3, when intelligence testing was brought from France to the United States, its original purposes and uses got lost at sea. In France, Binet's test had been given to each child individually, so the test-giver could see whether a child was ill or nervous, had poor vision, or was not trying. In America, the Wechsler tests and the revised Binet test were also given to individuals, but other intelligence tests were given to huge groups of people, usually students or soldiers, and the advantages of individualized testing were lost. Americans used the tests not to bring slow learners up to the average, but to categorize people in school and in the armed services according to their presumed "natural ability." The testers overlooked

TABLE 8.2 *Sample Items from the Stanford–Binet Intelligence Test, Form L-M*

The older the test-taker is, the more the test requires in the way of verbal comprehension and fluency.

Age	Task
4	Fills in the missing word when asked, "Brother is a boy; sister is a ____________." Answers correctly when asked, "Why do we have houses?"
9	Answers correctly when examiner says, "In an old graveyard in Spain they have discovered a small skull which they believe to be that of Christopher Columbus when he was about 10 years old." What is foolish about that? Examiner presents folded paper; child draws how it will look unfolded.
12	Completes "The streams are dry . . . there has been little rain." Tells what is foolish about statements such as "Bill Jones's feet are so big that he has to put his trousers on over his head."
Adult	Can describe the difference between *misery* and *poverty, character* and *reputation, laziness* and *idleness.* Explains how to measure 3 pints of water with a 5-pint and a 2-pint can.

Source: From Lewis M. Terman & Maud A. Merrill, *Stanford–Binet Intelligence Scale* (1972 norms ed.). Boston: Houghton Mifflin, 1973. (Currently published by The Riverside Publishing Company.) Items are copyright 1916 by Lewis M. Terman, 1937 by Lewis M. Terman and Maud A. Merrill, © 1960, 1973 by The Riverside Publishing Company. Reproduced or adapted by permission of the publisher.

Figure 8.2
Performance Tasks on the Wechsler Tests

Nonverbal items such as these are particularly useful for measuring the abilities of those who have poor hearing, are not fluent in the tester's language, have limited education, or resist doing classroom-type problems. A large gap between a person's verbal score and performance score on a Wechsler test sometimes indicates a specific learning problem. (Object assembly, digit symbol, and picture completion adapted from Cronbach, 1990.)

Picture arrangement
(Arrange the panels to make a meaningful story)

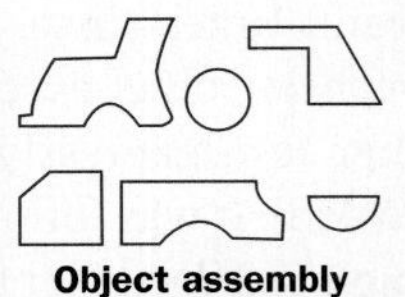

Object assembly
(Put together a jigsaw puzzle)

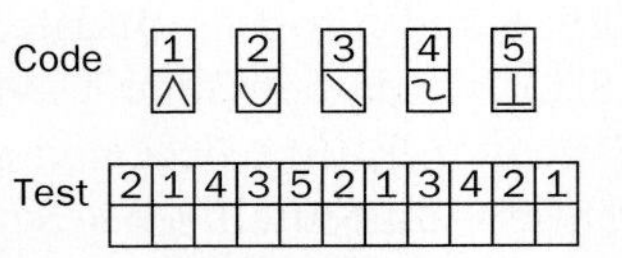

Digit symbol
(Using the key at the top, fill in the appropriate symbol beneath each number)

Picture completion
(Supply the missing feature)

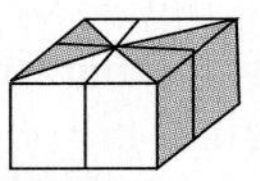

Block design
(Copy the design shown, using another set of blocks)

TABLE 8.3 *Verbal Items Similar to Those on the Wechsler Tests*

For each subtest, the first example illustrates the level of difficulty of the Wechsler Intelligence Scale for Children–Revised. The second example illustrates the level of difficulty of the Wechsler Adult Intelligence Scale–Revised. Digit-span items are similar on the two tests.

Subtest	Examples
Information	Who was Thomas Jefferson? Who wrote *Huckleberry Finn?*
Comprehension	Why is it important to use zip codes when you mail letters? Why do married people who want a divorce have to go to court?
Similarities	In what way are corn and macaroni alike? In what way are a book and a movie alike?
Vocabulary	What do we mean by *protect?* What does *formulate* mean?
Arithmetic	Dick had 13 pieces of candy and gave away 8. How many did he have left? How many hours will it take to drive 140 miles at the rate of 30 miles an hour?
Digit Span	I am going to say some numbers. Listen carefully, and when I am through, say them right after me: 3-6-1-7-5-8. Now I am going to say some more numbers, but this time when I stop, I want you to say them backward: 1-9-3-2-7.

Source: Adapted from Cronbach, 1990, and based on items from the Wechsler scales, published by The Psychological Corporation, 1958.

the fact that in America, with its many ethnic groups, people did not all share the same background and experience (Gould, 1981/1996).

Intelligence tests developed between World War I and the 1960s for use in schools favored city children over rural ones, middle-class children over poor ones, and white children over minority children. One item, for example, asked whether the Emperor Concerto was written by Beethoven, Mozart, Bach, Brahms, or Mahler. (The answer is Beethoven.) Critics complained that the tests did not measure the kinds of knowledge and skills that are intelligent in a minority neighborhood or in the hills of Appalachia (Scarr, 1984). They also pointed out that because teachers thought IQ scores revealed the limits of a child's potential, low-scoring children would not get the educational attention or encouragement they needed; only high-scoring children would. When teachers expect a child to do well, they respond more warmly, give more feedback, teach more material, and give the child more chances to ask and answer questions (Rosenthal, 1994; Rosenthal & Jacobson, 1992).

ANALYZE ASSUMPTIONS AND BIASES

When tests find IQ differences between groups of children, most people assume there must be something inherently deficient in the children who score lower. But could there also be something wrong with the test or the educational system?

CULTURE-FREE AND CULTURE-FAIR TESTS In the 1970s, group intelligence testing became a public issue. School boards and employers were sued for restricting the opportunities of low scorers. Some states prohibited the use of group tests for classifying children. Several test-makers responded by trying to construct tests that were *culture-free.* Such tests were usually nonverbal; in some, instructions were even pantomimed. Test constructors soon found, however, that culture can affect performance in unexpected ways. In one case, children who had emigrated from Arab countries to Israel were asked to show which detail was missing from a picture of a face with no mouth (Ortar, 1963). The children, who were not used to thinking of a drawing of a head as a complete picture, said that the *body* was missing!

Psychologists then tried to design tests that were *culture-fair.* Their aim was not to eliminate the influence of culture, but to find items that incorporate knowledge and skills common to many different cultures. This approach, too, was less successful than originally hoped, because cultural values affect a person's attitude toward taking tests, comfort in the settings required for testing, motivation, rapport with the test-giver, competitiveness, and experience in solving problems independently rather than with others (Anastasi, 1988; López, 1995). Moreover, cultures differ in the problem-solving strategies they emphasize (Serpell, 1994). For example, in the West, children from white, middle-class families typically learn to classify things by category—to say that an apple and a peach are similar because they are both fruits, and that a saw and a rake are

An intelligence test is useful only if it is used intelligently. Army intelligence testing during World War I often occurred under noisy, crowded, and confusing conditions, and many items were culturally loaded. Nevertheless, many people concluded from the results that a high proportion of army recruits were "morons."

"You can't build a hut, you don't know how to find edible roots and you know nothing about predicting the weather. In other words, you do terribly on our IQ test."

similar because they are both tools. But children who are not trained in middle-class ways of sorting things may classify objects according to their function. They will say that an apple and a peach are similar because they taste good. That's a charming and innovative answer, but it is one that test-givers interpret as less intelligent (Miller-Jones, 1989).

In theory, it should be possible to establish test norms that are not based on white urban children, by throwing out items on which such children get higher scores than others. A similar strategy was actually used years ago to eliminate sex differences in IQ. On early tests, girls scored higher than boys at every age (Samelson, 1979). No one was willing to conclude that males were intellectually inferior, so in the 1937 revision of the Stanford–Binet test, Lewis Terman simply deleted the items on which boys had done poorly. Poof! No sex differences.

But few people seem willing to do for cultural differences what Terman did for sex differences, and the reason reveals a dilemma at the heart of intelligence testing. Intelligence tests put some groups of children at a disadvantage, yet they also measure skills and knowledge useful in the classroom. How can educators recognize and accept cultural differences and, at the same time, require students to demonstrate mastery of the skills, knowledge, and attitudes that will help them succeed in school and in the larger society? How can they eliminate bias from tests, while preserving the purpose for which the tests were designed? Anne Anastasi (1988), an eminent testing specialist, has argued that concealing the effects of cultural disadvantage by rejecting conventional tests is "equivalent to breaking a thermometer because it registers a body temperature of 101." Instead, she believes, special help should be given to any child who needs it. Others feel that conventional mental tests do more harm than good. Sociologist Jane Mercer (1988) tried for years to get testers to understand that children can be *ignorant* of information required by IQ tests without being *stupid*, but she finally gave up, resolving instead to "kill the IQ test."

BEYOND THE IQ TEST The resolution of this debate may depend on whether test-users can learn to use intelligence tests more intelligently. Most educators feel that the tests have value, as long as a person's background is kept in mind and the results are interpreted cautiously. IQ tests are well standardized, and they predict school performance fairly well. Correlations between IQ scores and current or future school grades, though far from perfect, are high, ranging between .40 and .60. IQ tests often identify not only the mentally retarded, but also gifted students who have not previously considered higher education.

In some schools, a child's placement in a special education program now depends not only on an IQ score, but also on tests of specific abilities, medical data, and the child's demonstrated inability to get along in the family and community. And some schools are returning to Binet's original concept. Instead of using group tests to label and categorize children, they give individual tests to identify a child's strengths and weaknesses so that teachers can design individualized programs that will boost the child's performance.

This change in emphasis reflects an increasing awareness that the intellect—and IQ scores—can be improved, even in the mentally retarded (Butterfield & Belmont, 1977; Feuerstein, 1980; Sternberg, 1986). Educators also now realize that a person may have a **learning disability**—a problem with a specific mental skill, such as reading or arithmetic—without having a general intellectual impairment. Many children with learning disabilities have normal or even superior intelligence and can overcome or compensate for their handicaps.

learning disability A difficulty in the performance of a specific mental skill, such as reading or arithmetic; sometimes linked to perceptual or memory problems.

Children with Down syndrome, who score low on standard IQ tests, are accomplishing more academically than anyone once thought they could. They show that intellectual performance is not as fixed and immutable as many people assume.

Critics of traditional approaches to measuring intelligence, however, argue that when a child's abilities don't match those expected by teachers and testers, the best solution may be to modify the classroom or the test. Anthropologist Shirley Brice Heath (1983) has shown how this approach can work. In a study of a small African-American community in a southern city, Heath found that black parents were less likely than white parents to ask their children "what," "where," "when," and "who" questions—the sorts of questions found on standardized tests and in schoolbooks ("What's this story about?" "Who is this?"). Black parents preferred to ask analogy questions ("What's that like?") and story-starter questions ("Did you hear about. . . ?"). Teachers in the community used this information to modify their teaching strategies. They encouraged their black pupils to ask "school-type questions," but they also incorporated analogy and story-starter questions into their lessons. Soon the black children, who had previously been uncomfortable and quiet, became eager, confident participants.

Critics also point out that standardized tests don't reveal *how* a person goes about answering questions and solving problems. Nor do they explain why people with low scores on IQ tests often behave intelligently in real life. For example, one study done at a racetrack found that successful handicappers used an exceedingly complicated statistical method to predict winners, and this ability was *not* related to the handicappers' IQs (Ceci & Liker, 1986). And shoppers in a supermarket can select the best buy even when they cannot do the formal mathematical computations that would allow them to compare prices of two brands (Lave, Murtaugh, & de la Roche, 1984). Some researchers, therefore, have rejected the psychometric approach to the study and measurement of intelligence in favor of a cognitive approach.

DISSECTING INTELLIGENCE: THE COGNITIVE APPROACH

In contrast to the psychometric approach to intelligence, which is concerned with how many answers a person gets right on a test, the cognitive approach emphasizes the *strategies* people use when thinking about problems and arriving at a solution. Intelligent behavior involves, among other things, encoding problems, noticing similarities and differences, spotting fallacies, and "reading" the environment and other people.

THE TRIARCHIC THEORY One well-known cognitive theory, Robert Sternberg's *triarchic theory of intelligence* (1988), distinguishes three aspects of intelligence:

1. *Componential intelligence* refers to the information-processing strategies that go on inside your head when you are thinking intelligently about a problem. These mental "components" include recognizing the problem, selecting a method for solving it, mastering and carrying out the strategy, and evaluating the result. People who are strong in componential intelligence tend to do well on conventional mental tests.

2. *Experiential intelligence* refers to how well you transfer skills to new situations. People with experiential intelligence cope well with novelty and learn quickly to make new tasks automatic; those who are lacking in this area perform well only under a narrow set of circumstances. For example, a student may do well in school, where assignments have specific due dates and feedback is immediate, but be less successful after graduation if her job requires her to set her own deadlines and her employer doesn't tell her how she is doing.

3. *Contextual intelligence* refers to the practical application of intelligence, which requires you to take into account the different contexts in which you find yourself. If you are strong in contextual intelligence, you know when to adapt to the environment (you are in a dangerous neighborhood, so you become more vigilant); when to change environments (you had planned to be a teacher but discover that you don't enjoy working with kids, so you switch to accounting); and when to fix the situation (your marriage is rocky, so you and your spouse go for counseling).

Most intelligence tests do not measure the experiential and contextual aspects of intelligence, yet these aspects, which together constitute what theorists often call *practical intelligence*, have a powerful effect on personal and occupational success. For example, without contextual intelligence, you won't have the kind of practical savvy that allows you to pick up **tacit knowledge**—action-oriented strategies for success that usually are not formally taught but must instead be inferred (Sternberg et al., 1995). Tacit knowledge can be measured by asking people to solve actual problems in the workplace. In studies of college professors, business managers, and salespeople, scores on tests of tacit knowledge do not correlate strongly with conventional ability-test scores, but they do predict effectiveness on the job (Sternberg, Wagner, & Okagaki, 1993). Tacit knowledge about how to be a student predicts college success as well as academic tests do (Sternberg & Wagner, 1989).

Some of the operations that make up Sternberg's componential intelligence require **metacognition,** the knowledge or awareness of your own cognitive processes and the ability to monitor and control those processes. Metacognitive skills play a major role in making intelligent decisions. For example, before you can solve a problem, you have to recognize that one exists—a metacognitive skill. Some students, however, fail to notice when a textbook contains incomplete or inconsistent information, or when a passage is especially difficult. As a result, they don't study the difficult material enough, and they spend more time than necessary on material they already know (Nelson & Leonesio, 1988). Poor learners also tend to go through the motions of reading without realizing when they have failed to understand the material; good students are better at assessing what they do and don't know. They check their comprehension by restating what they have read, backtracking when necessary, and questioning what they are reading (Bereiter & Bird, 1985). (If they are reading this textbook, they also take the Quick Quizzes!)

tacit knowledge Strategies for success that are not explicitly taught but that instead must be inferred.

metacognition The knowledge or awareness of one's own cognitive processes.

GET INVOLVED

How good is your tacit knowledge about how to be a student? List as many strategies for success as you can think of. Consider what the successful student does when listening to lectures, participating in class discussions, communicating with professors, preparing for exams, writing term papers, and dealing with an unexpectedly low grade. Many of these strategies are never explicitly taught. How many could you think of? You may want to do this exercise with a friend and compare lists. Are there some strategies that one of you thought of and the other didn't?

Intelligence is more than what IQ tests measure. A singer has musical intelligence, a surveyor has spatial intelligence, and a compassionate friend has emotional intelligence.

DOMAINS OF INTELLIGENCE In other ways, too, cognitive approaches are expanding our understanding of what it means to be intelligent. Howard Gardner (1983), in his *theory of multiple intelligences,* suggests that there are seven "intelligences," or domains of talent: *linguistic, logical–mathematical, spatial, musical, bodily–kinesthetic* (which actors, athletes, and dancers have), *intrapersonal* (insight into yourself), and *interpersonal* (understanding of others). These talents are relatively independent, and each may even have its own neural structures. People with brain damage often lose one of the seven without losing their competence in the others. And some autistic and retarded individuals, known by the unfortunate label "idiot savants" (*savant* means "learned" in French), have exceptional talents in one area—such as music, art, or rapid mathematical computation—despite poor functioning in all others.

Gardner's last two "intelligences" correspond to what some psychologists call *emotional intelligence:* the ability to identify your own and other people's emotions accurately, express your emotions clearly, and regulate emotions in yourself and others (Goleman, 1995; Mayer & Salovey, 1997). People with high emotional intelligence use their emotions in beneficial ways, to motivate themselves and others, to spur creative thinking, and to deal empathically with others. People who are low in emotional intelligence are often unable to identify their own emotions; they may insist that they're not depressed when a relationship ends, for example, but meanwhile they start drinking too much, become extremely irritable, and stop going out with friends. They express emotions inappropriately, such as by acting violently or impulsively when they are angry or worried. And they misread nonverbal signals from others; for example, they will give a long-winded account of all their problems even when the listener is obviously bored.

People with emotional intelligence are skilled at reading nonverbal emotional cues. Which of these boys do you think feels the cockiest, and which is most anxious? What cues are you using to answer?

Emotional intelligence contributes to school achievement. Children who have difficulty in interpreting nonverbal emotional signals from others are less likely to do well academically, and this is especially true of boys (Nowicki & Duke, 1989). One study compared children whose parents had taught them to analyze and manage feelings of anger with children who had comparable IQs and socioeconomic backgrounds but whose parents were not good "emotional coaches." Those who had learned to understand their own emotions as preschoolers tended at age 8 to score higher on math and reading tests and to have longer attention spans (Hooven, Gottman, & Katz, 1995). Perhaps children who can't read emotional cues from their teachers and classmates, or who can't regulate their own emotions, have trouble learning because they feel anxious, confused, or angry (Goleman, 1995).

Studies of brain-damaged adults, too, show that using your head also involves your heart. Neuroscientist Antonio Damasio (1994) tells of patients with prefrontal-lobe damage that made them incapable of experiencing strong feelings. Although they scored in the normal range on mental tests, these patients persistently made "dumb," irrational decisions in their lives because they couldn't assign values to different options or read emotional cues from others. (As we will see again in Chapter 10, feeling and thinking aren't necessarily incompatible processes, as many people assume.)

Cognitive research on "intelligences" is starting to have practical benefits. Robert Sternberg and Howard Gardner have worked together with others to develop a practical intelligence curriculum being used in hundreds of classrooms (Sternberg, Okagaki, & Jackson, 1990; Williams et al., 1996). Children are taught three kinds of tacit knowledge necessary for success in school: how to manage themselves (e.g., by avoiding procrastination); how to manage tasks (e.g., by using different strategies when studying for multiple-choice and essay exams); and how to get along with others (e.g., by convincing a teacher that an idea is worthwhile). Children receiving the curriculum have shown greater improvement in reading, writing, homework performance, and test-taking ability than those not receiving it (Sternberg et al., 1995). Future research will assess the effectiveness of these new approaches.

Quick Quiz

How intelligent are you about intelligence?

1. In a sense, all mental tests are (aptitude/achievement) tests.
2. *True or false:* Culture-fair tests have eliminated group differences that show up on traditional IQ tests.
3. What goal do cognitive theories of intelligence have that psychometric theories do not?
4. Logan understands the material in his statistics class, but on tests, he plans his time poorly, spending the entire period on the most difficult problems and never even getting to the problems he can solve easily. According to the triarchic theory of intelligence, which aspect of intelligence does he need to improve?
5. Tracy does not have an unusually high IQ and she was not an A student in school, but at work, she was quickly promoted because she knew how to set priorities, communicate with management, and make others feel valued. Tracy has ____________ intelligence, characterized by the possession of ____________ knowledge.

6. What's wrong with defining intelligence as "whatever intelligence tests measure"?

Answers:

1. achievement 2. false 3. to understand people's strategies for solving problems and use this information to improve mental performance 4. componential intelligence (which involves metacognition) 5. practical, tacit 6. The definition is circular. How do we know someone is intelligent? Because he or she scored high on an intelligence test. Why did the person score high? Because the person is intelligent. The definition also discourages criticisms of the tests and efforts to improve them. People are led to assume that a low score must be entirely the scorer's fault rather than the test's. But the test-taker may be intelligent in ways that the test fails to measure, and the test may be measuring traits other than intelligence.

BELIEFS, MOTIVES, AND INTELLIGENCE

You could have a high IQ, think logically, have emotional intelligence, be talented, and "know your way around," but without a few other qualities, you might still get nowhere at all. Talent, unlike cream, does not inevitably rise to the top; success depends on drive and determination.

Consider a finding from one of the longest-running psychological studies ever conducted. Since 1921, researchers at Stanford University have been following 1,528 people with childhood IQ scores in the top 1 percent of the distribution. As boys and girls, these subjects were nicknamed "Termites," after Lewis Terman, who originally directed the research. The Termites started out bright, physically healthy, sociable, and well adjusted. As they entered adulthood, most became successful in the traditional ways of the times: men in careers and women as homemakers (Sears & Barbee, 1977; Terman & Oden, 1959). However, some gifted men failed to live up to their early promise, dropping out of school or drifting into low-level work. When the researchers compared the 100 most successful men in the Stanford study with the 100 least successful, they found that motivation made the difference. The successful men were ambitious, were socially active, had many interests, and were encouraged by their parents. The least successful drifted casually through life. There was *no* average difference in IQ between the two groups.

In another study, researchers interviewed 120 of America's top artists, athletes, and scholars, along with their families and teachers, to learn what had made them so successful (Bloom, 1985). The research team expected to hear tales of extraordinary natural talent. Instead, they heard tales of extraordinary dedication. Musicians had practiced several hours a day for years. Swimmers told of rising early every morning to swim for two hours before school started. These high achievers were perfect illustrations of the old joke: A young man walking down a New York street asks an old woman, "How do I get to Carnegie Hall?" Her reply: "Practice, young man. Practice."

Yes, you say, but where do you get the discipline to practice? One factor has to do with your beliefs about the origins of intelligence and the reasons for achievement. For nearly two decades, Harold Stevenson and his colleagues have been studying attitudes toward achievement in Japan, China, and the United States. The researchers began in 1980 by comparing large samples of first- and fifth-grade children, their parents, and their teachers in Minneapolis, Sendai (Japan), and Taipei (Taiwan). In another project, they compared children from 20 schools in Chicago and 11 schools in Beijing (Stevenson & Stigler, 1992). In 1990, Stevenson, along with Chuansheng Chen and Shin-Ying Lee (1993), revisited the original schools to collect new data on fifth-graders, and they also retested many of the children who had been in the 1980 study and who were now in the eleventh grade. Their results have much to teach us about the cultivation of intellect.

In 1980, the Asian children far outperformed the American children on a broad battery of mathematical tests. (A similar gap existed between the Chinese and American children on reading tests.) On computations and word problems, there was virtually no overlap between schools, with the lowest-scoring Beijing schools doing better than the highest-scoring Chicago schools. By 1990, the gap between the Asian and American children had grown even greater (see Figure 8.3). Only 4 percent of the Chinese children and 10 percent of the Japanese children had scores as low as those of the *average* American child. These differences could not be accounted for by educational resources: The Chinese had worse facilities and larger classes than the Americans. On the average, the American children's parents were far better-off financially and were better educated than the parents of the Chinese children. Nor could the test differences be accounted for by differences in the children's fondness

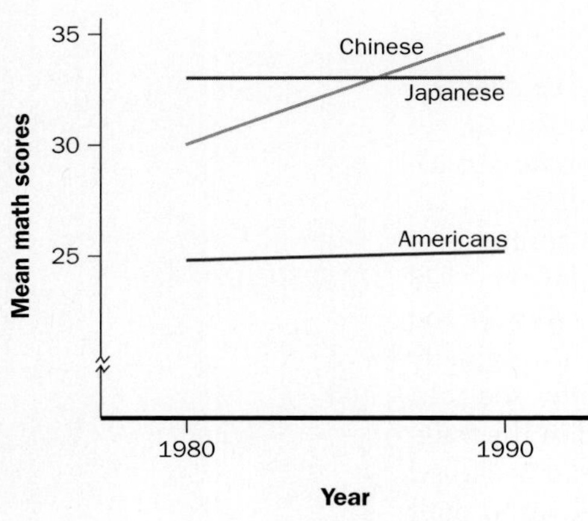

Figure 8.3
Mathematical Performance of Asian and American Children

In 1980 and again in 1990, the math performance of fifth-graders in Taiwan and Japan far outstripped that of children in the United States. This graph shows the gap on one of the tests given (Stevenson, Chen, & Lee, 1993). The performance differences were associated with differences in attitudes, standards, and effort.

for math: 85 percent of the Chinese kids said they liked math, but so did almost 75 percent of the American children. Nor did it have anything to do with intellectual ability in general, because the American children were just as knowledgeable and capable as the Asian children on tests of general information.

But the Asians and the Americans were worlds apart, so to speak, in their attitudes, expectations, and efforts:

- *Beliefs about intelligence.* American parents, teachers, and children were far and away more likely than Asians to believe that mathematical ability is innate. They thought that if you "have it," you don't have to work hard, and if you don't have it, there's no point in trying. When Japanese teachers were asked to choose the most important factor in math performance, 93 percent of them chose "studying hard," compared with only 26 percent of the American teachers. Students picked up these attitudes: 72 percent of the Japanese but only 27 percent of the American eleventh-graders thought studying hard was the key to success in math.
- *Standards.* American parents had far lower standards for their children's performance. They said they would be satisfied with scores barely above average on a 100-point test; most felt that their children were doing fine in math and that the schools were doing a good or excellent job. In contrast, the Chinese and Japanese parents said they would be happy only with very high scores, and most were not highly satisfied with their children's schools or even with their children's excellent performance.
- *Conflicts.* American students had more stressful, conflicting demands on their time than their Asian counterparts did. Chinese and Japanese students were expected to devote themselves to their studies, but American students were expected to be "well-rounded"—to have after-school jobs (74 percent of them did, compared with only 21 percent of the Asians), to have dates and active social lives (85 percent to 37 percent), and to have time for sports and other activities. Contrary to the stereotype of the stressed and overworked Japanese student, it was the American students who were most likely to report that school was a source of stress and academic anxiety (Crystal et al., 1994). The Japanese eleventh-graders actually had the lowest incidence of stress, depression, insomnia, aggression, and physical symptoms.
- *Values.* American students did not value education as much as Asian students did and were more complacent about mediocre work. When asked what they would wish for if a wizard could give them anything they wanted, more than 60 percent of the Chinese fifth-graders named something related to their education. Can you guess what the American children wanted? A majority said money or possessions.

The moral is clear: It's not just what you've got that counts, but what you do with it.

ANIMAL MINDS

How smart is this otter?

A green heron swipes some bread from a picnicker's table and scatters the crumbs on a nearby stream. When a minnow rises to the bait, the heron strikes, swallowing its prey before you can say "hook, line, and sinker." A sea otter, floating calmly on its back, bangs a mussel shell against a stone that is resting on its stomach. When the shell cracks apart, the otter devours the tasty morsel inside, tucks the stone under its flipper, and dives for another shell, which it will open in the same way. In Africa, a lioness appears behind a herd of wildebeests and chases them toward a ditch. Another lioness, lying in wait at the ditch, leaps up and kills one of the passing wildebeests. The first lioness then joins her companion for the feast.

Incidents such as these, summarized nicely in Donald Griffin's *Animal Minds* (1992), have convinced some biologists, psychologists, and ethologists that we are not the only animals with cognitive abilities—that "dumb beasts" are far smarter than we may think. For many years, any scientist who claimed that animals could think was likely to get laughed at, or worse; today, the interdisciplinary field of **cognitive ethology,** the study of cognitive processes in nonhuman animals, is gaining increased attention (Gould & Gould, 1995; Ristau, 1991). Cognitive ethologists argue that some animals can anticipate future events, make plans and choices, and coordinate their activities with those of their comrades. The versatility of these animals in meeting new challenges in the environment, say these researchers, suggests that they are, indeed, capable of thought.

Other scientists are not so sure, noting that even complex behavior can be genetically prewired. The assassin bug of South America catches termites by gluing nest material on its back as camouflage, but it is hard to imagine how the bug's tiny dab of brain tissue could enable it to plan this strategy consciously. Even trees and plants, which few people credit with consciousness, do things that *appear* intelligent. When willow trees are attacked by insects, they release into the air a chemical that causes leaves on nearby healthy willow trees to change chemically and become less palatable to the insects (Rhoades, 1985). This "communication" does not imply thought; it is a genetically controlled adaptation to the environment.

Even many cognitive ethologists are cautious about how much cognition they are willing to read into an animal's behavior. An animal could be conscious, they argue, in the sense of being aware of its environment and knowing some things, without knowing that it knows and without being able to think about its own thoughts in the way that human beings do (Cheney & Seyfarth, 1990; Crook, 1987).

But explanations of animal behavior that leave out any sort of consciousness at all and that attribute animal's actions entirely to instinct leave many questions unanswered. Like the otter who uses a stone to crack mussel shells, many animals are capable of using objects in the natural environment as rudimentary tools. For example, mother chimpanzees occasionally show their young how to use stone tools to open hard nuts (Boesch, 1991). In the laboratory, too, nonhuman primates have accomplished some truly surprising things. In one study, chimpanzees compared two pairs of food wells containing chocolate chips. One pair might contain, say, five chips and three chips, the other four chips and three chips. Allowed to choose which pair they wanted, the chimps almost always chose the one with the higher total, showing some sort of summing ability (Rumbaugh, Savage-Rumbaugh, & Pate, 1988). Other chimps have learned to use numerals to label quantities of items and simple sums (Boysen & Berntson, 1989; Washburn & Rumbaugh, 1991).

A primary ingredient in human cognition is *language,* the ability to combine elements that are themselves meaningless into an infinite number of utterances that convey meaning. Language is often regarded as the last bastion of human unique-

cognitive ethology The study of cognitive processes in nonhuman animals.

ness, a result of evolutionary forces that produced our species (see Chapter 3). Do animals have anything comparable? To qualify as a language, a communication system must meet three criteria (Hockett, 1960):

1. *Meaningfulness.* In any language, reference to things, ideas, and feelings is achieved by the arbitrary but consistent combination of sounds or gestures into meaningful units such as words or signs. There must be enough words (or signs) to express all the concepts that a community might want or need to express.
2. *Displacement.* Languages permit communication about objects and events that are not present here and now—that are displaced in time or space. Merely pointing to things is not language.
3. *Productivity.* A language has a set of grammatical rules that allows the expression and comprehension of an infinite number of novel utterances.

By these criteria, no nonhuman species has its own language. Of course, animals do communicate, using gestures, body postures, facial expressions, vocalizations, and odors. And some of these signals have highly specific meanings. For example, vervet monkeys seem to have separate calls to warn about leopards versus eagles versus snakes (Cheney & Seyfarth, 1985). But vervets can't combine these sounds to produce entirely novel utterances, as in "Look out, Harry, that eagle-eyed leopard is a real snake-in-the-grass."

Perhaps, however, some animals could acquire language if they got a little help from their human friends. Dozens of researchers have tried to provide chimpanzees with just such help. Because the vocal tract of a chimpanzee does not permit speech, early efforts to teach chimpanzees spoken language were failures, though some comprehension on the part of the animals did occur. During the 1960s and 1970s, researchers tried innovative approaches that relied on visual symbols or gestures, rather than speech. In one project, chimpanzees learned to use as words various geometric plastic shapes arranged on a magnetic board (Premack & Premack, 1983). In another, they learned to punch symbols on a computer-monitored keyboard (Rumbaugh, 1977). In yet another, they learned hundreds of signs from American Sign Language (ASL) (Fouts & Rigby, 1977; Gardner & Gardner, 1969). All these animals learned to follow instructions, answer questions, and make requests. More important, they combined individual signs or symbols into longer utterances that they had never seen before. In general, their linguistic abilities resembled those of a 2-year-old child.

As you can imagine, accounts of the apes' abilities caused quite a stir. The animals were apparently using their newfound skills to apologize for being disobedient, scold their trainers, and even talk to themselves. Koko, a lowland gorilla, reportedly used signs to say that she felt happy or sad, to refer to past and future events, to mourn for her dead pet kitten, and to convey her yearning for a baby. She even lied on occasion, when she did something naughty (Patterson & Linden, 1981).

AVOID EMOTIONAL REASONING

It's hard not to fall in love with apes who use rudimentary tools, appear able to add sums, and use symbols to request food, apologize, or lie. But emotion can sometimes get in the way of objectivity. What does research that controls for the researcher's affection show about the ability of animals to think and use language?

The animals in these studies were lovable, the findings appealing. But soon skeptics and some of the researchers themselves began to point out serious problems (Seidenberg & Petitto, 1979; Terrace, 1985). In their desire to talk to the animals and their affection for their primate friends, researchers had not always been objective. They had overinterpreted the animal's utterances, reading all sorts of meanings and intentions into a single sign or symbol. In videotapes, they could be seen unwittingly giving nonverbal cues that might enable the apes to respond correctly. Further, the animals appeared to be stringing signs and symbols

none exists; and to overestimate their ability to have made accurate predictions (the *hindsight bias*). The theory of *cognitive dissonance* holds that people are also motivated to reduce the tension that exists when two cognitions are in conflict—by rejecting or changing a belief, changing their behavior, or rationalizing. People are not always rational, but once we understand a bias, we may be able to reduce or eliminate it.

INTELLIGENCE

9) Although we all wish to think intelligently, intelligence is hard to define. Some theorists believe that a general ability (a *g factor*) underlies the many specific abilities tapped by intelligence tests, whereas other theorists do not.

10) The traditional approach to intelligence, the *psychometric* approach, focuses on how well people perform on standardized mental tests. The *intelligence quotient*, or *IQ*, represents how a person has done on an intelligence test, compared to other people. Alfred Binet designed the first widely used intelligence test for the purpose of identifying children who could benefit from remedial work. But in the United States, people assumed that intelligence tests revealed "natural ability," and they used the tests to categorize people in school and in the armed services.

11) IQ tests have been criticized for being biased in favor of white, middle-class people. However, efforts to construct culture-free and culture-fair tests have been disappointing. Some critics would like to dispense with IQ tests because they are so often interpreted unintelligently. Critics also argue that when a child's abilities don't match those expected by teachers and testers, the best solution may be to modify the classroom or the test. Others believe that the tests are useful for predicting school performance and diagnosing learning difficulties, as long as test scores are combined with other information.

12) In contrast to the psychometric approach, *cognitive approaches* to intelligence emphasize the strategies people use to solve problems and not just whether they get the right answers. Sternberg's *triarchic theory of intelligence* proposes three aspects of intelligence: componential, experiential, and contextual. Most intelligence tests do not measure experiential and contextual intelligence, or people's *tacit knowledge*, yet these help determine a person's personal and occupational success. *Metacognition*, which is part of componential intelligence, also plays an important role in intelligent behavior.

13) Howard Gardner's *theory of multiple intelligences* holds that there are actually seven "intelligences": linguistic, logical–mathematical, spatial, musical, bodily–kinesthetic, intrapersonal, and interpersonal. The last two correspond roughly to *emotional intelligence*, which is related to personal and academic success.

14) Achievement also depends on motivation and attitudes. Cross-cultural work shows that beliefs about the origins of mental abilities, parental standards, and attitudes toward education can help account for differences in academic performance.

ANIMAL MINDS

15) Some researchers argue that nonhuman animals have greater cognitive abilities than is usually thought. Some animals can use objects as rudimentary tools. Chimpanzees have learned to use numerals to label quantities of items and symbols to refer to objects. Several researchers have used visual symbol systems or American Sign Language (ASL) to teach primates language skills, and some animals (even some nonprimates) seem able to use simple grammatical ordering rules to convey meaning. However, scientists are still divided as to how to interpret these findings.

KEY TERMS

thinking 298
concept 299
basic concept 299
prototype 299
proposition 299
cognitive schema 299
mental image 298
subconscious processes 300
nonconscious processes 301
mindlessness 301
reasoning 302
algorithm 302
heuristics 302
premise 303
deductive reasoning 303
syllogism 303
inductive reasoning 303
informal versus formal reasoning 305
dialectical reasoning 305
reflective judgment 306
- prereflective stages 307
- quasi-reflective stages 308
- reflective stages 308

availability heuristic 310
avoidance of loss 311
confirmation bias 312
mental set 313
hindsight bias 314
cognitive dissonance 314
justification of effort 316
intelligence 317
factor analysis 318
g factor 318
psychometric approach to intelligence 318
achievement versus aptitude tests 318
mental age (MA) 318
intelligence quotient (IQ) 318
Stanford–Binet Intelligence Scale 319
Wechsler Adult Intelligence Scale (WAIS) 319
Wechsler Intelligence Scale for Children (WISC) 319
culture-free tests 321
culture-fair tests 321
learning disability 322
cognitive approaches to intelligence 323
triarchic theory of intelligence 323
- componential intelligence 323
- experiential intelligence 324
- contextual intelligence 324

practical intelligence 324
tacit knowledge 324
metacognition 324
theory of multiple intelligences 325
emotional intelligence 325
cognitive ethology 329
anthropomorphism 332
anthropocentrism 332
convergent versus divergent thinking 333

Answer to the Get Involved problem on page 312:
You need to turn over the cards that say "Drinking beer" and "16 years old."

Answers to the creativity test on page 333:
back, party, book, match, cheese

Some solutions to the nine-dot problem in the Get Involved exercise on page 313 (from Adams, 1986):

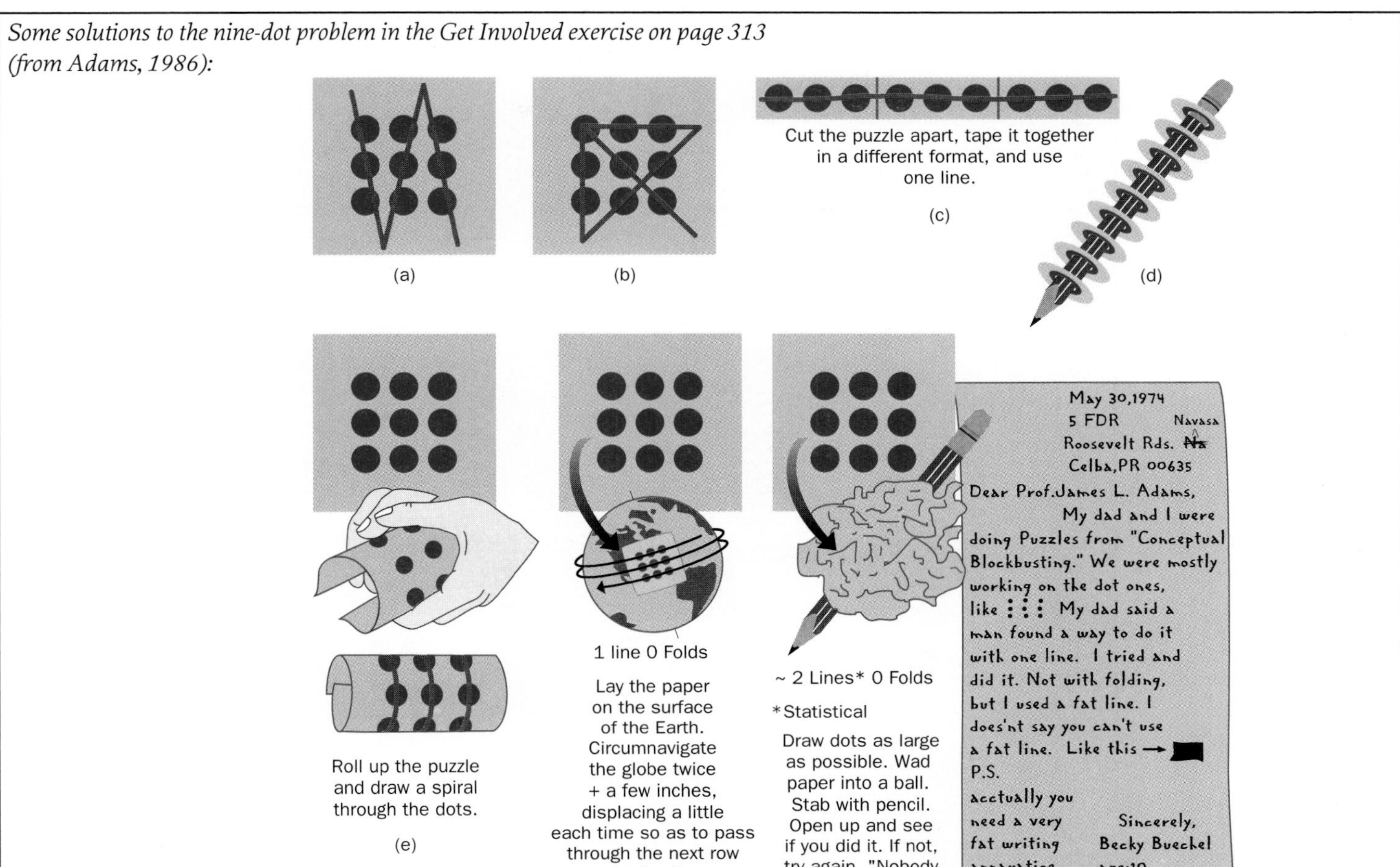

(a)
(b)
Cut the puzzle apart, tape it together in a different format, and use one line.
(c)
(d)
Roll up the puzzle and draw a spiral through the dots.
(e)
1 line 0 Folds
Lay the paper on the surface of the Earth. Circumnavigate the globe twice + a few inches, displacing a little each time so as to pass through the next row on each circuit as you "Go West, young man."
(f)
~ 2 Lines* 0 Folds
*Statistical
Draw dots as large as possible. Wad paper into a ball. Stab with pencil. Open up and see if you did it. If not, try again. "Nobody loses: play until you win."
(g)
May 30,1974
5 FDR
Roosevelt Rds. Navasa
Celba,PR 00635
Dear Prof.James L. Adams,
My dad and I were doing Puzzles from "Conceptual Blockbusting." We were mostly working on the dot ones, like ⁝⁝⁝ My dad said a man found a way to do it with one line. I tried and did it. Not with folding, but I used a fat line. I does'nt say you can't use a fat line. Like this →
P.S.
acctually you need a very fat writing apparatice.
Sincerely,
Becky Buechel
age:10
(h)

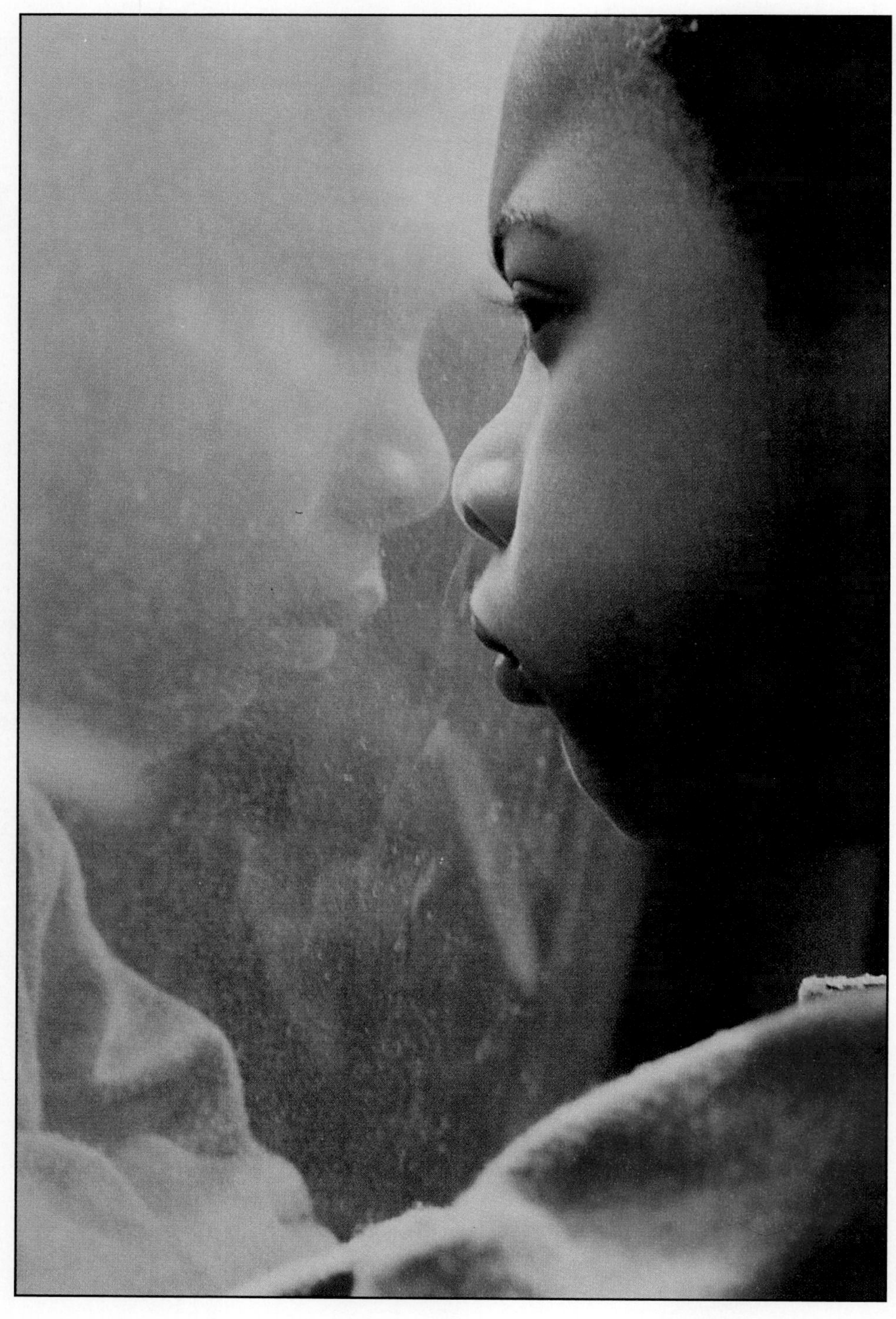

Better by far that you should forget and smile
Than that you should remember and be sad.

Christina Rossetti

CHAPTER NINE

Memory

IN 1983, A WRITER WE KNOW took a trip to Italy with her husband and spent a few days exploring the beautiful city of Florence. Not long afterward, she saw the film of E. M. Forster's novel *Room with a View,* which is set in Florence. Years went by, and a decade after her Italian vacation, she sat down on a winter's eve to rewatch the film of *Room with a View.* During the movie, a long camera shot of the Piazza Signoria suddenly brought back a flood of memories, one of them violent. Our friend remembered that while she and her husband had been in that piazza, a wild fight had broken out, and a young man had been seriously injured. In her mind's eye, she once again saw the crowd, the commotion, the blood on the man's shirt. "At that moment," she says, "I would have sworn in a court of law that we had seen a fight in the Piazza Signoria."

The fight scene from Room with a View.

Then, suddenly, she found herself watching, right up there on her television screen, the very same fight that she recalled witnessing a decade earlier. The fight she was so sure she had observed firsthand was a scene from the novel! Perhaps, she thought, some other violent event had occurred during her visit. Checking her journal of the trip, she found that when she and her husband were in the Piazza Signoria, they had spent some time admiring the sculptures, had sipped lemonade at a sidewalk cafe, and had watched a prostitute idly solicit business. But there had been no fight, no disturbance—only a typical, peaceful Florentine morning in the Piazza Signoria.

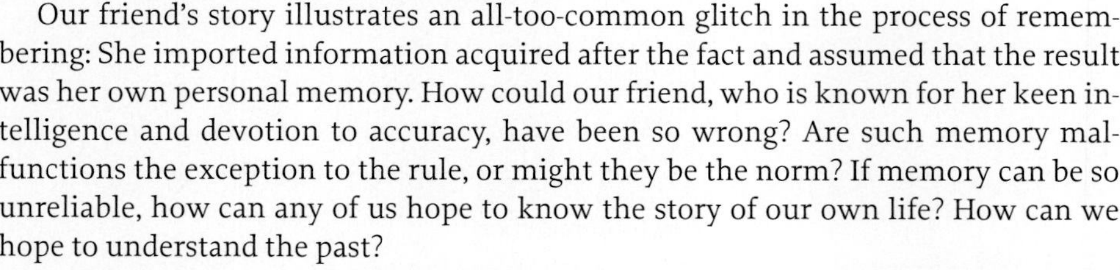

Our friend's story illustrates an all-too-common glitch in the process of remembering: She imported information acquired after the fact and assumed that the result was her own personal memory. How could our friend, who is known for her keen intelligence and devotion to accuracy, have been so wrong? Are such memory malfunctions the exception to the rule, or might they be the norm? If memory can be so unreliable, how can any of us hope to know the story of our own life? How can we hope to understand the past?

In this chapter, we will see how psychologists investigate these uncomfortable questions. Cognitive researchers want to know how a person can "remember" things that never happened. They also want to know why, despite our best efforts, we all forget many (perhaps most) events that did take place. They want to know why even recent memories can evaporate like the morning dew: why we watch the evening news and half an hour later can't recall the main story; why we enjoy a meal and quickly forget what we ate; why, as students, we may study our heads off for an exam, only to find that some of the information we studied isn't there when we need it most.

But psychologists also study the many astonishing feats of memory that all human beings are capable of. Who fought whom in World War II? When are presidential elections held? What is the tune of your national anthem? How do you use an automated teller machine? What's the most embarrassing thing that ever happened to you? You can probably answer most of these questions, and hundreds of thousands of others, without hesitation. A mathematician once calculated that over the course of a lifetime, we store 500 times as much information as there is in the entire *Encyclopaedia Britannica* (Griffith, in Horn & Hinde, 1970). Memory confers competence; without it we would be as helpless as newborns, unable to negotiate even the most trivial of our daily tasks. It also confers a sense of personal identity; we are each the sum total of our personal recollections, which is why we feel so threatened when others challenge our memories. Individuals and cultures alike rely on a remembered history for a sense of coherence and meaning; memory preserves the past and guides the future.

RECONSTRUCTING THE PAST

In ancient times, philosophers compared memory to a tablet of hot wax that would preserve anything that chanced to make an imprint on it. Then, with the advent of the printing press, they began to think of a memory as a sheet of paper, with specific events and facts filed away in a sort of giant mental filing cabinet, awaiting retrieval. Today, in the audiovisual age, many people think of memory as a mental tape recorder or movie camera, automatically recording each and every moment of their lives. One psychotherapist, who apparently never studied introductory psychology, expressed the modern pop-psych vision of memory this way (Fiore, 1989): "The subconscious mind has a memory bank of everything we ever experienced, exactly as we perceived it. Every thought, emotion, sound of music, word, taste and sight. Everything is faithfully recorded somehow in your mind. Your sub-conscious mind's memory is perfect, infallible."

Popular and appealing though this belief about memory is, however, it is utterly, absolutely wrong. *Not* everything that happens to us or impinges on our senses is tucked away for later use. If it were, our minds would be cluttered with all sorts of mental junk—the temperature at noon Thursday, the price of turnips two years ago, a phone number needed only once. Memory must be selective. And recovering a memory, as we are about to see, is not at all like replaying a film of an event; it is more like watching a few unconnected frames and then figuring out what the rest of the scene must have been like.

THE MANUFACTURE OF MEMORY

In 1932, the British psychologist Sir Frederic Bartlett asked people to read lengthy, unfamiliar stories from other cultures and then tell the stories back to him. Bartlett found that as the volunteers tried to recall the stories, they made interesting errors: They often eliminated or changed details that didn't make sense to them, and they added other details to make the story coherent, sometimes even adding a moral to the story. Memory, Bartlett concluded, must therefore be largely a *reconstructive* process. (Psychologists today sometimes call this process *confabulation.*) We may reproduce some kinds of simple information by rote, said Bartlett, but when we remember complex information, we typically alter it in ways that help us make sense of the material, based on what we already know, or think we know. Since Bartlett's time, hundreds of studies have found his conclusion to be true for everything from stories to conversations (Schacter, 1996).

You can see the process of reconstruction at work in the tragic case of H. M., whom we described briefly in Chapter 4 (page 140). Ever since 1953, when much of H. M.'s hippocampus and the adjacent cortex were surgically removed, he

Patients who cannot form new memories are helping researchers understand how memory normally works. K. P. (left) developed amnesia when her brain was robbed of oxygen for several minutes, possibly because of an accidental overdose of barbiturates. Although she is fluent in three languages, she has trouble remembering events for more than 10 minutes. Working with researcher and clinician Bonnie Olsen, K. P. has been able to acquire new skills and habits. Mnemonic techniques, such as cue cards and an electronic voice reminder, have helped her to become more self-sufficient.

GET INVOLVED

Select an incident in your childhood that stands out in your memory, and write down as much as you can about it. Now ask a friend or family member who was present at the time to write a description of the same event. Compare the two accounts; do they differ? If so, can one of you convince the other that his or her recollection is the "right" one? What does this exercise tell you about the nature of memory?

has suffered from the inability to form lasting memories for new events and facts. He cannot learn new words, songs, stories, or faces, and therefore he does not remember much of anything that has happened since 1953 (Hilts, 1995; Ogden & Corkin, 1991). To cope with his devastating condition, H. M. will sometimes try to reconstruct events. On one occasion, after eating a large chocolate Valentine's Day heart, H. M. stuck the shiny red wrapping in his shirt pocket. Two hours later, while searching for his handkerchief, he pulled out the paper and looked at it in puzzlement. When researcher Jenni Ogden asked why he had the paper in his pocket, he replied, "Well, it could have been wrapped around a big chocolate heart. It must be Valentine's Day!" Ogden could hardly contain her excitement about H. M.'s apparent recall of a recent episode. But a short time later, when she asked him to take out the paper again and say why he had it in his pocket, he replied, "Well, it might have been wrapped around a big chocolate rabbit. It must be Easter!"

Of course, H. M. *had* to reconstruct the past; his damaged brain could not recall it in any other way. But those of us with normal memory abilities also reconstruct, far more often than we realize. Suppose someone asks you to describe one of your early birthday parties. You may have some direct recollection of the event, especially if it was emotionally significant. But you have also stored information gleaned from family stories, photographs, or home videos. You may take all these bits and pieces and build one integrated account from them, and later you may not be able to separate your original experience from what you added after the fact—a phenomenon called **source amnesia** or *source misattribution.* Like the writer who "remembered" a fight in the peaceful piazza, you may even think you recall an event that never happened.

THE CONDITIONS OF CONFABULATION People are especially likely to have false memories of events or experiences under particular circumstances (Garry, Manning, & Loftus, 1996; Hyman & Pentland, 1996; Johnson, 1995). These include the following:

- *The person has thought about the imagined event many times.* Suppose that at family gatherings you keep hearing about the time when Uncle Sam scared everyone at a New Year's party by pounding a hammer into the wall with such force that the wall collapsed. It's such a colorful story that you can practically see Uncle Sam in your mind's eye. The more you think about this event, the more likely you are to believe that you were actually there, even if you were sound asleep in another house altogether.
- *The image of the event contains a lot of details.* Ordinarily, we can distinguish an imagined event from a real one by the amount of detail in our recollection of the event; real events tend to produce more detailed memories. However, the more you think about an imagined event, the more details you are likely to add—what Sam was wearing, the fact that he'd had too much to drink, the crumbling plaster, people standing around in party hats—and these details may in turn persuade you that the event really happened and that you have a direct memory of it.

source amnesia The inability to distinguish what you originally experienced from what you heard or were told about an event later.

- *The event is easy to imagine.* If forming an image of an event takes little effort (for example, it is easy to visualize a man pounding a wall with a hammer), then we tend to think our memory of the event is real. In contrast, when we have to make an effort to form an image—for example, of being in a place we have never seen or doing something that is utterly foreign to us—the cognitive operations we perform apparently serve as a cue that the event did not really take place, or that we were not there.
- *The rememberer focuses on his or her emotional reactions to the event rather than on what actually happened.* Emotional reactions to an imagined event can resemble those that would have occurred in response to a real event; therefore, the fact that a person has a strong feeling about an event is not a reliable cue to the event's reality. Consider again our Sam story, which happens to be true. A woman we know believed for years that she had been present in the room as an 11-year-old child when her uncle destroyed the wall. Because the story was so vivid and upsetting to her, she felt angry at him for what she thought was his mean and violent behavior, and she assumed that she must have been angry at the time as well. Then, as an adult, she learned that she wasn't at the party at all but had merely heard about it repeatedly over the years; and that Sam hadn't pounded the wall in anger, but as a joke—to inform the assembled guests that he and his wife were about to remodel their home. Nevertheless, our friend's family has had a hard time convincing her that her "memory" of this event is entirely wrong, and they aren't sure she believes them yet.

As the Sam story illustrates, and as laboratory research demonstrates, false memories can be as stable over time as true ones, or even more so (Brainerd, Reyna, & Brandse, 1995; Poole, 1995; Roediger & McDermott, 1995). Yet despite the wealth of evidence for the reconstructive nature of memory, some people still believe that memories are permanently stored somewhere in the brain with perfect accuracy. As evidence, they may cite studies of recall under hypnosis, or cases in which electrical brain stimulation prior to surgery has seemed to evoke memories of events thought by the patient to be long forgotten (Penfield & Perot, 1963). Hypnotically induced memories, however, are as vulnerable to confabulation and error as are any other memories (see Chapter 5). And the "memories" that result from brain stimulation are usually fragmentary reconstructions that draw in part on actual memories and in part on current thoughts or bits of conversation heard just before the operation (Loftus, 1980).

THE FADING FLASHBULB But, you may say, what about those surprising, shocking, or tragic events that hold a special place in memory? Such experiences seem frozen in time, with all the details intact (Conway et al., 1994). Years ago, Roger Brown and James Kulik (1977) labeled these vivid recollections *flashbulb memories* because that term captures the surprise, illumination, and seemingly photographic detail that characterize them. Brown and Kulik speculated that the capacity for flashbulb memories may have evolved because such memories had survival value. Remembering the details of a surprising or dangerous experience could have helped our ancestors avoid similar situations.

Despite their intensity, however, even flashbulb memories are not always complete or accurate records of the past (Wright, 1993). Many people who were alive when John F. Kennedy was killed swear that they saw the assassination on television, as he was riding in his motorcade. In reality, no television cameras were present, and the only film of the event, made by a bystander, was not shown until much later. Similarly, many

THE FAR SIDE By GARY LARSON

More facts of nature: All forest animals, to this very day, remember exactly where they were and what they were doing when they heard that Bambi's mother had been shot.

people over the age of 25 say that they know exactly where they were and what they were doing when they learned of the 1986 explosion of the space shuttle *Challenger*, as well as who told them the news and what their own reactions were. Yet even "unforgettable" memories such as these often grow dim with time (Bohannan, 1988; McClosky, Wible, & Cohen, 1988). In one study, college students, on the morning after the *Challenger* tragedy, reported how they had heard the news. Three years later, when they again recalled how they learned of the incident, not one student was entirely correct, and a third of them were *completely wrong*, although they felt confident that they were remembering accurately (Neisser & Harsch, 1992).

To be sure, some shocking or surprising events—such as earthquakes—do remain extremely memorable, especially when you are personally involved in the event (Neisser, Winograd, & Weldon, 1991). Even with flashbulb memories, however, facts tend to get mixed with a little fiction. These findings remind us, once again, that remembering is an *active* process; it involves not only dredging up stored information but also putting two and two together to reconstruct the past.

THE EYEWITNESS ON TRIAL

The reconstructive nature of memory helps the mind work efficiently. Instead of cramming our brains with zillions of specific details, we can store the essentials of an experience, then use our knowledge of the world to figure out the specifics when we need them. But sometimes the same process gets us into hot water, and this raises some thorny problems in legal cases that involve eyewitness testimony.

The legal system relies on the memories of eyewitnesses, but sometimes witnesses make mistakes. Seven people identified Father Bernard Pagno (top) as having committed a series of armed robberies, but Robert Clouser (bottom) later confessed to the crimes.

Imagine that as you leave an office building, you see a man running in the direction of a blue Dodge. You glance away for a moment, and when you look back, you see that someone in the Dodge is pulling away from the curb. You are not paying much attention to this chain of events; why should you? Just then, a woman emerges from the building, points wildly at the receding car, and shouts, "Stop that man, he stole my purse!" Soon the police arrive and ask you to tell what you saw.

If we again compare memory to a film, you have actually seen only some of the frames: a man running toward a car, the car pulling away. Asked now for a description of what happened, you are likely to fill in the frames that are missing, the ones that would presumably show the man climbing into the car. In other words, you *infer* (deduce) that the man you saw is the one who stole the purse. To make matters worse, some aspects of this episode were undoubtedly hazy or incomplete, so you have probably gone back and "retouched" them, adding a little color here, a little detail there: "I saw a brown-haired man, about 5 feet 10 inches tall, with a mustache, and wearing a blue shirt, run over to the blue Dodge, get in, and drive away." What has happened is something like perceptual closure, discussed in Chapter 6, except that in this case the closure has occurred in memory.

Will any harm result from your reconstruction? Perhaps the man you saw really did drive off in the car. But because memory is reconstructive, eyewitness testimony is not always reliable, even when the witness feels entirely confident about the accuracy of his or her report (Bothwell, Deffenbacher, & Brigham, 1987; Sporer et al., 1995). Of course, the accounts of eyewitnesses play a vital role in any justice system; without them, many guilty people would go free. But convictions based solely or mostly on such testimony occasionally turn out to be tragic mistakes. Errors are especially likely to occur when the suspect's ethnicity differs from that of the witness, perhaps because prejudices or lack of familiarity prevent people from attending to the distinctive features of members of other groups (Brigham & Malpass, 1985; Chance & Goldstein, 1995).

To complicate matters further, our reconstructions of past events are heavily in-

How Leading Questions Can Affect Recall

Students saw the face of a young man with straight hair, then heard a description of the face supposedly written by another witness—one that wrongly mentioned light, curly hair. When they reconstructed the face using a kit of facial features, 33 percent of their reconstructions contained the misleading detail, whereas only 5 percent contained it when curly hair was not mentioned. On the left is one person's reconstruction in the absence of the misleading information; on the right is another person's reconstruction of the same face after exposure to the misleading information (Loftus & Greene, 1980).

fluenced by the way in which questions about those events are put to us. In a classic study of leading questions, Elizabeth Loftus and John Palmer (1974) showed people short films depicting car collisions. Afterward, the researchers asked some of the viewers, "About how fast were the cars going when they hit each other?" Other viewers were asked the same question, but with the verb changed to *smashed, collided, bumped,* or *contacted.* These words imply different speeds, with *smashed* implying the greatest speed and *contacted* the least. Sure enough, the estimates of how fast the cars were going varied, depending on which word was used. *Smashed* produced the highest average speed estimates (40.8 mph), followed by *collided* (39.3 mph), *bumped* (38.1 mph), *hit* (34.0 mph), and *contacted* (31.8 mph).

In a similar study, the researchers asked some participants, "Did you see a broken headlight?" but asked of others "Did you see the broken headlight?" (Loftus & Zanni, 1975). Two other pairs of questions also differed only in the use of *a* or *the.* Note that the question with *the* presupposes a broken headlight and merely asks whether the witness saw it, whereas the question with *a* makes no such presupposition. People who received questions with *the* were far more likely to report having seen something that had not really appeared in the film than were those who received questions with *a.* If a tiny word like *the* can lead people to "remember" what they never saw, you can imagine how the leading questions of police detectives and lawyers might influence a witness's recall.

AVOID OVERSIMPLIFICATION

Some people claim that children's memories of sexual abuse are always accurate; other people claim that children can't distinguish fantasy from reality, so their memories shouldn't be trusted. How can we avoid either–or thinking on this emotional issue? Is the question "Are children's memories accurate?" even the right one to be asking?

Many people are especially concerned about the impact of leading questions on children's memories, especially when children are asked to tell whether they have been sexually abused. For many decades most adults believed that children's memories could not be trusted—that children confuse fantasy with reality and tend to say whatever adults expect. Then, as the issue of child abuse came to public attention in the 1970s and 1980s, some people began to argue that no child would ever lie about or misremember such a traumatic experience. This debate, which continues today, is one in which research on memory can have a tremendous impact.

After carefully reviewing the more than 100 studies of children's eyewitness testimony done since 1979, Stephen Ceci and Maggie Bruck (1993, 1995) concluded that extremists on both sides are wrong. Ceci and Bruck found that most young children *do* recollect accurately most of what they've observed or experienced, including potentially embarrassing experiences such as genital examinations at a doctor's office. More specifically, most children do not report that their genitals were touched if they were not touched, even when the children are asked leading questions (Goodman et al., 1990; Saywitz et al., 1991). This finding is important, because without a few leading questions, some young children who have been abused will not volunteer information that they feel is embarrassing or shameful. On the other hand, some children *will* say that something happened when it did not. Like adults, they can be influenced to report an event in a certain way, depending on the frequency of the suggestions and the insistence of the person making them.

Therefore, instead of asking "Are children suggestible?" or "Are children's memories accurate?" Ceci and Bruck suggest that a more useful question is "Under what conditions are children apt to be suggestible?" One such condition is age; preschoolers' memories are more vulnerable to suggestion than are those of school-aged children and adults. In addition, the boundary between reality and fantasy may blur for young children, especially in emotionally charged situations, making it more likely that their accounts will include confabulations of imagined events.

Moreover, children's memories can be as influenced as adults' memories are by leading questions, by pressure to conform to the interviewer's expectations, and by the desire to please the interviewer. In one study, 3- and 6-year-old children played with an unfamiliar man for five minutes while seated across the table from him. Four *years* later, the researchers interviewed the children, telling them that they were being questioned about "an important event" and that they would "feel better once they told about it." Of course, few children actually remembered the episode. Yet 5 of the 15 children, in response to a leading question, said that the man had hugged or kissed them; two "remembered" that he had taken pictures of them in the bathroom; and one little girl agreed that he had given her a bath (Goodman et al., 1989).

At present, then, the wisest course to take about children's memories is to be open-minded but cautious and to avoid extreme positions. Children, like adults, can be accurate in what they report; and, also like adults, they can distort, forget, fantasize, and be misled. As research shows, their memory processes are only human.

Quick Quiz

See whether you can reconstruct what you have read to answer these questions.

1. Memory is like (a) a wax tablet, (b) a giant file cabinet, (c) a video recorder, (d) none of these.
2. In the children's game "telephone," one person tells another person a story, the second person relates the story to a third, and so on. By the end of the game, the story will have changed considerably, which illustrates the principle that memory is __________.

3. In psychotherapy, hundreds of people have claimed to recall long-buried memories of having taken part in satanic rituals involving animal and human torture and sacrifice. Yet law-enforcement investigators and psychologists have been unable to confirm any of these reports (Goodman et al., 1995). Based on what you have learned so far, how might you explain such "memories"?

Answers:

1. d 2. reconstructive 3. Therapists who uncritically assume that satanic abuse cults are widespread may ask leading questions and make leading comments to their patients (Ganaway, 1991; Ofshe & Watters, 1994). Patients, who are susceptible to their therapists' interpretations, may then confabulate and "remember" experiences that did not happen, borrowing details from fictionalized accounts or from other traumatic experiences in their lives. If the therapist continues to probe for more details and emotions associated with the alleged experience, the result may be source amnesia and the mistaken conviction on the part of the patient that the memory is real.

MEASURING MEMORY

Now that we have seen how memory *doesn't* work—namely, like a tape recorder, an infallible filing system, or a journal written in indelible ink—we turn to studies of how it *does* work. The ability to remember is not an absolute talent; it depends on the type of performance being called for. Students who express a preference for multiple-choice, essay, or true–false exams already know this.

Conscious recollection of an event or an item of information is called **explicit memory.** It is usually measured using one of two methods. The first tests for **recall,** the ability to retrieve and reproduce information encountered earlier. Essay and fill-in-the-blank exams and memory games such as Trivial Pursuit or Jeopardy require recall. The second tests for **recognition,** the ability to identify information you have previously observed, read, or heard about. The information is given to you, and all you have to do is say whether it is old or new, or perhaps correct or incorrect, or pick it out of a set of alternatives. The task, in other words, is to compare the information you are given with the information stored in your memory. True–false and multiple-choice tests call for recognition.

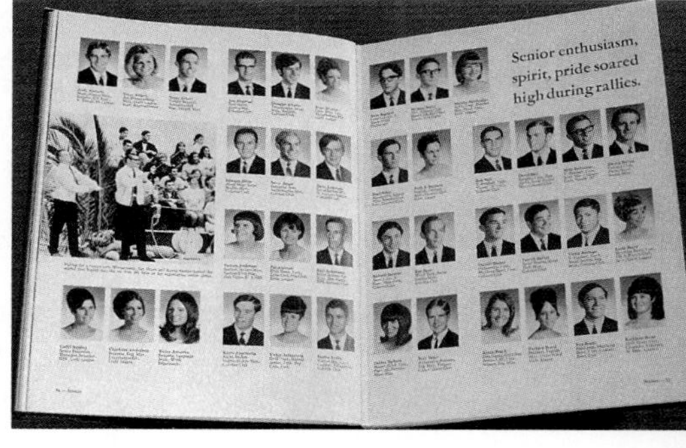

How many of your high school classmates can you recall by name? Would you do better at recognizing their pictures or their names?

As all students know, recognition tests can be tricky, especially when false items closely resemble correct ones. Under most circumstances, however, recall is the greater challenge. This difference was once demonstrated in a study of people's memories of their high school classmates (Bahrick, Bahrick, & Wittlinger, 1975). The subjects, ages 17 to 74, first wrote down the names of as many classmates as they could remember. Recall was poor; most recent graduates could write only a few dozen names, and those out of school for 40 years or more recalled an average of only 19. Even when prompted with yearbook pictures, the youngest participants failed to name almost 30 percent of their classmates, and the oldest ones failed to name more than 80 percent. Recognition, however, was far better. The task was to look at ten cards, each containing five photographs, and to say which picture on each card was that of a former classmate. Recent graduates were right 90 percent of the time, but so were people who had graduated 35 years earlier! Even those out of high school for *more than 40 years* could identify three-fourths of their classmates, and the ability to recognize names was nearly as impressive.

Sometimes information that we have retained affects our thoughts and actions even when we do not consciously or intentionally remember it—a phenomenon known as **implicit memory** (Graf & Schacter, 1985; Schacter, Chiu, & Ochsner, 1993). To get at this subtle sort of knowledge, researchers must rely on indirect methods. One common technique asks you to read or listen to some information and then

explicit memory Conscious, intentional recollection of an event or of an item of information.

recall The ability to retrieve and reproduce from memory previously encountered material.

recognition The ability to identify previously encountered material.

implicit memory Unconscious retention in memory, as evidenced by the effect of a previous experience or previously encountered information on current thoughts or actions.

GET INVOLVED

You can try this test of recall if you are familiar with the Christmas song "Rudolph the Red-Nosed Reindeer." In the song, Rudolph has eight reindeer friends; name as many of them as you can. After you've done your best, turn to the Get Involved exercise on the next page for a recognition test on the same information.

GET INVOLVED

If you took the recall test in the Get Involved exercise on page 347, now try a recognition test. From the following list, see whether you can identify the correct names of Rudolph the Red-Nosed Reindeer's eight reindeer friends:

Blitzen	*Dander*	*Dancer*	*Masher*
Cupid	*Dasher*	*Prancer*	*Comet*
Kumquat	*Donder*	*Flasher*	*Pixie*
Bouncer	*Blintzes*	*Trixie*	*Vixen*

Which was easier, recall or recognition? Can you speculate on the reason?

tests you later to see whether the information affects your performance on another type of task. With this method, called **priming,** you might read a list of words, for example, then later try to complete word stems (such as *def-*) with the first word that comes to mind (such as *define* or *defend*). Even when recognition or recall for the original list is poor, people who see the original list are more likely than control subjects to complete the word fragments with words from the list. The fact that the original words "prime" (make more available) certain responses on the word-completion task shows that people can retain more implicit knowledge about the past than they realize. They know more than they know that they know (Richardson-Klavehn & Bjork, 1988; Roediger, 1990).

Researchers have shown great ingenuity in uncovering elusive evidence of implicit memory. One group played a taped list of word pairs (such as *ocean–water*) while surgical patients were apparently unconscious. After their operations, the patients could not recall the word pairs, but when they were given the first word from each pair and were asked to say any word that popped into mind, they were somewhat more likely than they would otherwise have been to respond with the associated words they had "heard" during surgery (Kihlstrom et al., 1990). Equally fascinating research has been done with patients who, because of damage to the brain, cannot identify familiar faces. In one study, two patients shown photographs of familiar and unfamiliar people could not consciously identify the faces of people they knew. Yet electrical conductance of the skin (a measure of autonomic nervous system arousal) changed while they were looking at the familiar faces, indicating that some sort of implicit, nonconscious recognition must have been taking place (Tranel & Damasio, 1985).

Yet another method of measuring memory, the **relearning method,** or *savings method*, straddles the boundary between implicit and explicit memory tests. Devised by Hermann Ebbinghaus (1885/1913) over a century ago, the relearning method requires you to relearn information or a task that you learned earlier. If you fail to recall or recognize some or all of the material yet you master it more quickly the second time around, you must be remembering something from the first experience. One eminent memory researcher whom we consulted said that he considers the relearning method to be a test of explicit memory. Another, however, maintained that it can sometimes function as a test of implicit memory, if the learner is unaware that the material being relearned was ever learned earlier.

priming A method for measuring implicit memory, in which a person reads or listens to information and is later tested to see whether the information affects performance on another type of task.

relearning method A method for measuring retention that compares the time required to relearn material with the time used in the initial learning of the material.

MODELS OF MEMORY

Although people usually refer to memory as if it were a single faculty, as in "I must be losing my memory" or "He has a memory like an elephant's," the term *memory* actually covers a complex collection of abilities, processes, and mental systems. If tape recorders or video cameras aren't accurate metaphors for capturing these diverse components of memory, what metaphor would be better? As we saw in Chapter 8, many cognitive psychologists liken the mind to an information processor, along the lines of a computer, though more complex. They have constructed *information-processing models* of cognitive processes, borrowing liberally from the language of computer programming such terms as *inputs, output, accessing,* and *information retrieval.*

In information-processing models of memory, remembering begins with **encoding,** the conversion of information to a form that the brain can process and store. Our memories are not exact replicas of experience. Sensory information is changed in form almost as soon as it is detected, and the form retained for the long run differs from the original stimulus. One reason is that whenever we encounter new information, we integrate it with what we already know or believe, incorporating it into an existing web of knowledge called a **cognitive schema** (see Chapter 8). Often such schemas are useful because they help us make sense of separate pieces of information and thus remember them better. For example, having an overall schema of a country's history, and of the major issues and conflicts involved, makes it easier to remember specific dates and events. However, cognitive schemas can also lead to misremembering because people may distort new information in order to make it fit their existing schemas. And if the new information doesn't fit, they may ignore it—or forget it.

Even when we don't distort, we simplify. When you hear a lecture, you may hang on every word, but you do not encode those words verbatim. Instead, you convert sentences to units of meaning, possibly in the form of propositions. Propositions, as we saw in Chapter 8, are similar to sentences, but they express unitary ideas and are made up of abstract concepts rather than words. Thus the sentence "The clever psychologist made an amazing discovery" contains three propositions: *the psychologist was clever, the psychologist made a discovery,* and *the discovery was amazing.* A man who emigrated from Germany at a young age and forgot all his German would still remember facts that he learned in Germany because such information was stored as propositions, not as strings of German words.

encoding The conversion of information into a form that can be stored in and retrieved from memory.

cognitive schema An integrated network of knowledge, beliefs, and expectations concerning a particular topic or aspect of the world.

We also encode information in the form of auditory or visual images—melodies, sounds, and "pictures in the mind's eye." Visual images are particularly memorable. In one study, students looked at 612 colored slides. Then those pictures were paired with new ones, and the students had to select the ones they had previously seen. Immediately after seeing the original slides, the students identified 96.7 percent of them, and four months later, they still recognized more than 50 percent (Shepard, 1967). In another study, recognition remained high even when the original set of slides contained 2,560 different photographs (Haber, 1970).

Other forms of encoding are also possible. For example, memories for specific motor skills, such as those involved in swimming or riding a bicycle, may be encoded and stored as sets of kinesthetic (muscular) instructions. Memories for motor skills are extremely long-lasting. If you learned to swim as a child, you will still know how to swim at age 30, even if you haven't been in a pool or lake for 22 years.

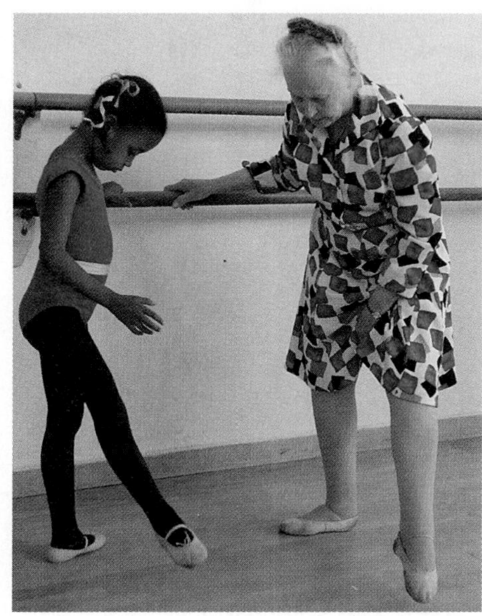

The motor skills we learn in our early years often last a lifetime.

With some kinds of information, encoding takes place automatically, without effort. Think about where you usually sit in your psychology class. When were you last there? You can probably provide this information easily, even though you never made a deliberate effort to encode it. In general, people automatically encode their location in space and time and the frequency with which they do certain things (Hasher & Zacks, 1984).

But other kinds of information require effortful encoding. To retain such information, you might have to label it, associate it with other material, or rehearse it until it is familiar. A friend of ours tells us that in her ballet class, she knows exactly what to do when asked to perform a *pas de bourrée,* yet she often has trouble recalling the term itself. Because she rarely uses it, she probably has not bothered to encode it well.

Unfortunately, people sometimes count on automatic encoding when effortful encoding is needed. For example, some students wrongly assume that they can encode the material in a textbook as effortlessly as they encode where they usually sit in the classroom. Or they assume that the ability to remember and perform well on tests is innate and that effort won't make any difference (Devolder & Pressley, 1989). As a result, they wind up in trouble at test time. Experienced students know that most of the information in a college course requires effortful encoding.

After encoding takes place, the next steps are *storage,* the maintenance of the material over time, and *retrieval,* the recovery of stored material. In most information-processing models, these processes occur in three separate, interacting systems: *sensory memory,* which retains incoming sensory information for a second or two, until it can be processed further; *short-term memory (STM),* which holds a limited amount of information for a brief period of time, perhaps up to 30 seconds or so, unless a conscious effort is made to keep it there longer; and *long-term memory (LTM),* which accounts for longer storage—from a few minutes to decades (Atkinson & Shiffrin, 1968, 1971). Information can pass from sensory memory to short-term memory and in either direction between short-term and long-term memory, as illustrated in Figure 9.1.

This model, which is sometimes informally called the "three-box model," has dominated research on memory for more than three decades. The three-box model, however, does not explain all the findings on memory, and competing information-processing models also exist. Advocates of these models disagree regarding how information passes from one kind of memory system to another and how information gets encoded and stored in each system. Some question the very notion of distinct memory systems. They argue that there is just one system, with different mental processes called on for different tasks.

Further, although many psychologists agree with Philip Johnson-Laird (1988) that "the computer is the last metaphor for the mind," others have expressed doubts about the usefulness of this metaphor. They argue that the human brain does not operate like your average computer. Most computers process instructions sequentially and work on a single stream of data, so information-processing models of memory have also represented mental processing as sequential. The human brain, however,

Figure 9.1
Three Memory Systems

In the "three-box model" of memory, information that does not transfer out of sensory memory or short-term memory is assumed to be forgotten forever. Once in long-term memory, information can be retrieved for use in analyzing incoming sensory information or performing mental operations in short-term memory.

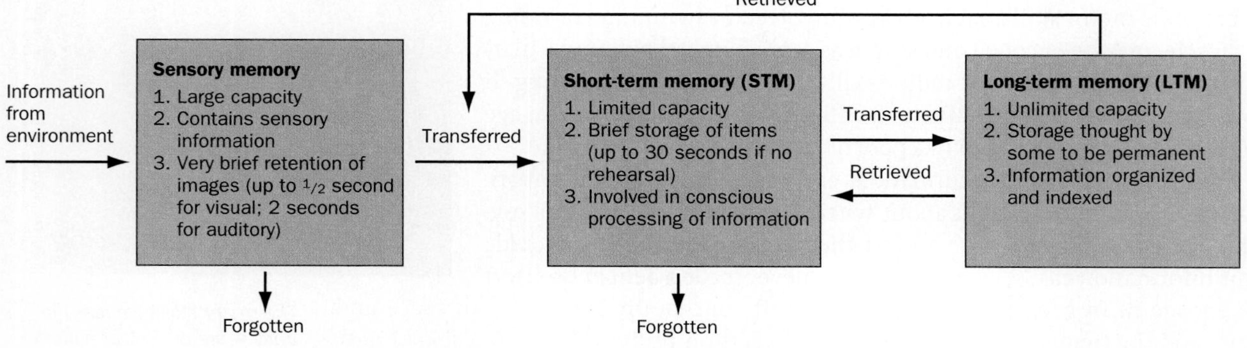

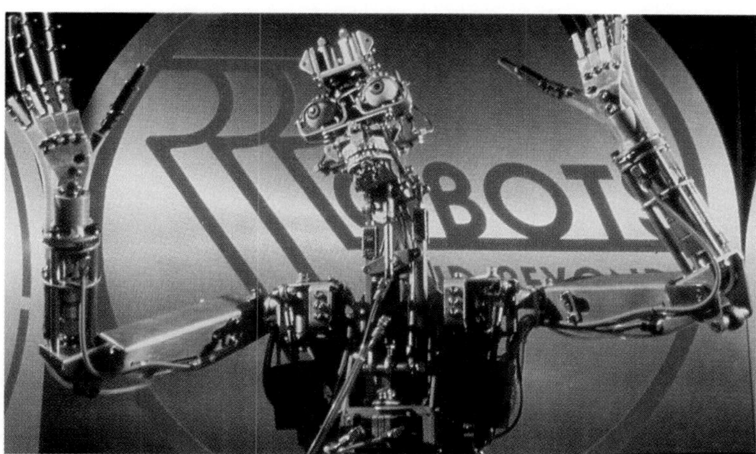

This cheerful piece of machinery informed visitors to the Boston Museum of Science, "Humans, you are witnessing the beginning of a great new era." Yet robots and their computer "brains" cannot contemplate the meaning of death, paint a great work of art, or know that it's time to prune the roses simply by looking at them. Most computers operate sequentially on previously stored information, whereas human brains make multiple connections all at once.

performs many operations simultaneously—that is, in parallel. It recognizes patterns all at once rather than as a sequence of information bits. It monitors bodily functions, perceives the environment, produces speech, and searches memory all at the same time. It can do this because millions of neurons are active at once, and each neuron communicates with thousands of others, which in turn communicate with millions more. Although no single neuron is terribly smart or terribly fast, millions of them working at the same time produce the complexities of cognition.

Some cognitive scientists, therefore, have rejected the traditional information-processing approach in favor of a **parallel distributed processing (PDP),** or *connectionist,* model (Bechtel & Abrahamsen, 1990; McClelland, 1994; Rumelhart, McClelland, & the PDP Research Group, 1986). In PDP models, knowledge is represented not as propositions or images but as connections among thousands and thousands of interacting processing units, distributed in a vast network and all operating in parallel—just like the neurons of the brain. As new information enters the system, the ability of these units to excite or inhibit each other is constantly adjusted to reflect new knowledge.

Although the details of PDP theory are beyond the scope of this book, we want to point out that it reverses the notion that the human brain can be modeled after a computer. PDP theorists say that for computers to be truly intelligent, they must be modeled after the human brain. Indeed, computer scientists are now designing machines called *neural networks* that attempt to imitate the brain's vast grid of densely connected neurons (Anderson & Rosenfeld, 1988; Levine, 1990). In these machines, thousands of simple processing units are linked up to one another in a weblike system, interacting with each other and operating in parallel. And researchers in the field of *artificial intelligence* have been writing programs that simulate the way in which PDP theorists believe the human mind works. Like human beings, these programs do not always find the best solution to a problem, but they do tend to find a good solution quickly. They also have the potential to learn from experience by adjusting the strengths of their "neural" connections in response to new information.

It is not clear whether the connectionist approach is an improvement on information-processing models. Both approaches can explain many findings about memory, but neither one can explain all the findings. PDP models have the virtue of resembling the brain's actual wiring, and they are applicable not just to memory but also to perception, language, and decision making. But traditional information-processing models do a better job, at least for now, of explaining memory for a single event (Schacter, 1990). They are also better at explaining why well-learned information is sometimes forgotten when new information is learned (Ratcliff, 1990).

In this chapter, we have decided to retain the information-processing model of three separate memory systems—sensory, short-term, and long-term—because it offers a convenient way to organize the major findings on memory, does a good job of

parallel distributed processing (PDP) An alternative to the information-processing model of memory, in which knowledge is represented as connections among thousands of interacting processing units, distributed in a vast network, and all operating in parallel.

accounting for these findings, and is consistent with biological facts about memory (to be described later). But keep in mind that the computer metaphor could one day be as outdated as the metaphor of memory as a camera.

Quick Quiz

How well have you encoded what you just learned?

1. Alberta solved a crossword puzzle a few days ago. She no longer has any conscious recollection of the words in the puzzle, but while playing a game of Scrabble with her brother, she unconsciously tends to form words that were in the puzzle, showing that she has __________ memories of some of the words.
2. The three basic memory processes are __________, storage, and __________.
3. Do the preceding two questions ask for recall, recognition, or relearning? (And what about *this* question?)
4. One objection to traditional information-processing theories of memory is that unlike most computers, which process information __________, the brain performs many independent operations __________.

Answers:

1. implicit 2. encoding, retrieval 3. The first two questions both measure recall; the third question measures recognition. 4. sequentially; simultaneously, or in parallel

THE THREE-BOX MODEL

The three systems described by the three-box model of memory can be viewed as clusters of mental processes that occur at different stages.

FLEETING IMPRESSIONS: SENSORY MEMORY

In the three-box model, all incoming sensory information must make a brief stop in **sensory memory,** the entryway of memory. Sensory memory includes a number of separate memory subsystems, or **sensory registers**—as many as there are senses. Information in sensory memory is short-lived. Visual images, or *icons,* remain in a visual register for a maximum of half a second. Auditory images, or *echoes,* remain in an auditory register for a slightly longer time, by most estimates up to two seconds or so.

sensory memory A memory system that momentarily preserves extremely accurate images of sensory information.

sensory registers Subsystems of sensory memory; most memory models assume a separate register for each sensory modality.

Sensory memory acts as a holding bin, retaining information just until we can select items for attention from the stream of stimuli bombarding our senses. *Pattern recognition,* the preliminary identification of a stimulus on the basis of information already contained in long-term memory, occurs during the transfer of information

GET INVOLVED

Go into a dark room or closet and swing a flashlight rapidly in a circle. You will see an unbroken circle of light instead of a series of separate points. The reason: The successive images remain briefly in sensory memory.

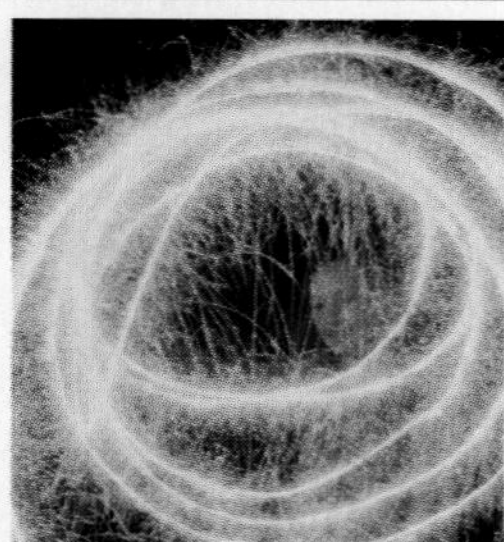

from sensory memory to short-term memory. Information that does not go on to short-term memory vanishes forever, like a message written in disappearing ink.

Images in sensory memory are fairly complete. How do we know that? In a clever experiment, George Sperling (1960) briefly showed people visual arrays of letters that looked like this:

X K C Q
N D X G
T F R J

In previous studies, subjects had been able to recall only four or five letters, no matter how many they initially saw. Yet many people insisted that they had actually seen more items. Some of the letters, they said, seemed to slip away from memory before they could report them. To overcome this problem, Sperling devised a method of "partial report." He had people report the first row of letters when they heard a high tone, the middle row when they heard a medium tone, and the third row when they heard a low tone:

X K C Q ← **High tone**
N D X G ← **Medium tone**
T F R J ← **Low tone**

If the tone occurred right after they saw the array, people could recall about three letters from a row. Because they did not know beforehand which row they would have to report, they therefore must have had most of the letters in sensory memory right after viewing them. However, if the tone occurred after a delay of even one second, people remembered very little of what they had seen. The letters had slipped away.

In normal processing, too, sensory memory needs to clear quickly to prevent sensory "double exposures." It also acts as a filter, keeping out extraneous and unimportant information. Our brains process billions of bits of information during our lifetimes. Storing everything detected by our senses, including irrelevancies, would lead to inefficiency and confusion.

If the visual sensory register did not clear quickly, multiple images might interfere with the accurate perception and encoding of information.

MEMORY'S WORK AREA: SHORT-TERM MEMORY

Like sensory memory, **short-term memory (STM)** retains information only temporarily—for up to about 30 seconds by most estimates, although some researchers think that the maximum interval may extend to a few minutes. In short-term memory, the material is no longer an exact sensory image but is an encoding of one, such as a word or a number. This material either transfers into long-term memory or decays and is lost forever.

Cases of brain injury demonstrate the importance of transferring new information from short-term memory into long-term memory. H. M.'s case is again instructive. H. M., you will recall, can store information on a short-term basis; he can hold a conversation and appears normal when you first meet him. He also retains implicit memories. However, for the most part, H. M. cannot retain information about new facts and events for longer than a few minutes. His terrible memory deficits involve a problem in transferring explicit memories from short-term storage into long-term storage. (If extraordinary measures are taken to get new visual information into H. M.'s long-term memory, he then remembers the material normally [McKee & Squire, 1992]. But usually information does not make it into his long-term memory in the first place.)

Besides retaining new information for brief periods, short-term memory also holds information that has been retrieved from long-term memory for temporary

short-term memory (STM) In the three-box model of memory, a limited-capacity memory system involved in the retention of information for brief periods; it is also used to hold information retrieved from long-term memory for temporary use.

use, providing the equivalent of a mental scratch pad. For this reason, short-term memory is often referred to as *working memory.* When you do an arithmetic problem, working memory contains the numbers and the instructions for doing the necessary operations ("Add the right-hand column, carry the 2"), plus the intermediate results from each step. The ability to bring information from long-term memory into working memory is not disrupted in patients such as H. M. They can do arithmetic, converse, relate events that occurred before their injury, and do anything else that requires retrieval of information from long-term into short-term memory.

People such as H. M. fall at the extreme end on a continuum of forgetfulness, but even those of us with normal memories know from personal experience how frustratingly brief short-term retention can be. We look up a telephone number, dial it, get a busy signal, and then find after only a moment that the number has vanished from our minds. We meet a woman at a party and two minutes later find ourselves groping unsuccessfully for her name. Is it any wonder that short-term memory has been called a "leaky bucket"?

According to most memory models, if the bucket did not leak, it would quickly overflow, because at any given moment, short-term memory can hold only so many items. Years ago, George Miller (1956) estimated its capacity to be "the magical number 7 plus or minus 2." Five-number zip codes and 7-number telephone numbers fall conveniently in this range; 15-digit credit card numbers do not. But some researchers have questioned whether Miller's magical number is so magical after all. Estimates of STM's capacity have ranged from 2 items to 20, with most of the estimates at the lower end. Some psychologists believe that it is not STM per se that is limited, but rather the processing capacity available to the entire memory system at any one time. Everyone agrees, however, that the number of items that short-term memory can handle at any one time is quite small.

If this is so, then how do we remember the beginning of a spoken sentence until the speaker reaches the end? After all, most sentences are longer than just a few words. According to most models of memory, we overcome this problem by grouping small bits of information into larger units, or **chunks.** The real capacity of STM, it turns out, is not a few bits of information but a few chunks. A chunk may be a word, a phrase, a sentence, or even a visual image, and it depends on previous experience. For most of us, the acronym *FBI* is one chunk, not three, and the date *1492* is one chunk, not four. In contrast, the number *9214* is four chunks and *IBF* is three—unless your address is 9214 or your initials are IBF. Take another, more visual example: If you are not familiar with football and look at a field full of players, you probably won't be able to remember their positions when you look away. But if you are a fan of the game, you may see a single chunk of information—say, a wishbone formation—and be able to retain it.

If you don't play chess, you probably won't be able to recall the positions of these chess pieces after looking away. But experienced chess players, in the middle of a game, can remember the position of every piece after glancing only briefly at the board. They are able to "chunk" the pieces into a few standard configurations, instead of trying to memorize where each piece is located.

Even chunking, however, cannot keep short-term memory from eventually filling up. Fortunately, much of the information we encounter during the day is needed for only a few moments. If you are multiplying two numbers, you need to remember them only until you have the answer. If you are talking to someone, you need to keep the person's words in mind only until you have understood them. But some information is needed for longer periods and must be transferred to long-term memory. Items that are particularly meaningful, have an emotional impact, or link up to

chunk A meaningful unit of information; it may be composed of smaller units.

something already in long-term memory may enter long-term storage easily, with only a brief stay in STM. The destiny of other items depends on how soon new information displaces them in short-term memory. Material in short-term memory is easily displaced unless we do something to keep it there—as we will discuss shortly.

FINAL DESTINATION: LONG-TERM MEMORY

The third box in the information-processing model of memory is the largest: **long-term memory (LTM).** The capacity of long-term memory seems to have no practical limits. The vast amount of information stored there enables us to learn, get around in the environment, and build a sense of identity and a personal history.

ORGANIZATION IN LONG-TERM MEMORY Because long-term memory contains so much information, we cannot search through it exhaustively, as we can through short-term memory. According to most models of memory, the information must be organized and indexed, just as items in a library are, so that we can find it. One way to index words (or the concepts they represent) is by the semantic categories to which they belong. *Chair*, for example, belongs to the category *furniture*. In a classic study, people had to memorize 60 words that came from four semantic categories: animals, vegetables, names, and professions. The words were presented in random order, but when people were allowed to recall the items in any order they wished, they tended to recall them in clusters corresponding to the four categories (Bousfield, 1953). This finding has since been replicated many times.

long-term memory (LTM) In the three-box model of memory, the memory system involved in the long-term storage of information.

Evidence on the storage of information by semantic category also comes from cases of people with brain damage. For example, one patient called M. D. appeared to have made a complete recovery two years after suffering several strokes, with one odd exception: He had trouble remembering the names of fruits and vegetables. M. D. could easily name a picture of an abacus or a sphinx but not a picture of an orange or a carrot. He could sort pictures of animals, vehicles, and other objects into their appropriate categories but did poorly with pictures of fruits and vegetables. On the other hand, when M. D. was *given* the names of fruits and vegetables, he immediately pointed to the corresponding pictures (Hart, Berndt, & Caramazza, 1985). Apparently, M. D. still had information about fruits and vegetables, but his brain lesion prevented him from using their names to get to the information when he needed it, unless the names were provided by someone else. This evidence suggests that information about a particular concept (such as *orange*) is linked in some way to information about the concept's semantic category (such as *fruit*).

Culture affects the encoding, storage, and retrieval of information. Navajo healers, who use stylized, symbolic sand paintings in their rituals, must commit to memory dozens of intricate designs because no exact copies are made and the painting is destroyed after each ceremony.

Many models of long-term memory represent its contents as a vast network or grid of interrelated concepts and propositions (Anderson, 1990; Collins & Loftus, 1975). A small part of a conceptual grid for *animals* might look something like the one in Figure 9.2. Network models assume that semantic networks are a universal way of organizing information. The way people use these networks, however, depends on experience and education. For example, studies of rural children in Liberia and Guatemala have shown that the more schooling children have, the more likely they are to use semantic categories in recalling lists of objects (Cole & Cole, 1993). This makes sense, because in school, children must memorize a lot of information in a short time, and

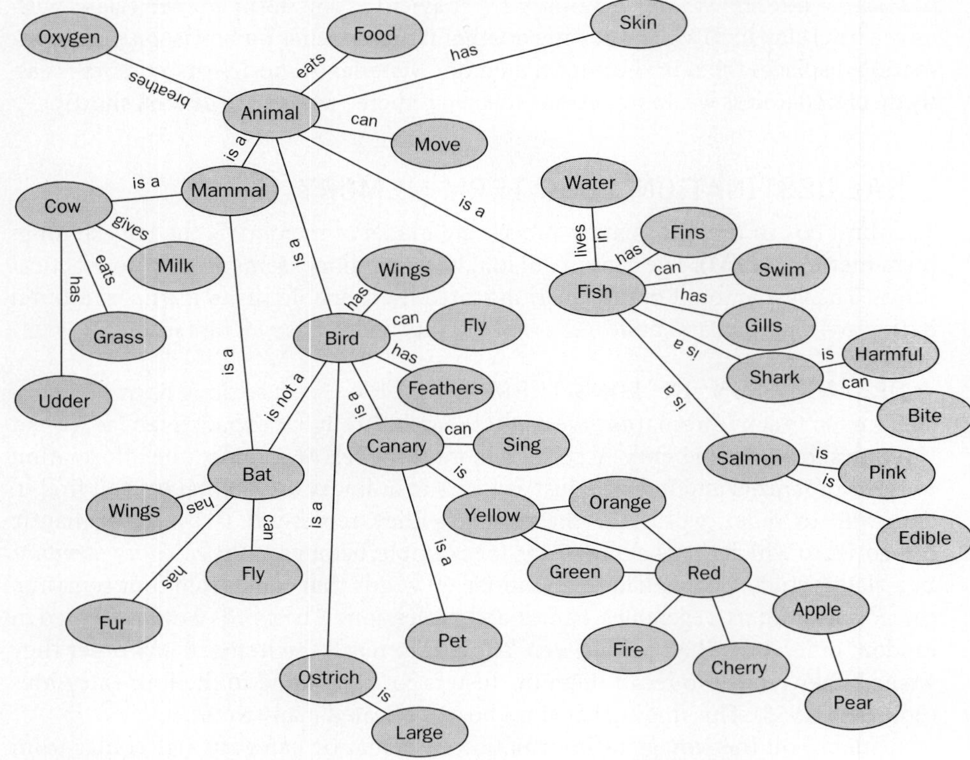

Figure 9.2
Part of a Conceptual Grid in Long-term Memory

Many models of memory represent the contents of long-term semantic memory as an immense network or grid of concepts and the relationships among them. This illustration shows part of a hypothetical grid for animals.

semantic grouping can help. Unschooled children, having less need to memorize lists, do not cluster items and do not remember them as well. But this does not mean that unschooled children have poor memories. When the task is meaningful to them—say, recalling objects that were in a story or a village scene—they remember extremely well (Mistry & Rogoff, 1994).

We organize information in long-term memory not only by semantic groupings but also in terms of the way words sound or look. Have you ever tried to recall some word that was on the "tip of your tongue"? Nearly everyone experiences such *tip-of-the-tongue (TOT) states,* especially when trying to recall the names of acquaintances or famous persons, the names of objects and places, or the titles of movies or books (Burke et al., 1991). TOT states are reported even by users of sign language, who call them tip-of-the-finger experiences! One way to study this frustrating state is to have people record tip-of-the-tongue episodes in daily diaries. Another is to give people the definitions of uncommon words and ask them to supply the words. When a word is on the tip of the tongue, people tend to come up with words that are similar in meaning to the right one before they finally recall it. For example, for "patronage bestowed on a relative, in business or politics" a person might say "favoritism" rather than the correct response, "nepotism." But verbal information in long-term memory also seems to be indexed by sound and form, and it is retrievable on that basis. Thus, incorrect guesses often have the correct number of syllables, the correct stress pattern, the correct first letter, or the correct prefix or suffix (A. Brown, 1991; R. Brown & McNeill, 1966). For example, for the target word *sampan* (an Asian boat), a person might say "Siam" or "sarong."

Information in long-term memory may also be organized by its familiarity, relevance, or association with other information. The method a person uses in any given instance probably depends on the nature of the memory; you would no doubt store information about the major cities of Europe differently from information about your first date. To understand the organization of long-term memory, then, we must know what kinds of information can be stored there.

THE CONTENTS OF LONG-TERM MEMORY Most theories of memory distinguish skills or habits ("knowing how") from abstract or representational knowledge ("knowing that"). **Procedural memories** are memories of knowing how—for example, knowing how to comb your hair, use a pencil, solve a jigsaw puzzle, knit a sweater, or swim. Some researchers consider procedural memories to be implicit rather than explicit, because once skills and habits are well learned, they do not require much conscious processing. **Declarative memories** are memories of "knowing that," and they are usually assumed to be explicit.

Declarative memories, in turn, come in two varieties, semantic memories and episodic memories (Tulving, 1985). **Semantic memories** are internal representations of the world, independent of any particular context. They include facts, rules, and concepts—items of general knowledge. On the basis of your semantic memory of the concept *cat*, you can describe a cat as a small, furry mammal that typically spends its time eating, sleeping, prowling, and staring into space, even though a cat may not be present when you give this description, and you probably won't know how or when you first learned it. **Episodic memories,** on the other hand, are internal representations of personally experienced events. When you remember how your cat once surprised you in the middle of the night by pouncing on your face as you slept, you are retrieving an episodic memory. You might draw on procedural memories to ride a bike, semantic memories to identify a bird, and episodic memories to recall your wedding. The following diagram summarizes these distinctions. Can you come up with some other examples for each type of memory?

procedural memories Memories for the performance of actions or skills ("knowing how").

declarative memories Memories of facts, rules, concepts, and events ("knowing that"); they include semantic and episodic memories.

semantic memories Memories of general knowledge, including facts, rules, concepts, and propositions.

episodic memories Memories of personally experienced events and the contexts in which they occurred.

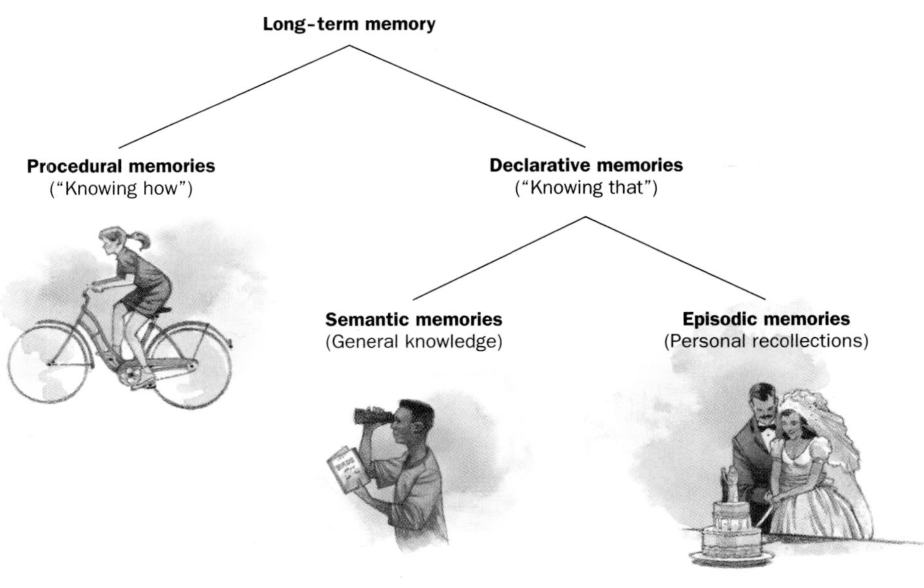

FROM SHORT-TERM TO LONG-TERM MEMORY: A RIDDLE The three-box model of memory has often been invoked to explain an interesting phenomenon called the **serial-position effect.** If you are shown a list of items and are then asked immediately to recall them, your retention of any particular item will depend on its position in the list (Glanzer & Cunitz, 1966). Recall will be best for items at the beginning of the list (the *primacy effect*) and at the end of the list (the *recency effect*). When retention of all the items is plotted, the result will be a U-shaped curve, as shown in Figure 9.3. A serial-position effect occurs when you are introduced to a roomful of people and find you can recall the names of the first few people and the last, but almost no one in the middle.

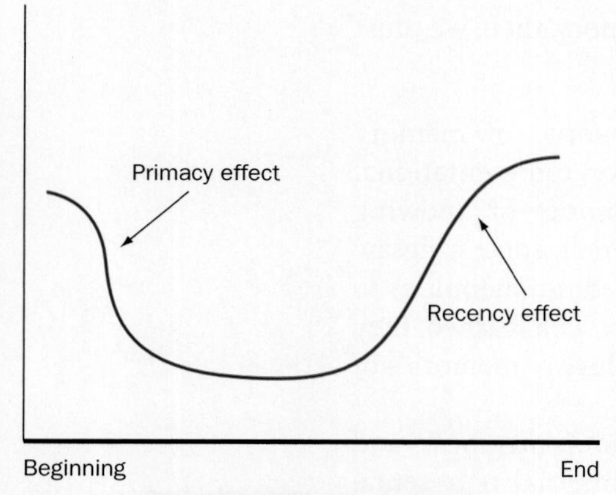

Figure 9.3
The Serial-Position Effect

When people try to recall a list of similar items immediately after learning it, they tend to remember the first and last items best and the ones in the middle worst.

According to the three-box model, the first few items on a list are remembered well because they have the best chance of getting into long-term memory. Because short-term memory was relatively "empty" when they entered, these items did not have to compete with other ones to make it into long-term memory. They were thoroughly processed (verbally encoded), so they remain memorable. The last few items are remembered for a different reason: At the time of recall, they are still sitting in short-term memory. The items in the middle of a list, however, are not so well retained because by the time they get into short-term memory, it is already crowded. As a result, many of these items drop out of short-term memory before they can be stored in long-term memory.

This explanation makes sense, except for two things. First, under some conditions, the last items on a list are well remembered even when the test is delayed past the time when short-term memory has presumably been "emptied" and filled with other information (Greene, 1986). In other words, the recency effect occurs even when, according to the three-box model, it should not. Second, serial-position curves occur in animals, including rats and birds, when they have to remember a series of places in a maze or cage (Crystal & Shettleworth, 1994; Kesner, Chiba, & Jackson-Smith, 1994). Therefore, the primacy effect can't be due just to the verbal processing of information (unless rats are miraculously muttering to themselves the rat equivalent of "two lefts, then a right . . . "). Whatever is producing these effects, researchers are not yet sure what it is—another puzzle of memory.

serial-position effect The tendency for recall of the first and last items on a list to surpass recall of items in the middle of the list.

Quick Quiz

Find out whether the findings just discussed have transferred from your short-term memory to your long-term memory.

1. __________ memory holds images for a fraction of a second.
2. For most people, the abbreviation *U.S.A.* consists of __________ informational chunk(s).
3. Suppose you must memorize a long list of words that includes the following: *desk, pig, gold, dog, chair, silver, table, rooster, bed, copper,* and *horse.* If you can recall the words in any order you wish, how are you likely to group them in recall? Why?
4. When you roller-blade, are you relying on procedural, semantic, or episodic memory? How about when you recall the months of the year? How about when you remember falling while roller-blading on an icy January day?
5. If a child is trying to memorize the alphabet, which sequence should present the greatest difficulty: *abcdefg, klmnopq,* or *tuvwxyz?* Why?

Answers:

1. sensory 2. one 3. *Desk, chair, table,* and *bed* would probably form one cluster; *pig, dog, rooster,* and *horse* a second; and *gold, silver,* and *copper* a third. Concepts tend to be organized in long-term memory in terms of semantic categories, such as *furniture, animals,* and *metals.* 4. procedural; semantic; episodic 5. *klmnopq,* because of the serial-position effect

HOW TO REMEMBER

Once we understand how memory works, we can use that understanding to remember better. One important technique for keeping information in short-term memory and increasing the chances of long-term retention is *rehearsal,* the review or practice of material. When people are prevented from rehearsing, the contents of their short-term memories quickly fade. In an early study of this phenomenon, people had to memorize meaningless groups of letters. Immediately afterward, they had to start counting backward by threes from an arbitrary number; this counting prevented them from rehearsing the letter groups. Within only 18 seconds, the subjects forgot most of the items (see Figure 9.4). But when they did not have to count backward, their performance was much better, probably because they were rehearsing the items to themselves (Peterson & Peterson, 1959). Similarly, if you repeat a telephone number over and over, you will be able to retain it in short-term memory for as long as you like; but if you look up a number and then get into a conversation with someone, you are apt to forget the number almost immediately.

A dramatic and poignant demonstration of the power of rehearsal once occurred during a session with H. M. (Ogden & Corkin, 1991). The experimenter gave H. M. five digits to repeat and remember, but then she was unexpectedly called away. When she returned after more than an hour, H. M. was able to repeat the five digits correctly. He had been rehearsing them the entire time!

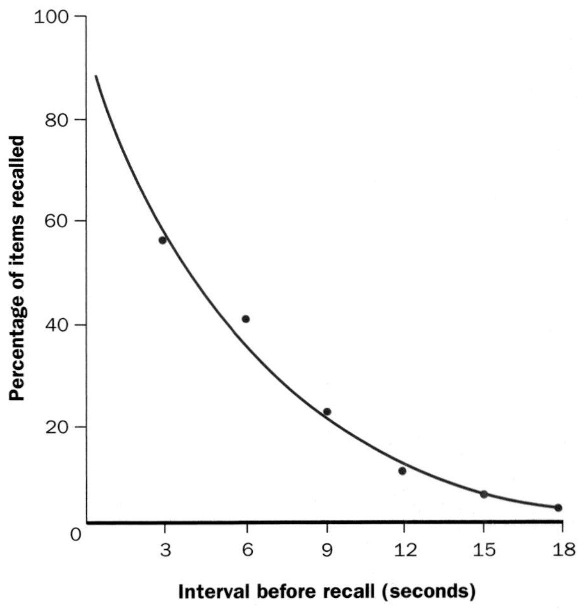

Figure 9.4
Going, Going, Gone
As this graph shows, without rehearsal, the ability to recall information in short-term memory quickly falls off. (From Peterson & Peterson, 1959.)

Short-term memory holds many kinds of information, including visual information and abstract meanings. In fact, some theorists believe that there are several STMs, each specializing in a particular type of information. But most people—or at least most hearing people—seem to favor speech for rehearsing the contents of short-term memory. The speech may be spoken aloud or to oneself. When people make errors on short-term memory tests that use letters or words, they often confuse items that sound the same or similar, such as *b* and *t,* or *bear* and *bare.* These errors suggest that they have been rehearsing verbally.

Some strategies for rehearsing are more effective than others. **Maintenance rehearsal** involves merely the rote repetition of the material. This kind of rehearsal is fine for keeping information in STM, but it will not always lead to long-term retention. A better strategy if you want to remember for the long haul is **elaborative rehearsal,** also called *elaboration of encoding* (Cermak & Craik, 1979; Craik & Tulving, 1975). Elaboration involves associating new items of information with material that has already been stored or with other new facts. It can also involve analyzing the physical, sensory, or semantic features of an item (see Figure 9.5).

Suppose, for example, that you are studying the concept of reinforcement in Chapter 7. Simply rehearsing the definition in a rote manner is unlikely to transfer the information you need from short-term to long-term memory. Instead, when go-

maintenance rehearsal Rote repetition of material in order to maintain its availability in memory.

elaborative rehearsal Association of new information with already stored knowledge and analysis of the new information to make it memorable.

Figure 9.5
Elaboration of Encoding

In elaborated encoding, you encode the features of an item and its associations with other items in memory. When you studied the hypothalamus in Chapter 4, was your encoding elaborated or impoverished?

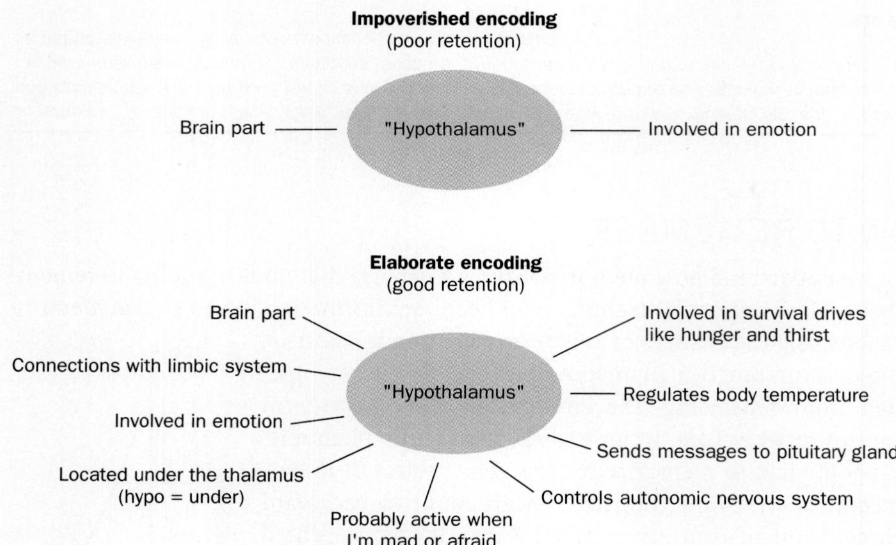

ing over (rehearsing) the concept, you could encode the information that a reinforcer follows a response, strengthens the response, and is similar to a reward. You might also note that the word *reinforcer* starts with the same two letters as *reward.* And you might think up some examples of reinforcement and of how you have used it in your own life and could use it in the future. The more you elaborate the concept of reinforcement, the better you will remember it.

A related strategy for prolonging retention is **deep processing,** or the processing of meaning. If you process only the physical or sensory features of a stimulus, such as how the word *reinforcement* is spelled and how it sounds, your processing will be shallow even if it is elaborated. If you recognize patterns and assign labels to objects or events ("Reinforcement is an operant procedure"), your processing will be somewhat deeper. If you fully analyze the meaning of what you are trying to remember, your processing will be deeper yet. Sometimes, shallow processing is useful; when you memorize a poem, for instance, you will want to pay attention to (and elaborately encode) the sounds of the words and the patterns of rhythm in the poem, and not just the poem's meaning. Usually, however, deep processing is more effective. Unfortunately, students (and other people) often try to memorize information that has little or no meaning for them, which explains why the information doesn't stick.

In addition to using elaborative rehearsal and deep processing, people who want to give their powers of memory a boost sometimes employ **mnemonics** [neh-MON-iks], formal strategies and tricks for encoding, storing, and retaining information. (Mnemosyne—neh-MOZ-eh-nee—was the ancient Greek goddess of memory; can you think of a mnemonic to remember her?) Some mnemonics take the form of easily memorized rhymes (e.g., "Thirty days hath September / April, June, and November . . . "). Others use formulas (e.g., "**E**very **g**ood **b**oy **d**oes **f**ine" for remembering which notes are on the lines of the treble clef in musical notation). Still others use visual images or word associations, which increase retention.

deep processing In the encoding of information, the processing of meaning rather than simply the physical or sensory features of a stimulus.

mnemonics Strategies and tricks for improving memory, such as the use of a verse or a formula.

The best mnemonics force you to encode material actively and thoroughly. They may also reduce the amount of information by chunking it (as in the phone number 466-3293, which corresponds to the letters in GOOD-BYE—appropriate, perhaps, for a travel agency). Or they may make the material meaningful and thus easier to store and retrieve; facts and words to be memorized are often more memorable, for example, if they are woven into a coherent story (Bower & Clark, 1969). If you needed to remember the parts of the digestive system for a physiology course, you could construct a narrative about what happens to a piece of food after it enters a person's mouth, then repeat the narrative out loud to yourself or to a study partner.

This customized license plate is much easier to remember than, say, 5LVP496.

Some stage performers with amazing recall rely on more complicated mnemonics. We are not going to spend time on them here, because for ordinary memory tasks, such tricks are often no more effective than rote rehearsal, and sometimes they are actually worse (Wang, Thomas, & Ouellette, 1992). Most memory researchers do not use such mnemonics themselves (Park, Smith, & Cavanaugh, 1990). After all, why bother to memorize a grocery list using a fancy mnemonic when you can write down what you need to buy? The fastest route to a good memory is to follow the principles suggested by the findings in this section and by other research on memory (see "Taking Psychology with You").

Very Quick Quiz

Camille is furious with her history professor. "I read the chapter three times, but I still failed the quiz," she fumes. "The quiz must have been unfair." What's wrong with Camille's reasoning, and what are some other possible explanations for her poor performance, based on principles of critical thinking and what you have learned so far in this chapter?

Answer:

Camille is reasoning emotionally and is not examining the assumptions underlying her explanations. Perhaps she relied on automatic rather than effortful encoding, used maintenance instead of elaborative rehearsal, and used shallow instead of deep processing when she studied. She may also have tried to encode everything, instead of being selective.

THE BIOLOGY OF MEMORY

So far we have been discussing memory solely in terms of information processing. But what is happening in the brain while all that processing is going on? What changes occur in neurons and synapses (the small gaps between neurons) when we store information about an event or a task? Where in the brain do these changes take place? And how might hormones and other substances regulate or improve memory? In work on these issues, researchers draw on many of the concepts already covered in this chapter and in Chapter 4. (It might help you to encode the following information in your own memory if you review the material in Chapter 4 first.)

CHANGES IN NEURONS AND SYNAPSES

Forming a memory involves chemical and structural changes at the level of neurons. But why do some memories last only a few seconds or minutes, whereas others persist for years or even a lifetime? Why, when a blow on the head or an electroconvulsive shock disrupts brain activity, do people often lose information stored during the past few minutes but not information stored weeks or years ago?

One answer is that short-term memory and long-term memory involve different kinds of brain changes. In short-term memory, changes occur within neurons that temporarily alter their ability to release neurotransmitters, the chemicals that carry messages from one cell to another. Evidence comes from studies with sea snails, sea slugs, and other organisms that have small numbers of easily identifiable neurons

(Alkon, 1989; Kandel & Schwartz, 1982). These primitive animals can be taught simple conditioned responses, such as withdrawing or not withdrawing parts of their bodies in response to a light touch. When the animal retains the skill only for the short term, the neuron or neurons involved temporarily show an increase or decrease in readiness to release neurotransmitter molecules, depending on the kind of response being learned.

In contrast, long-term memory involves permanent structural changes in the brain. To mimic what they think may happen during the formation of a long-term memory, researchers apply brief, high-frequency electrical stimulation to groups of neurons in the brains of animals. In various areas, especially the hippocampus, this stimulation leads to a long-lasting increase in the strength of synaptic responsiveness, known as **long-term potentiation** (McNaughton & Morris, 1987; Teyler & DiScenna, 1987). In other words, some synaptic pathways become more excitable. Long-term potentiation seems to occur as a result of two events: (1) an increase in the release of the neurotransmitter glutamate from transmitting neurons, and (2) a complex sequence of chemical reactions in receiving neurons, which increases or alters ion channels in glutamate receptors, making the neurons more receptive to stimulation (Bliss & Collingridge, 1993). One result is that the tiny spines (projections) that cover the dendrites of the receiving neuron change shape, becoming rounder. This change in turn causes decreased electrical resistance and increased responsiveness of the receiving neuron to the next signal that comes along. It is a little like what would happen if you increased the diameter of a funnel's neck to permit greater flow through the funnel.

Other related changes also occur in long-term potentiation and, presumably, the formation of long-term memories. For example, dendrites grow and branch out, and certain types of synapses increase in number (Greenough, 1984). At the same time, in a less well understood process, some neurons become *less* responsive than they were previously (Bolshakov & Siegelbaum, 1994). These changes all take time, which may explain why long-term memories remain vulnerable to disruption for a while after they are stored. Just as concrete takes time to set, the neural and synaptic changes in the brain that underlie long-term memory take time to develop; memories, therefore, require a period of **consolidation,** or stabilization, before they solidify. This process appears to be a gradual rather than an all-or-nothing process. If an animal gets electrical shock within the first hour after learning a task, it will forget what it has learned, which indicates that little if any consolidation has occurred. If the shock is delivered several hours or a few days after learning, the memory will be unaffected, which implies that consolidation has taken place by then. But *repeated* sessions of shock during this period will again disrupt the memory, showing that the process is not yet complete (Squire, 1987). Consolidation can continue in animals for weeks and in human beings for several years.

LOCATING MEMORIES

In 1996 a little study made big headlines: Researchers had their first clue that true memories might actually be located in a different part of the brain from false memories. PET scans showed that false and true memories for words heard in lists triggered different patterns of brain activity: Only true memories produced activity in left-hemisphere areas involved in processing sounds and speech; only false memories activated frontal-lobe areas thought to be involved in conscious attempts to remember information (Schacter et al., 1996). Some writers wondered whether these

long-term potentiation A long-lasting increase in the strength of synaptic responsiveness, thought to be a biological mechanism of long-term memory.

consolidation The process by which a long-term memory becomes durable and stable.

results would lead to a "litmus test" for distinguishing real memories from phony ones. (Think of all the family quarrels that could finally be resolved, such as the one about whether Sam's niece was really at that New Year's party!)

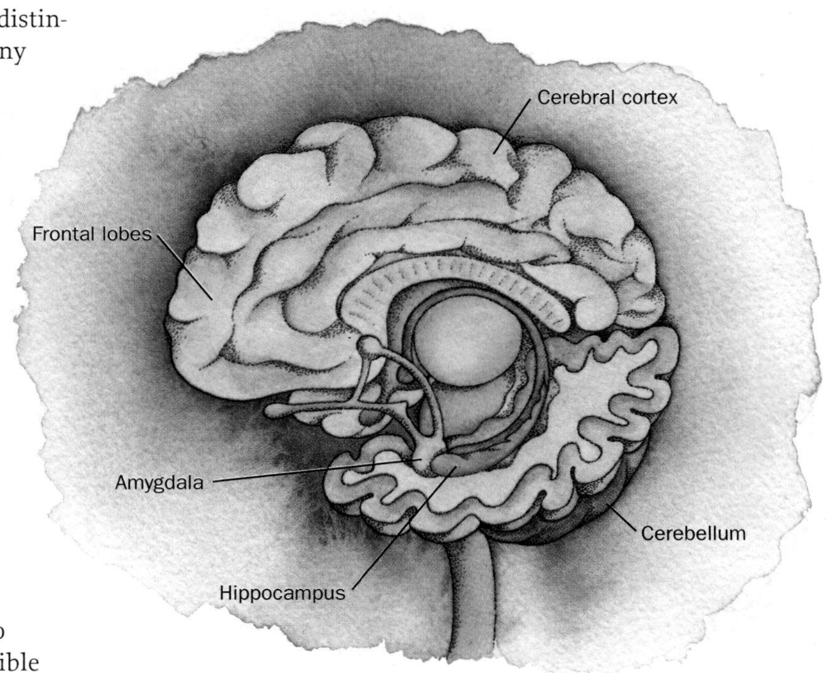

Figure 9.6
Brain Areas Critical for Memory

The regions shown are particularly important in the formation or storage of memories.

Such a test is a long way off and may never be possible; no one knows yet whether these results from a study of list learning will generalize to memories for real events and experiences. Nevertheless, this research illustrates one of the most important modern developments in the biological study of memory: the ability to use microelectrodes, brain-scan technology, and other laboratory techniques to identify the brain structures responsible for the formation and location of specific types of memories (see Figure 9.6). Work in this area shows that during short-term memory tasks, when STM functions as a working memory, specific areas in the prefrontal cortex of the brain are especially active (Goldman-Rakic, 1992, 1996). And during the formation of long-term declarative memories (memory for facts and events, or "knowing that"), the hippocampus and adjacent parts of the temporal lobe play a critical role (Squire & Zola-Morgan, 1991). The hippocampus is especially important: Damage that is limited to this structure results in amnesia for facts and events (Press, Amaral, & Squire, 1989).

In contrast, the formation of procedural memories (memory for skills and habits, or "knowing how") seems to involve other brain structures and pathways. For example, in work with rabbits, Richard Thompson (1983, 1986) has shown that one kind of procedural memory—a simple, classically conditioned response to an unpleasant stimulus—is associated with specific changes in the cerebellum. After Thompson conditioned rabbits to blink in response to a tone, he discovered changes in electrical activity in parts of the cerebellum. If he removed or destroyed the affected brain tissue, the animals immediately forgot the response and could not relearn it. In another study, Thompson and his colleagues used a drug to temporarily deaden either a specific part of the cerebellum or a specific part of the midbrain. In both cases, the rabbits failed to blink during training. When the drug wore off, the rabbits whose midbrain areas had been deadened blinked away when the tone sounded, but the rabbits whose cerebellums had been drugged showed no sign of having learned the response (Krupa, Thompson, & Thompson, 1993).

The formation of declarative and procedural memories in different brain areas could explain a curious finding about H. M. and other patients like him. Despite their inability to form new declarative memories, such patients can, with sufficient practice, acquire new procedural memories that enable them to perform manual, perceptual, and problem-solving tasks. They can learn to solve a puzzle, read mirror-reversed words, or play tennis—even though they do not recall the training sessions

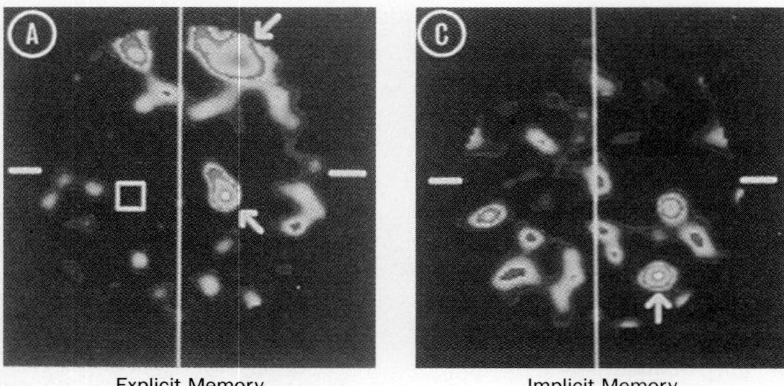

Figure 9.7
Brain Activity in Explicit and Implicit Memory

These PET scans reveal average changes in blood flow (and thus, neural activity) for several individuals as they took tests of memory (Squire et al., 1992). In scan A, yellow and red represent increased blood flow, but in scan C, the same colors represent decreased blood flow. Scan A shows that when people recalled words from a list—a test of explicit memory—neural activity increased in the right part of the hippocampus (lower arrow) and the right prefrontal cortex (upper arrow). (The right hemisphere may have been more active than the left because the task emphasized the visual form of the words rather than their sound or meaning.) In contrast, scan C shows that when people read the list and later said the first words that came to mind in response to word stems—a test of implicit memory—activity in the hippocampus increased much less. In addition, activity in the right part of the visual cortex decreased (see arrow), presumably because seeing the initial list reduced the visual processing necessary for the word stems. These findings support the view that explicit and implicit memory tasks involve different areas of the brain.

in which they learned these skills. Apparently, the parts of the brain involved in acquiring new procedural memories have remained intact.

Patients such as H. M. also retain some implicit memory for verbal material. For example, if H. M. sees the word *define* on a list and later has to complete the stem *def-* with the first word that comes to mind, he is more likely to say "define" than some other word, just as people with normal memories are (Keane, Gabrieli, & Corkin, 1987). Some psychologists conclude that there must be separate systems in the brain for implicit and explicit tasks (Sherry & Schacter, 1987; Tulving & Schacter, 1990). As Figure 9.7 shows, this view has been bolstered by PET scans, which reveal differences in the location of brain activity when normal subjects perform explicit versus implicit memory tasks (Squire et al., 1992).

The brain circuits that take part in the *formation* of long-term memories, however, are probably not the same as those involved in long-term *storage* of those memories. The role of the hippocampus, for example, appears to be only temporary, and the ultimate destinations of declarative memories seem to lie in parts of the cerebral cortex. More specifically, long-term storage may take place in the same cortical areas that were involved in the original perception of the information (Mishkin & Appenzeller, 1987). As we saw in Chapter 4, the typical "memory" is a complex cluster of information. When you recall meeting a man yesterday, you remember his greeting, his tone of voice, how he looked, and where he was. These different pieces of information are probably processed separately and stored at different locations that are distributed across wide areas of the brain, with all the sites participating in the representation of the event as a whole. The role of the hippocampus may be to somehow "bind together" the diverse aspects of a memory at the time it is formed, so that even though these aspects are stored in different cortical sites, the memory can be retrieved as one coherent entity (Squire & Zola-Morgan, 1991).

HORMONES AND MEMORY

Have you ever smelled fresh cookies and recalled a tender scene from your childhood? Do you have a vivid memory of the first time you fell in love? Emotional memories such as these are often especially vivid and intense. The explanation may reside in our hormones.

Hormones released by the adrenal glands during stress and emotional arousal, including epinephrine (adrenaline) and certain steroids, appear to enhance memory. If you give people a drug that prevents their adrenal glands from producing these hormones, they will remember less about emotional stories they have heard than will control subjects (Cahill et al., 1994). Conversely, if you give epinephrine to animals right after learning, their memories will improve (McGaugh, 1990). This effect occurs, however, only when the hormones are at moderate levels. If the dosages are too high, memory suffers. Thus a moderate level of arousal is probably best when you are learning and need to encode events in memory. If you want to remember information well, you should aim for an arousal level somewhere between "hyper" and "laid back."

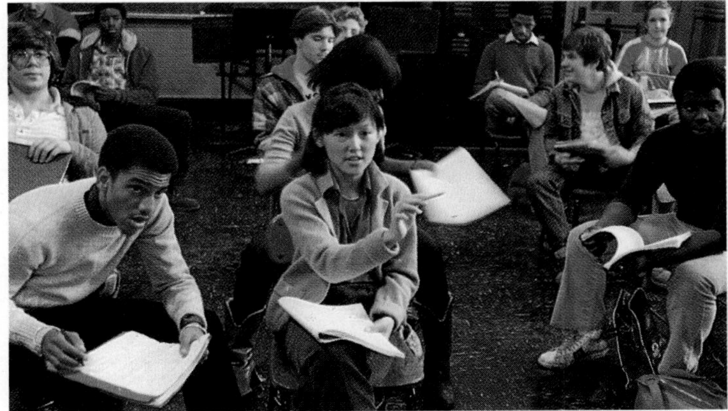

Which of these students will remember best? Keep in mind that retention appears to be enhanced when hormones associated with emotional arousal are at a moderate level.

The link between emotional arousal and memory makes good evolutionary sense: Arousal tells the brain that an event or piece of information is important enough to attend to or store for future use. But how can hormones produced in the adrenal glands affect storage of information in the brain? One possibility is that epinephrine causes the level of glucose (a sugar) to rise in the bloodstream, which carries it to the brain. Once in the brain, glucose may enhance memory either directly or by altering the effects of neurotransmitters (Gold, 1987). This "sweet memories" effect occurs both in aged rats and mice and in elderly human beings. In one fascinating study, healthy older people fasted overnight, drank a glass of lemonade sweetened with either glucose or saccharin, and then took two memory tests. The saccharin-laced drink had no effect on their performance, but lemonade with glucose greatly boosted their ability to recall a taped passage 5 or 40 minutes after hearing it and also their long-term ability to recall words from a list (Manning, Hall, & Gold, 1990). Glucose also enhances the ability of Alzheimer's patients to recognize words, prose passages, and faces (Manning, Ragozzino, & Gold, 1993).

However, the exact mechanisms involved in the hormone–memory link remain unclear and controversial. In this area, as in others in the biology of memory, we still have much to learn. New discoveries are being made at a tremendous rate, but many of these findings are provisional. We do not yet know how the brain actually stores information, how distributed circuits link up with one another, or how a student is able to locate and retrieve information at the drop of a multiple-choice item. And, as we will see next, there is as much to be learned about why we forget as about how we remember.

Quick Quiz

Find out whether your brain has recorded what you just read.

1. Is long-term potentiation associated with (a) increased responsiveness of a receiving neuron to a transmitting neuron, (b) a decrease in receptors on a receiving neuron, or (c) reaching your true potential?
2. The cerebellum has been associated with __________ memories; the hippocampus has been associated with __________ memories.
3. True or false: Hormone research suggests that if you want to remember well, you should be as relaxed as possible while learning.
4. After reading the findings on glucose and memory, should you immediately start gulping down lemonade? Why or why not?

Answers:

1. a 2. procedural, declarative 3. false 4. You probably shouldn't pig out on sugar yet. Results from elderly people, using measures of memory on which older people show deficits, will not necessarily generalize to younger people with normal memories (although they might). Even if the results do generalize, you would need to know how much glucose is effective; in the elderly, there is an optimal dose (Parsons & Gold, 1992). Also, in some people, frequent glucose consumption may have adverse health consequences that could outweigh the cognitive benefits.

WHY WE FORGET

Have you ever, in the heat of some deliriously happy moment, said to yourself, "I'll never forget this, never, *never,* NEVER"? Do you find that you can more clearly remember saying those words than the deliriously happy moment itself? Sometimes you encode an event, you rehearse it, you analyze its meaning, you tuck it away in long-term storage—and still you forget it. As we suggest in "Puzzles of Psychology" on page 369, not all forgetting is bad. Most of us, however, would like to remember better than we do.

Over a century ago, in an effort to measure pure memory loss independent of personal experience, Hermann Ebbinghaus (1885/1913) memorized long lists of nonsense syllables—such as *bok, waf,* or *ged*—and then tested his retention over a period of several weeks. Most of his forgetting occurred soon after the initial learning and then leveled off (see Figure 9.8a). Ebbinghaus's method of studying memory was adopted by generations of psychologists, even though it didn't tell them much about the kinds of memories that people care about most.

A century later, Marigold Linton decided to find out how people forget real events rather than nonsense syllables. Like Ebbinghaus, she used herself as a subject, but she charted the curve of forgetting over years rather than days. Every day for 12 years she recorded on a 4- × 6-inch card two or more things that had happened to her that day. Eventually, she accumulated a catalogue of thousands of discrete events, both trivial ("I have dinner at the Canton Kitchen: delicious lobster dish") and significant

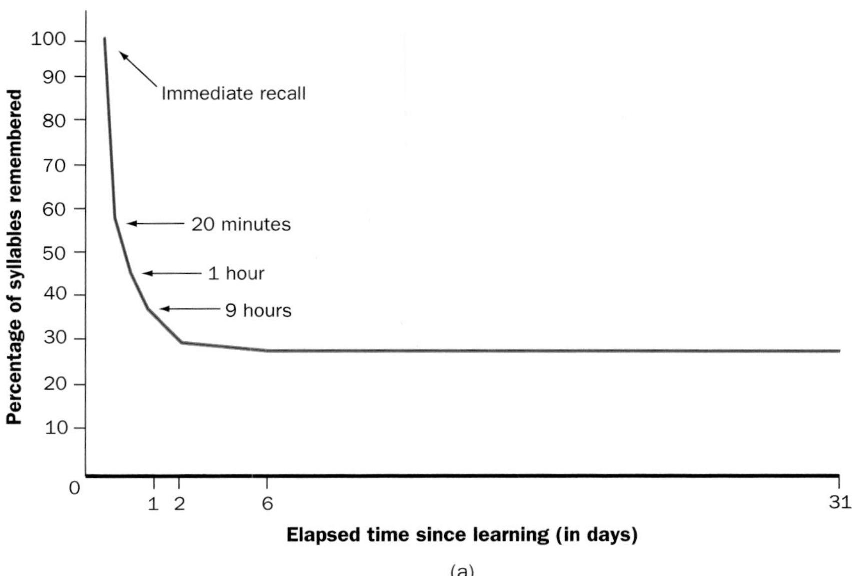

(a)

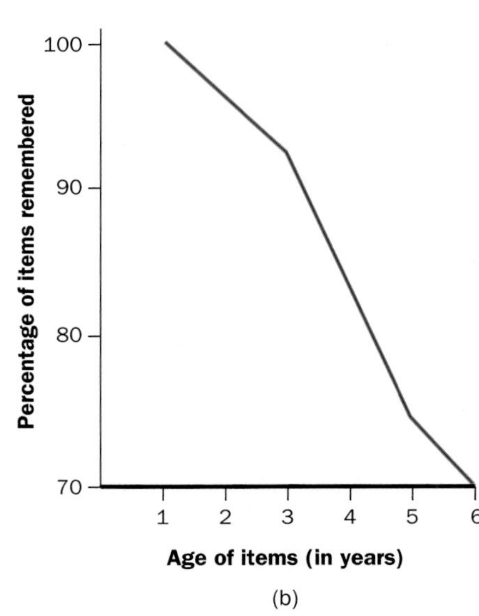

(b)

Figure 9.8
Two Kinds of Forgetting Curves
When Hermann Ebbinghaus tested his own memory for nonsense syllables, forgetting was rapid at first and then tapered off (a). In contrast, when Marigold Linton tested her own memory for personal events over a period of several years, her retention was excellent at first, but then it fell off at a gradual but steady rate (b).

("I land at Orly Airport in Paris"). Once a month, she took a random sampling of all the cards accumulated to that point, noted whether she could remember the events on them, and tried to date the events. Reporting on the results from the first six years of the study, Linton (1978) told how she had expected the kind of rapid forgetting reported by Ebbinghaus. Instead, as you can see in Figure 9.8b, she found that long-term forgetting was slower and proceeded at a much more constant pace, as details gradually dropped out of her memories.

Of course, some memories never lose their distinctiveness. Events that mark important transitions (marriage, getting a first job) are more memorable than others. But why did Marigold Linton, like the rest of us, forget so many details? Psychologists have proposed five mechanisms to account for forgetting: decay, replacement of new memories for old, interference, motivated forgetting, and cue-dependent forgetting.

THE DECAY THEORY

One commonsense view, the **decay theory,** holds that memory traces fade with time if they are not "accessed" now and then. We have already seen that decay occurs in sensory memory, and that it occurs in short-term memory as well, if we don't rehearse the material. However, the mere passage of time does not account so well for forgetting in long-term memory. People commonly forget things that happened only yesterday while remembering events from many years ago. Indeed, some knowledge remains accessible decades after learning. One study found that people did well on a Spanish test as long as 50 years later after taking Spanish in high school, even though most had hardly used Spanish at all in the intervening years (Bahrick, 1984). Decay alone, then, cannot explain lapses in long-term memory.

NEW MEMORIES FOR OLD

Another explanation holds that new information can completely wipe out old information, just as rerecording on an audiotape or videotape will obliterate the original material. In one of the many studies supporting this view, researchers showed people slides of a traffic accident and used leading questions to get them to think that

decay theory The theory that information in memory eventually disappears if it is not accessed; it applies more to short-term than to long-term memory.

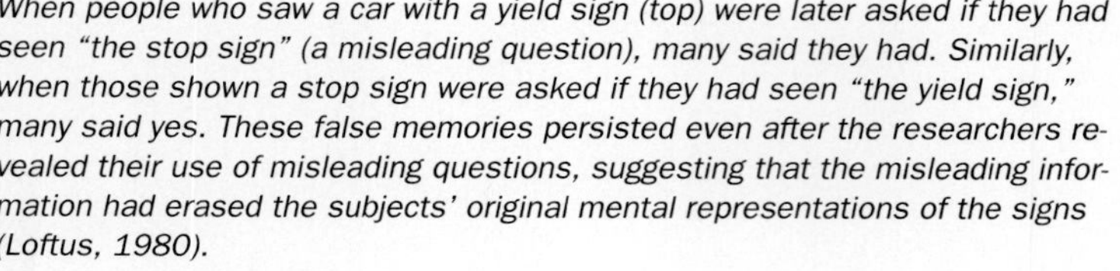

When people who saw a car with a yield sign (top) were later asked if they had seen "the stop sign" (a misleading question), many said they had. Similarly, when those shown a stop sign were asked if they had seen "the yield sign," many said yes. These false memories persisted even after the researchers revealed their use of misleading questions, suggesting that the misleading information had erased the subjects' original mental representations of the signs (Loftus, 1980).

they had seen a stop sign when they had really seen a yield sign, or vice versa. People in a control group who were not misled in this way were able to identify accurately the sign they had actually seen. Later, all the subjects were told the purpose of the study and were asked to guess whether they had been misled. Almost all of those who had been misled continued to insist that they had *really, truly* seen the sign whose existence had been planted in their minds (Loftus, Miller, & Burns, 1978). These findings suggest that the subjects' original perception was "erased" by the misleading information.

INTERFERENCE

A third theory holds that forgetting occurs because similar items of information interfere with one another in either storage or retrieval; the information is in memory, but it becomes confused with other information. This type of forgetting, which occurs in both short- and long-term memory, is especially common when you have to recall isolated facts.

Suppose you are at a party and you meet someone named Julie. A half-hour later you meet someone named Judy. You go on to talk to other people, and after an hour, you again bump into Julie, but by mistake you call her Judy. The second name has interfered with the first. This type of interference, in which new information interferes with the ability to remember old information, is called **retroactive.** Retroactive interference is sometimes illustrated by a story about an absent-minded professor of ichthyology (the study of fish) who complained that whenever he learned the name of a new student, he forgot the name of a fish.

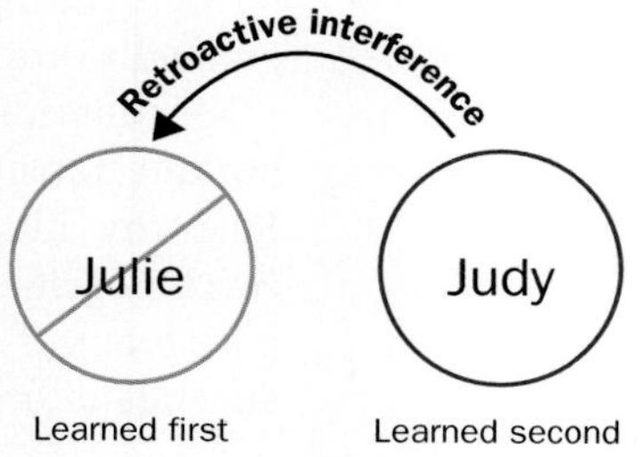

Because new information is constantly entering memory, we are all vulnerable to the effects of retroactive interference—or at least most of us are. H. M.'s memories of childhood and adolescence are unusually detailed and clear, and they rarely change. H. M. can remember actors and singers famous when he was a child, as well as the films they were in and who their costars were. He knows the names of friends from the second grade. Presumably, these declarative memories from early in life have not been subject to interference from memories acquired since the operation—because there have been no new memories!

Interference also works in the opposite direction. Old information (such as the Spanish you learned in high school) may interfere with the ability to remember new information (such as the French you're trying to learn now). This type of interference is called **proactive.** Over a period of weeks, months, and years, proactive interference may cause more forgetting than retroactive interference does because we have stored up so much information that can potentially interfere with anything new. Fortunately, we can also use our old information to elaboratively encode new information and thus improve our ability to remember.

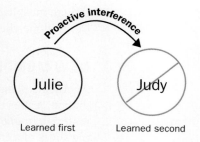

Proactive interference

Julie Judy

Learned first Learned second

retroactive interference Forgetting that occurs when recently learned material interferes with the ability to remember similar material stored previously.

proactive interference Forgetting that occurs when previously stored material interferes with the ability to remember similar, more recently learned material.

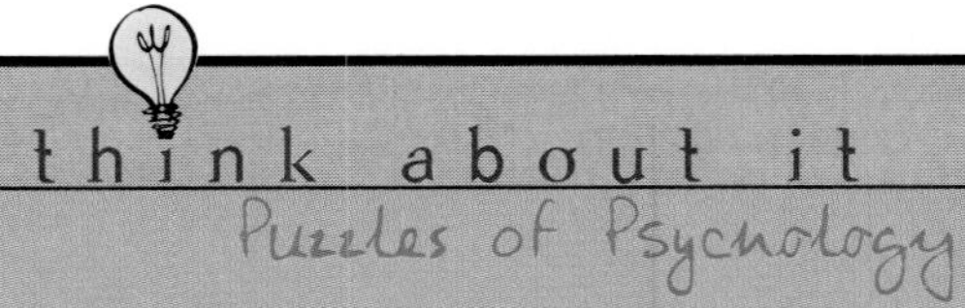

The Benefits of Forgetting

Who has not wished, at some time or other, for a "photographic memory"? It's bad enough that we forget so much that we have worked diligently to learn in school. How can we formulate a realistic assessment of ourselves if our recollection of the past is inaccurate and incomplete?

Yet a perfect memory is not the blessing that you might suppose. The Russian psychologist Alexander Luria (1968) once told of a journalist, S., who could remember giant grids of numbers and long lists of words, and could reproduce them both forward and backward, even after the passage of 15 years. S. also remembered the exact circumstances under which he had originally learned the material. He used mnemonics involving the formation of visual images to accomplish his astonishing feats. But you shouldn't envy him, for he had a serious problem: He could not forget even when he wanted to. Images he had formed in order to remember kept creeping into consciousness, distracting him and interfering with his ability to concentrate. At times, he even had trouble holding a conversation because the other person's words would set off a jumble of associations. In fact, Luria called him "rather dull-witted." Eventually, unable to work at his profession, S. took to supporting himself by traveling from place to place as a performer, demonstrating his mnemonic abilities for audiences.

Perhaps you still think a perfect memory would be a terrific thing to have. Imagine, then, for a moment, what it would be like to remember everything. Along with the diamonds of experience, you would keep dredging up the pebbles. Remembering might take hours instead of seconds. With a perfect memory, you might also remember things better off forgotten. Think back: Would you really want to recall every angry argument, every embarrassing episode, every painful moment of your life? How would total recall affect your relationships with relatives and friends? Could it be that the success of a close relationship depends on a little forgiving forgetfulness? Could it be that self-confidence and optimism are possible only if we lock some follies and grievances in a back drawer of memory and stop ruminating on them?

Like remembering, a degree of forgetting contributes to our survival and our sanity. Where is the line between adaptive forgetting and disruptive forgetting? If you had the choice, what would you recollect with greater clarity, and what would you allow to fade? Think about it.

MOTIVATED FORGETTING

Sigmund Freud maintained that people forget because they block from consciousness those memories that are too threatening or painful to live with, and he called this self-protective process *repression* (see Chapter 12). Today, many psychologists prefer a more general term, **motivated forgetting,** and they argue that people might be motivated to forget events for many reasons, including embarrassment, guilt, shock, and a desire to protect their own pride. (In Chapter 15 we will discuss *dissociative amnesia,* in which people selectively forget a stressful or traumatic experience that is threatening to the self.)

The concepts of repression and motivated forgetting are based mostly on clinical reports of people in psychotherapy who appear to recall long-buried memories, typically of traumatic events in childhood. Only rarely, however, have such memories been corroborated by objective evidence, so it is difficult and often impossible to determine their accuracy. Moreover, it is difficult to empirically distinguish "repression" from other kinds of forgetting or from a simple refusal to think about an upsetting experience.

Because of what psychologists have learned about the reconstructive nature of memory, claims of "recovered" memories of early trauma raise unsettling issues. Should the validity of memories that are recovered in therapy be accepted in a court of law? To what extent are these memories contaminated by what a person has heard from others since the event occurred, or by subsequent experiences? In "Issues in Popular Culture," we discuss the bitter debate over repressed memories of childhood sexual abuse.

motivated forgetting Forgetting that occurs because of a desire to eliminate awareness of painful, embarrassing, or otherwise unpleasant experiences.

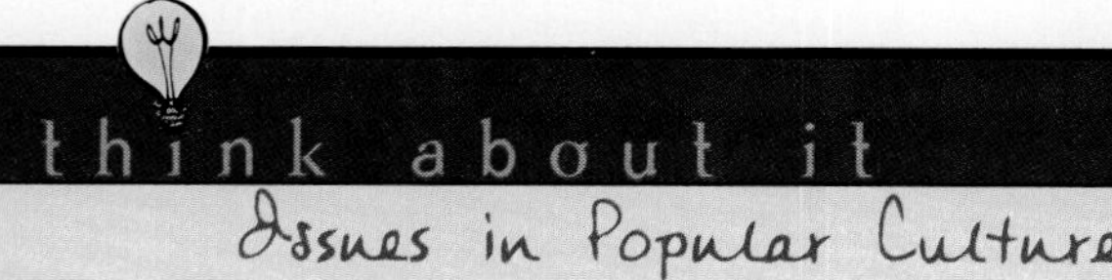

The Debate over Repressed Memories of Sexual Abuse

In 1989, a woman named Eileen Franklin Lipsker was playing with her young daughter when suddenly, according to her later account, a shocking memory returned. Her daughter reminded her of a close childhood friend named Susan Nason, who was murdered at the age of 8. The case had never been solved, but in that moment Eileen remembered who had killed Susan because she remembered being there: It was her own father, George Franklin. A few months later, she also remembered that her father had committed incest with her, starting when she was 3.

Eileen's recovered memories resulted in her father's conviction for murder. Thousands of other recovered memories of sexual abuse have since been reported all over North America, and many have led to lawsuits. In one typical case, Laura B. sued her father, claiming that he had molested her from the ages of 5 to 23, even raping her just days before her wedding. She had no memories of these events, she said, until therapy (Loftus, 1995). (We'll tell you what happened in Laura B.'s case and in Eileen's later.)

A controversy has been raging about whether such accusations should be believed, and whether they provide sufficient evidence, in the absence of other corroboration, to convict alleged perpetrators. Emotions run high because much is at stake: finding justice for people who were abused as children, while also protecting adults from false charges that can destroy their lives.

Some psychologists (we'll call them the *recovered-memory school*) believe that virtually all memories recovered in therapy should be taken seriously (Harvey & Herman, 1994). They argue that false memories are rare; thus, they fear that people who raise doubts about recovered memories are betraying victims and abetting child molesters. Other psychologists (we'll call them the *pseudomemory school*) argue that many false memories of abuse are being manufactured by naïve, unscrupulous, or uninformed therapists. They know that real abuse occurs, but they worry about a rising tide of spurious accusations (Loftus & Ketcham, 1994).

In general (with some notable exceptions), this is an argument between mental-health practitioners who do therapy and empirical psychologists and clinicians who do research. The polarization between the two schools results in part from their differing assumptions about scientific research and clinical evidence (Lindsay & Read, 1995). Here are just a few of the issues that divide them:

- *What is the nature and meaning of repression?* In the clinical view, people cope with traumatic events by repressing the memory of them. Later, if anxiety about the event is removed, an accurate memory of it will return. Proponents of this view insist that it is common for patients to repress abusive experiences, and that laboratory studies are irrelevant because they are artificial and the memories studied are trivial (Harvey & Herman, 1994; Wylie, 1993).

  But research on memory, as we have seen in this chapter, disputes the belief that memories can be stored in a pristine state of "repression," uncontaminated for years; all memories, even of shocking experiences, are subject to distortion, error, and influence by others. And research shows that although people can and do forget details of traumatic experiences, they do not forget the fact that they experienced the trauma at all, as the recovered-memory school claims; no one forgets that they were in a war or a concentration camp, for instance. Moreover, as we discuss later in this chapter, forgetting of events from the first few years of life is universal—a result of physiological and cognitive immaturity. Thus claims of recovered memories of events that happened "in the crib" should be regarded as highly doubtful.

- *How reliable are clinical methods of recovering memories?* A significant minority of therapists—between one-fourth and one-third—are using hypnosis and other suggestive techniques to try to uncover their

CUE-DEPENDENT FORGETTING

Often, when we need to remember, we rely on *retrieval cues,* items of information that can help us find the specific information we're looking for. When we lack such cues, we may feel as if we have lost the call number for an entry in the mind's library. This type of memory failure, called **cue-dependent forgetting,** may be the most common type of all. Willem Wagenaar (1986), who, like Marigold Linton, recorded critical details about events in his life, found that within a year, he had forgotten 20 percent of those details, and after five years, he had forgotten 60 percent. However, when he gathered cues from witnesses about ten events that he thought he had forgotten, he was able to recall something about all ten, which suggests that some of his forgetting was cue dependent.

cue-dependent forgetting The inability to retrieve information stored in memory because of insufficient cues for recall.

clients' supposedly repressed memories, without knowing much about the limitations of these methods (Poole et al., 1995). In Chapter 5, we described a study of family therapists, many of whom were ignorant of the research on hypnosis and memory (Yapko, 1994). Half mistakenly believed that "hypnosis can be used to recover memories from as far back as birth"; a third agreed that "the mind is like a computer, accurately recording events that actually occurred."

- *Can therapists "implant" false memories in their clients?* The recovered-memory school maintains that it is just about impossible to implant a memory of a traumatic event in a client. Yet several researchers have demonstrated how traumatic memories might indeed be implanted in some people through the use of leading questions. In one study, 7 out of 24 subjects were induced to "remember" being lost in a shopping mall or other public place at the age of about 5, even though the event never happened (Loftus & Pickrell, 1995). Other researchers have implanted false memories of such distinctive events as being hospitalized for a high fever (Hyman & Pentland, 1996). Those who came to hold these false memories were confident about their accuracy and filled their accounts with vivid details. But the recovered-memory school counters that these experimental findings do not apply to memories for something as horrible as childhood incest.

Today, more people have become cautious in evaluating claims of recovered memories. Across North America, people are winning malpractice lawsuits against therapists for creating false memories. In an important ruling in the case of Laura B., the judge wrote that her recovered memories would not be admissible evidence because "the phenomenon of memory repression, and the process of therapy used in these cases to recover the memories, have not gained general acceptance in the field of psychology; *and are not scientifically reliable*" (*State of New Hampshire* v. *Joel Hungerford,* May 23, 1995).

Most dramatically, the case that launched the recovered-memory phenomenon in the first place has fallen apart. George Franklin's conviction was reversed on the grounds that Eileen's testimony could have been based on information she read in the newspapers. Moreover, her "memories" emerged under hypnosis in therapy, *not* spontaneously. Later, Eileen "remembered" her father murdering two other girls, but an investigation completely exonerated him.

How, then, should a person evaluate a given claim of recovered memory? The answer depends on the specific evidence in each case. Here, for example, are some indications that skepticism is warranted: (1) The person says that, thanks to therapy, he or she now clearly remembers being molested in the first year or two of life. (2) Over time, the memories of abuse become more implausible—for instance, that the abuse continued day and night for 15 years without ever being remembered and without anyone else in the household noticing. (3) The therapist's diagnosis of sexual abuse was made quickly, based on problems a client could have for many other reasons (e.g., depression, low self-esteem, or an eating disorder). (4) The therapist used suggestive techniques such as hypnosis or guided imagery to "help" a patient recall the alleged abuse.

In contrast, the following would suggest that a person's recollections are trustworthy: (1) corroborating evidence from school or medical records or the recollections of other family members; (2) signs of trauma, such as nightmares and disturbed behavior, at the time the abuse is said to have occurred; and (3) spontaneous recall of the event or events, without pressure from others or the use of suggestive techniques in therapy.

This issue demands our best efforts to avoid either–or thinking, an ability to apply the rules of critical thinking and empirical evidence, and the willingness to retain compassion both for abused children and for unjustly accused adults.

Retrieval cues may work by getting us into the general area of memory where an item is stored, or by making a match with information that is linked in memory with the item in question. Thus, if you are trying to remember the last name of an actor, it might help to know the person's first name or the name of a recent movie the actor starred in. Cues that were present at the time you learned a new fact or had an experience are apt to be especially useful as retrieval aids. That may explain why remembering is often easier when you are in the same physical environment as you were when an event occurred: Cues in the present context match those from the past. Many people have suggested that the overlap between present and past cues may also lead to a *false* sense of having been in exactly the same situation before; this is the eerie phenomenon of *déjà vu* (which means "already seen" in French). Ordinarily, however, contextual cues help us remember the past more accurately.

Because of this finding, many police departments have altered the way they interview witnesses to a crime. The old way was to direct a set of "then what" questions at the witness: "Then what did he do? And then what happened after that?" The new way is to encourage witnesses to reconstruct the circumstances of the crime and to recall without interruption everything they can about what they saw, even details that seem unimportant. Such "cognitive interview" strategies often increase the number of available retrieval cues and produce better recall than standard "and-then-what-did-he-do" techniques (Fisher & Geiselman, 1992).

Your mental or physical state may also act as a retrieval cue, evoking a **state-dependent memory.** For example, if you are intoxicated when something happens, you may remember it better when you once again have had a few drinks than when you are sober. (This is not an endorsement of drunkenness! Your memory will be best if you are sober during both encoding and recall.) Likewise, if your emotional arousal is especially high or low at the time of an event, you may remember that event best when you are once again in the same emotional state. When victims of violent crimes have trouble recalling details of the experience, it may be in part because they are far less emotionally aroused than they were at the time of the crime (Clark, Milberg, & Erber, 1987).

Charlie Chaplin's film City Lights *provides a classic illustration of state-dependent memory. After Charlie saves the life of a drunken millionaire, the two spend the rest of the evening in boisterous merrymaking. But the next day, after sobering up, the millionaire fails to recognize Charlie and gives him the cold shoulder. Then, once again, the millionaire gets drunk—and once again he greets Charlie as a pal.*

Retrieval of a memory may also be more likely when your *mood* is the same as it was when you first encoded and stored the memory, presumably because mood serves as a retrieval cue. Findings on this notion, however, have been frustratingly inconsistent, possibly because the effect depends on many factors, such as the strength of the mood, the nature of the event, and the way the memory is retrieved (Eich, 1995). What really counts is probably the match between your current mood and the *kind of material* you are trying to remember, especially when you are feeling happy. In other words, you are likely to remember happy events better when you are feeling happy than when you are sad (Mayer, McCormick & Strong, 1995).

Quick Quiz

If you haven't repressed what you just read, try these questions.

1. Ever since she read *Even Cowgirls Get the Blues* many years ago, Wilma has loved the novels of Tom Robbins. Nowadays, one of her favorite actors is Tim Robbins, but every time she tries to recall his name she calls him "Tom." Why?
2. When a man at his twentieth high school reunion sees his old friends, he recalls incidents he had thought were long forgotten. Why?

Answers:

1. proactive interference 2. The sight of his friends provides retrieval cues for the incidents.

AUTOBIOGRAPHICAL MEMORIES: THE WAY WE WERE

Memory provides each of us with a sense of identity that evolves and changes as we build up a store of episodic memories about events we have experienced firsthand. For most of us, the memories we have of our own lives are by far the most fascinating. We use them as entertainment ("Did I ever tell you about the time. . . ?"); we manipulate them—some people even publish them—in order to create an image of ourselves; we analyze them to learn more about who we are (Ross, 1989).

state-dependent memory The tendency to remember something when the rememberer is in the same physical or mental state as during the original learning or experience.

be organized by semantic categories. Many models of LTM represent its contents as a network of interrelated concepts. The way people use these networks depends on experience and education. Words are also indexed in LTM in terms of sound and form.

11) *Procedural memories* ("knowing how") are memories for how to perform specific actions; *declarative memories* ("knowing that") are memories for abstract or representational knowledge. Declarative memories include *semantic memories* and *episodic memories.*

12) The three-box model has often been invoked to explain the *serial-position effect* in memory, but it cannot explain why a *recency effect* sometimes occurs when it shouldn't and why even rats and birds show the serial-position effect.

HOW TO REMEMBER

13) Rehearsal of information keeps it in short-term memory and increases the chances of long-term retention. *Elaborative rehearsal* is more likely to result in transfer to long-term memory than is *maintenance rehearsal,* and *deep processing* is usually a more effective retention strategy than *shallow processing. Mnemonics* can also enhance retention by promoting elaborative encoding and making material meaningful, but for ordinary memory tasks, complex memory tricks are often ineffective or even counterproductive.

THE BIOLOGY OF MEMORY

14) Short-term memory appears to involve temporary changes within neurons that alter their ability to release neurotransmitters. In contrast, long-term memory involves permanent structural changes in neurons and synapses. *Long-term potentiation,* an increase in the strength of synaptic responsiveness, seems to be an important mechanism of long-term memory. Neural changes associated with long-term potentiation take time to develop, which may explain why long-term memories require a period of *consolidation.*

15) Scientists are learning where specific memory processes take place. When short-term memory functions as a working memory, areas of the prefrontal cortex are especially active. During the initial formation of long-term declarative memories, the hippocampus and adjacent parts of the temporal lobe play a critical role; in contrast, the formation of procedural memories involves other brain areas, including the cerebellum. Studies of patients with amnesia suggest that different brain systems are active during explicit and implicit memory tasks. Finally, the long-term storage of declarative memories may take place in the cortical areas that were active during the original perception of the information or event. The various components of a memory are probably stored at different sites distributed across wide areas of the cortex, with all of these sites participating in the representation of the event as a whole.

16) Hormones released by the adrenal glands during stress or emotional arousal, including epinephrine and some steroids, may enhance memory at moderate levels. Epinephrine causes the level of glucose to rise in the bloodstream, and glucose may enhance memory either directly or by altering the effects of neurotransmitters. Hormonal effects may explain why moderate emotional arousal is an essential ingredient in learning and memory.

WHY WE FORGET

17) Forgetting can occur for several reasons. Information in sensory and short-term memory appears to *decay* if it does not receive further processing. New information may "erase" old information in long-term memory. *Proactive* and *retroactive interference* may take place. Some lapses in memory may be due to *motivated forgetting,* although it is difficult to confirm the validity of "repressed" memories that are then "recovered." (The validity of recovered memories of past abuse is the subject of bitter debate, as we discussed in "Issues in Popular Culture.") Finally, *cue-dependent forgetting* may occur when retrieval cues are inadequate. The most effective retrieval cues are those that were present at the time of the initial experience. A person's mood or physical state may also act as a retrieval cue, evoking a *state-dependent memory.*

AUTOBIOGRAPHICAL MEMORIES: THE WAY WE WERE

18) Because of *childhood amnesia,* most people cannot recall any events from earlier than the third or fourth year of life. The reason may be partly biological, but many cognitive explanations have also been proposed: the lack of a sense of self in the first few years of life; the child's reliance on cognitive schemas that differ from the schemas used later; the fact that young children encode experiences less elaboratively than older people do; and children's focus on routine rather than distinctive aspects of an experience.

19) A person's narrative or "life story" organizes the events of his or her life and gives it meaning. Narratives change as people build up a store of episodic memories. Many memories seem to be based on people's current traits and beliefs, and also on their *implicit theories* of how much particular traits or beliefs can change. Life stories are, to some degree, works of interpretation and imagination.

KEY TERMS

memory 340
reconstruction in memory 341
source amnesia 342
flashbulb memories 343
leading question 345
explicit memory 347
recall 347
recognition 347
implicit memory 347
priming 348
relearning method 348
information-processing models 349
encoding 349
cognitive schema 349
proposition 349
effortful versus automatic encoding 350
storage 350
retrieval 350
"three-box model" 350
parallel distributed processing (PDP) models 351
neural network 351
artificial intelligence 351
sensory memory 352
sensory register 352
  icons 352
  echoes 352
pattern recognition 352
short-term memory (STM) 353
working memory 354

The beauty of the world has two edges, one of laughter,
one of anguish, cutting the heart asunder.

Virginia Woolf

CHAPTER TEN

Emotion

FOR THE FIRST SEVEN YEARS OF HER LIFE, Chelsea Thomas was a happy, cheerful, normal child with just one problem. Chelsea had been born with Möbius syndrome, in which a nerve that transmits commands from the brain to the facial muscles is missing. As a result, the child had a perpetually grumpy look. She could not convey delight at being given a present, amusement at watching a favorite TV show, or friendliness at meeting another child. In 1996, surgeons transplanted nerves from Chelsea's leg to both sides of her mouth, and today Chelsea can finally do what most people in the world take for granted—smile.

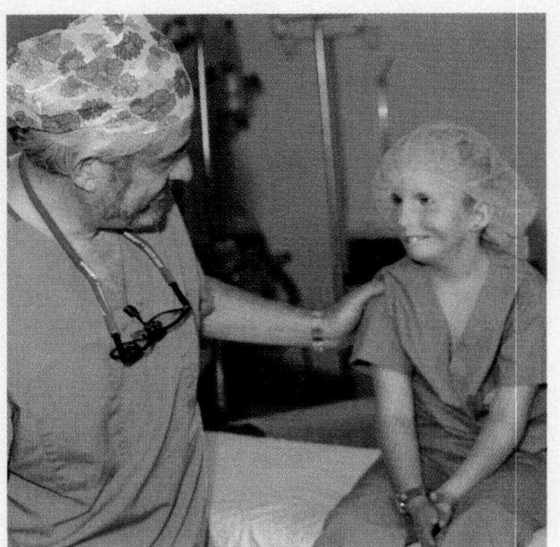

Chelsea Thomas after the first of two surgeries that enabled her to smile.

Temple Grandin is a biologist whose empathic understanding of animal suffering has enabled her to design improved livestock facilities in use all over the United States. She is a successful scientist and writer in spite of a condition that can be debilitating—a form of autism. Grandin (1996) observes that her emotions differ in quality and kind from those of normal people: She can feel the anguish of animals, but not of human beings. She has never known romantic love or been moved by the beauty of a sunset. Unable to feel the array of normal emotions, she is unable to read the emotions of others; she is "out of sync" with the flow of humanity.

Cases like these, and those of other people who suffer a wide range of emotional problems and deficiencies, illustrate poignantly the importance of the ability to feel emotions and the ability to communicate them. In Chapter 4, we met Phineas Gage, who suffered frontal-lobe damage that made him ill-tempered and undependable, while "flattening out" the emotions necessary to organize and plan his life. In Chapter 8, we discussed the problems faced by people who are low in "emotional intelligence"—the ability to identify one's own and other people's feelings and to regulate emotions appropriately. And in Chapter 15, we will look at the problems that occur when people suffer emotions they cannot seem to control, such as unrelenting anxiety or depression, and when they lack normal emotions entirely, such as empathy and guilt.

Emotions, then, are the heart and soul of human experience. If you lacked emotion, you would never again worry about a test result, a job interview, or a first date, and you would never be riled by injustice. But you would also be unmoved by the magic of music. You would never feel the grief of losing someone you love, not only because you wouldn't know sadness but also because you wouldn't know love. You would never laugh, because nothing would strike you as funny.

Yet people often curse their emotions, wishing to be freed from anger, jealousy, shame, guilt, grief, and unrequited love. The paradox of emotions is that we can't live with them, and we can't live without them. That's why viewers of the original *Star Trek* series are ambivalent about Mr. Spock, that unemotional, hyperrational Vulcan. He is so wise, so sensible, so mature, so . . . cold.

For many centuries, emotion was regarded as the opposite of thinking, and an inferior opposite at that. The heart (emotion) was said to go its own way, in spite of what the head (reason) wanted. The division between thinking and feeling has provoked some of the longest-running either–or debates in intellectual history. Are emotions and cognitions two separate processes that often conflict with each other, or are they inextricably connected? Can we control our emotions, or do they control us? Is thinking always "rational" and emotion "irrational"?

Psychologists have made great strides in answering these questions. They are investigating the role of emotions in every domain of life—including motivation, stress, memory, moral development, personality traits, decision making and reasoning, mental disorders, prejudice, and perception. They are learning that the full expe-

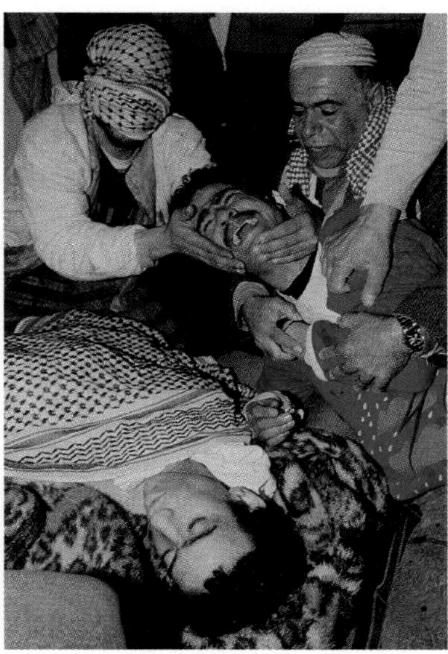

Israeli parents (left) and an Arab father (right) react to the death of their children in the Middle Eastern conflict. Their grief involves a physiological response to loss, the cognition that a young life has been unfairly cut short, and a cultural rule about whether they should "let it out" or "keep a stiff upper lip." Your own culture may affect how you are reacting to these scenes: Is the Israeli father "cold and uptight" or "mature and manly"? Is the Arab father being "hysterical" or "humanly expressive"?

rience of **emotion** involves three influences: *physiological* changes in the face and body, *cognitive* processes such as interpretations of events, and *cultural* influences that shape the experience and expression of emotion. Human emotions can be compared to a tree: The biological capacity for emotion is the trunk and root system; thoughts and explanations create the many branches; and culture is the gardener that shapes the tree and prunes it, cutting off some limbs and cultivating others.

ELEMENTS OF EMOTION 1: THE BODY

Early philosophers thought our personalities depended on mixes of four basic body fluids, or "humors": blood, phlegm, choler, and bile. If you were an angry, irritable sort of person, you supposedly had an excess of choler; even now, the word *choleric* describes a hothead. If you were slow-moving and unemotional, you supposedly had an excess of phlegm; the word for such people is *phlegmatic. Bilious* and *sanguine* still describe personality traits too—peevish and optimistic. The theory of the four humors is far-fetched, and yet the questions it was trying to answer remain with us. What is the physiology of emotion? Where in the body does an emotion occur?

One of the first modern answers to these questions came from William James (1884/1968), who challenged everyone who thought the chicken comes first to think about the egg. Common sense, then as now, assumed that (1) something happens, (2) you feel an emotion, and (3) you do something. In James's own examples, you lose your fortune, you feel miserable, and you cry; or your rival insults you, you feel angry, and you hit him. But James argued that this seemingly logical sequence was out of order, and he turned it around. The correct sequence, he said, should be (1) something happens, (2) your body reacts with a specific set of physiological responses, and (3) you interpret and experience those responses as an emotion. If a slimy alien appeared in your room as you were reading this, your heart would start pounding and you would escape as fast as you could; then you would realize you were feeling fear. "We feel sorry *because* we cry," James wrote, "angry *because* we strike, afraid *because* we tremble." At about the same time that James was writing, a Danish researcher named Carl Lange came up with a similar theory, and the two names were soon linked in the **James–Lange theory of emotion:** the idea that events trigger specific bodily changes and responses—for example, running away if you are frightened—and that emotion follows from your awareness of those physical changes.

The James–Lange theory was not quite right, but it produced animated debate and spurred a wave of research. During the past few decades, psychologists, armed

emotion A state of arousal involving facial and bodily changes, brain activation, cognitive appraisals, subjective feelings, and tendencies toward action.

James–Lange theory of emotion The theory, proposed independently by William James and Carl Lange, that emotion results from the perception of one's own bodily reactions.

with new ways to study the physiology of emotion, have explored the contributions to emotion of facial expressions, brain processes, and the autonomic nervous system.

THE FACE OF EMOTION

The most obvious place to look for emotion is on the face, where its expression is usually most visible. "There are characteristic facial expressions which are observed to accompany anger, fear, erotic excitement, and all the other passions," wrote Aristotle. Centuries later, in his classic book *The Expression of the Emotions in Man and Animals* (1872/1965), Charles Darwin argued that certain human facial expressions—the smile, the frown, the grimace, the glare—are as "wired in" as the wing flutter of a frightened bird, the purr of a contented cat, and the snarl of a threatened wolf. Such expressions may have evolved because they allowed our forebears to tell the difference immediately between a friendly stranger and a hostile one.

Modern psychologists have supported Darwin's idea by showing that certain emotional expressions are recognized the world over (see Figure 10.1). For more than 25 years, Paul Ekman and his colleagues have been gathering evidence for the universality of seven basic facial expressions of emotion: anger, happiness, fear,

Figure 10.1
Some Universal Expressions

Can you tell what feelings are being conveyed here? Most people around the world can readily identify expressions of surprise, disgust, happiness, sadness, anger, fear, and contempt—no matter what the age, culture, or historical epoch of the person conveying the emotion.

surprise, disgust, sadness, and contempt (Ekman, 1994; Ekman & Heider, 1988; Ekman et al., 1987). In every culture they have studied—in Brazil, Chile, Estonia, Germany, Greece, Hong Kong, Italy, Japan, New Guinea, Scotland, Sumatra, Turkey, and the United States—a large majority of people recognize the emotional expressions portrayed by those in other cultures. Even most members of isolated tribes that have never watched a movie or read *People* magazine, such as the Foré of New Guinea or the Minangkabau of West Sumatra, can recognize the emotions expressed in pictures of people who are entirely foreign to them, and we can recognize theirs.

These findings do not mean, however, that everybody in a society can recognize the same expressions in all situations. Ekman called his theory *neurocultural* to emphasize the two factors involved in facial expression: a universal *neurophysiology* in the facial muscles associated with certain emotions, and *culture-specific* variations in the expression of emotion. Thus, while most people in most cultures do recognize basic emotions as portrayed in photographs, sometimes a large minority does not. Across 20 studies of Western cultures, for example, fully 95 percent of the participants agreed in their judgments of happy faces, but only 78 percent agreed on expressions of sadness and anger; and across 11 non-Western societies, 88 percent recognized happiness, but only 74 percent agreed on sadness and 59 percent on anger (Ekman, 1994).

One emotion that nicely illustrates the "neuro-cultural" approach to facial expression is disgust. Make an expression of disgust and notice what you are doing: You are probably wrinkling your nose, dropping the corners of your mouth, or retracting your upper lip. These universal reactions may have originated in the "distaste" response of infants to bitter tastes and may serve as a warning against eating tainted food. But the *content* of what produces disgust changes as the infant matures, and it varies from culture to culture. In the course of growing up, people may acquire feelings of disgust in response to certain foods, as well as to bugs, sex, gore, dirt, and death; "contamination" by contact with undesirable strangers; or violations of moral rules, such as those governing incest (Rozin, Lowery, & Ebert, 1994).

Of course, people do not always display their emotions on their faces. Most of us do not go around scowling and clenching our jaws whenever we are angry. We can grieve and feel enormously sad without weeping. We can feel worried and tense, yet put on a happy face. We use facial expressions, in short, to lie about our feelings as well as to express them. To get around the human ability to mask emotions, Paul Ekman and his associates developed a way to peek under the mask. The Facial Action Coding System (FACS) allows researchers to analyze and identify each of the nearly 80 muscles of the face, as well as the combinations of muscles that are associated with various emotions. When people try to hide their real emotions, Ekman finds, they use different groups of muscles. For example, when people try to pretend that they feel grief, only 15 percent manage to get the eyebrows, eyelids, and forehead wrinkle exactly right, mimicking the way grief is expressed spontaneously. Authentic smiles last only two seconds; false smiles may last ten seconds or more (Ekman, 1994; Ekman, Friesen, & O'Sullivan, 1988).

Facial expressions don't always convey the emotion being felt. A posed, social smile like this one may have nothing to do with true feelings of happiness. Cover this woman's smile with your hand, and you'll see that her "smile" doesn't reach her eyes.

Facial expressions seem to have evolved for two purposes: They express internal states, and they help us communicate to others. This communication starts in infancy; a baby's expressions of misery, angry frustration, happiness, and disgust are apparent to most parents (Izard, 1994b; Stenberg & Campos, 1990)—and babies, in turn, react to the facial expressions of their parents. American, German, Greek, Japanese, Trobriand Island, and Yanomamo mothers all "infect" their babies with happy moods by displaying happy expressions (Keating, 1994). Starting at the end of their first year, babies begin to alter their own behavior by observing their parents' emotions and reactions, and this ability has survival value. Do you recall the visual-cliff studies described in Chapter 6 (see p. 238)? These studies were originally designed to test for depth perception, which emerges quite early in infancy. But in one experiment, 1-year-old babies were put on a more ambiguous visual cliff that didn't drop off sharply and thus didn't automatically evoke fear, as the original did. In this case, 74 percent of the babies crossed the cliff when their mothers showed a happy, reassuring expression, but *none* crossed when their mothers showed an expression of fear (Sorce et al., 1985). If you have ever watched a toddler take a tumble and then look at his or her parent before deciding whether to cry or to forget it, you will understand the influence of parental facial expressions!

Great moms have always understood the importance of facial feedback.

Interestingly, facial expressions may help people communicate with themselves, so to speak, by enabling them to identify their own emotions. As William James might have said, we not only frown because we are angry; sometimes we feel angry because we are frowning. In the process of *facial feedback,* the facial muscles send messages to the brain about the basic emotion being expressed (Izard, 1990; Tomkins, 1981). When people are asked to contort their facial muscles into various patterns, therefore, they often report changed emotions to fit the pattern. As one young man put it, "When my jaw was clenched and my brows down, I tried not to be angry but it just fit the position" (Laird, 1974). Voluntary expressions even seem to affect the involuntary nervous system. If you put on an "angry" face, your heart rate will rise faster than if you put on a "happy" face (Levenson, Ekman, & Friesen, 1990). When people are told to contract the facial muscles involved in smiling (though not actually instructed to smile) and then to look at cartoons, they find the cartoons funnier than if they are contracting their muscles in a way that is incompatible with smiling (Strack, Martin, & Stepper, 1988). See whether smiling affects your reactions to the cartoon on the left.

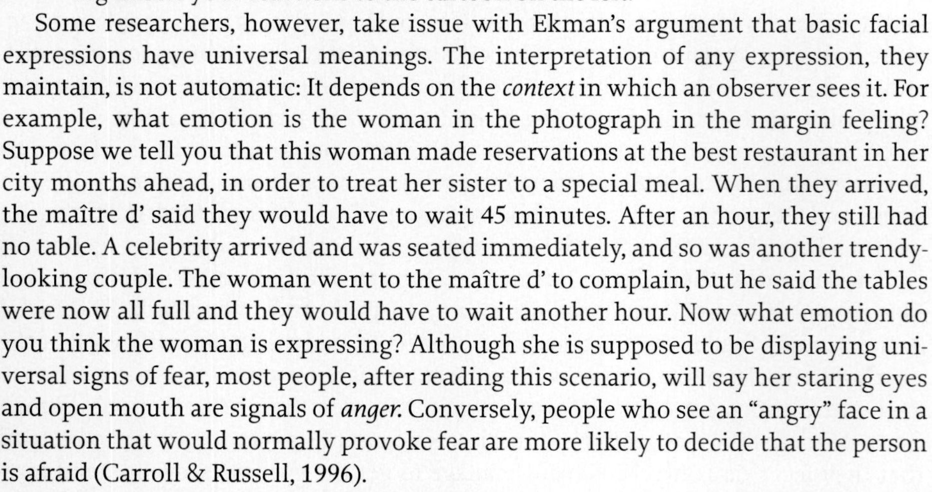

Some researchers, however, take issue with Ekman's argument that basic facial expressions have universal meanings. The interpretation of any expression, they maintain, is not automatic: It depends on the *context* in which an observer sees it. For example, what emotion is the woman in the photograph in the margin feeling? Suppose we tell you that this woman made reservations at the best restaurant in her city months ahead, in order to treat her sister to a special meal. When they arrived, the maître d' said they would have to wait 45 minutes. After an hour, they still had no table. A celebrity arrived and was seated immediately, and so was another trendy-looking couple. The woman went to the maître d' to complain, but he said the tables were now all full and they would have to wait another hour. Now what emotion do you think the woman is expressing? Although she is supposed to be displaying universal signs of fear, most people, after reading this scenario, will say her staring eyes and open mouth are signals of *anger.* Conversely, people who see an "angry" face in a situation that would normally provoke fear are more likely to decide that the person is afraid (Carroll & Russell, 1996).

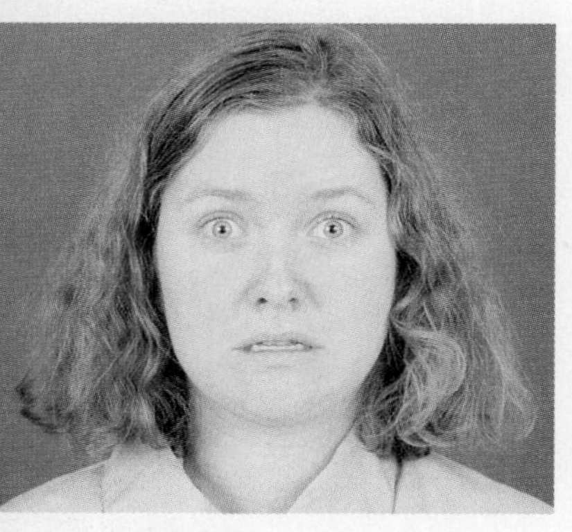

What emotion is this woman expressing?

Other researchers argue that facial expressions may or may not correspond with our internal emotional states, and that they evolved primarily to signal our intentions to others (Fridlund, 1994). When you are sitting at home by yourself, for example, you may be feeling perfectly happy, but it's unlikely that you will be smiling. You'll save your smiles until you have an audience—and even then your smile might not mean "I'm happy," but rather "I'm glad to meet you" or "Don't be mad at me." A study of 22 Olympic gold medalists, observed as they stood on the podium during the awards ceremonies, found that the athletes smiled only when they were interacting with officials or the public, not when they were standing alone—though presumably they were equally happy the whole time! (Fernández-Dols & Ruiz-Belda, 1995). As we will see later in this chapter, cultures and circumstances do play an important role in when and how people express their feelings.

GET INVOLVED

See if "facial feedback" works for you. Next time you are feeling sad or afraid, try purposely smiling—even if no one is around. Keep smiling. Does your facial expression affect your mood? Is it true, as Anna sings in The King and I, *that when we fool the people we meet—by wearing a happy smile or whistling a happy tune to disguise fear—we fool ourselves as well?*

Facial expressions thus have many functions, but they are only part of the emotional picture. Even Ekman, who has been studying them for years, concludes, "There is obviously emotion without facial expression and facial expression without emotion." In Shakespeare's play *Henry VI,* the villain who will become the evil King Richard III says,

Why, I can smile, and murder while I smile;
And cry content to that which grieves my heart;
And wet my cheeks with artificial tears,
And frame my face to all occasions.

EMOTION AND THE BRAIN

Another line of physiological research seeks to identify parts of the brain responsible for the many aspects of emotional experience: recognizing another person's emotion, feeling intensely aroused, labeling the emotion, deciding what to do about it, and so on. This research is finding that many components of emotion are quite specifically localized in the brain. For example, people with the rare disease of *prosopagnosia* are often able to recognize facial *expressions* even when they can't identify *faces* (Sacks, 1985). Both abilities are located in the right hemisphere but in different areas (Damasio, 1994). By following the instructions in Figure 10.2, you can verify that your own right hemisphere becomes activated when you identify facial expressions.

In recent years research has focused on the amygdala, a small structure in the limbic system that appears to be responsible for evaluating sensory information and

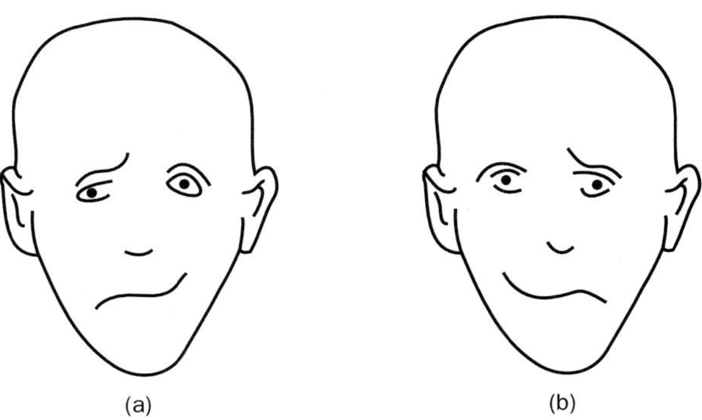

Figure 10.2
Hemispheric Activation and Emotion

These faces have expressions of happiness on one side and sadness on the other. Look at the nose of each face and decide which face looks happier and which sadder. You are likely to see face (b) as the happier one and face (a) as the sadder one. The most likely reason is that in most people the left side of a picture is processed by the right side of the brain, where recognition of emotional expression primarily occurs (Oatley & Jenkins, 1996).

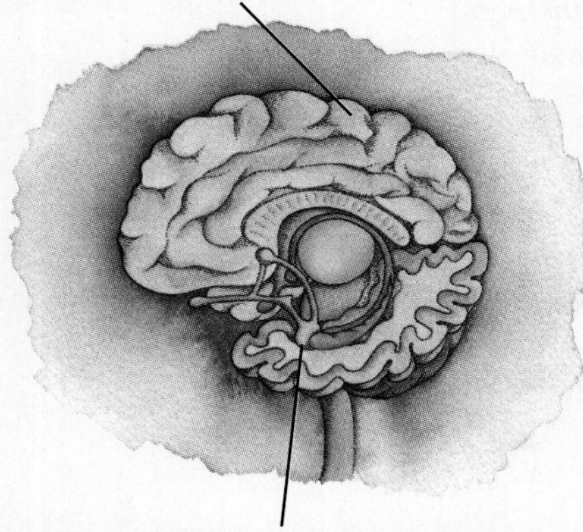

Second, the cerebral cortex generates a more complete picture; it can override signals sent by the amygdala ("It's only Mike in a down coat").

First, the amygdala scrutinizes information for its emotional importance ("It's a bear! Be afraid! Run!").

quickly determining its emotional importance, and also for the initial decision to approach or withdraw from a person or situation (LeDoux, 1994, 1996). The amygdala quickly assesses danger or threat, which is a good thing, because otherwise you could be standing in the street asking, "Is it wise to cross now, while that very large truck is coming toward me?" The amygdala's initial response may then be "overridden" by a more accurate appraisal from the cerebral cortex (LeDoux, 1996). This is why you jump with fear when you suddenly feel a hand on your back in a dark alley, and why your fear evaporates when the cortex registers that the hand belongs to a friend. If either the amygdala or critical areas of the cortex are damaged, emotional abnormalities result. A rat with a damaged amygdala "forgets" to be afraid when it should be; people with damage to the amygdala often have difficulty recognizing fear in themselves or others (Damasio, 1994). But rats or people with damage to certain areas of the cortex often lose the capacity to override their fear when it is no longer necessary. The result can be constant, irrational feelings of impending doom and anxiety, and obsessive thoughts of danger—as we will see in more detail in Chapter 15 (Schulkin, 1994; Schwartz et al., 1996).

The two cerebral hemispheres play different roles not only in the recognition of facial expression, but also in the experience of positive and negative emotions. This specialization is apparent in infants (Davidson, 1992). Regions of the left hemisphere appear to be specialized for the processing of such positive emotions as happiness, whereas regions of the right hemisphere are specialized for such negative emotions as fear and sadness. Damage to the left hemisphere tends to produce excessive anger or depression; damage to the right hemisphere is associated with excessive displays of mania and laughing. Even in people without brain damage, those who are clinically depressed have less activation in the left frontal regions than nondepressed people do (Henriques & Davidson, 1991).

THE ENERGY OF EMOTION

A third line of physiological research focuses on hormones, which produce the energy of emotion. In particular, the inner part of the adrenal gland, the medulla, sends out two hormones, *epinephrine* and *norepinephrine* (see Chapter 4). These hormones activate the sympathetic division of the autonomic nervous system and thus produce a state of *arousal,* a level of alertness that allows the body to respond quickly. During arousal the pupils dilate, widening to allow in more light; the heart beats faster; breathing speeds up; blood sugar rises, providing the body with more energy to act; and digestion slows down, so that blood flow can be diverted from the stomach and intestines to the muscles and surface of the skin. This is why, when you are excited, scared, furious, or wildly in love, you may not want to eat. In addition, your memory, concentration, and performance improve—up to a point. If hormone levels become too high, concentration and performance worsen. This is why a little nervousness when you take an exam is a good thing, but hand-trembling anxiety is not.

The adrenal glands produce epinephrine and norepinephrine in response to many challenges in the environment. These hormones will surge if you are laughing at a funny movie, playing a video game, worrying about an exam, cheering at a sports event, or responding to an insult. They will also rise in response to nonemotional conditions, such as heat, cold, pain, injury, and physical exercise; in response to some drugs, such as caffeine and nicotine; and in response to stress.

Epinephrine in particular provides the *energy* of an emotion—that familiar tingle, excitement, and sense of animation. At high levels, it can create the sensation of being "seized" or "flooded" by an emotion that is out of one's control. In a sense, the release of epinephrine does cause us to lose control, because few people can consciously alter their heart rates, blood pressures, and digestive tracts. (But people can learn to control their actions when they are emotionally aroused, as we discuss in "Taking Psychology with You.") As arousal subsides, a "hot" emotion usually turns into its "cool" counterpart. Anger may pale into annoyance, ecstasy into contentment, fear into suspicion, past emotional whirlwinds into calm breezes.

Although some emotions produce common reactions that mobilize the body to cope with the environment, many emotions differ chemically and anatomically. As we noted in Chapter 4, the brain has a variety of chemical messengers at its disposal—neurotransmitters, hormones, and neuromodulators—and these play different roles in different emotions (Oatley & Jenkins, 1996). In one series of experiments, subjects were induced, in a variety of ways, to experience fear, disgust, anger, sadness, surprise, and happiness. Each emotion was associated with a somewhat different pattern of autonomic activity, involving such measures as heart rate, electrical conductivity of the skin (galvanic skin responses, or GSR), and finger temperature. Indeed, the researchers found 14 distinctions among emotions in autonomic nervous system activity (Levenson, 1992; Levenson, Ekman, & Friesen, 1990). These distinctive patterns may be why people say they feel "hot and bothered" when they are angry, but "cold and clammy" when they are afraid.

Some psychologists believe that the ultimate purpose of emotion is to produce an overt response. Most emotions involve some change in *action readiness* (Frijda, 1988; Lang, 1995); they prepare the body to cope with danger or threat, excitement or opportunity. When you feel an emotion, you generally will feel motivated to do something specific: embrace the person who instills joy in you, yell at the person who is angering you, or run from the situation that is frightening you. This disposition to approach or withdraw, so closely linked with emotional states, is evident in infancy. In one study, 10-month-old babies were briefly separated from their mothers, then monitored during the happy reunion. The babies smiled, their left hemispheres were active, and they reached out to their moms. But when the babies were only smiling socially at strangers, their left hemispheres showed no increased activation, and the babies didn't reach out (Fox & Davidson, 1988).

As we have seen, the physiology of emotion involves facial expressions; activity in specific parts of the brain, notably the amygdala; activity in the two cerebral hemispheres during positive or negative emotions; and sympathetic nervous system activity that prepares the body to take action during an emotional state. Certain primitive emotions occur independently of higher cognitive processes, which is why people can be afraid for no "rational" reason or can have pleasant feelings about a familiar object without knowing why (Izard, 1994a; Murphy, Monahan, & Zajonc, 1995). Even so, the physical changes involved in emotion cannot explain why, of two students about to take an exam, one feels psyched up and the other feels overwhelmed by anxiety. They cannot explain why drugs that *lower* heart rate have no effect on people's subjective reports of anxiety (Neiss, 1988). Different patterns of hemispheric activation in cheerful and depressed people don't tell us why the former see the world through rose-tinted glasses, and the latter through foggy gray ones.

One consequence of the mistaken assumption that physiological changes tell the whole story of emotion has been the widespread use of "lie detectors" designed to read a person's "true" feelings (see "Puzzles of Psychology"). But physiological changes are usually not enough to create an emotional experience. Are you thrilled or frightened? Sick or just in love? Your hormones alone won't tell you.

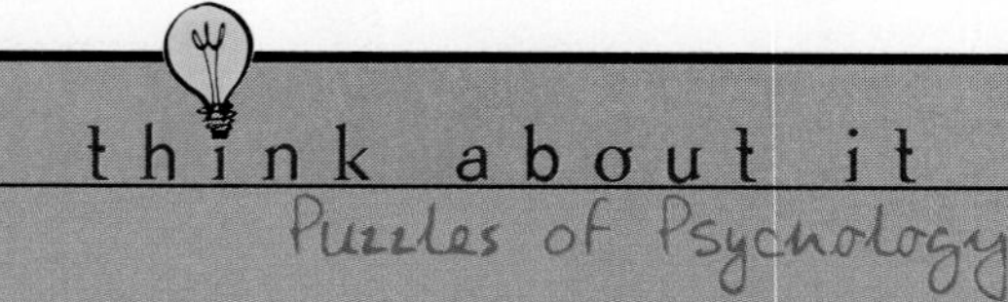

Can Lies Be Detected?

"The truth will out," goes an old saying, but the truth is that most human beings are not very good at detecting the lies of others. Many people think that liars won't smile or look you in the eye, for instance, but plenty of liars do exactly that. Many people assume that some body signs (such as facial animation) reflect truthfulness, whereas other signals (such as nervous gestures) indicate deception, but neither assumption is true. "There is no one cue that always indicates that a person is lying," says Bella DePaulo (1994), who has been looking for such cues in years of research. Even professionals commonly thought to be skilled at detecting lies—customs officers, police, polygraphers, judges, psychiatrists, and lawyers—are no better than amateurs at detecting deceit . . . which is to say, they aren't very good at it (DePaulo, 1994; Ekman & O'Sullivan, 1991). Of numerous professions tested, only the Secret Service does particularly well.

Is it possible to design a test that would let you know for sure whether a person is lying? In Asia, for many centuries, the "rice method" of lie detection was used on people suspected of a crime. The suspect had to chew on a handful of dry rice and then spit it out. The belief was that an innocent person would be able to do this easily, while a guilty person would have grains of rice stuck to the tongue and the roof of the mouth.

The rice method may seem primitive, but its rationale is not much removed from that of the modern polygraph machine, commonly called the lie detector. Both methods are based on the belief that a person who is guilty and fearful will have increased activity in the autonomic nervous system. In the case of the guilty rice-eater, such arousal should dry the saliva in the mouth and cause grains to stick to the tongue. In the case of the guilty suspect taking a polygraph test, a lie should be revealed by increased heart rate, respiration rate, and GSR as the person responds with incriminating answers to questions.

The appeal of the lie detector is that it is supposed to do better than people at finding out who is innocent of a crime or of lying and who is not. A few psychologists still lobby enthusiastically on behalf of the polygraph, arguing that it can be used reliably to identify liars (Raskin, Honts, & Kircher, 1997). However, they represent a minority view. Most researchers regard polygraph tests as being dangerously unreliable because *no physiological patterns of responses are specific to lying* (Iacono & Lykken, 1997; Lilienfeld, 1993; Saxe, 1994). Machines cannot tell whether you are feeling guilty, angry, nervous, amused, or revved up from an exciting day. Innocent people may be tense and nervous about the whole procedure. They may react to the word *bank* not because they robbed a bank, but because they recently bounced a check. In either case, the machine will record a "lie." The reverse mistake is also common. Some suave, practiced liars can lie without flinching, and others learn to "beat the machine" by tensing muscles or thinking about an exciting experience during neutral questions (Lykken, 1981). A few years ago, for example, Aldrich Ames, a high-level CIA official, was convicted of spying for the former Soviet Union and selling national secrets. During the investigation, Ames passed two polygraph tests designed to detect his treasonous acts.

Moreover, the people who administer the polygraph test often make many errors in reading the results. They do not reliably agree with one another's judgments, and, worst of all, they are more likely to accuse the innocent of lying than to let the guilty go free (Kleinmuntz & Szucko, 1984; Saxe, 1994). Because of such findings, in 1988 the

Quick Quiz

Which aspects of the physiology of emotion are involved in the following reactions to events?

1. A 3-year-old sees her dad dressed as a gorilla and runs away in fear. What brain structure is probably involved in her withdrawal from him?
2. Casey is watching *Hatchet Murders in the Dorm: Sequel XVII.* What hormones cause his heart to pound and his palms to sweat when the murderer is stalking an unsuspecting victim?
3. Melissa is watching an old Laurel and Hardy film, which makes her chuckle and puts her in a good mood. Which hemisphere of her brain is likely to be most activated?

Answers:

1. the amygdala 2. epinephrine, norepinephrine 3. left

U.S. Congress passed a law prohibiting employers from using lie detectors to screen job applicants or randomly test employees, and most courts do not admit polygraph evidence in trials. However, police departments continue to use them for various purposes, and polygraph tests are still used for obtaining security clearances in the U.S. government even though test accuracy is very low. In experiments in which federal employees were given knowledge of acts of mock espionage and told to try to hide this knowledge from investigators, many of the "guilty" respondents were able to pass polygraph tests with flying colors (Honts, 1994).

Nevertheless, efforts to measure physiological signs of lying continue. The Guilty Knowledge Test (Lykken, 1991) is based on the assumption that autonomic arousal will be higher in guilty subjects who are asked about aspects of a crime that only they could know about. Some researchers are using measures of brain activity, commonly called *event-related potentials,* to see whether they can infer whether a person possesses guilty knowledge of a crime or is lying (Bashore & Rapp, 1993). But because of the normal variability among people in their autonomic and brain reactivity, innocent but highly reactive people are still likely to be misdiagnosed as "guilty" by these tests.

When students and community members are asked to keep diaries of lies in their everyday lives, most people report telling one or two lies a day (DePaulo et al., 1996). They lie to protect themselves from embarrassment, loss of face, or looking bad. They lie to flatter or protect the feelings of the other person. They lie for personal gain. They lie about what they really believe, where they really went, or what they really did. Are all these lies equally wrong or bad? Paul Ekman, who has studied emotions and deception for many years, offers some thoughtful questions to consider when thinking about lie detection: "What would life be like if we couldn't lie? If we had something that was the equivalent of the dog's tail? . . . What a terrible life; there would be no privacy! On the other hand, imagine a world in which everyone could lie perfectly; [in which] anyone could mislead you without your knowing it. Basically, the world we live in—where we can lie, but not perfectly—is probably the best" (quoted in Howell, 1993).

Do you agree? When would it be desirable or disastrous to detect another person's lies—and would you want everyone to be able to detect yours? How reliable does a test need to be before its widespread use can be justified: Is it acceptable if it misidentifies "only" 1 innocent person in 10? in 100? in 1,000? What do you think?

"WE CAN'T DETERMINE IF YOU'RE TELLING THE TRUTH, BUT YOU SHOULD HAVE A DOCTOR CHECK YOUR PRESSURE."

ELEMENTS OF EMOTION 2: THE MIND

Let's say that you have had a crush for weeks on a fellow student in your history class. Finally you get up the nerve to start a conversation. Heart pounding, palms sweating, you cheerfully say, "Hi, there!" Before you can continue, the student has walked past you without even a nod. What emotion do you feel? Your answer will depend on how you explain the student's behavior:

Angry: "What a rude thing to do, to ignore me like that!"
Sad: "I knew it; I'm no good. No one will ever like me."
Embarrassed: "Oh, no! Everyone saw how I was humiliated!"
Relieved: "Thank goodness; I wasn't sure I wanted to get involved, anyway."

As we noted in Chapter 1, in the first century A.D., the Stoic philosophers suggested that people do not become angry or sad or anxious because of actual events, but because of their explanations of those events. Modern psychologists have been verifying the Stoics' ideas experimentally and identifying the specific mental processes involved in emotions.

HOW THOUGHTS CREATE EMOTIONS

In 1924, a Spanish physician named Gregorio Marañon wondered if he could generate emotions in his subjects simply by injecting them with epinephrine (see Cornelius, 1991). He got a curious result. Nearly 30 percent of the 210 people in his research reported feeling genuine emotions, usually sadness, often accompanied by weeping. But more than 70 percent merely reported physical changes ("My heart is beating fast," "My throat feels tight") or what Marañon called "as if" emotions: "I feel *as if* I were angry," "I feel *as if* I were happy."

What caused the difference between the two groups? Marañon reported that he was able to induce genuine emotions by asking the first group to think about their sick children or their deceased parents. In short, the people who reported genuine emotions had a reason for them! Marañon concluded that emotions involve a *physical* component, consisting of the bodily changes that accompany arousal, and a psychological or *mental* component, consisting of the interpretation the individual gives them, within the context in which those changes occur.

Marañon's research languished in a French journal of endocrinology until the 1960s, when Stanley Schachter and Jerome Singer advanced similar ideas with their **two-factor theory of emotion** (Schachter, 1971; Schachter & Singer, 1962). Like Marañon, they argued that bodily changes are necessary to experience an emotion, but they are not enough. Emotion, they said, depends on two factors: *physiological arousal* and the *cognitive interpretation* of that arousal. Your body may be churning away in high gear, but unless you can interpret, explain, and label those changes, you won't feel a true emotion. Conversely, if all your friends are worried about an upcoming exam, you may decide that the pounding of your heart is a sign that you are nervous, too. You may not realize that your heart is pounding because you have been partying late, losing sleep, and drinking too much coffee.

Schachter and Singer's own experiments, which were widely cited, were not successfully replicated. Their idea that arousal was necessary to feel an emotion proved overstated; and, as we just saw, the physiology of emotion turned out to involve more than the activation of hormones. But their work was important for two reasons. First, it helped explain why people often mislabel their own physical states. For example, when people are aroused and they don't know why (perhaps, as in one

two-factor theory of emotion The theory that emotions depend on both physiological arousal and a cognitive interpretation of that arousal.

GET INVOLVED

Put your finger on the dot, and smile. How do you feel at this moment, amused or irritated? If you followed our instructions and touched the dot, you probably feel more amused than angry. You may be laughing at yourself for doing such a silly thing, and that will make you feel happy. If you didn't put your finger on the dot, you probably feel more angry than amused. "Why are the authors of this book asking me to play stupid games?" you may be asking yourself. Notice that it is not our request that produced your emotion; it is your interpretation of what we asked you to do. Such interpretations are critical to all emotions.

study, because of residual arousal following exercise), they are more emotionally affected by cues in the environment than they are when they have an obvious explanation for their arousal (Sinclair et al., 1994). Second, their work launched scores of studies designed to identify the kinds of cognitions that are involved in the experience of emotion. Psychologists went on to study the thought patterns and perceptions that are typical of many emotions, from gradations of joy to degrees of sadness.

For example, most people assume that success on a project brings happiness, and failure brings unhappiness. In fact, however, people's emotions depend on how they *explain* their success or failure. In a series of experiments, students reported times when they had done well on or failed an exam for a particular reason, such as help from others or lack of effort, and described the emotions they felt on each of these occasions. Their emotions were more closely associated with their explanations than with the outcome of the test (Weiner, 1986). Students who believed they did well because of their own efforts and abilities tended to feel proud, competent, and satisfied. Those who believed they did well because of a lucky fluke or chance tended to feel gratitude, surprise, or guilt ("I don't deserve this"). Those who believed their failures were their own fault tended to feel regretful, guilty, or resigned. And those who blamed others tended to feel angry or hostile.

Here is another surprising example of how thoughts affect emotions. Of two Olympic medalists—one who wins a second-place silver and one who wins a third-place bronze—which will feel happier? Won't it be the silver medalist? Nope. In a study of athletes' reactions to placing second and third in the 1992 Olympics and the 1994 Empire State games, the bronze medalists were happier than the silver medalists (Medvec, Madey, & Gilovich, 1995). The reason, according to the researchers, is that the athletes were comparing their performance to "what might have been": The second-place winners, comparing themselves to the gold medalists, were unhappy that they didn't get the gold; but the third-place winners, comparing themselves to those who did worse than they, were happy that they earned a medal at all! As William James observed in 1892:

> So we have the paradox of a man shamed to death because he is only the second pugilist [boxer] or the second oarsman in the world. That he is able to beat the whole population of the globe minus one is nothing; he has 'pitted' himself to beat that one; and as long as he doesn't do that nothing else counts.

In general, negative emotions differ from positive ones in the kinds of perceptions that generate them. We observed this fact for ourselves when some friends returned from a mountain-climbing trip to Nepal. One said, "It was wonderful! The crystal-clear skies, the millions of stars, the friendly people, the majestic mountains, the harmony of the universe!" The other said, "It was horrible! The bedbugs and fleas, the lack of toilets, the yak-butter tea, the awful food, the unforgiving mountains!" Guess which traveler was ecstatic while traveling and which was unhappy?

Surprisingly, third place winners tend to be happier about their performance than those who come in second. Certainly Olympic fencing bronze-medalist Jean-Michel Henry of France (left) is happier than silver-medalist Pavel Kolobkov of the Unified Team (right)! (Eric Strecki, center, won the gold for France.)

To understand the mental processes involved in emotion, consider the feelings of sadness involved in loneliness and depression. National surveys show that the loneliest people in the United States are adolescents and college students; fortunately, loneliness declines as people get older (Perlman, 1990). Loneliness, however, is not the same thing as solitude or being alone. Many people live alone and do not feel lonely because they have close ties to good friends and family. Others live in large families and feel desperately lonely, because they think that no one understands them or cares about them. Feelings of loneliness, therefore, cannot be understood by studying only actual isolation. Similarly, stressful events—the breakup of a relationship, moving away from home, being fired from a job—make everyone temporarily unhappy, but a person's recovery depends on how he or she interprets and reacts to these events over time (Anderson et al., 1994; Forgas, 1994; Snodgrass, 1987; Weiner, 1986). Three aspects of a person's cognitions—internality, stability, and control—are especially important in prolonging depression:

1. *Internality.* Do you believe that the reason for your sad feelings is *internal* (something in you, an entrenched aspect of your personality) or *external* (something in the outside world)? Internal reasons for loneliness include "I'm unattractive" and "I don't know how to make friends." External explanations look outward: "The people I work with are unfriendly," "I'm having a run of bad luck," or "This school is so big and impersonal it's hard to meet new people." People who attribute their failures and woes to internal causes are sadder and lonelier than those who do not (Anderson et al., 1994).
2. *Stability.* Do you believe that the reason for your feelings is permanent ("This is just an unfriendly place and always will be") or temporary? People who think that their negative emotions are hopelessly stable and unchangeable create a vicious cycle for themselves. Expecting nothing to improve, they do nothing to improve their circumstances, and therefore remain lonely and sad.
3. *Control.* Do you believe you have control over the causes of your feelings? The belief that you can do nothing to change a bad situation ("I'm ugly and horrible and I can't do anything about it") often prolongs loneliness and despair.

These three dimensions help account for people's emotional reactions in a wide variety of situations, from school to marriage. For example, in numerous laboratory and field studies, when happy or depressed people are asked to describe and account for conflicts in their close relationships, the depressed people's explanations are more internal, stable, and global—leading them to feel more bitter and pessimistic about their relationships—than the happy people's (Fincham, 1994; Forgas, 1994).

Emotions occur, cognitive researchers believe, because people are constantly appraising the events that befall them for their personal implications: Do I care about what is happening? Is it good or bad for me? Can I do anything about it? Is this mat-

GET INVOLVED

Next time you get an exam grade back, write down the reasons you think you got the grade you did. Are the reasons internal (e.g., you worked hard or failed to study enough) or external (the test was too easy or unfair)? Are they stable (you think you're just "naturally" smart or dumb and always will be) or temporary (you worked hard or didn't study for this one exam)? Are they uncontrollable (your grade was out of your hands) or under your control (a result of something you did or failed to do)? How are these explanations related to your feelings about your grade?

ter going to get better or worse? These appraisals provide the emotional "heat" in our encounters (Smith et al., 1993). If you decide that being stuck in a traffic jam is trivial and you can't do anything about it anyway, you may take it calmly. If you are on the way to, say, your wedding, and you see that the traffic is getting worse, and being late is *really* going to be bad for you, you are likely to feel hopping mad at those stupid cars that are blocking your way.

Many emotions are distinguished by the particular thoughts and perceptions that generate them. For example, most people assume that envy and jealousy are much alike; but when students write about their actual experiences with either emotion, the two emotions prove to be cognitively different (Parrott & Smith, 1993). *Envy* is characterized by thoughts of inferiority, longing, and resentment; *jealousy* is characterized by fear of rejection or loss, distrust, anxiety, and anger.

Two other distinct emotions that are often confused are *shame* and *guilt*, either or both of which may occur when you do something you know you shouldn't have. The two emotions differ in the cognitions that provoke them and in the behavior they motivate (Lewis, 1971; Tangney et al., 1996). In shame, the focus is on the bad self; in guilt, the focus is on the bad behavior. The shamed person regards his or her failure or bad behavior as evidence of a global and enduring personality defect; he or she feels small, worthless, and powerless. The resulting motive is to hide or sink into the floor. In contrast, the guilty person regards the bad behavior or failure as just that—a bad act, but one that does not affect the overall worthiness of the self; the resulting motive is to apologize and make amends. Interestingly, studies of hundreds of children and adults find that shame is related to anger, hostility, resentment, and blame—but guilt is not (Tangney et al., 1996). The reason seems to be that guilty people think about their behavior this way: "Gee, if I did that bad thing, I should try to help fix it." But shamed people make cognitive appraisals that lead to blaming the person who they feel shamed them: "Gee, if I did that bad thing, what a horrible person I am! And how could you have put me in such a bind and made me feel so terrible, you skunk?"

Are these children feeling shame or guilt for breaking that vase? Guilt arises from the perception that you did something bad; shame arises from the perception that you are bad.

As the shame–anger link shows, one challenge of studying emotion is the sheer complexity of emotional experiences. Psychologists usually study one emotion or another, but most people feel one emotion *and* another; emotions often occur in bunches, like grapes. People's perceptions, beliefs, expectations, and appraisals of a situation help explain the reason for such mixed emotions. In one study, college students described their thoughts and feelings just before taking a midterm exam and again after they got their grades (Smith & Ellsworth, 1987). At both times, students reported mixed feelings, such as hope and fear before the exam or anger and guilt after the exam. These emotional blends were reliably related to the students' appraisals of their performance, the importance of the test, their own effort in studying, and so on. The students who felt angriest about their poor grades, for example, interpreted the exam as being unfair. This anger, though, was often combined with guilt ("I should have studied harder"), fear ("What if I don't pass?"), or apathy ("I don't care about this course anyway").

Studies of the cognitive element in emotion suggest that depressed or anxious people can learn how their thinking affects their emotions and change their thinking accordingly. (As we will see in Chapter 16, cognitive therapy is based on this assumption.) They can ask themselves what the evidence is for their belief that the world will collapse if they get a C in biology, that no one loves them, or that they will be lonely forever. In such cases, it is not emotional reasoning that prevents critical thinking; it is the failure to think critically that creates the emotion!

These cognitive skills can be taught, even to children, and the effects are long lasting. A remarkable intervention program targeted 69 fifth- and sixth-grade children

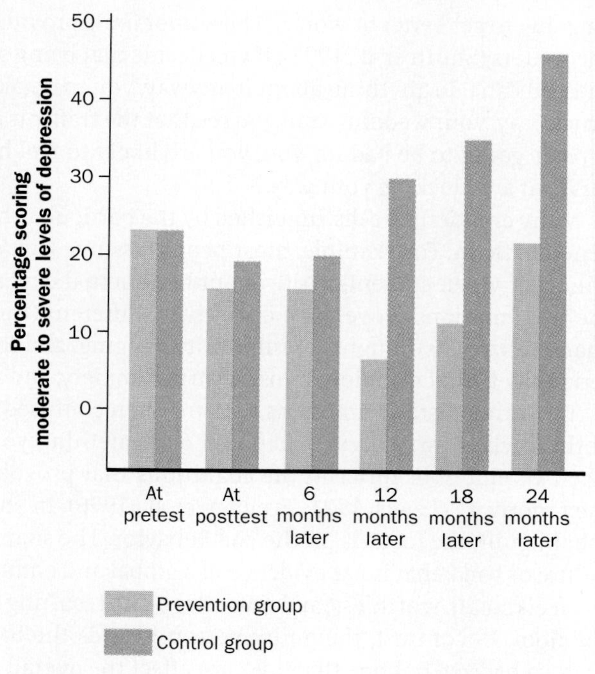

Figure 10.3
Inoculation Against Depression
This graph shows the percentage of children who were at moderate to high risk of depression on a pretest; again after completion of a cognitive intervention (posttest); and during four follow-up assessments. Notice that the effects of the intervention were still strong two years later, as the children entered adolescence (Gillham et al., 1995).

who were at risk of depression; they scored high on a children's depression inventory, came from homes with high levels of parental conflict, or both. The children were taught to identify pessimistic beliefs, to examine the evidence for and against those beliefs, and to generate more realistic alternatives. A control group of children at risk of depression did not get this training. As you can see in Figure 10.3, after the training, children in the intervention group consistently had lower depression scores than did those in the control group in all four follow-up sessions. The differences still held two years later, when the children were entering adolescence and when depression rates in the control group really shot up (Gillham et al., 1995).

In sum, the cognitions involved in emotion range from your immediate perceptions of a specific event to your general philosophy of life. If you believe that winning is everything and trying your best counts for nothing, you may feel depressed rather than happy if you "only" come in second—like those silver medalists. If you think a friend's criticism is intentionally mean rather than well meaning, you may respond with anger rather than gratitude. This is why almost all theories of emotion hold that cognitive appraisals—the *meanings* people give to events—are essential to the creation of emotion (Frijda, 1988; Lazarus, 1991; Oatley & Jenkins, 1996). Our emotions cannot be separated from our mental lives.

Quick Quiz

How are your thoughts affecting your feelings about this quiz?

1. Chronically lonely and unhappy people tend to believe that the reasons for their unhappiness are (a) controllable, (b) internal, (c) temporary, (d) caused by the situation.
2. Given that shame and guilt tend to motivate people differently, which emotion would you want your best friend or partner to feel if she or he behaved badly toward you, and why?
3. At a party, you see a stranger flirting with your date. Suddenly, you are flooded with jealousy. What cognitions might be causing this emotion? *Be specific.* What alternative thoughts might reduce the jealousy?

Answers:

1. b 2. guilt, because your friend is likely to be motivated to apologize and make amends rather than become angry and blame you, as shamed people tend to do. 3. Possible thoughts causing jealousy are "My date finds other people more attractive," "That person is trying to steal my date," or "My date's behavior is humiliating me." But you could be saying, "It's a compliment to me that other people find my date attractive" or "It pleases me that my date is getting such deserved attention."

THE MIND–BODY CONNECTION

Research on emotion has moved us a long way toward resolving the historic division between the mind ("reason") and the body ("emotion"). Rather than regarding reason and emotion as separate, often conflicting processes, researchers now emphasize the ways in which physiological and cognitive processes interact:

DON'T OVERSIMPLIFY

Many people believe that emotions are the downfall of our species because they are the opposite of reason. But are emotion and cognition really independent of each other? How can we avoid thinking about reason and emotion in either–or ways?

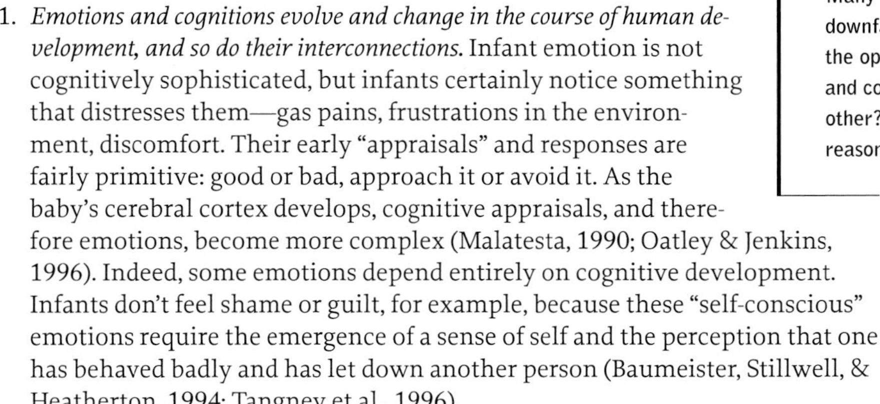

1. *Emotions and cognitions evolve and change in the course of human development, and so do their interconnections.* Infant emotion is not cognitively sophisticated, but infants certainly notice something that distresses them—gas pains, frustrations in the environment, discomfort. Their early "appraisals" and responses are fairly primitive: good or bad, approach it or avoid it. As the baby's cerebral cortex develops, cognitive appraisals, and therefore emotions, become more complex (Malatesta, 1990; Oatley & Jenkins, 1996). Indeed, some emotions depend entirely on cognitive development. Infants don't feel shame or guilt, for example, because these "self-conscious" emotions require the emergence of a sense of self and the perception that one has behaved badly and has let down another person (Baumeister, Stillwell, & Heatherton, 1994; Tangney et al., 1996).
2. *Relationships between cognition and emotion work in both directions.* Emotion results from appraisals and other thoughts; but emotions themselves can impair or interfere with subsequent thoughts and feelings. For example, you decide that a friend has intentionally stood you up for lunch, so you feel angry. But once you feel angry, you may be unwilling to listen to anyone who tries to correct your way of thinking about your friend's tardiness. Similarly, a perception such as "This person is out to hurt me" can produce emotional arousal, but being physiologically aroused for nonemotional reasons—exercise, stress, crowds, or noise, for example—can make emotions more intense. If you are at a noisy, crowded concert and you believe that someone has insulted you, you are likely to feel very angry, very quickly. You will feel angrier than if you had been listening to a clarinet, lying on the sofa, or watching a romantic comedy when the insult occurred (Averill, 1982; Zillmann, 1983).

This baby will not feel an ounce of remorse for keeping her parents up all night—or gratitude for their care. Remorse and gratitude require the capacity for complex cognitive appraisals.

3. *Cognitions need not be conscious and voluntary to create emotions.* As we saw in previous chapters, some modes of cognitive activity operate nonconsciously and without voluntary control. Some emotions, too, involve simple nonconscious reactions, such as a conditioned emotional response to a symbol of patriotism or a positive feeling toward a familiar object (Murphy, Monahan, & Zajonc, 1995). Others require complex cognitive capacity, such as being able to appreciate wordplay or subtle puns in order to find them funny. Some emotions are almost instantaneous, processed quickly by the amygdala, but others require the cerebral cortex, the center of reason, symbols, and logic. This part of the brain gives us the capacity for deciding we have been

betrayed, for reanalyzing our fears, for interpreting someone else's actions—in short, for generating complex emotions. Appraisals may conflict at these different levels, which is why you can simultaneously believe that airplanes are safe and feel worried about getting in one.

4. *Both emotion and cognition can be "rational" or "irrational."* As we saw in the chapters on thinking (Chapter 8) and memory (Chapter 9), human cognition is not always rational. It involves many "irrational" biases, including the confirmation bias, biases due to cognitive dissonance, and biases in the construction of memories. Conversely, emotions are not always irrational. They bind people together, regulate relationships, and motivate people to achieve their goals. Without the capacity to feel emotion, people have difficulty making ethical decisions and planning for the future (Damasio, 1994). "The appropriate way to see emotions is not as irrational elements in our lives," observes emotion researcher Keith Oatley (1990), "but as a clever biological solution to problems . . . that have no fully rational solutions." When you are faced with a decision between two appealing and justifiable career alternatives, for example, your sense of which one "feels right" emotionally may help you make the best choice.

An individual's experience of emotion, then, combines mind and body. But all individuals live in a social world. Thoughts may influence emotion, but where do these thoughts come from? You may decide you are wildly jealous, but where do you get your ideas of jealousy? You may feel angry enough to punch the walls, but where do you learn what to do when you are that enraged? To answer these questions, we turn to the third major aspect of emotional experience: the role of culture.

ELEMENTS OF EMOTION 3: THE CULTURE

A young wife leaves her house one morning to draw water from the local well as her husband watches from the porch. On her way back from the well, a male stranger stops her and asks for some water. She gives him a cupful and then invites him home to dinner. He accepts. The husband, wife, and guest have a pleasant meal together. The husband, in a gesture of hospitality, invites the guest to spend the night—with his wife. The guest accepts. In the morning, the husband leaves early to bring home breakfast. When he returns, he finds his wife again in bed with the visitor.

The question is: At what point in this story does the husband feel angry? The answer is: It depends on the culture to which he belongs (Hupka, 1981, 1991). A North American husband would feel rather angry at a wife who had an extramarital affair, and a wife would feel rather angry at being offered to a guest as if she were a lamb chop. But these reactions are not universal. A Pawnee husband of the nineteenth century would be enraged at any man who dared ask his wife for water. An Ammassalik Inuit husband finds it perfectly honorable to offer his wife to a stranger, but only once. He would be angry to find his wife and the guest having a second encounter. And a Toda husband at the turn of the century in India would not be angry at all, because the Todas allowed both husband and wife to take lovers. Both spouses might feel angry, though, if one of them had a *sneaky* affair, without announcing it publicly.

People in most cultures experience anger as a response to insult and the violation of social rules. It's just that they disagree about what an insult or the correct rule is. In this section, we will explore some cultural influences on emotion.

THE VARIETIES OF EMOTION

Are emotions universal, or do some of them have national boundaries? One problem in answering this question is that some languages have words for emotional states that other languages lack (Mesquita & Frijda, 1993). The Germans have *schadenfreude*, a feeling of joy at another's misfortune. The Japanese have *ijirashii*, a feeling associated with seeing an admirable person overcoming an obstacle, and *hagaii*, helpless anguish tinged with frustration. *Litost* is a Czech word that combines grief, sympathy, remorse, and longing; the Czech writer Milan Kundera used it to describe "a state of torment caused by a sudden insight into one's own miserable self." On the island of Java, *isin* is a complex anxiety and shame reaction involving fear and lowered self-esteem.

Anthropologist Robert Levy (1984) reports that Tahitians lack the Western concept of and word for sadness. If you ask a Tahitian who is grieving over the loss of a lover what is wrong, he will say, "A spirit has made me ill." In contrast, Tahitians have a word for an emotion that most Westerners do not experience: *Mehameha* refers to "a sense of the uncanny," a trembling sensation that Tahitians feel when ordinary categories of perception are suspended—at twilight, in the brush, watching fires glow without heat. To Westerners, an event that cannot be categorized and identified is usually greeted with fear. Yet *mehameha* does not describe what Westerners call fear or terror.

Likewise, most Westerners say that *love* refers to a positive emotion. However, in the People's Republic of China, "sad love" is considered a negative emotion, consisting of unrequited affection, infatuation, nostalgia, and sorrow. The researchers describe this emotion as "the fleeting passion you feel for an attractive person you see on a train and will never meet again" (Shaver, Wu, & Schwartz, 1992). Most Westerners would surely recognize this feeling, but it's not generally one they would define or experience as "love."

Do these interesting examples mean that Germans are more likely than others actually to feel *schadenfreude*, the Japanese to feel *hagaii*, the Javanese to feel *isin*, and the Czechs to feel *litost*—or are they just more willing to give these emotions a single name? Do the Tahitians experience sadness the way Westerners do even though they identify it as illness? Do the Chinese experience love differently?

Certain emotions are universal, but the rules for expressing them are not. The rule for a formal Japanese wedding portrait is "no expressions of emotion"—but not every member of this family has learned that rule yet.

Many psychologists believe that it is possible to identify a number of **primary emotions** that are experienced universally. Depending on the method of measuring emotion, the list of the primary ones varies somewhat, but it typically includes fear, anger, sadness, joy, surprise, disgust, and contempt. In contrast, **secondary emotions** are culture-specific. They include cultural variations such as *schadenfreude* or *hagaii;* blends of feeling such as *litost* or *isin;* and degrees of intensity and nuance.

This father is clearly proud of his family. Is pride a distinct emotion, or just a variation of happiness?

Those who argue on behalf of the universality of primary emotions draw on four lines of evidence:

1. *Physiological research on the brain and central nervous system,* which suggests that primary emotions are linked with specific survival tendencies, as in running from something fearful. Some physiological researchers, such as Joseph LeDoux (1996), argue that we should distinguish basic, hard-wired emotions from "feelings," which include all the higher-level human varieties influenced by cognition and culture.
2. *The existence of facial expressions that seem to be recognizable all over the world.* As we have seen, these expressions first appear, without learning, in infancy.
3. *The existence of emotion prototypes in most languages.* We saw in Chapter 8 that a *prototype* is a typical representative of a class of things. According to the prototype approach, basic emotions are those that people everywhere consider the core examples of the concept *emotion;* for example, most people will say that "anger" and "sadness" are more representative of an emotion than "irritability" and "nostalgia" are. Basic emotions are reflected in the emotion words that young children learn first: *happy, sad, mad,* and *scared.* As children develop, they begin to draw emotional distinctions that are less prototypical and more specific to their language and culture, such as *ecstatic, depressed, hostile,* or *anxious* (Russell, 1991; Russell & Fehr, 1994; Storm & Storm, 1987).
4. *The fact that certain emotions are evoked by the same situations everywhere.* For people everywhere, sadness follows perception of loss, fear follows perception of threat and bodily harm, anger follows perception of insult or injustice, and so forth. Moreover, people's physical descriptions of these emotions are similar, such as feeling hot in response to anger and a "lump in the throat" in response to sadness (Mesquita & Frijda, 1993; Oatley & Duncan, 1994). A massive cross-cultural project, involving 37 countries on five continents, found remarkable commonalities in people's reported experiences with fear, anger, joy, sadness, disgust, shame, and guilt (Scherer & Wallbott, 1994).

Other psychologists, however, think that the effort to find basic, primary, or universal emotions is misleading. They point out that most people don't think of surprise, disgust, or contempt as true emotions, although all three are registered on the face (Ortony & Turner, 1990; Shaver et al., 1987). Conversely, according to these researchers, shame, hope, guilt, pride, pity, love, and empathy are as much a part of human emotional experience as sadness and anger, but these feelings fail to make the list of primary emotions because they can't be measured in the brain or identified on the face (Roseman, Wiest, & Swartz, 1994).

primary emotions Emotions that are considered to be universal and biologically based; they generally include fear, anger, sadness, joy, surprise, disgust, and contempt

secondary emotions Emotions that are either "blends" of primary emotions or specific to certain cultures.

Critics of the universalist argument maintain that the effort to find biological universals in emotion masks the profound influence of culture on every aspect of emotional experience, starting with which feelings a culture even considers "basic." For example, anger is a basic emotion in the United States, which emphasizes independence and personal rights, but it is caused and experienced quite differently in community-oriented cultures, where shame and loss of face are more central and basic emotions (Kitayama & Markus, 1994). On the tiny Micronesian atoll of Ifaluk, everyone would say that *fago* is the most fundamental emotion. *Fago,* translated as "compassion/love/sadness," reflects the sad feeling one has when a loved one is absent or in need, and the pleasurable sense of compassion in being able to care and help (Lutz, 1988). What, then, would theories of primary emotions look like from a non-Western perspective? They might start with shame and *fago,* which are just blips on the radar screen of Western emotion research.

Even if certain basic emotions prove to be hard-wired biologically, it is clear that cultures determine much of what people feel angry, sad, lonely, happy, ashamed, or disgusted *about.* Among the Bedouins, shame is produced by any violations of a complex code of honor; on Bali and Java, shame and embarrassment are generated by perceived challenges to one's status (Mesquita & Frijda, 1993). In Ifaluk, it is cause for anger if someone next to you is smoking without offering you the cigarette; it means the smoker is unwilling to share—a terrible offense (Lutz, 1988). Increasingly in the United States, it is cause for anger if someone is smoking at all. To nonsmokers, smoking means an infringement on their right to clean air.

As you can see, answers to the question "Are emotions universal?" depend on whether researchers are focusing on the common elements in all emotions or on cultural differences.

THE COMMUNICATION OF EMOTION

On Sunday, April 25, in the year 1227, a knight named Ulrich von Lichtenstein disguised himself as the goddess Venus. Wearing an ornate white gown, waist-length braids, and heavy veils, Ulrich traveled from Venice to Bohemia, challenging all local warriors to a duel. By his own count (which may have been exaggerated), Ulrich broke 307 lances, unhorsed four opponents, and completed his five-week journey with an undefeated record. The reason for Ulrich's knightly performance was his passion for a princess, nameless to history, who barely gave poor Ulrich the time of day. Ulrich trembled in her presence, suffered in her absence, and constantly endured feelings of longing, misery, and melancholy—a state of love that apparently made him very happy (M. Hunt, 1959/1967).

What some of us do for love: Ulrich von Lichtenstein disguised as Venus.

We'll have a lot more to say about love in the next chapter, but for the moment consider only Ulrich's *expression* of his passion. If someone tried to win your heart by performing a modern version of such acts of bravery, would you be charmed or irritated?

Your answer will depend in part on what your culture has taught you about the **display rules** that govern how and when emotions may be expressed (Ekman et al., 1987). In some cultures, for example, people would find Ulrich's extravagant demonstration of love exciting and appropriate; in others, people would find it weird and lunatic—they would be suspicious of Ulrich's real motives. Likewise, in some cultures, grief is expressed by noisy wailing and weeping; in others, by stoic, tearless resignation; in still others, by merry dance, drink, and song. Once you feel an emotion, how you express it is rarely a simple matter of "I say (or show) what I feel." You may be obliged to disguise what you feel. You may wish you could feel what you say. You may convey an emotion unintentionally, through nonverbal signals.

For example, the smile seems simple and unmistakable; as we saw, it is generally recognized the world over as a sign of friendliness. Yet it has many meanings and uses that are not universal. Americans smile more frequently than Germans; this does not mean that Americans are friendlier than Germans, but that they differ in their notions of when a smile is appropriate. After a German–American business session, Americans often complain that their German counterparts are cold and aloof. For their part, Germans often complain that Americans are excessively cheerful, hid-

display rules Social and cultural rules that regulate when, how, and where a person may express (or must suppress) emotions.

GET INVOLVED

What are your culture's display rules for showing emotion in public places? Visit several different locations—a supermarket checkout line, a bus stop, your student union, an elevator in an apartment or office building—and notice people's emotional expressions. In general, are they showing much emotion, or are they "blank"? Do they make eye contact with strangers and smile at them, or avoid looking at anyone? If you do see someone expressing an emotion, such as anger or happiness, what is the person doing that conveys this feeling? To whom is the person expressing it? Under what conditions?

ing their real feelings under the mask of a smile (Hall & Hall, 1990). The Japanese smile even more than Americans, to disguise embarrassment, anger, or other negative emotions whose public display is considered rude and incorrect.

Body language is important in the communication of emotion. Have you ever been in a cheerful mood, had lunch with a depressed friend, and come away feeling vaguely depressed yourself? Have you ever stopped to have a chat with a friend who was nervous about an upcoming exam, and ended up feeling anxious yourself? Moods can indeed be highly contagious, especially when two people's body languages are in harmony (Hatfield, 1995; see Figure 10.4). For example, in a study of 96 pairs of college roommates, roommates of depressed students became more depressed themselves over the course of the three-week study, even when the researchers controlled for upsetting life events that might be affecting them (Joiner, 1994). An ability to synchronize moods through nonverbal gestures is crucial to smooth interaction and rapport between people (Bernieri et al., 1996; Hatfield, Cacioppo, & Rapson, 1992). (As we will see in Chapter 13, synchrony appears in the very first relationship a baby has, with his or her parents.) Conversely, a mismatch of body languages makes conversation feel "out of sync"; it can be as confusing and emotionally upsetting as verbal misunderstandings. An absence of synchrony occurs in people who have learning disabilities and emotional problems such as depression (Tronick, 1989).

CONSIDER OTHER EXPLANATIONS

A European who behaves in a way that conveys good manners and dignified restraint may seem cold to the average American. An American who smiles effusively may seem superficial and childish to the average European. How might each of them explain the other's behavior more constructively?

People learn their culture's display rules as effortlessly as they learn its language. Just as they can speak without knowing the rules of grammar, most people express or suppress their emotions without being aware of the rules they are following (Keating, 1994). Consider the display rules for the stages of an angry dispute (Hall, 1976). Suppose your neighbor builds a fence on what you believe is your property. If you are an American or Canadian, your anger is likely to move from small steps to large ones. You start by dropping hints ("Gee, Mort, are you sure that fence is on your side of the line?"). Next, you talk to friends. Then you get a third person to intervene. Eventually you confront Mort directly. If none of this works, you may go to court and sue him. If that strategy fails, you may burn the fence down.

There is, however, nothing "natural" about this course of action. Worldwide, it is not even typical. In many cultures, especially those of the Middle East and Latin America, the first thing you do when your neighbor builds a fence that angers you is . . . nothing. You think about it. You brood over your grievances and decide what to do. This brooding may last for weeks, months, or even years. The second step is . . . you burn the fence down. This is only to draw your neighbor's attention to the fact that you two have a problem, and now you are ready for negotiations, lawyers, third-party interventions, and so on. Notice how cultures

Figure 10.4
The Contagion of Emotion

These volunteers, videotaped in a study of conversational synchrony, are obviously "in sync" with one another, even though they have just met. The degree to which two people's gestures and expressions are synchronized determines how much rapport they will feel with one another. Such synchrony can also create a "contagion" of moods (Bernieri et al., 1991).

misunderstand the same action: Burning the fence down is the last resort in one, but the start of the conversation in another.

Display rules tell us not only what to do when we are feeling an emotion, but also how and when we should show an emotion we do not feel. Acting out an emotion we don't really feel, or trying to create the right emotion for the occasion, has been called **emotion work.** People are expected to demonstrate sadness at funerals, happiness at weddings, and affection toward relatives. If they don't really feel such emotions, they may playact to convince others that they do.

Sometimes emotion work is a job requirement, as a study of flight attendants and bill collectors found (Hochschild, 1983). Flight attendants must "put on a happy face" to convey cheerfulness, even if they are angry about a rude or drunken passenger. Bill collectors must put on a stern face to convey threat; they must withhold sympathy, even if they are feeling sorry for the poor person in debt. Other employees do emotion work when they express agreement with an employer's infuriating decision or when they display cheerfulness to annoying customers. The effort to interpret a situation in a positive light, and to generate real feelings of warmth and friendliness toward others, not only makes social relations more pleasurable but also may actually generate positive emotions.

Smiling to convey friendliness is part of the job description for flight attendants, whether they are male or female—but not necessarily for the passengers they serve.

Quick Quiz

The following example of cultural miscommunication occurred in an English class for foreign students. An Arab student was describing a tradition of his home country, when he inadvertently said something that embarrassed a Japanese student. To disguise his shame, the Japanese student smiled, and the Arab demanded to know what was so funny about Arab customs. The Japanese, now feeling publicly humiliated, giggled. The Arab, enraged, hit him. What concepts from the previous section explain this misunderstanding?

emotion work Expression of an emotion, often because of a role requirement, that the person does not really feel.

Answer:

Arab and Japanese cultures have different display rules regarding the expression of anger, the appropriate response to feeling shamed, and the management of embarrassment in public. The two students also misread each other's nonverbal communication. To the Arab, the Japanese student's smile meant he was being laughed at, but the Japanese intended merely to disguise his discomfort.

PUTTING THE ELEMENTS TOGETHER: THE CASE OF EMOTION AND GENDER

"Women are too emotional," men often complain. "Men are too repressed," women often reply. People hold strong beliefs about gender differences in emotion and about whether the male or female style is better (Fischer, 1993; Shields, 1991). But what do they mean by "emotional"? "Being emotional" can refer to an internal emotional state, to a cognitive tendency to make mountains out of molehills, to the way an emotion is displayed, or to emotion work. Because emotion has so many aspects, it is necessary to define our terms before we can understand whether or how the sexes differ.

THE EXPERIENCE OF EMOTION To begin with, there is little evidence that, around the world, one sex feels emotions more often than the other (Baumeister, Stillwell, & Wotman, 1990; Fischer et al., 1993; Oatley & Duncan, 1994; Shaver & Hazan, 1987; Shields, 1991). Both sexes are equally likely, on the average, to feel anxious in new situations; to feel jealousy, love, and loneliness; to feel angry when they are frustrated or believe they have been insulted or treated unfairly; to feel embarrassed when they make goofy mistakes; and to grieve when attachments break up (Hatfield & Rapson, 1996). So it seems we must look elsewhere for gender differences in emotion.

DEFINE YOUR TERMS

People say that women are the "emotional" sex, but they often fail to define their terms. What, for example, does "emotional" mean? Why is it "arguing" when he does it but "getting emotional" when she does it?

THE PHYSIOLOGY OF EMOTION If we define emotionality in terms of physiological reactivity to provocation, it seems that men are more emotional than women. John Gottman and his colleagues, in longitudinal studies of hundreds of married couples, have found that conflict and dissension are physiologically and psychologically more upsetting for men than for women, which may be why many men try to avoid conflict entirely (Gottman, 1994; Levenson, Carstensen, & Gottman, 1994). The researchers monitored the heart rates of husbands and wives before and during actual quarrels, and they found that the men's heart rates, unlike the women's, soared to a very fast rate as soon as signs of conflict began—and stayed high longer. Moreover, the husbands reported feeling more negative and hostile the more they were physiologically aroused, but the wives did not show such a correlation between arousal and negative feeling. Other studies, too, suggest that hostility and anger are more closely linked with marital distress and conflict for husbands than for wives (Smith, Sanders, & Alexander, 1990).

Gottman (1994) suggests two possible explanations for the physiological differences between men and women in response to conflict. One is that the male's autonomic nervous system may be more sensitive and hyperreactive than the female's. Indeed, when men are under stress or in a competitive situation, many show a more pronounced elevation in blood pressure, heart rate, and the secretion of epinephrine than women do (Polefrone & Manuck, 1987; Smith et al., 1996). Another reason, however, may be that men are more likely than women to rehearse negative thoughts—such as "I don't have to take this" or "It's all her fault"—that keep them riled up. This explanation brings us to the next factor that might produce gender differences in emotion.

COGNITIONS THAT GENERATE EMOTION Men and women often differ in the perceptions and expectations that generate certain emotions, within particular situations (Lakoff, 1990; Stapley & Haviland, 1989). Their different interpretations of the same event, in turn, can create different emotional responses to it. If a male teacher compliments a female student on her new outfit, is that a sign of flattery or sexual harassment? If a woman touches a male friend on his arm, is she signaling affection or sexual interest? Under such circumstances, it is not that one sex is "more emotional," but that the two parties disagree on what an action means. This disagreement produces an emotional response in one person that the other does not share or understand.

NONVERBAL COMMUNICATION Sometimes women are considered more emotional because of their supposed sensitivity to other people's emotional states and because of their own greater nonverbal expressiveness. Women in North America do smile more than men do, gaze at their listeners more, have more emotionally expressive faces, use more expressive hand and body movements, and tend to touch others more and be touched more (DePaulo, 1992). On a test called the Profile of Nonverbal Sensitivity, which measures a person's ability to detect emotions revealed in tones of voice, movements of the body, and facial expressions, women have scored slightly better than men (J. Hall, 1987). But sensitivity to another person's emotional state—as in reading a person's facial expression—often depends more on the context in which the two people are interacting than on their gender. In particular, the ability to "read" emotional signals depends on the following:

Does this woman's touch signify affection, dominance, harassment, sexual interest, sympathy, or simple friendliness? How do you think this man is reacting? Men and women often disagree on the meaning of another's touch. Depending on their perceptions, they may react with anger, happiness, disgust, fear, or desire.

1. *The sex of the sender and of the receiver.* People do better reading the emotional signals, facial expressions, and gestures of members of their own sex than those of the other sex (Buck, 1984).
2. *How well the two people know each other.* Dating and married couples can interpret each other's facial expressions and other emotional signs better than strangers can (Hatfield, Cacioppo, & Rapson, 1992). However, close partners are no better than strangers at detecting one another's *deceits*, unless they have already lost their trust in one another (DePaulo, 1994).
3. *Who has the power.* Less powerful people learn to read the powerful person's signals, usually for self-protection (Fiske, 1993; Henley, 1995; Lakoff, 1990). This fact helps explain apparent gender differences in the ability to read emotions. For example, in two experiments, Sara Snodgrass (1985, 1992) found that "women's intuition" should more properly be called "subordinate's intuition." In male–female pairs in which one person was assigned to be the leader and the other the follower, the person in the subordinate (follower) position was more sensitive to the leader's nonverbal signals than the leader was to the follower's cues. This difference occurred whether a man or a woman was the leader or the follower. The social positions that people are in, Snodgrass found, almost totally overrode any gender differences.

THE DISPLAY RULES FOR EMOTIONAL EXPRESSION Finally, we come to a significant gender difference that contributes to the stereotype of women's greater emotionality. In numerous studies in North America, women say that they express

Both sexes feel emotionally attached to their friends and loved ones, but often they express their affections differently. From childhood on, girls tend to prefer "face to face" friendships, based on shared feelings; boys tend to prefer "side by side" friendships, based on shared activities.

their feelings more often than men do, and they also report a greater tendency to talk about their emotions—especially emotions that reveal vulnerability and helplessness, such as fear, sadness, loneliness, shame, and guilt (Fischer, 1993; Grossman & Wood, 1993; Nolen-Hoeksema, 1990).

In contrast, most North American men are permitted to express only one emotion more freely than women: anger in public. Men are more likely than women to reveal anger to strangers, especially other men, when they believe they have been challenged or insulted. Men are also more likely to express anger, fear, or hurt pride in the form of aggressive action (Fischer, 1993). Otherwise, men are expected to control negative feelings. If they express "unmanly" emotions at all, many men tend to do so only to their intimate partners, and rarely to casual male friends (Gottman, 1994). Thus, although both sexes are equally likely to feel lonely, women are much more likely to admit it. One reason is that both sexes are more likely to reject and dislike a man who admits he is lonely than a woman who does. Men face greater negative consequences than women, it seems, when they reveal emotions of "weakness" (Borys & Perlman, 1985).

One consequence of the social taboo on male expression of vulnerability may be difficulty in recognizing when men are unhappy. In fact, some researchers believe that many boys and men fail to be diagnosed as depressed because the tests for depression are based on typically female reactions such as crying, staying in bed, and talking about one's unhappiness (Riessman, 1990; Stapley & Haviland, 1989). Because many men do not express grief this way, some people wrongly infer that men suffer less than women when relationships end or that men are incapable of deep feeling.

Catherine Riessman (1990) began to question these assumptions while she was interviewing a large sample of wives and husbands about their divorces. The men were suffering as much as the women, Riessman learned; they just didn't say so. In fact, most of the men claimed they felt sad only "some or a little of the time" and that they felt depressed or lonely "none of the time." However, these men were expressing grief in ways that are acceptably masculine: working too much, drinking heavily, driving too fast, singing sentimental songs. Many of the men reported trouble concentrating at work, difficulties on the job, restlessness and hyperactivity, and numerous physical ailments and stress symptoms. One man confessed that for four months after his separation he "threw up every morning," but he firmly denied that he was

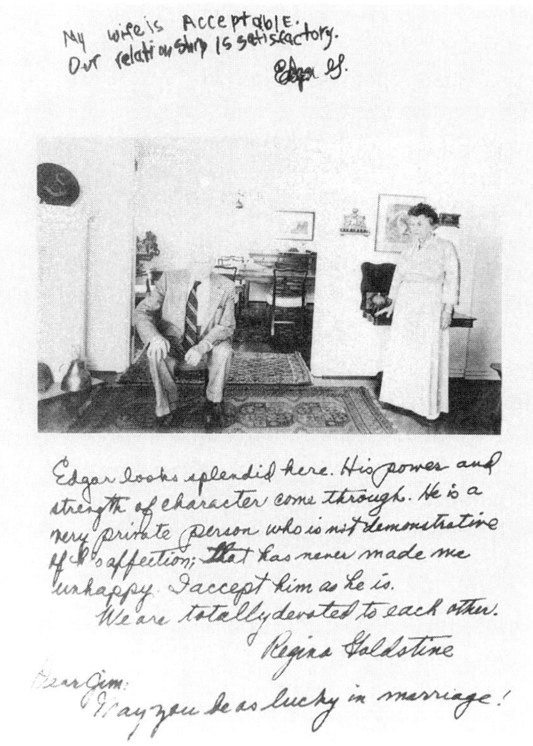

Photographer Jim Goldberg took photos of couples and asked them to write their comments on the prints. What do you think about the marriage portrayed in this picture? Do Edgar and Regina have different feelings about each other, or do they just express their feelings differently?

actually depressed. Another denied feeling sad, but in the six months since his divorce he had racked up a long list of criminal charges.

Gender differences in emotional expressiveness, however, are affected strongly by social roles and cultural norms (Grossman & Wood, 1993). In many Asian cultures, both sexes are taught to control emotional expression (Buck & Teng, 1987). In cultures throughout Europe, the Middle East, and South America, the display rules for women and men often depend on the emotion in question. In one large international study, for example, Israeli and Italian men were much more likely than women to control feelings of sadness, but British, Spanish, Swiss, and German women were more likely than their male counterparts to inhibit this emotion. Overall, European women were not more emotionally expressive than men; the differences were greater between cultures than between sexes (Wallbott, Ricci-Bitti, & Bänninger-Huber, 1986).

Even within a culture, the influence of a particular situation often overrides gender rules. An American man will be as likely as an American woman to control his temper when the target of anger is someone with higher status or power; few people, no matter how angry, will readily sound off at a professor, police officer, or employer. In the home, when a man and a woman feel angry they are both likely to express it by sulking, discussing matters outright, or being verbally abusive (Averill, 1982; Gelles & Straus, 1988; Thomas, 1993). And you won't find gender differences in emotional expressiveness at a football game!

So if emotionality is defined in terms of display rules, we find that North American women tend to be "more emotional" than men in revealing and talking about their negative feelings; men are "more emotional" than women in displaying negative feelings in aggressive or self-destructive ways. And in some situations—such as an exciting sports event or a conflict with an employer—neither sex is more expressive than the other.

EMOTION WORK Both sexes know the experience of having to hide emotions they feel and to show emotions they do not feel. Yet their emotion work, on the job and at home, is often different. On the whole, women tend to be involved in the flight-attendant side of emotion work, persuading others that they are friendly, happy, and warm, and making sure others are happy (DePaulo, 1992). Men tend to be involved in the bill-collection side, persuading others that they are stern, aggressive, and unemotional. Care-oriented emotion work—tending to other people's feelings, as well as managing or disguising one's own—is typically part of the woman's role more than the man's (Fischer, 1993; Grossman & Wood, 1993).

Perhaps women in North America smile more often than men do as part of their emotion work—not necessarily because they feel happier, but to pacify, nurture, and convey deference (Henley, 1995). If women don't smile when others expect them to, they are often disliked, even if they are actually smiling as often as men would. Children learn this lesson early; 6- to 10-year-olds show a steady increase in knowledge about where and when they should disguise feelings and put on a "polite smile"—for instance, when they are given a gift they don't like (Saarni, 1989). From childhood on, girls are more likely than boys to mask their negative feelings with positive expressions. As adults, women often express anger with a smile, a mixed message that can be puzzling to their friends, spouses, and children (Deutsch, LeBaron, & Fryer, 1987). The smile requirement for women is not universal, though. In Taiwan and China, for example, women do not differ from men in facial expressiveness (Buck & Teng, 1987).

Thus, with regard to emotion work and display rules, it appears that, in some cultural groups at least, women are expected to be more emotional than men, in terms of managing their own and other people's feelings. But if we define emotionality in terms of physiological reactivity, emotion-generating perceptions, expressiveness, or nonverbal sensitivity, we see that the answer to "who is more emotional" is sometimes men, sometimes women, and sometimes neither. It depends on the individual, the situation, the particular emotion, and the culture.

As we have seen in this chapter, the full experience and expression of emotion involve physiology, cognitive processes, and cultural rules. The case of gender and emotion shows that if we look at just one component, we come up with an incomplete or misleading picture. And it shows, too, that emotions have many purposes: They allow us to establish close bonds, threaten and warn, get help from others, reveal or deceive. The many varieties and expressions of emotion suggest that although we feel emotions physically, we use them socially. As we explore further issues in the study of motivation, personality, development, well-being, and mental disorders, we will see again and again how emotions involve thinking and feeling, perception and action—head and heart.

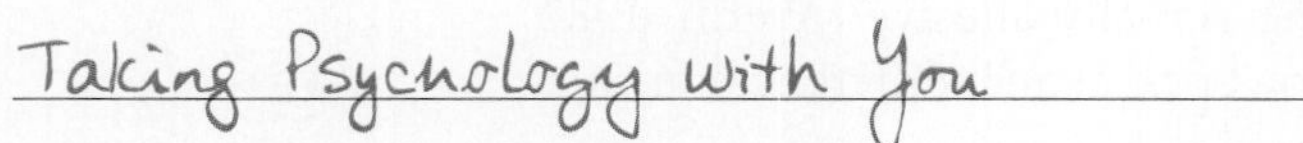

"Let It Out" or "Bottle It Up"? The Dilemma of Anger

What do you do when you feel angry? Do you tend to brood and sulk, collecting your righteous complaints like acorns for the winter, or do you erupt, hurling your wrath upon anyone or anything at hand? Do you discuss your feelings when you have calmed down? Does "letting anger out" get rid of it for you, or does it only make it more intense? The answer is crucial for how you get along with your family, neighbors, employers, and strangers. Increasingly, people are freely venting their anger in the home and in public with rude gestures and insulting remarks. Strangers shoot each other over trivial infractions, and public debate about serious issues often degenerates into name-calling and the exchange of hostilities.

Although some schools of therapy once advised people to "get it out of your system," psychologists have found that this advice often backfires. Chronic feelings of anger and an inability to control anger can be as emotionally devastating and unhealthy as chronic problems with depression, panic, or anxiety (Deffenbacher, 1994; Williams, 1989). In contrast to much pop-psych advice, research shows that expressing anger does not always get rid of anger; often it prolongs it. When people talk about their anger or act on that feeling, they tend to rehearse their grievances, create a hostile disposition, and pump up their blood pressure (Averill, 1982; Tavris, 1989). Conversely, when people learn to control their tempers and express anger constructively, they usually feel better, not worse; calmer, not angrier. Charles Darwin (1872/1965) observed this fact more than a century ago. "The free expression by outward signs of an emotion intensifies it," he wrote. "On the other hand, the repression, as far as this is possible, of all outward signs softens our emotions. He who gives way to violent gestures will increase his rage."

Some people behave aggressively when they are angry, but others behave in a friendly, cooperative way to try to solve the problem that is causing their anger. When people are feeling angry, after all, they can do many things: write letters, play the piano, jog, bake bread, kick the sofa, abuse their friends or family, or yell. If a particular action soothes their feelings or gets the desired response from other people, they are likely to acquire a habit. Soon that habit feels "natural," as if it could never be changed; indeed, many people justify their violent tempers by saying, "I just couldn't help myself." But they can. If you have learned an abusive or aggressive habit, the research in this chapter offers practical suggestions for relearning constructive ways of managing anger:

• *Don't sound off in the heat of anger; let bodily arousal cool down.* Whether your arousal comes from background stresses such as heat, crowds, or loud noise, or from conflict with another person, take time to relax. Time allows you to decide whether you are "really" angry or just tired and tense. This is the reason for that sage old advice to count to 10, count to 100, or sleep on it. Other cooling-off strategies include taking a time-out in the middle of an argument, meditating or relaxing, and calming yourself with a distracting activity.

• *Remember that anger depends on the perception of insult; check your perceptions for accuracy, and then see whether you can rethink the problem.* People who are quick to feel anger tend to interpret other people's actions as intentional offenses. People who are slow to anger tend to give others the benefit of the doubt, and they are not as focused on their own injured pride. Empathy ("Poor guy, he's feeling rotten") is usually incompatible with anger, so practice seeing the situation from the other person's perspective (Miller & Eisenberg, 1988; Tangney, 1992).

• *If you decide that expressing anger is appropriate, think carefully about how to do it so that you will get the results you want.* As we saw, different cultures have different display rules. Be sure the recipient of your anger understands what you are feeling and what complaint you are trying to convey—and this is true whether the recipient is your parent, a friend, an annoying neighbor, an employer, or city hall.

Ultimately, the decision about whether to express anger depends not only on whether you will feel good if you do, but also on what you hope to accomplish. Do you want to restore your rights, change the other person, improve a bad situation, or achieve justice? If those are your goals, then learning how to express anger so the other person will listen and respond is essential. People who have been the targets of injustice have learned that outbursts of anger may draw society's attention to a problem—but real change requires sustained political effort, challenges to unfair laws, and the use of tactics that persuade rather than alienate the opposition.

Of course, if you just want to blow off steam, go right ahead; but you risk becoming a hothead.

"I'm very angry. What do you suggest?"

SUMMARY

ELEMENTS OF EMOTION 1: THE BODY

1) The complex experience of *emotion* involves physiological changes in the brain, face, and body; cognitive processes; and culture. In the late nineteenth century, the *James–Lange theory of emotion* proposed that awareness of bodily reactions to an event gives rise to the experience of emotion. "We feel sorry *because* we cry, angry *because* we strike," wrote James. His work inspired modern efforts to study the relationship between physiology and cognition in emotion.

2) Some basic facial expressions—anger, fear, sadness, happiness, disgust, surprise, contempt—are widely recognized across cultures. Distinctive facial expressions are apparent in infancy, and infants recognize adult expressions of fear, anger, and happiness. But culture interacts with physiology to influence when and how emotions are displayed, as the example of disgust illustrates. Facial expressions probably evolved to foster communication and survival, but as studies of *facial feedback* show, they also send messages to the brain identifying our own emotional states. Because people can disguise their emotions, however, facial expressions do not always communicate accurately.

3) Some researchers study structures of the brain in order to identify biological components of emotion: particularly the *amygdala,* which is responsible for immediate processing of incoming stimuli that are perceived as dangerous or threatening, and the *cerebral cortex*, which provides the ability to confirm or override incoming information. Biological research is identifying the specific areas of the brain that are involved in various aspects of emotional experience; for example, different regions of the right hemisphere specialize in recognizing faces and facial expressions. The right hemisphere seems to be specialized for the experience of negative emotions, the left hemisphere for positive emotions.

4) *Epinephrine* and *norepinephrine* are hormones that produce physiological arousal to prepare the body to cope with environmental stimuli, nonemotional but physically taxing events, and all emotional states. These hormones produce changes in heart rate, respiration, pupil dilation, blood-sugar levels, digestion, memory, and performance. Arousal takes several forms, which involve different areas of the brain. The autonomic nervous system produces different patterns of physiological changes that correspond to certain basic emotions.

ELEMENTS OF EMOTION 2: THE MIND

5) Schachter and Singer's *two-factor theory of emotion* held that emotions result from arousal and the labeling or interpretation of that arousal. Their research launched many studies designed to identify the cognitive processes involved in emotion, such as the way people interpret and evaluate events. For example, people who feel depressed and lonely tend to think that the reasons for their unhappiness are *internal*, *stable*, and *uncontrollable*. Envy and jealousy, and shame and guilt, can be distinguished by the perceptions and beliefs that generate them.

6) New approaches help resolve the age-old "reason-versus-emotion" debate, showing how physiological and cognitive processes interact. Developmental research shows that emotions and cognitions change and become more complex with age; cognition and emotion influence each other; the cognitions involved in emotion can be nonconscious as well as conscious, with different degrees of cognitive complexity; both emotion and cognition can be rational or irrational, and both are necessary for making plans and wise decisions.

ELEMENTS OF EMOTION 3: THE CULTURE

7) Some researchers distinguish *primary* emotions, which are thought to be universal, from *secondary* emotions, which include blends and variations that are specific to cultures. Research on brain physiology, facial expressions, emotion prototypes, and the similarity of situations that evoke emotions supports the existence of basic primary emotions. Other psychologists criticize efforts to find primary emotions. They doubt that surprise and disgust, which produce typical facial expressions, are true emotions; they also think the list of "primary" emotions omits such universal feelings as love, hope, empathy, shame, and pride, which are difficult to measure through facial expressions or brain activity.

8) Cultures profoundly influence the experience and expression of emotions. They determine what their members feel emotional about and what people do when they feel an emotion. *Display rules* are the culture's way of regulating how, when, and where a person may express or must suppress an emotion. *Emotion work* is the effort a person makes to display an emotion he or she doesn't really feel but feels obliged to convey.

PUTTING THE ELEMENTS TOGETHER: THE CASE OF EMOTION AND GENDER

9) Women and men are equally likely to feel a wide array of emotions, from love to anger. Men seem to be more physiologically reactive to conflict than women are, however, and the sexes sometimes differ in the perceptions and expectations that generate emotion and emotional intensity. Although on the average, women are more nonverbally expressive than men and are thought to be better at reading another person's emotional state, this ability depends on whether the two individuals are of the same gender and culture, on their familiarity with each other, and, most of all, on which one has more power in the situation.

10) Men and women differ primarily in the display rules that govern the expression of emotions, a reason for the stereotype of female "emotionality." In North America, women are more likely to talk about feelings of fear, sadness, guilt, and loneliness than men are; men are more likely to deny they have such feelings or to reveal them in aggressive acts. But these gender differences are in turn affected by cultural norms and the influence of a particular situation. Role requirements often specify different emotion work for the two sexes. The example of gender and emotion shows that understanding the full experience and expression of emotion involves biology, cognitive perceptions, and cultural rules.

KEY TERMS

emotion 384
James–Lange theory of emotion 385
facial feedback 388
amygdala 389
epinephrine 390
norepinephrine 390
arousal 390
two-factor theory of emotion 394
cognitions and depression (internality, stability, control) 396
prototypes and emotion 402
primary emotions 402
secondary emotions 402
display rules 403
emotion work 405

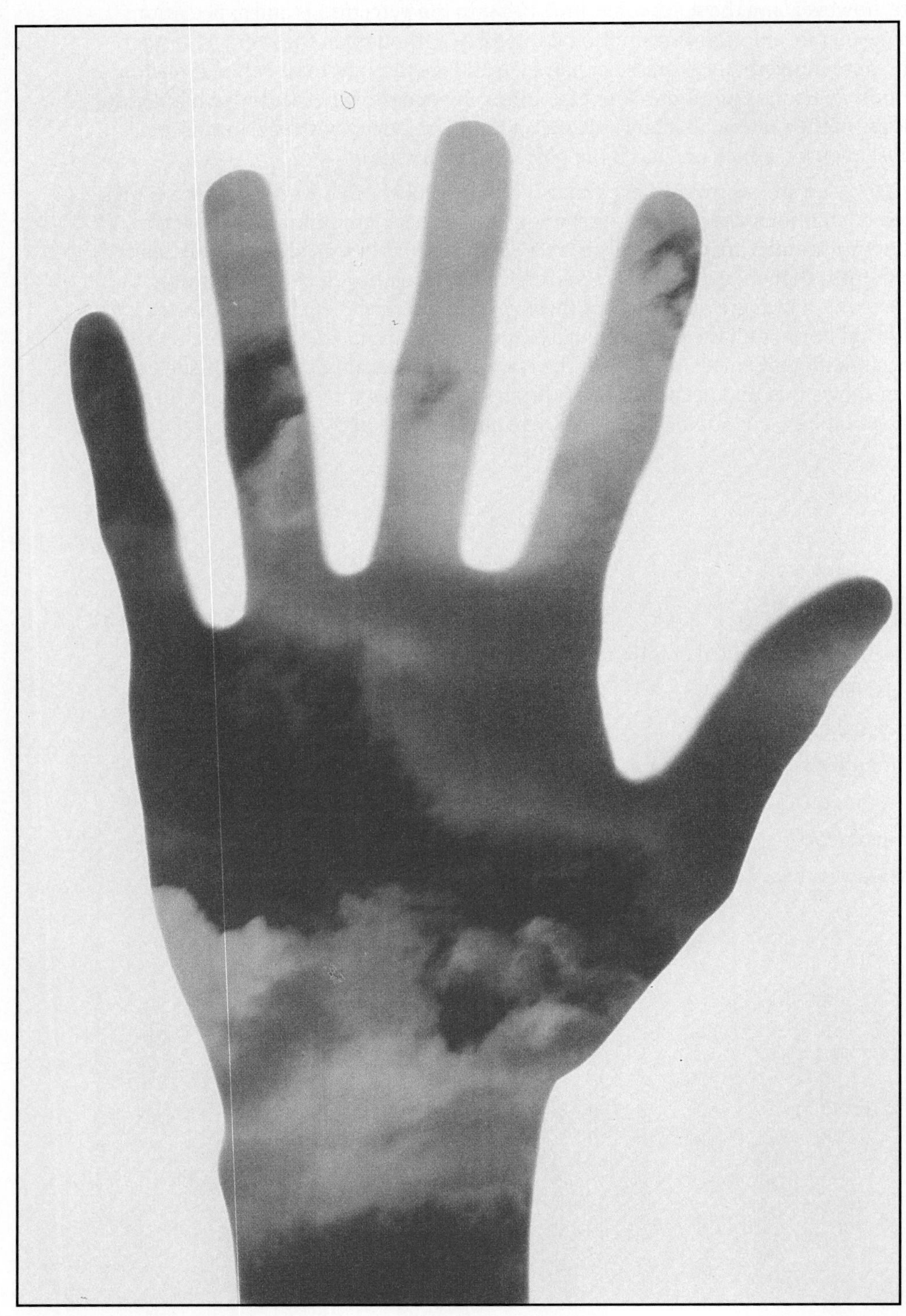

No limits but the sky.

Miguel de Cervantes

Gay men and lesbians follow sexual scripts, too. In terms of number of sexual partners, sexual behavior, and acceptance of casual sex, gay men are generally similar to heterosexual men, and lesbians are similar to heterosexual women. But most gay men and lesbians tend to be more idiosyncratic and innovative than heterosexuals in establishing rules for their relationships (Peplau, 1991; Rose, Zand, & Cini, 1993). An American study of lesbian courtship scripts—as revealed by analysis of lesbian romance novels, "how-to" books on dating and relationships, first-person accounts, and empirical research on lesbian sexuality—found that emotional intimacy, rather than physical attraction or sexuality, is the basis for most lesbian courtship scripts. These scripts are more ambiguous and varied than heterosexual dating and sexual scripts because neither partner is clearly the pursuer or the pursued or the one who makes the sexual overtures. "Whereas heterosexual women generally make the decision about when to 'let' sex happen," the researchers found, "lesbians indicated a more mutual decision-making process for initiating physical intimacy" (Rose, Zand, & Cini, 1993).

Simon and Gagnon (1986) have also argued that in addition to cultural scripts, people follow two other kinds. *Interpersonal scripts* include the rules of behavior that a couple develops in the course of their relationship. For example, will one be dominant and one passive? The answer differs depending on the relationship, and may change as the relationship changes. Individuals also follow their own *intrapsychic scripts*, scenarios for ideal or fantasized sexual behavior that develop out of their unique history.

As we saw in Chapter 3, evolutionary psychologists and sociobiologists think that the processes of natural selection and sexual selection best account for sex differences in courtship and mating practices. These processes, they say, explain why men often pressure women for sex, women tend to reject casual sex, and women "give in" and men "make a move" when they don't really want to (Buss, 1994; Oliver & Hyde, 1993). Certainly, one key biological difference has always affected gender differences in sexual attitudes and behavior: the fact that only one sex gets pregnant. However, social and cultural psychologists maintain that most of the differences between women and men can best be understood as a result of gender roles, which in turn reflect a culture's economic and social arrangements. When those arrangements change, so do people's attitudes and behavior, as we saw in the case of love.

In this view, because women have traditionally been concerned with finding and keeping a relationship that was the basis of their financial security, they have regarded sex as a bargaining chip—an asset to be rationed rather than an activity to be enjoyed for its own sake (Cassell, 1984). Women cannot afford to "let themselves go" and enjoy sex when such behavior means that they will get pregnant when they don't want to, or that they will lose the economic haven of marriage, their reputations in society, or their physical safety. When women become self-supporting and able to control their own fertility, however, they are more likely to want sex for pleasure rather than as a means to another goal. Indeed, as we will see in Chapter 18, all over the world, the processes of industrialization and modernization are transforming the roles and sexual scripts of women and men (Hatfield & Rapson, 1996). Although this transformation is slow and uneven, and although change always brings protest and confusion in its wake, social scientists have documented a growing endorsement, worldwide, of birth control, premarital sex, sexual freedom in general, and the entitlement of both sexes to love and sexual pleasure.

THE RIDDLE OF SEXUAL ORIENTATION

Why do some people become exclusively heterosexual, others exclusively homosexual, and still others bisexual? Although same-sex sexual behavior has existed

Many heterosexual people think that all gay men and lesbians live unconventional, flamboyant lives. In reality, as much diversity exists among gays as among straights, and just about everyone, regardless of sexual orientation, seeks the pleasures of love and companionship.

throughout history, the words *homosexual* and *heterosexual* were not invented until the mid-nineteenth century (Katz, 1995). Only then did homosexuality become a "problem" to be studied, an entity distinct from heterosexuality. Today, researchers are hotly debating the causes of sexual orientation—and even whether it is possible to identify "the" causes, because homosexuality has varied so much across time and culture (Baumrind, 1995).

Many of the researchers who are looking for the origins of sexual orientation are persuaded that biology holds the answer. They believe that sexual orientation has a genetic basis, and they point to evidence that certain brain areas, hormones, and neuroendocrine processes differ in homosexual and heterosexual men and women (Bailey & Pillard, 1995; Gladue, 1994). For example, women with a history of prenatal exposure to high levels of androgen, caused in some cases by a genetic variation, are more likely than others to become bisexual or lesbian (Collaer & Hines, 1995), and so are women with a history of prenatal exposure to synthetic estrogen (Meyer-Bahlburg et al., 1995). Simon LeVay (1991) made national headlines when he announced that he had found a difference in specific brain structures of homosexual and heterosexual men (see also Allen & Gorski, 1992). Others have reported that sexual orientation is moderately heritable, both in men and in women (Bailey & Pillard, 1995; Hershberger, Lykken, & McGue, 1995; Whitam, Diamond, & Martin, 1993). And Dean Hamer and his team (1993) caused a stir when they reported a genetic linkage study that found a shared stretch of DNA on the X chromosome in 33 of 40 pairs of gay brothers—a rate significantly above what one would expect to occur in siblings by chance. Two years later, another study by the same group got similar results (Hu et al., 1995).

These scientists are excited about such biological findings because exclusively *psychological* theories of homosexuality have never been supported: Homosexuality is unrelated to bad mothering, absent fathering, psychopathology, socialization practices, or parental role models (Bailey et al., 1995; Bell, Weinberg, & Hammersmith, 1981; Patterson, 1992). But other researchers are skeptical of biological explanations (Baumrind, 1995; Byne & Parsons, 1993; Kitzinger & Wilkinson, 1995). Some argue that biology cannot be the major explanation because sexual identity is so incredibly complex and varied: Not everybody is exclusively homosexual or heterosexual, for instance, and people's behavior is often at odds with their fantasies. Other critics point to serious limitations in studies that report differences in the brain or evidence of heritability. Dean Hamer's genetics study (Hamer et al., 1993) was based on a sample of gay brothers; but the vast majority of gay men and lesbians do *not* have a close gay relative. Likewise, the majority of women with histories of abnormal prenatal exposure to adrogens or estrogen do *not* become homosexual. And a key problem in LeVay's study was that the gay men in his sample had died of AIDS. AIDS itself, and also some of the medicines given for the disease, create endocrine abnormalities that can affect brain structures. The differences LeVay observed, therefore, might have been a result of AIDS rather than a cause of sexual orientation (Byne, 1993).

At present, the most reasonable conclusions may be that sexual identity and behavior involve an interaction of biology, culture, experiences, and opportunities; and that the route to sexual identity for one person may not be the same as for another (Gladue, 1994; Patterson, 1995). As Dean Hamer told *The New York Times* (July 16, 1993), "Sexual orientation is too complex to be determined by a single gene. The main value of this work is that it opens a window into understanding how genes, the brain and the environment interact to mold human behavior."

AVOID EMOTIONAL REASONING

Many people, straight and gay, have strong emotional reactions to biological research on homosexuality. Why? How do people's emotions and political views affect their interpretations of the research? Are their interpretations warranted?

What is your response to these findings? Your reactions are probably affected by your feelings about homosexuality and gay rights. Many gay men and lesbians themselves welcome the new biological research on the grounds that it supports what they have been saying all along: Sexual orientation is not a matter of choice, but a fact of nature. But people who are prejudiced against homosexuals can use the same research as evidence that gay people have a biological "defect" that should be eradicated or "cured." Other gay men and lesbians strongly oppose biological arguments and their implication of built-in differences between gays and straights; but so do many antigay people, who argue that homosexuality is a "preference" or "choice" that can and should be "unchosen."

Similarly, evidence about the rates of homosexuality in the general population has been interpreted differently by pro- and antigay groups, for different reasons. The national survey we described earlier, confirming surveys done in Europe, reported that gay men do not constitute 10 percent of the total population, as Kinsey had estimated, but more like 2 to 4 percent, and the percentage of lesbians is smaller yet (Laumann et al., 1994). (The percentages are significantly higher in big cities, where gay men and lesbians feel safer.) About 7.5 percent of men reported having had same-sex fantasies and attraction, still less than 10 percent. And when people were asked whether they had *ever* engaged in any sexual activities with a member of the same sex, again the numbers were lower than Kinsey's: 4 percent of the women and 9 percent of the men. Moreover, for many of those men, the same-sex activity occurred only between the ages of 13 and 18.

These statistics, like evidence of biological factors in sexual orientation, can be used for different purposes. Gay-rights activists welcomed Kinsey's 10 percent estimate as evidence that homosexuality is a common sexual variation and should be accepted as such; thus they tend to discount the new statistics, fearing the loss of power that a loss of numbers might produce. Antigay people used the 10 percent estimate to lament the decline of morality; thus they tend to welcome the lower numbers as evidence that homosexuality is such an aberration that gay people should be denied their civil rights.

Whatever research eventually reveals about the origins and prevalence of homosexuality, however, the scientific question of the origins of homosexuality is logically unrelated to political and moral questions of the rights of gay men and lesbians (Strickland, 1995). In a democracy, civil rights do not depend on whether one's beliefs or practices are a matter of choice, nor do they depend on how popular those beliefs are. A person's religion is not biologically inherited, yet America and Canada guarantee freedom of religion to everyone—whether your religion is shared by 75 percent of the population or 2 percent.

As you can see, research on sexuality can be used for many contradictory purposes and political goals, depending on the values and attitudes of the popular culture in which such findings emerge. As long as a society is uncomfortable about homosexuality, preconceptions and prejudice are likely to cloud its reactions to anything that psychologists learn about it.

Quick Quiz

Were you motivated to learn about sexual motivation?

1. Biological research finds that (a) male and female sexual responses are physiologically very different, (b) vaginal orgasms are healthier than clitoral ones, (c) testosterone promotes sexual desire in both sexes, (d) all women have multiple orgasms.
2. Research on the motives of rapists finds that rape is usually (a) a matter of sexual desire, (b) the result of hostility or a need for power, (c) a matter of crossed signals.
3. According to Simon and Gagnon, people follow three kinds of sexual scripts; what are they?
4. *True or false:* Exclusively psychological theories of the origins of homosexuality have never been supported.

Answers:

1. c 2. b 3. cultural, interpersonal, and intrapsychic (Now, can you define each of these types of scripts?) 4. true

THE COMPETENT ANIMAL: MOTIVES TO WORK

Almost every adult works. Most people spend more time at work than they do at play or with their families. "Work" does not mean only paid employment. Students work at studying. Homemakers work, often more hours than salaried employees, at running a household. Artists, poets, and actors work, even if they are paid only erratically. What keeps everybody doing it? The obvious answer, of course, is the need for food and shelter. Yet survival does not explain what motivates LeRoy to work for caviar on his table and Duane to work for peanut butter on his. It doesn't explain why some people want to do their work well and others just want to get it done. It doesn't explain the difference between Aristotle's view ("All paid employments absorb and degrade the mind") and Noël Coward's ("Work is more fun than fun").

Psychologists, particularly those in the field of *industrial/organizational psychology,* have studied work motivation in the laboratory, where they have measured internal motives such as the desire for achievement, and in organizations, where they study the conditions that influence productivity and satisfaction. Their results give us a fuller answer to "What keeps everybody working?"

THE EFFECTS OF MOTIVATION ON WORK

Several independent forces keep you working: your expectation of success, the goals you set for yourself, your need to achieve, opportunities in the environment, and the nature of your work. These factors apply to any form of achievement, from running a household to running a marathon.

EXPECTATIONS AND VALUES How hard you work for something depends partly on what you expect to accomplish. If you are fairly certain of success, you will work much harder to reach your goal than if you are fairly certain of failure.

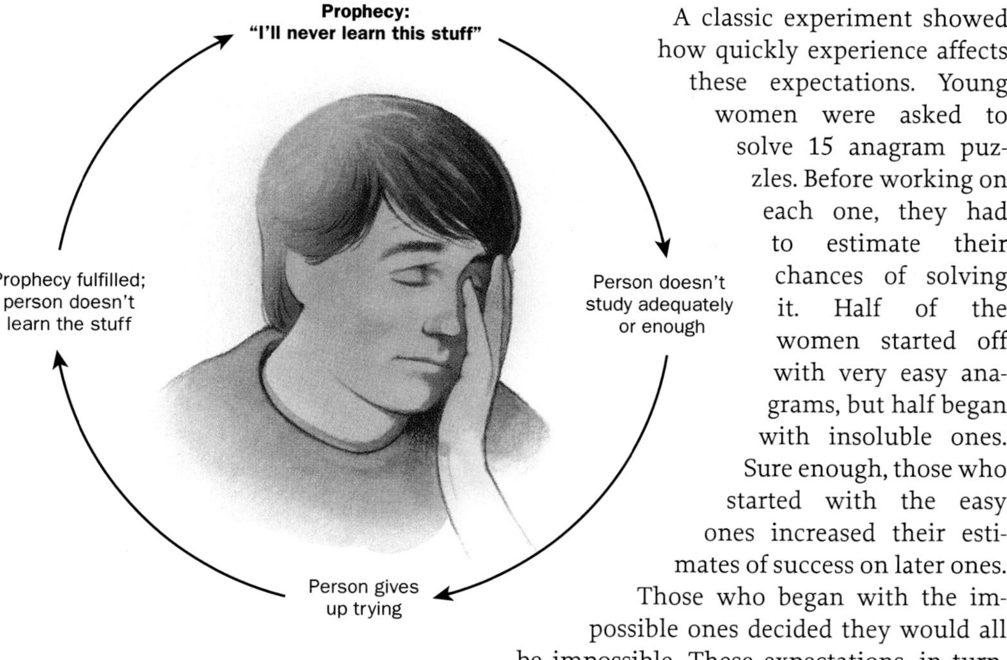
Prophecy:
"I'll never learn this stuff"
Person doesn't study adequately or enough
Person gives up trying
Prophecy fulfilled; person doesn't learn the stuff

A classic experiment showed how quickly experience affects these expectations. Young women were asked to solve 15 anagram puzzles. Before working on each one, they had to estimate their chances of solving it. Half of the women started off with very easy anagrams, but half began with insoluble ones. Sure enough, those who started with the easy ones increased their estimates of success on later ones. Those who began with the impossible ones decided they would all be impossible. These expectations, in turn, affected the young women's ability to actually solve the last ten anagrams, which were the same for everyone. The higher the expectation of success, the more anagrams the women solved (Feather, 1966).

Once acquired, therefore, expectations can create a **self-fulfilling prophecy,** in which a person predicts how he or she will do and then behaves in such a way as to make the prediction come true (Jones, 1977; Maddux, 1995). You expect to do well, so you study hard, and then you do well. You expect to fail, so you don't do much work, and then you do poorly. In either case, you have fulfilled your expectation of yourself.

How hard you work for something, of course, also depends on how much you want it, which in turn depends on your general value system (Feather, 1982). A *value* is a central motivating belief, reflecting a person's fundamental goals and ideals: freedom, beauty, equality, friendship, fame, wisdom, and so on (Rokeach & Ball-Rokeach, 1989). The values that motivate people can themselves have psychological consequences. For example, American culture puts a high value on wealth and financial success. But the pursuit of material wealth for its own sake has a dark side. Young adults whose central value is the acquisition of wealth have poorer overall emotional adjustment and lower well-being than do people whose primary values are self-acceptance, affiliation with others, or community feeling (wanting to make the world a better place for others) (Kasser & Ryan, 1993).

GOALS AND ASPIRATIONS One of the strongest findings about work motivation is the importance of having goals. Goals are most likely to improve performance when three conditions are met (Locke & Latham, 1990; Smither, 1994):

- *The goal is specific.* Defining a goal as "doing your best" is as ineffective as having no goals at all.
- *The goal has a time limit.* If you know you have to meet a goal in a specific amount of time, you are more likely to succeed than if you give yourself an indefinite amount of time ("by next year").
- *The goal is challenging but achievable.* You are apt to work harder for tough but realistic goals that make you feel gratified when you reach them, than for easy goals that pose no challenge or impossible goals that can never be attained.

self-fulfilling prophecy An expectation that comes true because of the tendency of the person holding it to act in ways that confirm it.

GET INVOLVED

Rank the following values in terms of their importance to you, with 1 the most important and 18 the least, being as honest as you can. Then ask some friends and relatives to do the same. How does your ranking differ from theirs? Do your values affect your goals, relationships, level of community activism, or decisions? Do any of your key values conflict with your daily actions—and if so, does that conflict motivate you to change in any way? (From Rokeach and Ball-Rokeach, 1989.)

________ *A world at peace*	________ *Accomplishment*
________ *Family security*	________ *True friendship*
________ *Freedom*	________ *National security*
________ *Happiness*	________ *Inner harmony*
________ *Self-respect*	________ *Mature love*
________ *Wisdom*	________ *A world of beauty*
________ *Equality*	________ *Social recognition*
________ *Salvation*	________ *Pleasure*
________ *A comfortable life*	________ *An exciting life*

But why do some people give up when a goal becomes difficult, whereas others become even more determined to succeed? Why do some people sink into helplessness, doing poorly at solving the problem and eventually giving up, whereas others keep going to master the problem and avoid failure? The crucial fact about these alternatives—helplessness or mastery—is that *they are unrelated to ability.* When people are faced with a frustrating problem, talent or ambition alone does not predict who will push on and who will give up. What does predict success is the way in which people think about the goals they set for themselves and how competent they feel about reaching them.

According to Carol Dweck (1990, 1992), people who are motivated by *performance goals* are concerned with doing well, being judged favorably, and avoiding criticism. When such people are focused on how well they are performing and then do poorly, they often decide the fault is theirs, and they stop trying to improve. Because their goal is to demonstrate their abilities, they set themselves up for grief when they temporarily fail—as all of us must if we are to learn anything new. In contrast, those who are motivated by *learning and mastery goals* are concerned with increasing their competence and skills. Therefore, they regard failure as a source of useful information that will help them improve. Failure and criticism do not discourage them because they know that learning takes time. In addition, when most people focus on mastery rather than on performance, they feel greater intrinsic pleasure in the task they are doing or the goal they are pursuing. (The opposite is true, however, among highly ambitious, performance-driven people, such as great athletes and musicians. For them, focusing on specific ways of improving their performance raises their intrinsic motivation and satisfaction [Elliot & Harackiewicz, 1994].)

self-efficacy A person's belief that he or she is capable of producing desired results, such as mastering new skills and reaching goals.

COMPETENCE AND SELF-EFFICACY When people accomplish their goals, they naturally feel competent, and competence is another key motive for everyone, child and adult alike (White, 1959). Albert Bandura (1990, 1994) argues that competence leads to **self-efficacy,** the conviction that you can accomplish what you set out to do. According to Bandura, self-efficacy is acquired from four sources:

People with high self-efficacy pursue their goals even in the face of great obstacles.

1. *Experiences in mastering new skills and overcoming obstacles on the path to achievement.* Occasional failures are necessary for self-efficacy because people who experience only success learn to expect quick results and tend to be easily discouraged by normal difficulties.

2. *Vicarious experiences provided by successful and competent people (models) who are similar to oneself.* For example, if an African-American boy learns that a black man, Garrett Morgan, invented the traffic light, his belief that he too could be an engineer may be strengthened. By observing the competence of persons similar to themselves, people learn both that the task is possible and how to do it. But negative modeling can undermine self-efficacy: If other people in their group seem to keep failing, people may come to doubt that they can succeed.

3. *Encouragement and persuasion from others.* People acquire a sense of self-efficacy when other people persuade them that they have what it takes to "make it," reward their capabilities, allow them to succeed, and do not subject them to repeated failure.

4. *Judgments of one's own physiological state.* People feel more competent when they are calm and relaxed than when they are tense or under extreme stress. But people who have high self-efficacy are able to use nervousness productively. For example, instead of interpreting normal feelings of stage fright as evidence that they are going to make fools of themselves when they give a talk, they regard these jitters as a source of energy that will help them perform better.

Research in North America, Europe, and Russia has found that self-efficacy affects just about every aspect of people's lives: how well they do on a task, how persistently they pursue their goals, the kinds of career choices they make, their ability to solve complex problems, their motivation to work for political and social goals, their health habits, and even their chances of recovery from a heart attack (Bandura, 1994, 1995; Ewart, 1995; Maddux, 1995). Fortunately, self-efficacy can be acquired through programs and experiences that provide skills and a sense of mastery.

THE NEEDS FOR ACHIEVEMENT AND POWER In the early 1950s, David McClelland and his associates (1953) speculated that some people have a **need for achievement** (often abbreviated *nAch*) that motivates them as much as hunger motivates people to eat. How could this motive be identified? McClelland (1961) later wrote that he and his colleagues sought the "'psychic x-ray' that would permit us to observe what was going on in a person's head in the same way that we can observe stomach contractions or nerve discharges in a hungry organism."

The solution came in the form of a method developed decades earlier by Christiana Morgan and Henry Murray (1935), called the **Thematic Apperception Test (TAT).** The TAT consists of a series of ambiguous pictures and drawings; all you have to do is make up a story about each scene. What is happening in the picture? What are the characters thinking and feeling? What will happen next? A standardized scoring system takes into account the themes raised in each story, the characters the test-taker identifies with, the motives and emotions attributed to the characters, and the endings given to the stories. The test can be scored for different motives, including the need for achievement, affiliation, and power. The strength of these internal motives, said McClelland (1961), is captured in the fantasies you tell. "In fantasy anything is at least symbolically possible," he explained. "A person may rise to great heights, sink to great depths, kill his grandmother, or take off for the South Sea Islands on a pogo stick."

need for achievement A learned motive to meet personal standards of success and excellence in a chosen area.

Thematic Apperception Test (TAT) A projective personality test that asks respondents to interpret a series of drawings showing ambiguous scenes of people.

The Many Motives of Accomplishment

PRODUCTIVITY

ISAAC ASIMOV
(1920–1992)
Scientist, writer

"If my doctor told me I had only six minutes to live, I wouldn't brood. I'd type a little faster."

KNOWLEDGE

HELEN KELLER
(1880–1968)
Blind/deaf author and lecturer

"Knowledge is happiness, because to have knowledge—broad, deep knowledge—is to know true ends from false, and lofty things from low."

JUSTICE

MARTIN LUTHER KING, JR.
(1929–1968)
Civil rights activist

"I have a dream . . . that my four little children will one day live in a nation where they will not be judged by the color of their skin but by the content of their character."

AUTONOMY

GEORGIA O'KEEFFE
(1887–1986)
Artist

"[I] found myself saying to myself—I can't live where I want to, go where I want to, do what I want to . . . I decided I was a very stupid fool not to at least paint as I wanted to."

Needless to say, people with high achievement motivation do not fantasize about taking off for the South Seas or sinking to great depths. They tell stories about working hard, becoming rich and famous, and clobbering the opposition with their wit and brilliance; if they don't succeed, they foresee devastation. For example, here is what two people wrote in response to a neutral illustration of a man named George at his desk (McClelland, 1985):

> High need for achievement: *George is an engineer who wants to win a competition in which the man with the most practicable drawing will be awarded the contract to build a bridge. He is taking a moment to think how happy he will be if he wins. He has been baffled by how to make such a long span strong, but remembers to specify a new steel alloy of great strength, submits his entry, but does not win and is very unhappy.*
>
> High need for affiliation: *George is an engineer who is working late. He is worried that his wife will be annoyed with him for neglecting her. She has been objecting that he cares more about his work than his wife and family. He seems unable to satisfy both his boss and his wife, but he loves her very much, and will do his best to finish up fast and get home to her.*

When high achievers are in situations that arouse their competitiveness and desire to succeed—when, for example, they believe that the TAT is measuring their

POWER

HENRY KISSINGER
(b. 1923)
Former Secretary of State

"Power is the ultimate aphrodisiac."

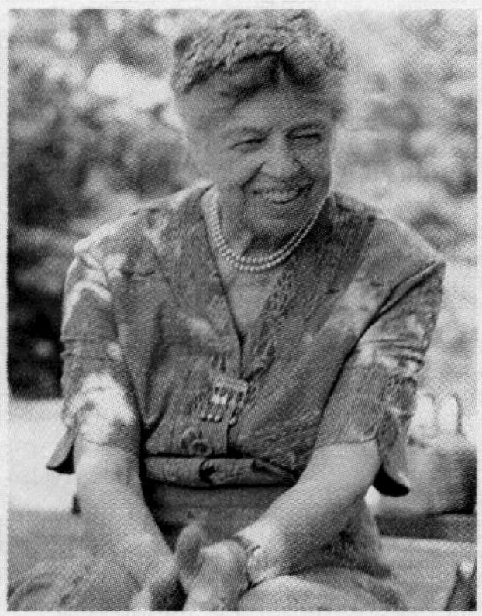

DUTY

ELEANOR ROOSEVELT
(1884–1962)
Humanitarian, lecturer, stateswoman

"As for accomplishments, I just did what I had to do as things came along."

EXCELLENCE

FLORENCE GRIFFITH JOYNER
(b. 1959)
Olympic gold medalist

"When you've been second best for so long, you can either accept it, or try to become the best. I made the decision to try and be the best."

GREED

IVAN BOESKY
(b. 1937)
Financier, convicted of insider trading violations

"Greed is all right . . . I think greed is healthy. You can be greedy and still feel good about yourself."

intelligence and leadership ability—their achievement-related themes increase (Atkinson, 1958). In the laboratory and real life, people who score high on the need for achievement consistently differ from those who score low. High scorers are more likely, for example, to start their own businesses. They set high personal standards and prefer to work with capable colleagues who can help them succeed rather than with co-workers who are merely friendly (McClelland, 1987).

The TAT has also been used to identify people motivated by a **need for power**—the desire to dominate others and to influence people (McClelland, 1975). Men and women who score high on this motive may try to win power by being aggressive and manipulative, or by being inspirational and charismatic (Winter, 1993). They seek prestige and visibility, enter powerful careers, and run for office. The need for power spurs some people to become leaders; but the *kind* of power that drives them distinguishes effective leaders from ineffective ones. Two researchers systematically examined the speeches, letters, and biographies of 39 U.S. presidents, from George Washington to Ronald Reagan (Spangler & House, 1991). Using complex measures of presidential performance, effectiveness, and greatness, they found that great presidents had a lower need for affiliation and even for achievement than mediocre ones, but a higher motivation to use power to improve society rather than to further their own ambitions—the difference between, say, Abraham Lincoln and Herbert Hoover.

In an innovative series of studies linking individual motives to national events, David Winter (1993) has measured power and achievement motivation in government by analyzing secret documents and official speeches by leaders. His work suggests that power motivation may be a crucial psychological cause of war. "When it rises," Winter reports, "war is likely; when it falls, war is less likely and ongoing wars are likely to end." The affiliation motive works in just the opposite fashion: When it rises, wars are averted.

This research raises fascinating questions. What causes power, achievement, and affiliation motives to rise and fall within a culture? Do we have any control over them? The evidence that these motives can be scored and measured on a national level—using historical documents, speeches, popular books, and indicators of achievement such as patents and discoveries—suggests not only that historical events can change people's motivations, but also that people's motivations can change historical events.

THE EFFECTS OF WORK ON MOTIVATION

Like the motives for affiliation and sexuality, the motives for achievement or power depend on what is going on in the culture at large. At one time, for example, many people believed that women had an internalized "fear of success"; but as opportunities for women improved, this apparent motive faded. Similarly, when the proportion of men and women in an occupation changes, so do people's motivations to work in that field (Kanter, 1977/1993). That is why some psychologists have criticized the whole idea that achievement depends solely on internal "motives"—enduring, unchanging qualities of the individual. This notion, they say, leads to the incorrect inference that if people don't succeed, it's their own fault because they lack the internal drive to make it (Morrison & Von Glinow, 1990). In fact, accomplishment depends not only on internal motives and cognitive processes; it can also be nurtured or reduced by the work you do and the conditions under which you do it.

need for power A learned motive to dominate or influence others.

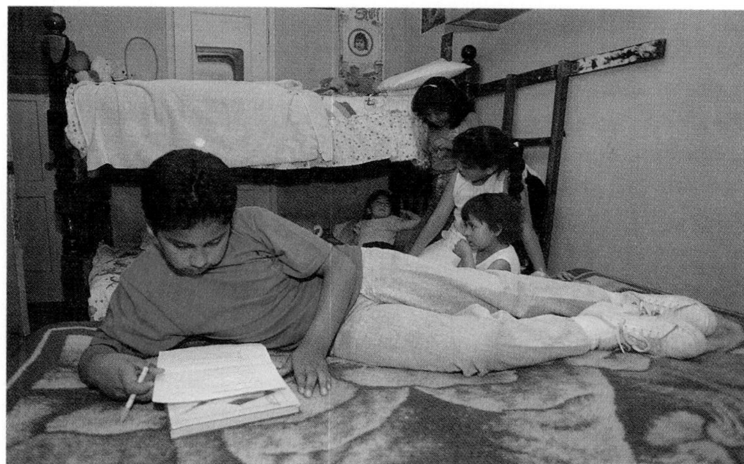

Like employees, students can have poor working conditions, such as having to study in crowded quarters or having small siblings who pester them.

WORKING CONDITIONS In a classic longitudinal study that followed a random sample of American workers for ten years, it turned out that aspects of the work (such as fringe benefits, complexity of daily tasks, pace, pressure, and how routine or varied the work was) significantly changed the workers' self-esteem, job commitment, and motivation (Kohn & Schooler, 1983). Meta-analyses show that two factors about a job are especially important in enhancing people's pleasure in and commitment to their work: the degree of flexibility and the autonomy that the job provides (Brown, 1996). People who have a chance to set their own hours, make decisions, vary their tasks, and solve problems are likely to rise to the challenge. They tend to become more flexible in their thinking and feel better about themselves and their work than if they feel stuck in a routine, boring job that gives them no control over what they do. As a result, their work motivation rises, and their level of stress drops (Karasek & Theorell, 1990; Locke & Latham, 1990). Conversely, when people with high power or achievement motivation are put in situations that frustrate their desire and ability to express these motives, they become dissatisfied and stressed, and their power and achievement motives decline (Jenkins, 1994).

American culture emphasizes money as the great motivator, but actually the research shows that work motivation is not related to the amount of money you get, but to how and when you get it. The strongest motivator is *incentive pay*—that is, bonuses that are given upon completion of a goal and not as an automatic part of salary (Locke et al., 1981). If you think about it, you can see why this might be so. Incentive pay increases people's feelings of self-efficacy and sense of accomplishment ("I got this raise because I deserved it"). This doesn't mean, however, that people should accept low pay so they will like their jobs better, or that they should never demand cost-of-living raises!

TEAMWORK One way to improve working conditions and work motivation is by creating cohesive, independent work teams. For example, an alternative to the standard boring assembly line is to have factory employees work in groups and handle different aspects of assembling the product instead of performing one repeated routine; this approach has been tried successfully by Sherwin-Williams, Volvo,

General Foods, and Saab (Sundstrom, De Meuse, & Futrell, 1990). Although some groups can be oppressive and stifle innovation, as we will see in Chapter 17, working in the right kind of group often raises workers' motivation and job satisfaction.

Organizational psychologists have identified several conditions that create these benefits (Smither, 1994): Employees have clear goals and prompt feedback on their performance; they work in a setting that permits informal interaction; everyone is encouraged to participate and feels responsible for his or her work; and rewards and recognition given to individual members depend on the whole team's performance.

GENDER, CULTURE, AND AMBITION Ultimately, achievement ambitions are related to people's *chances* of achieving. Men and women who work in dead-end jobs with no prospect of promotion tend to behave the same way: They play down the importance of achievement, fantasize about quitting, and emphasize the social benefits of their jobs instead of the intellectual benefits (Kanter, 1977/1993). Consider some comments from a man who realized in his mid-30s that he was never going to be promoted to top management and who scaled down his ambitions accordingly (Scofield, 1993). As organizational psychologists would predict, he began to emphasize the benefits of not achieving: "I'm freer to speak my mind," "I can choose not to play office politics," and "I don't volunteer for lousy assignments." He had time, he learned, for coaching Little League and could stay home when the kids were sick. "Of course," he wrote, "if I ever had any chance for upward corporate mobility it's gone now. I couldn't take the grind. Whether real or imagined, that glass ceiling has become an invisible shield."

Many women and members of minority groups encounter a "glass ceiling" in management—a barrier to promotion that is so subtle as to be transparent, yet strong enough to prevent advancement. For example, in a study of the banking industry, the three most significant problems that African-Americans reported were not being "in the network," and therefore not being told what was going on; racism; and an inability to find a mentor (Irons & Moore, 1985). Among Asian-Americans in professional and managerial positions, education and work experience do not predict advancement as they do for white American men (Cabezas et al., 1989).

Many people believe that women are underrepresented in leadership positions because of something about women—their style of managing is different from men's, or they have lower self-esteem and feelings of competence than men, or they have less commitment to the job than men. None of these popular beliefs has been supported by research. For example, after conducting a field study of 2,000 male and female managers, two researchers concluded that "The disproportionately low numbers of women in management can no longer be explained away by the contention that women practice a different brand of management from that practiced by men" (Donnell & Hall, 1980). And marketing researcher Robert Snyder (1993) found "absolutely no reliable empirical evidence" that women's commitment to work and their self-esteem are lower than men's. In fact, Snyder reported, when you compare women and men who are at the same organizational level, women's self-esteem and organizational commitment are usually higher than those of men. It is true that women managers are about twice as likely as men to leave an organization—but the reason, Snyder found, is not that they are leaving the workplace: They leave for better jobs, often because of lack of career advancement at the first one.

Work motivation and satisfaction, in sum, depend on the right fit between qualities of the individual and conditions of the work. This fact raises a host of questions about how best to structure work so that the increasing diversity of workers will result in greater worker satisfaction, achievement, and effectiveness rather than more conflict, bitterness, and prejudice. When should people be required to fit into the dominant culture, and when should companies become more multicultural, changing themselves to fit their employees?

Quick Quiz

Work on your understanding of work motivation.

1. Expecting to fail at work and then making no effort to do well can result in a ____________.
2. Ramon and Ramona are learning to ski. Every time she falls, Ramona says, "This is the most humiliating experience I've ever had! Everyone is watching me behave like a clumsy dolt!" When Ramon falls, he says, "&*!!@$@! I'll show these dratted skis who's boss!" Why is Ramona more likely than Ramon to give up? (a) She *is* a clumsy dolt. (b) She is less competent at skiing. (c) She is focused on performance. (d) She is focused on learning.
3. Which of these factors significantly increase work motivation? (a) specific goals, (b) regular pay, (c) feedback, (d) general goals, (e) being told what to do, (f) being able to make decisions, (g) the chance of promotion, (h) having routine, predictable work

4. Phyllis works at an umbrella company. Her work is always competent, but she rarely arrives on time, she doesn't seem as motivated to do well as others, and she has begun to take an unusual number of sick days. Phyllis's employer is irritated by this behavior and is thinking of firing her. What guidelines of critical thinking is the boss overlooking, and what research should the boss consider before taking this step?

Answers:

1. self-fulfilling prophecy 2. c 3. a, c, f, g 4. The boss is jumping to the conclusion that Phyllis has low achievement motivation. This may be true, but because her work is competent, the boss should consider other explanations and examine the evidence. Perhaps the work conditions are unsatisfactory: There may be few opportunities for promotion; she may get no feedback; perhaps the company does not provide day care, so Phyllis arrives late because she has child-care obligations. What other possible explanations come to mind?

WHEN MOTIVES CONFLICT

As we have seen, human beings are motivated by physical needs for food, water, and contact comfort, as well as by psychological needs for achievement, power, or success. But motives rarely coexist in perfect harmony. Two motives are in conflict when the satisfaction of one leads to the inability to act on the other—when, that is, you want to eat your cake and have it, too. Researchers have identified four kinds of motivational conflicts (Lewin, 1948):

1. *Approach–approach conflicts* occur when you are equally attracted to two or more possible activities or goals. For example, you would like to go out with Tom, Dick, *and* Harry, all at the same time; you would like to be a veterinarian *and* a rock singer; you would like to go out with friends on Sunday night (an affiliation motive) *and* study like mad for an exam (an achievement motive).

2. *Avoidance–avoidance conflicts* require you to choose between "the lesser of two evils" because you dislike both alternatives. Novice parachute jumpers, for example, must choose between the fear of jumping and the fear of losing face if they don't jump.

"C'mon, c'mon—it's either one or the other."

3. *Approach–avoidance conflicts* occur when one activity or goal has both a positive and a negative aspect. For example, you want to be a powerful executive but you worry about losing your friends if you succeed. You want power and yet you fear it at the same time. In culturally diverse nations such as the United States, differing cultural values produce many approach–avoidance conflicts, such as the following examples, which our students have described:

- A Chicano student says he wants to succeed and do well in the "white" culture, but the community in which he grew up values family closeness. His parents worry that if he goes to college, he will become too independent and eventually leave them behind.
- A Pakistani student says she desperately wants an education and a career, but she also doesn't want to be disobedient to her parents, who have arranged a marriage for her back home.
- An African-American student from a poor neighborhood is in college on a prestigious scholarship. He is torn between wanting to leave his ghetto background behind him forever and returning to help the family and community who have supported him.
- A white student wants to be a marine biologist, but her friends tell her that only nerds and dweebs go into science.

In many situations in which an approach–avoidance conflict occurs, both attraction and repulsion are strongest when you are nearest the goal. The closer you are to something appealing, the stronger your desire to approach; the closer you are to something unpleasant, the stronger your desire to flee. However, as you step away from the goal, the two motives change in strength. The attractive aspects of the goal still seem appealing, but the negative ones seem less unpleasant. This may be one reason people often have trouble resolving their ambivalence: When they leave a situation that has some benefits but many problems, and they consider it from a distance, they see its good aspects and overlook the bad ones. So they approach it again. Up close, the problems appear more clearly, motivating them to avoid the situation once more.

4. *Multiple approach–avoidance conflicts* occur in situations that offer several possible choices, each containing advantages and disadvantages. For example, you might want to marry and settle down while you're still in school, and you think you have found the right person. On the other hand, you also may want to establish a career and have some money in the bank, and lately you and the right person have been quarreling a lot.

Internal conflict is inevitable, unless you are a tree sloth. But over time, unresolved conflicts have a physical and mental cost. In a series of studies, students listed their main "personal strivings": *approach* goals such as "trying to be attractive" or "trying to seek new experiences," and *avoidance* goals such as "trying to avoid being noticed by others" or "trying to avoid being dependent on my boyfriend." Students rated these objectives on the amount of conflict they caused and on how ambivalent they felt about them. For example, a student might say that striving "to appear more intelligent than I am" conflicted with striving "to always present myself in an honest light." High levels of conflict and ambivalence were associated with anxiety, depression, headaches and other physical symptoms, and more visits to the student health center (Emmons & King, 1988).

Conflict and ambivalence, in turn, are affected by how people frame their goals. Those who do so in approach terms (e.g., "I'm going to lose weight by jogging three times a week") feel better about themselves, and are more optimistic and less depressed, than people who frame the same goals in avoidance terms (e.g., "I'm going to lose weight by staying away from rich foods"). The former way of thinking about a goal focuses on what the person can actively do to accomplish it, whereas the latter way focuses on what the person has to give up—resulting in big differences in well-being (Coats, Janoff-Bulman, & Alpert, 1996).

Another way of thinking about the varied, often competing motives in our lives comes from a theory proposed by humanist psychologist Abraham Maslow (1954/1970). Maslow envisioned people's "motivational strivings" on a pyramid that he called a *hierarchy of needs.* At the bottom level of the pyramid were basic physical survival needs, such as for food, sleep, and water; at the next level were security needs, such as protection against danger; at the third level were social needs, such as for belonging and affection; at the fourth level were esteem needs for self-respect and the respect of others; and at the top level were needs for "self-actualization" and "self-transcendence." Maslow argued that your needs must be met at each level before you can even think of the matters posed by the level above it. You can't worry about achievement, for instance, if you are hungry, cold, and poor. You can't become self-actualized if you haven't satisfied your needs for self-esteem and love. Human beings behave badly, he argued, only when their lower needs are frustrated.

This theory, which is intuitively logical and optimistic about human nature, became immensely popular, but it has not been supported by research (Smither, 1994). People have *simultaneous* needs for comfort and safety and for attachments, self-esteem, and competence. Individuals who have met their "lower" needs do not inevitably seek "higher" ones, nor is it the case that people behave badly only when their lower needs are frustrated. "Higher" needs may take precedence over "lower" ones. Human history is full of examples of people who would rather starve than be humiliated; who would rather die of torture than sacrifice their convictions; who would rather explore, risk, or create new art than stay safe and secure in their homes.

ANALYZE ASSUMPTIONS

Maslow's notion that motives can be ranked from basic physical needs to higher psychological ones is intuitively appealing. What is wrong with this assumption? How else might we think about the diversity of human motives?

Think of Jim Abbott, Dian Fossey, and all the other men and women who have done remarkable things with their lives. They may have been "self-actualized," but not necessarily because they had overcome lower needs or reached a resolution of all conflicts. Perhaps the wisest conclusion, therefore, is that each of us develops an individual hierarchy of motives in the course of our development from childhood to old age. For some people, the need for love, security, and safety will dominate. For others, the need for achievement or power will rule. Some will wrestle with conflicting motives; for others, one consuming passion, one driving motive, will hold sway over all others. This diversity is an inevitable part of human personality and cultural experience.

Taking Psychology with You

Improving Your Work Motivation

Why are you in school? What do you hope to accomplish in your life? Are you motivated primarily by the intrinsic goals of a job well done and the satisfaction of the work itself or by extrinsic goals such as getting a degree, a job, and a salary—or by both? Do you have a burning ambition, or are you burned out? If you are feeling unmotivated these days, research on work motivation suggests some steps you might take:

• *Seek activities that are intrinsically pleasurable, even if they don't "pay off."* If you really, really want to study Swahili or Swedish, even though these languages are not in your prelaw requirements, try to find a way to do it. You might also ask yourself whether your major in school or the kind of work you do is right for you. Are you in this field because you are drawn to it or because others think you should be in it? Remember, though, that even when you are doing the work you most want to do, you will have difficult or boring days.

• *Focus on learning goals rather than performance goals.* In general, you will be better able to cope with inevitable setbacks if your goal is to learn rather than to show off how good you are. It is important to be able to regard failure as a learning experience rather than as a sure sign of incompetence. Ironically, the more you are able to focus on learning, mastery, and improvement, the better your performance will be. Once you are an accomplished performer, focusing on polishing that performance will become intrinsically pleasurable.

• *Get accurate feedback on your performance.* Once you have specified a goal, continued motivation depends in part on getting feedback about your performance. Your employer needs to tell you that you are almost number one in sales. Your piano teacher needs to tell you that your playing has improved. Your statistics instructor needs to tell you what you need to do to raise a grade. When people work or study in environments that do not provide constructive feedback, their motivation to do well is often weakened. If you are not getting enough feedback, ask for it.

• *Assess your working conditions.* How is your job or academic situation structured? Are you getting support from co-workers, employers, or instructors? Do you have opportunities to develop ideas and vary your routine, or are you expected to toe the line and do the same thing day after day? Do you perceive a "glass ceiling" that might limit your advancement in your chosen field, and are you accurate in your perceptions? If you have entered school or a job with enthusiasm, optimism, and expectations of success, only to have these feelings slowly dwindle and dissipate, you might want to consider whether your working conditions are causing your burnout. And then you might consider whether changing some of those conditions could recharge your batteries.

• *Take steps to resolve motivational conflicts.* Many students in an approach–avoidance conflict tend to think a great deal about their conflicts but not do anything to resolve them. A student in one study, for instance, remained unhappily stuck between his goal of achieving independence and his desire to be cared for by his parents. The reconciliation of motivational conflicts, the researchers concluded, is "a premier goal of human development" and a cornerstone of well-being (Emmons & King, 1988).

What psychology cannot tell you, of course, is which goals and values to choose in the first place: love, wealth, security, freedom, fame, beauty, the desire to improve the world, or anything else. In a commencement address some years ago, Mario Cuomo, the former governor of New York, had these words of wisdom for the graduating students: "When you've parked the second car in the garage, and installed the hot tub, and skied in Colorado, and wind-surfed in the Caribbean, when you've had your first love affair and your second and your third, the question will remain: Where does the dream end for me?"

SUMMARY

THE SOCIAL ANIMAL: MOTIVES FOR CONNECTION

1) *Motivation* refers to an inferred process within a person or animal that causes that organism to move toward a goal or away from an unpleasant situation. A few primary motivating drives are based on physiological needs, but people's cognitive abilities permit them to plan and work for goals that stem from *social motives.*

2) People are motivated to *affiliate* with others for contact comfort, reassurance, and friendship. Individuals and cultures differ in how much affiliation they seek and in the importance they place on attachments. *Contact comfort* is essential in human development in early childhood, where it provides a secure base, and throughout life. Infants and caregivers become attached to each other after a few months; by the age of 7 to 12 months, babies often feel *stranger anxiety* and *separation anxiety.* Studies of the *Strange Situation* have identified three kinds of infant attachment: *secure, avoidant, and anxious–ambivalent.* Parents who are hostile, neglectful, rejecting, or simply uncomfortable handling their babies may create insecurely attached children, with long-term negative consequences for the children's cognitive, emotional, and social development. Babies may also become insecurely attached because they are temperamentally difficult. Being in day care does not affect a child's attachment style.

3) Psychologists have developed different theories to describe the varieties of love: a theory describing *six styles of love;* the *attachment theory* of love (love as secure, avoidant, or anxious–ambivalent); and the *triangle theory* of love (love as consisting of different combinations of passion, intimacy, and commitment). Adults' attachment styles are related to how their parents cared for them and predict how they get along in their own close relationships. Men and women are equally likely to feel love and need attachment, but gender roles affect how they experience and express love.

THE EROTIC ANIMAL: MOTIVES FOR SEX

4) Biological research finds that testosterone influences sexual desire in both sexes, that there is no "right" kind of orgasm for women to have, and that both sexes are capable of sexual arousal and response. Kinsey and, later, Masters and Johnson were the first modern researchers to show that physiologically, male and female sexuality are more similar than different.

5) Psychological approaches to sexual motivation emphasize the ways that a person's values, beliefs, perceptions, and fantasies affect sexual desire and response. Although most men and women have sexual intercourse for reasons of intimacy, pleasure, and procreation, they sometimes have negative motives as well: to seek revenge, to gain benefits, to dominate or bind the other person. Both sexes may agree to intercourse for nonsexual motives: Men sometimes feel obligated to "make a move" to prove their masculinity, and women sometimes feel obliged to "give in" to preserve the relationship. A major gender difference in sexuality has to do with rape and perceptions of sexual coercion. Men who rape do so for diverse reasons, including anger at women, sadism, and opportunity. Sexually aggressive males typically have a set of qualities called "hostile masculinity" and a history of impersonal sexual promiscuity.

6) Sexual attitudes and behavior are affected by *gender roles* and *sexual scripts.* For straight and gay people alike, cultural scripts specify appropriate behavior during courtship and sex. Scripts for heterosexual women and men often lead to misunderstandings over the meaning of sexual signals and the purpose of sex. People also follow interpersonal and intrapsychic scripts.

7) The origins of sexual orientation are still unknown. Traditional psychological explanations (such as bad mothers or absent fathers) do not account for why some people become heterosexual and others homosexual. Growing evidence suggests that genetic and hormonal factors are involved. However, biology, culture, learning, and circumstance interact in complex ways to produce a given person's orientation. Research on this issue is politically sensitive because people often confuse scientific questions about the origins of homosexuality with political and moral questions about the rights of gay men and lesbians.

THE COMPETENT ANIMAL: MOTIVES TO WORK

8) The motivation to work depends on a person's expectations of success, which can create *self-fulfilling prophecies* of success or failure, and on the value the person places on a goal. Success or failure depend not only on ability, but also on whether people set *learning goals*, which can lead to mastery, or *performance goals*, which can lead to helplessness if the person temporarily fails. People are also motivated by a need to feel competent at what they do and to have *self-efficacy* about their abilities to reach their goals. Self-efficacy comes from experience in mastering new skills, having successful role models, encouragement from others, and constructive interpretations of one's own emotional state.

9) People who are motivated by a high *need for achievement* set their own standards for success and excellence. People who are motivated by a *need for power* seek to dominate and influence others. They may use a variety of methods to gain this power, from persuasion to aggression. Patterns of social motives can help predict individual behavior, including presidential greatness, and national events, such as the outbreak of war.

10) Work motivation also depends on having the right *working conditions*—such as job flexibility, control, incentive pay, and teamwork—and on having the opportunity to be promoted and have good work rewarded and recognized.

WHEN MOTIVES CONFLICT

11) Human motives often conflict. In an *approach–approach conflict*, a person is equally attracted to two goals. In an *avoidance–avoidance conflict*, a person is equally repelled by two goals. An *approach–avoidance* conflict is the most difficult to resolve because the person is both attracted to and repelled by the same goal. Prolonged conflict can lead to physical symptoms and reduced well-being.

12) Abraham Maslow believed that human motives could be ranked from basic biological needs to higher psychological needs, but this popular theory is not supported by evidence. People can have simultaneous motives; "higher" motives can outweigh "lower" ones; and people do not always become kinder or more self-actualized when their needs for safety and love are met.

KEY TERMS

motivation 416
social motives 416
need for affiliation 417
attachment 417
contact comfort 418
stranger anxiety 418
separation anxiety 418
Strange Situation 418
secure attachment 419
insecure attachment (avoidant, anxious–ambivalent) 419
passionate and companionate love 420
six styles of love 421
attachment theory of love 421
triangle theory of love 422
gender roles 430
sexual scripts 430
cultural, interpersonal, intrapsychic scripts 431
self-fulfilling prophecy 435
values 435
performance and learning goals 436
self-efficacy 436
need for achievement (*nAch*) 438
Thematic Apperception Test (TAT) 438
need for power 440
working conditions 441
incentive pay 441
teamwork 441
approach–approach conflicts 443
avoidance–avoidance conflicts 443
approach–avoidance conflicts 444
Maslow's hierarchy of needs 445

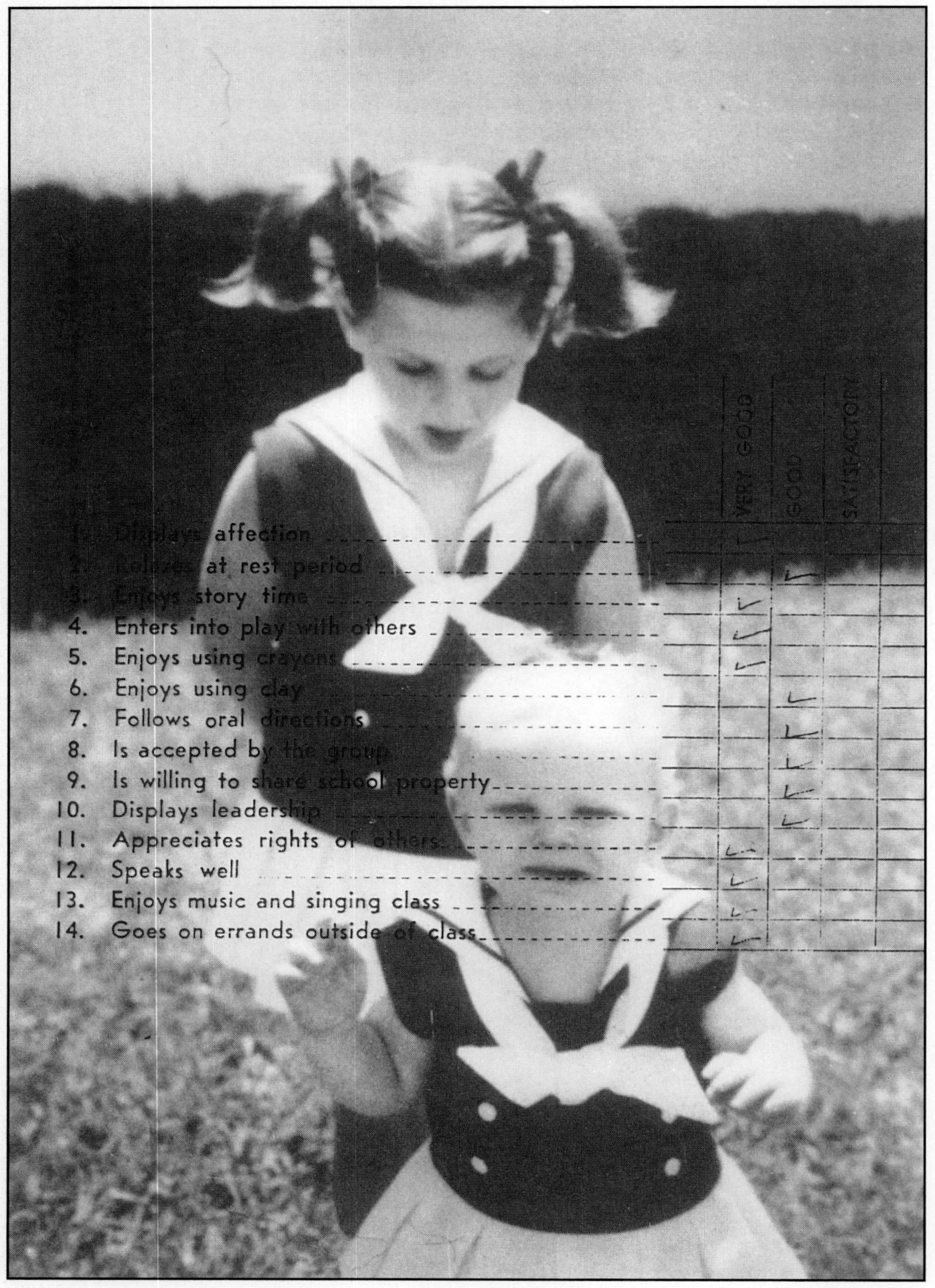

The tough-minded . . . respect difference.

Their goal is a world made safe for differences.

Ruth Benedict

CHAPTER TWELVE

Theories of Personality

A PSYCHOLOGIST WE KNOW once gave a lecture to the faculty of the first school she ever went to—her nursery school. Her topic was an optimistic report on adult life. "People are not prisoners of childhood," she said. "They change their attitudes, philosophies of life, self-esteem, ambitions, values, and looks. They have new experiences that change their outlook. Most recover from early traumas." In the audience was one of her original teachers, now 96 years old, and as clear-minded as ever. "A nice speech, dear," she said when it was over, "but as far as I'm concerned, you haven't changed a bit since you were 3. You're a bit taller is all."

What made our friend appear unchanged to her nursery-school teacher was, undoubtedly, her "personality." In psychology, the word doesn't refer to enthusiasm or a set of positive qualities, as in "he's got a lot of personality." **Personality** is a distinctive and stable pattern of behavior, thoughts, motives, and emotions that characterizes an individual over time. This pattern reflects a particular constellation of **traits,** characteristics that are assumed to describe the person across many situations: shy, brave, reliable, friendly, hostile, confident, sullen, and so on.

Psychologists differ, however, in which traits they consider the most important, and in their views of the origins and stability of personality. Biological psychologists seek evidence for genetically influenced qualities that remain entrenched throughout life. Psychodynamic psychologists look for personality in the dark, unconscious motives of the mind. Behaviorists argue that personality is really only an illusion because people are far more influenced by their immediate circumstances than by any individual qualities. And humanists regard personality as the private self, the "true self" behind the masks that people wear in daily life.

In this chapter, we will describe the major approaches to the study of personality, especially as they try to answer four puzzles of personality: Is personality stable, or are some qualities and traits changeable? What is "human nature"—are we, "by nature," aggressive, loving, cooperative, or hostile, or are these qualities learned? To what extent are we conscious of the motives and conflicts that shape our personalities? And which has more influence on behavior, our personality or the situation we are in?

Does personality change, or only superficial qualities? Marilyn Monroe changed significantly when she became a star—or did she?

THE ELEMENTS OF PERSONALITY

Personality consists of a complex interaction of traits, habits, tendencies, preferences, and moods, so no one test can possibly summarize all of them. But tests and assessment methods do provide information about aspects of personality, such as needs, values, interests, and typical ways of responding to situations. Using objective tests, psychologists have identified many fascinating traits, from sensation seeking (the enjoyment of risk) to "erotophobia" (the fear of sex). Some researchers have tried to identify the many individual traits that make up personality. Other researchers, unhappy with this piece-by-piece approach, look for a few organizing traits of personality.

One of the most influential trait theorists was Gordon Allport (1897–1967). Allport observed that most members of a society share certain common traits that their culture expects and rewards. To understand why two people differ, said Allport (1937, 1961), we must look at the individual traits that make each of them unique. *Cardinal traits* are of overwhelming importance to an individual and influence almost everything the person does. We might say that Mohandas Gandhi (called

personality A distinctive and relatively stable pattern of behavior, thoughts, motives, and emotions that characterizes an individual.

trait A descriptive characteristic of an individual, assumed to be stable across situations and time.

Mahatma, or wise one) and Martin Luther King, Jr., had the cardinal trait of nonviolence. But few people, said Allport, have cardinal traits. Instead, most of us have five to ten *central* (or *global*) *traits* that reflect a characteristic way of behaving, dealing with others, and reacting to new situations. Allport (1961) wrote, "For some the world is a hostile place where men are evil and dangerous; for others it is a stage for fun and frolic. It may appear as a place to do one's duty grimly; or a pasture for cultivating friendship and love." *Secondary traits,* in contrast, are more changeable aspects of personality. They include preferences (for foods, colors, movies), habits, casual opinions, and the like.

THE FAR SIDE By GARY LARSON

The four basic personality types

Another important personality theorist, Raymond B. Cattell, advanced the study of personality traits by applying a statistical method called *factor analysis,* which we discussed in Chapter 8. Performing a factor analysis on traits is like adding water to flour: It causes the material to clump up into little balls. Using questionnaires, life descriptions, and observations, Cattell (1965, 1973) measured dozens of personality traits in hundreds of people. He called these descriptive qualities *surface traits* because they are visible in a person's words or deeds. He believed that factor analysis, which identifies traits that are correlated with each other, would identify *source traits,* the underlying causes of surface qualities. For example, you might have the surface traits of assertiveness, courage, and ambition; the source trait linking all three might be dominance. Cattell and his associates investigated many aspects of personality, including humor, intelligence, creativity, leadership, and emotional disorder. Out of these he developed a 16 Personality Factors (PF) Questionnaire. Later in his career, he noted that only six of these factors had been repeatedly confirmed, but the 16 PF personality test was popular for many years (Digman, 1996).

By the mid-1980s, researchers, using diverse methods to reduce surface traits into basic clusters, had identified five "robust factors," sometimes called the *Big Five* (Digman, 1990, 1996; Goldberg, 1993; McCrae & Costa, 1996; Wiggins, 1996):

1. *Introversion versus extroversion* describes the extent to which people are outgoing or shy. It includes such traits as being talkative or silent, sociable or reclusive, adventurous or cautious, eager to be in the limelight or inclined to stay in the shadows. Extroversion is associated with *positive emotionality,* the inclination to be enthusiastic, lively, and cheerful.

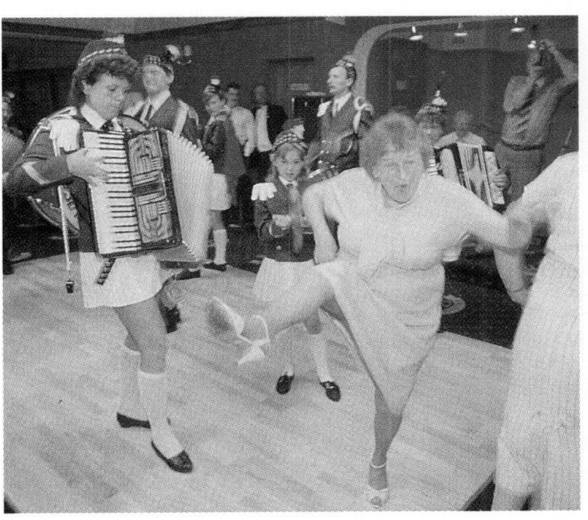

Extroversion–introversion is a stable dimension of personality. This merry dancer kicking up her heels has probably been outgoing and demonstrative since childhood.

2. *Neuroticism,* or emotional instability, includes such traits as anxiety and inability to control impulses, a tendency to have unrealistic ideas, and general emotional instability and negativity. Neurotic individuals are worriers, complainers, and defeatists, even in the absence of any major problems. They complain about different things at different ages, but they are always ready to see the sour side of life and none of its sweetness. Neuroticism is sometimes called *negative emotionality* because of the neurotic person's tendency to feel anger, scorn, revulsion, guilt, anxiety, and other negative moods (Watson & Clark, 1992).

3. *Agreeableness* describes the extent to which people are good-natured or irritable, gentle or headstrong, cooperative or abrasive, secure or suspicious and jealous. It reflects the capacity for friendly relationships or the tendency to have hostile ones.

4. *Conscientiousness* describes the degree to which people are responsible or undependable, persevering or likely to quit easily, steadfast or fickle, tidy or careless, scrupulous or unscrupulous.

5. *Openness to experience*, which in some personality measures is called *imagination*, describes the extent to which people are original, imaginative, questioning, artistic, and capable of divergent (creative) thinking—or are conforming, unimaginative, and predictable.

Not everyone subscribes to the Big Five model. Some researchers, conducting studies in North America, Israel, and Spain, argue for the Big Seven, which includes two additional dimensions that people use in everyday language when they evaluate themselves and each other: "positive valence" (outstanding, charismatic vs. ordinary, mediocre) and "negative valence" (evil, corrupt, pretentious vs. decent, sincere, honest) (Tellegen, 1993; Waller, 1996). Others have proposed the Giant Three (Eysenck, 1994), the Fundamental Four (Cloninger, Svrakic, & Przybeck, 1993), and even the Big Nine (Bouchard, 1995). Some agree that there are five factors, but they highlight different ones (Saucier, 1994; Zuckerman, 1995). Finally, some theorists argue that although the Big Five model captures certain simple qualities of the person, it is not a rich enough portrayal of the entire personality. Dan McAdams (1992) calls it a "psychology of the stranger," because, he says, it includes only the superficial qualities you would use to describe someone you didn't know.

In the midst of these continuing debates, evidence for the Big Five is turning up from many sources, including studies of children and adults in other cultures, using Chinese, Dutch, Japanese, Spanish, Filipino, Hawaiian, German, Tagalog, Russian, and Australian samples (Benet & Waller, 1995; Digman & Shmelyov, 1996; Katigbak, Church, & Akamine, 1996; Yang & Bond, 1990). Moreover, the Big Five traits are as

GET INVOLVED

Using the Big Five, rate your own personality traits along a five-point scale, mentally marking the appropriate space with an X. (Refer to the text for a description of the specific qualities that make up each dimension.)

Introverted ____ / ____ / ____ / ____ / ____ Extroverted
Neurotic ____ / ____ / ____ / ____ / ____ Emotionally stable
Agreeable ____ / ____ / ____ / ____ / ____ Stubborn
Conscientious ____ / ____ / ____ / ____ / ____ Undependable
Open to experience ____ / ____ / ____ / ____ / ____ Prefer the familiar

How did you come out? Are there some traits on which you fall at one end of the scale or the other?

Now choose one of these traits and find out how well it actually predicts your behavior. Over a period of time—a day may be enough, or you may need several days—keep notes about when your behavior is consistent with the trait and when it is not. For example, if you rated yourself as introverted, notice whether you are as introverted when you are with your friends as you are in class. In which situations, if any, are your actions at odds with the way you described yourself? What might be the explanation?

Here's something else to try. Have a friend or relative rate you on the Big Five. How closely does this rating match your own? If there's a discrepancy, what might be the reason?

persistent as crabgrass. You might think (and hope) that people would become more open-minded and agreeable and less neurotic as they mature. But longitudinal studies of men and women ages 21 to 96 find that no matter how you measure them, these traits remain stable year after year (Costa & McCrae, 1994).

Researchers are investigating the way each personality trait interacts with circumstances to foster or inhibit well-being. For example, the qualities of openness to experience, agreeableness, and extroversion are positively related to well-being (Demakis & McAdams, 1994; Magnus et al., 1993). One reason seems to be that when individuals with these traits are under stress or have problems, they respond by seeking help from others, trying new solutions, and maintaining optimism. In contrast, people who are high in neuroticism react by indulging in wishful thinking ("the problem will go away soon") or self-blame—two strategies that further increase their anxiety and other negative feelings (Bolger, 1990). A seven-year longitudinal study of 296 adults concluded that "Temperamental dispositions are more powerful than environmental factors in predicting psychological distress" (Ormel & Wohlfarth, 1991). Emotional difficulties and crises occur for everyone, of course, but people high in neuroticism bring their pessimism and negativity with them, making the situation worse.

Measures of the essential dimensions of personality are useful in probing the origins of human diversity, and psychologists have identified some of the key qualities that form the foundation of an individual's character. The logical next question is "Where do those traits come from?" We turn now to the major theories and the answers they offer.

Quick Quiz

1. Raymond Cattell advanced the study of personality through his method of (a) case-study analysis, (b) factor analysis.
2. Which of the following traits are *not* among the five "robust factors" in personality? (a) introversion, (b) agreeableness, (c) psychoticism, (d) openness to experience, (e) intelligence, (f) neuroticism, (g) conscientiousness

Answers:

1. b 2. c, e

THE BIOLOGICAL TRADITION: YOU ARE WHAT YOU'RE BORN

A mother we know was describing her two children. "My daughter has always been emotionally intense and a little testy," she said, "but my son is the opposite, placid and good-natured. They came out of the womb that way." Is it possible to be born touchy or easygoing? What aspects of personality might have an inherited component? And if some of them do, does that mean that people are stuck with those traits forever?

Psychologists who take a biological view of personality try to answer these questions in two ways: by studying temperaments in children and by doing heritability studies on adult personality traits. They hope that the actual genes underlying these traits will one day be discovered. Already geneticists have announced some early candidates. One group thought it had found a gene involved in novelty-seeking, but this work was not replicated. Another believes it has found one of several genes involved in neuroticism, pessimism, and anxiety (Murphy et al., 1996). This work is preliminary and the findings are tentative, but the search for genes involved in heritable aspects of personality is a hot area of research and you will undoubtedly be hearing more findings like these in the years to come.

HEREDITY AND TEMPERAMENT

Temperaments are relatively stable, characteristic styles of responding to the environment that appear in infancy or early childhood and have some genetic basis (Kagan, 1994). If personality has some genetic basis, temperaments ought to emerge early in life and affect subsequent development. This is, in fact, the case. Even in the first weeks after birth, infants differ in activity level, mood, responsiveness, and attention span. Some are irritable and cranky. Others are placid and sweet-natured. Some cuddle up in any adult's arms and snuggle. Others squirm and fidget, as if they can't stand being held. Babies differ in activity level (squirming and kicking), smiling and laughing, fussing and showing signs of distress, soothability (the time it takes a baby to calm down after distress), cooing and burbling in reaction to people or things, and amount of crying (Belsky, Hsieh, & Crnic, 1996; Kagan, 1994).

Jerome Kagan and his colleagues have been studying the physiological correlates of two specific temperamental styles, which they call "inhibited" and "uninhibited." (These temperaments are extremes; most children fall somewhere in between.) Inhibited and uninhibited temperaments are detectable in infancy and, in the absence of intervention, tend to remain stable throughout childhood (Kagan, 1994; Kagan & Snidman, 1991). (See Figure 12.1.) Inhibited children are shy and timid; they react negatively to novel situations, such as being introduced to a group of unfamiliar children. In contrast, uninhibited children are talkative and spontaneous. Kagan's group has found that shy, socially inhibited 5-year-olds are more likely than uninhibited children to show signs of sympathetic nervous system activity during mildly stressful mental tasks. These signs include increased heart rate, dilation of the pupils, characteristic patterns of brain activity, and high levels of norepineph-

temperaments Characteristic styles of responding to the environment that are present in infancy and are assumed to be innate.

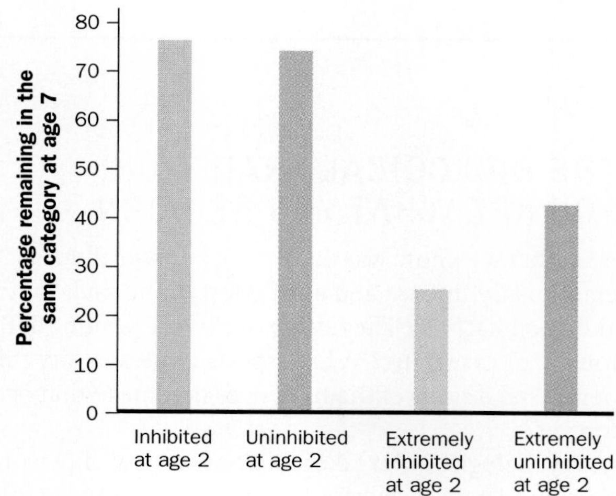

Figure 12.1
The Persistence of Temperament

Three-fourths of 2-year-old children classified as inhibited or uninhibited remained in those categories at the age of 7. Of those children who at age 2 were extremely inhibited, 25 percent remained so five years later; of those who were extremely uninhibited, 42 percent remained at that extreme (Kagan, 1994).

rine and cortisol, hormones associated with physiological arousal during stress. In white children (most of the children studied have been white), inhibition is associated to some extent with having blue eyes and allergies, or having close relatives with these characteristics (Kagan & Snidman, 1991).

Interestingly, Stephen Suomi (1987, 1991) has found exactly the same physiological attributes in shy, anxious infant rhesus monkeys (except for the blue eyes). Suomi calls the inhibited monkeys "uptight" and the uninhibited ones "laid back." Starting early in life, uptight monkeys, like Kagan's inhibited children, respond with anxiety to novelty and challenge. Like Kagan's human subjects, Suomi's monkeys have high heart rates and elevated levels of cortisol, and they are more likely to have allergic reactions starting in infancy. When uptight rhesus monkeys grow up, they usually continue to be anxious when challenged. They act traumatized even though they have experienced no traumas. When they are under stress, like humans, they tend to turn to alcohol (which the researchers make available), and they drink more alcohol than other monkeys do (Higley et al., 1991).

Some aspects of temperament lead to characteristic habits and mannerisms in adults. Identical twins reared apart will often have unnerving similarities in gestures, movements, and speech—for instance, one pair of male twins both flicked their fingers when unable to think of an answer, and a pair of female twins both rubbed their noses and rocked when tired (Farber, 1981). Separated identical twins also tend to have similar moods and emotions; if one is optimistic, glum, or excitable, so probably is the other (Braungert et al., 1992). The Minnesota Twins project, described in Chapter 3, has discovered the same resemblances in mood and mannerisms.

HEREDITY AND TRAITS

Another way to study the genetics of personality is to estimate the **heritability** of personality traits, by comparing identical and fraternal twins reared apart with twins reared together (see Chapter 3). With this method, whether the trait in question is altruism, aggression, one of the Big Five, overall well-being, or even religious attitudes, heritability is typically between .40 and .60 (Bouchard, 1995; Lykken & Tellegen, 1996; Loehlin, 1992; Tellegen et al., 1988; Waller et al., 1990). This means that within a group of people, 40 to 60 percent of the variance in such traits is attrib-

heritability A statistical estimate of the proportion of the total variance in some trait within a group that is attributable to genetic differences among individuals within the group.

Identical twins often unconsciously arrange their arms and legs in the same way and assume similar expressions. Such physical mannerisms seem to have a genetic basis.

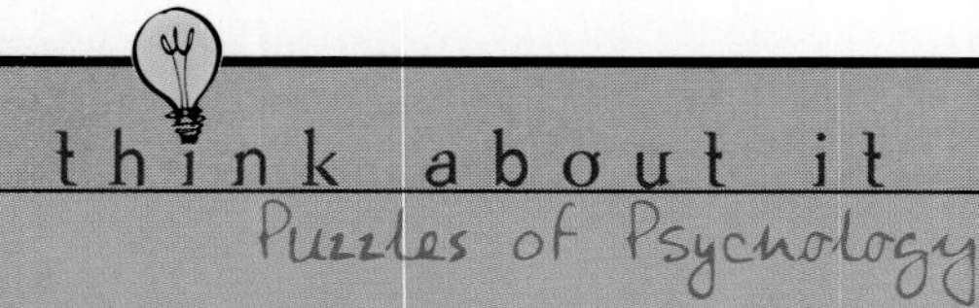

Can You Change Your Personality—and Would You If You Could?

Which of your personality traits, if any, would you like to change? And what would you be willing to do to change them?

Biological researchers have long been predicting that research in the biology of personality will transform psychology (Wender & Klein, 1981). Thanks to the success of research in behavioral genetics and drug treatments, they claim, people will no longer be doomed to suffer from unpleasant personality traits or emotional disorders such as depression and anxiety. In 1993, a book called *Listening to Prozac* reaffirmed these predictions. Its author, psychiatrist Peter Kramer, had begun administering Prozac—an antidepressant that we will discuss in more detail in Chapter 16—to his patients. "Spending time with patients who responded to Prozac had transformed my views about what makes people the way they are," Kramer wrote. "I had come to see inborn, biologically determined temperament where before I had seen slowly acquired, history-laden character."

Kramer reported the seemingly miraculous effects of Prozac on all sorts of traits: compulsiveness, perfectionism, low self-esteem, shyness, irritability, anxiety, hypersensitivity to rejection, need for attention, lack of assertiveness and inability to take risks, inhibition of pleasure, sluggishness of thought, and *dysthymia*, a condition of chronic melancholy. While admitting that scientists really don't know much about the brain, depression, or drugs at the moment, Kramer endorsed the biological model of personality and its prediction that drugs will one day "modify inborn predisposition" and "repair traumatic damage to personality." "As we have access to yet more specific drugs," he wrote, "our accuracy in targeting individual traits will improve."

As we discuss in this chapter, some key traits in personality are partly heritable. Suppose that drugs can be developed that would make a shy person more extroverted, a neurotic person more positive and optimistic, or a melancholy person happier. If you could take a pill to correct some part of your personality that you don't like, would you take it? And where would you draw the line? Would you take the pill if you were just mildly unhappy, or only if you were devastatingly depressed?

Before you answer, consider a few troubling issues. Kramer himself admits that the possibility of reaching into the personality to alter a single trait—to perk up low self-esteem, perhaps, or mental agility—"has worrisome implications." One is that doctors are already inclined to overprescribe medication for even mild or transitory personality problems, without considering alternative explanations and treatments. Another is what Kramer calls the "coercive power of convention." If most people in your social circle are extroverts and you are not, will you feel undue pressure to be like them? Why should you be like them?

Another issue concerns the social and cultural context of personality. A trait such as perfectionism might be normal and desirable in one society or relationship, but a problem or liability in another. Which should be fixed—the person or the environment? "Should a person with a personality style that might succeed in a different social setting," Kramer asks, "have to change her personality (by means of drugs!) in order to find fulfillment?" Suppose a person has a cooperative, agreeable way of getting along with others but works in a company or goes to a school that rewards aggressive, combative, and competitive behavior. Is it a good

utable to genetic differences. Some researchers have even reported high heritability estimates for getting divorced (McGue & Lykken, 1992) and watching a lot of television in childhood (Plomin et al., 1990)!

These results are astounding; how can religious attitudes, divorce, and TV watching be heritable? Our prehistoric ancestors didn't get married, let alone divorced, and they certainly didn't watch TV. What could be the personality traits or temperaments underlying these behaviors? But even more startling is the finding that the only environmental contribution to personality differences comes from experiences not shared with family members, such as having had a particular teacher in the fourth grade or having won the lead in the school play. *Shared environment and parental child-rearing practices seem to have no significant effect on adult personality traits* (Bouchard, 1995; Loehlin, 1992).

Understandably, researchers doing this research are excited about their results. They believe that the evidence for the heritability of personality traits represents an overwhelming attack on the conventional wisdom that child-rearing practices are central to personality development. "Our retrospective study showed only meager idea for such a person to take a drug to help him or her succeed in such a setting? Or would it be better to change the institution to make it possible for people with diverse personality traits to succeed?

As this example suggests, people will disagree about which traits are desirable and which should be "fixed." It isn't always easy to tell, again because *traits always interact with situations.* For instance, the most common behavioral disorder diagnosed in American children is "attention deficit hyperactivity disorder" (ADHD), a condition often diagnosed in children (and adults) who are full of energy, can't sit still, have trouble concentrating, and are messy and impulsive. The usual treatment for ADHD is Ritalin, a drug that helps modify these symptoms. Many people with ADHD and many parents of children with ADHD regard the drug as a lifesaver. But is the problem always in the children, or is it sometimes in the situations that require energetic children to sit still too long? In America, ADHD is diagnosed at ten times the rate that it is in Europe, leading some critics to wonder whether America is less tolerant of normally obstreperous children who won't accommodate to boring surroundings (Armstrong, 1993). Further, where do we draw the line between the positive and negative aspects of ADHD? "Kids with ADHD are wild, funny, effervescent," a psychiatrist told *Time* magazine (July 16, 1994). "They have a love of life. The rest of us sometimes envy them." Are those traits "cured" along with the rest of the disorder?

Finally, it is essential to consider the unforeseen *social* consequences of thousands of otherwise rational *individual* decisions to improve one's personality through medication. Do we want a world in which no one ever feels miserable or has chronic complaints? At first glance the answer might seem to be yes. But as Kramer points out, "Much of the insight and creative achievement of the human race is due to the discontent, guilt, and critical eye of dysthymics." Will people be able to resist a pill that eliminates their discontent, guilt, and critical observations? Who will want to make the effort to fix institutions, protest injustice, create art, and spend years working on new inventions if they can take a drug to help them adjust to the world as it is? Think about it.

"Before Prozac, she loathed company."

associations between parent–child relations and adult personality," wrote McCrae and Costa (1988). "It will doubtless seem incredible to many readers that variables such as social class, educational opportunities, religious training, and parental love and discipline have no substantial influence on adult personality, but imagine for a moment that it is correct. What will it mean for research in developmental psychology? How will clinical psychology and theories of therapy be changed?"

Good questions! What would these findings, if true, mean for education, for raising children, or for psychotherapy? In addition, as discussed in "Puzzles of Psychology," what would these findings mean for our views of personality and the treatment of personality problems? Should we really conclude that the environment counts for nothing?

EVALUATING GENETIC THEORIES

Before we can conclude that differences in personality are based almost entirely on differences in heredity, we need to consider some of the complexities of measuring heritability.

One problem is that measures of environmental factors are still quite crude, often relying on vague, grab-bag categories such as "social class" or "religious training." Thus they probably fail to detect some important environmental influences. Because heritability tells us only the *relative* impact of genetics and the environment on any trait, underestimating the influence of the environment inevitably means overestimating the influence of heritability. Another problem is that most separated twins have grown up in fairly similar settings, in terms of opportunities, stimulation, and experiences. When environmental differences are few, heritability estimates will automatically be inflated.

DON'T OVERSIMPLIFY

Some personality traits, such as shyness and aggressiveness, are partly heritable. Does that mean that shy 5-year-olds will inevitably grow up to become wallflowers or that all 8-year-old bullies will become criminals? What is a better way to think about the impact of heredity on personality?

In evaluating genetic influences on personality, keep in mind too that although temperaments appear early in life and can influence later personality traits, they do not provide a fixed, unchangeable blueprint. Consistency in a given temperament depends in part on how extreme that trait is in infancy. Jerome Kagan (1994) found that children who are shy at age 2 tend to be quiet, cautious, and inhibited at age 7; those who are sociable and uninhibited at age 2 are usually talkative and sociable at age 7. But most children fall somewhere in the middle and show far less consistency over time.

Even children at the extremes of a temperament may change as they grow older, and such change seems to depend on how parents and others respond to the child. In his work with monkeys, Stephen Suomi (1989) has shown that a highly inhibited infant is likely to overcome its timidity if it is reared by an extremely nurturant foster mother (see Figure 12.2). In human beings, the "fit" between a child's nature and the parents' is critical: Not only do parents affect the baby, but the baby also affects the parents. Imagine a high-strung parent with a child who is difficult and sometimes slow to respond to affection. The parent may begin to feel desperate, angry, or rejected. Over time, the parent may withdraw from the child or use excessive punishment, which in turn makes the child even more difficult to live with. In contrast, a more easygoing parent may have

Figure 12.2
Don't Be Shy

On the left, a timid infant rhesus monkey cowers behind a friend in the presence of an outgoing stranger. Such socially inhibited behavior seems to be biologically based, both in monkeys and in human beings (Kagan, 1994; Suomi, 1989). But a nurturant foster mother (center) can help an infant overcome its timidity. At first, the infant clings to her, but a few days later (right) the same young monkey has become more adventurous.

a calming effect on a difficult child or may persist in showing affection even when the child holds back, causing the child to become more responsive.

Finally, we must consider the diminishing effect of genes over time. A meta-analysis of 103 studies of twins found that over the years, correlations between twins in most personality traits tended to decrease (McCartney, Harris, & Bernieri, 1990). For some traits, experiences at certain periods in life become particularly influential. For example, an analysis of data from nearly 15,000 Finnish twins, ages 18 to 59, found that the heritability of extroversion *decreases* (and thus the impact of the environment *increases*) from the late teens and early 20s to the late 20s—a time when young people tend to leave home, marry, and establish independent adult lives (Viken et al., 1994).

In sum, even if some traits have a heritable component, this does not mean that all human qualities are rigidly fixed. As Kagan (1994) observes in his own research with temperamentally inhibited children, "A fearful child can learn to control the urge to withdraw from a stranger or a large dog. . . . The role of the environment is more substantial in helping a child overcome the tendency to withdraw than in making that child timid in the first place." Every child, he reminds us, is always part of a context in which biology and experience are inextricably intertwined.

Quick Quiz

Do you have the trait of conscientiousness to motivate you to take this quiz?

1. What two broad lines of research support the hypothesis that personality differences are due in part to genetic differences?
2. A newspaper headline announces "Couch Potatoes Born, Not Made: Kids' TV Habits May Be Hereditary." Why is this headline misleading? What other explanations of the finding are possible? What aspects of TV watching could have a hereditary component?

Answers:

1. Research on temperaments and on heritability of traits. 2. The headline implies that there is a "TV-watching gene," but the writer is failing to consider other explanations; e.g., perhaps some temperaments may dispose people to be sedentary or passive, and this disposition may lead to a lot of TV watching.

THE LEARNING TRADITION: YOU ARE WHAT YOU DO

On a hot summer day, James Peters shot and killed his next-door neighbor, Ralph Galluccio. Peters had reached the end of his patience in a ten-year dispute with Galluccio over their common property line. Shocked friends said that the intensity of this feud was not predictable from the men's personalities. Galluccio, his employer reported, was "a likable person with a good, even disposition." Peters, said his employer, was a "very mild-mannered, cooperative" man, "an all-around good guy."

A biological psychologist might say that this violent episode demonstrates the aggressive capacity of human nature in general and of violence-prone personalities in particular. A learning theorist, however, would emphasize each man's past learning and present environment. Within the learning tradition, some *radical behaviorists* take the extreme view that "personality" is an illusion. To understand human behavior, they say, we need only consider the environment in which the behavior occurs, not mental processes or biological factors. In contrast, *cognitive social-learning theorists* argue that we acquire personality patterns as we learn to deal with the environment, and that personality and situation are constantly influencing each other in an unending chain of interaction.

THE BEHAVIORAL SCHOOL

In 1913, while Sigmund Freud was busy formulating psychoanalysis in Vienna, John B. Watson was founding the behavioral tradition in the United States. The two men represented the north and south poles of personality theory, with Freud talking about instincts and unconscious motives and Watson dismissing these concepts as vague and unscientific. To Watson, all elements of personality were classically conditioned responses, just as salivation was in Pavlov's dogs.

In the learning view, life experiences are constantly affecting our personality traits. For example, many individuals lose self-esteem and ambition when they are fired from their jobs, or when they work in environments that give them no support.

The best-known American behaviorist, B. F. Skinner, shared with Watson a belief that behavior is primarily learned, but he rejected Watson's emphasis on classical conditioning as the major form of learning. Noting that many kinds of behavior were not classically conditioned, he turned to operant (instrumental) conditioning as the fundamental form of learning. (To refresh your memory on these terms, see Chapter 7.) For Skinner, personality was a collection of behavioral patterns. Labels such as "aggressive," "ambitious," or "conscientious" were merely shorthand descriptions of responses in particular situations.

This doesn't mean that all situations produce the same responses in all individuals. Imagine two people being interviewed for a job: One is calm and confident, another is anxious and shy. Skinner would say that if we looked into the behavioral histories of these two people, we would find different patterns of reinforcement. For one, calm confidence was reinforced; for the other, anxiety and shyness were reinforced. What could possibly reward such painful feelings? Shyness and anxiety are encouraged when they serve as a *self-handicapping strategy.* When shy people or people with low self-esteem are in situations in which they believe they will be evaluated, they learn to use their anxiety as an excuse for poor performance (Snyder, 1990). Self-handicappers place obstacles in the path of their own success. If they then fail, they can blame the failure on the handicap ("I'm shy" or "I have writer's block") instead of a lack of ability. If they succeed anyway, they can claim additional credit for doing well despite the handicap. In this way apparently self-defeating habits are acquired as learned strategies to protect self-esteem and maintain the intrinsic pleasure of an activity (Deppe & Harackiewicz, 1996).

Behaviorists do not deny that people have feelings, thoughts, or values. However, they believe that these mental states are as subject to the laws of learning as, say, nail biting is. Skinner believed that when people talk about "values," they are describing a history of reinforcers. It is unscientific and imprecise, he said, to say that "Pat values fame." Rather, fame is positively reinforcing to Pat, which is why Pat continues to strive for it. Someone else might find fame unpleasantly punishing and thus would hold different values. If we want a peaceful world, behaviorists say, we had better not wait around for people's personalities to change. We had better change circumstances so that cooperation is rewarded, cheaters don't win, and aggressors don't stay in power.

THE COGNITIVE SOCIAL-LEARNING SCHOOL

As we saw in Chapter 7, modern cognitive social-learning theories of personality depart from classic behaviorism in their emphasis on three things: (1) observational learning and the role of models; (2) cognitive processes such as perceptions and interpretations of events; and (3) motivating values, emotions, and beliefs, such as enduring expectations of success or failure and confidence in your ability to achieve goals. Where behaviorists see personality as a set of habits and beliefs that have been rewarded over a person's lifetime, cognitive social-learning theorists maintain that these habits and beliefs eventually acquire a life of their own, coming to exert their own effects on behavior. They may even supersede the power of reinforcers, which is why some people persist in their pursuit of fame, glory, or other goals without ever receiving external reinforcement of their efforts.

According to cognitive social-learning theorists, then, much of human behavior and personality is *self-regulated*—shaped by our thoughts, values, emotions, and goals (Bandura, 1994; Mischel & Shoda, 1995). For example, in the previous chapter, we discussed the importance of having what Albert Bandura calls *self-efficacy*—the belief that you can accomplish what you set out to do. Self-efficacy is learned, and once it is internalized, it begins to affect people's expectations of success and their efforts to carry those expectations out.

Another important personality trait that influences behavior, in the cognitive social-learning view, is the extent to which people believe they have control over their lives. Much of the original work on people's sense of control was done by Julian Rotter (1966, 1982, 1990), who started out as a behaviorally oriented experimentalist. During the 1950s, Rotter was working both as a psychotherapist and a researcher, trying to apply behavioral principles to his patients' troubling emotions and irrational beliefs (Hunt, 1993). Rotter saw that his clients had formed entrenched attitudes as a result of their lifetimes of experience, and these attitudes were affecting their decisions and actions.

Over time, Rotter concluded, people learn that some acts will be rewarded and others punished, and thus they develop *generalized expectancies* about which situations and acts will be rewarding. A child who studies hard and gets good grades, attention from teachers, admiration from friends, and loving praise from parents will come to expect that hard work in other situations will also pay off. A child who studies hard and gets poor grades, is ignored by teachers, is rejected by friends for being a grind, or earns no support or praise from parents will come to expect that hard work isn't worth it. One child may learn that if she speaks her mind, she can expect praise and attention. Another may learn that if she speaks her mind, she can expect to irritate her parents, who want her to be quiet and obedient. Once acquired, as we saw in Chapter 11, these expectations often create a *self-fulfilling prophecy*.

Rotter and his colleagues demonstrated the power of expectancies in many experiments. At the same time, both in his private practice and in his research, Rotter was observing people whose expectations of success never went up *even when they were actually successful*. "Oh, that was just a fluke," they would say, or "I was lucky; it will never happen again." Rotter concluded that people's feelings or beliefs about the factors that govern their behavior are as important as the actual reinforcers and punishers in the environment. He chose the term **locus of control** to refer to people's beliefs about whether the results of their actions are under their own control. People who have an *internal locus of control* ("internals") tend to believe they are responsible for what happens to them, that they control their own destinies. People who have an *external locus of control* tend to believe they are victims (or sometimes beneficiaries) of luck, fate, or other people. To measure these traits, Rotter (1966) developed an Internal/External (I/E) Scale consisting of pairs of statements. People had to choose the statement in each pair with which they most strongly agreed, as in these two items:

1. a. Many of the unhappy things in people's lives are partly due to bad luck.
   b. People's misfortunes result from mistakes they make.
2. a. Becoming a success is a matter of hard work; luck has little or nothing to do with it.
   b. Getting a good job depends mainly on being in the right place at the right time.

locus of control A general expectation about whether the results of your actions are under your own control (internal locus) or beyond your control (external locus).

GET INVOLVED

Think back to the last time you did well on a test, or on some task you set yourself. Which of the following phrases best describes how you explained your success to yourself?

- *I'm really competent (or smart, skillful, etc.).*
- *I worked hard, and it paid off.*
- *I was lucky.*
- *The test (or task) was pretty easy.*
- *I did well, but only because someone else helped me.*

Now think about a time you did not *do well on a test or task. Which phrase best describes how you accounted for your disappointing performance?*

- *I'm just not good at this.*
- *I didn't work (or try) hard enough.*
- *I was unlucky.*
- *I did poorly, but the test (or task) wasn't fair.*
- *I did poorly, but only because I got bad instruction or too little help.*

What do your answers tell you about your own locus of control? Do you tend to be internal or external for success? What about for failure? Do your beliefs about the results of your actions motivate you to further effort, or discourage you?

Research on locus of control took off like a shot, and over the years more than 2,000 studies based on the I/E Scale (including a version for children) have been published, with people of all ages and from many different ethnic groups (Hunt, 1993). Internal locus of control emerges at an early age, and it affects many aspects of life—including health (as we will see in Chapter 14), academic achievement, and political activism (Nowicki & Strickland, 1973; Strickland, 1989).

But a person's locus of control can change, depending on his or her position and experiences in society. As Rotter was developing his theory in the 1960s, the civil-rights movement was gathering steam. At that time, civil-rights activists and black student leaders were more likely to score at the "internal" end of the scale than control groups who were uninvolved in civil-rights efforts (Gore & Rotter, 1963; Strickland, 1965). By the 1970s, however—after the assassinations of Martin Luther King, Jr., Malcolm X, and John and Robert Kennedy, after riots had devastated many black communities, and with the nation embroiled in the Vietnam War—American self-confidence in social progress had been deeply shaken. Accordingly, scores on the locus-of-control scale changed. Civil-rights leaders and college students became less internal—that is, less confident that they, as individuals, could improve social conditions (Phares, 1976; Strickland, 1989).

Where would you place your own locus of control today? How do you think it reflects your actions? Does it affect your beliefs about the possibility of personal and social change?

These members of the Communications Workers Union have an internal locus of control, motivating them to protest their city's budget cuts. What social forces might increase people's sense of efficacy and internal locus of control, and what might extinguish these traits?

EVALUATING LEARNING THEORIES

Why did James Peters kill Ralph Galluccio? Instead of assuming that Galluccio and Peters were driven by biologically determined temperaments or genes promoting aggressiveness, cognitive social-learning psychologists would investigate the environmental conditions of their quarrel and each man's perceptions about it. The two men found themselves in an increasingly difficult situation that seemed to offer no way out. Learning psychologists would investigate why these two men lacked the skills to negotiate their differences, and how each had learned over time that aggressive actions would make other people knuckle under.

Learning approaches emphasize the ways in which personality and situation interact. In the learning view, you may have a skill, such as pie baking or hog calling, and find yourself in a place that never gives you the chance to reveal it. On the other hand, you may find yourself in a new environment that gives you an opportunity to learn skills you never dreamed you could master. Likewise, specific situations either allow us to express aspects of our personalities or prevent us from doing so. If George is assertive at home but meek at work, or if Georgina is independent at work but clingy with her friends, it is because George and Georgina are reinforced differently in different situations.

Some psychologists criticize behaviorism for implying that individuals are as soft as jellyfish, and that with the right environment, anyone can become anything. They also complain that behaviorism treats people as passive recipients of environmental events. These common charges are not really fair. Skinner, for instance, often stated that people have limits in what they can learn because of their genetic constitutions and temperaments, and he argued that people can choose to change their environments and thus their own behavior.

A more valid criticism is that social-learning approaches to personality sometimes attribute behavior to the "environment" without defining its contents or the process by which the environment affects people. For example, many people assume that images of women and men in the media strongly influence what people learn about femininity and masculinity. Principles of observational learning would seem to make this point obvious. Yet not everyone reacts to the same images in the same way. Therefore it is difficult to specify *which* media images are having an effect, and on whom; and it is difficult to disentangle the effects of the media from all the other events that influence people's ideas about how men and women should behave.

Learning researchers tend to explore one influence on learning at a time: a parental model, a teacher's reactions, the pattern of reinforcers in a given situation, media images, self-efficacy, locus of control, and so forth. In real life, though, people are surrounded by hundreds of interacting influences. This fact poses a serious problem for learning theories of personality: When nearly anything can have an influence on you, it can be frustratingly difficult to show that any one thing actually *is* having an influence. It's like trying to grab a fistful of fog; you know it's there, but somehow it keeps getting away from you.

Nevertheless, the learning approach to personality makes an essential point: In the most general sense, people must learn by observation and reinforcement what the rules of their culture and community are, how their parents expect them to behave, and which personality traits are encouraged or disparaged.

We turn now to approaches to personality that depart from mainstream empirical psychology, in both theory and methods. Psychodynamic and humanist views of the person regard the objective measurement of traits and the piece-by-piece approach of biological and learning theories of personality as being too cold, mechanical, and incomplete. Instead, they propose global theories of personality that emphasize the development of the whole person.

THE PSYCHODYNAMIC TRADITION: YOU ARE WHAT YOU WERE

Of all the theories of personality, the psychodynamic approach is the one most embedded in popular culture, particularly in people's ways of talking and thinking. A man apologizes for "displacing" his frustrations at work onto his family. A woman suspects that she is "repressing" a childhood trauma. An alcoholic reveals that he is no longer "in denial" about his dependence on drinking. A newspaper columnist advises readers to "sublimate" their anger or risk becoming ill. A teacher informs a divorcing couple that their 8-year-old child is "regressing" to immature behavior.

All of this language—about displacing, repressing, denying, sublimating, and regressing; about the unconscious—can be traced to the first psychodynamic theory of personality, Sigmund Freud's **psychoanalysis.** Freud's theory and the theories of his followers are called **psychodynamic** because they are based on the movement of psychological energy within the person, in the form of attachments, conflicts, and motivations. Today many psychodynamic theories exist, differing from Freudian theory and from one another, but they all share five general elements:

1. An emphasis on unconscious **intrapsychic** dynamics, the movement of psychic forces within the mind.
2. An assumption that adult behavior and ongoing problems are determined primarily by experiences in early childhood.
3. A belief that psychological development occurs in fixed stages, during which predictable mental events occur and unconscious issues or crises must be resolved.
4. A focus on fantasies and symbolic meanings of events as the unconscious mind perceives them—a person's *psychic reality*—as the main motivators of personality and behavior.
5. A reliance on subjective rather than objective methods of getting at the truth of a person's life—for example, through analysis of dreams, myths, folklore, symbols, and, most of all, the revelations uncovered in psychotherapy.

In this section, we will introduce you to Freud's ideas, to the variations of Freudian theory offered by some of his dissenting colleagues, and to the contemporary approaches that have added new rooms and levels to the original Freudian edifice.

FREUD AND PSYCHOANALYSIS

No one disputes the profound influence that Sigmund Freud (1856–1939) had on this century. But many people dispute the value of his work, as reflected in three current attitudes toward Freud and his ideas. The first, held by Freud himself and by his devoted followers to this day, is that Freud was one of the rare geniuses of history, an intellectual revolutionary like Copernicus, Darwin, and Newton. The second view, probably the most common among clinical psychologists, is that Freud was a great thinker and that many of his ideas have lasting value, but some are dated and others are plain wrong. The third view, held by many scientists and experimental psychologists, is that Freud was a fraud. The British scientist and Nobel laureate Peter Medawar (1982) called psychoanalysis a dinosaur in the history of ideas, doomed to

psychoanalysis A theory of personality and a method of psychotherapy developed by Sigmund Freud; it emphasizes unconscious motives and conflicts.

psychodynamic theories Theories that explain behavior and personality in terms of unconscious energy dynamics within the individual.

intrapsychic Within the mind (psyche) or self.

extinction. For good measure, he added that it is "the most stupendous intellectual confidence trick of the twentieth century."

In order to understand the kind of theory that could produce such wildly different reactions, let us enter the world of Freud—a realm of unconscious motives, conflicts, and fears. These unseen forces, Freud believed, have far more power over human behavior than consciousness does, so psychology must probe beneath the surface of a person's mental life. The unconscious reveals itself, said Freud, in dreams, in *free association*—talking about anything that pops into your head, without worrying about what anyone will think of you—and in slips of the tongue. A slip of the tongue was no random flub to Freud. The British member of Parliament who referred to the "honourable member from Hell" when he meant to say "Hull," said Freud (1920/1960), was revealing his actual, unconscious appraisal of his colleague.

THE STRUCTURE OF PERSONALITY In Freud's theory, personality is made up of three major systems: the id, the ego, and the superego. Any particular action we take or problem we have results from the interaction and degree of balance among them (Freud, 1905b, 1920/1960, 1923/1962).

The **id,** which is present at birth, is the reservoir of all psychological energies and inherited instincts. To Freud, the id was the true psychic reality because it represents the inner world of subjective experience. It is unconcerned with objective reality and is unaffected by the environment. The id operates according to the *pleasure principle,* seeking to reduce tension, avoid pain, and obtain pleasure. It contains two competing groups of instincts: the life, or sexual, instincts (fueled by psychic energy called the **libido**) and the death, or aggressive, instincts. As energy builds up in the id, tension results. The id may discharge this tension in the form of reflex actions, physical symptoms, or wishful thinking—uncensored mental images and unbidden thoughts.

The **ego,** the second system to emerge, is a referee between the needs of instinct and the demands of society. It obeys the *reality principle,* putting a rein on the id's desire for pleasure until a suitable outlet can be found. The ego, said Freud, represents "reason and good sense."

The **superego,** the last system of personality to develop, represents morality, the rules of parents and society, and the power of authority. The superego consists of the *ego ideal,* those moral and social standards you learn are right, and the *conscience,* the inner voice that says you did something wrong. The superego judges the activities of the id, handing out good feelings (pride, satisfaction) when you do something well and handing out miserable feelings (guilt, shame) when you break the rules.

An old joke summarizes the role of the id, ego, and superego this way: The id says, "I want, and I want it now"; the superego says, "You can't have it; it's bad for you"; and the ego, the rational mediator, says, "Well, maybe you can have some of it—later." According to Freud, the healthy personality must keep all three in balance. Someone who is too controlled by the id is governed by impulse and selfish desires. Someone who is too controlled by the superego is rigid, moralistic, and bossy. Someone who has a weak ego is unable to balance personal needs and wishes with social duties and realistic limitations.

If a person feels anxious or threatened when the wishes of the id conflict with social rules, the ego has weapons at its command to relieve the tension. These weapons, called **defense mechanisms,** have two characteristics: They deny or distort reality, and they operate unconsciously. According to Freud, ego defenses are necessary to protect us from conflict and the stresses of reality; they become unhealthy only when they cause self-defeating behavior and emotional problems. Freud described 17 defense mechanisms; later, other psychoanalysts expanded and

id In psychoanalysis, the part of personality containing inherited psychological energy, particularly sexual and aggressive instincts.

libido In psychoanalysis, the psychic energy that fuels the life or sexual instincts of the id.

ego In psychoanalysis, the part of personality that represents reason, good sense, and rational self-control.

superego In psychoanalysis, the part of personality that represents conscience, morality, and social standards.

defense mechanisms Methods used by the ego to prevent unconscious anxiety or threatening thoughts from entering consciousness.

"I'm sorry, I'm not speaking to anyone tonight. My defense mechanisms seem to be out of order."

modified his list. Following are some of the primary defenses identified by Freud's daughter Anna (1946), who became a psychoanalyst herself, and by most contemporary psychodynamic psychologists (Vaillant, 1992):

1. *Repression* occurs when a threatening idea, memory, or emotion is blocked from becoming conscious. A woman who had a frightening childhood experience that she cannot remember, for example, is said to be repressing her memory of it. Repression doesn't mean that you consciously bite your tongue rather than reveal a guilty secret. It refers to the mind's effort to keep a lid on unacceptable feelings and thoughts in the unconscious, so that you aren't even aware of them. In the psychodynamic view, people who say they never remember their dreams or they have never had an emotional crisis are likely to be repressing.

2. *Projection* occurs when a person's own unacceptable or threatening feelings are repressed and then attributed to someone else. A boy who dislikes his father, for instance, may feel anxious about disliking someone he depends on. So he may project his feelings onto his father, concluding that "he hates me." A person who is embarrassed about having sexual feelings toward members of a different ethnic group may project this discomfort onto them, saying, "Those people are dirty-minded and oversexed."

3. *Displacement* occurs when people direct their emotions (especially anger) toward things, animals, or other people that are not the real object of their feelings. People use displacement when they perceive the real target as being too threatening to confront directly. A boy who is forbidden to express anger at his father, for example, may "take it out" on his toys or his younger sister. Freud believed that the aggressive and sexual instincts of the id, if blocked from direct expression, would be displaced onto a substitute. Thus aggressive impulses might be displaced in sports competition instead of directly expressed in war; sexual impulses might be displaced in the creation of passionate poetry and literature. When displacement serves a higher cultural or socially useful purpose, as in the creation of art or inventions, it is called *sublimation.* Freud himself thought that for the sake of civilization and survival, sexual and aggressive energies could and should be displaced or sublimated into socially appropriate and constructive forms.

4. *Reaction formation* occurs when a feeling that produces unconscious anxiety is transformed into its opposite in consciousness. A woman who is afraid to admit to herself that she doesn't love her husband may cling to the belief that she deeply loves him. A person who is aroused by erotic images may angrily assert that pornography is disgusting. How does such a transformed emotion differ from a true emotion? In reaction formation the professed feeling is excessive: The person "protests too much" and is extravagant and compulsive about demonstrating it. ("Of course I love him! I *never* have any bad thoughts about him! He's perfect!")

5. *Regression* occurs when a person reverts to a previous phase of psychic development. As we will see, Freud believed that personality develops in a series of stages from birth to maturity. Each new step, however, produces a certain amount of frustration and anxiety. If these become too great, normal development may be halted, and the child may remain *fixated* at the current stage; for instance, a toddler may fail to outgrow clinging dependence. People may also regress to an earlier stage if they suffer a traumatic experience in a later one. An 8-year-old boy who is anxious about his parents' divorce may regress to earlier habits of thumb sucking or clinging. Adults may regress to immature behavior when they are under pressure—for example, by having a temper tantrum if they don't get their way.

6. *Denial* occurs when people refuse to admit that something unpleasant is happening or that they are experiencing a "forbidden" emotion. Some people deny that they are angry; alcoholics may deny that they depend on liquor. In the psychodynamic view, people who assert that they never have negative feelings or never feel disgusted by anything are revealing denial, for these are universal emotions. Denial protects the illusion of invulnerability—"It will never happen to me"—which is why people often behave in self-destructive and risky ways.

In Freud's view, different personalities emerge because people differ in the defenses they use, in how rigid their defenses are, and in whether their defenses lead to healthy or disturbed functioning. Table 12.1 summarizes Freud's model of the mind.

THE DEVELOPMENT OF PERSONALITY Freud maintained that personality develops in a series of five stages. He called these stages *psychosexual* because he believed that psychological development depends on the changing expression of sexual energy in different parts of the body as the child matures.

TABLE 12.1 ***Summary of Freud's Model of the Mind***

	Id	Ego	Superego
What it does	Expresses sexual and aggressive instincts; follows the pleasure principle	Mediates between desires of the id and demands of the superego; follows the reality principle; uses defense mechanisms to ward off unconscious anxiety	Represents conscience and the ego ideal; follows internalized moral standards
How conscious it is	Entirely unconscious	Partly conscious, partly unconscious	Partly conscious, mostly unconscious
When it develops	Present at birth	Emerges after birth, with early formative experiences	Last system to develop; becomes internalized after the Oedipal stage
Example	"I'm so mad I could kill you" (felt unconsciously)	Might make a conscious choice ("Let's talk about this") or resort to an unconscious defense mechanism, such as denial ("What, me angry? Never")	"Thou shalt not kill"

Is she fixated at the oral stage?

1. *The oral stage* marks the first year of life. Babies take in the world, as well as their nourishment, through their mouths, so the mouth, said Freud, is the focus of sensation at this stage. People who remain fixated at the oral stage may, as adults, seek constant oral gratification in smoking, drinking, overeating, nail biting, chewing on pencils, and the like.

2. *The anal stage,* at about ages 2 to 3, marks the start of ego development, as the child becomes aware of the self and of the demands of reality. The major issue at this stage, said Freud, is control of bodily wastes, a lesson in self-control that the child learns during toilet training. People who remain fixated at this stage, he thought, become "anal retentive," holding everything in, obsessive about neatness and cleanliness. Or they become just the opposite, "anal expulsive"—that is, messy and disorganized.

3. *The phallic (or Oedipal) stage* lasts roughly from ages 3 to 5 or 6. Now sexual sensation is located in the penis, for boys, and in the clitoris, for girls. The child, said Freud, unconsciously wishes to possess the parent of the other sex and to get rid of the parent of the same sex. Children of this age often announce proudly that "I'm going to marry Daddy (or Mommy) when I grow up," and they reject the same-sex "rival." Freud (1924a, 1924b) labeled this phenomenon the **Oedipus complex,** after the Greek legend of King Oedipus, who unwittingly killed his father and married his mother.

Boys and girls, Freud believed, go through the Oedipal stage differently. Boys at this stage are discovering the pleasure and pride of having a penis. When they see a naked girl for the first time, they are horrified. Their unconscious exclaims (in effect), "Her penis has been cut off! Who could have done such a thing to her? Why, it must have been her powerful father. And if he could do it to her, my father could do it to me!" This realization, said Freud, causes the boy to repress his desire for his mother, accept the authority of his father, and identify with him. **Identification** is the process by which boys take in, as their own, the father's standards of conscience and morality. The superego has emerged.

Freud admitted that he didn't quite know what to make of girls, who, lacking the penis, couldn't go through the same steps. He speculated that a girl, upon discovering male anatomy, would panic that she had only a puny clitoris instead of a stately penis. She would conclude, said Freud, that she already had lost her penis. As a result, girls don't have the powerful motivating fear that boys do to give up their Oedipal feelings; they have only a lingering sense of "penis envy." Thus, Freud concluded, women do not develop the strong moral superegos that men do.

By about age 5 or 6, when the Oedipus complex is resolved, said Freud, the child's personality patterns are formed. Unconscious conflicts with parents, unresolved fixations and guilts, and attitudes toward the same and the other sex will continue to replay themselves throughout life.

4. *The latency stage* lasts from the end of the phallic stage until puberty. According to Freud, the mental conflicts of the Oedipal complex are repressed. The child settles down, goes to school, makes friends, develops self-confidence, and learns the social rules for appropriate male or female behavior.

5. *The genital stage* begins at puberty and marks the beginning of what Freud considered mature adult sexuality. Sexual energy is now located in the genitals and eventually is directed toward sexual intercourse.

Oedipus complex In psychoanalysis, a conflict in which a child desires the parent of the other sex and views the same-sex parent as a rival; this is the key issue in the phallic stage of development.

identification A process by which the child adopts an adult's standards of morality, values, and beliefs as his or her own; in psychoanalysis, identification with the same-sex parent is said to occur at the resolution of the Oedipus complex.

As you might imagine, Freud's ideas were not exactly received with yawns. Sexual feelings in infants and children! Repressed longings in the most respectable adults! Unconscious meanings in dreams! Penis envy! Sexual sublimation! This was strong stuff, and before long psychoanalysis had captured the public imagination in Europe and America. But it also produced a sharp rift with the emerging schools of empirical psychology (Hornstein, 1992).

This rift continues to divide psychologists today. Many of Freud's followers revere Freud as they would the founder of a new religion, regarding him as a man who bravely battled public censure and ridicule in his unwavering pursuit of scientific truth (Gay, 1988). They think that even if some of his ideas have proved faulty, the overall framework of his theory is timeless and brilliant. Others think psychoanalysis is, frankly, nonsense, and that Freud himself was nothing like the brilliant theoretician and clinician he claimed to be. They cite new scholarship on Freud, based on previously unpublished papers, revealing that Freud himself manufactured the myth that he was a poor misunderstood genius in order to gain sympathy and credibility; that, far from being an impartial scientist, Freud often pressured his patients into accepting his explanations of their symptoms; and even that he was an incompetent therapist whose most famous patients would today have every ground to sue him for malpractice and unethical behavior (Cioffi, 1974; Crews, 1995; Esterson, 1993; Powell & Boer, 1994, 1995; Sulloway, 1992; Webster, 1995).

One such patient was "Dora" (Ida Bauer), an 18-year-old who had been spurning the explicit sexual advances made by her father's friend, "Herr K," since she was 14 (Lakoff & Coyne, 1993). Dora finally complained to her father. But her father wanted her to accept Herr K's overtures, perhaps because he himself was having an affair with Herr K's wife; so he sent her off to Freud, who attempted to cure her of her "hysterical" refusal to have sex with Herr K. Freud tried to convince Dora that it was not the ugly situation involving her father and his friend that was distressing her, but her own *repressed desires* for sex. "I should without question consider a person hysterical," Freud (1905a) wrote, "in whom an occasion for sexual excitement elicited feelings that were preponderantly or exclusively unpleasurable." Dora angrily left treatment after three months, and Freud was never able to accept her "obstinate" refusals to believe his analysis of her symptoms. If only Herr K had learned, said Freud, "that the slap Dora gave him by no means signified a final 'No' on her part," and if he had resolved "to press his suit with a passion which left room for no doubts, the result might very well have been a triumph of the girl's affection for him over all her internal difficulties."

Sigmund Freud was thus a man of contradictions—a mix of intellectual vision and blindness, sensitivity and arrogance (Hunt, 1993). His provocative ideas and his approach to therapy left a powerful legacy to psychology. And it was one that others began to tinker with immediately.

Quick Quiz

Which Freudian concepts do these events suggest?

1. A 4-year-old girl wants to snuggle on Daddy's lap but refuses to kiss her mother.
2. A celibate priest writes poetry about sexual passion.
3. A man who is angry at his boss shouts at his kids for making noise.
4. A woman who was molested by her stepfather for many years assures her friends that she adores him and thinks he is perfect.
5. A racist justifies segregation by saying that black men are only interested in sex with white women.
6. A 9-year-old boy who moves to a new city starts having tantrums.

Answers:

1. Oedipus complex 2. sublimation 3. displacement 4. reaction formation 5. projection 6. regression

FREUD'S DESCENDANTS

Some of Freud's followers stayed in the psychoanalytic tradition and modified Freud's theories from within. One of the most notable of these early dissenters was *Karen Horney* [HORN-eye] (1885–1952), who was one of the first analysts to challenge Freud's notions of penis envy and female inferiority. Horney (1967) argued that it is insulting philosophy and bad science to claim that half the human race is dissatisfied with its anatomy. When women feel inferior to men, she said, we should look for explanations in the disadvantages that women live with and their second-class status. Freudian theory, she feared, would be used to justify discrimination against women by making it seem that inferiority was in their nature and not in the conditions of their lives. In fact, said Horney, if anyone has an envy problem, it is men. Men have "womb envy": They envy women's ability to bear and nurse children. Men glorify their genitals, she said, because they are unable to give birth and unconsciously fear women's sexual power over them. Later psychoanalysts, such as Bruno Bettelheim (1962), argued that both sexes envy the reproductive abilities of the other.

Other members of Freud's circle broke away from Freud or were actively rejected by him, and they went off to start their own schools. One was *Alfred Adler* (1870–1937), who had a more positive view of humanity than Freud did. Whereas Freud held that personality development pretty much stops after the resolution of the Oedipal complex, Adler was one of the first psychologists to emphasize growth and change over the entire life span. Unlike Freud, Adler thought we are the directors of our lives, not merely victims of unconscious forces. He believed that people have a desire for self-improvement, an "upward drive" for perfection. This impulse, said Adler (1927/1959), stems from the natural feelings of inferiority that all of us have, first as children, when we are weak and powerless compared to adults, and then later, when we have to recognize limitations on our abilities. But some individuals, he wrote, develop an *inferiority complex*, because their parents failed to encourage their abilities. Unable to accept their limitations, they try to mask them by pretending to be strong and capable. They become overly concerned with protecting their self-esteem.

Alfred Adler believed that unless individuals are thwarted by social conditions, they strive to excel—as did champion skaters Jayne Torvill and Christopher Dean, who achieved perfect scores at the 1984 Olympics.

We turn now to two other psychodynamic approaches that remain especially popular today: the work of Carl Jung and of the object-relations theorists.

JUNGIAN THEORY Carl Jung (1875–1961) was originally one of Freud's closest friends, but by 1914 he had left Freud's inner circle. His greatest difference with Freud concerned the nature of the unconscious. In addition to the individual's own unconscious, said Jung (1967), there is a **collective unconscious** containing the universal memories and history of humankind. From his observation of myths, art, and folklore in cultures all over the world, Jung was impressed by common, repeated images, which he called **archetypes.** An archetype can be a picture, such as the "magic circle," called a *mandala* in Eastern religions, which Jung thought symbolizes the unity of life and "the totality of the self." Or it can be a mythical figure, such as the Hero, the Nurturing Mother, the Powerful Father, or the Wicked Witch. Other powerful archetypes are the persona and the shadow. The *persona* is the public personality, the aspects of yourself that you reveal to others, the role that society expects you to play. The *shadow* archetype reflects the prehistoric fear of wild animals and represents the animal side of human nature. Although most psychologists feel that Jung's idea of the collective unconscious is a mystical concept rather than a scientific one (indeed, that may be why it became popular with nationalist political movements and New Age religions), they recognize that some basic archetypes—such as the

collective unconscious To Carl Jung, the universal memories and experiences of humankind, represented in the unconscious images and symbols of all people.

archetypes [AR-ki-tipes] To Carl Jung, universal, symbolic images that appear in myths, art, dreams, and other expressions of the collective unconscious.

Hero, the Evil Beast, and the Earth Mother—do appear in virtually every society (Campbell, 1949/1968; Neher, 1996).

To Jungians, the reason that Dracula can't ever be killed is that he represents a classic archetype of evil.

Two of the most important archetypes, in Jung's view, are those of men and women themselves. Jung (like Freud) recognized that human beings are psychologically bisexual—that "masculine" and "feminine" qualities exist in both sexes. The *anima* represents the feminine archetype in men; the *animus* represents the masculine archetype in women. Problems can arise, however, if a person tries to repress his or her internal, opposite archetype—that is, if a man totally denies his softer "feminine" side or if a woman denies her "masculine" aspects. People also create problems in relationships when they expect the partner to behave like the ideal archetypal man or woman, instead of the real human being who has both sides (Young-Eisendrath, 1993).

Although Jung shared with Freud a fascination with the unconscious side of the personality, he shared with Adler a belief in the positive, forward-moving strengths of the ego. For Jung, people are motivated not only by past conflicts, as Freud thought, but also by their future goals and their desire to fulfill themselves. This emphasis anticipated the humanist movement in psychology by several decades. Jung also accurately anticipated modern trait research by many years when he identified introversion–extroversion as a central personality orientation.

Some Jungians, drawing on the cognitive concepts of *schema* and *narrative*, are interested in how universal images and stories affect the way people see their own lives. When Dan McAdams (1988) asked 50 people to tell their life stories in a two-hour session, he found that people tended to report a common archetype, a mythic character, at the heart of their life narratives. For example, many individuals told stories that could be symbolized by the myth of the Greek god Dionysus, the pleasure seeker who escapes responsibility. Archetypes, says McAdams, represent "the main characters in the life stories we construct as our identities."

THE OBJECT-RELATIONS SCHOOL In the late 1950s, John Bowlby (1958), a British psychoanalyst, contested the Freudian view that an infant's attachment to the mother can be explained solely in terms of her ability to gratify the baby's oral needs. Bowlby observed that infants who were deprived of normal contact with parents and other adults suffered catastrophically, and he argued for the primacy of attachment needs—social stimulation, warmth, and contact. Bowlby's work influenced other psychoanalysts to acknowledge the fundamentally *social* nature of human development. Although the need for social contact now seems obvious, this change in emphasis was a significant departure from the classic Freudian view, for Freud essentially regarded the baby as if it were an independent little organism ruled by its own instinctive desires.

Today an emphasis on relationships is associated with the **object-relations school,** which was developed in Great Britain by Melanie Klein, W. Ronald Fairbairn, and D. W. Winnicott (Horner, 1991; Hughes, 1989). In contrast to Freud's emphasis on the Oedipal period, object-relations theory holds that the first two years of life are the most critical for development of the inner core of personality. Freud emphasized the child's fear of the powerful father; object-relations analysts emphasize the child's need for the powerful mother, who is usually the baby's caregiver in the first critical years. Freud's theory was based on the dynamics of inner drives and impulses; object-relations theory holds that the basic human drive is not impulse gratification but the need to be in relationships.

object-relations school A psychodynamic approach that emphasizes the importance of the infant's first two years of life and the baby's formative relationships.

The reason for the clunky word "object" in object-relations theory (instead of the warmer word "human" or even "parent") is that the infant's attachment isn't only to

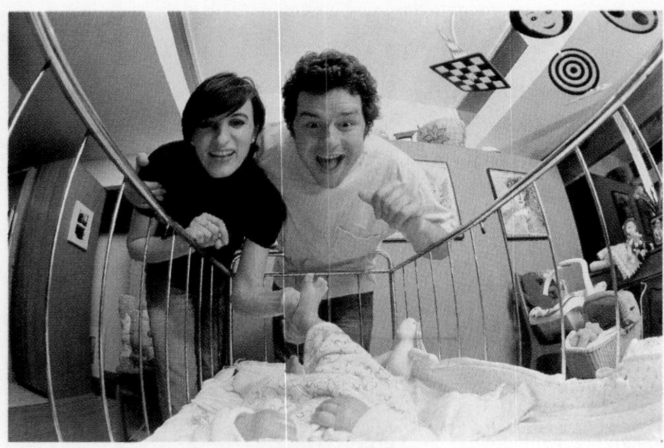

According to object-relations theory, a baby constructs unconscious representations of his or her parents—representations that will later influence the child's relations with others.

a person but also to the infant's evolving perception of the person. In this theory, the child "takes in" a *representation* of the mother—someone who is kind or fierce, protective or rejecting—that is not literally the same as the woman herself. A representation is a complex cognitive schema that the child constructs unconsciously. "Object relations" reflect the numerous representations of the self and others, and the psychodynamic interplay among them (Horner, 1991). These representations may unconsciously affect the individual throughout his or her life.

In Freudian theory, as we saw, the central dynamic tension is the shifting of psychic energy—sexual and aggressive energy in particular—within the individual. Other people are relevant only insofar as they gratify our drives or block them. But to object-relations theorists, other people are important as sources of attachment. Therefore the central dynamic tension is the constantly changing balance between independence and connection to others. This balance requires constant adjustment to separations and losses: small ones that occur during quarrels, moderate ones such as leaving home for the first time, and major ones such as divorce or death. In object-relations theory, the way we react to these separations is largely determined by our experiences in the first two years of life, and some theorists would say in the first months of life.

The object-relations school also departs from Freudian theory on the nature of male and female development. Whereas Freud thought that female development was the problem to be explained, many proponents of the object-relations school regard male development as the problem (Chodorow, 1978; Sagan, 1988; Winnicott, 1957/1990). In their view, children of both sexes identify first with the mother. Girls, who are the same sex as the mother, do not need to separate from her; the mother treats a daughter as an extension of herself. But boys, if they are to develop a masculine identity, must break away from the mother; the mother encourages a son to be independent and separate. To some object-relations theorists, this process is inevitable because women are biologically suited to be the primary nurturers. But others, such as Nancy Chodorow (1978, 1992), believe the process is culturally determined, and that if men played a greater role in the nurturing of infants and small children, the sex difference in the need for separation from the mother would fade.

In either case, in the object-relations view, a man's identity is more insecure than a woman's identity because it is based on *not* being like women. Men develop more rigid *ego boundaries* between themselves and other people, whereas women's boundaries are more permeable. Later in life, runs this argument, the typical psychological problem for women is how to increase their autonomy and independence, so they can assert their own abilities in their close relationships. In contrast, the typical problem for men is permitting close attachments (Gilligan, 1982).

Quick Quiz

Match each idea with the analyst(s) who proposed it.

1. Sigmund Freud	a. collective unconscious
2. Karen Horney	b. inferiority complex
3. Alfred Adler	c. womb envy
4. Carl Jung	d. Oedipus complex
5. object-relations theorists	e. superego
	f. archetype
	g. representation of mother

Answers:

1. d, e 2. c 3. b 4. a, f 5. g

EVALUATING PSYCHODYNAMIC THEORIES

Although modern psychodynamic theorists differ in many ways, they share Freud's general approach to personality and his assumptions about unconscious dynamics. Many psychologists in other fields, however, regard most psychodynamic ideas as descriptive metaphors, more poetic than scientific, that cannot be evaluated with traditional empirical methods. Freud saw penis envy; Horney saw womb envy. Freud emphasized the unconscious conflicts of the Oedipal period; object-relations theorists emphasize the unconscious conflicts of the infant. Freud saw evidence in his patients of a private unconscious, full of individualistic motives; Jung saw evidence of a collective unconscious, full of universal archetypes.

EXAMINE THE EVIDENCE

Psychodynamic theories are provocative. But what kind of evidence would you need to decide whether they are accurate? How would you choose, say, between Freud's notion of penis envy and Horney's notion of womb envy?

Critics point out that because so many psychodynamic claims depend on the subjective interpretation of the analyst, they can never be scientifically evaluated. The difference between objective and subjective approaches to personality continues to divide empirical and psychodynamic psychologists.

PROBLEMS WITH PSYCHODYNAMIC THEORIES To critics, psychodynamic theories are guilty of three scientific failings:

1. *Violating the principle of falsifiability.* As we saw in Chapter 2, a theory that is impossible to disconfirm in principle is not a scientific theory. Many psychodynamic ideas about unconscious motivations are, in fact, impossible to confirm or disprove. If your experience seems to support these ideas, it is taken as evidence of their correctness, but if you doubt their veracity or offer disconfirming evidence, you must be "revealing defensiveness," or you have "faulty observational skills," or (a favorite accusation) you are "in denial." This way of responding to criticism is neither scientific nor fair!

2. *Drawing universal principles from the experiences of a few atypical patients.* Freud and most of his followers generalized from a very few individuals, often patients in therapy, to all human beings. Of course, the problem of overgeneralizing from small samples occurs in other areas of psychology too, and sometimes valid insights about human behavior can be obtained from case studies. The problem occurs when the observer fails to *confirm* these observations by studying other samples and incor-

Some psychoanalytic ideas can be tested empirically. To Freudians, for example, aggressive sports such as football and soccer permit the displacement of aggressive energy into a socially accepted activity. But behavioral research repeatedly finds that aggressive sports actually stimulate hostility and violence among players and spectators.

rectly infers that what applies to some individuals must apply to all. For example, to confirm Freud's ideas about penis envy, you would need to observe or talk to many young children. Freud himself did not do this; however, when research psychologists interview preschool-age children, they typically find that many children of *both* sexes envy one another. In one charming study of 65 preschool-age boys and girls, 45 percent of the girls had fantasized about having a penis or being male in other ways—and 44 percent of the boys had fantasized about being pregnant (Linday, 1994).

3. *Basing theories of development on the retrospective accounts and fallible memories of patients.* Most psychodynamic theorists have not observed random samples of children at different ages, as modern cognitive and child psychologists do, to construct their theories of development. Instead they have worked backward, creating theories based on themes in adults' recollections.

The analysis of memories can be an illuminating way to achieve insights about our lives; in fact, it is the only way we can think about our own lives because none of us can be our own control group. But as we saw in Chapter 9, memory is often inaccurate, influenced as much by what is going on in a person's current life as by what actually happened. If you are currently not getting along with your mother, you may remember all the times in your childhood she seemed to treat you unkindly and forget the counterexamples of her kindness.

Retrospective analysis has another problem: It creates an *illusion of causality* between events. We assume that if A came before B, then A must have caused B. For example, if your mother spent three months in the hospital when you were 5 and today you are having trouble in school, you might draw a connection between the two facts. (An object-relations analyst probably would.) Perhaps these events are connected, but a lot of other things in your present circumstances might be causing your school difficulties. Indeed, when researchers have done *prospective* studies in which people are followed from childhood to adulthood, their findings often contradict the retrospective assumption of causality.

For example, most psychodynamic therapists believe that sexual abuse in childhood inevitably causes long-term trauma and predictable symptoms in all victims, a conclusion they draw from the clients they see in therapy. But a review of 45 longitudinal studies of children who had been sexually abused revealed quite a different picture. These children indeed had more emotional and behavioral symptoms than nonabused children. Yet one-third of the children had no symptoms at all, and about two-thirds recovered during the first 12 to 18 months after the abuse, especially if they had family support (Kendall-Tackett, Williams, & Finkelhor, 1993).

ASSESSING PSYCHODYNAMIC TESTS Psychodynamic concepts have been widely used in the creation of measures of personality. For example, the concept of projection provided the basis for the development of **projective tests** that attempt to measure unconscious motives, feelings, and conflicts—aspects of personality that may not be apparent in a person's overt behavior. (As we saw in Chapter 11, one widely used projective test, the Thematic Apperception Test, or TAT, has been used reliably to measure a specific aspect of personality, achievement motivation.) The tests present ambiguous pictures, patterns, or stories for the test-taker to interpret or complete. A child or adult may be asked to draw a person, a house, or other object, or to complete a sentence (such as "My mother . . ." or "Women are . . ."). Young children may be given toys or anatomically detailed dolls, and their play may be analyzed for evidence of emotional problems or sexual abuse. The assumption behind all projective tests is that the person's unconscious thoughts and feelings will be "projected" onto the test materials, and revealed in the person's drawings or interpretations of the image.

projective tests Psychological tests used to infer a person's motives, conflicts, and unconscious dynamics on the basis of the person's interpretations of ambiguous or unstructured stimuli.

Clinicians who use projective techniques maintain that they are a rich source of information because test-takers cannot fake answers or lie as easily as on objective tests. Projective tests can help a clinician establish rapport with a client and encour-

GET INVOLVED

This drawing was made by a young man who had bludgeoned his girlfriend with a hammer in a jealous rage. A psychologist has interpreted the drawing as follows:

Upraised hands: *Represent aggression, preparation to strike*

Short legs: *Represent feelings of inadequacy, possible feelings of sexual inadequacy*

Red shirt: *Represents passion, violence, impulsivity*

Rank the plausibility of this analysis, on the following scale:

Very high ____ / ____ / ____ / ____ / ____ *Very low*

What other features of the drawing seem to reflect the young man's personality? Consider movement, color, form, and content.

When you have finished this exercise, turn the page—but not before!

GET INVOLVED

This drawing was made by a young man recently hospitalized following a suicide attempt. A psychologist has interpreted the drawing as follows:

Upraised hands: *Represent helplessness, loss*

Short legs: *Represent diminished stature, inability to "measure up"*

Red shirt: *Represents anger turned toward himself*

Rank the plausibility of this analysis, on the following scale.

Very high ____ / ____ / ____ / ____ / ____ *Very low*

What other features of the drawing seem to reflect the young man's personality? Consider movement, color, form, and content.

What does this exercise, combined with the one on the previous page, tell you about how prior knowledge about a person might affect the interpretation of the person's performance on a projective test?

age a person to open up about anxieties, conflicts, and problems; very young children may reveal feelings in their play or drawings that they cannot express verbally (Anastasi, 1988). And the tests may help clinicians determine when someone is defensively attempting to hide worries or mental problems (Shedler, Mayman, & Manis, 1993).

But while projective tests may have these *therapeutic* uses, the evidence is mounting that they are too unreliable to be used, as they often currently are, for *assessment* purposes—to decide, say, whether a mother is psychologically fit enough to keep her children, whether a patient has an emotional disorder, or whether a child has been sexually abused (Dawes, 1994). For instance, some therapists in the child-protection field have argued that they can tell whether a child has been sexually abused by observing how the child plays with anatomically detailed dolls. The assumption is that an abused child will "project" what happened by playing with the dolls in a sexual manner. However, when researchers have studied how abused children play with the dolls, *compared with a control group of nonabused children,* they have learned that this method is not reliable. Nonabused children too are fascinated by the dolls' genitals, and independent raters cannot distinguish abused and nonabused children on the basis of how they play with the dolls (Ceci & Bruck, 1993; Koocher et al., 1995).

With preschoolers, who have difficulty understanding that a doll can represent a person, the use of dolls may even increase memory errors (DeLoache, 1995).

Most other projective tests also have low *reliability*—that is, different clinicians often interpret the same person's scores differently, perhaps because the clinicians themselves are "projecting" when they decide what a specific response means. The tests also have low *validity*—that is, they often do not measure what they claim to measure. For example, the tests are supposed to measure unconscious personality dynamics, but a person's response to a projective test is significantly affected by sleepiness, hunger, drugs, worry, verbal ability, the clinician's instructions about how to take the test, the clinician's own personality (friendly and warm, cool, or neutral), and what else is going on in the person's life that day (Anastasi, 1988).

All of these problems are apparent in the **Rorschach Inkblot Test,** which was devised by Swiss psychiatrist Hermann Rorschach in 1921. It consists of ten cards with symmetrical abstract patterns, originally formed by spilling ink on paper and folding the paper in half. The test-taker reports what he or she sees in the inkblots, and clinicians interpret the answers subjectively, taking into account the symbolic meanings emphasized by psychodynamic theories.

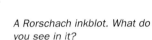

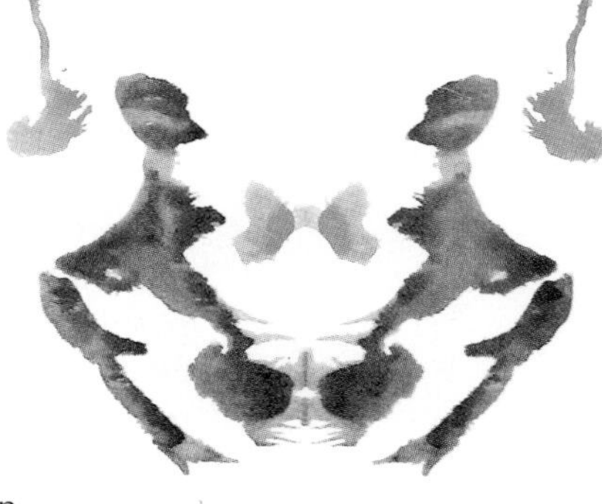

A Rorschach inkblot. What do you see in it?

Although the Rorschach is enormously popular among many clinicians, efforts to confirm its reliability and validity have repeatedly failed. As early as 1956, Lee Cronbach, one of the world's leading experts on testing, observed that "The test has repeatedly failed as a prediction of practical criteria"; and another testing expert, Raymond McCall, concluded, "Though tens of thousands of Rorschach tests have been administered . . . and while many relationships to personality dynamics and behavior have been hypothesized, the vast majority of these relationships *have never been validated empirically,* despite the appearance of more than 2000 publications about the test" (emphasis in original; quoted in Dawes, 1994). In recent years, a different scoring method for the Rorschach, called the Comprehensive System, has become widely used (Exner, 1993). But a critical examination found significant problems with this method too. Many scores are of questionable validity (again, they don't measure the personality traits they claim to measure, such as dependency). And claims of the system's success come from Rorschach workshops where clinicians are taught how to use the new method, which is not an impartial way of assessing its reliability or validity (Wood, Nezworski, & Stejskal, 1996).

The critical assessment of projective methods is important because of the real-life uses of their results. James Wood, who is both a clinician and a research psychologist, told us about a woman who reported to Child Protection Services (CPS) that her ex-husband was sexually molesting their 4-year-old son. Because the boy's answers were ambiguous when CPS interviewed him, CPS thought that perhaps the mother was "deranged" in making her accusation. So they had her tested by a psychologist who administered the Rorschach Inkblot Test. The mother said that one blot looked like "a Thanksgiving turkey already eaten"—and the psychologist, ignoring the fact that the test was being given shortly after Thanksgiving, scored this "food response" as evidence of the woman's "dependency." CPS, accepting the psychologist's conclusion that the mother had mental problems, refused to investigate her claims further. A year later, the boy was brought to the emergency room after a visit with his father. This time, sperm was found in his rectum.

Rorschach Inkblot Test A projective personality test that asks respondents to interpret abstract, symmetrical inkblots.

CONTRIBUTIONS OF PSYCHODYNAMIC IDEAS In response to the concerns of critics, many psychodynamic psychologists are turning to empirical methods and research findings to reformulate and refine their theories and clinical assessments. Some draw on cognitive findings on schemas, narratives, consciousness, and infant mental abilities (Schafer, 1992; Stern, 1985); sociocultural findings on gender roles and the impact of culture; or biological findings on the hereditary aspects of personality traits. For their part, some scientific psychologists are investigating psychodynamic concepts. Cognitive psychologists are integrating the psychodynamic notion of the unconscious with research on nonconscious processes (Epstein, 1994; Kihlstrom, Barnhardt, & Tataryn, 1992). Other researchers have developed objective tests of defense mechanisms to find out how defenses protect self-esteem and reduce anxiety (Margo et al., 1993; Plutchik et al., 1988).

Such research highlights the contributions of psychodynamic approaches. People are indeed often unaware of the motives behind their own puzzling actions. Some childhood experiences can have a lasting effect on personality. Rational thoughts and behavior can be distorted by guilt, anxiety, and shame. The mind does defend itself against information that is threatening, unpleasant, or shocking. Prolonged emotional conflict may indeed play itself out in physical symptoms, immature habits, and self-defeating actions.

Psychodynamic theorists have encouraged researchers to tackle large, fascinating, but difficult questions, such as why some symbols are universal, why men and women regard each other as often with envy and animosity as with love, and why people unconsciously repeat patterns of behavior that seem irrational to others. Psychodynamic psychologists have made imaginative use of qualitative sources of information, such as cultural rituals, literature, fairy tales, jokes, and art. Psychodynamic ideas have thus enriched psychology in many respects.

Quick Quiz

Try projecting the correct response to each question.

1. A 6-year-old boy is behaving aggressively in class, hitting other children and refusing to obey the teacher. Match each explanation of his behavior with the appropriate theorist: psychoanalyst, object-relations analyst, behaviorist, or cognitive social-learning theorist.
   a. The boy's aggressive behavior is being reinforced by attention from the teacher and the other children.
   b. The boy is expressing the aggressive energy of the id and has not developed enough ego control.
   c. The boy's behavior is a result of an interaction between his own high energy level and what he believes, based on his own experience and observation, about the consequences of aggression.
   d. The boy is having unusual difficulty separating emotionally from his mother and is compensating by behaving aggressively.
2. Which statement about the Rorschach Inkblot test is *true?* The test (a) has high reliability, (b) has high validity, (c) can be best used to help people in therapy reveal their feelings, (d) can be used to accurately diagnose sexual abuse.

3. In the 1950s and 1960s, many psychoanalysts, based on their observations of unhappy gay men who had sought therapy, concluded that homosexuality was a mental illness. What violation of the scientific method were they committing?

Answers:

1. a. behaviorist b. psychoanalyst c. cognitive social-learning theorist d. object-relations analyst
2. c 3. The analysts were drawing inappropriate conclusions from atypical patients in therapy, failing to test them with a sample of gay men who were not in therapy or with a sample of heterosexuals. When such research was actually done, by the way, it turned out that gay men were not more mentally disturbed or depressed than heterosexuals (Hooker, 1957).

THE HUMANIST AND EXISTENTIAL TRADITIONS: YOU ARE WHAT YOU CAN BECOME

A final way to look at personality starts from the person's own view of the world—his or her subjective interpretation of what is happening right now. Psychologists who take a *humanist* or *existential* approach to personality believe that personality is influenced less by our genes, past learning, or unconscious conflicts than by our uniquely human capacity to shape our own futures. It is defined, they say, by the human abilities that separate us from other animals: freedom of choice and free will.

THE INNER EXPERIENCE

Humanist psychology was launched as a movement within psychology in the early 1960s. Humanist psychologists rejected the psychoanalytic emphasis on hostility, instincts, and conflict. They also rejected the fragmented approach of behaviorism, with its emphasis on pieces of the person. The movement's chief leaders—Abraham Maslow (1908–1970), Rollo May (1909–1994), and Carl Rogers (1902–1987)—argued instead that it was time for a "third force" in psychology, one that dealt with people's real problems and drew a full picture of human potential.

The trouble with psychology, said Maslow (1971), was that it had forgotten many of the good things in human nature, such as joy, laughter, love, happiness, and *peak experiences* (rare moments of rapture caused by the attainment of excellence or the drive toward higher values). The traits that Maslow thought most important to personality were not the Big Five, but rather the qualities of the self-actualized person—the person who strives for a life that is meaningful, challenging, and productive. Personality development could be viewed, he thought, as a gradual progression toward a state of self-actualization.

humanist psychology A psychological approach that emphasizes personal growth and the achievement of human potential, rather than the scientific understanding and assessment of behavior.

Abraham Maslow regarded self-actualization as a lifelong process, one that you're never too old to begin. Hulda Crooks, shown here at the age of 91 climbing Mt. Fuji, took up mountain climbing in her 60s.

Carl Rogers, like Freud, derived many of his ideas from observing his clients in therapy. As a clinician, Rogers (1951, 1961) was interested not only in why some people cannot function well, but also in what he called the fully functioning individual. Rogers's theory of personality is based on the relationship between the *self* (your conscious view of yourself, the qualities that make up "I" or "me") and the *organism* (the sum of all your experiences, including unconscious feelings, perceptions, and wishes). This experience is known only to you, through your own frame of reference. How you behave depends on your own subjective reality, Rogers said, not on the external reality around you. Fully functioning people show a *congruence*, or harmony, between self and organism. Such people are trusting, warm, and open. They aren't defensive or intolerant. Their beliefs about themselves are realistic. When the self and the organism are in conflict, however, the person is said to be in a state of incongruence.

To become fully functioning people, Rogers maintained, we all need **unconditional positive regard,** love and support for the people we are, without strings (conditions) attached. This doesn't mean that Winifred should be allowed to kick her brother when she is angry with him or that Wilbur may throw his dinner out the window because he doesn't like pot roast. In these cases, a parent can correct the child's behavior without withdrawing love from the child. The child can learn that the behavior, not the child, is what is bad. "House rules are 'no violence,' Winifred," is a very different message from "You are a horrible person, Winifred."

Unfortunately, Rogers observed, many children are raised with *conditional* positive regard. The condition is "I'll love you if you behave well, and I won't love you if you behave badly." Adults often treat each other this way, too. People treated with conditional regard begin to suppress or deny feelings or actions that they believe are unacceptable to those they love. The result, said Rogers, is incongruence, which creates the sensation of being "out of touch with your feelings," of not being true to your "real self." The suppression of feelings and parts of oneself produces low self-regard, defensiveness, and unhappiness. The result is an individual who scores high on neuroticism—who is bitter, unhappy, and negative.

Not all humanists have been optimistic about human nature. Rollo May emphasized some of the inherently difficult and tragic aspects of the human condition, including loneliness, anxiety, and alienation. In books such as *The Meaning of Anxiety, Existential Psychology,* and *Love and Will,* May brought to American psychology elements of the European philosophy of *existentialism.* This doctrine holds that we have free will and freedom of choice, which confers on us responsibility for our actions. Freedom, and its burden of responsibility, carries a price in anxiety and despair, which is why so many people try to escape from freedom into narrow certainties and blame others for their misfortunes. May popularized the humanist idea that people can choose to make the best of themselves because of such inner resources as love and courage. But his writings also were a major influence on the development of **existential psychology.**

unconditional positive regard To Carl Rogers, love or support given to another person, with no conditions attached.

existential psychology An approach to psychology that emphasizes free will, personal responsibility, and the inevitable anxieties of existence, such as the need to find meaning in life and to accept suffering and death.

Existential psychologists argue that mainstream psychology overlooks the important dilemmas of existence—such as the universal struggle to find meaning in life, to live by moral standards, and to come to an understanding of suffering and death (Becker, 1973; Schneider & May, 1995; Vandenberg, 1993). According to Irvin Yalom (1989), the primal conflicts and concerns of life do not stem, as Freud thought, from repressed instinctual desires or traumatic childhood experiences. Rather, he argues, anxiety emerges from a person's efforts, conscious and unconscious, to cope with the harsh realities of life, "the 'givens' of existence." Those givens are "the inevitability of death for each of us and those we love; the freedom to make our lives as we will; our ultimate aloneness; and, finally, the absence of any obvious meaning or sense to life. However grim these givens may seem, they contain the seeds of wisdom and redemption." Perhaps the most remarkable example of a man able to find seeds of wisdom in a barren landscape was Victor Frankl (1955), who developed a form of existential therapy after surviving a Nazi concentration camp. In that pit of horror, he observed, some people maintained their sanity because they were able to find meaning in the experience, shattering though it was.

Existential and humanist psychologists depart from many other schools of psychology in maintaining that our lives are not inevitably determined by our parents, our pasts, or our present circumstances; we have the power to choose our own destinies, even when fate delivers us into tragedy.

EVALUATING HUMANIST AND EXISTENTIAL THEORIES

As with psychodynamic theories, the major criticism of these approaches is that many of their assumptions cannot be tested. How can we know whether existential anxiety characterizes everyone just by virtue of being human? How would you tell whether a person is "self-fulfilled" or "self-actualized"? Unconditional positive regard certainly sounds like a good thing, but can people really be expected to give it to their children and relatives at all times, no matter what the loved ones do? Humanists tend to use warm, intuitively appealing terms such as this one, but critical thinkers would want to know how they are defining their terms and how these concepts would be translated into actual practice. If unconditional positive regard is defined as unquestioned support of a child's efforts at mastering a new skill, or as assurance that the child is loved in spite of his or her mistakes, "unconditional positive regard" is a good idea. If it is defined as an unwillingness ever to say no to a child, offer constructive criticism, or set limits, then, as we will see in Chapter 13, research suggests it is not such a good idea.

DEFINE YOUR TERMS

Unconditional positive regard sounds like a good thing, but what does it mean? Does it mean giving loved ones your total support and approval, no matter what they do? Does it permit setting limits and offering constructive criticism?

Critics also say that humanist and existential psychologies are closer to philosophy than to science. Humanism happens to be a cheerier view of human nature than, say, Freud's vision, but it is just as difficult to verify. Freud looked at humanity and saw destructive drives, selfishness, and lust. Maslow and Rogers looked at humanity and saw cooperation, altruism, and love. Existentialists look at humanity and see fear of death, loneliness, and the struggle for meaning. These differences may tell us more about the observers than about the observed.

Despite such concerns, the issues raised by humanist and existential psychology have added balance to psychology's view of personality. Stress researchers have discovered the healing powers of humor and hope. Developmental psychologists have shown how parental treatment can foster or crush a child's empathy and creativity. Psychologists are even incorporating existential ideas about anxiety and the fear of death into their theories of behavior. Jean Lipman-Blumen (1994), for example, has argued that existential anxiety—"our human inability either to know or control our destiny"—is at the root of unequal relationships: People try to reduce such anxiety either by dominating others or by submitting to stronger individuals or institutions. And influenced by humanism, psychologists now study positive emotions and experiences—such as love, altruism, cooperation, and creativity—along with the troubling ones.

Quick Quiz

1. According to Carl Rogers, a man who loves his wife only when she is looking her best is giving her positive regard that is (a) conditional or (b) unconditional.
2. The humanist who described the importance of having peak experiences was (a) Rollo May, (b) Abraham Maslow, (c) Carl Rogers.

3. A humanist and a psychoanalyst are arguing about human nature. What underlying assumptions about psychology and human potential are they likely to bring to their discussion, and what do their assumptions overlook?

Answers:

1. a 2. b 3. The analyst assumes that human nature is basically selfish and destructive; the humanist, that it is basically loving and life-affirming. Their assumptions overlook the facts that human beings have both capacities, and the situation often determines which capacity is expressed.

THE PUBLIC AND PRIVATE PERSONALITY

The four approaches to personality that we have discussed in this chapter together portray a complex constellation of qualities that make up a human being. Biological research offers us an appreciation of the genetic influences on a person's typical ways of behaving in the world. Learning theories remind us that people do not be-

TABLE 12.2 ***Competing Explanations of Personality***

		Basic method of inquiry	Basic units of study	Basic view of human nature	Possibility of personal change	Influence of culture on behavior
Biological theories		Empirical	Genes, traits, temperament	Neutral	Limited by temperament and genetically influenced traits	Interacts with genetic dispositions
Learning theories	Behaviorism	Empirical	Behavior in a given situation	Neutral	Good, if environment changes	Affects what a society wants its members to learn and value
	Cognitive social-learning	Empirical	Behavior, cognitions, internalized beliefs and values	Neutral	Good, because of ability for self-regulation	
Psychodynamic theories	Freud	Subjective	Unconscious dynamics	Pessimistic	Limited by unconscious motives and early formative experiences	Largely irrelevant to universal unconscious forces
	Modern schools	Usually subjective, some empirical research	Unconscious dynamics	Varies; some more optimistic than classical psychoanalysis		
Humanist and existential theories		Subjective, but some ideas have influenced empirical research	Conscious self	Optimistic	Good, if person exercises free will and takes responsibility for change	All human beings share basic needs and must face the inherent dilemmas of life

Personality includes temperament, characteristics acquired through learning, and the inner sense of self that exists beneath the external masks we present to the world.

have the same way across all situations or throughout their lives. Psychodynamic theories contribute an appreciation of the unconscious motives and defenses that affect people's behavior and create distinctive, sometimes destructive, ways of coping with life. And humanist and existential approaches draw our attention to the uplifting possibilities of human nature, as well as to the universal struggle to make sense of what it means to be human. (For a summary of these four approaches to personality, see Table 12.2.)

One way to integrate these perspectives lies in recognizing that "personality" has two dimensions. Each of us has a public personality that we present to the world, consisting of our characteristic mannerisms, temperamental dispositions, and basic traits. This is the personality that biological and learning theories address. But we also have a private personality that reflects our interior sense of self, consisting of the subjective experience of emotions, memories, dreams, wishes, and worries (Hermans, 1996; Singer, 1984). This is the personality that psychodynamic and humanistic theories address. Each of us weaves these two dimensions of personality together in the narratives we tell to explain our lives, our inconsistencies, our failures and successes—to explain, in short, why we are the way we are. The combination of genetic influences, learned habits, unconscious fears, and visions of possibility, filtered through our interior sense of self and our life story, gives each of us the stamp of our personality . . . one that is as distinctive as a fingerprint.

How to Avoid the Barnum Effect

How well does the following paragraph describe you?

Some of your aspirations tend to be pretty unrealistic. At times you are extroverted, affable, sociable, while at other times you are introverted, wary, and reserved. You have found it unwise to be too frank in revealing yourself to others. You pride yourself on being an independent thinker and do not accept others' opinions without satisfactory proof. You prefer a certain amount of change and variety, and you become dissatisfied when hemmed in by restrictions and limitations. At times you have serious doubts as to whether you have made the right decision or done the right thing.

When people believe that this description was written just for them—the result of a personalized horoscope, "personality profile," or handwriting analysis—they all say the same thing: "It's me! It describes me *exactly!*" The reason is that this description is vague enough to apply to almost everyone and flattering enough to get almost anyone to accept it (French et al., 1991). The magician James Randi often gives audiences of college students a similar "personalized profile" and asks them to rate it for its accuracy. Audience members invariably rate their profiles as being highly accurate—until Randi asks them to exchange profiles with a neighbor, and they realize that all the profiles are identical.

It is sad but true that people are more willing to believe flattering statements about themselves than statements that are scientifically accurate (Thiriart, 1991). And if they must pay money for a profile, take the time to write away for it, or give detailed information about themselves, they are all the more likely to believe that the profile is "eerily accurate."

A French psychologist once advertised himself as an astrologer. In reply to the hundreds of people who wrote to him for his services, he sent out the same vague horoscope. More than 200 recipients sent him thank-you notes praising his accuracy and perceptiveness (Snyder & Shenkel, 1975).

This is why many psychologists worry about people who fall prey to the "P. T. Barnum effect." Barnum was the great circus showman who said "There's a sucker born every minute." He knew that the formula for success was to "have a little something for everybody"—which is what unscientific personality profiles, horoscopes, and handwriting tests have in common. To help you avoid the Barnum effect, research offers a few strategies:

- *Beware of all-purpose descriptions that could apply to anyone.* We know a couple who were terribly impressed when an astrologer told them that "Each of you needs privacy and time to be independent," along with "but don't become too independent, or you will lose your bond." Such observations, which play it safe by playing it both ways, apply to just about all couples.

- *Beware of your own selective perceptions.* Most of us are so impressed when a horoscope or supposed psychic gets something right that we overlook all the descriptions that are plain wrong.

- *Resist flattery.* This is the hard one. Most of us would reject a profile that described us as being nasty, sullen, and stupid, or unoriginal and eager to steal other people's ideas. But many of us fall for profiles that tell us how wonderful, considerate, and smart we are, or how modest we are about our abilities.

- *Beware of the confirmation bias.* It is normal to notice and remember anything that confirms your belief, and to ignore or forget evidence that doesn't fit.

If you keep your critical faculties with you, you won't end up paying hard cash for soft answers, pawning the piano because Geminis should invest in gold this month, or taking a job you despise because it fits your "type." In other words, you will prove Barnum wrong.

SUMMARY

THE ELEMENTS OF PERSONALITY

1) *Personality* is usually defined as an individual's distinctive and relatively stable pattern of behavior, motives, thoughts, and *traits,* characteristics that describe a person across situations.

2) Gordon Allport argued that personality consists of cardinal, central, and secondary traits. Raymond Cattell used *factor analysis* to distinguish *surface traits* from *source traits,* which he considered the basic components of personality. Although researchers are debating how many basic components there are, one leading theory proposes the *Big Five:* extroversion versus introversion, neuroticism (negative emotionality versus emotional stability), agreeableness, conscientiousness, and openness to experience.

THE BIOLOGICAL TRADITION

3) Some personality characteristics appear to be heritable to some degree. Individual differences in *temperaments* or ways of reacting to the environment emerge early in life and can influence subsequent development. Temperamental differences in shyness and inhibition, found in children and monkeys, may be due to variations in the responsiveness of the sympathetic nervous system to change and novelty. Data from twin studies suggest that the heritability of many adult personality traits is around .40 to .60. But caution is warranted in drawing conclusions about the heritability of traits because of the vagueness with which environment has been measured, the similarity of environments of even separated twins, the interaction of a child's temperament and the environment, and the diminishing effect of genes over time.

THE LEARNING TRADITION

4) Learning theories of personality emphasize the behavioral principles by which traits are acquired. *Radical behaviorists* argue that personality is only a convenient fiction because behavior depends on environmental reinforcers and punishers. *Cognitive social-learning theorists* also believe that personality consists of learned patterns, but they emphasize cognitive factors and social-learning principles, such as observation and self-reinforcement. They argue that learned expectations, habits, and beliefs come to influence and regulate behavior, even when external reinforcers are no longer present. One of the most important self-regulating traits that influence behavior is the extent to which people believe they have control over their lives (*locus of control*).

5) One problem with learning theories of personality is that behavior is sometimes attributed to a vague category called "the environment" without specifying which aspects of it are having effects. Another problem is that so many situational factors influence people's behavior that it can be difficult to single out the impact of any one of them.

THE PSYCHODYNAMIC TRADITION

6) Sigmund Freud was the founder of *psychoanalysis*, which emphasizes unconscious aspects of personality; it was the first *psychodynamic* theory, based on the movement of energy within the person. Modern psychodynamic theories share an emphasis on intrapsychic dynamics, the formative role of childhood experiences and conflicts, the idea that psychological development occurs in stages, a person's "psychic reality" as determined by the unconscious, and subjective methods of understanding a person's life and personality.

7) To Freud, the personality consists of the *id* (the source of *libido* or sexual energy and the aggressive instinct), the *ego* (the source of reason), and the *superego* (the source of conscience). *Defense mechanisms* protect the ego from unconscious anxiety. They include repression, projection, displacement (one form of which is sublimation), reaction formation, regression, and denial.

8) Freud believed that personality develops in a series of *psychosexual stages:* oral, anal, phallic (Oedipal), latency, and genital. During the phallic stage, Freud believed, the *Oedipus complex* occurs, in which the child desires the parent of the other sex and feels rivalry with the same-sex parent. When the complex is resolved, the child will *identify* with the same-sex parent and settle into the latency stage, but females retain a lingering sense of inferiority and "penis envy." At puberty, the genital stage of adult sexuality begins.

9) Karen Horney dissented from Freud's notion of inherent female inferiority and envy of the male, countering that men envied women's ability to bear children. Alfred Adler, another early dissenter, emphasized psychological development over the life span, self-determination, and the need for self-improvement, which, if thwarted, can lead to an *inferiority complex.*

10) Carl Jung believed that people share a *collective unconscious* that contains universal memories and images. Personality includes many universal *archetypes*, including the persona and the shadow, and anima and animus. Jung also identified extroversion–introversion as a key personality trait.

11) The contemporary *object-relations school* differs from classical Freudian theory in emphasizing the importance of the first two years of life, rather than the Oedipal phase; the infant's relationships to important figures, especially the mother, rather than sexual needs and drives; and the problem in male development of breaking away from the mother.

12) Psychodynamic theories have been criticized on several scientific grounds: for violating the principle of falsifiability; for overgeneralizing from atypical patients to everyone; and for being based on the unreliable memories and retrospective accounts of patients, rather than on prospective studies. In addition, subjective methods based on psychodynamic assumptions, such as *projective tests* (including the *Rorschach Inkblot Test*) are low in reliability and validity. But some psychodynamic ideas, especially about nonconscious processes and defenses, have made an important contribution to psychology.

THE HUMANIST AND EXISTENTIAL TRADITIONS

13) *Humanist and existential psychologists* focus on the person's subjective sense of self and free will to change. Humanists emphasize human potential and the strengths of human nature, as in Abraham Maslow's concepts of *peak experiences* and *self-actualization.* Carl Rogers stressed the importance of *unconditional positive regard* in creating a "fully functioning" person. Rollo May and other existentialists emphasize the inherent dilemmas of the human condition, including loneliness, anxiety, the search for meaning in life, and the fear of death. Critics observe that these ideas are subjective, elusive, and difficult to measure, but they have added depth to the field of psychology.

THE PUBLIC AND PRIVATE PERSONALITY

14) Biological and learning theories of personality tend to emphasize the public personality that we present to the world, consisting of mannerisms, temperamental dispositions, and basic traits. Psychodynamic and humanist theories tend to emphasize the private, "interior" personality. Together, these approaches portray a complex vision of human personality.

KEY TERMS

personality 452
trait 452
Gordon Allport 452
Raymond Cattell 453
factor analysis 453
"Big Five" personality traits 453
temperaments 456
heritability 457
radical behaviorism 461
cognitive social-learning theory 461
self-handicapping strategy 462
locus of control (internal vs. external) 463
Sigmund Freud 466
psychoanalysis 466
psychodynamic theories 466
intrapsychic dynamics 466
psychic reality 466
id 467
pleasure principle 467
libido 467
ego 467

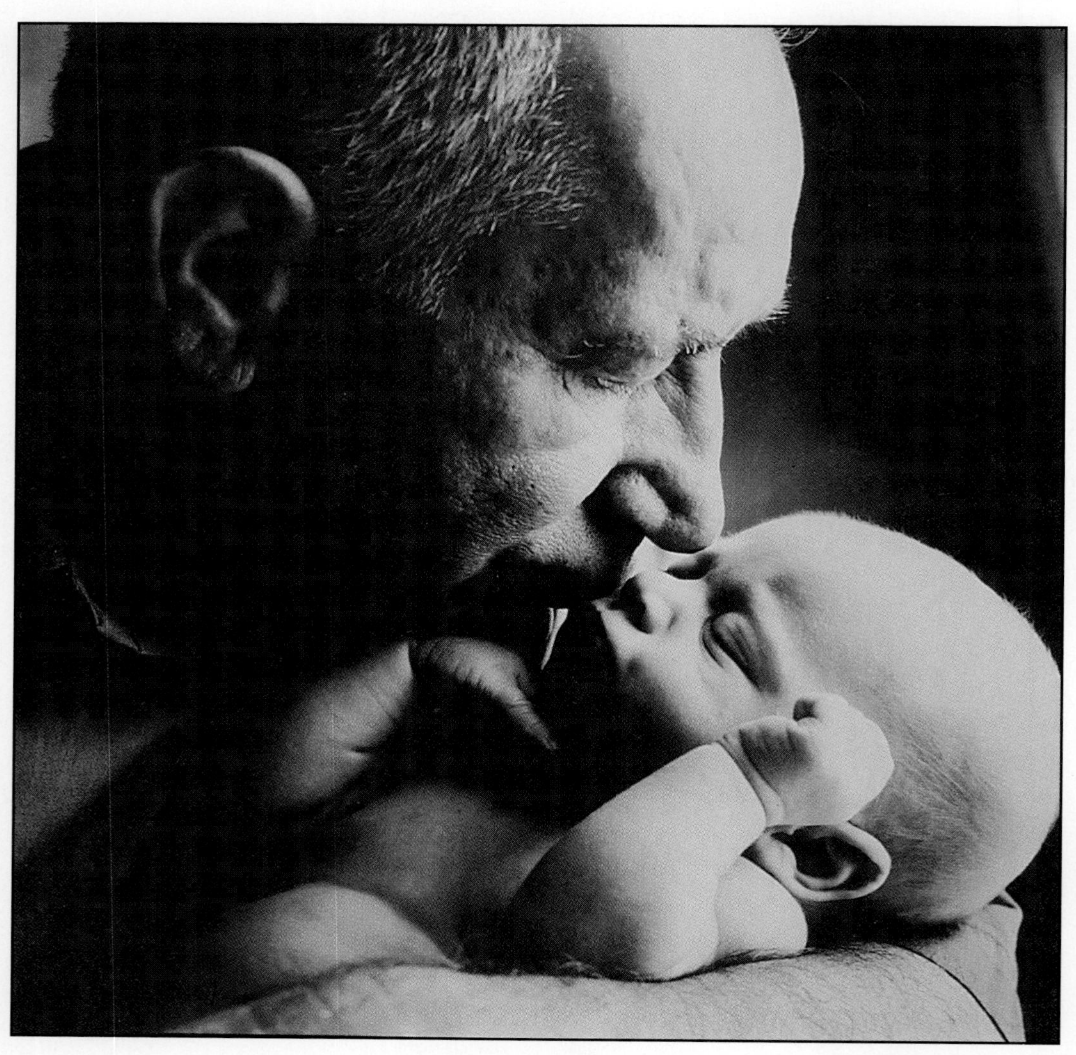

Time is a dressmaker specializing in alterations.

Faith Baldwin

CHAPTER THIRTEEN

Development over the Life Span

From Conception to the First Year
- *Prenatal Development*
- *The Infant's World*

Cognitive Development
- *The Ability to Think*
- *The Ability to Speak*

Gender Development

Moral Development
- *Moral Judgments: Reasoning About Morality*
- *Moral Emotions: Acquiring Empathy, Guilt, and Shame*
- *Moral Action: Learning to Behave Morally*

Adolescence
- *The Physiology of Adolescence*
- *The Psychology of Adolescence*

Adulthood
- *The Biological Clock*
- *The Social Clock*

Are Adults Prisoners of Childhood?

Think About It: Puzzles of Psychology
- *How Long Should We Prolong Life?*

Taking Psychology with You
- *Bringing Up Baby*

HOW OLD ARE YOU? Does it matter? Are you aware of your age—being "too old" for some things, such as playing hopscotch, and "too young" for others, such as managing an office? If so, you hold a thoroughly modern view. Before the start of the Industrial Revolution in the late nineteenth century, people of all ages often inhabited the same social world. Children of all ages were educated together. Children and teenagers worked alongside adults on farms and in factories. Several generations often shared one household. Neither children nor old people were set apart from the rest of society on the grounds that they were too young or too old to participate (Chudacoff, 1990).

In some eras, children have been regarded as "little adults," as this painting of Sir Walter Raleigh and his son shows. The idea of childhood as a developmentally special time is a relatively new one.

By the middle of the twentieth century, "age consciousness" had emerged, and people in developed cultures had become accustomed to thinking of life as a progression of distinct stages. Medical schools had established *pediatrics*, the treatment of children, and *geriatrics*, the treatment of old people. Birthday celebrations had become a commercial enterprise. "Childhood" had become a special time of life, when powerful formative experiences were thought to determine the kind of adult a child would become. "Adolescence," the years between the physical events of puberty and the social markers of adulthood, had become longer, regarded as a special stage with distinctive characteristics. "Adulthood" was said to be marked by a series of predictable events, from marriage and parenthood to retirement. And "old age" had come to mean a time of physical and mental deterioration; elderly people were increasingly separated from the rest of society on the grounds that they could not keep up with the fast-moving world.

Today, age consciousness remains a part of Western culture. But as a result of sweeping economic and demographic changes since World War II, people's development over the life span is no longer as predictable as it was only a few generations ago. Many people still have their first child in their 20s, but others have their first child in their 40s. Most college students are still in their late teens or their 20s, but many are in their 30s or 40s, or older. These changes show that the study of development cannot be separated from the culture and the historical moment in which a person's life unfolds.

Developmental psychologists study universal aspects of development, cultural variations, and individual differences. In this chapter, we will start from the very beginning—the periods from conception to birth, and from birth to the first year. Next we will examine children's physical, cognitive, social, and moral development; then the physical and psychological events of adolescence; and finally, the changes of adulthood and old age.

FROM CONCEPTION TO THE FIRST YEAR

A baby's development, before and after birth, is a marvel of *maturation*, the sequential unfolding of genetically influenced behavior and physical characteristics. In only 9 months of a mother's pregnancy, a cell grows from a dot this big (.) to a squalling bundle of energy that looks just like Aunt Sarah. In another 15 months, that bundle of energy grows into a babbling toddler who is curious about everything. No other time in human development brings so many changes, so fast.

PRENATAL DEVELOPMENT

Prenatal development is divided into three stages: the germinal, the embryonic, and the fetal. The *germinal stage* begins at conception, when the male sperm unites with the female ovum (egg). A day or so after conception, the fertilized egg, or *zygote*, begins to divide into two parts and in 10 to 14 days, it attaches itself to the wall of the uterus. The outer portion of the zygote will form part of the placenta and umbilical cord, and the inner portion becomes the embryo. The placenta will be the growing embryo's link for food from the mother, connected to the embryo itself through the umbilical cord. The placenta allows nutrients to enter the embryo and wastes to exit, and it screens out some, but not all, harmful substances.

Once implantation of the zygote is completed, about two weeks after conception, the germinal stage is over and the *embryonic stage* begins, lasting until the eighth week after conception. The embryo develops webbed fingers and toes, a tail, eyes, ears, a nose, a mouth, a heart and circulatory system, and a spinal cord—although at 8 weeks, the embryo is only $1\frac{1}{2}$ inches long. During the fourth to eighth weeks, the male hormone testosterone is secreted by the rudimentary testes in embryos that are genetically male; without this hormone, the embryo will develop as a female.

After 8 weeks, the *fetal stage* begins. The organism, now called a *fetus*, further develops the organs and systems that existed in rudimentary form in the embryonic stage. By 28 weeks, the nervous and respiratory systems are developed enough to allow most fetuses to live if born prematurely. (New technology allows many to survive if born even earlier, but the risks are much higher.) The greatest gains in brain and nervous system development and in fetal weight occur during the last 12 weeks of a full-term pregnancy.

Although the womb is a fairly sturdy protector of the growing fetus, some harmful influences, collectively called **teratogens**, can cross the placental barrier. These influences, which are particularly damaging during the embryonic stage, include the following:

- *German measles* (rubella), especially early in the pregnancy, often affects the fetus's eyes, ears, and heart. The most common consequence is deafness. Rubella is preventable if the mother has been vaccinated, which can be done in adulthood, up to three months before pregnancy.
- *X-rays or other radiation*, or *toxic chemicals* such as lead, can cause fetal abnormalities and deformities.
- *Sexually transmitted diseases*, such as syphilis, can cause mental retardation, blindness, and other physical disorders. Genital herpes can affect the fetus only if the mother has an outbreak at the time of delivery, which exposes the newborn to the virus as the baby passes through the birth canal. This risk can be avoided by having a cesarean section, in which the baby is removed surgically through the uterus. Although the AIDS virus can be transmitted to the fetus, not all babies born to HIV-infected mothers themselves become infected; estimates range from 13 percent in a European study to 30 percent in U.S. studies (Bee, 1997).
- *Cigarette smoking* during pregnancy increases the likelihood of miscarriage, premature birth, abnormal fetal heartbeat, and a low birth weight baby. The negative effects may last long after birth, showing up in increased rates of infant sickness, sudden infant death syndrome (SIDS), and, in later childhood, hyperactivity and difficulties in school.
- *Heavy alcohol consumption*—several drinks a day—increases by 30 percent the risk of a baby having **fetal alcohol syndrome (FAS).** FAS infants are smaller than normal, have smaller brains, have facial deformities, are more uncoordinated, and are mentally retarded. Even when babies do not have FAS, exposure to alcohol during pregnancy can affect their mental abilities and concentration as children (Streissguth et al., 1991).

teratogen An external agent, such as a disease or chemical, that increases the risk of abnormalities in prenatal development.

fetal alcohol syndrome (FAS) A pattern of physical and intellectual abnormalities in infants whose mothers drank an excessive amount of alcohol during pregnancy.

The effects of alcohol on the fetus are different at different stages of pregnancy; the most dangerous stage is the first trimester (12 weeks), but a little alcohol later in pregnancy is sometimes recommended as a way to prevent premature contractions. In a longitudinal British study, the children of mothers who did not drink at all during pregnancy were no different from those of mothers who had had fewer than 10 drinks a week during pregnancy (Forrest et al., 1991). In contrast, a similar American study, in which more than 500 children have been followed from birth to age 14, found small but significant differences in the children's intellectual performance when the mothers had had a drink or two of alcohol per day during their pregnancies (Hunt et al., 1995; Streissguth et al., 1991). So most American researchers conclude that the safest course of action for pregnant women is to abstain entirely.

- *Drugs* can be harmful to the fetus, whether they are illicit drugs such as morphine, cocaine, and heroin, or commonly used substances such as antibiotics, antihistamines, tranquilizers, acne medication, and diet pills. (Fathers' drug use can also cause fetal defects; cocaine, for example, does so by binding to sperm [Yazigi, Odem, & Polakoski, 1991].) Women should also guard against prescribed drugs that have not been adequately tested. In the 1960s, pregnant women who took the tranquilizer thalidomide gave birth to fetuses with missing or deformed limbs. Until 1971, many women were given the hormone diethylstilbestrol (DES) to prevent miscarriages; daughters of these women had an unusually high risk of developing vaginal cancer during adolescence, and sons were prone to testicular problems.

The lesson is clear. A pregnant woman does well to quit smoking completely, to avoid alcohol or drink very little of it, and to take no other drugs of any kind unless they are medically necessary and tested for safety (and then to accept the fact that her child will never be properly grateful for all that sacrifice!).

THE INFANT'S WORLD

Newborn babies could never survive on their own, but they are far from being passive and inert. They have several *motor reflexes,* automatic behaviors that are necessary for survival. They can see, hear, touch, smell, and taste (bananas and sugar water are in, rotten eggs are out). They even have rudimentary "conversations" with the adults who tend them. Let's consider some of these baby abilities:

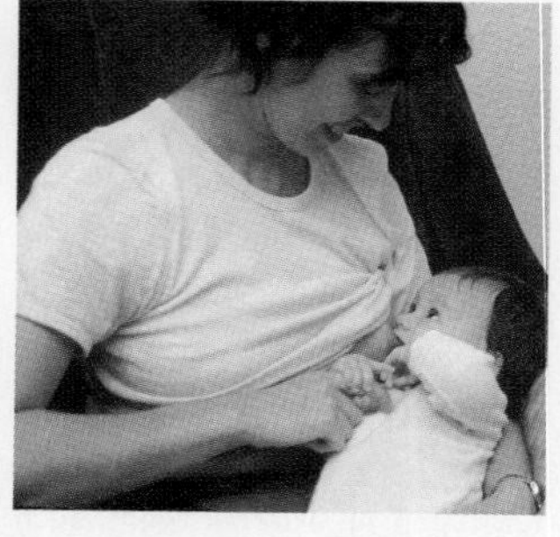

The sucking and grasping reflexes at work.

1. *Reflexes.* Table 13.1 shows the primary reflexes that babies are born with. Babies will turn their heads toward a touch on the cheek or corner of the mouth and search for something to suck on, a handy "rooting reflex" that allows them to find the breast or bottle. They suck vigorously on a nipple, finger, or pacifier placed in their mouths. They grasp tightly a finger pressed on their palms. They are startled by loud noises or shocks. They follow a moving light with their eyes and turn toward a familiar sound, such as the mother's voice or the thump-thump of a heartbeat (both of which they heard in the womb). Many of these reflexes eventually disappear, but others, such as the knee-jerk, eye-blink, and sneeze reflexes, remain.

2. *Vision.* At birth, a baby is very, very nearsighted. The focus range is about 8 inches, the average distance between the baby and the face of the person holding the baby. But visual ability develops rapidly. Newborns open their eyes wide to investigate what is around them, even in the dark. They can distinguish contrasts, shadows, and edges. They can discriminate their mother or other primary caregiver on the basis of smell, sight, or sound almost immediately (Bee, 1997). Within a couple of months, they show evidence of depth perception (see Chapter 6).

TABLE 13.1 *Reflexes of the Newborn Baby*

Reflex	Description
Rooting	An infant touched on the cheek or corner of the mouth will turn toward the touch and search for something to suck on.
Sucking	An infant will suck on anything suckable, such as a nipple or a finger.
Swallowing	An infant can swallow, though this reflex is not yet well coordinated with breathing.
Moro or "startle"	In response to a loud noise or a physical shock, an infant will throw its arms outward and arch back.
Babinski	In response to a touch on the bottom of the foot, the infant's toes will splay outward and then curl in. (In adults, the toes curl in.)
Grasp	In response to a touch on the palm of the hand, an infant will grasp.
Stepping	If held so that the feet just touch the ground, an infant will show "walking" movements, alternating the feet in steps.

By observing what infants look at, given a choice, and how long they gaze at it, psychologists have identified many infant preferences. For instance, infants are primed to respond to faces. Babies who are only *9 minutes old* will turn their heads to watch a drawing of a face if it moves in front of them, but they will not turn if the "face" consists of scrambled features or is only the outline of a face (Goren, Sarty, & Wu, 1975; Johnson et al., 1991). A preference for faces over other stimuli in the environment may have survival value because it helps babies recognize where their next meal is likely to come from.

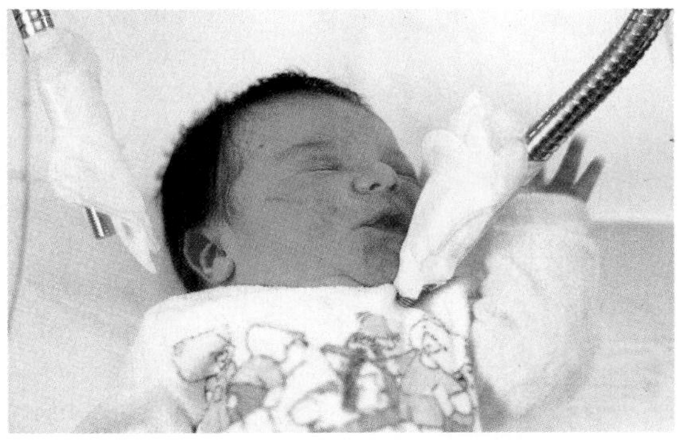

Researchers use imaginative methods to study the remarkable abilities of newborn babies. One study found that infants as young as 3 days old are calmer when they get a whiff of gauze worn by their mothers than when they smell gauze worn by other women (Montagner, 1985).

3. *Social skills.* Newborns are sociable from the start. By the age of 4–6 weeks, babies are smiling regularly, even when they haven't the foggiest notion of whom they are smiling at. Babies also have rudimentary "conversations" with those who tend them. Like many social exchanges, a baby's first conversation with its mother or primary caregiver often takes place over a good meal: During nursing, babies and their mothers often play little games with each other, exchanging nonverbal signals in a rhythmic pattern (see Figure 13.1). This rhythmic dialogue illustrates a crucial aspect of all human exchanges: **synchrony,** the adjustment of one person's nonverbal behavior to coordinate with another's (Bernieri et al., 1994; Condon, 1982). Just as adults unconsciously modify their rhythms of speech, their gestures, and their expressions to be "in sync" with each other, newborns synchronize their behavior and attention to adult speech but not to other sounds, such as street noise or tapping. Parents too coordinate their movements and rhythms with those of their baby.

During their first two years, babies grow as fast as weeds. Most infants double their birth weight in five months. By 1 year of age, on the average, they have tripled their birth weight and grown 10 to 12 inches in length. (The custom of talking about a baby's "length" but a child's "height" is charming; the language changes as soon as the baby is upright!) By age 2, most toddlers are half the height they will be as adults.

synchrony The adjustment of one person's nonverbal behavior to coordinate with another's.

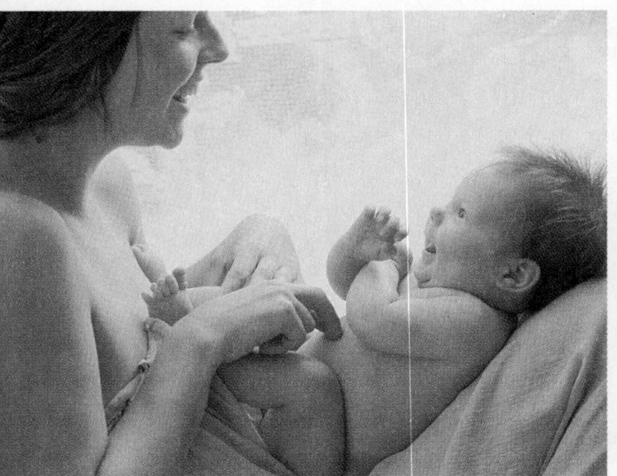
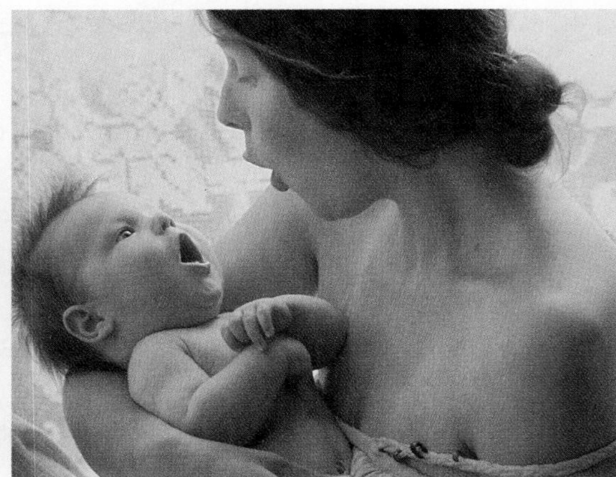
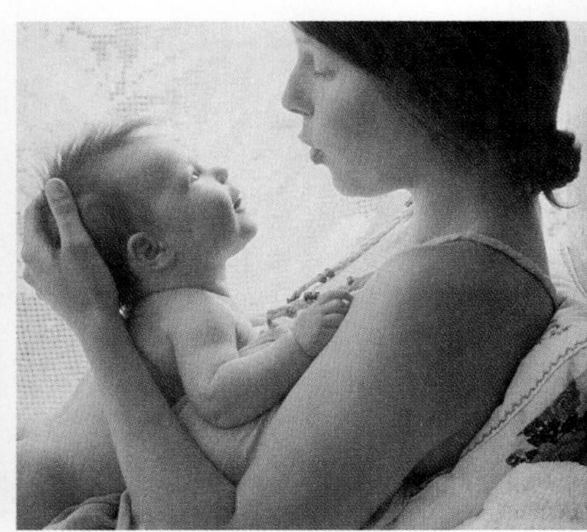

Figure 13.1
Look Who's Talking

This mother and infant illustrate synchrony in action, exchanging giggles, gestures, coos, and smiles. Most babies are able to imitate adult facial expressions within a few weeks.

The baby not only grows in height and weight but also changes the proportion of head to body. An infant's head is nearly one-third of the whole body; a 2-year-old's head is about one-fourth; an adult's head is only one-eighth to one-tenth of total height.

A baby's motor skills develop accordingly. At about 1 month, infants can hold their chins up when lying on their stomachs. At about 2 months, they can raise the upper body. At 4 months, they can sit if someone supports them. At about 7 months, they can sit upright without support. From then on, parents have to look sharp. Babies soon crawl and stand with help (9 months), walk with help (10 months), and toddle off on their own (13 months). These milestones are only averages, however; some babies develop more quickly, others more slowly.

Although infants everywhere develop according to the same maturational sequence, many aspects of their development depend on cultural customs that govern how their parents hold, touch, feed, and talk to them (Super & Harkness, 1994). For example, in the United States, babies are expected to sleep for eight uninterrupted hours by the age of 4 or 5 months. This milestone is considered a sign of neurological maturity, although many babies weep and wail when the parent puts them in the crib at night and leaves the room. But among Mayan Indians, rural Italians, African villagers, and urban Japanese, this nightly clash of wills never occurs because the infant sleeps with the mother for the first few years of life. Mothers have no incentive to get their babies to sleep through the night, and infants continue to wake and nurse about every four hours. Cultural differences in babies' sleep arrangements in turn reflect cultural values. Mayan mothers believe it is important to sleep with the baby in order to forge a close bond with the child; many American parents, in contrast, believe it is important to foster the child's independence as soon as possible (Morelli et al., 1992).

EXAMINE ASSUMPTIONS

Some child-rearing manuals advise parents to teach their 5-month-old infants to sleep through the night by not responding to the babies' cries for attention. What assumptions about babies and about the parent–child relationship are these books making? Are these assumptions the same everywhere?

Similarly, although attachment between infant and caregiver is a universal human need (see Chapter 11), cultures differ in whether they expect that attachment to occur between infant and mother, infant and both parents, or infant and extended family. Among the Efe of Africa, babies spend about half their time, and 3-year-olds spend fully 70 percent of their time, away from their mothers, in the care of older children and other adults (Tronick, Morelli, & Ivey, 1992). Efe children do not experience the one-on-one intense attachment that Western children do, and thus they develop a sense of self that incorporates many other people.

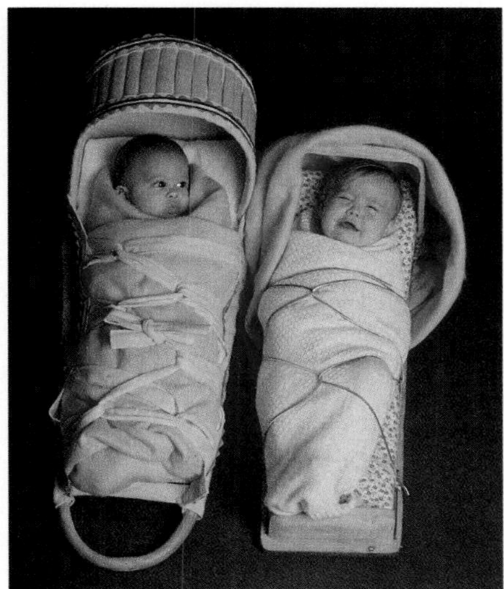

Maturation and culture both influence physical development. Most Navaho babies (left) calmly accept the custom of being strapped to a cradle board, whereas a Caucasian baby (right) will protest vigorously when confined in one. Yet despite cultural differences in such practices, babies in every culture eventually sit, crawl, and walk.

Cultural customs even influence physical development. Infants in many African cultures routinely surpass American infants in their rate of learning to sit and to walk, but not in learning to crawl or climb stairs. The reason is that the African parents routinely bounce babies on their feet, exercise the newborn's walking reflex, prop young infants in sitting positions, and discourage crawling (Cole & Cole, 1993).

Some psychologists argue that no year of life is as important as the first. If the baby doesn't start out well, they warn, and if the parents (especially the mother) do not tend to the baby's every need in the "right" way, the baby's whole life may be influenced for the worse. This is indeed true in the sad cases of babies deprived of secure attachment to caregivers. And newborns who start off with sickness or premature birth do have more physical problems than full-term babies who start off healthy. But study after study show that the events of the first year do not necessarily have permanent effects (Kagan, 1996).

For example, researchers who followed the development of 643 poor and biologically vulnerable children, from birth to age 32, found that supportive home environments totally overcame any initial biological weakness. Problems that emerged were related more to stressful home lives than to biological vulnerabilities in infancy, and even those problems proved temporary. "As we watched these children grow from babyhood to adulthood," the researchers reported, "we could not help but respect the self-righting tendencies within them that produced normal development under all but the most persistently adverse circumstances" (Werner, 1989; Werner & Smith, 1982). Even babies born with the debilitating effects of having been exposed to cocaine in the womb can recover fully, if moved to a healthy environment (Newman & Buka, 1991).

The lesson is that given adequate stimulation, attention, and nourishment, normal babies, and even those with difficulties, will develop normally. Moreover, "adequate" covers a lot of territory. Babies get along fine on cradle boards or unbound, at home with caregivers or, as we saw in Chapter 11, in good child-care centers (Mott, 1991; NICHD Early Child Care Research Network, 1996).

By the end of the first year, infants everywhere have made tremendous progress in their physical abilities (see Table 13.2). Now the story becomes even more interesting.

Quick Quiz

Is your understanding of early development developing normally?

1. Name as many potentially harmful influences on fetal development as you can.
2. Almost all newborn babies can (a) focus at about 16 inches, (b) identify scrambled features of a face, (c) synchronize their behavior with that of a caregiver.
3. *True or false:* Neurologically normal children will sleep through the night by age 4 or 5 months.

Answers:

1. German measles early in pregnancy; exposure to radiation or toxic chemicals; sexually transmitted diseases; the mother's use of cigarettes, alcohol, or other drugs. 2. c 3. false; it depends on the culture.

TABLE 13.2 *Developmental Changes During the First Year*

Average age	Motor	Cognitive	Emotional
0–2 months	Turns head; lifts chin when lying on stomach	Prefers looking at faces; likes familiar sounds; is interested in novelty; tracks *where* things are	Can imitate adult facial expressions; cries when distressed
3–4 months	Lifts chest; holds head erect; reaches for an object; sits with support	Becomes interested in *what* things are; recognizes different faces and details of objects	Smiles and shows interest in slightly unfamiliar objects; may be distressed by objects that are too unfamiliar
5–6 months	Holds head steady; transfers an object from one hand to another	Demonstrates depth perception; understands object identity (that a thing is the same each time it is encountered)	Apparent fear when on visual cliff (see Chapter 6); facial expressions of anger may appear in response to frustration
7–8 months	Sits alone; gets into sitting position	Develops retrieval memory (can recall a familiar face) and larger "working memory"; understands object permanence	Shows first signs of stranger and separation anxiety
9–10 months	Stands with help; crawls	Understands some words and concepts	
11–12 months	Pulls self to standing position; walks with support	Begins symbolic play; utters first meaningful words	Shows sadness at loss of an attachment figure

COGNITIVE DEVELOPMENT

Our friend Joel reports how thrilled he was when his 13-month-old daughter Alison looked at him one day and said, for the first time, "Daddy!" His delight was deflated somewhat, though, when the doorbell rang and she ran to the door, calling, "Daddy!" And his delight was completely shattered when the phone rang and Alison ran to it, shouting, "Daddy!" Later Joel learned that there was a 2-year-old child in Alison's day-care group whose father would call her on the telephone during the day and ring the doorbell when he picked her up. Alison acquired her friend's enthusiasm for phones and doorbells but didn't quite get the hang of "Daddy." She will, though, and that is the mystery of language. Further, she will eventually be able to imagine, reason, and see the world from Daddy's viewpoint, and that is the mystery of thought.

THE ABILITY TO THINK

The ability to think and reason begins in early infancy. But as anyone who has ever observed a young child knows, children do not think the way adults do. At age 2, they may call all large animals by one name (say, *horsie*) and all small animals by another (say, *bug*). At 4, they may protest that a sibling has "more" fruit juice when it is only the shapes of the glasses that differ, not the amount of juice.

In the 1920s, the Swiss psychologist Jean Piaget [Zhan Pee-ah-ZHAY] (1896–1980) proposed a new theory of cognitive development to explain these childish mistakes. Piaget was to child development what Freud was to psychoanalysis and Skinner to behaviorism: a figure of towering influence (Brainerd, 1996). He was a keen observer of children and a brilliant experimentalist who devised ingenious ways of measuring children's abilities. His theory and methods have produced thousands of studies by investigators all over the world.

Piaget's great insight was that children's errors are as interesting as their correct responses; children will say things that are cute or wildly illogical to adults, but which make perfect sense to them because their concepts and reasoning differ from an adult's. The strategies children use to solve problems, said Piaget, are not random or meaningless; they reflect a predictable interaction between the child's developmental stage and experience in the world. Although many of Piaget's ideas have since been challenged and modified, they caused a revolution in thinking about how thinking develops.

PIAGET'S COGNITIVE STAGES Piaget (1929/1960, 1952, 1984) proposed that mental functioning depends on two inborn processes. One is *organization:* All human beings are designed to organize their observations and experiences into a coherent set of meanings. The other is *adaptation* to new observations and experiences. Adaptation, said Piaget, takes two forms, which he called assimilation and accommodation.

Assimilation is what you do when you fit new information into your present system of knowledge and beliefs or into your mental *schemas* (categories of things and people). Suppose that little Harry learns the schema for "dog" by playing with the family schnauzer. If he then sees the neighbor's collie and says "doggie!" he has assimilated the new information about the neighbor's pet into his schema for dogs. **Accommodation** is what you do when, as a result of undeniable new information, you must change or modify your existing schemas. If Harry sees the neighbor's Siamese cat and still says "doggie!" his parents are likely to laugh and correct him. Harry will have to modify his schema for *dogs* to exclude cats, and he will have to create a schema for *cats.* In this way, he accommodates the new information that a Siamese cat is not a dog.

assimilation In Piaget's theory, the process of absorbing new information into existing cognitive structures.

accommodation In Piaget's theory, the process of modifying existing cognitive structures in response to experience and new information.

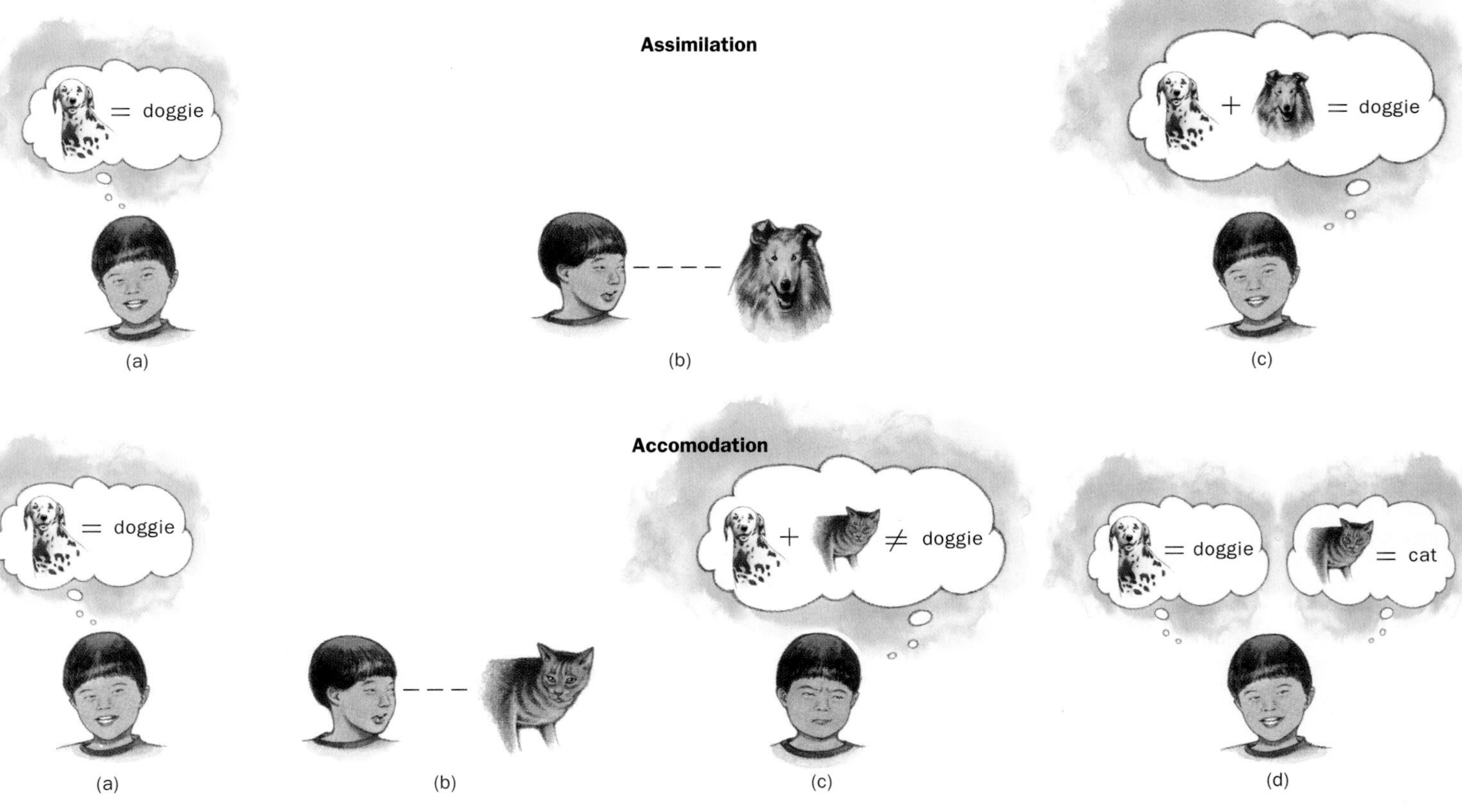

Using these concepts, Piaget proposed that all children go through four stages of cognitive development:

1. *The sensorimotor stage (birth to age 2):* In this stage, the infant learns through concrete actions: looking, touching, hearing, putting things in the mouth, sucking, grasping. "Thinking" consists of coordinating sensory information with bodily movements. Soon these movements become more purposeful, as the child actively explores the environment and learns that specific movements will produce specific results. Swatting a cloth away will reveal a hidden toy; releasing one's grasp of a fuzzy duck will cause the duck to drop out of reach; banging on the table with a spoon will produce dinner (or Mom, taking the spoon away).

One of the baby's major accomplishments at this stage, said Piaget, is **object permanence,** the understanding that something continues to exist even if you can't see it or touch it. In their first few months, he observed, infants seem to follow the motto "out of sight, out of mind." They will look intently at a little toy, but if you hide it behind a piece of paper they will not look behind the paper or make an effort to get the toy. By about 6 months of age, infants begin to grasp the idea that a toy exists and the family cat exists, whether or not they can see the toy or the cat. If a baby of this age drops a toy from her playpen, she will look for it; she also will look under a cloth for a toy that is partially hidden. By 1 year of age, most babies have developed an awareness of the permanence of (some) objects. This is when they love to play peekaboo.

Object permanence, said Piaget, represents the beginning of *representational thought,* the capacity for using mental imagery and other symbolic systems. The child is able for the first time to hold a concept in mind, to learn that the word *fly* represents an annoying, buzzing creature, and that *Daddy* represents a friendly, playful one.

2. *The preoperational stage (ages 2 to 7):* In this stage, the use of symbols and language accelerates, in play and in imitation of adult behavior. A 2-year-old is able to pretend, for instance, that a large box is a house, table, or train. But Piaget described this stage largely in terms of what (he thought) the child cannot do. Children can think, said Piaget, but they cannot reason. They do not yet have the kinds of mental abilities that allow them to understand abstract principles or cause and effect. Piaget called these missing abilities **operations,** by which he meant reversible actions that the child performs in the mind. An operation is a sort of "train of thought" that can be run backward or forward. Multiplying 2 times 6 to get 12 is an operation; so is the reverse operation, dividing 12 by 6 to get 2.

Children at the preoperational stage, Piaget believed, rely on primitive reasoning based on the evidence of their own senses, which can be misleading. If a tree moves in the wind, it must be alive. If the wind blows while the child is walking, then walking must make the wind blow. Piaget also believed—mistakenly, as we will see—that children of this age cannot take another person's point of view because their thinking is **egocentric.** They see the world only from their own frame of reference. They cannot imagine that you see things differently, that events happen to others that do not happen to them, or that the world does not exist solely for them. "Why are there mountains [with lakes]?" Piaget asked a preoperational Swiss child. "So that we can skate," answered the child.

Further, said Piaget, preoperational children cannot grasp the concept of **conservation**—the notion that physical properties do not change when their forms or appearances change. These children are unable to understand that an amount of liquid, a number of pennies, or a length of rope remains the same even if you pour the liquid from one glass to another, stack the pennies, or coil the rope (see Figure 13.2). If you pour liquid from a short, fat glass into a tall, narrow glass, preoperational chil-

object permanence The understanding, which develops late in the first year, that an object continues to exist even when you can't see it or touch it.

operations In Piaget's theory, mental actions that are cognitively reversible.

egocentric thinking Seeing the world from only your own point of view; the inability to take another person's perspective.

conservation The understanding that the physical properties of objects—such as the number of items in a cluster or the amount of liquid in a glass—can remain the same even when their form or appearance changes.

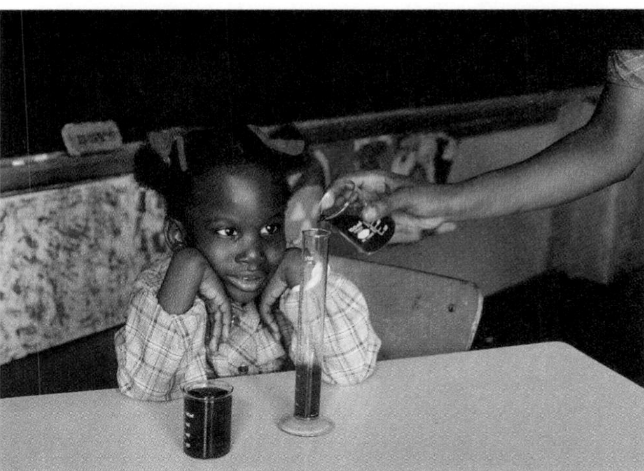

Figure 13.2
Piaget's Principle of Conservation

In a typical test for conservation of number (left), the child must say whether one of the sets of blocks has "more." His answer shows whether he understands that the two sets contain the same number, even though the larger blocks in one set take up more space. In a test for conservation of quantity (right), the child is shown two short, fat glasses with equal amounts of liquid. Then the contents of one glass are poured into a tall, narrow beaker, and the child is asked whether one container now has more. Her answer shows whether she understands that pouring liquid from a short, fat glass into a tall, narrow one leaves the amount of liquid unchanged.

dren will say there is more liquid in the second glass. They attend to the appearance of the liquid (its height in the glass) instead of its fixed quantity.

3. *The concrete operations stage (about age 6 or 7 to 11):* During this stage, the nature and quality of children's thought change significantly. According to Piaget, during these years children come to understand the principles of conservation, reversibility, and cause and effect. They understand the nature of *identity;* for example, they know that a girl doesn't turn into a boy by wearing a boy's hat, and that a brother will always be a brother, even if he grows up. They learn mental operations, such as addition, subtraction, multiplication, division, and categorization—not only of numbers, but also of people, events, and actions. They learn a few abstract concepts, such as *serial ordering,* the idea that things can be ranked from smallest to largest, lightest to darkest, shortest to tallest. But, according to Piaget, children's thinking at this age is "concrete" because it is still grounded primarily in concrete experiences and concepts, rather than in abstractions or logical deductions.

GET INVOLVED

If you know any young children, try one of Piaget's conservation experiments. A simple one is to make two rows of seven buttons or pennies, aligned identically. Ask the child whether one row has more. Now simply spread out the buttons in one row, and ask the child again whether one row has more. If the child says yes, ask which row does and why. Try to do this experiment with a 3-year-old and a 7- or 8-year-old. You will see a big difference in their answers.

TABLE 13.3 Summary of Piaget's Stages of Cognitive Development

Stage	Major Accomplishments
Sensorimotor (0–2)	Object permanence Beginning of representational thought
Preoperational (2–7)	Accelerated use of symbols and language
Concrete operations (6–11)	Understanding of conservation Understanding of identity Understanding of serial ordering
Formal operations (12–)	Abstract reasoning Ability to compare and classify ideas

4. *The formal operations stage (age 12 to adulthood):* This stage, said Piaget, marks the beginning of abstract reasoning. Teenagers understand that ideas can be compared and classified, as objects can. They are able to reason about situations they have not experienced firsthand, and they can think about future possibilities. They are able to search systematically for answers to problems. They are able to shift from concrete operations to deductive reasoning, using premises common to their culture and experience. (Table 13.3 summarizes Piaget's four stages of cognitive development.)

EVALUATING PIAGET Piaget transformed the field of developmental psychology, providing an entirely new vision of the nature of children (Flavell, 1996). Before summarizing the lasting contributions of his theory, however, we want to consider the findings from later research that modified his ideas:

Possible event

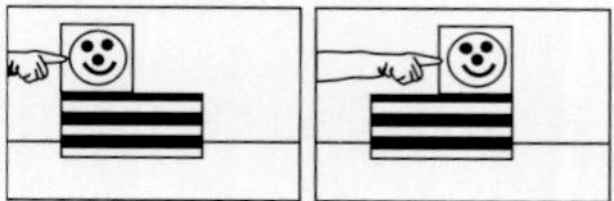

Impossible event

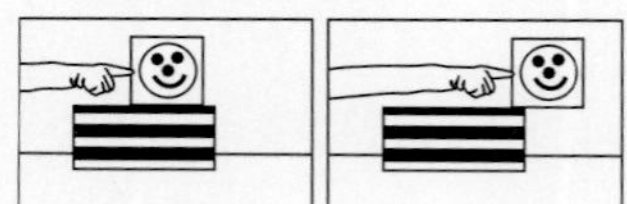

Figure 13.3
Testing Infants' Knowledge

In one method for studying infants' understanding of whether an object needs physical support, a hand pushes a colorful box from left to right along a striped platform. The box is pushed until it reaches the end of the platform—a possible event, or until only a bit of it rests on the platform—an impossible event. Babies look longer at the impossible event, suggesting that it surprises them (Baillargeon, 1994).

1. *The changes from one stage to another are neither as clear-cut nor as sweeping as Piaget implied;* in particular, there is no abrupt shift from preoperational to concrete-operational thought. At any given age, a child may use several different strategies in trying to solve a problem, some more complex or accurate than others—a finding that has prompted one researcher to suggest that cognitive ability develops in overlapping waves rather than discrete steps (Siegler, 1996). Moreover, children's reasoning ability often depends on the circumstances—who is asking them questions, the specific words used, the materials used, and what they are reasoning *about*—not just on the stage they are in.

2. *Children can understand more than Piaget gave them credit for.* Taking advantage of the well-documented fact that infants look longer at novel than at familiar stimuli, psychologists have designed delightfully imaginative methods of testing what babies know. In a typical experiment, infants are shown a possible event and an impossible event that violates expectations of reality (see Figure 13.3). The idea is that if infants possess the belief or expectation being tested—for example, "It is impossible for a box to float on air"—they will perceive the impossible event as being more unusual and surprising than the possible event and, thus, will look at it longer. And so they do.

Using this method, Elizabeth Spelke and her colleagues (1992) learned that infants as young as 4 months seem to understand some basic principles of physics! The babies look longer at a ball if it seems to roll through a solid barrier, or leap between two platforms, or hang in midair, than they do when an action obeys the laws of

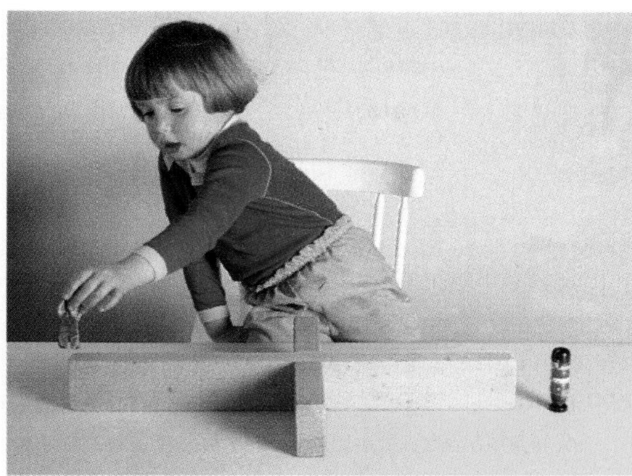

This 3-year-old girl was asked to place the doll where the policeman could not find him. According to Piaget, she should be "egocentric" and therefore hide the doll from herself as well (left). On several occasions, however, she placed the doll where she, but not the policeman, could see him, suggesting that she was able to take the policeman's point of view (right).

physics. Spelke believes that babies are biologically programmed with a certain "core knowledge" about how the world works (evolutionary psychologists would agree, as we saw in Chapter 3). Similarly, Renée Baillargeon (1994) found that infants as young as $2\frac{1}{2}$ to $3\frac{1}{2}$ months understand some of the physical properties of objects. Even at this age, she summarizes, babies "are aware that objects continue to exist when masked by other objects, that objects cannot remain stable without support, that objects move along spatially continuous paths, and that objects cannot move through the space occupied by other objects."

Children also advance rapidly in their symbolic abilities earlier than Piaget thought—between the ages of $2\frac{1}{2}$ and 3. Within that six-month period, as one experiment showed, toddlers become able to think of a miniature model of a room in two ways at once: as a room in its own right and as a symbol of the larger room it represents (DeLoache, 1995). This ability is a big step toward adult symbolic thought, in which anything can stand for anything else—a flag for a country, a logo for a company.

3. *Preschoolers are not as egocentric as Piaget thought, nor as fooled by appearances.* A large body of evidence shows that most 3- and 4-year-olds *can* take another person's perspective. When 4-year-olds play with 2-year-olds, for example, they modify and simplify their speech so the younger children will understand (Shatz & Gelman, 1973). As we will see later, even very young children are capable of charming acts of empathy.

John Flavell (1992, 1993) has proposed that children go through two levels of perspective-taking ability: at level one, about ages 2 to 3, the child knows *that* another person experiences things differently. At level two, about ages 4 to 5, the child begins to figure out *what* another person is seeing or experiencing (Flavell, Green, & Flavell, 1990). One 5-year-old we know showed her teacher a picture she had drawn of a cat and an unidentifiable blob. "The cat is lovely," said the teacher, "but what is this thing here?" "That has nothing to do with you," said the child. "That's what the *cat* is looking at."

This shift in perspective taking, says Flavell, is part of a broader change in how the child understands appearance and reality. Two- and 3-year-olds judge by appearance: If you put a dog mask on a cat, they will say it's a dog. By age 5, children know it's still a cat. Even more important, at 4 or 5 they understand that someone else might be fooled into thinking it's a dog and even act on that false belief. In addition, they understand that you can't predict what a person will do just by observing a situation or knowing the "facts"; you have to know what the person is feeling and thinking. In short, they have developed a **theory of mind,** a theory about how their own and other people's minds work and how people are affected by their beliefs and feelings (Astington, 1993; Flavell, Green, & Flavell, 1990).

Psychologists are debating how and why the 4- or 5-year-old child's emerging theory of mind occurs. Some think it is an "innate module," of the sort proposed by evolutionary psychologists (see Chapter 3). Others examine the cognitive and social factors in the child's life—such as having high verbal ability or many siblings—that hasten its development (Jenkins & Astington, 1996). In any case, the accumulating evidence shows that Piaget was clearly wrong in assuming that children of this age are egocentric and literal minded. They are capable of forms of logic and inference about other people's behavior, which Piaget thought impossible.

4. *Children's cognitive development, like their biological development, occurs in a social and cultural context.* The development of concrete operations, for example, varies in timing and content from one culture to another. Pierre Dasen (1994) spent years testing Piaget's theory in different cultures: among the Aborigines in Australia, the Inuit in Canada, the Ebri and the Baoulé in the Ivory Coast, and the Kikuyu in Kenya. Traditional nomadic hunting peoples, such as the Inuit and the Aborigines, do not quantify things and do not need to. The Aborigines have number words only up to five; after that, all quantities are described as "many." In such cultures, the cognitive ability to understand the conservation of quantity or number develops late, if at all. But nomadic hunting tribes rely on their spatial orientation—knowing where water holes and successful hunting routes are—and so spatial abilities develop rapidly. In contrast, children who live in settled agricultural communities, such as the Baoulé, develop rapidly in the domain of quantification and much more slowly in spatial reasoning. Experiences with school affect cognitive development too: Many unschooled children of the Wolof, a rural group in Senegal, do not acquire an understanding of conservation, as do their peers who attend school. But a brief training program can speed its development (Greenfield, 1976).

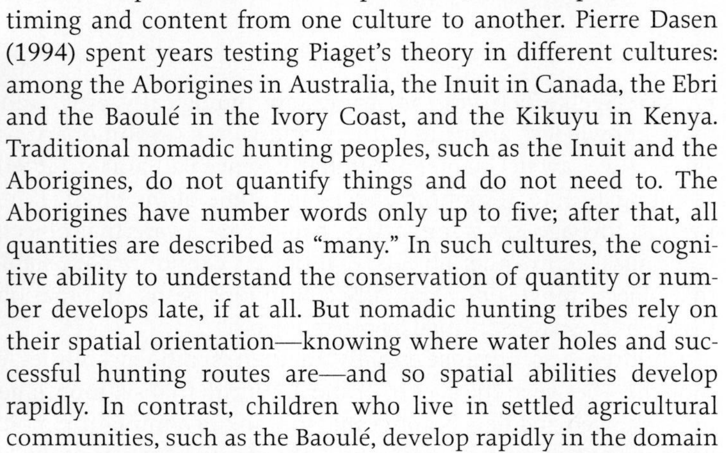

Experience affects cognitive development. This young potter in India, and other children who work with materials such as clay, understand the concept of conservation of quantity sooner than children who do not have this practical experience.

5. *Just as Piaget underestimated the cognitive skills of young children, he also overestimated those of many adults.* As we saw in Chapter 8, not all adolescents and adults develop the ability for formal reasoning and reflective judgment. Many continue to show the magical thinking typical of preoperational children (such as "If X precedes Y, then X must have caused Y"). Some people never develop the capacity for formal operations, and others continue to think concretely unless a specific problem requires abstract thought.

Although these important findings have required significant modifications of Piaget's theory, the general sequence of cognitive development that he described does hold up across cultures. Most psychologists today accept his major point, that new reasoning abilities depend on the emergence of previous ones: You can't learn algebra before you can count, and you can't learn philosophy before you understand logic. Piaget's assimilation–accommodation model correctly emphasizes the ongoing interaction between the cognitive structures that children are born with and the child's continuing adaptation to the environment (Flavell, 1996). It is largely due to Piaget that developmental psychologists (and parents) now understand that children are not passive vessels into which education and experience are poured. Children actively interpret their worlds, using their perceptions and developing schemas to assimilate new information and to try to figure things out.

theory of mind A theory about the way your own mind and other people's minds work, and of how people are affected by their beliefs and feelings; children develop a theory of mind by age 4 or 5.

THE ABILITY TO SPEAK

In Chapter 3 we saw that the ability to use language is an evolutionary adaptation of the human species. In only a few years of life, children are able to understand thousands and thousands of words; use rules of syntax to string them together in meaningful sentences; and produce and understand an infinite number of new word combinations.

In the first months, babies cry and coo. They are highly responsive to the pitch, intensity, and sound of language. They are responsive to emotions in the voice before they respond to facial expressions. Anne Fernald (1990) finds that for a baby, "The melody is the message." When most people speak to babies, their pitch is higher and more varied than usual and their intonation is more exaggerated. Babies as young as two days old prefer to hear adults talk this way. Speaking to infants in "baby talk" is not universal, but it is widespread, as investigators in France, Italy, Japan, rural South Africa, Britain, Canada, and China have found.

By 4 to 6 months, babies have learned many of the key sounds of their native language, even before they can utter a word of it. They can recognize their own names and other words that are regularly spoken with emotion, such as "mommy" and "daddy." In a study of 64 infants in Sweden and the United States, 6-month-olds could distinguish the typical consonant and vowel sounds (phonemes) of their parents' language from those of a foreign language (Kuhl et al., 1992). Over time, exposure to the baby's native language reduces his or her ability to perceive speech sounds in other languages. Thus Japanese infants can hear the difference between the English sounds "la" and "ra," but Japanese adults cannot because this contrast does not exist in their language.

Between 6 months and 1 year, infants become increasingly familiar with the sound structure of their native language, and soon they are able to distinguish words from the unbroken flow of speech. They will listen longer to native words that violate their expectations of what words should sound like (Jusczyk, 1993; Jusczyk et al., 1993). They start making many "ba-ba" and "goo-goo" sounds, endlessly repeating sounds and syllables. This *babbling phase* lasts until about 1 year of age, when the child begins to name things. One-year-olds already have some concepts in their minds—they can recognize favorite objects and people—and their first words are those that represent familiar concepts ("mama," "doggie," "bug").

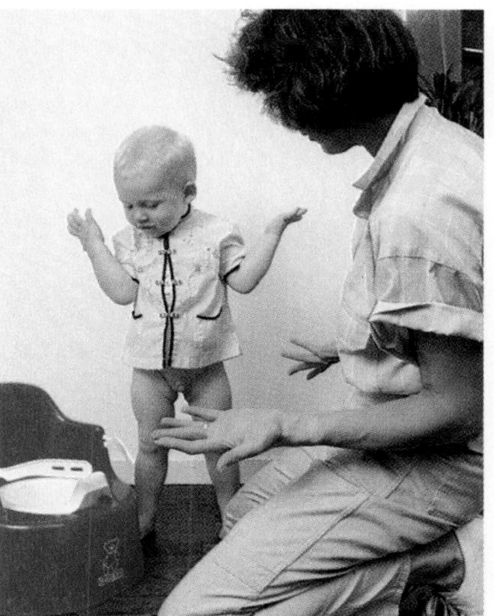

Symbolic gestures emerge early! This mother and her son are clearly having a "conversation."

Starting at about 11 months, babies begin to develop a repertoire of symbolic *gestures*, another important tool of communication. They use gestures to refer to objects (sniffing to indicate "flower"), to request something (smacking the lips for "food," moving the hands up and down for "play the piano"), to describe an object (blowing or waving a hand for "hot," raising the arms for "big"), and to reply to questions (opening the palms or shrugging the shoulders for "I don't know"). One baby baseball fan used a clapping sign in response to baseball games, pictured or real. Parents who encourage their babies to use gestures like these actually spur their child's language learning; their babies turn out to be more alert, better listeners, and less frustrated in their efforts to communicate than babies who are not encouraged to use gestures (Goodwyn & Acredolo, 1993).

Between the ages of 18 months and 2 years, toddlers begin to produce words in two- or three-word combinations ("Mama here," "go 'way bug," "my toy"). The child's first combinations of words have a common quality in most languages: They are **telegraphic.** When people had to pay for every word in a telegram, they quickly learned to drop unnecessary articles (*a, an,* or *the*) and auxiliary verbs (such as *is* or

telegraphic speech A child's first combination of words, which omits (as a telegram does) unnecessary words.

are), but they still conveyed the message. Similarly, the two-word sentences of toddlers omit articles, auxiliary verbs, other parts of speech, and word endings, but are remarkably accurate in conveying meaning. Here are some functions and examples of children's two-word "telegrams" (Slobin, 1985):

- *To locate or name something:* there toy, that chair, see doggie
- *To demand something:* more milk, give candy
- *To negate an action:* no wet, no want, not hungry, allgone milk
- *To describe an event:* Bambi go, mail come, hit ball
- *To show possession:* my shoe, Mama dress
- *To modify an object:* pretty dress, big boat
- *To question:* where ball, where Daddy

Pretty good for a little kid, don't you think? At about this age, children reveal another impressive talent. They begin to acquire new words rapidly, a phenomenon called the *naming explosion.* They absorb the new words as they encounter them in conversation, forming a quick impression of the likely meaning of the word by using their knowledge of grammatical contexts and the rules for formulating words. The cognitive ability to understand meanings of words seems to precede the rapid acquisition of vocabulary: Even 13-month-old infants, who have six to eight months to go before the naming explosion begins, are able to comprehend new names for objects after hearing them only nine times in a five-minute training session (Woodward, Markman, & Fitzsimmons, 1994). This process of understanding new words continues throughout childhood.

Quick Quiz

Please use language (and thought) to answer these questions.

1. Understanding that two rows of six pennies are equal in number, even if one row is flat and the other is stacked up, is an example of __________.
2. Understanding that a toy exists even after Mom puts it in her purse is an example of __________, which develops during the __________ stage.
3. The belief that a car moves because you are riding in it shows __________ thinking.
4. Name five modifications of Piaget's theory.
5. "More cake!" and "Mommy come" are examples of __________ speech.
6. *True or false:* Children acquire most new words without explicit training.

Answers:

1. conservation 2. object permanence, sensorimotor 3. egocentric 4. The changes from one stage to another are not as clear as Piaget implied; children know more and know it earlier than Piaget thought; they are less egocentric than Piaget thought; their cognitive development is affected by their culture; not all adolescents and adults achieve the ability for formal operations. 5. telegraphic 6. true

GENDER DEVELOPMENT

This conversation was overheard in the infant department of a large store between a female clerk and a customer buying a receiving blanket for her friend's newborn baby:

Buyer: I'd like this receiving blanket, please.

Clerk: Is the baby a boy or girl?

cathy® by Cathy Guisewite

Sex typing starts early.

Buyer: A boy.

Clerk: In that case, I'd suggest a different pattern. How about this one, with the little cowboys and guns?

Buyer: But I like the clowns—they're so colorful and cute.

Clerk: Trust me, honey. I get lots of dads in here, and you can't imagine how much time they spend choosing colors and patterns. They all say the cowboys are more masculine.

Most babies, unless they have rare abnormalities, are born unambiguously male or female—a biological distinction. But developmental psychologists want to know how children learn to be masculine or feminine—a psychological distinction. This learning starts at the moment of birth, when the newborn is enveloped in the clothes, colors, and toys the parents think are appropriate for its sex. No parent ever excitedly calls a relative to exclaim, "It's a baby! It's a seven-and-a-half-pound, black-haired baby!"

To distinguish what is anatomically given from what is learned, many psychologists differentiate *sex* and *gender* (Deaux, 1985; Lott & Maluso, 1993; Unger, 1990). *Sex* refers to the anatomical and physiological attributes of the sexes; thus they would speak of a "sex difference" in frequencies of baldness and color blindness. But they use *gender* to refer to the cultural and psychological attributes that children learn are appropriate for the sexes; thus they would speak of a "gender difference" in sexual attitudes, dishwashing, and fondness for romance novels. (In Chapter 18 we will take up this distinction again, in considering how culture shapes the rules of gender.)

By the age of 4 or 5, children have developed a secure **gender identity,** a fundamental sense of maleness or femaleness that exists regardless of what one wears or does. They understand that a girl remains a girl even if she can climb a tree, and a boy remains a boy even if he has a ponytail. **Gender socialization,** sometimes called **sex typing,** is the psychological process by which boys and girls learn what it means to be masculine or feminine, including the abilities, interests, personality traits, actions, and self-concepts that their culture says are appropriate for males or females. A person can have a strong gender identity and not be sex typed: A man may be confident in his maleness and not feel threatened by doing "unmasculine" things such as needlepointing a pillow; a woman may be confident in her femaleness and not feel threatened by doing "unfeminine" things such as serving in combat.

gender identity The fundamental sense of being male or female, regardless of whether the person conforms to the rules of sex typing.

gender socialization (sex typing) The process by which children learn the behaviors, attitudes, and expectations associated with being masculine or feminine in their culture.

Look familiar? This scene is typical of many nursery schools and homes—the boy builds a gun out of anything he can, and the girl dresses up in any pretty thing she can find. Psychologists (and parents) debate whether such sex-typed behaviors are biologically based or are a result of subtle reinforcements and the emergence of gender schemas.

Developmental psychologists study gender identity and socialization by considering biological factors, principles of learning, cognitive processes, and situational influences.

BIOLOGICAL FACTORS Biological psychologists and sociobiologists hold that some differences between the sexes are largely a matter of hormones, genes, and possibly brain lateralization: especially differences in aggression, occupational interests (e.g., math or nursing), and skills (e.g., flying airplanes or knitting sweaters). Girls who were exposed to prenatal androgens (masculinizing hormones) in the womb, they note, are later more likely than nonexposed girls to prefer "boys' toys" such as cars, fire engines, and Lincoln logs (Berenbaum & Snyder, 1995). And in all primate species, young males are more likely than females to go in for physical roughhousing.

Biologically oriented researchers are critical of learning theories of gender socialization, which emphasize the rewards and punishments that children get for behaving appropriately or inappropriately for their sex. For one thing, they argue, some sex differences emerge regardless of what parents and teachers do; parents may treat their sons and daughters equally, or try to, yet their sons will still prefer mechanical toys and their daughters will want tea sets. Many parents say they are merely *responding* to their children's interests when they give their children sex-typed toys, and indeed, children express preferences for what they want to play with at a very early age (Snow, Jacklin, & Maccoby, 1983). Moreover, a meta-analysis of 172 studies showed that in 18 domains of parental treatment of children—including responsiveness and warmth, encouragement of achievement or dependency, use of reasoning, restrictiveness, and amount of interaction—parents treated sons and daughters no differently (Lytton & Romney, 1991). Yet the children often acted out gender stereotypes anyway, leading the researchers to conclude that toy and play preferences have a biological basis.

Is this a "mailman"? Learning theorists study subtle influences on gender socialization. For example, they find that masculine nouns and pronouns promote the assumption that some jobs are suited only to men (Hyde, 1984a). This finding has led to the increased use of gender-neutral terms, such as police officer *and* mail carrier.

LEARNING INFLUENCES Behavioral and social-learning theorists agree that traditional learning principles cannot account for all aspects of gender socialization, but they have identified many of the subtle reinforcers that do affect behavior. For example, even at 1 year of age, boys and girls *whose behavior is the same* are treated differently by adults. Beverly Fagot and her colleagues (1985) observed the reactions of teachers to "assertive acts" (such as efforts to get an adult's attention) and "communicative acts" of 12- to 16-month-old children. Although the boys and girls did not differ in the frequency of these acts, the teachers responded far more often to assertive boys than to shy ones, and to verbal girls than to less verbal ones. When the researchers observed the same children a year later, a gender difference was now apparent, with boys behaving more assertively and girls talking more to teachers.

Similarly, the aggressiveness of boys gets more attention and other rewards from teachers and peers than does aggressiveness in girls, again even when the children start out being equally aggressive. In one observational study of preschool children, peers or teachers paid attention to the aggression of boys 81 percent of the time, compared to only 24 percent of the time for the girls' aggression. When girls and boys behaved dependently, however, such as by calling for help from the teacher, the girls got attention far more often than did the boys (Fagot, 1984).

The hidden messages conveyed by parents, teachers, and other adults affect older children as well, as a longitudinal study of seventh- and ninth-grade children's math achievement revealed (Jacobs & Eccles, 1985). At the start of the study, the children were equal in math ability, as determined by test scores and teachers' evaluations. But over time, parents who believed that boys have a natural superiority in math unintentionally communicated this message to their children. For instance, parents would say of their sons' good math grades, "You're a natural math whiz, Johnny!" But if their daughters got identically good grades, the parents would say, "Wow, you really worked hard in math, Janey, and it shows!" The implication, not lost on the children, was clear: When girls do well, it is because of concerted effort; when boys do well, it is because they have a natural gift. This attitude was related to the reduced likelihood that the girls would take further math courses, remain interested in math, and value math in general. Why should they, if the subject is going to be so hard and isn't natural to females anyway? Parents' stereotypical expectations about their children's talents in math, English, and sports also strongly influence their children's performance and feelings of competence in these areas (Eccles, 1993; Eccles, Jacobs, & Harold, 1990).

By their actions, parents convey all sorts of lessons about gender to their children. This family's group effort to make dinner is teaching the children that (1) both sexes belong in the kitchen, (2) group cooking may be messy but it's fun, and (3) the person who frosts the cake gets to lick the spoon.

GENDER SCHEMAS Another approach to gender socialization examines the role of children's unfolding cognitive abilities. As children mature, they develop a **gender schema,** a mental network of beliefs and expectations about what it means to be male or female (Bem, 1985, 1993; Fagot, 1985; Spence, 1985). Before you can have a gender schema, though, you have to be able to recognize that there are two genders—an ability that develops well before children can speak! By the age of only 9 months, most babies can discriminate male and female faces, even if they vary according to clothing, hairstyle, and facial expression (Fagot & Leinbach, 1993), and they can match female faces with female voices (Poulin-Dubois et al., 1994).

Once children acquire the ability to distinguish male and female, they soon label themselves as "boy" or "girl." And once they can do that, they begin to prefer same-sex playmates and sex-typed toys, without having been explicitly taught to do so. In her studies, Beverly Fagot (1993) found that 18-month-old boys and girls *did not differ* on several behavioral measures in which sex differences are often taken for granted: large motor activity (running, jumping, climbing), play with sex-typed toys (e.g., trucks for boys, dolls for girls), aggression, and verbal skills. Nine months later, at age 27 months, half of the children could correctly distinguish boys from girls on a test in which they had to assign gender labels to pictures of boys and girls, and men and

gender schema A cognitive schema (mental network) of knowledge, beliefs, metaphors, and expectations about what it means to be male or female.

GET INVOLVED

If you woke up tomorrow and found that you had been transformed into a member of the other sex, how would your life change, if at all? Would anything be different about your attitudes, behavior, habits, experiences, choices, preferences, and feelings? Write down your first reactions, and then ask a few of your male and female friends the same question. If possible, ask young children, too. Do their answers differ depending on their sex? If so, how? What does this exercise reveal about gender socialization?

women. That is, they had acquired a gender schema. These "early-labeling" children were now more sex-typed in their toy play and the other categories than were children who still could not consistently label males and females. Most notably, early-labeling girls showed less aggression than late-labeling girls. It was as if the girls were going along, behaving like the boys, until they knew they were girls. At that moment, but not until then, they seemed to decide: "Girls don't do this; I'm a girl; I'd better not either." The late-labeling children eventually caught up in their ability to distinguish males and females, and then their behavior, too, became more sex-typed.

The period between ages 2 and 4 is especially important for the development of gender schemas. Later, these schemas expand far beyond preferences for dolls or jungle gyms to include all sorts of meanings and associations (Fagot & Leinbach, 1993). Children between the ages of 4 and 7, for instance, will usually say that the following things are masculine: bears, fire, anger, the color black, spiky and angular shapes, dogs, and rough textures. Feminine things include butterflies, hearts, the color pink, flowers, cats, birds, rabbits, and soft textures. (Crayons, maple trees, cameras, and telephones are neutral.) Children at this age are learning the *metaphors of gender,* associating qualities such as strength or dangerousness with males, and gentler qualities with females. By age 5 all children can differentiate male from female solely on the basis of these qualities.

With increasing experience, knowledge, and cognitive sophistication, children construct their own standards of what boys and girls may or may not do. However, boys express stronger preferences for "masculine" toys and activities than girls do for "feminine" ones, and boys are harsher on themselves if they fail to behave in sex-typed ways (see Figure 13.4). One reason for this gender difference may be that masculine activities, occupations, and traits hold more value in society than feminine ones. So when boys behave like (or play with) girls, they lose status, and when girls behave like boys they gain status (Serbin, Powlishta, & Gulko, 1993). Indeed, preschoolers are already aware of gender differences in status. When asked to watch two furry rabbit puppets acting out a story, 4- and 5-year-olds thought the rabbit that was deferent, had its opinions overruled, and was less likely to have its advice followed was . . . a female (Ward, 1994).

As their abilities mature, children understand the exceptions to their gender schemas—for instance, that women can be engineers and men can be cooks. From middle childhood through adolescence, they become more flexible both about what they will be able to do as women or men, and about people who are nontraditional, especially if they have friends of the other sex and if their families or cultures encourage such flexibility (Katz & Ksansnak, 1994). But internalized beliefs about gender continue to have an effect throughout adulthood. When a man or a woman behaves in a way or takes a job that violates an observer's gender schema, the observer is often uncomfortable and reacts negatively (Eagly, Makhijani, & Klonsky, 1990). Gender schemas can and do change throughout our lives as they accommodate to new experiences, but they continue to influence us.

THE SPECIFIC SITUATION Although most people think of feminine and masculine qualities as being stable aspects of personality, boys and girls, like adult men and women, often behave in feminine ways *and* in masculine ways (Deaux & Major, 1990). Thus a fourth key influence on gender socialization is *social context.* Some situations, such as a date, evoke sex-typed behavior: Which partner pays? Who asks whom out? Who makes the sexual overtures? In other situations, such as working on an assembly line, gender is irrelevant, and sex-typed behavior disappears.

The effects of the situation on sex-typed behavior are apparent in early childhood. For example, boys and girls do not consistently differ in the traits of passivity or

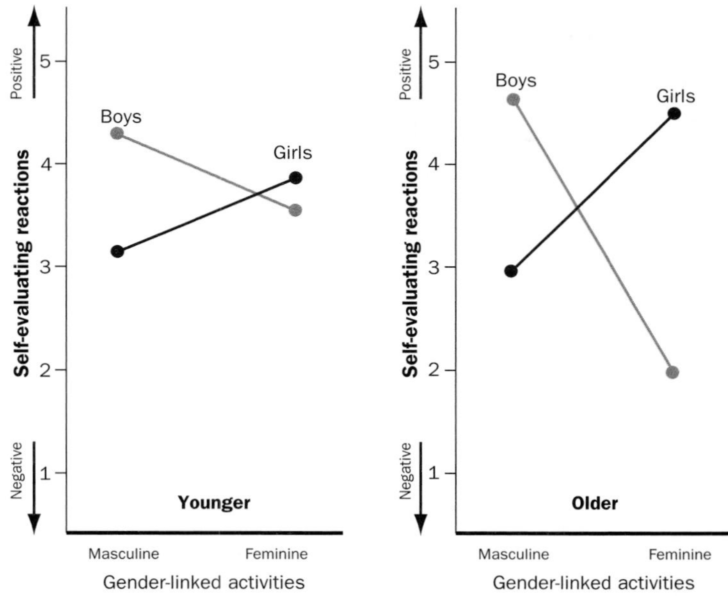

Figure 13.4
The Internalization of Gender Roles

In a study of sex-typing, 3-year-old children (left graph) did not expect to feel significantly different about themselves if they played with "masculine" or "feminine" toys. But 4-year-olds, especially boys (right graph), anticipated feeling much better about playing with toys associated with their own sex than those associated with the other sex. These self-evaluations accurately predicted which toys the children actually played with (Bussey & Bandura, 1992).

activity; *their behavior often depends on the sex of the child they are playing with* (Maccoby, 1990). Among preschoolers, girls are seldom passive with each other; however, when paired with boys, girls typically stand on the sidelines and let the boys monopolize the toys. The reason, it seems, is that when a boy and girl compete for a shared toy, the boy dominates—unless an adult is in the room. Girls in mixed classrooms may stay nearer to the teacher not because they are more dependent but because they want a chance at the toys! Girls play as independently as boys when they are in all-girl groups, and they will actually sit farther from the teacher than boys in all-boy groups do (Maccoby, 1990).

Because of the importance of situations in evoking or minimizing sex-typed behavior, gender differences in personality and behavior that are acquired in childhood do not necessarily last. Consider the fascinating results of a meta-analysis of 65 studies, involving more than 9,000 people, of gender differences in personality, moral reasoning, "maturity of thought," conformity, and other characteristics (Cohn, 1991). Differences were greatest among junior- and senior-high-school students, largely because girls mature earlier than boys. But most of these differences declined significantly among college-age adults, and disappeared entirely among older men and women. The reason, it seems, is that as people have new experiences, their behavior changes. This is why children can grow up in an extremely sex-typed family and, as adults, find themselves in careers or relationships they might never have imagined for themselves.

Quick Quiz

Are you socialized yet into the habit of taking quizzes?

1. A 7-year-old girl who is quiet and passive in class, but active and independent in her all-girl Brownie troop, illustrates which type of influence on gender development? (a) gender schemas, (b) subtle reinforcers, (c) social context, (d) biological factors
2. Which statement about gender schemas is *false?* (a) They are present in early form by 1 year of age; (b) they are permanent conceptualizations of what it means to be masculine or feminine; (c) they eventually expand to include metaphors associated with male and female.
3. Herb really wants to be a doctor, but he doesn't get into medical school. A friend suggests he become a nurse. "Yipes!" says Herb. "Real men aren't nurses." Herb (a) has a strong gender identity and is sex typed, (b) has a strong gender identity but isn't sex typed, (c) is strongly sex-typed but has a weak gender identity, (d) isn't sex typed and has a weak gender identity.

Answers:

1. c 2. b 3. a

MORAL DEVELOPMENT

Do you think it is morally acceptable to steal something you desperately need if you can't afford to pay for it? If you visited your lonely grandmother, but only because you hoped to inherit her estate, would your act be moral? If you could help a friend cheat on a test, would you do it? How would you feel about it? As these questions suggest, "morality" is a complex phenomenon involving empathy for others, the cognitive ability to evaluate moral dilemmas, the inner voice of conscience, and behaving in considerate and responsible ways (Kurtines & Gewirtz, 1995).

The study of moral development in children focuses on three areas: (1) how children make moral judgments (is stealing candy right or wrong?); (2) how children develop moral emotions (how will they feel if they steal that candy?); and (3) how children learn to behave morally (they may know it is wrong to steal, and even feel guilty if they do, but will they do it anyway?).

MORAL JUDGMENTS: REASONING ABOUT MORALITY

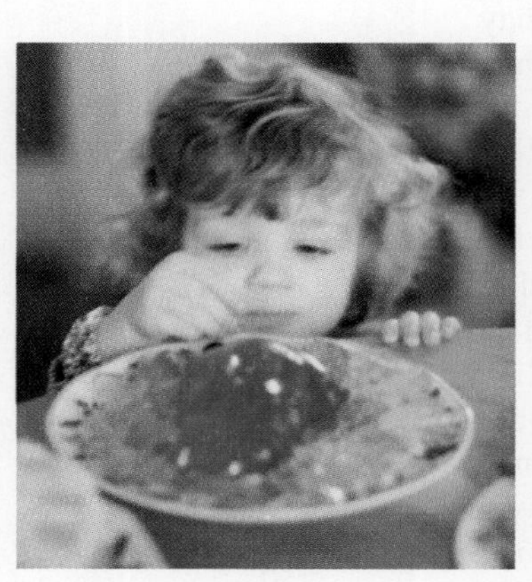

How do children learn to make moral judgments, resist temptation, and understand right from wrong?

Piaget (1932) was the first psychologist to divide the development of moral reasoning into stages. Children's moral reasoning, said Piaget, follows the increasing cognitive complexity of their reasoning in general. Young children, he said, see right and wrong in terms of results rather than intentions. They might tell you that a child who accidentally breaks two dishes is naughtier than a child who intentionally breaks one. They think that rules are set by a higher authority and are inflexible: You can't change the rules of a game, of family tradition, or of life. Not until about age 7, said Piaget, do children begin to understand that rules are social contracts that can be changed. Older children believe that good intentions, fair play, and reciprocity ("You do for me and I do for you") are the standards of moral action.

In the 1960s, Lawrence Kohlberg (1964, 1966) outlined his own theory of stages in moral reasoning, which became highly influential both for the research it generated and for its applications. Like Piaget, Kohlberg focused on moral reasoning, not on behavior. Your moral stage, said Kohlberg, can be determined by the answers you give to hypothetical moral dilemmas. For example, suppose a man's wife is dying and needs a special drug. The man can't afford the drug, and the druggist won't lower his price. Should the man steal the drug? What if he no longer loves his wife? If the man is caught, should the judge be lenient? Again, the reasoning behind the answers was more important than the decisions themselves.

Kohlberg (1964, 1976, 1984) proposed three levels of moral development, each divided into two stages. He believed that the stages were universal and occurred in invariant order; a person would not reach the highest stages, however, without having certain key experiences. At Kohlberg's first level, *preconventional morality*, young children obey rules early on because they fear being punished if they disobey (Stage 1), and later because they think it is in their best interest to obey (Stage 2). Stage 2 reasoning is also hedonistic, self-centered, and lacking in empathy; what is "right" is what feels good. At about ages 10 or 11, according to Kohlberg, children shift to the second level, the *conventional morality* of adult society. At Stage 3, conventional morality is based on trust, conformity, and loyalty to others; morality means "Don't hurt others; don't rock the boat." Most people then advance to Stage 4, a "law-and-order" orientation, based on understanding the social order, law, justice, and duty.

Late in adolescence and early adulthood, said Kohlberg, some people realize that some laws—such as those that segregate ethnic groups or that legitimize the systematic mistreatment of minorities—are themselves immoral. Such awareness moves them to the highest level, *postconventional ("principled") morality*. At Stage 5, they realize that values and laws are relative, that people hold different standards, that laws are important but can be changed. Kohlberg thought that only a few great individuals reach Stage 6, developing a moral standard based on universal human rights. When faced with a conflict between law and conscience, such people follow conscience, even at personal risk.

Hundreds of studies have been done, on samples all over the world, to test Kohlberg's theory (Eckensberger, 1994; Shweder, Mahapatra, & Miller, 1990; Snarey, 1985). The results show that Stages 5 and 6 are rare, but the others indeed develop sequentially in many cultures. Some developmental psychologists are persuaded therefore that children's moral reasoning does evolve according to Kohlberg's stages (Bee, 1997).

In the early 1980s, Carol Gilligan (1982) countered Kohlberg's theory of moral reasoning with one of her own. She argued that men tend to base their moral choices on abstract principles of law and justice, asking questions such as "Whose rights should take precedence here?" whereas women tend to base their moral decisions on principles of compassion and caring, asking questions such as "Who will be hurt least?" Some studies have supported Gilligan's view, finding that men care more about justice and women care more about caring (Bussey & Maughan, 1982; Gilligan & Wiggins, 1987; Walker, 1989). Most research, however, finds no gender differences, especially when people are allowed to rank *all* the reasons behind their moral judgments (Clopton & Sorell, 1993; Cohn, 1991; Friedman, Robinson, & Friedman, 1987; Thoma, 1986). Both sexes usually say that they base their moral decisions on compassion *and* on abstract principles of justice; they worry about feelings *and* fairness.

DON'T OVERSIMPLIFY

People go through stages of moral reasoning as their cognitive abilities mature. But is moral reasoning all there is to morality? Does it predict moral behavior? At what stage is a human-rights activist who treats his or her own family in a callous manner?

Kohlberg's and Gilligan's theories of moral reasoning have generated much research and animated discussion. Many people enjoy speculating about which stage they might be at and whether the sexes really differ in how they think about moral problems. Some psychologists, however, regard all stage theories of moral judgment as inherently limited, for three reasons:

1. *Stage theories tend to overlook cultural and educational influences on moral reasoning.* Many critics argue that Kohlberg's hierarchy of stages

reflects verbal ability and education, not moral judgment, and it ignores cultural differences (Shweder, Mahapatra, & Miller, 1990). In Iceland and Germany, for example, concern for others is far more important than the theory would predict among children supposedly at only the Stage 2 level; and because Stage 4 is heavily based on formal legal conceptions, unschooled members of many cultures do not achieve it (Eckensberger, 1994). College-educated people give "higher-level" explanations of moral decisions than people who have not attended college, but all that shows, say Kohlberg's critics, is that they are more verbally sophisticated.

Likewise, a child who thinks the judge should be lenient because the husband acted unselfishly will score lower than the adult who says "The judge should be lenient because he or she can find a precedent or rule that reflects what is right." As two critics note, in Kohlberg's system the cruelest lawyer could get a higher score than the kindest 8-year-old (Schulman & Mekler, 1994). And the fact that many people become more verbally skilled as they get older doesn't necessarily mean that their reasons for moral decisions really change. As Jerome Kagan (1993) has pointed out, a 7-year-old, when asked why he should not steal, will typically reply that he wants to avoid punishment, whereas a 15-year-old will typically say that the stability of society would be destroyed if everyone stole. Yet, says Kagan, fear of punishment is not the only reason that 7-year-olds don't steal; as we will see, very young children are capable of moral feelings and of behaving considerately. Conversely, adolescents are by no means indifferent to being punished by their parents or the police!

2. *People's moral reasoning is often inconsistent across situations.* Once people reach a higher stage, they don't necessarily stay there. On the contrary, in most people's lives moral reasoning depends on the situation and on what they are reasoning *about* (Bee, 1997; Wark & Krebs, 1996). You might show conventional morality by overlooking a racial slur at a dinner party because you don't want to upset everyone else, but reveal postconventional reasoning by protesting a governmental policy you regard as immoral. In one study in which 110 college students evaluated three of Kohlberg's moral dilemmas, 85 percent made judgments that spanned three to six substages, and only one young man based all his judgments on the same stage (Wark & Krebs, 1996). And in studies of Gilligan's theory, women *and* men tend to use "justice" reasoning when they are thinking about highly abstract ethical dilemmas, and "care" reasoning when they are thinking about intimate dilemmas in their own lives (Clopton & Sorell, 1993; Walker, deVries, & Trevethan, 1987).

People's moral behavior, like their moral reasoning skills, is also inconsistent: You might do something charitable out of sympathetic feelings one day, and not another; behave selflessly in one situation, and not another. Even those admirable people who reach Kohlberg's sixth stage are not consistent. Mohandas Gandhi, for example, reached the highest moral stage because of his commitment to universal principles of peace, justice, and nonviolence. But as Gandhi's biographers have pointed out, he was also aloof from his family and followers, whom he often treated in the harshest and most callous manner. Vietnam war hero John Vann performed astonishing feats of bravery during the war, time and again rescuing soldiers from certain death. Yet he was also an obsessive seducer who abandoned his wife and five children without supporting them, and he lied to avoid being court-martialed for seducing a 15-year-old girl (Sheehan, 1988).

3. *People's moral reasoning and their behavior are often unrelated.* The third and most important criticism of cognitive theories of moral development is that these theories do not predict whether people will actually *behave* in kind, fair, and responsible ways. People can know what is right and come up with all sorts of highfalutin rationalizations for not doing it. College students usually draw on "higher" levels—principles of justice and fair play—to justify moral decisions, yet about one-third of American and Canadian college men say they would force a woman into sexual acts if they could "get away with it" (Malamuth & Dean, 1990), an admission that reveals the lowest form of moral reasoning. Indeed, as Kagan (1993) observes, "Although the quality of moral reasoning increases dramatically from school entrance to high school graduation, so, too, do cheating and cruelty." But no one has proposed a stage theory of "immoral development," based on the child's increasing cognitive abilities to rationalize immoral acts!

MORAL EMOTIONS: ACQUIRING EMPATHY, GUILT, AND SHAME

A different approach to moral development concentrates on the emergence of conscience and the development of a "moral sense" based on empathy, shame, and guilt. The capacity for moral feeling, like that for language, seems to be inborn. As Kagan (1984) wrote, "Without this fundamental human capacity, which nineteenth-century observers called a *moral sense*, the child could not be socialized." The "moral sense" stems from children's attachment to their parents, which motivates them to adopt the parents' standards of good and bad behavior. Children shift from obeying rules for external reasons, such as fear of punishment, to obeying rules for internal reasons, because they will feel guilty or ashamed of behaving badly or disappointing the loved parent (Bandura, 1991).

The internalization of moral standards begins with *empathy*, the ability to feel bad about another person's unhappiness and to feel good about another's joy. Empathy is related to moral reasoning skills *and* to behaving in helpful and compassionate ways, starting in early childhood (Eisenberg et al., 1996). According to research by Martin Hoffman (1987, 1990), empathy takes different forms, depending on a child's age and cognitive abilities:

- *Global empathy.* In the first year, before they even have a sense of themselves as distinct from others, infants feel general distress at another person's misery. One 11-month-old girl in Hoffman's research, seeing an older child fall and cry, behaved as if she had been hurt. She looked about to cry, put her thumb in her mouth, and buried her head in her mother's lap.

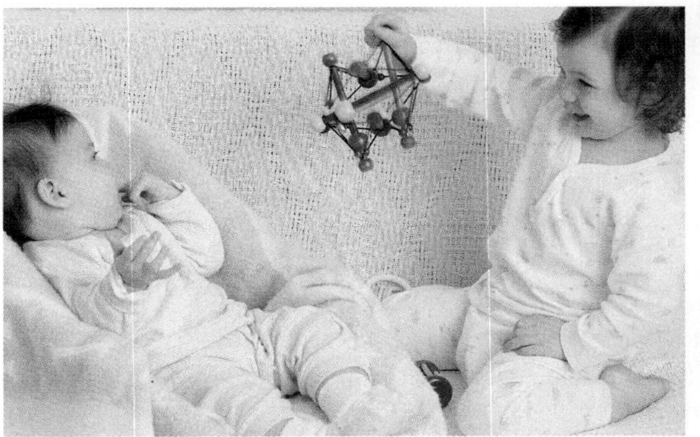

Children have an innate ability to form attachments, but experience determines whether they will develop empathy for or rivalry with others. In the photo on the left, 21-month-old Shifra happily offers a toy to her 4-month-old sister. A child who learns how to care for a new sibling, as in the photo on the right, is likely to acquire feelings of protectiveness and concern instead of rivalry.

- *Egocentric empathy.* As toddlers develop a sense of self (ages 1 to 2), they can understand that someone else is in distress and feel sad themselves when another child or adult is unhappy. In one touching instance Hoffman described, a 13-month-old child offered her own beloved doll to a sad adult. However, children at this stage still assume that other people always feel as they do.
- *Empathy for another's feelings.* By the age of 2 or 3, children are capable of understanding that another person has feelings that are different from their own. They can empathize with another child's feelings of shame without feeling ashamed themselves. They know when another child is sad and wants to be left alone. They are able to feel angry on someone else's behalf. One little boy, seeing a doctor give another child a painful injection, swatted the doctor in protest.
- *Empathy for another's life condition.* In late childhood, many children are able to feel empathy toward whole groups of individuals who are less fortunate than they.

Although people might like to have a life without shame or guilt, these emotions, too, are essential to the emotional underpinnings of morality. They help maintain rules and standards, and they encourage moral action. *Shame* is a wound to the self-concept. It comes from perceiving that others have seen you doing something wrong and that they will like you less for having done it. As soon as the toddler has a sense of self, shame is quick to follow (Lewis, 1992). *Guilt,* in contrast, is the emotion you feel when you have not lived up to your own internal standard of behavior; it is remorse for real or imagined wrongdoings, a kind of self-inflicted punishment. Of course, guilt can also be maladaptive and self-defeating. Children who live with a chronically depressed or deeply troubled parent, for example, often develop unhealthy patterns of empathy and guilt, a result of having an unrealistic feeling that they are somehow responsible for the parent's misery (Zahn-Waxler et al., 1990).

By the age of 2, children are aware of standards of behavior, and at this tender age they react with anxious concern or distress when a standard has been violated. By the age of 3 or 4, children associate a bad act with being a "bad boy" or "bad girl," and they begin to regulate their own behavior. In all cultures, children now judge their thoughts, feelings, and behavior against the standards they know are right (Edwards, 1987; Kagan, 1994). In turn, adults treat children differently, expecting them to do the right thing.

MORAL ACTION: LEARNING TO BEHAVE MORALLY

Unfortunately, moral reasoning and emotions are not always related to moral behavior. "We can reach high levels of moral reasoning," said Thomas Lickona (1983), "and still behave like scoundrels." And we can feel really miserable about treating each other horribly, and do it anyway. In Chapter 17 we will look at some social forces, such as conformity and obedience, that affect moral behavior. Here we want to consider how children become helpful members of society. How do they learn to avoid the temptations to steal, lie, cheat, and otherwise behave as they might like to?

Learning theorists answer that children's moral actions depend on the rewards, punishments, and examples they get as they grow up. When children are rewarded for aggressive, selfish, and competitive acts, such behavior will prevail over cooperation and altruism. Children also learn about moral behavior by observing the behavior of public figures—what they do, and what they "get away with." Does a person commit an illegal act and then earn a fortune from movie deals? Does a sports hero get away with cheating because it helped the team win?

Although role models and cultural norms set standards for the moral behaviors a culture values, children also learn as much from how their parents interact with them as from the content of their parents' lessons. When you did something wrong as a child, for example, what did the adults in your family do about it? Did they shout at you, punish you, or explain the error of your ways?

One of the most common methods that parents use to enforce standards is **power assertion,** which includes threats, physical punishment, depriving the child of privileges, and generally taking advantage of being bigger, stronger, and more powerful ("Do it because I say so"). Yet power assertion, which is based on the child's fear of punishment, is associated with a lack of moral feeling and behavior in children; as we saw in Chapter 7, fear of punishment often interferes with learning self-control and internalizing values.

But perhaps aggressive children are simply hard to discipline consistently, so the parent must respond with efforts to assert power. For years, Gerald Patterson and his colleagues have been conducting longitudinal and observational studies of parents and children, often in the family's home, to try to separate the causes and effects of parental practices (Patterson, 1994; Patterson, DeBaryshe, & Ramsey, 1989; Patterson, Reid, & Dishion, 1992). Parents of aggressive children use a great deal of punishment (shouting, scolding, spanking), yet they fail to clearly connect the punishment with the child's behavior. They do not state clear rules, require compliance, consistently punish violations, or praise good behavior. Instead, they nag and shout at the child, occasionally and unpredictably tossing in a slap or a loss of privileges. This combination of power assertion with a pattern of intermittent discipline causes the children's aggressiveness to increase and eventually get out of hand. The child becomes withdrawn, manipulative, and difficult to control, which causes the parents to try to assert their power even more forcefully, which makes the child angrier . . . and a vicious cycle is generated.

Child-rearing practices based on power assertion have been linked to a wide variety of negative outcomes for children's moral behavior (Eisenberg & Murphy, 1995; Hoffman, 1994). In a study of male delinquency, for example, the factors that predicted which boys would avoid a life of crime included consistent discipline, parental affection, a low level of aggressiveness in the father, restrictions on the son's behavior, and high parental standards and expectations (McCord, 1990). In the families that scored below the median on these factors, 58 percent of the sons eventually went on to commit serious crimes, compared to only 15 percent of those who came from families above the median.

In contrast to power assertion, a far more successful method for teaching moral behavior is **induction,** in which the parent appeals to the child's own resources, helpful nature, affection for others, and sense of responsibility. For example, a mother will explain to her child that the child's actions would harm, inconvenience, or disappoint another person ("You made Doug cry; it's not nice to bite," or "You must never poke anyone's eyes because that could hurt them seriously"). Or the parent will appeal to the child's own helpful inclinations ("I know you're a person who likes to be good to others"), which is far more effective than using external reasons to be good ("Do this to please me" or "You'd better be nice or you won't get dessert") (Eisenberg, 1995). Induction tends to produce children who behave morally on five different measures. They feel guilty if they hurt others; they internalize standards of right and wrong, instead of simply following orders; they confess rather than lie if they misbehave; they accept responsibility for their misbehavior; and they are considerate of others (Hoffman & Saltzstein, 1967; Radke-Yarrow, Zahn-Waxler, & Chapman, 1983).

power assertion A method of child rearing in which the parent uses punishment and authority to correct the child's misbehavior.

induction A method of child rearing in which the parent appeals to the child's own resources, abilities, sense of responsibility, and feelings for others in correcting the child's misbehavior.

Power Assertion

Parent uses threats, physical force, or other kinds of power to get child to obey.

Example:
"Do it because I say so"; "Stop that right now."

Result:
Child obeys, but only when parent is present; child often feels resentful.

Induction

Parent appeals to child's good nature, empathy, love of parent, and sense of responsibility to others; offers *explanation* of rules.

Example:
"You're too grown-up to behave like that"; "Fighting hurts your little brother."

Result:
Child tends to internalize reasons for good behavior.

In a program of research spanning three decades, Diana Baumrind (1966, 1971, 1973, 1989, 1991), expanding on the concepts of induction and power assertion, has identified three overall styles of child rearing and their results:

1. *Authoritarian* parents exercise too much power and give too little nurturance. Communication is all one way: The parent issues orders ("Stop that!" "Do it because I say so!"), and the child is expected to listen and obey. The children of these parents tend to be less socially skilled than other children, have lower self-esteem, and do more poorly in school. Some are overly timid, and others are overly aggressive.

2. *Permissive* parents are nurturant, but they exercise too little control and don't make strong demands for mature and responsible behavior on the part of their children. They fail to state rules clearly and consistently, and they have poor communication with their kids. Their children, compared with the offspring of other kinds of parents, are likely to be impulsive, immature, irresponsible, and academically unmotivated.

3. *Authoritative* parents travel a middle road, knowing when and how to discipline their children. They set high but reasonable expectations and teach their children how to meet them. They also give their children emotional support and encourage two-way communication; they use induction. Their children tend to have good self-control, high self-esteem, and high self-efficacy; to be independent yet cooperative; to do better than average in school; and to be socially mature, cheerful, thoughtful, and helpful.

Parental techniques, however, can have different results in different social and economic contexts. A parent may seem harsh and "authoritarian" in an impoverished or dangerous community, but the child may interpret the parent's behavior as evidence of love and concern (Baumrind, 1991). And some parents may become "authoritarian" because they are dealing with a difficult child whose temperament is aggressive and antisocial from the outset (Henry et al., 1996). So the parent's methods of discipline always interact with the child's temperament, cognitive abilities (such

In many cultures, children are expected to contribute to the family income and to take care of their younger siblings. These experiences encourage helpfulness and empathy.

as an understanding of rules and another person's feelings), and perceptions of the parent's intentions (Fabes et al., 1994; Grusec & Goodnow, 1994). (We discuss methods of child rearing further in "Taking Psychology with You.")

Ultimately, the greatest influence on children's moral behavior is what others expect of them (Eisenberg, 1995). In a cross-cultural study of children in Kenya, India, Mexico, Okinawa, the Philippines, and the United States, Beatrice and John Whiting (1975) measured how often children behaved altruistically (offering help, support, or unselfish suggestions) or egoistically (seeking help and attention or wanting to dominate others). This research was later reanalyzed, and five new cultures were added to it (Whiting & Edwards, 1988). American children were the least altruistic on all three measures and the most egoistic. Altruistic children come from societies in which children are assigned many tasks, such as caring for younger children and gathering and preparing food. The children know that their work makes a genuine contribution to the well-being or economic survival of the family. Mothers have many responsibilities inside and outside the home, and children respect the parents' authority to set rules and limits.

In summary, in accounting for how children learn to become (or fail to become) kind, helpful, and responsible members of society, developmental psychologists direct us to four factors: (1) the importance of children's emerging cognitive capacities to evaluate complex moral issues; (2) the moral emotions of empathy, shame, and guilt; (3) the styles of child rearing that foster or inhibit moral standards and behavior; and (4) the behavior that is expected and required of children in everyday situations.

Quick Quiz

To raise children who are kind and helpful, parents and parents-to-be should be able to answer the following questions.

1. LaVerne, age 14 months, feels sad when she sees her mother crying during a tear-jerker, and she starts to cry too. LaVerne has developed (a) global empathy, (b) egocentric empathy, (c) empathy for another's feelings.

2. Shame and guilt are (a) unconscious emotions in infancy, (b) necessary in internalizing moral standards, (c) destructive emotions that should be stamped out as soon as possible.
3. Which method of parental discipline tends to create children who have internalized values of helpfulness and empathy? (a) induction, (b) punishment, (c) power assertion
4. Which form of family life tends to create helpful children? (a) Every family member "does his or her own thing," (b) parents insist that children obey, (c) children contribute to the family welfare, (d) parents remind children often about the importance of being helpful.

5. In Chapter 12 you read that the Big Five personality traits have a genetic component, are resistant to change, and emerge almost regardless of what parents do. Now here we are offering evidence that what parents do often does make a difference. How might these two lines of research be reconciled?

Answers:

1. b 2. b 3. a 4. c 5. We can avoid either–or thinking by asking which qualities may be due largely to temperament (such as extroversion) and which are strongly affected by parental lessons (such as aggressiveness and empathy). Also, how a child turns out depends on the interactions between a child's temperament and the parents' reactions. And perhaps the relative impact of temperament and parental techniques changes as the child matures.

ADOLESCENCE

Adolescence refers to the period of development between **puberty,** the age at which a person becomes capable of sexual reproduction, and adulthood. In some cultures, the time span between puberty and adulthood is only a few months; a sexually mature boy or girl is expected to marry and assume adult tasks. In modern Western societies, adolescence lasts several years. Teenagers are not considered emotionally mature enough to be full-fledged adults with all the rights, responsibilities, and roles of adulthood. The long span of adolescence is new to this century. In the past, societies needed the labor of young people and could not afford to have them spend a decade in school or in "self-discovery."

THE PHYSIOLOGY OF ADOLESCENCE

Until puberty, boys and girls produce roughly the same amount of male hormones (androgens) and female hormones (estrogens). At puberty, the pituitary gland begins to stimulate hormone production in the adrenal and other endocrine glands and in the reproductive glands. In boys, the reproductive glands are the testes (testicles), which produce sperm; in girls, the reproductive glands are the ovaries, which release eggs, or ova. Now boys have a higher level of androgens than girls do, and girls have a higher level of estrogens than boys do.

During puberty, the sex organs mature and the individual becomes capable of reproduction. In girls, the onset of menstruation, called **menarche,** and the development of breasts are signs of sexual maturity. In boys, the signs are the onset of nocturnal emissions and the growth of the testes, scrotum, and penis. Hormones are also responsible for the emergence of *secondary sex characteristics,* such as a deepened voice and facial and chest hair in boys and pubic hair in both sexes.

puberty The age at which a person becomes capable of sexual reproduction.

menarche [men-ARE-kee] The onset of menstruation.

The dramatic physical changes of puberty are part of the last "growth spurt" on the child's road to adulthood. For girls, the adolescent growth spurt begins, on the average, at age 10, peaks at 12 or 13, and stops at about age 16, by which time most girls are sexually mature. For boys, the average adolescent growth spurt starts at about age 12 and ends at about age 18. This difference in the rates of development is often a source of misery to adolescents, for most girls mature sooner than most boys.

The timing of the changes of puberty depends on both genetic and environmental factors. The onset of menarche, for example, can be affected by nutrition, stress, and exercise; indeed, better nutrition may be one reason that the average age of menarche has been declining in Europe and North America for the past 150 years. The onset of puberty seems to be occurring earlier for males, too. Decades ago, the average American man did not reach his maximum height until the age of 26; today this marker of the end of puberty occurs, on the average, at age 18 (Cole & Cole, 1993).

Individuals vary enormously, however, in the onset and length of puberty. Some girls first menstruate as early as age 8 and others as late as 16. One 15-year-old male may be as developed as an adult man and another may still be a boy. In addition, mischievous nature has made growth a jumpy, irregular business, with different parts of the body maturing at different rates. A girl may have undeveloped breasts but adult-sized hands and feet. A boy may be tall and gangly but have no trace of a longed-for beard. Eventually, everything catches up.

Children typically reach puberty at different times, often to their embarrassment. These girls are all the same age, but they differ considerably in physical maturity.

If you entered puberty before most of your classmates, or if you matured much later than they did, you know that your experience of adolescence was different from that of the average teenager (whoever that is). Some psychologists believe that the *timing* of puberty is more important in an adolescent's development than the specific biological events themselves. Early-maturing boys generally have a more positive view of their bodies, and their relatively greater size and strength gives them a boost in sports and the prestige that being a good athlete brings young men. But they are also more likely to smoke, drink, use drugs, and break the law than later-maturing boys, and to have less self-control and emotional stability (Duncan et al., 1985). Late-developing boys feel the worst about themselves in the seventh grade, but by the twelfth grade they usually end up as the healthiest group (Petersen, 1989).

Likewise, some early-maturing girls have the prestige of being socially popular, but, partly because others regard them as being sexually precocious, they are also more likely to have conflict with their parents, have behavioral problems, drop out of school, have a negative body image, and have emotional problems (Caspi & Moffitt, 1991; Stattin & Magnusson, 1990). Girls who go through puberty relatively late, in contrast, have a more difficult time at first, but by the end of adolescence many are happier with their appearance and more popular than their early-maturing classmates.

A longitudinal study of 501 girls in New Zealand found that girls who entered menarche before the age of 12 subsequently had the most problems (Caspi & Moffitt, 1991). Because the researchers had been observing these teenagers since childhood, however, they were able to show that early menarche itself wasn't the problem; rather, it tended to accentuate the *existing* behavioral problems and family conflicts the girls had had in childhood. The group with the most troubles throughout adolescence were early maturers who had a history of behavioral problems in childhood.

During times of transition—whether a biological change such as puberty or a social change such as starting college—existing personality traits and problems are magnified. Biological changes alone, even the hormonal changes of adolescence, do not produce the same psychological consequences for everyone (Eccles et al., 1993; Jessor, 1993).

THE PSYCHOLOGY OF ADOLESCENCE

Recently we came across a high-school textbook on adolescence that painted the bleakest picture of teenage life we've ever seen. To be an adolescent, according to this book, is to suffer depression, anxiety, insecurity, horrible fights with parents, loneliness, identity conflicts, and all-around misery. Reading this book, you wouldn't have a clue that teenagers ever felt good about themselves, held jobs, did well in school, had friends, or got along with their parents.

It is certainly true that adolescence can be difficult for teenagers, who must learn the rules of adult sexuality, morality, work, and family. Teenagers are beginning to develop their own standards and values, and often they do so by trying on the styles, actions, and attitudes of their peers, in contrast to those of their parents. They are questioning adult life, even as they are rehearsing for it. For some teenagers, these changes can feel overwhelming and can lead to loneliness, depression, and anxiety. Some succumb to psychological problems typical of their gender as they struggle to fit their peers' and society's views of masculinity or femininity: In adolescence, "externalizing" problems (such as aggression and other antisocial behavior) become substantially higher in boys than in girls, and "internalizing" problems (such as depression and eating disorders) become higher in girls than in boys (Zahn-Waxler, 1996). For adolescent males, rates of suicide are a serious, growing problem in North America and Europe (Garland & Zigler, 1994).

EXAMINE THE EVIDENCE

Rebellious-teenager movies and studies of troubled teens depict adolescence as a time of turmoil and misery, conflict and hostility toward parents, and a desire for separation. What is missing from this portrait of adolescence?

Yet among representative samples of teenagers, extreme turmoil and unhappiness are the exception, not the rule; they are not an inevitable part of adolescence (Bee, 1997; Offer & Sabshin, 1984; Steinberg, 1990). Most teenagers have supportive families, a sense of purpose and self-confidence, good friends, and the skill to cope with their problems. Others have a bumpier ride, having suffered parental divorce, the death of a close relative, or serious illness. But only a minority conform to the stereotype of the troubled, angry, unhappy adolescent.

Nevertheless, the transition for teenagers from childhood to adulthood is sometimes filled with conflicts and misunderstandings with adults, often over the adoles-

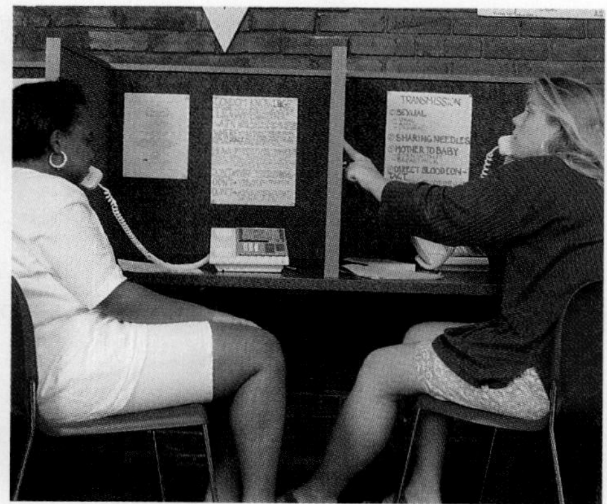

The Varieties of Adolescence

The stereotype of adolescence emphasizes teenage turmoil and rebellion (left). But most teens feel good about themselves and their communities, as do these students volunteering at an AIDS hot line service (center), and many hold jobs to earn income (right).

cent's increased desire for autonomy. The Michigan Study of Adolescent Life Transitions followed some 1,500 adolescents as they moved from the sixth grade (elementary school) to the seventh (junior high). The preteens whose motivation dwindled and misconduct increased were reacting to specific changes in their environments: Their teachers were no longer encouraging active classroom participation and decision making as they had in elementary school, but used rote learning instead; and their parents, perhaps worried about their maturing children's sexuality and possible drug use, were using increasingly punitive measures of controlling them. Thus, the researchers conclude, just when adolescents want more say in making their own rules, and just when their cognitive abilities are maturing to enable them to do more complex academic tasks and make personal decisions, some teachers and parents are stifling these needs. When adolescents are given a say in family decisions and in classroom activities, they feel better about themselves and are more enthusiastic about their schoolwork (Eccles et al., 1993).

A need for autonomy, however, doesn't mean total separation from or rejection of the parent. Early theories of adolescent development assumed that a child who did not separate sufficiently, who maintained a close bond with the parents, was "immature." This idea ignored the pattern that is common in most cultures: continued love and connection between child and parent. Today it is clear that two meanings of separation had been confused: *individuation,* the process of becoming a distinct individual with your own values and needs; and a complete *rift,* a severing of affection and an effort to replace the parent with other mentors (Apter, 1990).

When teenagers have conflicts with their parents, the reason is usually to "individuate," to develop their own opinions and values, rather than to sever the connection. In one major study, adolescents listed complaints like these: "Why my mother manipulates the conversation to get me to hate her"; "How much of a bastard my father is to my sister"; "How ugly my mom's taste is"; "How pig-headed my mom and dad are" (Csikszentmihalyi & Larson, 1984). But these fights—over what is important, who should set the rules, differences of opinion and taste, and the like—rarely reflected a true rift between parent and adolescent. Likewise, in a study of 65 ethnically diverse mother–daughter pairs in Britain and the United States, Terri Apter (1990) found that most of the teenage girls said the person they felt closest to, who offered them the greatest support, was their mother. They had plenty of quarrels with her—over clothes, school, chores—but these were, said Apter, "little puff balls" that did not indicate a serious break in the relationship, but an effort to get the mother to *understand.* For young men and women in Western societies, the familiar quarrels they have with their parents tend to signify a change from one-sided parental authority to a more reciprocal, adult relationship (Laursen & Collins, 1994; Steinberg, 1990).

Quick Quiz

If you're not feeling rebellious, try these questions.

1. The onset of menstruation is called ___________.
2. In boys, a deepening voice and a new mustache are examples of ___________.

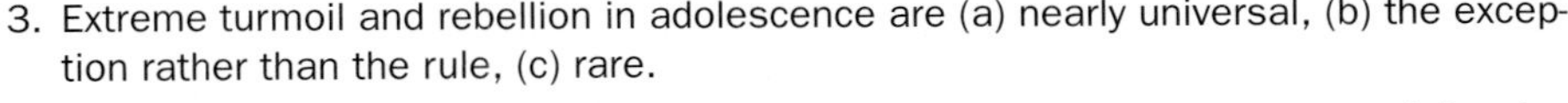

3. Extreme turmoil and rebellion in adolescence are (a) nearly universal, (b) the exception rather than the rule, (c) rare.

4. A TV reporter asserts that teenagers must separate from their parents and develop independent selves. What assumption is implicit in this claim, and can it be challenged? What are some possible definitions of "separation"?

Answers:

1. menarche 2. secondary sex characteristics 3. b 4. The reporter assumes that independence from parents is normal, universal, and good. But many people hold other values, such as continued attachment to family and respect for elders. The reporter also assumes that it is always economically feasible for adolescents to break away from their families; this is not always so. Finally, it is important to define terms: Does separation mean a complete severing of connection, putting yourself first, or developing your own identity and wishes?

ADULTHOOD

According to ancient Greek legend, the Sphinx was a monster—half lion, half woman—who terrorized passersby on the road to Thebes. The Sphinx would ask each traveler a question and then murder those who failed to answer correctly. (The Sphinx was a pretty tough grader.) The question was this: What animal walks on four feet in the morning, two feet at noon, and three feet in the evening? Only one traveler, Oedipus, knew the solution to the riddle. The animal, he said, is Man, who crawls on all fours as a baby, walks upright as an adult, and limps in old age with the aid of a staff.

The Sphinx was the first life-span theorist. Since then, many philosophers, writers, and scientists have speculated on the course of adult life, expanding the Sphinx's three stages into seven, eight, or ten. The idea of stages is terrifically appealing. Everyone can see that children go through stages of physical and mental maturation, so people have assumed that adults go through stages too. But do they? In this section, we will consider this question, as we examine the biological and psychological influences on adult development.

THE BIOLOGICAL CLOCK

The biology of aging affects people all through life, as a 27-year-old "aging" tennis champion can tell you. For most people, though, after puberty the next significant chiming of the biological clock rings at midlife, when women go through the allegedly traumatic experience of menopause and men are said to go through the emotional equivalent, a "midlife crisis." And many people believe that the older you get, the more you lose, biologically speaking—your memory, your brain cells, your intelligence. Let's examine the scientific evidence for these ideas.

MENOPAUSE AND MIDLIFE **Menopause** is the midlife cessation of menstruation, which is brought on when the ovaries stop producing estrogen and progesterone. Many people think that the typical menopausal woman suffers from a "syndrome" or "deficiency disease" that makes her depressed, irritable, and irrational. (One student asked us if it was like "being in a constant state of PMS"—which is certainly what the media often imply!)

Menopause does produce physical symptoms in many women, notably "hot flashes," as the vascular system adjusts to the decrease in estrogen. But only about 10 percent of all women have severe physical symptoms. The negative view of menopause as a syndrome that causes depression and other emotional reactions is based on women who have had an early menopause following a hysterectomy (removal of the uterus) or who have had a lifetime history of depression. But these women are not typical. In a large survey of more than 8,000 healthy, randomly chosen women, most viewed menopause positively (with relief that they no longer had to worry about pregnancy or menstrual periods) or with no particular feelings at all. Only 3 percent reported regret at having reached menopause. The vast majority had only a

menopause The cessation of menstruation and of the production of ova; usually a gradual process lasting up to several years.

few "temporarily bothersome symptoms" and did not suffer from depression. In short, most women said that menopause is no big deal (McKinlay, McKinlay, & Brambilla, 1987). Other large-scale studies of normal populations have confirmed that menopause itself has no effect on most women's mental and emotional health (Matthews et al., 1990). In fact, the women who have the most positive attitudes toward menopause are the women who have been through it (Gannon & Ekstrom, 1993).

Moreover, for most educated women, the midlife years are the best and happiest. American women in their 50s today are more likely than those in any other age group to describe their lives as being "first-rate" and to report having a high quality of life (Mitchell & Helson, 1990). They tend to have higher incomes than women in other age groups; their children are grown and launched; and they are more likely than other women to have struck a balance between their needs for intimacy and for autonomy—feeling close to others yet also in charge of their lives.

What about men? Although testosterone does seem to peak during adolescence, men lack a biological equivalent to menopause: Testosterone never drops as sharply in men as estrogen does in women, and men do not lose their fertility, although their sperm count may slowly decline. For both sexes, the physical changes of midlife and the biological fact of aging do not predict how people will feel about aging or how they will respond to it (Ryff & Keyes, 1995). Whether a man or a woman will have a "midlife crisis" has little to do with their hormones and more to do with how satisfied they are with their lives.

THE COMING OF AGE What does it mean to be old? The popular image is of a person who is forgetful, somewhat senile, and physically and mentally feeble. On television and in the movies, old people are usually portrayed as objects of amusement, sympathy, or scorn. But *gerontologists*—people who study aging and the old—have been challenging these stereotypes. By distinguishing the processes that are part of normal aging from those due to preventable conditions, they have dramatically changed our understanding of old age, in these ways:

CONSIDER OTHER EXPLANATIONS

For many years, people assumed that aging inevitably produced senility, brittle bones, forgetfulness, loss of skills, and a decline in mental abilities. What other explanations for these aspects of old age are possible?

1. *The definition of "old" has gotten older.* Not long ago, you would have been considered old in your 60s. Today the fastest-growing segment of the population in North America consists of people over the age of 85, and many of them are doing fine. So "old age" is no longer just a matter of chronological years, but of how well a person is able to function. The fact that people are living longer and better, however, raises crucial ethical and legal concerns about death—in particular, how and when to draw the line between death that is inevitable, and death that can be delayed with technological interventions (see "Puzzles of Psychology").

2. *Aging has been separated from illness.* People used to think that all bodily functions declined with age. Some conditions, such as osteoporosis (having extremely brittle bones) or senility (the loss of mental abilities), were assumed to be inevitable. Today we know that many such conditions are a result of malnutrition, overmedication, disease, or cellular damage from too much sun. For example, an alarmingly

GET INVOLVED

Ask five people—each about a decade apart in age, and one of whom is at least 70—how old they feel. (You may include yourself.) What is the gap, if any, between their chronological age and their psychological age? Is the gap larger among the oldest individuals? Ask them why they perceive an "age gap" between their actual years and how old they feel.

high number of older people are given too many drugs for different problems, and the combination can cause confusion, senility, or even psychosis. So can over-the-counter drugs, such as sleeping pills and antihistimines.

3. *The biology of aging has been separated from its psychology.* Many problems once thought to be an inherent part of aging are actually a result of social losses, not physical ones—the loss of loved ones, close friends, meaningful activity, intellectual stimulation, and control over what happens to you (Langer, 1989; Schaie, 1994). Imagine that you are taken from your home, your friends, and your work, and put in a residence where you know no one and have nothing to do. Your relatives live too far away to visit. You aren't allowed to make decisions, decorate your room, keep a pet, have a lover, or choose your food. What would happen to you? Probably you would become depressed, bored, and forgetful. You would become, in a word, "old."

At the same time, researchers are hot on the trail of genes that might be involved in some of the physical deterioration of old age. Recently they found the gene for Werner's syndrome, a rare inherited disorder that causes its victims to age prematurely (Yu et al., 1996). Werner's sufferers develop cataracts, wrinkled skin, and thin bones in their 20s, and most die from heart attacks or cancer in their 40s. Although it is unlikely that this gene or any other is solely responsible for the normal aging process, this discovery may lead to an understanding of the cellular changes that bring on age-related changes and diseases.

4. *The benefits of aging have been recognized.* Aging often brings wisdom, tolerance, and maturity (Baltes & Graf, 1996). In societies that value youth and the new, it is easy to overlook the value of experience and the traditional.

The picture of old age that emerges from research is not entirely positive, of course; some aspects of intelligence, memory, and other forms of mental functioning do decline (Craik & Salthouse, 1992). As people age, it takes them longer to retrieve names, dates, and other facts, such as who starred with Humphrey Bogart in *Casablanca.* And, on average, older adults score lower on tests of reasoning and complex problem solving than do younger adults. But gerontologists disagree about exactly which cognitive abilities decline with age, and what the reasons for this decline might be.

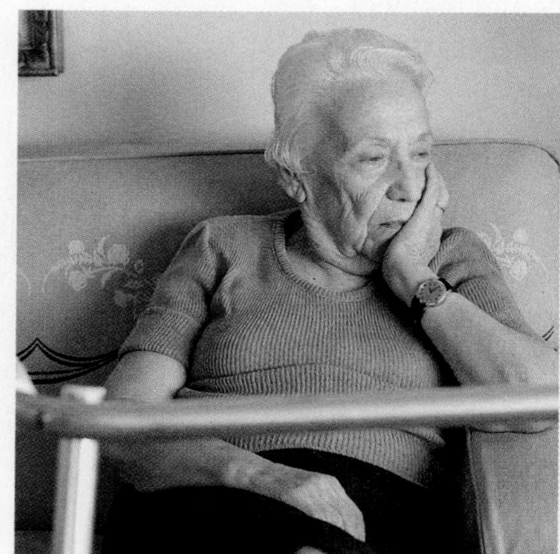

The Varieties of Old Age

Stereotypes about older people are breaking down as more and more people are living longer, healthier lives. Some people in their 80s are ailing and infirm, or suffering from Alzheimer's disease (left). But most are healthy and active (center), and some are exceptionally energetic and strong (right).

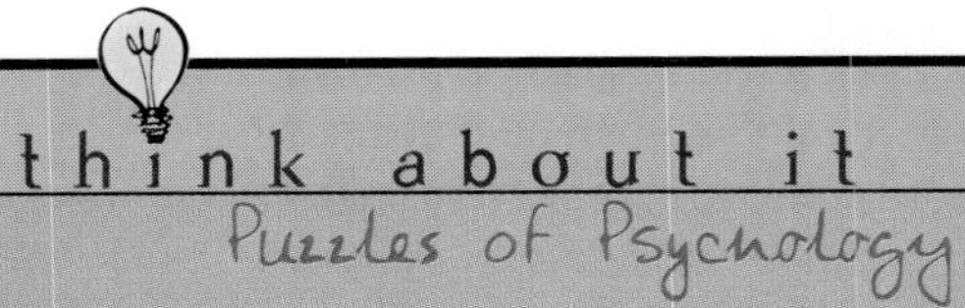

How Long Should We Prolong Life?

• In a medical journal, physician Timothy Quill revealed that he had helped a dying leukemia patient to commit suicide, which was her carefully considered wish. A grand jury in New York was summoned to determine whether to indict Quill for his role in his patient's death. They decided not to.

• A 76-year-old Florida man shot and killed his beloved wife who was dying of Alzheimer's disease. He was convicted of first-degree murder.

• In 1994, Oregon became the first state to permit doctors to help terminally ill patients, or patients living in chronic unendurable pain, to end their lives—but the following year the law was overturned by a federal judge. In Michigan, Dr. Jack Kevorkian has been tried three times for helping terminal patients die, and thus far has won acquittal each time.

When is it time to "pull the plug," and who decides? As these conflicting examples illustrate, North America is extremely divided about *euthanasia,* the act of painlessly putting to death someone who is suffering an incurable and agonizing disease. (Euthanasia means "easy death"—from the Greek *eu,* "good" or "well," as in euphoria; and *thanatos,* "death.") Some people think it is humane and merciful to help a person who is dying in pain to end life quickly. Others fear that such license will be abused—for example, that it will open the door to the unnecessary deaths of people who are not dying, but who are depressed, disabled, or a financial burden to their families.

Some people who reject *active* euthanasia—intentionally doing something to end a sufferer's life, as Dr. Kevorkian does—accept the idea of *passive* euthanasia, allowing a person to die by forgoing medical measures, such as intravenous feeding, that might keep the person alive. But doctors, lawyers, families, and clergy often disagree with each other on the right time to let an ailing person die. Doctors, trained to prolong life, often want to keep the dying person alive as long as possible, even when that goal produces pain and suffering. They also fear malpractice suits if they let someone die who the family thinks could have lived longer. Religious groups differ too. Some believe that death is natural and inevitable and that doctors should not interfere with its course. Others believe that death is to be fought with all the weapons of modern medicine.

Because of the ongoing and emotional controversy about this matter, medical ethicists and consumer advocates recommend that people sign an *advance directive* that specifies their wishes about the use of heroic measures to keep them alive. (The sad cases of young accident victims living in comas for many years, while their lovers, families, and doctors fight over who gets to decide what should happen to them, are a reminder that everyone should do this, regardless of age.) A "living will" specifies your wishes about being kept alive if you are permanently unconscious or terminally ill. A "durable power of attorney for health care" gives a person you designate the power to make this decision for you, not only if you are permanently unconscious or dying but also if you become mentally incapacitated.

Societies must also struggle with the question of who will care for people who are dying of protracted illnesses, such as Alzheimer's disease, AIDS, or cancer, which can last months or even years. Hospitals are often cold institutions that deprive a dying person of dignity and individuality, the company of friends and family, and choices about life-prolonging techniques. One alternative is the *hospice,* a center for the dying person and his or her family. Hospices offer the medical care of hospitals, but they are homier, allow families to live with the patient, and help the patient die with little pain. Some hospice services are provided in the patient's home.

Concerns about the high costs of life-sustaining equipment, long-term hospital or hospice care, and organ transplants complicate these questions. Who should pay for expensive new technologies? Families? Taxpayers? Insurance companies? If someone else can afford an organ transplant and you can't, should that person be allowed to live and you to die?

These issues reflect one abiding philosophical question: How much control do we have over illness and death, and when is it time to let go? Is the Western belief in fighting sad but inevitable events such as death beneficial or harmful? In *What Kind of Life: The Limits of Medical Progress,* Daniel Callahan (1989) argued that Americans must curb their insatiable appetite for a longer life. They should, he says, be "creatively and honorably accepting aging and death, not struggling to overcome them." Do you agree? Should a society set limits on efforts to extend life? Think about it.

In terms of the intellectual abilities and knowledge measured over the life span, "intelligence" generally takes two forms: *fluid intelligence*, the capacity for deductive reasoning and the ability to use new information to solve problems, and *crystallized intelligence*, the knowledge and skills that are built up over a lifetime—the kind that gives us the ability to solve math problems, define words, or summarize the president's policy on the environment (Horn & Donaldson, 1980). Fluid intelligence is relatively independent of education and experience; it reflects an inherited predisposition, and it parallels other biological capacities in its growth and, in later years, decline (Baltes & Graf, 1996). Crystallized intelligence, in contrast, depends heavily on culture, education, and experience, and it tends to remain stable or even improve over the life span. This is why physicians, lawyers, teachers, farmers, musicians, insurance agents, politicians, and people in many other occupations can continue working well into old age. Fortunately, a person's crystallized intelligence may compensate for the brain's declining efficiency late in life (Baltes & Graf, 1996).

Some of the decline in fluid intelligence stems from physical changes that occur because of illness, medication, or normal deterioration. But the decline may also appear to be steeper than it really is because of *generational* differences in nutrition, education, and current levels of intellectual stimulation. Someone who is 70 years old today may do worse on a test than a 30-year-old because the 70-year-old did not have as much education when younger or is currently living a less mentally challenging life. That may be why *cross-sectional* studies, which compare people of different ages at the same time, often find a steady decline in mental abilities, whereas *longitudinal* studies, which compare the same people as they age, often do not find this decline until extreme old age. The Seattle Longitudinal Study, for example, has been assessing the intellectual abilities of more than 5,000 adults, following some of them for 35 years (Schaie, 1994). So far, the results suggest that people who have complex and challenging occupations and interests are most likely to maintain their cognitive abilities in later life. So are those who are flexible—who adapt easily to change and who enjoy learning new things.

Moreover, years of schooling and current enrollment in school are better predictors of differences in memory ability than age is (Zivian & Darjes, 1983). And just as training programs can boost the intelligence scores of children, they can boost the memory skills of older people. Older adults can do as well on memory tests as people in their 20s, when given guidance and cues for retrieving memories—for example, when they are taught to use encoding strategies rather than making lists (Loewen, Shaw, & Craik, 1990). Short-term training programs for people between 60 and 80 produce gains in mental test scores that are as large as the losses typical for that age group (Baltes, Sowarka, & Kliegl, 1989; Willis, 1987).

Many researchers who study cognition and aging are therefore optimistic. From studies of healthy rats and people who live in stimulating, enriched environments, they conclude that brain function does not significantly and inevitably decay (Diamond, 1993; Kolb, 1996). Others are more cautious. They note that although most older people, in the absence of disease, function well intellectually, in extreme old age the rates of cognitive impairment and dementia rise dramatically (Baltes & Graf, 1996). The challenge for society, and for us as individuals, is to make sure that the many people who will be living into their 90s can keep using their brains instead of losing them.

THE SOCIAL CLOCK

Since the 1970s, best-selling books have tried to identify the predictable "passages," "seasons," and "transformations" of adult life. It is always fun for readers to figure out what stage they are in and to have a guide through the uncharted territory of the future. Adult development, however, is not comparable to the stages of child development. Children's maturation is dictated by genes; but as children and adolescents mature, genes become less of a driving influence, and environmental demands and individual experiences have greater impact (Neugarten & Neugarten, 1986).

STAGES AND AGES As we saw in Chapter 12, Freud believed that the personality is formed by age 5 or 6, when the Oedipus complex is resolved. A fuller theory of development, stretching from birth to death, was proposed by psychoanalyst Erik H. Erikson (1902–1994). Erikson called his theory *psychosocial*, instead of "psychosexual" as Freud had, because he believed that people are propelled by many kinds of psychological and social forces, not just by sexual motives. Erikson (1950/1963, 1982, 1987) wrote that all individuals go through eight stages in their lives, resolving an inevitable "crisis" at each one:

1. *Trust versus mistrust* is the crisis that occurs during the baby's first year, when the baby depends on others to provide food, comfort, cuddling, and warmth. If these needs are not met, the child may never develop the essential trust necessary to get along in the world, especially in relationships.

2. *Autonomy (independence) versus shame and doubt* is the crisis that occurs when the child is a toddler. The young child is learning to be independent and must do so without feeling too ashamed or doubtful of his or her actions.

3. *Initiative versus guilt* is the crisis that occurs as the preschooler develops. The child is acquiring new physical and mental skills, setting goals, and enjoying newfound talents, but must also learn to control impulses and energies. The danger lies in developing too strong a sense of guilt over his or her fantasies, growing abilities, and childish instincts.

4. *Competence versus inferiority* is the crisis for school-age children, who are learning to make things, use tools, and acquire the skills for adult life. Children who fail these lessons of mastery and competence risk feeling inadequate and inferior.

5. *Identity versus role confusion* is the crisis of adolescence, when teenagers must decide what they are going to be and what they hope to make of their lives. Those who resolve this crisis will come out of this stage with a strong identity, ready to plan for the future. Those who do not will sink into confusion, unable to make decisions. The term *identity crisis* describes what Erikson considered to be the primary conflict of this stage.

6. *Intimacy versus isolation* is the crisis of young adulthood. Once you have decided who you are, said Erikson, you must share yourself with another and learn to make commitments. No matter how successful you are in work, you are not complete until you are capable of intimacy.

According to Erikson, children must resolve the crisis of competence and older adults must resolve the crisis of generativity. This child and her grandmother are certainly meeting their respective developmental tasks! But do these psychological needs occur only during one stage of life?

7. *Generativity versus stagnation* is the crisis of the middle years. Now that you know who you are and have an intimate relationship, will you sink into complacency and selfishness, or will you experience generativity, the pleasure of creativity and renewal? Parenthood is the most common means for the successful resolution of this stage, but people can be productive, creative, and nurturant in other ways, in their work or their relationships with the younger generation.

8. *Ego integrity versus despair* is the crisis of old age. As they age, people strive to reach the ultimate goal—wisdom, spiritual tranquility, an acceptance of their lives. Just as the healthy child will not fear life, said Erikson, the healthy adult will not fear death.

Erikson recognized that cultural and economic factors affect psychological development. Some societies, for example, make the transition between stages relatively easy. If you know you are going to be a farmer like your mother and father and you have no alternative, then moving from adolescence into young adulthood is not a very painful step (unless you hate farming). If you have many choices, however, as adolescents in urban societies often do, the transition can become prolonged. Some people put off making choices indefinitely and never resolve their "identity crisis." Similarly, cultures that place a high premium on independence and individualism will make it difficult for many of their members to resolve Erikson's sixth crisis, that of intimacy versus isolation.

Erikson showed that development is never finished; it is an ongoing process, and the unconscious issues of one stage may be reawakened during another. Erikson's work was important because he placed adult development in the context of family and society, and he specified the essential concerns of adulthood: trust, competence, identity, generativity, and the ability to enjoy life and accept death.

However, Erikson's stages are far from universal, nor do they occur in the same order for everyone. Although in Western societies adolescence *is* often a time of confusion about identity and aspirations, an "identity crisis" is not limited to the teen years. A man who has worked in one job all his life and then is laid off may have an identity crisis too. Likewise, competence is not mastered once and for all in childhood. People learn new skills and lose old ones throughout their lives, and their sense of competence rises and falls accordingly. Erikson omitted women from his original work, and when they were later studied they seemed to be doing things out

People don't always progress steadily through life's stages. Some relapse to earlier ones.

of order—for example, going through "generativity" by having families before they faced the matter of professional "identity" (Peterson & Stewart, 1993).

Many of the psychological qualities Erikson thought essential to adult well-being are indeed important, but they are important no matter how old you are. A study based on a representative sample of 1,108 American adults showed that well-being in adulthood rests on six dimensions: *autonomy,* or feeling independent and in charge of your life; *environmental mastery,* feeling able to master the complex demands being made on you; *personal growth,* having a sense of continuing development and self-realization; *positive relations with others;* having a *purpose in life* that provides meaning to what you do; and *self-acceptance,* coming to terms with yourself and your past (Ryff & Keyes, 1995). None of these needs is fulfilled, once and for all, at some critical stage; all are constantly being renegotiated as our lives change.

THE TRANSITIONS OF LIFE When Erikson was first writing about the life cycle, people's lives were fairly consistent and orderly; stage theories made sense. But nowadays many people are departing from the once-traditional order. Growing numbers of young people are delaying marriage and parenthood, if they marry at all, or they do one without the other. Many young adults are remaining at home with their parents for financial reasons, long past the time they would once have been expected to be on their own. Many older adults are still working, long past the time they planned to retire.

For these reasons, theories of adult development now emphasize the *transitions* and milestones that mark adult life instead of a rigid developmental sequence (Baltes, 1983; Schlossberg, 1984). According to these theories, having a child has stronger effects on you than when you have a child; entering the workforce affects self-esteem and ambition regardless of when you start work.

In spite of the growing unpredictability of changes in adult life, most people still unconsciously evaluate their transitions according to a *social clock* that determines whether they are "on time" for their age or "off time" (Helson & McCabe, 1993; Neugarten, 1979). The social clock creates special pressures for young adults, who are often making many transitions in a short span—from family to college, from college to work, from work to close relationships— and who often feel "under the gun" in comparison to their peers: "I'm a junior and haven't declared a major," "I'm almost 30 and not even in a serious relationship" (Helson & McCabe, 1993).

What is your reaction to these two first-time mothers? One is in her teens, the other in her 40s. Does either seem to be "on time" or "off time" for motherhood—and does your answer affect your feelings about them?

GET INVOLVED

Do you feel "on time" or "off time" regarding any major milestones of importance to you? If you think you are off time, what is the reason? How does it make you feel? Might an unanticipated transition or a nonevent transition be causing it?

All cultures have social clocks that define the right time to marry, start work, and have children, but these clocks may vary greatly. In some societies young men and women are supposed to marry and start having children right after puberty, and work responsibilities come later. In others, a man may not marry until he has demonstrated his ability to support a family, which might not be until his 30s. Society's reactions to people who are "off time" vary as well, from amused tolerance ("Oh, when will he grow up?") to pity, scorn, and outright rejection.

Doing the right thing at the right time, compared to your friends and age-mates, can make you feel satisfied and "normal." When nearly everyone in your group goes through the same experience or enters a new role at the same time—going to school, driving a car, voting, marrying, having a baby, retiring—adjusting to these *anticipated transitions* is relatively easy. Increasingly, though, you may have to face *unanticipated transitions*—the things that happen without warning, such as being fired from a job or becoming too ill to finish school. In addition, you are likely to have to deal with "*nonevent transitions*"—the changes you expect to happen that don't: For example, you don't get married at the age you expected to; you learn that you can't have children; you aren't promoted; you hoped to retire but can't afford to (Schlossberg & Robinson, 1996). People who wish to do things "on time" and cannot, for reasons out of their control, may feel inadequate, depressed, and anxious.

In sum, being a certain age has few if any inevitable consequences; in adulthood, age is what we make of it. The sheer diversity of life-cycle transitions and experiences in modern life means that it is no longer possible to describe key milestones or life stages that will apply to everyone, and probably not even to a majority. As one developmental psychologist put it, "There is not one process of aging, but many; there is not one life course followed, but multiple courses. . . . The variety is as rich as the historic conditions people have faced and the current circumstances they experience" (Pearlin, 1982).

Quick Quiz

By now these quizzes should be anticipated transitions for you.

1. Most women react to menopause by (a) feeling depressed, (b) regretting the loss of femininity, (c) feeling relieved or neutral, (d) going a little crazy.
2. Almost overnight, your 80-year-old grandmother has become confused and delusional. Before concluding that old age has made her senile, what other explanations should you rule out?
3. Which of these statements about the decline of mental abilities in old age is *false?* This decline (a) can often be reversed with training programs, (b) inevitably happens to all old people, (c) is often a result of malnutrition or disease rather than aging, (d) is slowed when people live in stimulating environments.
4. The key psychological issue during adolescence, said Erikson, is a(n) __________ crisis.
5. Frank wants to go to law school but is failing his prelaw classes. Frank is about to undergo a(n) __________ transition.

6. You are reading a best-seller called *Levels,* which describes five levels of adult development: preconscious, barely aware, conscious, hyperconscious, and, for a select few, "evolved." What is likely to be a problem with the assumptions of this book, and how might you critically evaluate its argument?

Answers:

1. c 2. You should rule out the possibility that she is taking too many medications, or taking drugs, such as sleeping pills, that can be hazardous in older people. 3. b 4. identity 5. nonevent 6. Adult development does not occur in predictable, clear-cut phases that apply to everyone. People may move back and forth between "stages," depending on changing circumstances. You would also want to know the evidence for this theory: Was it based on a representative sample of men and women from different cultures? How does the author define and measure vague terms like "evolved"?

ARE ADULTS PRISONERS OF CHILDHOOD?

Of all the controversial issues in the study of human development, perhaps the most controversial is this: How straight is the path from childhood to adolescence to adulthood? All of us acquire attitudes, habits, and deep emotional feelings from our families, and many adults carry with them the scars of abuse they suffered as children. But do the experiences of childhood lead in a straight and inflexible line to the future?

Certainly, many adults today account for their current problems in terms of the traumatic experiences of their early years. Certainly, children who are beaten or neglected, or who live with the continuous risk of violence from their parents, strangers, or gangs, are more likely than nonabused children to become delinquent and violent themselves, to commit crimes, to have low IQs, and to attempt suicide (Malinosky-Rummell & Hansen, 1993; Widom, 1989). Remarkably, however, studies that follow people from childhood to adulthood do not confirm the widespread belief that childhood traumas always have specific and inescapable effects (Kagan, 1996):

- After World War II, many European children, made homeless by the war, were adopted by American families. About 20 percent of the children initially showed signs of anxiety (e.g., overeating and nightmares), but over the years these symptoms vanished. All of the children made good progress in school; none had psychiatric problems; and all established happy, affectionate relationships with their new parents (Rathbun, DiVirgilio, & Waldfogel, 1958).
- Among children who have had psychological disorders ranging from delinquency to depression, the majority recover completely by late adolescence or young adulthood (Thomas & Chess, 1984). Except for the most seriously disturbed children, said the researchers who did one of these studies, "There seems to be little continuity between child and adult disturbances" (Cass & Thomas, 1979).
- Although more children of abusive parents become abusive as adults than do children of nonviolent parents, as we noted in Chapter 2, the majority of them do not (Kaufman & Zigler, 1987). Likewise, a meta-analysis of studies of children of alcoholic parents found that although "parental alcoholism is undoubtedly disruptive to family life," the majority of these children were not "inevitably doomed to psychological disorder" (West & Prinz, 1987).

Because of these heartening discoveries, some psychologists are looking for the origins of *resilience* in the children of violent, neglectful, or alcoholic parents (Cowen et al., 1990; Garmezy, 1991; Werner, 1989). Resilient children often get love and attention from the nondisturbed parent or another doting adult. They have an informal

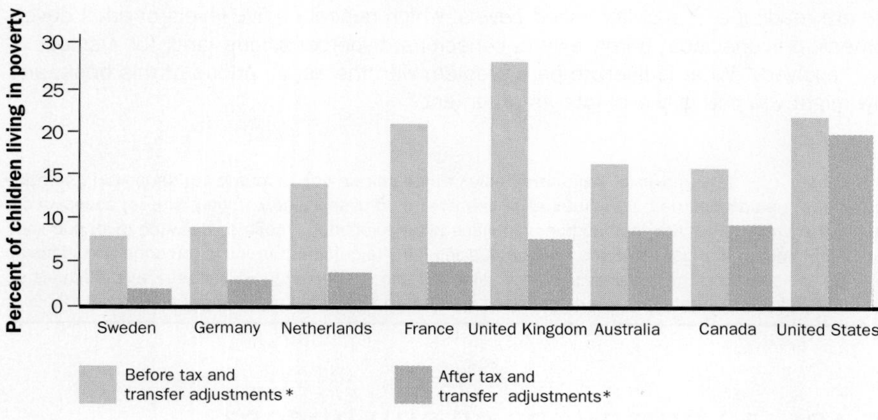

Figure 13.5
Living Conditions for Children Around the World

Twenty percent of American children live in poverty—two to three times as many as in other industrialized nations. Some developed countries, notably the United Kingdom and France, have many low-income families too, but their social welfare programs sharply reduce rates of actual poverty. (Data from the *United Nations Children's Fund Progress of Nations Report;* graph adapted from the *San Francisco Chronicle,* September 23, 1993.)

support network for advice and aid. They have good experiences in school. They have activities and hobbies that they do well at, that provide solace and self-esteem. They have acquired a sense of meaning about life. Most of all, they make the conscious determination not to repeat their histories.

This optimistic news does not mean that it is easy to recover from a painful or traumatic childhood. Nor does it mean that childhood experiences are insignificant or that society can afford to be indifferent to children's welfare. Unlike Canada and most European nations, the United States places a low priority on child-care services and education; one in five American children lives in poverty, more than in any other industrialized nation (see Figure 13.5). The abuse and neglect of children continues to be widespread (Finkelhor & Dziuba-Leatherman, 1994).

But as children develop, they are subject to other influences, too. As we saw in Chapter 12, they have some genetically influenced temperaments that affect how they respond to adversity and challenge throughout life, which may be why some people can roll with fairly severe punches, and others crumple under the smallest setbacks. Children outgrow certain habits and attitudes, even as they cling to others that have been rewarded and encouraged. Events happen to children and adults that can overturn the effects of earlier experiences. Perhaps the most powerful reason for the resilience of so many children, and for the changes that adults make throughout their lives, is that human beings are constantly interpreting their experiences. Children, like adults, have minds of their own—which is why the link between childhood and adulthood is more like a dotted curve than a straight line.

Taking Psychology with You

Bringing Up Baby

How should you treat your children? Should you be strict or lenient, powerful or permissive? Should you require your child to stop having tantrums, to clean up his or her room, to be polite? How can parents learn to rear children who are competent, kind, responsible, and emotionally healthy? According to the research described in this chapter, the following guidelines are effective in teaching children to control aggressive impulses; have good self-control, high self-esteem, and confidence; and be considerate and helpful:

• *Set high expectations that are appropriate to the child's age,* and teach the child how to meet them (Damon, 1995). Some parents make few demands on their children, either unintentionally or because they believe a parent should not impose standards. Others make many demands, such as requiring children to be polite, help with chores, control their anger, be thoughtful of others, and do well in school. The children of parents who make few demands tend to be aggressive, impulsive, and immature. The children of parents who have high expectations tend to be helpful and above average in competence and self-confidence. Of course, the demands must be appropriate for the child's age. You can't expect 2-year-olds to dress themselves, and before you can expect children to get up on time, they have to know how to work an alarm clock.

• *Explain, explain, explain.* Induction—telling a child why you have applied a rule—is an essential guideline. Punitive methods ("Do it because I say so") may result in compliance, but the child will tend to disobey as soon as you are out of sight. Explanations also teach children how to reason and understand; they reward curiosity and open-mindedness. This doesn't mean you have to argue with a 4-year-old about the merits of table manners. But, while setting standards for your children, you can also allow them to express disagreements and feelings.

• *Use induction and empathy.* Call the child's attention to the effect of his or her actions on others, appeal to the child's own sense of fair play and of being a good person, and teach the child to take another person's point of view. Vague orders, such as "Don't fight," are less effective than showing the child how fighting disrupts and hurts others. For boys especially, aggression and empathy are strongly and negatively related: the higher the one, the lower the other (Eisenberg et al., 1996; Feshbach & Feshbach, 1986).

• *Notice, approve of, and reward good behavior.* Many parents tend to punish the behavior they dislike, a form of attention that may actually be rewarding to the child (see Chapter 7). It is much more effective to praise the behavior you do want, which teaches the child what is right.

We know that many people get huffy at the notion of using induction with their children, saying "My parents hit me and I turned out okay, so why shouldn't I do the same with my kids?" Some people scoff at the idea of explaining the reasons for family rules to a 6-year-old. People often care deeply for even the most authoritarian of parents, and they may equate criticisms of the authoritarian approach with criticisms of their parents, who, after all, may only have been doing their best. But if we are willing to examine the evidence and question some assumptions, we will be open to the lessons that developmental psychology has to offer.

Finally, all of these guidelines depend on how the child reacts to them and how the child interprets your actions. You cannot create the "ideal child," that is, one who is an exact replica of you. But you can expect the best from your children—their best, not yours.

SUMMARY

FROM CONCEPTION TO THE FIRST YEAR

1) Prenatal development consists of the *germinal, embryonic,* and *fetal stages.* Certain drugs and diseases can cross the placental barrier and affect the fetus's development, including measles, toxic chemicals, some sexually transmitted diseases, cigarettes, alcohol (which in excess can cause *fetal alcohol syndrome*), illegal drugs, and even over-the-counter medications.

2) Babies are born with motor reflexes that are necessary for survival, including the grasping, startle, sucking, and rooting reflexes. At first, babies can focus at a distance of only 8 inches, but within a few weeks they can distinguish where something is and what it is. Soon after birth, babies develop *synchrony* of pace and rhythm with their caregivers.

3) Physical development is rapid during the first year. On the average, babies sit without support at 7 months, crawl at 9 months, and take their first steps at 13 months. But many aspects of maturation depend on cultural practices, such as whether the baby sleeps alone or with the mother.

COGNITIVE DEVELOPMENT

4) Jean Piaget argued that children's cognitive development depends on an interaction between their current developmental stage and their experience in the world. Children's thinking changes and adapts through *assimilation* and *accommodation.* Piaget proposed four stages of cognitive development: *sensorimotor* (birth to age 2), during which the child learns object permanence; *preoperational* (ages 2 to 7), during which language and symbolic thought develop; *concrete operations* (ages 6 or 7 to 11), during which the child comes to understand *conservation,* identity, and serial ordering; and *formal operations* (age 12 to adulthood), during which abstract reasoning develops.

5) In evaluating Piaget's theory, researchers find that the changes from one stage to another are not as clear-cut as Piaget implied; young children have more cognitive abilities, at earlier ages, than Piaget thought; they are not always egocentric in their thinking; and by the age of 4 or 5 they have developed a *theory of mind* to account for their own and other people's behavior. Further, cultural practices affect the pace and content of cognitive development; and not all adults develop the ability for formal operations. But the general sequence of development that Piaget observed does hold up.

6) Infants are responsive to the pitch, intensity, and sound of language, which may be why adults in many cultures speak to babies in higher-pitched tones, with exaggerated intonation. At 4 to 6 months of age, babies begin to recognize the sounds of their own language; and they go through a "babbling phase" from age 6 months to 1 year. At about 1 year, one-word utterances begin, as do symbolic gestures. At age 2, children speak in two- or three-word telegraphic sentences that convey a variety of messages, and they begin to acquire new words rapidly (the *naming explosion*).

GENDER DEVELOPMENT

7) *Gender socialization* (*sex typing*) is the process by which boys and girls learn what it means to be "masculine" or "feminine," as distinct from acquiring a *gender identity,* which is the cognitive understanding of being biologically male or female.

8) Biological psychologists account for gender differences in behavior and sex-typed activities in terms of genetics, hormones, and brain lateralization. Learning theorists study the subtle rewards, punishments, and models that cause children to become sex typed. Cognitive psychologists study how children develop *gender schemas* of "male" and "female" categories and qualities, which in turn shape their sex-typed behavior. Gender schemas tend to be inflexible at first but often assimilate new information as the child cognitively matures. A fourth important influence on gender socialization is *context and situation.*

MORAL DEVELOPMENT

9) Lawrence Kohlberg's theory of moral development proposes three levels of moral reasoning, each with two stages: *preconventional morality* (based on rules, punishment, and self-interest), *conventional morality* (based on relationships and rules of justice and law), and *postconventional ("principled") morality* (based on higher principles of human rights). Carol Gilligan has argued that women tend to base moral decisions on principles of compassion, whereas men tend to base theirs on abstract principles of justice. Most research, however, finds no gender differences in moral reasoning.

10) Evidence supports the universality of Kohlberg's first four stages, but cognitive theories of moral reasoning have three limitations: They tend to overlook the influence of culture and education, which means that people who are verbally sophisticated may score higher than those less well educated or verbally skilled; moral reasoning is often inconsistent, and people often "regress" to a lower stage of reasoning, depending on the situation; and, most important, moral reasoning and moral behavior are often unrelated.

11) Moral development also depends on the moral emotions of empathy, shame, and guilt. Empathy takes different forms, depending on the child's age and cognitive abilities: *global* empathy, *egocentric* empathy, *empathy for another's feelings*, and *empathy for another's life condition*. Shame develops with the sense of self, around age 2; guilt develops when children have an internal standard of behavior, about age 3 or 4.

12) Parental methods of discipline, such as *power assertion* and *induction*, have different consequences for a child's moral behavior. Power assertion is associated with children who have a sense of external control, are aggressive and destructive, and show a lack of empathy and moral behavior. Induction is associated with children who develop empathy and internalized moral standards and who can resist temptation. In general, *authoritative* parents have better results with their children than do *authoritarian* or *permissive* parents. Altruistic (helpful) children tend to come from families in which they contribute to the family's well-being, carry out many tasks, and respect parental authority, and in which parents set limits without being arbitrary.

ADOLESCENCE

13) *Adolescence* begins with *puberty*. In girls, puberty is signaled by *menarche* and the development of breasts; in boys, it begins with the onset of nocturnal emissions and the development of the testes and scrotum. Hormones are responsible for *secondary sex characteristics*. Boys and girls who enter puberty early tend to have a more difficult later adjustment than do those who enter puberty later than average. One reason may be that early puberty intensifies already existing problems from childhood.

14) Although adolescence is difficult for many teenagers, most do not go through extreme emotional turmoil, anger, or rebellion. One of the main challenges at this stage is developing autonomy and a balanced, adult relationship with parents. "Separation" from parents usually means becoming an individual, not having a complete rift with them.

ADULTHOOD

15) In women, the *menopause* begins in the late 40s or early 50s. Many women have a few physical symptoms, such as hot flashes, but most do not regret the end of fertility, do not become depressed and irritable, and do not feel unfeminine. In middle-aged men, hormone production slows down, but fertility continues.

16) Ideas about old age have been revised now that old people are living longer and healthier lives. Many supposedly inevitable results of aging, such as senility and cognitive decline, are often the result of disease, overmedication, poor nutrition, lack of education, and lack of stimulation and control of one's environment. *Fluid intelligence*, which is relatively independent of education and experience, parallels other biological capacities in its eventual decline. *Crystallized intelligence*, in contrast, depends heavily on culture, education, and experience, and tends to remain stable or even improve over the life span.

17) Erik Erikson proposed an influential *psychosocial theory* of development over the life span. He argued that life consists of eight stages, each with its unique psychological crisis that must be resolved, such as an *identity crisis* in adolescence. Although research disputes the idea that psychological development occurs in predictable stages, Erikson made an important contribution by recognizing the essential concerns of adulthood and showing that development is a lifelong process.

18) Adult "stages" are not universal or biologically driven, like stages of child development. The *transitions* approach emphasizes the changes in people's lives regardless of when they occur: *anticipated transitions*, *unanticipated transitions*, and *"nonevent" transitions.* Adults evaluate their development according to a *social clock* that determines whether they are "on time" or "off time" for a particular event.

ARE ADULTS PRISONERS OF CHILDHOOD?

19) With the exception of serious disorders, many childhood problems are outgrown by late adolescence or adulthood, and most children of alcoholic or abusive parents do not become alcoholic or abusive parents themselves. Psychologists are now studying the origins of children's resilience, as well as the consequences of poverty and trauma.

KEY TERMS

maturation 492
germinal, embryonic, fetal stages 492
teratogen 493
fetal alcohol syndrome (FAS) 493
motor reflexes 494
synchrony 495
Jean Piaget 498
assimilation 499
accommodation 499
sensorimotor stage 500
object permanence 500
representational thought 500
preoperational stage 500
operations 500
egocentric thinking 500
conservation 500
concrete operations stage 501
formal operations stage 502
theory of mind 504
telegraphic speech 505
sex versus gender 507
gender identity 507
gender socialization (sex typing) 507
gender schema 509
preconventional, conventional, and postconventional stages of moral reasoning (Kohlberg) 512
care-based versus justice-based types of moral reasoning (Gilligan) 513

empathy 515
shame and guilt 516
power assertion 517
induction 517
authoritarian, permissive, and authoritative parenting styles 518
puberty 520
menarche 520
secondary sex characteristics 520
menopause 524
gerontology 525
fluid versus crystallized intelligence 527
Erik Erikson 529
psychosocial theory of development 529
identity crisis 530
social clock 531
transitions: anticipated, unanticipated, and nonevent 531
resilience 533

The process of living is the process of reacting to stress.

Stanley Sarnoff

CHAPTER FOURTEEN

The Psychology of Health and Well-being

A stressful day at work?

- Bill and his father have been battling for years. Bill feels that his father is always ready to criticize him for the slightest flaw. After Bill left home he gained some perspective on their relationship, but every time his father comes to visit, Bill breaks out in a rash.
- Tanya lost her apartment and most of her possessions in a hurricane. Months later, she finds it difficult to talk about her continuing anxieties, sure that no one will understand or sympathize.
- Josh is working two jobs to make ends meet. Neither pays much or offers any chance for promotion, but he needs the money. His supervisor at one job is making his life miserable, but Josh can't afford to offend him, so he says nothing. His blood pressure is too high and lately he's been having awful stomachaches, but he can't see a way of improving his situation.
- Lucy gets stuck in a massive traffic jam and is late for class. As she walks in the door, her instructor reprimands her for being late. Later, rushing to get her notes together for an overdue research paper, Lucy spills coffee all over herself and the documents. By noon she has a splitting headache and feels exhausted.

All of these people are certainly under "stress," but, as you see, their experiences are far from the same. Stress can be caused by recurring conflicts (Bill and his father), a traumatic experience that shatters your sense of safety (Tanya), a continuing set of pressures you feel you can't control (Josh), or a collection of small irritations that wear you down (Lucy). The question that most fascinates laypeople and professionals alike, though, is what, if any, is the link between these stressors and illness? Can we, by our own actions, prevent illness and maintain good health?

In this chapter, we will explore these questions by looking at findings from *health psychology,* which is concerned with the psychological factors that influence how people stay healthy, why they become ill, and how they respond when they do get ill. Health psychologists study the sources of wellness and illness, to learn why some people succumb to stress and disease and others do not.

STRESS AND THE BODY

An early approach to psychological factors in illness came from the field of *psychosomatic medicine,* which developed in psychiatry at the turn of the twentieth century. The word **psychosomatic** refers to the interaction of mind (*psyche*) and body (*soma*). Sigmund Freud promoted the view that physical symptoms are often the result of unconscious conflicts, and other psychodynamic theorists maintained that many disorders—such as rheumatoid arthritis, hypertension, asthma, ulcers, and migraine headaches—are caused by neurotic personality patterns. (We now know that they aren't.) Freud's ideas led to the popular but mistaken view that a "psychosomatic" illness is one that is "all in the mind." The modern field of psychosomatic medicine examines psychological as well as somatic origins of disease and the interaction between them.

THE PHYSIOLOGY OF STRESS

In his 1956 book *The Stress of Life,* Canadian physician Hans Selye (1907–1982) greatly advanced the study of stress. Selye noted that many environmental factors—heat, cold, pain, toxins, viruses, and so on—can throw the body out of balance. These factors, called *stressors,* force the body to respond by mobilizing its resources and preparing the individual to fight or flee. Using data from many animal studies, Selye

psychosomatic A term that describes the interaction between a physical illness or condition and psychological states; literally, mind (*psyche*) and body (*soma*).

concluded that "stress" consists of a series of physiological reactions that occur in three phases:

1. *The alarm phase,* in which the organism mobilizes to meet the threat with a package of biological responses that allow the person or animal to escape from danger no matter what the stressor is: crossing a busy street or having deadline pressures at work.

2. *The resistance phase,* in which the organism attempts to resist or cope with a threat that cannot be avoided. During this phase, the body's physiological responses are in high gear—a response to the original stressor—but this very mechanism makes the body more susceptible to other stressors. For example, when your body has mobilized to fight off the flu, you may find that you are more easily annoyed by minor frustrations. In most cases, the body will eventually adapt to the stressor and return to normal.

3. *The exhaustion phase,* which occurs if the stressor persists. Over time, the body's resources may be overwhelmed. Depleted of energy, the body becomes vulnerable to fatigue, physical problems, and eventually illness. The same reactions that allow the body to resist short-term stressors—a boost in energy, tensed muscles, reduced sensitivity to pain, the shutting down of digestion, elevated blood pressure—are unhealthy as long-range responses. Tense muscles can cause headache and neck pain. Increased blood pressure can become chronic hypertension. The closing off of digestion can eventually lead to digestive disorders.

Not all stress is bad, however. Some stress, which Selye called *eustress* (YOO-stress), is positive and feels good, even if it also requires the body to produce short-term energy: competing in an athletic event, falling in love, working hard on a project you enjoy. Selye did not believe that all stress could be avoided or that people should aim for a stress-free life, which is an impossible goal anyway. The goal is to minimize wear and tear on the system.

Who has more "stress": corporate managers and white-collar workers or assembly-line workers and blue-collar laborers? People in highly competitive and complicated jobs, or people in boring and predictable jobs? Researchers find that "It is not the bosses but the bossed who suffer most from job stress" (Karasek & Theorell, 1990).

Selye recognized that psychological stressors, such as fighting with a loved one or grief over loss, can have as great an impact on health as do physical stressors, such as heat, crowds, or noise. He also observed that some factors *mediate,* or act as buffers, between the stressor and the stress. A comfortable climate or a nutritious diet, for example, can soften the impact of an environmental stressor such as pollution. Conversely, a harsh climate or a poor diet can make such stressors worse. But by and large, Selye concentrated on the biological responses that result from a person's or animal's attempt to adapt to environmental demands. A diagram of his view would look like this:

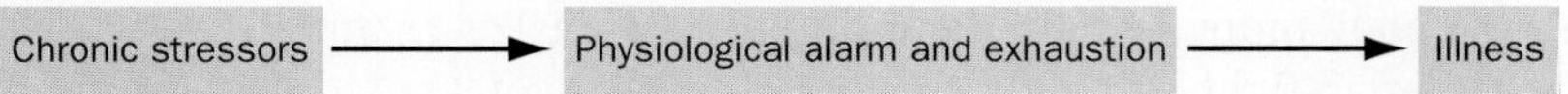

Health psychologists have since expanded on Selye's model of stressors and illness, hoping to find out why individuals differ so much in their susceptibility to stress and vulnerability to disease (Basic Behavioral Science Task Force, 1996). They want to know why, of two people who are exposed to a flu virus, one is sick all winter and the other doesn't even get the sniffles; or why, of two people who have high-pressure jobs, one gets heart disease and the other doesn't. They want to know how external stressors "get under the skin" and make trouble for some people but not others (Taylor, Repetti, & Seeman, 1997).

One approach has been to study individual variation in the body's cardiovascular, digestive, reproductive, and immune systems. For example, some individuals respond to stressors with much greater elevation in blood pressure, heart rate, and hormones than other individuals do (Smith et al., 1996). Over time, as Selye said, that constant exertion of the cardiovascular system may result in heart disease.

One of the most intensively studied bodily systems in relation to stress is the immune system. In the 1980s, scientists created an interdisciplinary field with the cumbersome name **psychoneuroimmunology,** or *PNI* for short: "psycho" for psychological processes such as emotions and perceptions, "neuro" for the nervous and endocrine systems, and "immunology" for the immune system (Andersen, Kiecolt-Glaser, & Glaser, 1994). The white blood cells of the immune system are designed to do two things: (1) recognize foreign substances (antigens), such as flu viruses, bacteria, and tumor cells; and (2) destroy or deactivate them. When an antigen invades the body, white blood cells called *phagocytes* are dispatched to ingest and eliminate the intruder. If this effort is unsuccessful, other white blood cells, called *lymphocytes,* and other processes of the immune system are summoned. To defend the body against antigens, the immune system deploys different cells as weapons, depending on the nature of the enemy.

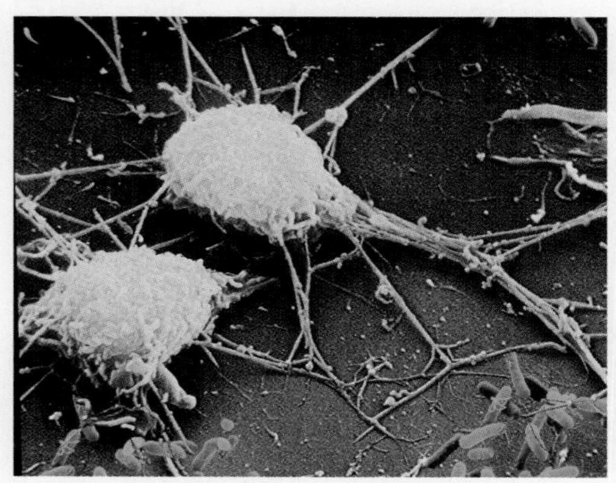

Like a fantastical Hollywood creature, a phagocyte reaches out with extended "arms" to ensnare unwitting bacteria.

Prolonged stress can suppress some or many of these cells that fight disease and infection. For instance, in one study of medical students who had the herpes virus, herpes outbreaks were more likely to occur when the students were feeling lonely or under exam pressure. Loneliness and tension apparently suppress the immune system's capabilities, permitting the existing herpes virus to erupt (Kiecolt-Glaser et al., 1985a). In another study, 420 people heroically volunteered to fight in the war against the common cold. Some were given nose drops containing viruses known to cause a cold's miserable symptoms and others received uncontaminated nose drops. Everyone was then quarantined for a week. The results: Contaminated people who were under high stress, who felt their lives were "unpredictable, uncontrollable, and overwhelming," were twice as likely to develop colds as those reporting low levels of stress (Cohen, Tyrrell, & Smith, 1993).

A second approach to studying individual vulnerability to stress focuses on *psychological factors*, such as personality traits, perceptions, and emotions. An event that is stressful or enraging for one person may be challenging for another and boring for a third. Likewise, losing a job, traveling to China, or having "too much" work is stressful to some people and not to others.

A third approach focuses on *how the individual behaves when under stress* and how he or she manages it. Not all individuals who are under stress behave in the same way. Some drink too much, drive recklessly, or fail to take care of themselves, all of which increases their risk of illness or accident. Others, in contrast, cope constructively and thereby reduce the effects of stress.

Thus, unlike Selye, who defined stress narrowly as the body's response to any environmental threat, health psychologists now define stress to include qualities of the individual (e.g., how the person perceives the stressor) and whether the individual feels able to cope with the stressor (Taylor, 1995):

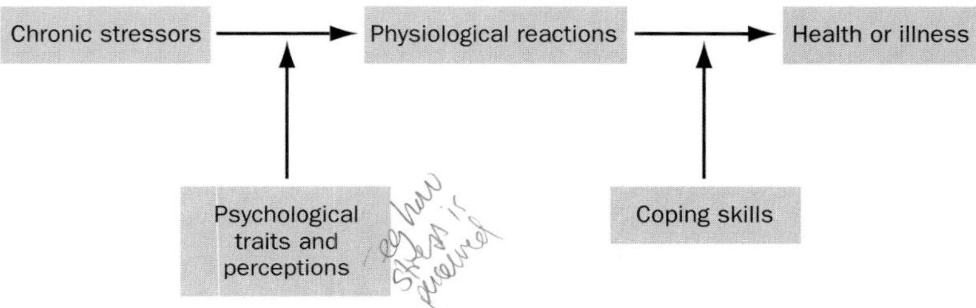

Psychological stress is caused by an interaction of the person and the environment, in which the person believes that the situation strains or overwhelms his or her resources and is endangering his or her ability to cope.

SOME SOURCES OF STRESS

Stressors, then, do not lead directly to illness. But are some more likely than others to affect the immune system and other bodily responses and thus lead eventually to poor health? To find out, psychologists have studied the significant events that disrupt our lives, the irritating nuisances that wear us down, and continuing pressures in the environment.

BEREAVEMENT AND LOSS One of the most powerful stressors in anyone's life is the loss of a loved one or a close relationship, especially through divorce or the death of a spouse. In the two years following bereavement, widowed people are more susceptible to illness and physical ailments, and their mortality rate is higher than expected. Divorce also often takes a long-term health toll: Divorced adults have higher rates of heart disease, pneumonia, and other diseases than comparable adults who are not divorced (Jacobson, 1983).

Bereaved and divorced people may be vulnerable to illness in part because, feeling unhappy, they don't sleep well, they stop eating properly, and they consume more drugs and cigarettes. In addition, broken attachments affect us at a basic cellular level; as we saw in Chapter 11, attachment is a biological need of the species. Bereavement, and the emotional loneliness it creates, produces cardiovascular changes, a lowered number of white blood cells, and other abnormal responses of the immune system (Laudenslager, 1988; Stroebe et al., 1996). The quality of the attachment is as important as its presence or absence. Unhappily married individuals

psychoneuroimmunology (PNI) The study of the relationships among psychology, the nervous and endocrine systems, and the immune system.

psychological stress The result of a relationship between the person and the environment, in which the person believes the situation is overwhelming and threatens his or her ability to cope.

show the same decline in immune function as unhappy divorced people (Kiecolt-Glaser et al., 1993).

These findings do not mean that everyone who loses a loved one gets sick or has an impaired immune system. In one study, 202 women with breast cancer were interviewed about stressful events in their lives at 4, 24, and 42 months after the initial diagnosis and treatment. The researchers found no relationship between stress and recurrence of the cancer. Half of the women had experienced a painful emotional event, but many of these women remained well, including all 13 who had suffered the death of a husband, child, or grandchild. And many women who did have a relapse of cancer had not experienced a traumatic event (Barraclough et al., 1992).

NOISE, CROWDS, AND HASSLES In everyday life, when people speak of being under stress they are often thinking of hassles—thoughtless friends, traffic jams, bad weather, endless paperwork, quarrels, broken plumbing, lost keys, a computer that dies when a deadline is near. Some researchers think that major life events, such as divorce, wreak their most stressful effects by forcing people to deal with a whole new set of everyday stressors (Pillow, Zautra, & Sandler, 1996). But do these aggravations affect health?

Everyday hassles are hazardous to health primarily for people who tend to be highly anxious and quick to overreact (Kohn, Lafreniere, & Gurevich, 1991). Every little thing, to them, feels like the last straw. For most people, however, hassles are short-term (*acute*) nuisances that may be annoying but that don't have any long-term risks, unless they turn into *chronic* (recurring or constant) stressors.

One unhealthy chronic stressor is loud noise, which impairs the ability to think and work, even when people believe they have adjusted to it. Children in noisy schools, such as those near airports, tend to have higher blood pressure and other elevated physiological responses, be more distractable, have poorer long-term memory, and have more difficulty with puzzles, reading, and math than do children in quieter schools (Cohen et al., 1980; Evans, Hygge, & Bullinger, 1995). In adults, noise contributes to cardiovascular problems, irritability, fatigue, and aggressiveness, probably because of overstimulation of the autonomic nervous system (Staples, 1996). The noise that is most stressful to people, however, is noise they cannot con-

Crowds can be fun or stressful, depending on whether you want to be in them and are involved in what they're doing.

trol. The rock song that you choose to listen to at jackhammer loudness may be pleasurable to you but intolerable—stressful—to anyone who does not share your musical taste.

Another chronic stressor is crowding, which, like noise, becomes most stressful when it curtails your sense of freedom and control. Crowds are detrimental to health and intellectual performance not when you *are* crowded but when you *feel* crowded or trapped. Thus people who work without interruptions in a densely packed room feel less crowded and are less stressed than those who work with fewer people but lots of interruptions (Taylor, 1995). Chronic residential crowding—whether in prisons, dorms, or households—is also associated with psychological distress, but this link occurs primarily when people feel they are having too many interactions that are unwanted, intrusive, and inescapable (Evans, Lepore, & Schroeder, 1996). Reactions to crowding also depend in part on culture. At one time, crowding was thought to be a direct cause of crime, juvenile delinquency, and other urban ills. But this theory did not hold up when researchers controlled for income, class, ethnicity, and cultural differences. In Tokyo, where population density exceeds that of any U.S. city, people are accustomed to crowding, and it is not associated with urban problems such as crime.

CONTINUING PROBLEMS In a classic study done more than two decades ago, two identical groups of mice, both carrying a virus known to produce a type of breast cancer, were housed in one of two different conditions: a high-stress environment, characterized by crowding, noise, temperature fluctuations, frequent handling by the experimenters, and other stressful events; or a comfortable low-stress environment. After 12 months, 92 percent of the stressed mice had developed cancerous tumors, compared to only 7 percent of the stress-free mice (Riley, Spackman, & Santisteban, 1975). The degree of stress can apparently affect a biological predisposition to disease: High stress can precipitate onset of the illness, and low stress can delay it, perhaps indefinitely.

The same finding is true for human beings, too. People at the lower end of the socioeconomic ladder have worse health and higher mortality rates for almost every disease and medical condition than do those on the upper rungs (Adler et al., 1994). One obvious reason is that poor people cannot afford good medical care, healthy food, and preventive examinations. But another has to do with the continuous stressors they live with: higher crime rates, fewer community services, dilapidated housing, fewer recreational facilities, and greater exposure to environmental hazards (Taylor, Repetti, & Seeman, 1997).

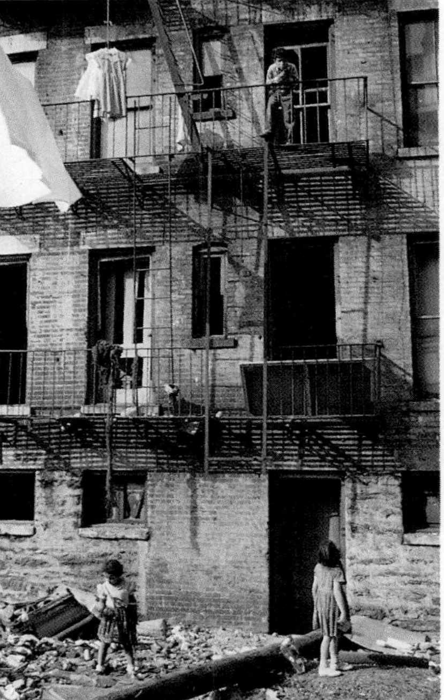

Middle-class stress is a luxury to people whose health is chronically jeopardized by poverty, exposure to toxic materials, malnutrition, and lack of access to medical care.

As we saw in the case of noise and crowds, the most serious threat to health occurs when stress becomes interminable and uncontrollable—when people feel caught in a situation they can't escape. Thus the employees who most suffer from job stress and who are at greatest risk of a variety of illnesses are not executives and managers, but those who have little opportunity to exercise initiative and who are trapped doing repetitive tasks (Karasek & Theorell, 1990). The women who are most at risk of heart disease are clerical workers who feel they have no support from their bosses, who are stuck in low-paying jobs without hope of promotion, and who have financial problems at home (Haynes & Feinleib, 1980). And a Swedish study found that people who reported a history of severe workplace problems over the preceding decade had 5.5 times the risk of developing colon or rectal cancers, even controlling for diet and other factors linked to these malignancies (Courtney et al., 1993).

Prolonged stress is also associated with *hypertension* (high blood pressure), which can lead to kidney disease, strokes, and heart attacks. Hypertension and heart disease have been called "diseases of civilization" because they occur largely in people living in fast-paced urban environments. Hypertension in the United States is far more prevalent among blacks than whites, in part because blacks often live with the stress of chronic discrimination and live in neighborhoods characterized by poor housing, drug use, high unemployment rates, crime, and exposure to chemical contamination (Anderson, 1991; Krieger & Sidney, 1996). But these environmental factors interact with diet, such as fast foods that are high in sodium, and with a genetic susceptibility to the negative effects of salt. African-Americans are more likely to be salt sensitive, possibly, as one leading theory holds, because over many centuries their ancestors adapted to living in a hot African climate. (When people sweat, they lose salt, which is necessary to regulate body systems. A mechanism that would permit retention of salt would therefore be adaptive in a hot climate.) When people with such a genetic vulnerability eat a high-salt diet *and* live in a high-stress environment, the result is high blood pressure (Weder & Schork, 1994).

In summary, the stressors we have discussed are related to health, yet they are not the whole story. Some people show impaired immune function as a result of bereavement, living with uncontrollable noise, and uncontrollable job tensions; yet many individuals show no immune changes at all (Manuck et al., 1991). Some show heightened blood pressure and heart rate when faced with an exam or other challenge, but others do not (Uchino et al., 1995). Something else, as we will see next, is going on between the stressful event and a person's physical response to it.

Quick Quiz

We hope these questions are not sources of stress for you.

1. Steve is unexpectedly called on in class to discuss a question. He hasn't the faintest idea of the answer, and he feels his heart start to pound and his palms to sweat. According to Selye, he is in the __________ phase of his stress response.
2. Which of these stressors has the strongest relationship to immune problems and illness? (a) listening to loud music in your room, (b) listening to your roommate's rotten choice of loud music in your room, (c) being swept up in a crowd of people celebrating New Year's Eve, (d) having a high-paying job that requires you to make many important but rapid decisions
3. Maria has worked as a file clerk for 17 years. Which aspect of the job is likely to be most stressful for her? (a) the speed of the work, (b) the predictable routine, (c) feeling trapped, (d) the daily demands from her boss

Answers:

1. alarm 2. b 3. c

PERSONALITY AND HEALTH

Some people seem to manufacture their own misery. Send them to a beach for a week to escape the pressures of civilization, and they bring along a suitcase full of worries and irritations. Others have a talent for staying serene in the midst of chaos and conflict. We now turn to three aspects of personality that affect how people respond to stressors: emotional styles, pessimism or optimism, and a sense of control.

EMOTIONS AND ILLNESS

Perhaps you have heard people say things like this: "She was so depressed, it's no wonder she got cancer" or "He worried himself into an ulcer over that job." Are negative emotions—anger, anxiety, and depression—hazardous to your health?

NEGATIVE EMOTIONS One of the first modern efforts to link emotions and illness was research on the *Type A behavior pattern,* a set of qualities proposed two decades ago as a predictor of heart disease (Friedman & Rosenman, 1974). The Type A pattern describes people who are determined to achieve, have a sense of time urgency, are irritable, and are impatient at anyone who gets in their way. Type B people are calmer and less intense. It seemed logical that Type As would be at greater risk of heart trouble than Type Bs.

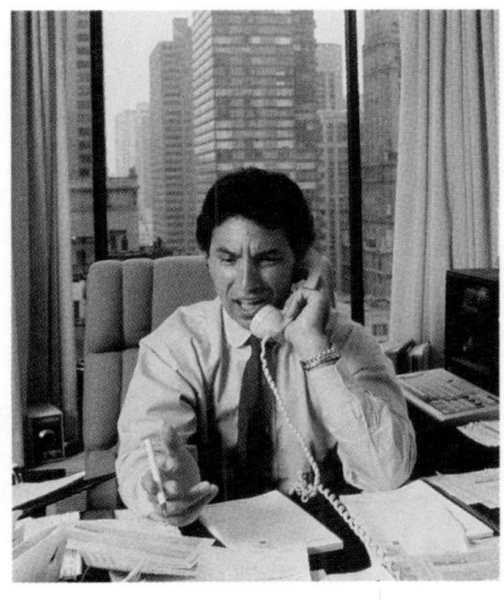

Which is more stressful for this Type A man—his workload or his emotional reaction to it?

It turned out, however, that being highly reactive to stress and challenge is not a risk factor in heart disease (Krantz & Manuck, 1984). Type A people do set themselves a fast work pace and a heavy workload, but many cope better than Type B people who have a lighter workload, and without paying a high physiological price. Further, people who are highly involved in their jobs, even if they work hard, have a low incidence of heart disease. "There'd be nothing wrong with us fast-moving Type As," said a friend of ours, "if it weren't for all those slow-moving Type Bs."

The next round of research uncovered what it was about Type A behavior that is dangerous to health: hostility. "Hostility" is not the irritability or anger that everyone feels on occasion. The toxic kind is *cynical* or *antagonistic hostility,* which characterizes people who are mistrustful of others and quick to have mean, furious arguments (Marshall et al., 1994; Miller, Smith, et al., 1996). Years ago, a longitudinal study that followed male medical students throughout their lives found that men who were chronically angry and resentful and who had a hostile attitude toward others were *five times as likely* as nonhostile men to get coronary heart disease, even after controlling for other risk factors such as smoking (Williams, Barefoot, & Shekelle, 1985). (See Figure 14.1.) This finding has since been replicated many times among men (Ewart & Kolodner, 1994). The relationship between hostility and heart disease in women is less clear, partly because women were omitted from many of the large longitudinal studies that began years ago (Miller, Smith et al., 1996; Thomas, 1993).

A second emotional suspect in the risk of illness is depression. Until recently it was difficult to sort out cause and effect in the link between depression and illness because illness often makes its sufferers deeply unhappy. But according to a recent longitudinal study of 1,551 people, those who had been clinically depressed at the start of the study were four times more likely to have a heart attack in

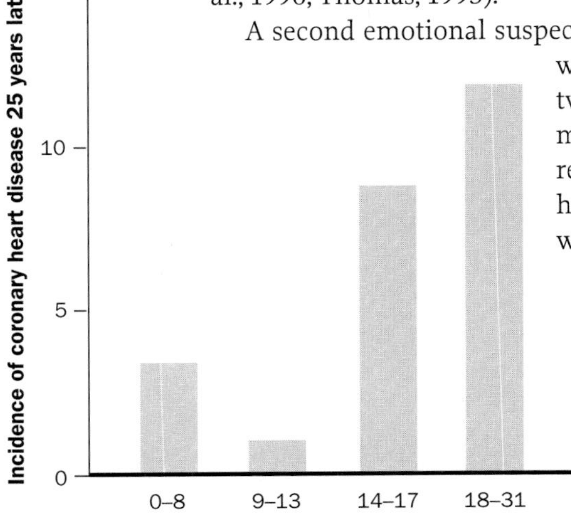

Figure 14.1
Hostility and Heart Disease
Men who had the highest hostility scores as young medical students were the most likely to have coronary heart disease 25 years later (Williams, Barefoot, & Shekelle, 1985).

the ensuing 13 years than nondepressed people—even after the researchers controlled for all other risk factors, including high blood pressure and smoking (Pratt et al., 1996). It is still not known, however, whether depression increases the risk of heart attack because many depressed people fail to take care of themselves or because depression has direct biochemical effects on the body.

There is a common belief that depression is associated with other diseases, notably cancer and AIDS, but here the evidence is conflicting. Some reviews of the literature, for example, find no links among depression, immune function, and cancer, or outbreaks of illness among men with HIV (Lyketsos et al., 1993; Zonderman, Costa, & McCrae, 1989). Yet other studies report that chronic depression *is* associated with numerous aberrations in the immune system and that it speeds the development of infection and AIDS-related diseases (Burack et al., 1993; Herbert & Cohen, 1993). At present, therefore, it seems that chronic depression is a risk factor for heart disease and possibly other diseases as well. We will consider some reasons why this might be so in other sections of this chapter.

DISCLOSURE AND REPRESSION Now pay attention: *Don't think of a white bear.* Are you not thinking of it? Anyone who has ever tried to banish an unwelcome thought knows how hard it can be to do this. In an actual study, people who were told not to think of a white bear mentioned it *nine times* in a five-minute stream-of-consciousness session (Wegner et al., 1987). In daily life, people often find it hard to erase the mental tape of worries, unhappy memories, or obsessions about failed relationships. The reason seems to be that when you are trying to avoid a thought, you are in fact processing the thought frequently—rehearsing it and making it more accessible to consciousness. When the subject of your obsession involves an old flame whom you still desire, trying not to think of him or her actually prolongs your emotional responsiveness to the person (Wegner & Gold, 1995).

Most people try to suppress feelings some of the time, but some people do so almost all of the time; they have the personality trait of *emotional inhibition* (Basic Behavioral Science Task Force, 1996). People who have this trait, called "repressors," tend to deny feelings of anxiety, anger, or fear (to themselves as well as others) and pretend that everything is fine. Yet, when they are in stressful or emotion-producing situations, their physiological responses, such as heart rate and blood pressure, rise sharply. Repressors are at greater risk of becoming ill than people who can acknowledge their fears, and once they contract a serious disease, repressors may even die sooner. In one study, 178 women diagnosed with breast cancer were divided according to their style of coping with the illness: positive/confronting, fatalistic, hopeless/helpless, and denial/avoidance. The "positive/confronting" style was associated with the greatest longevity, regardless of severity of the illness (Burgess, Morris, & Pettingale, 1988).

Why should this be so? According to James Pennebaker and his associates, the *prolonged* inhibition of thoughts and emotions requires physical effort that is stressful to the body (Pennebaker, 1995; Pennebaker & Harber, 1993). Yet many people try to inhibit private thoughts and feelings that make them ashamed or depressed. The inability or unwillingness to confide important or traumatic events, the researchers maintain, places continuing stress on the immune system and can thereby lead to long-term health problems. (This finding is not true in all cultures, however, especially those in which the experience and expression of anger and sadness are normally avoided for the sake of group harmony [Wellenkamp, 1995].)

In one of Pennebaker's studies, college students were assigned to write about either a personal, traumatic experience or a trivial topic for 20 minutes a day for four days. Those who were asked to reveal "their deepest thoughts and feelings" about a

GET INVOLVED

To see whether the research on the benefits of confession will benefit you, take a moment to jot down your "deepest thoughts and feelings" about being in college, your past, a secret, your future . . . anything you've never told anyone. Do this again tomorrow, and again for a few days in a row. Note your feelings after writing. Are you upset? Troubled? Sad? Relieved? Does your account change over time? James Pennebaker predicts that if you do this exercise now, you will have fewer colds, headaches, and trips to the medical clinic in the coming year.

traumatic event all had something to talk about. Many told stories of sexual coercion, physical beatings, humiliation, and parental abandonment. Yet most had never discussed these feelings with anyone. The researchers took blood samples from the students to test for the immune activity of lymphocytes. They also collected data on the students' physical symptoms, emotions, and visits to the health center. On every measure, the students who wrote about traumatic experiences were better off than those who did not (Pennebaker, Kiecolt-Glaser, & Glaser, 1988). Some of them showed short-term increases in anger and depression; writing about an unpleasant experience was disturbing. But over time, their health and well-being improved.

Writing about the same experience for several days may be beneficial because it often produces insight and distance, breaking the stressful repetition of obsessive thoughts and unresolved feelings. One woman, who had been molested at the age of 9 by a boy a year older, at first wrote about her feelings of embarrassment and guilt. By the third day, she was writing about how angry she felt at the boy. By the last day, she had begun to see the whole event differently; he was young too, after all. When the study was over, she said, "Before, when I thought about it, I'd lie to myself. . . . Now, I don't feel like I even have to think about it because I got it off my chest. I finally admitted that it happened."

Confession even seems able to speed up the normal coping process associated with significant transitions. In another study, freshmen wrote either about their feelings associated with going to college or their feelings on superficial topics. The experimental group reported higher feelings of homesickness and anxiety in the short run, but by the end of the school year they had had far fewer bouts of flu and visits to the infirmary than the control group (Pennebaker, Colder, & Sharp, 1990).

Some researchers maintain that personality traits involving the expression or suppression of emotion play a key role in the onset of illness, and even that specific emotions can be tied to particular illnesses, such as cancer or heart disease (Eysenck, 1993; Grossarth-Maticek et al., 1991). Others caution against exaggerating the role of emotional styles in health, arguing that we must not overlook the stronger influences of chronic stressors, the biology of the disease, and the individual's health habits, such as diet and smoking (Greenwald, 1992; Jorgensen et al., 1996).

DON'T OVERSIMPLIFY

Research suggests that negative emotions contribute to illness, and that ventilating and suppressing them can both be unhealthy. What are some other ways of looking at the relationship between emotions and health?

This is a lively and continuing debate in health psychology, although both sides agree that it is important to avoid oversimplifying the link between emotions and health. Living in a constant state of negative emotions that are never resolved can be stressful to the body, but a life of constant stress also tends to foster negative emotions. Depression and anxiety may contribute to illness in some individuals, but illness also makes some people severely depressed or anxious. The effort to suppress a secret or a negative emotion may be stressful for some individuals, but sometimes such suppression is socially, culturally, or morally necessary. Indeed, sometimes when people reveal their secrets and fears, their listeners become uncomfortable and angry with them, making the revealer feel worse rather than better (Kelly & McKillop, 1996). Chronic emotional inhibition is hazardous to health, but so is constant emotional ventilation (see Chapter 10). Health psychology suggests a middle path: learning to identify and resolve our negative emotions and not let them dominate our lives.

OPTIMISM AND PESSIMISM

How do you react when bad things happen to you? Do you usually expect that you can make the best of a bad situation, and come through it okay? Or do you have the attitude that "If something can go wrong for me, it will"?

These two characteristic responses to bad events reflect *pessimistic* and *optimistic explanatory styles* (Scheier & Carver, 1992; Seligman, 1991). The pessimistic style is associated with lower self-esteem, less achievement, more illness, and slower emotional recovery from trauma. For example, among a group of people in Florida who had suffered devastating losses as a result of Hurricane Andrew, pessimism was a significant predictor of continued distress six months after the disaster, whereas loss of resources was not (Carver et al., 1993a). It's not how much you lose, apparently, but how you think about that loss that makes the most difference to your state of mind.

Pessimists will probably complain that optimism is just a result of good health or good fortune; it's easy to think positively when you feel good. But optimism may actually produce good health as well as reflect it. In one imaginative study of baseball Hall-of-Famers who had played between 1900 and 1950, 30 players were rated according to their explanatory style. A pessimist would attribute a bad performance to a permanent failing in himself, as in, "We didn't win because my arm is shot, and it'll never get better." An optimist would attribute the same performance to external and changing conditions, as in, "We didn't win because we got a couple of lousy calls, just bad luck in this game, but we'll be great tomorrow." The optimists were significantly more likely to have lived into old age than were the pessimists (Seligman, 1991). Another study followed 1,719 men and women with heart disease who had undergone a procedure to check the arteries for clogging. Twelve percent of the pessimists—people who doubted they would recover enough to lead normal lives—died within a year, compared to only 5 percent of the optimists (Mark, 1994). This difference was not related to differences in severity of the disease, either: Some of the people with the mildest heart disease were the most pessimistic.

Many pessimists, naturally, think that optimists are just poor judges of reality. Sometimes this pessimistic assertion is right—but that turns out to be a good

Studies suggest that explanatory style affects longevity. Zack Wheat, an outfielder for the Brooklyn Dodgers, had an optimistic explanatory style: "I'm a better hitter than I used to be because my strength has improved and my experience has improved." Wheat lived to be 83.

thing! Shelley Taylor and Jonathon Brown (1988, 1994) have found that health and well-being often depend on having "positive illusions"—"overly positive self-evaluations, exaggerated perceptions of control or mastery, and unrealistic optimism." Positive illusions underlie many of the conditions of good mental health, such as the ability to care about others, to be contented, to be happy with your choice of partner, and to work productively.

People who are optimistic and have positive illusions do not *deny* that they have problems. They acknowledge bad news when it comes, but they are more likely to be active problem solvers, and more likely to seek information that can help them (Aspinwall & Taylor, 1997). When faced with a problem, such as a risky operation or a serious continuing struggle with alcoholism, optimists focus on what they can do about it. They have a higher expectation of being successful, so they don't give up at the first sign of a setback. They keep their senses of humor, plan for the future, and reinterpret the situation in a positive light (Aspinwall & Brunhart, 1996; Carver et al., 1993a). They may have better health than pessimists because they take better care of themselves when they have minor ailments, such as colds, and also when they have life-threatening illnesses, such as AIDS (Taylor, 1995). Pessimists and people who refuse to acknowledge their vulnerabilities, in contrast, often do self-destructive things: They drink too much, smoke, fail to wear seat belts, or refuse to take medication for illness. They also may be more likely to become ill because they give in to negative emotions, or give up.

Pessimism, however, is not associated with poor coping for everyone. Some people adopt a stance called "defensive pessimism": "I expect the worst, but I'll work hard to avoid it, so if it happens anyway, it won't be my fault." Edward Chang (1996) finds that this attitude is more common in Asian cultures than in Western ones. Whereas pessimism is associated with poorer coping strategies among Westerners, his studies show, it is associated with stronger problem-solving strategies among Asians. By anticipating the worst, Chang argues, many Asians paradoxically take action to avoid it.

Can the risky form of pessimism be "cured"? Optimists, naturally, think so! In Chapter 10, we discussed an effective intervention program that inoculates elementary-school children against pessimism and depression by teaching them optimistic explanatory styles (Gillham et al., 1995). And in Chapter 16 we will see that cognitive therapy is also effective. Yet another approach worked for psychologist Rachel Hare-Mustin, whose mother cured her childhood pessimism with humor. "Nobody likes me," Rachel lamented. "Don't say that," her mother said. "Everybody hasn't met you yet."

Walter Johnson, a star pitcher for the Washington Senators, had a pessimistic explanatory style: "I can't depend on myself to pitch well. I'm growing old. I have had my day." Johnson died at the age of 59.

THE SENSE OF CONTROL

Optimism, in turn, is related to another important ingredient of psychological and physical health: having an internal locus of control (Marshall et al., 1994). **Locus of control,** described in Chapter 12, refers to your general expectation of whether you can control the things that happen to you (Rotter, 1966). People who have an *internal* locus of control ("internals") tend to believe that they are responsible for what happens to them; those who have an *external* locus of control ("externals") tend to believe that they are the victims of circumstance.

When adversity strikes, many people restore a sense of control by taking action. Others feel overwhelmed by events or accept them fatalistically.

THE BENEFITS OF CONTROL As we noted earlier, the most debilitating aspect of chronically stressful situations is a feeling of powerlessness. People can tolerate years of difficulty if they believe they can control events or at least predict them and thereby be prepared for them. Feeling in control of events helps to reduce pain, improve adjustment to surgery and illness, and speed up recovery from some diseases (Shapiro, Schwartz, & Astin, 1996; E. Skinner, 1996). In a group of patients recovering from heart attack, for example, those who thought their illness was due to bad luck or fate—factors outside their control—were less likely to generate active plans for recovery and more likely to resume their old unhealthy habits. In contrast, those who thought the heart attack occurred because they smoked, didn't exercise, or had a stressful job were more likely to change their bad habits and recover more quickly (Affleck et al., 1987; Ewart, 1995).

A sense of control actually affects the neuroendocrine and immune systems, which may explain why it is so beneficial to old people, whose immune systems normally decline (Rodin, 1988). When elderly residents of nursing homes are given more choices over their activities and environment and given more control over day-to-day events—even small but engrossing activities such as tending plants—the results are dramatic: They become more alert, more active, happier, and even less likely to die (Langer, 1983).

Cultures differ in their degree of fatalism and in their beliefs about whether it is possible to take control of one's health. Might these cultural attitudes be related to mortality rates? The answer, remarkably, is yes. Researchers examined the deaths of 28,169 adult Chinese-Americans and 412,632 randomly selected, matched control subjects whose death certificates identified them as "white." In traditional Chinese astrology, certain birth years are considered bad luck, and people born in those years often become fatalistic, expecting bad fortune. This expectation can become a self-fulfilling prophecy. Chinese-Americans who had been born in a year traditionally considered to be ill-fated died significantly earlier—one to five years earlier!—than whites who had been born in the same year and who had the same disease. The more strongly traditional the Chinese were, the more years of life they lost. These results held for nearly all causes of death studied, even when the researchers controlled for how well the patients took care of themselves and which treatments they were given (Phillips, Ruth, & Wagner, 1993).

THE LIMITS OF CONTROL Overall, then, a sense of control is a good thing. But the question must always be asked: control over what? If an unrealistically confident person tries to control the uncontrollable ("I'm going to be a movie star in 60 days!"), the inevitable failure may lead to a sense of helplessness or incompetence. It also doesn't help people to believe they had control over a past traumatic event when they did not. Victims of rape or other crimes, for example, often suffer because they blame themselves for having provoked their attackers, as if they could have controlled the criminals' behavior (Janoff-Bulman, 1989).

locus of control A general expectation about whether the results of your actions are under your own control (internal locus) or beyond your control (external locus).

"Control," therefore, has different meanings, and not all of them are related to health (E. Skinner, 1996). In one study that dissected the various meanings of control, the only one that was related to health was *self-efficacy:* the belief that you are basically in charge of your own life and well-being, and that if you become sick you can take steps to improve your health (Marshall, 1991). (You may recall the discussion of self-efficacy in the context of achievement motivation in Chapter 11.) Other, more unrealistic kinds of control did not affect health and well-being, such as self-blame ("Whatever goes wrong with my health is my fault") and the belief that all disease can be prevented by doing the right thing ("If I eat right, I'll never get sick").

DEFINE YOUR TERMS

In general, it's good to feel in control of your life, but what does that mean exactly? Control over what? How much of your life? Can too much control ever be a bad thing?

Research on self-efficacy has had many practical benefits. For example, media campaigns to encourage people to eat healthier meals, wear seat belts, take medication, practice safe sex, perform breast self-examinations, and so forth are most likely to succeed when they enhance people's perceptions of their self-efficacy in managing their own health. In contrast, campaigns based only on providing factual information, scaring the public ("You'll die if you don't do this!"), or trying to persuade people of the risks of some activity are far less effective (Meyerowitz & Chaiken, 1987; Miller, Shoda, & Hurley, 1996).

Ideas about control, as we have seen, are strongly influenced by culture. Eastern and Western cultures tend to hold different attitudes toward the ability and desirability of controlling our own lives. In general, the Western approach celebrates **primary control,** in which people try to influence existing reality by changing other people, events, or circumstances: If you have a problem, you should change it, fix it, or fight it. The Eastern approach emphasizes **secondary control,** in which people try to accommodate to reality by changing their own aspirations or desires: If you have a problem, learn to live with it or act in spite of it (Rothbaum, Weisz, & Snyder, 1982). These two perspectives influence a culture's practices in child rearing, religion, work, psychotherapy, and medicine (Weisz, Rothbaum, & Blackburn, 1984).

A Japanese psychologist offered some examples of Japanese proverbs that teach the benefits of yielding to the inevitable (Azuma, 1984): *To lose is to win* (giving in, to protect the harmony of a relationship, demonstrates the superior trait of generosity); *willow trees do not get broken by piled-up snow* (no matter how many problems pile up in your life, flexibility will help you survive them); and *the true tolerance is to tolerate the intolerable* (some "intolerable" situations are facts of life that no amount of protest will change). You can imagine how long "to lose is to win" would survive on an American football field, or how long most Americans would be prepared to tolerate the intolerable!

Both primary and secondary control have benefits. One way that people who are ill or under stress can combine these two forms of control is to take responsi-

primary control An effort to modify reality by changing other people, the situation, or events; a "fighting back" philosophy.

secondary control An effort to accept reality by changing your own attitudes, goals, or emotions; a "learn to live with it" philosophy.

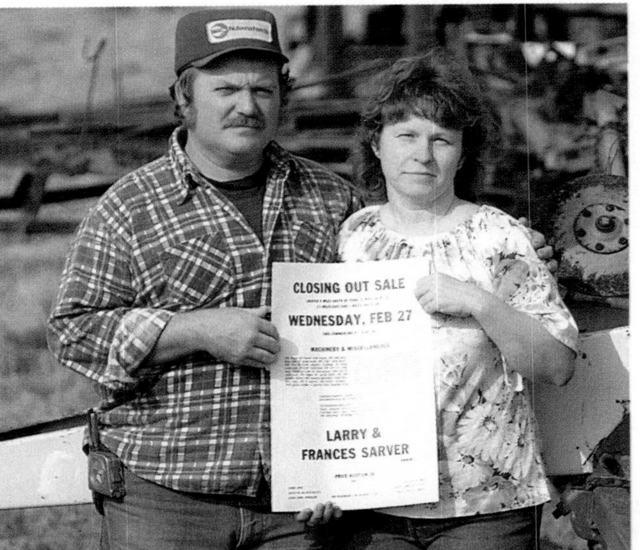

Sometimes life serves up a disaster, as it has for many farm families who have lost their lands and livelihoods because of the changing economy. When is it helpful to believe we can control everything that happens to us, and when is it harmful?

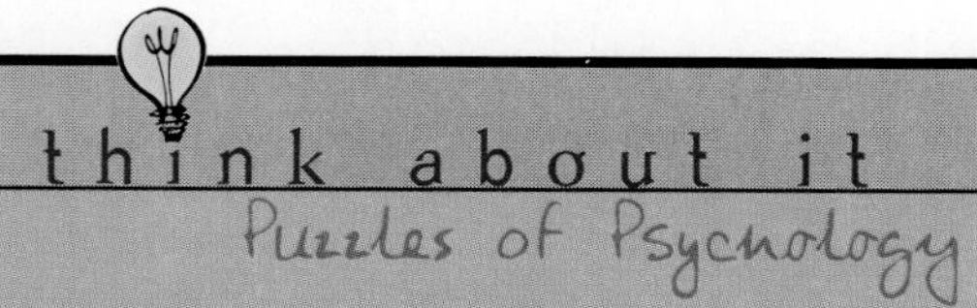

How Much Control Do We Have Over Our Health?

To hear some people talk, health is almost entirely a matter of "mind over matter"—even the worst diseases, they say, can be cured with jokes and positive thinking. This attitude is actually quite modern, a result of historical and medical changes that have occurred in this century. As industrialized societies conquered many of the environmental sources of infectious diseases—for example, through innovations in water treatment, sewage disposal, and food storage—public attention turned to "diseases of lifestyle," such as heart disease and emphysema, which are affected by what people eat and how they live. Accordingly, the focus of health prevention has shifted from changing the environment to changing individuals (Taylor, Repetti, & Seeman, 1997).

Health psychologists agree that people's behavior has a tremendous impact on their health. For example, a study done at the Harvard School of Public Health found that smoking, diet, and lack of exercise cause 65 percent of all deaths from cancer, while only 2 percent of cancer deaths are due to environmental pollution and 10 percent to genetics (Trichopoulos, Li, & Hunter, 1996). Most researchers also agree that psychological factors such as emotional style and optimism are involved in the connection between stress and illness, although, as we saw in the text, they disagree about how strong these factors are (Andersen, Kiecolt-Glaser, & Glaser, 1994).

However, many health psychologists are worried about the rise of a "pop-health" industry that oversimplifies findings from health research, encouraging people to believe that individuals are always to blame when they become ill (Becker, 1993). And they worry that the public is starting to think in either–or terms about medical treatment: *Either* you get traditional medical procedures to treat a disease *or* you go for alternative psychological ones, such as visual imagery, meditation, and support groups. These aren't antithetical choices, of course. In fact, most physicians today, while endorsing traditional medical treatments, also recognize the role of psychological and social factors in their patients' recovery and well-being—the importance of their patients' having optimistic attitudes, good support systems, and effective coping strategies. The danger is that people will put off medical procedures that they need in favor of "alternative" treatments that have no demonstrated validity.

Psychologists are also concerned about the many unscrupulous marketers who prey on people's worries by selling them worthless programs, pills, and devices. The health-care marketplace in North America is overflowing with quacks and pseudoprofessionals with meaningless but impressive-looking "credentials," often from unaccredited "universities" that offer mail-order degrees. At

bility for future actions, while not blaming themselves for past ones. People who view control in this way adjust better than people who believe they can control everything—or nothing—about their disease (Thompson, Nanni, & Levine, 1994). In a study of women coping with cancer, for instance, adjustment was related to a woman's belief that she was not to blame for getting sick but that she was in charge of taking care of herself from now on (Taylor, Lichtman, & Wood, 1984). "I felt that I had lost control of my body somehow," said one woman, "and the way for me to get back some control was to find out as much as I could." This way of thinking about illness allows people to avoid guilt and self-blame while retaining a sense of self-efficacy. Indeed, most problems require us to decide what we can change and accept what we cannot. As we discuss in "Puzzles of Psychology," perhaps the secret of healthy control lies in knowing the difference.

Quick Quiz

You can increase your sense of control over the material in this section by answering these questions:

1. Which of the following aspects of Type A behavior seems most hazardous to men's health? (a) working hard, (b) being in a hurry, (c) cynical hostility, (d) high physical reactivity to work, (e) general grumpiness

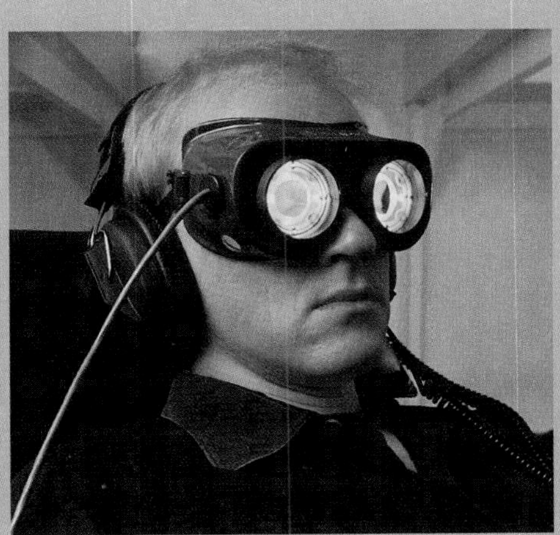

In this electronic route to stress reduction, goggles flash lights in the eyes and headphones play soothing tones. What would you predict about the long-term success of such methods?

one of these schools you can study "nutrimedical dentistry," for example, or "therapeutic nutrimedicine." Jack Raso (1996), a dietician who became alarmed by the many people claiming to be experts in nutrition, did a survey of such mail-order programs and found them to be dominated by "fast-buck artists, charlatans, and propagators of mysticism, pseudoscience, and supernaturalism."

When it comes to taking control of our health, therefore, we need to avoid the traps of oversimplifying, either–or thinking, and emotional reasoning. Take the example of exercise, an activity that individuals can do for themselves that has many benefits for mind and body. "Quick fix" alternatives (such as "passive exercise" machines that allegedly exercise your muscles while you flop in front of the TV) are emotionally appealing, but they are no substitute for the real thing. Further, exercise is not a cure-all: People who exercise in order to *avoid* solving their problems are not necessarily reducing their stress load; you can't jog away from everything. And *excessive* exercise has been linked to infertility, damage to the immune system, and premature aging (Becker, 1993).

Moreover, although individual approaches to maintaining health are indisputably beneficial, societies today face many complex and costly health problems that call for community, not individual, solutions—such as eradicating hazardous wastes and assuring basic health care for everyone. Are we focusing so much on steps that individuals can take that we are forgetting about societal causes of illness, such as unemployment, poverty, and discrimination? How can we take responsibility for our health without falling for exaggerated pop-health claims that disease is "all in the mind" or that a magic pill or potion will cure all our problems? What do you think?

2. "I'll never find anyone else to love because I'm not good-looking; that one romance was a fluke" illustrates a(n) ____________ explanatory style.
3. Valerie has many private worries about being in college, but she is afraid to tell anyone. What might be the healthiest solution for her? (a) exercise, (b) writing down her feelings in a diary, (c) talking frequently to strangers who won't judge her, (d) trying not to think about her fears
4. Adapting yourself to the reality that you are getting older is an example of (primary/secondary) control; joining a protest to make a local company clean up its hazardous wastes is an example of (primary/secondary) control.
5. On television, a self-described health expert explains that "No one gets sick if they don't want to be sick," because we all can have psychological control over our bodies. How should a critical thinker assess this claim?

Answers:

1. c 2. pessimistic 3. b 4. secondary, primary 5. Skeptically. First, you would want to define your terms: What does "control" mean, and what kind of control? People can control some things, such as the decision to exercise and quit smoking, and they can control some aspects of treatment once they become ill; but they don't have control over everything that happens to them. Second, this "expert" assumes that control is always a good thing, but the belief that we have total control over our lives could lead to depression and unwarranted self-blame when illness strikes.

COPING WITH STRESS

Remarkably, most people who are under stress—even those living in the toxic environments of war and poverty, or living through long episodes of anger or grief—do not become ill. Why not? What helps people cope with and recover from the most awful adversity?

Coping is the process of adapting to demands, in the environment or in yourself, that you believe are straining your resources or abilities (Lazarus & Folkman, 1984). Coping is not a single strategy that applies to all circumstances; people cope differently with hassles, losses, dangers, and challenges. And the techniques they use change over time and circumstance, depending on the nature of the stressor and the particular situation (Carver & Scheier, 1994; Terry, 1994). We will describe three general kinds of techniques: (1) solving the problem, (2) rethinking the problem, and (3) learning to live with the problem. The first deals with the stressor, the second involves the person's interpretation of the stressor, and the third addresses the physical effects of stress.

SOLVING THE PROBLEM

A woman we know, whom we will call Nancy, was struck by tragedy when she was 22. She and her new husband were driving home one evening when a car went out of control and crashed into them. When Nancy awoke in a hospital room, she learned that her husband had been killed and that she herself had permanent spinal injury and would never walk again. For many months, Nancy reacted with understandable rage and despair. "Get it out of your system," her friends said. "You need to get in touch with your feelings." "But I know I'm miserable," Nancy lamented. "What do I *do?*"

Children are a famous source of delight—and stress. If you were in this weary mother's place, how would you cope with your children's behavior?

What should Nancy do, indeed? Her friends' advice and her reply illustrate the difference between emotion-focused and problem-focused coping (Lazarus & Folkman, 1984). *Emotion-focused coping* concentrates on the emotions the problem has caused, whether anger, anxiety, or grief. For a period of time after any personal tragedy or traumatic natural disaster, it is normal to give in to these emotions and feel overwhelmed by them. In this stage, people often need to talk obsessively about the event in order to come to terms with it, make sense of it, and decide what to do about it (Pennebaker & Harber, 1993). Eventually, though, most people become ready to move beyond their emotional state and concentrate on the problem itself. The specific steps in *problem-focused coping* depend on the nature of the problem: whether it is a pressing but one-time decision; a continuing difficulty, such as living with a disability; or an anticipated event, such as having an operation.

"Defining the problem" may seem an obvious first step, especially when the problem is standing there yelling at you. However, people often define a problem incorrectly and then set off down a wrong coping road. For example, unhappy couples typically blame each other for their misery. Sometimes, of course, they are right; but sometimes marital misery is a result of misdiagnosis. A husband who is under great pressure at his office may decide that his problem is an unsupportive wife. A wife who is feeling too many conflicting demands may decide that her problem is her lazy husband. If this couple tries to cope with their unhappiness by attacking each other, they merely increase their difficulties. If they correctly diagnose the problem ("I'm worried about my job"; "I don't have enough leisure time to myself"), different coping solutions become apparent (Karney et al., 1994).

Once the problem is identified, the coper can learn as much as possible about it from professionals, friends, books, and others in the same predicament. In Nancy's case, she can begin by learning more about her medical condition and prognosis. What can she do for herself? What kind of exercise will help her? How do other accident victims cope? What occupations are possible for her? By the way, Nancy stayed in school, remarried, got a Ph.D. in psychology, and now does research and counseling with disabled people.

Problem-focused coping has a large psychological benefit: It tends to increase a person's sense of self-efficacy, control, and effectiveness (D'Zurilla & Sheedy, 1991). Problem-focused coping requires components of critical thinking, such as considering alternatives and resisting emotional reasoning. When under stress, people who think creatively about their problems are better able to solve them, avoid negative emotions such as anger and anxiety, and even reduce physiological arousal (Katz & Epstein, 1991).

RETHINKING THE PROBLEM

A second way of coping with problems is to think about them in new ways. Such cognitive strategies have three purposes (Taylor, 1989). First, they help the person find meaning in the experience: Why did this event happen to me? What does it mean for my life now? Second, they help the person regain a sense of mastery over the event and the future: What can I do about it now? How can I keep this from happening again? Third, they help the person regain self-esteem after a devastating setback. Let's consider some of the most effective strategies that people use for rethinking their problems.

REAPPRAISAL: "IT'S NOT SO BAD." When people cannot eliminate a stressor, they can choose to reassess its meaning. Problems can be turned into challenges, losses into unexpected gains. You lost your job; maybe it wasn't such a good job, but you were too afraid to quit to look for another, and now you can do so. Even life-shattering events can be viewed in more than one light. A study of 100 spinal-cord-injured people found that two-thirds of them felt the disability had had positive side effects (Schulz & Decker, 1985). Benefits included becoming "a better person," "seeing other people as more important," and having an "increased awareness of self" and a new appreciation of "brain, not brawn." People can also reappraise the actions of others. Instead of becoming enraged at someone's distressing behavior, for example, the empathic person tries to see the situation from the other person's standpoint in order to avoid misunderstandings.

The ultimate example of rethinking your problems.

GET INVOLVED

Most days we encounter stressful events: a traffic jam, a cat that gets sick on the carpet, a power outage, a surprise exam in class, an irritating call from a family member. The next time you feel stressed by a situation you can't control, observe your thoughts. What are you saying to yourself? Are your thoughts adding to your stress ("That stupid driver just tried to kill me!")? Try to apply the lessons on "rethinking the problem" to your own situation, and see whether they help. For example, can you think of another explanation for a family member's behavior? Can you think of something humorous about your predicament—and will it make a good story later? Can you think of something good about the situation?

SOCIAL COMPARISONS: "I'M BETTER OFF THAN SOME PEOPLE, AND I CAN LEARN FROM THOSE WHO ARE DOING BETTER THAN I AM." When successful copers are sick or in a difficult situation, they often compare themselves to others who are (they feel) less fortunate. No matter how bad off they are, even if they have fatal diseases, they find someone who is even worse off (Taylor & Lobel, 1989). For example, one AIDS sufferer said in an interview, "I made a list of all the other diseases I would rather not have than AIDS. Lou Gehrig's disease, being in a wheelchair; rheumatoid arthritis, when you are in knots and in terrible pain. So I said, 'You've got to get some perspective on this, and where you are on the Great Nasty Disease List.'" Another said, "I really have an advantage in a sense over other people. I know there is a possibility that my life may not go on for as many years as other people's. I have the opportunity to look at my life, to make changes, and to deeply appreciate the time that I have" (Reed, 1990).

Sometimes successful copers also compare themselves to those who are doing *better* than they are (Collins, 1996). Such comparisons are beneficial when they provide a person with information about ways of coping or managing the illness, and when the person feels able to take advantage of such information. Comparisons in either direction can be inspiring or detrimental, depending on what the coper is looking for and what lesson he or she draws from the experiences of others. People with low self-esteem, for example, seem to feel insecure when they compare themselves to others who are doing better than they; they cope better with setbacks when they compare themselves to others who are worse off (Aspinwall & Taylor, 1993).

VIGILANCE VERSUS AVOIDANCE: "TELL ME EVERYTHING" VERSUS "IT'S NOT IMPORTANT; LET'S GO TO THE MOVIES." Suppose you are going to the hospital for surgery. Should you get as much information as you can about every detail and risk of the procedure, or, having decided to go ahead, should you avoid thinking about it?

People who are "vigilant" scan all information for evidence of threat, whereas "avoidant" individuals try to elude threatening information by distracting themselves. As with primary and secondary control, each style has benefits and disadvantages. Vigilant individuals, for example, are overly sensitive to their bodily symptoms and take longer to recover from them (Miller, Brody, & Summerton, 1988). But a moderate amount of preoperative anxiety and vigilance actually protects against the stressfulness of surgery and speeds recovery, perhaps by helping the person mentally prepare for the operation (Manyande et al., 1992). When women need to have a biopsy for breast cancer—a scary situation—those who use avoidance or other "escape" tactics later show greater distress if they are diagnosed with cancer than do women who accept the possibility of a positive test (Carver et al., 1993b; Stanton & Snider, 1993). In such cases, vigilant individuals apparently do better than avoiders because they face the situation, get information about what to do, and then do it.

Vigilance is called for when action is possible and necessary, but once you have all the necessary information and have made your decision, avoidance and distraction can be excellent coping tactics. In a hospital, patients do best if they refuse to dwell on every little thing that could go wrong and distract themselves as much as possible. They also get well faster—and protect themselves—when they are vigilant about the care they are getting, and when they protest incorrect or thoughtless treatment. The benefits of distraction do not mean you should lie there like a flounder and passively accept every decision made for you.

HUMOR: "PEOPLE ARE FUNNY." "A merry heart doeth good like a medicine," says Proverbs in the Old Testament, and so it does. Once thought too frivolous a topic for serious study, humor has made its way into the laboratory.

"Sense of humor" includes the ability to respond with humor in real situations, to like humor and witty people, and to use humor in coping with stress.

The actor Bert Lahr, shown here as the lovable Cowardly Lion in The Wizard of Oz, *began using humor as a way to cope with unhappiness and stress early in his life.*

What can possibly be funny about misery? "He who laughs," thundered the German poet and dramatist Bertolt Brecht, "has not heard the terrible news." But people who can transform the "terrible news" into a sense of the absurd or the whimsical are less prone to depression, anger, tension, and fatigue than are people who give in to gloom. Research with many groups—including students, female executives, and old people—finds that individuals who use humor to cope with unfortunate events and daily hassles feel fewer negative emotions and unhappiness than do people who don't have a sense of humor or who instead succumb to moping and tears (P. Fry, 1995; Nezu, Nezu, & Blissett, 1988; Solomon, 1996). And among people with serious illnesses, humor reduces distress, improves immune functioning, and hastens recovery from surgery (Carver et al., 1993b; Martin & Dobbin, 1988).

Some theories of laughter emphasize its ability to reduce tension and emotion. You have probably been in a tense group situation when someone suddenly made a remark that made everyone laugh and defused the mood. Laughter seems to produce some beneficial biological responses, possibly stimulating the immune system or starting a flow of endorphins, the painkilling chemicals in the brain (W. Fry, 1994). Other theories emphasize the cognitive components of humor. When you laugh at a problem, you are putting it in a new perspective—seeing its silly or absurd aspects—and gaining control over it (Dixon, 1980). Humor also allows you to express indirectly feelings that are hazardous to express directly, which is why it is so often the weapon of the powerless. An old joke tells of a Jewish man who accidentally bumped into a Nazi on a street. "Swine!" bellowed the Nazi. "And I'm Cohen," replied the Jew, "pleased to meet you."

Having a sense of humor, however, is not the same as smiling all the time or "putting on a happy face." For humor to be effective in coping with stress, a person must actually use it during a specific, stressful situation—by noticing or inventing the funny or absurd aspects of the situation and laughing at them. For example, one therapist we know helps motorists reduce their stress and rage when they are caught in traffic jams by having them visualize other drivers as donkeys (a better technique than calling another driver a donkey!). The humor must also be good-natured; hostile humor misses the point. Vicious, rude jokes at another person's expense only create more tension and anger.

LIVING WITH THE PROBLEM

Stress is called the bane of modern civilization because our physiological alarm mechanism, which is so adaptive in helping us fight or flee from short-term danger, now chimes too often and stays on too long without a turn-off switch. Today, when the typical stressor is a mammoth traffic jam and not a mammoth mammal, the fight-or-flight response frequently gets revved up with nowhere to go. A third approach to coping, therefore, concentrates on reducing the physical effects of stress itself, and on establishing healthy habits that will reduce the chances of becoming ill.

STRESS-REDUCTION STRATEGIES Several techniques reduce symptoms of stress, improve immune function, and enhance the quality of a person's life. These techniques are effective for coping with the everyday stresses of life, as well as with serious, even terminal illnesses (Anderson, 1995; Taylor, 1995).

1. *Relaxation.* One of the simplest but most important ways to reduce symptoms of stress, such as high blood pressure and rapid breathing, is to relax. *Relaxation training*—learning to alternately tense and relax the muscles, to lie or sit quietly, to meditate by clearing your mind and banishing worries of the day—has beneficial effects on the body, lowering stress hormones and enhancing immune function (Baum, Herberman, & Cohen, 1995). In a study of 45 elderly people living in retirement homes, those who reduced stress with relaxation techniques showed significantly improved immune activity (Kiecolt-Glaser et al., 1985b). And in a study of 13 women with first-stage breast cancer, the women who received relaxation training during a nine-week intervention study showed no decline in their white-blood-cell count and a beneficial increase in cells that fight disease, in contrast to the control subjects (Gruber et al., 1993).

2. *Massage and "contact comfort."* We noted in Chapter 11 the importance of contact comfort to all human beings and other mammals, and indeed massage can be helpful in reducing stress, depression, and anxiety. Tiffany Field (1995), in a series of wide-ranging studies, is finding remarkable effects of periodic massage on preterm infants, who gain weight faster than unmassaged infants do; on normal full-term infants, who fall asleep faster and cry less than babies who are only rocked; and on children and adolescents with eating disorders, emotional disorders such as depression, and medical problems such as asthma and diabetes, who feel better and improve more quickly in contrast to controls who do not get the massage.

3. *Exercise.* Physical exercise, such as walking, jogging, dancing, biking, and swimming, is an important buffer between stressors and physical symptoms. A low level of physical activity is associated with decreased life expectancy for both sexes and contributes independently to the development of many chronic diseases (Dubbert, 1992). As you can see in Figure 14.2, when people are experiencing the same objective pressures, those who are physically fit have fewer health problems than people who are less fit; they show less physiological arousal to stressors and pay fewer visits to the doctor (Brown, 1991). These benefits of exercise apply to adults, adolescents, and even preschoolers. Preschoolers who did aerobic exercises daily for eight weeks, compared with children who spent the same time each day in free play, had better cardiovascular fitness and agility, and their self-esteem improved (Alpert et al., 1990). Similarly, the more that employees exercise, the fewer physical symptoms and colds they have—and they also are less anxious, depressed, and irritable (Hendrix et al., 1991).

4. *Looking outward.* Julius Segal (1986), a psychologist who worked with Holocaust survivors, prisoners of war, hostages, refugees, and other survivors of catastrophe, wrote that a key element in their recovery was compassion, "healing through helping." People gain strength, he said, by giving it to others. In fact, people who are highly empathic and cooperative are healthier and happier than those who are self-involved (Crandall, 1984). Why? The ability to look outside yourself, to be concerned with helping others, is related to virtually all of the successful coping mechanisms we have discussed so far. It tends to lead to

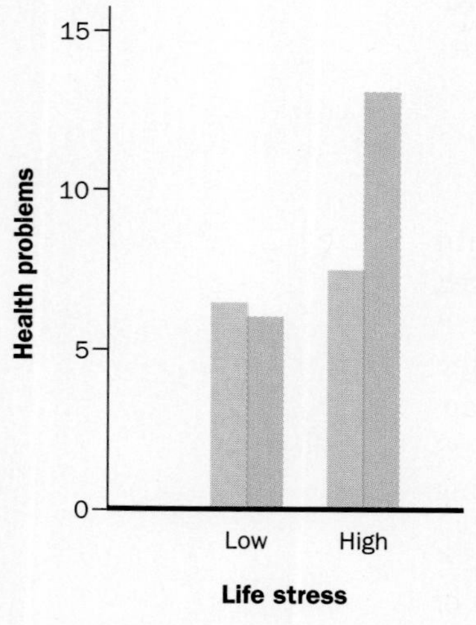

Figure 14.2
Fitness and Health

Among people under low stress, aerobically fit individuals had about the same number of health problems as those who were less fit. But among people under high stress, fit individuals had fewer health problems (Roth & Holmes, 1985).

Exercise has many health benefits, which is why some Western companies are adopting the Japanese practice, shown here, of scheduling exercise breaks for workers. Should exercise be a required part of the workday?

solving problems instead of blaming others; helps you reappraise a conflict by trying to see the conflict as others do, instead of taking it personally; and allows you to get perspective on a problem instead of exaggerating its importance. Because of its elements of forgiveness, tolerance, and empathy, "looking outward" helps you live with situations that are facts of life.

HEALTHY HABITS We bet you $100 that you already know the rules for protecting your health: Get enough sleep, exercise regularly, eat a nutritious diet, drink alcohol only in moderation if you drink at all, do not overeat or go on starvation diets, wear seat belts, and do not smoke cigarettes. According to a 10-year longitudinal study of nearly 7,000 people in Alameda County, California, each of these practices is independently related to good health and a lack of stress symptoms (Matarazzo, 1984). The more of these practices that people follow, the better their health.

So, why aren't you following all of them? Why, when people know what is good for them, don't they always do it? An important goal of health psychology is to help people reduce or eliminate the risk factors for illness before it has a chance to develop. But health psychologists have discovered several obstacles in their pursuit of prevention (Taylor, 1995):

- *Many health habits become entrenched during childhood.* Parents and extended families play a powerful role in determining a child's health habits and attitudes, by the lessons they teach, the meals they provide, and the examples they set. It is hard for people to give up a high-fat diet if they associate it with love and hearty home-cooked dinners.
- *People often have little incentive to change unhealthy habits.* Smoking, eating rich food, and not exercising have few immediate negative consequences; their effects do not become apparent for years. Many people therefore feel invulnerable.
- *Health habits are largely independent of one another.* Some people exercise every day and continue to smoke. Some people eat nutritious meals and take a lot of drugs.
- *Health habits are unstable over time.* Some people quit smoking for a year, and then take it up again. Others lose 50 pounds, and then gain 60.

Health psychologists have identified many factors that influence your ability to overcome the obstacles to good health. Some, as we have seen in this section, are in your personality and beliefs, such as whether you feel fatalistic about illness or in charge of your health. Some are in your *social system:* Do all your friends smoke and

GET INVOLVED

How do you score on following the seven basic rules of good health?

	Almost always or always	Sometimes	Hardly ever or never
I get enough sleep	______	______	______
I get regular exercise	______	______	______
I eat a nutritious diet	______	______	______
I drink alcohol only in moderation (or not at all)	______	______	______
I eat moderately and avoid crash diets	______	______	______
I wear seat belts	______	______	______
I do not smoke cigarettes	______	______	______

Now, for each answer that falls in the middle or right-hand column, what is the reason? Is it psychological—for example, not sleeping enough because you feel under pressure, going on crash diets because you think you look fat, or not wearing seat belts because you think they are nerdy? Is the reason social—for example, smoking or binge drinking because everyone you know does, and they think it's cool? Is the reason a matter of your culture and upbringing—for example, eating too much junk food because your family always did? What would have to change, in your mind or your environment, to cause you to improve your health habits?

drink themselves into a stupor on weekends? Chances are that you will join them. Some are in your larger *cultural environment:* Does your culture think it is appropriate for women to exercise or for men to stop eating red meat? Finally, some factors are determined by your *access to health-care services and information:* In the United States, unlike Canada, Europe, and Japan, many people lack medical insurance and cannot afford to visit a doctor. Maintaining good health depends not only on your personality, then, but also on your access to medical care and, as we will see next, on your social networks.

Quick Quiz

Can you cope with these refresher questions?

1. You accidentally broke your glasses. Which response is an example of cognitive reappraisal? (a) "I am such a stupid clumsy idiot!" (b) "I never do anything right." (c) "What a shame, but I've been wanting new frames anyway." (d) "I'll forget about it in aerobics class."
2. Finding out what your legal and financial resources are when you have been victimized by a crime is an example of (a) problem-focused coping, (b) emotion-focused coping, (c) distraction, (d) reappraisal.
3. Learning deep-breathing techniques to reduce anxiety about poor performance in a course is an example of (a) problem-focused coping, (b) emotion-focused coping, (c) avoidance, (d) reappraisal.
4. "This class drives me crazy, but I'm better off than my friends who aren't in college" is an example of (a) distraction, (b) social comparison, (c) denial, (d) empathy.
5. Your roommate has turned your room into a garbage dump, filled with rotten leftover food and unwashed clothes. Assuming that you don't like living with rotting food and dirty clothes, what coping strategies described in this section might help you?

Answers:

1. c 2. a 3. b 4. b 5. You might attack the problem by finding a compromise (clean the room together). You might reappraise the seriousness of the problem ("I only have to live with this person until the end of the term") or compare your roommate to others ("At least mine is generous and friendly"). You might also apply humor (e.g., pile everything into a heap, put a flag on top, and add a sign: "Monument to the Battle of the Bilge").

SOCIAL NETWORKS AND HEALTH

Everyone lives in a network of family, friends, neighbors, co-workers, and extended relations. Think of all the ways that members of your friendship network help you: They offer concern and affection. They help you evaluate problems and plan a course of action. They offer resources and services such as lending money or the car, or taking notes in class for you when you have to go to the doctor. Most of all, they are sources of attachment and connection, which everyone needs throughout life. Perhaps this is why old people who have dogs as companions visit medical clinics less often than their comparable peers who have no pets—or who have cats! Dogs provide companionship and attachment, the two ingredients of a truly best friend (Siegel, 1990).

WHEN FRIENDS HELP YOU COPE . . .

The Alameda County health study that we mentioned earlier, which followed nearly 7,000 adults for a decade, also investigated the importance of relationships to health. The researchers considered four kinds of social ties: marriage, contact with friends and relatives, church membership, and participation in other groups. People who had few social networks were more likely to have died at the time of the 10-year follow-up than those who had many (Berkman & Syme, 1979).

Perhaps the people who died were sicker to begin with or had poorer health habits, which kept them from socializing? No. The importance of social networks was unrelated to physical health at the time the study began, to socioeconomic status, and to such risk factors as smoking.

Perhaps the people who died had some undiagnosed illness at the beginning of the study? This interpretation was possible because the study was based on the participants' self-reports. So the research was repeated with nearly 3,000 people in Tecumseh, Michigan, and this time the investigators collected everyone's medical exams. Ten years later, those who had few relationships were more likely to have died than the people who had many, even after age, health, and other risk factors were taken into account (House, Landis, & Umberson, 1988).

One explanation for these findings is that social support somehow affects the body. In fact, one meta-analysis of 81 studies found that social support is related to many beneficial effects on the cardiovascular, endocrine, and immune systems (Uchino, Cacioppo, & Kiecolt-Glaser, 1996). Indeed, people who score high on the need for affiliation actually have higher levels of white blood cells that fight disease (Jemmott et al., 1990). Perhaps this is why lonely people have poorer immune function than people who are not lonely; why students in a network of friends have better immune function before, during, and after exam periods than students who are more solitary; and why spouses of cancer patients, although under considerable stress themselves, do not show a drop in immune function if they have lots of social support (Baron et al., 1990).

In some cases, social-support groups can even extend the survival time of people with serious illnesses. In a study of 194 older men and women who had had heart at-

Friends can be our greatest source of warmth, support, and fun . . .

tacks, 58 percent of those who reported having no close contacts died within the year, compared with only 27 percent of those who said they had two or more people they could count on (Berkman, Leo-Summers, & Horwitz, 1992). And in a study of 84 women with terminal breast cancer, researchers compared the survival rates of those who had cancer treatment plus weekly group support sessions with other patients, and those who had cancer treatment alone. Overall, a striking survival difference emerged between the women in the support group, who lived an average of 36.6 months from the start of the study, and those in the control group, who lived an average of 18.9 months (Spiegel et al., 1989).

Other studies have gotten similar results. Interventions that provide social support, improve patients' coping skills, and increase their optimism and self-efficacy may prolong the length of remissions in some kinds of cancer (Fawzy et al., 1993). Even when social support does not lengthen their lives, it lessens the suffering and pain of people with terminal illnesses, and it enhances their ability to come to terms with death.

. . . AND COPING WITH FRIENDS

As psychologists explored the benefits of friends and family, however, they noticed something else: Sometimes friends and family are themselves the source of hassles, unhappiness, and conflicts. When disaster or serious illness strikes, friends and relatives may blunder around, not knowing what to do or say. They may abandon you, or say something stupid and hurtful. In a study of more than 1,000 people who had recently lost their jobs, having a partner was not always beneficial. The laid-off workers who felt unwanted, criticized, or attacked by their partners were in worse mental health than those who felt that their spouses offered useful advice and emotional support (Vinokur & van Ryn, 1993).

Moreover, relationships impose the burdens of care. The work of caring for a chronically sick child, partner, or parent, a task that disproportionately falls on women in midlife, can become extremely stressful (Shumaker & Hill, 1991). In a study of 34 people who were taking care of a relative with Alzheimer's disease, the caregivers had more immune-system abnormalities than the control group did (Kiecolt-Glaser et al., 1987b).

Do the benefits of friendship outweigh these costs, or do they balance each other out? Several factors affect whether support helps or hurts (Dakof & Taylor, 1990):

. . . and also sources of exasperation, headaches, and pressure.

1. *Amount of support.* Too much help and sympathy offered to someone in trouble can actually backfire, creating dependency and low self-esteem.

2. *Timing of support.* After bereavement, divorce, or loss, a person needs lots of understanding. Friends who try to stem grief prematurely are not helping the sufferer. Later, however, they can prove helpful by trying to get the friend back into a social life.

3. *Kind of support.* For a friend's advice and sympathy to be effective, the sufferer must feel that the friend understands and has been in the same boat. Sometimes well-meaning friends and family members offer the wrong kind of support because they don't know what to do. People with cancer, for example, often report that their closest friends and relatives are willing to help them with *physical* tasks, for example by lifting or carrying things for them if they are too weak to do so, but frequently let them down *emotionally,* by being unwilling to listen to their expressions of fear or unhappiness (Bolger et al., 1996).

4. *Density of support.* In dense social networks, friends all know one another. Dense networks are good for a person's sense of stability and identity, but being in such a web can get sticky if the individual wants to get out. In a study of women going back to college, for example, those who were in a tight group of friends who were not in school showed worse adjustment, more physical symptoms, and lower self-esteem than women who were not in dense networks (Hirsch, 1981). "Good old friends" want you to stay put, and they can make you feel guilty for trying to change.

In close relationships, the person who is the source of support can also become the source of stress, especially if the two parties frequently argue. Constant fights can elevate both partners' blood pressures and can affect the immune system, too. In a study of 90 married couples, those who behaved in a negative and hostile fashion during a 30-minute discussion of marital problems (criticizing, interrupting, or insulting the other person, and becoming angry and defensive) showed significant elevations of stress hormones and impairments on four measures of immune function over the next 24 hours. Couples who argued in a positive fashion (trying to find common ground, compromising, listening to each other's concerns, and using humor to defuse tension) did not show these impairments (Kiecolt-Glaser et al., 1993; Malarkey et al., 1994). As one student of ours observed, "This study gives new meaning to the accusation 'You make me sick'!" It also suggests that learning to argue fairly and constructively may have physical as well as psychological benefits.

Quick Quiz

Maybe a friend will help you reduce the stress of this quiz.

1. Isabel has been diagnosed with diabetes. Her family is trying to be helpful, but they are reluctant to listen to her talk about her fears and worries. Which problem with social support is her family illustrating, and what might Isabel do about it?
2. Isadore wants to go away to graduate school, but his close friends want him to stay in town with them. Which problem with social support are they illustrating?

Answers:

1. Isabel's family is not offering her the right kind of support, because they don't understand her worries and can't provide emotional comfort. She might seek a support group of other people with diabetes who can meet this need. 2. dense network

It should be clear by now that the line between stress and illness is not a straightforward, direct one. Many factors—including personality traits, emotional styles, perceptions and attitudes, coping strategies, social networks, and biological vulnerability—are links in the long chain that connects continuing environmental stressors and poor health (see Figure 14.3). If people understood the importance of all of these factors, they might be less vulnerable to the inflated promises and programs in popular culture—the kind that offer simple solutions (at high prices). If you are under stress at work because you feel trapped by the job and mistreated by your employer, taking a "stress-reduction relaxation" course certainly might help, but ultimately you will have to figure out what to do about the job. Similarly, if you are under stress at home because you are having constant angry quarrels with your partner, joining a social-support group to talk about the problem might make you feel temporarily better, but ultimately you and your partner will have to figure out why you are fighting so much and how you can argue without hostility.

CONSIDER OTHER INTERPRETATIONS

"Boy, I've been under a lot of stress lately," you think. "I think I'll get one of those stress-reduction tapes." Before you jump to the conclusion that this is the best coping strategy, what alternatives might you consider?

As we discuss in "Taking Psychology with You," research in health psychology suggests many interventions that promote good health, and many effective strate-

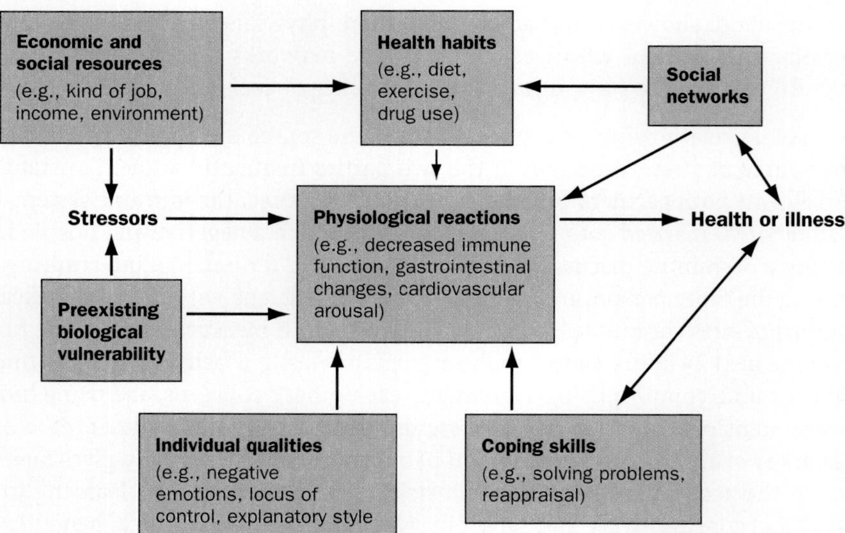

Figure 14.3
A Model of Stress and Illness

This chart shows some of the many factors that affect the path between stressors and illness. Complex as it is, it does not reflect all the possible interactions among contributing factors. For example, good health habits may counteract an existing biological vulnerability to disease. Can you think of other links?

gies for coping with problems. Keep in mind, however, that successful coping does not mean eliminating all stress. It does not mean constant happiness or a life without pain. The healthy person faces problems, deals with them, and gets beyond them, but the problems are necessary if the person is to acquire coping skills that endure. To wish for a life without stress would be like wishing for a life without friends. The result might be calm, but it would be joyless and ultimately hazardous to your health. The stresses of life—the daily hassles and the occasional tragedies—force us to grow, and to grow up.

Taking Psychology with You

Health Habits You Can Live With

The findings from health psychology offer practical guidelines for maintaining good health and coping with stressors or illness when they occur. Here are some suggestions based on the research in this chapter:

• *Take control of what you can, such as finding the best treatment for a medical problem or the best solution to a psychological one.* The effects of stress are worsened when you feel helpless. Many things happen that are out of your control: accidents, being born to particular parents, flu epidemics, natural disasters, and countless other events. But you do have control over how you cope with them. Building self-efficacy—by learning to monitor the behavior you wish to change, setting incentives for success, and finding social support—can help you increase control over your health and emotional well-being (Bandura, 1992).

• *Remember that some ways of coping are better than others.* If the situation requires action, it's better to use problem-solving techniques than to wallow around indecisively or simply vent emotions. But if the situation is a fact of life, people who can use humor, reappraisal, and constructive social comparisons will be better off than those who are overcome by depression and pessimism.

• *Don't try to "go it alone"; get the social support you need.* Find individuals who understand your problems and those who can offer practical as well as moral support. Whether your stress results from a one-time upsetting event or a chronic situation, try to find people who have "been there" and who can advise you on the best ways to cope, without keeping you mired in self-defeating patterns. The right kind of social support can offset emotional stressors, such as loneliness, and their physical effects, such as impaired immune function (Uchino, Cacioppo, & Kiecolt-Glaser, 1996).

• *Don't remain stuck in a network that isn't being helpful; get rid of the "social support" you don't need!* Are your friends or colleagues encouraging you to maintain unhealthy practices that you would like to change—such as smoking, abusing alcohol or other drugs, or going on crash diets? Are they preventing you from making improvements in your life? If so, you may need to think about finding new friends or new ways of sticking to your changed habits in spite of your old friends' efforts.

• *Follow "good old-fashioned motherly advice" and practice those habits associated with health.* These include not smoking, not drinking excessively or in binges, eating a healthful diet, wearing seat belts, walking or doing other forms of regular exercise at least several times a week, and getting enough sleep. Healthful habits are important not only for prevention of illness, but also for its treatment. When people become ill, they often stop taking care of themselves. They drink too much, become couch potatoes, misuse medication, and don't eat well, which in turn can speed the course of the disease (Taylor, 1995).

• *Learn when and how to disclose your emotions and upsetting experiences.* The complete suppression of feelings and secrets can be stressful to the body and can lead to illness. Research from psychoneuroimmunology suggests healthy alternatives to the suppression of traumatic experiences, embarrassing episodes, or emotional worries.

Start, paradoxically, by letting go of the effort to suppress the troubling thought, memory, or feeling. As we saw in this chapter, the very effort to suppress a thought makes you more likely to think and obsess about it, and living with unresolved secrets can be physiologically stressful (Pennebaker, 1995; Wegner, 1994). Instead of trying repeatedly to escape stressful feelings of worry, sadness, or anger, therefore, accept their existence. Then you will be ready to take steps to understand and resolve them.

According to James Pennebaker (1995), an effective way to understand and resolve any unfinished business that worries you is to write or talk about your deepest thoughts and feelings. Writing in a journal or talking into a tape recorder will both work. This process can help you assimilate the experience and come to a sense of completion about it. But confession must not turn to obsession. Confessing your deepest thoughts and feelings is not therapeutic if you keep rehearsing and confessing them endlessly to all who will listen (Nolen-Hoeksema, 1991). The key to reducing stress is physiological release *and* cognitive reappraisal.

These suggestions are only a few of the practical implications of health psychology. Perhaps you can find others mentioned in this chapter, such as the importance of maintaining primary control under some circumstances, of looking outward and helping other people, and of modifying the environment when you can. But if you find that you aren't perfectly able to control every aggravation, hassle, and crisis that comes your way, don't get upset. After all, that will only add to your stress!

SUMMARY

STRESS AND THE BODY

1) Hans Selye argued that environmental stressors such as heat, pain, and toxins cause the body to respond with fight-or-flee responses, occurring in three stages: *alarm, resistance,* and *exhaustion.* If a stressor persists, it may overwhelm the body's ability to cope, and fatigue and illness may result. Health psychologists today study the psychological and physical differences that make some individuals more vulnerable to stress and illness. Researchers in the field of *psychoneuroimmunology* (PNI) are studying how psychological factors, the nervous and endocrine systems, and the immune system interact to produce illness. Others study the psychological factors that mediate between the stressor and the stress, especially qualities of the individual (personality traits and perceptions) and how the individual copes with problems.

2) Certain major events, such as divorce or bereavement, are extremely stressful. Daily hassles—such as traffic jams, loud noise, and crowding—are stressful primarily when people cannot control these annoyances. Continuing, uncontrollable situations of powerlessness and poverty are far more stressful, and have greater cumulative effects on the body and health, than any one event.

PERSONALITY AND HEALTH

3) Researchers have sought links between personality traits and illness. Having a competitive, impatient *Type A personality* is not itself related to heart disease, but cynical *hostility,* which is often part of the Type A pattern, is. Depression seems to be an independent risk factor in heart disease, but the link between depression and other illnesses remains unclear. "Repressors," people who are emotionally inhibited, are at greater risk of illness than people who can acknowledge and cope with negative emotions. The effort to suppress thoughts, worries, secrets, and memories of upsetting experiences can paradoxically lead to obsessively ruminating on these thoughts and can be stressful to the body.

4) Other important personality factors that affect health are having an *optimistic explanatory style* (in contrast to a pessimistic one) and a *sense of control,* or self-efficacy. Optimism and control affect a person's ability to tolerate pain, live with ongoing illness and stress, and recover from disease. People can sometimes have too strong a sense of control; the healthiest balance is taking responsibility for solving problems without blaming yourself for things you can't do anything about. Health and well-being may depend on the right combination of *primary control,* trying to change the stressful situation, and *secondary control,* learning to accept the stressful situation. Cultures differ in the kind of control they emphasize and value.

COPING WITH STRESS

5) *Coping* involves a person's active and adaptive efforts to manage demands that he or she feels are stressful. Methods of coping include *solving the problem; rethinking the problem* (reappraising the situation to find meaning in the experience, comparing yourself to others with the problem, finding a balance between vigilance and distraction in attending to the problem, and seeing the humor in the situation); and *living with the problem* (reducing the physical effects of stress through relaxation, massage, exercise, and working on behalf of other people).

6) *Healthy habits* can prevent certain illnesses and can speed recovery when illness does occur. Some problems in getting people to acquire good habits and drop bad ones are that health habits are often established in childhood; people have little immediate incentive to change them; health habits are independent of one another; and health practices are unstable. Whether people practice good health habits depends not only on their personality traits but also on their social system, culture, and access to health care.

SOCIAL NETWORKS AND HEALTH

7) Friends, family, and other sources of social support are important in maintaining physical health and emotional well-being. They provide emotional support, advice, financial help, companionship, and attachment. However, parents, partners, spouses, and friends can also be stressful—a source of conflicts, burdens, and betrayals. They sometimes provide the wrong kind of support or too much support. A *dense network,* in which many friends know each other, is good for a person's stability but can make change difficult if one member wants to break away. In close relationships, couples who fight in a hostile and negative way show impaired immune function.

8) Psychological factors and social networks are links in a long chain that connects stress and illness. Coping with stress does not mean trying to live without pain, problems, or nuisances. It means learning how to live *with* them.

KEY TERMS

health psychology 542

psychosomatic medicine 542

stressor 542

alarm, resistance, and exhaustion phases of stress 543

eustress 543

psychoneuroimmunology (PNI) 544

psychological stress 545

Type A behavior pattern 549

cynical (antagonistic) hostility 549

pessimistic versus optimistic explanatory styles 552

positive illusions 553

defensive pessimism 553

locus of control (internal vs. external) 554

primary control 555

secondary control 555

coping 558

emotion-focused coping 558

problem-focused coping 558

reappraisal 559

social comparisons 560

avoidance and vigilance 560

humor (as way of coping) 560

dense network 567

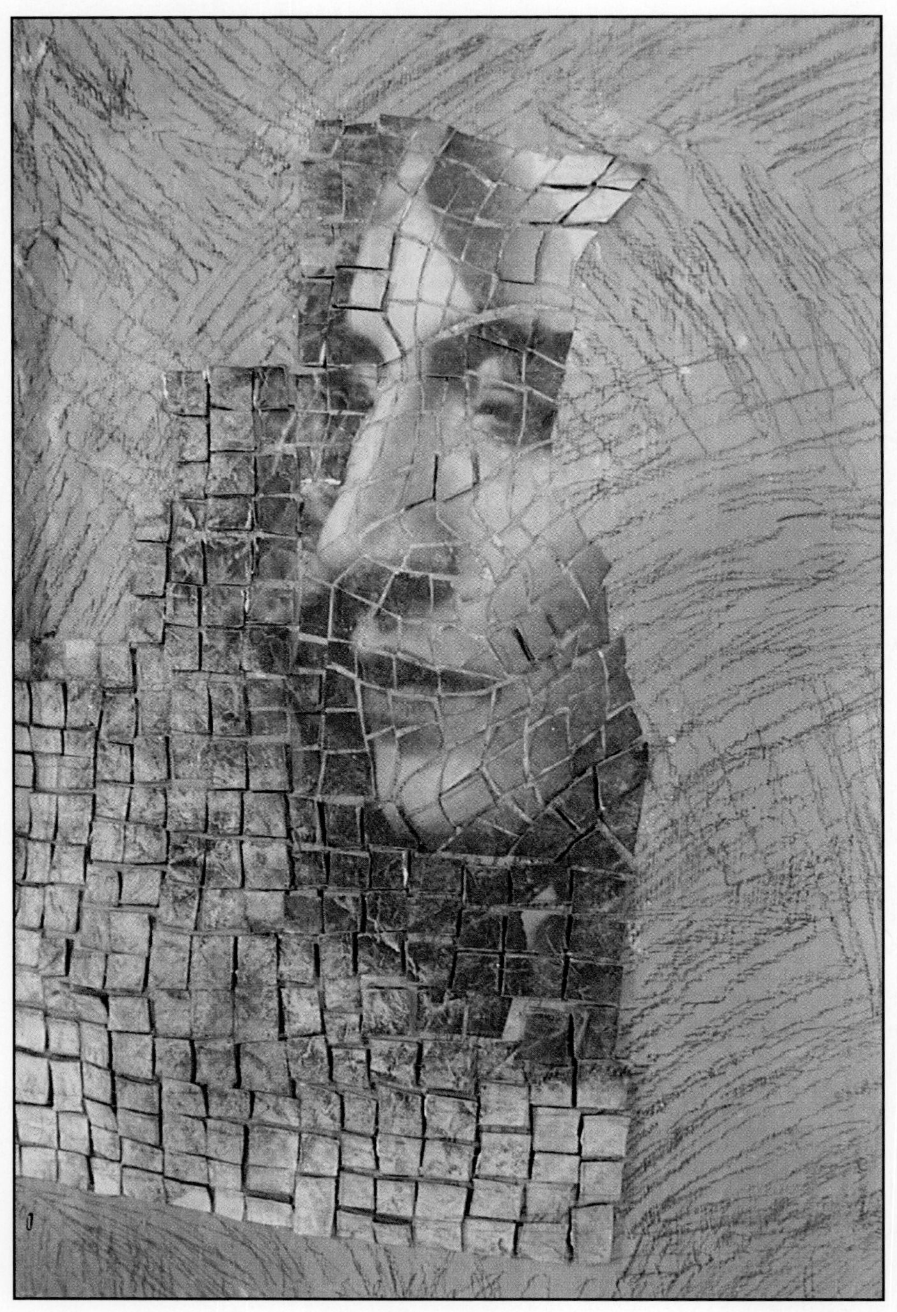

Who in the rainbow can draw the line where the violet tint ends
and the orange tint begins? . . . So with sanity and insanity.
In pronounced cases there is no question about them.
But in [less obvious cases, few people are willing]
to draw the exact line of demarcation
. . . though for a fee some professional experts will.

Herman Melville, *Billy Budd*

CHAPTER FIFTEEN

Psychological Disorders

Joan of Arc heard voices that inspired her to martyrdom. Was she sane and saintly—or mad?

YOU DON'T HAVE TO BE A PSYCHOLOGIST to recognize extreme forms of abnormal behavior. A homeless woman stands on a street corner every night between midnight and 3:00 A.M., screaming obscenities and curses; by day, she is calm. A man in a shop tells you confidentially that his shoes have been bugged by the FBI, his phone is wiretapped, and his friends are spying on him for the CIA. An old man has kept every one of his daily newspapers going back to 1945, and, although he has no room in his house for anything else, he panics at the thought of giving them up.

When most people think of "mental illness," they think of odd individuals like these, whose stories fill the newspapers. But most of the psychological problems that trouble people are far less dramatic and would never make the nightly news. They occur when an individual cannot cope effectively with the stresses and problems of life. The person may become so anxious and worried that work is impaired, or become severely depressed for months, or begin to abuse drugs. In most cases, as the quote that opens this chapter says, no "exact line of demarcation" indicates when normal behavior ends and abnormal behavior begins.

You will have noticed by now that we have tried to avoid traps of either–or thinking in this book, whether the subject is right-brain versus left-brain differences or nature versus nurture. It is the same with *normality* and *abnormality,* concepts that include a rainbow of behaviors, with many shadings of color and brightness. A given problem is not a fixed point on the rainbow. A person may go through episodes of inability to function, yet get along fine between those episodes. Problems also vary in intensity; they may be mildly uncomfortable, serious but endurable, or completely incapacitating. Psychologists and psychiatrists diagnose and treat a wide range of "abnormal" behavior.

One of the most common worries that people have is "Am I normal?" It is normal to fear being abnormal. We all occasionally have difficulties that seem too much to handle, that make us feel we can't cope. It is also normal to experience "medical students' syndrome": deciding that you suffer from whatever disorder you are reading about. Precisely because many psychological problems are so common, differing only in shades of intensity on the rainbow, you may start thinking that you have them all. (We are tempted to add that this faulty conclusion is a pigment of the imagination.)

DEFINING DISORDER

Many people tend to confuse the terms *abnormal behavior*—behavior that deviates from the norm—and *mental disorder,* but the two are not the same. A person may behave in ways that are statistically rare without having a mental illness. Some of this behavior is destructive, such as murder; some is charmingly unique, such as collecting ceramic pigs; and some is desirable, such as genius. Conversely, some mental difficulties, such as depression or anxiety, can be statistically common in a society; and some thoughts or behaviors that would usually be called disordered, such as paranoid delusions or sadism, may even be considered desirable qualities in certain cults and organizations, such as the neo-Nazi Aryan Nation.

DEFINE YOUR TERMS

A sect believes that it is being persecuted by nonbelievers, that a secret cabal controls the world, and that World War III is imminent. The group is stockpiling weapons and building bunkers for protection. These beliefs and actions are "normal" to all members of the sect, but would you call them signs of mental disorder? Why or why not?

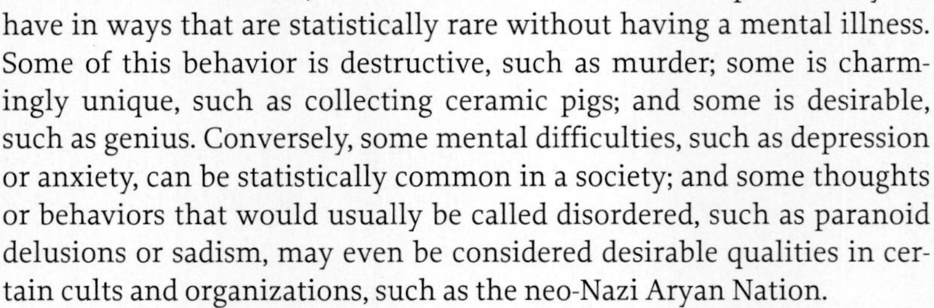

Moreover, the same symptom may be normal in one context but a sign of a disorder in another. For example, it is normal for people to hallucinate when they have a high fever, are isolated from all external sensation (see Chapter 5), are physically and mentally exhausted or stressed, are under the influence of various drugs, or are waking from deep sleep or falling into sleep. These conditions can produce "waking dreams" in which people report seeing ghosts, demons, space aliens, or other terrifying images. These normal hallucinations may be bizarre, but they are not signs of disorder; they arise from reactions of the brain to excessive stimulation or deprivation (Siegel, 1992).

Thus defining mental disorder is not an easy task. It depends in part on who is doing the defining and for what purpose, and it depends on understanding the context of the individual's symptoms and behavior. Here are several criteria in current use:

1. *Violation of cultural standards.* One definition of a mental disorder is that it involves a violation of group standards and cultural rules. Every society sets up standards of behavior that its members are expected to follow, and those who break the rules will be considered deviant or abnormal. Some standards are nearly universal, such as wearing clothes. If you run around naked in New Hampshire, most people (and the police) will think something is the matter with you.

But behavior that reflects normal conformity to a standard in one culture might seem to be abnormal in another setting. For example, seeing visions might be interpreted as a sign of schizophrenia in a twentieth-century farmer, but as a sign of healthy religious fervor in a thirteenth-century monk. For most North American cultural groups, hearing the voice or having visions of a deceased relative is thought to be abnormal; but the Chinese, the Hopi, and several other cultures regard such hallucinations as normal. (Actually, hallucinations are fairly common among whites too during bereavement; it is just that they don't tell anyone because they fear being considered "crazy" [Bentall, 1990].)

2. *Maladaptive behavior.* Many psychologists define mental disorder in terms of behavior that is maladaptive for the individual or society. This definition would apply to the behavior of a woman who is so afraid of crowds that she cannot leave her house, the behavior of a man who drinks so much that he cannot keep a job, and the behavior of a student who is so anxious about failure that he cannot write term

People all over the world paint their bodies, but what is normal in one culture often is abnormal or eccentric in another. Hiromi Nakano (left), whose body has been completely tattooed, has taken body painting to an extreme rare in most societies; but the Samburu tribesman of Kenya (center) is painted and adorned in ways typical of his culture. And the tattoos of the American bikers (right) are abnormal to most Americans but perfectly normal in the biking subculture. How are you reacting to these examples of body decoration? Do you think they are beautiful, amusing, disgusting, or creepy?

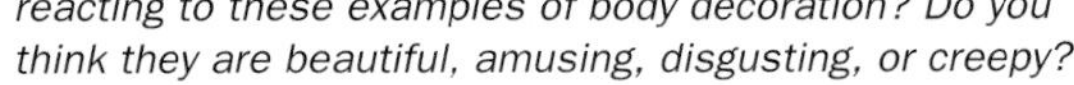

GET INVOLVED

You don't need to read a text on abnormal psychology to find cases of psychopathology; just open any magazine or newspaper! You will discover stories of violence, suicide, sexual obsession, delusion ("I was abducted by aliens"), and paranoia ("The government is spying on me from black helicopters"). As you look through an issue of your local paper, ask yourself whether the behavior in such stories seems clearly disturbed, normal, or somewhere in between. What are your criteria: cultural violations, maladaptive behavior, emotional distress, or legal judgments of impaired judgment? Can you identify cases in which it is hard to pinpoint where normality ends and disorder begins?

papers or take exams. It also covers the actions of individuals who say they feel fine and deny that anything is wrong but who behave in ways that are disruptive or dangerous to the community, or who are out of touch with reality—the child who sets fires, the compulsive gambler who loses the family savings, or the man who hears voices telling him to kill.

3. *Emotional distress.* A third definition identifies mental disorder in terms of a person's suffering. A person may conform to the rules of his or her community, working and getting along adequately, yet privately feel unreasonably anxious, afraid, angry, depressed, or guilty. By these criteria, according to a nationwide study of 20,000 randomly selected adults, in any given year about 28 percent of all Americans have one or more disorders—such as depression, anxiety, incapacitating fears, and alcohol or other drug problems (Regier et al., 1993; see also Kessler et al., 1994). The benefit of this definition is that it takes the person's own distress as a measure of disorder instead of imposing a single standard for everyone. A behavior that is unendurable or upsetting for one person, such as lack of interest in sex, may be acceptable and thus not distressful to another. One problem with this definition is that some people may be mentally disturbed and harmful to others, yet not feel troubled or conflicted about their behavior.

4. *The legal definition: impaired judgment and lack of self-control.* In law, the definition of mental disorder rests primarily on whether a person is aware of the consequences of his or her actions and can control his or her behavior. If not, the person may be declared insane—that is, incompetent to stand trial. But *insanity* is a legal term only; psychologists and psychiatrists do not use the terms *sanity* or *insanity* in relation to mental disorders.

Each of these definitions is useful, and no one of them is enough. In this chapter we will define **mental disorder** broadly, as any behavior or emotional state that causes an individual great suffering or worry; is self-defeating or self-destructive; or is maladaptive and disrupts either the person's relationships or the larger community. By these criteria, many people will have some mental-health problem in the course of their lives. This is normal.

DILEMMAS OF DIAGNOSIS

Even armed with a broad definition of mental disorder, psychologists have found that agreeing on a specific diagnosis is easier said than done. As George Albee (1985), a past president of the American Psychological Association, put it, "Appendicitis, a brain tumor and chicken pox are the same everywhere, regardless of culture or class; mental conditions, it seems, are not." In this section we will examine the difficulties of measuring and diagnosing some of those mental conditions.

mental disorder Any behavior or emotional state that causes an individual great suffering or worry; is self-defeating or self-destructive; or is maladaptive and disrupts the person's relationships or the larger community.

MEASURING MENTAL DISORDERS

Clinical and personality psychologists often use psychological tests to help them decide whether a person has a mental disorder. In Chapter 12 we discussed *projective tests*, which are based on the assumption that the test-taker will project his or her unconscious conflicts and motivations onto the stimulus materials. (You may recall the problems with these tests; see pages 478–479.) Most clinicians also rely on *objective tests*, or **inventories,** to diagnose their clients' problems. These tests are standardized questionnaires that require written responses, typically to multiple-choice or true-false items. Usually the test-taker is asked to report how she or he feels or acts in certain circumstances. For example, the Beck Depression Inventory is widely used to measure the severity of depression and distress; the Spielberger State–Trait Anger Inventory and the Taylor Manifest Anxiety Scale assess degrees and expressions of anger and anxiety. Objective tests have better *reliability* (they are more consistent over time) and *validity* (they are more likely to measure what they say they measure) than do projective methods or clinicians' subjective judgments (Anastasi, 1988; Dawes, 1994).

The most famous and widely used objective test of personality is the **Minnesota Multiphasic Personality Inventory (MMPI).** The MMPI was developed in the 1930s by Starke Hathaway and J. Charnley McKinley, who wanted a way to screen people with psychological disorders. They administered 1,000 potential test items to 200 people with various mental disorders and to a control group of 1,500 people who were not in treatment; the two groups differed in their answers to 550 items, and these were retained. The items were then assigned to ten clinical categories, or *scales*, that identified such problems as depression, paranoia, schizophrenia, and introversion. Four *validity scales* indicated whether a test-taker was likely to be lying, careless, defensive, or evasive while answering the items. For example, if a person tried to present an overall favorable but unrealistic image on nearly every item, the person's score on the lie scale would be high.

Since the original MMPI was devised, hundreds of additional scales have been added, and thousands of books and articles have been written on the test (Cronbach, 1990). The inventory has been used in some 50 countries, on everyone from ordinary job applicants to Russian cosmonauts. In 1989, a major revision of the MMPI was released, the MMPI-2, with norms based on a sample that was more representative in terms of region, ethnicity, age, and gender (Butcher et al., 1989).

Despite its popularity, the MMPI has many critics. Some have observed that the test is biased because its standards of normalcy do not reflect cultural differences. Although the sample used for establishing test norms in the MMPI-2 was an improvement, it still underrepresented minorities, the elderly, the poor, and the poorly educated. Some of the scales are still based on inadequate and outdated norms, and some items are affected by the respondent's tendency to give the socially appropriate answer rather than an honest one (Edwards & Edwards, 1991; Helmes & Reddon, 1993). One review concluded that the MMPI is adequate if the test is used for its original purpose—identifying people with emotional disorders (Parker, Hanson, & Hunsley, 1988). Yet in practice, the MMPI is often used in business, industry, and education for inappropriate reasons by persons who are not well trained in testing. Two psychologists who reviewed the history and validity of both MMPIs concluded that the correct interpretation of these tests requires "substantial experience and sophistication" by the clinician who administers them (Helmes & Reddon, 1993).

The debate about the MMPI reflects a deeper issue: whether mental disorder can be diagnosed objectively at all. The debate about testing is a whisper compared with the noisy controversy about the diagnosis of mental disorder itself.

inventories Standardized objective questionnaires requiring written responses; they typically include scales on which people are asked to rate themselves.

Minnesota Multiphasic Personality Inventory (MMPI) A widely used objective personality test.

Harriet Tubman (far left) with some of the people she helped to escape from slavery on her "underground railroad." Slaveholders welcomed the idea that Tubman and others who insisted on their freedom had a "mental disorder" called "drapetomania."

DIAGNOSIS: ART OR SCIENCE?

In the early years of the nineteenth century, a physician named Samuel Cartwright argued that many slaves were suffering from two forms of mental illness: *drapetomania*, an uncontrollable urge to escape from slavery, and *dysathesia aethiopica*, the symptoms of which included destroying property on the plantation, being disobedient, talking back, refusing to work, and fighting back when beaten. "Sanity for a slave was synonymous with submission," noted Hope Landrine (1988), "and protest and seeking freedom were the equivalent of psychopathology." Thus doctors could assure slaveowners that a mental illness, not the intolerable condition of slavery, made slaves seek freedom.

Today, "drapetomania" sounds foolish and cruel, and most people assume that the bad old days of psychiatric misdiagnosis are past. Yet cultural factors and subjective interpretations still affect the process of diagnosis, a fact that raises many important issues for those who define and treat mental disorders.

In theory, diagnostic categories must meet a set of solid scientific criteria to be included in the "bible" of psychological and psychiatric diagnosis, the *Diagnostic and Statistical Manual of Mental Disorders* (DSM), which is published by the American Psychiatric Association. The first edition of the DSM, in 1952, was only 128 pages long and contained brief descriptions of organic brain disorders, severe mental disorders, and personality problems. The second edition, the DSM-II, appeared in 1968; it too was short. The third edition, DSM-III, published in 1980, began to include ordinary difficulties such as tobacco dependence, marital conflicts, and sexual problems. The revised third edition, DSM-III-R, in 1987, was 567 pages long and listed more than 200 kinds of mental disorder. The fattest edition yet, the DSM-IV, published in 1994, is nearly 900 pages long and contains more than 300 mental disorders.

The primary aim of the DSM is *descriptive:* to provide clear criteria of diagnostic categories, so that clinicians and researchers can agree on which disorders they are talking about, study them, and treat them. (For a list of its major categories, see Table 15.1.) The DSM makes few assumptions about the causes of the disorders it describes; in many cases, the causes are not known. Where possible, information is provided about typical age of onset, predisposing factors, course of the disorder, prevalence of the disorder, sex ratio of those affected, and cultural issues that might affect diagnosis. The DSM also classifies each disorder on five *axes*, or factors:

1. The primary diagnosis of the problem, such as depression.
2. Ingrained aspects of the client's personality that are likely to affect his or her behavior and ability to be treated, such as narcissism or dependency.
3. General medical conditions that are relevant to the disorder, such as respiratory or digestive problems.
4. Social and environmental problems that can make the disorder worse, such as job and housing troubles or loss of a support group.
5. A global assessment of the client's overall level of functioning in work, relationships, and leisure time, including whether the problem is of recent origin or of long duration, and how incapacitating it is.

The DSM has had an extraordinary impact worldwide. It has standardized the categories of what is, and what is not, a mental disorder. Its categories and terminology have become the common language of most clinicians and researchers. Virtually all textbooks in psychiatry and psychology base their discussions of mental disorders on the DSM. Insurance companies require clinicians to assign their clients the appropriate DSM code number of the diagnosed disorder, which puts pressure on com-

TABLE 15.1 *Major Diagnostic Categories in the DSM-IV*

Disorders usually first diagnosed in infancy, childhood, or adolescence include mental retardation, attention-deficit disorders (such as hyperactivity or an inability to concentrate), eating disorders, and developmental problems.

Delirium, dementia, amnesia, and other cognitive disorders are those resulting from brain damage, degenerative diseases such as syphilis or Alzheimer's, toxic substances, or drugs.

Substance-related disorders are problems associated with excessive use of or withdrawal from alcohol, amphetamines, caffeine, cocaine, hallucinogens, nicotine, opiates, or other drugs.

Schizophrenia and other psychotic disorders are disorders characterized by delusions, hallucinations, and severe disturbances in thinking and emotion.

Mood disorders include major depression, bipolar disorder (manic-depression), and dysthymia (chronic depressed mood).

Anxiety disorders include generalized anxiety disorder, phobias, panic attacks with or without agoraphobia, posttraumatic stress disorder, and obsessive thoughts or compulsive rituals.

Somatoform disorders involve individual reports of physical symptoms (e.g., paralysis, heart palpitations, or dizziness) for which no organic cause can be found. This category includes hypochondria, extreme preoccupation with health and the unfounded conviction that one is ill; and conversion disorder, in which a physical symptom (such as a paralyzed arm or blindness) serves a psychological function.

Dissociative disorders include dissociative amnesia, in which important events cannot be remembered after a traumatic event; and dissociative identity disorder (formerly "multiple personality disorder"), characterized by the presence of two or more distinct identities or personality states.

Sexual and gender identity disorders include problems of sexual (gender) identity, such as transsexualism (wanting to be the other gender); problems of sexual performance (such as premature ejaculation, lack of orgasm, or lack of desire); and paraphilias, which involve unusual or bizarre imagery or acts that are necessary for sexual arousal, as in fetishism, sadomasochism, or exhibitionism.

Impulse control disorders involve an inability to resist an impulse to perform some act that is harmful to the individual or to others, as in pathological gambling, stealing (kleptomania), setting fires (pyromania), or having violent rages.

Personality disorders are inflexible and maladaptive patterns that cause distress to the individual or impair the ability to function; they include paranoid, narcissistic, and antisocial personality disorders.

Additional conditions that may be a focus of clinical attention include "problems in living" such as bereavement, academic difficulties, religious or spiritual problems, and acculturation problems.

pilers of the manual to add more diagnoses so that physicians and psychologists will be compensated. Attorneys and judges often refer to the manual's list of mental disorders, even though the DSM warns that its categories "may not be wholly relevant to legal judgments."

Because of the power of the DSM to define mental disorders, it is important to know its limitations. Critics point to the following concerns about the scientific basis of diagnosis in general and the DSM in particular:

1. *The fostering of overdiagnosis.* When people have a tool, they will use it, a tendency that Abraham Kaplan (1967) called "The Law of the Instrument." "If you give a small boy a hammer," Kaplan wrote, "it will turn out that everything he runs into needs pounding." So it is, some say, with clinicians. Give them the instruments to diagnose disorders, and everything they run into will need treatment. For example, before 1980, fewer than 200 cases of dissociative identity disorder (commonly known as "multiple personality disorder") had ever been diagnosed. Since 1980, when the DSM-III included new criteria for this diagnosis, thousands and thousands of cases have been reported, most of them in North America (Nathan, 1994; Piper, 1997). Does this mean that the disorder is being better identified, or that it is being overdiagnosed by American and Canadian clinicians who are looking for it? Clinicians are also more likely to diagnose a disorder once they have a treatment for it. As medication was promoted to treat obsessive–compulsive disorder, for example, the rate of diagnosis of this problem rose significantly (Stoll, Tohen, & Baldessarini, 1993).

2. *An increased risk of self-fulfilling prophecies.* The very act of diagnosing a disorder can create a self-fulfilling prophecy for both the client and the clinician: The client tries to conform to the assigned diagnosis, and the clinician interprets everything the client does as further confirmation of the diagnosis (Maddux, 1996; Rosenhan, 1973). Moreover, as we will see in Chapter 17, once a person has acquired a label—for example, once an impulsive, troubled teenager is given the diagnosis of "oppositional defiant disorder"—others often become oblivious to changes in the individual's behavior or to other possible reasons for it, continuing to see him or her only in terms of the diagnosis.

3. *The confounding of serious mental disorders with normal problems in living.* The DSM is not called "The Diagnostic and Statistical Manual of Mental Disorders and a Whole Bunch of Everyday Problems." Yet the compilers of the DSM keep adding everyday problems. The latest version actually contains "disorder of written expression" (having trouble writing clearly), "mathematics disorder" (not doing well in math), and "caffeine-induced sleep disorder." Some critics fear that by lumping together such normal difficulties with true mental illnesses, such as schizophrenia, the DSM implies that everyday problems are comparable to disorders—and equally likely to require professional treatment (Dumont, 1987; Maddux, 1993; Szasz, 1961/1967).

4. *Misuse of diagnoses for social and political purposes.* Some critics are concerned that once people are given a formal diagnosis for their problems, they may feel absolved of responsibility for their behavior or use the label to claim diminished responsibility for criminal acts. This concern was a major reason that the task force revising the DSM-III decided to drop a proposed diagnosis called "paraphilic coercive disorder," describing the behavior of men who rape. The task force agreed with women who were concerned that rapists diagnosed as having such a "disorder" would not be held responsible.

5. *A false implication that diagnosis can be purely objective.* Finally, some critics argue that the whole enterprise of the DSM is a foolhardy effort to impose a veneer of science on the inherently arbitrary process of defining mental disorder. They maintain that the DSM wants to look like an objective set of disorders, as if no bias or choice were involved in deciding what to include and what to leave out (Dumont, 1987; Maddux, 1993; Tiefer, 1995). In fact, say the critics, many such decisions have been based not on empirical evidence, but on group consensus or on the pressure to have more diagnosable categories that insurance companies will compensate (Kirk & Kutchins, 1992).

For example, when the American Psychiatric Association decided in the early 1970s to remove homosexuality from the DSM, it did not base its decision on the research showing that homosexuals were no more disturbed than heterosexuals.

If people have a disorder, are they still responsible for their actions? Which disorders described in this chapter do you think should excuse people's behavior or merit the legal defense of "diminished responsibility"?

Rather, *it took a vote of its members* (Bayer, 1981). Over the years, psychiatrists have quite properly rejected many other "disorders" that reflected cultural prejudices, such as drapetomania, lack of vaginal orgasm, childhood masturbation disorder, masochism, and nymphomania (Wakefield, 1992). But they have also voted in new "disorders" that reflect today's prejudices and values, such as "hypoactive sexual desire disorder"—not wanting to have sex often enough. Compilers of the DSM-III-R, amid much controversy, voted in a diagnosis called "self-defeating personality disorder," which would have applied mainly to women who adopted the extreme self-sacrificing qualities of the female role; compilers of the DSM-IV voted it out. But they kept, in an appendix, "premenstrual dysphoric disorder," even though, as we saw in Chapter 5, this alleged syndrome lacks an agreed-on definition, and men have as many symptoms and mood changes over the month as women do.

The point to underscore is that *as times change, so does the cultural consensus about what is normal—and thus what is abnormal.* And that, in turn, means that clinicians must be aware of how their own beliefs and leanings affect their clinical judgments, even when they are trying to follow objective criteria. In one study, for example, 47 therapists were randomly assigned to view one of two videotapes of a depressed male client. The tapes were identical except for the man's job and family roles: He was portrayed as either a traditional breadwinner or a nontraditional househusband whose wife earned the family income. Later, when the therapists evaluated the man's mental health, assigned a diagnosis, and outlined a proposed treatment, they judged nontraditional men as being more disturbed than traditional men (Robertson & Fitzgerald, 1990).

Advocates of the DSM argue that when the manual is used correctly, diagnoses are more accurate and bias is reduced, and that new field studies are improving the empirical basis of the clinical categories (Barlow, 1991; Spitzer & Williams, 1988; Wittchen et al., 1995). A study of psychiatric patients in Maryland, for instance, found better accuracy in the diagnosis of schizophrenia and mood disorders than other studies had, apparently because the physicians were more closely following DSM criteria (Pulver et al., 1988). Other advocates argue that the correct labeling of a disorder helps people identify the source of their unhappiness and leads them to proper treatment (Kessler et al., 1994). They respond to the criticisms of subjectivity in diagnosis by pointing out that some mental disorders, such as schizophrenia, anxiety, and depression, occur in all societies. The fact, they say, that *some* diagnoses reflect society's biases doesn't mean that *all* diagnoses do (Wakefield, 1992). In cultures around the world, from the Inuit of Alaska to the Yorubas of Nigeria, there are individuals who have delusions, who are severely depressed, or who can't control their behavior; in every culture, they are considered to have mental illnesses (Kleinman, 1988).

We will return to these controversies as we examine some of the major categories of disorder in the DSM.

Quick Quiz

Your mental health will improve if you can answer these questions.

1. What is the advantage of inventories, compared with clinical judgment and projective tests, in diagnosing mental disorders?
2. The primary purpose of the DSM is to (a) provide descriptive criteria for diagnosing mental disorders, (b) help psychologists assess normal as well as abnormal personality traits, (c) describe the causes of common mental disorders, (d) keep the number of diagnostic categories of mental disorders to a minimum.
3. List five concerns about the DSM and its uses.

4. Two psychologists are discussing an anxious and depressed Japanese-American man who, along with 112,000 other Japanese-Americans in World War II, lost his job and home and was sent to an internment camp. Dr. Smith diagnoses "posttraumatic stress disorder." Dr. Jones believes that because the man's symptoms resulted from an act of governmental injustice, the diagnosis should be something like "post-oppression disorder" (Loo, 1991). Can you identify the main assumption in the kind of label each psychologist is using and the solution it implies?

Answers:

1. In general, they have better reliability and validity. 2. a 3. Fostering overdiagnosis; increasing the risk of self-fulfilling prophecies; confounding normal problems in living with mental disorders; using diagnoses for undesirable social and political purposes; and creating a scientific veneer to disguise the essentially subjective process of diagnosis. 4. Dr. Smith assumes that the origins of the man's unhappiness lie within him, in his own personal reaction to the trauma of imprisonment; the implied solution is psychotherapy. Dr. Jones assumes that the man's unhappiness is a result of a miscarriage of justice; the implied solution, in addition to psychotherapy, might involve a social remedy, such as reparations.

ANXIETY DISORDERS

The body, sensibly, prepares us to feel anxiety (a general state of apprehension or psychological tension) or fear (apprehension about a specific threat) when we are facing dangerous, unfamiliar, or stressful situations, such as making a first parachute jump or waiting for important news. In the short run, these are adaptive emotions that enable us to cope with danger. But some individuals are prone to irrational fear or to a chronic state of anxiety. In clinical terms, such fear and anxiety can take several forms: *generalized anxiety disorder*, marked by long-lasting, continuous feelings of apprehension and doom; *phobias*, unrealistic fears of specific things or situations; and *obsessive–compulsive disorder,* in which people develop irrational thoughts and rituals designed to ward off anxious feelings.

Is this woman feeling normal fear or unreasonable panic? (To find out, turn the page.)

ANXIETY AND PHOBIAS

The chief characteristic of **generalized anxiety disorder** is continuous, uncontrollable anxiety or worry—a feeling of foreboding and dread—that occurs more days than not in a six-month period and that is not brought on by physical causes such as disease, drugs, or drinking too much coffee. Symptoms include restlessness or feeling keyed up, being easily fatigued, having difficulty concentrating, irritability, muscle tension and jitteriness, and sleep disturbance.

Chronic anxiety has no single cause. *Predisposing factors* include having a hereditary predisposition, having poor coping methods, living through a traumatic event, and having unrealistic goals or unreasonable beliefs that foster worry and fears. *Precipitating factors* are the immediate events that produce anxiety and keep it going. You are likely to feel anxious when you are in a situation in which others continually express their disapproval of you, or when you have to adapt yourself to an environment that doesn't fit your personality, such as being a slow-paced person in a fast-moving job.

When anxiety results from experiencing an uncontrollable and unpredictable danger or a natural disaster, it may produce *posttraumatic stress disorder* (*PTSD*) or *acute stress disorder.* PTSD consists of emotional symptoms that are common in people who have suffered traumatic experiences such as war, rape, other assaults, and natural disasters such as hurricanes, fire, or earthquake. The reaction might occur immediately or it might be delayed for months. In contrast, acute stress disorder typically occurs right after the traumatic event and subsides within several months. In both disorders, typical symptoms include reliving the trauma in recurrent, intrusive thoughts or dreams; "psychic numbing," a sense of detachment from others and an inability to feel happy or loving; and increased physiological arousal, reflected in difficulty concentrating, insomnia, and irritability. A random survey of 5,877 Americans found that PTSD is more common and more persistent than previously assumed: Nearly 1 in 12 has suffered from PTSD in his or her life, and in more than one-third of the cases, the symptoms lasted for at least ten years (Kessler et al., 1995).

A **phobia** is an unrealistic fear of a specific situation, activity, or thing. Some phobias are extremely common, such as fear of heights (acrophobia); fear of closed spaces (claustrophobia); fear of dirt and germs (mysophobia); and fear of animals, especially snakes, dogs, insects, and mice (zoophobia). Others are rarer, such as fear of purple (porphyrophobia), fear of the number 13 (triskaidekaphobia), and fear of thunder (brontophobia).

generalized anxiety disorder A continuous state of anxiety marked by feelings of worry and dread, apprehension, difficulties in concentration, and signs of motor tension.

phobia An unrealistic fear of a specific situation, activity, or object.

GET INVOLVED

Everyone fears something. Stop for a moment to think about what you fear most. Is it heights? Snakes? Speaking in public? Ask yourself these questions:

- *How long have I feared this thing or situation?*
- *How would I respond if I could not avoid this thing or situation?*
- *How much would I be willing to rearrange my life (my movements, schedule, activities) to avoid this feared thing or situation?*

After considering these questions, would you regard your fear as a full-blown phobia or merely a normal source of apprehension? What are your criteria for deciding?

It is normal to feel afraid when you jump out of a plane for the first time. But people with anxiety disorders feel as if they are jumping out of planes all the time.

People who have a *social phobia* have a persistent, irrational fear of situations in which they will be observed by others. They worry that they will do or say something that will humiliate or embarrass them. Common social phobias are fears of speaking or performing in public, using public restrooms, eating in public, and writing in the presence of others. (Notice that these phobias are more severe forms of the occasional shyness and social anxiety that everyone experiences.)

By far the most disabling fear disorder is **agoraphobia,** which accounts for more than half of the phobia cases for which people seek treatment. Disregard the dictionary and popular definition of agoraphobia as "fear of open spaces." In ancient Greece, the *agora* was the social, political, business, and religious center of town. It was the public meeting place away from home. The essential feature in what agoraphobics fear is being alone in a public place from which escape might be difficult or help unavailable. They may report a great variety of specific fears—of public buses, driving in traffic or tunnels, eating in restaurants, or going to parties—but the underlying fear is of being away from a safe place, usually home, or a safe person, usually a parent or spouse.

Agoraphobia may begin with a series of panic attacks that seem to come out of the blue. A **panic attack** is a sudden onset of intense fear or terror, with feelings of impending doom. It may last from a few minutes to (more rarely) several hours, and it involves such intense symptoms as trembling and shaking; dizziness; chest pain or discomfort; feelings of unreality; hot and cold flashes; sweating; and a fear of dying, going crazy, or losing control. The attack is so unexpected and so scary that the agoraphobic-to-be begins to avoid situations that he or she thinks may provoke another one. After a while, any sort of emotional arousal, from whatever source, feels too much like anxiety, and the person with agoraphobia will try to avoid it. Because so many of the actions associated with this phobia are designed to help the person avoid a panic attack, researchers often describe agoraphobia as a "fear of fear" rather than a fear of places (Chambless, 1988).

People who have panic attacks are found throughout the world, in both industrial and nonindustrial societies (Barlow, 1990). The common symptoms are heart palpitations, dizziness, and faintness, but culture influences the likelihood of other telltale signs. Feelings of choking or being smothered, numbness, and fear of dying are most common in Latin America and southern Europe; fear of public places is most common in northern Europe and America; and a fear of going crazy is more common in the Americas than in Europe. In Greenland, some fishermen suffer from "kayak-angst": a sudden attack of dizziness and fear that occurs while they are fishing in small, one-person kayaks (Amering & Katschnig, 1990).

Studies of twins suggest a heritable component in panic disorder, a tendency for the body to respond to stress with a sudden "alarm" reaction. (For other people, the response may be headaches or hives.) Although panic attacks seem to come from nowhere, they are in fact often related to the physical arousal of stress, prolonged emotion, exercise, drugs such as caffeine or nicotine, or specific worries (Barlow, 1990; Beck, 1988). Panic attacks are not uncommon. The essential difference between people who go on to develop a disorder and those who don't lies in *how they interpret their bodily reactions* (Barlow, 1990; McNally, 1994). Healthy people who have occasional panic attacks see them correctly as a result of a passing crisis or period of stress, comparable to another person's migraines. But people who develop a full-fledged panic disorder regard the attack as a sign of impending death or disaster, and they begin to worry about possible future ones. Agoraphobia develops when they begin to avoid any situation that they fear will set off another attack.

agoraphobia A set of phobias, often set off by a panic attack, involving the basic fear of being away from a safe place or person.

panic attack A brief feeling of intense fear and impending doom or death, accompanied by intense physiological symptoms, such as rapid breathing and pulse, and dizziness.

OBSESSIONS AND COMPULSIONS

Obsessive–compulsive disorder (OCD) is characterized by recurrent, persistent, unwished-for thoughts or images (*obsessions*) and by repetitive, ritualized, stereotyped behaviors that the person feels must be carried out to avoid disaster (*compulsions*). The disorder can begin in childhood, and it occurs in both sexes. Of course, many people have trivial compulsions and superstitious rituals; as we noted in Chapter 7, baseball players are famous for them. Obsessions and compulsions become serious—a disorder—when they trouble the individual and interfere with his or her life.

A person with obsessive thoughts often finds them frightening and repugnant. For example, the person may have repetitive thoughts of killing a child, of becoming contaminated by shaking hands, or of having unknowingly hurt someone in a traffic accident. Obsessive thoughts take many forms, but they are alike in reflecting maladaptive ways of reasoning and processing information. Some people may develop obsessions because they have difficulty managing anger. In one case, a man had repeated images of hitting his 3-year-old son with a hammer. Unable to explain his horrible thoughts about his beloved son, he assumed he was going insane. Most parents, in fact, have occasional negative feelings about their children and may even entertain a fleeting thought of murder, but they recognize that these are not the same as actions. The man, it turned out, felt that his son had usurped his place in his wife's affections, but he was unable to reveal his anger and hurt to his wife directly (Carson, Butcher, & Mineka, 1996).

What is a normal concern with hygiene in one culture could seem an abnormal compulsion in another. This Lysol ad played on Americans' fears of disease by warning about the "unseen menace—more threatening, more fatal, more cruel than a million mad dogs— . . . the disease germ."

People who suffer from compulsions likewise feel they have no control over them. For example, a woman *must* check the furnace, lights, locks, oven, and fireplace three times before she can sleep; a man *must* wash his hands and face precisely eight times before he leaves the house. The most common compulsions are hand washing, counting, touching, and checking. Most sufferers of OCD do not enjoy these rituals and realize that the behavior is senseless. But if they try to break the ritual, they feel mounting anxiety that is relieved only by giving in to the compulsion. They are like the man who constantly snaps his fingers to keep tigers away. "But there aren't any tigers here," says a friend. "You see! It works!" answers the man.

PET scans find that several parts of the brain are hyperactive in people with OCD. One area, the orbital cortex (which lies just above the eye sockets), apparently sends messages of impending danger to the caudate nucleus, an area involved in controlling the movement of the limbs, and to other structures involved in preparing the body to feel afraid and respond to external threats. Normally, once danger is past or a person realizes there is no real cause for fear, the caudate nucleus switches off the alarm signals. In people with OCD, however, the orbital cortex sends out repeated false alarms; the emotional networks send out mistaken "fear!" messages, and the caudate nucleus fails to turn them off. The sufferer feels in a constant state of danger and tries repeatedly to reduce the resulting anxiety (Schwartz et al., 1996).

Anxiety disorders, uncomfortable or painful as they can be, are at least a sign of commitment to the future. They mean a person can anticipate the future enough to worry about it. But sometimes people's hopes for the future become extinguished. They are no longer anxious that something may go wrong; they are convinced it *will* go wrong, so there is no point in trying. This belief is a sign of the disorder of depression.

obsessive–compulsive disorder (OCD) An anxiety disorder in which a person feels trapped in repetitive, persistent thoughts (obsessions) and repetitive, ritualized behaviors (compulsions) designed to reduce anxiety.

Quick Quiz

We hope you don't feel anxious about matching the term on the left with its description on the right:

1. social phobia
2. generalized anxiety disorder
3. posttraumatic stress disorder
4. agoraphobia
5. compulsion
6. obsession

a. need to perform ritual
b. fear of fear; of being trapped in public
c. continuing sense of doom and worry
d. repeated, unwanted thoughts
e. fear of meeting new people
f. anxiety following severe shock

Answers:

1. e 2. c 3. f 4. b 5. a 6. d

MOOD DISORDERS

In everyday talk, we all use the word *depression* to describe sadness, gloom, and loss of pep. By that definition, everyone feels depressed at times. Psychologists, however, consider depression to be a disorder only when it goes beyond normal sadness over life's problems, or even the wild grief that may accompany tragedy or bereavement. Serious depression is so widespread that it has been called the common cold of psychiatric disturbances.

The hallmarks of depression are despair and a sense of isolation.

DEPRESSION AND MANIA

Major depression is severe enough to disrupt a person's ordinary functioning. It differs from chronic depressed mood, a condition called *dysthymia* [dis-THIGH-me-a], in the intensity and duration of symptoms. In dysthymia, the depressive symptoms are milder, and they *are* the person's customary way of functioning.

Major depression brings emotional, behavioral, and cognitive changes. Depressed people report despair and hopelessness. They are tearful and weepy. They think often of death or suicide. They lose interest or pleasure in their usual activities. They feel unable to get up and do things; it takes an enormous effort just to get dressed. Their thinking patterns feed their bleak moods. They exaggerate minor failings, ignore or discount positive events ("She didn't mean that compliment; she was only being polite"), and interpret any little thing that goes wrong as evidence that nothing will ever go right. Unlike normal sadness or grief, major depression involves low self-esteem. Emotionally healthy grieving people do not see themselves as completely worthless and unlovable, and they know at some level that grief will pass. Depressed people interpret losses as signs of personal failure and conclude that they will never be happy again.

Depression is accompanied by physical changes as well. The depressed person may stop eating or overeat, have difficulty falling asleep or sleeping through the night, lose sexual desire, have trouble concentrating, and feel tired all the time. Some sufferers have other physical reactions, such as inexplicable pain or headaches. (Anyone with these symptoms should have a medical exam because they can also be signs of physical illness.) About half of all those who go through a period of major depression will do so only once. Others have recurrent bouts. Some people have episodes that are many years apart; others have clusters of depressive episodes over a few years. Alarmingly, depression and suicide rates among young people have increased rapidly in recent years. (See "Taking Psychology with You.")

major depression A mood disorder involving disturbances in emotion (excessive sadness), behavior (loss of interest in one's usual activities), cognition (thoughts of hopelessness), and body function (fatigue and loss of appetite).

At the opposite pole from depression is *mania*, an abnormally high state of exhilaration. You might think it's impossible to feel too good, but mania is not the normal joy of being in love or winning the Pulitzer Prize. Someone in a manic phase is expansive to an extent that is out of character. The symptoms are exactly the opposite of those in depression. Instead of feeling fatigued and listless, the manic person is full of energy. Instead of feeling unambitious, hopeless, and powerless, the manic person feels full of ambitions, plans, and power. The depressed person speaks slowly, monotonously, with no inflections. The manic person speaks rapidly, dramatically, often with many jokes and puns. The depressed person has no self-esteem. The manic person has inflated self-esteem. Although people may experience major depressions without manic episodes, they rarely have only manic episodes. Most manic episodes are a sign of **bipolar disorder** (formerly called *manic–depressive disorder*), in which depression alternates with mania.

Although bipolar disorder is equally common in both sexes, major depression is overrepresented among women of all ethnicities (McGrath et al., 1990). Some psychologists think that women actually are more likely to become depressed than men are, but others think the difference is more apparent than real. As we saw in Chapter 10, the sexes often express feelings differently, so men's depression may be overlooked or misdiagnosed. Men, for instance, have higher rates of drug abuse and violent behavior than women do, and some researchers believe that this behavior masks depression or anxiety (Canetto, 1992; Kessler et al., 1994).

THEORIES OF DEPRESSION

Explanations of depression generally fall into five categories, emphasizing biological predispositions, social conditions, problems with close attachments, cognitive habits, or a combination of individual vulnerability and stress.

1. *Biological explanations* account for depression in terms of genetics and brain chemistry. As we saw in Chapter 4, neurotransmitters permit messages to be transmitted from one neuron to another in the brain. Two neurotransmitters that seem to be implicated in depressive disorders are norepinephrine and serotonin. In the view of some researchers, depression is caused by a deficient production of one or both of these neurotransmitters, and manic moods are caused by an excessive production (see Figure 15.1). Biological theories seem especially applicable in cases of depression that do not involve reactions to real-life crises or losses, but which instead seem to come from nowhere or occur in response to minor stresses.

bipolar disorder A mood disorder in which depression alternates with mania (excessive euphoria).

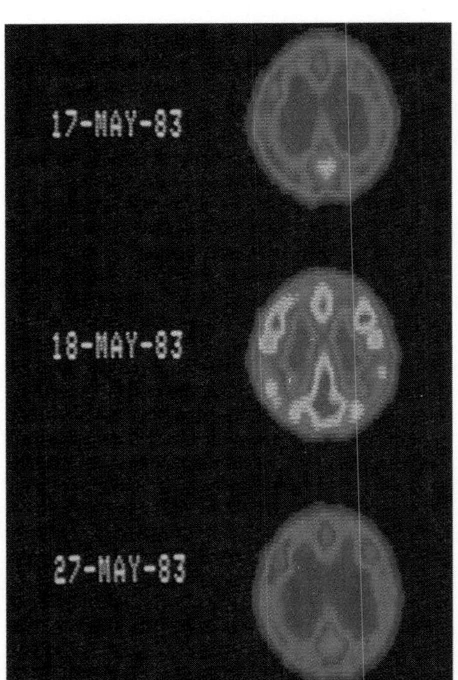

Figure 15.1
The Depressed Brain

These PET scans show changes in the metabolism of glucose, the brain's energy supply, in a patient with bipolar disorder. On May 17 and 27, the patient was depressed, and glucose metabolism throughout the brain was lower than normal. On May 18, the patient became manic, and metabolic activity increased to near normal levels. Keep in mind that such changes do not show the direction of cause and effect: A drop in glucose might bring on depression, but depression might also cause a drop in glucose levels.

Biological theories are supported by studies showing that when animals are given drugs that diminish the body's ability to produce serotonin, the animals become sluggish and inactive—a symptom of depression (Kramer, 1993; Wender & Klein, 1981). Conversely, drugs that increase the levels of serotonin and norepinephrine sometimes alleviate symptoms of depression; hence they are called "antidepressants." The early success of these drugs provoked great interest in the search for the biological origins of depression. However, as we will see in the next chapter, drugs are not universally effective, and even when they help some individuals, this does not necessarily mean that the depression had an organic basis. Studies of adopted twins suggest that major depression and bipolar disorder may have a genetic component, but the search for the gene or genes involved has so far proved fruitless. A decade ago, several highly publicized studies raised the possibility that a specific gene might be linked with bipolar disorder, but subsequent research failed to confirm these results (Faraone, Kremen, & Tsuang, 1990; Kelsoe et al., 1989).

2. *Social explanations* of depression consider the conditions of people's lives. In the social view, for example, the reason that women are more likely than men to suffer from depression is that women are more likely to lack fulfilling jobs or family relations. Men are nearly twice as likely as women to be married and working full time, a combination of activities that is strongly associated with mental health (Brown, 1993; Golding, 1988). In a random sample of 1,111 men and women in Boston, virtually all of the differences between men and women in their reported levels of depression could be accounted for by their different states of marriage and employment (Gore & Mangione, 1983). Mothers are especially vulnerable to depression: The more children they have, the more likely women are to become depressed (McGrath et al., 1990).

Another social factor in the origins of depression may be sexual abuse and other forms of violence. In a study of women in a psychiatric inpatient hospital, over half reported a history of such abuse. Moreover, the number and severity of their depressive symptoms were greater than those of women who reported no sexual trauma (Bryer et al., 1987). A community survey of 3,125 white, Latino, and black women found that depression, anxiety, and panic attacks were significantly more frequent among women who had been sexually molested or raped (Burnam et al., 1988). And in the United States, inner-city adolescents of both sexes who are exposed to high rates of violence report higher levels of depression and more thoughts of, and efforts to commit, suicide than those who are not subjected to violence in their lives or communities (Mazza, Reynolds, & Grover, 1995).

Social and economic explanations may help account for the rise of depression among young people all over the world, many of whom are struggling economically, have delayed making family commitments, or live with violence in their families and communities. Social analyses, though, fail to explain why most people who have these experiences do not become clinically depressed, while others stay locked in the grip of despair. Nor do they explain why some people become depressed even though they seem to "have it all."

3. *Attachment explanations* emphasize the importance to well-being of affiliation and attachment. In this view, depression results from disturbed relationships and separations, both past and present, and from a history of insecure attachments (Roberts, Gotlib, & Kassel, 1996). One important attachment theory, the *interpersonal theory of depression*, recognizes the role of biological and social factors, but it emphasizes the depressed person's disputes, losses, anxieties, feelings of incompetence, and disturbed relationships (Klerman et al., 1984).

The one thing that most often sets off a depressive episode is, in fact, the end of a close relationship, which is hardest on people who lack social support and coping skills (Barnett & Gotlib, 1988). However, attachment theories raise an interesting cause-and-effect problem. Disturbed or broken relationships may make some people severely depressed; but depressed people are also demanding and "depressing" to family and friends, who often feel angry or sad around them and may eventually break away (Gotlib & Hooley, 1988; Joiner & Metalsky, 1995).

4. *Cognitive explanations* propose that depression results from, or is maintained by, particular habits of thinking and interpreting events. Two decades ago, the theory of "learned helplessness" held that people become depressed when their efforts to avoid pain or to control the environment fail (Seligman, 1975). The fatal flaw in this theory was that not all depressed people have actually failed in their lives; many merely believe, without evidence, that nothing they do will be successful. Thus the theory evolved into its current form, which is that some depression results from having a hopeless and *pessimistic explanatory style* (see Chapter 14). People with this habitual way of thinking believe that nothing good will ever happen to them and that they cannot do anything to change this bleak future (Abramson, Metalsky, & Alloy, 1989; Seligman, 1991).

Other cognitive bad habits are associated with depression. People who focus inward and brood endlessly about their negative feelings—who have a "ruminating response style"—tend to have longer and more intense periods of depression than do those who are able to distract themselves, look outward, and seek solutions to problems. Women are more likely than men to develop this introspective style, beginning in adolescence, and this tendency may contribute both to longer-lasting depressions in women and to the sex difference in reported rates (Bromberger & Matthews, 1996; Nolen-Hoeksema, 1991; Nolen-Hoeksema & Girgus, 1994).

Although the evidence is strong that negative thoughts can cause depression, it is also true that depression causes negative thoughts; when you are feeling sad, gloomy ideas come more easily. Negative thinking, therefore, is both a cause and a result of depression (Hilsman & Garber, 1995).

5. *"Vulnerability–stress" explanations* draw on all four explanations just discussed. They hold that depression (and, as we will see throughout this chapter, many other psychological problems and mental disorders) result from an *interaction* between individual vulnerabilities—in personality traits, habits of thinking, genetic predispositions, and so forth—and environmental stress or sad events. In one study of more than 1,000 pairs of female twins, the women most likely to suffer major depression following the death of a close relative, assault, serious marital problems, or divorce were those who had a genetic susceptibility (Kendler et al., 1995).

Interaction models of depression are an improvement over theories implying that everyone is equally vulnerable to depression, given a certain experience or biological disposition. Vulnerability–stress theories try to specify which personality traits interact with which events to produce depression. According to one approach, some depression-prone individuals are excessively dependent on other people for acceptance, understanding, and support. If their relationships fail, they become preoccupied with feelings of loss and abandonment (as the interpersonal theory of depression would predict). Other depression-prone individuals are excessively focused on achievement. If they fail to achieve their goals, they become preoccupied with feelings of inadequacy and incompetence (Coyne & Whiffen, 1995).

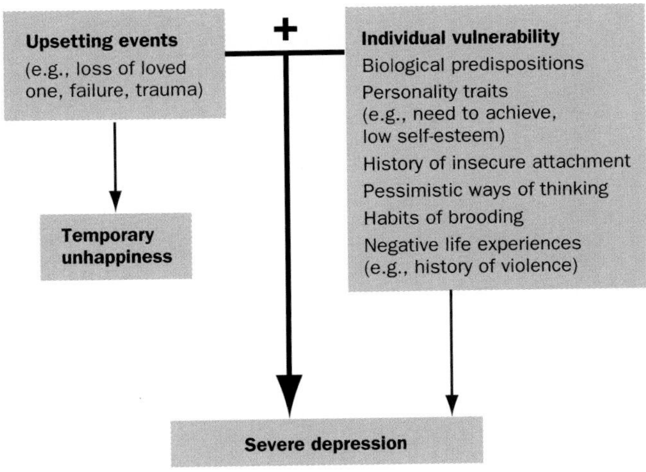

Other vulnerability–stress models are trying to specify which cognitive factors are likely to cause or prolong depression. One study found that students who got worse grades than they expected reported feeling depressed (not a surprise), but this mood persisted only in those who *also* had a depressive attributional style ("I'm stupid and always will be") *and* low self-esteem. In this case, depression resulted from a combination of having a pessimistic explanatory style, low self-esteem, an experience with failure, and a resulting sense of hopelessness (Metalsky et al., 1993).

DON'T OVERSIMPLIFY

Countless studies of depression have been done. What do their contradictory results suggest about the search for a single cause of the disorder? How can we make the most sense of conflicting results and explanations?

In assessing these different approaches, we should keep in mind that depression comes in degrees of severity, from tearful tiredness to an inability to get out of bed. Further, depression may have different causes in different people. One person may have been abandoned in childhood and may therefore feel insecurely attached in current relationships; another may have a pessimistic cognitive style that fosters depressive interpretations of events; a third may have a biological predisposition to respond to stress with depression; a fourth may lack satisfying work or love, or may have been subjected to violence or other trauma. By understanding depression as an interaction between an individual's personality and experiences, we can see why the same precipitating event, such as the loss of a loved one or even a minor setback, might produce different degrees of depression in different people.

Quick Quiz

A newspaper headline announces that a single gene has been identified as the cause of depression, but when you read the fine print you learn that other studies have failed to support this research. What explanations can you think of to explain these contradictory findings?

Answers:

The conflicting evidence may mean, among other possibilities, that if a genetic predisposition for depression does exist, it is not due to a single specific gene, but involves several genes working in the context of environmental events. It may mean that the right gene has not yet been identified. Or it may mean that genes are not a factor in all forms of depression.

PERSONALITY DISORDERS

Personality disorders involve rigid, maladaptive traits that cause great distress or an inability to get along with others. The DSM-IV describes a personality disorder as "an enduring pattern of inner experience and behavior that deviates markedly from the expectations of the individual's culture." This pattern is not caused by depression, a drug reaction, or a situation that temporarily induces a person to behave in ways that are out of character.

personality disorders Rigid, maladaptive personality patterns that cause personal distress or an inability to get along with others.

paranoid personality disorder A disorder characterized by habitually unreasonable and excessive suspiciousness, jealousy, or mistrust. Paranoid symptoms may also occur in schizophrenia and other psychoses.

narcissistic personality disorder A disorder characterized by an exaggerated sense of self-importance and self-absorption.

PROBLEM PERSONALITIES

People with **paranoid personality disorder** suffer from a pervasive, unfounded suspiciousness and mistrust of other people, irrational jealousy, secretiveness, and doubt about the loyalty of others. They have delusions of being persecuted by everyone from their closest relatives to government agencies, and their beliefs are immune to disconfirming evidence. People who have **narcissistic personality disorder** share an exaggerated sense of self-importance and self-absorption. Narcissism gets its name from the Greek myth of Narcissus, a beautiful boy who fell in love with his own image. Individuals with narcissistic personality disorder are preoccupied with fantasies of unlimited success, power, brilliance, or ideal love. They demand constant attention and admiration and feel entitled to special favors, without being willing to reciprocate. They fall in love quickly and out of love just as fast, when the beloved proves to have some human flaw.

Notice that these descriptions are both specific and vague. They are specific, in that they evoke flashes of recognition ("I know that type!"), but vague in that they involve general qualities that depend on subjective labels and value judgments (Maddux & Mundell, 1997). Culture influences the decision to classify an individual as having one of these disorders. For example, American society often encourages people to pursue dreams of unlimited success and ideal love, but such dreams might be considered signs of serious disturbance in a more group-oriented society. Where would you draw the line between having a "narcissistic personality disorder" and being a normal member of a group or culture that encourages "looking out for number one" and places high values on youth and physical beauty?

Narcissus fell in love with his own image, and now he has a personality disorder named after him—just what a narcissist would expect!

One personality disorder in particular has provoked interest and study because of its consequences for society: the disorder of the individual who lacks conscience, morality, and emotional attachments. In the 1830s this disorder was called "moral insanity." By 1900 it had become the "psychopathic personality," a phrase that some researchers and most newspapers still use. More recently the word "sociopath" was coined. The DSM now uses the term *antisocial personality disorder.* By any name, this disorder, which has been around forever, has troubling characteristics.

THE ANTISOCIAL PERSONALITY

- Two teenage boys held a teacher down while a third poured gasoline over him and set him on fire. Fortunately, another teacher intervened in time for a rescue, but the boys showed no remorse, did not consider their actions wrong, and were disappointed that they had not actually murdered the teacher (whom they did not know). "Next time we'll do it right," said the ringleader, "so there won't be nobody left around to identify us."
- Giovanni Vigliotto was, by all accounts, warm and charming; by too many accounts, in fact. Vigliotto married 105 women in an elaborate con game. He would find a wealthy woman, charm her into marriage, steal her assets, and vanish. Finally, one wife charged him with fraud, and he was convicted. Vigliotto admitted the many marriages, but not deception or theft. He didn't think he had done anything wrong (Carson, Butcher, & Mineka, 1996).

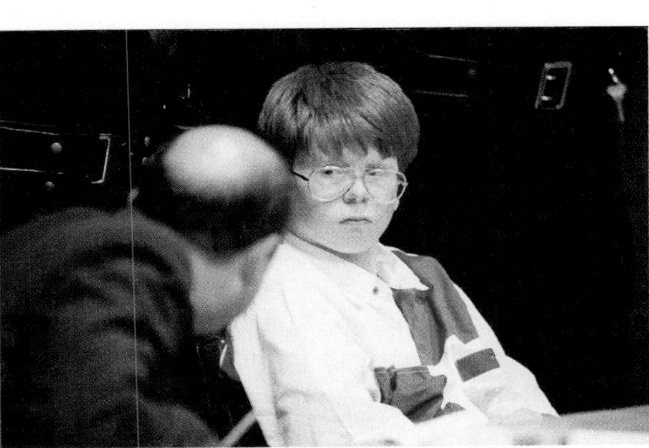

Some people with antisocial personalities use charm and elaborate con tricks to deceive others. Giovanni Vigliotto (left) married 105 women over 33 years, seized their assets, and then abandoned them. But other people with APD are sadistic and violent, starting in childhood. At age 13, Eric Smith (right) bludgeoned and strangled a 4-year-old boy to death. He was tried as an adult and sentenced to a prison term of nine years to life.

People like these, who have **antisocial personality disorder,** are fascinating and frightening because they lack the emotions that link people to one another: empathy, the ability to take another person's perspective; shame for actions that hurt others; and guilt, the ability to feel remorse or sorrow for immoral actions. They have no conscience. They can lie, charm, seduce, and manipulate others, and then drop them without a qualm. If caught in a lie or a crime, they may seem sincerely sorry and promise to make amends, but it is all an act. They are often sexually promiscuous, unable to maintain attachments, and irresponsible in their obligations to others. Some antisocial persons, like the teenagers who set a teacher on fire, are sadistic, with a history of criminal or cruel behavior that began in childhood. They can kill anyone—an intended victim, a child, a bystander—without a twinge of regret. Others direct their energies into con games or career advancement, abusing other people emotionally rather than physically. Understandably, more attention is devoted to the antisocial individuals who commit violent crimes than to those who gain power and fortune while wreaking devastation on their families or employees, but the latter also do great harm.

For unknown reasons, antisocial personality disorder is far more common in males than in females; according to the DSM-IV and survey evidence, it occurs in 3 to 5 percent of all males and fewer than 1 percent of all females (Robins, Tipp, & Przybeck, 1991). Although these percentages are small, antisocial individuals create a lot of havoc; they may account for more than half of the serious crimes committed in the United States (Hare, 1993).

It is important to distinguish antisocial *behavior* from antisocial *personalities.* Most antisocial behavior (as defined by crime statistics on homicide, rape, robbery, assault, burglary, and auto theft) is carried out by young men whose criminal activities peak in late adolescence and drop off sharply by their late 20s. Their behavior seems to be influenced by their age, situation, and peer group, and it does not necessarily reflect a personality disorder. But a smaller number of men begin displaying antisocial behavior in early childhood, are drawn to criminal environments, and end up with confirmed antisocial personalities (Henry et al., 1996). In a review of longitudinal research, Terrie Moffitt (1993) found that the behavior of such individuals might include "biting and hitting at age 4, shoplifting and truancy at age 10, selling drugs and stealing cars at age 16, robbery and rape at age 22, and fraud and child abuse at age 30 . . . [Such] persons lie at home, steal from shops, cheat at school, fight in bars, and embezzle at work."

Some people with antisocial personality disorder can be very "sociable," charming everyone around them, but they have no emotional connection to others or guilt about their wrongdoing. Their inability to feel emotional arousal—empathy, guilt, fear of punishment, anxiety under stress—suggests some abnormality in the central nervous system. Antisocial individuals do not respond to punishments that would affect other people, such as threat of physical harm or loss of approval (Hare, 1965, 1993). This fact may explain why antisocial persons fail to learn that their actions will have unpleasant consequences. Normally when a person is anticipating danger, pain, or shock, the electrical conductance of the skin changes—a classically conditioned response that indicates anxiety or fear. But in several experiments, people with antisocial personality disorder were slow to develop such responses. As you can see in Figure 15.2, it is as if they aren't able to feel the anxiety necessary for avoidance learning.

antisocial personality disorder
A disorder (sometimes called psychopathy or sociopathy) characterized by antisocial behavior such as lying, stealing, manipulating others, and sometimes violence; a lack of social emotions (guilt, shame, and empathy); and impulsivity.

One theory, based on animal and human studies, maintains that people who are antisocial, hyperactive, addicted, or impulsive have a common inherited disorder (Luengo et al., 1994; Newman, Widom, & Nathan, 1985). These conditions all involve

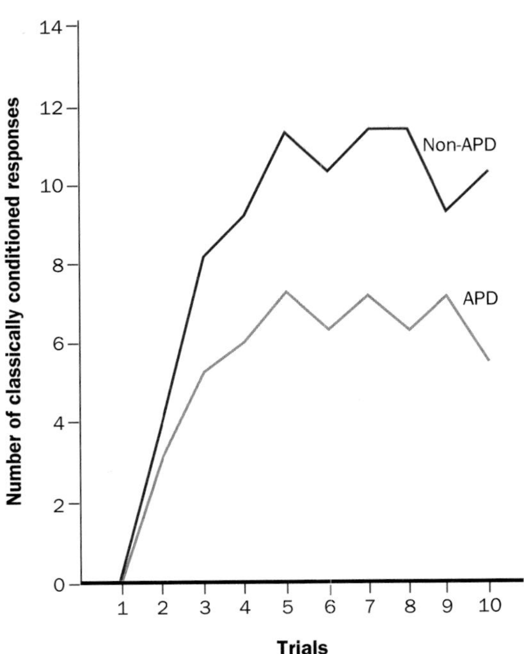

Figure 15.2
The Antisocial Personality

In several experiments, people with antisocial personality disorder (APD) were slow to develop classically conditioned responses to anticipated danger, pain, or shock—responses that indicate normal anxiety (Hare, 1965). This deficit may be related to the ability of people with APD to behave in destructive ways without remorse or regard for the consequences (Hare, 1993).

problems in *behavioral inhibition*—the ability to control responses to frustration or to inhibit a pleasurable action that may have unpleasant repercussions. The biological children of parents with antisocial personality disorder, substance-abuse problems, or impulsivity disorders are at greater than normal risk of developing these disorders themselves, even when they are reared by others (Nigg & Goldsmith, 1994).

Many children who become violent and antisocial have suffered neurological impairments, a result not of genetics but of physical battering and subsequent brain injury (Milner & McCanne, 1991; Moffitt, 1993). Consider the chilling results of a study that compared two groups of delinquents: violent boys who had been arrested for repeated incidents of vicious assault, rape, or murder; and boys whose violence was limited to fistfights. Nearly all of the extremely violent boys (98.6 percent) had at least one neurological abnormality, and many had more than one, compared with 66.7 percent of the less violent boys. More than three-fourths of the violent boys had suffered head injuries as children, had had serious medical problems, or had been beaten savagely by their parents, compared with "only" one-third of the others (Lewis, 1981).

Other research supports a *vulnerability–stress model,* which holds that brain damage can interact with social deprivation and other experiences to produce individuals who are impulsively violent. A study of 4,269 boys, followed from birth to age 18, found that many of those who became violent offenders had had a combination of two risk factors: birth complications (with resulting damage to the prefrontal cortex, as noted in Chapter 4) and early maternal rejection. Their mothers hadn't wanted the pregnancy, and the babies were put in public institutional care for at least four months during their first year. Although only 4.4 percent of the boys had both risk factors, they accounted for 18 percent of all violent crimes committed by the sample as a whole (Raine, Brennan, & Mednick, 1994).

Clearly, cultures and environments can make antisocial behavior more likely or less so (Moffitt, 1993; Patterson, 1994; Persons, 1986). Some societies and subcultures cultivate the qualities of selfishness, professional ruthlessness, and emotional hardheartedness. In contrast, small, close-knit cultures that depend on each member's cooperation and consideration for others would find selfishness and emotional coldness intolerable.

It seems, then, that several routes lead to the development of antisocial personality disorder: Having a genetic disposition toward impulsivity, addiction, or hyperactivity, which leads to rule breaking and crime; being neglected or rejected by parents; having brain damage as a result of birth complications or physical abuse in childhood; and living in a culture or environment that rewards and fosters antisocial traits. These multiple origins may explain why the incidence of antisocial personality disorder varies within and across societies and history.

Quick Quiz

Can you diagnose each of the following disorders?

1. Ann can barely get out of bed in the morning. She feels that life is hopeless and despairs of ever feeling good about herself.
2. Brad lacks guilt, empathy, and moral standards.
3. Connie constantly feels a sense of impending doom; for many weeks, her heart has been beating rapidly and she can't relax.
4. Damon is totally absorbed in his own feelings and wishes.
5. Edna believes that everyone is out to get her and no one can be trusted.

Answers:

1. major depression 2. antisocial personality disorder 3. generalized anxiety disorder 4. narcissistic personality disorder 5. paranoid personality disorder

DISSOCIATIVE DISORDERS

Stress or shock can make any of us feel temporarily dissociated—that is, cut off from ourselves, feeling strange, dazed, or "unreal." In **dissociative disorders,** consciousness, behavior, and identity are split or altered. Unlike normal, short-lived states of dissociation, these symptoms are extremely intense, last a long time, and appear to be out of the individual's control. Like posttraumatic stress disorder, dissociative disorders are often responses to shocking events. But in the former case, people can't get the trauma out of their minds and waking thoughts. In the latter, people apparently escape the trauma by putting it out of their minds, erasing it from memory (Cardeña et al., 1994).

AMNESIA AND FUGUE

On a Hawaiian beach in the spring of 1996, a man was found lying face down, fading in and out of consciousness and complaining of a thumping headache. "His pockets were empty," wrote a reporter from *The New York Times* (July 18, 1996), "and so was his memory." Taken to a local hospital, where tests showed signs of brain swelling but no external bruises or cuts, the man said his name was William Charles D'Souza, that the year was 1988, and that he lived in Wantagh, New York. He was wrong on all counts. After three months of investigation, an enterprising detective learned that D'Souza's real name was Philip Charles Cutajar, that he was from Massapequa, New York, and that he had been living in Maryland and planning a trip to Brazil. But even after calls from his mother and brother, Cutajar wasn't really sure

dissociative disorders Conditions in which consciousness or identity is split or altered.

he recognized them, wasn't really sure who he was, and had no recollection of how he ended up in Hawaii.

Amnesia, according to the DSM-IV, is an inability to remember important personal information, usually of a traumatic or stressful nature, that cannot be explained by ordinary forgetfulness. Amnesia can result from organic conditions, such as head injury, as was probably the case with Cutajar. When no organic causes are apparent, and when the person forgets only selective information that is threatening to the self, the amnesia is considered *dissociative.* In one case of dissociative amnesia, a young man appeared at a hospital complaining that he did not know who he was. After a few days, he awoke in great distress, eventually remembering that he had been in an automobile accident in which a pedestrian was killed. The shock of the experience and his fear that he might have been responsible set off the amnesia.

Dissociative fugue states are even more fascinating. A person in a fugue state not only forgets his or her identity but also gives up customary habits and wanders far from home—as also might have happened to Cutajar. The person may take on a new identity, remarry, get a new job, and live contentedly until he or she suddenly "wakes up"—puzzled and often with no memory of the fugue experiences. The fugue state may last anywhere from a few days to many years. James McDonnell, Jr., left his family in New York in 1971 and wandered to New Jersey, where he took a new name and a new job. Fifteen years later, he "woke up" and made his way back to his wife—who (apparently) greeted him with open arms.

As you might imagine, it is often difficult to determine when people in fugue states have a true disorder and when they are faking. This problem is also apparent in the curious disorder of multiple personality.

amnesia (dissociative) When no organic causes are present, a dissociative disorder involving partial or complete loss of memory for threatening information or traumatic experiences.

dissociative identity disorder A controversial dissociative disorder marked by the appearance within one person of two or more distinct personalities, each with its own name and traits; also called *multiple personality disorder.*

DISSOCIATIVE IDENTITY DISORDER ("MULTIPLE PERSONALITY")

The DSM-IV has replaced the familiar term "multiple personality disorder" (MPD) with **dissociative identity disorder** to describe the appearance, within one person, of two or more distinct identities. (In our discussion, however, we will retain the more commonly used term.) In this disorder, each identity appears to have its own memories, preferences, handwriting, and even medical problems. In a case study of one person with four identities, for example, the researcher concluded that it was "as if four different people had been tested" (Larmore, Ludwig, & Cain, 1977).

Cases of multiple personality are extremely dramatic: Those portrayed in the films *The Three Faces of Eve* and *Sybil* fascinated audiences for years, and so do the legal cases that make the news. A woman charges a man with rape, claiming that only one of her personalities consented to having sex with him while another objected; a man commits murder and claims his "other personality"

In the 1950s the book and film The Three Faces of Eve, *based on a reported case of multiple personality, spawned dozens of imitators, such as* Lizzie. *Stories about MPD then faded from the public eye, and so did individuals who claimed to have the disorder. In the 1980s, MPD returned in the form of several highly publicized books and case studies, and since then thousands of cases have been reported. Controversy exists about whether this increase is due to better diagnosis, or to unwitting therapist influence and sensational stories in the media.*

did it. Among mental-health professionals, however, two competing and totally incompatible views of MPD currently exist. Some think it is a real disorder, common but often underdiagnosed. Others are skeptical: They think that most cases are generated by clinicians, in unwitting collusion with vulnerable and suggestible clients, and that if it exists at all it is extremely rare.

Those in the MPD-is-real camp believe the disorder originates in childhood, as a means of coping with unspeakable, continuing traumas, such as torture (Gleaves, 1996; Kluft, 1993; Ross, 1995). In this view, the trauma produces a mental "splitting"; one personality emerges to handle everyday experiences and another emerges to cope with the bad ones. MPD patients are frequently described as having lived for years with several personalities of which they were unaware, until hypnosis and other techniques in therapy revealed them. Clinicians who endorse MPD argue that diagnoses can be made more accurately now because the physiological changes that occur within each personality cannot be faked.

Those who are skeptical about MPD, however, have shown that most of the research used to support the diagnosis is seriously flawed (Merskey, 1995; Piper, 1997). A review of the claims that MPD patients have different physiological patterns associated with each personality concluded that most of the studies are anecdotal, have many methodological problems, and have failed to be replicated (Brown, 1994). Most important, research in this area has been marred by that familiar research mistake, the missing control group. When one research team corrected this flaw by comparing the EEG activity of two MPD patients with that of a normal person who merely role-played different personalities, they found EEG differences between "personalities" to be *greater* in the normal person (Coons, Milstein, & Marley, 1982). Other studies comparing MPD patients with control subjects who were merely role-playing have not found any reliable differences (Miller & Triggiano, 1992). Because normal people can create EEG changes by changing their moods, energy levels, and concentration, brain-wave activity cannot be used to verify the existence of MPD.

ASK QUESTIONS; EXAMINE THE EVIDENCE

A man charged with murder claims that one of his "other personalities" committed the crime. You are on the jury, and you know that psychologists disagree about the validity of his defense. What questions would you want to ask about this man's claim, and what evidence would help you reach a decision about it?

Clinicians and researchers who are doubtful about this diagnosis also point out that cases of MPD seem to turn up only in people who go to therapists who believe in it and are looking for it (McHugh, 1993a; Merskey, 1992, 1995; Piper, 1997; Spanos, 1996). Critics fear that clinicians who are convinced of the widespread existence of MPD may actually be creating the disorder in their clients through the power of suggestion. For example, here is the way one psychologist questioned the Hillside Strangler, Kenneth Bianchi, a man who killed more than a dozen young women:

> I've talked a bit to Ken, but I think that perhaps there might be another part of Ken that I haven't talked to, another part that maybe feels somewhat differently from the part that I've talked to. . . . And I would like that other part to come to talk to me. . . . Part, would you please come to communicate with me? (Quoted in Holmes, 1994)

Notice that the psychologist repeatedly asked Bianchi to produce another "part" of himself and even addressed the "part" directly. Before long, Bianchi was maintaining that the murders were really committed by another personality called Steve Walker. Did the psychologist in this case *permit* another personality to reveal itself, or did he actively *create* such a personality by planting the suggestion that one existed?

Proponents of the view that MPD is real and widespread often seem unaware of the difference. One of the best-known advocates of the MPD diagnosis, Richard Kluft

(1987), maintains that efforts designed to determine the presence of MPD—that is, to get the person to reveal a dissociated personality—may require "between $2\frac{1}{2}$ and 4 hours of continuous interviewing. Interviewees must be prevented from taking breaks to regain composure, averting their faces to avoid self-revelation, etc. In one recent case of singular difficulty, the first sign of dissociation was noted in the 6th hour, and a definitive spontaneous switching of personalities occurred in the 8th hour." After eight hours of "continuous interviewing" without a single break, how many of us *wouldn't* do what the interviewer wanted?

An alternative, *sociocognitive explanation* of multiple personality disorder is that it is an extreme form of the ability we all have to present different aspects of our personalities to others (Merskey, 1995; Spanos, 1996). In this view, the diagnosis of multiple personality disorder provides a way for some troubled people to understand and legitimize their problems—or to account for embarrassing, regretted, or even criminal behavior that they commit ("My other personality did it"). In turn, therapists who believe in MPD reward such patients by paying attention to their symptoms and "personalities," thus further influencing the patients to reorganize their memories and make them consistent with the diagnosis (Ofshe & Watters, 1994). Canadian psychiatrist Harold Merskey (1992) reviewed several famous cases of MPD, including those of Eve and Sybil, and was unable to find a single case in which a patient developed MPD without being influenced by the therapist's suggestions or reports about the disorder in books and the media. Sybil's psychiatrist, Cornelia Wilbur, first diagnosed Sybil as being schizophrenic, but later encouraged her to produce multiple personalities and report memories of sexual abuse in childhood (reports that were never corroborated). Some investigators think that this change of diagnosis was part of a marketing strategy for the psychiatrist's book (see Nathan, 1994).

Of course, the fact that MPD is a controversial diagnosis with little empirical evidence to support it does not mean that no legitimate cases exist. It does mean that caution is warranted, especially because diagnoses of MPD have implications regarding responsibility for criminal acts. In the case of the Hillside Strangler, a determined and skeptical prosecutor discovered that Bianchi had read numerous psychology textbooks on multiple personality and had modeled "Steve" on a student he knew! When another psychologist purposely misled Bianchi by telling him that "real" multiple personalities come in packages of at least three, Bianchi suddenly produced a third personality. Bianchi was convicted of murder and sentenced to life in prison. But Paul Miskamen, who battered his wife to death, convinced psychiatrists and a jury that the man who killed his wife was a separate personality named Jack Kelly. Judged insane, Miskamen was committed to a mental hospital and released after 14 months. (For further discussion of the relationship between mental illness and legal responsibility for one's crimes, see "Puzzles of Psychology.")

DRUG ABUSE AND ADDICTION

Perhaps no topic in this chapter better illustrates the problem of finding the shade of the spectrum in which normal blurs into abnormal than that of drug abuse and addiction. Most people use drugs—legal, illegal, or prescription—in moderation, for short-lived effects, but some people overuse them. The consequences of drug abuse for society are costly: loss of productive work, high rates of violence and crime, and family disruption. And the consequences for individuals and their families are tragic: unhappiness, illness, and the increased likelihood of early death from accident or disease.

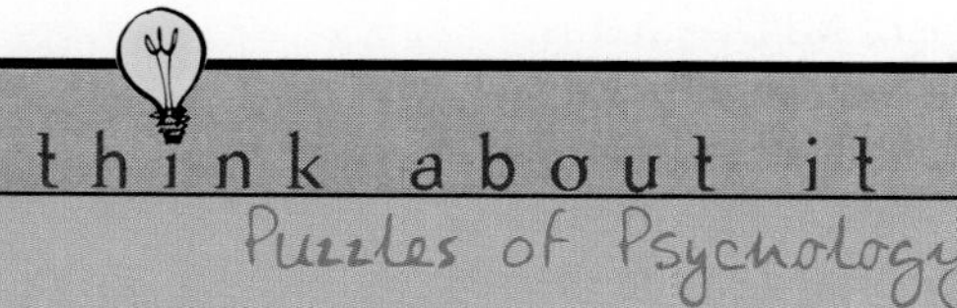

When Does a Mental Disorder Cause Diminished Responsibility?

No one disputes the fact that Lyle and Erik Menendez shot their parents to death in a barrage of gunfire, as their parents sat watching television and eating ice cream. After the initial volley, Lyle reloaded his gun and shot their mother several more times because, he later told his therapist, "She was trying to sneak away." At first the brothers maintained their innocence, while spending extravagant amounts of their $14 million inheritance; then, faced with incontrovertible evidence, they confessed. Many months later they explained why they had committed this crime: They were victims of sexual molestation by their father and believed they were in imminent danger of being killed by him. Their first trial ended in hung juries for both defendants. At the second trial, they were convicted of murder and sentenced to life in prison without parole.

Were the Menendez brothers responsible for murdering their parents? "No," say some people, "not if they were abused and humiliated by their parents; no wonder they eventually broke down and lost control. Society must be sympathetic to children who are treated brutally." "Yes," say others; "because that sex-abuse excuse seems awfully unlikely, and everything about their actions was premeditated. And even if they were abused, so are plenty of people who don't commit murder. These young men had all the resources of wealth and class to have simply left home."

The Menendez case raises some fascinating questions for law and psychology. What mental conditions and disorders warrant a defense of diminished responsibility or exoneration of one's actions? What is the proper penalty for someone who temporarily or habitually cannot control his or her actions: treatment or prison? If someone is sentenced to spend time in a mental institution, how can we know when he or she is "cured"? How do we know whether someone is "insane" or just faking?

Insanity is a legal term, not a psychological one. In 1834, a Scot named Daniel M'Naghten tried to assassinate the prime minister of England, killing the prime minister's secretary by mistake. M'Naghten was acquitted of murder on the grounds that he had a "mental defect" that prevented him from understanding what he was doing at the time of the act. The "M'Naghten rule" meant that people could be acquitted "by reason of insanity" and sentenced not to prison, but to mental institutions (or set free). In the United States, the 1954 Durham decision recognized this principle by specifying that "An accused is not criminally responsible if his unlawful act was the product of a mental disease or defect."

Today, because of sensational cases in the news, the public has the impression that hordes of crazed and violent criminals are "getting off" by reason of insanity. Public outrage has caused some states to abolish the insanity defense altogether or to permit only a defense of "insane but guilty." Actually, public perceptions are not accurate. Surveys indicate that the public thinks the insanity defense is raised in 37 percent of all felony cases; in fact, it is raised in only 0.9 percent. The public believes that 44 percent of all those who claim this defense are acquitted; the actual rate is 26 percent. The public believes that only about half of those acquitted actually spend time in mental hospitals; in fact, about 81 percent do (Silver, Cirincione, & Steadman, 1994). And it is getting tougher to claim an insanity defense at all. The defense must show "clear and convincing evidence" that the defendant had a severe, abnormal mental condition and not just a personality defect.

Nevertheless, many defense attorneys, aided by the testimony of psychiatrists and psychologists, keep trying to expand the legal grounds for diminished responsibility, searching for "the mental disease or defect" that might mitigate the sentence a guilty person receives. Because of the differing views within psychology and psychiatry—and because of the subjective nature of many diagnoses—many trials end up as a battle of the experts, and the jury must decide which side to believe. Some psychologists think that the Menendez brothers were suffering from a form of posttraumatic stress disorder resulting from years of abuse. Others think that if the brothers have any mental disorder at all, their cold-bloodedness indicates psychopathy—antisocial personality disorder. How can a jury decide between such competing views when the experts can't?

In a sizzling indictment of the ability of psychologists to determine legal insanity or to predict the future behavior of individuals, psychologists David Faust and Jay Ziskin (who is also a lawyer) reviewed hundreds of studies (Faust & Ziskin, 1988). They learned that clinicians were wrong more often than they were right. In one study, for example, military recruits who were kept in the service, despite psychiatrists' recommendations that they be discharged for "severe psychiatric liabilities," turned out to be as successful and well adjusted as the control group. Overall, clinicians were not very good at detecting efforts to fake insanity, and they were dismal at predicting future violence.

Most legal and mental-health professionals believe that in a humane society, people who are mentally incompetent, delusional, or disturbed should not be held entirely responsible for their actions. But where do we draw the line of responsibility? Should being physically beaten or sexually abused, having experiences with racism, or living in a violent subculture be treated as legitimate reasons for taking violent revenge? What should the treatment or punishment for such individuals be? And if psychologists cannot agree on the answers, how should juries do so? Think about it.

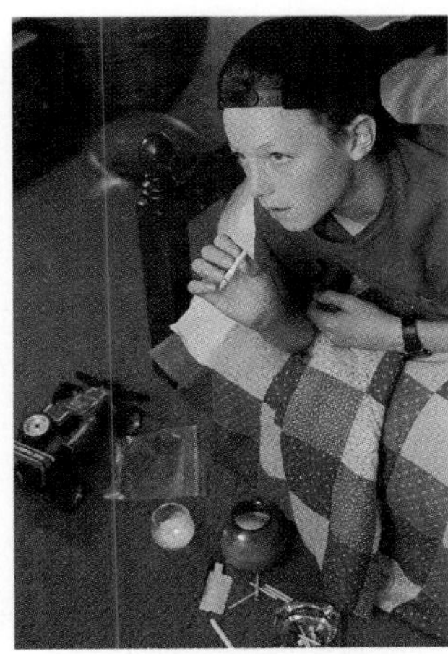
When and why does drug use become abuse?

Every drug—including aspirin, cough medicine, and coffee—can be dangerous and even lethal if taken in excess. As we saw in Chapter 5, with many drugs, light or moderate use has different medical and psychological consequences than heavy or excessive use. The problem lies in defining "excess." The DSM-IV definition of *substance abuse* is "a maladaptive pattern of substance use leading to clinically significant impairment or distress." Symptoms of such impairment include the failure to fulfill role obligations at work, home, or school (the person cannot hold a job, care for children, or complete schoolwork because of excessive drug use); use of the drug in hazardous situations (such as driving a car or operating machinery); recurrent arrests for drug use; and persistent conflicts with others about use of the drug or as a result of using the drug.

Why are some people able to use drugs moderately, while others abuse them? In this section, focusing on the example of alcoholism, we will consider the two dominant approaches to addiction and drug abuse—the biological model and the learning model—and conclude with an effort to integrate the contributions of both.

THE BIOLOGICAL MODEL

In 1960, a book was published that profoundly changed the way most people thought about alcoholics. In *The Disease Concept of Alcoholism,* E. M. Jellinek argued that alcoholism is a disease over which an individual has no control and from which he or she never recovers. Drunkenness is not an inevitable property of alcohol, he said, but a characteristic of some people who have an inbred vulnerability to liquor; for them, complete abstinence is the only solution. The disease theory of alcoholism was tremendously important because it transformed the moral condemnation of the addict as a bad and sinful person into concern for someone who is sick. Today the *biological model* of addiction is widely accepted by researchers and the public, and many people continue to regard alcoholism as a disease. The biological model holds that addiction, whether to alcohol or any other drug, is due primarily to a person's biochemistry, metabolism, or genetic predisposition.

In the biological view, how people respond to drugs begins with their own physiological responses to it. Just as some individuals and ethnic groups cannot physically tolerate the lactose in milk, some individuals and ethnic groups have a low tolerance for alcohol. Women generally will get drunker than men on the same amount of alcohol because women are smaller, on average, and their bodies metabolize alcohol differently (Fuchs et al., 1995). Many Asians have a genetically determined adverse reaction to even small amounts of alcohol, which can cause severe headaches and diarrhea (Cloninger, 1990).

But why are some people in every group more likely than others to become alcoholic? Because having biological relatives who are alcoholic contributes to a person's risk of becoming alcoholic, proponents of the biological model believe that alcoholism involves an inherited predisposition (Cloninger, 1990; Schuckit & Smith, 1996). Researchers are trying to identify the key genes or biological anomalies that might be involved in alcoholism, or at least in some kinds of alcoholism (Blum, 1991; Kendler et al., 1992; Polich, Pollock, & Bloom, 1994). *Type I alcoholism* begins in adulthood, and it is not associated with genetic factors. But *Type II alcoholism,* which begins in adolescence and is linked to impulsivity, antisocial behavior, and violent criminality, does seem to have a hereditary component (Bohman et al., 1987; McGue, Pickens, & Svikis, 1992). Type II alcoholics also have a lowered activity of the enzyme MAOB (monoamine oxidase-B) in their blood cells, compared with nonalcoholics. Low levels of MAOB are not a direct cause of addiction, but they may reflect an underlying physiological deficiency leading to severe alcoholism and other psychiatric problems (Devor et al., 1994).

Genes may also affect a person's *level of response* to alcohol, which is an independent risk factor in becoming alcoholic. In a ten-year longitudinal study of 450 young men (half had alcoholic fathers and half did not), the men who at age 20 had a low response to alcohol—meaning they needed to drink more than most people to feel any effect—were at increased risk of becoming alcoholic within the decade. This was true regardless of their current drinking habits or family history (Schuckit & Smith, 1996).

As with so many other disorders, however, it has been difficult to track down specific genes that might contribute to addiction. Several studies have found that a certain gene, which affects the function of key dopamine receptors on brain cells, is more likely to be present in the DNA of alcoholics than in that of nonalcoholics (Noble et al., 1991). Dopamine helps regulate pleasure-seeking actions, so researchers suspect that this gene might explain why alcoholics drink. However, other studies, using different measurements, have found no difference between alcoholics and controls in the presence of this gene (Baron, 1993; Bolos et al., 1990; Gelernter et al., 1991). Similarly, some researchers, comparing alcoholism rates among identical and fraternal twins, conclude that genetic factors play a part in alcoholism in women (Kendler et al., 1992); but other studies find evidence of genetic factors only in men (McGue, Pickens, & Svikis, 1992).

At present, then, we cannot conclude that a single gene causes alcoholism (or any other addiction) in any direct way. It is possible that several genes in combination may affect the response to alcohol, the compulsive use of alcohol (or other mood-altering drugs), or the progression of alcohol-related diseases such as cirrhosis of the liver. It is possible that genes contribute to temperament or personality traits that predispose some people to become alcoholics. And it is possible that genes affect how the liver metabolizes alcohol. But it is also possible that genes have little to do with alcoholism, and that alcoholism results, basically, from alcohol! Heavy drinking alters brain function, reduces the level of painkilling endorphins, produces nerve damage, shrinks the cerebral cortex, and wrecks the liver. In the view of some researchers, these changes then create biological dependence, an inability to metabolize alcohol, and psychological problems.

THE LEARNING MODEL

The biological model, popular though it is, has been challenged by another approach, which holds that we cannot understand addiction and drug abuse without also taking learning and cultural factors into account. Its proponents note that biological theories of addiction cannot adequately account for the often rapid rise and fall in addiction rates within a country, or for the fact that people can become "addicted" to activities, exercise, television, or the Internet as well as to drugs; what "disease" are they catching?

CONSIDER OTHER EXPLANATIONS

Addiction is often considered a biological problem or a disease, but people can become addicted to jogging, love, work, and the Internet. What "disease" are they catching? What other explanations of addiction are possible?

According to the *learning model,* addiction to any drug is neither a sin nor a disease but "a central activity of the individual's way of life" (Fingarette, 1988). Proponents of this model marshal four arguments in support:

1. *Addiction patterns vary according to cultural practices and the social environment.* In colonial America, the average person actually drank two to three times the amount of liquor that is consumed today, yet alcoholism was

not the serious social problem it is now. Drinking was a universally accepted social activity. Families drank and ate together. Alcohol was believed to produce pleasant feelings and relaxation. The Puritan minister Cotton Mather even called liquor "the good creature of God." If a person committed a crime or became violent while drunk, the colonials did not conclude that liquor was to blame. Rather, they assumed that the person's own immoral tendencies led to drunkenness *and* crime (Critchlow, 1986).

Between 1790 and 1830, when the American frontier was expanding, drinking came to symbolize masculine independence, high-spiritedness, and toughness. The saloon became the place for drinking away from home, and alcoholism rates shot up. Why? The reason, according to the learning model, is that when people do not learn how to drink moderately, they are more likely to drink irresponsibly and in binges (unless they are committed to a cultural or religious rule that forbids all psychoactive drugs).

In fact, alcoholism is much more likely to occur in societies that forbid children to drink but condone drunkenness in adults (as in Ireland) than in societies that teach children how to drink responsibly but condemn adult drunkenness (as in Italy, Greece, France, and colonial America). In cultures with low rates of alcoholism, adults demonstrate correct drinking habits to their children, gradually introducing them to alcohol in safe family settings. These lessons are maintained by adult customs. Alcohol is not used as a rite of passage into adulthood, nor is it associated with masculinity and power (Peele & Brodsky, 1991; Vaillant, 1983). Drinking is considered neither a virtue nor a sin. Abstainers are not sneered at, and drunkenness is not considered charming, comical, or manly; it's considered stupid or obnoxious.

Substance abuse and addiction problems increase not only when people fail to learn how to take drugs in a moderate cultural context, but also when they move from their own culture of origin into another that has different drinking rules (Westermeyer, 1995). For example, in most Latino cultures, such as those of Mexico and Puerto Rico, drinking and drunkenness are considered male activities. Thus Latina women tend to drink little, if at all, and they have few drinking problems—until they move into an Anglo environment, when their rates of alcoholism rise (Canino, 1994).

Some cultures of drinking or other drug abuse are much smaller than a nationality or ethnic group. Colleges and companies create their own subcultures, which may forbid drinking entirely, permit moderate drinking, or encourage drunken

In cultures in which people drink moderately with meals and children learn the rules of social drinking from their families, alcoholism rates are much lower than in cultures in which drinking occurs mainly in bars, in binges, or in privacy.

binges. In a survey of 140 American colleges, rates of heavy and binge drinking ranged from a low of only 1 percent of all students at some colleges to a high of 70 percent at others (Wechsler et al., 1994). In the United States, binge drinking among college students is strongly associated with living in a fraternity or a sorority (Baer, Kivlahan, & Marlatt, 1995).

2. *Policies of total abstinence tend to increase rates of addiction rather than reduce them.* Further compelling evidence for a learning explanation of drug abuse comes from the history of Prohibition in America. The temperance movement of the early twentieth century argued that drinking inevitably led to drunkenness, and drunkenness to crime. The solution it proposed, and won for the Prohibition years (1920 to 1933), was national abstinence. Temperance advocates were not trying to do a scientific study, but they created the perfect conditions for one. As the learning model would predict, Prohibition actually increased rates of alcoholism: Because people were denied the opportunity to learn to drink moderately, they drank excessively when given the chance. Men who were teenagers at the time of Prohibition were far and away more likely to become serious problem drinkers in adulthood than were older men, who had learned how to drink alcohol before it became illegal (McCord, 1989). Similarly, the Inuit of British Columbia were forbidden from drinking alcohol until 1951, when they were permitted to drink only in licensed bars. As a result, the Inuit would drink as much as they could while in a bar. It was a policy virtually guaranteed to create drunkenness.

3. *Not all addicts go through withdrawal symptoms when they stop taking the drug.* During the Vietnam War, nearly 30 percent of American soldiers were taking heroin in doses far stronger than those available on the streets of U.S. cities. These men believed themselves to be addicted. Experts predicted a drug-withdrawal disaster among the returning veterans; it never materialized. Over 90 percent of the men simply gave up the drug, without withdrawal pain, when they came home to new circumstances (Robins, Davis, & Goodwin, 1974). Likewise, the majority of people who are addicted to cigarettes, tranquilizers, or painkillers are also able to stop taking these drugs, without outside help and without withdrawal symptoms (Prochaska, Norcross, & DiClemente, 1994).

Many people go through phases of heavy drinking, yet cut back to social drinking levels once their environments change—again, without withdrawal symptoms. (As we will see, though, there is much dispute about whether true alcoholics can do this.) In a 40-year study, many of the men in the sample went through a period of severe problem drinking but eventually healed themselves. Their drinking was not progressive, permanently incapacitating, or a downward spiral to skid row (Vaillant, 1983).

4. *Addiction does not depend on the drug alone but also on the reason the person is taking it.* Addicts use drugs to escape from the real world, but, as we saw in Chapter 5, people living with chronic pain use some of the same drugs, including opiates, in order to function in the real world; they don't become addicted (Portenoy, 1994). In a study of 100 hospital patients who had been given strong doses of narcotics for postoperative pain, 99 had no withdrawal symptoms upon leaving the hospital (Zinberg, 1974). And of 10,000 burn patients who received narcotics as part of their hospital care, not one became an addict (Perry & Heidrich, 1982).

Although we often think of drug abuse as the cause of psychological problems, having psychological problems is more often the cause of drug abuse. In a surprising study that followed a large sample of children from preschool through age 18, adolescents who had experimented moderately with alcohol and marijuana were the *best* adjusted. Those who had never experimented with any drug were the most anxious, emotionally constricted, and lacking in social skills. And those teenagers who abused drugs were the most maladjusted, alienated, impulsive, and emotionally distressed (Shedler & Block, 1990). Because this study followed these young people over time, the researchers were able to show that drug abuse was largely a *result*, not a *cause*, of psychological maladjustment and other difficulties. The best-adjusted students were able to use drugs moderately *because* they were well adjusted.

To understand why people abuse drugs, therefore, the learning model focuses on the reasons that people take a drug. For example, most people drink simply to be sociable or to conform to the group they are with, but many people drink in order to regulate their emotions. Some drink to reduce negative feelings when they are anxious, depressed, or tense ("coping" drinkers); others to increase positive feelings when they are tired, bored, or stressed ("enhancement" drinkers). Coping drinkers have significantly more drinking problems than enhancement drinkers do (Cooper et al., 1995). Drinking thus has psychologically distinct functions; to understand why some people abuse alcohol, in this view, you would need to know what function drinking serves for them. The same principle applies to other forms of substance abuse.

DEBATING THEORIES OF ADDICTION

The biological and learning models both contribute to our understanding of drug abuse and addiction. Yet among most researchers and public-health professionals these views are quite polarized, as you can see in this summary of the two approaches (adapted from Peele & Brodsky, 1991):

The Biological Model	**The Learning Model**
Addiction is genetic, biological.	Addiction is a way of coping.
Once an addict, always an addict.	A person can grow beyond the need for alcohol or other drugs.
An addict must abstain from the drug forever.	Most problem drinkers can learn to drink in moderation.
A person is either addicted or not.	The degree of addiction will vary, depending on the situation.
The solution is medical treatment and membership in groups that reinforce one's permanent identity as a recovering addict.	The solution involves learning new coping skills and changing one's environment.
An addict needs the same treatment and group support forever.	Treatment lasts only until the person no longer abuses the drug.

As this table suggests, what we have here is a case of either–or thinking on a national scale, and the reason has to do with the serious, real-world consequences of each model for the treatment of alcoholics and other addicts. The argument is most heated in the debate over controlled drinking—whether it is possible for former alcoholics to drink moderately without showing signs of dependence and intoxication and without causing harm to themselves or others.

To those who hold the biological or disease model, there is no such thing as a "former" alcoholic and controlled drinking is impossible; once an addict has even a single drink, he or she cannot stop. Daniel Flavin, medical and scientific director of the National Council on Alcoholism and Drug Dependence, observes that "In general, it's not a good idea under any circumstances to encourage an alcoholic to moderate [his or her drinking], or the heavy drinker whose natural history would be to go on to alcoholism. How do you tease those people out?" (quoted in Foderaro, 1995). He and others believe that problem drinkers who learn to cut back to social-drinking levels were never true alcoholics in the first place.

To those who adopt a learning model, however, controlled drinking is possible; once a person no longer needs to become drunk, he or she can learn to drink socially and in moderation (Marlatt, 1996). Across North America, alternatives to the total-abstinence program of Alcoholics Anonymous have emerged, such as Rational Recovery, Moderation Management, and DrinkWise. As Frederick Rotgers, director of research at the Center of Alcohol Studies at Rutgers University, says: "Unfortunately, in this country, for many, many years even to talk about people with a drinking problem simply cutting down has been anathema. . . . It is heresy. Among pragmatic people who are reading the scientific literature, it's no longer heresy" (quoted in Foderaro, 1995).

How can we assess these two positions critically? Can we locate a common ground between them? Because alcoholism and problem drinking occur for many and varied reasons, neither model offers the only solution. Many alcoholics, perhaps most, cannot learn to drink moderately, especially if they have had drinking problems for many years (Vaillant, 1995). On the other hand, although Alcoholics Anonymous has unquestionably saved lives, it doesn't work for everyone. According to its own surveys, one-third to one-half of those who join AA drop out, and many of those dropouts benefit from programs that teach people how to drink moderately and keep their drinking under control (Marlatt, 1996; Peele & Brodsky, 1991; Rosenberg, 1993).

According to meta-analyses, the factors that predict whether an addict or problem drinker will be able to learn to control excessive drinking are these: previous severity of dependence on the drug; social stability (not having a criminal record, having a stable work history, being married); and beliefs about the necessity of maintaining abstinence (Rosenberg, 1993). Alcoholics who believe that one drink will set them off—those who accept the alcoholics' creed, "first drink, then drunk"—are in fact more likely to behave that way, compared with those who believe that controlled

GET INVOLVED

If you drink, why? Check all of the motives that apply to you:

- ________ *to relax*
- ________ *to be sociable*
- ________ *to escape from worries, stress*
- ________ *to handle feelings of depression*
- ________ *to enhance a good meal*
- ________ *to get drunk and lose control*
- ________ *to conform to peer pressure*
- ________ *to rebel against authority*
- ________ *to relieve boredom*
- ________ *other (specify)*

Do your reasons for drinking promote abuse or responsible use? How do you respond physically to alcohol? What have you learned about drinking from your family, your friends, and cultural messages? What do your answers tell you about your own vulnerability to addiction?

drinking is possible. Ironically, then, the course that alcoholism takes may reflect, in part, a person's belief in the disease model or the learning model.

Taken together, this evidence suggests that drug abuse and addiction reflect an interaction of physiology and psychology, person and culture. They occur when an individual who is emotionally and physically vulnerable to abusing drugs finds a culture and environment that support such abuse. More specifically, drug addiction and abuse are likely to occur when:

- People have a genetic or physiological vulnerability to the drug.
- People believe the drug is stronger than they are—that is, they believe they are addicted and will always be.
- People learn (or laws or customs encourage them) to take a drug in binges rather than in moderation.
- People learn that drugs can be used to justify behavior that would not otherwise be socially tolerated.
- People come to rely on a drug as a way of coping with problems, relieving pain, avoiding stress, or providing a sense of power and self-esteem.
- "Everyone" in a person's peer group drinks heavily or uses other drugs excessively.
- Moderate use is neither taught nor encouraged.

Researchers who hold a biological model of addiction hope to discover a medical solution to drug abuse, such as a nonaddictive drug that will break an addict's craving. But researchers who hold a learning model think that this effort is probably doomed. If someone is desperate to escape from reality, they say, he or she will find a way to do it. They believe that the search for a perfect drug that has no addictive qualities is futile; instead, we should look at the human qualities that make a drug seem perfect.

Quick Quiz

If you are addicted to passing exams, try these questions:

1. What seems to be the most reasonable conclusion about the role of genes in alcoholism? (a) Without a key gene, a person cannot become alcoholic; (b) the presence of a key gene or genes will almost always cause a person to become alcoholic; (c) genes may work in combination to increase a person's vulnerability to some kinds of alcoholism.
2. Which cultural practice is associated with *low* rates of alcoholism? (a) drinking in family or group settings, (b) infrequent but binge drinking, (c) drinking as a rite of passage, (d) regarding alcohol as a sinful drink

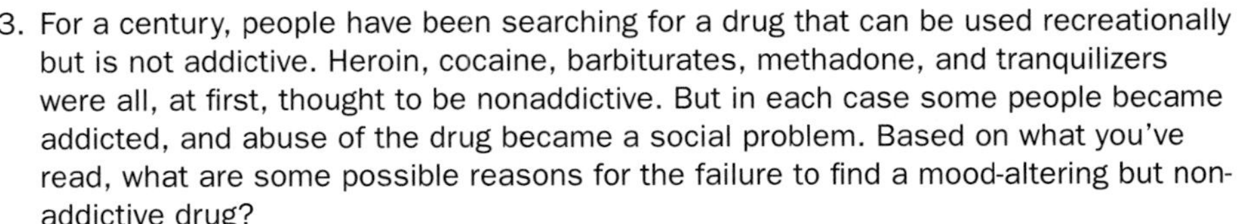

3. For a century, people have been searching for a drug that can be used recreationally but is not addictive. Heroin, cocaine, barbiturates, methadone, and tranquilizers were all, at first, thought to be nonaddictive. But in each case some people became addicted, and abuse of the drug became a social problem. Based on what you've read, what are some possible reasons for the failure to find a mood-altering but nonaddictive drug?

Answers:

1. c 2. a 3. Perhaps some people are biologically vulnerable to any mind-altering drug. Perhaps the psychological need for addiction exists in the individual and not in the chemical properties of the drug. Perhaps the chemistry of the drug is less important than the cultural practices that encourage drug abuse among some groups. If that is so, we will never find a recreational drug that has no addictive properties for *some* people.

SCHIZOPHRENIA

> To be schizophrenic is best summed up in a repeating dream that I have had since childhood. In this dream I am lying on a beautiful sunlit beach but my body is in pieces. This fact causes me no concern until I realize that the tide is coming in and that I am unable to gather the parts of my dismembered body together to run away. The tide gets closer and just when I am on the point of drowning I wake up screaming in panic. This to me is what schizophrenia feels like; being fragmented in one's personality and constantly afraid that the tide of illness will completely cover me. (Quoted in Rollin, 1980)

In 1911, Swiss psychiatrist Eugen Bleuler coined the term **schizophrenia** to describe cases in which the personality loses its unity: words are split from meaning, actions from motives, perceptions from reality. Schizophrenia is not the same as "split" or "multiple personality." As the quotation illustrates, schizophrenia refers to a fragmented condition, not the coexistence of several different personalities. It is an example of a **psychosis,** a mental condition that involves distorted perceptions of reality and an inability to function in most aspects of life.

THE NATURE OF THE "SCHIZOPHRENIAS"

If depression is the common cold of psychological disorder, said psychiatrist Donald Klein (1980), schizophrenia is its cancer: a baffling and complex problem. Schizophrenia produces *active or positive symptoms* that involve an exaggeration or distortion of normal thinking processes and behavior, and more subtle *negative symptoms* that involve the loss of former traits and abilities. The most common active symptoms include the following:

1. *Bizarre delusions,* such as the belief that dogs are anthropologists from another planet, disguised as pets to infiltrate human families. Some people with schizophrenia have paranoid delusions, taking innocent events—a stranger's cough, a helicopter overhead—as evidence that the world is plotting against them. Some have "delusions of identity," believing that they are Moses, Jesus, Joan of Arc, or some other famous person.

2. *Hallucinations* that usually take the form of voices and consist of garbled, odd words; a running conversation in the head; or two or more voices conversing with each other. Unlike the hallucinations that might occur in a normal person on a drug high, schizophrenic hallucinations feel intensely real and believable to the sufferer (Bentall, 1990). Most are voices, but some are tactile (feeling insects crawling over the body) or visual (seeing Elizabeth Taylor in the mirror).

3. *Disorganized, incoherent speech* consisting of an illogical jumble of ideas and symbols, linked by meaningless rhyming words or by remote associations called *word salads.* A patient of Bleuler's wrote, "Olive oil is an Arabian liquor-sauce which the Afghans, Moors and Moslems use in ostrich farming. The Indian plantain tree is the whiskey of the Parsees and Arabs. Barley, rice and sugar cane called artichoke, grow remarkably well in India. The Brahmins live as castes in Baluchistan. The Circassians occupy Manchuria and China. China is the Eldorado of the Pawnees" (Bleuler, 1911/1950). The story goes that the great novelist James Joyce once asked Carl Jung to explain the difference between Joyce's own stream-of-consciousness writing and the odd associations of his schizophrenic daughter. Jung supposedly replied, "You dive—she falls" (Wender & Klein, 1981).

schizophrenia A psychotic disorder or group of disorders marked by positive symptoms (e.g., delusions, hallucinations, disorganized and incoherent speech, and inappropriate behavior) and negative symptoms (e.g., emotional flatness and loss of motivation).

psychosis An extreme mental disturbance involving distorted perceptions and irrational behavior; it may have psychological or organic causes. (Plural: *psychoses.*)

4. *Grossly disorganized and inappropriate behavior* that may range from childlike silliness to unpredictable and violent agitation. The person may wear three overcoats and gloves on a hot day, start collecting garbage, or hoard scraps of food. Some people with schizophrenia completely withdraw into a private world, sitting for hours without moving, a condition called *catatonic stupor.* In *Autobiography of a Schizophrenic Girl,* Marguerite Sechehaye wrote, "A wall of brass separates me from everybody and everything. In the midst of desolation, in indescribable distress, in absolute solitude, I am terrifyingly alone."

Negative symptoms may appear months before these active ones and often persist when the active symptoms are in remission. Negative symptoms include loss of motivation; poverty of speech (making only brief, empty replies in conversation, because of diminished thought rather than an unwillingness to speak); and, most notably, *emotional flatness*—unresponsive facial expressions, poor eye contact, and diminished emotionality (see Figure 15.3). One man set fire to his house and then sat down calmly to watch TV.

Figure 15.3
Emotions and Schizophrenia

When people with schizophrenia are asked to draw pictures, their drawings are often distorted, lack color, include words, and reveal flat emotion. One patient was asked to copy a picture of flowers from a magazine (left). The initial result is shown bottom left. The drawing on bottom right shows how much the patient improved after several months of treatment.

Some people recover from schizophrenia and others learn to manage its symptoms, the way diabetics learn to live with their disease. Joseph Rogers overcame the symptoms of schizophrenia and became director of the National Mental Health Consumers' Association.

Cases of schizophrenia vary in the severity and duration of symptoms. In some individuals, the symptoms appear abruptly and eventually disappear with the passage of time, with or without treatment. In others, the onset is more gradual and insidious. Friends and family report a slow change in personality. The person may stop working or bathing, become isolated and withdrawn, and start behaving in peculiar ways.

As for prognosis, again schizophrenia is unpredictable. Psychiatrists often speak of the "rule of thirds": Of all people diagnosed and hospitalized with schizophrenia, one-third will recover completely, one-third will improve significantly, and one-third will not get well. The more breakdowns and relapses the individual has had, the poorer the chances for complete recovery (Eaton et al., 1992a, 1992b). Yet many people suffering from this illness learn to live with it, are able to work and have warm family relationships, and eventually outgrow their symptoms (Eaton et al., 1992b; Harding, Zubin, & Strauss, 1992).

The mystery of schizophrenia is that we could go on listing symptoms and variations all day and not finish. Some people with schizophrenia are almost completely impaired in all spheres; others do extremely well in certain areas. Some have normal moments of lucidity in otherwise withdrawn lives. One adolescent crouched in a rigid catatonic posture in front of a television for the month of October; later, he was able to report on all the highlights of the World Series he had seen. A middle-aged man, hospitalized for 20 years, believing he was a prophet of God and that monsters were coming out of the walls, was able to interrupt his ranting to play a good game of chess (Wender & Klein, 1981). People with brain damage usually cannot interrupt their madness to watch the World Series or play chess. How can those with schizophrenia do so?

THEORIES OF SCHIZOPHRENIA

As you might imagine, any disorder that has so many variations and symptoms will pose many problems for diagnosis and explanation. One psychologist concluded that the concept of schizophrenia is "almost hopelessly in tatters" (Carson, 1989), and others think we should drop the label entirely (Sarbin, 1992). The idea that schizophrenia is a single, stable, diagnostic disorder, critics maintain, is simply a convenient myth.

Of course, these critics recognize that some people do behave in bizarre ways and that *something* is wrong with them. In their view, however, "schizophrenia" is a lot of different somethings, and its name is a grab-bag term for rule-breaking actions that must be understood by the cultural context in which they occur. Robert Carson (1989) noted that it is impossible to define a "delusion" without reference to a culture's norms. In every society, he observed, perfectly sane individuals hold patently "false or absurd beliefs" with conviction and zeal. Why do we think a person has schizophrenia if he believes he is the Prophet Ezekiel now, but not if he believes he was the Prophet Ezekiel in a past life?

Other psychologists (and the compilers of the DSM) reply to these criticisms by arguing that in cultures around the world, the same core signs of schizophrenia appear: hallucinations, delusions that are far more disturbed than mere "false beliefs," inappropriate behavior, and disorders of thought. That is why almost everyone studying this disorder believes that schizophrenia is a brain disease of some sort (Heinrichs, 1993; Torrey et al., 1994). "If schizophrenia is a myth," said Seymour Kety (1974) many years ago, "it is a myth with a strong genetic component."

Using brain-imaging techniques, longitudinal studies, and dissections of brains, researchers are unraveling the mysteries of this troubling and fascinating disorder. They are searching for genetic factors, for abnormalities in the brain and in prenatal development, and for the interaction between biological vulnerabilities and a person's life experiences.

1. *Brain abnormalities.* Some individuals with schizophrenia (but not all of them) have decreased brain weight, a decrease in the volume of the temporal lobe or limbic regions, reduced numbers of neurons in specific layers of the prefrontal cortex, or enlargement of the *ventricles,* the spaces in the brain filled with cerebrospinal fluid; these may all be signs of cerebral damage (Andreasen et al., 1994; Heinrichs, 1993; Raz & Raz, 1990). (See Figure 15.4.) Many people who have schizophrenic symptoms have abnormal eye movements, which some researchers regard as a biological marker of the disease (Clementz & Sweeney, 1990). Men with schizophrenia are more likely than controls to have abnormalities in the thalamus, the traffic-control center for incoming sensations (Andreasen et al., 1994). This finding might explain why the brains of some people with schizophrenia are overly sensitive to everyday stimuli, causing them to retreat into an inner world.

2. *Genetic predispositions.* Children have a greater risk of schizophrenia if an identical twin develops the disorder, if one parent has the disorder, and especially if both parents are schizophrenic—even if the child is reared apart from the affected relative (Gottesman, 1991, 1994). In the general population, the risk of developing schizophrenia is 1–2 percent, but children with one schizophrenic parent have a lifetime risk of 12 percent; and for children with two schizophrenic parents, the risk jumps to 35–46 percent (Goldstein, 1987).

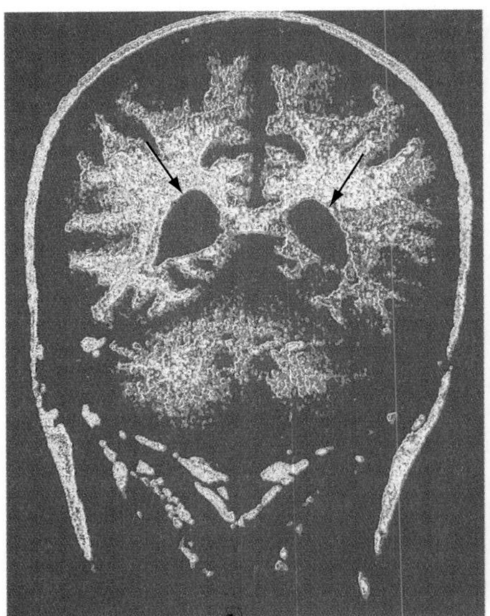

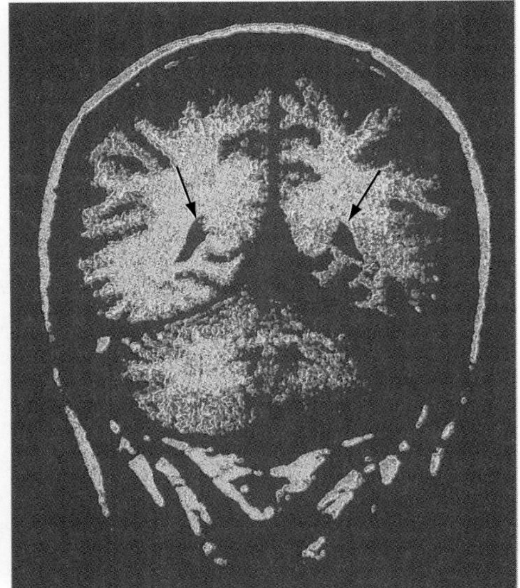

Figure 15.4
Schizophrenia and the Brain

MRI scans show that a person with schizophrenia (left) is more likely than a healthy person (right) to have enlarged ventricles, or spaces, in the brain (see arrows) (Andreasen et al., 1994).

Just as with alcoholism and bipolar disorder, however, it has been hard to track down specific genes or determine the extent of their influence (Holzman & Matthysse, 1990). Great excitement arose when a research team found a link between schizophrenic symptoms and abnormalities on chromosome 5; disappointment followed when other research failed to confirm it (Kennedy et al., 1988). One problem with genetic-origin theories is that even among identical twins, when one twin develops schizophrenia, the chances that the other will do so range from 28 percent to 40 percent—not even half of them (Torrey et al., 1994). Moreover, nearly 90 percent of all persons with schizophrenia do *not* have a schizophrenic parent, and nearly 90 percent of all children with one such parent do not develop the disorder.

3. *Prenatal abnormalities.* In recent years the evidence has mounted that damage to the fetal brain increases the likelihood of schizophrenia (and some other mental disorders). The damage may occur because of severe malnutrition. Babies conceived during times of famine have twice the schizophrenia rate as babies conceived when their mothers ate normal diets during pregnancy (Susser et al., 1996). Or the problem may be a mismatch between the mother's antibodies and the infant's, such as Rh incompatibilities (Hollister, Laing, & Mednick, 1996).

Another culprit in the origins of schizophrenia may be, remarkably, an infectious virus during prenatal development (Torrey, 1988; Torrey et al., 1994). In fact, a longitudinal study that began decades ago found a significant association between exposure to influenza virus during the second trimester of gestation and adult schizophrenia 20 to 30 years later (Mednick, Huttunen, & Machón, 1994). The virus theory accounts for many odd aspects of schizophrenia. It explains why schizophrenic symptoms may not emerge until a person reaches adolescence or young adulthood: Viruses can attack specific areas of the brain, leaving other areas untouched, yet remain latent for many years before causing symptoms to appear. It explains why the births of schizophrenic children show seasonal fluctuations; viruses too are seasonal. And it explains why sometimes only one twin of a genetically identical pair later becomes schizophrenic: Only one was affected prenatally by a virus.

The second trimester of prenatal development is critical because the brain is forming crucial connections during this time. Neurologist H. Stefan Bracha reasoned that if a viral infection or other prenatal trauma (such as lack of oxygen) affected the fetal brain and led to the subsequent development of schizophrenia, its effects should appear elsewhere in the body as well. Bracha's team conducted an ingenious study of 24 pairs of identical twins in which only one twin suffered from schizophrenia. They discovered that the twins who had schizophrenia, unlike their healthy counterparts, were significantly more likely to have abnormalities in their hands, such as fewer ridges in their fingerprints (Bracha et al., 1991). Of course, hand abnormalities do not cause schizophrenia! But hands are formed during the second trimester, so the same environmental accident might have affected the development of both the brain and the hands.

Other evidence also points to the role of abnormalities in fetal brain development. In the second trimester of fetal development, cells migrate to the cortex. If this migration is disrupted, by a virus or a faulty genetic mechanism, cells end up in the wrong place or have faulty connections. This seems to be precisely the problem in many schizophrenics, whose brains are more likely to contain neurons in the prefrontal cortex that are "out of place" (Akbarian et al., 1996; Bunney, Potkin, & Bunney, 1995). By studying the medical records of children who eventually became schizophrenic, and, cleverly, by scrutinizing the home movies their parents took of these children as infants and toddlers, researchers have been able to identify a lifelong pattern of delayed maturation in such individuals. For example, at 6 months, about one-third of all babies are two weeks or more late in sitting up; but of those who later develop schizophrenia, two-thirds are late (Weinberger, 1995).

4. *The vulnerability–stress model.* Although the evidence for brain abnormalities in schizophrenia is compelling, many researchers believe that the onset and course of this disorder—as in the cases of depression, antisocial personality disorder, and addiction—are best explained by an interactive theory (Gottesman, 1991). In this view, genes or brain damage alone will not inevitably produce schizophrenia, and a vulnerable person who lives in a good environment may never show full-fledged signs of it.

For many years, the Copenhagen High-Risk Project has followed 207 children at high risk for schizophrenia (because of having a schizophrenic parent) and a control group of 104 low-risk children. The project has identified factors that, *in combination,* increase the likelihood of schizophrenia: the existence of schizophrenia in the family; physical trauma during childbirth that might damage the brain; exposure to the flu virus or other prenatal trauma during the second trimester of gestation; unstable, stressful environments in childhood and adolescence; and having emotionally disturbed parents (Mednick, Parnas, & Schulsinger, 1987; Olin & Mednick, 1996).

Some researchers hope that a common source of all the schizophrenias may yet be discovered. They note that rheumatic fever can appear as a disease of the nervous system, of the heart, of the joints, or of the skin. It seemed to be four diseases until bacteriologists identified the common source. But other investigators believe that the "schizophrenias" include several unrelated disorders with different causes and that no single culprit is likely to be found. "The likelihood that researchers are studying different illnesses without being able to specify these differences," concluded researcher Walter Heinrichs (1993), ". . . is the major obstacle to scientific progress."

We have come to the end of a long walk along the spectrum of mental disorders. The writer William Styron, who recovered from severe and debilitating depression, used the beginning of Dante's beautiful classic poem, *The Divine Comedy,* to convey his experience of mental illness:

In the middle of the journey of our life
I found myself in a dark wood.
For I had lost the right path.

"For those who have dwelt in depression's dark wood," wrote Styron, "and known its inexplicable agony, the return from the abyss is not unlike the ascent of the poet, trudging upward and upward out of hell's black depths and at last emerging into what he saw as 'the shining world.'" Dante wrote,

And so we came forth, and once again beheld the stars.

Taking Psychology with You

When a Friend Is Suicidal

Suicide is a scary subject, surrounded by mystery and myth. It can be frightening to those who find themselves fantasizing about it, and it is devastating to the family, friends, and acquaintances of those who go through with it. In the United States and Canada, most people who commit suicide are over the age of 45, but suicide rates are rapidly increasing among young people. Between 1960 and 1988, the suicide rate among adolescents rose by more than 200 percent, increasing especially among white males (Garland & Zigler, 1994).

People who attempt suicide have different motives. Some believe they have no reason to live; some feel like failures in a world where they think everyone else is happy and successful; some want revenge against those who they think have made them suffer. In the African-American community, where suicide attempts have been rising, risk factors include parental drug abuse, family losses and low levels of family cohesion, exposure to violence, and being a teenage mother (Summerville, Kaslow, & Doepke, 1996). All suicidal people share the belief that life is unendurable. This belief may be rational in the case of people who are terminally ill and in pain, but more often it reflects the distorted thinking of someone suffering from depression. Often, the suicidal person doesn't really want to die; rather, he or she wants to escape intolerable emotions and despair (Baumeister, 1990).

Friends and family members can help prevent a suicide by recognizing the danger signs.

- *Don't assume you can identify a "suicidal type."* Most adolescents who try to commit suicide are isolated and lonely. Many are children of divorced or alcoholic parents. Some have problems in school and feel like failures. But others who are vulnerable to suicide attempts are college students who are perfectionistic and self-critical. The former may feel like ending their lives because they can foresee no future. The latter may feel suicidal because they do not like the futures they foresee for themselves.

- *Take all suicide threats seriously.* Many people fail to take action when a friend talks about committing suicide. Some believe the friend's intention but think they can't do anything about it. "He'll just do it at another place, another time," they think. In fact, most suicides occur during an acute crisis; once the person gets through the crisis, the desire to die fades. One researcher tracked down 515 people who had attempted suicide by jumping off the Golden Gate Bridge many years earlier. After those attempts, fewer than 5 percent had actually committed suicide in the subsequent decades (Seiden, 1978).

Some people believe that if a friend is talking about suicide, he or she won't really do it. This belief is also false. Few people commit suicide without signaling their intentions. Most are ambivalent: "I want to kill myself, but I don't want to be dead—at least not forever." Most suicidal people want relief from the terrible pain of feeling that nobody cares, that life is not worth living. Getting these thoughts and fears out in the open is an important first step.

- *Know the danger signs.* A depressed person may be at risk of trying to commit suicide if he or she has tried to commit suicide before; has become withdrawn, apathetic, and isolated, or has a history of depression; reveals specific plans for carrying out the suicide or begins to give away cherished possessions; expresses no concern about the usual deterrents to suicide, such as consideration for one's family, adherence to religious rules, or the fact that suicide is irreversible; and has access to a lethal method, such as a gun (Garland & Zigler, 1994).

- *Take constructive action.* If you believe a friend is in danger of suicide, do not be afraid to ask, "Are you thinking of suicide?" This question does not "put the idea" in anyone's mind. If your friend is contemplating the action, he or she will probably be relieved to talk about it, and you will know that it is time to get help. Let your friend talk without argument or disapproval. Don't try to talk your friend out of it by debating whether suicide is right or wrong, and don't put on phony cheerfulness. If your friend's words or actions scare you, say so. By listening nonjudgmentally, you are showing that you care. By allowing your friend to unburden his or her grief, you help the person get through the immediate crisis.

Most of all, don't leave your friend alone. If necessary, get the person to a counselor, health professional, or emergency room of a hospital; or call a local suicide hot line. Don't worry about doing the wrong thing. In an emergency, the worst thing you can do is nothing at all.

SUMMARY

DEFINING DISORDER

1) "Mental disorder" is not necessarily the same as behavior that is statistically abnormal. *Mental disorder* has been defined as a violation of cultural standards; as maladaptive or destructive behavior; as emotional distress; and as "insanity," the legal term for incompetence to stand trial.

DILEMMAS OF DIAGNOSIS

2) Diagnosing psychological disorders is a complicated process. Clinicians typically use *projective tests* and also *objective tests or inventories* such as the *MMPI*. Reliability and validity are better with objective tests than with projective ones. *The Diagnostic and Statistical Manual of Mental Disorders* (DSM) tries to provide objective criteria for the diagnosis of mental disorder. But some critics argue that the manual fosters overdiagnosis and creates self-fulfilling prophecies; inflates normal problems in living into disorders; can be misused to absolve people of responsibility for their actions; and implies that diagnosis is scientific when really it is a subjective process. Because of human bias and judgment, reliability in diagnosing most mental disorders is low. Supporters of the DSM reply that when the DSM criteria are used correctly, reliability in diagnosis improves; and that although some diagnoses are subjective and culture-specific, certain mental disorders (such as depression and delusion) occur in all societies.

ANXIETY DISORDERS

3) *Generalized anxiety disorder* is a condition of continuous anxiety, with signs of nervousness, worry, and physiological arousal. Other anxiety disorders include *post-traumatic stress disorder* and *acute stress disorder* (anxiety symptoms that may follow traumatic or stressful experiences), *phobias*, *panic attack*, *agoraphobia*, and *obsessive–compulsive disorder*.

MOOD DISORDERS

4) *Mood disorders* include major depression, dysthymia, and bipolar disorder. Symptoms of *major depression* include distorted thinking patterns, low self-esteem, physical ailments such as fatigue and loss of appetite, and prolonged grief and despair. *Dysthymia* is chronic depressed mood. In *bipolar disorder*, depression alternates with mania or euphoria. Women are more likely than men to be treated for depression, but it is not clear whether the sex difference is real or is a result of differences in expressing emotions and willingness to seek help.

5) *Biological* explanations of depression emphasize a depletion of neurotransmitters in the brain and the role of specific genes in mood disorders. *Social* explanations consider the conditions of people's lives that might generate depression (and cause gender differences), such as work and family life, motherhood, and sexual abuse. *Attachment* or *interpersonal theories* argue that depression results from broken or conflicted relationships. *Cognitive* explanations emphasize having a pessimistic explanatory style, distorted thoughts, and habits of brooding or rumination that cause depressive symptoms to last. *Vulnerability–stress models* look at how specific interactions between individual characteristics (biological, cognitive, or personality traits) and environmental stress can produce depression.

PERSONALITY DISORDERS

6) *Personality disorders* are characterized by rigid, self-destructive traits that cause distress or an inability to get along with others. They include *paranoid*, *narcissistic*, and *antisocial* personality disorders. A person with *antisocial personality disorder* (sometimes also called a psychopath or sociopath) shows extreme forms of antisocial behavior; lacks guilt, shame, and empathy; and is impulsive and lacks self-control. The disorder may involve a neurological defect that is genetic or caused by brain or central nervous-system damage at birth or during childhood; parental rejection and abuse; and living in environments that reward some antisocial traits and behaviors.

DISSOCIATIVE DISORDERS

7) *Dissociative disorders* involve a split in consciousness or identity. They include *amnesia, fugue* states, and *dissociative identity disorder* (*multiple personality disorder,* or MPD), in which two or more distinct personalities and identities appear within one person. Considerable controversy surrounds the validity and nature of MPD. Some clinicians think it is a common but often undiagnosed disorder, originating in childhood trauma; others hold a *sociocognitive* explanation, arguing that most cases of MPD are manufactured in unwitting collusion between therapists who believe in the disorder and suggestible patients who find it a congenial explanation for their problems.

DRUG ABUSE AND ADDICTION

8) The effects of drugs depend on whether they are used moderately or are abused. Signs of *substance abuse* include impaired ability to work or get along with others, use of the drug in hazardous situations, recurrent arrests for drug use, and conflicts with others caused by drug use. According to the *biological or disease model* of addiction, some people have a biological vulnerability to addictions such as alcoholism. The vulnerability may result from a genetic factor or from years of heavy drinking or other drug use. Advocates of the *learning model* of addiction point out that addiction patterns vary according to culture, learning, and accepted practice; that many people can stop taking a drug, even a narcotic, with no withdrawal symptoms; that drug abuse depends on the reasons people take a drug; and that drug abuse increases when people are not taught moderate use. Addiction and abuse appear to reflect an interaction of individual vulnerability (because of genetics, physiology, or psychological need) and a person's culture, learning history, and situation.

SCHIZOPHRENIA

9) *Schizophrenia* is a psychotic disorder involving *positive* or *active symptoms*—delusions, hallucinations, disorganized speech (*word salads*), and grossly inappropriate behavior—and *negative symptoms*—loss of motivation, poverty of speech, and emotional flatness. The "schizophrenias" vary in severity, duration, and prognosis. Research on their causes is focusing on brain abnormalities; genetic predispositions; abnormalities of prenatal development, resulting from viral infection or other trauma during the second trimester; and, in the *vulnerability–stress model,* interactions between such factors and a person's environment during childhood or young adulthood.

KEY TERMS

insanity 576

mental disorder 576

objective tests (inventories) 577

Minnesota Multiphasic Personality Inventory (MMPI) 577

Diagnostic and Statistical Manual of Mental Disorders (DSM) 578

generalized anxiety disorder 583

posttraumatic stress disorder (PTSD) 583

acute stress disorder 583

phobia 583

social phobia 584

agoraphobia 584

panic attack 584

People often say that this or that person has not yet found himself.
But the self is not something that one finds.
It is something that one creates.

Thomas Szasz

CHAPTER SIXTEEN
Approaches to Treatment and Therapy

Psychotherapists use many techniques to help people resolve their problems, including the use of art. In this drawing, a child expresses her grief over a classmate's suicide.

- Murray is a smart fellow with just one problem: He procrastinates. He can't seem to settle down and write his term papers. He keeps getting incompletes, swearing he'll do those papers soon, but before long the incompletes turn to Fs. Why does Murray do this, manufacturing his own misery? What kind of therapy might help him?
- Sally complains of anxieties, irritability, and continuing problems in her marriage. Although she is successful at work, she feels like a fraud, a useless member of society, and a burden to her family. She weeps often. Why is Sally so unhappy, and what can she do about it?
- Jerry, a college student, is brought to the hospital by the campus police, who found him wandering around, dazed and confused. He is anxious and talkative, and he reports hearing angry voices that accuse him of being a spy. What treatment can help Jerry?
- Margaret's parents were drug addicts who abandoned her when she was a baby. She lived in four foster homes before finding a family that truly cared for her. Margaret is married and loves her husband, but she has many inhibitions and insecurities. What can Margaret do to get over them?

People seek professional help for many difficulties and disorders. These range from "problems in living," such as family conflicts and procrastination, to the delusions of schizophrenia. In this chapter we will evaluate three major approaches to treatment. *Biological treatments* include drugs or direct intervention in brain function, with or without additional therapy; they are prescribed by psychiatrists or other physicians in a hospital or on an outpatient basis. *Psychotherapy* covers an array of psychological approaches to treating problems, including psychodynamic therapies, cognitive-behavioral therapies, family therapy, and humanist therapies. Finally, *self-help and community alternatives* include support groups, skills training, rehabilitation counseling, and community interventions.

Each of these approaches can successfully treat some problems but not others. Each can help some individuals but may harm others. Finding the right treatment depends not only on having a good practitioner but also on being an educated consumer. What does research show about the effectiveness of drugs, psychotherapy, and self-help? What works best and for what problem? When do therapies fail, and when do they do harm?

BIOLOGICAL TREATMENTS

Over the centuries, efforts to understand and treat psychological disorders have taken either a biological (*organic*) approach, regarding such disorders as diseases that can be treated surgically or with drugs; or a *psychological* approach, regarding psychological problems as difficulties stemming from people's experiences and relationships. Today organic approaches are enjoying a resurgence for two reasons: the evidence, discussed in Chapter 15, that some disorders have a genetic component or involve a biochemical or neurological abnormality; and the failure of traditional psychotherapies to help chronic sufferers of some disorders.

antipsychotic drugs Major tranquilizers used primarily in the treatment of schizophrenia and other psychotic disorders.

antidepressant drugs Drugs used primarily in the treatment of mood disorders, especially depression and anxiety.

THE QUESTION OF DRUGS

Because drugs are so widely prescribed these days, both for severe disorders such as schizophrenia and for more common problems such as anxiety and depression, it is important for consumers to understand what these drugs are, how they can best be used, and their often overlooked limitations. The main classes of drugs used in the treatment of mental and emotional disorders are these:

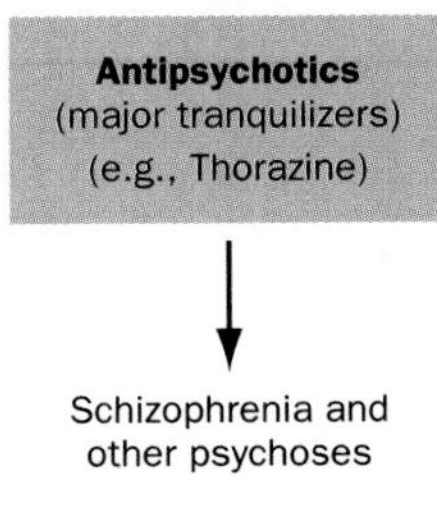

1. **Antipsychotic drugs,** or *major tranquilizers,* include chlorpromazine (Thorazine), haloperidol (Haldol), and clozapine (Clozaril). These drugs have transformed the treatment of schizophrenia and other psychoses. Before they were introduced, hospital staffs controlled patients with physical restraints, including straitjackets, or put them in padded cells to keep them from hurting others or themselves during states of extreme agitation and delusion. Some people on clozapine have "awakened" after a decade of illness and resumed their former lives. When given to people who are acutely ill with schizophrenia and likely to improve spontaneously within a few weeks or months, antipsychotic drugs can reduce agitation and delusions, and they can shorten the schizophrenic episode (Kane, 1987).

However, antipsychotic drugs are not a cure. For some patients, they remove or lessen the most dramatic symptoms, such as word salads and hallucinations, but they usually cannot restore normal thought patterns or relationships. They allow many people to be released from hospitals, but often these individuals cannot care for themselves or they fail to take their medication because of its unpleasant unintended effects. The overall success of these drugs is modest, and some individuals diagnosed as schizophrenic deteriorate when they take them (Breggin, 1991; Karon, 1994).

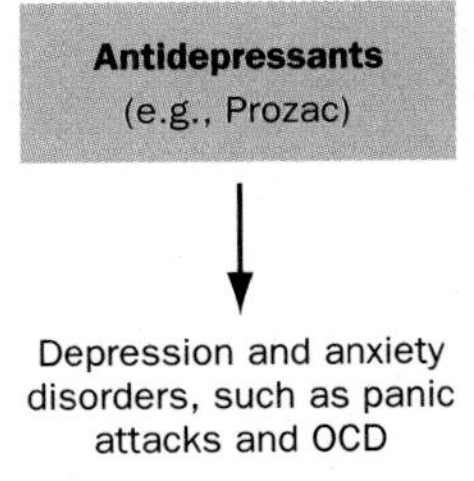

2. **Antidepressant drugs** are used primarily in treating mood disorders such as depression, anxiety, phobias, and obsessive-compulsive disorder (Swedo & Rapoport, 1991). There are three types of antidepressants. *Monoamine oxidase (MAO) inhibitors,* such as Nardil, elevate the level of norepinephrine and serotonin in the brain by blocking or inhibiting the enzyme that deactivates these neurotransmitters. *Tricyclic antidepressants,* such as Elavil, prevent the normal reabsorption, or "reuptake," of norepinephrine and serotonin by the cells that have released them. *Selective seratonin reuptake inhibitors (SSRIs),* such as Prozac, work on the same principle as the tricyclics but specifically target serotonin, boosting its levels. Antidepressants are nonaddictive, but they can produce unpleasant physical reactions, including dry mouth, headaches, constipation, nausea, restlessness, gastrointestinal problems, weight gain, and, in as many as one-third of all patients, decreased sexual desire and blocked or delayed orgasm.

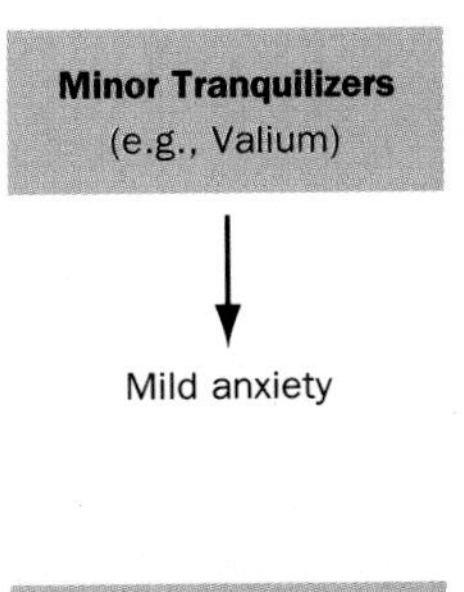

3. **"Minor" tranquilizers,** such as Valium and Xanax, are classified as depressants and are the drugs most often prescribed by physicians for patients who complain of unhappiness, panic, or anxiety. Unfortunately, they are the least effective drugs for these emotional disorders. A small but significant percentage of people who take tranquilizers overuse the drugs and develop problems with *tolerance* (i.e., they need larger and larger doses) and withdrawal (Lader & Morton, 1991). Xanax can also result in rebound panic attacks if it is not taken exactly on schedule. Thus antidepressants are preferable to tranquilizers in treating mood disorders.

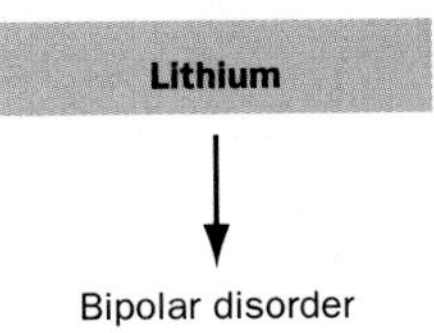

4. A special category of drug, a salt called *lithium carbonate,* is often successful in helping people who suffer from bipolar disorder (depression alternating with manic euphoria). It must be given in exactly the right dose, and the patient's blood levels of lithium must be carefully monitored, because too little won't help and too much is toxic.

The increasing popularity of drugs as a method of treatment poses a problem for clinical psychologists, who, unlike psychiatrists, are not currently licensed to prescribe medication. Many psychologists are now lobbying for prescription rights, ar-

These photos show the effects of antipsychotic drugs on the symptoms of a young man with schizophrenia. In the photo on the left, he was unmedicated; in the photo on the right, he had taken medication. However, these drugs do not help all people with psychotic disorders.

guing that they should have access to the full range of treatment possibilities (DeLeon & Wiggins, 1996). But they have run into resistance, both from the medical profession, which argues that even with increased training psychologists will not be qualified to prescribe medication, and from other psychologists who are concerned about the medicalizing of their field and who want psychology to remain a distinct alternative to psychiatry (DeNelsky, 1996).

Drugs have helped many people who have gone from therapy to therapy without relief (Shuchman & Wilkes, 1990). Although medication cannot magically eliminate people's problems, it can be a useful first step in treatment. By improving sleep patterns, appetite, and energy, it may help people concentrate on solving their problems. Yet, despite these benefits, some words of caution are in order. Many psychiatrists and drug companies are trumpeting the benefits of medication without informing the public of its limitations. Here are some of them:

1. *The placebo effect.* New drugs, like new psychotherapies, often promise quick and effective cures, as was the case with the arrival of Clozaril, Xanax, and Prozac. Yet the placebo effect ensures that some people will respond positively to new drugs just because of the enthusiasm surrounding them. After a while, when placebo effects decline, many drugs turn out to be neither as effective as promised nor as widely applicable. This has happened repeatedly with each new generation of tranquilizer and is happening again with antidepressants.

EXAMINE THE EVIDENCE

A magazine announces that Prozac is "A breakthrough drug for depression." Other headlines announce that Clozaril is a miracle cure for people with schizophrenia. Why should the public be cautious before concluding that these drugs are really miracle cures?

The belief nowadays that antidepressants are the treatment of choice for depression is widespread, so we were as surprised as anybody to discover the large amount of evidence calling that belief into question. For example, a meta-analysis of 22 studies that compared new antidepressants to older kinds of antidepressants and to placebos found that although clinicians thought the drugs were helpful, the patients did not: "Patient ratings revealed no advantage for antidepressants beyond the placebo effect," the researchers reported, and this was true for men and women regardless of their age, dosage level of the drug, and length of treatment (Greenberg et al., 1992). A more recent meta-analysis of 39 studies involving more than 3,000 depressed patients treated with medication, placebo drugs, or psychotherapy, found *no differences* in the effectiveness of medication versus psychotherapy. Moreover, 73 percent of the effectiveness of the antidepressant was due to the placebo effect or other

"minor" tranquilizers
Depressants commonly but often inappropriately prescribed for patients who complain of unhappiness or worry.

nonchemical factors (Sapirstein & Kirsch, 1996). Studies of the much-heralded Prozac show that even it is no more effective than the older generation of antidepressants (Greenberg et al., 1994).

Even when drugs do show a positive effect, another problem can occur: In supposedly double-blind studies of new drugs, patients can usually tell whether they are being given an active drug or a placebo. The reason is that virtually all of the drugs we have described produce physical effects, whereas inert placebos do not. Patients and researchers therefore often figure out who is getting the genuine drug, and this knowledge can affect the patients' responses and the researchers' judgments of the treatment's success (Carroll, Rounsaville, & Nich, 1994). When true double-blind studies are done, using *active placebos* that mimic the physical effects of real drugs, researchers have found, again, little difference in effectiveness between the placebos and the antidepressants (Fisher & Greenberg, 1993; Sapirstein & Kirsch, 1996).

2. *Relapse and dropout rates.* A person may have short-term success with antipsychotic or antidepressant drugs. However, in part because these medications have some unpleasant physical effects, the percentage of people who stop taking them is very high—between 50 and 67 percent (McGrath et al., 1990; Torrey, 1988). People who take antidepressants without learning how to cope with their problems are also more likely to relapse and again become depressed (Antonuccio, Danton, & DeNelsky, 1995).

3. *Dosage problems.* The challenge with drugs is to find the "therapeutic window," the amount that is enough but not too much. Some people have taken drugs for years without improvement, which is as useless as staying in psychotherapy for years without improvement. Some critics are concerned that drug therapy creates a "delusion of precision" in treatment, when in fact many questions remain about which drug best suits which problem, what the proper dose should be, how long the drug should and can be taken, and so forth (Gutheil, 1993).

In addition, the same dose of a drug may be metabolized differently in men and women, old people and young people, and different ethnic groups (Strickland et al., 1991, 1995; Willie et al., 1995). When psychiatrist Keh-Ming Lin moved from Taiwan to the United States, he was amazed to learn that the dosage of antipsychotic drugs given to American patients with schizophrenia was often 10 times higher than the dose for Chinese patients. In subsequent research comparing 13 white and 16 Asian schizophrenics, Lin and his colleagues confirmed that the Asian patients required significantly lower doses of the medication for optimal treatment (Lin, Poland, & Chien, 1990; Lin et al., 1989). African-Americans suffering from depression or bipolar disorder also seem to need lower dosages of tricyclic antidepressants and lithium than other ethnic groups do (Strickland et al., 1991, 1995). Groups may differ in the dosages they can tolerate because of variations in metabolic rates, amount of body fat, the number or type of drug receptors in the brain, or cultural practices such as smoking and eating habits.

4. *Long-term risks, known and unknown.* Antipsychotic drugs are among the safest in medicine, but they can have some dangerous effects if they are taken over many years. One is the development of a neurological disorder called *tardive* (late-appearing) *dyskinesia,* which is characterized by involuntary muscle movements. About one-fourth of all adults who take antipsychotics develop this disorder, and fully one-third of elderly patients do (Saltz et al., 1991). In a small percentage of cases, antipsychotic drugs cause *neuroleptic malignant syndrome,* which produces fever, delirium, coma, and sometimes death (Keck, McElroy, & Pope, 1991). Clozapine has produced, in about 2 percent of cases, a sharp decrease in white blood cells that is potentially fatal.

Antidepressants are assumed to be safe, but the effects of taking them for many years are simply unknown. No one knows the long-term effects of Prozac, for example, although it is prescribed widely, especially to women of childbearing age (Kramer, 1993). The general public and even many physicians do not realize that new drugs are often tested on only a few hundred people for only a few weeks, even when the drug is one that patients might take for many years. For example, the Food and Drug Administration (FDA) warns that "Because clomipramine [for obsessive-compulsive disorder] has not been systematically evaluated for long-term use (more than ten weeks), physicians should periodically reevaluate the long-term usefulness of the drug for individual patients." Clozapine, the neuroleptic now often prescribed for people with schizophrenia, was tested in controlled trials that lasted only six weeks (*FDA Drug Bulletin,* 1990). Many psychiatrists, relying on these short-term tests, overlook the possibility of negative long-term effects.

As we will see later in this chapter, certain psychotherapies work as well as drugs do, or even better, for most people who have panic attacks, phobias, anxiety, or depression. And unlike drug treatments, psychotherapies teach people how to cope with recurrences of their disorder, so the relapse rate for people in psychotherapy is much lower than that for people who take medication exclusively.

Moreover, we want to emphasize that *the fact that a disorder may have biological origins does not mean that the only appropriate treatment is biological.* Researchers used PET scans to examine cerebral glucose metabolism in 18 patients with obsessive–compulsive disorder, before and after treating them with either Prozac or behavior therapy. They found that glucose metabolic rates changed equally in response to both treatments (Baxter et al., 1992). Another study, comparing drugs with cognitive-behavior therapy, got the same results (Schwartz et al., 1996). These studies offer yet another vivid reminder that although the brain affects behavior, behavior also affects the brain (see Figure 16.1).

Without question, drugs have rescued some people from emotional despair, suicide, or years in a mental hospital. But it is essential to think critically about drug therapies because many doctors prescribe them *routinely,* often without accompanying psychotherapy for the person's problems. The overprescription of drugs is partly a result of pressure from managed-care organizations, which prefer to pay for one patient visit for a prescription rather than for ten visits for psychotherapy, and from drug companies, which are spending fortunes to market and promote these highly profitable medications (Antonuccio, Danton, & DeNelsky, 1995; Critser, 1996). (Most of the major drug companies have actually bought managed-care groups and others are forming "mental-health group alliances"—without any national debate, according to one investigator, over the potential conflict of interest that might occur when a company that makes pills owns the companies that oversee their use [Critser, 1996].) At one conference we attended, a psychiatrist warned that because of the ease of prescribing antidepressants and tranquilizers, "It is not unusual for [psychiatrists] to see anywhere from six

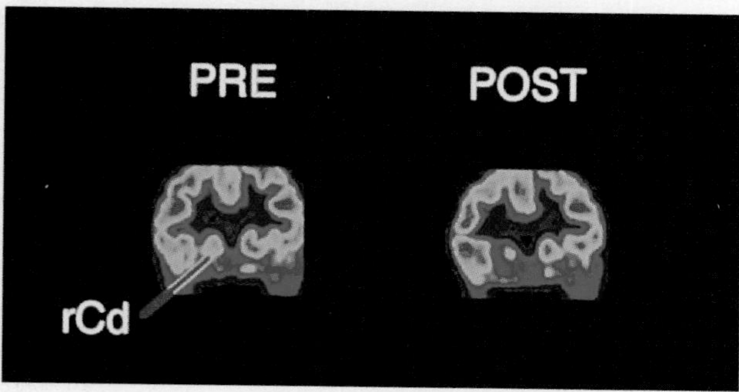

Figure 16.1
Psychotherapy and the Brain

These PET scans show the brain of a person with obsessive-compulsive disorder before and after treatment with behavior therapy. Before therapy, the glucose metabolic rates in the right caudate nucleus (rCd) were elevated, but after therapy they "calmed down," becoming less active (Schwartz et al., 1996).

to eight patients per client hour. This is not being involved with your patient in any meaningful way."

In sum, consumers should avoid the tendency to think about drugs in a simplistic way, as either totally miraculous or totally worthless. Their proper use depends on the individual, the problem, and whether drugs are combined with psychotherapy.

PROBING THE BRAIN: SURGERY AND ELECTROSHOCK

For centuries, physicians treated mental illness by trying to change brain function directly. In the seventeenth century, for example, doctors drilled holes in the skull (a method called *trepanning*), which supposedly released the "psychic pressures" thought to be causing the person's symptoms. **Psychosurgery**—surgery designed to destroy selected areas of the brain thought to be responsible for emotional disorders or disturbed behavior—continued well into this century.

The most famous form of modern psychosurgery was invented in 1935, when a Portuguese neurologist, Egas Moniz, drilled two holes into the skull of a mental patient and used a specially designed instrument to cut or crush nerve fibers running from the prefrontal lobes to other areas. The operation, called a *prefrontal lobotomy*, was supposed to reduce the patient's emotional symptoms without impairing intellectual ability. This procedure (which, incredibly, was never assessed or validated scientifically) was performed on tens of thousands of people. In America, the lobotomy was popularized by Walter Freeman, who personally performed more than 3,500 operations. Tragically, lobotomies left many patients apathetic, withdrawn, and unable to care for themselves (Valenstein, 1986). Yet Moniz won a Nobel Prize for his work.

With the advent of antipsychotic drugs in the 1950s, the number of lobotomies declined, but other forms of psychosurgery took their place. These surgeries, like lobotomies, also had unpredictable and often devastating consequences for the patient (Breggin, 1991; Valenstein, 1986). Psychosurgery is rarely used anymore, although the rapid development of new technologies for probing the brain may mean that we will see its resurgence in the future.

psychosurgery Any surgical procedure that destroys selected areas of the brain believed to be involved in emotional disorders or violent, impulsive behavior.

electroconvulsive therapy (ECT) A procedure occasionally used for cases of prolonged major depression, in which a brief brain seizure is induced to alter brain chemistry.

Another controversial procedure that *has* made a dramatic return is **electroconvulsive therapy (ECT)**, or "shock treatment," which is used for the treatment of severe depression. An electrode is placed on one or both sides of the head, and a brief current is turned on. The current triggers a seizure that typically lasts one minute, causing the body to convulse. A colleague told us about a man who was given ECT

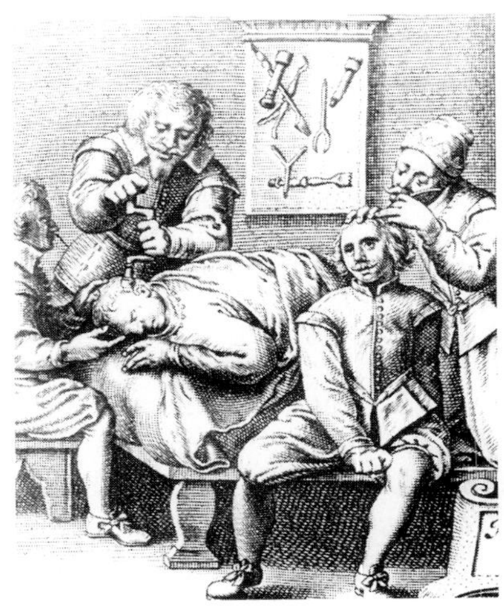

Throughout history, healers have tried literally to root out behavior they considered abnormal. An engraving from 1634 shows trepanning, an ancient method of drilling holes in the skull to release "psychic pressures" supposedly causing mental illness.

in the early 1950s: The convulsions sent him flying off the table and shattered his legs. Cases such as this reinforced the public impression of ECT as a barbaric and painful practice, and the method lost favor, especially when drugs seemed so promising. Then, when drugs proved to have limited effectiveness and to take time to work, and when new ways of measuring brain activity appeared, researchers began to reexamine ECT.

Today, the technique has been vastly modified and the voltage reduced. Patients are given muscle relaxants and anesthesia, so their convulsions are minimized and they can sleep through the procedure (Malitz & Sackeim, 1986). ECT is most effective with suicidally depressed people, for whom there is a risk in waiting until antidepressants or psychotherapy can take effect, but no one knows how or why ECT works. It is *ineffective* with other disorders, such as schizophrenia or alcoholism, though it is sometimes misused for these conditions. MRI studies of patients given ECT find no evidence that the treatment causes brain damage (Coffey, 1993; Endler, 1991). ECT does produce brief memory loss, but the question of the extent and permanence of that memory loss is still being debated (Holmes, 1994).

ECT's supporters argue that it is foolish to deny suffering, depressed patients a way out of their misery, especially if that misery is making them suicidal. Critics reply that the application of 150 volts of electrical current to the brain is "a crime against humanity," and one psychiatrist has called its use "like hitting [someone] with a two-by-four" (Fisher, 1985). ECT continues to inspire passion, pro and con.

Quick Quiz

A. Match these treatments with the problems for which they are typically used.

1. antipsychotic drugs
2. antidepressant drugs
3. lithium carbonate
4. electroconvulsive therapy

a. suicidal depression
b. bipolar disorder
c. schizophrenia
d. depression and anxiety
e. obsessive–compulsive disorder

B. Give four reasons why the public should be cautious about concluding that drugs for psychological disorders are miracle cures.

C. Jezebel has had occasional episodes of depression that seem to be getting worse. Her physician prescribes an antidepressant for her. Before taking it, what questions should Jezebel ask herself—and the doctor?

Answers:

A. 1. c 2. d, e 3. b 4. a B. Placebo effects are common; dropout and relapse rates are high; appropriate dosages must be given, which can vary by sex, age, and ethnicity; and some drugs have unkown or long-term risks. C. Jezebel might want to ask these questions: Has the physician taken her full medical and psychological history, or prescribed the drug casually? Has he or she explored with her the possible reasons for her depression, or referred her to a mental-health professional who will do so? Would psychotherapy be appropriate, either with or without medication? Does the medication have any unpleasant physical effects or long-term risks? Will the doctor continue to monitor her reactions to the drug on a regular basis?

THE HOOFBEATS OF A ZEBRA

One rainy afternoon a young woman named Sheila Allen went to a community hospital and asked for psychiatric help. Sheila Allen had virtually no strength left. She couldn't walk; she could barely sit up. For years she had been going to doctors, getting sicker and sicker. The doctors didn't take her physical complaints seriously, and finally she agreed to enter the "kook hospital." Upon admission, her diagnosis was "bizarre behavior, with looseness of thought associations and severe depression associated with suicidal thoughts." Sheila Allen was lucky. She met a neurologist who suspected, correctly, that she had an uncommon disease called *myasthenia gravis*, which weakens the muscles. He treated her for this illness, and she recovered.

In California in 1995, however, a psychiatrist was convicted of malpractice because he failed to diagnose a patient who was suffering from the same disease. For *12 years* she had gotten steadily worse, until she couldn't even lift her hand to brush her teeth. The reason, said the psychiatrist who had treated her all that time, was her "repressed rage" at her parents.

Why have some doctors failed to consider that their patients might be suffering from a disease rather than a psychological problem? Sheila Allen's neurologist said, "There is a saying about diagnosis—about why doctors often fail to recognize one of the less common diseases. It goes, 'When you hear hoofbeats, you don't necessarily think of a zebra.' I recognized the hoofbeats of a zebra" (Roueché, 1984).

All researchers learn to recognize the hoofbeats that make the most noise in their profession. "Mind-oriented" people listen for one beat, "body-oriented" people for another. Throughout history, both sides have made terrible errors. In the nineteenth century, people thought that tuberculosis was caused by a "tubercular personality" until the bacillus that causes the disease was discovered (Sontag, 1978). In this century, people have been subjected to months or years of psychoanalytic therapy when their real problem was a brain tumor, a disease, or another organic condition. But many psychologists are concerned about an equally troubling mistake: reducing complex psychological problems to matters of biochemistry. As we noted, some physicians prescribe drugs indiscriminately, without finding out why the patient is distressed and without helping the patient learn to cope with adversities. As long as people think that hoofbeats indicate only one animal, disagreements about biological and psychological models of mental illness will continue.

DON'T OVERSIMPLIFY

Psychologically minded researchers and biologically minded researchers often interpret the same behavior differently. How can we avoid the diagnostic errors that occur because of this either–or thinking?

KINDS OF PSYCHOTHERAPY

All psychotherapists share one goal: They want to help clients think about their lives in new ways, to find solutions to the problems that plague them. In this section we will consider the major schools of psychotherapy and some of their offshoots. To illustrate the philosophy and methods of each of the therapeutic schools that follow, we will use the example of our procrastinating friend Murray, whom we met at the start of this chapter. But keep in mind that these therapies can be applied to many problems, including emotional disorders, difficult decisions, conflicts in relationships, and traumatic experiences.

PSYCHODYNAMIC THERAPY

Sigmund Freud was the father of the "talking cure," as one of his patients called it. He believed that intensive probing of the past and of the mind would produce *insight*—the patient's moment of truth, the awareness of the reason for his or her symptoms and anguish. With insight and emotional release, the symptoms would disappear. Freud's original method of *psychoanalysis* has evolved into many different forms of therapy, which are called *psychodynamic* because they share the goal of exploring the unconscious dynamics of personality, such as defenses and conflicts (see Chapter 12). These approaches are considered by their proponents to be "depth" therapies because the goal is to delve for unconscious processes rather than "superficial" symptoms and conscious beliefs.

Freud (1910/1957) believed that Leonardo da Vinci's paintings of Madonnas were a sublimated expression of his longing for his mother, from whom he had been separated early in life. One goal of psychoanalysis is to help clients "sublimate" their energies constructively.

Traditional, orthodox psychoanalysis is a method for those who have money and time. The client usually meets with the analyst three to five times a week, often for many years. One such analyst, John Gedo (1979), reported that in 20 years he treated only 36 people, each one requiring "more than 600 sessions, sometimes as many as 1,000, spread over 3 to 7 years." (In the old film *Sleeper,* Woody Allen's character lies in suspended animation for two centuries. When he awakes, his first thought is: "I haven't seen my analyst in 200 years! He was a strict Freudian—if I'd been going all this time I'd probably almost be cured by now.")

In analysis and some other psychodynamic therapies, the client lies on a couch, facing away from the analyst, and uses **free association** to say whatever comes to mind. For example, by free associating to his dreams, his fantasies about work, and his early memories, Murray might gain the insight that he procrastinates as a way of expressing anger toward his parents. He might realize that he is angry because they insist that he study for a career he dislikes. Ideally, Murray will come to this insight by himself. If the analyst suggests it, Murray might feel too defensive about displeasing his parents to accept it.

The second major element of psychodynamic therapy is **transference,** the patient's transfer (displacement) of emotional elements of his or her inner life—usually feelings about the parents—outward onto the analyst. Have you ever found yourself responding to a new acquaintance with unusually quick affection or dislike, and later realized it was because the person reminded you of a loved or loathed relative? That experience is similar to transference. In this view, a woman who failed to resolve her Oedipal love for her father might seem to fall in love with the analyst. A man who is unconsciously angry at his mother for rejecting him might now become furious with his analyst for going on vacation. Through transference, psychodynamic therapists believe, patients can resolve their emotional conflicts.

Psychodynamic therapy, and especially psychoanalysis, does not expressly aim to solve an individual's immediate problem. In fact, a person may come in complaining of a symptom such as anxiety or headaches, and the therapist may not get around to that symptom for months or even years. The therapist views the symptom as only the tip of the mental iceberg. Some traditional analysts don't attempt cures at all. The goal, they say, is understanding, not change.

Many psychodynamic therapists use Freudian principles but reject traditional psychoanalytic methods. They face the client; they participate more; and they are more goal-directed. Time-limited or *brief psychodynamic therapy* consists of 15, 20, or 25 sessions. Without delving into the client's entire history, the therapist listens to the client's problems and formulates the main issue or *dynamic focus* (Strupp & Binder, 1984). The rest of the therapy focuses on the person's self-defeating habits and recurring problems. The therapist looks for clues in the client's behavior in therapy to identify and change these patterns.

BEHAVIORAL AND COGNITIVE THERAPY

Psychologists who practice behavioral or cognitive therapy (or a combination of the two) would focus on helping Murray change his current behavior and attitudes rather than on striving for insight. "Mur," they would say, "you have lousy study habits. And you have a set of beliefs about studying, writing papers, and success that are woefully unrealistic." Such therapists would not worry much about Murray's past, his parents, or his unconscious anxieties.

In Chapter 7 we discussed the major principles of learning theory and some of their applications. *Behavior therapies* are based on techniques derived from behavioral principles:

free association In psychoanalysis, a method of uncovering unconscious conflicts by saying freely whatever comes to mind.

transference In psychodynamic therapies, a critical step in which the patient transfers unconscious emotions or reactions, such as emotional feelings about his or her parents, onto the therapist.

1. *Behavioral records and contracts* are used to help clients identify the rewards that keep an unwanted habit going and make commitments to better forms of behavior. For example, a man who wants to curb his overeating may not be aware of how much he eats throughout the day; a behavioral record might show that he eats more junk food than he realized in the late afternoon. Once the unwanted behavior is identified, along with the reinforcers that keep it going, a treatment program can be designed to change it. The therapist helps the person set *behavioral goals,* small step by small step. A husband and wife who fight over housework, for instance, might be asked to draw up a contract indicating who will do what, with specified rewards for carrying out their duties. With such a contract, they can't fall back on accusations such as "You never do anything around here!"

2. *Systematic desensitization* is a step-by-step process of desensitizing a client to a feared object or experience. It combines relaxation training with a systematic hierarchy of stimuli, sometimes in imagined situations and sometimes in real ones, leading gradually to the one that is most feared. The sequence for a person who is terrified of flying might be to read about airplane safety, visit an airport, sit in a plane while it is on the ground, take a short flight, and then take a long flight. At each step the person must become comfortable before going on.

3. *Aversive conditioning* substitutes punishment for the reinforcement that has perpetuated a bad habit. Suppose a woman who bites her nails is reinforced each time she does so by relief from her anxiety and a brief good feeling. A behavior therapist might have her wear a rubber band around her wrist and ask her to snap it (hard!) each time she bites her nails or feels the desire to do so. The goal is to make sure that she receives no continuing rewards for the undesirable behavior.

4. *Flooding or exposure treatments* take the client right into a feared situation, but the therapist goes along to show that the situation isn't going to kill either of them. For example, a person suffering from agoraphobia would be taken into the very situation that he or she fears most—a procedure called "in vivo" exposure—and would remain there, with the therapist, until the panic and anxiety decline. Notice how different this approach is from a psychodynamic one, in which the goal would be to uncover the presumably unconscious reason that the agoraphobic feels afraid of going out.

Exposure therapy at work.

Batters overcoming *bonkinogginophobia,* a fear of the ball.

GET INVOLVED

If you read Chapter 15, perhaps you already did the exercise that asked you to identify your greatest fear. What was it? Spiders? Speaking in front of a large group of strangers? Now see whether systematic-desensitization procedures will help you conquer your fear. Write down a list of situations that can evoke your fear, starting with one that produces the least anxiety (e.g., seeing a photo of a tiny brown spider) and ending with the most frightening one you can think of (e.g., looking at live tarantulas at the pet store). Now, find a quiet room where you will have no distractions or interruptions, sit in a comfortable reclining chair, and relax all the muscles of your body. Breathe slowly and deeply. Imagine the first, easiest scene, remaining as relaxed as possible. Do this until you can confront the image without becoming anxious. When that happens, go on to the next scene in your hierarchy. Don't try this all at once; space out your sessions over time. Does it work?

5. *Skills training* provides practice in specific acts that are necessary for achieving the person's goals. It's not enough to tell someone "Don't be shy" if the person doesn't know how to make small talk when meeting other people. Countless skills-training programs are available—for parents who don't know how to discipline children, for people with social anxieties, for children and adults who don't know how to express themselves, and so on.

A behaviorist would treat Murray's procrastination in several ways. Murray might not be aware of how he actually spends his time when he is avoiding his studies. Afraid that he hasn't time to do everything, he does nothing. Keeping a behavioral diary would let Murray know exactly how he spends his time, and how much time he can realistically allot to a project. (Procrastinators often are poor judges of how much time it takes to do things.) Instead of having a vague, impossibly huge goal, such as "I'm going to reorganize my life," Murray would establish specific small goals, such as reading the two books necessary for an English paper and writing one page of an assignment. The therapist might also offer skills training to make sure Murray knows how to reach those goals.

Poet Michael Casey described the first daffodil that bravely rises through the snow as "a gleam of laughter in a sullen face." Are you more inclined to focus on the lingering icy clutch of winter or the early sunny signs of spring?

Of course, people's thoughts, feelings, and motivations can influence their behavior. In discussing emotion (Chapter 10) and emotional disorders (Chapter 15), we saw that distorted thoughts and perceptions are related to mood problems. *Cognitive therapy* aims to help clients identify the beliefs and expectations that might be unnecessarily prolonging their unhappiness, conflicts, and other problems (Beck, 1976, 1991; Ellis & Dryden, 1987; Greenberger & Padesky, 1995). Albert Ellis founded one of the earliest and still best-known forms of cognitive therapy, rational emotive therapy, which he now calls *rational emotive behavior therapy* (Ellis, 1993). In this approach, the therapist challenges the client's illogical and self-defeating beliefs directly with rational arguments. Other forms of cognitive therapy encourage clients to test their beliefs against the evidence.

A cognitive therapist might treat Murray's procrastination problem by having Murray write down his thoughts about work, read the thoughts as if someone else had said them, and then write a rational response to each one. This technique is useful because many people have unrealistic notions of what they must or should do in their lives, and often they do not examine the validity of these notions. Many procrastinators are perfectionists; if they can't do something perfectly, they won't do it at all. Unable to accept their limitations, they set impossible standards and "catastrophize":

Negative thought	**Rational response**
This paper isn't good enough; I'd better rewrite it for the twentieth time.	Good enough for what? It won't win a Pulitzer Prize, but it is a pretty good paper.
If I don't get an A+ on this paper, my life will be ruined.	My life will be a lot worse if I keep getting incompletes. It's better to get a B or even a C than to do nothing at all.
My professor is going to think I'm an idiot when he reads this. I'll feel humiliated by his criticism.	He's not accused me of being an idiot yet. If he makes some criticisms, I can learn from them and do better next time.

Strict behaviorists consider thoughts to be "behaviors" that are modifiable by learning principles. But most psychologists believe that thoughts and behavior influence each other, which is why cognitive-behavioral therapy is more common than either form alone.

TABLE 16.1 *The Major Schools of Therapy Compared*

	Primary goal	Methods
Psychodynamic	Insight into unconscious motives and feelings	Probing the unconscious through dream analysis, free association, transference, other forms of "talk therapy"
Cognitive-Behavioral	Modification of behavior and irrational beliefs	Behavioral techniques such as systematic desensitization and flooding; exercises to identify and change faulty beliefs
Humanist	Insight; self-acceptance and self-fulfillment	Providing a safe, nonjudgmental setting in which to discuss life issues
Family	Modification of individual habits and family patterns	Working with couples, families, and sometimes individuals to identify and change patterns that perpetuate problems

In addition, therapists from all schools may take advantage of a method from family therapy—namely, that some problems respond best to treatment in groups. In *group therapy*, people with the same or different problems are put together to find solutions. Members learn that their problems are not unique. They also learn that they cannot get away with their usual excuses because others in the group have tried them all (Yalom, 1995). Group therapies are commonly used in institutions, such as prisons and mental hospitals. But they are also popular among people who have a range of social difficulties, such as shyness and anxiety, or who share a common traumatic experience, such as sexual assault (Becker et al., 1984). Keep in mind that group therapy is not the same as self-help groups, which we will discuss in the next section, or programs designed for personal growth rather than psychotherapy.

All successful therapies seem to share common elements (Lambert & Hill, 1994; Mahoney, 1991; Orlinsky & Howard, 1994). One has to do with the stories, or narratives, that people tell about themselves. Good therapists try to replace a client's self-defeating, pessimistic, or unrealistic life story with one that is more hopeful and attainable. As George Howard (1991) put it, therapy is an exercise in "story repair."

Some therapists are making this "story repair" an explicit focus of treatment, using the *narrative method* to help clients form new stories about themselves (Freedman & Combs, 1996; White & Epston, 1990). The therapist may write a letter to the client, framing the problem as the therapist sees it and inviting the client to write a reply. Letter writing allows people to identify their problems more clearly and see their own behavior in new ways. One proponent of the narrative method, David Epston, wrote a long letter to Marisa, an immigrant woman who had been abused and rejected all her life. It said, in part, "Telling me, a virtual stranger, your life story, which turned out to be a history of exploitation, frees you to some extent from it. To tell a story about your life turns it into a history, one that can be left behind, and makes it easier for you to create a future of your own design" (quoted in O'Hanlon, 1994). Marisa replied that his letter helped her to tell a new story about her life and future. Instead of seeing the tragedies that had befallen her as evidence that she was a worthless victim, as she always had, she now saw the same events as evidence of her strength and endurance. In short, she transformed her victim narrative into a story of triumph. "My life has a future now," she wrote back to him. "It will never be the same again."

ALTERNATIVES TO PSYCHOTHERAPY

Psychotherapy is popular for people with all sorts of problems, but sometimes it is not enough and sometimes it is too much. *Community programs* aim to help people who are seriously mentally ill or who have disabilities and need more than psychotherapy. *Self-help groups* are designed for people who have problems that do not require individual or group therapy.

THE COMMUNITY AND REHABILITATION MOVEMENTS

Many people assume that individuals who are seriously mentally ill are in hospitals and other institutions, but this is not so. The vast majority of those with severe mental disorders spend most of their lives in the community, in boarding houses, hotel rooms, hostels, jails, hallways, abandoned buildings, halfway houses, or the streets. The question of how best to treat them is crucial to these individuals, their families, and society (see "Puzzles of Psychology").

Rehabilitation psychologists are concerned with the assessment and treatment of people who are physically or mentally disabled, either temporarily or permanently.

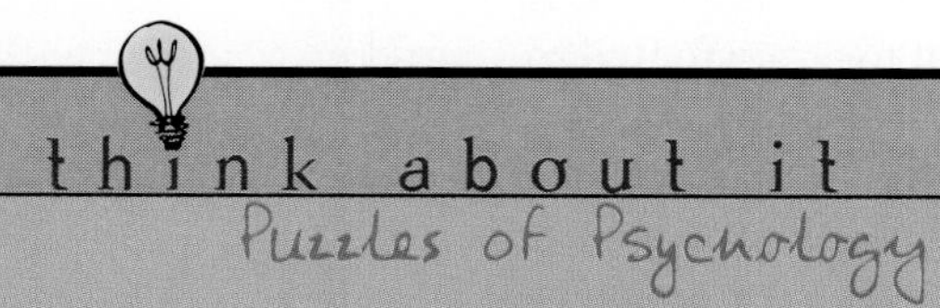

Mental Illness and the Limits of Liberty

In January 1996, in the small town of Waterville, Maine, the parents of Mark Bechard became alarmed at their son's growing agitation and paranoia—symptoms that had caused him to be hospitalized in the past. They called the local mental-health center, but the center, lacking funds for weekend staff, was closed. The next day, Mark Bechard went to the chapel where he often attended mass, and bludgeoned two elderly nuns to death.

For most of this century, people like Mark Bechard would have been involuntarily committed to mental hospitals indefinitely. But in the 1960s and 1970s, three trends resulted in the closing of many institutions and the release of most disturbed patients:

1. New antipsychotic medications calmed most of the extreme symptoms, so people were released with the expectation that they would be able to return to their families and communities.
2. Patients'-rights groups protested the abuses of involuntary confinement. Many mentally ill people were being warehoused without treatment; people were being committed without sufficient cause; and hospitals had no review procedures to determine when a person should be released. Many disturbed individuals were spending far longer in mental hospitals for committing minor crimes than they would have spent in prison. Some people were confined by mistake because they could not speak English or were mildly retarded. A woman named Gladys Burr was involuntarily confined in 1936, with an incorrect diagnosis of mental retardation and psychosis. No one paid attention to her pleas for freedom for 42 years.
3. The U.S. government began a program of deinstitutionalizing mentally disturbed people, sending them back to their communities for treatment. The public, wanting more cuts in taxes, supported this effort. In 1963, Congress passed the Community Mental Health Centers Act, designed to set up a nationwide network of mental-health centers that would provide services for the mentally ill.

Sadly, efforts to eliminate the warehousing of the mentally ill backfired. Hospital administrators, anxious to avoid legal charges of violating patients' rights, began discharging patients as soon as possible without regard for where they might go. Some state regulations made it very difficult to hospitalize people involuntarily for longer than a few weeks. Although this meant that hospitals couldn't confine harmless or misdiagnosed people such as Gladys Burr, it also meant they had to release people who were dangerous to themselves or others, such as Mark Bechard.

Further, having pressured the states to close their mental hospitals and release disturbed people, the government then cut financial aid for mental-health care and for housing the poor and homeless. The Community Mental Health Centers Act was never funded. Thousands of patients were simply "dumped" onto the streets. Between 1955 and 1992 the number of people in mental institutions plummeted from 559,000 to 90,000 (Shogren, 1994).

They work with people with mental retardation, epilepsy, chronic pain, severe physical injuries, arthritis, cancer, addictions, and psychiatric problems. They conduct research to find the best ways to teach disabled people to work and live independently, overcome motivational slumps, improve their sex lives, and follow healthy regimens. Rehabilitation psychologists' approach to treatment is eclectic, often including behavior therapy, group counseling, job training, and community intervention. Because more people are surviving traumatic injuries and living long enough to develop chronic medical conditions, rehabilitation is one of the fastest-growing areas of health care (Frank, Gluck, & Buckelew, 1990).

Community psychologists and other mental-health workers have been successful in setting up programs to help many people who are mentally ill or who have disabilities (Dion & Anthony, 1987; Orford, 1992). In a follow-up study of people with schizophrenia who had been hospitalized 20 years earlier, researchers found that the greatest predictor of successful functioning was community support, including outpatient services at local clinics and close contact with family and friends. The course of schizophrenia, they found, depends less on any "inherent natural outcome" than on the individual's family and support systems (Harding, Zubin, & Strauss, 1987).

Today the care of chronic mental patients has shifted to profit-making, private nursing homes and board-and-care homes, which are often unregulated and poorly staffed. For the most part, mental patients are no better off in these facilities than they were in state institutions (Shadish, Lurigio, & Lewis, 1989). General hospitals have been burdened with people who have mental problems. Many patients are given medication and released with no services and families to care for them. Back on the street, patients stop taking their medication because of its negative effects and long-term risks, or because they don't see a need for it. Their psychotic symptoms return, they are rehospitalized, and the revolving-door cycle continues.

For all these reasons, the pendulum is swinging back toward some forms of involuntary commitment, particularly if a person is potentially violent. About 35 states in the United States have policies of involuntary commitment to an *outpatient* program instead of to a hospital, in an effort to give patients as much liberty as possible while compelling them to take part in treatment programs. People can be compelled to enter treatment if they meet certain standards of being dangerous, or if they have a troubled psychiatric history and show evidence of being "obviously ill" (Shogren, 1994). The idea behind involuntary outpatient commitment is that patients can be monitored regularly so that they don't slip through the cracks; only if they violate the program's rules are they committed to an institution. However, there is little agreement on what should be done when a patient contests involuntary commitment.

Opponents of any form of involuntary treatment argue that, in practice, patients often end up being policed, like parolees from prison, without actually getting treatment. They worry about granting the state too much power to invade the privacy of the mentally ill. To make sure a person is taking medication, for example, would you require urine tests? Exactly what aspects of the person's life would you monitor for treatment—the patient's family life? Sexual relationships? Friends? Drinking? And who should do the monitoring?

Moreover, society must decide what to do about the emotionally disturbed people who live on the streets—the ones who aren't violent, but who are distressing to observers. Should people who have obvious signs of mental illness be forced to receive treatment, or do they have an absolute right to refuse therapy and medication if they have committed no crime? If you think society should impose treatment on the mentally ill, what behaviors would warrant such intrusion on their liberty: if the person is dangerous to others, or "only" dangerous to himself or herself? What if the person is annoying, dirty, and unpleasant, but is breaking no law and is insisting on the right to live on the street?

You are the public. What services should governments provide for disturbed people? How can communities protect the rights of the mentally ill while responding to the public's desire to be shielded from disturbed people? How can a community balance the values of compassion and individual liberty? What do you think?

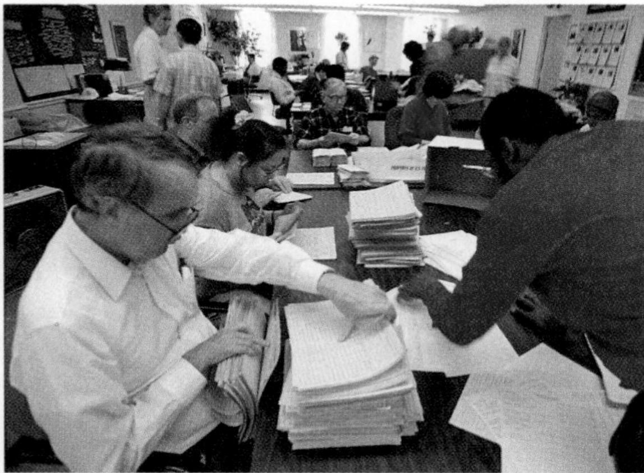

At halfway houses such as Fountain House in New York City, people with mental disorders live "halfway" between hospitalization and complete independence. They learn to take care of themselves and others, they get job training, and they receive some therapy until they are able to live on their own.

But what kind of community support? People with schizophrenia need a comprehensive program. Traditional psychotherapies are not effective for most of them. Although drugs are helpful, even essential, they are not sufficient; a drug can reduce symptoms but cannot teach a person how to get a job. Psychologists have experimented with many different solutions. One successful approach is the *clubhouse model,* a program for mentally ill people that provides rehabilitation counseling, job and skills training, and a support network. Members may live at the clubhouse until they are ready to be on their own, and they may visit the clubhouse at any time. New York City's Fountain House, one of the oldest such programs in the country, has an excellent track record, helping its members find work, return to school, and establish friendships (Beard, Propst, & Malamud, 1982; Foderaro, 1994). Other community approaches include the establishment of support systems, family therapy, foster care and family home alternatives, and family support groups (Hatfield & Lefley, 1987; Orford, 1992). The success of these programs often depends on the dedication of the people running them, which is why it can be difficult to transplant a program from one place to another. To solve this problem, some psychologists are developing ways of teaching the staff who work with psychiatric patients how to set rehabilitation goals, how to teach skills, and how to evaluate patients' progress (Anthony, Cohen, & Kennard, 1990).

Rehabilitation psychologists do not work only with the mentally ill. We know a secretary who permanently injured her back and was no longer able to sit long hours at a desk. She entered a program run by rehabilitation psychologists who were helping people find new careers when they could no longer work at their old ones. Now she has a new career. She's a rehabilitation psychologist.

THE SELF-HELP MOVEMENT

Long before there were psychotherapists, there were sympathetic advisers. Long before there were psychologists, there was psychological help. Nowadays, there are literally thousands of books and programs designed to help people help themselves. (See "Issues in Popular Culture.") More than 2,000 self-help books are published every year, and estimates of people in self-help groups range from 7 to 15 million adults (Christensen & Jacobson, 1994; Jacobs & Goodman, 1989). *Self-help groups* are organized around a common concern; there are countless groups for alcoholics, people who live with alcoholics, abusive parents, people suffering from depression or schizophrenia, gay fathers, divorced people, women who have had mastectomies, parents of murdered children, rape victims, widows, stepparents, cancer patients, and relatives of patients. A survey of 1,900 randomly selected Americans found that about 40 percent participate regularly in a small group that provides emotional support for its members. About two-thirds of these groups are organized around prayer or Bible study, and the others around shared problems or interests. But regardless of the kind of group, members say that the primary benefits they get are the awareness that they are not alone, encouragement when they are feeling down, and help in feeling better about themselves (Wuthnow, 1995).

think about it

Issues in Popular Culture

The Self-help Society

If you wander through the psychology section of your local bookstore (perhaps called "psychology and self-help" or "personal growth"), you may conclude that psychology is only about changing yourself. You will find rows of books promising to fix anything that ails you: books that tell you how to make money, how to use your mind to cure your body, and how to recover from heartbreak. You can learn to stop being too independent, too dependent, or too codependent. You can learn to find a relationship, fix a relationship, or end a relationship. You can learn to change your bad habits, or maybe live with them.

The United States and Canada, countries with long historical traditions of self-improvement and do-it-yourself attitudes, consume self-help books like peanuts—by the handful. Which are helpful, harmful, or just innocuous?

Self-help books, if they propose a specific program for the reader to follow, can be as effective as treatment administered by a therapist (Christensen & Jacobson, 1994). And of course we must not forget that plenty of people solve their problems on their own. Fifty studies, involving more than 30,000 people, found that most, without professional help, successfully quit smoking, stopped abusing alcohol, lost weight and kept it off, or resolved emotional problems and family disputes (Prochaska, Norcross, & DiClemente, 1994). The major drawback to self-help books and programs is that many individuals, on their own, don't follow through. For example, one study found that procedures for teaching parents to toilet-train their children were more effective and had fewer "emotional side effects" when a therapist was involved than when the parents got the same advice from a self-help book (Matson & Ollendick, 1977).

Gerald Rosen (1993) cautions consumers that the fact that a book has been written by a psychologist or even endorsed by the American Psychological Association is no guarantee of the book's merit. After serving as chair of the APA's Task Force on Self-Help Therapies, which investigated the proliferation and promises of self-help books and tapes, Rosen (1981) concluded, "Unfortunately, the involvement of psychologists in the development, assessment, and marketing of do-it-yourself treatment programs has often been less than responsible. Psychologists have published untested materials, advanced exaggerated claims, and accepted the use of misleading titles that encourage unrealistic expectations regarding outcome." Rosen recognizes that self-help books and programs can be effective in helping people, however, and thus offers consumers some research-based criteria for evaluating a self-help book:

- The authors must be qualified, either because they have conducted good research or are thoroughly versed in the field. Personal testimonials by people who have survived tragedy can be helpful and inspirational, of course, but an author's own experience is not grounds for generalizing to everyone.
- The book's advice must be based on sound scientific theory, not on the author's hunches, pseudoscientific theories, or armchair observations. This criterion lets out, among other books, all the weight-loss manuals based on crash diets or goofy nutritional advice ("Eat popcorn and watermelon for a week").
- The book must include evidence of the program's effectiveness and not simply the author's assertions that it works. Many self-help books offer programs that have not been tested for efficacy; they are just the author's idea of what will work.
- The book must not promise the impossible. This lets out books that promise you perfect sex, total love, or high self-esteem in 30 days. And it lets out books, programs, or tapes that promote techniques whose effectiveness has been disconfirmed by psychological research, such as "subliminal" tapes, discussed in Chapter 5 (Moore, 1995).
- The advice should be organized in a systematic program, step by step, not as a vague pep talk to "take charge of your life" or "find love in your heart"; and the reader must be told how to evaluate his or her progress.

Some books do meet all these criteria. One is *Changing for Good* (Prochaska, Norcross, & DiClemente, 1994), which describes the common ingredients of effective change, described in this chapter, that apply to people in and out of therapy. Yet as long as people yearn for a magic bullet to cure their problems—a pill, a book, a subliminal tape—quick-fix solutions will continue to sell.

By uniting people with common problems and interests, support groups offer their members three ingredients of feeling better: understanding, empathy, and advice. Others in the group have been there, know what you are going through, and may have found solutions you never would have imagined. For people who fear that no one else has ever suffered what they have or felt what they feel, such groups can be reassuring in ways that family, friends, and even psychotherapists are not (Dunkel-Schetter, 1984; Wyatt & Mickey, 1987). For example, people with disabilities face unique concerns that involve not only coping with their physical problems but also coping with the condescension, hostility, and prejudice of many nondisabled people (Robertson, 1995).

Although self-help groups can be immensely therapeutic, however, they are not the same as psychotherapy that focuses on specific problems, and they are not designed to help people with serious psychological difficulties. Unlike most group therapies, which are generally supervised by a licensed therapist, self-help groups are not regulated by law or by professional standards. As a result, they vary widely in their philosophies and methods. Some are accepting and tolerant, offering support, cohesiveness, and spiritual guidance. Others can become quite confrontational and coercive, and members who disagree with the premises of the group may be made to feel deviant, crazy, or "in denial."

EVALUATING PSYCHOTHERAPY AND ITS ALTERNATIVES

Poor Murray! He's getting a little tired by now, having tried so many therapies. That last weekend with the Nature Walk "Trek to Truth" self-help group was especially fun, but now he's really behind. All of these choices are enough to make a person procrastinate about getting help. Which therapy is the right one?

THE SCIENTIST–PRACTITIONER GAP

Is it possible to measure the effectiveness of therapy, or is this human exchange too varied and complex to be captured by the researcher's empirical arsenal? Many psychotherapists assume that measuring psychotherapy is a futile task. Psychotherapy is an art, not a science, they say, and research is thus irrelevant to what they do. Most believe that clinical experience is more valuable than research, and that laboratory and survey studies capture only a small and shadowy image of the real person. They wish that academic psychologists would pay more attention to clinical evidence and observations in the research they do (Edelson, 1994). A survey of 400 clinical psychologists found that the great majority paid little attention to empirical research at all, stating that they gained their most useful information from "clinical work with clients." The majority also believed that research on therapy's effectiveness fails to incorporate the complexities of psychotherapy, obscures essential differences among therapies, and ignores the importance of the relationship between therapist and client (Elliott & Morrow-Bradley, 1994).

EXAMINE ASSUMPTIONS AND BIASES

Some psychotherapists think that the effectiveness of therapy cannot be measured empirically; researchers disagree. What assumptions and biases does each side bring to this debate? How can it be resolved?

Certainly, research has little or nothing to say about some of the existential aims of therapy, such as helping people come to terms with illness and death or helping them choose which values to live by (Cushman, 1995). But scientific psychologists are concerned that when therapists fail to keep up with empirical findings in the field—about the most beneficial methods for particular problems, about ineffective or potentially harmful techniques, and about basic research on topics relevant to their practice, such as memory, hypnosis, and normal child development—their clients may pay the price (Dawes, 1994). Over the years, the breach between scientists and therapists has widened on just this issue of the relevance and importance of research findings, leading to what some psychologists call *the scientist–practitioner gap.* This gap can have powerful individual and social consequences, as we saw in Chapter 9, in discussing the controversy about repressed memories of sexual abuse; in Chapter 12, in assessing popular but unvalidated projective tests; and in Chapter 13, in discussing the varied consequences of childhood trauma.

Economic pressures and the rise of managed-care health programs are now forcing psychotherapists to produce clear guidelines for which therapies are most effective, which therapies are best for which disorders, and which therapies are ineffective or potentially harmful (Barlow, 1996; Chambless, 1995). To develop these guidelines, researchers conduct *controlled clinical trials,* in which patients with a given problem or disorder are randomly assigned to one or more treatment groups or to a control group. To date, hundreds of studies have been designed to test the effectiveness of different kinds of therapy, counseling, and self-help groups (Lambert & Hill, 1994). Here are the overall results to date:

1. *Psychotherapy is better than doing nothing at all.* People who receive almost any professional treatment improve more than people who do not get help (Lambert & Bergin, 1994; Lipsey & Wilson, 1993; Maling & Howard, 1994; Robinson, Berman, & Neimeyer, 1990; Smith, Glass, & Miller, 1980; Weisz et al., 1995). However, as we will see, some kinds of psychotherapy are demonstrably more effective than others for particular problems.

2. *The people who do the best in psychotherapy have less serious problems and are motivated to improve.* Emotional disorders, self-defeating habits, and problems coping with crises are more successfully treated by psychotherapy than are long-standing personality problems and psychotic disorders (Kopta et al., 1994). The people who make best use of therapy tend to have more adaptive levels of functioning to begin with, are prepared for treatment, and are ready to change (Orlinsky & Howard, 1994; Strupp, 1982).

3. *For many common mild disorders and everyday problems, paraprofessional therapists may be as effective as professional therapists.* Numerous meta-analyses of studies of therapist effectiveness find no difference in overall success rates between professional and paraprofessional therapists—that is, people without graduate training in any mental-health field (Christensen & Jacobson, 1994; Dawes, 1994; Shapiro & Shapiro, 1982; Smith, Glass, & Miller, 1980; Strupp, 1982; Weisz et al., 1987, 1995). A meta-analysis of 150 psychotherapy studies with children and adolescents, for example, found no overall difference in effectiveness among professional therapists, graduate-student therapists, and paraprofessional therapists (Weisz et al., 1995).

4. *For people who have one of the common emotional problems of life, short-term treatment is usually all that is necessary.* Most psychodynamic therapists believe that the longer therapy goes on, the more successful it will be. Research does not support this claim: About half of all people in therapy improve within 8 to 11 sessions (according to their self-reports and on objective measures of improvement), and 76 percent improve within six months to a year; after that, further change is minimal (Howard et al., 1986; Kopta et al., 1994) (see Figure 16.3). Of course, people who have severe mental disorders often require and benefit from continued therapeutic care.

5. *In some cases, psychotherapy is harmful because of the therapist's incompetence, bias against the client, or unethical behavior* (Brodsky, 1982; Garnets et al., 1991; Lambert & Bergin, 1994; López, 1989; McHugh, 1993b; Peterson, 1992). Individual therapists can do great harm by behaving unethically or prejudicially. Some psychologists are con-

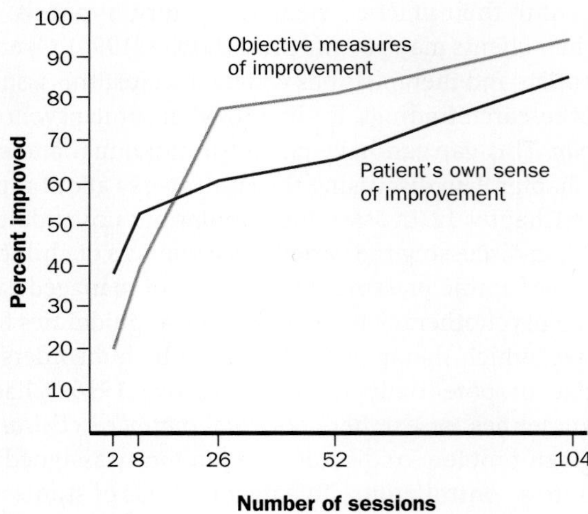

Figure 16.3
Is More Therapy Better?

In one study, about half of all patients improved in only 8 sessions and about three-fourths improved by the 26th session (Howard et al., 1986). Subsequent research confirmed that the benefits of therapy occur within 8 to 11 sessions for half of all clients, and most of the rest need no more than a year of treatment (Kopta et al., 1994).

cerned that therapeutic malpractice may be increasing because of the recent surge in the number of poorly trained, unlicensed therapists who use unvalidated methods (Dawes, 1994; Poole et al., 1995).

Given this pattern of findings, most of the new research on psychotherapy is directed toward three questions: What are the common ingredients in all successful therapies? Which kinds of therapy are best suited for which problems? Under what conditions can therapy be harmful?

WHEN THERAPY HELPS

Psychotherapy is a social exchange. Like all relationships, its success depends on qualities of both participants and on the fit between them (Frank, 1985; Lambert & Hill, 1994; Orlinsky & Howard, 1994).

The clients who are most likely to do well in therapy have a strong sense of self and also sufficient distress to motivate them to change. For example, one study of depressed elderly people found that cognitive, behavioral, and brief dynamic therapy were equally likely to be successful. What made the difference between good outcomes and poor ones were the clients' commitment to the therapy, their willingness to work on their problems, and their expectations of success. Successful clients also had support from their families and a personal style of dealing actively with problems instead of avoiding them (Gaston et al., 1989).

As we saw in Chapter 12, some people are temperamentally negative and bitter; others, even in the midst of emotional crises, are temperamentally more agreeable and positive. These personality differences often influence the success of therapy and how much a person can be expected to change (Costa & Widiger, 1994). The strongest predictors of successful therapy, in terms of the client's qualities, are the client's cooperativeness with suggested interventions and positive feelings during the therapy session. Hostile, negative individuals are more resistant to treatment and less likely to benefit from it (Orlinsky & Howard, 1994).

The personality of the therapist is also important to the success of any therapy, particularly the qualities that Carl Rogers praised: empathy, warmth, and genuineness. The great teachers who establish new schools of therapy often have high success rates because of their own charisma. They make their clients feel respected, accepted, and understood. Therapists whose efforts are most successful tend to be empathic, expressive, and actively invested in the interaction with the client, as opposed to being a detached observer in the manner of Freud (Orlinsky & Howard, 1994). These qualities are not limited to professional psychologists, which may be one reason for the finding that paraprofessionals are often as effective as trained psychologists in treating most everyday problems.

Finally, apart from the individual qualities of the client and the therapist, successful therapy depends on the bond they establish between them, called the **therapeutic alliance.** (For an example of such an alliance in action, see Figure 16.4.) In a good therapeutic alliance, both parties respect and understand one another, feel reaffirmed, and work toward a common goal. Establishing a successful therapeutic alliance does not mean that the therapist and client must share the same ethnicity, sex, sexual orientation, or religion (Howard, 1991). It does mean that both parties must try to identify and avoid potential misunderstandings that might result from ignorance, dissimilar qualities, or prejudice on either side (Comas-Díaz & Greene, 1994; Cross & Fhagen-Smith, 1996; Franklin, 1993).

therapeutic alliance The bond of confidence and mutual understanding established between therapist and client, which allows them to work together to solve the client's problems.

Figure 16.4
Psychotherapy in Action

Robert Hobson (1985) spent many weeks trying to communicate with Stephen, a troubled 15-year-old boy who refused to speak or even look at him. One day, in frustration, Hobson took an envelope and drew a squiggly line (a), inviting Stephen to add to the picture. Stephen drew a ship (b), thereby turning Hobson's meaningless line into a tidal wave. Was Stephen, Hobson wondered, afraid of being emotionally "drowned"? Hobson next drew a landing pier (c), representing safety, but Stephen was not interested in safety. On his boat, he put a person waving goodbye (d). Hobson, suspecting that Stephen's problem might stem from emotional separation from his mother, drew a woman waving goodbye (e). Ignoring the woman, Stephen added a creature caught in the wave (f), and spoke for the first time: "A flying fish." Hobson added an octopus (g). Stephen, suddenly sad, marked up the entire sketch with lines (h), adding, "It's raining." Hoping to convey optimism, Hobson drew a sun (i), its rays shining through the rain. Stephen paused and looked at Hobson intently for the first time. He drew large arcs embracing the whole illustration (j). "A rainbow," said Stephen. He smiled.

For example, some white therapists not only misunderstand their black clients' psychological concerns, but also their body language. They regard lack of eye contact and frequent glancing around as the client's attempt to avoid revelations, instead of as signs of discomfort and an effort to get oriented (Brodsky, 1982). For their part, African-American clients often misunderstand or distrust the white therapist's demand for self-disclosure. A lifetime of experience with racism often makes them reluctant to reveal feelings that they believe a white person wouldn't understand or accept. As for black therapists, they frequently have to deal with clients and co-workers who are bigoted or uncomfortable with them, or who fail to understand or accept them (Boyd-Franklin, 1989; Markowitz, 1993).

In establishing a bond with clients, therapists must distinguish normal cultural patterns from individual psychological problems (Pedersen et al., 1996). Monica McGoldrick and John Pearce (1982), Irish-American clinicians, described some problems that are typical of Irish-American families. For example, many Irish parents believe that it is wrong to praise a child directly, on the grounds that the child will think that he or she is better than others and get a "swelled head." (You can imagine what human therapists, such as Carl Rogers, would make of this failure to give children "unconditional positive regard.") In response to McGoldrick's question about whether she ever praised her children, one Irish-American mother in family therapy said, "Why, sure. Kevin, here, he's not so bad."

These customs arose from Irish history and religious beliefs, and they are deeply ingrained. "In general, the therapist cannot expect the family to turn into a physically affectionate, emotionally intimate group, or to enjoy being in therapy very much," they observed. "The notion of Original Sin—that you are guilty before you are born—leaves them with a heavy sense of burden. Someone not sensitized to these issues may see this as pathological. It is not. But it is also not likely to change and the therapist should help the family tolerate this inner guilt rather than try to get rid of it."

More and more psychotherapists are becoming "sensitized to the issues" caused by cultural differences. For example, Latino and Asian clients are likely to react to a formal interview with a therapist with relative passivity and deference, leading some therapists to diagnose a shyness problem that is only a cultural norm. Latinos may respond to catastrophic stress with an *ataque nervioso,* a nervous attack of screaming, swooning, and agitation. It is a culturally determined response, but an uninformed clinician might label it as a sign of pathology (Malgady, Rogler, & Costantino, 1987). Similarly, *susto,* or "loss of the soul," is a syndrome common in Latin American cultures as a response to extreme grief or fright; the person believes his or her soul has departed along with that of the deceased relative. A psychiatrist unfamiliar with this culturally determined response might conclude that the sufferer was delusional or psychotic.

As a result of the growing understanding of the importance of culture, the American Psychiatric Association (1994) now recommends that therapists consider a person's cultural background when making a diagnosis or suggesting treatment. For example, one New York psychiatrist, originally from Peru, treated a woman suffering from *susto* by prescribing a tradition important in her culture: a mourning ritual to help her accept the loss of her uncle. This wake "was quite powerful for her," the psychiatrist told *The New York Times* (December 5, 1995). "She didn't need any antidepressants, and within a few meetings, including two with her family, her symptoms lifted and she was back participating fully in life once again."

Being aware of cultural differences, however, doesn't mean that the therapist should stereotype all clients from a particular culture or tailor the therapy to fit a stereotype of cultural rules (Sue, 1991). Some Asians, after all, do have problems with excessive shyness, some Latinos do have emotional disorders, and some Irish don't feel the burden of guilt! It does mean that therapists must do what is necessary

Some psychotherapists fit their approach to a client's cultural background. The therapists below are using traditional Puerto Rican stories, such as the tales of Juan Bobo (left), to teach Puerto Rican children to control aggression, understand right from wrong, and delay gratification. The children and their mothers watch a videotape of the folktale, discuss it together, and later role play its major themes. This method has been more successful than traditional therapies in reducing children's anxiety and improving their attention spans and imaginations (Costantino, Malgady, & Rogler, 1986).

to ensure that the client will find the therapist to be trustworthy and effective, and clients must be aware of their prejudices too (Sue & Zane, 1987).

WHICH THERAPY FOR WHICH PROBLEM?

Murray has found a therapist who is sympathetic, he's motivated to change, and he thinks that he and the therapist will form a nice therapeutic alliance. But which therapeutic approach, if any, will be best for him?

To answer this question, the APA's Division of Clinical Psychology convened a task force to assess research evaluating specific methods for specific problems (Barlow, 1996; Chambless, 1995; Chambless et al., 1996). To qualify as a well-established, *empirically validated treatment,* the method had to meet stringent criteria, including having been repeatedly tested against a placebo or another treatment and having its efficacy demonstrated by at least two different investigators. Although the task force could not assess every therapy now in existence, let alone all the variations within each major school of therapy, one key finding clearly emerged: *For many specific problems and emotional disorders, behavioral and cognitive therapies are the method of choice* (see also Lambert & Bergin, 1994; Lazarus, 1990; Rachman & Wilson, 1980;

Weisz et al., 1995). These treatments are particularly effective for the following psychological problems:

- *Anxiety disorders,* including panic attacks, phobias, and obsessive-compulsive disorder. For example, a meta-analysis of 88 studies found that exposure techniques for reducing severe phobias were more effective than any other treatment (Kaplan, Randolph, & Lemli, 1991). Systematic desensitization is most effective with simple phobias, such as fear of speaking to a group. Cognitive-behavioral therapy is recommended for panic disorder, generalized anxiety disorder, and obsessive-compulsive disorder (Schwartz et al., 1996).
- *Depression.* Cognitive therapy's greatest success has been in the treatment of mood disorders, notably depression (Black et al., 1993; Greenberger & Padesky, 1995). Cognitive therapy is often more effective than treatment with antidepressant drugs alone, and is more likely to prevent relapses of depression (Antonuccio, Danton, & DeNelsky, 1995; McNally, 1994; Robinson, Berman, & Neimeyer, 1990; Whisman, 1993).
- *Health problems,* including chronic pain, chronic fatigue syndrome, headaches, irritable bowel syndrome, and eating disorders such as bulimia (J. Skinner et al., 1990; Butler et al., 1991; Wilson & Fairburn, 1993).
- *Childhood and adolescent behavior problems.* Researchers who conducted a meta-analysis of more than 100 outcome studies of children and adolescents reported that "Behavioral treatments proved more effective than nonbehavioral treatments regardless of client age, therapist experience, or treated problem" (Weisz et al., 1987).

Of course, as the APA task force acknowledges, these important findings don't tell the whole story (nor have we listed every effective therapy the task force identified, such as couples therapy for marital discord). Cognitive-behavioral therapies are designed for specific identifiable problems, but sometimes people seek therapy for less clearly defined reasons—they may wish to introspect about their feelings and lives, find solace and courage, or explore moral issues. "Depth" approaches may be well suited for such individuals. Moreover, in spite of their many successes, behavior and cognitive therapies have had their failures, especially with personality disorders and psychoses (Brody, 1990; Foa & Emmelkamp, 1983). They are not particularly helpful for people recovering from trauma. They are not highly effective with people who do not really want to change and who are not motivated to carry out a behavioral or cognitive program.

Further, some problems, and some clients, are immune to any single kind of therapy but may respond to *combined* methods. Some people who have mood disorders, obsessive-compulsive disorder, or drug-abuse problems respond better to a combination of antidepressants and cognitive-behavioral therapy than to either method alone (Bowers, 1990; Carroll et al., 1994; Leonard et al., 1993). Aggressive or depressed adolescents are best helped by the multidimensional family therapy programs we mentioned earlier; these often include skills training, family therapy, and highly structured treatments that set clear behavioral limits (Liddle, 1995; Pinsof & Wynne, 1995). The most promising treatment for sex offenders combines cognitive therapy, aversive conditioning, sex education, group therapy, reconditioning of sexual fantasies, and social-skills training (Abel et al., 1988; Kaplan, Morales, & Becker, 1993). Young adults with schizophrenia often do best with a combination of medication *and* family therapy to help parents learn to cope with their children's illness constructively and to communicate without hostility or criticism (Goldstein & Miklowitz, 1995). And, as we also saw earlier, adults with schizophrenia need medication and community-support programs.

In summary, then, the factors contributing to successful therapy look like this:

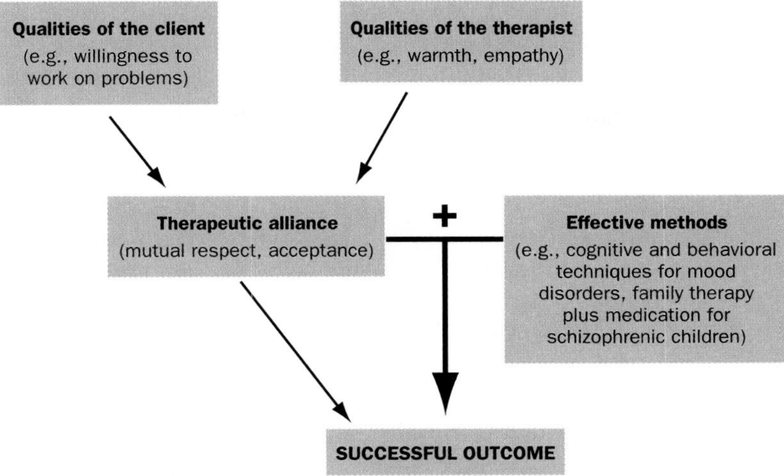

WHEN THERAPY HARMS

Every treatment and intervention carries risks, and so does psychotherapy. Some people in therapy are seriously harmed or unduly influenced by the treatment or by the therapist. Their emotional states may deteriorate and their symptoms may worsen. Some clients become excessively dependent, relying on the therapist for all decisions; some therapists actively foster this dependency for financial or psychological motives (Johnson, 1988). Clients can also be harmed for the following reasons:

- *Coercion* by the therapist to accept the therapist's advice, sexual intimacies, or other unethical behavior (Gabbard, 1989; Peterson, 1992). Some therapists abuse their clients' trust, convincing them that the therapy requires them to behave in ways the clients find reprehensible. Coercion can be subtle as well as overt. Some therapy groups acquire cultlike attributes, persuading their members that their mental health depends on staying in the group and severing their connections to their families (Mithers, 1994). Such "psychotherapy cults" are created by the therapist's use of techniques that foster the client's dependency and isolation, prevent the client from terminating therapy, and reduce the client's ability to think critically (Temerlin & Temerlin, 1986).
- *Bias* on the part of a therapist who doesn't understand the client because of the client's gender, culture, religion, or sexual orientation. The therapist may try to induce the client to conform to the therapist's standards and values, even if they are not appropriate to the client or in the client's best interest (Brodsky, 1982; López, 1989). For example, for many years gay men and lesbians who entered therapy were told that homosexuality is a mental illness that should be "cured," and some of the so-called treatments were quite savage (Bayer, 1981).
- *Therapist-induced disorders.* In a healthy therapeutic alliance, therapists and clients seek a common explanation for the client's problems. Of course, the therapist will influence this explanation, according to his or her training and

philosophy. This is why Freudian patients have dreams of phallic symbols, and patients in Jungian therapy have dreams of archetypes! However, some therapists so zealously believe in the prevalence of certain problems that they inadvertently induce the client to produce the symptoms they are looking for (Merskey, 1995; McHugh, 1993b; Ofshe & Watters, 1994). Indeed, recent evidence suggests that Freud himself induced his patients to report memories and symptoms that confirmed his beliefs about psychoanalytic processes (Powell & Boer, 1994, 1995).

In Chapter 15 we discussed how such therapist influence might be one reason for the growing number of patients diagnosed with multiple personality disorder. It is also the mechanism by which people create *pseudomemories*, constructed memories about events that did not happen—why people in primal-scream therapy "remember" being born, people in fetal therapy "remember" their lives in the womb, and people in past-lives therapy "remember" being Julius Caesar (or whomever) (Spanos, 1996; Spanos, Burgess, & Burgess, 1994). The risk of therapist influence is increased when a therapist uses hypnosis, sodium amytal (a barbiturate misleadingly called "truth serum"), guided imagery, and other techniques that enhance the client's suggestibility. As we noted in Chapter 9, a significant minority of therapists—between one-fourth and one-third—are using one or more of these techniques (Poole et al., 1995).

For all of these reasons, it is important for people to become educated consumers of psychotherapeutic services (see "Taking Psychology with You").

Quick Quiz

How insightful are you feeling about psychotherapy?

1. The most important predictor of successful therapy is (a) how long it lasts, (b) the insight it provides the client, (c) the bond between therapist and client, (d) whether the therapist and client are matched according to gender, ethnicity, and culture.
2. The most important attribute of a good therapist is (a) years of training, (b) warmth and empathy, (c) objective detachment, (d) intellectual ability.
3. In general, mood disorders such as anxiety and depression are most effectively treated by which type of therapy?
4. What are three possible sources of harm in psychotherapy?
5.  Ferdie, who spends all his free time playing softball, joins a self-help group called "Sportaholics Anonymous" (SA). The group tells him he is suffering from sport addiction and that the only cure is SA. After a few months, Ferdie announces that the group doesn't seem to be helping him and he's going to quit. The other members reply with personal testimonials of how SA has helped them. They tell Ferdie that he is in denial, and that his very doubts about the group are a sign that it's working. What are some problems with their argument?

Answers:

1. c 2. b 3. cognitive-behavioral 4. coercion, bias, and therapist-induced disorders 5. The group members have violated the principle of falsifiability (see Chapter 2): That is, they will accept no evidence that disproves their claims. If a person is helped by the group, they say it works; if a person is not helped by the group, they still say it works, but the person doesn't know it yet or is denying its benefits. They are also arguing by anecdote: Ferdie is not hearing testimonials from people who have dropped out of the group and were not helped by it. Arguing by anecdote is not scientific reasoning, nor is it a way to determine a group's or a therapy's effectiveness.

THE VALUE AND VALUES OF PSYCHOTHERAPY

In the midst of the rapid growth in the number and kinds of therapists in North America, social critics and psychotherapists themselves have begun to raise questions about the larger place and purpose of psychotherapy. Has the professional support of psychotherapy replaced, for too many people, the informal but essential support of friends and family? Should therapists really try to be value free and morally neutral about their clients' problems, or should the moral dimension of people's choices be a central focus of the therapeutic encounter? How much personal change is possible, and do some therapies promise too much? Does psychotherapy foster a preoccupation with the self?

In *The Shrinking of America*, Bernie Zilbergeld (1983) argued that psychotherapy, while unquestionably beneficial in most cases, promotes three myths that increase dissatisfaction: People should always be happy, and if they aren't, they need fixing; almost any change is possible; and change is relatively easy. In contrast, as you may remember from Chapter 14, Eastern cultures have a less optimistic view of change, and they tend to be more tolerant of events they regard as being outside of human control. In the Japanese practice of Morita therapy, clients are taught to accept and live with their most troubling emotions, instead of trying to eradicate these psychological weeds from the lawn of life (Reynolds, 1987). Some Western psychotherapists now teach techniques of mindful meditation and greater self-acceptance instead of constant self-improvement (Kabat-Zinn, 1994).

ASK QUESTIONS

The benefits of psychotherapy are well documented, but we can ask questions about its larger place in society and its implicit messages. For example, does psychotherapy foster unrealistic expectations of personal change? Does it promote individualism at the expense of community and relationships?

Other psychotherapists have begun to question Western psychotherapy's focus on fixing the self, and on the idea that fulfillment can be achieved by paying attention only to the self (Cushman, 1995). In *We've Had a Hundred Years of Psychotherapy—And the World's Getting Worse*, family therapists James Hillman and Michael Ventura (1992) argued that therapy often reflects outdated values from nineteenth-century individualism, which celebrated the lone inventor, achiever, pioneer, and entrepreneur and the idea that the "self" has priority over other people. Such values are inappropriate today, these therapists maintain, because, more than ever, modern life demands active social involvement in our communities and our world.

How much can therapy change a person?

Given these concerns, what can we reasonably expect of psychotherapy, and what are its limitations? Psychotherapy cannot transform you into someone you're not. It cannot cure you overnight. It cannot provide a life without problems. But it can help you make decisions and clarify your values and goals. It can teach you new skills and new ways of thinking. It can help you get along better with your family and break out of repetitive, destructive family patterns. It can get you through bad times when no one seems to care or understand. Psychotherapy is not intended to substitute for experience—for work that is satisfying, relationships that are sustaining, activities that are enjoyable. As Socrates said, the unexamined life is not worth living. But as an anonymous philosopher added, the unlived life is not worth examining.

Taking Psychology with You

Becoming a Smart Consumer of Therapy

In North America today, a vast and bewildering array of therapies fills the marketplace. The word *therapy* is unregulated; anyone can set up any kind of program and call it "therapy." To protect themselves as well as to get the best possible help, consumers need to be informed and know how to choose wisely. Some people spend more time looking for a good dentist than for a good therapist. They fail to remember that their consumer rights apply to buying mental-health services as well as to buying any other professional service. You would not be likely to keep going to a dentist, year after year, if your toothache got worse and the dentist merely kept promising to make it go away. Yet some people stay in therapy, year after year, with no resolution of their problems.

In order for consumers to make the best use of therapy, research suggests the following guidelines:

• *Knowing when to start.* In general, if you have a persistent problem that you do not know how to solve, one that causes you considerable unhappiness and that has lasted six months or more, it may be time to look for help. Everyone gets caught in an emotional maze from time to time. It may take the clear-eyed observations of a perceptive bystander to see a way out.

• *Setting goals.* Try to identify exactly what you expect from therapy, and discuss your goals with the therapist. Do you want to solve a problem in your relationships or in your emotional life? Are your goals realistic? Some therapies, as we saw in this chapter, are designed not for solving problems but for exploring ideas and insights. If you know what you want from therapy, you are less likely to feel disappointed later. You will also be better able to select a therapist who can meet your needs.

• *Choosing a therapist.* As we saw in Chapter 1, a person must have an advanced degree and a period of supervised training to become a licensed psychologist, psychiatrist, counselor, or social worker. Unfortunately, the fact that someone has a license does not guarantee that he or she is competent, reputable, or ethical. Your school counseling center is a good place to start if you are looking for a reputable therapist. Your local mental-health association or psychological association chapter (check your phone book) can also provide information on nearby therapists.

A therapist or counselor should be someone you trust and like. Never trust anyone who suggests that a sexual relationship will help your problem; this is unethical conduct and is illegal in many states. The basic rule is this: If the therapist does not treat you with the same attention and respect that you give him or her, find someone else.

• *The question of fees.* The amount of payment does not affect the success of the therapy (Orlinsky, 1994). In one study, in fact, college students in paid versus free therapy did not differ in self-reports of improvement, but the students who paid no fee had *lower* levels of distress when the therapy ended (Yoken & Berman, 1984). As a consumer, you can often negotiate a fee, depending on what you can afford. If you have medical insurance that covers psychotherapy, find out whether your policy covers the kind of therapist you are seeking.

• *Knowing when to stop.* If you are in time-limited treatment, such as 12 sessions of brief therapy or a seven-session airplane-phobia program, you ought to stick with it to the end. In unlimited therapy, however, you have the right to determine when enough is enough. Breaking with a therapist or self-help group can be painful and difficult, but it can also be a sign that the treatment has been successful (Johnson, 1988). You may need to consider ending therapy, changing therapists, or leaving a group if therapy dominates your life and nothing else seems important; the therapist keeps finding new reasons for you to stay, although the original problems were solved long ago; you have become so dependent on the therapist that you won't make a move without consulting him or her; or your therapist has been unable to help you with your problem.

As we saw in this chapter, not all therapies are appropriate for all problems. If you are not improving, the reason could be as much in the treatment as in you. If you have made a real effort to work with a therapist and there has been no result after ample time and effort, it is time to think about alternatives.

SUMMARY

BIOLOGICAL TREATMENTS

1) Approaches to the diagnosis and treatment of psychological problems have alternated throughout history between biological or *organic* ones and *psychological* ones.

2) The medications most commonly prescribed for mental disorders are *antipsychotic drugs,* used in treating schizophrenia and other psychotic disorders; *antidepressants,* used in treating depression, anxiety disorders, and obsessive-compulsive disorder; *minor tranquilizers,* often prescribed for emotional problems; and *lithium,* a salt used to treat bipolar disorder. Antidepressants are more effective for mood disorders than are minor tranquilizers, which have little or no effect and can become addictive.

3) Some difficulties with drug treatment include the problem of the *placebo effect,* including the need to use *active placebos* in double-blind studies; the high dropout and relapse rates among people who take medications without also learning how to cope with problems; finding the correct dose (the *therapeutic window*) for each individual, especially considering that a person's ethnicity, sex, and age can influence a drug's effectiveness; and the long-term risks of medication. Antipsychotic drugs can have some dangerous effects if they are taken for many years; the long-term effects of antidepressants are unknown. Medication can be helpful and even save lives, but it should not be prescribed mindlessly and routinely, especially when nondrug therapies can work as well as drugs for many mood and behavioral problems.

4) When drugs or psychotherapy failed to help seriously disturbed people, some psychiatrists intervened directly in the brain. *Psychosurgery,* one form of which was the *lobotomy,* destroys selected areas of the brain thought to be responsible for a psychological problem; it is rarely done today. *Electroconvulsive therapy* (ECT), in which a brief current is sent through the brain, has been used successfully to treat suicidal depressives. However, controversy exists about its effects on memory and the appropriateness of its use.

5) Errors of diagnosis and treatment occur on both sides of the mind–body debate. Some people with organic disorders have been mistakenly treated with psychotherapy; some people with psychological problems have been mistakenly treated solely with drugs.

KINDS OF PSYCHOTHERAPY

6) The hundreds of existing psychotherapies basically fall into four schools: (1) *Psychodynamic ("depth") therapies* include Freudian psychoanalysis and its modern variations, which explore unconscious dynamics. Brief psychodynamic therapy is a time-limited version that focuses on one major dynamic issue. (2) *Therapies based on cognitive and behavioral techniques* draw on cognitive and learning principles. *Behavior therapies* use such methods as behavioral contracts, systematic desensitization, aversive conditioning, flooding or exposure, and skills training. *Cognitive therapies* aim to change the irrational thoughts involved in negative emotions and self-defeating actions. (3) *Humanist and existential therapies* aim to help people feel better about themselves by focusing on here-and-now issues and learning to cope with philosophical dilemmas, such as the meaning of life and the fear of death. (4) *Family therapies* share the view that individual problems do not exist by themselves but develop in the context of the whole family network. Family therapists may use a *genogram* to document generational patterns in a family or *solution-focused techniques* to solve a client's problems. In practice, most therapists are *eclectic*, using many methods and ideas, and good therapies share certain features, such as helping clients form more adaptive "life narratives."

ALTERNATIVES TO PSYCHOTHERAPY

7) People who have severe mental disorders, such as schizophrenia, or who have physical disabilities resulting from disease or injury, may benefit from alternatives to individual psychotherapy. *Rehabilitation psychologists* offer job training, support, and community treatment programs such as the clubhouse model. *Community psychologists* set up programs in the community to treat social and mental-health problems. *Self-help groups* are organized around a specific problem or common interest; they can be immensely helpful, but they vary widely in their methods and results.

EVALUATING PSYCHOTHERAPY AND ITS ALTERNATIVES

8) *The scientist–practitioner gap* refers to the different assumptions held by researchers and many clinicians regarding the value of research in assessing psychotherapy. Controlled clinical trials to evaluate the effectiveness of psychotherapy show that overall, psychotherapy is better than no treatment at all; it is most effective with people who have the least serious disorders and who are motivated to improve; for many everyday problems, paraprofessionals are as effective as professionals; for problems other than chronic mental disorders, short-term treatment is as effective as long-term therapy; and sometimes therapy can be harmful.

9) Successful therapy requires a good relationship between the therapist and the client. Clients who benefit most are motivated to solve their problems and are willing to take responsibility for them. Good therapists are empathic, warm, and constructive. A *therapeutic alliance* between client and therapist depends on their ability to understand each other and work together. They do not need to be matched in terms of gender or ethnicity, but both parties must try to avoid bias, stereotyping, and cultural misunderstandings.

10) Some therapies are demonstrably better than others for specific problems. Behavioral and cognitive-behavioral therapies are the most effective for anxiety disorders, depression, certain health problems and eating disorders, and childhood and adolescent behavior problems. Depth therapies may be most effective for people who want to introspect about their lives. And some problems, such as sex offenses and schizophrenia, respond best to combined techniques.

11) In some cases, therapy is harmful. The therapist may foster the client's dependency; be coercive, biased, or unethical; or actually create disorders in the client—delusions, other symptoms of mental disorder, or *pseudomemories*—through the process of suggestion.

THE VALUE AND VALUES OF PSYCHOTHERAPY

12) Some critics and psychotherapists themselves have raised important questions about the implicit values of psychotherapy in North America, worrying about psychotherapy's assumptions that change is easy and desirable, and about the consequences of unduly focusing on the self rather than on the community. Therapy can help in many ways, but it cannot transform you into something you are not, and it cannot substitute for the family, friends, and work that everyone needs.

KEY TERMS

antipsychotic drugs (major tranquilizers) 619
antidepressant drugs 619
"minor" tranquilizers 620
lithium carbonate 620
active placebo 621
therapeutic window 621
psychosurgery 623
lobotomy 623
electroconvulsive therapy (ECT) 623
psychoanalysis 625
psychodynamic ("depth") therapies 625
free association 626
transference 626
brief psychodynamic therapy 626
behavior therapies 626
behavioral records and contracts 627
systematic desensitization 627
aversive conditioning 627
flooding (exposure) 627
skills training 628
cognitive therapies 628
rational emotive behavior therapy 628
humanist therapies 629
client-centered therapy 629
unconditional positive regard 629
existential therapy 629
family therapy 629
genogram 630
solution-focused (strategic) family therapy 631
family-systems approach 632
eclectic approaches 632
group therapy 633
narrative method 633
rehabilitation psychologists 634
community psychologists 635
self-help groups 636
scientist–practitioner gap 639
therapeutic alliance 641

We are all fragile creatures caught in a cobweb of social constraints.

Stanley Milgram

CHAPTER SEVENTEEN
Principles of Social Life

During the Nazi occupation of France, people living in the Protestant village of Le Chambon, led by their pastor André Trocmé and his wife Magda, rescued some 5,000 Jewish children from being sent to their deaths.

IN 1942, WLADYSLAW MISIUNA, A YOUNG MAN from Radom, Poland, was ordered by the Germans to supervise inmates at a concentration camp. Misiuna stuffed his pockets with bread, milk, and potatoes and smuggled the food to the 30 women in his charge. One day, one of his workers, Devora Salzberg, came to see him about an infection that had covered her arms with open lesions. Misiuna knew that if the Germans discovered her illness, they would kill her; but there was no way he could get a doctor to the camp to treat her. So Misiuna did the only thing he could think to do: He infected himself with her blood, contracted the lesions himself, and went to a doctor. Then he shared with Devora the medication he was given. Both were cured, and both survived the war (Fogelman, 1994).

Why do some people behave so generously? Thanks to the much-publicized story of Oskar Schindler, the Polish entrepreneur who used his entire fortune to save more than 1,100 Jews who worked for him (Keneally, 1982/1993), people are becoming aware of those remarkable individuals who, in times of adversity, put themselves in danger to rescue others—rising above the temptation to walk away and save their own skins.

Rescuers always raise our hopes for humanity, but the fact is that they are a minority. The historical record shows, sadly, that most people will go along with the crowd, even when the crowd is performing immoral or brutal acts. The Nazis, for good reason, have come to symbolize the evil potential in human nature; the Holocaust was unique because the Nazis so systematically used technology and ideology to exterminate 6 million Jews, as well as millions of Catholics, Gypsies, homosexuals, disabled people, and anyone else not of the "pure" Aryan "race." But the Nazis are not an aberration that can safely be buried in the past; virtually no nation can claim to have bloodless hands. Torture, genocide, and massacre are all too common in human history: Americans slaughtered native peoples, Turks slaughtered Armenians, the Khmer Rouge slaughtered millions of fellow Cambodians, the Spanish conquistadors slaughtered native Mexicans, Idi Amin waged a reign of terror against his own people in Uganda, the Japanese slaughtered Koreans and Chinese, Iraqis slaughtered Kurds, Iranians slaughtered members of the Baha'i religion, despotic regimes in Argentina and Chile launched mass killings ("disappearances") of dissidents and rebels. In a 1994 bloodbath in Rwanda, hundreds of thousands of Tutsis were shot or hacked to death with machetes by members of the rival Hutu tribe; and in the former Yugoslavia, Bosnian Serbs exterminated entire villages of Bosnian Muslims in the name of "ethnic cleansing." The systematic destruction of people defined as the enemy has been and continues to be a widespread practice (Staub, 1990).

Why do so many human beings commit such atrocities, and why do some individuals behave bravely, even at the risk of their lives? The fields of *social psychology* and *cultural psychology* explore these and many other questions by examining the individual in a social and cultural context. In this chapter, we will examine some of the major areas of research in social psychology: roles, attitudes, and the behavior of groups, including the conditions under which people conform or dissent. In the next chapter, we will consider findings from cultural psychology that illuminate some of the reasons for group conflict, prejudice, and war.

The "psychology" part of social psychology concerns a person's perceptions, attitudes, emotions, and behavior. The "social" part concerns a person's group, situation, and relationships. In previous chapters, we have already reported on many topics in social psychology, including love and attachment; how "set and setting" affect the use of drugs; how roles and scripts affect sexual behavior; how emotions communicate; why friends are necessary for health; and social processes in psychotherapy. Social psychology covers a lot of territory, from first impressions on meeting a stranger to international diplomacy.

THE OBEDIENCE STUDY

In the early 1960s, Stanley Milgram (1963, 1974) designed a study that was to become one of the most famous in all of psychology. Milgram wanted to know how many people would obey an authority figure when ordered to violate their own ethical standards. Participants in the study, however, thought they were part of an experiment on the effects of punishment on learning. Each was assigned, apparently at random, to the role of "teacher." Another person, introduced as a fellow volunteer, was the "learner." Whenever the learner, seated in an adjoining room, made an error in reciting a list of word pairs he was supposed to have memorized, the teacher had to give him an electric shock by depressing a lever on a machine (see Figure 17.1). With each error, the voltage (marked from 0 to 450) was to be increased by another 15 volts. The shock levels on the machine were labeled from SLIGHT SHOCK to DANGER—SEVERE SHOCK and, finally, ominously, XXX. In reality, the learners were confederates of Milgram and did *not* receive any shocks, but none of the teachers ever realized this during the experiment. The actor-victims played their parts convincingly: As the study continued, they shouted in pain and pleaded to be released, all according to a prearranged script.

When Milgram first designed this experiment, he asked a number of psychiatrists, students, and middle-class adults how many people they thought would "go all the way" to XXX on orders from the experimenter. The psychiatrists predicted that most people would refuse to go beyond 150 volts, the point at which the learner first demanded to be freed, and that only one person in a thousand—someone who was emotionally disturbed and sadistic—would administer the highest voltage. The nonprofessionals agreed with this prediction, and all of them said that they personally would disobey early in the experiment.

ASK QUESTIONS

Jot down your best guess in answering these three questions: (1) What percentage of people are sadistic? (2) If told by an authority to harm an innocent person, what percentage of people would do it? (3) If *you* were instructed to harm an innocent person, would you do it, or would you refuse?

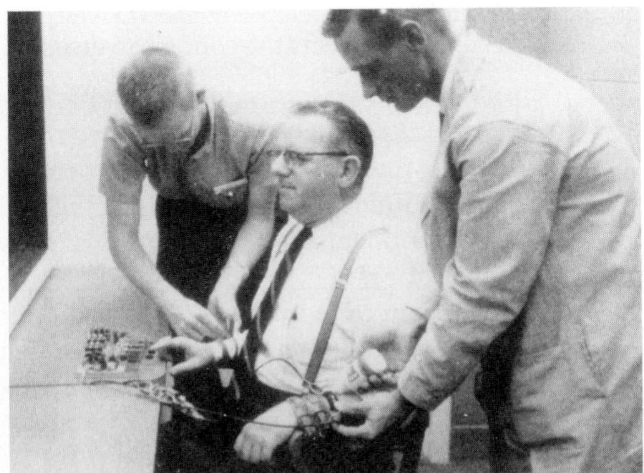

Figure 17.1
The Milgram Obedience Experiment

On the left is Milgram's original shock machine; in 1963, it looked pretty ominous. On the right, the "learner" is being strapped into his chair by the experimenter and the "teacher."

In fact, however, every subject administered some shock to the learner, and about two-thirds, of all ages and from all walks of life, obeyed the experimenter to the fullest extent. They obeyed no matter how much the victim shouted for them to stop and no matter how painful the shocks seemed to be. They obeyed even when they themselves were anguished about the pain they believed they were causing. They obeyed even as they wept, implored the experimenter to release them from further participation, and argued with themselves. Milgram (1974) noted that many would "sweat, tremble, stutter, bite their lips, groan, and dig their fingernails into their flesh"; many protested to the experimenter, but they backed down when he merely asserted, "The experiment requires that you continue."

More than 1,000 participants at several universities eventually went through the Milgram experiment. Most of them, men and women equally, inflicted what they thought were dangerous amounts of shock to another person. (Seven of eight subsequent American replications of the study also found the obedience rates of men and women to be identical [Blass, 1993].) Researchers in at least eight other countries have likewise found high percentages of obedience, ranging to more than 90 percent in Spain and the Netherlands (Meeus & Raaijmakers, 1995; Smith & Bond, 1994).

Milgram and his team subsequently set up several variations of the basic experiment to determine the conditions under which people might disobey the experimenter. They found that virtually *nothing the victim did or said changed the likelihood of the person's compliance*—even when the victim said he had a heart condition, screamed in agony, or stopped responding entirely, as if he had collapsed. However, people were more likely to disobey under the following conditions:

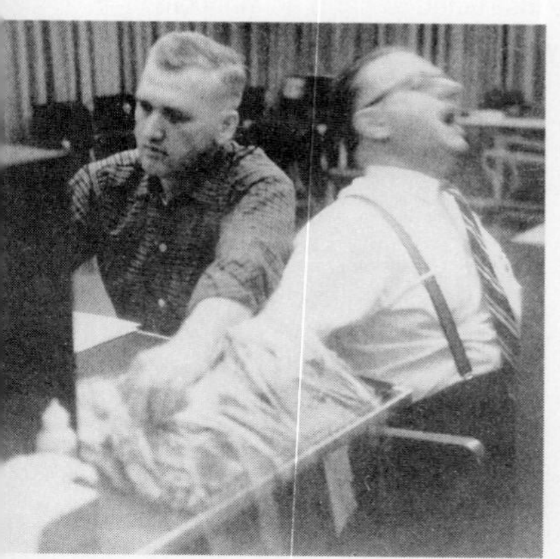

In the "touch-proximity" variation of Milgram's experiment, the "teacher" had to administer shock directly to the learner. Here, a subject continues to obey, but most in this condition did not.

- *When the experimenter left the room.* Many people then subverted authority by giving low levels of shock but reporting that they had followed orders.
- *When the victim was right there in the room,* and the teacher had to administer the shock directly to the victim's body.
- *When two experimenters issued conflicting demands* to continue the experiment or to stop at once. In this case, no one kept inflicting shock.
- *When the person ordering them to continue was an ordinary man,* apparently another volunteer, instead of the authoritative experimenter.
- *When the subject worked with peers who refused to go further.* Seeing someone else rebel gave subjects the courage to disobey.

Obedience, then, was more a function of the situation than of the particular personalities of the participants. "The key to the behavior of subjects," Milgram (1974) summarized, "lies not in pent-up anger or aggression but in the nature of their relationship to authority. They have given themselves to the authority; they see themselves as instruments for the execution of his wishes; once so defined, they are unable to break free."

The Milgram experiment, too, has had its critics. Some believe it was unethical, both because of Milgram's deception in not telling subjects what was really happening until after the session was over (of course, such honesty in advance would have invalidated the findings) and because the study caused so many of the subjects such emotional pain (Milgram countered that the subjects wouldn't have felt pain if they had disobeyed instructions). Others question Milgram's assertion that the situation often overrules personality; certain personality traits, such as hostility and authoritarianism, do predict obedience to authority in real life (Blass, 1993). Some psychologists strenuously disagree with those who have equated the behavior of Milgram's participants with that of Nazi doctors, concentration-camp executioners, and soldiers who perpetrate massacres. As John Darley (1995) put it, Milgram's subjects obeyed only when the experimenter was hovering right there, and many of them felt enormous discomfort and pain; in contrast, he notes, the defining characteristics of those who commit atrocities is that they do so without supervision by authorities, without external pressure, and without feelings of anguish.

Nevertheless, this experiment had a tremendous influence on public awareness of the dangers of uncritical obedience. As Darley himself observed, "Milgram shows us the beginning of a path by means of which ordinary people, in the grip of social forces, become the origins of atrocities in the real world."

THE POWER OF ROLES

In spite of their limitations, the three imaginative studies we have described vividly demonstrate the power of social roles and obligations to influence the behavior of individuals. The behavior of the prisoners and guards varied; some prisoners were more rebellious than others, some guards were more abusive than others. But, ultimately, what the students did depended on the roles they were assigned. Regardless of their personal feelings, staff members at the mental hospitals, from psychiatrists at the top to ward attendants at the bottom, had to adapt to the structure of the institution. And whatever their personal traits, when people in the Milgram experiment believed they had to follow the legitimate orders of authority, most of them put their private values aside.

Obedience, of course, is not always harmful or bad. A certain amount of routine compliance with rules is necessary for any group to function, and obedience to authority can have constructive results as well as destructive ones (Darley, 1995). That is why all societies set penalties, from a mild fine to life in prison, on those who fail to obey the law—indeed, some societies impose the death penalty. All groups impose consequences, from mild censure to outright banishment, on those who fail to obey the group's everyday norms and rules. A nation could not operate if all its citizens ignored traffic signals, cheated on their taxes, dumped garbage wherever they chose, or assaulted each other. An organization could not function if its members "did their own thing," working only when they felt like it. But obedience also has a darker aspect. Throughout history, the plea "I was only following orders" has been offered to excuse actions carried out on behalf of orders that were foolish, destructive, or illegal. The writer C. P. Snow observed that "More hideous crimes have been committed in the name of obedience than in the name of rebellion."

Most people follow orders because of the obvious consequences of disobedience: They can be suspended from school, fired from their jobs, or arrested. In addition, they obey because they respect the authority who is giving the orders; because they want to be liked; or because they hope to gain personal advantages. They obey without thinking critically about the authority's right to issue orders or in the confidence that the authority knows more than they do. But what about those obedient people in Milgram's experiment who felt they were doing wrong, who wished they were free, but who could not untangle themselves from the cobweb of social constraints? Why do people obey when it is not in their interests, or when obedience requires them to ignore their own values or even commit a crime?

Social psychologists Herbert Kelman and Lee Hamilton (1989) have studied "crimes of obedience," ranging from military massacres of civilians to bureaucratic crimes such as Watergate and the Iran-Contra scandal (in which Ronald Reagan's administration, against the express wishes of Congress, illegally sold arms to Iran in order to fund the Contra forces in Nicaragua). They and other researchers draw our attention to several factors that cause people to obey when they would rather not:

1. *Legitimization of the authority* allows people to feel absolved of responsibility for their actions. In Milgram's experiment, many people who administered the highest levels of shock gave up their own accountability to the demands of the experiment. A 37-year-old welder explained that the experimenter was responsible for any pain the victim might suffer "for the simple reason that I was paid for doing this. I had to follow orders. That's how I figured it." In contrast, the people who refused to give high levels of shock took credit for their actions and refused to grant the authority legitimacy. "One of the things I think is very cowardly," said a 32-year-old engineer, "is to try to shove the responsibility onto someone else. See, if I now turned around and said, 'It's your fault . . . it's not mine,' I would call that cowardly" (Milgram, 1974).

2. *Routinization* is the process of defining the activity in terms of routine duties and roles so that one's behavior becomes normalized, a job to be done, and there is little opportunity to raise doubts or ethical questions. In the Milgram study, some people became so fixated on the "learning task" that they shut out any moral concerns about the learner's demands to be let out. Routinization is typically the mechanism by which governments enlist citizens to aid and abet programs of genocide: German bureaucrats kept meticulous records of every Nazi victim, and in Cambodia, the Khmer Rouge recorded the names and histories of the millions of victims they tortured and killed. "I am not a violent man," said Sous Thy, one of the clerks who recorded these names, to a reporter from *The New York Times*. "I was just making lists."

3. *The rules of good manners.* Good manners, of course, are the honey of relationships and the grease of civilization; they smooth over the rough spots of interaction and protect good feelings. But once people are caught in what they perceive to be legitimate roles and obeying a legitimate authority, good manners further ensnare them into obedience. Most people don't like to rock the boat, appear to doubt the experts, or be rude, because they know they will be disliked for doing so (Sabini & Silver, 1985). Indeed, when students watch a videotape of the Milgram procedure, they are much more favorably inclined toward dissenters who politely disobey than those who get furiously riled up and morally indignant. The psychologist who reported these findings, Barry Collins (1993), observes that they dispel the typical fantasy that people have about "What *I* would have liked to have done as a Milgram subject."

The routinization of horror enables people to commit or collaborate in atrocities. More than 16,000 political prisoners were tortured and killed at Tuol Sleng prison by members of Cambodia's Khmer Rouge. Prison authorities kept meticulous records and photos of each victim. This man, Ing Pech, was one of only seven survivors, spared because he had skills useful to his captors. He now runs a museum at the prison, exhibiting the barbarous acts of Pol Pot's regime.

Because of good manners, many people lack a *language of protest.* To have gotten up from your chair in the Milgram study and walked out would have been embarrassing, and you would have had to explain and justify your "rudeness." Many could not find the words to do so. One woman kept apologizing to the experimenter, trying not to offend him with her worries for the victim: "Do I go right to the end, sir? I hope there's nothing wrong with him there." (She did go right to the end.) A man repeatedly protested and questioned the experimenter, but he too obeyed, even when the victim had apparently collapsed in pain. "He thinks he is killing someone," Milgram (1974) commented, "yet he uses the language of the tea table."

4. *Entrapment.* Although obedience often seems to be an either–or matter—you obey or you do not—the fact is that obedience usually escalates through a process called **entrapment.** In entrapment, individuals increase their commitment to a course of action in order to justify their investment in it (Brockner & Rubin, 1985). You are trapped at the point at which you are heavily invested in an activity and it costs too much to get out. The first steps of entrapment pose no difficult choices. But one step leads to another, and before the person realizes it, he or she has become committed to a course of action that does pose problems. In Milgram's study, once subjects had given a 15-volt shock, they had committed themselves to the experiment. The next level was "only" 30 volts. Before they knew it, they were administering what they believed were dangerously high shocks. At that point, it was difficult to explain a sudden decision to quit. In contrast, the earlier in the experiment that Milgram's participants began to resist (questioning or disagreeing with the procedure), the less likely they were to become entrapped by it—and the more likely they were ultimately to disobey (Modigliani & Rochat, 1995).

Because of the principle of entrapment, slot machines make millions for casinos. A person vows to spend only a few dollars, but, after losing them, says, "Well, maybe another couple of tries" or "I've spent so much, now I really have to win something to get back my loss."

Everyone is vulnerable to the process of entrapment. A job requires, at first, only a "little" cheating, and, besides, "Everyone else is doing it," and before long, you are enmeshed in the company's dishonest policies. You start dating someone you like moderately. Before you know it, you have been together so long that you can't break up, although you don't want to become committed, either. Or you visit Las Vegas and quickly lose the $50 you allotted yourself for gambling, so you decide to keep going "just a little longer" in hopes of recovering the lost money. Before long, you're out $500 and have to go home a day early.

Entrapment can lead to aggressive and violent actions by individuals and nations, and examples of it appear frequently in the news. A young man decides to ride along with some gang members but does not intend to do anything illegal. Soon he is scrawling graffiti, then stealing tires, then dealing drugs, although he would rather not do any of these things. Government leaders start a war they think will end quickly. Years later, the nation has lost so many soldiers and so much money that the leaders believe they cannot retreat without losing face.

A chilling study of entrapment was conducted with 25 men who had served in the Greek military police during the authoritarian regime that ended in 1974 (Haritos-Fatouros, 1988). A psychologist who interviewed the men identified the steps used in training them to use torture in questioning prisoners. First, the men were ordered to stand guard outside the interrogation and torture cells. Then they stood guard in the detention rooms, where they observed the torture of prisoners. Then they "helped" beat up prisoners. Once they had obediently followed these orders and became actively involved, the torturers found their actions easier to carry out.

Many people expect the solutions to moral problems to fall into two clear categories, with right on one side and wrong on the other. Yet in everyday life, as in the Milgram study, people often set out on a path that is morally ambiguous, only to find that they have traveled a long way toward violating their own principles. From

entrapment A gradual process in which individuals escalate their commitment to a course of action to justify their investment of time, money, or effort.

Greece's "bad" torturers to the Khmer Rouge's "dutiful" clerks to Milgram's "well-meaning" subjects, people share the difficult task of drawing a line beyond which they will not go. People who mindlessly succumb to the power of roles are less likely to hear the voice of conscience.

Quick Quiz

Step into your role as student to answer these questions.

1. About what percentage of the people in Milgram's obedience study administered the highest levels of shock? (a) two-thirds, (b) one-half, (c) one-third, (d) one-tenth
2. Which of the following actions by the "learner" reduced the likelihood of being shocked by the "teacher"? (a) protesting noisily, (b) screaming in pain, (c) complaining of having a heart ailment, (d) nothing he did made a difference
3. In the Milgram, Zimbardo, and Rosenhan studies, people's behaviors were predicted most strongly by (a) their personality traits, (b) the dictates of conscience, (c) their assigned roles, (d) norms codified in law
4. What social-psychological concepts does each story illustrate?
   a. A friend of yours, who is moving, asks you to bring over a few boxes. Since you are there anyway, he asks you to fill them with books. Before you know it, you have packed up his entire kitchen, living room, and bedroom.
   b. Sam is having dinner with a group of fellow students when one of his friends tells a joke about how dumb women are. Sam is angry and disgusted but doesn't say anything. Later, in the shower, he thinks of what he should have said.

Answers:

1. a 2. d 3. c 4. a. entrapment b. the rules of good manners and lacking a language of protest

SOCIAL COGNITION: ATTRIBUTIONS AND ATTITUDES

Social psychologists are interested not only in what people do in social situations, but also in what goes on in their heads while they are doing it. Researchers in the area of **social cognition** examine how the social environment influences thoughts, beliefs, and memories; how people perceive one another and the effects of those perceptions on their relationships; and how their cognitive schemas about relationships affect the way they process information (A. Fiske & Haslam, 1996). We will consider two important topics in this area: explanations about behavior and the formation and change of attitudes.

EXPLANATIONS AND EXCUSES

One theme of this book has been that human beings are active, problem-solving creatures, forever trying to make sense of the world and understand what is going on around them. Although detective stories are called "whodunits," detective work in fiction and real life is really more a "*why*dunit"—everyone wants to know *why* the villain did the dirty deed. Was it something in the villain's nature, background, or current predictment? According to **attribution theory,** all of us are constantly seeking to attribute causes to the behavior of themselves and others. These explanations generally fall into two categories. When we make a *situational attribution,* we are identifying the cause of an action as something in the environment: "Joe stole the money because his family is starving." When we make a *dispositional attribution,* we are identifying the cause of an action as something in the person, such as a trait or a motive: "Joe stole the money because he is a born thief."

social cognition An area in social psychology concerned with social influences on thought, memory, perception, and other cognitive processes.

attribution theory The theory that people are motivated to explain their own and others' behavior by attributing causes of that behavior to a situation or a disposition.

GET INVOLVED

Read the following passage, and then, before reading further, list a few reasons why you think the motorcycle driver acted as he did. Ask several of your friends or relatives, and possibly people from other cultural backgrounds than yours, to do the same thing.

> The back wheel burst on the motorcycle, and the passenger sitting on the rear was thrown, hitting his head on the pavement. The driver of the motorcycle, an attorney, took the passenger to a local hospital and went on to court to do his work. The driver left without consulting the doctor about the seriousness of the passenger's injury or whether the passenger should be moved. Ultimately, the passenger died. (Adapted from J. Miller, 1984)

Why did the driver behave as he did? Westerners will tend to give dispositional *answers: "He was obviously irresponsible" or "He was aggressive in pursuing his career interests." Easterners will tend to give* situational *answers: "It was his duty to be in court for the client he was representing" or "The injured man might not have looked as seriously injured as he was." What do you and your respondents say?*

In other chapters, we have already noted the psychological effects of certain attributions: In Chapter 10, for example, we saw that attributions influence emotions (did that man intend to insult you or not?), and in Chapter 14, we saw that attributions influence how much control people think they have over their health. Attributions even affect the happiness of marriage partners and the long-term success of their marriages. Unhappy spouses are more likely than happy ones to attribute marital problems to their partner's stable *dispositions,* blaming the person's selfishness, meanness, or thoughtlessness. Happy spouses, in contrast, are more likely to attribute marital problems to the *situation,* blaming the stress the partner is under, a lack of time together because of work and family obligations, and so forth (Fincham & Bradbury, 1993; Karney et al., 1994).

Through experimental research, social psychologists have specified some of the conditions under which people prefer certain attributions to others. For example, when people try to find reasons for someone else's behavior, they tend to overestimate personality factors and underestimate the influence of the situation (Nisbett & Ross, 1980). This tendency has been called the **fundamental attribution error.** Were the student guards in the prison study basically mean and the prisoners basically cowardly? Were the staff members in the hospital study lazy, thoughtless, or selfish? Were the hundreds of people who obeyed Milgram's experimenters sadistic by nature? People who think so are committing the fundamental attribution error. They are especially likely to make this mistake when they are distracted or preoccupied and don't have time to stop and ask themselves, "Why, exactly, *is* Aurelia behaving like a dork today?" Instead, they leap to the easiest attribution, which is dispositional: Aurelia simply has a dorky personality (Gilbert, Pelham, & Krull, 1988).

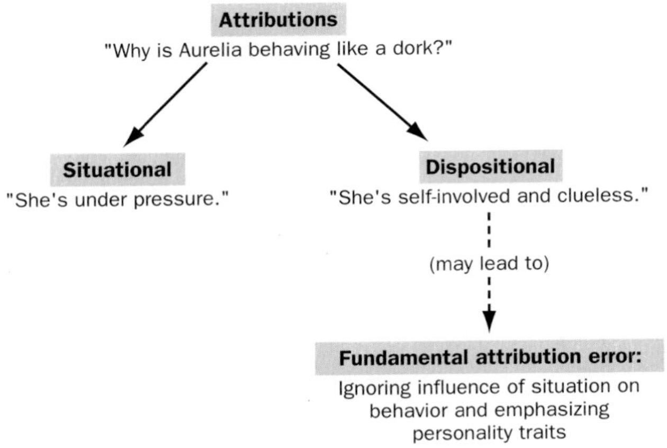

Attributions
"Why is Aurelia behaving like a dork?"

Situational
"She's under pressure."

Dispositional
"She's self-involved and clueless."

(may lead to)

Fundamental attribution error:
Ignoring influence of situation on behavior and emphasizing personality traits

The fundamental attribution error is prevalent in Western nations, where middle-class people tend to believe that individuals are responsible for their own actions. But this error is by no means universal. In countries such as

fundamental attribution error The tendency, in explaining other people's behavior, to overestimate personality factors and underestimate the influence of the situation.

India, for example, where everyone is deeply embedded in caste and family networks, and in Japan, China, and Hong Kong, where people are more group oriented than they are in the West, people are more likely to recognize situational constraints on behavior (Lee, Hallahan, & Herzog, 1996; J. G. Miller, 1984; Morris & Peng, 1994). If someone is behaving oddly, makes a mistake, or plays badly in a soccer match, an Indian or Chinese, unlike a Westerner, is more likely to make a situational attribution of the person's behavior than a dispositional one.

When it comes to explaining their *own* behavior, however, most Westerners have a **self-serving bias:** They tend to choose attributions that are favorable to them, taking credit for their good actions (a dispositional attribution) and letting the situation account for their bad ones. For instance, most of us will say, "I am furious for good reason—this situation is intolerable." We are less likely to say, "I am furious because I am an ill-tempered grinch." If we do something admirable, though, such as donating $100 to charity, we attribute our motives to personality ("I'm the generous type") instead of to the situation ("That guy on the phone pressured me into it").

The self-serving bias is also apparent in the excuses people make to justify their mistakes. C. R. Snyder, Raymond Higgins, and Rita Stucky (1983) have observed that self-protecting excuses have been part of human life since Adam blamed Eve for giving him the apple—and Eve blamed the serpent. The researchers identified several categories of excuses: "I didn't do it"; "I did it, but it wasn't so bad"; "I didn't mean to"; and "I couldn't help it." A psychotherapy client of one of the researchers put it best. "It's like this," she said. "If it's not my fault, it's her fault, and if it's not her fault, it's still not my fault."

Excuses have several social purposes. They allow people to assert their good qualities, reduce their responsibility, and minimize the badness of the action itself (Snyder, 1989). Excuses also make it possible for people to maintain self-esteem, soften the other person's anger, and change the other person's attributions about their own actions (Weiner, Figueroa-Muñoz, & Kakihara, 1991). Unfortunately, excuses are also used to justify the destructive things that people do and to rationalize their failure to take helpful action.

Culture affects not only the fundamental attribution error, but also self-serving attributions and excuses. In Japan, for example, heads of companies are expected to take responsibility not only for their own failings, but also for the failings of their employees or products—and they do (Hamilton & Sanders, 1992; Markus & Kitayama, 1991). In the United States, in contrast, the common practice is for heads of corporations to get huge salaries and bonuses even when the company is doing

self-serving bias The tendency, in explaining one's own behavior, to take credit for one's good actions and rationalize one's mistakes.

Children learn the value of excuses at an early age.

poorly, and to blame the economy, government policies, or their employees if something goes wrong. (Of course, many Americans also deny responsibility for their mistakes because they fear lawsuits.)

People also make attributions for events that have little to do with their self-esteem or even their own behavior. According to the **just-world hypothesis,** most people all over the world need to believe that the world is fair, that good people are rewarded and villains punished (Lerner, 1980). The belief in a just world helps people make sense out of senseless events and feel safe in the presence of threatening events. If a friend loses his job, if a woman is raped, if a prisoner is tortured, it is reassuring to believe that they all must have done something to deserve what happened or at least to cause it. The need to believe in a just world often leads to a dispositional attribution called *blaming the victim.* When everyone agrees that A did something to harm B, A can argue that B deserved the treatment, provoked the treatment, or wanted the treatment. "Many subjects harshly devalue the victim as a consequence of acting against him," wrote Milgram (1974). "Such comments as, 'He was so stupid and stubborn he deserved to get shocked,' were common."

Of course, most human actions are determined both by personality and by environment. In that case, is the fundamental attribution error always an error? Sometimes dispositional attributions accurately predict how a person will behave. Moreover, is the self-serving bias always a bias? Maybe we know more about our own behavior and intentions than we do about the actions of others. The point to keep is mind is that attributions, whether accurate or not, have important consequences for emotions and actions, for legal decisions, and for everyday relations.

Quick Quiz

To what do you attribute your success in answering these questions?

A. What kind of attribution is being made in each case, situational (S) or dispositional (D)?

1. A jury decides that a congressman accepted a bribe because FBI agents set up a sting operation to trap him.
2. A jury decides that a congressman accepted a bribe because he is dishonest.
3. A man says, "My wife has sure become a grouchy person."
4. The same man says, "I'm grouchy because I've had a bad day at the office."
5. A woman reads that unemployment is very high in inner-city communities. "Well, if those people weren't so lazy, they would find work," she says.

B. What principles of attribution theory are suggested by Items 3, 4, and 5 in the preceding question?

Answers:

A. 1. S 2. D 3. D 4. S 5. D B. Item 3 illustrates the fundamental attribution error; 4, the self-serving bias; and 5, blaming the victim, because of the just-world hypothesis.

THE SOCIAL ORIGINS OF ATTITUDES

People have attitudes about all sorts of things—politics, people, food, children, movies, sports heroes, you name it. An *attitude* is a relatively stable opinion containing a cognitive element (your perceptions and beliefs about the topic) and an emotional element (your feelings about the topic, which may range from negative and hostile to positive and loving). Attitudes range from shallow, changeable opinions to deeply held convictions. Many public-opinion polls do not discriminate between

just-world hypothesis The notion that most people need to believe that the world is fair and that justice is served; that bad people are punished and good people rewarded.

these extremes; they just ask for a person's attitude, not how strongly it is felt. The results, therefore, may be misleading; public opinion often seems easily swayed—and it is. But the public's convictions are less swayable.

CONSIDER OTHER EXPLANATIONS

Most people think that their attitudes are a result of thinking and clear reasoning. But are all your attitudes carefully thought out? What are some other origins of attitudes, and why is it important for critical thinkers to be aware of them?

Most people think that their attitudes are based on thinking, a reasoned conclusion about how things work. Sometimes, of course, that's true. But social psychologists have found that some attitudes are a result of not thinking at all. They are a result of conformity, habit, rationalization, economic self-interest, and many subtle social and environmental influences.

For example, some attitudes arise by virtue of the "cohort effect." Each generation, or age *cohort*, has its own experiences and economic concerns, and therefore its own characteristic attitudes. The ages of 16 to 24 appear to be critical for the formation of a *generational identity* that lasts throughout adulthood (Inglehart, 1990). In one survey of the American population, researchers found that the major political events and social changes that occur during these years make deeper impressions and exert more lasting influence than those that happen later in a person's life (Schuman & Scott, 1989). Some of the key events that have affected generational cohorts in this century include the Great Depression (1930s), World War II (1940s), the dropping of the atomic bomb on Hiroshima (1945), the rise of the civil rights movement (1950s–1960s), the assassination of John F. Kennedy (1963), the Vietnam War (1965–1973), the rebirth of the women's rights movement (1970s), and the legalization of abortion (1973). People who were between 16 and 24 when these events occurred regard them as "peak memories" that have shaped their political philosophy, values, and attitudes about life. What do you think might be the critical generational events affecting the attitudes of your cohort?

Psychologists have argued for years about which comes first, attitudes or behavior, and whether they need even be related. Of course, attitudes do dispose people to behave in certain ways (Kraus, 1995); if you have a positive attitude toward martial-arts movies, you'll go to as many as you can, and if you hate them, you'll stay away from them. Yet all too often, attitudes and behavior are as unrelated as grapefruit and shoes. For example, in a study of 5,500 Canadian college students, the majority knew which sexual acts increase the risk of AIDS transmission and also had a favorable attitude about safe sexual practices. Yet that attitude, the researchers reported, "was not typically translated into safer behavior" (MacDonald et al., 1990).

Although it is commonly believed that the way to change behavior is first to change attitudes, it also works the other way around: Changing behavior can lead to a change in attitude because the new behavior alters our knowledge or experience. For example, suppose you dislike exercise and have always avoided it, but your friend persuades you to begin jogging with her; once

LIFESTYLE

Lounging: Have an hour? Make it happy hour.

Young Fogies

Bored with the present and uneasy about the future, Gen X toasts the good old days

By Kendall Hamilton and T. Trent Gegax

Alex Klenert may only be 22, but he's already acquired a taste for the finer things in life. He loves big-band music, a bracing round on the links, all-night card games with the guys. And when it's time for a haircut, Klenert knows just the place. Up a short flight of granite steps, just a few blocks off New York's Wall Street, lies John Allan's, a dark-paneled paradise. Young Alex settles back in a green leather chair, leafing through the latest issue of the glossy cigar monthly Smoke, as Mary Ann, an attractive stylist in a very short skirt, runs her fingers through his hair, snipping it just so. Another woman holds his hand, administering a glistening manicure. Yet a third brings him a glass of beer, fresh from the tap, and sets it atop a svelte black metal stand. "You kinda get hooked on it," says Klenert, a marketing writer who clears barely $20,000 a year, but finds the budgetary headroom to find a haircut, manicure, shoeshine and hot-towel treatment at John Allan's every six weeks. It's 44 bucks plus tip—but, hey, it's worth it. "With the hot towel, you just lose yourself in the heat, it just radiates through your body."

Mary Ann's proximity may have something to do with that particular sensation, but the appeal of a place like John Allan's extends far beyond the boundaries of Klenert's leather chair. In every corner of the culture, it seems, people in their 20s—and not just men—are embracing the good life, old style. Indeed, if Generation Xers are skipping the Clinton-Dole debates, it's because they're too busy immersing themselves in the accouterments of the Eisenhower era. There are the precocious connoisseurs, like Klenert, with their cigars, single malts and men's-club mentalities. Others seek high style in the low culture of yore. Cocktail-happy "lounge" devotees, with their rat-packy, Foster

64 NEWSWEEK OCTOBER 28, 1996

Your "generational identity" refers to psychological characteristics that arise out of the shared experiences and values of your generation. What, if any, are the defining experiences of Generation X, those who are in their twenties today? The news media keep trying to identify them!

you get the hang of it, you find you enjoy it and that your attitude is completely changed. Attitudes also change to conform to our behavior because of the need for consistency. In Chapter 8, we discussed **cognitive dissonance,** the uncomfortable feeling that people have when two attitudes, or an attitude and behavior, are in conflict (are dissonant). People are often motivated to resolve the conflict by changing the attitude or changing their behavior.

Many influences on attitudes are external; they result from the intentional efforts of others, not always benign, to get us to change our minds. That's not necessarily a bad thing, but when persuasive tactics go beyond the use of reasoned argument, people become vulnerable to manipulation. The best protection against being manipulated is not rigid thinking and the refusal to accept new ideas; it is critical thinking, and the ability to identify the social forces that influence the formation and change of attitudes. (In "Taking Psychology with You," we discuss some ways to protect yourself from manipulation.)

FRIENDLY PERSUASION All around you, every day, advertisers, politicians, and friends are trying to get you to change your attitudes. One weapon they use is the drip, drip, drip of a repeated idea. In fact, repeated exposure even to a nonsense syllable such as *zug* is enough to make a person feel more positive toward it (Zajonc, 1968). The effectiveness of familiarity has long been known to politicians and advertisers: Repeat something often enough, even the basest lie, and eventually the public will believe it. The effect of familiarity on attitudes is the reason that advertisements are repeated so often. Many people will spend four times as much for a familiar brand of aspirin as for an unfamiliar one, although the cheaper product is just as good.

The formal name for this phenomenon is the **validity effect.** In a series of experiments, Hal Arkes and his associates demonstrated how the validity effect operates (Arkes, 1991; Arkes, Boehm, & Xu, 1991). In one typical study, people read a list of statements, such as "Mercury has a higher boiling point than copper" or "Over 400 Hollywood films were produced in 1948." They had to rate each statement for its validity, where "1" meant that the rater thought the statement was definitely false and "7" that it was definitely true. A week or two later, subjects again rated the validity of some of these statements and also rated others that they hadn't seen previously. The result: Mere repetition increased the perception that the familiar statements were true. The validity effect also occurred for other kinds of statements, including unverifiable opinions (e.g., "At least 75 percent of all politicians are basically dishonest"), for opinions that subjects initially felt were true, and even for those they initially felt were false. "Note that no attempt has been made to persuade," wrote Arkes (1991). "No supporting arguments are offered. We just have subjects rate the statements. Mere repetition seems to increase rated validity. This is scary." Further experiments ruled out competing explanations, confirming that the simple familiarity of an argument is sufficient to make many people believe that it is valid (Boehm, 1994).

When Arkes discussed this research with a student from the People's Republic of China, she was not surprised. She told him how her government made use of the validity effect by distributing posters claiming, for example, that the protest for democracy in Tiananmen Square had been organized by a small band of traitors. At first, no one believed these lies; but over time, with repetition, the government's assertions became more plausible.

People are also more easily persuaded to change their minds when they hear arguments from someone they admire or think is attractive, which is why advertisements are full of beautiful models, sports heroes, and "experts" (Cialdini, 1993). Persuaders will also try to link their message with a good feeling. In one classic study,

cognitive dissonance A state of tension that occurs when a person simultaneously holds two cognitions that are psychologically inconsistent, or when a person's belief is incongruent with his or her behavior.

validity effect The tendency of people to believe that a statement is true or valid simply because it has been repeated many times.

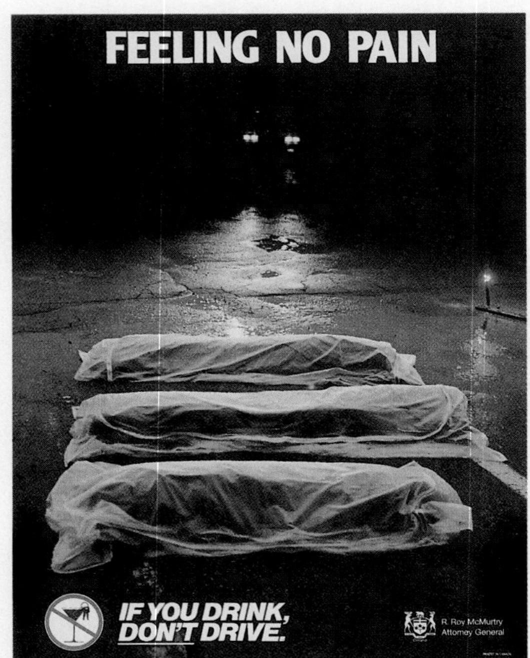

FEELING NO PAIN
IF YOU DRINK, DON'T DRIVE.
R. Roy McMurtry
Attorney General

Would this ad keep you from drinking and driving? Why or why not? Successful campaigns to prevent drunk driving have not relied solely on fear campaigns. They have involved increased penalties, changing social norms to make drunk driving "uncool," promoting the use of a designated driver, and giving people alternatives to driving after drinking—such as free cab rides.

students who were given peanuts and Pepsi while listening to a speaker's point of view were more likely to be convinced by it than were students who listened to the same words without the pleasant munchies and soft drinks (Janis, Kaye, & Kirschner, 1965). Perhaps this is why so much business is conducted over lunch, and so many courtships over dinner!

The emotion of fear, in contrast, can cause people to resist arguments that are in their own best interest (Pratkanis & Aronson, 1992). Fear tactics are often used to try to persuade people to quit smoking or abusing other drugs, drive only when sober, use condoms, check for signs of cancer, and prepare for earthquakes. However, fear works only if people are moderately anxious, not scared to death, *and* if the message also provides information about how to avoid the danger (Leventhal & Nerenz, 1982). When messages about a potential disaster are too terrifying and when people believe that they can do nothing to avoid it, they tend to deny the danger.

COERCIVE PERSUASION Sometimes, efforts to change attitudes go beyond exposing people to a new idea and persuading them to accept it. The manipulator uses harsh tactics, not just hoping that people will change their minds, but attempting to force them to. These tactics are sometimes referred to as *brainwashing,* a term first used during the Korean War to describe techniques used on American prisoners of war to get them to collaborate with their Chinese Communist captors and to endorse anti-American propaganda. Most psychologists, however, prefer the phrase *coercive persuasion.* "Brainwashing," they argue, implies that a person has a sudden change of mind and is unaware of what is happening. It sounds mysterious and powerful. In fact, the methods involved are neither mysterious nor unusual. The difference between "persuasion" and "brainwashing" is often only a matter of degree and the observer's bias, just as a group that is a crazy cult to one person is a group of devoutly religious people to another.

How, then, might we distinguish coercive persuasion from the usual techniques of persuasion that occur in daily life? Persuasion techniques become coercive when they suppress an individual's ability to reason and make choices in his or her own best interests. Studies of religious, political, and other cults have identified some of the processes by which individuals, whether singly or in groups, can be coerced (Galanter, 1989; Mithers, 1994; Ofshe & Watters, 1994; Singer, Temerlin, & Langone, 1990; Zimbardo & Leippe, 1991):

1. *The person is put under physical or emotional distress.* The individual may not be allowed to eat, sleep, or exercise. He or she may be isolated in a dark room with no stimulation or food prior to joining the group. In the group, the person may be induced into a trancelike state through repetitive chanting, hypnosis, deep relaxation, or fatigue. A participant who is already under stress, perhaps feeling lonely or troubled, is especially likely to be primed to accept the ideas of the leader or group.

2. *The person's problems are defined in simplistic terms, and simple answers are offered repeatedly.* There are as many of these answers as there are persuasive groups, but here are some actual examples: Are you afraid or unhappy? It all stems from the pain of being born. Are you worried about homeless earthquake victims? It's not your problem; victims are responsible for everything that happens to them. Are your parents giving you a hard time? Reject them completely. Are you struggling financially? It's your fault for not wanting to be rich fervently enough.

3. *The leader offers unconditional love, acceptance, and attention.* The new recruit may be given a "love bath" from the group—constant praise, support, applause, and affection. Positive emotions of euphoria and well-being are generated. In exchange, the leader demands everyone's attachment, adoration, and idealization.

4. *A new identity based on the group is created.* The recruit is told that he or she is part of the chosen, the elite, the redeemed. To foster this new identity, many cults require a severe initiation rite; require their members to wear identifying clothes or eat special diets; and assign each new member a new name. All members of the Philadelphia group MOVE were given the last name "Africa"; all members of the Church of Armageddon took the last name "Israel." Conversely, members are taught to hate certain "evil" enemies: parents, capitalists, blacks, whites, nonbelievers.

5. *The person is subjected to entrapment.* "There is no contract up front that says 'I agree to become a beggar and give up my family,' " says Philip Zimbardo. Instead, the person agrees to small things: to spend a weekend with the group, then another weekend, then take weekly seminars, then advanced courses. During the Korean War, the Chinese first got the American POWs to agree with mild remarks, such as "The United States is not perfect." Then the POWs had to add their own examples of the imperfections. At the end, they were signing their names to anti-American broadcasts (Schein, Schneier, & Barker, 1961).

6. *The person's access to information is severely controlled.* As soon as a person is a committed believer or follower, the group limits his or her choices, denigrates critical thinking, makes fun of doubts, defines the outside world as evil, and insists that any private distress is due to lack of belief in the group. The person may be isolated from the outside world and thus from antidotes to the leader's ideas. Total conformity is demanded.

All of these techniques were apparent in the Branch Davidian cult led by David Koresh. By moving his group to a virtually self-sufficient compound in Waco, Texas, Koresh physically isolated his followers from their families and from other people who would have offered them a different interpretation of Koresh's paranoid beliefs. He subjected them to exhausting all-night vigils and lectures. He offered them simple answers for their complex lives: "Believe in me; you will be saved; you will no longer be unhappy; I will take care of you." He entrapped them in an escalating

These members of the Aum Shinrikyo ("Supreme Truth") sect in Japan, wearing masks of their leader's face, take the uniformity of cult identity to an extreme. The sect was founded by Shoko Asahara, who calls himself "The Savior of This Century," and who instructed his devotees to place a nerve gas in a Japanese subway, killing ten and sickening thousands of other passengers. One former member said of the sect, "Their strategy is to wear you down and take control of your mind. They promise you heaven, but they make you live in hell."

series of obligations and commitments. Koresh never said to new recruits, "Follow me, and you will have to give up your marriages, your homes, your children, and your lives"; but by the end, that is just what they did.

Some people may be more vulnerable than others to coercive tactics. But these techniques are powerful enough to overwhelm even strong individuals. Unless people understand how these methods work, few can resist their combined effects.

Quick Quiz

How can we persuade you to take this quiz?

1. Candidate Carson spends $3 million to make sure his name is seen and heard frequently, and to repeat unverified charges that his opponent is a thief. What psychological process is he relying on to win?

2. Your best friend urges you to join a "life-renewal" group called "The Feeling Life." Your friend has been spending increasing amounts of time with her fellow Feelies, and you have some doubts about them. What questions would you want to have answered before joining up?

Answers:

1. the validity effect 2. A few things to consider: Is there a single autocratic leader who tolerates no dissent or criticism, while rationalizing this practice as a benefit for members? ("Doubt and disbelief are signs that your feeling side is being repressed.") Have long-standing members given up their friends and families, their interests and ambitions, for this group? Does the leader offer simple but unrealistic promises to repair your life and all that troubles you? Are members required to make extreme personal sacrifices by donating large amounts of money and breaking off their outside relationships? You might also examine the dissonance you are feeling between loyalty to your friend and doubts about your friend's enthusiasm for this group.

INDIVIDUALS AND GROUPS

Something happens to individuals when they collect in groups. They act differently than they would on their own; this is true for every social species. It is true when the group exists to solve problems and make decisions; when it has gathered to have fun, as at a soccer game; when it consists of anonymous bystanders; or when it is just a loose collection of individuals in a room. A group's actions, research suggests, depend less on the personalities of its members than on the structure and dynamics of the group itself.

CONFORMITY

One thing that happens in groups is that people *conform*, taking action or adopting attitudes as a result of real or imagined group pressure. Suppose that you are required to appear at your professor's laboratory for an experiment on perception. You join seven other students seated in a room. You are shown a 10-inch line and asked which of three other lines is identical to it. The correct answer, line A, is obvious, so you are amused when the first person in the group chooses line B. "Bad eyesight," you say to yourself. "He's off by 2 whole inches!" The second person also chooses line B. "What a dope," you think. But by the time the fifth person has chosen line B, you are beginning to doubt yourself. The sixth and seventh students also choose line B, and now you are worried about *your* eyesight. The experimenter looks at you. "Your turn," he says. Do you follow the evidence of your own eyes or the collective judgment of the group?

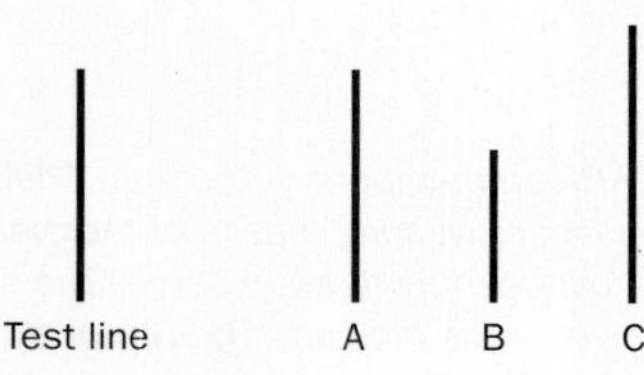

Sometimes people like to conform in order to feel part of the group . . .

. . . and sometimes they like to rebel a little in order to assert their individuality.

This was the design for a series of famous studies of conformity conducted by Solomon Asch (1952, 1965). The seven "nearsighted" students were actually Asch's confederates. Asch wanted to know what people would do when a group unanimously contradicted an obvious fact. He found that when people made the line comparisons on their own, they were almost always accurate. But in the group, only 20 percent of the students remained completely independent on every trial, and they were often apologetic for not agreeing with the group. One-third conformed to the group's incorrect decision more than half the time, and the rest conformed at least some of the time. Conformers and independents often felt uncertain regardless of their decision. As one participant later said, "I felt disturbed, puzzled, separated, like an outcast from the rest."

Asch's experiment has been replicated many times over the years, in the United States and many other countries. A meta-analysis of 133 studies in 17 countries revealed three general findings (Bond & Smith, 1996). First, in America, conformity has declined since the 1950s, when Asch first did his work, suggesting that conformity reflects prevailing social norms. Second, people in individualistic cultures, such as the United States, are less likely to conform than are people in group-oriented cultures, where social harmony is considered more important than individual assertiveness (as we will see in the next chapter). Third, regardless of culture, conformity increases under certain conditions: as the stimulus becomes more ambiguous, as the number of people who disagree with the subject increases, and as the majority becomes more homogenous.

Like obedience, conformity has both its positive and its negative sides. It allows people to feel connected to one another. Society runs more smoothly when people know how to behave in a given situation, when they go along with the rules of dress and manners. But conformity can also suppress critical thinking and creativity. Many people will, in a group, deny their private beliefs, agree with silly notions, and violate their own values (Aronson, 1995; Cialdini, 1993). Some do so because they identify with group members and want to be like them in dress, attitudes, or behavior. Some conform because they believe the group has knowledge or abilities that are superior to their own. Some conform in order to keep their jobs, win promotions, or win votes. Some conform for the same reason they obey; they wish to be liked and know that disagreeing with a group can make them unpopular. For their part, groups are often uncomfortable with nonconformists, and their members will try to persuade a deviant to conform. If pleasant persuasion fails, the group may punish, isolate, or reject the deviant altogether (Moscovici, 1985).

Just as people are often led to commit crimes of obedience, they can be induced to commit crimes of conformity. They commit or cover up illegal acts, or do destructive and even self-destructive things, because "everyone else does it," and they assume, often correctly, that they won't be held accountable. In a cross-cultural study of attributions of responsibility in situations of organizational wrongdoing (e.g., covering up an auto defect or causing a toxic waste spill in an effort to cut company costs), residents of Moscow, Tokyo, and Washington, DC, attributed the *least* responsibility to employees who were "only following orders" and the next least to those who were "going along" with their co-workers. They attributed the *most* responsibility to managers or authorities who made the decision (Hamilton & Sanders, 1995).

THE ANONYMOUS CROWD

Many years ago, in a case that received much public attention, a woman named Kitty Genovese was stabbed repeatedly in front of her apartment building. She screamed for help for more than half an hour, but not one of the 38 neighbors who heard her, who came to their windows to watch, even called the police.

Kitty Genovese was a victim of a process called the **diffusion of responsibility,** in which responsibility for an outcome is diffused, or spread, among many people. Individuals fail to take action because they believe that someone else will do so. The many reports of *bystander apathy* in the news—people watching as a woman is attacked, as a man struggles with a stalled car on a freeway, as a child is eventually beaten to death by disturbed parents—reflect the diffusion of responsibility on a large scale.

In work groups, the diffusion of responsibility sometimes takes the form of *social loafing:* Each member of a team slows down, letting others work harder (Karau & Williams, 1993; Latané, Williams, & Harkins, 1979). This slowdown of effort and abdication of personal responsibility does not happen in all groups. It occurs primarily when individual group members are not accountable for the work they do; when people feel that working harder would only duplicate their colleagues' efforts; when workers feel exploited; or when the work itself is uninteresting (Shepperd, 1995). When the challenge of the job is increased or when each member of the group has a different, important job to do, the sense of individual responsibility rises, and loafing declines. Loafing also declines when people know they will have to evaluate their own performance later, or when they know their group's performance will be evaluated against that of another group (Harkins & Szymanski, 1989). And if people are working on a group project that really matters to them, they may even work harder than they would on their own, in order to compensate for some of their loafing buddies (Williams & Karau, 1991).

The most extreme instances of the diffusion of responsibility occur in groups in which people lose all awareness of their individuality and sense of self, a state called **deindividuation** (Festinger, Pepitone, & Newcomb, 1952). Deindividuated people do not take responsibility for their own actions; they "forget themselves" in responding to the immediate situation. They are more likely to act mindlessly, and their behavior becomes disconnected from their values. They may do destructive things: break store windows, loot, get into fights, riot at a sports event, or commit rape. But sometimes deindividuated people become more friendly; think of all the chatty people on buses and planes who reveal things to their seatmates they would never tell anyone they knew.

diffusion of responsibility In organized or anonymous groups, the tendency of members to avoid taking responsibility for actions or decisions, assuming that others will do so.

deindividuation In groups or crowds, the loss of awareness of one's own individuality and the abdication of mindful action.

GET INVOLVED

For this exercise in deindividuation, choose two situations: one in which you are one of many people, perhaps hundreds (as in a large classroom or a concert audience); and one in which you are one of a few (as in a small discussion group). In both situations, close your eyes and pretend to fall asleep. Is this easier to do in one context than in the other? Why? In each case, what is the reaction of other people around you?

Deindividuation increases under conditions of anonymity. It is more likely to occur, for instance, when a person is in a large city rather than a small town, in a faceless mob rather than an intimate group; when signs of individuality are covered by uniforms or masks; or in a large and impersonal class of hundreds of students rather than a small class of only 15.

The power of the situation to influence what deindividuated people do has been demonstrated repeatedly in experiments. In one, women who wore Ku Klux Klan-like white disguises delivered twice as much apparent electric shock to another woman as did women who were not only undisguised but also wore large name tags (Zimbardo, 1970). In a second, women who were wearing nurses' uniforms gave *less* shock than did women in regular dress (Johnson & Downing, 1979). Evidently, the KKK disguise was a signal to behave aggressively; the nurses' uniforms were a signal to behave nurturantly.

Deindividuation promotes mindlessness—and sometimes cruelty—as the experiment in the text describes (Zimbardo, 1970).

As these studies suggest, deindividuated women are perfectly capable of behaving aggressively, in spite of the stereotype that women are less aggressive than men. Indeed, the commonly observed sex difference in aggressiveness has more to do with *gender roles* than with supposedly natural male and female inclinations. When women are provoked and insulted, they "forget themselves" just as men do. Indeed, a meta-analysis of 64 studies found that the sex difference in aggressiveness drops to almost zero when women are provoked (Bettencourt & Miller, 1996). This drop also occurs when women are deindividuated. In two studies, men behaved more aggressively than women in a competitive video war game when they were individuated—that is, when their names and background information about them were spoken aloud, heard by all subjects, and recorded publicly by the experimenter. But when the men and women believed they were anonymous to their fellow students and to the experimenter—when they were deindividuated—they did not differ in how aggressively they played the game (Lightdale & Prentice, 1994). (The social consequences of deindividuation, and the problem of individual responsibility, are the subject of "Issues in Popular Culture.")

In summary, here are the main causes and consequences of deindividuation and individuation:

	Deindividuation	**Individuation**
Factors that promote:	Being in a crowd Uniforms Anonymity	Being in a small group Having a distinctive appearance Standing out in a group
Consequences:	Social loafing Loss of inhibition Feeling no responsibility for actions	Participation Self-awareness Feeling responsible for actions

think about it

Issues in Popular Culture

Swept Away: Mob Violence and the Law

The research on people's behavior in crowds poses an interesting moral and legal issue: What is the personal responsibility of individuals who are swept away by mob violence and group pressure? Should the law treat them as harshly as it would treat persons acting alone, or is their responsibility diminished by virtue of being in a crowd? The psychology of mob violence made the news during the 1992 Los Angeles riots that followed the acquittal of four white police officers who had beaten the black motorist Rodney King. In the ensuing violence and looting, Damian Williams and three other black men attacked and nearly killed a white man, Reginald Denny. Did their anger at the acquittal of the police officers, and the understandable community outrage that followed, justify their loss of self-control? The jury that served at the men's trial seemed to think so.

In the late 1980s, British social psychologist Andrew Colman (1991a, 1991b) appeared as an expert witness in two murder trials in South Africa. In one, eight black railway workers had pleaded guilty to the murder of four black strike-breakers during a bitter industrial dispute. In the other, six black residents of an impoverished township were accused of murdering an 18-year-old black woman who was having an affair with a hated black police officer. She was "necklaced"—a tire was placed around her neck and set afire—during a community protest against the police that got out of control. The crowd danced and sang as she burned to ashes.

Colman testified about the social-psychological processes that he believed should be considered extenuating circumstances in these cases, including conformity, obedience to authority, deindividuation, and other aspects of crowd psychology. "Each of these social forces on its own," he wrote (1991b), "is powerful and can lead people to behave in ways that are not characteristic of their normal behaviour. . . . Anything that helps to explain a person's behaviour could potentially have a bearing on the moral blameworthiness of that behaviour."

Colman's testimony was not intended to acquit the defendants, who had all been found guilty, but to keep them from being executed. In this, he was successful. In the first case, only four of the eight workers were sentenced to death, and an appeals court commuted those sentences on the grounds that the psychological evidence of extenuating circumstances had not been disproved by the prosecutor. In the second case, all six defendants had their death sentences commuted to 20 months of imprisonment.

Colman regards the successful use of social-psychological findings as a breakthrough for law and justice, but other psychologists and social critics are worried that such findings could also be used to exonerate the guilty. Pumla Gobodo-Madikizela (1994), an African social scientist, interviewed some of the men accused of the necklacing and didn't find them quite so "deindividuated" after all. Some were tremendously upset, were well aware of their actions and choices, had actively debated the woman's guilt, had thought about running away, and consciously tried to rationalize their behavior. More important, she adds, "If nobody can be held culpable, it would be an open invitation to resort to vigilante justice. Surely, the thugs of the world who prefer to act in groups should be found guilty when they knowingly and willingly kill their declared 'enemies.'"

This issue alerts us to the problem, raised elsewhere this book, between understanding behavior and excusing it. Deindividuation certainly helps us understand why people in crowds do things they would never do on their own, but should they therefore be exempt from punishment? If not, what punishment is appropriate?

Just as extreme deindividuation has its hazards, however, so does extreme individuation. People can become *too* self-aware and self-focused, and forget their dependence on others. The very notion of whether deindividuation is good or bad is influenced by culture. Some cultures emphasize the importance of individual action; others emphasize the importance of social harmony. Asians are on the average less individuated than whites, blacks, and Latinos, reflecting the Asian cultural emphasis on social harmony (Maslach, Stapp, & Santee, 1985).

GROUPTHINK AND GROUP THINKING

Group members who like each other and share attitudes often work well together. But close, friendly groups face the problem of getting the best ideas and efforts of

Before you answer, you might consider that if you support a "deindividuation defense" because you sympathize with the defendants, you will need to support the same defense when you are unsympathetic to the defendants. Deindividuation may characterize a mob of oppressed people rioting to protest living conditions, but it also characterizes members of the Ku Klux Klan out on a raid, soldiers committing mass rapes in Bosnia, and the South African whites who went on bloody rampages before the 1994 elections, shooting black civilians. As Gobodo-Madikizela (1994) says, "Psychologists must separate scientific findings from our political preferences, no matter how distasteful the political consequences."

Finally, remember that in every crowd, some people don't go along; they remain individuated. During the riot in which Reginald Denny was attacked, two African-Americans, Terri Barnett and Gregory Alan Williams, rescued a white man from the same fate, and many other black people came to the aid of white and Latino passersby. Does that information affect your reaction to the deindividuation defense? We can be sure that the issue of personal responsibility and psychological understanding will return frequently in the news.

Millions remember the sight of Reginald Denny being bludgeoned by Damian Williams during the 1992 Los Angeles riots. Yet even under extreme conditions, many people retain their individuality and courage. Terri Barnett and Gregory Alan Williams were honored at City Hall for rescuing white people in danger.

their members while reducing the risk of social loafing and conformity. In particular, they must avoid a problem called **groupthink,** the tendency for all members of the group to think alike and to suppress dissent.

According to Irving Janis (1982, 1989), groupthink occurs when a group's need for total agreement overwhelms its need to make the wisest decision, and when the members' needs to be liked and accepted overwhelm their ability to disagree with a bad decision. At least two instances of groupthink in American history resulted in disastrous military decisions. In 1961, President John F. Kennedy, after meeting with his advisers, approved a CIA plan to invade Cuba at the Bay of Pigs and overthrow the government of Fidel Castro; the invasion was a humiliating disaster. In the mid-1960s, President Lyndon Johnson and his cabinet escalated the war in Vietnam in spite of obvious signs that further bombing and increased troops were not bringing the war to an end.

groupthink In close-knit groups, the tendency for all members to think alike for the sake of harmony and to suppress dissent.

To analyze groupthink, Janis (1982) examined the historical records pertaining to these two decisions. He argued that groups that are susceptible to groupthink have several typical features: They are highly cohesive, are isolated from other viewpoints, feel under pressure from outside forces, and have a strong, directive leader. Under these conditions, the symptoms of groupthink tend to appear. These symptoms include:

- *An illusion of invulnerability.* The group believes that it can do no wrong, that it is 100 percent correct in its decisions.
- *Self-censorship.* Dissenters decide to keep quiet in order not to rock the boat, offend their friends, or risk being ridiculed. Arthur Schlesinger, one of Kennedy's advisers, later reported that he had grave doubts about the Bay of Pigs invasion, but he did not express them out of fear that "Others would regard it as presumptuous of him, a college professor, to take issue with august heads of major government institutions."
- *Direct pressure on dissenters to conform,* either by the leader or other group members. For example, President Johnson, who favored increased bombing of North Vietnam, ridiculed his adviser Bill Moyers by greeting him with "Well, here comes Mr. Stop-the-Bombing."
- *An illusion of unanimity.* Group members create an illusion of consensus by not inviting disagreement or calling on suspected dissenters. For example, Schlesinger did voice his doubts to the secretary of state, who passed them along to Kennedy, who was not pleased. When it came time to vote on whether to invade, Kennedy asked each of his advisers for their opinion—except Schlesinger.

The result of these symptoms of groupthink is faulty decision making. Group members not only suppress dissent within the group, but they also avoid getting any outside information from experts that might challenge their views. They avoid thinking of alternatives to the leader's initial preference, in order to stay in the leader's good graces. Instead of generating as many solutions to a problem as possible, they stick with the first one and then fail to examine this initial preference closely for errors or flaws. The result is that everyone remains in a "tight little ship," even if the ship is about to sink.

Groupthink can sometimes be counteracted, however, if conditions explicitly encourage and reward the expression of doubt and dissent (Janis, 1989); if group members are not worried about how others are evaluating them (Paulus & Dzindolet, 1993); and if the group's decision is based on majority rule instead of a demand for unanimity (Kameda & Sugimori, 1993). President Kennedy apparently learned a lesson from the Bay of Pigs decision. In his next major foreign policy decision, the Cuban missile crisis, he brought in outside experts to advise his inner circle, and he often absented himself from the group so as not to inhibit or influence their discussion (Aronson, Wilson, & Akert, 1997).

Some researchers dislike the term *groupthink* because, catchy and compelling though it is, they believe it oversimplifies the complexities of group decision making and implies that conformity and group cohesiveness are always bad. It is easy to see *retrospectively* how conformity contributes to making a bad decision, as Janis did. If we want to predict whether a group *will* make good or bad decisions in the future, however, we need to know a lot more about the group. We need to know, among other things, its history of decision making, the nature of the decision to be made, the characteristics of the leader, the context in which the group is making the decision, whether the group is permanent or temporary, and whether the group is subject to outside pressures (Aldag & Fuller, 1993). Nevertheless, Janis certainly put his finger on a phenomenon that many people have experienced in groups: individual members suppressing their real opinions and doubts so as to be good team players.

Many people assume that when it comes to making decisions, groups have a conservative influence on their members, isolating the extremists and imposing a moderate consensus. Yet, as the Bay of Pigs decision showed, sometimes groups make more extreme decisions than individuals do, a phenomenon called **group polarization.** Polarization does not mean that a group becomes split between two poles. It means that a group's *average decision* is more extreme than its members' *individual* decisions would be (Lord, Ross, & Lepper, 1979; Miller et al., 1993). Polarization, like groupthink, occurs partly because of social pressure to conform and to be liked. But it also occurs for several cognitive reasons, as people are exposed to others' views and new evidence, and as they become mentally engaged in arguing about a topic. First, some people intensify their opinions once they realize that others not only agree with them but also are even stronger in their convictions. Second, as people talk in a group, they may become aware of inconsistencies in their own thinking and resolve them in favor of a stronger, more extreme position (Chaiken & Yates, 1985). However, some people are initially neutral toward the topic in question; as they listen to the discussion, their own views may shift from neutral to moderate. This shift, which appears to add to the "group polarization" effect, actually reflects only the formation of an opinion (Kuhn & Lao, 1996).

One kind of group whose decisions have especially important consequences is the jury, 12 individuals who must agree on conviction or acquittal. What are the effects of group discussion on their collective decision? Usually, the verdict initially favored by a majority of the members is the one that eventually wins, as group polarization would predict. When the group is equally split, however, most juries show a *leniency bias:* The more the group talks, the more lenient its verdict. One reason is that jurors who favor acquittal are more influential than jurors who favor conviction. Why might this be so? The "reasonable doubt" standard—a person is innocent unless proven guilty beyond a reasonable doubt—favors acquittal; it is easier to raise one doubt than to refute all doubts. But when juries are instructed to arrive at a verdict based on "a preponderance of evidence that the defendant committed the crime," the leniency bias vanishes (MacCoun & Kerr, 1988). If you ever serve on a jury, you might keep these findings in mind.

Other researchers remind us that just as groups influence individuals, individuals influence groups (Wood et al., 1994). Considering, as Serge Moscovici (1985) put it, that the minority usually starts off being viewed as "deviant, incompetent, unreasonable, unappealing, and unattractive," how *does* it influence the group? Some effective methods have already been mentioned in this chapter; can you think of them? One is repetition. As repeated minority arguments become familiar, they seem less outrageous—an instance of the validity effect, perhaps, but also, sometimes, a sign that the idea does have validity. Recycling, for example, was once thought to be a weirdo radical extremist proposal, but today it is practiced by countless households and is an integral part of many cities' waste-management programs. Another strategy is to find allies in the group, which makes minority members seem less deviant or rebellious and their ideas more legitimate (Wood et al., 1994). By undermining the majority's complacency, dissenters may move the group to more independent and innovative ideas.

group polarization The tendency for a group's decision to be more extreme than its members' individual decisions.

COMPETITION AND COOPERATION

If you want to make some money, play the dollar auction with a few people you know. Everyone must bid for your dollar in 5-cent increases, and the auction is over when no one bids for 30 seconds. The catch is this: The second-highest bidder must also pay you, although he or she will get nothing in return. Usually, the bidding soon narrows to two competitors. After one of them has bid $1.00, the other decides to bid $1.05, because she would rather pay $1.05 for your dollar than give you $.95 for nothing. Following the same logic, the person who bid $1.00 decides to go to $1.10. By the time they quit, you may have won $5 or $6. Your bidders will have been sucked in by the nature of competition—and entrapment. Both will want to win; both will fear losing; both will try to save face. Had they thought of cooperation, however, they both would have won. The bidders could have agreed to set a limit on the bidding, say 45 cents, and split the profits.

During a competitive game, participants and spectators are involved and energized, and they have a good time. Competition in business and science can lead to better services and products and new inventions. Yet competition has some psychological hazards. When winning is everything, competitors may find no joy in being second or even in being in the activity at all. After reviewing the huge number of studies on the effects of competition, Alfie Kohn (1992) concluded that "The phrase *healthy competition* is a contradiction in terms." Competition, research shows, often decreases work motivation. It makes people feel insecure and anxious, even if they win; it fosters jealousy and hostility; and it can stifle achievement. In practice, businesses depend on cooperation among employees, and cooperation is often economically beneficial to all participants. In 1993, the three rival companies that had been competing for the right to develop high-definition television (HDTV) agreed to join forces to design a single approach. With that decision, they avoided litigation and disputes that would have delayed HDTV for years.

QUESTION ASSUMPTIONS

In the United States, most people assume that competition, in everything from the Little League to big business, is a good thing. Why, then, do some psychologists think that "healthy competition" is a contradiction in terms?

Years ago, Muzafer Sherif and his colleagues used a natural setting, a Boy Scout camp called Robbers Cave, to conduct an experiment on the effects of cooperation and competition (Sherif, 1958; Sherif et al., 1961). Sherif randomly assigned 11- and 12-year-old boys to two groups, the Eagles and the Rattlers. To build team spirit, he had each group work on communal projects, such as making a rope bridge and building a diving board. Sherif then put the teams in competition for prizes. During fierce games of football, baseball, and tug-of-war, the boys whipped up a competitive fever that spilled off of the playing fields. They began to raid each other's cabins, call each other names, and start fistfights. No one dared to have a friend from the opposite group. Before long, the Rattlers and the Eagles were as hostile toward each other as any two rival gangs fighting for turf, any two siblings fighting for a parent's attention, and any two nations fighting for dominance. Their hostility continued even when they were just sitting around together watching movies.

Then Sherif determined to undo the hostility he had created and to make peace between the Eagles and the Rattlers. The experimenters set up a series of predicaments in which both groups needed to work together to reach a desired goal. The boys had to cooperate to get the water-supply system working. They had to pool their resources to get a movie they all wanted to see. When the staff truck broke down on a camping trip, they all had to join forces to pull the truck up a steep hill and get it started again. This policy of *interdependence in reaching mutual goals* was highly successful in reducing the boys' competitiveness and hostility. The boys eventually made friends with their former enemies.

In the first stage of the Robbers Cave study, a harmonious atmosphere was created through cooperation and teamwork. On the left, the Rattlers build group solidarity by carrying canoes to the lake. In the second stage, competitive games such as tug-of-war (center) fostered stereotyping and hostility between the Rattlers and the Eagles. Finally, in stage three, cooperation was again established when the two groups had to work together to solve various problems, such as repairing the camp's water-supply system (right).

Interdependence has a similar effect in adult groups. When adults work together in a cooperative group in which teamwork is rewarded, they often like each other better and are less hostile than when they are competing for individual success (Deutsch, 1949, 1980). Cooperation causes people to think of themselves as members of one big group instead of two opposed groups, *us* and *them* (Gaertner et al., 1990). Organizational psychologists have found that in many companies, employees do better and their motivation is higher when they work in cooperative teams than when they work competitively or alone. For example, as we saw in Chapter 11, a successful alternative to the standard boring assembly line is to have factory employees work in groups and handle different aspects of assembling the product instead of one repeated routine.

Quick Quiz

You may cooperate with a classmate or assert your individuality in answering this quiz.

A. Identify which phenomenon—deindividuation, group polarization, diffusion of responsibility, or groupthink—is represented in each of the following situations.

1. The president's closest advisers are afraid to disagree with his views on arms negotiations.
2. You are at a Halloween party wearing a silly gorilla suit. When you see a chance to play a practical joke on the host, you do it.
3. You invite four friends out for pizza to help you decide the merits of a new job offer. After talking things over with them, you agree to quit your safe job for a new one that offers greater challenge but has a risk of failure.
4. Walking down a busy street, you see that fire has broken out in a store window. "Someone must have called the fire department," you say.

B. What strategy does the Robbers Cave study suggest for reducing hostility between groups?

Answers:

A. 1. groupthink 2. deindividuation 3. group polarization 4. diffusion of responsibility B. the fostering of interdependence in reaching mutual goals

Sometimes a lone dissenter can change history. In 1956 in Montgomery, Alabama, Rosa Parks, weary after a hard day's work, refused to give up her seat and move to the back of a bus as the segregation laws of the time required. She was arrested, fingerprinted, and convicted of violating the law. Her calm defiance touched off a boycott in which the black citizens of Montgomery refused to ride city buses. It took them over a year, but they won—and the civil rights movement began.

ALTRUISM AND DISSENT: THE CONDITIONS OF INDEPENDENT ACTION

Throughout history, men and women have often obeyed orders or conformed to ideas that they believed to be misguided or immoral; sometimes, however, as we noted at the beginning of this chapter, people have disobeyed such orders or gone against prevailing beliefs, and their actions have changed the course of history. Many blacks and whites disobeyed the laws of segregation. Many individuals have stopped conforming to traditional gender roles. Many men and women "blow the whistle" on practices they consider immoral or unfair, risking their jobs and friendships to do so (Glazer & Glazer, 1990).

Altruism, the willingness to take selfless or dangerous action on behalf of others, is in part a matter of personal belief and conscience. The Quakers and other white abolitionists who risked their lives to help blacks escape their captors before the Civil War did so because they believed in the inherent evil of slavery. In the former Soviet Union, a KGB officer named Viktor Orekhov secretly informed political dissidents of planned KGB action against them, thereby saving hundreds of people from arrests and grueling interrogations. Orekhov was eventually caught and spent eight years in a Soviet jail. On his release, he explained why he felt he had to help the protesters: "I was afraid that [unless I acted] my children would be ashamed of me" (Fogelman, 1994).

Studies of individuals who have saved the lives of others find that two motives sustained the rescuers: deeply held moral values or personal feelings for the victim (Fogelman, 1994; Oliner & Oliner, 1988). The second motive is obviously at work when someone rescues a friend or colleague whom they know and like. Sometimes, however, rescuers save people whom they consider boring, demanding, or otherwise unpleasant. In such cases, the rescuers' moral values—their belief in the importance of saving a human being in danger—supersede their personal feelings about the person being rescued.

However, just as there are many social and situational reasons for obedience and conformity, so there are many such influences on a person's decision to dissent, speak up for an unpopular opinion, or help a stranger in trouble. Instead of condemning bystanders and conformists for their laziness or cowardice, social psychologists investigate the social and situational factors that predict independent action.

For example, some have set up experimental situations in which they can vary the conditions under which a bystander observes another person in trouble: alone or with other people, when the victim is anonymous or when the bystander empathizes with the victim, and so forth (Dovidio, Allen, & Schroeder, 1990; Latané & Darley, 1976). Others have gone into the field and interviewed people in actual work settings. In one study, 8,587 federal government employees were asked whether they had observed any wrongdoing at work, whether they had told anyone about it, and what happened if they had told (Graham, 1986). Nearly half of the sample had observed some serious cases of wrongdoing, such as someone stealing federal funds, accepting bribes, or creating a situation that was dangerous to public safety. Of that half, 72 percent had done nothing at all. What made the rest different?

According to evidence from field and laboratory research, several factors predict independent action such as whistle-blowing and altruism:

1. *The individual perceives the need for intervention or help.* Many bystanders see no need to help someone in trouble. Sometimes this willful blindness is used to justify inaction. During World War II, the German citizens of Dachau didn't "see" the local concentration camp, although it was in plain view. Similarly, many employees choose not to see flagrant examples of bribery and other illegal actions.

Sometimes, however, the blindness is an inevitable result of screening out too many demands on attention. People who live in a big city cannot stop to offer help to everyone who seems to need it; people who have many demands on their time at work cannot stop to correct every problem they notice. A study of 36 small, medium, and large American cities found that the strongest predictor of whether people would help strangers with small favors (such as making change for a quarter or helping a person with a leg brace pick up a heavy stack of spilled magazines) was not population *size*, but population *density* (Levine et al., 1994). Density both increases the sensory overload on people and makes them more deindividuated.

Whether people interpret a situation as requiring their aid also depends on cultural rules. In northern European nations and in the United States, husband–wife disputes are considered strictly private; neighbors intervene at their peril. In one field study, bystanders observed a (staged) fight between a man and a woman. When the woman yelled, "Get away from me; I don't know you!" two-thirds of the bystanders went to help her. When she shouted, "Get away from me; I don't know why I ever married you!" only 19 percent tried to help (Shotland & Straw, 1976). In Mediterranean and Latin cultures, however, a dispute between any two people is considered fair game for anyone who is passing by. In fact, two people in a furious dispute might even rely on bystanders to intervene (Hall & Hall, 1990).

2. *The individual decides to take responsibility.* In a large crowd of observers or in a large organization, it is easy for people to avoid action. Crowds of anonymous people encourage the diffusion of responsibility because everyone assumes that someone else will take charge. When people are alone and hear someone call for help, they usually do intervene (Latané & Darley, 1976). Bystanders are also more likely to take responsibility when they are in a good mood—and when they are thinking of themselves as kind people (Brown & Smart, 1991). Similarly, whistle-blowers take personal responsibility for doing something about the ethical violations they observe.

3. *The individual decides that the costs of doing nothing outweigh the costs of getting involved.* The cost of helping or protesting might be embarrassment and wasted time or, more seriously, lost income, loss of friends, and even personal danger. The cost of not helping or remaining silent might be guilt, blame from others, loss of honor, or, in some tragic cases, responsibility for the injury or death of others. Although three courageous whistle-blowers from Rockwell International tried to inform NASA that the space shuttle *Challenger* was not safe, the NASA authorities remained silent. No one was prepared to take responsibility for the costly decision to postpone the launch. The price of their silence was an explosion that caused the deaths of the entire crew.

4. *The individual has an ally.* In Asch's conformity experiment, the presence of one other person who gave the correct answer was enough to overcome agreement with the incorrect majority. In Milgram's experiment too, the presence of a peer who disobeyed the experimenter's instruction to shock the learner sharply increased the number of subjects who also disobeyed. One dissenting member of a group may be viewed as a troublemaker, but two dissenting members are a coalition, and enough dissenting members can become a majority. Having an ally reassures a person of the rightness of the protest, and their combined efforts may eventually persuade others.

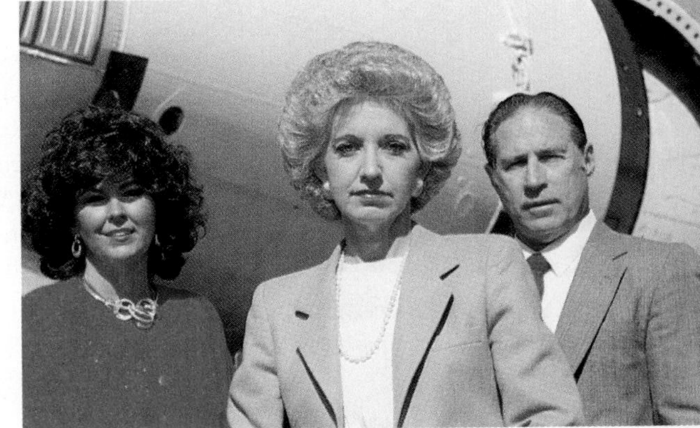

Three courageous whistle-blowers from Rockwell International—Ria Solomon, Sylvia Robins, and Al Bray—tried to inform NASA that the space shuttle Challenger *was not safe.*

5. *The individual becomes entrapped.* Once having taken the initial step of getting involved, most people will increase their commitment. In the study of federal employees who had witnessed wrongdoing, 28 percent reported the problem to their immediate supervisors. Once they had taken that step, nearly 60 percent eventually took the matter to higher authorities (Graham, 1986). Many non-Jewish rescuers of Jews said that once they had taken action to aid one person, even in a small way, they could not avoid helping others. Because they could be arrested or shot for helping one Jew, they reasoned, they might as well rescue as many as possible (Fogelman, 1994).

As you can see, independent action is not just a spontaneous or selfless expression of a desire to do the right thing. Certain social conditions make altruism and dissent more likely to occur, just as certain conditions suppress them. Some psychologists believe that all acts of helpfulness and moral protest are ultimately selfish, even if one person helps another in order to feel like a moral and decent soul. Others argue that life is full of countless illustrations of true altruism, in which people help others out of empathy and concern, without weighing costs or benefits at all (Batson, 1990). Are you suspicious of the motives of rescuers, whistle-blowers, and others who follow conscience over safety? How do you think you would behave if you were faced with a conflict between social pressure and conscience? Could you ever be a hero? (For a discussion of this question, see "Puzzles of Psychology.")

Quick Quiz

Imagine that you are chief executive officer of a new electric-car company. You want your employees to feel free to offer suggestions and criticisms, and to inform managers if they find any evidence that your cars are unsafe, even if that means delaying production. What concepts from this chapter could you use in setting company policy?

Answers:

Some possibilities: Set up cooperative production teams based on teamwork rather than competition; reward individual innovation and suggestions by paying attention to them and implementing the best ones; encourage and acknowledge deviant ideas; stimulate commitment to the task (building a car that will solve the world's pollution problem); establish a written policy to protect whistle-blowers. What else can you think of?

Adolf Eichmann at his trial. Was he a "monster"?

THE QUESTION OF HUMAN NATURE

A man was on trial for murder, although he personally had never killed anyone. Six psychiatrists examined him and pronounced him sane. His family life was normal, and he had deep feelings of love for his wife, children, and parents. Two observers, after reviewing transcripts of his 275-hour interrogation, described him as "an average man of middle class origins and normal middle class upbringing, a man without identifiable criminal tendencies" (Von Lang & Sibyll, 1984).

The man was Adolf Eichmann, a high-ranking officer of the Nazi SS (an elite military unit of storm troopers). Eichmann supervised the deportation and death of millions of Jews during World War II. He was proud of his efficiency and his ability to resist the temptation to feel pity for his victims. But he insisted he was not anti-Semitic: He had had a Jewish mistress, and he personally arranged for the protection of his Jewish half-cousin—two dangerous crimes for an SS officer. Shortly before his execution by hanging, Eichmann said, "I am not the monster I am made out to be. I am the victim of a fallacy" (R. Brown, 1986).

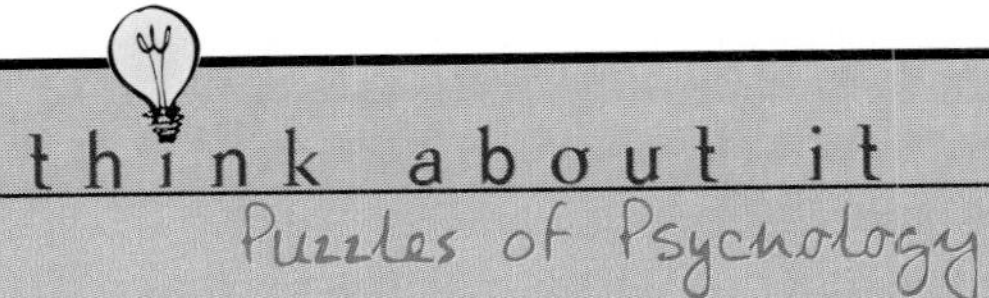

Could You Be a Hero—and Should You Be?

• You are working for an organization that you like very much. Your job is to supervise the safe installation of toxic-waste cleanup systems. But after a while, you learn that your immediate supervisor is taking bribes from companies that do not want to pay the cost of cleaning up their wastes. What will you do?

• You are witness to a violent crime in a grocery store. The robber sees you and threatens your life if you identify him. When the police arrive to question witnesses, what will you do?

• You are home one evening watching TV and hear a commotion in the street outside. You look outside and see a man attacking a woman. What will you do?

In truth, none of us knows how we would behave in an emergency or when faced with a moral dilemma. The lesson of social psychology is that in many situations, group pressure, conformity, and the power of social roles will influence people's behavior more than their attitudes or preferences will. This is why psychiatrists and laypeople alike were so wildly wrong in their predictions about how many people would "go all the way" in the Milgram experiment: They overlooked the compelling nature of social roles and obedience to authority. If you were to predict your behavior based on the statistics for most people, you would keep quiet about your employer's illegal behavior, lie to the police, and go back to watching television without even calling 911.

Perhaps for this reason, many people question the motives of rescuers, Good Samaritans, whistle-blowers, and others who take action in a crisis. When Eva Fogelman (1994) began lecturing on the non-Jewish rescuers of Jews during the Holocaust, she noticed that her stories "had a disquieting effect on many listeners. Rescuers' altruistic behavior throws people off balance by calling into question their own vision of themselves as good people. As they listen, they cannot help but wonder: What would I have done? Would I have had the courage to defy authority? Would I have risked my life? My family's lives?" She added,

> *General audiences listened, they wondered, and they doubted their own capacity for selfless action. This discomfort, in turn, led to a disbelief that anyone could engage in altruistic behavior. People looked for ulterior motives. . . . "What's the angle?" they want to know. Many young people simply do not believe that there were then, or are today, individuals who do not put their own concerns first.*

The decision to rescue someone in trouble, blow the whistle on wrongdoing, or help the needy is not an easy matter of right or wrong. In big cities across the nation and increasingly in small towns, helping strangers in trouble can sometimes be dangerous, even fatal. A passerby in San Francisco intervened in an angry dispute between two men in the street and was stabbed to death as a consequence; he had interrupted a quarrel between drug dealers. In cities where homeless persons number in the thousands, many people are feeling "compassion fatigue": How many can they help? What kind of help is best? It is easier to be a whistle-blower or to protest a company policy when you know it will be easy to find another job, but what if jobs in your field are scarce and you have a family to support?

As this chapter shows, people can end up doing all sorts of harmful things they would never have predicted doing, and then call on self-serving attributions, excuses, and belief in a just world to rationalize their behavior. On the other hand, people can also end up doing all sorts of helpful and courageous things they would never have imagined doing. What anyone does in a given situation depends on a particular constellation of personal beliefs and perceptions, personality traits, and aspects of the situation itself. This is why a man may leap into a frozen river to rescue a child on Monday and embezzle money from his company on Friday.

So: *Would* you blow the whistle on your boss, tell the truth to the police although worried about your safety, and call 911 when you see a fight? What aspects of the situation would influence your responses, and what aspects of your own personality and beliefs? Can you imagine situations in which you could not live with yourself if you failed to help, and if so, what are they? Do you agree with Eva Fogelman that some people truly are humanitarian and selfless in their willingness to rescue others in distress, or do you side with the skeptics who want to know "What's the angle?" Think about it.

The fallacy to which Eichmann referred was the widespread belief that a person who does monstrous deeds must be a monster—someone sick and evil. But as we have seen, otherwise good people can and do behave in monstrous ways. When philosopher Hannah Arendt (1963) wrote about the trial of Adolf Eichmann, she used the phrase "the banality of evil" to describe this phenomenon. (*Banal* means "commonplace" or "unoriginal.") Eichmann and his fellow Nazis were ordinary men, Arendt wrote, just doing their jobs.

DEFINE YOUR TERMS

People often disagree about whether human beings are basically cooperative and good or selfish and cruel. With the question stated that way, the only answer is both—or neither. What would be a better question and a more useful answer?

The compelling evidence for the banality of evil is, perhaps, the hardest lesson in psychology. Most people want to believe that harm to others is done only by evil people who are bad down to their bones. It is reassuring to divide the world into those who are good or bad, kind or cruel, moral or immoral. Yet perfectly nice people often behave in brutal, conforming, and mindless ways if the situation demands it. From the standpoint of social psychology, such universal problems as mob violence, bystander apathy, and groupthink are not a result of human nature but of human social organization. They are a result of the *normal psychological processes* discussed in this chapter, such as adherence to roles, obedience to authority, vulnerability to self-serving biases, conformity, entrapment, deindividuation, and competition.

This is good news and bad news. The bad news is that bad behavior cannot be eliminated by getting rid of a few "bad" people or nations, because the conditions that produce deindividuation, groupthink, and war will always be with us. The good news is that situations can be created that encourage considerate and helpful behavior, independent action, and constructive dissent. If social conditions have created the banality of evil, others can be used to foster the "banality of virtue"—everyday acts of kindness, selflessness, and generosity.

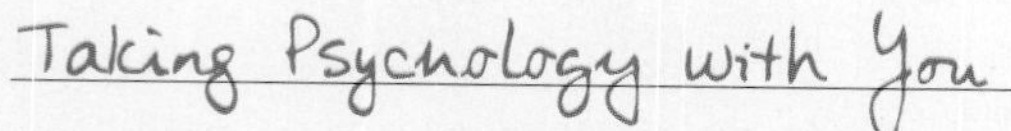

Swimming in a Sea of Ads

From time to time, we ask our classes to do a seemingly simple field study: From the time you get up to the time you go to sleep, count the number of ads you see or hear. Include television and radio, junk mail, newspaper ads, and telemarketers who call you up, of course, but also hidden ads such as posters on the sides of buses and giant product names on T-shirts and on the walls surrounding sports arenas. If you try this assignment, chances are that you won't finish it: There are just too many ads to count. Indeed, in a single day, the average American encounters hundreds of them.

In a nation dominated by advertising, where so many groups are trying to get you to buy their product—whether their product is soap, cereal, a candidate for political office, a ballot proposition, or support for a cause—how can you determine which ads are useful and which are manipulative? Social psychologists have discovered not only which kinds of ads are effective and for which people, but also how you can resist manipulation (Aronson, Wilson, & Akert, 1997; Cialdini, 1993; Pratkanis & Aronson, 1992):

- *Beware of the validity effect.* Are you feeling favorably inclined toward a product or candidate simply because you have heard the name a zillion times? Test yourself by asking what you actually know about the product's unique benefits or the candidate's actual voting record. For example, is there any difference in the ingredients of generic drugs and brand-name drugs? Are you as informed about the voting record and political goals of candidates who don't have as much money to spend on their campaigns as the most familiar candidate does?

- *Assess your actual need for the product.* Early in this century, a man named Gerald Lambert inherited a company that made an antiseptic for treating throat infections. The product was called Listerine. Lambert decided to expand the market for Listerine by promoting it as a mouthwash. Trouble was, nobody used mouthwash in those days, so Lambert had to invent a reason for them to do it. He made up a medical-sounding term to describe bad breath—"halitosis"—and advertised Listerine as the cure for it. His ads played on people's insecurities about their personal hygiene, health, and attractiveness. So do many ads today. For example, ads for "rejuvenation" creams, which often claim to contain miracle ingredients with scientific-sounding labels, take advantage of people's fears of aging.

- *Beware of emotion-based advertising and political campaigns.* Many ads for practical products such as computers, air conditioners, and cameras are useful; they tell you about the product's price, reliability, and quality. But choosing a particular brand of jeans, perfume, athletic shoes, or cola is mostly a matter of personal taste. So, to win your allegiance, advertisers associate these products with happy emotions, a cool lifestyle, sexiness, and good looks. In other words, they try to generate emotional responses in you that have nothing to do with the product itself. One ad campaign was designed to get young men to drink diet cola. This was a challenge: Diet cola is not a macho drink! So the ad showed a handsome, suitably macho construction worker with an officeful of women ogling him as he took his diet-cola break.

Many political campaigns increasingly are based on invoking emotions—fear of crime, fear and hatred of outsiders, passionate reactions to hot-button topics such as the death penalty—rather than providing information. Often, these ads tell a single inflammatory story, such as one about a paroled felon who commits rape or murder, to accuse the opposition of being "soft on crime." But critical thinkers should be wary of arguing by anecdote and should not be swayed by one story, no matter how sensational or infuriating it is.

• *Think critically about conformity and peer pressure.* As we have seen, the desire to feel part of a group is universal and necessary in human societies. Some ads, however, play on people's insecurities about being outsiders. The result is that many people buy products they don't need or can't afford in the hopes that the product will help them fit in.

• *Be mindful.* The bottom line in evaluating any message designed to persuade you to change your mind, buy a product, or vote for a candidate is to keep your wits about you. In *The Age of Propaganda,* Anthony Pratkanis and Elliot Aronson (1992) suggest the kinds of mindful questions people can ask that will help inoculate them against manipulative messages: "What does the source of the communication have to gain? Why are these choices being presented to me in this manner? Are there other options and other ways of presenting those options? What would happen if I chose something other than the recommended option? What are the arguments for the other side?"

We do not wish to imply that all advertising is misleading or fraudulent, and that you should believe nothing you hear. On the contrary, many ads contain useful information. Without ads, new products could never get a foothold in the noisy marketplace, and unknown candidates could never become visible to voters. The effort to persuade is itself neither good nor bad. Persuasive tactics can be used to twist the facts or to expose the facts. The goal is to use ads wisely, and not to let them use you.

SUMMARY

ROLES AND RULES

1) Social psychology is the study of people in social context, including the influence of *norms, roles,* and groups on behavior and cognition. Three classic studies illustrate the power of roles to affect individual actions. In Zimbardo's prison study, college students quickly fell into the role of "prisoner" or "guard." In Rosenhan's mental-hospital study, the role of staff member caused nurses and psychiatrists to *depersonalize* patients and sometimes treat them harshly. In Milgram's obedience study, most people in the role of "teacher" inflicted what they thought was extreme shock on another person because of the authority of the experimenter.

2) Obedience to authority has many important positive functions for the smooth running of society, but obedience can lead to actions that are deadly, foolish, or illegal. People follow orders because of the obvious consequences of disobedience, out of respect for authority, and to gain advantages. Even when they would rather not, they may obey because they believe the authority is *legitimate;* because the role is *routinized* into duties that are performed mindlessly; because they are embarrassed to break the rules of good manners and lack a *language of protest* to do so; or because they have been *entrapped.* Entrapment can lead to increasingly aggressive or self-defeating actions by individuals and nations.

SOCIAL COGNITION: ATTRIBUTIONS AND ATTITUDES

3) According to *attribution theory,* people are motivated to search for causes to which they attribute their own and other people's behavior. These attributions may be *situational* or *dispositional.* The *fundamental attribution error* occurs when people overestimate personality traits as a cause of behavior and underestimate the influence of the situation. A *self-serving bias* allows people to take credit for their good deeds and excuse their own mistakes by blaming the situation. According to the *just-world hypothesis,* most people need to believe that the world is fair and that people get what they deserve. To preserve this belief, they may blame the victim for inviting injustice.

4) People have many *attitudes*, which include cognitions and feelings about a subject. Some attitudes are casual opinions; others are based on carefully elaborated convictions. One important influence on attitudes is a person's age *cohort* and the corresponding experiences that shape the person's *generational identity*. Another influence is the *validity effect:* Simply hearing a statement over and over again makes it seem more believable. Techniques of attitude change include associating a product or message with someone who is famous, attractive, or expert, and linking the product with good feelings. Fear tactics tend to backfire. Attitudes dispose people to behave in certain ways, but sometimes a change of behavior causes attitudes to change.

5) Some methods of attitude change are intentionally manipulative rather than persuasive. Tactics of *coercive persuasion* include putting a person under extreme distress; defining problems simplistically; offering the appearance of unconditional love and acceptance in exchange for unquestioning loyalty; creating a new identity for the person; using entrapment; and controlling access to outside information.

INDIVIDUALS AND GROUPS

6) In groups, individuals often behave differently than they would on their own. They may conform to social pressure because they identify with a group, trust the group's judgment or knowledge, hope for personal gain, or wish to be liked. But they also may conform mindlessly and self-destructively, violating their own preferences and values because "Everyone else is doing it."

7) *Diffusion of responsibility* in a group can lead to inaction on the part of individuals—to *bystander apathy*, and, in work groups, *social loafing*. The most extreme instances of the diffusion of responsibility occur in *deindividuation*, when people lose awareness of their individuality. Deindividuation increases under conditions of anonymity.

8) Groups that are isolated from different views, are under outside pressure, have strong leaders, and are cohesive are vulnerable to *groupthink*, the tendency of group members to think alike, censor themselves, actively suppress disagreement, and feel that their decisions are invulnerable. Groupthink often produces faulty decisions because group members fail to seek disconfirming evidence for their ideas. In *group polarization*, the group's collective decision is more extreme than its members' private decisions. However, groups can be structured to counteract these processes. Also, people who hold minority opinions can influence the larger group by repeating their arguments persuasively and by finding allies.

9) Competition can lead to better services and products and new inventions, but it can also increase hostility, stereotyping, and aggression between groups; decrease work motivation; and make people feel insecure. Conflict and hostility between groups can be reduced by teamwork and by *interdependence* in working for mutual goals.

ALTRUISM AND DISSENT: THE CONDITIONS OF INDEPENDENT ACTION

10) In the social-psychological view, mob violence, bystander apathy, groupthink, and deindividuation stem from the structure of groups, and so solutions must involve restructuring groups and situations rather than just fixing individuals. Although the willingness to speak up for an unpopular opinion, blow the whistle, or help a stranger in trouble is in part a matter of personal belief and conscience, several social and situational factors are also important. These include seeing a need for help, deciding to take responsibility, having an ally, weighing the costs of getting involved, and becoming entrapped in a commitment.

THE QUESTION OF HUMAN NATURE

11) Although it is commonly believed that only bad people do bad deeds, the principles of social psychology show that under certain conditions, good people can be induced to do bad things. By themselves, roles, obedience, conformity, self-serving biases, entrapment, deindividuation, groupthink, and competition are neutral; they can be used for good or ill.

KEY TERMS

social psychology 654
cultural psychology 654
norms (social) 655
role 655
depersonalization 658
routinization 662
"language of protest" 663
entrapment 663
social cognition 664
attribution theory 664
situational attributions 664
dispositional attributions 664
fundamental attribution error 665
self-serving bias 666
just-world hypothesis 667
blaming the victim 667
attitude 667
cohort 668
generational identity 668
cognitive dissonance 669
validity effect 669
coercive persuasion 670
diffusion of responsibility 674
bystander apathy 674
social loafing 674
deindividuation 674
groupthink 677
group polarization 679
leniency bias 679
altruism 682
banality of evil 685

As the traveler who has once been from home
is wiser than he who has never left his own doorstep,
so a knowledge of one other culture should sharpen our ability
to scrutinize more steadily, to appreciate more lovingly, our own.

Margaret Mead

CHAPTER EIGHTEEN
The Cultural Context

Yoshihiro Hattori and his friends.

IN A SUBURB OF BATON ROUGE, LOUISIANA, in October 1992, Yoshihiro Hattori, a 16-year-old Japanese exchange student, went along with his friend Webb Haymaker to a Halloween party. They mistakenly stopped in front of a house covered in Halloween decorations and rang the bell. Hearing no answer, Yoshihiro went around the side of the house to see whether the party might be in the backyard. The home owner, Bonnie Peairs, opened the front door, saw Webb (in a Halloween costume), and then saw Yoshihiro running back toward her waving an object (which turned out to be a camera). She panicked and called for her husband to get his gun. Rodney Peairs grabbed a loaded .44 Magnum and shouted at Yoshihiro to "freeze." Yoshihiro, not understanding the word, did not stop. Peairs shot him in the heart, killing him instantly. Little more than a minute passed between the time that Yoshihiro Hattori rang the doorbell and the time that Rodney Peairs shot him to death.

When the case came to trial, the jury acquitted Rodney Peairs of manslaughter after only three hours of deliberation.

If ever a tragic misunderstanding illustrated the power of cultural differences, this one is it. To the Japanese news media, the story illustrated everything that is wrong with America. In their view, it is a nation rife with guns and violence—a "developing nation," as one commentator put it, that is still growing out of its Wild-West past. Japanese television reporters, in amazement, showed their viewers American gun stores, restaurants that display guns on the walls, and racks of gun magazines. The Japanese cannot imagine a nation in which private individuals are allowed to keep guns. In the entire nation of Japan each year, only some 70 people are killed with guns, almost all of them members of organized crime; in the United States, a person is fatally shot every 16 minutes.

"I think for Japanese the most remarkable thing is that you could get a jury of Americans together, and they could conclude that shooting someone before you even talked to him was reasonable behavior," Masako Notoji, a professor of American cultural studies in Tokyo, told *The New York Times* (May 25, 1993). "We are more civilized. We rely on words." Yet the citizens of Baton Rouge were surprised that the case came to trial at all. What is more right and natural, they said, than protecting yourself and your family from intruders? "A man's home is his castle," said one potential juror, expressing puzzlement that Peairs had even been arrested. "That's my question—why [was he arrested]?" A local man, joining the many sympathizers of Rodney Peairs, said, "It would be to me what a normal person would do under those circumstances."

Bonnie Peairs wept on the witness stand. "There was no thinking involved," she said. "I wish I could have thought. If I could have just thought."

The clash of American and Japanese cultures, which is so clear in this sad case, shows why it is important to understand what culture means and how it influences us. Although we have been describing research on culture throughout this book—for example, in discussions of thinking and intelligence (Chapter 8), emotion (Chapter 10), child development (Chapter 13), and psychotherapy (Chapter 16)—actually defining it is easier said than done. As cross-cultural psychologist Walter Lonner (1995) observes, "It ranks right up there with truth, beauty, justice, and intelligence as abstract and fuzzy constructs whose precise definitions challenge even the most insightful thinkers."

culture A program of shared rules that govern the behavior of members of a community or society, and a set of values, beliefs, and attitudes shared by most members of that community.

Lonner himself and most other researchers, however, would agree that **culture** can be defined as (1) a program of shared rules that govern the behavior of members of a community or society, and (2) a set of values, beliefs, and attitudes shared by most members of that community. Every culture includes a system of rules, passed from one generation to another, for just about everything in the human-made environment: for getting along with other people, for raising children, for making decisions, and for using artifacts (e.g., an ax or a computer) and symbols (e.g., written words, gestures, or painted images) (Cole, 1990; Lonner, 1995; Lonner & Malpass, 1994; Shweder, 1990).

Cultural psychologists study the many ways in which people are affected by the rules of the culture in which they live; for example, they might study how American cultural values such as independence or youthfulness affect people's behavior, beliefs, and self-esteem. *Cross-cultural psychologists* compare different societies, searching for both their commonalities and their distinctive cultural differences (Berry et al., 1997). For example, they might study several cultures to determine whether Piaget's stages of cognitive development are universal (see Chapter 13), or compare cultural attitudes toward math ability in Japan and in the United States to see whether these attitudes result in different levels of math performance (they do, as we saw in Chapter 8). Both of these fields overlap somewhat with *cultural anthropology*, the study of customs within and across human cultures, and indeed we will be reporting some research from anthropologists. Anthropologists, however, tend to study the economy and customs of a cultural unit as a whole, whereas cultural psychologists are more interested in how culture affects individual psychological processes such as reasoning abilities, child development, or motivation.

Until recently, most Western psychologists were uninterested in the influence of culture on individuals. In contrast to biology, which they treated as real and tangible, they regarded culture as merely a light veneer on human behavior, or perhaps a source of information for tourist travel ("In Spain, people eat dinner at 10 P.M."). As a result, students and teachers knew little about the psychological characteristics of people living in other societies, and they assumed that they could generalize from studies of people in their own culture to people everywhere (Berry et al., 1997; Matsumoto, 1996).

Today most psychologists recognize that culture is just as powerful an influence on human behavior as is any biological process. In fact, culture affects biological processes. Everyone needs to eat, for instance, but culture affects how often people eat, what they eat, and with whom they eat. Depending on your culture, you might eat lots of little meals throughout the day or only one large meal. You will eat food that your culture calls delicious—whale meat in Inuit communities, lizards in South America, locusts in Africa, horses in France, dogs in Asia—and you are likely to find everyone else's food preferences disgusting. You won't eat foods that your culture calls taboo: pigs among Muslims and Orthodox Jews, cows in India, horses in America, deer among the Tapirapé (Harris, 1985). And your culture affects your choice of dining companions. People don't eat with those they consider their social inferiors, which in various cultures includes servants, employees, women, or children.

These cultural influences on a process as essential as eating can cause people to eat when they aren't hungry (to be sociable) or not to eat when they *are* hungry (because the company or food is culturally "unappetizing"). Sometimes, cultural pressures conflict directly with biological dispositions. Evolution has programmed women to maintain a reserve of fat necessary for healthy childbearing, nursing, and, after menopause, the production and storage of the hormone estrogen. And, as we saw in Chapter 3, genes influence body shape and weight. Yet the contemporary cultural ideal for many American women is a boyishly slim body, an ideal that is by no means universal across cultures or across historical epochs. The result of the battle between biological design and cultural standards is that many women are obsessed with weight, continually dieting, excessively exercising, or suffering from eating disorders such as *anorexia nervosa* (self-starvation) or *bulimia* (bingeing and vomiting) (Rodin, Silberstein, & Striegel-Moore, 1990; Silverstein & Perlick, 1995).

Trying to understand a culture other than your own poses interesting problems. You are by definition an outsider, with different clothes, customs, and attitudes. Researchers must find a balance between empathizing with the people they are studying and retaining their own objectivity.

If culture can so powerfully affect a person's beliefs about what is proper behavior, you can imagine why misunderstandings between cultures are so frequent. "Many people have the well-meaning delusion that if they could only get to know people in another culture, they would realize how alike they are," said anthropologist Edward T. Hall. "The truth is that the more you get to know people from another culture, the more you realize how *different* they are" (quoted in Tavris, 1987). In this chapter, we will try to show you what Hall meant.

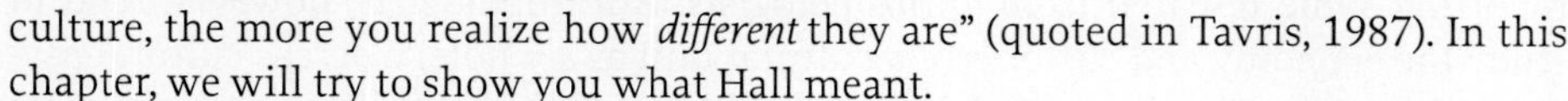

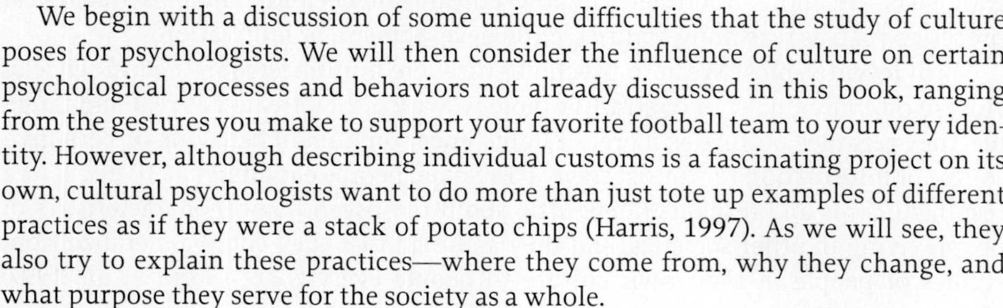

We begin with a discussion of some unique difficulties that the study of culture poses for psychologists. We will then consider the influence of culture on certain psychological processes and behaviors not already discussed in this book, ranging from the gestures you make to support your favorite football team to your very identity. However, although describing individual customs is a fascinating project on its own, cultural psychologists want to do more than just tote up examples of different practices as if they were a stack of potato chips (Harris, 1997). As we will see, they also try to explain these practices—where they come from, why they change, and what purpose they serve for the society as a whole.

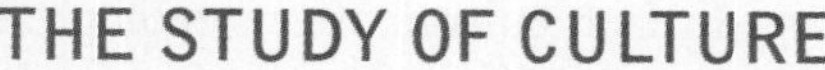

THE STUDY OF CULTURE

The study of culture is challenging for methodological and psychological reasons. Four issues in particular make this kind of research different from other methods and approaches in psychology (van de Vijver & Leung, 1996).

1. *The problem of methods and samples.* Devising good methods and getting good samples is difficult enough when you are studying just one culture; these tasks are even more daunting when you are dealing with many societies and hope to make cultural comparisons. Right off the bat, you have to worry about linguistic equivalence: You must make sure that your questionnaires and interviews convey the same meanings in every language. This is hard to do. The meaning of "Mary had a little lamb" is obvious to an English speaker, who knows that she owned the lamb and did not give birth to it, eat it, or have an affair with it! But translations can be difficult. Sometimes a concept that is tremendously important in one culture cannot easily be translated into an equivalent term in another culture. The Chinese Value Survey, for instance, contains items that seem strange to many Westerners, such as "filial piety," defined as "honoring of ancestors and obedience to, respect for, and financial support of parents" (Hofstede & Bond, 1988).

Further, cross-cultural psychologists must consider more complex criteria in selecting their samples than researchers working within one culture: societal (How many societies or cultures should I have?), community (How many groups within each society do I need?), individual (How many individuals within each community shall I select?), and behavioral (Which specific actions or attitudes should I measure?) (Lonner & Malpass, 1994).

Some cultural differences can be measured indirectly, by drawing inferences from data about collective behavior, such as the frequency of domestic violence, traffic accidents, or suicides (Smith & Bond, 1994). In New York, for example, almost everyone jaywalks, but in German cities almost no one jaywalks, a finding that implies a cultural difference in attitudes toward breaking a law governing public behavior. However, indirect measurements can be ambiguous: Perhaps the jaywalking difference doesn't reflect attitudes toward the law but the density of pedestrians and the number of cars per clogged street. For this reason, many cross-cultural psychologists prefer to use direct measures, such as questionnaires or observations of *matched samples* of respondents from different countries. Matching means that an effort is made to study samples of individuals who are similar in all aspects of their lives except their nationality, including age, socioeconomic status, and education.

2. *The problem of interpreting results.* Once you have your findings from two or more cultures, you then have to think about how to interpret them. A custom in one culture might not have the same meaning or purpose as the same practice elsewhere. For example, the circumcision of male babies has a religious purpose among Jews and serves to strengthen identification with the group, but the same practice became widespread in Europe and America during the Victorian era for a very different reason: It was (mistakenly) believed that circumcised boys wouldn't masturbate and thus succumb to "masturbatory insanity" (Paige & Paige, 1981). In addition, a custom may persist long after its original function or intention has been abandoned. Circumcision continued in North America, but not in Europe, decades after masturbatory insanity was forgotten as its rationale, because the medical establishment endorsed the procedure in the name of hygiene.

3. *The problem of stereotyping.* A third problem in studying culture is how to describe average differences across societies without stereotyping. As one student of ours put it, "How come when we students speak of 'the' Japanese or 'the' blacks or 'the' whites or 'the' Latinos, it's called stereotyping, and when you do it, it's called 'cross-cultural psychology'?" This question shows excellent critical thinking! The study of culture does not rest on the assumption, implicit in stereotypes, that *all* members of a culture behave the same way. (Later in this chapter, we will discuss the nature of stereotypes.) As we have seen in this book, individuals vary according to their temperaments, beliefs, and learning histories, and this variation occurs within every culture (see Figure 18.1). Just as people play their social roles differently, they read their cultural scripts differently. But the fact that individuals vary within a culture does not negate the

ASK QUESTIONS

Cultural psychologists often use terms such as "the" Japanese or "the" Canadians. What is the difference, if any, between such convenient generic labels and stereotyping?

The same behavior may have different functions in different cultures. For the Yanomamo Indians, nose piercing is a part of normal facial decoration and display, but a Westerner might do it to be unusual, rebellious, or shocking.

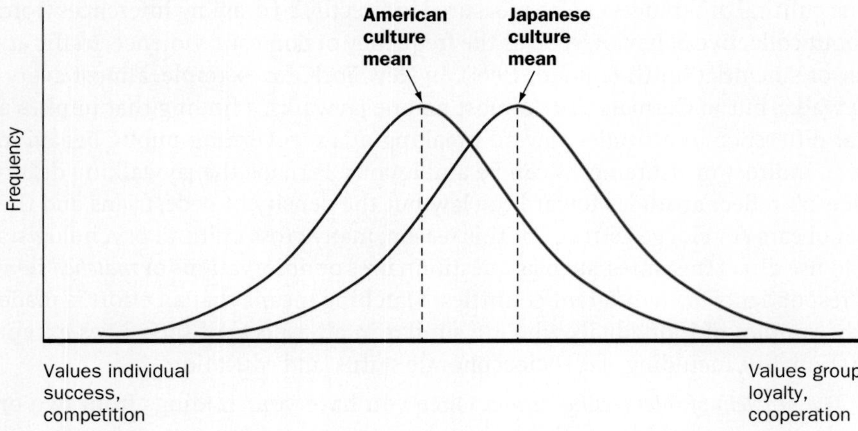

Figure 18.1
Hypothetical Distributions of Values in Two Cultures

Whenever cultural psychologists speak of differences between two cultures, they are really describing average differences. There is always overlap among individuals.

existence of cultural rules that, *on the average*, make Swedes different from Bedouins or Cambodians different from Italians.

However, if researchers bring preexisting stereotypes to their studies, what they expect to find may be what they get. For example, all over the world, men are more physically violent and aggressive than women (we will discuss some cultural explanations for this difference later in this chapter). Yet the stereotype that "men are aggressive" and "women are nurturant" has caused numerous researchers to overlook the many examples of male nurturance and female aggression in every culture. When David Gilmore (1990) examined how cultures define manhood, he expected to find masculinity equated with selfishness and hardness. Yet by resisting this stereotype, he was able to see that masculinity frequently entails generosity and sacrifice. Men nurture their families and society, he observed, by "bringing home food for both child and mother . . . and by dying if necessary in faraway places to provide a safe haven for their people." Similarly, people who have a stereotype of women as nurturant may miss evidence of female aggressiveness. Women are as aggressive as men when aggression is defined as saying intentionally hurtful things; slapping, kicking, biting, or throwing objects during disputes; abusing and humiliating their children; having bellicose attitudes toward their perceived enemies; and supporting and participating in war, in whatever ways their societies have permitted (Campbell, 1993; Crick & Grotpeter, 1995; Elshtain, 1987; Gelles & Straus, 1988).

The moral is that we can study and talk about average differences between groups, but we should try to do so without implying that the groups are as different as chocolate and cheese—or, as one pop-psych book title grandiosely asserts, that *Men Are from Mars, Women Are from Venus.*

4. *The reification of culture.* To *reify* means to regard an intangible process, such as a feeling, as if it were a literal object. For example, when people say, "I have a lot of anger buried in me," they are reifying anger—treating it as a thing that sits inside them like a kidney, instead of as a cluster of mental and physical reactions that come and go. Those who study culture must avoid the tendency to reify it—that is, to regard "culture" as an explanation without identifying the specific mechanisms or aspects of culture that influence behavior. To say "The Japanese work hard because of their culture" or "The Americans are violent because of their culture" shows circular reasoning. Using a label as an explanation, observe Lonner and Malpass (1994), is like telling a man with a leg injury that he can't walk because he is lame. We may observe that Culture A behaves more aggressively than Culture B, but we don't get to say that Culture A frequently attacks its neighbors because it is a warlike culture. Instead, we need to ask what is going on in Culture A that makes it different from Culture B. "To say that the difference is cultural," say Lonner and Malpass, "just means that we have to look for the explanation in the details of how people live."

As if these methodological problems in the study of culture were not enough, we then have to deal with the political and emotional sensitivity of many cross-cultural findings. It is often difficult for people to talk about cultural differences when they feel uncomfortable and suspicious about other groups and defensive about their own. Emotions run high. For example, some time ago, we were talking with students about average differences in the kinds of questions that southern African-American adults and white adults ask children. (This interesting study was discussed in Chapter 8.) Later, a white student came up to us and asked why we had "trashed" the white parents, and a black student argued that the study was invalid because no one *she* knew in *her* southern community talked to children that way. Both of these students were letting their tensions about race get in the way of their ability to hear the point of the research. Of course we weren't trashing the white parents or the black parents; neither was the study's author. But the students were unable to distinguish an objective difference from a value judgment. No one said that one parental style was better than the other, but these students heard it that way.

Social and cultural psychologists have studied why discussions of culture so often deteriorate into judgmental and emotional language, and why so many people assume that their own culture is the best. Must cultural differences always be sources of conflict and misunderstanding, or can people learn to accept them? And must differences always be evaluated in terms of better and worse, or can they just be . . . differences?

Quick Quiz

Students from all cultures should be able to answer this quiz.

1. Dr. Livingston does research on Americans' habit of moving frequently and how it affects their attitudes toward friendship and sociability. Dr. Livingston can best be described as a (cultural/cross-cultural) psychologist.
2. Like eating, sleeping is a biological process that is influenced in many ways by culture. Can you think of some of those ways?

3. Several decades ago, a study compared arranged marriages in Japan with marriages for love in the United States; after 10 years of married life, the groups did not differ in their self-rankings of marital satisfaction and marital love. What might be a problem in interpreting these findings?

Answers:

1. cultural 2. Culture affects what time people go to sleep and get up in the morning; the kind of bed, cot, or mat they sleep on; what they wear (if anything); whether they rely on an artificial signal (e.g., an alarm clock) to wake them up; whether they permit their infants or older children to sleep with them; and whether they take afternoon naps. (This list is not exhaustive.) 3. One problem is that "satisfaction" and "love" might have had different meanings in the two cultures or might have been measured in different ways.

THE RULES OF CULTURE

People learn their culture's rules as effortlessly as they learn its language. Just as they can speak without being able to state the rules of grammar, most people follow their culture's prescriptions without being consciously aware of them. In this section, we will consider some of those invisible rules.

CONTEXT AND COMMUNICATION

Fiorello LaGuardia, who was mayor of New York from 1933 to 1945, was fluent in three languages: English, Italian, and Yiddish. LaGuardia knew more than the words of those languages; he also knew the gestures that went along with each one. Researchers who studied films of his speeches could tell which language he was speaking with the sound turned off! They could do so by reading his *body language*, the nonverbal signals of body movement, posture, gesture, and gaze that people constantly express (Birdwhistell, 1970). Italians and Jews embellish their speech with circular movements of their arms and hands, and by measuring the radius of those movements you can actually predict whether a speaker is of Italian or Jewish descent: The larger the radius, the more likely the speaker is Italian (Keating, 1994).

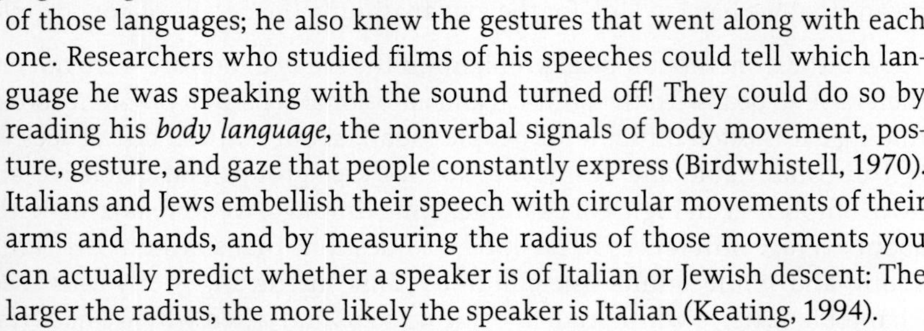

Some signals of body language, like some facial expressions, seem to be "spoken" universally. Across cultures, people generally recognize body movements that reveal pleasure or displeasure, liking or dislike, tension or relaxation, high status or low status, and the basic emotions described in Chapter 10 (Buck, 1984; Keating, 1994). When people are depressed, it shows in their walk, stance, and head position. However, most aspects of body language are specific to particular spoken languages and cultures, which makes even the simplest gesture subject to misunderstanding and offense. The sign of the University of Texas football team, the Longhorns, is to extend the second finger and the pinkie. In Italy and other parts of Europe, this gesture means a man's wife has been unfaithful to him—a serious insult! Anita Rowe, a consultant who advises businesses on cross-cultural customs, tells of a newly hired Asian engineer in a California company who left his office to lead the first meeting of his project team. His secretary crossed her fingers and wished him luck. Instead of reassuring him, her gesture left him thoroughly confused: In his home country, crossing your fingers is a sexual proposition (Gregor, 1993)

Culture influences body language. Arabs stand much closer to each other in conversation than Westerners do, close enough to feel one another's breath and "read" one another's eyes. In many societies, men greet men with an embrace and a kiss, behavior that is taboo in most of the United States and Canada. In Asian cultures, body contact in a public greeting is considered insulting or disgraceful. The Japanese have developed a complex system of bowing that varies with the status and gender of the greeters.

When a nonverbal rule is broken, a person is likely to feel extremely uncomfortable without knowing why. One such rule governs *conversational distance*—how close people normally stand to one another when they are speaking (Hall, 1959, 1976). Arabs like to stand close enough to feel your breath, touch your arm, and see your eyes—a distance that makes white Americans, Canadians, and northern Europeans uneasy, unless they are talking intimately with a lover. The English and the Swedes stand farthest apart when they converse; southern Europeans stand closer; and Latin Americans and Arabs stand the closest (Keating, 1994; Sommer, 1969).

Knowing about cultural differences, though, doesn't make it easier to change your own rules. Caroline Keating (1994), an American cross-cultural psychologist, tells of walking with a Pakistani colleague: "I found myself clumsily stepping off the sidewalk. Without realizing it, the closer my Muslim colleague moved toward me (seeking the interpersonal closeness he was comfortable with) the more I moved over streetside (seeking the interpersonal distance I was comfortable with). . . . I would suddenly disappear from his view, having fallen into the street; perhaps not 'the ugly American,' but a clumsy one!"

GET INVOLVED

To find out what your own comfortable "conversational distance" is, talk to a friend of the same sex. While you are standing or sitting at a comfortable distance from your friend, measure the distance between you (nose to nose, or shoulder to shoulder). Now, the next time you talk to a friend, step closer to the person or step farther away. What happens? Which one of you will restore "comfortable" space first? If you know people from other cultures or ethnic groups, measure the conversational distance they feel comfortable with.

People from different cultures differ in how attentive they are to body language and other nonverbal signals, and they differ in how much attention they pay to the *context* of a conversation (Ambady et al., 1996; Goldman, 1994; Gudykunst & Ting-Toomey, 1988; Hall, 1983). In **high-context cultures,** which are generally homogeneous and close-knit, people pay close attention to nonverbal signs such as posture, gestures, and distance between speakers. They also assume a shared knowledge and history, so things don't have to be spelled out directly. In Japan, for instance, people will rarely say "No, I can't do that" right to your face; it would be considered too direct and too insulting. They are more likely to say, "That is difficult" or "We will see."

In **low-context cultures,** such as Germany and most regions of the United States and Canada, people pay far more attention to words than to nonverbal signals. They assume little or no shared knowledge and history, so everything has to be explained and stated directly. When low-context Americans talk to high-context Japanese, both sides may come away dissatisfied. Americans will have difficulty knowing what their Japanese colleagues meant, and why they meandered around the subject instead of getting to the point. The Japanese, who think that intelligent human beings should be able to discover the point of a conversation from its context, will think the direct-speaking Americans are talking down to them.

The importance of knowing the difference between high- and low-context cultures cannot be overestimated: Misunderstandings between them can lead to war (Triandis, 1994). On January 9, 1991, the foreign minister of Iraq, Tariq Aziz, met with the American secretary of state, James Baker, to discuss Iraq's invasion of Kuwait. Seated next to Aziz was the half-brother of Iraq's president, Saddam Hussein. Baker said, "If you do not move out of Kuwait we will attack you." An unmistakable statement, right? But his *nonverbal* language was that of a low-context American diplomat, moderate and polite. He didn't roar, stamp his feet, or wave his hands. Saddam Hussein's brother, for his part, behaved like a normal, high-context Iraqi. He paid attention to Baker's nonverbal language, which he considered the important form of communication. He reported to Saddam Hussein that Baker was "not at all angry. The Americans are just talking, and they will not attack." Saddam therefore instructed Aziz to be inflexible and to yield nothing. This misunderstanding contributed to the outbreak of a bloody war in which untold thousands of children, women, and men died.

THE ORGANIZATION OF TIME

Imagine that you have arranged to meet a friend for lunch at noon. The friend has not arrived at 12:15, 12:30, or even 12:45. Please answer these questions: What time would *you* have arrived? Would you have been "on time"? How long would you wait for your friend before you started to feel annoyed or worried? When would you leave?

In most parts of North America, the answers are obvious. You would have been there pretty close to noon and would not have waited much past 12:30. That is because Canada and the United States, along with northern European nations, are

high-context cultures Cultures in which people pay close attention to nonverbal forms of communication and assume a shared context for their interactions—a common history and set of attitudes.

low-context cultures Cultures in which people do not take a shared context for granted, and instead emphasize direct verbal communication.

monochronic cultures: Time is organized into linear segments in which people do one thing "at a time" (Hall, 1983; Hall & Hall, 1990). The day is divided into appointments, schedules, and routines, and because time is a precious commodity, people don't like to "waste" time or "spend" too much time on any one activity. In such cultures, therefore, it is considered the height of rudeness (or high status) to keep someone waiting. But the farther south you go in Europe, South America, and Africa, the more likely you are to find **polychronic cultures.** Here, time is organized along parallel lines. People do many things at once, and the needs of friends and family supersede those of the appointment book. People in Latin America and the Middle East think nothing of waiting all day, or even a week, to see someone. The idea of having to be somewhere "on time," as if time were more important than a person, is unthinkable. (Table 18.1 summarizes the differences between the two cultural styles.)

The Japanese have one of the few cultures to combine elements of both systems. With the American occupation that followed World War II, they started being monochronic as a way of creating harmony with the *gaijin* (foreigners). Today, they are extremely monochronic about appointments and schedules, but in every other way they are high context and polychronic. For instance, they are loyal to long-term relationships and customers, and employees and managers share office space and information freely (Hall & Hall, 1990).

monochronic cultures Cultures in which time is organized sequentially; schedules and deadlines are valued over people.

polychronic cultures Cultures in which time is organized horizontally; people tend to do several things at once and value relationships over schedules.

In culturally diverse North America, the two time systems keep bumping into each other. Business, government, and other institutions are organized monochronically, but Native Americans, Chicanos, Latinos, African-Americans, and others tend to operate on polychronic principles. The result is repeated misunderstandings. A white judge in Miami got into hot water when he observed that "Cubans always

TABLE 18.1 ***Cross-Cultural Differences in the Uses and Structure of Time***

Monochronic People	Polychronic People
Use low-context communication	Use high-context communication
Do one thing at a time	Do many things at once
Concentrate on the job	Are highly distractible and subject to interruptions
Take time commitments seriously	Consider time commitments secondary to relationships
Give the job first priority	Give people first priority
Adhere religiously to plans	Change plans often and easily
Are concerned about not disturbing others; value privacy	Are more concerned with relationships than with privacy; may not even have a word for privacy
Like "own space" or private office to work in	Freely share working space, which increases flow of information
Show great respect for private property; seldom borrow or lend	Borrow and lend things often
Emphasize promptness	Care less about own promptness than about other people's needs; are almost never "on time"
Develop many short-term relationships	Build lifetime relationships

Source: Hall & Hall, 1990.

show up two hours late for weddings"—late in his culture's terms, that is. The judge was accurate in his observation; the problem was his implication that something was wrong with Cubans for being "late." And "late" compared to what, by the way? The Cubans were perfectly on time for Cubans.

A culture's way of organizing time does not develop arbitrarily. It stems from the culture's economic system, social organization, political history, and ecology. The monochronic structure of time emerged as a result of the Industrial Revolution in England (Hall, 1983). That makes sense: When thousands of people began working in factories and assembly lines, their efforts had to become coordinated. Moreover, factories have no intrinsic rhythms; people can and do work day or night in them.

But in rural economies, where work is based on the rhythms of nature, people think of time differently. When Hall (1983) worked on a Hopi reservation many decades ago, he noticed that the Hopi behaved in ways that mystified the whites; for example, the Hopi would start to build a dam, a house, or a road, and stop in the middle of the project. To the whites, this meant the Hopi were shiftless and lazy. To the Hopi, the whites were arbitrary and compulsive. What was so important about building dams, houses, and roads? Unlike the maturing of a sheep or the ripening of corn, said the Hopi, building a house has no inherent timetable. What did matter to the Hopi was working in their fields and completing religious ceremonies, activities that indeed had to be done "on time"—nature's time, not human time.

THE SELF AND SELF-IDENTITY

Who are you? Take as much time as you like to complete this projective test: "I am ______________________."

One of the most important ways in which cultures differ has to do with whether the individual or the group is given the greater emphasis (Hofstede & Bond, 1988; Markus & Kitayama, 1991; Triandis, 1995). **Individualist cultures** emphasize the independent individual over the needs of the group, and the "self" is defined as a collection of stable personality traits ("I am outgoing, agreeable, and ambitious"). **Collectivist cultures** emphasize the harmony of the group over the wishes of the individual, and the "self" is defined in the context of relationships and the larger community ("I am descended from three generations of storytellers on my mother's side and five generations of farmers on my father's side, and their ancestors came to this village 200 years ago . . .").

In a revealing study comparing Japanese and Americans, the Americans reported that their sense of self changes only 5 to 10 percent in different situations, whereas the Japanese said that 90 to 99 percent of their sense of self changes (de Rivera, 1989). For the Japanese, it is important to enact *tachiba*, to perform one's social roles correctly so that there will be harmony with others. (As we just noted, this was one reason they adopted the American monochronic system of time after World War II.) Americans, in contrast, tend to value "being true to your self" and having a "core identity." Similarly, people from collectivist cultures typically respond to the "I am . . ." cue in terms of family (e.g., "I am an uncle, a cousin, a son") or ethnic group, whereas people from individualist cultures tend to answer in terms of personality traits or occupation (Triandis, 1995, 1996). The way that people define the self affects many aspects of individual psychology, including which personality traits are valued, how emotions are expressed, and how much value people place on having relationships or individual freedom (Campbell et al., 1996; Kashima et al., 1995).

individualist cultures Cultures in which the self is regarded as autonomous, and individual goals and wishes are prized above duty and relations with others.

collectivist cultures Cultures in which the self is regarded as embedded in relationships, and harmony with the group is prized above individual goals and wishes.

In collectivist cultures, the strongest human bond is usually not between husband and wife, but between parent and child or among siblings (Triandis, 1995). In China, the most valued and celebrated relationship is the father–son bond; in India, Mexico, Ireland, and Greece, it is mother–son; in parts of Africa, it is older brother–

In collectivist societies, such as China, group harmony is prized over individual wishes; in individualist societies, such as the United States, personal preferences are celebrated. Chinese workers in Beijing do their morning T'ai Chi exercises in identical, harmonious fashion; individualistic Americans exercise by running or walking in different directions, in different ways, in different clothes.

younger brother; among the Tiwi of North Australia, it is mother-in-law and son-in-law (no mother-in-law jokes among the Tiwi!). In individualist cultures, child rearing is considered a private parental matter, and neighbors and friends intervene at their peril. But child rearing in collectivist cultures is a communal matter; everyone has a say in correcting the child's behavior (a value expressed in the African proverb, "It takes a whole village to raise a child"). The idea of privacy for children is unknown, and the goal is to raise children who are obedient, hardworking, and dutiful toward their parents. Some of the differences between the two kinds of culture are summarized in Table 18.2.

TABLE 18.2 *Some Average Differences Between Individualist and Collectivist Cultures*

Members of Individualist Cultures	Members of Collectivist Cultures
Define the self as autonomous, independent of groups	Define the self as an interdependent part of groups
Give priority to individual, personal goals	Give priority to the needs and goals of the group
Value independence, leadership, achievement, "self-fulfillment"	Value group harmony, duty, obligation, security
Give more weight to an individual's attitudes and preferences than to group norms as explanations of behavior	Give more weight to group norms than to individual attitudes as explanations of behavior
Attend to the benefits and costs of relationships; if costs exceed advantages, a person is likely to drop a relationship	Attend to the needs of group members; if a relationship is beneficial to the group but costly to the individual, the individual is likely to stay in the relationship

Source: Triandis, 1996.

GET INVOLVED

Rank the following 12 values in order of their importance to you, with 1 being most important and 12 being least important:

_____ *Pleasure (gratification of desires)*

_____ *Honor of parents and elders (showing respect)*

_____ *Creativity (uniqueness, imagination)*

_____ *Social order (stability of society)*

_____ *A varied life (filled with challenge and change)*

_____ *National security (protection of my nation from enemies)*

_____ *Being daring (seeking adventure, risk)*

_____ *Self-discipline (self-restraint, resistance to temptation)*

_____ *Freedom (freedom of action and thought)*

_____ *Politeness (courtesy, good manners)*

_____ *Independence (self-reliance, choice of own goals)*

_____ *Obedience (fulfilling duties, meeting obligations)*

Individualist and collectivist values are listed in alternating order (e.g., "pleasure" is an individualist value and "honor of parents and elders" is a collectivist value). Do items from one set of values tend to rank high on your list, and the others low, or do they overlap? If you know classmates from other cultures, how do they rank these values? (From Chan, 1994, and Franzoi, 1996.)

Can you predict what will happen if a collectivist man marries an individualist woman? The chances are high that the husband will regard his relationship with one or both of his parents as being most important, whereas his wife will expect his relationship with her to be most important. And they are likely to disagree intensely, without knowing why, about such matters as letting their children have their own rooms, speak their minds, make their own choices, talk back, and become independent.

Everyone develops a *personal identity*—a sense of who they are—that is based on their particular traits and unique history. But people also develop **social identities** based on their nationality, ethnicity, religion, and social roles (Brewer & Gardner, 1996; Hogg & Abrams, 1988; Tajfel & Turner, 1986). Social identities are important because they give people a feeling of place and position in the world. Without them, most people would feel like loose marbles rolling around in an unconnected universe. The social identity that comes from belonging to a distinctive group satisfies two important motives: the individual's need for inclusion in a larger collective, and the individual's need to feel different from others (Brewer, Manzi, & Shaw, 1993).

In modern societies, many social identities are possible. People face the dilemma of balancing an **ethnic identity,** a close identification with their own religious or ethnic group, with **acculturation,** identifying with and feeling part of the dominant culture (Cross, 1971; Phinney, 1996; Spencer & Dornbusch, 1990). Ethnic-identity formation and acculturation are separate processes. Some people learn to alternate easily between their culture of origin and the majority culture, slipping into the customs and language of each as circumstances dictate. They are comfortable and competent in both cultures, just as bilingual people are in two languages, without feeling that they must choose one culture over another (LaFromboise, Coleman, & Gerton, 1993). Others, however, struggle to find a balance between their culture of origin and the dominant culture of the society.

social identity The part of a person's self-concept that is based on his or her identification with a nation, culture, or ethnic group or with gender or other roles in society.

ethnic identity A close identification with your own racial, religious, or ethnic group.

acculturation The process by which members of groups that are minorities in a given society come to identify with and feel part of the mainstream culture.

The tension in America between ethnic identity and acculturation came to a boil during the 1996 Hispanic March on Washington, when thousands of Hispanic Americans demanded rights for immigrants—while waving flags from their countries of origin. To the demonstrators, the flags symbolized pride in their heritage, but many other Americans regarded them as evidence of the demonstrators' lack of commitment to the United States. How can people find a balance between preserving their ethnic heritage and becoming an integral part of the larger society?

For any individual, four outcomes are possible, depending on whether ethnic identity is strong or weak, and whether identification with the larger culture is strong or weak (Berry, 1994; Phinney, 1990). People who are *bicultural* have strong ties both to their ethnicity and to the larger culture: They say, "I am proud of my ethnic heritage, but I identify just as much with my country." People who choose *assimilation* have weak feelings of ethnicity but a strong sense of acculturation: Their attitude, for example, might be, "I'm an American, period." *Ethnic separatists* have a strong sense of ethnic identity but weak feelings of acculturation: They might say, "My ethnicity comes first; if I join the mainstream, I'm betraying my origins." And some people feel *marginal,* connected to neither their ethnicity nor the dominant culture: They may say, "I'm an individual and don't identify with any group" or "I don't belong anywhere." (See Table 18.3.)

Some of the conflicts between cultural groups in North America, as well as within these groups, arise because people have different ideas about the relative benefits of acculturation versus ethnic identity and how (and whether) these should be balanced. The issue becomes more complicated when an ethnic group is a minority that is struggling to gain recognition and equality (Phinney, 1996). The resulting tension is reflected in the touchy subject of what groups should be called, and why their names change (see "Issues in Popular Culture").

For example, *Hispanic* is a label used by the U.S. government to include all Spanish-speaking groups. But many "Hispanics" dislike the term, pointing out that Spaniards, Mexican-Americans (Chicanos), Latin Americans (Latinos), Cubans, and Puerto Ricans differ in their culture and history, and therefore in their ethnic identity (Vasquez & Barón, 1988). Other Hispanics, however, dislike the term Latino. The 1992 Latino National Political Survey found that most Latinos don't think of themselves as such, preferring national-origin labels such as Mexican-American or just

TABLE 18.3 *Patterns of Ethnic Identity and Acculturation*

		Ethnic Identity Is	
		Strong	**Weak**
Acculturation Is	**Strong**	Bicultural	Assimilated
	Weak	Separatist	Marginal

This 10-year-old is African-American, Native American, and Mexican. What is her "ethnic identity"? The growing number of multiethnic combinations is making this question hard for many people to answer. For example, this photo is part of a series of multiethnic children, including one who is Chinese/Native American/Filipino/Scottish and another who is Dutch/Jamaican/Irish/African-American/Russian-Jewish. What should they be called?

American (de la Garza et al., 1992). Likewise, Koreans, Japanese, Chinese, and Vietnamese are all Asian, but many individuals in these groups resent being lumped into a single category. The Hopi, Navajo, Cheyenne, Lakota (Sioux), Ojibwa, Iroquois, and hundreds of other groups are all considered Native American, but they differ culturally in many ways. For that matter, not all white Americans want to be called Anglos, which refers to a British heritage, or European-American, as if all European countries, from Greece to Norway, France to Poland, were the same. And growing numbers of people of multiethnic backgrounds are exasperated and irritated by society's efforts to squeeze them into only one category.

The tension between personal and social identity will continue, as ethnic groups struggle to define their place and raise their status in a medley of cultures.

As we have seen, an appreciation of the rules of culture expands our understanding of human behavior. Among other things, culture affects people's sense of time, the priorities they assign to people and schedules, the ways they process information and communicate meaning, their nonverbal language and even whether they pay much attention to nonverbal language, their notions of the self and their relationships, and their fundamental identities.

Quick Quiz

Are you assimilated into the culture of test-takers?

A. Provide the term that describes each of the following cultural characteristics:

1. Cultures whose members pay close attention to nonverbal signs and often don't spell things out directly.
2. Cultures whose members do things one at a time and consider time a precious commodity.
3. Cultures whose members regard the "self" as a collection of stable personality traits.

B. Which of the terms in Item 1 apply to the majority culture in the United States and Canada?

C. Frank, an African-American student, finds himself caught between two philosophies on his campus. One holds that blacks should shed their identity as victims of racism and move toward full integration into mainstream culture. The other favors Afrocentric education, holding that blacks should immerse themselves in the history, values, and contributions of African culture. Frank is caught between his __________ and __________.

Answers:

A. 1. high context 2. monochronic 3. individualist B. monochronic and individualist C. ethnic identity, acculturation

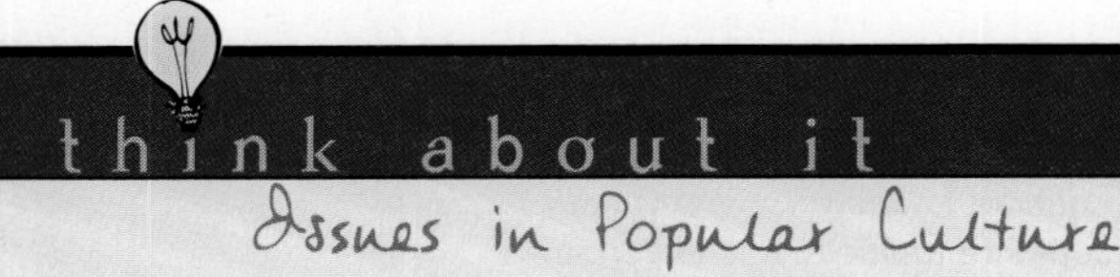

What's in a Name? The Debate over "Political Correctness"

Across the United States and Canada, many universities, companies, government agencies, and newspapers have tried to come up with regulations about what different groups should be called. When does a term become offensive, and why? One college, in a leaflet distributed to all students, defined "ableism" as "oppression of the differently abled by the temporarily able." Was that a wise effort to make people think about the terms they use to describe people with disabilities, or was it plain silliness? "Sexual preference," with its implication that people can choose to be homosexual or heterosexual, has been widely replaced by "sexual orientation," but some homosexuals prefer the term "affectional orientation" so that they will not be labeled solely according to their sexual behavior. Will such a change in terms affect straight people's prejudices?

The question of what groups should be called and what terms are offensive evokes much controversy. One side argues that because language shapes attitudes and prejudices, we must be ever vigilant about the mindless use of labels or phrases that offend or perpetuate untruths. Although most North Americans do not realize the derivation of the term "to welsh" on a bet, for example, the term is as offensive to people from Wales as the expression "to Jew him down" is to Jews.

The opposing side argues that efforts to legislate "political correctness" (P.C.) in language produce tedious or comical gobbledygook, impede clear thinking, and don't change anyone's prejudices anyway. Moreover, in this view, when everyone is focused on the correct word and quick to take offense if someone uses the "wrong" one, it becomes easy to forget the bottom line—how people are actually being treated. Nancy Mairs (1986), a writer who suffers from multiple sclerosis, said,

> *I am a cripple. I choose this word to name me.... "cripple" seems to me a clean word, straightforward and precise.... As a lover of words, I like the accuracy with which it describes my condition: I have lost the full use of limbs. "Disabled," by contrast, suggests any incapacity, physical or mental.... Most remote is the recently coined euphemism "differently abled," which partakes of the same semantic hopefulness that transformed countries from "undeveloped" to "underdeveloped," then to "less developed," and finally to "developing" nations. People have continued to starve in those countries during the shift. Some realities do not obey the dictates of language.*

The one thing everyone can agree on is that labels have great symbolic and emotional significance. Around the world, many ethnic groups are rejecting names that were imposed on them by the majority culture, insisting instead on a name that reflects their own cultural identity. This is why the Eskimos of Canada are now called the Inuit, their own name for themselves, and the Sioux are now the Lakota. In addition, a group's name reflects its history, status, and self-concept. In the early 1970s, William Cross (1971) analyzed "The Negro-to-Black conversion experience," arguing that this change was critical for "the psychology of Black liberation." In the 1980s, Halford Fairchild (1985) analyzed the significance of labels that are based on skin color ("black"), race ("Negro"), or national origin ("Afro-American"), for each term has different historical and emotional connotations. Only a

THE ORIGINS OF CULTURE

When most people read about the customs of other cultures, they are inclined to say, "Oh, boy, I like the attitudes of the Gorks but I hate the habits of the Zorks." Yet a culture's practices cannot easily be exported elsewhere, like cheese, or surgically removed, like a tumor. The reason is that a culture's attitudes and practices are deeply embedded in its history, environment, economy, and survival needs.

To explain the origins of cultural customs, cultural researchers study a culture's political system and its economy, and how these systems are affected by geography, natural resources, and even the weather. They find out who controls and distributes the resources, and how safe a society is from interlopers. They study the kinds of work that people do. They observe whether there is environmental pressure on a group to produce more children or to have fewer of them. To illustrate this approach, few years after that article appeared, African-American became a popular term to identify people of African descent living in the Americas; those who like the term argue that it is analogous to Polish-American or Italian-American.

Nevertheless, as psycholinguist Stephen Pinker (1994a) observes, there is a difference between changing a word that is blatantly incorrect or offensive and changing a word in the hopes of changing its connotations. Pinker argues that when terms that are acceptable are nearly synonymous with those that are now offensive—such as colored people versus people of color; Afro-American versus African-American; Negro (which is Spanish for "black") versus black—something else is going on besides identity politics. Pinker calls this something the "euphemism treadmill." People invent new words to try to escape emotional associations with the old words. In the absence of social change, the new word acquires the same emotional association, and soon another word must be invented. "We will know we have achieved equality and mutual respect," Pinker concludes, "when names for minorities stay put."

Moreover, says Pinker, "Despite the appeal of the theory that language determines thought, no cognitive scientist believes it. People coin new words, grapple for *le mot juste* [the right word], translate from other languages and ridicule or defend P.C. terms. None of this would be possible if the ideas expressed by the words were identical to the words themselves. This should alleviate anxiety on both sides, reminding us that we are talking about style manuals, not brain programming."

Because language and ethnic identities are constantly changing processes, it is impossible to designate a single P.C. term that everyone will know about immediately, let alone agree on. Many blacks, feeling no kinship to Africa, do not consider themselves African-American. Supreme Court Justice Thurgood Marshall preferred the word Negro for most of his life, and social critic Henry Louis Gates, Jr., called his autobiography *Colored People*, the term he grew up with and still likes. A decade ago, activist American Indian groups sought to replace the term *American Indian* with *Native American*, and the latter term caught on with colleges and other organizations wanting to support a group's right to self-designation. Ironically, according to Joseph Trimble and Beatrice Medicine (1993), Indian political groups then decided to keep the term *American Indian*, as in the American Indian Movement and the National Congress of American Indians. Today, despite the stance of American Indian groups themselves, it is non-Indians who tend to prefer the term Native American!

This story contains a lesson for people on both sides of the debate about being P.C. Words do matter, but words are not everything. Pinker worries about people who, unaware of the current "correct" term (because they are older or do not travel in university, media, and government circles), find themselves accused of being bigots when they innocently use the "wrong" word.

But if Nancy Mairs considers herself a cripple, and Thurgood Marshall favored the word Negro, and members of the American Indian Movement call themselves Indians, how rigid should we all be about names? And if the goal is tolerance for all groups, how can we make sure that a focus on words does not replace a commitment to deeds?

we will take a look at sociocultural explanations for the origins of gender roles and why those roles often vary across cultures.

Let's start with a story: A young boy notices, at an early age, that he seems different from other boys. He prefers playing with girls. He is attracted to the work adult women do, such as cooking and sewing. He often dreams at night of being a girl, and he even likes to put on the clothes of girls. As the boy enters adolescence, people begin to whisper that he's "different," that he seems feminine in his movements, posture, and language. One day, the boy can hide his secret feelings no longer and reveals them to his parents.

How do his parents respond? It depends on their culture. In the United States today, many parents would react with tears, anger, or guilt. They might haul their son off to a psychiatrist, who would diagnose him as having a "gender identity disorder" and begin intensive treatment. But these reactions are not universal. Until the late

Throughout history, a person's anatomical sex *and the culturally assigned duties of* gender *have not always corresponded. Some men have chosen to wear the clothes and play the roles of women, as in the case of the Native American* berdache. *In the photo on the left, taken about 1885, We-wha, a Zuni Indian man, wears the traditional earrings, jewelry, and dress of a woman. Likewise, some women have worn the clothes and played the roles of men, as did the eighteenth-century pirate Mary Read (right).*

1800s, in a number of Plains Indians and western American Indian tribes, parents and other elders reacted with sympathy when a young man wanted to live the life of a woman. A man in this role (whom whites called a *berdache*) was often given an honored status as a shaman, a person with the power to cure illness and to act as an intermediary between the natural and spiritual worlds, and he was permitted to dress as and perform the duties of a woman. In some tribes, he was even permitted to marry another man (Williams, 1986).

In the Sambian society of Papua New Guinea, parents would react still differently (Herdt, 1984). In Sambia, all adolescent boys are *required* to engage in oral sex with older males as part of their initiation into manhood. Sambians believe that a boy cannot mature physically or emotionally unless he ingests another man's semen over a period of several years. However, Sambian parents would react with shock and disbelief if a son said he wanted to live as a woman. Every Sambian man and woman marries someone of the other sex and performs the work assigned to his or her own sex.

These diverse reactions support the view of cultural psychologists that a person's anatomical *sex* does not automatically impose universal rules of *gender.* (As we saw in discussing gender socialization in Chapter 13, social-learning theorists also make this distinction.) In this view, sex is genetically determined and unchangeable, unless extraordinary surgical procedures are used; but gender, which encompasses all the duties, rights, and behaviors a culture considers appropriate for males and females, is learned. In contrast, evolutionary psychologists believe that sex heavily influences gender—that is, that the biological fact of being male or female constrains the fundamental tasks and gender roles that men and women will play (Archer, 1996). By comparing and contrasting different cultures around the world, cross-cultural psychologists are trying to identify which aspects of gender roles seem to be universally male or female, as well as those that are culturally specific.

GENDER AND CULTURE: THEMES AND VARIATIONS

First, let's consider the commonalities. In general, men have had, and continue to have, more status and power than women, especially in public affairs. Men traditionally fight the wars, and they commit more acts of physical aggression and violence than women do. If a society's economy includes hunting large game, traveling a long way from home, or making weapons, men typically handle these activities. Women have had the primary responsibility for cooking, cleaning, and taking care of children. Corresponding with this division of tasks, in many cultures around the world masculinity is regarded as something that boys must achieve through strenuous effort. Males must pass physical tests, endure pain, confront danger, suppress their emotions, and separate themselves psychologically and even physically from their mothers and the world of women. Sometimes they have to prove their self-reliance and courage in harsh initiation rites. Femininity, in contrast, is generally associated with responsibility, obedience, and nurturance, and it is seen as something that develops without any special intervention from others (Archer, 1996).

Those are the common themes. Now for some variations:

- The status of women worldwide is not uniformly low (di Leonardo, 1991); it is highest in Scandinavian countries and lowest in Bangladesh, with tremendous variation in between. Women's status has been assessed by measures of economic security, educational opportunities, access to birth control and medical care, degree of self-determination, participation in public and political life, power to make decisions in the family, and physical safety. In some places, women are completely under the rule of men. Women in Saudi Arabia are not allowed to drive a car; many girls in India submit to arranged marriages as early as age 9. Yet elsewhere, women are attaining greater power, influence, education, and independence. In this century, women have been elected heads of state in Israel, India, Norway, England, Iceland, Pakistan, Nicaragua, Bangladesh (where women otherwise have the lowest status), Poland, Turkey . . . and the list keeps growing.
- The content of what is considered "men's work" and "women's work" varies from culture to culture. In some places, dentistry and teaching are men's work; in others, they are women's work. In many cultures, women do the shopping and marketing, but in others, marketing is men's work.
- Cultures differ in the degree of daily contact that is permitted between the sexes. In many farm communities and in most modern occupations in North America and Europe, men and women work together. At the other end of the continuum, men and women are forbidden to work, pray, or socialize together. Some Middle Eastern societies practice *purdah,* the custom of veiling women and secluding them from all male eyes except those of their close relatives.

- In some cultures, particularly those of East Asia, Southeast Asia, and Muslim societies, female chastity is highly prized. Women are expected to suppress all sexual feeling and behavior until marriage, and premarital or extramarital sex is cause for the woman's ostracism from the community or even her death. In other cultures, such as those of Polynesia, Scandinavia, and northern Europe, female chastity is considered unimportant (Buss et al., 1990; Hatfield & Rapson, 1996). Women are expected to have sex before marriage and even extramarital sex is not necessarily cause for alarm.
- In some cultures, men and women regard one another as opposite in nature, ability, and personality, a view that reflects their separate domains. In other cultures, such as those of the Ifaluk, the Tahitians, and people who live on Sudest Island southeast of New Guinea, men and women do not regard each other as opposites or even as being very different. For example, men are not raised to be more aggressive than women, nor are women supposed to be gentler or more nurturant than men (Gilmore, 1990; Lepowsky, 1994; Lutz, 1988).

GENDER AND CULTURE: EXPLAINING THE DIFFERENCES

Cultural researchers believe that evolutionary and biological explanations cannot account for the wide variation in gender roles around the world. They emphasize instead two other fundamental factors: *production* (matters pertaining to the economy and the creation of food, clothing, and shelter) and *reproduction* (matters pertaining to the bearing, raising, and nurturing of children).

One important finding is that strict concepts of manhood tend to exist wherever there is a great deal of competition for resources and especially when war is frequent—which is to say, in most places (Gilmore, 1990; Harris, 1997). For the human species, life has usually been harsh. Consider a tribe trying to survive in the wilds of a South American forest; or in the dry and unforgiving landscape of the desert; or in an icy arctic terrain that imposes limits on the number of people who can survive by fishing. When conditions such as these exist, men are taught to hunt for large game, compete with each other for work, and fight off enemies. (This division of labor may originally have occurred because of men's relatively greater upper-body muscular strength and the fact that they do not become pregnant or nurse children.) Men are socialized to face confrontation and to resist the impulse to retreat from danger. They are "toughened up" and pushed to take risks, even with their lives.

CONSIDER OTHER EXPLANATIONS

Around the world, men tend to commit more acts of violence than women do. Many people assume that the universality of this difference means it must be biologically based. What are some alternative explanations?

How do you get men to wage war and risk death, go off on long treks for food, and be willing to get bloodied defending the homestead? Far from being natural to men, some cultural researchers argue, aggressiveness has to be constantly rewarded (Gilmore, 1990). To persuade men to wage war and risk death, societies have to give

In most cultures, men are required to do the dangerous, life-threatening work . . . but it's not easy to get all of them to do it.

them something; and the something is prestige and power—and women (Harris, 1997). That, in turn, means you have to raise obedient women; if the king is going to offer his daughter in marriage to the bravest warrior, she has to agree to be handed over. In contrast, in societies such as Tahiti and Sudest Island, where resources are abundant and people have no serious hazards or enemies to worry about, men don't feel they have to prove themselves or set themselves apart from women (Lepowsky, 1994).

A culture's economy also helps account for the variations in how aggressive men are required and expected to be. In a fascinating analysis of the rates of violence in different regional cultures of the United States, Richard Nisbett (1993) set out to explain why the American South, and some western regions of the country originally settled by southerners, have much higher rates of homicide by whites than the rest of the country has. Southerners are more likely to endorse the use of violence for protection (recall the reactions to Rodney Peairs's shooting of the Japanese exchange student) and as the proper response to perceived insults. "Violence has been associated with the South since the time of the American Revolution," begins an essay in the *Encyclopedia of Southern Culture*, and it goes on to devote 39 pages to bloodcurdling accounts of feuds, duels, lynchings, violent sports, and murder.

Nisbett ruled out explanations based on poverty and racial tensions. Although both factors are associated with violence, "southernness" remains a predictor of homicide even when he controlled for regional differences in poverty and percentage of blacks in the population.

Nisbett argues that the South "is heir to a culture, deriving ultimately from economic determinants, in which violence is a natural and integral part." The New England and the middle Atlantic states were settled by Puritans, Quakers, and Dutch farmers and artisans who had an advanced agricultural economy. For them, the most adaptive policy was one of cooperation with others for the common good. In contrast, the South was settled largely by immigrants from Scotland and Ireland, whose economies were based on herding and hunting, activities that continued to provide their economic base in America.

Why should herding, as opposed to farming, make such a difference in rates of violence? People who depend economically on their herds are extremely vulnerable; their livelihoods can be lost in an instant by the theft of their animals. To reduce the likelihood of theft, says Nisbett, herders "cultivate a posture of extreme vigilance toward any act that might be perceived as threatening in any way, and respond with sufficient force to frighten the offender and the community into recognizing that they are not to be trifled with." This is why cattle rustling and horse thievery were capital crimes in the Old West, and why Mediterranean and Middle Eastern herding cultures, as well as those of the southern United States, place a high value on male aggressiveness. When Nisbett examined agricultural practices within the South, he found that homicide rates were more than twice as high in the hills and plains regions (where herding occurs) as in farming regions.

Cultures based on herding foster male aggressiveness as a means of protecting livestock. That is why cattle rustlers and horse thieves have often been summarily hanged, as this one was in Colorado in 1888.

Herding cultures, in turn, foster a "culture of honor," in which even apparently small disputes and trivial insults (trivial to people from other cultures, that is) put a man's reputation for toughness on the line, requiring him to respond with violence to restore his status. Although the herding economy has become less important in the South and the West, the legacy of its culture of honor remains. Nisbett and his colleagues conducted three experiments with male students who had grown up in the North or the South. In each, students were insulted by a confederate and called an offensive name. Northerners were relatively unaffected by the insult, but southerners reacted strongly. They felt that their masculine reputation was threatened, and they were more upset (as shown by a rise in their stress hormones), more physiologically primed for aggression (as shown by a rise in testosterone levels), and more likely to retaliate aggressively than northerners were (Cohen et al., 1996).

Cultural theories predict that gender differences in occupations, personality traits, and involvement in child care will decline as jobs that both sexes can perform become both commonplace and necessary for society and for families. In modern societies around the world, these changes are already occurring.

Because of research like this, cultural psychologists conclude that male biology does not inevitably dictate aggressive behavior. Males are raised to be aggressive in cultures of honor, which promote violence as a way to restore a man's reputation and protect society's economic interests.

In terms of the kinds of gender roles they promote, cultures fall along a continuum from traditional to modern (egalitarian). In a cross-cultural study of 100 men and women from each of 14 countries in North and South America, Europe, and Asia, Deborah Best and John Williams (1993) asked people to fill out an inventory concerning ideal role relationships between women and men. Sample items included, "The husband should be regarded as the legal representative of the family group in all matters of law" (a traditional attitude) and "A woman should have exactly the same freedom of action as a man" (a modern attitude). Gender-role ideologies are significantly related to a culture's social and economic development. As countries become industrialized and urban, their gender roles also become more modern. Why might this be so?

One answer is that industrialization eliminates the traditional reasons for a sexual division of labor. Most jobs in industrial nations, including military jobs, now involve service skills and brainwork that both sexes can do—a situation that has never existed before in human history. And another profound change has also occurred in this century for the first time: Reproduction has been revolutionized. Although women in many countries still lack access to safe and affordable contraceptives, it is now technologically possible for women to limit reliably the number of children they will have and to plan when to have them. Along with these changes, ideas about the "natural" qualities of men and women are being transformed. It is no longer news that a woman can be a police officer or a miner, walk in space or run a country. And it is no longer news that many men, whose own fathers would no more have diapered a baby than jumped into a vat of boiling oil, are now actively involved fathers (Barnett & Rivers, 1996; Gerson, 1993).

What cross-cultural research shows, then, is that many of our gender arrangements, and the qualities associated with being male and female, are affected by economic, ecological, and other practical conditions. This research also suggests that no matter how entrenched our own cultural habits and attitudes are, they change depending on the kind of work we do, technological advances, and the needs of society. Understanding the forces that generate and sustain cultural practices may even help us better evaluate customs we think are morally reprehensible, in our own culture or elsewhere (see "Puzzles of Psychology").

Quick Quiz

Your gender won't affect your ability to answer these questions.

1. Which of the following is most common in cultures around the world? (a) Women do the weaving, marketing, and teaching; (b) men have more status and power in public affairs than women do; (c) men and women are physically separated while working.
2. What two general factors do cultural researchers emphasize in explaining variations in gender roles around the world?
3. Nisbett's analysis of regional differences in violence showed that an important factor in predicting male aggressiveness is (a) how people earn their livings, (b) racial tensions, (c) poverty, (d) male biology.

Answers:

1. b 2. production and reproduction 3. a

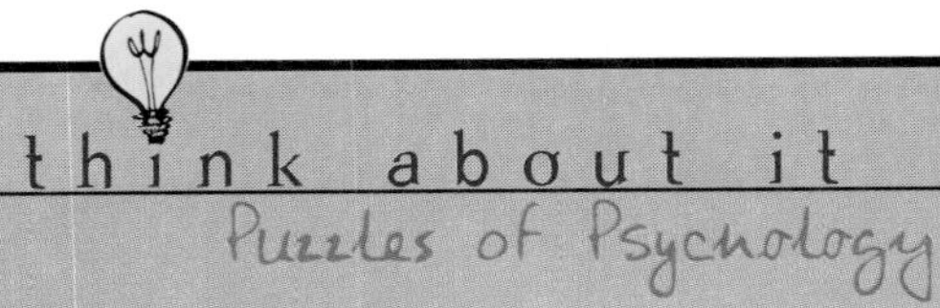

What Are the Limits of Tolerance?

Fauziya Kasinga fled her West African homeland of Togo and sought asylum in the United States, hoping to escape a cultural tradition that was about to be inflicted on her: genital mutilation. An immigration judge, saying her story was "not credible," rejected her request. Kasinga spent 18 months in prison while her case was appealed. After publicity about her caused a public outcry, an appeals court freed her, and she is now living in America.

The tradition that Kasinga escaped is practiced in more than 25 countries throughout Africa, the Middle East, and Indonesia. Performed on an estimated 2 million female children every year, ranging in age from infancy to late adolescence, the operation takes one of three forms: in *circumcision*, part of the clitoris is removed; in *excision*, the entire clitoris and all or part of the vaginal lips (labia) are removed; and in *infibulation*, the clitoris and the inner and outer labia are removed and the sides of the vaginal opening are stitched together, leaving only a small hole for urination and menstruation. These operations, usually performed without anesthesia or even an antiseptic, are excruciatingly painful and hazardous; some girls bleed to death. Most women who have been excised or infibulated develop lifelong medical and reproductive problems, and many have severe problems in childbirth (Bardach, 1993).

People in cultures that practice infibulation believe that it will ensure a girl's chastity before marriage and her fidelity afterward. Most people in other cultures believe it is barbaric—hence their insistence on calling it "genital mutilation." But what, if anything, should outsiders do? Should they say, "Well, it's their custom, and it's up to them to change it; we must be tolerant," or "It is a violation of human rights, and we should do what we can to eradicate it"? This is not just an intellectual matter in European countries and North America, which have growing numbers of immigrants who subject their daughters to the surgery. The result is a clash between the law of the majority, which forbids the practice, and the immigrants' determination to continue adhering to their tradition. (The United States Congress outlawed the procedure in 1996.)

Every day brings more examples of such clashes between the law or custom of the majority and a minority's tradition. In California, a man from Laos killed a puppy, a sacrifice he believed would help his wife recover from an illness, but one that enraged his neighbors and violated the animal-cruelty laws. In Nebraska, two Iraqi men, ages 34 and 28, married 13-year-old Iraqi girls—a normal custom for them, but statutory rape under Nebraska law.

Cultural psychologists have described problems with both "absolutist" and "relativist" positions on such issues (Adamopoulos & Lonner, 1994). In reacting to the absolutist assumptions of traditional psychology, which holds that there are universal truths and a common human nature, relativists conclude that every culture differs from every other and that each can be judged only on its own terms. Extreme relativists take a nonjudgmental view of all cultural practices, even those that cause suffering and death.

It is not necessary to be utterly relativist, but it is important to prevent indignation from getting in the way of understanding why and how certain practices emerged or eventually faded. Cultural psychologists try to find out why certain customs have survived and what their adaptive consequences might be. This does *not* mean that any custom that survives must therefore be right and good. It *does* mean that because cultural customs are embedded in the larger structure of society, efforts to outlaw them often fail. (Egypt and many African countries prohibit or officially discourage infibulation, for example, but villagers defiantly continue it.)

Infibulation works like a marriage contract, guaranteeing a woman a place in society. When efforts to make the practice illegal ignore the system of kinship and economic arrangements that support it, they can backfire, condemning women to even more hardship. African women who are working to eliminate female genital mutilation know this (Dawit & Mekuria, 1993). They know that the custom cannot just be outlawed without making other changes to raise the social status and economic security of women.

The study of culture does not require us to abandon the concern for human rights, but it does alert us to the dangers of climbing up on an ethnocentric high horse, galloping off in the certainty that our own ways are always right and normal and everyone else's are wrong.

Alice Walker, whose novel *Possessing the Secret of Joy* is a haunting indictment of infibulation as a crime against women, pointed out in a television interview that plenty of American women mutilate themselves with breast implants, plastic surgery, and liposuction to fit their culture's standards of being beautiful. How would they like it if outsiders pressured the U.S. government to make plastic surgery for cosmetic purposes illegal? Or consider this: Among the developed nations of the world, only the United States continues to execute criminals in increasing numbers. To most other nations, the death penalty is barbaric, a violation of human rights. But many Americans would counter that it's their cultural custom, and no one has the right to interfere.

Obviously, then, emotional reasoning should not be the only guide in evaluating practices you find reprehensible or immoral. What criteria would you use in deciding when to be tolerant of other cultures' practices and when to take a stand against them? If you take an opposing stand, what actions would you be willing to ask your own country to take—moral persuasion, education, military intervention, sanctions, or something else? And when might it be wise to let yourself be influenced by another culture's customs? Think about it.

CROSS-CULTURAL RELATIONS

By now, you should be persuaded that cultures differ in countless ways and that a culture's customs do not arise for some arbitrary or foolish reason. But it has probably also been difficult for you to turn off your mental moral evaluator, the little voice that says, "Boy, a culture that does *that* must really be dumb/weird/uncivilized." That little voice, which everyone hears to one degree or another, is the echo of **ethnocentrism,** the belief that your own culture or ethnic group is superior to all others.

Ethnocentrism is so pervasive that it is even embedded in some languages: The Chinese word for China means "the center of the world," and the Navajo and the Inuit call themselves simply "The People." Ethnocentrism is probably universal because it aids survival by making people feel attached to their own group and willing to work on the group's behalf. But does the fact that people feel good about their own culture or nationality mean that prejudice toward other groups is inevitable? Does it mean we are destined to a world of ethnic separatism? Can't people say, "Well, I'm happy being an Agfloyp, and I love our customs, but I also am grateful to the people who invented jazz, small cars, chicken soup, movies, paper, the tango, democracy, penicillin . . ."?

ETHNOCENTRISM AND STEREOTYPES

Ethnocentrism rests on a fundamental social identity: Us. As soon as people have created a category called "us," however, they invariably perceive everybody else as "not-us." The experiment at Robbers Cave (described in the previous chapter) showed how easy it is to activate *us–them thinking* when any two groups perceive themselves to be in competition. Although competition is sufficient to stimulate ethnocentrism, however, it isn't necessary. Just being a member of an in-group will do it.

Who is the chemical engineer, and who is the assistant? The Western stereotype holds that (1) women aren't engineers in the first place, but (2) if they are, they are Western. Actually, the engineer at this refinery is the Kuwaiti woman on the left.

In fact, ethnocentrism can be manufactured in a minute in a laboratory, as Henri Tajfel and his colleagues (1971) first demonstrated in a classic experiment with British schoolboys. Tajfel showed the boys slides with varying numbers of dots on them and asked the boys to guess how many dots there were. The boys were arbitrarily told they were "overestimators" or "underestimators" and were then asked to work on another task. In this phase, they had the chance to allocate points to other boys known to be overestimators or underestimators. The researchers had created in-group favoritism: Although each boy worked alone in his cubicle, almost every single one assigned far more points to other boys he thought were like him, an overestimator or an underestimator. As the boys emerged from their rooms, they were asked, "Which were you?"—and the answers received a mix of cheers and boos.

Even the collective pronouns that apply to *us* and *them* are powerful emotional signals. In one experiment, which students believed was testing their verbal skills, nonsense syllables such as *xeh, yof, laj,* or *wuh* were randomly paired with either an in-group word (*us, we,* or *ours*), an out-group word (*them, they,* or *theirs*), or, for a control measure, another pronoun (such as *he, hers,* or *yours*). The students then had to rate the syllables on how pleasant or unpleasant they were. Why, you might ask, would anyone have an emotional reaction to the nonsense word *yof*? Yet students liked the nonsense syllables significantly more when they had been paired with in-group words. Not one student guessed why; none was aware of how the words had been paired (Perdue et al., 1990).

ethnocentrism The belief that your own ethnic group, nation, or religion is superior to all others.

stereotype A cognitive schema or a summary impression of a group, in which a person believes that all members of the group share a common trait or traits (positive, negative, or neutral).

Us–them thinking both creates and reflects stereotyping. A **stereotype** is a summary impression of a group of people in which a person believes that all members of that group share a common trait or traits. Stereotypes are among the cognitive schemas by which we map the world. They may be negative, positive, or neutral. There are stereotypes of people who drive Volkswagens or BMWs, of men who wear earrings and of women who wear business suits, of engineering students and art students, of feminists and fraternities.

The fact that everyone occasionally thinks in stereotypes is itself neither good nor bad. Stereotypes help us process new information and retrieve old memories. They allow us to organize experience, make sense of the differences among individuals and groups, and predict how people will behave. They are, as some psychologists have called them, useful "tools in the mental toolbox"—energy-saving devices that allow us to make efficient decisions (Macrae, Milne, & Bodenhausen, 1994). For example, as one study found, people remember the qualities associated with stereotypes such as "prude" or "politician" better than they remember a list of specific traits ("reserved"; "extroverted"). The researchers concluded that "categorization by stereotype provides a virtually instantaneous, detailed, and memorable portrait of an individual" (Andersen, Klatzky, & Murray, 1990).

Although stereotypes do help us put the world together, they lead to three distortions of reality (Judd et al., 1995). First, *stereotypes accentuate differences between groups,* leading people to overlook the common features between groups. As a result, the stereotyped group may seem odd, unfamiliar, or dangerous—"not like us." Second, *stereotypes produce selective perceptions.* People tend to see only what fits the stereotype and to reject any perceptions that do not fit. Third, *stereotypes underestimate differences within other groups.* People realize that their own groups are heterogeneous—that is, made up of all kinds of individuals. But stereotypes create the impression that all members of other groups (say, all Texans or all teenagers) are the same. One rude French waiter means that all French people are rude; one Greek thief means that all Greeks are thieves. But if someone in their own group is rude or steals, most people draw no such conclusions. This cognitive habit starts early. Social psychologist Marilynn Brewer reports that her daughter returned from kindergarten one day with the observation that "Boys are crybabies." The child's evidence was that she had seen two boys crying on their first day away from home. Brewer asked whether any little girls had also cried. Oh yes, said her daughter. "But," she insisted, "only *some* girls cry; *I* didn't cry."

Stereotypes are not always entirely wrong. Many have a grain of truth, capturing with some accuracy something about the group (Allport, 1954/1979). The problems occur when people assume that the grain of truth is the whole seashore. For example, many American whites have a stereotype about blacks that is based on the troubling statistics that are in the news, such as the number of young black men who are in prison. But in recent decades there has also been an enormous expansion of blacks into the middle class and into integrated occupations and communities. Many whites, however, have not assimilated these positive statistics into their racial stereotypes.

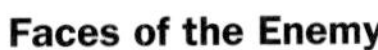

Faces of the Enemy

In every country, propaganda posters stereotype "them," the enemy, as ugly, aggressive, brutish, and greedy; "we," the heroes, are beautiful and virtuous. These examples show the Soviet view of the United States in the 1930s as a greedy capitalist; an American depiction of the German enemy in World War I as a "mad brute"; and an IRA poster of bloody "English pigs."

For their part, many blacks have negative stereotypes about whites, whom they often see as unvarying in their attributes and prejudices (Judd et al., 1995).

When people like a group, their stereotype of the group's behavior tends to be positive. When they dislike a group, their stereotype of the same behavior tends to be negative (Peabody, 1985). For example, if you like a woman who is careful with money, you might call her *thrifty*, but if you dislike her, you might call her *stingy*. Likewise, someone who is friendly toward strangers could be *trusting* or *gullible;* someone who enjoys spending time with relatives could be *family-loving* or *clannish*.

Positive and negative stereotypes, in turn, depend on the values, cultural norms, and attributions of the observer. For example, Mexican students are significantly more accepting of fat people and less concerned about their own weight than are American students. Americans tend to have strongly negative stereotypes about fat people, which stem from a cultural ideology that individuals are responsible for what happens to them and for how they look (Crandall & Martinez, 1996).

Such differences in ideology and values may affect how people from different cultures evaluate the same event (Taylor & Porter, 1994). Is coming late to class good, bad, or neutral? Is it good or bad to argue with your parents about grades? Chinese students in Hong Kong, where communalism and respect for one's elders are highly valued, and students in Australia, where individualism is highly valued, give entirely different interpretations of these two actions (Forgas & Bond, 1985). It is a small step from different interpretations to negative stereotypes: "Australians are selfish and disrespectful of adults"; "The Chinese are mindless slaves of authority." And it is a small step from negative stereotyping to prejudice.

The Many Faces of Prejudice

WANTS, &c.

WANTED A COOK—She must not be an Irish woman, and must bring unexceptionable recommendations. Apply at 33 Grove street, Greenwich. j5 3t

WANTED—A FARM in Westchester county, with a good water prospect. One in the vicinity of Throg's Neck would be preferred. Apply at 250 Pearl-street. d20 d&ctf

WANTED.—Young Ladies as apprentices wanted at the Mantua-making Establishment of A. C. SMETS & CO. 258 Broadway. n30

BOARD WANTED—by a gentleman and lady in a private family, in the vicinity of Cliff-street. A family where there are no other boarders would be preferred. Address A. B. at this Office. J6 3t*

These photos reveal the history of prejudice in the United States. In 1831, a newspaper boldly reflected the then popular dislike of the Irish. Hotels and want ads used to make it clear that "Gentiles only" were wanted, and anti-Semitism is on the rise again today.

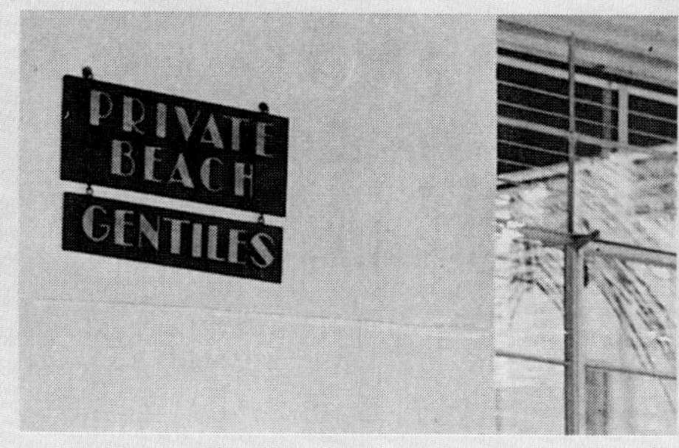

PREJUDICE

A *prejudice* is an unreasonable negative feeling toward a category of people or a cultural practice. Prejudice consists of a negative stereotype of a group and a strong emotional dislike of, or outright hatred of, its members. Feelings of prejudice violate the spirit of critical thinking and the scientific method because they resist rational argument and evidence. In his classic book *The Nature of Prejudice*, social psychologist Gordon Allport (1954/1979) described the responses characteristic of a prejudiced person when confronted with evidence contradicting his or her beliefs:

Mr. X: The trouble with Jews is that they only take care of their own group.

Mr. Y: But the record of the Community Chest campaign shows that they give more generously, in proportion to their numbers, to the general charities of the community, than do non-Jews.

Mr. X: That shows they are always trying to buy favor and intrude into Christian affairs. They think of nothing but money; that is why there are so many Jewish bankers.

Mr. Y:: But a recent study shows that the percentage of Jews in the banking business is negligible, far smaller than the percentage of non-Jews.

Mr. X: That's just it; they don't go in for respectable business; they are only in the movie business or run night clubs.

Notice that Mr. X doesn't respond to Mr. Y's evidence; he just moves along to another reason for his dislike of Jews. That is the nature of prejudice. Elliot Aronson

Anti-Japanese feelings ran high in the 1920s and during World War II, and returned in the 1990s with America's economic recession. Iranians and other "aliens" have been the target of political hostilities.

(1995) gives another example: Suppose Mr. Y tried to persuade you to eat boiled insects. "Ugh," you might say, "they are so ugly." "But so are lobsters," he says, "and lots of people love lobsters." "Well, insects have no food value," you say. "Actually, they are a good source of protein," he answers. He might try other arguments, but the fact is that you have a food prejudice against eating insects, a reaction that does not exist in all cultures.

THE SOURCES OF PREJUDICE One powerful reason for prejudice lies in its ability to ward off feelings of inadequacy, doubt, and fear. Often, prejudiced persons project their fears onto the target group, using it as a *scapegoat.* Prejudice also reduces anxiety in uncertain times by allowing people to reduce complex problems to one cause: "Those people are the source of all my troubles." Most important, as research on samples from many nations has repeatedly confirmed, prejudice is a tonic for low self-esteem: People puff up their own low feelings of self-worth by disliking or hating groups they see as inferior (Islam & Hewstone, 1993; Stephan et al., 1994; Tajfel & Turner, 1986).

In a demonstration of the link between low self-esteem and prejudice, students participated in what they believed were two separate studies (Fein & Spencer, 1997). In the first, they got positive or negative feedback about their performance on a test of "social perceptiveness" and verbal skills. In the second, they were asked to evaluate the résumé of a woman who had applied for a job as personnel manager. All the subjects were shown the same résumé and photograph of the candidate, but half were told her name was "Julie Goldberg" and that she did volunteer work for a

Native Americans have been objects of hatred since Europeans first arrived on the continent. Animosity toward blacks resulted in segregated facilities, a legal practice until the 1950s, and today many neighborhoods and schools remain separate and unequal.

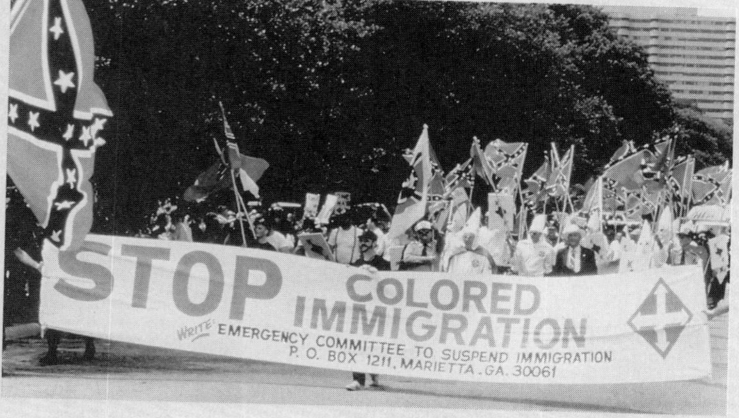

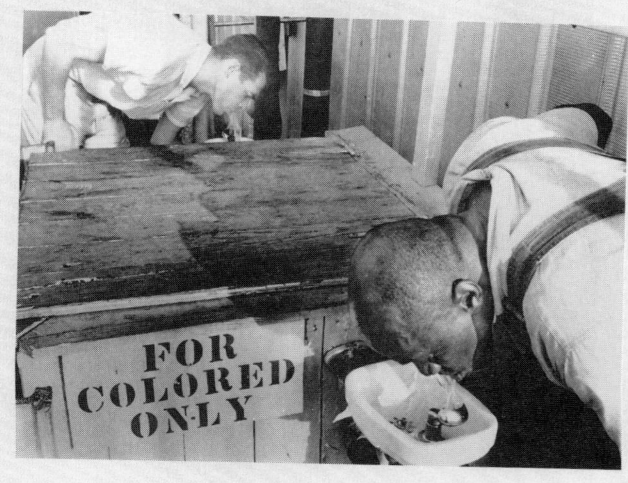

Jewish organization, and half were told her name was "Maria D'Agostino" and that she volunteered at a Catholic organization. (Data from the few Jewish students in the sample were excluded from analysis.) The students who were feeling good about their test scores did not evaluate the "Jewish" woman differently from the "Italian" woman. But those who had received a blow to their self-esteem evaluated the woman they believed to be Jewish more harshly than the Italian candidate. Their denigration of her, in turn, had the effect of raising their own self-esteem. The same results occurred when heterosexual students evaluated a man they believed to be gay: Their evaluations of him were harsher only when their self-esteem had been threatened (Fein & Spencer, 1997).

Not all prejudices have deep-seated psychological roots. Some are acquired mindlessly in the process of socialization; parents may communicate subtle messages to their children that say "We don't associate with people like that," sometimes without either generation having ever met the object of their dislike. And, as social-learning theorists have shown, some people acquire prejudices from advertising, entertainment shows, and news reports that perpetuate derogatory images and stereotypes of groups such as old people and fat people.

Social and cultural psychologists have also identified factors *outside* the individual that contribute to the persistence of prejudice and discrimination. For one thing, prejudices often bring support from others who share them, as well as the threat of losing that support by abandoning the prejudice. The pressures to conform make it difficult for most people to break away from the prejudices of their friends, families, and associates.

Prejudice against women also remains widespread, as does virulent anger against gay men and lesbians. Why do new prejudices keep emerging, and why do some old ones persist?

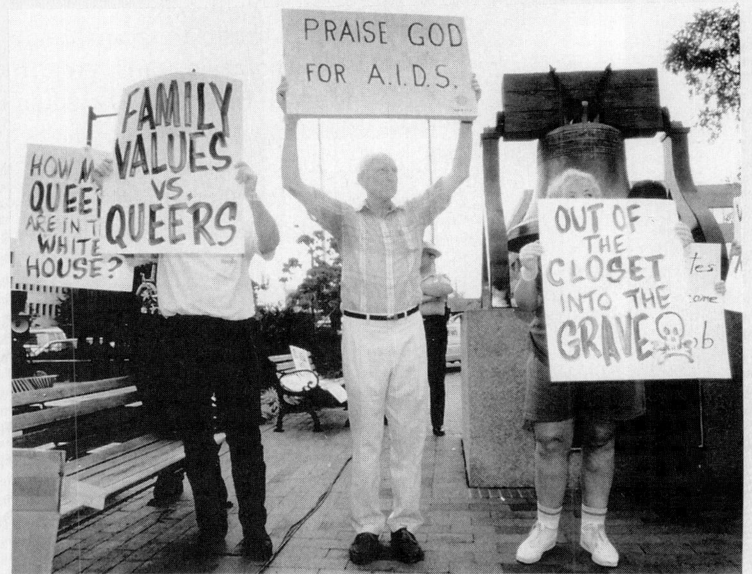

GET INVOLVED

Are you prejudiced against a specific group of people? Is it a group defined by gender, ethnicity, sexual orientation, nationality, religion, physical appearance, or political views? Write down your deepest thoughts and feelings about this group. Take as long as you want, and do not censor yourself or say what you think you ought to say. Now reread what you have written. Which of the many reasons for prejudice discussed in the text might be supporting your views? Do you feel that your attitudes toward the group are legitimate, or are you uncomfortable about having them?

But perhaps the most important reason for prejudice, in the sociocultural view, is that it brings *economic benefits and justifies the majority group's dominance* (Sidanius, Pratto, & Bobo, 1996). That's why prejudice always rises when groups are in direct competition for jobs. In the nineteenth century, when Chinese immigrants in the United States were working in the gold mines, they were described by the local whites as being depraved and vicious, bloodthirsty and inhuman. Just a decade later, when the Chinese began working on the transcontinental railroad—doing difficult and dangerous jobs that few white men would do—prejudice against them declined. They were considered hardworking, industrious, and law-abiding. But after the railroad was finished, jobs dwindled. The Chinese had to compete with Civil War veterans for scarce jobs, and white attitudes toward the Chinese changed again. Chinese workers were considered "criminal," "crafty," "conniving," and "stupid" (Aronson, 1995). Thus prejudice served to justify the whites' treatment of the Chinese, as it continues to justify any dominant group's ill treatment of a minority. In a series of experiments in Bangladesh, Muslims (who are the majority there) and Hindus (a minority) both revealed strong in-group favoritism, but only the Muslims also denigrated the minority Hindus (Islam & Hewstone, 1993).

Years ago, a classic study confirmed the link between economic conditions and scapegoating in America. Data from 14 states in the American South revealed a strong negative correlation between the number of black lynchings and the economic value of cotton: the poorer the economic conditions for whites, the greater the number of lynchings (Hovland & Sears, 1940). These data were later reanalyzed to assess other possible explanations, but the correlation remained (Hepworth & West, 1988). Another research project used many different measures of economic threat and social insecurity (including the unemployment rate, the rate of serious crimes, the number of work stoppages, and personal income levels) and of prejudice (including the number of anti-Semitic incidents, activities by the Ku Klux Klan, and attitudes toward other groups). Again, during times of high social and economic threat, prejudice increased significantly (Doty, Peterson, & Winter, 1991).

DEFINE YOUR TERMS

How would you define a racist? Are people racist if they privately dislike members of another group, but never actually treat them unfairly? Are people racist if they are opposed to racism but feel uncomfortable being around a member of another group?

THE VARIETIES OF PREJUDICE One problem in studying prejudice is that not all prejudiced people are prejudiced in the same way or to the same extent. Gordon Allport (1954/1979) astutely observed that "defeated intellectually, prejudice lingers emotionally." That is, a person might want to lose a prejudice against a certain group and realize that his or her feelings are unwarranted, yet still feel uncomfortable with members of the group. Should we put this person in the same category as one who is outspokenly bigoted or who actively discriminates against others by virtue of their sex, culture, sexual orientation, or skin color? Do good intentions count? What if a person is ignorant of another culture and mindlessly blurts out a remark that reflects that ignorance? Does that count as prejudice or merely as thoughtlessness?

Studies that define prejudice according to people's expressed attitudes find that prejudice in the United States and Canada is declining: White attitudes toward integration have become steadily more favorable, and beliefs that blacks are inferior to whites have markedly dropped (Devine, 1995). Similarly, men's endorsement of gender equality has steadily increased; the number of men openly expressing prejudice toward women executives, for example, declined from 41 percent in 1965 to only 5 percent in 1985 (Tougas et al., 1995), and between 1970 and 1995 antiwoman attitudes in general dropped sharply (Twenge, 1996).

On the other hand, many people hold remnants of prejudices that were acquired in childhood but that, as adults, they are consciously trying to eradicate. Thus some whites and heterosexuals may feel uncomfortable when they are with blacks or homosexuals, but they also feel guilty about having these feelings and struggle to overcome them (Devine et al., 1991). According to Patricia Devine (1995), people who are actively trying to break their "prejudice habit" should not be accused of being bigots. The discomfort could reflect an honest effort to put old prejudices aside or simple unfamiliarity with the other group's ways.

A similar argument holds that the main problem dividing blacks and whites is not prejudice but differing cultural values. Surveys find that many white Americans place a high value on equality but also on individualism and self-reliance (Katz & Hass, 1988). Their support of equality leads many whites to feel sympathy toward blacks because of the disadvantages and discrimination they know that blacks have suffered. But the values of individualism and self-reliance lead many of the same whites to accuse blacks of not taking enough responsibility for solving their own problems. Most African-Americans, however, place their highest value on equality and justice. They argue that their lower status and income are not a result of a failure of self-reliance but of the systematic injustice they have suffered at the hands of whites. As reactions to the acquittal of O. J. Simpson and to other divisive events have shown, the gap in perceptions of racism and injustice in America is large, and it confirms to many African-Americans that white Americans just "don't get it."

Other social scientists believe that racial animosity and sexism are undiminished. Overt attitudes, they say, are not an accurate measure of these prejudices, because people know they should not admit these feelings (Bell, 1992; Tougas et al., 1995). These observers maintain that prejudice toward blacks, for example, lurks behind a mask of *symbolic racism*, in which whites focus not on dislike of black individuals but on racial issues such as "reverse discrimination," "hard-core criminals," or "welfare abuse." In their view, these issues have become code words for the continuing animosity that many whites have for blacks.

The way to measure racism, according to this argument, is by using unobtrusive measures rather than direct attitude questionnaires. You might observe how people behave when they are with a possible object of prejudice; do they sit farther away than they normally would? You might observe how quickly people come up with positive or negative associations to stimulus pictures, for instance of black versus white faces—a possible measure of unconscious prejudice (Fazio et al., 1995). You might observe how people who say they are unprejudiced behave when they are emotionally upset (Jones, 1991). In one such experiment in which students administered shock to confederates in an apparent study of biofeedback, whites showed *less* aggression toward blacks than toward whites. But as soon as the whites were angered by overhearing derogatory remarks about themselves, they showed *more* aggression toward blacks than toward whites (Rogers & Prentice-Dunn, 1981). This finding implies that whites may be willing to control their negative feelings toward blacks (or, if you recall the "Julie Goldberg" study, toward Jews or other targets of prejudice) under normal conditions. But as soon as they are angry, stressed, provoked, or suffer a blow to their self-esteem, their real prejudice reveals itself.

As if these complexities of prejudice were not enough, there is another. Peter Glick and Susan Fiske (1996) argue that sexism is "a special case of prejudice" that is often marked by "a deep ambivalence, rather than a uniform antipathy, toward women." Using a questionnaire they call the Ambivalent Sexism Inventory, which has been administered to more than 2,000 individuals of both sexes, they have identified two kinds of sexism that are empirically distinct. The first is *hostile sexism*, which involves strongly negative feelings about women, such as anger, hatred, and contempt; this kind of sexism is comparable to any other negative prejudice toward an entire group. The second is *benevolent sexism*, which involves positive feelings about women, along with paternalistic, protective, and stereotyped attitudes toward them—a prejudice that says "I like women, as long as they stay in their proper place."

As you can see, the definition and study of racism and other forms of prejudice are not easy. How does covert discomfort or a patronizing sense of superiority differ from explicit hostility? Can a woman hold sexist attitudes toward men, or should sexism refer only to prejudice and discrimination against women? Is a black person who dislikes all whites or Asians a racist, or is racism an attribute only of institutions and of those in power? Because people differ in their premises, such as the definitions of *racist* and *sexist*, and in their values, such as equality or self-reliance, their conclusions about prejudice will also differ.

REDUCING PREJUDICE How can prejudice and conflict between groups be reduced? As we have seen, prejudice can stem from low self-esteem or other psychological needs, mindlessly acquired attitudes prevalent in your family or larger society, the desire to maintain group dominance or to preserve economic interests, conflicts over values, or unfamiliarity with another group's ways. Given the many sources and definitions of prejudice, no one solution will fit all kinds (Monteith, 1996).

Efforts to reduce prejudice and cultural conflicts must also distinguish between strongly prejudiced people who lack any motivation to change, and people who are unfamiliar or uncomfortable with members of another culture but who feel guilty about their discomfort. For example, a "cycle of distrust" and animosity can emerge in a group when members actually start off with the best intentions to get along. Some majority-group members are highly motivated to work well with minorities, but they are self-conscious and anxious about doing "the wrong thing." Their anxiety makes them behave awkwardly, for instance, by blurting out dumb remarks and avoiding eye contact with minority-group members. The minority members, based on their own history of discrimination, interpret the majority-group members' behavior as evidence of hostility—and thus respond with withdrawal, aloofness, or anger. The majority members, not understanding that their own anxieties have been interpreted as evidence of prejudice, regard the minority members' behavior as unreasonable or mysterious, so they reciprocate the hostility or withdraw. This behavior confirms the minority members' suspicions about the majority's true feelings and prejudices (Devine, Evett, & Vasquez-Suson, 1996).

By understanding the cycle, people can learn to break it. Majority members can become aware of the discrepancy between their good intentions and their actual behavior. They can learn to reduce their discomfort with people unlike themselves, and to acquire the skills that will lessen their anxiety. But breaking the cycle of distrust and hostility, Patricia Devine and her colleagues argue, is not only a majority-group problem. Minorities must become part of the solution too, for example, by recognizing their possible biases in seeing the majority members' behavior only in a negative light. Both sides, Devine (1995) emphasizes, should remember that reduc-

Some doubts and insecurities felt by minority-group members.

Some doubts and insecurities felt by majority-group members.

ing prejudice is a *process*, not an "all or none event." It doesn't happen overnight. It is important, she argues, to reward people who are making the effort to change their biases, rather than condemning them for not being perfect.

But what happens when two groups really do bear enormous animosity toward each other, for historical, economic, or emotional reasons? How then might their conflicts be reduced? Solutions based on sociocultural findings emphasize *changing people's social and cultural circumstances*, rather than waiting around for individuals to have a moral or psychological conversion.

One line of attack on prejudice is to change the laws that make discrimination—the official endorsement of prejudice against certain groups—acceptable. Integration of public facilities in the American South would never have occurred if civil-rights advocates had waited for segregationists to have a change of heart. Women would never have gotten the right to vote, attend college, or do "men's work" without persistent challenges to the laws that permitted discrimination. But laws do not necessarily change attitudes if all they do is produce unequal contact between two former antagonists or if economic competition for jobs continues. Even with legal reforms, de facto segregation of schools and neighborhoods is still the rule in the United States and other countries, and racial prejudices are still deeply felt.

Another approach, the *contact hypothesis*, holds that the best way to end prejudice is to bring members of both sides together and let them get acquainted; in this way, they will discover their shared humanity. The contact hypothesis had a moment of glory during the 1950s and 1960s. In some settings, such as newly integrated housing projects, contact between blacks and whites did reduce hostility (Deutsch & Collins, 1951; Wilner, Walkley, & Cook, 1955). However, as is apparent at most big-city high schools today, desegregation and opportunities to socialize are often unsuccessful (Stephan, 1985). Ethnic groups still form cliques and gangs, fighting other groups and defending their own ways.

A third approach is to go directly into desegregated schools and businesses and set up *cooperative situations* in which antagonistic groups have to work together for a common goal (as the Eagles and the Rattlers had to do in the Robbers Cave study, discussed in Chapter 17). For example, years ago, researchers tried to reduce ethnic conflict among white, Chicano, and black children in Texas elementary schools by designing a "jigsaw method" to build cooperation (Aronson et al., 1978). Classes were divided into groups of six students of mixed ethnicity, and every group worked together on a shared task that was broken up like a jigsaw puzzle. Each child needed the contributions of the others to put the assignment together; for instance, each child might be given one paragraph of a six-paragraph biography and be asked to learn the whole story. The cooperative students, in comparison to classmates in regular classes, had greater self-esteem, liked their classmates better, showed a decrease in prejudice, and improved their grades. These findings, and studies of other versions of cooperative learning, have been replicated in many different classrooms (Aronson, Wilson, & Akert, 1997; Johnson and Johnson, 1989). But cooperation does not work when members of a group have unequal status, blame one another for loafing or "dropping the ball," or perceive that their teachers or employers are playing favorites.

Because of the complex reasons for the tensions between unequal groups in today's world, no single-arrow effort to hit the bull's-eye of prejudice is likely to hit its target. The zinger is that for any of these strategies to have its greatest impact, you have to have all of them. In combination, they have a powerful effect on reducing prejudice and conflict (Amir, 1994; Fisher, 1994; Rubin, 1994; Staub, 1996; Stephan & Brigham, 1985):

1. *Both sides must have equal status and equal economic standing.* If one side has more power or greater economic opportunity, prejudice can continue. Thus, simply putting blacks and whites in the same situation won't necessarily reduce conflict if the whites have all the decision-making authority and higher status. Indeed, in such cases, white stereotypes about blacks tend to be reinforced rather than weakened (Amir, 1994). But when blacks have equal or higher status, white attitudes typically change in a much more favorable direction.

2. *Both sides must cooperate, working together for a common goal,* an enterprise that reduces us–them thinking and creates an encompassing social identity. Both sides must work together to find solutions, in a spirit of collaboration and joint problem solving. If one side tries to bully and dominate the other, if one side passively capitulates or withdraws, or if both sides compete to see who will win, the conflict will continue (Rubin, 1994).

3. *Both sides must have the moral, legal, and economic support of authorities,* such as teachers, employers, the judicial system, government officials, and the police. In other words, the larger culture must support the goal of equality in its laws and in the actions of its officials.

4. *Both sides must have opportunities to work and socialize together, formally and informally.* The contact hypothesis is right in predicting that prejudice is reduced when people have the chance to get used to one another's food, music, customs, attitudes, and everyday preferences (Fisher, 1994).

Perhaps one reason that cultural conflicts have been so persistent around the world is that these four conditions are rarely met all at the same time.

Quick Quiz

Try to overcome your prejudice against quizzes and take this one.

A. Identify which concept—ethnocentrism, stereotyping, or prejudice—is illustrated by the following three statements.

1. Juan believes that all Anglos are uptight and cold, and he won't listen to any evidence that contradicts his belief.

2. John knows and likes the Chicano minority in his town, but he privately believes that Anglo culture is superior to all others.
3. Jane believes that Honda owners are thrifty and practical. June believes that Honda owners are stingy and dull.

B. A 1994 survey found that large percentages of African-Americans, Asian-Americans, and Latinos hold negative stereotypes of one another and resent other minorities almost as much as they resent whites. What are some of the reasons that people who have themselves been victims of stereotyping and prejudice would hold the same attitudes toward others?

Answers:

A. 1. prejudice 2. ethnocentrism 3. stereotypes B. socialization by parents and messages in the larger society; conformity with friends who share these prejudices; and economic competition for jobs and other resources

CAN CULTURES GET ALONG?

The whole world is festering with unhappy souls—
The French hate the Germans, the Germans hate the Poles,
Italians hate Yugoslavs, South Africans hate the Dutch;
And I don't like anybody very much.

Sheldon Harnick, "Merry Little Minuet"

Sometimes the possibility of harmonious relations between cultures looks bleak indeed. All over the world, animosities erupt in bloody battles, and new wars emerge even where groups had been living together companionably. When cultures with different customs, values, and nonverbal gestures collide, misunderstandings can even be fatal. In Stockton, California, a driver used a hand signal to alert a car behind him at a stoplight that his headlights were off. The driver of the second car, taking this gesture as a sign of disrespect, shot at the first car, killing a passenger.

Cultural psychology, which has identified the continuing reasons for international and multicultural conflict, also gives us hope for reducing such conflict. The knowledge of how cultures differ, even in the smallest rules of time management and eye contact, benefits everyone who has to deal with another culture—which, on this shrinking planet, is all of us: neighbor, tourist, business executive, or diplomat. The study of culture suggests that conflict and aggression are not determined solely by human biology, but also by our circumstances. Therefore, as circumstances change, so does the need for violence; and indeed, throughout history, societies have changed from being warlike to being peaceful, and vice versa. The Swedes were once one of the most warlike nations on earth, but today they are among the most pacifistic and egalitarian (Groebel & Hinde, 1989).

Yet cultural research, which has done so much to make people aware of the dangers of ethnocentrism and the reasons for differences among groups, is sometimes misused or misunderstood. The study of difference is not meant to foster cultural separatism, in which people glorify only their own group and regard other cultures or the other gender as inherently inferior—or so hopelessly different that there's no point in trying to get along with them (Fowers & Richardson, 1996).

As groups that were once excluded from psychological research and theory have become aware of the injustice of this omission, they have done much to remedy matters. But some psychologists and social critics are concerned about tendencies to replace old biases with new ones (Appiah, 1994; Crawford & Marecek, 1989; Gates,

These eloquent paintings were created by children of the former Yugoslavia during the war that shattered their lives and bitterly divided their country along ethnic lines. Dinko, age 12, called his drawing of war "Horror and Scream." Nikoleta, age 10, dreamed of peace. Can the findings of cross-cultural psychology help us create a world in which conflicts and differences, though inevitable, need not erupt in horrors and screams?

AVOID EMOTIONAL REASONING

Ethnocentrism—the emotionally gratifying feeling that your own culture is best—often blinds people to the evidence that no human group is naturally "nicer" or "kinder" than all others. Can people learn to take pride in their own culture or gender without feeling superior to others?

1992; Hughes, 1993; Yoder & Kahn, 1993). Thus, some women want to replace the view that women are the deficient sex with the view that women are the better sex, the sex that will save the world (Eisler, 1987). Some Native Americans promulgate a romantic view that before the advent of Europeans, native cultures lived in complete harmony with each other and with the environment (actually, some of them waged war, pillaged the countryside, and enslaved captured enemies). Some African-Americans argue that Africans are the "sun people," who have a "humanistic, spiritualistic value system," whereas Europeans are the "ice people," who are "egoistic, individualistic, and exploitative" (Traub, 1993). However, as Kwame Appiah (1994), a professor of Afro-American studies who is himself from Ghana, writes, "Cruelty and kindness are not Western prerogatives, any more than intelligence and creativity. . . . The proper response to Eurocentrism is surely not a reactive Afrocentrism, but a new understanding that humanizes all of us by learning to think beyond race."

Cultural psychology shows that no culture has always and everywhere been superior to every other in its dealings with humanity. This is because all of us are subject to the same psychological, cultural, and economic factors that foster tolerance or animosity. But cultural psychology *can* help us formulate more realistic goals for living in a diverse world. At one unrealistic extreme, some people would persuade or force every other group and religion to become just like them. At the other unrealistic extreme, some people dream of all cultures living together in perfect harmony, respecting their differences. Cultural research suggests, on the contrary, that we would do better to recognize that conflicts will always occur, because of economic inequities and cultural misunderstandings, and then turn our attention to finding nonviolent ways of resolving these conflicts. Ethnocentrism may always be with us, as long as people live in different groups. But if we can think of ways to reduce the payoffs of prejudice, perhaps we can also reduce the tendency for good feelings about our own culture to create hostile feelings toward others. That would be the best way of all to "take psychology with us."

Taking Psychology with You

Travels Across the Cultural Divide

A French salesman worked for a company that was bought by Americans. When the new American manager ordered him to step up his sales within the next three months, the employee quit in a huff, taking his customers with him. Why? In polychronic France, it takes years to develop customers; in family-owned businesses, relationships with customers may span generations. The monochronic American wanted instant results, as Americans usually do, but the French salesman knew this was impossible and quit. The American view was, "He wasn't up to the job; he's lazy and disloyal, so he stole my customers." The French view was, "There is no point in explaining anything to a person who is so stupid as to think you can acquire loyal customers in three months" (Hall & Hall, 1987).

As this story shows, when monochronic and polychronic people try to do business with one another, they often make unintentional mistakes. Many corporations are beginning to realize that such cultural differences are not trivial and that their business success depends on understanding them. You, too, can benefit from the research on cultures, whether you plan to do business abroad, visit as a tourist, or just want to get along better in our own increasingly diverse society.

• *Be sure you understand the other culture's rules,* not only of manners and customs but also of nonverbal gestures and methods of communication. If you find yourself getting angry over something a person from another culture is doing, try to find out whether your expectations and perceptions of that person's behavior are appropriate. For example, Koreans typically do not shake hands when greeting strangers, whereas African-Americans and whites do. People who shake hands as a gesture of friendship and courtesy are likely to feel insulted if another person refuses to do the same, unless they understand that what is going on is a cultural difference.

• *When in Rome, do as the Romans do—as much as possible.* Most of the things you really need to know about a culture are not to be found in the guidebooks or travelogues, but in the kind of information reported in this chapter. To learn the unspoken rules of a culture, keep your eyes open and your mouth shut: Look, listen, and observe. What is the pace of life like? Which is more valued in this culture, relationships or schedules? Are business transactions based on bargaining and negotiation or on a fixed exchange? When customers enter a shop, do they greet and chat with the shopkeeper or ignore the person as they browse?

For example, you can't do business across cultures unless you understand a culture's rules of negotiation. If you are not used to bargaining, shopping in Morocco or Mexico will be exasperating. You won't know the unstated rules, you won't know whether you got "taken" or got "a great buy," and you will walk away wishing for a system of fixed prices. If you are used to bargaining, you will be just as exasperated when a seller offers you a flat price. "Where's the fun in this?" you'll say. "The whole human transaction of shopping is gone!" It will help to find a cultural "translator" who can show you the ropes.

Remember, though, that even when you know the rules, you may find it difficult to carry them out. For example, cultures differ in their tolerance for prolonged gazes (Keating, 1994). In the Middle East, two men will look directly at one another as they talk, but such direct gazes would be deeply uncomfortable to most Japanese or white Americans, and a sign of insult to some African-Americans. Knowing this fact about gaze rules can help people accept the reality of different customs, but most of us will still feel uncomfortable trying to change our own entrenched ways.

• *Nevertheless, avoid stereotyping.* Try not to let your awareness of cultural differences cause you to overlook individual variations within cultures. During a dreary Boston winter, social psychologist Roger Brown (1986) went to the Bahamas for a vacation. To his surprise, he found the people he met unfriendly, rude, and sullen. He decided that the reason was that Bahamians had to deal with spoiled, critical foreigners, and he tried out this hypothesis on a cab driver. The cab driver looked at Brown in amazement, smiled cheerfully, and told him that Bahamians don't mind tourists; just *unsmiling* tourists.

And then Brown realized what had been going on. "Not tourists generally, but this tourist, myself, was the cause," he wrote. "Confronted with my unrelaxed wintry Boston face, they had assumed I had no interest in them and had responded non-committally, inexpressively. I had created the Bahamian national character. Everywhere I took my face it sprang into being. So I began smiling a lot, and the Bahamians changed their national character. In fact, they lost any national character and differentiated into individuals."

Perhaps the best advice is to *use cultural explanations to expand your understanding of human behavior, not to reduce behavior to culture.* Any one-factor explanation can lead to an abdication of individual responsibility, which is why "The system made me do it" or "My culture made me do it" is no more valid than "My hormones made me do it" or "My upbringing made me do it." Cultural psychology teaches us to appreciate the countless explicit and implicit cultural rules that govern our behavior, values, and attitudes. Yet we should not forget Roger Brown's lesson that every human being is an individual—one who shares the common concerns of all humanity.

SUMMARY

THE STUDY OF CULTURE

1) *Culture* is a program of shared rules that govern the behavior of members of a community or society, and a set of values, beliefs, and attitudes shared by most members of that community. The study of culture is challenging because of difficulties in devising effective methods and getting samples from many societies in order to make valid cultural comparisons; the difficulty of interpreting results when the same custom may have different meanings and functions across cultures; the risk of stereotyping; the common tendency to *reify* "culture" as an explanation without identifying the mechanisms or aspects of culture that influence behavior; and the political sensitivity of many findings.

THE RULES OF CULTURE

2) Some signals of *body language* seem to be universal, but most, such as *conversational distance* and notions of when a smile is appropriate, are specific to particular cultures. This fact creates many possibilities for misunderstanding and offense. In *high-context cultures,* people pay close attention to nonverbal signs; they assume a shared knowledge and history, so things need not be spelled out. In *low-context cultures,* people pay more attention to words than to nonverbal language; everything must be explained and stated directly.

3) *Monochronic cultures* organize time into linear segments in which people do one thing at a time, and they value promptness. *Polychronic cultures* organize time along parallel lines; people do many things at once, and the demands of friends and family supersede those of the appointment book. A culture's way of organizing time stems from its economic system, social organization, political history, and ecology.

4) *Individualist cultures* define the "self" as a collection of personality traits and tend to value the rights of the individual over the needs of the group; *collectivist cultures* see the "self" as embedded in a community and place group needs first. The way that people define the self affects many aspects of individual psychology, including people's personalities, emotions, and relationships. In collectivist cultures, the strongest human bond is usually not between husband and wife but between parent and child, and child rearing is communal.

5) People develop *social identities* based on their nationality, ethnicity, religion, and other roles in society. One important social identity is an *ethnic identity.* In culturally diverse societies, many people face the problem of balancing their ethnic identity with *acculturation* into the larger society. Depending on whether ethnic identity and identification with the larger culture are strong or weak, a person may become bicultural; choose assimilation; become an ethnic separatist; or feel marginal. Ethnic labels have great symbolic and emotional significance, which is why they are so politically volatile (as discussed in "Psychology and Popular Culture").

THE ORIGINS OF CULTURE

6) In the cultural view, a culture's attitudes and practices are embedded in its history, environment, economy, and survival needs; thus most gender differences are learned rather than determined by anatomical sex. For example, although some gender differences appear to be universal, there are many variations in women's status, the work that men and women do, the degree of male–female contact, the value placed on female chastity, and the salience of gender differences. Factors pertaining to *production* (the economy) and *reproduction* (availability of birth control and the need for many or few children) help explain these variations.

7) Economic and social factors are also involved in the variations among men in aggressiveness and in the status of women. High rates of male violence and homicide in the American South and West are related to a history of reliance on herding, which produces a "culture of honor," rather than on farming. As countries become industrialized and urban, their gender roles also become more egalitarian; access to reliable birth control and the growth of jobs involving service skills and brainwork are eliminating the traditional reasons for a sexual division of labor.

CROSS-CULTURAL RELATIONS

8) *Ethnocentrism,* the belief that your own group or nation is superior to all others, promotes "us–them" thinking. *Stereotypes* help people rapidly process new information, retrieve memories, organize experience, and predict how others will behave. But they distort reality in three ways: (1) They emphasize differences between groups; (2) they underestimate the differences within groups; and (3) they produce selective perception. The values and rules of culture determine how people see and interpret the same event. When they like a group, their stereotypes of the group's behavior are positive; when they dislike a group, their stereotypes of the same behavior are often negative.

9) A *prejudice* is an unreasonable negative feeling toward a category of people or a cultural practice. Prejudice has several psychological functions: It reduces anxiety by allowing people to feel superior; it bolsters self-esteem when a person feels threatened; and it provides a simple explanation of complex problems. But prejudice also has social and financial functions. People acquire prejudices through childhood socialization, the social support they receive, and the economic benefits they gain as a result. During times of economic difficulty, prejudice rises significantly.

10) Prejudice occurs in many varieties and degrees, a fact that causes debates about definitions of racism, sexism, and other prejudices. Blacks and whites often disagree on their definitions of racism and on the question of whether racism is declining or has merely taken new forms (e.g., *symbolic racism*). Similarly, *hostile sexism*—dislike of and contempt for women—is different from *benevolent sexism*—an attitude of "I like women, as long as they stay in their place."

11) Efforts to reduce prejudice and group conflict must be based on the reasons for people's prejudices, which include psychological needs, economic motives, social benefits, and unfamiliarity with another group's ways. In groups where members of majority and minority groups work together, participants need to assess each other's behavior accurately, to avoid inferring prejudice or hostility when none is intended. Social and cultural psychologists emphasize the external factors involved in reducing prejudice and conflict, starting with the importance of making discrimination illegal. However, laws do not inevitably change attitudes, especially if economic competition continues. Prejudice decreases when people from different groups work together for a common goal; have equal status and economic standing; have the legal and moral support of authorities; and have opportunities to work and socialize together (the *contact hypothesis*).

CAN CULTURES GET ALONG?

12) Cultural psychologists have identified many reasons for cultural conflicts and have sought solutions for reducing them. But they also are concerned that cultural research, which has done much to make people aware of the dangers of ethnocentrism and the differences among groups, can be used to foster ethnocentrism and ethnic separatism and to inflame intolerance rather than reduce it.

KEY TERMS

culture 692
cultural psychologists 693
cross-cultural psychologists 693
reification 696
body language 698
conversational distance 698
high-context versus low-context cultures 699
monochronic versus polychronic cultures 700
individualist versus collectivist cultures 701
social identity 703
ethnic identity 703
acculturation 703
bicultural identity 704
assimilation 704
ethnic separatism 704
marginal identity 704
sex versus gender 708
production 710
reproduction 710
ethnocentrism 714
us–them thinking 714
stereotype 714
prejudice 717
symbolic racism 721
hostile versus benevolent sexism 722
contact hypothesis 723

EPILOGUE
Taking Psychology with You

We [human beings] never stop investigating.
We are never satisfied that we know enough to get by.
Every question we answer leads on to another question.
This has become the greatest survival trick of our species.

Desmond Morris

YOU'VE COME A LONG WAY since the beginning of this book. It is now time to stand back and ask yourself where you've been and what you've learned from the many studies, topics, and controversies that you have read about. What fundamental principles emerge, and how can you take them with you into your own life? You probably won't be surprised that different psychologists would answer these questions differently; as we noted back in Chapter 1, psychology is a patchwork quilt of ideas. Still, even a patchwork quilt has an overall pattern. We believe that a "big picture" exists in the study of psychology, and that it reveals five fundamental determinants of human behavior.

THE FIVE STRANDS OF HUMAN EXPERIENCE

If you look back at the chapters in this book, you will see that our focus began within the individual—with neurons and hormones—and gradually expanded to include the physical environment, the social environment, and entire cultures. In Chapter 1, we described five general perspectives on human behavior that guide the assumptions and methods of psychologists. Each of these perspectives on human experience offers questions to ask when you are trying to understand or change a particular aspect of your own life:

1. *Biological influences.* As physical creatures, we are influenced by our bodies and our brains. Physiology affects the rhythms of our lives, our perceptions of reality, our ability to learn, the intensity of our emotions, our temperaments, and in some cases our vulnerability to emotional disorder.

Thus, when you are distressed, you might want to start by asking yourself what might be going on in your body. Do you have a physical condition that might be affecting your behavior? Do you have a temperamental tendency to be easily aroused or to be calm? Are alcohol or other drugs altering your ability to make decisions or behave as you would like? Might an irregular schedule be disrupting your physical functions and impairing your efficiency? Are you under unusual pressures that increase your physical stress?

2. *Cognitive influences.* Our species is, above all, the animal that explains things. These explanations may not always be realistic or sensible, but they continually influence our actions and choices. To solve problems, you need to ask yourself how you are framing the situation you are in. Are your explanations of what is causing the problem reasonable? Have you tested them? Are you wallowing in negative thoughts? Do you attribute your successes to luck but take all the blame for your failures—or do you take credit for your successes and blame everyone else for your failures? Do you assume the worst about others? Do you make external attributions or internal ones? Are you responding to other people's expectations or rules in a mindless way?

3. *Learning influences.* From the moment of birth, we begin learning and are exquisitely sensitive to our environments. What we do and how we do it are often a result of our learning histories and the specific situations we are in. We respond to the environment, and, in turn, our acts have consequences that influence future behavior. The right environment and rewards can help us cope better with disabilities, get along better with others, and even become more creative and happy. The wrong kind can foster boredom, hostility, and discontent.

So, as you analyze a situation, you would want to examine the contingencies and consequences governing your behavior and that of others. What rewards are maintaining your behavior? Of the many messages being aimed at you by television, books, parents, and teachers, which have the greatest influence? Who are your role models, the people you most admire and wish to emulate?

4. *Psychodynamic influences.* People are often unaware of the reasons they are getting themselves in trouble, just as they are unaware of the defense mechanisms they use to rationalize mistakes and protect self-esteem. If you find that you are repeating self-defeating patterns, expectations, and emotional reactions that you acquired in childhood, you might want to consider the reasons. Do other people "push your buttons" for reasons you cannot explain? Are you displacing feelings about your parents onto your friends or intimates? Are you carrying around "unfinished business" from childhood losses and hurts?

5. *Social and cultural influences.* Although most Westerners think of themselves as independent creatures, everyone conforms to some extent to the expectations and demands of others. Spouses, lovers, friends, bosses, parents, and perfect strangers "pull our strings" in ways we may not recognize. We conform to group pressures, obey authorities, and blossom or wilt in close relationships. Throughout life, we need "contact comfort"—sometimes in the literal touch or embrace of others and sometimes in shared experience or conversation. Although many universals of behavior unite humanity, "human nature" also varies from one culture to another. Culture dictates norms and roles for how employers and employees, strangers and friends, and men and women are supposed to act. Whenever you find yourself wondering irritably why "*those* people are behaving that way," chances are that a cultural difference is at work.

So, in solving problems, you will want to think about the people in your life who affect your attitudes and behavior. Do your friends and relatives support you or hinder you in achieving your goals? How do your ethnicity and nationality affect you? What gender roles do they specify for you and your partners in close relationships? What would happen if you ignored the norms of your role? Are your conflicts with other people a result of cultural misunderstandings—due, for instance, to differing rules for expressing emotion?

Keep in mind, though, that no single one of these factors operates in isolation from the others. The forces that govern our behavior are as intertwined as strands of ivy on a wall, and it can be hard to see where one strand begins and another ends. This message, if enough people believed it, would probably put an end to the pop-psych industry, which promotes single, simple answers to real-life complexities. (Anxious about the state of the world? Just jog some more, or fix your diet. Not doing so well at work? Just learn to dress for success.) Some simplifiers of psychology try to reduce human problems to biochemical imbalances or genetic defects. Others argue that anyone can "fulfill any potential," regardless of biology or environment, and that solving problems is merely a matter of having enough determination.

In this book, we have tried to show that the concerns and dilemmas of life do not divide up neatly according to the chapters of an introductory psychology text (even ours). For example, to understand shyness or loneliness, you might need to consider your learning history; childhood experiences and what you observed from adult role models; temperamental tendencies; the autobiographical memories that make up your story; how stress, diet, drugs, and sleep patterns might be affecting your mood; and whether you come from a culture that encourages or prohibits assertiveness. It may seem daunting to keep so many factors in mind. But once you get into the habit of seeing a situation from many points of view, relying on single-answer approaches will feel like wearing blinders. And it's a habit that will inoculate you against appealing pop-psych ideas that are unsupported by evidence.

PSYCHOLOGY IN YOUR LIFE

If the theories and findings in this book are to be of long-lasting value to you, they must jump off the printed page and into your daily life. In previous chapters, we have tried to point out ways in which you can apply what you have learned. However, you must select those particular aspects of psychological knowledge that can benefit you.

To give you some practice in doing so, we will take two common problems and offer some ideas about where to look in this book for principles and findings that may shed light on them. If you are serious about wanting to use psychology, we recommend that you turn to the specified pages and think about how the information there can best be applied, even if you don't have the particular problems we have selected. Our brief lists of hints are far from exhaustive, and we have not attempted to touch on every topic in this book that might be relevant to each problem. You should feel free to make the remote associations that are the heart of creativity and come up with additional ideas that could be brought to bear on a particular problem. These hypothetical situations do not have a single correct solution, any more than the actual problems you encounter do.

SITUATION 1: WHEN LOVE HAS GONE

You have been romantically involved with someone for a year. When the relationship began, you felt very much in love, and you thought your feelings were returned. But for a long time now, your partner's treatment of you has been anything but loving. In fact, your partner makes fun of your faults in front of others, yells at you about the slightest annoyance, and insults and humiliates you. Sometimes your partner ignores you for days on end, as if to punish you for some imagined wrong. Your friends advise you to leave the relationship, yet you can't shake the feeling that your partner must really love you. You still occasionally have a great time together, and your partner appears distressed whenever you threaten to leave. You wish you could either improve the relationship or get out, and your inability to act leaves you feeling angry and depressed.

How might each of the following topics help you resolve this problem? We suggest that you try to come up with your own answers, aided by these text references, before you look at ours:

- Approach–avoidance conflicts (Chapter 11, page 444)
- Intermittent reinforcement (Chapter 7, page 273)
- Observational learning (Chapter 7, page 285)
- Locus of control (Chapter 12, page 463, and Chapter 14, page 554)
- Cognitive-dissonance theory (Chapter 8, page 314)
- Gender differences in emotion and love (Chapter 10, page 406, and Chapter 11, page 423)
- Attribution theory (Chapter 17, page 664)

Here are a few reasons why these topics might apply, but feel free to think of others:

- Research on *approach–avoidance conflicts* may help explain why you are both attracted to and repelled by this relationship, and why the closer you approach, the more you want to leave (and vice versa). When a goal is both attractive and painful, it is not unusual to feel uncertain and to vacillate about the possible courses of action.

- *Intermittent reinforcement* may explain why you persist in apparently self-defeating behavior. If staying in the relationship brought only punishment or if your partner always ignored you, it would be easier to leave. But your partner intermittently gives you good times, and when behavior is occasionally rewarded, it becomes resistant to extinction.
- Past *observational learning* may help account for your present behavior. Perhaps your parents have a relationship like the one you are in, and their way of interacting is what you have learned to expect in your own relationships.
- If you have an *external locus of control*, you may feel that you cannot control what is happening to you, that you are merely a victim of fate, chance, or the whims and wishes of others. People with an internal locus of control feel more in charge of their lives and are less inclined to blame outside circumstances for their difficulties.
- *Cognitive-dissonance theory* suggests that you may be trying to keep your attitudes and behavior consistent. The cognition "I am in this relationship and choose to be with this person" is dissonant with "This person ignores and mistreats me." Because you are still unable to break up and alter the first cognition, you are working on the second cognition, hoping that your partner will change for the better.
- Research on *gender differences* finds that men and women often have different unstated rules about expressing emotion and different definitions of love. Perhaps traditional gender roles are preventing you and your partner from communicating your true preferences and feelings.
- *Attribution theory* addresses the consequences of explaining another person's behavior as *dispositional* (due to something about the person) or *situational* (due to something about the circumstances). Unhappy couples tend to make dispositional attributions when the partner does something wrong or thoughtless ("My partner is mean"); happy couples look for situational attributions ("My partner is under a lot of pressure at work"). You might test different possible reasons that your partner is treating you badly. Is the behavior characteristic of your partner in many situations, or might it be a result of stress, particular problems with you, or other difficulties?

Understanding your situation, of course, does not lead automatically to a solution. Depending on the circumstances, you might choose to cope with the ongoing stress of the situation (Chapter 14); change your perceptions of the situation and your attributions about your partner (Chapter 17); use learning principles to try to alter your own or your partner's behavior (Chapter 7); find a support group of people in the same situation (Chapter 16); seek psychological therapy or counseling, with or without your partner (Chapter 16); or leave the relationship.

SITUATION 2: JOB STRESS

You are an up-and-coming computer programmer. You like your job, but you feel overwhelmed by the amount of work you have to do. You never seem to be able to meet your deadlines, and you find yourself worrying about work at night and on weekends; you are unable to relax. Your friends accuse you of being a grind and a workaholic, though you would like to work less if you could. You believe you deserve a promotion, but your boss is curt and abrupt, rarely accepts your good ideas, and never gives you any feedback about your work, let alone praise. You assume that your boss has some grudge against you. You are beginning to feel isolated from your co-workers, too. Lately, you find that your motivation is sagging, and creative ideas are slow in coming. The occasional evening drink to calm your nerves has turned into steady drinking at home and several belts during the day, too, as you try to blot out your worries. What can you do to improve this situation? Here are some psychological topics that may yield insights:

- Sources of stress (Chapter 14, page 545)
- Work motivation (Chapter 11, page 434)
- Attributions (Chapter 17, page 664)
- Defense mechanisms (Chapter 12, page 467)
- Drug use and abuse (Chapter 5, page 181, and Chapter 15, page 597)
- Conformity and dissent (Chapter 17, pages 672 and 682)

Again, here are a few reasons why these topics might apply:

- Research on *sources of stress* may alert you to the reasons for your harried condition. You may need to analyze how much of the pressure you feel is due to the demands of the job and how much is a product of your own internal standards. You can't cope with stress appropriately until you know what is causing it.
- Research on *work motivation* shows that achievement motivation can be a part of personality but is also affected by the work environment. Burnout, for instance, often occurs because of the way a job is structured; co-workers or employers may offer little support, infrequent feedback, and few opportunities for developing innovative ideas. Workers are most productive when the conditions of the job—such as flexibility, variation in routine, and the power to make decisions—encourage intrinsic motivation.
- *Attribution theory* states that attributions, whether accurate or not, guide our responses to a situation. Your assumption that your employer dislikes you may not be valid. Perhaps he or she is under unusual pressure and is therefore distracted. Perhaps he or she is unaware of your contributions. A talk with the boss may be in order.
- Some clinicians would say your overwork is a *defense mechanism*, a way to channel thoughts away from some other area of your life that is troubling you. Would you really work less if you could, or is your constant preoccupation with your job a sign of denial—an unwillingness to face problems at home?
- Research on *drug use* shows that drug effects and the likelihood of abuse depend on mental set and situational setting, your physical tolerance, your cultural experience with the use of the drug, and your social environment when taking the drug. You may also have a vulnerability to alcohol's physical effects, which may explain your gradual slide into a serious alcohol problem. Or alcohol may offer you a convenient excuse for relaxing your standards of performance on the job ("I can't help it; it's the booze"). Because excessive drinking affects brain function and judgment, it probably does impair your performance, creating a vicious cycle of drug use and excuse.
- Finally, research on *conformity* and *dissent* suggests that you may not be alone in your problems at work. Perhaps your co-workers share your problems and would like to make improvements, but they fear rocking the boat. You might work out a solution with them that would be difficult to achieve on your own.

Our two examples have been individual problems, but the applications of psychology extend beyond personal concerns to social ones, as we have seen throughout this book: disputes between neighbors and nations; prejudice and cross-cultural relations; the best ways to rear moral, considerate, and competent children; the formulation of social policies; and countless other issues.

On the other hand, research findings often change as new questions are asked, new methods become available, and new theories evolve. Indeed, some findings become dated in a year, thanks to the speed of the information explosion. That is why the one chapter that may ultimately be most useful to you is the one you may have assumed to be least useful: Chapter 2, "How Psychologists Know What They Know." The best way to take psychology with you is to understand its basic ways of approaching problems and questions—that is, its principles of critical and scientific thinking. Old theories give way to new ones, dated results yield to contemporary ones, dead-end investigations halt, and new directions are taken. But the methods of psychology continue, and critical thinking is their hallmark.

"I still don't have all the answers, but I'm beginning to ask the right questions."

APPENDIX

Statistical Methods

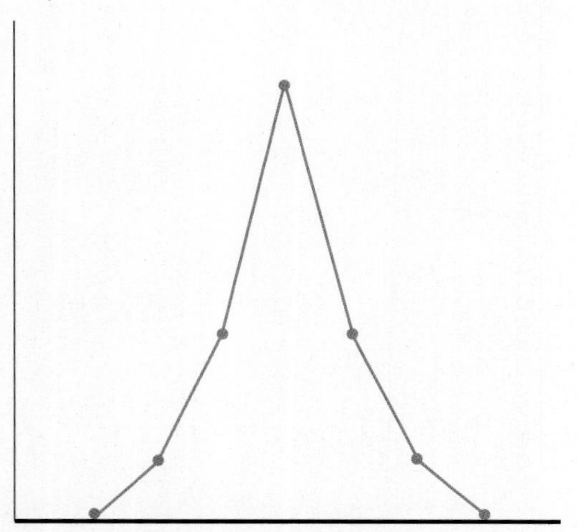

NINETEENTH-CENTURY ENGLISH STATESMAN Benjamin Disraeli reportedly once named three forms of dishonesty: "lies, damned lies, and statistics." It is certainly true that people can lie with the help of statistics. It happens all the time: Advertisers, politicians, and others with some claim to make either use numbers inappropriately or ignore certain critical ones. (When hearing that "four out of five doctors surveyed" recommended some product, have you ever wondered just how many doctors were surveyed and whether they were representative of all doctors?) People also use numbers to convey a false impression of certainty and objectivity when the true state of affairs is uncertainty or ignorance. But it is people, not statistics, that lie. When statistics are used correctly, they neither confuse nor mislead. On the contrary, they expose unwarranted conclusions, promote clarity and precision, and protect us from our own biases and blind spots.

If statistics are useful anywhere, it is in the study of human behavior. If human beings were all alike, and psychologists could specify all the influences on behavior, there would be no need for statistics. But any time we measure human behavior, we are going to wind up with different observations or scores for different individuals. Statistics can help us spot trends amid the diversity.

This appendix will introduce you to some basic statistical calculations used in psychology. Reading the appendix will not make you into a statistician, but it will acquaint you with some ways of organizing and assessing research data. If you suffer from a "number phobia," relax: You do not need to know much math to understand this material. However, you should have read Chapter 2, which discussed the rationale for using statistics and described various research methods. You may want to review the basic terms and concepts covered in that chapter. Be sure that you can define *hypothesis, sample, correlation, independent variable, dependent variable, random assignment, experimental group, control group, descriptive statistics, inferential statistics* and *test of statistical significance.* (Correlation coefficients, which are described in some detail in Chapter 2, will not be covered here.)

To read the tables in this appendix, you will also need to know the following symbols:

N = the total number of observations or scores in a set

X = an observation or score

Σ = the Greek capital letter sigma, read as "the sum of"

$\sqrt{}$ = the square root of

(*Note:* Boldfaced terms in this appendix are defined in the glossary at the end of the book.)

ORGANIZING DATA

Before we can discuss statistics, we need some numbers. Imagine that you are a psychologist and that you are interested in that most pleasing of human qualities, a sense of humor. You suspect that a well-developed funny bone can protect people from the negative emotional effects of stress. You already know that in the months following a stressful event, people who score high on sense-of-humor tests tend to feel less tense and moody than more sobersided individuals do. You realize, though, that this correlational evidence does not prove cause and effect. Perhaps people with a healthy sense of humor have other traits, such as flexibility or creativity, that act as the true stress buffers. To find out whether humor itself really softens the impact of stress, you do an experiment.

First, you randomly assign subjects to two groups, an experimental group and a control group. To keep our calculations simple, let's assume there are only 15 people per group. Each person individually views a silent film that most North Americans find fairly stressful, one showing Australian aboriginal boys undergoing a puberty rite involving physical mutilation. Subjects in the experimental group are instructed to make up a humorous monologue while watching the film. Those in the control group are told to make up a straightforward narrative. After the film, each person answers a mood questionnaire that measures current feelings of tension, depression, aggressiveness, and anxiety. A person's overall score on the questionnaire can range from 1 (no mood disturbance) to 7 (strong mood disturbance). This procedure provides you with 15 "mood disturbance" scores for each group. Have people who tried to be humorous reported less disturbance than those who did not?

CONSTRUCTING A FREQUENCY DISTRIBUTION

Your first step might be to organize and condense the "raw data" (the obtained scores) by constructing a **frequency distribution** for each group. A frequency distribution shows how often each possible score actually occurred. To construct one, you first order all the possible scores from highest to lowest. (Our mood disturbance scores will be ordered from 7 to 1.) Then you tally how often each score was actually obtained. Table A.1 gives some hypothetical raw data for the two groups, and Table A.2 shows the two frequency distributions based on these data. From these distributions you can see that the two groups differed. In the experimental group, the extreme scores of 7 and 1 did not occur at all, and the most common score was the middle one, 4. In the control group, a score of 7 occurred four times, the most common score was 6, and no one obtained a score lower than 4.

TABLE A.1 *Some Hypothetical Raw Data*

These scores are for the hypothetical humor-and-stress study described in the text.

Experimental group	4,5,4,4,3,6,5,2,4,3,5,4,4,3,4
Control group	6,4,7,6,6,4,6,7,7,5,5,5,7,6,6

TABLE A.2 *Two Frequency Distributions*

The scores are from Table A.1.

Experimental Group			Control Group		
Mood Disturbance Score	**Tally**	**Frequency**	**Mood Disturbance Score**	**Tally**	**Frequency**
7		0	7	////	4
6	/	1	6	~~////~~ /	6
5	///	3	5	///	3
4	~~////~~ //	7	4	//	2
3	///	3	3		0
2	/	1	2		0
1		0	1		0
		$N = 15$			$N = 15$

Because our mood scores have only seven possible values, our frequency distributions are quite manageable. Suppose, though, that your questionnaire had yielded scores that could range from 1 to 50. A frequency distribution with 50 entries would be cumbersome and might not reveal trends in the data clearly. A solution would be to construct a *grouped frequency distribution* by grouping adjacent scores into equal-sized *classes* or *intervals.* Each interval could cover, say, five scores (1–5, 6–10, 11–15, and so forth). Then you could tally the frequencies within each *interval.* This procedure would reduce the number of entries in each distribution from 50 to only 10, making the overall results much easier to grasp. However, information would be lost. For example, there would be no way of knowing how many people had a score of 43 versus 44.

GRAPHING THE DATA

As everyone knows, a picture is worth a thousand words. The most common statistical picture is a **graph,** a drawing that depicts numerical relationships. Graphs appear at several points in this book, and are routinely used by psychologists to convey their findings to others. From graphs, we can get a general impression of what the data are like, note the relative frequencies of different scores, and see which score was most frequent.

In a graph constructed from a frequency distribution, the possible score values are shown along a horizontal line (the *x-axis* of the graph) and frequencies along a vertical line (the *y-axis*), or vice versa. To construct a **histogram,** or **bar graph,** from our mood scores, we draw rectangles (bars) above each score, indicating the number of times it occurred by the rectangle's height (Figure A.1 on the next page).

A slightly different kind of "picture" is provided by a **frequency polygon,** or **line graph.** In a frequency polygon, the frequency of each score is indicated by a dot placed directly over the score on the horizontal axis, at the appropriate height on the vertical axis. The dots for the various scores are then joined together by straight lines, as in Figure

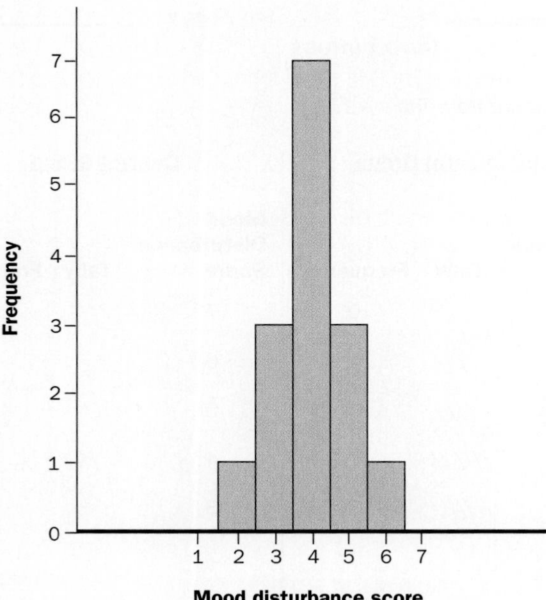

Figure A.1
A histogram

This graph depicts the distribution of mood disturbance scores shown on the left side of Table A.2.

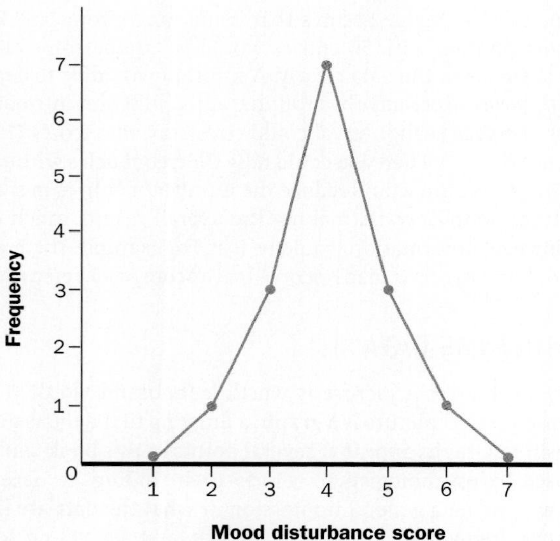

Figure A.2
A frequency polygon

This graph depicts the same data as Figure A.1.

A.2. When necessary an "extra" score, with a frequency of zero, can be added at each end of the horizontal axis, so that the polygon will rest on this axis instead of floating above it.

A word of caution about graphs: They may either exaggerate or mask differences in the data, depending on which units are used on the vertical axis. The two graphs in Figure A.3, although they look quite different, actually depict the same data. Always read the units on the axes of a graph; otherwise, the shape of a histogram or frequency polygon may be misleading.

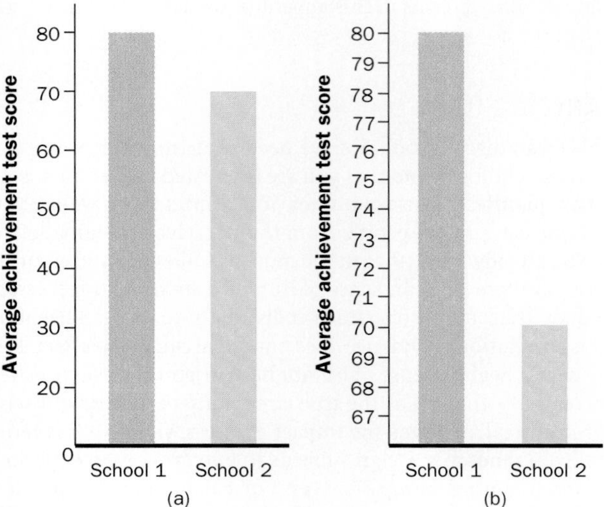

Figure A.3
Same data, different impressions

These two graphs depict the same data, but have different units on the vertical axis.

DESCRIBING DATA

Having organized your data, you are now ready to summarize and describe them. As you will recall from Chapter 2, procedures for doing so are known as *descriptive statistics.* In the following discussion, the word *score* will stand for any numerical observation.

MEASURING CENTRAL TENDENCY

Your first step in describing your data might be to compute a **measure of central tendency** for each group. Measures of central tendency characterize an entire set of data in terms of a single representative number.

THE MEAN The most popular measure of central tendency is the arithmetic mean, usually called simply the **mean.** It is often expressed by the symbol *M.* Most people are thinking of the mean when they say "average." We run across means all the time: in grade point averages, temperature averages, and batting averages. The mean is valuable to the psychologist because it takes all the data into account and it can be used in further statistical analyses. To compute the mean, you simply add up a set of scores and divide the total by the number of scores in the set. Recall that in mathematical notation, Σ means "the sum of," X stands for the individual scores, and N represents the total number of scores in a set. Thus the formula for calculating the mean is:

$$M = \frac{\Sigma X}{N}$$

Table A.3 shows how to compute the mean for our experimental group. Test your ability to perform this calculation by computing the

TABLE A.3 *Calculating a Mean and a Median*

The scores are from the left side of Table A.1.

Mean (*M*)

$$M = \frac{4+5+4+4+3+6+5+2+4+3+5+4+4+3+4}{15}$$

$$= \frac{60}{15}$$

$$= 4$$

Median

Scores, in order: 2, 3, 3, 3, 4, 4, 4, [4], 4, 4, 4, 5, 5, 5, 6

↑ Median

mean for the control group yourself. (You can find the answer, along with other control group statistics, on page 744.) Later, we will describe how a psychologist would compare the two means statistically to see if there is a significant difference between them.

THE MEDIAN Despite its usefulness, sometimes the mean can be misleading, as we noted in Chapter 2. Suppose you piled some children on a seesaw in such a way that it was perfectly balanced, and then a 200-pound adult came and sat on one end. The center of gravity would quickly shift toward the adult. In the same way, one extremely high score can dramatically raise the mean (and one extremely low score can dramatically lower it). In real life, this can be a serious problem. For example, in the calculation of a town's mean income, one millionaire would offset hundreds of poor people. The mean income would be a misleading indication of the town's actual wealth.

When extreme scores occur, a more representative measure of central tendency is the **median,** or midpoint in a set of scores or observations ordered from highest to lowest. In any set of scores, the same *number* of scores falls above the median as below it. The median is not affected by extreme scores. If you were calculating the *median* income of that same town, the one millionaire would offset only one poor person.

When the number of scores in the set is odd, calculating the median is a simple matter of counting in from the ends to the middle. However, if the number of scores is even, there will be two middle scores. The simplest solution is to find the mean of those two scores and use that number as the median. (When the data are from a grouped frequency distribution, a more complicated procedure is required, one beyond the scope of this appendix.) In our experimental group, the median score is 4 (see Table A.3). What is it for the control group?

THE MODE A third measure of central tendency is the **mode,** the score that occurs most often. In our experimental group, the modal score is 4. In our control group, it is 6. In some distributions, all scores occur with equal frequency, and there is no mode. In others, two or more scores "tie" for the distinction of being most frequent. Modes are used less often than other measures of central tendency. They do not tell us anything about the other scores in the distribution; they often are not very "central"; and they tend to fluctuate from one random sample of a population to another more than either the median or the mean.

MEASURING VARIABILITY

A measure of central tendency may or may not be highly representative of other scores in a distribution. To understand our results, we also need a **measure of variability** that will tell us whether our scores are clustered closely around the mean or widely scattered.

THE RANGE The simplest measure of variability is the **range,** which is found by subtracting the lowest score from the highest one. For our hypothetical set of mood disturbance scores, the range in the experimental group is 4 and in the control group it is 3. Unfortunately, though, simplicity is not always a virtue. The range gives us some information about variability but ignores all scores other than the highest and lowest ones.

THE STANDARD DEVIATION A more sophisticated measure of variability is the **standard deviation (SD).** This statistic takes every score in the distribution into account. Loosely speaking, it gives us an idea of how much, on the average, scores in a distribution differ from the mean. If the scores were all the same, the standard deviation would be zero. The higher the standard deviation, the more variability there is among scores.

To compute the standard deviation, we must find out how much each individual score deviates from the mean. To do so we simply subtract the mean from each score. This gives us a set of *deviation scores.* Deviation scores for numbers above the mean will be positive, those for numbers below the mean will be negative, and the positive scores will exactly balance the negative ones. In other words, the sum of the deviation scores will be zero. That is a problem, since the next step in our calculation is to add. The solution is to *square* all the deviation scores (that is, to multiply each score by itself). This step gets rid of negative values. Then we can compute the average of the *squared* deviation scores by adding them up and dividing the sum by the number of scores (N). Finally, we take the square root of the result, which takes us from squared units of measurement back to the same units that were used originally (in this case, mood disturbance levels).

The calculations just described are expressed by the following formula:

$$SD = \sqrt{\frac{\Sigma(X-M)^2}{N}}$$

Table A.4 shows the calculations for computing the standard deviation for our experimental group. Try your hand at computing the standard deviation for the control group.

Remember, a large standard deviation signifies that scores are widely scattered, and that therefore the mean is not terribly typical of the entire population. A small standard deviation tells us that most scores are clustered near the mean, and that therefore the mean is representative. Suppose two classes took a psychology exam, and both classes had the same mean score, 75 out of a possible 100. From the means alone, you might conclude that the classes were similar in performance. But if Class A had a standard deviation of 3 and Class B had a standard deviation of 9, you would know that there was much more

TABLE A.4 *Calculating a Standard Deviation*

Scores (X)	Deviation scores ($X-M$)	Squared deviation scores $(X-M)^2$
6	2	4
5	1	1
5	1	1
5	1	1
4	0	0
4	0	0
4	0	0
4	0	0
4	0	0
4	0	0
4	0	0
3	−1	1
3	−1	1
3	−1	1
2	−2	4
	0	14

$$SD = \sqrt{\frac{\Sigma(X-M)^2}{N}} = \sqrt{\frac{14}{15}} = \sqrt{.93} = .97$$

Note: When data from a sample are used to estimate the standard deviation of the population from which the sample was drawn, division is by $N-1$ instead of N, for reasons that will not concern us here.

variability in performance in Class B. This information could be useful to an instructor in planning lectures and making assignments.

TRANSFORMING SCORES

Sometimes researchers do not wish to work directly with raw scores. They may prefer numbers that are more manageable, such as when the raw scores are tiny fractions. Or they may want to work with scores that reveal where a person stands relative to others. In such cases, raw scores can be transformed to other kinds of scores.

PERCENTILE SCORES One common transformation converts each raw score to a *percentile score* (also called a *centile rank*). A percentile score gives the percentage of people who scored at or below a given raw score. Suppose you learn that you have scored 37 on a psychology exam. In the absence of any other information, you may not know whether to celebrate or cry. But if you are told that 37 is equivalent to a percentile score of 90, you know that you can be pretty proud of yourself; you have scored as well as, or higher than, 90 percent of those who have taken the test. On the other hand, if you are told that 37 is equivalent to a percentile score of 50, you have scored only at the median—only as well as, or higher than, half of the other students. The highest possible percentile rank is 99, or more precisely, 99.99, because you can never do better than 100 percent of a group when you are a member of the group. (Can you say what the lowest possible percentile score is? The answer is on page 744.) Standardized tests such as those described in previous chapters often come with tables that allow for the easy conversion of any raw score to the appropriate percentile score, based on data from a larger number of people who have already taken the test.

Percentile scores are easy to understand and easy to calculate. However, they also have a drawback: They merely rank people and do *not* tell us how far apart people are in terms of raw scores. Suppose you scored in the 50th percentile on an exam, June scored in the 45th, Tricia scored in the 20th, and Sean scored in the 15th. The difference between you and June may seem identical to that between Tricia and Sean (five percentiles). But in terms of *raw* scores you and June are probably more alike than Tricia and Sean, because exam scores usually cluster closely together around the midpoint of the distribution and are farther apart at the extremes. Because percentile scores do not preserve the spatial relationships in the original distribution of scores, they are inappropriate for computing many kinds of statistics. For example, they cannot be used to calculate means.

Z-SCORES Another common transformation of raw scores is to **z-scores,** or **standard scores.** A z-score tells you how far a given raw score is above or below the mean, using the standard deviation as the unit of measurement. To compute a z-score, you subtract the mean of the distribution from the raw score and divide by the standard deviation:

$$z = \frac{X-M}{SD}$$

Unlike percentile scores, z-scores preserve the relative spacing of the original raw scores. The mean itself always corresponds to a z-score of zero, since it cannot deviate from itself. All scores above the mean have positive z-scores and all scores below the mean have negative ones. When the raw scores form a certain pattern called a *normal distribution* (to be described shortly), a z-score tells you how high or low the corresponding raw score was, relative to the other scores. If your exam score of 37 is equivalent to a z-score of +1.0, you have scored 1 standard deviation above the mean. Assuming a roughly normal distribution, that's pretty good, because in a normal distribution only about 16 percent of all scores fall at or above 1 standard deviation above the mean. But if your 37 is equivalent to a z-score of −1.0, you have scored 1 standard deviation below the mean—a poor score.

Z-scores are sometimes used to compare people's performance on different tests or measures. Say that Elsa earns a score of 64 on her first psychology test and Manuel, who is taking psychology from a different instructor, earns a 62 on his first test. In Elsa's class, the mean score is 50 and the standard deviation is 7, so Elsa's z-score is (64 − 50)/7 = 2.0. In Manuel's class, the mean is also 50, but the standard deviation is 6. Therefore, his z-score is also 2.0 [(62 − 50)/6]. Compared to their respective classmates, Elsa and Manuel did equally well. *But be careful:* This does *not* imply that they are equally able students. Perhaps Elsa's instructor has a reputation for giving easy tests and Manuel's for giving hard ones, so Manuel's instructor has attracted a more industrious group of students. In that case, Manuel faces stiffer competition than Elsa does, and even though he and Elsa have the same z-score, Manuel's performance may be more impressive.

You can see that comparing z-scores from different people or different tests must be done with caution. Standardized tests, such as IQ tests and various personality tests, use z-scores derived from a large sample of people assumed to be representative of the general population taking the tests. When two tests are standardized for similar populations, it is safe to compare z-scores on them. But z-scores derived from special samples, such as students in different psychology classes, may not be comparable.

CURVES

In addition to knowing how spread out our scores are, we need to know the *pattern* of their distribution. At this point we come to a rather curious phenomenon. When researchers make a very large number of observations, many of the physical and psychological variables they study have a distribution that approximates a pattern called a **normal distribution.** (We say "approximates" because a *perfect* normal distribution is a theoretical construct and is not actually found in nature.) Plotted in a frequency polygon, a normal distribution has a symmetrical, bell-shaped form known as a **normal curve** (see Figure A.4).

A normal curve has several interesting and convenient properties. The right side is the exact mirror image of the left. The mean, median, and mode all have the same value and are at the exact center of the curve, at the top of the "bell." Most observations or scores cluster around the center of the curve, with far fewer out at the ends, or "tails" of the curve. Most important, as Figure A.4 shows, when standard deviations (or z-scores) are used on the horizontal axis of the curve, the percentage of scores falling between the mean and any given point on the horizontal axis is always the same. For example, 68.26 percent of the scores will fall between plus and minus 1 standard deviation from the mean; 95.44 percent of the scores will fall between plus and minus 2 standard deviations from the mean; and 99.74 percent of the scores will fall between plus and minus 3 standard deviations from the mean. These percentages hold for any normal curve, no matter what the size of the standard deviation. Tables are available showing the percentages of scores in a normal distribution that lie between the mean and various points (as expressed by z-scores).

The normal curve makes life easier for psychologists when they want to compare individuals on some trait or performance. For example, since IQ scores from a population form a roughly normal curve, the mean and standard deviation of a test are all the information you need in order to know how many people score above or below a particular score. On a test with a mean of 100 and a standard deviation of 15, about 68.26 percent of the population scores between 85 and 115—1 standard deviation below and 1 standard deviation above the mean (see Chapter 3).

Not all types of observations, however, are distributed normally. Some curves are lopsided, or *skewed,* with scores clustering at one end or the other of the horizontal axis (see Figure A.5). When the "tail" of the curve is longer on the right than on the left, the curve is said to be positively, or right, skewed. When the opposite is true, the curve is said to be negatively, or left, skewed. In experiments, reaction times typically form a right-skewed distribution. For example, if people must press a button whenever they hear some signal, most will react quite quickly; but a few will take an unusually long time, causing the right "tail" of the curve to be stretched out.

Knowing the shape of a distribution can be extremely valuable. Paleontologist and biologist Stephen Jay Gould (1985) has told how such information helped him cope with the news that he had a rare and serious form of cancer. Being a researcher, he immediately headed for the library to learn all he could about his disease. The first thing he found was that it was incurable, with a median mortality of only eight months after discovery. Most people might have assumed that a "median mortality of eight months" means "I will probably be dead in eight months." But Gould realized that although half of all patients died within eight months, the other half survived longer than that. Since his disease had been diagnosed in its early stages, he was getting top-notch medical treatment, and he had a strong will to live, Gould figured he

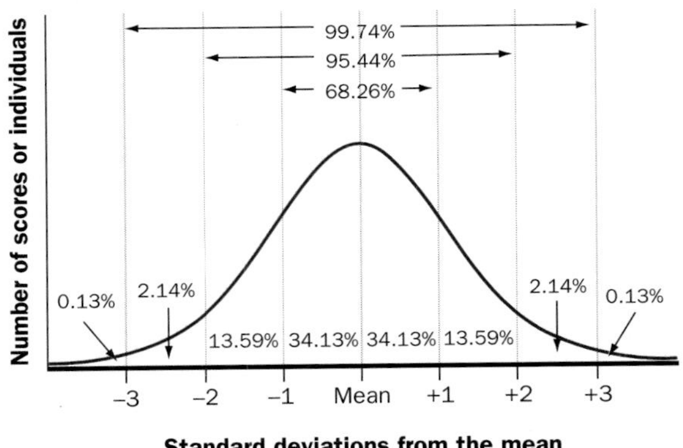

Figure A.4
A normal curve

When standard deviations (or z-scores) are used along the horizontal axis of a normal curve, certain fixed percentages of scores fall between the mean and any given point. As you can see, most scores fall in the middle range (between +1 and –1 standard deviations from the mean).

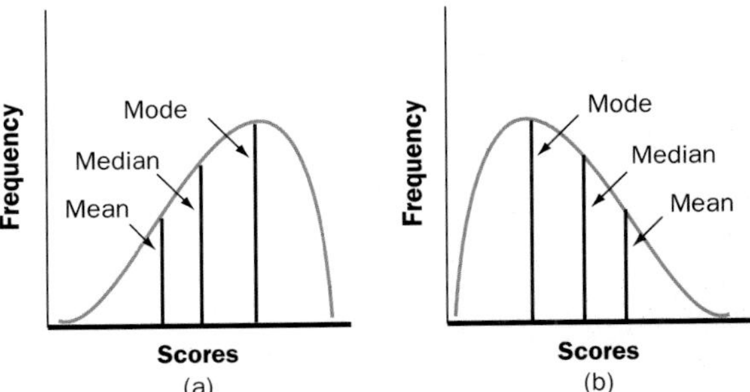

Figure A.5
Skewed curves

Curve (a) is skewed negatively, to the left. Curve (b) is skewed positively, to the right. The direction of a curve's skewness is determined by the position of the long tail, not by the position of the bulge. In a skewed curve, the mean, median, and mode fall at different points.

could reasonably expect to be in the half of the distribution that survived beyond eight months. Even more cheering, the distribution of deaths from the disease was right-skewed: The cases to the left of the median of eight months could only extend to zero months, but those to the right could stretch out for years. Gould saw no reason why he should not expect to be in the tip of that right-hand tail.

For Stephen Jay Gould, statistics, properly interpreted, were "profoundly nurturant and life-giving." They offered him hope and inspired him to fight his disease. Today, Gould is as active professionally as he ever was. The initial diagnosis was made in July of 1982.

Answers:

Control group statistics:

Mean $= \frac{\Sigma X}{N} = \frac{87}{15} = 5.8$

Median = 6

Standard Deviation $= \sqrt{\frac{\Sigma(X - M)^2}{N}} = \sqrt{\frac{14.4}{15}}$

$= \sqrt{.96} = .98$

Lowest possible percentile score: 1 (or, more precisely, .01)

DRAWING INFERENCES

Once data are organized and summarized, the next step is to ask whether they differ from what might have been expected purely by chance (see Chapter 2). A researcher needs to know whether it is safe to infer that the results from a particular sample of people are valid for the entire population from which the sample was drawn. *Inferential statistics* provide this information. They are used in both experimental and correlational studies.

THE NULL VERSUS THE ALTERNATIVE HYPOTHESIS

In an experiment, the scientist must assess the possibility that his or her experimental manipulations will have no effect on the subjects' behavior. The statement expressing this possibility is called the **null hypothesis.** In our stress-and-humor study, the null hypothesis states that making up a funny commentary will not relieve stress any more than making up a straightforward narrative will. In other words, it predicts that the difference between the means of the two groups will not deviate significantly from zero. Any obtained difference will be due solely to chance fluctuations. In contrast, the **alternative hypothesis** (also called the experimental or research hypothesis) states that on the average the experimental group will have lower mood disturbance scores than the control group.

The null hypothesis and the alternative hypothesis cannot both be true. Our goal is to reject the null hypothesis. If our results turn out to be consistent with the null hypothesis, we will not be able to do so. If the data are inconsistent with the null hypothesis, we will be able to reject it with some degree of confidence. Unless we study the entire population, though, we will never be able to say that the alternative hypothesis has been proven. No matter how impressive our results are, there will always be some degree of uncertainty about the inferences we draw from them. Since we cannot prove the alternative hypothesis, we must be satisfied with showing that the null hypothesis is unreasonable.

Students are often surprised to learn that in traditional hypothesis testing it is the null hypothesis, not the alternative hypothesis, that is tested. After all, it is the alternative hypothesis that is actually of interest. But this procedure does make sense. The null hypothesis can be stated precisely and tested directly. In the case of our fictitious study, the null hypothesis predicts that the difference between the two means will be zero. The alternative hypothesis does not permit a precise prediction because we don't know how much the two means might differ (if, in fact, they do differ). Therefore, it cannot be tested directly.

TESTING HYPOTHESES

Many computations are available for testing the null hypothesis. The choice depends on the design of the study, the size of the sample, and other factors. We will not cover any specific tests here. Our purpose is simply to introduce you to the kind of *reasoning* that underlies hypothesis testing. With that in mind, let us return once again to our data. For each of our two groups we have calculated a mean and a standard deviation. Now we want to compare the two sets of data to see if they differ enough for us to reject the null hypothesis. We wish to be reasonably certain that our observed differences did not occur entirely by chance.

What does it mean to be "reasonably certain"? How different from zero must our result be to be taken seriously? Imagine, for a moment, that we had infinite resources and could somehow repeat our experiment, each time using a new pair of groups, until we had "run" the entire population through the study. It can be shown mathematically that if only chance were operating, our various experimental results would form a normal distribution. This theoretical distribution is called "the sampling distribution of the difference between means," but since that is quite a mouthful, we will simply call it the *sampling distribution* for short. If the null hypothesis were true, the mean of the sampling distribution would be zero. That is, on the average, we would find no difference between the two groups. Often, though, because of chance influences or *random error,* we would get a result that deviated to one degree or another from zero. On rare occasions, the result would deviate a great deal from zero.

We cannot test the entire population, though. All we have are data from a single sample. We would like to know whether the difference between means that we actually obtained would be close to the mean of the theoretical sampling distribution (if we *could* test the entire population) or far away from it, out in one of the "tails" of the curve. Was our result highly likely to occur on the basis of chance alone or highly unlikely?

Before we can answer that question, we must have some precise way to measure distance from the mean of the sampling distribution. We must know exactly how far from the mean our obtained result must be to be considered "far away." If only we knew the standard deviation of the sampling distribution, we could use it as our unit of measurement. We don't know it, but fortunately, we can use the standard deviation of our *sample* to estimate it. (We will not go into the reasons that this is so.)

Now we are in business. We can look at the mean difference between our two groups and figure out how far it is (in terms of standard deviations) from the mean of the sampling distribution. As mentioned earlier, one of the convenient things about a normal distribution is that a certain fixed percentage of all observations falls between the mean of the distribution and any given point above or below the mean. These percentages are available from tables. Therefore, if we know the "distance" of our obtained result from the mean of the theoretical sampling distribution, we automatically know how likely our result is to have occurred strictly by chance.

To give a specific example, if it turns out that our obtained result is 2 standard deviations above the mean of the theoretical sampling distribution, we know that the probability of its having occurred by chance is less than 2.3 percent. If our result is 3 standard deviations above the mean of the sampling distribution, the probability of its having occurred by chance is less than .13 percent—less than 1 in 800. In either case, we might well suspect that our result did not occur entirely by chance after all. We would call the result *statistically significant.* (Psychologists usually consider any highly unlikely result to be of interest, no matter which direction it takes. In other words, the result may be in either "tail" of the sampling distribution.)

To summarize: Statistical significance means that if only chance were operating, our result would be highly improbable, so we are fairly safe in concluding that more than chance was operating—namely, the influence of our independent variable. We can reject the null hypothesis, and open the champagne. As we noted in Chapter 2, psychologists usually accept a finding as statistically significant if the likelihood of its occurring by chance is 5 percent or less (see Figure A.6). This cutoff point gives the researcher a reasonable chance of confirming reliable results as well as reasonable protection against accepting unreliable ones.

Some cautions are in order, though. As noted in Chapter 2, conventional tests of statistical significance have drawn serious criticisms in recent years. Statistically significant results are not always psychologically interesting or important. Further, statistical significance is related to the size of the sample. A large sample increases the likelihood of reliable results. But there is a trade-off: The larger the sample, the more probable it is that a small result having no practical importance will reach statistical significance. On the other hand, with the sample sizes typically used in psychological research, there is a good chance of falsely concluding that an experimental effect has *not* occurred when one actually has (Hunter, 1997). For these reasons, it is always useful to know how much of the total variability in scores was accounted for by the independent variable (the *effect size*). (The computations are not discussed here.) If only 3 percent of the variance was accounted for, then 97 percent was due either to chance factors or to systematic influences of which the researcher was unaware. Because human behavior is affected by so many factors, the amount of variability accounted for by a single psychological variable is often modest. But sometimes the effect size is considerable even when the results don't quite reach significance.

Oh, yes, about those humor findings: Our fictitious study is similar to two more-complicated ones done by Herbert M. Lefcourt and Rod A. Martin (1986). Women who tried to be funny reported less mood disturbance than women who merely produced a straightforward narrative. They also grimaced and fidgeted less during the film, suggesting that they really did feel less stress. The results were not statistically significant for men, possibly because men did not find the film all that stressful. Other findings, however, suggest that humor can shield both sexes from stress (see Chapter 14). *The moral:* When gravity gets you down, try a little levity.

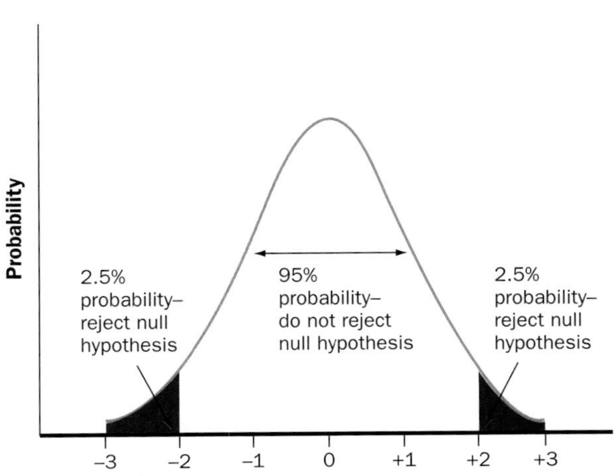

Figure A.6
Statistical significance

This curve represents the theoretical sampling distribution discussed in the text. The curve is what we would expect by chance if we did our hypothetical stress-and-humor study many times, testing the entire population. If we used the conventional significance level of .05, we would regard our obtained result as significant only if the probability of getting a result that far from zero by chance (in either direction) totaled 5 percent or less. As shown, the result must fall far out in one of the tails of the sampling distribution. Otherwise, we cannot reject the null hypothesis.

SUMMARY

1) When used correctly, statistics expose unwarranted conclusions, promote precision, and help researchers spot trends amid diversity.

2) Often, the first step in data analysis is to organize and condense data in a *frequency distribution,* a tally showing how often each possible score (or interval of scores) occurred. Such information can also be depicted in a *histogram* (bar graph) or a *frequency polygon* (line graph).

3) Descriptive statistics summarize and describe the data. *Central tendency* is measured by the *mean, median,* or, less frequently, the *mode.* Since a measure of central tendency may or may not be highly representative of other scores in a distribution, it is also important to analyze variability. A large *standard deviation* means that scores are widely scattered about the mean; a small one means that most scores are clustered near the mean.

4) Raw scores can be transformed into other kinds of scores. *Percentile scores* indicate the percentage of people who scored at or below a given raw score. *Z-scores* (*standard scores*) indicate how far a given raw score is above or below the mean of the distribution.

5) Many variables have a distribution approximating a *normal distribution,* depicted as a *normal curve.* The normal curve has a convenient property: When standard deviations are used as the units on the horizontal axis, the percentage of scores falling between any two points on the horizontal axis is always the same. Not all types of observations are distributed normally, however. Some distributions are *skewed* to the left or right.

6) Inferential statistics can be used to test the *null hypothesis* and to tell a researcher whether a result differed significantly from what might have been expected purely by chance. Basically, hypothesis testing involves estimating where the obtained result would have fallen in a theoretical *sampling distribution* based on studies of the entire population in question. If the result would have been far out in one of the "tails" of the distribution, it is considered statistically significant. A statistically significant result may or may not be psychologically interesting or important, so many researchers also compute the *effect size.*

KEY TERMS

GLOSSARY

absolute threshold The smallest quantity of physical energy that can be reliably detected by an observer.

accommodation In Piaget's theory, the process of modifying existing cognitive structures in response to experience and new information.

acculturation The process by which members of groups that are minorities in a given society come to identify with and feel part of the mainstream culture.

activation–synthesis theory The theory that dreaming results from the cortical synthesis and interpretation of neural signals triggered by activity in the lower part of the brain.

adrenal hormones Hormones produced by the adrenal glands, which are involved in emotion and stress; they include cortisol, epinephrine, and norepinephrine.

agoraphobia A set of phobias, often set off by a panic attack, involving the basic fear of being away from a safe place or person.

algorithm A problem-solving strategy guaranteed to produce a solution even if the user does not know how it works.

alpha waves Relatively large, slow brain waves characteristic of relaxed wakefulness.

altered state of consciousness A state of consciousness that differs from ordinary wakefulness or sleep.

alternative hypothesis An assertion that the independent variable in a study will have a certain predictable effect on the dependent variable; also called an *experimental* or *research hypothesis.*

amnesia (dissociative) When no organic causes are present, a dissociative disorder involving partial or complete loss of memory for threatening information or traumatic experiences.

amygdala A brain structure involved in the arousal and regulation of emotion and the initial emotional response to sensory information.

antidepressant drugs Drugs used primarily in the treatment of mood disorders, especially depression and anxiety.

antipsychotic drugs Major tranquilizers used primarily in the treatment of schizophrenia and other psychotic disorders.

antisocial personality disorder A disorder (sometimes called psychopathy or sociopathy) characterized by antisocial behavior such as lying, stealing, manipulating others, and sometimes violence; a lack of social emotions (guilt, shame, and empathy); and impulsivity.

applied psychology The study of psychological issues that have direct practical significance and the application of psychological findings.

archetypes [AR-ki-tipes] To Carl Jung, universal, symbolic images that appear in myths, art, dreams, and other expressions of the collective unconscious.

arithmetic mean An average that is calculated by adding up a set of quantities and dividing the sum by the total number of quantities in the set.

assimilation In Piaget's theory, the process of absorbing new information into existing cognitive structures.

attribution theory The theory that people are motivated to explain their own and others' behavior by attributing causes of that behavior to a situation or a disposition.

autonomic nervous system The subdivision of the peripheral nervous system that regulates the internal organs and glands.

availability heuristic The tendency to judge the probability of a type of event by how easy it is to think of examples or instances.

axon A neuron's extending fiber that conducts impulses away from the cell body and transmits them to other neurons.

basic concepts Concepts that have a moderate number of instances and that are easier to acquire than those having few or many instances.

basic psychology The study of psychological issues in order to seek knowledge for its own sake rather than for its practical application.

behavioral genetics An interdisciplinary field of study concerned with the genetic bases of behavior and personality.

behaviorism A psychological approach that emphasizes the study of observable behavior and the role of the environment as a determinant of behavior.

behavior modification The application of conditioning techniques to teach new responses or to reduce or eliminate maladaptive or problematic behavior.

binocular cues Visual cues to depth or distance requiring two eyes.

biological perspective A psychological approach that emphasizes bodily events and changes associated with actions, feelings, and thoughts.

biological rhythm A periodic, more or less regular fluctuation in a biological system; it may or may not have psychological implications.

bipolar disorder A mood disorder in which depression alternates with mania (excessive euphoria).

brain stem The part of the brain at the top of the spinal cord; it is responsible for automatic functions such as heartbeat and respiration.

brightness Lightness or luminance; the dimension of visual experience related to the amount of light emitted from or reflected by an object.

case study A detailed description of a particular individual being studied or treated.

cell body The part of the neuron that keeps it alive and determines whether it will fire.

central nervous system (CNS) The portion of the nervous system consisting of the brain and spinal cord.

cerebellum A brain structure that regulates movement and balance, and that is involved in the learning of certain kinds of simple responses.

cerebral cortex A collection of several thin layers of cells covering the cerebrum; it is largely responsible for higher mental functions. *Cortex* is Latin for "bark" or "rind."

cerebral hemispheres The two halves of the cerebrum.

cerebrum [suh-REE-brum] The largest brain structure, consisting of the upper part of the forebrain; it is in charge of most sensory, motor, and cognitive processes. From the Latin for "brain."

childhood (infantile) amnesia The inability to remember events and experiences that occurred during the first two or three years of life.

chromosomes Within every body cell, rod-shaped structures that carry the genes.

chunk A meaningful unit of information; it may be composed of smaller units.

circadian [sur-CAY-dee-un] rhythm A biological rhythm with a period (from peak to peak or trough to trough) of about 24 hours; from the Latin *circa*, "about," and *dies*, "a day."

classical conditioning The process by which a previously neutral stimulus acquires the capacity to elicit a response through association with a stimulus that already elicits a similar or related response; also called *Pavlovian* and *respondent conditioning*.

cochlea (KOCK-lee-uh) A snail-shaped, fluid-filled organ in the inner ear, containing the receptors for hearing.

coefficient of correlation A measure of correlation that ranges in value from −1.00 to +1.00.

cognitive dissonance A state of tension that occurs when a person simultaneously holds two cognitions that are psychologically inconsistent, or when a person's belief is incongruent with his or her behavior.

cognitive ethology The study of cognitive processes in nonhuman animals.

cognitive map A mental representation of the environment.

cognitive perspective A psychological approach that emphasizes mental processes in perception, memory, language, problem solving, and other areas of behavior.

cognitive schema An integrated mental network of knowledge, beliefs, and expectations concerning a particular topic or aspect of the world.

collective unconscious To Carl Jung, the universal memories and experiences of humankind, represented in the unconscious images and symbols of all people.

collectivist cultures Cultures in which the self is regarded as embedded in relationships, and harmony with the group is prized above individual goals and wishes.

complexity of light Refers to the number of different wavelengths contained in light from a particular source.

concept A mental category that groups objects, relations, activities, abstractions, or qualities having common properties.

conditioned response (CR) The classical-conditioning term for a response that is elicited by a conditioned stimulus; occurs after the conditioned stimulus is associated with an unconditioned stimulus.

conditioned stimulus (CS) The classical-conditioning term for an initially neutral stimulus that comes to elicit a conditioned response after being associated with an unconditioned stimulus.

conditioning A basic kind of learning that involves associations between environmental stimuli and the organism's responses.

cones Visual receptors involved in color vision.

confirmation bias The tendency to look for or pay attention only to information that confirms one's belief.

consciousness Awareness of the environment and of one's own existence, sensations, and thoughts.

conservation The understanding that the physical properties of objects—such as the number of items in a cluster or the amount of liquid in a glass—can remain the same even when their form or appearance changes.

consolidation The process by which a long-term memory becomes durable and stable.

contact comfort In primate infants, the innate need for close physical contact; it is the basis of an infant's first attachment.

continuous reinforcement A reinforcement schedule in which a particular response is always reinforced.

control condition In an experiment, a comparison condition in which subjects are not exposed to the same treatment as in the experimental condition.

corpus callosum The bundle of nerve fibers connecting the two cerebral hemispheres.

correlation A measure of how strongly two variables are related to one another.

correlational study A descriptive study that looks for a consistent relationship between two phenomena.

counterconditioning In classical conditioning, the process of pairing a conditioned stimulus with a stimulus that elicits a response that is incompatible with an unwanted conditioned response.

critical thinking The ability and willingness to assess claims and to make objective judgments on the basis of well-supported reasons, and to be creative and constructive in explaining events.

cross-sectional study A study in which subjects of different ages are compared at a given time.

cue-dependent forgetting The inability to retrieve information stored in memory because of insufficient cues for recall.

culture A program of shared rules that govern the behavior of members of a community or society, and a set of values, beliefs, and attitudes shared by most members of that community.

dark adaptation A process by which visual receptors become maximally sensitive to dim light.

decay theory The theory that information in memory eventually disappears if it is not accessed; it applies more to short-term than to long-term memory.

declarative memories Memories of facts, rules, concepts, and events ("knowing that"); they include semantic and episodic memories.

deductive reasoning A form of reasoning in which a conclusion follows necessarily from certain premises; if the premises are true, the conclusion must be true.

deep processing In the encoding of information, the processing of meaning rather than simply the physical or sensory features of a stimulus.

defense mechanisms Strategies used by the ego to prevent unconscious anxiety or threatening thoughts from entering consciousness.

deindividuation In groups or crowds, the loss of awareness of one's own individuality and the abdication of mindful action.

delta waves Slow, regular brain waves characteristic of Stage 3 and Stage 4 sleep.

dendrites A neuron's branches that receive information from other neurons and transmit it to the cell body.

dependent variable A variable that an experimenter predicts will be affected by manipulations of the independent variable.

depersonalization Treating another person without regard for the person's individuality as a human being.

depressants Drugs that slow down activity in the central nervous system.

descriptive methods Methods that yield descriptions of behavior but not necessarily causal explanations.

descriptive statistics Statistics that organize and summarize research data.

dialectical reasoning A process in which opposing facts or ideas are weighed and compared, with a view to determining the best solution or to resolving differences.

difference threshold The smallest difference in stimulation that can be reliably detected by an observer when two stimuli are compared; also called *just noticeable difference (jnd).*

diffusion of responsibility In organized or anonymous groups, the tendency of members to avoid taking responsibility for actions or decisions, assuming that others will do so.

discriminative stimulus A stimulus that signals when a particular response is likely to be followed by a certain type of consequence.

display rules Social and cultural rules that regulate when, how, and where a person may express (or suppress) emotions.

dissociative disorders Conditions in which consciousness or identity is split or altered.

dissociative identity disorder A controversial dissociative disorder marked by the appearance within one person of two or more distinct personalities, each with its own name and traits; also called *multiple personality disorder.*

dizygotic twins *See* fraternal twins.

DNA (deoxyribonucleic acid) The chromosomal molecule that transfers genetic characteristics by way of coded instructions for the structure of proteins.

double-blind study An experiment in which neither the subjects nor the individuals running the study know which subjects are in the control group and which are in the experimental group until after the results are tallied.

ego In psychoanalysis, the part of personality that represents reason, good sense, and rational self-control.

egocentric thinking Seeing the world from only your own point of view; the inability to take another person's perspective.

elaborative rehearsal Association of new information with already stored knowledge and analysis of the new information to make it memorable.

electroconvulsive therapy (ECT) A procedure occasionally used for cases of prolonged major depression, in which a brief brain seizure is induced to alter brain chemistry.

electroencephalogram (EEG) A recording of neural activity detected by electrodes.

emotion A state of arousal involving facial and bodily changes, brain activation, cognitive appraisals, subjective feelings, and tendencies toward action.

emotion work Expression of an emotion, often because of a role requirement, that the person does not really feel.

empirical Relying on or derived from observation, experimentation, or measurement.

encoding The conversion of information into a form that can be stored in and retrieved from memory.

endocrine glands Internal organs that produce hormones and release them into the bloodstream.

endorphins [en-DOR-fins] Chemical substances in the nervous system that are similar in structure and action to opiates; they are involved in pain reduction, pleasure, and memory, and are known technically as *endogenous opioid peptides.*

entrainment The synchronization of biological rhythms with external cues, such as fluctuations in daylight.

entrapment A gradual process in which individuals escalate their commitment to a course of action to justify their investment of time, money, or effort.

episodic memories Memories of personally experienced events and the contexts in which they occurred.

equilibrium The sense of balance.

ethnic identity A close identification with your own racial, religious, or ethnic group.

ethnocentrism The belief that your own ethnic group, nation, or religion is superior to all others.

evoked potentials Patterns of brain activity produced in response to specific events.

evolution A change in gene frequencies within a population over many generations; a mechanism by which genetically influenced characteristics of a population change.

evolutionary psychology A field of psychology emphasizing evolutionary mechanisms that may help explain human commonalities in cognition, development, emotion, social practices, and other areas of behavior.

existential psychology An approach to psychology that emphasizes free will, personal responsibility, and the inevitable anxieties of existence, such as the need to find meaning in life and to accept suffering and death.

experiment A controlled test of a hypothesis in which the researcher manipulates one variable to discover its effect on another.

experimenter effects Unintended changes in subjects' behavior due to cues inadvertently given by the experimenter.

explicit memory Conscious, intentional recollection of an event or of an item of information.

extinction The weakening and eventual disappearance of a learned response. In classical conditioning, it occurs when the conditioned stimulus is no longer paired with the unconditioned stimulus; in operant conditioning, it occurs when a response is no longer followed by a reinforcer.

extrinsic reinforcers Reinforcers that are not inherently related to the activity being reinforced, such as money, prizes, and praise.

factor analysis A statistical method for analyzing the intercorrelations among various measures or test scores; clusters of measures or scores that are highly correlated are assumed to measure the same underlying trait, ability, or aptitude (factor).

feature detectors Cells in the visual cortex that are sensitive to specific features of the environment.

feminist psychology A psychological approach that analyzes the influence of social inequities on gender relations and on the behavior of the two sexes.

fetal alcohol syndrome (FAS) A pattern of physical and intellectual abnormalities in infants whose mothers drank an excessive amount of alcohol during pregnancy.

fixed-interval (FI) schedule An intermittent schedule of reinforcement in which a reinforcer is delivered for the first response made after a fixed period of time has elapsed since the last reinforcer.

fixed-ratio (FR) schedule An intermittent schedule of reinforcement in which reinforcement occurs only after a fixed number of responses.

flashbulb memory A vivid, detailed recollection of a significant or startling event, or of the circumstances in which the rememberer learned of such an event.

fraternal (dizygotic) twins Twins that develop from two separate eggs fertilized by different sperm; they are no more alike genetically than are any other pair of siblings.

free association In psychoanalysis, a method of uncovering unconscious conflicts by saying freely whatever comes to mind.

frequency (of a sound wave) The number of times per second that a sound wave cycles through a peak and low point.

frequency distribution A summary of how frequently each score in a set occurred.

frequency polygon (line graph) A graph showing a set of points obtained by plotting score values against score frequencies; adjacent points are joined by straight lines.

functionalism An early psychological approach that stressed the function or purpose of behavior and consciousness.

fundamental attribution error The tendency, in explaining other people's behavior, to overestimate personality factors and underestimate the influence of the situation.

ganglion cells Neurons in the retina of the eye that gather information from receptor cells (by way of intermediate bipolar cells); their axons make up the optic nerve.

gate-control theory The theory that the experience of pain depends in part on whether pain impulses get past a neurological "gate" in the spinal cord and thus reach the brain.

gender identity The fundamental sense of being male or female, regardless of whether the person conforms to the rules of sex typing.

gender role A set of rules and norms that defines socially approved attitudes and behavior for men and women.

gender schema A cognitive schema (mental network) of knowledge, beliefs, metaphors, and expectations about what it means to be male or female.

gender socialization (sex typing) The process by which children learn the behaviors, attitudes, and expectations associated with being masculine or feminine in their culture.

generalized anxiety disorder A continuous state of anxiety marked by feelings of worry and dread, apprehension, difficulties in concentration, and signs of motor tension.

genes The functional units of heredity; they are composed of DNA and specify the structure of proteins.

genome The full set of genes in each cell of an organism (with the exception of sperm and egg cells).

g factor A general intellectual ability assumed by some theorists to underlie specific mental abilities and talents.

glial cells Cells that hold neurons in place, insulate neurons, and provide neurons with nutrients.

graph A drawing that depicts numerical relationships.

group polarization The tendency for a group's decision to be more extreme than its members' individual decisions.

groupthink In close-knit groups, the tendency for all members to think alike for the sake of harmony and to suppress dissent.

heritability A statistical estimate of the proportion of the total variance in some trait within a group that is attributable to genetic differences among individuals within the group.

heuristic A rule of thumb that suggests a course of action or guides problem solving but does not guarantee an optimal solution.

high-context cultures Cultures in which people pay close attention to nonverbal forms of communication and assume a shared context for their interactions—a common history and set of attitudes.

higher-order conditioning In classical conditioning, a procedure in which a neutral stimulus becomes a conditioned stimulus through association with an already established conditioned stimulus.

hindsight bias The tendency to overestimate one's ability to have predicted an event once the outcome is known; the "I knew it all along" phenomenon.

hippocampus A brain structure involved in the storage of new information in memory.

histogram (bar graph) A graph in which the heights (or lengths) of bars are proportional to the frequencies of individual scores or classes of scores in a distribution.

hormones Chemical substances, secreted by organs called *glands*, that affect the functioning of other organs.

hue The dimension of visual experience specified by color names and related to the wavelength of light.

humanist psychology A psychological approach that emphasizes personal growth and the achievement of human potential rather than the scientific understanding and assessment of behavior.

hypnosis A procedure in which the practitioner suggests changes in the sensations, perceptions, thoughts, feelings, or behavior of the subject.

hypothalamus A brain structure involved in emotions and drives vital to survival, such as fear, hunger, thirst, and reproduction; it regulates the autonomic nervous system.

hypothesis A statement that attempts to predict or to account for a set of phenomena; scientific hypotheses specify relationships among events or variables and are supported or disconfirmed by empirical investigation.

id In psychoanalysis, the part of personality containing inherited psychological energy, particularly sexual and aggressive instincts.

identical (monozygotic) twins Twins that develop when a fertilized egg divides into two parts that become separate embryos.

identification A process by which the child adopts an adult's standards of morality, values, and beliefs as his or her own; in psychoanalysis, identification with the same-sex parent is said to occur at the resolution of the Oedipus complex.

implicit memory Unconscious retention in memory, as evidenced by the effect of a previous experience or previously encountered information on current thoughts or actions.

independent variable A variable that an experimenter manipulates.

individualist cultures Cultures in which the self is regarded as autonomous, and individual goals and wishes are prized above duty and relations with others.

induction A method of child rearing in which the parent appeals to the child's own resources, abilities, sense of responsibility, and feelings for others in correcting the child's misbehavior.

inductive reasoning A form of reasoning in which the premises provide support for a conclusion, but it is still possible for the conclusion to be false.

infantile amnesia *See* childhood amnesia.

inferential statistics Statistical tests that allow researchers to assess how likely it is that their results occurred merely by chance.

infradian [in-FRAY-dee-un] rhythm A biological rhythm that occurs less frequently than once a day; from the Latin for "below a day."

insight A form of problem solving that appears to involve the (often sudden) understanding of how elements of a situation are related or can be reorganized to achieve a solution.

instinctive drift The tendency of an organism to revert to an instinctive behavior over time; it can interfere with learning.

intelligence An inferred characteristic of an individual, usually defined as the ability to profit from experience, acquire knowledge, think abstractly, act purposefully, or adapt to changes in the environment.

intelligence quotient (IQ) A measure of intelligence originally computed by dividing a person's mental age by his or her chronological age and multiplying the result by 100; it is now derived from norms provided for standardized intelligence tests.

intermittent (partial) schedule of reinforcement A reinforcement schedule in which a particular response is sometimes but not always reinforced.

intrapsychic Within the mind (psyche) or self.

intrinsic reinforcers Reinforcers that are inherently related to the activity being reinforced, such as enjoyment of the task and the satisfaction of accomplishment.

inventories Standardized objective questionnaires requiring written responses; they typically include scales on which people are asked to rate themselves.

James–Lange theory of emotions The theory, proposed independently by William James and Carl Lange, that emotion results from the perception of one's own bodily reactions.

just-world hypothesis The notion that many people need to believe that the world is fair and that justice is served; that bad people are punished and good people rewarded.

kinesthesis (KIN-es-THEE-sis) The sense of body position and movement of body parts; also called *kinesthesia.*

language A system that combines meaningless elements such as sounds or gestures to form structured utterances that convey meaning.

latent learning A form of learning that is not immediately expressed in an overt response; it occurs without obvious reinforcement.

lateralization Specialization of the two cerebral hemispheres for particular psychological operations.

learning A relatively permanent change in behavior (or behavioral potential) due to experience.

learning disability A difficulty in the performance of a specific mental skill, such as reading or arithmetic; sometimes linked to perceptual or memory problems.

learning perspective A psychological approach that emphasizes the role of experience in acquiring new behaviors; the perspective encompasses *behaviorism* and *social-learning theories.*

libido In psychoanalysis, the psychic energy that fuels the sexual or life instincts of the id.

limbic system A group of brain areas involved in emotional reactions and motivated behavior.

linkage studies Studies that look for patterns of inheritance of genetic markers in large families in which a particular condition is common; the markers consist of DNA segments that vary considerably among individuals and that have known locations on the chromosomes.

localization of function Specialization of particular brain areas for particular functions.

locus of control A general expectation about whether the results of your actions are under your own control (internal locus) or beyond your control (external locus).

longitudinal study A study in which subjects are followed and periodically reassessed over a period of time.

long-term memory (LTM) In the three-box model of memory, the memory system involved in the long-term storage of information.

long-term potentiation A long-lasting increase in the strength of synaptic responsiveness, thought to be a biological mechanism of long-term memory.

loudness The dimension of auditory experience related to the intensity of a pressure wave.

low-context cultures Cultures in which people do not take a shared context for granted, and instead emphasize direct verbal communication.

lucid dream A dream in which the dreamer is aware of dreaming.

maintenance rehearsal Rote repetition of material in order to maintain its availability in memory.

major depression A mood disorder involving disturbances in emotion (excessive sadness), behavior (loss of interest in one's usual activities), cognition (thoughts of hopelessness), and body function (fatigue and loss of appetite).

magnetic resonance imaging *See* MRI.

mean *See* arithmetic mean.

measure of central tendency A number intended to characterize an entire set of data.

measure of variability A number that indicates how dispersed scores are around the mean of the distribution. *See also* variance.

median A measure of central tendency; the value at the midpoint of a distribution of scores when the scores are ordered from highest to lowest.

medulla A structure in the brain stem responsible for certain automatic functions, such as breathing and heart rate.

melatonin A hormone, secreted by the pineal gland, that is involved in the regulation of daily biological rhythms.

menarche [men-ARE-kee] The onset of menstruation.

menopause The cessation of menstruation and of the production of ova; usually a gradual process lasting up to several years.

mental age (MA) A measure of mental development expressed in terms of the average mental ability at a given age. A child with a mental age of 8 performs on a test of mental ability at the level of the average 8-year-old.

mental disorder Any behavior or emotional state that causes an individual great suffering or worry; is self-defeating or self-destructive; or is maladaptive and disrupts the person's relationships or the larger community.

mental image A mental representation that mirrors or resembles the thing it represents; mental images can occur in many and perhaps all sensory modalities.

mental set A tendency to solve problems using procedures that worked before on similar problems.

meta-analysis A procedure for combining and analyzing data from many studies; it determines how much of the variance in scores across all studies can be explained by a particular variable.

metacognition The knowledge or awareness of one's own cognitive processes.

Minnesota Multiphasic Personality Inventory (MMPI) A widely used objective personality test.

"minor" tranquilizers Depressants commonly but often inappropriately prescribed for patients who complain of unhappiness or worry.

mnemonics Strategies and tricks for improving memory, such as the use of a verse or a formula.

mode A measure of central tendency; the most frequently occurring score in a distribution.

monochronic cultures Cultures in which time is organized sequentially; schedules and deadlines are valued over people.

monocular cues Visual cues to depth or distance that can be used by one eye alone.

monozygotic twins *See* identical twins.

motivated forgetting Forgetting that occurs because of a desire to eliminate awareness of painful, embarrassing, or otherwise unpleasant experiences.

motivation An inferred process within a person or animal, which causes that organism to move toward a goal or away from an unpleasant situation.

MRI (magnetic resonance imaging) A method for studying body and brain tissue, using magnetic fields and special radio receivers.

multiple personality disorder *See* dissociative identity disorder.

myelin sheath A fatty insulation that may surround the axon of a neuron.

narcissistic personality disorder A disorder characterized by an exaggerated sense of self-importance and self-absorption.

natural selection The evolutionary process in which individuals with genetically influenced traits that are adaptive in a particular environment tend to survive and to reproduce in greater numbers than do other individuals; as a result, their traits become more common in the population over time.

need for achievement A learned motive to meet personal standards of success and excellence in a chosen area; often abbreviated *nAch.*

need for affiliation The motive to associate with other people, as by seeking friends, moral support, contact comfort, or companionship.

need for power A learned motive to dominate or influence others.

negative correlation An association between increases in one variable and decreases in another.

negative reinforcement A reinforcement procedure in which a response is followed by the removal, delay, or decrease in intensity of an unpleasant stimulus; as a result, the response becomes stronger or more likely to occur.

nerve A bundle of nerve fibers (axons and sometimes dendrites) in the peripheral nervous system.

neuromodulators Chemical messengers in the nervous system that increase or decrease the action of specific neurotransmitters.

neuron A cell that conducts electrochemical signals; the basic unit of the nervous system; also called a *nerve cell.*

neuropsychology The field of psychology concerned with the neural and biochemical bases of behavior and mental processes.

neurotransmitter A chemical substance that is released by a transmitting neuron at the synapse and that alters the activity of a receiving neuron.

nonconscious processes Mental processes occurring outside of and not available to conscious awareness.

normal curve A symmetrical, bell-shaped frequency polygon representing a normal distribution.

normal distribution A theoretical frequency distribution having certain special characteristics. For example, the distribution is symmetrical; the mean, mode, and median all have the same value; and the farther a score is from the mean, the less the likelihood of obtaining it.

norms In test construction, established standards of performance.

norms (social) Social conventions that regulate human life, including explicit laws and implicit cultural standards.

null hypothesis An assertion that the independent variable in a study will have no effect on the dependent variable.

object permanence The understanding, which develops late in the first year, that an object continues to exist even when you can't see it or touch it.

object-relations school A psychodynamic approach that emphasizes the importance of the infant's first two years of life and the baby's formative relationships.

observational learning A learning process in which an individual learns new responses by observing the behavior of another (a model) rather than through direct experience; sometimes called *vicarious conditioning.*

observational study A study in which the researcher carefully and systematically observes and records behavior without interfering with the behavior; it may involve either naturalistic or laboratory observation.

obsessive-compulsive disorder (OCD) An anxiety disorder in which a person feels trapped in repetitive, persistent thoughts (obsessions) and repetitive, ritualized behaviors (compulsions) designed to reduce anxiety.

Oedipus complex In psychoanalysis, a conflict in which a child desires the parent of the other sex and views the same-sex parent as a rival; this is the key issue in the phallic stage of development.

operant conditioning The process by which a response becomes more likely to occur or less so, depending on its consequences.

operational definition A precise definition of a term in a hypothesis; it specifies the operations for observing and measuring the process or phenomenon being defined.

operations In Piaget's theory, mental actions that are cognitively reversible.

opiates Drugs, derived from the opium poppy, that relieve pain and commonly produce euphoria.

opponent-process theory A theory of color perception that assumes that the visual system treats pairs of colors as opposing or antagonistic.

panic attack A brief feeling of intense fear and impending doom or death, accompanied by intense physiological symptoms, such as rapid breathing and pulse, and dizziness.

papillae [pa-PILL-ee] Knoblike elevations on the tongue, containing the taste buds. (Singular: *papilla.*)

parallel distributed processing (PDP) An alternative to the information-processing model of memory, in which knowledge is represented as connections among thousands of interacting processing units, distributed in a vast network, and all operating in parallel.

paranoid personality disorder A disorder characterized by habitually unreasonable and excessive suspiciousness, jealousy, or mistrust. Paranoid symptoms may also occur in schizophrenia and other psychoses.

parapsychology The study of purported psychic phenomena such as ESP and mental telepathy.

parasympathetic nervous system The subdivision of the autonomic nervous system that operates during relaxed states and that conserves energy.

perception The process by which the brain organizes and interprets sensory information.

perceptual constancy The accurate perception of objects as stable or unchanged despite changes in the sensory patterns they produce.

perceptual illusion An erroneous or misleading perception of reality.

perceptual set A habitual way of perceiving, based on expectations.

peripheral nervous system (PNS) All portions of the nervous system outside the brain and spinal cord; it includes sensory and motor nerves.

personality A distinctive and relatively stable pattern of behavior, thoughts, motives, and emotions that characterizes an individual.

personality disorders Rigid, maladaptive personality patterns that cause personal distress or an inability to get along with others.

PET scan (positron-emission tomography) A method for analyzing biochemical activity in the brain, using injections of a glucoselike substance containing a radioactive element.

phobia An unrealistic fear of a specific situation, activity, or object.

pitch The dimension of auditory experience related to the frequency of a pressure wave; height or depth of a tone.

pituitary gland A small endocrine gland at the base of the brain, which releases many hormones and regulates other endocrine glands.

placebo An inactive substance or fake treatment used as a control in an experiment or given by a medical practitioner to a patient.

polychronic cultures Cultures in which time is organized horizontally; people tend to do several things at once and value relationships over schedules.

pons A structure in the brain stem involved in, among other things, sleeping, waking, and dreaming.

positive correlation An association between increases in one variable and increases in another.

positive reinforcement A reinforcement procedure in which a response is followed by the presentation of, or increase in intensity of, a reinforcing stimulus; as a result, the response becomes stronger or more likely to occur.

positron emission tomography *See* PET scan.

power assertion A method of child rearing in which the parent uses punishment and authority to correct the child's misbehavior.

primary control An effort to modify reality by changing other people, the situation, or events; a "fighting back" philosophy.

primary emotions Emotions that are considered to be universal and biologically based; they generally include fear, anger, sadness, joy, surprise, disgust, and contempt.

primary punisher A stimulus that is inherently punishing; an example is electric shock.

primary reinforcer A stimulus that is inherently reinforcing, typically satisfying a physiological need; an example is food.

priming A method for measuring implicit memory, in which a person reads or listens to information and is later tested to see whether the information affects performance on another type of task.

principle of falsifiability The principle that a scientific theory must make predictions that are specific enough to expose the theory to the possibility of disconfirmation; that is, the theory must predict not only what will happen, but also what will not happen.

proactive interference Forgetting that occurs when previously stored material interferes with the ability to remember similar, more recently learned material.

procedural memories Memories for the performance of actions or skills ("knowing how").

projective tests Psychological tests used to infer a person's motives, conflicts, and unconscious dynamics on the basis of the person's interpretations of ambiguous or unstructured stimuli.

proposition A unit of meaning that is made up of concepts and expresses a single idea.

prototype An especially representative example of a concept.

psychedelic drugs Consciousness-altering drugs that produce hallucinations, change thought processes, or disrupt the normal perception of time and space.

psychiatry The medical specialty concerned with mental disorders, maladjustment, and abnormal behavior.

psychoactive drug A drug capable of influencing perception, mood, cognition, or behavior.

psychoanalysis A theory of personality and a method of psychotherapy, originally formulated by Sigmund Freud, that emphasizes unconscious motives and conflicts.

psychodynamic perspective A psychological approach, originating with Freud's theory of psychoanalysis, that emphasizes unconscious energy dynamics within the individual, such as inner forces, conflicts, or the movement of instinctual energy.

psychological stress The result of a relationship between the person and the environment, in which the person believes the situation is overwhelming and threatens his or her ability to cope.

psychological tests Procedures used to measure and evaluate personality traits, emotional states, aptitudes, interests, abilities, and values.

psychology The scientific study of behavior and mental processes and how they are affected by an organism's physical state, mental state, and external environment; the term is often represented by Ψ, the Greek letter psi (usually pronounced "sy").

psychometrics The measurement of mental abilities, traits, and processes.

psychoneuroimmunology (PNI) The study of the relationships among psychology, the nervous and endocrine systems, and the immune system.

psychophysics The area of psychology concerned with the relationship between physical properties of stimuli and sensory experience.

psychosis An extreme mental disturbance involving distorted perceptions and irrational behavior; it may have psychological or organic causes. (Plural: *psychoses.*)

psychosomatic A term that describes the interaction between a physical illness or condition and psychological states; literally, mind (*psyche*) and body (*soma*).

psychosurgery Any surgical procedure that destroys selected areas of the brain believed to be involved in emotional disorders or violent, impulsive behavior.

puberty The age at which a person becomes capable of sexual reproduction.

punishment The process by which a stimulus or event weakens or reduces the probability of the response that it follows.

random assignment A procedure for assigning people to experimental and control groups, in which each individual has the same probability as any other of being assigned to a given group.

range A measure of the spread of scores, calculated by subtracting the lowest score from the highest score.

rapid eye movement (REM) sleep Sleep periods characterized by eye movement, loss of muscle tone, and dreaming.

reasoning The drawing of conclusions or inferences from observations, facts, or assumptions.

recall The ability to retrieve and reproduce from memory previously encountered material.

recognition The ability to identify previously encountered material.

reflex An automatic response to a stimulus.

reinforcement The process by which a stimulus or event strengthens or increases the probability of the response that it follows.

relearning method A method for measuring retention that compares the time required to relearn material with the time used in the initial learning of the material.

reliability In test construction, the consistency, from one time and place to another, of scores derived from a test.

REM sleep *See* rapid eye movement (REM) sleep.

representative sample A sample that matches the population in question on important characteristics, such as age and sex.

reticular activating system (RAS) A dense network of neurons found in the core of the brain stem; it arouses the cortex and screens incoming information.

retina Neural tissue lining the back of the eyeball's interior, which contains the receptors for vision.

retinal disparity The slight difference in lateral separation between two objects as seen by the left eye and the right eye.

retroactive interference Forgetting that occurs when recently learned material interferes with the ability to remember similar material stored previously.

rods Visual receptors that respond to dim light but are not involved in color vision.

role A given social position that is governed by a set of norms for proper behavior.

Rorschach Inkblot Test A projective personality test that asks respondents to interpret abstract, symmetrical ink blots.

sample A group of subjects selected from a population for study in order to estimate characteristics of the population.

saturation Vividness or purity of color; the dimension of visual experience related to the complexity of light waves.

schizophrenia A psychotic disorder or group of disorders marked by positive symptoms (e.g., delusions, hallucinations, disorganized and incoherent speech, and inappropriate behavior) and negative symptoms (e.g., emotional flatness and loss of motivation).

secondary control An effort to accept reality by changing your own attitudes, goals, or emotions; a "learn to live with it" philosophy.

secondary emotions Emotions that are either "blends" of primary emotions or specific to certain cultures.

secondary punisher A stimulus that has acquired punishing properties through association with other punishers.

secondary reinforcer A stimulus that has acquired reinforcing properties through association with other reinforcers.

selective attention The focusing of attention on selected aspects of the environment and the blocking out of others.

self-efficacy A person's belief that he or she is capable of producing desired results, such as mastering new skills and reaching goals.

self-fulfilling prophecy An expectation that comes true because of the tendency of the person holding it to act in ways that confirm it.

self-serving bias The tendency, in explaining one's own behavior, to take credit for one's good actions and rationalize one's mistakes.

semantic memories Memories of general knowledge, including facts, rules, concepts, and propositions.

semicircular canals Sense organs in the inner ear that contribute to equilibrium by responding to rotation of the head.

sensation The detection of physical energy emitted or reflected by physical objects; it occurs when energy in the external environment or the body stimulates receptors in the sense organs.

sense receptors Specialized cells that convert physical energy in the environment or the body to electrical energy that can be transmitted as nerve impulses to the brain.

sensory adaptation The reduction or disappearance of sensory responsiveness that occurs when stimulation is unchanging or repetitious.

sensory deprivation The absence of normal levels of sensory stimulation.

sensory memory A memory system that momentarily preserves extremely accurate images of sensory information.

sensory registers Subsystems of sensory memory; most memory models assume a separate register for each sensory modality.

serial-position effect The tendency for recall of the first and last items on a list to surpass recall of items in the middle of the list.

set point According to one theory, the genetically influenced weight range for an individual, thought to be maintained by a biological mechanism that regulates food intake, fat reserves, and metabolism.

sex hormones Hormones that regulate the development and functioning of reproductive and sex organs and that stimulate the development of male and female sexual characteristics; they include androgens (such as testosterone), estrogens, and progesterone.

sex-typing *See* gender socialization.

shaping An operant-conditioning procedure in which successive approximations of a desired response are reinforced; used when the desired response has a low probability of occurring spontaneously.

short-term memory (STM) In the three-box model of memory, a limited-capacity memory system involved in the retention of information for brief periods; it is also used to hold information retrieved from long-term memory for temporary use.

signal-detection theory A psychophysical theory that divides the detection of a sensory signal into a sensory process and a decision process.

single-blind study An experiment in which subjects do not know whether they are in an experimental or a control group.

social cognition An area in social psychology concerned with social influences on thought, memory, perception, and other cognitive processes.

social constructionism The view that there are no universal truths about human nature because people construct reality differently, depending on their culture, the historical moment, and the power arrangements within their society.

social identity The part of a person's self-concept that is based on his or her identification with a nation, culture, or ethnic group or with gender or other roles in society.

social-learning theories Theories of learning that emphasize how behavior is learned and maintained through observation and imitation of others, positive consequences, and cognitive processes such as plans, expectations, and motivating beliefs.

sociobiology An interdisciplinary field of study that emphasizes evolutionary explanations of social behavior in animals, including human beings.

sociocultural perspective A psychological approach that emphasizes social and cultural influences on behavior.

somatic nervous system The subdivision of the peripheral nervous system that connects to sensory receptors and to skeletal muscles; sometimes called the *skeletal nervous system*.

source amnesia The inability to distinguish what you originally experienced from what you heard or were told about an event later.

spinal cord A collection of neurons and supportive tissue running from the base of the brain down the center of the back, protected by a column of bones (the spinal column).

spontaneous recovery The reappearance of a learned response after its apparent extinction.

standard deviation A commonly used measure of variability that indicates the average difference between scores in a distribution and their mean; more precisely, the square root of the average squared deviation from the mean.

standardize In test construction, to develop uniform procedures for giving and scoring a test.

state-dependent memory The tendency to remember something when the rememberer is in the same physical or mental state as during the original learning or experience.

states of consciousness Distinctive and discrete patterns in the functioning of consciousness, characterized by particular modes of perception, thought, memory, or feeling.

statistically significant A term used to refer to a result that is extremely unlikely to have occurred by chance.

stereotype A cognitive schema or a summary impression of a group, in which a person believes that all members of the group share a common trait or traits (positive, negative, or neutral).

stimulants Drugs that speed up activity in the central nervous system.

stimulus control Control over the occurrence of a response by a discriminative stimulus.

stimulus discrimination The tendency to respond differently to two or more similar stimuli. In classical conditioning, it occurs when a stimulus similar to the conditioned stimulus fails to evoke the conditioned response; in operant conditioning, it occurs when an organism learns to make a response in the presence of one stimulus but not in the presence of other, similar stimuli that differ from it on some dimension.

stimulus generalization After conditioning, the tendency to respond to a stimulus that resembles one involved in the original conditioning. In classical conditioning, it occurs when a stimulus that resembles the conditioned stimulus elicits the conditioned response; in operant conditioning, it occurs when a response that has been reinforced (or punished) in the presence of one stimulus occurs (or is suppressed) in the presence of other, similar stimuli.

stress *See* psychological stress.

structuralism An early psychological approach that stressed analysis of immediate experience into basic elements.

subconscious processes Mental processes occurring outside of conscious awareness but accessible to consciousness when necessary.

successive approximations In the operant-conditioning procedure of shaping, behaviors that are ordered in terms of increasing similarity or closeness to the desired response.

superego In psychoanalysis, the part of personality that represents conscience, morality, and social standards.

surveys Questionnaires and interviews that ask people directly about their experiences, attitudes, or opinions.

sympathetic nervous system The subdivision of the autonomic nervous system that mobilizes bodily resources and increases the output of energy during emotion and stress.

synapse The site where transmission of a nerve impulse from one nerve cell to another occurs; it includes the axon terminal, the synaptic cleft, and receptor sites in the membrane of the receiving cell.

synchrony The adjustment of one person's nonverbal behavior to coordinate with another's.

tacit knowledge Strategies for success that are not explicitly taught but that instead must be inferred.

taste buds Nests of taste-receptor cells.

telegraphic speech A child's first combination of words, which omits (as a telegram does) unnecessary words.

temperaments Characteristic styles of responding to the environment that are present in infancy and are assumed to be innate.

teratogen An external agent, such as a disease or chemical, that increases the risk of abnormalities in prenatal development.

thalamus A brain structure that relays sensory messages to the cerebral cortex.

Thematic Apperception Test (TAT) A projective personality test that asks respondents to interpret a series of drawings showing ambiguous scenes of people.

theory An organized system of assumptions and principles that purports to explain a specified set of phenomena and their interrelationships.

theory of mind A theory about the way your own mind and other people's minds work, and of how people are affected by their beliefs and feelings; children develop a theory of mind by age 4 or 5.

therapeutic alliance The bond of confidence and mutual understanding established between therapist and client, which allows them to work together to solve the client's problems.

timbre The distinguishing quality of a sound; the dimension of auditory experience related to the complexity of the pressure wave.

token economy A behavior-modification technique in which secondary reinforcers called *tokens*, which can be collected and exchanged for primary or other secondary reinforcers, are used to shape behavior.

tolerance Increased resistance to a drug's effects accompanying continued use; as tolerance develops, larger doses are required to produce effects once brought about by smaller ones.

trained introspection A form of self-observation in which individuals examine and report the contents of their own consciousness.

trait A descriptive characteristic of an individual, assumed to be stable across situations and time.

transduction The conversion of one form of energy to another; sensory receptors are biological transducers.

transference In psychodynamic therapies, a critical step in which the patient transfers unconscious emotions or reactions, such as emotional feelings about his or her parents, onto the therapist.

trichromatic theory A theory of color perception that proposes three mechanisms in the visual system, each sensitive to a certain range of wavelengths; their interaction is assumed to produce all the different experiences of hue.

two-factor theory of emotion The theory that emotions depend on both physiological arousal and a cognitive interpretation of that arousal.

ultradian [ul-TRAY-dee-un] rhythm A biological rhythm that occurs more frequently than once a day; from the Latin for "beyond a day."

unconditional positive regard To Carl Rogers, love or support given to another person, with no conditions attached.

unconditioned response (UR) The classical-conditioning term for a reflexive response elicited by a stimulus in the absence of learning.

unconditioned stimulus (US) The classical-conditioning term for a stimulus that elicits a reflexive response in the absence of learning.

validity The ability of a test to measure what it was designed to measure.

validity effect The tendency of people to believe that a statement is true or valid simply because it has been repeated many times.

variable-interval (VI) schedule An intermittent schedule of reinforcement in which a reinforcer is delivered for a response made after a variable period of time has elapsed since the last reinforcer.

variable-ratio (VR) schedule An intermittent schedule of reinforcement in which reinforcement occurs after a variable number of responses.

variables Characteristics of behavior or experience that can be measured or described by a numeric scale; variables are manipulated and assessed in scientific studies.

variance A measure of the dispersion of scores around the mean.

volunteer bias A shortcoming of findings derived from a sample of volunteers instead of a representative sample.

Weber's law A law of psychophysics stating that the change necessary to produce a just noticeable difference is a constant proportion of the original stimulus.

withdrawal symptoms Physical and psychological symptoms that occur when someone addicted to a drug stops taking it.

z-score (standard score) A number that indicates how far a given raw score is above or below the mean, using the standard deviation of the distribution as the unit of measurement.

BIBLIOGRAPHY

Abel, Gene G.; Mittelman, Mary; Becker, Judith V.; Rathner, Jerry; et al. (1988). Predicting child molesters' response to treatment: Conference of the New York Academy of Sciences. Human sexual aggression: Current perspectives. *Annals of the New York Academy of Sciences, 528*, 223–234.

Abramovitch, Henry (1995). The nightmare of returning home: A case of acute onset nightmare disorder treated by lucid dreaming. *Israel Journal of Psychiatry and Related Sciences, 32*, 140–145.

Abrams, David B., & Wilson, G. Terence (1983). Alcohol, sexual arousal, and self-control. *Journal of Personality and Social Psychology, 45*, 188–198.

Abramson, Lyn Y.; Metalsky, Gerald I.; & Alloy, Lauren B. (1989). Hopelessness depression: A theory-based subtype of depression. *Psychological Review, 96*, 358–372.

Adamopoulos, John, & Lonner, Walter J. (1994). Absolutism, relativism, and universalism in the study of human behavior. In W. J. Lonner & R. S. Malpass (eds.), *Psychology and culture*. Needham Heights, MA: Allyn & Bacon.

Adams, Gerald R.; Ryan, John H.; Hoffman, Joseph J.; Dobson, William R.; & Nielsen, Elwin C. (1985). Ego identity status, conformity behavior, and personality in late adolescence. *Journal of Personality and Social Psychology, 47*, 1091–1104.

Adams, James L. (1986). *Conceptual blockbusting: A guide to better ideas* (3rd ed.). Boston: Addison-Wesley.

Adams, M. J. (1990). *Learning to read: Thinking and learning about print.* Cambridge, MA: MIT Press.

Ader, Robert, & Cohen, Nicholas (1993). Psychoneuroimmunology: Conditioning and stress. *Annual Review of Psychology, 44*, 53–85.

Adler, Alfred (1927/1959). *Understanding human nature.* New York: Premier.

Adler, Nancy E.; Boyce, Thomas; Chesney, Margaret A.; Cohen, Sheldon; Folkman, Susan; Kahn, Robert L.; & Syme, S. Leonard (1994). Socioeconomic status and health: The challenge of the gradient. *American Psychologist, 49*, 15–24.

Affleck, Glenn; Tennen, Howard; Croog, Sydney; & Levine, Sol (1987). Causal attribution, perceived control, and recovery from a heart attack. *Journal of Social and Clinical Psychology, 5*, 339–355.

Ainsworth, Mary D. S. (1973). The development of infant mother attachment. In B. M. Caldwell & H. N. Ricciuti (eds.), *Review of child development research* (Vol. 3). Chicago: University of Chicago Press.

Ainsworth, Mary D. S. (1979). Infant mother attachment. *American Psychologist, 34*, 932–937.

Ainsworth, Mary D. S.; Blehar, Mary L.; Waters, Everett; & Wall, Sally (1978). *Patterns of attachment.* Hillsdale, NJ: Erlbaum.

Akbarian, Schahram; Kim, J. J.; Potkin, Steven G.; Hetrick, W. P.; et al. (1996). Maldistribution of interstitial neurons in prefrontal white matter of the brains of schizophrenic patients. *Archives of General Psychiatry, 53*, 425–436.

Alagna, Sheryle W., & Hamilton, Jean A. (1986). *Science in the service of mythology: The psychopathologizing of menstruation.* Paper presented at the annual meeting of the American Psychological Association, Washington, DC.

Albee, George W. (1985, February). The answer is prevention. *Psychology Today*, 60–64.

Aldag, Ramon J., & Fuller, Sally R. (1993). Beyond fiasco: A reappraisal of the groupthink phenomenon and a new model of group decision processes. *Psychological Bulletin, 113*, 533–552.

Alkon, Daniel L. (1989). Memory storage and neural systems. *Scientific American, 261*, 42–50.

Allen, Laura S., & Gorski, Robert A. (1992). Sexual orientation and the size of the anterior commissure in the human brain. *Proceedings of the National Academy of Sciences, 89*, 7199–7202.

Allison, David B., & Heshka, Stanley (1993). Emotion and eating in obesity? A critical analysis. *International Journal of Eating Disorders, 13*, 289–295.

Allison, David B.; Heshka, Stanley; Neale, Michael C.; Lykken, David T.; et al. (1994). A genetic analysis of relative weight among 4,020 twin pairs, with an emphasis on sex effects. *Health Psychology, 13*, 362–365.

Allport, Gordon W. (1937). *Personality: A psychological interpretation.* New York: Holt, Rinehart and Winston.

Allport, Gordon W. (1954/1979). *The nature of prejudice.* Reading, MA: Addison-Wesley.

Allport, Gordon W. (1961). *Pattern and growth in personality.* New York: Holt, Rinehart and Winston.

Alpert, Bené; Field, Tiffany; Goldstein, Sheri; & Perry, Susan (1990). Aerobics enhances cardiovascular fitness and agility in preschoolers. *Health Psychology, 9*, 48–56.

Amabile, Teresa M. (1983). *The social psychology of creativity.* New York: Springer-Verlag.

Amabile, Teresa M. (1985). Motivation and creativity: Effects of motivational orientation on creative writers. *Journal of Personality and Social Psychology, 48*, 393–399.

Amabile, Teresa M.; Phillips, Elise D.; & Collins, Mary Ann (1993). *Creativity by contract: Social influences on the creativity of professional artists.* Paper presented at the annual meeting of the American Psychological Association, Toronto, Canada.

Ambady, Nalini; Koo, Jasook; Lee, Fiona; & Rosenthal, Robert (1996). More than words: Linguistic and nonlinguistic politeness in two cultures. *Journal of Personality and Social Psychology, 70*, 996–1011.

American Psychiatric Association (1994). *The diagnostic and statistical manual of mental disorders* (4th ed.). Washington, DC: Author.

American Psychological Association (1984). *Survey of the use of animals in behavioral research at U.S. universities.* Washington, DC: Author.

Amering, Michaela, & Katschnig, Heinz (1990). Panic attacks and panic disorder in cross-cultural perspective. *Psychiatric Annals, 20*, 511–516.

Amir, Yehuda (1994). The contact hypothesis in intergroup relations. In W. J. Lonner & R. Malpass (eds.), *Psychology and culture*. Needham Heights, MA: Allyn & Bacon.

Anastasi, Anne (1988). *Psychological testing* (6th ed.). New York: Macmillan.

Andersen, Barbara L.; Kiecolt-Glaser, Janice K.; & Glaser, Ronald (1994). A biobehavioral model of cancer stress and disease course. *American Psychologist, 49,* 389–404.

Andersen, Susan M.; Klatzky, Roberta L.; & Murray, John (1990). Traits and social stereotypes: Efficiency differences in social information processing. *Journal of Personality and Social Psychology, 59,* 192–201.

Anderson, Barbara (1995). *Surviving cancer: Do psychological interventions play a role?* Paper presented at the annual meeting of the American Psychological Association, New York.

Anderson, Craig A.; Miller, Rowland S.; Riger, Alice L.; Dill, Jody C.; & Sedikides, Constantine (1994). Behavioral and characterological attributional styles as predictors of depression and loneliness: Review, refinement, and test. *Journal of Personality and Social Psychology, 66,* 549–558.

Anderson, James A., & Rosenfeld, Edward (eds.) (1988). *Neurocomputing: Foundations of research.* Cambridge, MA: MIT Press.

Anderson, John R. (1990). *The adaptive nature of thought.* Hillsdale, NJ: Erlbaum.

Anderson, Norman B. (1991). *Addressing ethnic minority health issues: Behavioral medicine at the forefront of research and practice.* Paper presented at the annual meeting of the Society of Behavioral Medicine, Washington, DC.

Andreasen, Nancy C.; Arndt, Stephan; Swayze, Victor, II; Cizadlo, Ted; et al. (1994). Thalamic abnormalities in schizophrenia visualized through magnetic resonance image averaging. *Science, 266,* 294–298.

Anliker, J. A.; Bartoshuk, L. M.; Ferris, A. M.; & Hooks, L. D. (1991). Children's food preferences and genetic sensitivity to the bitter taste of PROP. *American Journal of Clinical Nutrition, 54,* 316–320.

Anthony, William A.; Cohen, Mikal; & Kennard, William (1990). Understanding the current facts and principles of mental health systems planning. *American Psychologist, 45,* 1249–1252.

Antonuccio, David; Danton, William G.; & DeNelsky, Garland Y. (1995). Psychotherapy vs. medication for depression: Challenging the conventional wisdom. *Professional Psychology: Research and Practice, 26,* 574–585.

APA Commission on Violence and Youth (1993). *Violence and youth: Psychology's response.* Washington, DC: American Psychological Association.

Appiah, Kwame A. (1994). Beyond race: Fallacies of reactive Afrocentrism. *Skeptic, 2*(4), 104–107.

Apter, Terri (1990). *Altered loves: Mothers and daughters during adolescence.* New York: St. Martin's Press.

Archer, John (1996). Sex differences in social behavior: Are the social role and evolutionary explanations compatible? *American Psychologist, 51,* 909–917.

Arendt, Hannah (1963). *Eichmann in Jerusalem: A report on the banality of evil.* New York: Viking.

Arkes, Hal R. (1991). *Some practical judgment/decision making research.* Paper presented at the annual meeting of the American Psychological Association, Boston.

Arkes, Hal R.; Boehm, Lawrence E.; & Xu, Gang (1991). The determinants of judged validity. *Journal of Experimental Social Psychology, 27,* 576–605.

Arkes, Hal R.; Faust, David; Guilmette, Thomas J.; & Hart, Kathleen (1988). Eliminating the hindsight bias. *Journal of Applied Psychology, 73,* 305–307.

Armstrong, Louise (1993). *And they call it help: The psychiatric policing of America's children.* Reading, MA: Addison-Wesley.

Aron, Arthur, & Westbay, Lori (1996). Dimensions of the prototype of love. *Journal of Personality and Social Psychology, 70,* 535–551.

Aronson, Elliot (1995). *The social animal* (7th ed.). New York: Freeman.

Aronson, Elliot, & Mills, Judson (1959). The effect of severity of initiation on liking for a group. *Journal of Abnormal and Social Psychology, 59,* 177–181.

Aronson, Elliot; Stephan, Cookie; Sikes, Jev; Blaney, Nancy; & Snapp, Matthew (1978). *The jigsaw classroom.* Beverly Hills, CA: Sage.

Aronson, Elliot; Wilson, Timothy D.; & Akert, Robin A. (1997). *Social psychology: The heart and the mind* (2nd ed.). New York: Longman.

Asch, Solomon E. (1952). *Social psychology.* Englewood Cliffs, NJ: Prentice-Hall.

Asch, Solomon E. (1965). Effects of group pressure upon the modification and distortion of judgments. In H. Proshansky & B. Seidenberg (eds.), *Basic studies in social psychology.* New York: Holt, Rinehart and Winston.

Aserinsky, Eugene, & Kleitman, Nathaniel (1955). Two types of ocular motility occurring in sleep. *Journal of Applied Physiology, 8,* 1–10.

Aspinwall, Lisa G., & Brunhart, Susanne M. (1996). Distinguishing optimism from denial: Optimistic beliefs predict attention to health threats. *Personality and Social Psychology Bulletin, 22,* 993–1003.

Aspinwall, Lisa G., & Taylor, Shelley E. (1993). Effects of social comparison direction, threat, and self-esteem on affect, self-evaluation, and expected success. *Journal of Personality and Social Psychology, 64,* 708–722.

Aspinwall, Lisa G., & Taylor, Shelley E. (1997). A stitch in time: Self-regulation and proactive coping. *Psychological Bulletin, 121,* 417–436.

Astington, Janet W. (1993). *The child's discovery of the mind.* Cambridge, MA: Harvard University Press.

Atkinson, John W. (ed.) (1958). *Motives in fantasy, action, and society.* Princeton, NJ: Van Nostrand.

Atkinson, Richard C., & Shiffrin, Richard M. (1968). Human memory: A proposed system and its control processes. In K. W. Spence & J. T. Spence (eds.), *The psychology of learning and motivation: Vol. 2. Advances in research and theory.* New York: Academic Press.

Atkinson, Richard C., & Shiffrin, Richard M. (1971, August). The control of short-term memory. *Scientific American, 225*(2), 82–90.

AuBuchon, Peter G., & Calhoun, Karen S. (1985). Menstrual cycle symptomatology: The role of social expectancy and experimental demand characteristics. *Psychosomatic Medicine, 47,* 35–45.

Averill, James R. (1982). *Anger and aggression.* New York: Springer-Verlag.

Azrin, Nathan H., & Foxx, Richard M. (1974). *Toilet training in less than a day.* New York: Simon & Schuster.

Azuma, Hiroshi (1984). Secondary control as a heterogeneous category. *American Psychologist, 39,* 970–971.

Baer, John S.; Kivlahan, Daniel R.; & Marlatt, G. Alan (1995). High-risk drinking across the transition from high school to college. *Alcoholism: Clinical and Experimental Research, 19,* 54–61.

Bahill, A. Terry, & Karnavas, William J. (1993). The perceptual illusion of baseball's rising fastball and breaking curveball. *Journal of Experimental Psychology: Human Perception & Performance, 19,* 3–14.

Bahrick, Harry P. (1984). Semantic memory content in permastore: Fifty years of memory for Spanish learned in school. *Journal of Experimental Psychology: General, 113,* 1–29.

Bahrick, Harry P.; Bahrick, Phyllis O.; & Wittlinger, Roy P. (1975). Fifty years of memory for names and faces: A cross-sectional approach. *Journal of Experimental Psychology: General, 104,* 54–75.

Bailey, J. Michael; Bobrow, David; Wolfe, Marilyn; & Mikach, Sarah (1995). Sexual orientation of adult sons of gay fathers. *Developmental Psychology, 31,* 124–129.

Bailey, J. Michael; Gaulin, Steven; Agyei, Yvonne; & Gladue, Brian A. (1994). Effects of gender and sexual orientation on evolutionarily relevant aspects of human mating psychology. *Journal of Personality and Social Psychology, 66,* 1081–1093.

Bailey, J. Michael, & Pillard, Richard C. (1995). Genetics of human sexual orientation. *Annual Review of Sex Research, 6,* 126–150.

Baillargeon, Renée (1994). How do infants learn about the physical world? *Current Directions in Psychological Science, 5,* 133–140.

Baker, Robert A. (1992). *Hidden memories: Voices and visions from within.* Buffalo, NY: Prometheus.

Baker, Robin (1996). *The sperm wars: The science of sex.* New York: Basic Books.

Baltes, Paul B. (1983). Life-span developmental psychology: Observations on history and theory revisited. In R. M. Lerner (ed.), *Developmental psychology: Historical and philosophical perspectives.* Hillsdale, NJ: Erlbaum.

Baltes, Paul, & Graf, Peter (1996). Psychological aspects of aging: Facts and frontiers. In D. Magnusson (ed.), *The lifespan development of individuals.* Cambridge, England: Cambridge University Press.

Baltes, Paul B.; Sowarka, Doris; & Kliegl, Reinhold (1989). Cognitive training research on fluid intelligence in old age: What can older adults achieve by themselves? *Psychology and Aging, 4,* 217–221.

Bandura, Albert (1973). *Aggression: A social learning analysis.* Englewood Cliffs, NJ: Prentice-Hall.

Bandura, Albert (1977). *Social learning theory.* Englewood Cliffs, NJ: Prentice-Hall.

Bandura, Albert (1986). *Social foundations of thought and action: A social cognitive theory.* Englewood Cliffs, NJ: Prentice-Hall.

Bandura, Albert (1990). Self-regulation of motivation through goal systems. In R. A. Dienstbier (ed.), *Nebraska Symposium on Motivation* (Vol. 38). Lincoln: University of Nebraska Press.

Bandura, Albert (1991). Social cognitive theory of moral thought and action. In W. M. Kurtines & J. L. Gewirtz (eds.), *Handbook of moral behavior and development: Vol. 1. Theory.* Hillsdale, NJ: Erlbaum.

Bandura, Albert (1992). Self-efficacy mechanism in psychobiologic functioning. In R. Schwarzer (ed.), *Self-efficacy: Thought control of action.* Washington, DC: Hemisphere.

Bandura, Albert (1994). Self-efficacy. *In Encyclopedia of human behavior* (Vol. 4). Orlando, FL: Academic Press.

Bandura, Albert (ed.) (1995). *Self-efficacy in changing societies.* New York: Cambridge University Press.

Bandura, Albert; Ross, Dorothea; & Ross, Sheila A. (1963). Vicarious reinforcement and imitative learning. *Journal of Abnormal and Social Psychology, 67,* 601–607.

Banks, Martin S. (in collaboration with Philip Salapatek) (1984). Infant visual perception. In P. Mussen (series ed.), M. M. Haith & J. J. Campos (vol. eds.), *Handbook of child psychology: Vol. II. Infancy and developmental psychobiology* (4th ed.). New York: Wiley.

Barber, Theodore X. (1979). Suggested ("hypnotic") behavior: The trance paradigm versus an alternative paradigm. In E. Fromm & R. E. Shor (eds.), *Hypnosis: Developments in research and new perspectives* (2nd ed.). New York: Aldine.

Bardach, Ann Louise (1993, August). Tearing the veil. *Vanity Fair,* 123–127, 154–158.

Barinaga, Marcia (1992). Challenging the "no new neurons" dogma. *Science, 255,* 1646.

Barkow, Jerome H.; Cosmides, Leda; & Tooby, John (eds.) (1992). *The adapted mind: Evolutionary psychology and the generation of culture.* New York: Oxford University Press.

Barlow, David H. (1990). *Disorders of emotion.* Paper presented at the annual meeting of the American Psychological Association, Boston.

Barlow, David H. (ed.) (1991). Special issue on diagnoses, dimensions, and DSM-IV: The science of classification. *Journal of Abnormal Psychology, 100,* 243–412.

Barlow, David H. (1996). Health care policy, psychotherapy research, and the future of psychotherapy. *American Psychologist, 51,* 1050–1058.

Barnett, Peter A., & Gotlib, Ian H. (1988). Psychosocial functioning and depression: Distinguishing among antecedents, concomitants, and consequences. *Psychological Bulletin, 104,* 97–126.

Barnett, Rosalind C., & Rivers, Caryl (1996). *She works, he works: How two-income families are healthier, happier, and better off.* San Francisco: HarperCollins.

Baron, Miron (1993). The D2 dopamine receptor gene and alcoholism: A tempest in a wine cup? *Biological Psychiatry, 34,* 821–823.

Baron, Robert S.; Cutrona, Carolyn E.; Hicklin, Daniel; Russell, Daniel W.; & Lubaroff, David M. (1990). Social support and immune function among spouses of cancer patients. *Journal of Personality and Social Psychology, 59,* 344–352.

Barraclough, J.; Pinder, P.; Cruddas, M.; Osmond, C.; Taylor, I.; & Perry, M. (1992). Life events and breast cancer prognosis. *British Medical Journal, 304*(6834), 1078–1081.

Bartlett, Frederic C. (1932). *Remembering.* Cambridge, England: Cambridge University Press.

Bartoshuk, Linda (1990, August/September). Psychophysical insights on taste. *APA Science Agenda,* 12–13.

Bartoshuk, Linda M. (1993). Genetic and pathological taste variation: What can we learn from animal models and human disease? In D. J. Chadwick, J. Marsh, & J. Goode (eds.), *The molecular basis of smell and taste transduction.* CIBA Foundation Symposia Series, No. 179. New York: Wiley.

Bartoshuk, Linda M., & Beauchamp, Gary K. (1994). Chemical senses. *Annual Review of Psychology, 45,* 419–449.

Bashore, Theodore R., & Rapp, Paul E. (1993). Are there alternatives to traditional polygraph procedures? *Psychological Bulletin, 113,* 3–22.

Basic Behavioral Science Task Force of the National Advisory Mental Health Council (1996). Basic behavioral science research for mental health: Vulnerability and resilience. *American Psychologist, 51,* 22–28.

Batson, C. Daniel (1990). How social an animal? The human capacity for caring. *American Psychologist, 45,* 336–346.

Bauer, Patricia J., & Dow, Gina Annunziato (1994). Episodic memory in 16- and 20-month-old children: Specifics are generalized but not forgotten. *Developmental Psychology, 30,* 403–417.

Baum, Andrew; Herberman, Holly; & Cohen, Lorenzo (1995). *Managing stress and managing illness: Survival and quality of life in chronic disease.* Paper presented at the annual meeting of the American Psychological Association, New York.

Baum, William M. (1994). *Understanding behaviorism: Science, behavior, and culture.* New York: HarperCollins.

Baumeister, Roy F. (1990). Suicide as escape from self. *Psychological Review, 97,* 90–113.

Baumeister, Roy F., & Leary, Mark R. (1995). The need to belong: Desire for interpersonal attachments as a fundamental human motivation. *Psychological Bulletin, 117,* 497–529.

Baumeister, Roy F.; Stillwell, Arlene M.; & Heatherton, Todd F. (1994). Guilt: An interpersonal approach. *Psychological Bulletin, 115,* 243–267.

Baumeister, Roy F.; Stillwell, Arlene M.; & Wotman, Sara R. (1990). Victim and perpetrator accounts of interpersonal conflict: Autobiographical narratives about anger. *Journal of Personality and Social Psychology, 59,* 994–1005.

Baumrind, Diana (1966). Effects of authoritative parental control on child behavior. *Child Development, 37,* 887–907.

Baumrind, Diana (1971). Current patterns of parental authority. *Developmental Psychology Monograph, 4* (1, Part 2).

Baumrind, Diana (1973). The development of instrumental competence through socialization. In A. D. Pick (ed.), *Minnesota Symposium on Child Psychology* (Vol. 7). Minneapolis: University of Minnesota Press.

Baumrind, Diana (1989). Rearing competent children. In W. Damon (ed.), *Child development today and tomorrow.* San Francisco: Jossey-Bass.

Baumrind, Diana (1991). Parenting styles and adolescent development. In R. Lerner, A. C. Petersen, & J. Brooks-Gunn (eds.), *The encyclopedia of adolescence.* New York: Garland.

Baumrind, Diana (1995). Commentary on sexual orientation: Research and social policy implications. *Developmental Psychology, 31,* 130–136.

Baxter, Lewis R.; Schwartz, Jeffrey M.; Bergman, Kenneth S.; Szuba, Martin P.; et al. (1992). Caudate glucose metabolic rate changes with both drug and behavior therapy for obsessive-compulsive disorder. *Archives of General Psychiatry, 49,* 681–689.

Bayer, Ronald (1981). *Homosexuality and American psychiatry.* New York: Basic Books.

Beard, John H.; Propst, Rudyard N.; & Malamud, T. J. (1982). The Fountain House model of psychiatric rehabilitation. *Psychosocial Rehabilitation Journal, 5,* 47–54.

Bechtel, William, & Abrahamsen, Adele (1990). *Connectionism and the mind: An introduction to parallel processing in networks.* Cambridge, MA: Basil Blackwell.

Beck, Aaron T. (1976). *Cognitive therapy and the emotional disorders.* New York: International Universities Press.

Beck, Aaron T. (1988). Cognitive approaches to panic disorder: Theory and therapy. In S. Rachman & J. D. Maser (eds.), *Panic: Psychological perspectives.* Hillsdale, NJ: Erlbaum.

Beck, Aaron T. (1991). Cognitive therapy: A 30-year retrospective. *American Psychologist, 46,* 368–375.

Becker, Ernest (1973). *The denial of death.* New York: Free Press.

Becker, Judith V.; Skinner, Linda J.; Abel, Gene G.; & Cichon, Joan (1984). Time-limited therapy with sexually dysfunctional sexually assaulted women. *Journal of Social Work and Human Sexuality, 3,* 97–115.

Becker, Marshall H. (1993). A medical sociologist looks at health promotion. *Journal of Health and Social Behavior, 34,* 1–6.

Bee, Helen (1997). *The developing child* (8th ed.). New York: Longman.

Bee, Helen; Barnard, Kathryn E.; et al. (1982). Prediction of IQ and language skill from perinatal status, child performance, family characteristics, and mother infant interaction. *Child Development, 53,* 1134–1156.

Begg, Ian M.; Needham, Douglas R.; & Bookbinder, Marc (1993). Do backward messages unconsciously affect listeners? No. *Canadian Journal of Experimental Psychology, 47,* 1–14.

Bekenstein, Jonathan W., & Lothman, Eric W. (1993). Dormancy of inhibitory interneurons in a model of temporal lobe epilepsy. *Science, 259,* 97–100.

Bell, Alan P.; Weinberg, Martin S.; & Hammersmith, Sue K. (1981). *Sexual preference: Its development in men and women.* Bloomington: Indiana University Press.

Belsky, Jay; Campbell, Susan B.; Cohn, Jeffrey F.; & Moore, Ginger (1996). Instability of infant parent attachment security. *Developmental Psychology, 32,* 921–924.

Belsky, Jay; Hsieh, Kuang-Hua; & Crnic, Keith (1996). Infant positive and negative emotionality: One dimension or two? *Developmental Psychology, 32,* 289–298.

Benbow, Camilla P., & Stanley, Julian C. (1983). Sex differences in mathematical reasoning: More facts. *Science, 222,* 1029–1031.

Benet, Verónica, & Waller, Niels G. (1995). The Big Seven factor model of personality description: Evidence for its cross-cultural generality in a Spanish sample. *Journal of Personality and Social Psychology, 69,* 701–718.

Benjamin, J.; Li, L.; Patterson, C.; et al. (1996). Population and familial association between the D4 dopamine receptor gene and measures of novelty seeking. *Nature Genetics, 12,* 81–84.

Bennett, Henry L. (1988). Perception and memory for events during adequate general anesthesia for surgical operations. In H. M. Pettinati (ed.), *Hypnosis and memory.* New York: Guilford Press.

Bentall, R. P. (1990). The illusion of reality: A review and integration of psychological research on hallucinations. *Psychological Bulletin, 107,* 82–95.

Bereiter, Carl, & Bird, Marlene (1985). Use of thinking aloud in identification and teaching of reading comprehension strategies. *Cognition and Instruction, 2,* 131–156.

Berenbaum, Sheri A., & Hines, Melissa (1992). Early androgens are related to childhood sex-typed toy preferences. *Psychological Science, 3,* 203–206.

Berkman, L. F.; Leo-Summers, L.; & Horwitz, R. I. (1992). Emotional support and survival after myocardial infarction: A prospective, population-based study of the elderly. *Annals of Internal Medicine, 117,* 1003–1009.

Berkman, Lisa, & Syme, S. Leonard (1979). Social networks, host resistance, and mortality: A nine-year follow-up study of Alameda County residents. *American Journal of Epidemiology, 109,* 186–204.

Berko, Jean (1958). The child's learning of English morphology. *Word, 14,* 150–177.

Bernieri, Frank J.; Davis, J.; Rosenthal, R.; & Knee, C. (1991). *Interactional synchrony and the social affordance of rapport: A validation study.* Unpublished manuscript, Oregon State University, Corvallis.

Bernieri, Frank J.; Gillis, John S.; Davis, Janet M.; & Grahe, Jon E. (1996). Dyad rapport and the accuracy of its judgment across situations: A lens model analysis. *Journal of Personality and Social Psychology, 71,* 110–129.

Berry, John W. (1994). Acculturative stress. In W. J. Lonner & R. S. Malpass (eds.), *Psychology and culture.* Needham Heights, MA: Allyn & Bacon.

Berry, John W.; Dasen, Pierre R.; Kagiticibasi, Cigdem; Pandey, Janak; Poortinga, Ype H.; Saraswathi, T.; & Segall, Marshall H. (eds.) (1997). *Handbook of cross-cultural psychology* (2nd ed.). Boston: Allyn & Bacon.

Berscheid, Ellen (1985). Interpersonal attraction. In G. Lindzey & E. Aronson (eds.), *Handbook of social psychology* (Vol. 2). New York: Random House/Erlbaum.

Best, Deborah L., & Williams, John E. (1993). Cross-cultural viewpoint. In A. E. Beall & R. J. Sternberg (eds.), *The psychology of gender.* New York: Guilford Press.

Betancourt, Hector, & López, Steven Regeser (1993). The study of culture, ethnicity, and race in American psychology. *American Psychologist, 48,* 629–637.

Bettelheim, Bruno (1962). *Symbolic wounds.* New York: Collier.

Bettelheim, Bruno (1967). *The empty fortress.* New York: Free Press.

Bettencourt, B. Ann, & Miller, Norman (1996). Gender differences in aggression as a function of provocation: A meta-analysis. *Psychological Bulletin, 119,* 422–447.

Biederman, Irving (1987). Recognition-by-components: A theory of human image understanding. *Psychological Review, 94,* 115–147.

Birdwhistell, Ray L. (1970). *Kinesics and context: Essays on body motion communication.* Philadelphia: University of Pennsylvania Press.

Bishop, Katherine M., & Wahlsten, Douglas (1997). Sex differences in the human corpus callosum: Myth or reality? *Neuroscience and Biobehavioral Reviews, 21.*

Bjork, Daniel W. (1993). *B. F. Skinner: A life.* New York: Basic Books.

Black, Donald W.; Wesner, Robert; Bowers, Wayne; & Gabel, Janelle (1993). A comparison of fluvoxamine, cognitive therapy, and placebo in the treatment of panic disorder. *Archives of General Psychiatry, 50,* 44–50.

Blakemore, Colin, & Cooper, Grahame F. (1970). Development of the brain depends on the visual environment. *Nature, 228,* 477–478.

Blass, Thomas (1991). Understanding behavior in the Milgram obedience experiment: The role of personality, situations, and their interactions. *Journal of Personality and Social Psychology, 60,* 398–413.

Bleuler, Eugen (1911/1950). *Dementia praecox or the group of schizophrenias.* New York: International Universities Press.

Bliss, T. V., & Collingridge, G. L. (1993). A synaptic model of memory: Long-term potentiation in the hippocampus. *Nature, 361*(6407), 31–39.

Bloom, Benjamin S. (ed.) (1985). *Developing talent in young people.* New York: Ballantine.

Bloom, Lois M. (1970). *Language development: Form and function in emerging grammars.* Cambridge, MA: MIT Press.

Blum, Kenneth, with James E. Payne (1991). *Alcohol and the addictive brain.* New York: Free Press/Science News Press.

Boehm, Lawrence E. (1994). The validity effect: A search for mediating variables. *Personality and Social Psychology Bulletin, 20,* 285–293.

Boesch, Cristophe (1991). Teaching among wild chimpanzees. *Animal Behavior, 41,* 530–532.

Bohannon, John N. (1988). Flashbulb memories for the space shuttle disaster: A tale of two theories. *Cognition, 29,* 179–196.

Bohannon, John N., & Stanowicz, Laura (1988). The issue of negative evidence: Adult responses to children's language errors. *Developmental Psychology, 24,* 684–689.

Bohannon, John N., & Symons, Victoria (1988). *Conversational conditions of children's imitation.* Paper presented at the biennial Conference on Human Development, Charleston, South Carolina.

Bohman, Michael; Cloninger, R.; Sigvardsson, S.; & von Knorring, Anne-Liis (1987). The genetics of alcoholisms and related disorders. *Journal of Psychiatric Research, 21,* 447–452.

Boivin, D. B.; Duffy, J. F.; Kronauer, R. E.; & Czeisler, C. A. (1996). Dose response relationships for resetting of human circadian clock by light. *Nature, 379,* 540–542.

Bolger, Niall (1990). Coping as a personality process: A prospective study. *Journal of Personality and Social Psychology, 59,* 525–537.

Bolger, Niall; Foster, Mark; Vinokur, Amiram D.; & Ng, Rosanna (1996). Close relationships and adjustment to a life crisis: The case of breast cancer. *Journal of Personality and Social Psychology, 70,* 283–294.

Bolos, Annabel M.; Dean, M.; Lucas-Derse, S.; Ramsburg, M.; et al. (1990, December 26). Population and pedigree studies reveal a lack of association between the dopamine D2 receptor gene and alcoholism. *Journal of the American Medical Association, 264,* 3156–3160.

Bolshakov, Vadim Y., & Siegelbaum, Steven A. (1994). Postsynaptic induction and presynaptic expression of hippocampal long-term depression. *Science, 264,* 1148–1152.

Bond, Rod, & Smith, Peter B. (1996). Culture and conformity: A meta-analysis of studies using Asch's (1952b, 1956) line judgment task. *Psychological Bulletin, 119,* 111–137.

Bonnet, Michael H. (1990). The perception of sleep onset in insomniacs and normal sleepers. In R. R. Bootzin, J. F. Kihlstrom, & D. L. Schacter (eds.), *Sleep and cognition.* Washington, DC: American Psychological Association.

Bootzin, Richard R.; Epstein, Dana; & Wood, James M. (1991). Stimulus control instruction. In P. Hauri (ed.), *Case studies in insomnia.* New York: Plenum.

Boring, Edwin G. (1953). A history of introspection. *Psychological Bulletin, 50,* 169–187.

Bornstein, Robert F.; Leone, Dean R.; & Galley, Donna J. (1987). The generalizability of subliminal mere exposure effects: Influence of stimuli perceived without awareness on social behavior. *Journal of Personality and Social Psychology, 53,* 1070–1079.

Borys, Shelley, & Perlman, Daniel (1985). Gender differences in loneliness. *Personality and Social Psychology Bulletin, 11,* 63–74.

Bothwell, R. K., Deffenbacher, K. A., & Brigham, J. C. (1987). Correlation of eyewitness accuracy and confidence: Optimality hypothesis revised. *Journal of Applied Psychology, 72,* 691–698.

Bouchard, Claude; Tremblay, A.; Despres, J. P.; Nadeau, A.; et al. (1990, May 24). The response to long-term overfeeding in identical twins. *New England Journal of Medicine, 322,* 1477–1482.

Bouchard, Thomas J., Jr. (1984). Twins reared together and apart: What they tell us about human diversity. In S. W. Fox (ed.), *Individuality and determinism.* New York: Plenum.

Bouchard, Thomas J., Jr. (1995). *Nature's twice-told tale: Identical twins reared apart—what they tell us about human individuality.* Paper presented at the annual meeting of the Western Psychological Association, Los Angeles.

Bouchard, Thomas J., Jr. (1997a). IQ similarity in twins reared apart: Findings and responses to critics. In R. J. Sternberg & E. Grigorenko (eds.), *Intelligence: Heredity and environment.* New York: Cambridge University Press.

Bouchard, Thomas J., Jr. (1997b). The genetics of personality. In K. Blum & E. P. Noble (eds.), *Handbook of psychiatric genetics.* Boca Raton, FL: CRC Press.

Bouchard, Thomas J., Jr.; Lykken, David T.; McGue, Matthew; Segal, Nancy L.; et al. (1990). Sources of human psychological differences: The Minnesota Study of Twins Reared Apart. *Science, 250,* 223–228.

Bouchard, Thomas J., Jr.; Lykken, David T.; McGue, Matthew; Segal, Nancy L.; et al. (1991). "Sources of human psychological differences: The Minnesota Study of Twins Reared Apart": Response. *Science, 252,* 191–192.

Bouchard, Thomas J., Jr.; Lykken, David T.; Segal, Nancy L.; & Wilcox, Kimerly J. (1986). Development in twins reared apart: A test of the chronogenetic hypothesis. In A. Demirjian (ed.), *Human growth: A multidisciplinary review.* London: Taylor & Francis.

Bouchard, Thomas J., Jr., & McGue, Matthew (1981). Familial studies of intelligence: A review. *Science, 212,* 1055–1058.

Bousfield, W. A. (1953). The occurrence of clustering in the recall of randomly arranged associates. *Journal of General Psychology, 49,* 229–240.

Bowen, Murray (1978). *Family therapy in clinical practice.* New York: Jason Aronson.

Bower, Gordon H., & Clark, M. C. (1969). Narrative stories as mediators of serial learning. *Psychonomic Science, 14,* 181–182.

Bowers, Kenneth S.; Regehr, Glenn; Balthazard, Claude; & Parker, Kevin (1990). Intuition in the context of discovery. *Cognitive Psychology, 22,* 72–110.

Bowers, Wayne A. (1990). Treatment of depressed in-patients: Cognitive therapy plus medication, relaxation plus medication, and medication alone. *British Journal of Psychiatry, 156,* 73–78.

Bowlby, John (1958). The nature of the child's tie to his mother. *International Journal of Psycho-Analysis, 39,* 350–373.

Bowlby, John (1969). *Attachment and loss. Vol. I: Attachment.* New York: Basic Books.

Bowlby, John (1973). *Attachment and loss. Vol. II: Separation.* New York: Basic Books.

Boyd-Franklin, Nancy (1989). *Black families in therapy: A multisystems approach.* New York: Guilford Press.

Boysen, Sarah T., & Berntson, Gary G. (1989). Numerical competence in a chimpanzee *(Pan troglodytes). Journal of Comparative Psychology, 103,* 23–31.

Bracha, H. Stefan; Torrey, E. Fuller; Bigelow, Llewellyn B.; Lohr, James B.; & Linington, Beverly B. (1991). Subtle signs of prenatal maldevelopment of the hand ectoderm in schizophrenia: A preliminary monozygotic twin study. *Biological Psychiatry, 30,* 719–725.

Braddock, Oliver; Atkinson, Janette; Hood, Bruce; Harkness, William; et al. (1992). Possible blindsight in infants lacking one cerebral hemisphere. *Nature, 360,* 461–463.

Bradley, Robert H., & Caldwell, Bettye M. (1984). 174 children: A study of the relationship between home environment and cognitive development during the first 5 years. In Allen W. Gottfried (ed.), *Home environment and early cognitive development: Longitudinal research.* Orlando, FL: Academic Press.

Brainard, David H.; Wandell, Brian A.; & Chichilnisky, Eduardo-Jose (1993). Color constancy: From physics to appearance. *Current Directions in Psychological Science, 2,* 165–170.

Brainerd, C. J. (1996). Piaget: A centennial celebration. *Psychological Science, 7,* 191–195.

Brainerd, C. J.; Reyna, V. F.; & Brandse, E. (1995). Are children's false memories more persistent than their true memories? *Psychological Science, 6,* 359–364.

Braungert, J. M.; Plomin, Robert; DeFries, J. C.; & Fulker, D. W. (1992). Genetic influence on tester-rated infant temperament as assessed by Bayley's Infant Behavior Record: Nonadoptive and adoptive siblings and twins. *Developmental Psychology, 28,* 40–47.

Breggin, Peter R. (1991). *Toxic psychiatry.* New York: St. Martin's Press.

Brehm, Sharon S. (1992). *Intimate relationships* (2nd ed.). New York: McGraw-Hill.

Breland, Keller, & Breland, Marian (1961). The misbehavior of organisms. *American Psychologist, 16,* 681–684.

Brennan, Kelly A., & Shaver, Phillip R. (1995). Dimensions of adult attachment, affect regulation, and romantic relationship functioning. *Personality and Social Psychology Bulletin, 21,* 267–283.

Brewer, Marilynn B., & Gardner, Wendi (1996). Who is this "we"? Levels of collective identity and self representations. *Journal of Personality and Social Psychology, 71,* 83–93.

Briggs, Jean (1970). *Never in anger: Portrait of an Eskimo family.* Cambridge, MA: Harvard University Press.

Briggs, John (1984, December). The genius mind. *Science Digest, 92*(12), 74–77, 102–103.

Brigham, John C., & Malpass, Roy S. (1985, Fall). The role of experience and contact in the recognition of faces of own- and other-race persons. *Journal of Social Issues, 41,* 139–155.

Brockner, Joel, & Rubin, Jeffrey Z. (1985). *Entrapment in escalating conflicts: A social psychological analysis.* New York: Springer-Verlag.

Brodie-Scott, Cheryl, & Hobbs, Stephen H. (1992). *Biological rhythms and publication practices: A follow-up survey, 1987–1991.* Paper presented at the Southeastern Psychological Association, Knoxville, Tennessee.

Brodsky, Annette M. (1982). Sex, race, and class issues in psychotherapy research. In J. H. Harvey & M. M. Parks (eds.), *Psychotherapy research and behavior change: Vol. 1. The APA Master Lecture Series.* Washington, DC: American Psychological Association.

Brody, D. J.; Pirkle, J. L.; Kramer, R. A.; et al. (1994). Blood lead levels in the US population: Phase 1 of the Third National Health and Nutrition Examination Survey (NHANES III, 1988 to 1991). *Journal of the American Medical Association, 272,* 277–283.

Brody, Nathan (1990). Behavior therapy versus placebo: Comment on Bowers and Clum's meta-analysis. *Psychological Bulletin, 107,* 106–109.

Bromberger, Joyce T., & Matthews, Karen A. (1996). A "feminine" model of vulnerability to depressive symptoms: A longitudinal investigation of middle-aged women. *Journal of Personality and Social Psychology, 70,* 591–598.

Brown, Alan S. (1991). A review of the tip-of-the-tongue experience. *Psychological Bulletin, 109,* 204–223.

Brown, George W. (1993). Life events and affective disorder: Replications and limitations. *Psychosomatic Medicine, 55,* 248–259.

Brown, Jonathon D. (1991). Staying fit and staying well. *Journal of Personality and Social Psychology, 60,* 555–561.

Brown, Jonathon D., & Smart, S. April (1991). The self and social conduct: Linking self-representations to prosocial behavior. *Journal of Personality and Social Psychology, 60,* 368–375.

Brown, Paul (1994). Toward a psychobiological study of dissociation. In S. J. Lynn & J. Rhue (eds.), *Dissociation: Clinical, theoretical and research perspectives.* New York: Guilford Press.

Brown, Robert, & Middlefell, Robert (1989). Fifty-five years of cocaine dependence [letter]. *British Journal of Addiction, 84,* 946.

Brown, Roger (1986). *Social psychology* (2nd ed.). New York: Free Press.

Brown, Roger; Cazden, Courtney; & Bellugi, Ursula (1969). The child's grammar from I to III. In J. P. Hill (ed.), *Minnesota Symposium on Child Psychology* (Vol. 2). Minneapolis: University of Minnesota Press.

Brown, Roger, & Kulik, James (1977). Flashbulb memories. *Cognition, 5,* 73–99.

Brown, Roger, & McNeill, David (1966). The "tip of the tongue" phenomenon. *Journal of Verbal Learning and Verbal Behavior, 5,* 325–337.

Brown, Steven P. (1996). A meta-analysis and review of organizational research on job involvement. *Psychological Bulletin, 120,* 235–255.

Brownell, Kelly D., & Rodin, Judith (1994). The dieting maelstrom: Is it possible and advisable to lose weight? *American Psychologist, 49,* 781–791.

Brunner, H. G.; Nelen, M. R.; & van Zandvoort, P. (1993). X-linked borderline mental retardation with prominent behavioral disturbance: Phenotype, genetic localization, and evidence for disturbed monoamine metabolism. *American Journal of Human Genetics, 52,* 1032–1039.

Bryant, Richard A., & McConkey, Kevin M. (1990). Hypnotic blindness and the relevance of cognitive style. *Journal of Personality and Social Psychology, 59,* 756–761.

Bryer, Jeffrey; Nelson, Bernadette; Miller, Jean; & Krol, Pamela (1987). Childhood sexual and physical abuse as factors in adult psychiatric illness. *American Journal of Psychiatry, 144,* 1426–1430.

Buck, Linda, & Axel, Richard (1991). A novel multigene family may encode odorant receptors: A molecular basis for odor recognition. *Cell, 65,* 175–187.

Buck, Ross (1984). *The communication of emotion.* New York: Guilford Press.

Buck, Ross, & Teng, Wan-Cheng (1987). *Spontaneous emotional communication and social biofeedback: A cross-cultural study of emotional expression and communication in Chinese and Taiwanese students.* Paper presented at the annual meeting of the American Psychological Association, New York.

Bunney, B. G.; Potkin, Steven G.; & Bunney, William E., Jr. (1995). New morphological and neuropathological findings in schizophrenia: A neurodevelopmental perspective. *Clinical Neuroscience, 3,* 81–88.

Burack, J. H.; Barrett, D. C.; Stall, R. D.; Chesney M. A.; Ekstrand, M. L.; & Coates, T. J. (1993). Depressive symptoms and CD4 lymphocyte decline among HIV-infected men. *Journal of the American Medical Association, 270,* 2568–2573.

Burgess, C.; Morris, T.; & Pettingale, K. W. (1988). Psychological response to cancer diagnosis II. Evidence for coping styles (coping styles and cancer diagnosis). *Journal of Psychosomatic Research, 32,* 263–272.

Burke, Deborah M.; Burnett, Gayle; & Levenstein, Peggy (1978). *Menstrual symptoms: New data from a double-blind study.* Paper presented at the annual meeting of the Western Psychological Association, San Francisco.

Burke, Deborah M.; MacKay, Donald G.; Worthley, Joanna S.; & Wade, Elizabeth (1991). On the tip of the tongue: What causes word finding failures in young and older adults? *Journal of Memory and Language, 30,* 237–246.

Burnam, M. Audrey; Stein, Judith; Golding, Jacqueline; Siegel, Judith; & Sorenson, Susan (1988). Sexual assault and mental disorders in a community population. *Journal of Counseling and Clinical Psychology, 56,* 843–850.

Burstyn, Linda (1995, October). Female circumcision comes to America. *The Atlantic Monthly,* 28–35.

Bushman, Brad J. (1993). Human aggression while under the influence of alcohol and other drugs: An integrative research review. *Psychological Science, 2,* 148–152.

Bushman, Brad J. (1995). Moderating role of trait aggressiveness in the effects of violent media on aggression. *Journal of Personality and Social Psychology, 69,* 950–960.

Buss, David M. (1994). *The evolution of desire: Strategies of human mating.* New York: Basic Books.

Buss, David M. (1995). Evolutionary psychology: A new paradigm for psychological science. *Psychological Inquiry, 6,* 1–30.

Buss, David M. (1996). Sexual conflict: Can evolutionary and feminist perspectives converge? In D. M. Buss & N. Malamuth (eds.), *Sex, power, conflict: Evolutionary and feminist perspectives.* New York: Oxford University Press.

Buss, David M.; Abbott, M.; Angleitner, Alois; et al. (1990). International preferences in selecting mates: A study of 37 cultures. *Journal of Cross-Cultural Psychology, 21,* 5–47.

Bussey, Kay, & Bandura, Albert (1992). Self-regulatory mechanisms governing gender development. *Child Development, 63,* 1236–1250.

Bussey, Kay, & Maughan, Betty (1982). Gender differences in moral reasoning. *Journal of Personality and Social Psychology, 42,* 701–706.

Butcher, James N.; Dahlstrom, W. Grant; Graham, John R.; Tellegen, Auke; & Kaemmer, Beverly (1989). *Minnesota Multiphasic Personality Inventory-II: Manual for administration and scoring.* Minneapolis: University of Minnesota Press.

Butler, S.; Chalder, T.; Ron, M.; Wessely, S.; et al. (1991). Cognitive behaviour therapy in chronic fatigue syndrome. *Journal of Neurology, Neurosurgery & Psychiatry, 54,* 153–158.

Butterfield, E. C., & Belmont, J. M. (1977). Assessing and improving the executive cognitive functions of mentally retarded people. In I. Bialer & M. Sternlict (eds.), *Psychological issues in mental retardation.* New York: Psychological Dimensions.

Buunk, Bram; Angleitner, Alois; Oubaid, Viktor; & Buss, David M. (1996). Sex differences in jealousy in evolutionary and cultural perspective: Tests from the Netherlands, Germany, and the United States. *Psychological Science, 7,* 359–363.

Byne, William (1993). *Sexual orientation and brain structure: Adding up the evidence.* Paper presented at the annual meeting of the International Academy of Sex Research, Pacific Grove, CA.

Byne, William, & Parsons, Bruce (1993). Human sexual orientation: The biologic theories reappraised. *Archives of General Psychiatry, 50,* 228–239.

Cabezas, A.; Tam, T. M.; Lowe, B. M.; Wong, A.; & Turner, K. (1989). Empirical study of barriers to upward mobility of Asian Americans in the San Francisco Bay area. In G. Nomura (ed.), *Frontiers of Asian American studies.* Pullman: Washington State University Press.

Cahill, Larry; Prins, Bruce; Weber, Michael; & McGaugh, James L. (1994). β-Adrenergic activation and memory for emotional events. *Nature, 371,* 702–704.

Callahan, Daniel (1989). *What kind of life: The limits of medical progress.* New York: Simon & Schuster.

Camera, Wayne J., & Schneider, Dianne L. (1994). Integrity tests: Facts and unresolved issues. *American Psychologist, 49,* 112–119.

Campbell, Anne (1993). *Men, women, and aggression.* New York: Basic Books.

Campbell, Frances A., & Ramey, Craig T. (1994). Effects of early intervention on intellectual and academic achievement: A follow-up study of children from low-income families. *Child Development, 65,* 684–698.

Campbell, Frances A., & Ramey, Craig T. (1995). Cognitive and school outcomes for high risk students at middle adolescence: Positive effects of early intervention. *American Educational Research Journal, 32,* 743–772.

Campbell, Jennifer; Trapnell, Paul D.; Heine, Steven J.; Katz, Ilana M.; et al. (1996). Self-concept clarity: Measurement, personality correlates, and cultural boundaries. *Journal of Personality and Social Psychology, 70,* 141–156.

Campbell, Joseph (1949/1968). *The hero with 1,000 faces* (2nd ed.). Princeton, NJ: Princeton University Press.

Cancian, Francesca M. (1987). *Love in America: Gender and self-development.* Cambridge, England: Cambridge University Press.

Canetto, Silvia S. (1992). Suicide attempts and substance abuse: Similarities and differences. *Journal of Psychology, 125,* 605–620.

Canino, Glorisa (1994). Alcohol use and misuse among Hispanic women: Selected factors, processes, and studies. [Special Issue: Substance use patterns of Latinas.] *International Journal of the Addictions, 29,* 1083–1100.

Caplan, Paula J. (1995). *They say you're crazy.* Reading, MA: Addison-Wesley.

Caramazza, Alfonso, & Hillis, Argye E. (1991, February 28). Lexical organization of nouns and verbs in the brain. *Nature, 349,* 788–790.

Cardeña, Etzel; Lewis-Fernández, Roberto; Bear, David; Pakianathan, Isabel; & Spiegal, David (1994). Dissociative disorders. In *DSM-IV Sourcebook.* Washington, DC: American Psychiatric Press.

Carducci, Bernardo J., & McGuire, Jay C. (1990). *Behavior and beliefs characteristic of first-, second-, and third-time lovers.* Paper presented at the annual meeting of the American Psychological Association, Boston.

Carpenter, William T., Jr.; Sadier, John H.; et al. (1983). The therapeutic efficacy of hemodialysis in schizophrenia. *New England Journal of Medicine, 308*(12), 669–675.

Carr, Edward G., & Durand, V. Mark (1985). Reducing behavior problems through functional communication training. *Journal of Applied Behavior Analysis, 18,* 111–126.

Carroll, James M., & Russell, James A. (1996). Do facial expressions signal specific emotions? Judging emotion from the face in context. *Journal of Personality and Social Psychology, 70,* 203–218.

Carroll, Kathleen M.; Rounsaville, Bruce J.; Gordon, Lynn T.; Nich, Charla; et al. (1994b). Psychotherapy and pharmacotherapy for ambulatory cocaine abusers. *Archives of General Psychiatry, 51,* 177–187.

Carroll, Kathleen M.; Rounsaville, Bruce J.; & Nich, Charla (1994a). Blind man's bluff: Effectiveness and significance of psychotherapy and pharmacotherapy blinding procedures in a clinical trial. *Journal of Consulting and Clinical Psychology, 62*, 276–280.

Carskadon, Mary A.; Mitler, Merrill M.; & Dement, William C. (1974). A comparison of insomniacs and normals: Total sleep time and sleep latency. *Sleep Research, 3*, 130 [Abstract].

Carson, Robert C. (1989). *What happened to schizophrenia? Reflections on a taxonomic absurdity.* Paper presented at the annual meeting of the American Psychological Association, New Orleans.

Carson, Robert C.; Butcher, James N.; & Mineka, Susan (1996). *Abnormal psychology and modern life* (10th ed.). New York: HarperCollins.

Carter, Betty, & McGoldrick, Monica (eds.) (1988). *The changing family life cycle: A framework for family therapy* (2nd ed.). New York: Gardner Press.

Cartwright, Rosalind D. (1990). A network model of dreams. In R. R. Bootzin, J. F. Kihlstrom, & D. L. Schacter (eds.), *Sleep and cognition.* Washington, DC: American Psychological Association.

Cartwright, Rosalind, & Lloyd, Stephen R. (1994). Early REM sleep: A compensatory change in depression? *Psychiatry Research, 51*, 245–252.

Carver, Charles S.; Ironson, G.; Wynings, C.; Greenwood, D.; et al. (1993a). *Coping with Andrew: How coping responses relate to experience of loss and symptoms of poor adjustment.* Paper presented at the annual meeting of the American Psychological Association, Toronto, Canada.

Carver, Charles S.; Pozo, Christina; Harris, Suzanne D.; Noriega, Victoria; et al. (1993b). How coping mediates the effect of optimism on distress: A study of women with early stage breast cancer. *Journal of Personality and Social Psychology, 65*, 375–390.

Carver, Charles S., & Scheier, Michael F. (1994). Situational coping and coping dispositions in a stressful transaction. *Journal of Personality and Social Psychology, 66*, 184–195.

Caspi, Avshalom, & Moffitt, Terrie E. (1991). Individual differences are accentuated during periods of social change: The sample case of girls at puberty. *Journal of Personality and Social Psychology, 61*, 157–168.

Cass, Loretta K., & Thomas, Carolyn (1979). *Childhood pathology and later adjustment.* New York: Wiley-Interscience.

Casswell, Sally (1993). Public discourse on the benefits of moderation: Implications for alcohol policy development. *Addiction, 88*, 459–465.

Cattell, Raymond B. (1965). *The scientific analysis of personality.* Baltimore, MD: Penguin.

Cattell, Raymond B. (1973). *Personality and mood by questionnaire.* San Francisco: Jossey-Bass.

Ceci, Stephen J., & Bruck, Maggie (1993). Suggestibility of the child witness: A historical review and synthesis. *Psychological Bulletin, 113*, 403–439.

Ceci, Stephen J., & Bruck, Maggie (1995). *Jeopardy in the courtroom: A scientific analysis of children's testimony.* Washington, DC: American Psychological Association.

Ceci, Stephen J., & Liker, Jeffrey K. (1986). Academic and nonacademic intelligence: An experimental separation. In R. J. Sternberg & R. K. Wagner (eds.), *Practical intelligence: Nature and origins of competence in the everyday world.* New York: Cambridge University Press.

Celis, William, III (1993, August 1). Down from the self-esteem high. *The New York Times*, Education Section.

Cermak, Laird S., & Craik, Fergus I. M. (eds.) (1979). *Levels of processing in human memory.* Hillsdale, NJ: Erlbaum.

Chaiken, Shelly, & Yates, Suzanne (1985). Affective cognitive consistency and thought-induced attitude polarization. *Journal of Personality and Social Psychology, 49*, 1470–1481.

Chambless, Dianne L. (1988). Cognitive mechanisms in panic disorder. In S. Rachman & J. D. Maser (eds.), *Panic: Psychological perspectives.* Hillsdale, NJ: Erlbaum.

Chambless, Dianne L. (1995). Training in and dissemination of empirically validated psychological treatments: Report and recommendations. *The Clinical Psychologist, 48*, 3–24.

Chambless, Dianne L., & members of the Division 12 Task Force (1996). An update on empirically validated therapies. *The Clinical Psychologist, 49*, 5–18.

Chan, Darius Kwan-Shing (1994). Colindex: A refinement of three collectivism measures. In U. Kim, H. Triandis, C. Kagitcibasi, S. Choi, & G. Yoon (eds.), *Individualism and collectivism: Theory, method, and applications.* Thousand Oaks, CA: Sage.

Chance, June E., & Goldstein, Alvin G. (1995). The other-race effect in eyewitness identification. In S. L. Sporer, G. Koehnken, & R. S. Malpass (eds.), *Psychological issues in eyewitness identification.* Hillsdale, NJ: Erlbaum.

Chance, Paul (1988, October). Knock wood. *Psychology Today*, 68–69.

Chance, Paul (1994). *Learning and behavior* (3rd ed.). Belmont, CA: Wadsworth.

Chang, Edward C. (1996). Cultural differences in optimism, pessimism, and coping: Predictors of subsequent adjustment in Asian American and Caucasian American college students. *Journal of Counseling Psychology, 43*, 113–123.

Chaves, J. F. (1989). Hypnotic control of clinical pain. In N. P. Spanos & J. F. Chaves (eds.), *Hypnosis: The cognitive-behavioral perspective.* Buffalo, NY: Prometheus Books.

Checkley, Stuart A.; Murphy, D. G.; Abbas, M.; Marks, M.; et al. (1993). Melatonin rhythms in seasonal affective disorder. *British Journal of Psychiatry, 163*, 332–337.

Cheney, Dorothy L., & Seyfarth, Robert M. (1985). Vervet monkey alarm calls: Manipulation through shared information? *Behavior, 94*, 150–166.

Cheney, Dorothy L., & Seyfarth, Robert M. (1990). *How monkeys see the world: Inside the mind of another species.* Chicago: University of Chicago Press.

Chipuer, Heather M.; Rovine, Michael J.; & Plomin, Robert (1990). LISREL modeling: Genetic and environmental influences on IQ revisited. *Intelligence, 14*, 11–29.

Chodorow, Nancy (1978). *The reproduction of mothering.* Berkeley: University of California Press.

Chodorow, Nancy (1992). *Feminism and psychoanalytic theory.* New Haven, CT: Yale University Press.

Chomsky, Noam (1957). *Syntactic structures.* The Hague, Netherlands: Mouton.

Chomsky, Noam (1980). Initial states and steady states. In M. Piatelli-Palmerini (ed.), *Language and learning: The debate between Jean Piaget and Noam Chomsky.* Cambridge, MA: Harvard University Press.

Chrisler, Joan C.; Johnston, Ingrid K; Champagne, Nicole M.; & Preston, Kathleen E. (1994). Menstrual joy: The construct and its consequences. *Psychology of Women Quarterly, 18*, 375–387.

Christensen, Andrew, & Jacobson, Neil S. (1994). Who (or what) can do psychotherapy: The status and challenge of nonprofessional therapies. *Psychological Science, 5*, 8–14.

Christensen, Larry, & Burrows, Ross (1990). Dietary treatment of depression. *Behavior Therapy, 21*, 183–194.

Chua, Streamson C., Jr.; Chung, Wendy K.; Wu-Peng, S. Sharon; et al. (1996). Phenotypes of mouse *diabetes* and rat *fatty* due to mutations in the OB (leptin) receptor. *Science, 271*, 994–996.

Chudacoff, Howard P. (1990). *How old are you? Age consciousness in American culture.* Princeton, NJ: Princeton University Press.

Cialdini, Robert B. (1993). *Influence: The psychology of persuasion.* New York: Quill/Morrow.

Cioffi, Delia, & Holloway, James (1993). Delayed costs of suppressed pain. *Journal of Personality and Social Psychology, 64*, 274–282.

Cioffi, Frank (1974, February 7). Was Freud a liar? *The Listener, 91*, 172–174.

Clark, Margaret S.; Milberg, Sandra; & Erber, Ralph (1987). Arousal state dependent memory: Evidence and some implications for understanding social judgments and social behavior. In K. Fiedler & J. P. Forgas (eds.), *Affect, cognition and social behavior.* Toronto, Canada: Hogrefe.

Clarke-Stewart, K. Alison; VanderStoep, Laima P.; & Killian, Grant A. (1979). Analyses and replication of mother child relations at two years of age. *Child Development, 50*, 777–793.

Clementz, Brett A., & Sweeney, John A. (1990). Is eye movement dysfunction a biological marker for schizophrenia? A methodological review. *Psychological Review, 108*, 77–92.

Cloninger, C. Robert (1990). *The genetics and biology of alcoholism.* Cold Springs Harbor, ME: Cold Springs Harbor Press.

Cloninger, C. Robert; Svrakic, Dragan M.; & Przybeck, Thomas R. (1993). A psychobiological model of temperament and character. *Archives of General Psychiatry, 50*, 975–990.

Clopton, Nancy A., & Sorell, Gwendolyn T. (1993). Gender differences in moral reasoning: Stable or situational? *Psychology of Women Quarterly, 17*, 85–101.

Coats, Erik J.; Janoff-Bulman, Ronnie; & Alpert, Nancy (1996). Approach versus avoidance goals: Differences in self-evaluation and well-being. *Personality and Social Psychology Bulletin, 22,* 1057–1067.

Coffey, C. E. (1993). Structural brain imaging and ECT. In C. E. Coffey (ed.), *The clinical science of electroconvulsive therapy.* Washington, DC: American Psychiatric Association.

Cohen, Dov; Nisbett, Richard E.; Bowdle, Brian F.; & Schwarz, Norbert (1996). Insult, aggression, and the Southern culture of honor: An "experimental ethnography." *Journal of Personality and Social Psychology, 70,* 945–960.

Cohen, Sheldon; Evans, Gary W.; Krantz, David S.; & Stokols, Daniel (1980). Physiological, motivational, and cognitive effects of aircraft noise on children. *American Psychologist, 35,* 231–243.

Cohen, Sheldon; Tyrrell, David A.; & Smith, Andrew P. (1993). Negative life events, perceived stress, negative affect, and susceptibility to the common cold. *Journal of Personality and Social Psychology, 64,* 131–140.

Cohn, Lawrence D. (1991). Sex differences in the course of personality development: A meta-analysis. *Psychological Bulletin, 109,* 252–266.

Cole, Michael (1990). Cultural psychology: A once and future discipline? In J. J. Berman (ed.), *Cross-cultural perspectives: Nebraska Symposium on Motivation, 1989.* Lincoln: University of Nebraska Press.

Cole, Michael, & Cole, Sheila R. (1993). *The development of children* (2nd ed.). New York: Freeman.

Collaer, Marcia L., & Hines, Melissa (1995). Human behavioral sex differences: A role for gonadal hormones during early development? *Psychological Bulletin, 118,* 55–107.

Collins, Allan M., & Loftus, Elizabeth F. (1975). A spreading-activation theory of semantic processing. *Psychological Review, 82,* 407–428.

Collins, Barry (1993). *Using person perception methodologies to uncover the meanings of the Milgram obedience paradigm.* Paper presented at the annual meeting of the American Psychological Association, Toronto, Canada.

Collins, Rebecca L. (1996). For better or worse: The impact of upward social comparison on self-evaluations. *Psychological Bulletin, 119,* 51–69.

Colman, Andrew (1991a). Crowd psychology in South African murder trials. *American Psychologist, 46,* 1071–1079.

Colman, Andrew (1991b, November). Psychological evidence in South African murder trials. *The Psychologist, 4,* 482–486.

Comas-Díaz, Lillian, & Greene, Beverly (1994). *Women of color: Integrating ethnic and gender identities in psychotherapy.* New York: Guilford Press.

Comstock, George; Chaffee, Steven; Katzman, Natan; McCombs, Maxwell; & Roberts, Donald (1978). *Television and human behavior.* New York: Columbia University Press.

Condon, William (1982). Cultural microrhythms. In M. Davis (ed.), *Interaction rhythms: Periodicity in communicative behavior.* New York: Human Sciences Press.

Considine, R. V.; Sinha, M. K.; Heiman, M. L.; et al. (1996). Serum immunoreactive-leptin concentrations in normal-weight and obese humans. *New England Journal of Medicine, 334,* 292–295.

Conway, Martin A.; Anderson, Stephen J.; Larsen, Steen F.; Donnelly, C. M.; et al. (1994). The formation of flashbulb memories. *Memory and Cognition, 22,* 326–343.

Conway, Michael, & Ross, Michael (1984). Getting what you want by revising what you had. *Journal of Personality and Social Psychology, 47,* 738–748.

Coons, Philip M.; Milstein, Victor; & Marley, Carma (1982). EEG studies of two multiple personalities and a control. *Archives of General Psychiatry, 39,* 823–825.

Cooper, M. Lynne; Frone, Michael R.; Russell, Marcia; & Mudar, Pamela (1995). Drinking to regulate positive and negative emotions: A motivational model of alcohol use. *Journal of Personality and Social Psychology, 69,* 990–1005.

Copi, Irving M., & Burgess-Jackson, Keith (1992). *Informal logic* (2nd ed.). New York: Macmillan.

Coren, Stanley (1996). Daylight saving time and traffic accidents. *New England Journal of Medicine, 334,* 924.

Corkin, Suzanne (1984). Lasting consequences of bilateral medial temporal lobectomy: Clinical course and experimental findings in H. M. *Seminars in Neurology, 4,* 249–259.

Cornelius, Randolph R. (1991). Gregorio Maraûon's two-factor theory of emotion. *Personality and Social Psychology Bulletin, 17,* 65–69.

Cose, Ellis (1994). *The rage of a privileged class.* New York: HarperCollins.

Cosmides, Leda; Tooby, John; & Barkow, Jerome H. (1992) Introduction: Evolutionary psychology and conceptual integration. In J. H. Barkow, L. Cosmides, & J. Tooby (eds.), *The adapted mind: Evolutionary psychology and the generation of culture.* New York: Oxford University Press.

Costa, Paul T., Jr., & McCrae, Robert R. (1994). "Set like plaster"? Evidence for the stability of adult personality. In R. Heatherton & J. Weinberger (eds.), *Can personality change?* Washington, DC: American Psychological Association.

Costa, Paul T., Jr., & Widiger, Thomas A. (eds.) (1994). *Personality disorders and the five-factor model of personality.* Washington, DC: American Psychological Association.

Costantino, Giuseppe; Malgady, Robert G.; & Rogler, Lloyd H. (1986). Cuento therapy: A culturally sensitive modality for Puerto Rican children. *Journal of Consulting and Clinical Psychology, 54,* 639–645.

Coupland, Scott K.; Serovich, Julianne; & Glenn, J. Edgar (1995). Reliability in constructing genograms: A study among marriage and family therapy doctoral students. [Special Section: Genograms in family therapy.] *Journal of Marital and Family Therapy, 21,* 251–263.

Courtney, J. G.; Longnecker, M. P.; Theorell, T.; & Gerhardsson de Verdier, M. (1993). Stressful life events and the risk of colorectal cancer. *Epidemiology, 4,* 407–414.

Cowen, Emory L.; Wyman, Peter A.; Work, William C.; & Parker, Gayle R. (1990). The Rochester Child Resilience Project (RCRP): Overview and summary of first year findings. *Development and Psychopathology, 2,* 193–212.

Coyne, James C., & Whiffen, Valerie E. (1995). Issues in personality as diathesis for depression: The case of sociotropy dependency and autonomy self-criticism. *Psychological Bulletin, 118,* 358–378.

Craik, F. I. M., & Salthouse, Timothy A. (eds.) (1992). *The handbook of aging and cognition.* Hillsdale, NJ: Erlbaum.

Craik, Fergus I. M., & Tulving, Endel (1975). Depth of processing and the retention of words in episodic memory. *Journal of Experimental Psychology: General, 104,* 268–294.

Crain, Stephen (1991). Language acquisition in the absence of experience. *Behavioral & Brain Sciences, 14,* 597–650.

Crandall, Christian S., & Martinez, Rebecca (1996). Culture, ideology, and antifat attitudes. *Personality and Social Psychology Bulletin, 22,* 1165–1176.

Crandall, James E. (1984). Social interest as a moderator of life stress. *Journal of Personality and Social Psychology, 47,* 164–174.

Crawford, Mary, & Marecek, Jeanne (1989). Psychology constructs the female: 1968–1988. *Psychology of Women Quarterly, 13,* 147–165.

Crews, Frederick, and his critics (1995). *The memory wars: Freud's legacy in dispute.* New York: A New York Review Book.

Crick, Francis, & Mitchison, Graeme (1995). REM sleep and neural nets. *Behavioural Brain Research, 69,* 147–155.

Crick, Nicki R., & Grotpeter, Jennifer K. (1995). Relational aggression, gender, and social-psychological adjustment. *Child Development, 66,* 710–722.

Critchlow, Barbara (1983). Blaming the booze: The attribution of responsibility for drunken behavior. *Personality and Social Psychology Bulletin, 9,* 451–474.

Critchlow, Barbara (1986). The powers of John Barleycorn: Beliefs about the effects of alcohol on social behavior. *American Psychologist, 41,* 751–764.

Critser, Greg (1996, June). Oh, how happy we will be: Pills, paradise, and the profits of the drug companies. *Harper's,* 39–48.

Cronbach, Lee J. (1956). Assessment of individual differences. *Annual Review of Psychology* (Vol. 7). Stanford, CA: Annual Reviews.

Cronbach, Lee J. (1990). *Essentials of psychological testing* (5th ed.). New York: Harper & Row.

Crook, John H. (1987). The nature of conscious awareness. In C. Blakemore & S. Greenfield (eds.), *Mindwaves: Thoughts on intelligence, identity, and consciousness.* Oxford: Basil Blackwell.

Cross, William E. (1971). The Negro-to-Black conversion experience: Toward a psychology of Black liberation. *Black World, 20,* 13–27.

Crystal, David S.; Chen, Chuansheng; Fuligni, Andrew J.; Stevenson, Harold W.; et al. (1994). Psychological maladjustment and academic achievement: A cross-cultural study of Japanese, Chinese, and American high school students. *Child Development, 65,* 738–753.

Crystal, Jonathon D., & Shettleworth, Sara J. (1994). Spatial list learning in black-capped chickadees. *Animal Learning and Behavior, 22,* 77–83.

Csikszentmihalyi, Mihaly, & Larson, Reed (1984). *Being adolescent: Conflict and growth in the teenage years.* New York: Basic Books.

Cubelli, Roberto (1991, September 19). A selective deficit for writing vowels in acquired dysgraphia. *Nature, 353,* 209–210.

Curtin, Brian J. (1985). *The myopias.* New York: Harper & Row.

Curtiss, Susan (1977). *Genie: A psycholinguistic study of a modern-day "wild child."* New York: Academic Press.

Curtiss, Susan (1982). Developmental dissociations of language and cognition. In L. Obler & D. Fein (eds.), *Exceptional language and linguistics.* New York: Academic Press.

Curtiss, Susan (1985). The development of human cerebral lateralization. In D. Frank Benson & Eran Zaidel (eds.), *The dual brain.* New York: Guilford Press.

Cushman, Philip (1995). *Constructing the self, constructing America: A cultural history of psychotherapy.* New York: Addison-Wesley.

Czeisler, C. A.; Shanahan, T. L.; Klerman, E. B.; et al. (1995). Suppression of melatonin secretion in some blind patients by exposure to bright light. *New England Journal of Medicine, 332,* 6–11.

Dabbs, James M., Jr., & Morris, Robin (1990). Testosterone, social class, and antisocial behavior in a sample of 4,462 men. *Psychological Science, 1,* 209–211.

Dagenbach, Dale; Carr, Thomas H.; & Wilhelmsen, AnneLise (1989). Task-induced strategies and near-threshold priming: Conscious influences on unconscious perception. *Journal of Memory and Language, 28,* 412–443.

Dahmer, Lionel (1994). *A father's story.* New York: Morrow.

Dakof, Gayle A., & Taylor, Shelley E. (1990). Victims' perceptions of social support: What is helpful from whom? *Journal of Personality and Social Psychology, 58,* 80–89.

Daly, Martin, & Wilson, Margo (1983). *Sex, evolution, and behavior* (2nd ed.). Belmont, CA: Wadsworth.

Damasio, Antonio R. (1990). Category-related recognition defects as a clue to the neural substrates of knowledge. *Trends in Neurosciences, 13,* 95–98.

Damasio, Antonio R. (1994). *Descartes' error: Emotion, reason, and the human brain.* New York: Grosset/Putnam.

Damasio, Hanna; Grabowski, Thomas; Frank, Randall; Galaburda, Albert M.; & Damasio, Antonio R. (1994). The return of Phineas Gage: Clues about the brain from the skull of a famous patient. *Science, 264,* 1102–1105.

Damasio, Hanna; Grabowski T. J.; Tranel, Daniel; Hichwa, R. D.; & Damasio, Antonio R. (1996). A neural basis for lexical retrieval. *Nature, 380,* 499–505.

Damon, William (1995). *Greater expectations.* New York: Free Press.

Danish, Paul (1994, February 13). Legalizing marijuana would allow regulation of its potency. *The New York Times,* letters page.

Darley, John M. (1995). Constructive and destructive obedience: A taxonomy of principal agent relationships. In A.G. Miller, B. E. Collins, & D. E. Brief (eds.), Perspectives on obedience to authority: The legacy of the Milgram experiments. *Journal of Social Issues, 51*(3), 125–154.

Darwin, Charles (1859). *On the origin of species.* [A facsimile of the first edition, edited by Ernst Mayer, 1964.] Cambridge, MA: Harvard University Press.

Darwin, Charles (1872/1965). *The expression of the emotions in man and animals.* Chicago: University of Chicago Press.

Darwin, Charles (1874). *The descent of man and selection in relation to sex* (2nd ed.). New York: Hurst.

Dasen, Pierre R. (1994). Culture and cognitive development from a Piagetian perspective. In W. J. Lonner & R. S. Malpass (eds.), *Psychology and culture.* Needham Heights, MA: Allyn & Bacon.

Davidson, Richard J. (1992). Anterior cerebral asymmetry and the nature of emotion. *Brain and Cognition, 20,* 125–151.

Davidson, Richard J.; Ekman, Paul; Saron, Clifford D.; Senulis, Joseph A.; & Friesen, Wallace V. (1990). Approach withdrawal and cerebral asymmetry: I. Emotional expression and brain physiology. *Journal of Personality and Social Psychology, 58,* 330–341.

Davis, Joel (1984). *Endorphins: New waves in brain chemistry.* Garden City, NY: Dial Press.

Dawes, Robyn M. (1994). *House of cards: Psychology and psychotherapy built on myth.* New York: Free Press.

Dawit, Seble, & Mekuria, Salem (1993, December 7). The West just doesn't get it (Let Africans fight genital mutilation). *The New York Times,* A13.

Dawson, Drew; Lack, Leon; & Morris, Mary (1993). Phase resetting of the human circadian pacemaker with use of a single pulse of bright light. *Chronobiology International, 10,* 94–102.

Dawson, Neal V.; Arkes, Hal R.; Siciliano, C.; et al. (1988). Hindsight bias: An impediment to accurate probability estimation in clinicopathologic conferences. *Medical Decision Making, 8*(4), 259–264.

Dean, Geoffrey (1986–1987, Winter). Does astrology need to be true? Part I: A look at the real thing. *The Skeptical Inquirer, 11,* 166–184.

Dean, Geoffrey (1987, Spring). Does astrology need to be true? Part II: The answer is no. *The Skeptical Inquirer, 11,* 257–273.

Deaux, Kay (1985). Sex and gender. *Annual Review of Psychology, 36,* 49–81.

Deaux, Kay, & Major, Brenda (1990). A social-psychological model of gender. In D. L. Rhode (ed.), *Theoretical perspectives on sexual difference.* New Haven, CT: Yale University Press.

de Bono, Edward (1985). *de Bono's thinking course.* New York: Facts on File.

Deci, Edward L., & Ryan, Richard M. (1987). The support of autonomy and the control of behavior. *Journal of Personality and Social Psychology, 53,* 1024–1037.

Defebvre, Philippe P.; Malgrange, Brigitte; Staecker, Hinrich; Moonen, Gustave; & Van De Water, Thomas R. (1993). Retinoic acid stimulates regeneration of mammalian auditory hair cells. *Science, 260,* 692–695.

Deffenbacher, Jerry L. (1994). *Anger and diagnosis: Where has all the anger gone?* Paper presented at the annual meeting of the American Psychological Association, Los Angeles.

de Lacoste-Utamsing, Christine, & Holloway, Ralph L. (1982). Sexual dimorphism in the human corpus callosum. *Science, 216,* 1431–1432.

de la Garza, Rodolfo O.; DeSipio, Luis; Garcia, F. Chris; Garcia, John; & Falcon, Angelo (1992). *Latino voices: Mexican, Puerto Rican, & Cuban perspectives on American politics.* Boulder, CO: Westview Press.

DeLeon, Patrick H., & Wiggins, Jack G., Jr. (1996). Prescription privileges for psychologists. *American Psychologist, 51,* 225–229.

DeLoache, Judy S. (1995). Early understanding and use of symbols: The model model. *Current Directions in Psychological Science, 4,* 109–113.

Demakis, George J., & McAdams, Dan P. (1994). Personality, social support and well-being among first year college students. *College Student Journal, 28,* 235–243.

Dement, William (1978). *Some must watch while some must sleep.* New York: Norton.

Dement, William (1992). *The sleepwatchers.* Stanford, CA: Stanford Alumni Association.

Dement, William, & Kleitman, Nathaniel (1957). The relation of eye movements during sleep to dream activity: An objective method for the study of dreaming. *Journal of Experimental Psychology, 53,* 339–346.

DeMyer, Marian K. (1975). Research in infantile autism: A strategy and its results. *Biological Psychiatry, 10,* 433–452.

DeNelsky, Garland Y. (1996). The case against prescription privileges for psychologists. *American Psychologist, 51,* 207–212.

Dennett, Daniel C. (1991). *Consciousness explained.* Boston: Little, Brown.

DePaulo, Bella M. (1992). Nonverbal behavior and self-presentation. *Psychological Bulletin, 111,* 203–243.

DePaulo, Bella M. (1994). Spotting lies: Can humans learn to do better? *Current Directions in Psychological Science, 3,* 83–86.

DePaulo, Bella M.; Kashy, Deborah A.; Kirkendol, Susan E.; Wyer, Melissa M.; & Epstein, Jennifer A. (1996). Lying in everyday life. *Journal of Personality and Social Psychology, 70,* 979–995.

Deppe, Roberta K., & Harackiewicz, Judith M. (1996). Self-handicapping and intrinsic motivation: Buffering intrinsic motivation from the threat of failure. *Journal of Personality and Social Psychology, 70,* 868–876.

de Rivera, Joseph (1989). Comparing experiences across cultures: Shame and guilt in America and Japan. *Hiroshima Forum for Psychology, 14,* 13–20.

de Shazer, Steve (1993). *Putting difference to work.* New York: Norton.

Desimone, Robert (1991). Face-selective cells in the temporal cortex of monkeys. *Journal of Cognitive Neuroscience, 3,* 1–8.

Deutsch, Francine M.; LeBaron, Dorothy; & Fryer, Maury M. (1987). What is in a smile? *Psychology of Women Quarterly, 11,* 341–352.

Deutsch, Morton (1949). An experimental study of the effects of cooperation and competition among group processes. *Human Relations, 2,* 199–231.

Deutsch, Morton (1980). Fifty years of conflict. In L. Festinger (ed.), *Retrospections on social psychology.* New York: Oxford University Press.

Devine, Patricia G. (1995). *Breaking the prejudice habit: Progress and prospects.* Award address paper presented at the annual meeting of the American Psychological Association, New York.

Devine, Patricia G.; Evett, Sophia R.; & Vasquez-Suson, Kristin A. (1996). Exploring the interpersonal dynamics of intergroup contact. In R. M. Sorrentino & E. T. Higgins (eds.), *Handbook of motivation and cognition: Vol. 3. The interpersonal context.* New York: Guilford Press.

Devine, Patricia G.; Monteith, Margo J.; Zuwerink, Julia R.; & Elliot, Andrew J. (1991). Prejudice with and without compunction. *Journal of Personality and Social Psychology, 60,* 817–830.

Devolder, Patricia A., & Pressley, Michael (1989). Metamemory across the adult lifespan. *Canadian Psychology, 30,* 578–587.

Devor, E. J.; Abell, C. W.; Hoffman, P. L.; Tabakoff, B.; & Cloninger, C. R. (1994). Platelet MAO activity in type I and type II alcoholism. *Annals of the New York Academy of Sciences, 708,* 119–128.

Dewsbury, Donald A. (1996). Animal research: Getting in and getting out. *The General Psychologist, 32,* 19–25.

Diamond, Guy, & Siqueland, Lynne (1995). Family therapy for the treatment of depressed adolescents. *Psychotherapy, 32,* 77–90.

Diamond, Jared (1994, November). Race without color. *Discover,* 82–89.

Diamond, Marian C. (1993, Winter–Spring). An optimistic view of the aging brain. *Generations, 17,* 31–33.

Diamond, Marian; Johnson, Ruth E.; Young, Daniel; & Singh, S. Sukhwinder (1983). Age related morphologic differences in the rat cerebral cortex and hippocampus: Male female; right left. *Experimental Neurology, 81,* 1–13.

Dickinson, Alyce M. (1989). The detrimental effects of extrinsic reinforcement on "intrinsic motivation." *The Behavior Analyst, 12,* 1–15.

DiFranza, Joseph R.; Winters, Thomas H.; Goldberg, Robert J.; Cirillo, Leonard; et al. (1986). The relationship of smoking to motor vehicle accidents and traffic violations. *New York State Journal of Medicine, 86,* 464–467.

Digman, John M. (1990). Personality structure: Emergence of the five-factor model. In M. R. Rosenzweig & L. W. Porter (eds.), *Annual Review of Psychology.* Palo Alto, CA: Annual Reviews.

Digman, John M. (1996). The curious history of the five-factor model. In J. S. Wiggins (ed.), *The five-factor model of personality: Theoretical perspectives.* New York: Guilford Press.

Digman, John M., & Shmelyov, Alexander G. (1996). The structure of temperament and personality in Russian children. *Journal of Personality and Social Psychology, 71,* 341–351.

di Leonardo, Micaela (1987). The female world of cards and holidays: Women, families, and the work of kinship. *Signs, 12,* 1–20.

di Leonardo, Micaela (1991). Introduction. In M. di Leonardo (ed.), *Gender at the crossroads of knowledge.* Berkeley: University of California Press.

Dinges, David F.; Whitehouse, Wayne G.; Orne, Emily C.; Powell, John W.; Orne, Martin T.; & Erdelyi, Matthew H. (1992). Evaluating hypnotic memory enhancement (hypermnesia and reminiscence) using multitrial forced recall. *Journal of Experimental Psychology: Learning, Memory, and Cognition, 18,* 1139–1147.

Dion, George L., & Anthony, William A. (1987). Research in psychiatric rehabilitation: A review of experimental and quasi-experimental studies. *Rehabilitation Counseling Bulletin, 30,* 177–203.

Dion, Kenneth L., & Dion, Karen K. (1993). Gender and ethnocultural comparisons in style of love. *Psychology of Women Quarterly, 17,* 463–474.

Dixon, N. F. (1980). Humor: A cognitive alternative to stress? In I. G. Sarason & C. D. Spielberger (eds.), *Stress and anxiety* (Vol. 7). Washington, DC: Hemisphere.

Doblin, R., & Kleiman, M. A. R. (1991). Marihuana as anti-emetic medicine: A survey of oncologists' attitudes and experiences. *Journal of Clinical Oncology, 9,* 1275–1280.

Doering, Charles H.; Brodie, H. K. H.; Kraemer, H. C.; Becker, H. B.; & Hamburg, D. A. (1974). Plasma testosterone levels and psychologic measures in men over a 2-month period. In R. C. Friedman, R. M. Richard, & R. L. Vande Wiele (eds.), *Sex differences in behavior.* New York: Wiley.

Doi, L. T. (1973). *The anatomy of dependence.* Tokyo: Kodansha International.

Dollard, John, & Miller, Neal E. (1950). *Personality and psychotherapy: An analysis in terms of learning, thinking, and culture.* New York: McGraw-Hill.

Dolnick, Edward (1990, July). What dreams are (really) made of. *The Atlantic Monthly, 226,* 41–45, 48–53, 56–58, 60–61.

Donnell, S. M., & Hall, J. (1980, Spring). Men and women as managers: A significant case of no significant difference. *Organizational Dynamics, 8,* 60–76.

Doty, Richard M.; Peterson, Bill E.; & Winter, David G. (1991). Threat and authoritarianism in the United States, 1978–1987. *Journal of Personality and Social Psychology, 61,* 629–640.

Dovidio, John F.; Allen, Judith L.; & Schroeder, David A. (1990). Specificity of empathy-induced helping: Evidence for altruistic motivation. *Journal of Personality and Social Psychology, 59,* 249–260.

Druckman, Daniel, & Swets, John A. (eds.) (1988). *Enhancing human performance: Issues, theories, and techniques.* Washington, DC: National Academy Press.

Dubbert, Patricia M. (1992). Exercise in behavioral medicine. *Journal of Consulting and Clinical Psychology, 60,* 613–618.

Dumont, Matthew P. (1987, December). A diagnostic parable (1st ed.–unrevised) [Review of DSM-III-R]. *Readings: A Journal of Reviews and Commentary in Mental Health,* 9–12.

Duncan, Paula D.; Ritter, Philip L.; Dornbusch, Sanford M.; Gross, Ruth T.; & Carlsmith, J. Merrill (1985). The effects of pubertal timing on body image, school behavior, and deviance. *Journal of Youth and Adolescence, 14,* 227–235.

Dunford, Franklyn; Huizinga, David; & Elliott, Delbert S. (1990). The role of arrest in domestic assault: The Omaha police experiment. *Criminology, 28,* 183–206.

Dunkel-Schetter, Christine (1984). Social support and cancer: Findings based on patient interviews and their implications. *Journal of Social Issues, 40*(4), 77–98.

Dunn, Judy, & Plomin, Robert (1990). *Separate lives: Why siblings are so different.* New York: Basic Books.

du Verglas, Gabrielle; Banks, Steven R.; & Guyer, Kenneth E. (1988). Clinical effects of fenfluramine on children with autism: A review of the research. *Journal of Autism and Developmental Disorders, 18,* 297–308.

Dweck, Carol S. (1990). Toward a theory of goals: Their role in motivation and personality. In R. A. Dienstbier (ed.), *Nebraska Symposium on Motivation* (Vol. 38). Lincoln: University of Nebraska Press.

Dweck, Carol S. (1992). The study of goals in psychology [Commentary to feature review]. *Psychological Science, 3,* 165–167.

Eagly, Alice H., & Carli, Linda L. (1981). Sex of researchers and sex-typed communications as determinants of sex differences in influencibility: A meta-analysis of social influence studies. *Psychological Bulletin, 90,* 1–20.

Eagly, Alice H.; Makhijani, M. G.; & Klonsky, B. G. (1990). Gender and the evaluation of leaders: A meta-analysis. *Psychological Bulletin, 111,* 3–22.

Eastman, C. I.; Steward, K. T.; Mahoney, M. P.; et al. (1994). Dark goggles and bright light improve circadian rhythm adaptation to night-shift work. *Sleep, 17,* 535–543.

Eaton, William W.; Bilker, Warren; Haro, Josep M.; Herrman, Helen; et al. (1992a). Long-term course of hospitalization for schizophrenia: II. Change with passage of time. *Schizophrenia Bulletin, 18,* 229–241.

Eaton, William W.; Mortensen, Preben B.; Herrman, Helen; Freeman, Hugh; et al. (1992b). Long-term course of hospitalization for schizophrenia: I. Risk for rehospitalization. *Schizophrenia Bulletin, 18,* 217–228.

Ebbinghaus, Hermann M. (1885/1913). *Memory: A contribution to experimental psychology* (H. A. Ruger & C. E. Bussenius, trans.). New York: Teachers College Press, Columbia University.

Eberlin, Michael; McConnachie, Gene; Ibel, Stuart; & Volpe, Lisa (1993). Facilitated communication: A failure to replicate the phenomenon. *Journal of Autism and Developmental Disorders, 23,* 507–530.

Ebstein, R. P.; Novick, O.; Umansky, R.; et al. (1996). Dopamine D4 receptor (D4DR) exon III polymorphism associated with the human personality trait of novelty seeking. *Nature Genetics, 12,* 78–80.

Eccles, Jacquelynne S. (1993). Parents and gender-role socialization during the middle childhood and adolescent years. In S. Oskamp & M. Costanzo (eds.), *The Claremont Symposium on Applied Social Psychology: Gender issues in contemporary society.* Newbury Park, CA: Sage.

Eccles, Jacquelynne S.; Jacobs, Janis E.; & Harold, Rena D. (1990). Gender role stereotypes, expectancy effects, and parents' socialization of gender differences. *Journal of Social Issues, 46,* 183–201.

Eccles, Jacquelynne S.; Midgley, Carol; Wigfield, Allan; Buchanan, Christy M.; et al. (1993). Development during adolescence: The impact of stage environment fit on young adolescents' experiences in schools and in families. *American Psychologist, 48,* 90–101.

Eccles, John C. (1981). In praise of falsification. In R. D. Tweney, M. E. Doherty, & C. R. Mynatt (eds.), *On scientific thinking.* New York: Columbia University Press.

Eckensberger, Lutz H. (1994). Moral development and its measurement across cultures. In W. J. Lonner & R. Malpass (eds.), *Psychology and culture.* Needham Heights, MA: Allyn & Bacon.

Edelson, Marshall (1994). Can psychotherapy research answer this psychotherapist's questions? In P. F. Talley, H. H. Strupp, & S. F. Butler (eds.), *Psychotherapy research and practice: Bridging the gap.* New York: Basic Books.

Edwards, Carolyn P. (1987). Culture and the construction of moral values. In J. Kagan & S. Lamb (eds.), *The emergence of morality in young children.* Chicago: University of Chicago Press.

Edwards, Kari, & Smith, Edward E. (1996). A disconfirmation bias in the evaluation of arguments. *Journal of Personality and Social Psychology, 71,* 5–24.

Edwards, Lynne K., & Edwards, Allen L. (1991). A principal-components analysis of the Minnesota Multiphasic Personality Inventory Factor Scales. *Journal of Personality and Social Psychology, 60,* 766–772.

Ehrenreich, Barbara (1978). *For her own good: 150 years of the experts' advice to women.* New York: Doubleday.

Eich, Eric (1995). Searching for mood dependent memory. *Psychological Science, 6,* 67–75.

Eich, E., & Hyman, R. (1992). Subliminal self-help. In D. Druckman & R. A. Bjork (eds.), *In the mind's eye: Enhancing human performance.* Washington, DC: National Academy Press.

Eisenberg, Nancy (1995). Prosocial development: A multifaceted model. In W. M. Kurtines & J. L. Gewirtz (eds.), *Moral development: An introduction.* Boston: Allyn & Bacon.

Eisenberg, Nancy, & Murphy, Bridget (1995). Parenting and children's moral development. In M. H. Bornstein (ed.), *Handbook of parenting* (Vol. 4). Mahwah, NJ: Erlbaum.

Eisenberger, Robert, & Cameron, Judy (1996). Detrimental effects of reward: Reality or myth? *American Psychologist, 51,* 1153–1166.

Eisler, Riane (1987). *The chalice and the blade.* San Francisco: HarperCollins.

Ekman, Paul (1994). Strong evidence for universals in facial expressions: A reply to Russell's mistaken critique. *Psychological Bulletin, 115,* 268–287.

Ekman, Paul; Friesen, Wallace V.; & O'Sullivan, Maureen (1988). Smiles when lying. *Journal of Personality and Social Psychology, 54,* 414–420.

Ekman, Paul; Friesen, Wallace V.; O'Sullivan, Maureen; et al. (1987). Universals and cultural differences in the judgements of facial expression of emotion. *Journal of Personality and Social Psychology, 53,* 712–717.

Ekman, Paul, & Heider, Karl G. (1988). The universality of a contempt expression: A replication. *Motivation and Emotion, 12,* 303–308.

Ekman, Paul, & O'Sullivan, Maureen (1991). Who can catch a liar? *American Psychologist, 46,* 913–920.

Elbert, Thomas; Pantev, Christo; Wienbruch, Christian; Rockstroh, Brigitte; & Taub, Edward (1995, October 13). Increased cortical representation of the fingers of the left hand in string players. *Science, 270,* 305–307.

Elliot, Andrew J., & Harackiewicz, Judith M. (1994). Goal setting, achievement orientation, and intrinsic motivation: A mediational analysis. *Journal of Personality and Social Psychology, 66,* 968–980.

Elliott, Diana M. (1995). *Delayed recall of traumatic events: Correlates and clinical implications.* Paper presented at the annual meeting of the American Psychological Association, New York.

Elliott, Robert, & Morrow-Bradley, Cheryl (1994). Developing a working marriage between psychotherapists and psychotherapy researchers: Identifying shared purposes. In P. F. Talley, H. H. Strupp, & S. F. Butler (eds.), *Psychotherapy research and practice: Bridging the gap.* New York: Basic Books.

Ellis, Albert (1993). Changing rational-emotive therapy (RET) to rational emotive behavior therapy (REBT). *Behavior Therapist, 16,* 257–258.

Ellis, Albert, & Dryden, Windy (1987). *The practice of rational emotive therapy.* New York: Springer.

Elshtain, Jean B. (1987). *Women and war.* New York: Basic Books.

Emmons, Robert A., & King, Laura A. (1988). Conflict among personal strivings: Immediate and long-term implications for psychological and physical well-being. *Journal of Personality and Social Psychology, 54,* 1040–1048.

Emmorey, Karen; Kosslyn, Stephen M.; & Bellugi, Ursula (1993). Visual imagery and visual-spatial language: Enhanced imagery abilities in deaf and hearing ASL signers. *Cognition, 46,* 139–181.

Endler, Norman S. (1991). *Electroconvulsive therapy: Myths and realities.* Paper presented at the annual meeting of the American Psychological Association, San Francisco.

Englander-Golden, Paula; Whitmore, Mary R.; & Dienstbier, Richard A. (1978). Menstrual cycle as focus of study and self-reports of moods and behavior. *Motivation and Emotion, 2,* 75–86.

Ennis, Robert H. (1985). Critical thinking and the curriculum. *National Forum, 65*(1), 28–30.

Entin, Alan D. (1992). *Family photographs: Visual icons and emotional history.* Paper presented at the annual meeting of the American Psychological Association, Washington, DC.

Epstein, Robert (1990). Generativity theory and creativity. In M. A. Runco & R. S. Albert (eds.), *Theories of creativity.* Newbury Park, CA: Sage.

Epstein, Robert; Kirshnit, C. E.; Lanza, R. P.; & Rubin, L. C. (1984, March 1). "Insight" in the pigeon: Antecedents and determinants of an intelligent performance. *Nature, 308,* 61–62.

Epstein, Seymour (1994). Integration of the cognitive and the psychodynamic unconscious. *American Psychologist, 49,* 709–724.

Erikson, Erik H. (1950/1963). *Childhood and society* (2nd ed.). New York: Norton.

Erikson, Erik H. (1982). *The life cycle completed.* New York: Norton.

Erikson, Erik H. (1987). *A way of looking at things: Selected papers from 1930 to 1980* (Stephen Schlein, ed.). New York: Norton.

Ernsberger, Paul, & Nelson, D. O. (1988). Refeeding hypertension in dietary obesity. *American Journal of Physiology, 154,* R47–55.

Eron, Leonard D. (1980). Prescription for reduction of aggression. *American Psychologist, 35,* 244–252.

Eron, Leonard D. (1982). Parent–child interaction, television violence, and aggression of children. *American Psychologist, 37,* 197–211.

Eron, Leonard D. (1995). *Media violence: How it affects kids and what can be done about it.* Invited address presented at the annual meeting of the American Psychological Association, New York.

Eron, Leonard D., & Huesmann, L. Rowell (1987). Television as a source of maltreatment of children. *School Psychology Review, 16,* 195–202.

Ervin-Tripp, Susan (1964). Imitation and structural change in children's language. In E. H. Lenneberg (ed.), *New directions in the study of language.* Cambridge, MA: MIT Press.

Escera, Carles; Cilveti, Robert; & Grau, Carles (1992). Ultradian rhythms in cognitive operations: Evidence from the P300 component of the event-related potentials. *Medical Science Research, 20,* 137–138.

Esterson, Allen (1993). *Seductive mirage: An exploration of the work of Sigmund Freud.* New York: Open Court.

Evans, Christopher (1984). *Landscapes of the night* (edited and completed by Peter Evans). New York: Viking.

Evans, Gary W.; Hygge, Staffan; & Bullinger, Monika (1995). Chronic noise and psychological stress. *Psychological Science, 6,* 333–338.

Evans, Gary W.; Lepore, Stephen J.; & Schroeder, Alex (1996). The role of interior design elements in human responses to crowding. *Journal of Personality and Social Psychology, 70,* 41–46.

Ewart, Craig K. (1995). Self-efficacy and recovery from heart attack. In J. E. Maddux (ed.), *Self-efficacy, adaptation, and adjustment: Theory, research, and application.* New York: Plenum.

Ewart, Craig K., & Kolodner, Kenneth B. (1994). Negative affect, gender, and expressive style predict elevated ambulatory blood pressure in adolescents. *Journal of Personality and Social Psychology, 66,* 596–605.

Exner, John E. (1993). *The Rorschach: A comprehensive system: Vol. 1. Basic foundations* (3rd ed.). New York: Wiley.

Eyferth, Klaus (1961). [The performance of different groups of the children of occupation forces on the Hamburg-Wechsler Intelligence Test for Children.] *Archiv für die Gesamte Psychologie, 113,* 222–241.

Eysenck, Hans J. (1993). Prediction of cancer and coronary heart disease mortality by means of a personality inventory: Results of a 15-year follow-up study. *Psychological Reports, 72,* 499–516.

Fabes, Richard A.; Eisenberg, Nancy; Karbon, Mariss; Bernzweig, Jane; Speer, Anna Lee; & Carlo, Gustavo (1994). Socialization of children's vicarious emotional responding and prosocial behavior: Relations with mothers' perceptions of children's emotional reactivity. *Developmental Psychology, 30,* 44–55.

Fagot, Beverly I. (1984). Teacher and peer reactions to boys' and girls' play styles. *Sex Roles, 11,* 691–702.

Fagot, Beverly I. (1985). Beyond the reinforcement principle: Another step toward understanding sex role development. *Developmental Psychology, 2,* 1097–1104.

Fagot, Beverly I. (1993, June). *Gender role development in early childhood: Environmental input, internal construction.* Invited address presented at the annual meeting of the International Academy of Sex Research, Monterey, CA.

Fagot, Beverly I.; Hagan, R.; Leinbach, Mary D.; & Kronsberg, S. (1985). Differential reactions to assertive and communicative acts of toddler boys and girls. *Child Development, 56,* 1499–1505.

Fagot, Beverly I., & Leinbach, Mary D. (1993). Gender-role development in young children: From discrimination to labeling. *Developmental Review, 13,* 205–224.

Fairchild, Halford H. (1985). Black, Negro, or Afro-American? The differences are crucial! *Journal of Black Studies, 16,* 47–55.

Falk, Ruma, & Greenbaum, Charles W. (1995). Significance tests die hard: The amazing persistence of a probabilistic misconception. *Theory & Psychology, 5*(1), 75–98.

Faraone, Stephen V.; Kremen, William S.; & Tsuang, Ming T. (1990). Genetic transmission of major affective disorders: Quantitative models and linkage analyses. *Psychological Bulletin, 108,* 109–127.

Farber, Susan L. (1981). *Identical twins reared apart: A reanalysis.* New York: Basic Books.

Faust, David, & Ziskin, Jay (1988, July 1). The expert witness in psychology and psychiatry. *Science, 241,* 31–35.

Fawzy, Fawzy I.; Fawzy, Nancy W.; Hyun, Christine S.; Elashoff, Robert; et al. (1993). Malignant melanoma: Effects of an early structured psychiatric intervention, coping, and affective state on recurrence and survival six years later. *Archives of General Psychiatry, 50,* 681–689.

Fazio, Russell H.; Jackson, Joni R.; Dunton, Bridget C.; & Williams, Carol J. (1995). Variability in automatic activation as an unobtrusive measure of racial attitudes: A bona fide pipeline? *Journal of Personality and Social Psychology, 69,* 1013–1027.

FDA Drug Bulletin (1990, April). Two new psychiatric drugs. *20*(1), 9.

Feather, N. T. (1966). Effects of prior success and failure on expectations of success and subsequent performance. *Journal of Personality and Social Psychology, 3,* 287–298.

Feather, N. T. (ed.) (1982). *Expectations and actions: Expectancy value models in psychology.* Hillsdale, NJ: Erlbaum.

Feeney, Dennis M. (1987). Human rights and animal welfare. *American Psychologist, 42,* 593–599.

Feeney, Judith A., & Noller, Patricia (1990). Attachment style as a predictor of adult romantic relationships. *Journal of Personality and Social Psychology, 58,* 281–291.

Fehr, Beverly (1993). How do I love thee . . . ? Let me consult my prototype. In S. Duck (ed.), *Individuals in relationships* (Vol. 1). Newbury Park, CA: Sage.

Fehr, Beverly, & Russell, James A. (1991). The concept of love viewed from a prototype perspective. *Journal of Personality and Social Psychology, 60,* 425–438.

Fein, Steven, & Spencer, Steven J. (1997). Prejudice as self-image maintenance: Affirming the self through derogating others. *Journal of Personality and Social Psychology,* in press.

Feingold, Alan (1988). Cognitive gender differences are disappearing. *American Psychologist, 43,* 95–103.

Ferguson, Thomas, & Rogers, Joel (1986, May). The myth of America's turn to the right. *Atlantic,* 43–53.

Fernald, Anne (1990). *Emotion in the voice: Meaningful melodies in mother's speech to infants.* Paper presented at the annual meeting of the American Psychological Association, Boston.

Fernald, L. D. (1984). *The Hans legacy: A story of science.* Hillsdale, NJ: Erlbaum.

Fernández-Dols, José-Miguel, & Ruiz-Belda, María-Angeles (1995). Are smiles a sign of happiness? Gold medal winners at the Olympic games. *Journal of Personality and Social Psychology, 69,* 1113–1119.

Feshbach, Norma; Feshbach, Seymour; Fauvre, Mary; & Ballard-Campbell, Michael (1983). *Learning to care: A curriculum for affective and social development.* Glenview, IL: Scott, Foresman.

Feshbach, Seymour, & Feshbach, Norma D. (1986). Aggression and altruism: A personality perspective. In C. Zahn-Waxler, E. M. Cummings, & R. Iannotti (eds.), *Altruism and aggression: Biological and social origins.* Cambridge, England: Cambridge University Press.

Festinger, Leon (1957). *A theory of cognitive dissonance.* Evanston, IL: Row, Peterson.

Festinger, Leon (1980). Looking backward. In L. Festinger (ed.), *Retrospections on social psychology.* New York: Oxford University Press.

Festinger, Leon, & Carlsmith, J. Merrill (1959). Cognitive consequences of forced compliance. *Journal of Abnormal and Social Psychology, 58,* 203–210.

Festinger, Leon; Riecken, Henry W.; & Schachter, Stanley (1956). *When prophecy fails.* Minneapolis: University of Minnesota Press.

Feuerstein, Reuven (1980). *Instrumental enrichment: An intervention program for cognitive modifiability.* Baltimore, MD: University Park Press.

Field, Tiffany (1995). *Massage therapy for infants and children.* Paper presented at the annual meeting of the American Psychological Association, New York.

Fields, Howard (1991). Depression and pain: A neurobiological model. *Neuropsychiatry, Neuropsychology, and Behavioral Neurology, 4,* 83–92.

Fiez, J. A. (1996). Cerebellar contributions to cognition. *Neuron, 16,* 13–15.

Fincham, Frank D. (1994). Cognition in marriage: Current status and future challenges. *Applied and Preventive Psychology: Current Scientific Perspectives, 3,* 185–198.

Fincham, Frank D., & Bradbury, Thomas N. (1993). Marital satisfaction, depression, and attributions: A longitudinal analysis. *Journal of Personality and Social Psychology, 64,* 442–452.

Fingarette, Herbert (1988). *Heavy drinking: The myth of alcoholism as a disease.* Berkeley: University of California Press.

Finkelhor, David, & Dziuba-Leatherman, Jennifer (1994). Victimization of children. *American Psychologist, 49,* 173–183.

Fiore, Edith (1989). *Encounters: A psychologist reveals case studies of abduction by extraterrestrials.* New York: Bantam.

Fischer, Agneta H. (1993). Sex differences in emotionality: Fact or stereotype? *Feminism & Psychology, 3,* 303–318.

Fischer, Pamela C.; Smith, Randy J.; Leonard, Elizabeth; Fuqua, Dale R.; et al. (1993). Sex differences on affective dimensions: Continuing examination. *Journal of Counseling and Development, 71,* 440–443.

Fischhoff, Baruch (1975). Hindsight is not equal to foresight: The effect of outcome knowledge on judgment under uncertainty. *Journal of Experimental Psychology: Human Perception and Performance, 1,* 288–299.

Fisher, Kathleen (1985, March). ECT: New studies on how, why, who. *APA Monitor, 16,* 18–19.

Fisher, Ronald J. (1994). Generic principles for resolving intergroup conflict. *Journal of Social Issues, 50,* 47–66.

Fisher, Ronald P., & Geiselman, R. Edward (1992). *Memory-enhancing techniques for investigative interviewing: The cognitive interview.* New York: C. C. Thomas.

Fiske, Alan P., & Haslam, Nick (1996). Social cognition is thinking about relationships. *Current Directions in Psychological Science, 5,* 143–148.

Fiske, Susan T. (1993). Controlling other people: The impact of power on stereotyping. *American Psychologist, 48,* 621–628.

Fitzgerald, Joseph M. (1988). Vivid memories and the reminiscence phenomenon: The role of a self narrative. *Human Development, 31,* 261–273.

Fivush, Robyn, & Hamond, Nina R. (1991). Autobiographical memory across the school years: Toward reconceptualizing childhood amnesia. In R. Fivush & J. A. Hudson (eds.), *Knowing and remembering in young children.* New York: Cambridge University Press.

Flavell, John H. (1992). Cognitive development: Past, present, and future. *Developmental Psychology, 28,* 998–1005.

Flavell, John H. (1993). Young children's understanding of thinking and consciousness. *Current Directions in Psychological Science, 2,* 40–43.

Flavell, John H. (1996). Piaget's legacy. *Psychological Science, 7,* 200–203.

Flavell, John H.; Green, F. L.; & Flavell, E. R. (1990). Developmental changes in young children's knowledge about the mind. *Cognitive Development, 5,* 1–27.

Flor, H.; Elbert, T.; Knecht, S.; Wienbruch, C., et al. (1995). Phantom-limb pain as a perceptual correlate of cortical reorganization following arm amputation. *Nature, 375,* 482–484.

Flor, Herta; Kerns, Robert D.; & Turk, Dennis C. (1987). The role of spouse reinforcement, perceived pain, and activity levels of chronic pain patients. *Journal of Psychosomatic Research, 31,* 251–259.

Flynn, James R. (1987). Massive IQ gains in 14 nations: What IQ tests really measure. *Psychological Bulletin, 95,* 29–51.

Foa, Edna, & Emmelkamp, Paul (eds.) (1983). *Failures in behavior therapy.* New York: Wiley.

Foderaro, Lisa W. (1994, November 8). 'Clubhouse' helps mentally ill find the way back. *The New York Times,* B1, B3.

Foderaro, Lisa W. (1995, May 28). Can problem drinkers really just cut back? *The New York Times,* National section, 15, 349–358.

Fogelman, Eva (1994). *Conscience and courage: Rescuers of Jews during the Holocaust.* New York: Anchor Books.

Foreyt, John P.; Goodrick, G. Ken; Reeves, Rebecca S.; Raynaud, A. Scott; et al. (1993). Response of free-living adults to behavioral treatment of obesity: Attrition and compliance to exercise. *Behavior Therapy, 24,* 659–669.

Forgas, Joseph (1994). Sad and guilty? Affective influences on the explanation of conflict in close relationships. *Journal of Personality and Social Psychology, 66,* 56–68.

Forgas, Joseph, & Bond, Michael H. (1985). Cultural influences on the perception of interaction episodes. *Personality and Social Psychology Bulletin, 11,* 75–88.

Forrest, F.; Florey, C. du V.; Taylor, D.; McPherson, F.; & Young, J. A. (1991, July 6). Reported social alcohol consumption during pregnancy and infants' development at 18 months. *British Medical Journal, 303,* 22–26.

Foulkes, David; Hollifield, Michael; Sullivan, Brenda; Bradley, Laura; et al. (1990). REM dreaming and cognitive skills at ages 5–8: A cross-sectional study. *International Journal of Behavioral Development, 13,* 447–465.

Fouts, Roger S.; Fouts, Deborah H.; & Van Cantfort, Thomas E. (1989). The infant Loulis learns signs from cross-fostered chimpanzees. In R. A. Gardner, B. T. Gardner, & T. E. Van Cantfort (eds.), *Teaching sign language to chimpanzees.* New York: State University of New York Press.

Fouts, Roger S., & Rigby, Randall L. (1977). Man–chimpanzee communication. In T. A. Seboek (ed.), *How animals communicate.* Bloomington: University of Indiana Press.

Fowers, Blaine J., & Richardson, Frank C. (1996). Why is multiculturalism good? *American Psychologist, 51,* 609–621.

Fox, Nathan A., & Davidson, Richard J. (1988). Patterns of brain electrical activity during facial signs of emotion in 10-month-old infants. *Developmental Psychology, 24,* 230–236.

Fox, Ronald E. (1994). Training professional psychologists for the twenty-first century. *American Psychologist, 49,* 200–206.

Frank, Jerome D. (1985). Therapeutic components shared by all psychotherapies. In M. J. Mahony & A. Freeman (eds.), *Cognition and psychotherapy.* New York: Plenum.

Frank, Robert G.; Gluck, John P.; & Buckelew, Susan P. (1990). Rehabilitation: Psychology's greatest opportunity? *American Psychologist, 45,* 757–761.

Frankl, Victor E. (1955). *The doctor and the soul: An introduction to logotherapy.* New York: Knopf.

Franklin, Anderson J. (1993, July/August). The invisibility syndrome. *The Family Therapy Networker,* 33–39.

Franzoi, Stephen L. (1996). *Adding a cross-cultural perspective to social psychology: The influence of individualism and collectivism.* Paper presented at the annual meeting of the National Institute on the Teaching of Psychology, St. Petersburg Beach, FL.

Frederich, R. C.; Hamann, A.; Anderson, S.; et al. (1995). Leptin levels reflect body lipid content in mice: Evidence for diet-induced resistance to leptin action. *Nature Medicine, 1,* 1311–1314.

Freed, C. R.; Breeze, R. E.; Rosenberg, N. L.; & Schneck, S. A. (1993). Embryonic dopamine cell implants as a treatment for the second phase of Parkinson's disease: Replacing failed nerve terminals. *Advances in Neurology, 60,* 721–728.

Freedman, Hill, & Combs, Gene (1996). *Narrative therapy.* New York: Norton.

Freedman, Jonathan L. (1988). Television violence and aggression: What the evidence shows. In S. Oskamp (ed.), *Applied social psychology annual: Vol. 8. Television as a social issue.* Newbury Park, CA: Sage.

French, Christopher C.; Fowler, Mandy; McCarthy, Katy; & Peers, Debbie (1991, Winter). Belief in astrology: A test of the Barnum effect. *Skeptical Inquirer, 15,* 166–172.

Freud, Anna (1946). *The ego and the mechanisms of defence.* New York: International Universities Press.

Freud, Sigmund (1905a). Fragment of an analysis of a case of hysteria. In J. Strachey (ed. and trans.), *The standard edition of the complete psychological works of Sigmund Freud* (Vol. 7). London: Hogarth Press and the Institute of Psycho-Analysis (1964 edition).

Freud, Sigmund (1905b). Three essays on the theory of sexuality. In Strachey, *Standard edition* (Vol. 7).

Freud, Sigmund (1910/1957). Leonardo da Vinci: A study in psychosexuality. In Strachey, *Standard edition* (Vol. 11).

Freud, Sigmund (1920/1960). *A general introduction to psychoanalysis* (Joan Riviere, trans.). New York: Washington Square Press.

Freud, Sigmund (1923/1962). *The ego and the id* (Joan Riviere, trans.). New York: Norton.

Freud, Sigmund (1924a). The dissolution of the Oedipus complex. In Strachey, *Standard edition* (Vol. 19).

Freud, Sigmund (1924b). Some psychical consequences of the anatomical distinction between the sexes. In Strachey, *Standard edition* (Vol. 19).

Fridlund, Alan J. (1994). *Human facial expression: An evolutionary view.* San Diego: Academic Press.

Friedman, Meyer, & Rosenman, Ray (1974). *Type A behavior and your heart.* New York: Knopf.

Friedman, William; Robinson, Amy; & Friedman, Britt (1987). Sex differences in moral judgments? A test of Gilligan's theory. *Psychology of Women Quarterly, 11,* 37–46.

Frijda, Nico H. (1988). The laws of emotion. *American Psychologist, 43,* 349–358.

Fry, P. S. (1995). Perfectionism, humor, and optimism as moderators of health outcomes and determinants of coping styles of women executives. *Genetic, Social, and General Psychology Monographs, 121,* 211–245.

Fry, William F. (1994). The biology of humor. *Humor: International Journal of Humor Research, 7,* 111–126.

Frye, Richard E.; Schwartz, B. S.; & Doty, Richard L. (1990). Dose-related effects of cigarette smoking on olfactory function. *Journal of the American Medical Association, 263,* 1233–1236.

Fuchs, C. S.; Stampfer, M. J.; Colditz, G. A.; Giovannucci, E. L.; et al. (1995, May 11). Alcohol consumption and mortality among women. *New England Journal of Medicine, 332,* 1245–1250.

Fussell, Paul (1989). *Wartime.* New York: Oxford University Press.

Gabbard, Glen O. (ed.) (1989). Sexual exploitation within professional relationships. Washington, DC: American Psychiatric Association.

Gaertner, Samuel L.; Mann, Jeffrey A.; Dovidio, John F.; Murrell, Audrey J.; & Pomare, Marina (1990). How does cooperation reduce intergroup bias? *Journal of Personality and Social Psychology, 59,* 692–704.

Gagnon, John, & Simon, William (1973). *Sexual conduct: The social sources of human sexuality.* Chicago: Aldine.

Galanter, Eugene (1962). Contemporary psychophysics. In R. Brown, E. Galanter, H. Hess, & G. Mandler (eds.), *New directions in psychology.* New York: Holt, Rinehart and Winston.

Galanter, Marc (1989). *Cults: Faith, healing, and coercion.* New York: Oxford University Press.

Gallant, Jack L.; Braun, Jochen; & Van Essen, David C. (1993). Selectivity for polar, hyperbolic, and Cartesian gratings in macaque visual cortex. *Science, 259,* 100–103.

Gallant, Sheryle J.; Hamilton, Jean A.; Popiel, Debra A.; Morokoff, Patricia J.; et al. (1991). Daily moods and symptoms: Effects of awareness of study focus, gender, menstrual-cycle phase, and day of the week. *Health Psychology, 10,* 180–189.

Gallo, Linda C., & Eastman, Charmane I. (1993). Circadian rhythms during gradually delaying and advancing sleep and light schedules. *Physiology and Behavior, 53,* 119–126.

Galotti, Kathleen (1989). Approaches to studying formal and everyday reasoning. *Psychological Bulletin, 105,* 331–351.

Ganaway, George K. (1991). *Alternative hypotheses regarding satanic ritual abuse memories.* Paper presented at the annual meeting of the American Psychological Association, San Francisco.

Gannon, Linda, & Ekstrom, Bonnie (1993). Attitudes toward menopause: The influence of sociocultural paradigms. *Psychology of Women Quarterly, 17,* 275–288.

Gao, Jia-Hong; Parsons, Lawrence M.; Bower, James M.; et al. (1996). Cerebellum implicated in sensory acquisition and discrimination rather than motor control. *Science, 272,* 545–547.

Garcia, John, & Koelling, Robert A. (1966). Relation of cue to consequence in avoidance learning. *Psychonomic Science, 4,* 23–124.

Gardner, Howard (1983). *Frames of mind: The theory of multiple intelligences.* New York: Basic Books.

Gardner, R. Allen, & Gardner, Beatrice T. (1969). Teaching sign language to a chimpanzee. *Science, 165,* 664–672.

Garfinkel, D.; Laudon, M.; Nof, D.; & Zisapel, N. (1995). Improvement of sleep quality in elderly people by controlled-release melatonin. *Lancet, 346*(8974), 541–544.

Garland, Ann F., & Zigler, Edward (1994). Adolescent suicide prevention: Current research and social policy implications. *American Psychologist, 48,* 169–182.

Garmezy, Norman (1991). Resilience and vulnerability to adverse developmental outcomes associated with poverty. *American Behavioral Scientist, 34,* 416–430.

Garnets, Linda; Hancock, Kristin A.; Cochran, Susan D.; Goodchilds, Jacqueline; & Peplau, Letitia A. (1991). Issues in psychotherapy with lesbians and gay men: A survey of psychologists. *American Psychologist, 46,* 964–972.

Garry, Maryanne; Manning, Charles G.; & Loftus, Elizabeth F. (1996). Imagination inflation: Imagining a childhood event inflates confidence that it occurred. *Psychonomic Bulletin & Review, 3,* 208–214.

Gaston, Louise; Marmar, Charles R.; Gallagher, Dolores; & Thompson, Larry W. (1989). Impact of confirming patient expectations of change processes in behavioral, cognitive, and brief dynamic psychotherapy. *Psychotherapy, 26,* 296–302.

Gates, Henry Louis (1992, July 20). Black demagogues and pseudo-scholars. *The New York Times,* opinion page.

Gauci, M.; Husband, A. J.; Saxarra, H.; & King, M. G. (1994). Pavlovian conditioning of nasal tryptase release in human subjects with allergic rhinitis. *Physiology & Behavior, 55,* 823–825.

Gay, Peter (1988). *Freud: A life for our time.* New York: Norton.

Gaziano, J. Michael, & Hennekens, Charles (1995, July 1). Royal colleges' advice on alcohol consumption [editorial]. *British Medical Journal, 311,* 3–4.

Gazzaniga, Michael S. (1967). The split brain in man. *Scientific American, 217*(2), 24–29.

Gazzaniga, Michael S. (1983). Right hemisphere language following brain bisection: A 20-year perspective. *American Psychologist, 38,* 525–537.

Gazzaniga, Michael S. (1985). *The social brain: Discovering the networks of the mind.* New York: Basic Books.

Gazzaniga, Michael S. (1988). *Mind matters.* Boston: Houghton Mifflin.

Geary, David C. (1995). Reflections of evolution and culture in children's cognition: Implications for mathematical development and instruction. *American Psychologist, 50,* 24–37.

Gedo, John (1979). A psychoanalyst reports at mid-career. *American Journal of Psychiatry, 136,* 646–649.

Geen, Russell G. (1978). Some effects of observing violence upon the behavior of the observer. In B. A. Maher (ed.), *Progress in experimental personality research.* New York: Academic Press.

Gelernter, Joel; O'Malley, S.; Risch, N.; Kranzler, H. R.; et al. (1991, October 2). No association between an allele at the D2 dopamine receptor gene (DRD2) and alcoholism. *Journal of the American Medical Association, 266,* 1801–1807.

Geller, E. Scott, & Lehman, Galen R. (1988). Drinking-driving intervention strategies: A person-situation-behavior framework. In M. D. Laurence, J. R. Snortum, & F. E. Zimring (eds.), *The social control of drinking and driving.* Chicago: University of Chicago Press.

Gelles, Richard J., & Straus, Murray A. (1988). *Intimate violence: The causes and consequences of abuse in the American family.* New York: Simon & Schuster/Touchstone.

Gerbner, George (1988). Telling stories in the information age. In B. D. Ruben (ed.), *Information and behavior* (Vol. 2). New Brunswick, NJ: Transaction Books.

Gergen, Kenneth J. (1985). The social constructionist movement in modern psychology. *American Psychologist, 40,* 266–274.

Gergen, Kenneth J. (1994). Exploring the postmodern: Perils or potentials? *American Psychologist, 49,* 412–416.

Gergen, Mary M. (1992). Life stories: Pieces of a dream. In G. Rosenwald & R. Ochberg (eds.), *Storied lives.* New Haven, CT: Yale University Press.

Gerson, Kathleen (1993). *No man's land: Men's changing commitments to family and work.* New York: Basic Books.

Gevins, A. S.; Le, J.; Martin, N.; et al. (1994). High resolution EEG: 124-channel recording, spatial enhancement and MRI integration methods. *Electroencephalographic Clinical Neurophysiology, 90,* 337–358.

Gibbons, Frederick X.; McGovern, Paul G.; & Lando, Harry A. (1991). Relapse and risk perception among members of a smoking cessation clinic. *Health Psychology, 10,* 42–45.

Gibson, Eleanor J. (1994). Has psychology a future? *Psychological Science, 5,* 69–76.

Gibson, Eleanor, & Walk, Richard (1960). The "visual cliff." *Scientific American, 202,* 80–92.

Gilbert, Daniel T.; Pelham, Brett W.; & Krull, Douglas S. (1988). On cognitive busyness: When person perceivers meet persons perceived. *Journal of Personality and Social Psychology, 54,* 733–739.

Gillham, Jane E.; Reivich, Karen J.; Jaycox, Lisa H.; & Seligman, Martin E. P. (1995). Prevention of depressive symptoms in schoolchildren: A two-year follow-up. *Psychological Science, 6,* 343– 351.

Gilligan, Carol (1982). *In a different voice.* Cambridge, MA: Harvard University Press.

Gilligan, Carol, & Wiggins, Grant (1987). The origins of morality in early childhood relationships. In J. Kagan & S. Lamb (eds.), *The emergence of morality in young children.* Chicago: University of Chicago Press.

Gillin, J. Christian; Sitaram, N.; Janowsky, D.; et al. (1985). Cholinergic mechanisms in REM sleep. In A. Wauquier, J. M. Gaillard, J. M. Monti, & M. Radulovacki (eds.), *Sleep: Neurotransmitters and neuromodulators.* New York: Raven Press.

Gilmore, David D. (1990). *Manhood in the making: Cultural concepts of masculinity.* New Haven, CT: Yale University Press.

Giordano, Magda; Ford, Lisa M.; Shipley, Michael T.; et al. (1990). Neural grafts and pharmacological intervention in a model of Huntington's disease. *Brain Research Bulletin, 25,* 453–465.

Gise, Leslie H. (ed.) (1988). *The premenstrual syndromes.* New York: Churchill Livingstone.

Gladue, Brian A. (1994). The biopsychology of sexual orientation. *Current Directions in Psychological Science, 3,* 150–154.

Glanzer, Murray, & Cunitz, Anita R. (1966). Two storage mechanisms in free recall. *Journal of Verbal Learning and Verbal Behavior, 5,* 351–360.

Glazer, Myron P., & Glazer, Penina M. (1990). *The whistleblowers: Exposing corruption in government and industry.* New York: Basic Books.

Gleaves, David H. (1996). The sociocognitive model of dissociative identity disorder: A reexamination of the evidence. *Psychological Bulletin, 120,* 42–59.

Glick, Peter, & Fiske, Susan T. (1996). The ambivalent sexism inventory: Differentiating hostile and benevolent sexism. *Journal of Personality and Social Psychology, 70,* 491–512.

Gobodo-Madikizela, Pumla (1994). *The notion of the "collective" in South African "political" murder cases: The "deindividuation" argument revisited.* Paper presented to the biennial conference of the American Psychology and Law Society, Santa Fe, NM.

Goddard, Henry H. (1917). Mental tests and the immigrant. *Journal of Delinquency, 2,* 243–277.

Gold, Paul E. (1987). Sweet memories. *American Scientist, 75,* 151–155.

Goldberg, Lewis R. (1993). The structure of phenotypic personality traits. *American Psychologist, 48,* 26–34.

Golding, Jacqueline M. (1988). Gender differences in depressive symptoms. *Psychology of Women Quarterly, 12,* 61–74.

Goldman, Alan (1994, Winter). The centrality of "Ningensei" to Japanese negotiating and interpersonal relationships: Implications for U.S.-Japanese communication. *International Journal of Intercultural Relations, 18*, 29–54.

Goldman-Rakic, Patricia S. (1992). Working memory and the mind. *Scientific American, 267*(3), 111–117.

Goldman-Rakic, Patricia S. (1996). *Opening the mind through neurobiology.* Invited address at the annual meeting of the American Psychological Association, Toronto, Canada.

Goldstein, Michael J. (1987). Psychosocial issues. *Schizophrenia Bulletin, 13*(1), 157–171.

Goldstein, Michael, & Miklowitz, David (1995). The effectiveness of psychoeducational family therapy in the treatment of schizophrenic disorders. *Journal of Marital and Family Therapy, 21*, 361–376.

Goleman, Daniel (1982, March). Staying up: The rebellion against sleep's gentle tyranny. *Psychology Today*, 24–25, 27–28, 31–32, 35.

Goleman, Daniel (1995). *Emotional intelligence.* New York: Bantam.

Golub, Sharon (1992). *Periods: From menarche to menopause.* Newbury Park, CA: Sage.

Goodison, Tina, & Siegel, Shephard (1995). Learning and tolerance to the intake suppressive effect of cholecystokinin in rats. *Behavioral Neuroscience, 109*, 62–70.

Goodman, Gail S.; Qin, Jianjian; Bottoms, Bette L.; & Shaver, Phillip R. (1995). *Characteristics and sources of allegations of ritualistic child abuse.* Final report to the National Center on Child Abuse and Neglect, Washington, DC. [Executive summary and complete report available from NCCAN, 1-800-394-3366.]

Goodman, Gail S.; Rudy, L.; Bottoms, B.; & Aman, C. (1990). Children's concerns and memory: Issues of ecological validity in the study of children's eyewitness testimony. In R. Fivush & J. Hudson (eds.), *Knowing and remembering in young children.* New York: Cambridge University Press.

Goodman, Gail S.; Wilson, M. E.; Hazan, C.; & Reed, R. S. (1989). *Children's testimony nearly four years after an event.* Paper presented at the annual meeting of the Eastern Psychological Association, Boston.

Goodwyn, Susan W., & Acredolo, Linda P. (1993). Symbolic gesture versus word: Is there a modality advantage for onset of symbol use? *Child Development, 64*, 688–701.

Gopnik, Myrna (1991). Familial aggregation of a developmental language disorder. *Cognition, 39*, 1–50.

Gopnik, Myrna (1994). Prologue. [Special Issue: Linguistic aspects of familial language impairment.] In J. Matthews (ed.), *McGill working papers in linguistics* (Vol. 10 [1&2]). Montreal: McGill University.

Gore, P. M., & Rotter, Julian B. (1963). A personality correlate of social action. *Journal of Personality, 31*, 58–64.

Gore, Susan, & Mangione, Thomas W. (1983). Social roles, sex roles and psychological distress. *Journal of Health and Social Behavior, 24*, 300–312.

Goren, C. C.; Sarty, J.; & Wu, P. Y. (1975). Visual following and pattern discrimination of face-like stimuli by newborn infants. *Pediatrics, 56*, 544–549.

Gorn, Gerald J. (1982). The effects of music in advertising on choice behavior: A classical conditioning approach. *Journal of Marketing, 46*, 94–101.

Gotlib, Ian H., & Hooley, J. M. (1988). Depression and marital functioning. In S. Duck (ed.), *Handbook of personal relationships: Theory, research and interventions.* Chichester, England: Wiley.

Gottesman, Irving I. (1991). *Schizophrenia genesis: The origins of madness.* New York: Freeman.

Gottesman, Irving I. (1994). *Perils and pleasures of genetic psychopathology.* Distinguished Scientist Award address presented at the annual meeting of the American Psychological Association, Los Angeles.

Gottfried, Adele Eskeles; Fleming, James S.; & Gottfried, Allen W. (1994). Role of parental motivational practices in children's academic intrinsic motivation and achievement. *Journal of Educational Psychology, 86*, 104–113.

Gottman, John (1994, May/June). Why marriages fail. *The Family Therapy Networker*, 40–48.

Gould, James L., & Gould, Carol G. (1995). *The animal mind.* San Francisco: Freeman.

Gould, Stephen Jay (1981/1996). *The mismeasure of man.* New York: Norton.

Gould, Stephen Jay (1985, June). The median isn't the message. *Discover, 6*(6), 40–42.

Gould, Stephen Jay (1987). *An urchin in the storm.* New York: Norton.

Gould, Stephen Jay (1990, April). The war on (some) drugs. *Harper's*, 24.

Gould, Stephen Jay (1994, November 28). Curveball. [Review of *The Bell Curve*, by Richard J. Herrnstein and Charles Murray.] *The New Yorker*, 139–149.

Gould, Stephen Jay, & Eldredge, Niles (1977). Punctuated equilibria: The tempo and mode of evolution reconsidered. *Paleobiology, 3*, 115–151.

Graf, Peter, & Schacter, Daniel A. (1985). Implicit and explicit memory for new associations in normal and amnesic subjects. *Journal of Experimental Psychology: Learning, Memory, and Cognition, 11*, 501–518.

Graham, Jill W. (1986). Principled organizational dissent: A theoretical essay. *Research in Organizational Behavior, 8*, 1–52.

Graham, Sandra (1994). Motivation in African Americans. *Review of Educational Research, 64*, 55–117.

Grandin, Temple (1996). *Thinking in pictures and other reports from my life with autism.* New York: Doubleday.

Greenberg, Roger P.; Bornstein, Robert F.; Greenberg, Michael D.; & Fisher, Seymour (1992). A meta-analysis of antidepressant outcome under "blinder" conditions. *Journal of Consulting and Clinical Psychology, 60*, 664–669.

Greenberg, Roger P.; Bornstein, Robert F.; Zborowski, Michael J.; Fisher, Seymour; et al. (1994). A meta-analysis of fluoxetine outcome in the treatment of depression. *Journal of Nervous and Mental Disease, 182*, 547–551.

Greenberger, Dennis, & Padesky, Christine A. (1995). *Mind over mood: A cognitive therapy treatment manual for clients.* New York: Guilford Press.

Greene, Robert L. (1986). Sources of recency effects in free recall. *Psychological Bulletin, 99*, 221–228.

Greenfield, Patricia (1976). Cross-cultural research and Piagetian theory: Paradox and progress. In K. F. Riegel & J. A. Meacham (eds.), *The developing individual in a changing world: Vol. 1. Historical and cultural issues.* The Hague, Netherlands: Mouton.

Greenfield, Patricia, & Beagles-Roos, Jessica (1988). Radio vs. television: Their cognitive impact on children of different socioeconomic and ethnic groups. *Journal of Communication, 38*, 71–92.

Greenough, William T. (1984). Structural correlates of information storage in the mammalian brain: A review and hypothesis. *Trends in Neurosciences, 7*, 229–233.

Greenough, William T. (1991). The animal rights assertions: A researcher's perspective. *Psychological Science Agenda* (American Psychological Association), *4*(3), 10–12.

Greenough, William T., & Anderson, Brenda J. (1991). Cerebellar synaptic plasticity: Relation to learning vs. neural activity. *Annals of the New York Academy of Sciences, 627*, 231–247.

Greenough, William T., & Black, James E. (1992). Induction of brain structure by experience: Substrates for cognitive development. In M. Gunnar & C. A. Nelson (eds.), *Behavioral developmental neuroscience: Vol. 24. Minnesota Symposia on Child Psychology.* Hillsdale, NJ: Erlbaum.

Greenwald, Anthony G. (1992). New look 3: Unconscious cognition reclaimed. *American Psychologist, 47*, 766–779.

Greenwald, Anthony G.; Draine, Sean C.; & Abrams, Richard L (1996). Three cognitive markers of unconscious semantic activation. *Science, 273*, 1699–1702.

Greenwald, Anthony G.; Spangenberg, Eric R.; Pratkanis, Anthony R.; & Eskenazi, Jay (1991). Double-blind tests of subliminal self-help audiotapes. *Psychological Science, 2*, 119–122.

Gregor, Anne (1993, June 1). Getting to root of cultural gaffes. *The Los Angeles Times*, D3, D10.

Gregory, Richard L. (1963). Distortion of visual space as inappropriate constancy scaling. *Nature, 199*, 678–679.

Gregory, Richard L., & Wallace, Jean G. (1963). Recovery from early blindness: A case study. *Monograph Supplement 2, Quarterly Journal of Experimental Psychology, No. 3.* (Reprinted in R. L. Gregory, *Concepts and mechanisms of perception.* New York: Scribners.)

Greven, Philip (1991). *Spare the child: The religious roots of punishment and the psychological impact of physical abuse.* New York: Knopf.

Griffin, Donald R. (1992). *Animal minds.* Chicago: University of Chicago Press.

Griggs, Richard A., & Cox, J. R. (1982). The elusive thematic-materials effect in Wason's selection task. *British Journal of Psychology, 73*, 407–420.

Grinspoon, Lester, & Bakalar, James B. (1993). *Marihuana, the forbidden medicine.* New Haven, CT: Yale University Press.

Groebel, Jo, & Hinde, Robert (eds.) (1989). The Seville statement on violence. In *Aggression and war: Their biological and social bases.* Cambridge, England: Cambridge University Press.

Gronbaek, M.; Deis, A.; Sorensen, T. I.; Becker, U.; Schnohr, P.; & Jensen, G. (1995, May 6). Mortality associated with moderate intakes of wine, beer, or spirits. *British Medical Journal, 310,* 1165–1169.

Gross, Paul R., & Levitt, Norman (1994). *Higher superstition: The academic left and its quarrels with science.* Baltimore, MD: Johns Hopkins University Press.

Grossarth-Maticek, Ronald; Eysenck, Hans J.; Gallasch, G.; Vetter, H.; & Frentzel-Beyme, R. (1991). Changes in degree of sclerosis as a function of prophylactic treatment in cancer-prone and CHD-prone probands. *Behavior Research and Therapy, 29,* 343–351.

Grossman, Michele, & Wood, Wendy (1993). Sex differences in intensity of emotional experience: A social role interpretation. *Journal of Personality and Social Psychology, 65,* 1010–1022.

Gruber, Barry L.; Hersh, Stephen P.; Hall, Nicholas R.; Waletzky, Lucy R.; et al. (1993). Immunological responses of breast cancer patients to behavioral interventions. *Biofeedback and Self-Regulation, 18,* 1–22.

Grusec, Joan E., & Goodnow, Jacqueline J. (1994). Impact of parental discipline methods on child's internalization of values: A reconceptualization of current points of view. *Developmental Psychology, 30,* 4–19.

Grusec, Joan E.; Saas-Kortsaak, P.; & Simutis, Z. M. (1978). The role of example and moral exhortation in the training of altruism. *Child Development, 49,* 920–923.

Guba, Egon G. (1990). The alternative paradigm dialog. In E. G. Guba (ed.), *The paradigm dialog.* Newbury Park, CA: Sage.

Gudykunst, W. B., & Ting-Toomey, S. (1988). *Culture and interpersonal communication.* Newbury Park, CA: Sage.

Guilford, J. P. (1988). Some changes in the structure-of-intellect model. *Educational and Psychological Measurement, 48,* 1–4.

Gutheil, Thomas G. (1993). The psychology of pharmacology. In M. Schacter (ed.), *Psychotherapy and medication.* Worthvale, NJ: Jason Aronson.

Gwiazda, Jane; Thorn, Frank; Bauer, Joseph; & Held, Richard (1993). Emmetropization and the progression of manifest refraction in children followed from infancy to puberty. *Clinical Vision Sciences, 8,* 337–344.

Haber, Ralph N. (1970, May). How we remember what we see. *Scientific American, 222,* 104–112.

Haier, Richard J.; Siegel, Benjamin V., Jr.; MacLachlan, Andrew; Soderling, Eric; et al. (1992). Regional glucose metabolic changes after learning a complex visuospatial/motor task: A positron emission tomographic study. *Brain Research, 570,* 134–143.

Haier, Richard J.; Siegel, Benjamin V., Jr.; Nuechterlein, Keith H.; Hazlett, Erin; et al. (1988). Cortical glucose metabolic rate correlates of abstract reasoning and attention studied with positron emission tomography. *Intelligence, 12,* 199–217.

Haimov, I., & Lavie, P. (1996). Melatonin—A soporific hormone. *Current Directions in Psychological Science, 5,* 106–111.

Halaas, Jeffrey L.; Gajiwala, Ketan S.; & Maffei, Margherita; et al. (1995). Weight-reducing effects of the plasma protein encoded by the *obese gene. Science, 269,* 543–546.

Haley, Jay (1984). *Ordeal therapy.* San Francisco: Jossey-Bass.

Hall, Edward T. (1959). *The silent language.* Garden City, NY: Doubleday.

Hall, Edward T. (1976). *Beyond culture.* New York: Anchor.

Hall, Edward T. (1983). *The dance of life: The other dimension of time.* Garden City, NY: Anchor Press/Doubleday.

Hall, Edward T., & Hall, Mildred R. (1987). *Hidden differences: Doing business with the Japanese.* Garden City, NY: Anchor Press/Doubleday.

Hall, Edward T., & Hall, Mildred R. (1990). *Understanding cultural differences.* Yarmouth, ME: Intercultural Press.

Hall, G. Stanley (1899). A study of anger. *American Journal of Psychology, 10,* 516–591.

Hall, Judith A. (1987). On explaining gender differences: The case of nonverbal communication. In P. Shaver & C. Hendrick (eds.), *Sex and gender: Review of Personality and Social Psychology* (Vol. 7). Beverly Hills, CA: Sage.

Halpern, Diane (1989). The disappearance of cognitive gender differences: What you see depends on where you look. *American Psychologist, 44,* 1156–1157.

Halpern, Diane (1995). *Thought and knowledge: An introduction to critical thinking* (3rd ed.). Hillsdale, NJ: Erlbaum.

Hamer, Dean H.; Hu, Stella; Magnuson, Victoria L.; et al. (1993). A linkage between DNA markers on the X chromosome and male sexual orientation. *Science, 261,* 321–327.

Hamilton, V. Lee, & Sanders, Joseph (1992). *Everyday justice: Responsibility and the individual in Japan and the United States.* New Haven, CT: Yale University Press.

Hamilton, V. Lee, & Sanders, Joseph (1995). Crimes of obedience and conformity in the workplace: Surveys of Americans, Russians, and Japanese. In A. G. Miller, B. E. Collins, & D. E. Brief (eds.), *Perspectives on obedience to authority: The legacy of the Milgram experiments. Journal of Social Issues, 51*(3), 67–88.

Haney, Craig; Banks, Curtis; & Zimbardo, Philip (1973). Interpersonal dynamics in a simulated prison. *International Journal of Criminology and Penology, 1,* 69–97.

Harding, Courtenay M.; Zubin, Joseph; & Strauss, John S. (1987). Chronicity in schizophrenia: Fact, partial fact, or artifact? *Hospital and Community Psychiatry, 38,* 477–486.

Harding, Courtenay M.; Zubin, Joseph; & Strauss, John S. (1992). Chronicity in schizophrenia: Revisited. *British Journal of Psychiatry, 161*(Suppl. 18), 27–37.

Hare, Robert D. (1965). Temporal gradient of fear arousal in psychopaths. *Journal of Abnormal Psychology, 70,* 442–445.

Hare, Robert D. (1993). *Without conscience: The disturbing world of the psychopaths among us.* New York: Pocket Books.

Hare-Mustin, Rachel T. (1991). Sex, lies, and headaches: The problem is power. In T. J. Goodrich (ed.), *Women and power: Perspectives for therapy.* New York: Norton.

Hare-Mustin, Rachel T., & Marecek, Jeanne (1990). Gender and the meaning of difference: Postmodernism and psychology. In R. Hare-Mustin & J. Marecek (eds.), *Psychology and the construction of gender.* New Haven, CT: Yale University Press.

Haritos-Fatouros, Mika (1988). The official torturer: A learning model for obedience to the authority of violence. *Journal of Applied Social Psychology, 18,* 1107–1120.

Harkins, Stephen G., & Szymanski, Kate (1989). Social loafing and group evaluation. *Journal of Personality and Social Psychology, 56,* 934–941.

Harlow, Harry F. (1958). The nature of love. *American Psychologist, 13,* 673–685.

Harlow, Harry F., & Harlow, Margaret K. (1966). Learning to love. *American Scientist, 54,* 244–272.

Harlow, Harry F.; Harlow, Margaret K.; & Meyer, D. R. (1950). Learning motivated by a manipulation drive. *Journal of Experimental Psychology, 40,* 228–234.

Harmon-Jones, Eddie; Brehm, Jack W.; Greenberg, Jeff; Simon, Linda; & Nelson, David E. (1996). Evidence that the production of aversive consequences is not necessary to create cognitive dissonance. *Journal of Personality and Social Psychology, 70,* 5–16.

Harris, Marvin (1985). *Good to eat: Riddles of food and culture.* New York: Simon & Schuster.

Harris, Marvin (1997). *Culture, people, nature* (7th ed.). New York: Longman.

Hart, John, Jr.; Berndt, Rita S.; & Caramazza, Alfonso (1985, August 1). Category-specific naming deficit following cerebral infarction. *Nature, 316,* 339–340.

Harter, Susan, & Jackson, Bradley K. (1992). Trait vs. nontrait conceptualizations of intrinsic/extrinsic motivational orientation. *Motivation and Emotion, 16,* 209–230.

Harvey, Mary R., & Herman, Judith L. (1994). Amnesia, partial amnesia and delayed recall among adult survivors of childhood trauma.[Special issue: The recovered memory/false memory debate.] *Consciousness and Cognition, 3,* 295–306.

Hasher, Lynn, & Zacks, Rose T. (1984). Automatic processing of fundamental information: The case of frequency of occurrence. *American Psychologist, 39,* 1372–1388.

Hastorf, Albert H., & Cantril, Hadley (1954). They saw a game: A case study. *Journal of Abnormal and Social Psychology, 49,* 129–134.

Hatfield, Agnes B., & Lefley, Harriet P. (eds.) (1987). *Families of the mentally ill: Coping and adaptation.* New York: Guilford Press.

Hatfield, Elaine (1995). *Emotional contagion.* Paper presented at the annual meeting of the American Psychological Association, New York.

Hatfield, Elaine; Cacioppo, John T.; & Rapson, Richard (1992). The logic of emotion: Emotional contagion. In M. S. Clark (ed.), *Review of Personality, and Social Psychology* (Vol. 12). Newbury Park, CA: Sage.

Hatfield, Elaine, & Rapson, Richard L. (1996). *Love and sex: Cross-cultural perspectives.* Boston: Allyn & Bacon.

Hawkins, Scott A., & Hastie, Reid (1990). Hindsight: Biased judgments of past events after the outcomes are known. *Psychological Bulletin, 107,* 311–327.

Haynes, Suzanne, & Feinleib, Manning (1980). Women, work, and coronary heart disease: Prospective findings from the Framingham heart study. *American Journal of Public Health, 70,* 133–141.

Hazan, Cindy, & Shaver, Phillip R. (1994). Attachment as an organizational framework for research on close relationships. *Psychological Inquiry, 5,* 1–22.

Heath, Shirley B. (1983). *Ways with words: Language, life, and work in communities and classrooms.* New York: Cambridge University Press.

Heinrichs, R. Walter (1993). Schizophrenia and the brain: Conditions for a neuropsychology of madness. *American Psychologist, 48,* 221–233.

Helmes, Edward, & Reddon, John R. (1993). A perspective on developments in assessing psychopathology: A critical review of the MMPI and MMPI-2. *Psychological Bulletin, 113,* 453–471.

Helson, Ravenna, & McCabe, Laurel (1993). The social clock project in middle age. In B. F. Turner & L. E. Troll (eds.), *Women growing older.* Newbury Park, CA: Sage.

Hendrick, Clyde, & Hendrick, Susan S. (1986). A theory and method of love. *Journal of Personality and Social Psychology, 50,* 392–402.

Hendrick, Susan S., & Hendrick, Clyde (1992). *Romantic love.* Newbury Park, CA: Sage.

Hendrick, Susan S.; Hendrick, Clyde; & Adler, Nancy L. (1988). Romantic relationships: Love, satisfaction, and staying together. *Journal of Personality and Social Psychology, 54,* 980–988.

Hendrix, William H.; Steel, Robert P.; Leap, Terry L.; & Summers, Timothy P. (1991). Development of a stress-related health promotion model: Antecedents and organizational effectiveness outcomes. [Special Issue: Handbook on job stress.] *Journal of Social Behavior and Personality, 6,* 141–162.

Henley, Nancy (1995). Body politics revisited: What do we know today? In P. J. Kalbfleisch & M. J. Cody (eds.), *Gender, power, and communication in human relationships.* Hillsdale, NJ: Erlbaum.

Henriques, Jeffrey B., & Davidson, Richard J. (1991). Left frontal hypoactivation in depression. *Journal of Abnormal Psychology, 100,* 535–545.

Henry, Bill; Caspi, Avshalom; Moffitt, Terrie E.; & Silva, Phil A. (1996). Temperamental and familial predictors of violent and nonviolent criminal convictions: Age 3 to age 18. *Developmental Psychology, 32,* 614–623.

Hepworth, Joseph T., & West, Stephen G. (1988). Lynchings and the economy: A time-series reanalysis of Hovland and Sears (1940). *Journal of Personality and Social Psychology, 55,* 239–247.

Herbert, Tracy B., & Cohen, Sheldon (1993). Depression and immunity: A meta-analytic review. *Psychological Bulletin, 113,* 472–486.

Herdt, Gilbert (1984). *Ritualized homosexuality in Melanesia.* Berkeley: University of California Press.

Herman, John H. (1992). Transmutative and reproductive properties of dreams: Evidence for cortical modulation of brainstem generators. In J. Antrobus & M. Bertini (eds.), *The neuropsychology of dreaming.* Hillsdale, NJ: Erlbaum.

Herman, Louis M. (1987). Receptive competencies of language-trained animals. In J. S. Rosenblatt, C. Beer, M. C. Busnel, & P. J. B. Slater (eds.), *Advances in the study of behavior* (Vol. 17). Petaluma, CA: Academic Press.

Herman, Louis M.; Kuczaj, Stan A.; & Holder, Mark D. (1993). Responses to anomalous gestural sequences by a language-trained dolphin: Evidence for processing of semantic relations and syntactic information. *Journal of Experimental Psychology: General, 122,* 184–194.

Hermans, Hubert J. M. (1996). Voicing the self: From information processing to dialogical interchange. *Psychological Bulletin, 119,* 31–50.

Heron, Woodburn (1957). The pathology of boredom. *Scientific American, 196*(1), 52–56.

Herrnstein, Richard J., & Murray, Charles (1994). *The bell curve: Intelligence and class structure in American life.* New York: Free Press.

Hershberger, Scott L.; Lykken, David T.; & McGue, Matt (1995). *A twin registry study of male and female sexual orientation.* Paper presented at the annual meeting of the American Psychological Association, New York.

Hicks, Robert D. (1991). The police model of satanism crime. In J. T. Richardson, J. Best, & D. G. Bromley (eds.), *The satanism scare.* New York: Aldine de Gruyter.

Higley, J. D.; Hasert, M. L.; Suomi, S. J.; & Linnoila, M. (1991). A nonhuman primate model of alcohol abuse: Effects of early experience, personality, and stress on alcohol consumption. *Proceedings of the National Academy of Science, 88,* 7261–7265.

Hilgard, Ernest R. (1977). *Divided consciousness: Multiple controls in human thought and action.* New York: Wiley-Interscience.

Hilgard, Ernest R. (1986). *Divided consciousness: Multiple controls in human thought and action* (2nd ed.). New York: Wiley.

Hilgard, Josephine R. (1979). *Personality and hypnosis: A study of imaginative involvement* (2nd ed.). Chicago: University of Chicago Press.

Hill, Harlan F.; Chapman, C. Richard; Kornell, Judy A.; Sullivan, Keith M.; et al. (1990). Self-administration of morphine in bone marrow transplant patients reduces drug requirement. *Pain, 40,* 121–129.

Hillman, James, & Ventura, Michael (1992). *We've had a hundred years of psychotherapy—and the world's getting worse.* San Francisco: HarperCollins.

Hilsman, Ruth, & Garber, Judy (1995). A test of the cognitive diathesis stress model of depression in children: Academic stressors, attributional style, perceived competence, and control. *Journal of Personality and Social Psychology, 69,* 370–380.

Hilts, Philip J. (1995). *Memory's ghost: The strange tale of Mr. M. and the nature of memory.* New York: Simon & Schuster.

Hirsch, Barton (1981). Social networks and the coping process: Creating personal communities. In B. H. Gottlieb (ed.), *Social networks and social support.* Beverly Hills, CA: Sage.

Hirsch, Helmut V. B., & Spinelli, D. N. (1970). Visual experience modifies distribution of horizontally and vertically oriented receptive fields in cats. *Science, 168,* 869–871.

Hirschel, J. David; Hutchinson, Ira W., III; Dean, Charles; et al. (1990). *Charlotte spouse assault replication project: Final report.* Washington, DC: National Institute of Justice.

Hirst, William; Neisser, Ulric; & Spelke, Elizabeth (1978, January). Divided attention. *Human Nature, 1,* 54–61.

Hite, Shere (1987). *Women and love: A cultural revolution in progress.* New York: Knopf.

Hobson, J. Allan (1988). *The dreaming brain.* New York: Basic Books.

Hobson, J. Allan (1990). Activation, input source, and modulation: A neurocognitive model of the state of the brain mind. In R. R. Bootzin, J. F. Kihlstrom, & D. L. Schacter (eds.), *Sleep and cognition.* Washington, DC: American Psychological Association.

Hobson, Robert F. (1985). *Forms of feeling: The heart of psychotherapy.* London: Tavistock.

Hochschild, Arlie (1983). *The managed heart.* Berkeley: University of California Press.

Hockett, Charles F. (1960). The origins of speech. *Scientific American, 203,* 89–96.

Hoffman, Martin L. (1987). The contribution of empathy to justice and moral judgment. In N. Eisenberg & J. Strayer (eds.), *Empathy and its development.* New York: Cambridge University Press.

Hoffman, Martin L. (1990). Empathy and justice motivation. [Special Issue: Empathy.] *Motivation and Emotion, 14,* 151–172.

Hoffman, Martin L. (1994). Discipline and internalization. *Developmental Psychology, 30,* 26–28.

Hoffman, Martin L., & Saltzstein, Herbert (1967). Parent discipline and the child's moral development. *Journal of Personality and Social Psychology, 5,* 45–57.

Hofstede, Geert, & Bond, Michael H. (1988). The Confucius connection: From cultural roots to economic growth. *Organizational Dynamics,* 5–21.

Hogg, Michael A., & Abrams, Dominic (1988). *Social identifications: A social psychology of intergroup relations and group processes.* New York: Routledge.

Hollister, J. Megginson; Laing, Peter; & Mednick, Sarnoff A. (1996). Rhesus incompatibility as a risk factor for schizophrenia in male adults. *Archives of General Psychiatry, 53,* 19–24.

Holmes, David S. (1994). *Abnormal psychology* (2nd ed.). New York: HarperCollins.

Holt, Jim (1994, October 19). Anti-social science? *The New York Times,* op-ed page.

Holzman, Philip S., & Matthysse, Steven (1990). The genetics of schizophrenia: A review. *Psychological Science, 1,* 279–286.

Honts, Charles R. (1994). Psychophysiological detection of deception. *Current Directions in Psychological Science, 3,* 77–82.

Hooker, Evelyn (1957). The adjustment of the male overt homosexual. *Journal of Projective Techniques, 21,* 18–31.

Hooven, Carole; Gottman, John M.; & Katz, Lynn F. (1995). Parental meta-emotion structure predicts family and child outcomes. *Cognition and Emotion, 9,* 229–269.

Hoptman, Matthew J., & Davidson, Richard J. (1994). How and why do the two cerebral hemispheres interact? *Psychological Bulletin, 116,* 195–219.

Horgan, John (1995, November). Get smart, take a test: A long-term rise in IQ scores baffles intelligence experts. *Scientific American, 273,* 12, 14.

Horm, J., & Anderson, K. (1993). Who in America is trying to lose weight? *Annals of Internal Medicine, 119,* 672–676.

Horn, G., & Hinde, R. A. (eds.) (1970). *Short-term changes in neural activity and behaviour.* New York: Cambridge University Press.

Horn, John L., & Donaldson, Gary (1980). Cognitive development in adulthood. In O. G. Brim, Jr., & J. Kagan (eds.), *Constancy and change in human development.* Cambridge, MA: Harvard University Press.

Horne, J. A. (1988). Sleep loss and "divergent" thinking ability. *Sleep, 11,* 528–536.

Horner, Althea J. (1991). *Psychoanalytic object relations therapy.* New York: Jason Aronson.

Horney, Karen (1967). *Feminine psychology.* New York: Norton.

Hornstein, Gail (1992). The return of the repressed: Psychology's problematic relations with psychoanalysis, 1909–1960. *American Psychologist, 47,* 254–263.

House, James S.; Landis, Karl R.; & Umberson, Debra (1988, July 19). Social relationships and health. *Science, 241,* 540–545.

Hovland, Carl I., & Sears, Robert R. (1940). Minor studies of aggression: Correlation of lynchings with economic indices. *Journal of Psychology, 9,* 301–310.

Howard, George S. (1991). Culture tales: A narrative approach to thinking, cross-cultural psychology, and psychotherapy. *American Psychologist, 46,* 187–197.

Howard, Kenneth; Kopta, S. Mark; Krause, Merton S.; & Orlinsky, David (1986). The dose-effect relationship in psychotherapy. *American Psychologist, 41,* 159–164.

Howe, Mark L., & Courage, Mary L. (1993). On resolving the enigma of infantile amnesia. *Psychological Bulletin, 113,* 305–326.

Howe, Mark L.; Courage, Mary L.; & Peterson, Carole (1994). How can I remember when "I" wasn't there? Long-term retention of traumatic experiences and emergence of the cognitive self. [Special Issue: The recovered memory/false memory debate.] *Consciousness and Cognition, 3,* 327–355.

Howell, Debi (1993, August 8). Detecting the dirty lie [Interview with Paul Ekman]. *San Francisco Examiner and Chronicle,* This World section, 7.

Hrdy, Sarah B. (1988). Empathy, polyandry, and the myth of the coy female. In R. Bleier (ed.), *Feminist approaches to science.* New York: Pergamon.

Hrdy, Sarah B. (1994). What do women want? In T. A. Bass (ed.), *Reinventing the future: Conversations with the world's leading scientists.* Reading, MA: Addison-Wesley.

Hu, S.; Pattatucci, A. M.; Patterson C; et al. (1995). Linkage between sexual orientation and chromosome Xq28 in males but not in females. *Nature Genetics, 11,* 248–256.

Hubbard, Ruth (1990). *The politics of women's biology.* New Brunswick, NJ: Rutgers University Press.

Hubbard, Ruth, & Wald, Elijah (1993). *Exploding the gene myth.* Boston: Beacon Press.

Hubel, David H., & Wiesel, Torsten N. (1962). Receptive fields, binocular interaction and functional architecture in the cat's visual cortex. *Journal of Physiology* (London), *160,* 106–154.

Hubel, David H., & Wiesel, Torsten N. (1968). Receptive fields and functional architecture of monkey striate cortex. *Journal of Physiology* (London), *195,* 215–243.

Hughes, Judith M. (1989). *Reshaping the psychoanalytic domain: The work of Melanie Klein, W. R. D. Fairbairn, & D. W. Winnicott.* Berkeley: University of California Press.

Hughes, Robert (1993). *The culture of complaint: The fraying of America.* New York: Oxford University Press.

Hunt, Earl; Streissguth, Ann P.; Kerr, Beth; & Olson, Heather C. (1995). Mothers' alcohol consumption during pregnancy: Effects on spatial-visual reasoning in 14-year-old children. *Psychological Science, 6,* 339–342.

Hunt, Morton M. (1959/1967). *The natural history of love.* New York: Minerva Press.

Hunt, Morton M. (1993). *The story of psychology.* New York: Doubleday.

Hunter, John E. (1996). *Significance tests should be banned.* Paper presented at the annual meeting of the American Psychological Society, San Francisco.

Hunter, John E. (1997). Needed: A ban on the significance test. *Psychological Science, 8,* 3–7.

Huntington's Disease Collaborative Research Group (1993). A novel gene containing a trinucleotide repeat that is expanded and unstable on Huntington's disease chromosomes. *Cell, 72,* 971–983.

Hupka, Ralph B. (1981). Cultural determinants of jealousy. *Alternative Lifestyles, 4,* 310–356.

Hupka, Ralph B. (1991). The motive for the arousal of romantic jealousy: Its cultural origin. In P. Salovey (ed.), *The psychology of jealousy and envy.* New York: Guilford Press.

Huston, Aletha, & Wright, John C. (1995). *Effects of educational TV viewing of lower-income preschoolers on academic skills, school readiness, and school adjustment 1 to 3 years later.* Report to Children's Television Workshop from the Center for Research on the Influences of Television on Children, University of Kansas, Lawrence.

Hyde, Janet S. (1981). How large are cognitive gender differences? A meta-analysis using w^2 and d. *American Psychologist, 36,* 892–901.

Hyde, Janet (1984a). Children's understanding of sexist language. *Developmental Psychology, 20,* 697–706.

Hyde, Janet S. (1984b). How large are gender differences in aggression? A developmental meta-analysis. *Developmental Psychology, 20,* 722–736.

Hyde, Janet S.; Fennema, Elizabeth; & Lamon, Susan J. (1990). Gender differences in mathematics performance: A meta-analysis. *Psychological Bulletin, 107,* 139–155.

Hyde, Janet S., & Linn, Marcia C. (1988). Gender differences in verbal ability: A meta-analysis. *Psychological Bulletin, 104,* 53–69.

Hyman, Ira E.; Husband, Troy H.; & Billings, F. James (1995). False memories of childhood experiences. *Applied Cognitive Psychology, 9,* 181–197.

Hyman, Ira E., Jr., & Pentland, Joel (1996). The role of mental imagery in the creation of false childhood memories. *Journal of Memory and Language, 35,* 101–117.

Hyman, Irwin A. (1994). *Is spanking child abuse? Conceptualizations, research and policy implications.* Paper presented at the annual meeting of the American Psychological Association, Los Angeles.

Hyman, Ray (1994). Anomaly or artifact? Comments on Bem and Honorton. *Psychological Bulletin, 115,* 25–27.

Inglehart, Ronald (1990). *Culture shift in advanced industrial society.* Princeton, NJ: Princeton University Press.

Inglis, James, & Lawson, J. S. (1981). Sex differences in the effects of unilateral brain damage on intelligence. *Science, 212,* 693–695.

Irons, Edward D., & Moore, Gilbert W. (1985). *Black managers: The case of the banking industry.* New York: Praeger/Greenwood.

Irvine, Janice M. (1990). *Disorders of desire: Sex and gender in modern American sexology.* Philadelphia: Temple University Press.

Isen, Alice M.; Daubman, Kimberly A.; & Nowicki, Gary P. (1987). Positive affect facilitates creative problem solving. *Journal of Personality and Social Psychology, 52,* 1122–1131.

Islam, Mir Rabiul, & Hewstone, Miles (1993). Intergroup attributions and affective consequences in majority and minority groups. *Journal of Personality and Social Psychology, 64,* 936–950.

Izard, Carroll E. (1990). Facial expressions and the regulation of emotions. *Journal of Personality and Social Psychology, 58,* 487–498.

Izard, Carroll E. (1994a). Four systems for emotion activation: Cognitive and noncognitive processes. *Psychological Review, 100,* 68–90.

Izard, Carroll E. (1994b). Innate and universal facial expressions: Evidence from developmental and cross-cultural research. *Psychological Bulletin, 115,* 288–299.

Jacobs, Janis E., & Eccles, Jacquelynne S. (1985). Gender differences in math ability: The impact of media reports on parents. *Educational Researcher, 14,* 20–25.

Jacobs, Marion K., & Goodman, Gerald (1989). Psychology and self-help groups: Predictions on a partnership. *American Psychologist, 44,* 536–545.

Jacobsen, Paul B; Bovbjerg, Dana H.; Schwartz, Marc D.; Hudis, Clifford A.; et al. (1995). Conditioned emotional distress in women receiving chemotherapy for breast cancer. *Journal of Consulting & Clinical Psychology, 63,* 108–114.

Jacobsen, Teresa; Edelstein, Wolfgang; & Hofmann, Volker (1994). A longitudinal study of the relation between representations of attachment in childhood and cognitive functioning in childhood and adolescence. *Developmental Psychology, 30,* 112–124.

Jacobson, Gerald (1983). *The multiple crises of marital separation and divorce.* New York: Grune & Stratton.

Jacobson, John W., & Mulick, James A. (1994). Facilitated communication: Better education through applied ideology. *Journal of Behavioral Education, 4,* 93–105.

James, William (1884/1968). What is an emotion? *Mind, 9,* 188–205. (Reprinted in M. Arnold [ed.], *The nature of emotion.* Baltimore, MD: Penguin.)

James, William (1890/1950). *Principles of psychology* (Vol. 1). New York: Dover.

James, William (1902/1936). *The varieties of religious experience.* New York: Modern Library.

Janis, Irving L. (1982). *Groupthink: Psychological studies of policy decisions and fiascoes* (2nd ed.). Boston: Houghton Mifflin.

Janis, Irving L. (1989). *Crucial decisions: Leadership in policymaking and crisis management.* New York: Free Press.

Janis, Irving L.; Kaye, Donald; & Kirschner, Paul (1965). Facilitating effects of "eating-while-reading" on responsiveness to persuasive communications. *Journal of Personality and Social Psychology, 1,* 181–186.

Janoff-Bulman, Ronnie (1989). The benefits of illusions, the threat of disillusionment, and the limitations of inaccuracy. [Special Issue: Self-illusions: When are they adaptive?] *Journal of Social and Clinical Psychology, 8,* 158–175.

Jellinek, E. M. (1960). *The disease concept of alcoholism.* New Haven, CT: Hillhouse Press.

Jemmott, John B.; Hellman, Caroline; McClelland, David C.; Locke, Steven E.; et al. (1990). Motivational syndromes associated with natural killer cell activity. *Journal of Behavioral Medicine, 13,* 53–73.

Jenkins, Jennifer M., & Astington, Janet W. (1996). Cognitive factors and family structure associated with theory of mind development in young children. *Developmental Psychology, 32,* 70–78.

Jenkins, John G., & Dallenbach, Karl M. (1924). Obliviscence during sleep and waking. *American Journal of Psychology, 35,* 605–612.

Jenkins, Sharon Rae (1994). Need for power and women's careers over 14 years: Structural power, job satisfaction, and motive change. *Journal of Personality and Social Psychology, 66,* 155–165.

Jensen, Arthur R. (1969). How much can we boost IQ and scholastic achievement? *Harvard Educational Review, 39,* 1–123.

Jensen, Arthur R. (1981). *Straight talk about mental tests.* New York: Free Press.

Jensen, J. P.; Bergin, Allen E.; & Greaves, D. W. (1990). The meaning of eclecticism: New survey and analysis of components. *Professional Psychology: Research and Practice, 21,* 124–130.

Jessor, Richard (1993). Successful adolescent development among youth in high-risk settings. *American Psychologist, 48,* 117–126.

John, E. R.; Tang, Y.; Brill, A. B.; Young, R.; & Ono, K. (1986). Double-labeled metabolic maps of memory. *Science, 233,* 1167–1175.

Johnson, Catherine (1988). *When to say goodbye to your therapist.* New York: Simon & Schuster.

Johnson, David W., & Johnson, Roger T. (1989). *A meta-analysis of cooperative, competitive, and individualistic goal structures.* Hillsdale, NJ: Erlbaum.

Johnson, Marcia K. (1995). *The relation between memory and reality.* Paper presented at the annual meeting of the American Psychological Association, New York.

Johnson, Mark H.; Dziurawiec, Suzanne; Ellis, Hadyn; & Morton, John (1991). Newborns' preferential tracking of face-like stimuli and its subsequent decline. *Cognition, 40,* 1–19.

Johnson, Robert, & Downing, Leslie (1979). Deindividuation and valence of cues: Effects of prosocial and antisocial behavior. *Journal of Personality and Social Psychology, 37,* 1532–1538.

Johnson-Laird, Philip N. (1988). *The computer and the mind: An introduction to cognitive science.* Cambridge, MA: Harvard University Press.

Joiner, Thomas E. (1994). Contagious depression: Existence, specificity to depressed symptoms, and the role of reassurance seeking. *Journal of Personality and Social Psychology, 67,* 287–296.

Joiner, Thomas E., Jr., & Metalsky, Gerald I. (1995). A prospective test of an integrative interpersonal theory of depression: A naturalistic study of college roommates. *Journal of Personality and Social Psychology, 69,* 778–788.

Jones, James M. (1991). Psychological models of race: What have they been and what should they be? In J. D. Goodchilds (ed.), *Psychological perspectives on human diversity in America.* Washington, DC: American Psychological Association.

Jones, Mary Cover (1924). A laboratory study of fear: The case of Peter. *Pedagogical Seminary, 31,* 308–315.

Jones, Russell A. (1977). *Self-fulfilling prophecies.* Hillsdale, NJ: Erlbaum.

Jones, Steve (1994). *The language of genes.* New York: Anchor/Doubleday.

Jorgensen, Randall S.; Johnson, Blair T.; Kolodziej, Monika E.; & Schreer, George E. (1996). Elevated blood pressure and personality: A meta-analytic review. *Psychological Bulletin, 120,* 293–320.

Judd, Charles M.; Park, Bernadette; Ryan, Carey S.; Brauer, Markus; & Kraus, Susan (1995). Stereotypes and ethnocentrism: Diverging interethnic perceptions of African American and white American youth. *Journal of Personality and Social Psychology, 69,* 460–481.

Jung, Carl (1967). *Collected works.* Princeton, NJ: Princeton University Press.

Jusczyk, Peter W. (1993). From general to language-specific capacities: The WRAPSA model of how speech perception develops. [Special Issue: Phonetic development.] *Journal of Phonetics, 21,* 3–28.

Jusczyk, Peter W.; Friederici, Angela D.; Wessels, Jeanine M.; Svenkerud, Vigdis Y.; et al. (1993). Infants' sensitivity to the sound patterns of native language words. *Journal of Memory and Language, 32,* 402–420.

Kabat-Zinn, Jon (1994). *Wherever you go, there you are: Mindfulness meditation in everyday life.* New York: Hyperion.

Kagan, Jerome (1984). *The nature of the child.* New York: Basic Books.

Kagan, Jerome (1989). *Unstable ideas: Temperament, cognition, and self.* Cambridge, MA: Harvard University Press.

Kagan, Jerome (1993). The meanings of morality. *Psychological Science, 4,* 353, 357–360.

Kagan, Jerome (1994). *Galen's prophecy: Temperament in human nature.* New York: Basic Books.

Kagan, Jerome (1996). Three pleasing ideas. *American Psychologist, 51,* 901–908.

Kagan, Jerome, & Snidman, Nancy (1991). Infant predictors of inhibited and uninhibited profiles. *Psychological Science, 2,* 40–44.

Kahneman, Daniel, & Treisman, Anne (1984). Changing views of attention and automaticity. In R. Parasuraman, D. R. Davies, & J. Beatty (eds.), *Varieties of attention.* New York: Academic Press.

Kalmijn, Ad. J. (1982). Electric and magnetic field detection in elasmobranch fishes. *Science, 218,* 916–918.

Kameda, Tatsuya, & Sugimori, Shinkichi (1993). Psychological entrapment in group decision making: An assigned decision rule and a groupthink phenomenon. *Journal of Personality and Social Psychology, 65,* 282–292.

Kamin, Allen; Houston, Susan E.; Axton, Ted R.; & Hall, Rosalie (1995). *Self-efficacy and race car driver performance: A field investigation.* Paper presented at the annual meeting of the American Psychological Association, New York.

Kandel, Eric R., & Schwartz, James H. (1982). Molecular biology of learning: Modulation of transmitter release. *Science, 218,* 433–443.

Kane, John M. (1987). Treatment of schizophrenia. *Schizophrenia Bulletin, 13,* 133–156.

Kanin, Eugene J. (1985). Date rapists: Differential sexual socialization and relative deprivation. *Archives of Sexual Behavior, 14,* 219–231.

Kanter, Rosabeth Moss (1977/1993). *Men and women of the corporation.* New York: Basic Books.

Kaplan, Abraham (1967). A philosophical discussion of normality. *Archives of General Psychiatry, 17,* 325–330.

Kaplan, Meg S.; Morales, Miguel; & Becker, Judith V. (1993). The impact of verbal satiation of adolescent sex offenders: A preliminary report. *Journal of Child Sexual Abuse, 2,* 81–88.

Karasek, Robert, & Theorell, Tores (1990). *Healthy work: Stress, productivity, and the reconstruction of working life.* New York: Basic Books.

Karau, Steven J., & Williams, Kipling D. (1993). Social loafing: A meta-analytic review and theoretical integration. *Journal of Personality and Social Psychology, 65,* 681–706.

Karney, Benjamin R.; Bradbury, Thomas N.; Fincham, Frank D.; & Sullivan, Kieran T. (1994). The role of negative affectivity in the association between attributions and marital satisfaction. *Journal of Personality and Social Psychology, 66,* 413–424.

Karni, Avi; Tanne, David; Rubenstein, Barton S.; Askenasy, Jean J. M.; & Sagi, Dov (1994). Dependence on REM sleep of overnight improvement of a perceptual skill. *Science, 265,* 679–682.

Karon, Bertram P. (1994). *Psychotherapy: The appropriate treatment of schizophrenia.* Paper presented at the annual meeting of the American Psychological Association, Los Angeles.

Kashima, Yoshihisa; Yamaguchi, Susumu; Kim, Uichol; Choi, Sang-Chin; Gelfand, Michele J.; & Yuki, Masaki (1995). Culture, gender, and self: A perspective from individualism-collectivism research. *Journal of Personality and Social Psychology, 69,* 925–937.

Kasser, Tim, & Ryan, Richard M. (1993). A dark side of the American dream: Correlates of financial success as a central life aspiration. *Journal of Personality and Social Psychology, 65,* 410–422.

Katigbak, Marcia S.; Church, A. Timothy; & Akamine, Toshio X. (1996). Cross-cultural generalizability of personality dimensions: Relating indigenous and imported dimensions in two cultures. *Journal of Personality and Social Psychology, 70,* 99–114.

Katz, Irwin, & Hass, R. Glen (1988). Racial ambivalence and American value conflict: Correlational and priming studies of dual cognitive structures. *Journal of Personality and Social Psychology, 55,* 893–905.

Katz, Joel, & Melzack, Ronald (1990). Pain "memories" in phantom limbs: Review and clinical observations. *Pain, 43,* 319–336.

Katz, Jonathan Ned (1995). *The invention of heterosexuality.* New York: Dutton.

Katz, Lilian G. (1993, Summer). All about me. *American Educator, 17*(2), 18–23.

Katz, Lori, & Epstein, Seymour (1991). Constructive thinking and coping with laboratory-induced stress. *Journal of Personality and Social Psychology, 61,* 789–800.

Katz, Phyllis A., & Ksansnak, Keith R. (1994). Developmental aspects of gender role flexibility and traditionality in middle childhood and adolescence. *Developmental Psychology, 30,* 272–282.

Katz, Stuart; Blackburn, A. Boyd; & Lautenschlager, Gary J. (1991). Answering reading comprehension items without passages on the SAT when items are quasi-randomized. *Educational and Psychological Measurement, 51,* 747–754.

Katz, Stuart, & Lautenschlager, Gary J. (1994). Answering reading comprehension items without passages on the SAT-I, the ACT, and the GRE. *Educational Assessment, 2,* 295–308.

Kaufman, Joan, & Zigler, Edward (1987). Do abused children become abusive parents? *American Journal of Orthopsychiatry, 57,* 186–192.

Keane, M. M.; Gabrieli, J. D. E.; & Corkin, S. (1987). Multiple relations between fact-learning and priming in global amnesia. *Society for Neuroscience Abstracts, 13,* 1454.

Keating, Caroline F. (1994). World without words: Messages from face and body. In W. J. Lonner & R. Malpass (eds.), *Psychology and culture.* Needham Heights, MA: Allyn & Bacon.

Keck, Paul E.; McElroy, Susan L.; & Pope, Harrison G. (1991). Epidemiology of neuroleptic malignant syndrome. *Psychiatric Annals, 21,* 148–151.

Keefe, Francis J., & Gil, Karen M. (1986). Behavioral concepts in the analysis of chronic pain syndromes. *Journal of Consulting and Clinical Psychology, 54,* 776–783.

Keirstead, Susan A.; Rasminsky, Michael; Fukuda, Y.; et al. (1989). Electrophysiologic responses in hamster superior colliculus evoked by regenerating retinal axons. *Science, 246,* 255–257.

Kelly, Anita E., & McKillop, Kevin J. (1996). Consequences of revealing personal secrets. *Psychological Bulletin, 120,* 450–465.

Kelly, Dennis D. (1981). Disorders of sleep and consciousness. In E. Kandel & J. Schwartz (eds.), *Principles of neural science.* New York: Elsevier-North Holland.

Kelman, Herbert C., & Hamilton, V. Lee (1989). *Crimes of obedience: Toward a social psychology of authority and responsibility.* New Haven, CT: Yale University Press.

Kelsoe, John R.; Ginns, Edward I.; Egeland, Janice A.; Gerhard, Daniela S.; et al. (1989). Re-evaluation of the linkage relationship between chromosome 11p loci and the gene for bipolar affective disorder in the Old Order Amish. *Nature, 342,* 238–243.

Kendall-Tackett, Kathleen A.; Williams, Linda Meyer; & Finkelhor, David (1993). Impact of sexual abuse on children: A review and synthesis of recent empirical studies. *Psychological Bulletin, 113,* 164–180.

Kendler, K. S.; Heath, A. C.; Neale, M. C.; Kessler, R. C.; & Eaves, L. J. (1992, October 14). A population-based twin study of alcoholism in women. *Journal of the American Medical Association, 268,* 1877–1882.

Kendler, Kenneth S.; Kessler, Ronald C.; Walters, Ellen E.; MacLean, Charles; et al. (1995). Stressful life events, genetic liability, and onset of an episode of major depression in women. *American Journal of Psychiatry, 152,* 833–842.

Keneally, Thomas (1982/1993). *Schindler's list.* New York: Simon & Schuster.

Kennedy, James; Giuffra, Luis; Moises, Hans; Cavalli-Sforza, L. L.; et al. (1988, November 10). Evidence against linkage of schizophrenia to markers on chromosome 5 in a northern Swedish pedigree. *Nature, 336*(6195), 167–169.

Kenrick, Douglas T., & Trost, Melanie R. (1993). The evolutionary perspective. In A. E. Beall & R. J. Sternberg (eds.), *The psychology of gender.* New York: Guilford Press.

Kephart, William M. (1967). Some correlates of romantic love. *Journal of Marriage and the Family, 29,* 470–474.

Kerr, Michael E., & Bowen, Murray (1988). *Family evaluation: An approach based on Bowen theory.* New York: Norton.

Kesner, Raymond P.; Chiba, Andrea A.; & Jackson-Smith, Pamela (1994). Rats do show primacy and recency effects in memory for lists of spatial locations: A reply to Gaffan. *Animal Learning and Behavior, 22,* 214–218.

Kessler, R. C.; DeLongis, Anita; Haskett, Roger F.; & Tal, Margalit (in press). Late luteal phase dysphoric disorder in a general population sample. In P. Leaf (ed.), *Research in community and mental health* (Vol. 9). Greenwich, CT: JAI Press.

Kessler, Ronald C.; McGonagle, Katherine A.; Zhao, Shanyang; Nelson, Christopher B.; et al. (1994). Lifetime and 12-month prevalence of DSM-III-R psychiatric disorders in the United States: Results from the National Comorbidity Study. *Archives of General Psychiatry, 51,* 8–19.

Kessler, Ronald C.; Sonnega, A.; Bromet, E.; Hughes, M.; & Nelson, C. B. (1995). Posttraumatic stress disorder in the National Comorbidity Survey. *Archives of General Psychiatry, 52,* 1048–1060.

Kety, Seymour S. (1974). From rationalization to reason. *American Journal of Psychiatry, 131,* 957–963.

Kiecolt-Glaser, Janice; Garner, Warren; Speicher, Carl; Penn, Gerald; Holliday, Jane; & Glaser, Ronald (1985a). Psychosocial modifiers of immunocompetence in medical students. *Psychosomatic Medicine, 46,* 7–14.

Kiecolt-Glaser, Janice; Glaser, Ronald; Shuttleworth, Edwin; Dyer, Carol; et al. (1987). Chronic stress and immunity in family caregivers of Alzheimer's disease victims. *Psychosomatic Medicine, 49,* 523–535.

Kiecolt-Glaser, Janice; Glaser, Ronald; Williger, D.; Stout, J. C; et al. (1985b). Psychosocial enhancement of immunocompetence in a geriatric population. *Health Psychology, 4,* 25–41.

Kiecolt-Glaser, Janice; Malarkey, William B.; Chee, MaryAnn; Newton, Tamara; et al. (1993). Negative behavior during marital conflict is associated with immunological down-regulation. *Psychosomatic Medicine, 55,* 395–409.

Kihlstrom, John F. (1994). Hypnosis, delayed recall, and the principles of memory. *International Journal of Clinical and Experimental Hypnosis, 40,* 337–345.

Kihlstrom, John (1995). *From a subject's point of view: The experiment as conversation and collaboration between investigator and subject.* Invited address presented at the seventh annual meeting of the American Psychological Society, New York.

Kihlstrom, John F., & Harackiewicz, Judith M. (1982). The earliest recollection: A new survey. *Journal of Personality, 50,* 134–148.

Kihlstrom, John F.; Schacter, Daniel L.; Cork, Randall C.; Hurt, Catherine A.; & Behr, Steven E. (1990). Implicit and explicit memory following surgical anesthesia. *Psychological Science, 1,* 303–306.

Kimble, Gregory A. (1993). A modest proposal for a minor revolution in the language of psychology. *Psychological Science, 4,* 253–255.

Kimble, Gregory A. (1994). A frame of reference for psychology. *American Psychologist, 49,* 510–519.

Kimble, Gregory A. (1996). *Psychology: The hope of a science.* Cambridge, MA: MIT Press.

King, Patricia M., & Kitchener, Karen S. (1994). *Developing reflective judgment: Understanding and promoting intellectual growth and critical thinking in adolescents and adults.* San Francisco: Jossey-Bass.

Kinsbourne, Marcel (1982). Hemispheric specialization and the growth of human understanding. *American Psychologist, 37,* 411–420.

Kinsey, Alfred C.; Pomeroy, Wardell B.; & Martin, Clyde E. (1948). *Sexual behavior in the human male.* Philadelphia: Saunders.

Kinsey, Alfred C.; Pomeroy, Wardell B.; Martin, Clyde E.; & Gebhard, Paul H. (1953). *Sexual behavior in the human female.* Philadelphia: Saunders.

Kirk, Stuart A., & Kutchins, Herb (1992). *The selling of DSM: The rhetoric of science in psychiatry.* Hawthorne, NY: Aldine de Gruyter.

Kirkpatrick, Lee A., & Davis, Keith A. (1994). Attachment style, gender, and relationship stability: A longitudinal analysis. *Journal of Personality and Social Psychology, 66,* 502–512.

Kirsch, Irving, & Lynn, Steven Jay (1995). The altered state of hypnosis: Changes in the theoretical landscape. *American Psychologist, 50,* 846–858.

Kirsch, Irving; Montgomery, G.; & Sapirstein, G. (1995). Hypnosis as an adjunct to cognitive behavioral psychotherapy: A meta-analysis. *Journal of Consulting and Clinical Psychology, 63,* 214–220.

Kirsch, Irving; Silva, Christopher E.; Carone, James E.; Johnston, J. Dennis; & Simon, B. (1989). The surreptitious observation design: An experimental paradigm for distinguishing artifact from essence in hypnosis. *Journal of Abnormal Psychology, 98,* 132–136.

Kirschenbaum, B.; Nedergaard, M.; Preuss, A.; et al. (1994). In vitro neuronal production and differentiation by precursor cells derived from the adult human forebrain. *Cerebral Cortex, 4,* 576–589.

Kitayama, Shinobu, & Markus, Hazel R. (1994). Introduction to cultural psychology and emotion research. In S. Kitayama & H. R. Markus (eds.), *Emotion and culture: Empirical studies of mutual influence.* Washington, DC: American Psychological Association.

Kitchener, Karen S., & King, Patricia M. (1990). The Reflective Judgment Model: Ten years of research. In M. L. Commons (ed.), *Models and methods in the study of adolescent and adult thought: Vol. 2. Adult development.* Westport, CT: Greenwood Press.

Kitchener, Karen S.; Lynch, Cindy L.; Fischer, Kurt W.; & Wood, Phillip K. (1993). Developmental range of reflective judgment: The effect of contextual support and practice on developmental stage. *Developmental Psychology, 29,* 893–906.

Kitzinger, Celia, & Wilkinson, Sue (1995). Transitions from heterosexuality to lesbianism: The discursive production of lesbian identities. *Developmental Psychology, 31,* 95–104.

Klatsky, Arthur L. (1994). Epidemiology of coronary heart disease—influence of alcohol. *Alcohol: Clinical and Experimental Research, 18,* 88–96.

Klein, Donald F. (1980). Psychosocial treatment of schizophrenia, or psychosocial help for people with schizophrenia? *Schizophrenia Bulletin, 6,* 122–130.

Klein, Raymond, & Armitage, Roseanne (1979). Rhythms in human performance: $1\frac{1}{2}$-hour oscillations in cognitive style. *Science, 204,* 1326–1328.

Kleinman, Arthur (1988). *Rethinking psychiatry: From cultural category to personal experience.* New York: Free Press.

Kleinmuntz, Benjamin, & Szucko, Julian J. (1984, March 29). A field study of the fallibility of polygraph lie detection. *Nature, 308,* 449–450.

Klerman, Gerald L.; Weissman, Myrna M.; Rounsaville, Bruce J.; & Chevron, Eve S. (1984). *Interpersonal psychotherapy of depression.* New York: Basic Books.

Klima, Edward S., & Bellugi, Ursula (1966). Syntactic regularities in the speech of children. In J. Lyons & R. J. Wales (eds.), *Psycholinguistics papers.* Edinburgh, Scotland: Edinburgh University Press.

Kluft, Richard P. (1987). The simulation and dissimulation of multiple personality disorder. *American Journal of Clinical Hypnosis, 30,* 104–118.

Kluft, Richard P. (1993). Multiple personality disorders. In D. Spiegel (ed.), *Dissociative disorders: A clinical review.* Lutherville, MD: Sidran.

Kluger, Richard (1996). *Ashes to ashes: America's hundred-year cigarette war, the public health, and the unabashed triumph of Philip Morris.* New York: Knopf.

Knight, George P.; Johnson, Lora G.; Carlo, Gustavo; & Eisenberg, Nancy (1994). A multiplicative model of the dispositional antecedents of a prosocial behavior: Predicting more of the people more of the time. *Journal of Personality and Social Psychology, 66,* 178–183.

Koch, Sigmund (1992). "Psychology" or "The psychological studies"? *American Psychologist, 48,* 902–904.

Koegel, Robert L.; Schreibman, Laura; O'Neill, Robert E.; & Burke, John C. (1983). The personality and family-interaction characteristics of parents of autistic children. *Journal of Consulting and Clinical Psychology, 51,* 683–692.

Koeske, Randi D. (1987). Premenstrual emotionality: Is biology destiny? In M. R. Walsh (ed.), *The psychology of women: Ongoing debates.* New Haven, CT: Yale University Press.

Kohlberg, Lawrence (1964). Development of moral character and moral ideology. In M. Hoffman & L. W. Hoffman (eds.), *Review of child development research.* New York: Russell Sage Foundation.

Kohlberg, Lawrence (1966). A cognitive-developmental analysis of children's sex-role concepts and attitudes. In E. E. Maccoby (ed.), *The development of sex differences.* Stanford, CA: Stanford University Press.

Kohlberg, Lawrence (1976). Moral stages and moralization: The cognitive-developmental approach. In T. Lickona (ed.), *Moral development and behavior.* New York: Holt, Rinehart and Winston.

Kohlberg, Lawrence (1984). *Essays on moral development: Vol. 2. The psychology of moral development: The nature and validity of moral stages.* San Francisco: Harper & Row.

Köhler, Wolfgang (1925). *The mentality of apes.* New York: Harcourt, Brace.

Köhler, Wolfgang (1959). *Gestalt psychology today.* Presidential address to the American Psychological Association, Cincinnati. [Reprinted in E. R. Hilgard (ed.), *American psychology in historical perspective: Addresses of the presidents of the American Psychological Association, 1892–1977.* Washington, DC: American Psychological Association, 1978.]

Kohn, Alfie (1992). *No contest: The case against competition* (rev. ed.). Boston: Houghton Mifflin.

Kohn, Alfie (1993). *Punished by rewards.* Boston: Houghton Mifflin.

Kohn, Melvin, & Schooler, Carmi (1983). *Work and personality: An inquiry into the impact of social stratification.* Norwood, NJ: Ablex.

Kohn, Paul M.; Lafreniere, Kathryn; & Gurevich, Maria (1991). Hassles, health, and personality. *Journal of Personality and Social Psychology, 61,* 478–482.

Kolb, B. (1996). *Neural plasticity and behavioural development.* [State of the art address.] Paper presented at the International Congress of Psychology, Montreal.

Kolbert, Elizabeth (1995, June 5). Public opinion polls swerve with the turns of a phrase. *The New York Times, 144,* A1.

Konishi, Masakazu (1993). Listening with two ears. *Scientific American, 268,* 66ff.

Koocher, Gerald (1990). *Self-help or hype?* Paper presented at the annual meeting of the American Psychological Association, Boston.

Koocher, Gerald P.; Goodman, Gail S.; White, C. Sue; Friedrich, William N.; et al. (1995). Psychological science and the use of anatomically detailed dolls in child sexual-abuse assessments. *Psychological Bulletin, 118,* 199–222.

Kopta, Stephen M.; Howard, Kenneth I.; Lowry, Jenny L.; & Beutler, Larry E. (1994). Patterns of symptomatic recovery in psychotherapy. *Journal of Consulting and Clinical Psychology, 62,* 1009–1016.

Koshland, Daniel E., Jr. (1988–1989). The future of biological research: What is possible and what is ethical? *MBL Science, 3,* 10–15.

Koss, Mary P.; Dinero, Thomas E.; Seibel, Cynthia A.; & Cox, Susan L. (1988). Stranger and acquaintance rape: Are there differences in the victim's experience? *Psychology of Women Quarterly, 12,* 1–24.

Kosslyn, Stephen M. (1980). *Image and mind.* Cambridge, MA: Harvard University Press.

Kosslyn, Stephen M.; Seger, Carol; Pani, John R.; & Hillger, Lynn A. (1990). When is imagery used in everyday life? A diary study. *Journal of Mental Imagery, 14,* 131–152.

Kramer, Peter (1993). *Listening to Prozac.* New York: Viking.

Krantz, David S., & Manuck, Stephen B. (1984). Acute psychophysiologic reactivity and risk of cardiovascular disease: A review and methodological critique. *Psychological Bulletin, 96,* 435–464.

Kraus, Stephen J. (1995). Attitudes and the prediction of behavior: A meta-analysis of the empirical literature. *Personality and Social Psychology Bulletin, 21,* 58–75.

Kreps, Bonnie (1990). *Authentic passion.* Toronto, Canada: McClelland & Stewart.

Krieger, Nancy, & Sidney, S. (1996, October). Racial discrimination and blood pressure: The CARDIA Study of young black and white adults. *American Journal of Public Health, 86,* 1370–1378.

Kripke, Daniel F. (1974). Ultradian rhythms in sleep and wakefulness. In E. D. Weitzman (ed.), *Advances in sleep research* (Vol. 1). Flushing, NY: Spectrum.

Kristof, Nicholas D. (1996, February 11). Who needs love? In Japan, many couples don't. *The New York Times,* International section, 1, 6.

Kroll, Barry M. (1992). *Teaching hearts and minds: College students reflect on the Vietnam War in literature.* Carbondale: Southern Illinois University Press.

Krupa, David J.; Thompson, Judith K.; & Thompson, Richard F. (1993). Localization of a memory trace in the mammalian brain. *Science, 260,* 989–991.

Kubey, Robert, & Csikszentmihalyi, Mihaly (eds.) (1990). *Television and the quality of life: How viewing shapes everyday experiences.* Hillsdale, NJ: Erlbaum.

Kuczmarski, R. J.; Flegal, K. M; Campbell, S. M.; & Johnson, C. L. (1994). Increasing prevalence of overweight among U.S. adults: The National Health and Nutrition Examination Surveys, 1960 to 1991. *Journal of the American Medical Association, 272,* 205–211.

Kuhl, Patricia K.; Williams, Karen A.; Lacerda, Francisco; Stevens, Kenneth N.; et al. (1992, January 31). Linguistic experience alters phonetic perception in infants by 6 months of age. *Science, 255,* 606–608.

Kuhn, Deanna, & Lao, Joseph (1996). Effects of evidence on attitudes: Is polarization the norm? *Psychological Science, 7,* 115–120.

Kuhn, Deanna; Weinstock, Michael; & Flaton, Robin (1994). How well do jurors reason? Competence dimensions of individual variation in a juror reasoning task. *Psychological Science, 5,* 289–296.

Kuhn, Thomas (1981). Unanswered questions about science. In R. D. Tweney, M. E. Doherty, & C. R. Mynatt (eds.), *On scientific thinking.* New York: Columbia University Press.

Kunda, Ziva (1990). The case for motivated reasoning. *Psychological Bulletin, 108,* 480–498.

Kurtines, William M., & Gewirtz, Jacob J. (eds.) (1995). *Moral development: An introduction.* Boston: Allyn & Bacon.

LaBerge, Stephen (1986). *Lucid dreaming.* New York: Ballantine Books.

LaBerge, Stephen, & Levitan, Lynne (1995). Validity established of DreamLight cues for eliciting lucid dreaming. *Dreaming: Journal of the Association for the Study of Dreams, 5,* 159–168.

Lachman, Sheldon J. (1996). Processes in perception: Psychological transformations of highly structured stimulus material. *Perceptual and Motor Skills, 83,* 411–418.

Lader, Malcolm, & Morton, Sally (1991). Benzodiazepine problems. *British Journal of Addiction, 86,* 823–828.

LaFromboise, Teresa; Coleman, Hardin L. K.; & Gerton, Jennifer (1993). Psychological impact of biculturalism: Evidence and theory. *Psychological Bulletin, 114,* 395–412.

Laird, James D. (1974). Self-attribution of emotion: The effects of expressive behavior on the quality of emotional experience. *Journal of Personality and Social Psychology, 29,* 475–486.

Lakoff, Robin T. (1990). *Talking power.* New York: Basic Books.

Lakoff, Robin T., & Coyne, James C. (1993). *Father knows best: The use and abuse of power in Freud's case of "Dora."* New York: Teachers College Press.

Lambert, Michael J., & Bergin, Allen E. (1994). The effectiveness of psychotherapy. In A. E. Bergin & S. L. Garfield (eds.), *Handbook of psychotherapy and behavior change* (4th ed.). New York: Wiley.

Lambert, Michael J., & Hill, Clara E. (1994). Assessing psychotherapy outcomes and processes. In A. E. Bergin & S. L. Garfield (eds.), *Handbook of psychotherapy and behavior change* (4th ed.). New York: Wiley.

Land, Edwin H. (1959). Experiments in color vision. *Scientific American, 200*(5), 84–94, 96, 99.

Landrine, Hope (1988). Revising the framework of abnormal psychology. In P. Bronstein & K. Quina (eds.), *Teaching a psychology of people.* Washington, DC: American Psychological Association.

Lane, Charles (1994, December 1). The tainted sources of "The Bell Curve." *New York Review of Books,* 14–18.

Lang, Peter (1995). The emotion probe: Studies of motivation and attention. *American Psychologist, 50,* 372–385.

Langer, Ellen J. (1983). *The psychology of control.* Beverly Hills, CA: Sage.

Langer, Ellen J. (1989). *Mindfulness.* Reading, MA: Addison-Wesley.

Langer, Ellen J.; Blank, Arthur; & Chanowitz, Benzion (1978). The mindlessness of ostensibly thoughtful action: The role of placebic information in interpersonal interaction. *Journal of Personality and Social Psychology, 36,* 635–642.

Langer, Ellen J., & Piper, Alison I. (1988). Television from a mindful/mindless perspective. In S. Oskamp (ed.), *Applied social psychology annual: Vol. 8. Television as a social issue.* Newbury Park, CA: Sage.

Larmore, Kim; Ludwig, Arnold M.; & Cain, Rolene L. (1977). Multiple personality: An objective case study. *British Journal of Psychiatry, 131,* 35–40.

Lashley, Karl S. (1950). In search of the engram. In *Symposium of the Society for Experimental Biology* (Vol. 4). New York: Cambridge University Press.

Latané, Bibb, & Darley, John (1976). Help in a crisis: Bystander response to an emergency. In J. Thibaut, J. Spence, & R. Carlson (eds.), *Contemporary topics in social psychology.* Morristown, NJ: General Learning Press.

Latané, Bibb; Williams, Kipling; & Harkins, Stephen (1979). Many hands make light the work: The causes and consequences of social loafing. *Journal of Personality and Social Psychology, 37,* 822–832.

Laumann, Edward O.; Gagnon, John H.; Michael, Robert T.; & Michaels, Stuart (1994). *The social organization of sexuality.* Chicago: University of Chicago Press.

Laurence, J. R., & Perry, C. (1988). *Hypnosis, will, and memory: A psycho-legal history.* New York: Guilford Press.

Laursen, Brett, & Collins, W. Andrew (1994). Interpersonal conflict during adolescence. *Psychological Bulletin, 115,* 197–209.

Lave, J.; Murtaugh, M.; & de la Roche, O. (1984). The dialectic of arithmetic in grocery shopping. In B. Rogoff & J. Lave (eds.), *Everyday cognition: Its development in social context.* Cambridge, MA: Harvard University Press.

Lavie, Peretz (1976). Ultradian rhythms in the perception of two apparent motions. *Chronobiologia, 3,* 21–218.

Lazarus, Arnold A. (1990). If this be research. . . . *American Psychologist, 58,* 670–671.

Lazarus, Richard S. (1991). Cognition and motivation in emotion. *American Psychologist, 46,* 352–367.

Lazarus, Richard S., & Folkman, Susan (1984). *Stress, appraisal, and coping.* New York: Springer.

Lebow, Jay, & Gurman, Alan S. (1995). Research assessing couple and family therapy. *Annual Review of Psychology, 46,* 27–57.

LeDoux, Joseph E. (1994, June). Emotion, memory, and the brain. *Scientific American, 220,* 50–57.

LeDoux, Joseph E. (1996). *The emotional brain.* New York: Simon & Schuster.

Lee, Fiona; Hallahan, Mark; & Herzog, Thaddeus (1996). Explaining real-life events: How culture and domain shape attributions. *Personality and Social Psychology Bulletin, 22,* 732–741.

Lee, John Alan (1973). *The colours of love.* Ontario, Canada: New Press.

Lee, John Alan (1988). Love-styles. In R. J. Sternberg & M. L. Barnes (eds.), *The psychology of love.* New Haven, CT: Yale University Press.

Lee, Tatia M. C., & Chan, Chetwyn C. H. (1996). *Phototherapy for seasonal affective disorder: A meta-analytic review.* Paper presented at the annual meeting of the American Psychological Association, Toronto, Canada.

Lefcourt, Herbert M., & Martin, Rod A. (1986). *Humor and life stress: Antidote to adversity.* New York: Springer-Verlag.

Lehman, Adam K., & Rodin, Judith (1989). Styles of self-nurturance and disordered eating. *Journal of Consulting and Clinical Psychology, 57,* 117–122.

Lehman, Darrin R.; Lempert, Richard O.; & Nisbett, Richard E. (1988). The effects of graduate training on reasoning. *American Psychologist, 43,* 431–442.

Leibel, Rudolph L.; Rosenbaum, Michael; & Hirsch, Jules (1995). Changes in energy expenditure resulting from altered body weight. *New England Journal of Medicine, 332,* 621–628.

Lenneberg, Eric H. (1967). *Biological foundations of language.* New York: Wiley.

Lent, James R. (1968, June). Mimosa cottage: Experiment in hope. *Psychology Today,* 51–58.

Leonard, Henrietta L.; Swedo, Susan E.; Lenane, Marge C.; Rettew, David C.; et al. (1993). A 2- to 7-year follow-up study of 54 obsessive-compulsive children and adolescents. *Archives of General Psychiatry, 50*, 429–439.

Lepowsky, Maria (1994). *Fruit of the motherland: Gender in an egalitarian society.* New York: Columbia University Press.

Lepper, Mark R.; Greene, David; & Nisbett, Richard E. (1973). Undermining children's intrinsic interest with extrinsic rewards. *Journal of Personality and Social Psychology, 28*, 129–137.

Lerner, Melvin J. (1980). *The belief in a just world: A fundamental delusion.* New York: Plenum.

LeVay, Simon (1991). A difference in hypothalamic structure between heterosexual and homosexual men. *Science, 253*, 1034–1037.

Levenson, Robert W. (1992). Autonomic nervous system differences among emotions. *Psychological Science, 3*, 23–27.

Levenson, Robert W.; Carstensen, Laura L.; & Gottman, John M. (1994). Influence of age and gender on affect, physiology, and their interrelations: A study of long-term marriages. *Journal of Personality & Social Psychology, 67*, 56–68.

Levenson, Robert W.; Ekman, Paul; & Friesen, Wallace V. (1990). Voluntary facial action generates emotion-specific autonomic nervous system activity. *Psychophysiology, 27*, 363–384.

Leventhal, Howard, & Nerenz, D. R. (1982). A model for stress research and some implications for the control of stress disorders. In D. Meichenbaum & M. Jaremko (eds.), *Stress prevention and management: A cognitive behavioral approach.* New York: Plenum.

Levine, Daniel S. (1990). *Introduction to cognitive and neural modeling.* Hillsdale, NJ: Erlbaum.

Levine, Joseph, & Suzuki, David (1993). *The secret of life: Redesigning the living world.* Boston: WGBH Educational Foundation.

Levine, Robert V.; Martinez, Todd S.; Brase, Gary; & Sorenson, Kerry (1994). Helping in 36 U.S. cities. *Journal of Personality and Social Psychology, 67*, 69–82.

Levinthal, Charles F. (1988). *Messengers of paradise: Opiates and the brain.* New York: Anchor.

Levitan, Alexander A., & Ronan, William J. (1988). Problems in the treatment of obesity and eating disorders. *Medical Hypnoanalysis Journal, 3*, 131–136.

Levy, Jerre (1985, May). Right brain, left brain: Fact and fiction. *Psychology Today*, 38–39, 42–44.

Levy, Jerre; Trevarthen, Colwyn; & Sperry, Roger W. (1972). Perception of bilateral chimeric figures following hemispheric deconnection. *Brain, 95*, 61–78.

Levy, Robert I. (1984). The emotions in comparative perspective. In K. R. Scherer & P. Ekman (eds.), *Approaches to emotion.* Hillsdale, NJ: Erlbaum.

Lewin, Kurt (1948). *Resolving social conflicts.* New York: Harper.

Lewis, Dorothy O. (ed.) (1981). *Vulnerabilities to delinquency.* New York: Spectrum Medical and Scientific Books.

Lewis, Helen B. (1971). *Shame and guilt in neurosis.* New York: International Universities Press.

Lewis, Marc D. (1993). Early socioemotional predictors of cognitive competency at 4 years. *Developmental Psychology, 29*, 1036–1045.

Lewis, Michael (1992). *Shame: The exposed self.* New York: Free Press.

Lewontin, Richard C. (1970). Race and intelligence. *Bulletin of the Atomic Scientists, 26*(3), 2–8.

Lewontin, Richard C. (1982). *Human diversity.* New York: Scientific American Library.

Lewontin, Richard C. (1993). *Biology as ideology: The doctrine of DNA.* New York: HarperPerennial.

Lewontin, Richard C.; Rose, Steven; & Kamin, Leon J. (1984). *Not in our genes: Biology, ideology, and human nature.* New York: Pantheon.

Lewy, Alfred J.; Ahmed, Saeeduddin; Jackson, Jeanne L.; & Sack, Robert L. (1992). Melatonin shifts human circadian rhythms according to a phase response curve. *Chronobiology International, 9*, 380–392.

Lewy, Alfred J.; Ahmed, Saeeduddin; & Sack, Robert L. (1996). Phase shifting the human circadian clock using melatonin. *Behavior and Brain Research, 73*, 131–134.

Lewy, Alfred J.; Sack, Robert L.; Miller, L. Steven; & Hoban, Tana M. (1987). Antidepressant and circadian phase-shifting effects of light. *Science, 235*, 352–354.

Lichtenstein, Sarah; Slovic, Paul; Fischhoff, Baruch; Layman, Mark; & Combs, Barbara (1978). Judged frequency of lethal events. *Journal of Experimental Psychology: Human Learning and Memory, 4*, 551–578.

Liddle, Howard A. (1995). Conceptual and clinical dimensions of multidimensional, multisystems engagement strategy in family-based adolescent treatment. [Special Issue: Adolescent treatment: New frontiers and new dimensions.] *Psychotherapy, 32*, 39–58.

Lightdale, Jenifer R., & Prentice, Deborah A. (1994). Rethinking sex differences in aggression: Aggressive behavior in the absence of social roles. *Personality and Social Psychology Bulletin, 20*, 34–44.

Lightfoot, Lynn O. (1980). *Behavioral tolerance to low doses of alcohol in social drinkers.* Unpublished doctoral dissertation, University of Waterloo, Waterloo, Ontario.

Likona, Thomas (1983). *Raising good children.* New York: Bantam.

Lilienfeld, Scott O. (1993, Fall). Do "honesty" tests really measure honesty? *Skeptical Inquirer, 18*, 32–41.

Lin, Keh-Ming; Poland, Russell E.; & Chien, C. P. (1990). Ethnicity and psychopharmacology: Recent findings and future research directions. In E. Sorel (ed.), *Family, culture, and psychobiology.* New York: Legas.

Lin, Keh-Ming; Poland, Russell E.; Nuccio, Inocencia; Matsuda, Kazuko; et al. (1989). A longitudinal assessment of haloperidol doses and serum concentrations in Asian and Caucasian schizophrenic patients. *American Journal of Psychiatry, 146*, 1307–1311.

Linday, Linda A. (1994). Maternal reports of pregnancy, genital, and related fantasies in preschool and kindergarten children. *Journal of the American Academy of Child and Adolescent Psychiatry, 33*, 416–423.

Lindsay, D. Stephen, & Read, J. Don (1995). "Memory work" and recovered memories of childhood sexual abuse: Scientific evidence and public, professional, and personal issues. *Psychology, Public Policy, and the Law, 1*, 846–908.

Lindvall, O.; Sawle, G.; Widner, H.; et al. (1994). Evidence for long-term survival and function of dopaminergic grafts in progressive Parkinson's disease. *Annals of Neurology, 35*, 172–180.

Linton, Marigold (1978). Real-world memory after six years: An in vivo study of very long-term memory. In M. M. Gruneberg, P. E. Morris, & R. N. Sykes (eds.), *Practical aspects of memory.* London: Academic Press.

Linz, Daniel; Donnerstein, Edward; & Penrod, Steven (1988). The effects of long-term exposure to violent and sexually degrading depictions of women. *Journal of Personality and Social Psychology, 55*, 758–767.

Lipman-Blumen, Jean (1994). The existential bases of power relationships: The gender role case. In H. L. Radtke & H. J. Stam (eds.), *Power/gender social relations in theory and practice.* London: Sage.

Lipsey, Mark W., & Wilson, David B. (1993). The efficacy of psychological, educational, and behavioral treatment: Confirmation from meta-analysis. *American Psychologist, 48*, 1181–1209.

Lipstadt, Deborah E. (1993). *Denying the Holocaust: The growing assault on truth and memory.* New York: Free Press.

Lipstadt, Deborah E. (1994, Spring). Denying the Holocaust: The fragility of memory. *Brandeis Review*, 30–33.

Lissner, L.; Odell, P. M.; D'Agostino, R. B.; Stokes, J., III; et al. (1991, June 27). Variability of body weight and health outcomes in the Framingham population. *New England Journal of Medicine, 324* (26), 1839–1844.

Locke, Edwin A., & Latham, Gary P. (1990). Work motivation and satisfaction: Light at the end of the tunnel. *Psychological Science, 1*, 240–246.

Locke, Edwin A., & Latham, Gary P. (1991). The fallacies of common sense "truths": A reply to Lamal. *Psychological Science, 2*, 131–132.

Locke, Edwin A.; Shaw, Karyll; Saari, Lise; & Latham, Gary (1981). Goal-setting and task performance: 1969–1980. *Psychological Bulletin, 90*, 125–152.

Loehlin, John C. (1992). *Genes and environment in personality development.* Newbury Park CA: Sage.

Loehlin, John C.,: Horn, J. M.; & Willerman, L. (1996). Heredity, environment, and IQ in the Texas adoption study. In R. J. Sternberg & E. Grigorenko (eds.), *Intelligence: Heredity and environment.* New York: Cambridge University Press.

Loewen, E. Ruth; Shaw, Raymond J.; & Craik, Fergus I. (1990). Age differences in components of metamemory. *Experimental Aging Research, 16*(1–2), 43–48.

Loftus, Elizabeth F. (1980). *Memory.* Reading, MA: Addison-Wesley.

Loftus, Elizabeth F. (1995). *Memories of childhood trauma or traumas of childhood memory.* Paper presented at the annual meeting of the American Psychological Association, New York.

Loftus, Elizabeth F., & Greene, Edith (1980). Warning: Even memory for faces may be contagious. *Law and Human Behavior, 4,* 323–334.

Loftus, Elizabeth F., & Ketcham, Katherine (1994). *The myth of repressed memory.* New York: St. Martin's Press.

Loftus, Elizabeth F.; Miller, David G.; & Burns, Helen J. (1978). Semantic integration of verbal information into a visual memory. *Journal of Experimental Psychology: Human Learning and Memory, 4,* 19–31.

Loftus, Elizabeth F., & Palmer, John C. (1974). Reconstruction of automobile destruction: An example of the interaction between language and memory. *Journal of Verbal Learning and Verbal Behavior, 13,* 585–589.

Loftus, Elizabeth F., & Pickrell, Jacqueline E. (1995). The formation of false memories. [Special Issue on false memories.] *Psychiatric Annals, 25,* 720–725.

Loftus, Elizabeth F., & Zanni, Guido (1975). Eyewitness testimony: The influence of the wording of a question. *Bulletin of the Psychonomic Society, 5,* 86–88.

Loftus, Geoffrey R. (1993). A picture is worth a thousand *p* values: On the irrelevance of hypothesis testing in the microcomputer age. *Behavior Research Methods, Instruments & Computers, 25,* 150–156.

Lonner, Walter J. (1995). Culture and human diversity. In E. Trickett, R. Watts, & D. Birman (eds.), *Human diversity: Perspectives on people in context.* San Francisco: Jossey-Bass.

Lonner, Walter J., & Malpass, Roy S. (1994). When psychology and culture meet: An introduction to cross-cultural psychology. In W. J. Lonner & R. S. Malpass (eds.), *Psychology and culture.* Needham Heights, MA: Allyn & Bacon.

Loo, Chalsa M. (1991). *An integrative-sequential treatment model for post-traumatic stress disorder: A case study of the Japanese American internment and redress.* Paper presented at the annual meeting of the American Psychological Association, San Francisco.

López, Steven R. (1989). Patient variable biases in clinical judgment: Conceptual overview and methodological considerations. *Psychological Bulletin, 106,* 184–203.

López, Steven R. (1995). Testing ethnic minority children. In B. B. Wolman (ed.), *The encyclopedia of psychology, psychiatry, and psychoanalysis.* New York: Henry Holt.

Lord, C. G.; Ross, L.; & Lepper, M. R. (1979). Biased assimilation and attitude polarization: The effects of prior theories on subsequently considered evidence. *Journal of Personality and Social Psychology, 37,* 2098–2109.

Lott, Bernice, & Maluso, Diane (1993). The social learning of gender. In A. E. Beall & R. J. Sternberg (eds.), *The psychology of gender.* New York: Guilford Press.

Lottes, Ilsa L., & Kuriloff, Peter J. (1994). Sexual socialization differences by gender, Greek membership, and religious background. *Psychology of Women Quarterly, 18,* 203–219.

Lovaas, O. Ivar (1977). *The autistic child: Language development through behavior modification.* New York: Halsted Press.

Lovaas, O. Ivar; Schreibman, Laura; & Koegel, Robert L. (1974). A behavior modification approach to the treatment of autistic children. *Journal of Autism and Childhood Schizophrenia, 4,* 111–129.

Luce, Gay Gaer, & Segal, Julius (1966). *Current research on sleep and dreams.* Bethesda, MD: U.S. Department of Health, Education, and Welfare.

Luengo, M. A.; Carrillo-de-la-Peña, M. T.; Otero, J. M.; & Romero, E. (1994). A short-term longitudinal study of impulsivity and antisocial behavior. *Journal of Personality and Social Psychology, 66,* 542–548.

Luepnitz, Deborah A. (1988). *The family interpreted: Feminist theory in clinical practice.* New York: Basic Books.

Lugaresi, Elio; Medori, R.; Montagna, P.; et al. (1986, October 16). Fatal familial insomnia and dysautonomia with selective degeneration of thalamic nuclei. *New England Journal of Medicine, 315,* 997–1003.

Luria, Alexander (1968). *The mind of a mnemonist* (L. Soltaroff, trans.). New York: Basic Books.

Luria, Alexander R. (1980). *Higher cortical functions in man* (2nd rev. ed.). New York: Basic Books.

Lutz, Catherine (1988). *Unnatural emotions.* Chicago: University of Chicago Press.

Lyketsos, C. G.; Hoover, D. R.; Guccione, M.; Senterfitt, W.; et al. (1993). Depressive symptoms as predictors of medical outcomes in HIV infection: Multicenter AIDS Cohort Study. *Journal of the American Medical Association, 270,* 2563–2567.

Lykken, David T. (1981). *A tremor in the blood: Uses and abuses of the lie detector.* New York: McGraw-Hill.

Lykken, David T. (1991). The lie detector controversy: An alternative solution. In J. R. Jennings, P. K. Ackles, & M. G. H. Coles (eds.), *Advances in psychophysiology.* London: Jessica Kingsley Publishers.

Lykken, David, & Tellegen, Auke (1996). Happiness is a stochastic phenomenon. *Psychological Science, 7,* 186–189.

Lynch, James J. (1985). *Language of the heart: The body's response to human dialogue.* New York: Basic Books.

Lynn, Steven Jay; Rhue, Judith W.; & Weekes, John R. (1990). Hypnotic involuntariness: A social cognitive analysis. *Psychological Review, 97,* 69–184.

Lytton, Hugh, & Romney, David M. (1991). Parents' differential socialization of boys and girls: A meta-analysis. *Psychological Bulletin, 109,* 267–296.

Maccoby, Eleanor E. (1990). Gender and relationships: A developmental account. *American Psychologist, 45,* 513–520.

MacCoun, Robert J., & Kerr, Norbert L. (1988). Asymmetric influence in mock jury deliberation: Jurors' bias for leniency. *Journal of Personality and Social Psychology, 54,* 21–33.

MacDonald, N. E.; Wells, G. A.; Fisher, W. A.; Warren, W. K; et al. (1990). High risk STD/HIV behavior among college students. *Journal of the American Medical Association, 263,* 3155–3159.

MacKavey, William R.; Malley, Janet E.; & Stewart, Abigail, J. (1991). Remembering autobiographically consequential experiences: Content analysis of psychologists' accounts of their lives. *Psychology and Aging, 6,* 50–59.

Mackenzie, Brian (1984). Explaining race differences in IQ: The logic, the methodology, and the evidence. *American Psychologist, 39,* 1214–1233.

MacKinnon, Donald W. (1962). The nature and nurture of creative talent. *American Psychologist, 17,* 484–495.

MacKinnon, Donald W. (1968). Selecting students with creative potential. In P. Heist (ed.), *The creative college student: An unmet challenge.* San Francisco: Jossey-Bass.

MacLean, Paul (1993). Cerebral evolution of emotion. In M. Lewis & J. M. Haviland (eds.), *Handbook of emotions.* New York: Guilford Press.

Macrae, C. Neil; Milne, Alan B.; & Bodenhausen, Galen V. (1994). Stereotypes as energy-saving devices: A peek inside the cognitive toolbox. *Journal of Personality and Social Psychology, 66,* 37–47.

Maddux, James E. (1993, Summer). The mythology of psychopathology: A social cognitive view of deviance, difference, and disorder. *The General Psychologist, 29,* 34–45.

Maddux, James E. (ed.) (1995). *Self-efficacy, adaptation, and adjustment: Theory, research, and application.* New York: Plenum.

Maddux, James E. (1996). The social-cognitive construction of difference and disorder. In D. F. Barone, J. E. Maddux, & C. R. Snyder (eds.), *Social cognitive psychology: History and current domains.* New York: Plenum.

Maddux, James E., & Mundell, Clare E. (1997). Disorders of personality. In V. Derlega, B. Winstead, & W. Jones (eds.), *Personality: Contemporary theory and research* (2nd ed.). Chicago: Nelson-Hall.

Maffei, M.; Halaas, J.; Ravussin, E.; et al. (1995). Leptin levels in human and rodent: Measurement of plasma leptin and ob RNA in obese and weight-reduced subjects. *Nature Medicine, 1,* 1155–1161.

Mahoney, Michael J. (1991). *Human change processes: The scientific foundations of psychotherapy.* New York: Basic Books.

Mairs, Nancy (1986). *Plaintext: Deciphering a woman's life.* New York: Harper & Row.

Malamuth, Neil, & Dean, Karol (1990). Attraction to sexual aggression. In A. Parrot & L. Bechhofer (eds.), *Acquaintance rape: The hidden crime.* Newark, NJ: Wiley.

Malamuth, Neil M.; Linz, Daniel; Heavey, Christopher L.; Barnes, Gordon; & Acker, Michele (1995). Using the confluence model of sexual aggression to predict men's conflict with women: A 10-year follow-up study. *Journal of Personality and Social Psychology, 69,* 353–369.

Malamuth, Neil M.; Sockloskie, Robert J.; Koss, Mary P.; & Tanaka, J. S. (1991). Characteristics of aggressors against women: Testing a model using a national sample of college students. [Special Section: Theories of sexual aggression.] *Journal of Consulting and Clinical Psychology, 59,* 670–681.

Malarkey, William B.; Kiecolt-Glaser, Janice K.; Pearl, Dennis; & Glaser, Ronald (1994). Hostile behavior during marital conflict alters pituitary and adrenal hormones. *Psychosomatic Medicine, 56*, 41–51.

Malatesta, Carol Z. (1990). The role of emotions in the development and organization of personality. In R. A. Thompson (ed.), *Socioemotional development: Nebraska Symposium on Motivation, 1988*. Lincoln: University of Nebraska Press.

Malgady, Robert G.; Rogler, Lloyd; & Costantino, Giuseppe (1987). Ethnocultural and linguistic bias in mental health evaluation of Hispanics. *American Psychologist, 42*, 228–234.

Maling, Michael S., & Howard, Kenneth I. (1994). From research to practice to research to. . . . In P. F. Talley, H. H. Strupp, & S. F. Butler (eds.), *Psychotherapy research and practice: Bridging the gap*. New York: Basic Books.

Malinosky-Rummell, Robin, & Hansen, David J. (1993). Long-term consequences of childhood physical abuse. *Psychological Bulletin, 114*, 68–79.

Malitz, Sidney, & Sackeim, Harold A. (eds.) (1986). *Electroconvulsive therapy: Clinical and basic research issues*. New York: New York Academy of Sciences.

Manning, Carol A.; Hall, J. L.; & Gold, Paul E. (1990). Glucose effects on memory and other neuropsychological tests in elderly humans. *Psychological Science, 1*, 307–311.

Manning, Carol A.; Ragozzino, Michael E.; & Gold, Paul E. (1993). Glucose enhancement of memory in patients with probable senile dementia of the Alzheimer's type. *Neurobiology of Aging, 14*, 523–528.

Manuck, Stephen B.; Cohen, Sheldon; Rabin, Bruce S.; Muldoon, Matthew F.; & Bachen, Elizabeth A. (1991). Individual differences in cellular immune response to stress. *Psychological Science, 2*, 111–115.

Manyande, Anne; Chayen, Susan; Priyakumar, Pooma; Smith, Christopher C.; et al. (1992). Anxiety and endocrine responses to surgery: Paradoxical effects of preoperative relaxation training. *Psychosomatic Medicine, 54*, 275–287.

Marcus, Gary F.; Pinker, Steven; Ullman, Michael; Hollander, Michelle; et al. (1992). Overregularization in language acquisition. *Monographs of the Society for Research in Child Development, 57* (Serial No. 228), 1–182.

Margo, Geoffrey M.; Greenberg, Roger P.; Fisher, Seymour; & Dewan, Mantosh (1993). A direct comparison of the defense mechanisms of nondepressed people and depressed psychiatric inpatients. *Comprehensive Psychiatry, 34*, 65–69.

Mark, Daniel (1994). Paper presented to the annual meeting of the Society of Behavioral Medicine, Boston.

Markowitz, Laura M. (1993, July/August). Walking the walk. *The Family Therapy Networker*, 19–31.

Marks, Gary, & Miller, Norman (1987). Ten years of research on the false-consensus effect: An empirical and theoretical review. *Psychological Bulletin, 102*, 72–90.

Markus, Hazel R., & Kitayama, Shinobu (1991). Culture and the self: Implications for cognition, emotion, and motivation. *Psychological Review, 98*, 224–253.

Marlatt, G. Alan (1996). Models of relapse and relapse prevention: A commentary. *Experimental and Clinical Psychopharmacology, 4*, 55–60.

Marlatt, G. Alan, & Rohsenow, Damaris J. (1980). Cognitive processes in alcohol use: Expectancy and the balanced placebo design. In N. K. Mello (ed.), *Advances in substance abuse* (Vol. 1). Greenwich, CT: JAI Press.

Marriott, Bernadette M. (ed.) (1994). *Food components to enhance performance*. Washington, DC: National Academy Press.

Marshall, Grant N. (1991). A multidimensional analysis of internal health locus of control beliefs: Separating the wheat from the chaff? *Journal of Personality and Social Psychology, 61*, 483–491.

Marshall, Grant N.; Wortman, Camille B.; Vickers, Ross R., Jr.; Kusulas, Jeffrey W.; & Hervig, Linda K. (1994). The five-factor model of personality as a framework for personality health research. *Journal of Personality and Social Psychology, 67*, 278–286.

Martin, Emily (1987). *The woman in the body: A cultural analysis of reproduction*. Boston: Beacon Press.

Martin, Rod A.; & Dobbin, James P. (1988). Sense of humor, hassles, and immunoglobulin A: Evidence for a stress-moderating effect of humor. *International Journal of Psychiatry in Medicine, 18*, 93–105.

Maslach, Christina; Stapp, Joy; & Santee, Richard T. (1985). Individuation: Conceptual analysis and assessment. *Journal of Personality and Social Psychology, 49*, 729–738.

Maslow, Abraham H. (1954/1970). *Motivation and personalit* (1st and 2nd eds.). New York: Harper & Row.

Maslow, Abraham H. (1971). *The farther reaches of human nature*. New York: Viking.

Masters, William H., & Johnson, Virginia E. (1966). *Human sexual response*. Boston: Little, Brown.

Matarazzo, Joseph (1984). Behavioral immunogens and pathogens in health and illness. In B. L. Hammonds & C. J. Scheirer (eds.), *Psychology and health: The master lecture series* (Vol. 3). Washington, DC: American Psychological Association.

Matson, Johnny L., & Ollendick, Thomas H. (1977). Issues in toilet training normal children. *Behavior Therapy, 8*, 549–553.

Matsumoto, David (1996). *Culture and psychology*. Pacific Grove, CA: Brooks-Cole.

Matthews, John (ed.) (1994). *McGill working papers in linguistics* (Vol. 10 [1&2]). [Special Issue: Linguistic aspects of familial language impairment.] Montreal, Quebec: McGill University.

Matthews, Karen A.; Wing, Rena R.; Kuller, Lewis H.; Meilahn, Elaine N.; et al. (1990). Influences of natural menopause on psychological characteristics and symptoms of middle-aged healthy women. *Journal of Consulting and Clinical Psychology, 58*, 345–351.

Mawhinney, T. C. (1990). Decreasing intrinsic "motivation" with extrinsic rewards: Easier said than done. *Journal of Organizational Behavior Management, 11*, 175–191.

May, Cynthia P.; Hasher, Lynn; & Stoltzfus, Ellen R. (1993). Optimal time of day and the magnitude of age differences in memory. *Psychological Science, 4*, 326–330.

Mayer, John D.; McCormick, Laura J.; & Strong, Sara E. (1995). Mood-congruent memory and natural mood: New evidence. *Personality and Social Psychology Bulletin, 21*, 736–746.

Mayer, John D., & Salovey, Peter (1997). What is emotional intelligence? In P. Salovey & D. Sluyter (eds.), *Emotional development and emotional intelligence: Implications for educators*. New York: Basic Books.

Mazur, Allen, & Lamb, Theodore A. (1980). Testosterone, status, and mood in human males. *Hormones and Behavior, 14*, 236–246.

Mazza, James J.; Reynolds, William M.; & Grover, Jennifer H. (1995). *Exposure to violence, suicidal ideation and depression in school-based adolescents*. Paper presented at the annual meeting of the American Psychological Association, New York.

McAdams, Dan P. (1988). *Power, intimacy, and the life story: Personological inquiries into identity*. New York: Guilford Press.

McAdams, Dan P. (1992). The five-factor model in personality: A critical appraisal. [Special Issue: The five-factor model: Issues and applications.] *Journal of Personality, 60*, 329–361.

McCartney, Kathleen; Harris, Monica J.; & Bernieri, Frank (1990). Growing up and growing apart: A developmental meta-analysis of twin studies. *Psychological Bulletin, 107*, 226–237.

McCauley, Elizabeth, & Ehrhardt, Anke (1980). Female sexual response. In D. D. Youngs & A. Ehrhardt (eds.), *Psychosomatic obstetrics and gynecology*. New York: Appleton-Century-Crofts.

McClearn, Gerald E. (1993). Behavioral genetics: The last century and the next. In R. Plomin & G. E. McClearn (eds.), *Nature, nurture, and psychology*. Washington, DC: American Psychological Association.

McClelland, David C. (1961). *The achieving society*. New York: Free Press.

McClelland, David (1975). *Power: The inner experience*. New York: Irvington.

McClelland, David (1985). *Human motivation*. Glenview, IL: Scott, Foresman.

McClelland, David C. (1987). Characteristics of successful entrepreneurs. *Journal of Creative Behavior, 3*, 219–233.

McClelland, David C.; Atkinson, John W.; Clark, Russell A.; & Lowell, Edgar L. (1953). *The achievement motive*. New York: Appleton-Century-Crofts.

McClelland, James L. (1994). The organization of memory: A parallel distributed processing perspective. *Revue Neurologique, 150*, 570–579.

McCloskey, Michael; Wible, Cynthia G.; & Cohen, Neal J. (1988). Is there a special flashbulb-memory mechanism? *Journal of Experimental Psychology: General, 117*, 171–181.

McConnell, James V. (1962). Memory transfer through cannibalism in planarians. *Journal of Neuropsychiatry, 3* (Monograph Supplement 1).

McCord, Joan (1989). *Another time, another drug.* Paper presented at the conference, Vulnerability to the Transition from Drug Use to Abuse and Dependence, Rockville, MD.

McCord, Joan (1990). Crime in moral and social contexts. *Criminology, 28,* 1–26.

McCord, Joan (1991). Questioning the value of punishment. *Social Problems, 38,* 167–179.

McCrae, Robert R. (1987). Creativity, divergent thinking, and openness to experience. *Journal of Personality and Social Psychology, 52,* 1258–1265.

McCrae, Robert R. (1993). Moderated analyses of longitudinal personality stability. *Journal of Personality and Social Psychology, 65,* 577–585.

McCrae, Robert R., & Costa, Paul T., Jr. (1988). Do parental influences matter? A reply to Halverson. *Journal of Personality, 56,* 445–449.

McCrae, Robert R., & Costa, Paul T., Jr. (1996). Toward a new generation of personality theories: Theoretical contexts for the five-factor model. In J. S. Wiggins (ed.), *The five-factor model of personality: Theoretical perspectives.* New York: Guilford Press.

McDonough, Laraine, & Mandler, Jean M. (1994). Very long-term recall in infancy. *Memory, 2,* 339–352.

McEwen, Bruce S. (1983). Gonadal steroid influences on brain development and sexual differentiation. *Reproductive Physiology IV (International Review of Physiology), 27,* 99–145.

McFarlane, Jessica; Martin, Carol L.; & Williams, Tannis M. (1988). Mood fluctuations: Women versus men and menstrual versus other cycles. *Psychology of Women Quarterly, 12,* 201–223.

McFarlane, Jessica M., & Williams, Tannis M. (1994). Placing premenstrual syndrome in perspective. *Psychology of Women Quarterly, 18,* 339–373.

McGaugh, James L. (1990). Significance and remembrance: The role of neuromodulatory systems. *Psychological Science, 1,* 15–25.

McGinnis, Michael, & Foege, William (1993, November 10). Actual causes of death in the United States. *Journal of the American Medical Association, 270,* 2207–2212.

McGlone, Jeannette (1978). Sex differences in functional brain asymmetry. *Cortex, 14,* 122–128.

McGlynn, Susan M. (1990). Behavioral approaches to neuropsychological rehabilitation. *Psychological Bulletin, 108,* 420–441.

McGoldrick, Monica; & Gerson, Randy. (1985). *Genograms in family assessment.* New York: Norton.

McGoldrick, Monica; Pearce, John K.; & Giordano, J. (eds.) (1982). *Ethnicity and family therapy.* New York: Guilford Press.

McGrath, Ellen; Keita, Gwendolyn P.; Strickland, Bonnie; & Russo, Nancy F. (eds.) (1990). *Women and depression: Risk factors and treatment issues.* Washington, DC: American Psychological Association.

McGue, Matt; Bouchard, Thomas J., Jr.; Iacono, William G.; & Lykken, David T. (1993). Behavioral genetics of cognitive ability: A life-span perspective. In R. Plomin & G. E. McLearn (eds.), *Nature, nurture, and psychology.* Washington, DC: American Psychological Association.

McGue, Matt, & Lykken, David T. (1992). Genetic influence on risk of divorce. *Psychological Science, 3,* 368–373.

McGue, Matt; Pickens, Roy W.; & Svikis, Dace S. (1992). Sex and age effects on the inheritance of alcohol problems: A twin study. *Journal of Abnormal Psychology, 101,* 3–17.

McGuinness, Diane (1993). Sex differences in cognitive style: Implications for math performance and achievement. In L. A. Penner, G. M. Batsche, & H. Knoff (eds.), *The challenge in mathematics and science education: Psychology's response.* Washington, DC: American Psychological Association.

McHugh, Paul R. (1993a). *History and the pitfalls of practice.* Unpublished paper, Johns Hopkins University.

McHugh, Paul R. (1993b, December). Psychotherapy awry. *American Scholar,* 17–30.

McKee, Richard D., & Squire, Larry R. (1992). Equivalent forgetting rates in long-term memory for diencephalic and medical temporal lobe amnesia. *Journal of Neuroscience, 12,* 3765–3772.

McKee, Richard D., & Squire, Larry R. (1993). On the development of declarative memory. *Journal of Experimental Psychology: Learning, Memory, and Cognition, 19,* 397–404.

McKinlay, John B.; McKinlay, Sonja M.; & Brambilla, Donald (1987). The relative contributions of endocrine changes and social circumstances to depression in mid-aged women. *Journal of Health and Social Behavior, 28,* 345–363.

McLeod, Beverly (1985, March). Real work for real pay. *Psychology Today,* 42–44, 46, 48–50.

McNally, Richard J. (1994). *Panic disorder: A critical analysis.* New York: Guilford Press.

McNaughton, B. L., & Morris, R. G. M. (1987). Hippocampal synaptic enhancement and information storage within a distributed memory system. *Trends in Neuroscience, 10,* 408–415.

McNeill, David (1966). Developmental psycholinguistics. In F. L. Smith & G. A. Miller (eds.), *The genesis of language: A psycholinguistic approach.* Cambridge, MA: MIT Press.

Mealey, Linda (1996). Evolutionary psychology: The search for evolved mental mechanisms underlying complex human behavior. In J. P. Hurd (ed.), *Investigating the biological foundations of human morality* (Vol. 37). Lewiston, NY: Edwin Mellen Press.

Medawar, Peter B. (1979). *Advice to a young scientist.* New York: Harper & Row.

Medawar, Peter B. (1982). *Pluto's republic.* Oxford, England: Oxford University Press.

Mednick, Martha T. (1989). On the politics of psychological constructs: Stop the bandwagon, I want to get off. *American Psychologist, 44,* 1118–1123.

Mednick, Sarnoff A. (1962). The associative basis of the creative process. *Psychological Review, 69,* 220–232.

Mednick, Sarnoff A.; Huttunen, Matti O.; & Machón, Ricardo (1994). Prenatal influenza infections and adult schizophrenia. *Schizophrenia Bulletin, 20,* 263–267.

Mednick, Sarnoff A.; Parnas, Josef; & Schulsinger, Fini (1987). The Copenhagen High-Risk Project, 1962–86. *Schizophrenia Bulletin, 13,* 485–495.

Medvec, Victoria H.; Madey, Scott F.; & Gilovich, Thomas (1995). When less is more: Counterfactual thinking and satisfaction among Olympic medalists. *Journal of Personality and Social Psychology, 69,* 603–610.

Meeus, Wim H. J., & Raaijmakers, Quinten A.W. (1995). Obedience in modern society: The Utrecht studies. In A.G. Miller, B. E. Collins, & D. E. Brief (eds.), *Perspectives on obedience to authority: The legacy of the Milgram experiments. Journal of Social Issues, 51*(3), 155–175.

Meltzoff, Andrew N., & Gopnik, Alison (1993). The role of imitation in understanding persons and developing a theory of mind. In S. Baron-Cohen, H. Tager-Flusberg, & D. Cohen (eds.), *Understanding other minds.* New York: Oxford University Press.

Melzack, Ronald (1973). *The puzzle of pain.* New York: Basic Books.

Melzack, Ronald, & Wall, Patrick D. (1965). Pain mechanisms: A new theory. *Science, 13,* 971–979.

Mercer, Jane (1988, May 18). *Racial differences in intelligence: Fact or artifact?* Talk given at San Bernardino Valley College, San Bernardino, CA.

Merikle, Philip M., & Skanes, Heather E. (1992). Subliminal self-help audiotapes: A search for placebo effects. *Journal of Applied Psychology, 77,* 772–776.

Merskey, Harold (1992). The manufacture of personalities: The production of MPD. *British Journal of Psychiatry, 160,* 327–340.

Merskey, Harold (1994). The artifactual nature of multiple personality disorder. *Dissociation, VII,* 173–175.

Merskey, Harold (1995). The manufacture of personalities: The production of multiple personality disorder. In L. M. Cohen, J. N. Berzoff, & M. R. Elin (eds.), *Dissociative identity disorder: Theoretical and treatment controversies.* Northvale, NJ: Jason Aronson.

Mesquita, Batja, & Frijda, Nico H. (1993). Cultural variations in emotions: A review. *Psychological Bulletin, 112,* 179–204.

Metalsky, Gerald I.; Joiner, Thomas E., Jr.; Hardin, Tammy S.; & Abramson, Lyn Y. (1993). Depressive reactions to failure in a naturalistic setting: A test of the hopelessness and self-esteem theories of depression. *Journal of Abnormal Psychology, 102,* 101–109.

Meyer-Bahlburg, Heino F. L.; Ehrhardt, Anke A.; Rosen, Laura R.; Gruen, Rhoda S.; Veridiano, Norma P.; Vann, Felix H.; & Neuwalder, Herbert F. (1995). Prenatal estrogens and the development of homosexual orientation. *Developmental Psychology, 31,* 12–21.

Meyerowitz, Beth E., & Chaiken, Shelley (1987). The effect of message framing on breast self-examination attitudes, intentions, and behavior. *Journal of Personality and Social Psychology, 52,* 500–510.

Middlebrooks, John C.; Clock, Ann E.; Xu, Li; & Green, David M. (1994). A panoramic code for sound location by cortical neurons. *Science, 264,* 842–844.

Mikulincer, Mario (1995). Attachment style and the mental representations of the self. *Journal of Personality and Social Psychology, 69,* 1203–1215.

Milavsky, J. Ronald (1988). Television and aggression once again. In S. Oskamp (ed.), *Applied social psychology annual: Vol. 8. Television as a social issue.* Newbury Park, CA: Sage.

Milgram, Stanley (1963). Behavioral study of obedience. *Journal of Abnormal and Social Psychology, 67,* 371–378.

Milgram, Stanley (1974). *Obedience to authority: An experimental view.* New York: Harper & Row.

Millar, Keith, & Watkinson, Neal (1983). Recognition of words presented during general anaesthesia. *Ergonomics, 26,* 585–594.

Miller, Arthur G.; McHoskey, John W.; Bane, Cynthia M.; & Dowd, Timothy G. (1993). The attitude polarization phenomenon: Role of response measure, attitude extremity, and behavioral consequences of reported attitude change. *Journal of Personality and Social Psychology, 64,* 561–574.

Miller, George A. (1956). The magical number seven, plus or minus two: Some limits on our capacity for processing information. *Psychological Review, 63,* 81–97.

Miller, George A. (1969, December). On turning psychology over to the unwashed. *Psychology Today,* 53–55, 66–68, 70, 72, 74.

Miller, Inglis J., & Reedy, Frank E. (1990). Variations in human taste bud density and taste intensity perception. *Physiology and Behavior, 47,* 1213–1219.

Miller, Joan G. (1984). Culture and the development of everyday social explanation. *Journal of Personality and Social Psychology, 46,* 961–978.

Miller, Jonathan (1983). *States of mind.* New York: Pantheon.

Miller, Neal E. (1978). Biofeedback and visceral learning. *Annual Review of Psychology, 29,* 421–452.

Miller, Neal E. (1985). The value of behavioral research on animals. *American Psychologist, 40,* 423–440.

Miller, Paul A., & Eisenberg, Nancy (1988). The relation of empathy to aggressive and externalizing/antisocial behavior. *Psychological Bulletin, 103,* 324–344.

Miller, Richard L.; Brickman, Philip; & Bolen, Diana (1975). Attribution versus persuasion as a means for modifying behavior. *Journal of Personality and Social Psychology, 31,* 430–441.

Miller, Scott D., & Triggiano, Patrick J. (1992). The psychophysiological investigation of multiple personality disorder: Review and update. *American Journal of Clinical Hypnosis, 35,* 47–61.

Miller, Suzanne M.; Brody, David; & Summerton, Jeffrey (1988). Styles of coping with threat: Implications for health. *Journal of Personality and Social Psychology, 54,* 142–148.

Miller, Suzanne M.; Shoda, Yuichi; & Hurley, Karen (1996). Applying cognitive-social theory to health-protective behavior: Breast self-examination in cancer screening. *Psychological Bulletin, 119,* 70–94.

Miller, Todd Q.; Smith, Timothy W.; Turner, Charles W.; Guijarro, Margarita L.; & Hallet, Amanda J. (1996). A meta-analytic review of research on hostility and physical health. *Psychological Bulletin, 119,* 322–348.

Miller-Jones, Dalton (1989). Culture and testing. *American Psychologist, 44,* 360–366.

Milner, Brenda (1970). Memory and the temporal regions of the brain. In K. H. Pribram & D. E. Broadbent (eds.), *Biology of memory.* New York: Academic Press.

Milner, J. S., & McCanne, T. R. (1991). Neuropsychological correlates of physical child abuse. In J. S. Milner (ed.), *Neuropsychology of aggression.* Norwell, MA: Kluwer Academic.

Minuchin, Salvador (1984). *Family kaleidoscope.* Cambridge, MA: Harvard University Press.

Mischel, Walter (1973). Toward a cognitive social learning reconceptualization of personality. *Psychological Review, 80,* 252–253.

Mischel, Walter, & Shoda, Yuichi (1995). A cognitive affective system theory of personality: Reconceptualizing situations, dispositions, dynamics, and invariance in personality structures. *Psychological Review, 102,* 246–268.

Mishkin, Mortimer, & Appenzeller, Tim (1987). The anatomy of memory. *Scientific American, 256,* 80–89.

Mistlberger, Ralph E. (1991). Scheduled daily exercise or feeding alters the phase of photic entrainment in Syrian hamsters. *Physiology and Behavior, 50,* 1257–1260.

Mistry, Jayanthi, & Rogoff, Barbara (1994). Remembering in cultural context. In W. J. Lonner & R. Malpass (eds.), *Psychology and culture.* Needham Heights, MA: Allyn & Bacon.

Mitchell, D. E. (1980). The influence of early visual experience on visual perception. In C. S. Harris (ed.), *Visual coding and adaptability.* Hillsdale, NJ: Erlbaum.

Mitchell, Valory, & Helson, Ravenna (1990). Women's prime of life: Is it the 50s? *Psychology of Women Quarterly, 14,* 451–470.

Mithers, Carol L. (1994). *Reasonable insanity: A true story of the seventies.* Reading, MA: Addison-Wesley.

Modigliani, Andre, & Rochat, François (1995). The role of interaction sequences and the timing of resistance in shaping obedience and defiance to authority. In A.G. Miller, B. E. Collins, & D. E. Brief (eds.), *Perspectives on obedience to authority: The legacy of the Milgram experiments. Journal of Social Issues, 51*(3), 107–125.

Moffitt, Terrie E. (1993). Adolescence-limited and life-course-persistent antisocial behavior: A developmental taxonomy. *Psychological Review, 100,* 674–701.

Monk, Timothy H., & Aplin, Lynne C. (1980). Spring and autumn daylight saving time changes: Studies of adjustment in sleep timings, mood, and efficiency. *Ergonomics, 23,* 167–178.

Montagner, Hubert (1985). Approache ethologique des systems à interaction du nouveau né et du jeune enfant. [An ethological approach of the interaction systems of the infant and the young child.] *Neuropsychiatrie de l'Enfance et de l'Adolescence, 33,* 59–71.

Monteith, Margo J. (1996). Contemporary forms of prejudice-related conflict: In search of a nutshell. *Personality and Social Psychology Bulletin, 22,* 461–473.

Moore, Robert Y. (1997). Circadian rhythms: Basic neurobiology and clinical applications. *Annual Review of Medicine, 48,* 253–266.

Moore, Timothy E. (1982, Spring). Subliminal advertising: What you see is what you get. *Journal of Marketing, 46,* 38–47.

Moore, Timothy E. (1989). Subliminal psychodynamic activation and the establishment of thresholds. *American Psychologist, 44,* 1420–1421.

Moore, Timothy E. (1992, Spring). Subliminal perception: Facts and fallacies. *Skeptical Inquirer, 16,* 273–281.

Moore, Timothy E. (1995). Subliminal self-help auditory tapes: An empirical test of perceptual consequences. *Canadian Journal of Behavioural Science, 27,* 9–20.

Moore, Timothy E. (1996, November/December). Scientific consensus and expert testimony: Lessons from the Judas Priest trial. *Skeptical Inquirer,* 32–38, 60.

Morelli, Gilda A.; Rogoff, Barbara; Oppenheim, David; & Goldsmith, Denise (1992). Cultural variation in infants' sleeping arrangements: Questions of independence. [Special Section: Cross-cultural studies of development.] *Developmental Psychology, 28,* 604–613.

Morgan, Arlene H.; Johnson, David L.; & Hilgard, Ernest R. (1974). The stability of hypnotic susceptibility: A longitudinal study. *International Journal of Clinical and Experimental Hypnosis, 22,* 249–257.

Morgan, Christiana D., & Murray, Henry A. (1935). A method for investigating fantasies: The Thematic Apperception Test. *Archives of Neurology and Psychiatry, 34,* 289–306.

Morris, Michael W., & Peng, Kaiping (1994). Culture and cause: American and Chinese attributions for social and physical events. *Journal of Personality and Social Psychology, 67,* 949–971.

Morrison, Ann M., & Von Glinow, Mary Ann (1990). Women and minorities in management. *American Psychologist, 45,* 200–208.

Moscovici, Serge (1985). Social influence and conformity. In G. Lindzey & E. Aronson (eds.), *Handbook of social psychology* (Vol. 2, 3rd ed.). New York: Random House.

Mott, Frank L. (1991). Developmental effects of infant care: The mediating role of gender and health. In S. L. Hofferth & D. A. Phillips (eds.), *Child care policy, research. Journal of Social Issues, 47*(2), 139–158.

Mozell, Maxwell M.; Smith, Bruce P., Smith, Paul E.; Sullivan, Richard L.; & Swender, Philip (1969). Nasal chemoreception in flavor identification. *Archives of Otolaryngology, 90,* 367–373.

Muehlenhard, Charlene L. (1988). "Nice women" don't say yes and "real men" don't say no: How miscommunication and the double standard can cause sexual problems. [Special Issue: Women and sex therapy.] *Women & Therapy, 7,* 95–108.

Muehlenhard, Charlene, & Cook, Stephen (1988). Men's self-reports of unwanted sexual activity. *Journal of Sex Research, 24,* 58–72.

Mulick, James (1994, November/December). The non-science of facilitated communication. *Science Agenda* (APA newsletter), 8–9.

Murphy, Sheila T.; Monahan, Jennifer L.; & Zajonc, R. B. (1995). Addivity of nonconscious affect: Combined effects of priming and exposure. *Journal of Personality and Social Psychology, 69*, 589–602.

Myers, David G. (1980). *The inflated self.* New York: Seabury.

Nadel, Lynn, & Zola-Morgan, Stuart (1984). Infantile amnesia: A neurobiological perspective. In M. Moscovitch (ed.), *Infantile memory: Its relation to normal and pathological memory in humans and other animals.* New York: Plenum.

Nadon, Robert; Hoyt, Irene, P.; Register, Patricia A.; & Kihlstrom, John (1991). Absorption and hypnotizability: Context effects reexamined. *Journal of Personality and Social Psychology, 60*, 144–153.

Nash, Michael R. (1987). What, if anything, is regressed about hypnotic age regression? A review of the empirical literature. *Psychological Bulletin, 102*, 42–52.

Nash, Michael R. (1994). Memory distortion and sexual trauma: The problem of false negatives and false positives. *International Journal of Clinical and Experimental Hypnosis, 42*, 346–362.

Nash, Michael R., & Nadon, Robert (1997). Hypnosis. In D. L. Faigman, D. Kaye, M. J. Saks, & J. Sanders (eds.), *Modern scientific evidence: The law and science of expert testimony.* St. Paul, MN: West.

Nathan, Debbie (1994, Fall). Dividing to conquer? Women, men, and the making of multiple personality disorder. *Social Text, 40*, 77–114.

National Academy of Sciences (National Research Council) (1989). *Diet and health: Implications for reducing chronic disease risk.* Washington, DC: National Academy Press.

National Victim Center & Crime Victims Research and Treatment Center (1992). *Rape in America: A report to the nation.* Fort Worth, TX: National Victim Center.

Needleman, Herbert L.; Riess, Julie A.; Tobin, Michael J.; et al. (1996). Bone lead levels and delinquent behavior. *Journal of the American Medical Association, 275*, 363–369.

Needleman, Herbert L.; Schell, Alan; Bellinger, David; Leviton, Alan; et al. (1990). The long-term effects of exposure to low doses of lead in childhood: An 11-year follow-up report. *New England Journal of Medicine, 322*, 83–88.

Neher, Andrew (1996). Jung's theory of archetypes: A critique. *Journal of Humanistic Psychology, 36*, 61–91.

Neiss, Rob (1988). Reconceptualizing arousal: Psychobiological states in motor performance. *Psychological Bulletin, 103*, 345–366.

Neisser, Ulric; Boodoo, Gwyneth; Bouchard, Thomas J., Jr.; et al. (1996). Intelligence: Knowns and unknowns. *American Psychologist, 51*, 77–101.

Neisser, Ulric, & Harsch, Nicole (1992). Phantom flashbulbs: False recollections of hearing the news about *Challenger.* In E. Winograd & U. Neisser (eds.), *Affect and accuracy in recall: Studies of "flashbulb memories."* New York: Cambridge University Press.

Neisser, Ulric; Winograd, Eugene; & Weldon, Mary Sue (1991). *Remembering the earthquake: "What I experienced" vs. "How I heard the news."* Paper presented at the annual meeting of the Psychonomic Society, San Francisco.

Nelson, Thomas O., & Dunlosky, John (1991). When people's judgments of learning (JOLs) are extremely accurate at predicting subsequent recall: The "delayed JOL effect." *Psychological Science, 2*, 267–270.

Nelson, Thomas O., & Leonesio, R. Jacob (1988). Allocation of self-paced study time and the "labor in vain effect." *Journal of Experimental Psychology: Learning, Memory, and Cognition, 14*, 676–686.

Neugarten, Bernice (1979). Time, age, and the life cycle. *American Journal of Psychiatry, 136*, 887–894.

Neugarten, Bernice, & Neugarten, Dail A. (1986, Winter). Age in the aging society. *Daedalus, 115*, 31–49.

Newman, Eric A., & Hartline, Peter H. (1982). The infrared "vision" of snakes. *Scientific American, 246*(3), 116–127.

Newman, Joseph P.; Widom, Cathy S.; & Nathan, Stuart (1985). Passive avoidance in syndromes of disinhibition: Psychopathy and extraversion. *Journal of Personality and Social Psychology, 48*, 1316–1327.

Newman, Leonard S., & Baumeister, Roy F. (1994). *"Who would wish for the trauma?" Explaining UFO abductions.* Paper presented at the annual meeting of the American Psychological Association, Los Angeles.

Newman, Lucille F., & Buka, Stephen (1991, Spring). Clipped wings. *American Educator,* 27–33, 42.

Nezu, Arthur M.; Nezu, Christine M.; & Blissett, Sonia E. (1988). Sense of humor as a moderator of the relation between stressful events and psychological distress: A prospective analysis. *Journal of Personality and Social Psychology, 54*, 520–525.

NICHD Early Child Care Research Network (1996, April 20). *Infant child care and attachment security: Results of the NICHD study of early child care.* Symposium paper presented at the International Conference on Infant Studies, Providence, RI.

Nickerson, Raymond A., & Adams, Marilyn Jager (1979). Long-term memory for a common object. *Cognitive Psychology, 11*, 287–307.

Niemi, G.; Katz, R. S.; & Newman, D. (1980). Reconstructing past partisanship: The failure of party identification recall questions. *American Journal of Political Science, 24*, 633–651.

Nigg, Joel T., & Goldsmith, H. Hill (1994). Genetics of personality disorders: Perspectives from personality and psychopathology research. *Psychological Bulletin, 115*, 346–380.

Nisbett, Richard E. (1993). Violence and U.S. regional culture. *American Psychologist, 48*, 441–449.

Nisbett, Richard E., & Ross, Lee (1980). *Human inference: Strategies and shortcomings of social judgment.* Englewood Cliffs, NJ: Prentice-Hall.

Noble, Ernest P.; Blum, Kenneth; Ritchie, T.; Montgomery, A.; & Sheridan, P. J. (1991). Allelic association of the D2 dopamine receptor gene with receptor-binding characteristics in alcoholism. *Archives of General Psychiatry, 48*, 648–654.

Noelle-Neumann, Elisabeth (1984). *The spiral of silence.* Chicago: University of Chicago Press.

Nolen-Hoeksema, Susan (1990). *Sex differences in depression.* Stanford, CA: Stanford University Press.

Nolen-Hoeksema, Susan (1991). Responses to depression and their effects on the duration of depressive episodes. *Journal of Abnormal Psychology, 100*, 569–582.

Nolen-Hoeksema, Susan, & Girgus, Joan S. (1994). The emergence of gender differences in depression during adolescence. *Psychological Bulletin, 115*, 424–443.

Norman, Donald A. (1988). *The psychology of everyday things.* New York: Basic Books.

Nowicki, Stephen, & Duke, Marshall P. (1989). *A measure of nonverbal social processing ability in children between the ages of 6 and 10.* Paper presented at the annual meeting of the American Psychological Society, Alexandria, VA.

Nowicki, Stephen, & Strickland, Bonnie R. (1973). A locus of control scale for children. *Journal of Consulting Psychology, 40*, 148–154.

Oatley, Keith (1990). Do emotional states produce irrational thinking? In K. J. Gilhooly, M. T. G. Keane, R. H. Logie, & G. Erdos (eds.), *Lines of thinking* (Vol. 2). New York: Wiley.

Oatley, Keith, & Duncan, Elaine (1994). The experience of emotions in everyday life. *Cognition and Emotion, 8*, 369–381.

Oatley, Keith, & Jenkins, Jennifer M. (1992). Human emotions: Function and dysfunction. *Annual Review of Psychology, 43*, 55–85.

Oatley, Keith, & Jenkins, Jennifer M. (1996). *Understanding emotions.* Cambridge, MA: Blackwell.

Offer, Daniel, & Sabshin, Melvin (1984). Adolescence: Empirical perspectives. In D. Offer & M. Sabshin (eds.), *Normality and the life cycle.* New York: Basic Books.

Ofshe, Richard J., & Watters, Ethan (1994). *Making monsters: False memory, psychotherapy, and sexual hysteria.* New York: Scribners.

Ogbu, John U. (1993). Differences in cultural frame of reference. *International Journal of Behavioral Development, 16*, 483–506.

Ogden, Jenni A., & Corkin, Suzanne (1991). Memories of H. M. In W. C. Abraham, M. C. Corballis, & K. G. White (eds.), *Memory mechanisms: A tribute to G. V. Goddard.* Hillsdale, NJ: Erlbaum.

O'Hanlon, Bill (1994, November/December). The third wave. *The Family Therapy Networker,* 18–29.

Olds, James (1975). Mapping the mind onto the brain. In F. G. Worden, J. P. Swazy, & G. Adelman (eds.), *The neurosciences: Paths of discovery.* Cambridge, MA: Colonial Press.

Olds, James, & Milner, Peter (1954). Positive reinforcement produced by electrical stimulation of septal area and other regions of the rat brain. *Journal of Comparative and Physiological Psychology, 47*, 419–429.

Olin, Su-Chin S., & Mednick, Sarnoff A. (1996). Risk factors of psychosis: Identifying vulnerable populations premorbidly. *Schizophrenia Bulletin, 22*, 223–240.

Oliner, Samuel P., & Oliner, Pearl M. (1988). *The altruistic personality: Rescuers of Jews in Nazi Europe.* New York: Free Press.

Oliver, Mary Beth, & Hyde, Janet S. (1993). Gender differences in sexuality: A meta-analysis. *Psychological Bulletin, 114,* 29–51.

Olsen, Bonnie J.; Starr, Arnold; & Parker, Elizabeth S. (in preparation). Learning in a patient with profound memory loss.

O'Neil, Harold F., Jr.; Sugrue, Brenda; & Baker, Eva L. (1995/1996). Effects of motivational interventions on the National Assessment of Educational Progress mathematics performance. *Educational Assessment, 3,* 135–157.

Orford, Jim (1992). *Community psychology: Theory and practice.* New York: Wiley.

Orlinsky, David E. (1994). Research-based knowledge as the emergent foundation for clinical practice in psychotherapy. In P. F. Talley, H. H. Strupp, & S. F. Butler (eds.), *Psychotherapy research and practice: Bridging the gap.* New York: Basic Books.

Ormel, Johan, & Wohlfarth, Tamar (1991). How neuroticism, long-term difficulties, and life situation change influence psychological distress: A longitudinal model. *Journal of Personality and Social Psychology, 60,* 744–755.

Ortar, G. (1963). Is a verbal test cross-cultural? *Scripts Hierosolymitana* (Hebrew University, Jerusalem), *13,* 219–235.

Ortony, Andrew, & Turner, Terence J. (1990). What's basic about basic emotions. *Psychological Review, 97,* 315–331.

Oskamp, Stuart (ed.) (1988). *Television as a social issue.* Newbury Park, CA: Sage.

Page, Gayle G.; Ben-Eliyahu, Shamgar; Yirmiya, Raz; & Liebeskind, John C. (1993). Morphine attenuates surgery-induced enhancement of metastatic colonization in rats. *Pain, 54,* 21–28.

Page, J. Bryan; Fletcher, Jack; & True, William R. (1988). Psychosociocultural perspectives on chronic cannabis use: The Costa Rican follow-up. *Journal of Psychoactive Drugs, 20,* 57–65.

Paige, Karen E., & Paige, Jeffery M. (1981). *The politics of reproductive ritual.* Berkeley: University of California Press.

Panksepp, Jack; Herman, B. H.; Vilberg, T.; Bishop, P.; & DeEskinazi, F. G. (1980). Endogenous opioids and social behavior. *Neuroscience and Biobehavioral Reviews, 4,* 473–487.

Park, Denise C.; Smith, Anderson D.; & Cavanaugh, John C. (1990). Metamemories of memory researchers. *Memory and Cognition, 18,* 321–327.

Parker, Elizabeth S.; Birnbaum, Isabel M.; & Noble, Ernest P. (1976). Alcohol and memory: Storage and state dependency. *Journal of Verbal Learning and Verbal Behavior, 15,* 691–702.

Parker, Kevin C. H.; Hanson, R. Karl; & Hunsley, John (1988). MMPI, Rorschach, and WAIS: A meta-analytic comparison of reliability, stability, and validity. *Psychological Bulletin, 103,* 367–373.

Parks, Randolph W.; Loewenstein, David A.; Dodrill, Kathryn L.; Barker, William W.; et al. (1988). Cerebral metabolic effects of a verbal fluency test: A PET scan study. *Journal of Clinical and Experimental Neuropsychology, 10,* 565–575.

Parlee, Mary Brown (1982). Changes in moods and activation levels during the menstrual cycle in experimentally naive subjects. *Psychology of Women Quarterly, 7,* 119–131.

Parlee, Mary B. (1994). The social construction of premenstrual syndrome: A case study of scientific discourse as cultural contestation. In M. G. Winkler & L. B. Cole (eds.), *The good body: Asceticism in contemporary culture.* New Haven, CT: Yale University Press.

Parrott, W. Gerrod, & Smith, Richard H. (1993). Distinguishing the experiences of envy and jealousy. *Journal of Personality and Social Psychology, 64,* 906–920.

Parsons, Michael W., & Gold, Paul E. (1992). Glucose enhancement of memory in elderly humans: An inverted-U dose response curve. *Neurobiology of Aging, 13,* 401–404.

Patterson, Charlotte J. (1992). Children of lesbian and gay parents. *Child Development, 63,* 1025–1042.

Patterson, Charlotte J. (1995). Sexual orientation and human development: An overview. *Developmental Psychology, 31,* 3–11.

Patterson, Francine, & Linden, Eugene (1981). *The education of Koko.* New York: Holt, Rinehart and Winston.

Patterson, Gerald R. (1994). *Developmental perspectives on violence.* Invited address presented at the annual meeting of the American Psychological Association, Los Angeles.

Patterson, Gerald R.; DeBaryshe, Barbara D.; & Ramsey, Elizabeth (1989). A developmental perspective on antisocial behavior. *American Psychologist, 44,* 329–335.

Patterson, Gerald R.; Reid, John; & Dishion, Thomas (1992). *Antisocial boys.* Eugene, OR: Castalia.

Paul, Richard W. (1984, September). Critical thinking: Fundamental to education for a free society. *Educational Leadership,* 4–14.

Paulus, Paul B., & Dzindolet, Mary T. (1993). Social influence processes in group brainstorming. *Journal of Personality and Social Psychology, 64,* 575–586.

Peabody, Dean (1985). *National characteristics.* Cambridge, England: Cambridge University Press.

Pearlin, Leonard (1982). Discontinuities in the study of aging. In T. K. Hareven & K. J. Adams (eds.), *Aging and life course transitions: An interdisciplinary perspective.* New York: Guilford Press.

Pedersen, Paul B.; Draguns, Juris G.; Lonner, Walter J.; & Trimble, Joseph E. (eds.) (1996). *Counseling across cultures* (4th ed.). Thousand Oaks, CA: Sage.

Peele, Stanton, & Brodsky, Archie, with Mary Arnold (1991). *The truth about addiction and recovery.* New York: Simon & Schuster.

Pellegrini, Anthony D., & Galda, Lee (1993). Ten years after: A reexamination of symbolic play and literacy research. *Reading Research Quarterly, 28,* 163–175.

Penfield, Wilder, & Perot, Phanor (1963). The brain's record of auditory and visual experience: A final summary and discussion. *Brain, 86,* 595–696.

Pennebaker, James W. (1995). Emotion, disclosure, and health: An overview. In J. W. Pennebaker (ed.), *Emotion, disclosure, and health.* Washington, DC: American Psychological Association.

Pennebaker, James W.; Colder, Michelle; & Sharp, Lisa K. (1990). Accelerating the coping process. *Journal of Personality and Social Psychology, 58,* 528–527.

Pennebaker, James W., & Harber, Kent D. (1993). A social stage model of collective coping: The Loma Prieta earthquake and the Persian Gulf War. *Journal of Social Issues, 49*(4), 125–145.

Pennebaker, James W.; Kiecolt-Glaser, Janice; & Glaser, Ronald (1988). Disclosure of traumas and immune function: Health implications for psychotherapy. *Journal of Consulting and Clinical Psychology, 56,* 239–245.

Peplau, Letitia A. (1991). Lesbian and gay relationships. In J. C. Gonsiorek & J. D. Weinrich (eds.), *Homosexuality: Research findings for social policy.* Newbury Park, CA: Sage.

Peplau, Letitia A., & Conrad, Eva (1989). Beyond nonsexist research: The perils of feminist methods in psychology. *Psychology of Women Quarterly, 13,* 379–400.

Peplau, Letitia A., & Gordon, Steven L. (1985). Women and men in love: Gender differences in close heterosexual relationships. In V. O'Leary, R. Unger, & B. Wallston (eds.), *Women, gender, and social psychology.* Hillsdale, NJ: Erlbaum.

Pepperberg, Irene M. (1990). Cognition in an African gray parrot (*Psittacus erithacus*): Further evidence for comprehension of categories and labels. *Journal of Comparative Psychology, 104,* 41–52.

Pepperberg, Irene M. (1994). Numerical competence in an African gray parrot (*Psittacus erithacus*). *Journal of Comparative Psychology, 108,* 36–44.

Perdue, Charles W.; Dovidio, John F.; Gurtman, Michael B.; & Tyler, Richard B. (1990). Us and them: Social categorization and the process of intergroup bias. *Journal of Personality and Social Psychology, 59,* 475–486.

Perlman, Daniel (1990). *Age differences in loneliness: A meta-analysis.* Paper presented at the annual meeting of the American Psychological Association, Boston.

Perloff, Robert (1992, Summer). "Where ignorance is bliss, 'tis folly to be wise." *The General Psychologist Newsletter, 28,* 34.

Perry, Samuel W., & Heidrich, George (1982). Management of pain during debridement: A survey of U.S. burn units. *Pain, 13,* 267–280.

Persons, Ethel S. (1986). Manipulativeness in entrepreneurs and psychopaths. In W. H. Reid, D. Dorr, J. I. Walker, & J. W. Bonner (eds.), *Unmasking the psychopath.* New York: Norton.

Pert, Candace B., & Snyder, Solomon H. (1973). Opiate receptor: Demonstration in nervous tissue. *Science, 179,* 1011–1014.

Pervin, Lawrence A. (1992). The rational mind and the problem of volition [feature review]. *Psychological Science, 3,* 162–164.

Petersen, Anne C. (1989). *Developmental transitions and their role in influencing life trajectories.* Paper presented at the annual meeting of the American Psychological Association, New Orleans.

Peterson, Bill E., & Stewart, Abigail J. (1993). Generativity and social motives in young adults. *Journal of Personality and Social Psychology, 65*, 186–198.

Peterson, Lloyd R., & Peterson, Margaret J. (1959). Short-term retention of individual verbal items. *Journal of Experimental Psychology, 58*, 193–198.

Peterson, Marilyn R. (1992). *At personal risk: Boundary violations in professional-client relationships.* New York: Norton.

Pfungst, Oskar (1911/1965). *Clever Hans (The horse of Mr. von Osten): A contribution to experimental animal and human psychology.* New York: Holt, Rinehart and Winston.

Phares, E. Jerry (1976). *Locus of control in personality.* Morristown, NJ: General Learning Press.

Phillips, D. P.; Ruth, T. E.; & Wagner, L. M. (1993, November 6). Psychology and survival. *Lancet, 342*(8880), 1142–1145.

Phinney, Jean S. (1990). Ethnic identity in adolescents and adults: Review of research. *Psychological Bulletin, 108*, 499–514.

Phinney, Jean S. (1996). When we talk about American ethnic groups, what do we mean? *American Psychologist, 51*, 918–927.

Piaget, Jean (1929/1960). *The child's conception of the world.* Paterson, NJ: Littlefield, Adams.

Piaget, Jean (1932). *The moral judgment of the child.* New York: Macmillan.

Piaget, Jean (1951). *Plays, dreams, and imitation in childhood.* New York: Norton.

Piaget, Jean (1952). *The origins of intelligence in children.* New York: International Universities Press.

Piaget, Jean (1984). Piaget's theory. In P. Mussen (series ed.) & W. Kessen (vol. ed.), *Handbook of child psychology: Vol. 1. History, theory, and methods* (4th ed.). New York: Wiley.

Pickens, Jeffrey (1994). Perception of auditory-visual distance relations by 5-month-old infants. *Developmental Psychology, 30*, 537–544.

Pillow, David R.; Zautra, Alex J.; & Sandler, Irwin (1996). Major life events and minor stressors: Identifying mediating links in the stress process. *Journal of Personality and Social Psychology, 70*, 381–394.

Pines, Maya (1983, September). The human difference. *Psychology Today*, 62–68.

Pinker, Steven (1994a, April 5). The game of the name. *The New York Times*, opinion page.

Pinker, Steven (1994b). *The language instinct: How the mind creates language.* New York: Morrow.

Pinsof, William M., & Wynne, Lyman C. (1995). The effectiveness and efficacy of marital and family therapy: Introduction to the special issue. [Special Issue: The effectiveness of marital and family therapy.] *Journal of Marital and Family Therapy, 21*, 341–343.

Pipe, Margaret-Ellen, & Goodman, Gail S. (1991). Elements of secrecy: Implications for children's testimony. *Behavioral Sciences and the Law, 9*, 33–41.

Piper, August, Jr. (1994). Multiple personality disorder. *British Journal of Psychiatry, 164*, 600–612.

Piper, August, Jr. (1997). *Hoax and reality: The bizarre world of multiple personality disorder.* Northvale, NJ: Jason Aronson.

Plomin, Robert (1989). Environment and genes: Determinants of behavior. *American Psychologist, 44*, 105–111.

Plomin, Robert; Corley, Robin; DeFries, J. C.; & Fulker, D. W. (1990). Individual differences in television viewing in early childhood: Nature as well as nurture. *Psychological Science, 1*, 371–377.

Plomin, Robert, & DeFries, John C. (1985). *Origins of individual differences in infancy: The Colorado Adoption Project.* New York: Academic Press.

Plous, Scott L. (1991). An attitude survey of animal rights activists. *Psychological Science, 2*, 194–196.

Plous, Scott L. (1996). Attitudes toward the use of animals in psychological research and education: Results from a national survey of psychologists. *American Psychologist, 51*, 1167–1180.

Plutchik, Robert; Conte, Hope R.; Karasu, Toksoz; & Buckley, Peter (1988, Fall/Winter). The measurement of psychodynamic variables. *Hillside Journal of Clinical Psychology, 10*, 132–147.

Polefrone, Joanna M., & Manuck, Stephen B. (1987). Gender differences in cardiovascular and neuroendocrine response to stressors. In R. C. Barnett, L. Biener, & G. K. Baruch (eds.), *Gender and stress.* New York: Free Press.

Polich, John; Pollock, Vicki E.; & Bloom, Floyd E. (1994). Meta-analysis of P300 amplitude from males at risk for alcoholism. *Psychological Bulletin, 115*, 55–73.

Pollak, Richard (1997). *The creation of Dr. B: A biography of Bruno Bettelheim.* New York: Simon & Schuster.

Pollitt, Katha (1991, Dec.). Reading books, great or otherwise. *Harper's, 34*, 36.

Poole, Debra A. (1995). Strolling fuzzy-trace theory through eyewitness testimony (or vice versa). *Learning and Individual Differences, 7*, 87–93.

Poole, Debra A.; Lindsay, D. Stephen; Memon, Amina; & Bull, Ray (1995). Psychotherapy and the recovery of memories of childhood sexual abuse: U.S. and British practitioners' opinions, practices, and experiences. *Journal of Consulting and Clinical Psychology, 63*, 426–437.

Pope, Harrison G., & Katz, David L. (1992). Psychiatric effects of anabolic steroids. *Psychiatric Annals, 22*, 24–29.

Portenoy, Russell K. (1994). Opioid therapy for chronic nonmalignant pain: Current status. In H. L. Fields & J. C. Liebeskind (eds.), *Progress in pain research and management. Pharmacological approaches to the treatment of chronic pain: Vol. 1.* Seattle: International Association for the Study of Pain.

Posada, German; Lord, Chiyoko; & Waters, Everett (1995). *Secure base behavior and children's misbehavior in three different contexts: Home, neighbors, and school.* Paper presented at the annual meeting of the Society for Research in Child Development, Indianapolis.

Postman, Neil (1985). *Amusing ourselves to death.* New York: Viking Penguin.

Poulin-Dubois, Diane; Serbin, Lisa A.; Kenyon, Brenda; & Derbyshire, Alison (1994). Infants' intermodal knowledge about gender. *Developmental Psychology, 30*, 436–442.

Poulos, Constantine X., & Cappell, Howard (1991). Homeostatic theory of drug tolerance: A general model of physiological adaptation. *Psychological Review, 98*, 390–408.

Powell, Russell A., & Boer, Douglas P. (1994). Did Freud mislead patients to confabulate memories of abuse? *Psychological Reports, 74*, 1283–1298.

Powell, Russell A., & Boer, Douglas P. (1995). Did Freud misinterpret reported memories of sexual abuse as fantasies? *Psychological Reports, 77*, 563–570.

Pratkanis, Anthony, & Aronson, Elliot (1992). *Age of propaganda: The everyday use and abuse of persuasion.* New York: Freeman.

Pratt, L. A.; Ford, D. E.; Crum, R. M.; et al. (1996, December 15). Depression psychotropic medication, and risk of myocardial infarction. Prospective data from the Baltimore ECA follow-up. *Circulation, 94,* 3123–3129.

Premack, David, & Premack, Ann James (1983). *The mind of an ape.* New York: Norton.

Press, Gary A.; Amaral, David G.; & Squire, Larry R. (1989, September 7). Hippocampal abnormalities in amnesic patients revealed by high-resolution magnetic resonance imaging. *Nature, 341*, 54–57.

Pribram, Karl H. (1971). *Languages of the brain: Experimental paradoxes and principles.* Englewood Cliffs, NJ: Prentice-Hall.

Pribram, Karl H. (1982). Localization and distribution of function in the brain. In J. Orbach (ed.), *Neuropsychology after Lashley.* Hillsdale, NJ: Erlbaum.

Prochaska, James O.; Norcross, John C.; & DiClemente, Carlo C. (1994). *Changing for good.* New York: Morrow.

Ptito, Alain; Lepore, Franco; Ptito, Maurice; & Lassonde, Maryse (1991). Target detection and movement discrimination in the blind field of hemispherectomized patients. *Brain, 114*, 497.

Pulver, Ann; Carpenter, William; Adler, Lawrence; & McGrath, John (1988). Accuracy of diagnoses of affective disorders and schizophrenia in public hospitals. *American Journal of Psychiatry, 145*, 218–220.

Putnam, Frank (1989). *Diagnosis and treatment of multiple personality disorder.* New York: Guilford Press.

Rachman, S. J., & Wilson, G. Terence (1980). *The effects of psychological therapy* (2nd ed.). Oxford, England: Pergamon.

Radetsky, Peter (1991, April). The brainiest cells alive. *Discover, 12*, 82–85, 88, 90.

Radke-Yarrow, Marian; Zahn-Waxler, Carolyn; & Chapman, M. (1983). Prosocial dispositions and behavior. In P. Mussen (ed.), *Manual of child psychology: Vol. 4. Socialization, personality, and social development.* New York: Wiley.

Raine, Adrian; Brennan, Patricia; & Mednick, Sarnoff A. (1994). Birth complications combined with early maternal rejection at age one year predispose to violent crime at age 18 years. *Archives of General Psychiatry, 51*, 984–988.

Raine, Adrian; Buchsbaum, Monte S.; Stanley, Jill; et al. (1994). *Selective reductions in prefrontal glucose metabolism in murderers.* Paper presented at the annual meeting of the American Psychological Association, Los Angeles.

Randi, James (1982, March). The 1980 divining tests. *The Skeptic,* 2–6.

Rapkin, Andrea J.; Chang, Li C.; & Reading, Anthony E. (1988). Comparison of retrospective and prospective assessment of premenstrual symptoms. *Psychological Reports, 62,* 55–60.

Raskin, David C.; Honts, Charles R.; & Kircher, John C. (1997). The scientific status of research on polygraph techniques: The case for polygraph tests. In David L. Faigman, David Kaye, Michael J. Saks, & Joseph Sanders (eds.), *Modern scientific evidence: The law and science of expert testimony.* St. Paul, MN: West.

Raso, Jack (1996, July/August). Alternative health education and pesudocredentialing. *Skeptical Inquirer,* 39–45.

Ratcliff, Roger (1990). Connectionist models of recognition memory: Constraints imposed by learning and forgetting functions. *Psychological Review, 97,* 285–308.

Rathbun, Constance; DiVirgilio, Letitia; & Waldfogel, Samuel (1958). A restitutive process in children following radical separation from family and culture. *American Journal of Orthopsychiatry, 28,* 408–415.

Ravussin, Eric; Lillioja, Stephen; Knowler, William; Christin, Laurent; et al. (1988). Reduced rate of energy expenditure as a risk factor for body-weight gain. *New England Journal of Medicine, 318,* 467–472.

Raz, Sarah, & Raz, Naftali (1990). Structural brain abnormalities in the major psychoses: A quantitative review of the evidence from computerized imaging. *Psychological Bulletin, 108,* 93–108.

Rechtschaffen, Allan; Gilliland, Marcia A.; Bergmann, Bernard M.; & Winter, Jacqueline B. (1983). Physiological correlates of prolonged sleep deprivation in rats. *Science, 221,* 182–184.

Redelmeier, Donald A., & Tversky, Amos (1996). On the belief that arthritis pain is related to the weather. *Proceedings of the National Academy of Sciences, 93,* 2895–2896.

Reed, Geoffrey M. (1990). *Stress, coping, and psychological adaptation in a sample of gay and bisexual men with AIDS.* Unpublished doctoral dissertation, University of California, Los Angeles.

Reedy, F. E.; Bartoshuk, L. M.; Miller, I. J.; Duffy, V. B.; Lucchina, L.; & Yanagisawa, K. (1993). Relationships among papillae, taste pores, and 6-n-propylthiouracil (PROP) suprathreshold taste sensitivity. *Chemical Senses, 18,* 618–619.

Regier, Darrel A.; Narrow, William E.; Rae, Donald S.; Manderscheid, Ronald W.; et al. (1993). The de facto US mental and addictive disorders service system: Epidemiologic Catchment Area prospective 1-year prevalence rates of disorders and services. *Archives of General Psychiatry, 50,* 85–94.

Rescorla, Robert A. (1968). Probability of shock in the presence and absence of CS in fear conditioning. *Journal of Comparative and Physiological Psychology, 66,* 1–5.

Rescorla, Robert A. (1988). Pavlovian conditioning: It's not what you think it is. *American Psychologist, 43,* 151–160.

Rescorla, Robert A., & Wagner, Allan R. (1972). A theory of Pavlovian conditioning: Variations in the effectiveness of reinforcement and nonreinforcement. In A. H. Black & W. F. Prokasy (eds.), *Classical conditioning: Vol 2: Current research and theory.* New York: Appleton-Century-Crofts.

Restak, Richard (1983, October). Is free will a fraud? *Science Digest, 91*(10), 52–55.

Restak, Richard M. (1994). *The modular brain.* New York: Macmillan.

Reynolds, Brent A., & Weiss, Samuel (1992). Generation of neurons and astrocytes from isolated cells of the adult mammalian central nervous system. *Science, 255,* 1707–1710.

Reynolds, David K. (1987). *Water bears no scars: Japanese lifeways for personal growth.* New York: Morrow.

Rhoades, David F. (1985). Pheromonal communication between plants. In G. A. Cooper-Driver, T. Swain, & E. E. Conn (eds.), *Research advances in phytochemistry* (Vol. 19). New York: Plenum.

Ricaurte, George A.; Forno, Lysia; Wilson, Mary; deLanney, Louis; Irwin, Ean; Mulliver, Mark; & Langston, J. William (1988). (+or–) 3, 4-Methylenedioxy-methamphetamine selectively damages central serotonergic neurons in nonhuman primates. *Journal of the American Medical Association, 260,* 51–55.

Rice, Mabel L. (1989). Children's language acquisition. *American Psychologist, 44,* 149–156.

Richards, Ruth L. (1991). *Everyday creativity and the arts.* Paper presented at the annual meeting of the American Psychological Association, San Francisco.

Richardson, John T. E. (ed.) (1992). *Cognition and the menstrual cycle.* New York: Springer-Verlag.

Richardson-Klavehn, Alan, & Bjork, Robert A. (1988). Measures of memory. *Annual Review of Psychology, 39,* 475–543.

Richmond, Barry J., & Optican, Lance M. (1990). Temporal encoding of two-dimensional patterns by single units in primate primary visual cortex: II. Information transmission. *Journal of Neurophysiology, 64,* 370–380.

Riessman, Catherine K. (1990). *Divorce talk: Women and men make sense of personal relationships.* New Brunswick, NJ: Rutgers University Press.

Riley, Vernon; Spackman, Darrel; & Santisteban, George (1975). The role of physiological stress on breast tumor incidence in mice. *Proceedings of the American Association of Cancer Research, 16,* 152.

Ristau, Carolyn A. (ed.) (1991). *Cognitive ethology: The minds of other animals.* Hillsdale, NJ: Erlbaum.

Roberts, John E.; Gotlib, Ian H.; & Kassel, Jon D. (1996). Adult attachment security and symptoms of depression: The mediating roles of dysfunctional attitudes and low self-esteem. *Journal of Personality and Social Psychology, 70,* 310–320.

Roberts, Susan B.; Savage, J.; Coward, W. A.; Chew, B.; & Lucas, A. (1988). Energy expenditure and intake in infants born to lean and overweight mothers. *New England Journal of Medicine, 318,* 461–466.

Robertson, Barbara A. (1995). *Creating a disability community.* Paper presented at the annual meeting of the American Psychological Association, New York.

Robertson, John, & Fitzgerald, Louise F. (1990). The (mis)treatment of men: Effects of client gender role and life-style on diagnosis and attribution of pathology. *Journal of Counseling Psychology, 37,* 3–9.

Robins, Lee N.; Davis, Darlene H.; & Goodwin, Donald W. (1974). Drug use by U.S. Army enlisted men in Vietnam: A follow-up on their return home. *American Journal of Epidemiology, 99,* 235–249.

Robins, Lee N.; Tipp, Jayson; & Przybeck, Thomas R. (1991). Antisocial personality. In L. N. Robins & D. A. Regier (eds.), *Psychiatric disorders in America.* New York: Free Press.

Robinson, Leslie A.; Berman, Jeffrey S.; & Neimeyer, Robert A. (1990). Psychotherapy for the treatment of depression: A comprehensive review of controlled outcome research. *Psychological Bulletin, 108,* 30–49.

Rodgers, Joann (1988, April). Pains of complaint. *Psychology Today,* 26–27.

Rodin, Judith (1988). *Control, health, and aging.* Invited address presented at the annual meeting of the Society of Behavioral Medicine, Boston.

Rodin, Judith; Silberstein, Lisa R.; & Striegel-Moore, Ruth H. (1990). Vulnerability and resilience in the age of eating disorders: Risk and protective factors for bulimia. In J. E. Rolf et al. (eds.), *Risk and protective factors in the development of psychopathology.* Cambridge, England: Cambridge University Press.

Roediger, Henry L., III (1990). Implicit memory: Retention without remembering. *American Psychologist, 45,* 1043–1056.

Roediger, Henry L., & McDermott, Kathleen B. (1995). Creating false memories: Remembering words not presented in lists. *Journal of Experimental Psychology; Learning, Memory, & Cognition, 21,* 803–814.

Rogers, Carl (1951). *Client-centered therapy: Its current practice, implications, and theory.* Boston: Houghton Mifflin.

Rogers, Carl (1961). *On becoming a person.* Boston: Houghton Mifflin.

Rogers, Ronald W., & Prentice-Dunn, Steven (1981). Deindividuation and anger-mediated interracial aggression: Unmasking regressive racism. *Journal of Personality and Social Psychology, 41,* 63–73.

Rogoff, Barbara, & Chavajay, Pablo (1995). What's become of research on the cultural basis of cognitive development? *American Psychologist, 50,* 859–877.

Rokeach, Milton, & Ball-Rokeach, Sandra (1989). Stability and change in American value priorities, 1968–1981. *American Psychologist, 44,* 775–784.

Rollin, Henry (ed.) (1980). *Coping with schizophrenia.* London: Burnett.

Rosaldo, Renato (1989). *Culture and truth: The remaking of social analysis.* Boston: Beacon Press.

Rosch, Eleanor H. (1973). Natural categories. *Cognitive Psychology, 4,* 328–350.

Rose, Suzanna; Zand, Debra; & Cini, Marie A. (1993). Lesbian courtship scripts. In E. D. Rothblum & K. A. Brehony (eds.), *Boston marriages.* Amherst: University of Massachusetts Press.

Roseman, Ira J.; Wiest, Cynthia; & Swartz, Tamara S. (1994). Phenomenology, behaviors, and goals differentiate discrete emotions. *Journal of Personality and Social Psychology, 67,* 206–221.

Rosen, B. R.; Aronen, H. J.; Kwong, K. K.; et al. (1993). Advances in clinical neuroimaging: Functional MR imaging techniques. *Radiographics, 13,* 889–896.

Rosen, Gerald M. (1981). Guidelines for the review of do-it-yourself treatment books. *Contemporary Psychology, 26,* 189–191.

Rosen, Gerald M. (1993). Self-help or hype? Comments on psychology's failure to advance self-care. *Professional Psychology: Research and Practice, 24,* 340–345.

Rosen, R. D. (1977). *Psychobabble.* New York: Atheneum.

Rosenberg, Harold (1993). Prediction of controlled drinking by alcoholics and problem drinkers. *Psychological Bulletin, 113,* 129–139.

Rosenhan, David L. (1973). On being sane in insane places. *Science, 179,* 250–258.

Rosenthal, Norman E.; Sack, David A.; et al. (1985). Antidepressant effects of light in seasonal affective disorder. *American Journal of Psychiatry, 142,* 163–169.

Rosenthal, Norman E.; Sack, David A.; Skwerer, R. G.; et al. (1989). Phototherapy for seasonal affective disorder. In N. E. Rosenthal & M. C. Blehar (eds.), *Seasonal affective disorders and phototherapy.* New York: Guilford Press.

Rosenthal, Robert (1966). *Experimenter effects in behavioral research.* New York: Appleton-Century-Crofts.

Rosenthal, Robert (1994). Interpersonal expectancy effects: A 30-year perspective. *Current Directions in Psychological Science, 3,* 176–179.

Rosenthal, Robert, & Jacobson, Lenore (1992). *Pygmalion in the classroom: Teacher expectation and pupils' intellectual development.* New York: Irvington.

Rosenzweig, Mark R. (1984). Experience, memory, and the brain. *American Psychologist, 39,* 365–376.

Ross, Colin (1995). The validity and reliability of dissociative identity disorder. In L. M. Cohen, J. N. Berzoff, & M. R. Elin (eds.), *Dissociative identity disorder: Theoretical and treatment controversies.* Northvale, NJ: Jason Aronson.

Ross, Lee (1977). The intuitive psychologist and his shortcomings: Distortions in the attribution process. In L. Berkowitz (ed.), *Advances in experimental social psychology* (Vol. 10). New York: Academic Press.

Ross, Michael (1989). Relation of implicit theories to the construction of personal histories. *Psychological Review, 96,* 341–357.

Roth, David L.; & Holmes, David S. (1985). Influence of physical fitness in determining the impact of stressful life events on physical and psychologic health. *Psychosomatic Medicine, 47,* 164–173.

Rothbaum, Fred M.; Weisz, John R.; & Snyder, Samuel S. (1982). Changing the world and changing the self: A two-process model of perceived control. *Journal of Personality and Social Psychology, 42,* 5–37.

Rotter, Julian B. (1966). Generalized expectancies for internal versus external control of reinforcement. *Psychological Monographs, 80* (Whole No. 609), 1–28.

Rotter, Julian B. (1982). *The development and applications of social learning theory: Selected papers.* New York: Praeger.

Rotter, Julian B. (1990). Internal versus external control of reinforcement: A case history of a variable. *American Psychologist, 45,* 489–493.

Roueché, Berton (1984, June 4). Annals of medicine: The hoof-beats of a zebra. *The New Yorker, LX,* 71–86.

Rovee-Collier, Carolyn (1993). The capacity for long-term memory in infancy. *Current Directions in Psychological Science, 2,* 130–135.

Rowe, Walter F. (1993, Winter). Psychic detectives: A critical examination. *Skeptical Inquirer, 17,* 159–165.

Rozin, Paul; Lowery, Laura; & Ebert, Rhonda (1994). Varieties of disgust faces and the structure of disgust. *Journal of Personality and Social Psychology, 66,* 870–881.

Rubin, Jeffrey Z. (1994). Models of conflict management. *Journal of Social Issues, 50,* 33–45.

Ruggiero, Vincent R. (1988). *Teaching thinking across the curriculum.* New York: Harper & Row.

Ruggiero, Vincent R. (1991). *The art of thinking: A guide to critical and creative thought* (3rd ed.). New York: HarperCollins.

Rumbaugh, Duane M. (1977). *Language learning by a chimpanzee: The Lana project.* New York: Academic Press.

Rumbaugh, Duane M.; Savage-Rumbaugh, E. Sue; & Pate, James L. (1988). Addendum to "Summation in the chimpanzee (*Pan troglodytes*)." *Journal of Experimental Psychology: Animal Behavior Processes, 14,* 118–120.

Rumelhart, David E., & McClelland, James L. (1987). Learning the past tenses of English verbs: Implicit rules or parallel distributed processing. In B. MacWhinney (ed.), *Mechanisms of language acquisition.* Hillsdale, NJ: Erlbaum.

Rumelhart, David E.; McClelland, James L.; & the PDP Research Group (1986). *Parallel distributed processing: Explorations in the microstructure of cognition* (Vols. 1 and 2). Cambridge, MA: MIT Press.

Rushton, J. Philippe (1988). Race differences in behavior: A review and evolutionary analysis. *Personality and Individual Differences, 9,* 1009–1024.

Rushton, J. Philippe (1993). *Cyril Burt: Victim of the scientific hoax of the century.* Paper presented at the annual meeting of the American Psychological Association, Toronto, Canada.

Russell, Diana E. H. (1990). *Rape in marriage* (rev. ed.). Bloomington: Indiana University Press.

Russell, James A. (1991). In defense of a prototype approach to emotion concepts. *Journal of Personality and Social Psychology, 60,* 37–47.

Russell, James A., & Fehr, Beverley (1994). Fuzzy concepts in a fuzzy hierarchy: Varieties of anger. *Journal of Personality and Social Psychology, 67,* 186–205.

Russell, Michael; Peeke, Harmon V. S.; et al. (1984). Learned histamine release. *Science, 225,* 733–734.

Ryff, Carol D., & Keyes, Corey L. M. (1995). The structure of psychological well-being revisited. *Journal of Personality and Social Psychology, 69,* 719–727.

Ryle, Gilbert (1949). *The concept of mind.* London: Hutchinson.

Rymer, Russ (1993). *Genie: An abused child's flight from silence.* New York: HarperCollins.

Saarni, Carolyn (1989). Children's understanding of strategic control of emotional expression in social transactions. In C. Saarni & P. L. Harris (eds.), *Children's understanding of emotion.* Cambridge, England: Cambridge University Press.

Sabini, John, & Silver, Maury (1985, Winter). Critical thinking and obedience to authority. *National Forum (Phi Beta Kappa Journal),* 13–17.

Sackett, Paul R. (1994). Integrity testing for personnel selection. *Current Directions in Psychological Science, 3,* 73–76.

Sacks, Oliver (1985). *The man who mistook his wife for a hat and other clinical tales.* New York: Simon & Schuster.

Sagan, Eli (1988). *Freud, women, and morality: The psychology of good and evil.* New York: Basic Books.

Sahley, Christie L.; Rudy, Jerry W.; & Gelperin, Alan (1981). An analysis of associative learning in a terrestrial mollusk: 1. Higher-order conditioning, blocking, and a transient US preexposure effect. *Journal of Comparative Physiology, 144,* 1–8.

Saltz, Bruce L.; Woerner, M. G.; Kane, J. M.; Lieberman, J. A.; et al. (1991, November 6). Prospective study of tardive dyskinesia incidence in the elderly. *Journal of the American Medical Association, 266*(17), 2402—2406.

Samel, Alexander; Wegmann, Hans-Martin; Vejvoda, Martin; Maass, Hartmut; et al. (1991). Influence of melatonin treatment on human circadian rhythmicity before and after a simulated 9-hr time shift. *Journal of Biological Rhythms, 6,* 235–248.

Samelson, Franz (1979). Putting psychology on the map: Ideology and intelligence testing. In A. R. Buss (ed.), *Psychology in social context.* New York: Irvington.

Sameroff, Arnold J., & Seifer, Ronald (1989). *Social regulation of developmental continuities.* Paper presented at the annual meeting of the American Association for the Advancement of Science, San Francisco.

Sameroff, Arnold J.; Seifer, Ronald; Barocas, Ralph; Zax, Melvin; & Greenspan, Stanley (1987). Intelligence quotient scores of 4-year-old children: Social-environmental risk factors. *Pediatrics, 79,* 343–350.

Sanberg, Paul R.; Koutouzis, Ted K.; Freeman, Thomas B.; et al. (1993). Behavioral effects of fetal neural transplants: Relevance to Huntington's disease. *Brain Research Bulletin, 32,* 493–496.

Sapirstein, Guy, & Kirsch, Irving (1996). *Listening to Prozac, but hearing placebo? A meta-analysis of the placebo effect of antidepressant medication.* Paper presented at the annual meeting of the American Psychological Association, Toronto, Canada.

Sapolsky, Robert M. (1987, July). The case of the falling nightwatchmen. *Discover, 8,* 42–45.

Sarbin, Theodore R. (1986). The narrative as a root metaphor for psychology. In T. R. Sarbin (ed.), *Narrative psychology: The storied nature of human conduct.* New York: Praeger.

Sarbin, Theodore R. (1991). Hypnosis: A fifty year perspective. *Contemporary Hypnosis, 8,* 1–15.

Sarbin, Theodore R. (1992). The social construction of schizophrenia. In W. Flack, D. R. Miller, & M. Wiener (eds.), *What is schizophrenia?* New York: Springer-Verlag.

Sarbin, Theodore R., & Coe, William C. (1972). *Hypnosis: A social psychological analysis of influence communication.* New York: Holt, Rinehart and Winston.

Sáry, Gyula; Vogels, Rufin; & Orban, Guy A. (1993). Cue-invariant shape selectivity of macaque inferior temporal neurons. *Science, 260,* 995–997.

Saucier, Gerard (1994). Separating description and evaluation in the structure of personality attributes. *Journal of Personality and Social Psychology, 66,* 141–154.

Savage-Rumbaugh, Sue, & Lewin, Roger (1994). *Kanzi: The ape at the brink of the human mind.* New York: Wiley.

Savage-Rumbaugh, Sue; Shanker, Stuart; & Taylor, Talbot (1996). *Apes, language and the human mind.* New York: Oxford University Press.

Saxe, Leonard (1994). Detection of deception: Polygraph and integrity tests. *Current Directions in Psychological Science, 3,* 69–73.

Saywitz, Karen; Goodman, Gail S.; Nicholas, Elissa; & Moan, Susan (1991). Children's memory for genital exam: Implications for child sexual abuse. *Journal of Consulting and Clinical Psychology, 59,* 682–691.

Scarborough, Elizabeth, & Furumoto, Laurel (1987). *Untold lives: The first generation of American women psychologists.* New York: Columbia University Press.

Scarr, Sandra (1984). Intelligence: What an introductory psychology student might want to know. In A. M. Rogers & C. J. Scheirer (eds.), *The G. Stanley Hall Lecture Series* (Vol. 4). Washington, DC: American Psychological Association.

Scarr, Sandra (1993). Biological and cultural diversity: The legacy of Darwin for development. *Child Development, 64,* 1333–1353.

Scarr, Sandra; Pakstis, Andrew J.; Katz, Soloman H.; & Barker, William B. (1977). Absence of a relationship between degree of white ancestry and intellectual skill in a black population. *Human Genetics, 39,* 69–86.

Scarr, Sandra, & Weinberg, Richard A. (1977). Intellectual similarities within families of both adopted and biological children. *Intelligence, 1,* 170–191.

Scarr, Sandra, & Weinberg, Robert A. (1994). Educational and occupational achievement of brothers and sisters in adoptive and biologically related families. *Behavioral Genetics, 24,* 301–325.

Schachter, Stanley (1971). *Emotion, obesity, and crime.* New York: Academic Press.

Schachter, Stanley, & Singer, Jerome E. (1962). Cognitive, social, and physiological determinants of emotional state. *Psychological Review, 69,* 379–399.

Schacter, Daniel L. (1990). Memory. In M. I. Posner (ed.), *Foundations of cognitive science.* Cambridge, MA: MIT Press.

Schacter, Daniel L. (1996). *Searching for memory: The brain, the mind, and the past.* New York: Basic Books.

Schacter, Daniel L.; Chiu, C.-Y. Peter; & Ochsner, Kevin N. (1993). Implicit memory: A selective review. *Annual Review of Neuroscience, 16,* 159–182.

Schacter, Daniel L.; Reiman, E.; Curran, T.; et al. (1996). Neuroanatomical correlates of veridical and illusory recognition memory: Evidence from positron emission tomography. *Neuron, 17,* 267–274.

Schafer, Roy (1992). *Retelling a life: Narration and dialogue in psychoanalysis.* New York: Basic Books.

Schaie, K. Warner (1993). The Seattle longitudinal studies of adult intelligence. *Current Directions in Psychological Science, 2,* 171–175.

Schaie, K. Warner (1994). *The course of adult intellectual development.* Distinguished scientific contribution award address presented at the annual meeting of the American Psychological Association, Toronto, Canada.

Schank, Roger, with Peter Childers (1988). *The creative attitude.* New York: Macmillan.

Schatzman, M.; Worsley, A.; & Fenwick, P. (1988). Correspondence during lucid dreams between dreamed and actual events. In J. Gackenbach & S. LaBerge (eds.), *Conscious mind, sleeping brain.* New York: Plenum.

Scheier, M. F., & Carver, C. S. (1992). Effects of optimism on psychological and physical well-being: Theoretical overview and empirical update. *Cognitive Therapy and Research, 16,* 201–228.

Schein, Edgar; Schneier, Inge; & Barker, Curtis H. (1961). *Coercive persuasion.* New York: Norton.

Scherer, Klaus R., & Wallbott, Harald G. (1994). Evidence for universality and cultural variation of differential emotion response patterning. *Journal of Personality and Social Psychology, 66,* 310–328.

Schlaug, Gottfried; Jäncke, Lutz; Huang, Yanxiong; & Steinmetz, Helmuth (1995, February 3). In vivo evidence of structural brain asymmetry in musicians. *Science, 267,* 699–701.

Schlossberg, Nancy K. (1984). Exploring the adult years. In A. M. Rogers & C. J. Scheirer (eds.), *The G. Stanley Hall Lecture Series* (Vol. 4). Washington, DC: American Psychological Association.

Schlossberg, Nancy K., & Robinson, Susan P. (1996). *Going to plan B.* New York: Simon & Schuster/Fireside.

Schmidt, Peter J.; Nieman, Lynnette K.; Grover, Gay N.; Muller, Kari L.; et al. (1991). Lack of effect of induced menses on symptoms in women with premenstrual syndrome. *New England Journal of Medicine, 324,* 1174–1179.

Schneider, Allen M., & Tarshis, Barry (1986). *An introduction to physiological psychology* (3rd ed.). New York: Random House.

Schneider, Kirk J., & May, Rollo (1995). *The psychology of existence: An integrative, clinical perspective.* New York: McGraw-Hill.

Schnell, Lisa, & Schwab, Martin E. (1990, January 18). Axonal regeneration in the rat spinal cord produced by an antibody against myelin-associated neurite growth inhibitors. *Nature, 343,* 269–272.

Schrader, Harald; Obelieniene, D.; Bovim, G.; et al. (1996). Natural evolution of late whiplash syndrome outside the medicolegal context. *Lancet, 347,* 1207–1211.

Schuckit, Marc A., & Smith, T. L. (1996). An 8-year follow-up of 450 sons of alcoholic and control subjects. *Archives of General Psychiatry, 53,* 202–210.

Schulkin, Jay (1994). Melancholic depression and the hormones of adversity: A role for the amygdala. *Current Directions in Psychological Science, 3,* 41–44.

Schulman, Michael, & Mekler, Eva (1994). *Bringing up a caring child* (rev. ed.). New York: Doubleday.

Schulz, Richard, & Decker, Susan (1985). Long-term adjustment to physical disability: The role of social support, perceived control, and self-blame. *Journal of Personality and Social Psychology, 48,* 1162–1172.

Schuman, Howard, & Scott, Jacqueline (1989). Generations and collective memories. *American Journal of Sociology, 54,* 359–381.

Schwartz, Barry, & Reilly, Martha (1985). Long-term retention of a complex operant in pigeons. *Journal of Experimental Psychology: Animal Behavior Processes, 11,* 337–355.

Schwartz, Jeffrey; Stoessel, Paula W.; Baxter, Lewis R.; Martin, Karron M.; & Phelps, Michael E. (1996). Systematic changes in cerebral glucose metabolic rate after successful behavior modification treatment of obsessive-compulsive disorder. *Archives of General Psychiatry, 53,* 109–113.

Scofield, Michael (1993, June 6). About men: Off the ladder. *The New York Times Magazine,* 22.

Scribner, Sylvia (1977). Modes of thinking and ways of speaking: Culture and logic reconsidered. In P. N. Johnson-Laird & P. C. Wason (eds.), *Thinking: Readings in cognitive science.* Cambridge, England: Cambridge University Press.

Seabrook, John (1994, March). Building a better human. [Book review of "The Gene Wars" by Robert Cook-Deegan.] *The New Yorker,* 109–114.

Sears, Pauline, & Barbee, Ann H. (1977). Career and life satisfactions among Terman's gifted women. In J. C. Stanley, W. C. George, & C. H. Solano (eds.), *The gifted and the creative: A fifty-year perspective.* Baltimore, MD: Johns Hopkins University Press.

Sebel, Peter, S.; Bonke, Benno; & Winograd, Eugene (1993). *Memory and awareness in anesthesia.* Englewood Cliffs, NJ: Prentice-Hall.

Segal, Julius (1986). *Winning life's toughest battles.* New York: McGraw-Hill.

Segall, Marshall H. (1994). A cross-cultural research contribution to unraveling the nativist/empiricist controversy. In W. J. Lonner & R. Malpass (eds.), *Psychology and culture.* Needham Heights, MA: Allyn & Bacon.

Segall, Marshall H.; Campbell, Donald T.; & Herskovits, Melville J. (1966). *The influence of culture on visual perception.* Indianapolis: Bobbs-Merrill.

Segall, Marshall H.; Dasen, Pierre R.; Berry, John W.; & Poortinga, Ype H. (1990). *Human behavior in global perspective: An introduction to cross-cultural psychology.* New York: Pergamon.

Seiden, Richard (1978). Where are they now? A follow-up study of suicide attempters from the Golden Gate Bridge. *Suicide and Life-Threatening Behavior, 8,* 203–216.

Seidenberg, Mark S., & Petitto, Laura A. (1979). Signing behavior in apes: A critical review. *Cognition, 7,* 177–215.

Seifer, Ronald; Schiller, Masha; Sameroff, Arnold; Resnick, Staci; & Riordan, Kate (1996). Attachment, maternal sensitivity, and infant temperament during the first year of life. *Developmental Psychology, 32,* 12–25.

Sekuler, Robert, & Blake, Randolph (1994). *Perception* (3rd ed.). New York: Knopf.

Seligman, Martin E. P. (1975). *Helplessness: On depression, development, and death.* San Francisco: Freeman.

Seligman, Martin E. P. (1991). *Learned optimism.* New York: Knopf.

Seligman, Martin E. P., & Hager, Joanne L. (1972, August). Biological boundaries of learning: The sauce-béarnaise syndrome. *Psychology Today,* 59–61, 84–87.

Selye, Hans (1956). *The stress of life.* New York: McGraw-Hill.

Sem-Jacobsen, C. W. (1959). Effects of electrical stimulation on the human brain. *Electroencephalography and Clinical Neurophysiology, 11,* 379.

Serbin, Lisa A.; Powlishta, Kimberly K.; & Gulko, Judith (1993). The development of sex typing in middle childhood. *Monographs of the Society for Research in Child Development, 58*(2, Serial No. 232), v-74.

Serdula, Mary K.; Collins, M. E.; Williamson, David F.; et al. (1993). Weight control practices of U.S. adolescents and adults. *Annals of Internal Medicine, 119,* 667–671.

Serpell, Robert (1994). The cultural construction of intelligence. In W. J. Lonner & R. S. Malpass (eds.), *Psychology and culture.* Needham Heights, MA: Allyn & Bacon.

Shadish, William R., Jr.; Lurigio, Arthur J.; & Lewis, Dan A. (1989). After deinstitutionalization: The present and future of mental health long-term care policy. *Journal of Social Issues, 45*(3), 1–16.

Shapiro, A. Eugene, & Wiggins, Jack G. (1994). A PsyD degree for every practitioner. *American Psychologist, 49,* 207–210.

Shapiro, David A., & Shapiro, Diana (1982). Meta-analysis of comparative therapy outcome studies: A replication and refinement. *Psychological Bulletin, 92,* 581–604.

Shapiro, Deane H.; Schwartz, Carolyn E.; & Astin, John A. (1996). Controlling ourselves, controlling our world. *American Psychologist, 51,* 1213–1230.

Shatz, Marilyn, & Gelman, Rochel (1973). The development of communication skills: Modifications in the speech of young children as a function of the listener. *Monographs of the Society for Research in Child Development, 38.*

Shaver, Phillip R. (1994). *Attachment and care giving in adult romantic relationships.* Paper presented at the annual meeting of the American Psychological Association, Los Angeles.

Shaver, Phillip, & Hazan, Cindy (1987). Romantic love conceptualized as an attachment process. *Journal of Personality and Social Psychology, 52,* 511–524.

Shaver, Phillip R., & Hazan, Cindy (1993). Adult romantic attachment: Theory and evidence. In D. Perlman & W. H. Jones (eds.), *Advances in personal relationships* (Vol. 4). London: Kingsley.

Shaver, Phillip; Schwartz, Judith; Krison, Donald; & O'Connor, Cary (1987). Emotion knowledge: Further exploration of a prototype approach. *Journal of Personality and Social Psychology, 52,* 1061–1086.

Shaver, Phillip R.; Wu, Shelley; & Schwartz, Judith C. (1992). Cross-cultural similarities and differences in emotion and its representation: A prototype approach. In M. S. Clark (ed.), *Review of Personality and Social Psychology* (Vol. 13). Newbury Park, CA: Sage.

Shaw, Daniel S.; Keenan, Kate; & Vondra, Joan I. (1994). Developmental precursors of externalizing behavior: Ages 1 to 3. *Developmental Psychology, 30,* 355–364.

Shaywitz, Bennett A.; Shaywitz, Sally E.; Pugh, Kenneth R.; et al. (1995). Sex differences in the functional organization of the brain for language. *Nature, 373,* 607–609.

Shea, Christopher (1996, August 16). Psychologists debate accuracy of "significance test." *Chronicle of Higher Education,* A16, A17.

Shedler, Jonathan, & Block, Jack (1990). Adolescent drug use and psychological health. *American Psychologist, 45,* 612–630.

Shedler, Jonathan; Mayman, Martin; & Manis, Melvin (1993). The illusion of mental health. *American Psychologist, 48,* 1117–1131.

Sheehan, Neil (1988). *A bright shining lie: John Paul Vann and America in Vietnam.* New York: Random House.

Shepard, Roger N. (1967). Recognition memory for words, sentences and pictures. *Journal of Verbal Learning and Verbal Behavior, 6,* 156–163.

Shepard, Roger N., & Metzler, Jacqueline (1971). Mental rotation of three-dimensional objects. *Science, 171,* 701–703.

Shepperd, James A. (1995). Remedying motivation and productivity loss in collective settings. *Current Directions in Psychological Science, 4,* 131–140.

Sherif, Carolyn Wood (1979). Bias in psychology. In J. Sherman & E. T. Beck (eds.), *The prism of sex.* Madison: University of Wisconsin Press.

Sherif, Muzafer (1958). Superordinate goals in the reduction of intergroup conflicts. *American Journal of Sociology, 63,* 349–356.

Sherif, Muzafer; Harvey, O. J.; White, B. J.; Hood, William; & Sherif, Carolyn (1961). *Intergroup conflict and cooperation: The Robbers Cave experiment.* Norman: University of Oklahoma Institute of Intergroup Relations.

Sherman, Bonnie R., & Kunda, Ziva (1989). *Motivated evaluation of scientific evidence.* Paper presented at the annual meeting of the American Psychological Society, Arlington, VA.

Sherman, Lawrence W. (1992). *Policing domestic violence.* New York: Free Press.

Sherman, Lawrence W., & Berk, Richard A. (1984). The specific deterrent effects of arrest for domestic assault. *American Sociological Review, 49,* 261–271.

Sherman, Lawrence W.; Schmidt, Janell D.; Rogan, Dennis P.; et al. (1991). From initial deterrence to long-term escalation: Short-custody arrest for poverty ghetto domestic violence. *Criminology, 29,* 821–849.

Shermer, Michael (1997). *Why people believe weird things: Pseudoscience, superstition, and other confusions of our time.* New York: Freeman.

Sherrington, R.; Rogaev, E. I.; Liang, Y.; et al. (1995). Cloning of a gene bearing missense mutations in early-onset familial Alzheimer's disease. *Nature, 375,* 754–760.

Sherry, David F., & Schacter, Daniel L. (1987). The evolution of multiple memory systems. *Psychological Review, 94,* 439–454.

Sherwin, Barbara B. (1988). A comparative analysis of the role of androgen in human male and female sexual behavior: Behavioral specificity, critical thresholds, and sensitivity. *Psychobiology, 16,* 416–425.

Shields, Stephanie A. (1975). Functionalism, Darwinism, and the psychology of women: A study in social myth. *American Psychologist, 30,* 739–754.

Shields, Stephanie A. (1991). Gender in the psychology of emotion: A selective research review. In K. T. Strongman (ed.), *International review of studies on emotion* (Vol. 1). New York: Wiley.

Shogren, Elizabeth (1994, August 18). Treatment against their will. *The Los Angeles Times,* A1, A14–16.

Shotland, R. Lance, & Straw, Margaret (1976). Bystander response to an assault: When a man attacks a woman. *Journal of Personality and Social Psychology, 34,* 990–999.

Shuchman, Miriam, & Wilkes, Michael S. (1990, October 7). Dramatic progress against depression. *The New York Times Magazine,* Pt. 2: *The Good Health Magazine,* 12, 30ff.

Shumaker, Sally A., & Hill, D. Robin (1991). Gender differences in social support and physical health. *Health Psychology, 10,* 102–111.

Shweder, Richard A. (1990). Cultural psychology—What is it? In J. W. Stigler, R. A. Shweder, & G. Herdt (eds.), *Cultural psychology: The Chicago Symposia on Human Development.* Cambridge, England: Cambridge University Press.

Shweder, Richard A.; Mahapatra, Manamohan; & Miller, Joan G. (1990). Culture and moral development. In J. W. Stigler, R. A. Shweder, & G. Herdt (eds.), *Cultural psychology: Essays on comparative human development.* Cambridge, England: Cambridge University Press.

Sidanius, Jim; Pratto, Felicia; & Bobo, Lawrence (1996). Racism, conservatism, affirmative action, and intellectual sophistication: A matter of principled conservatism or group dominance? *Journal of Personality and Social Psychology, 70,* 476–490.

Siegel, Alan B. (1991). *Dreams that can change your life.* Los Angeles: Jeremy Tarcher.

Siegel, Ronald K. (1989). *Intoxication: Life in pursuit of artificial paradise.* New York: Dutton.

Siegel, Ronald K. (1992). *Fire in the brain: Clinical tales of hallucination.* New York: Dutton.

Siegel, Shepard (1990). Classical conditioning and opiate tolerance and withdrawal. In D. J. K. Balfour (ed.), *Psychotropic drugs of abuse.* New York: Pergamon.

Siegel, Shepard; Hinson, Riley E.; Krank, Marvin D.; & McCully, Jane (1982). Heroin "overdose" death: Contribution of drug-associated environmental cues. *Science, 216,* 436–437.

Siegler, Robert (1996). *Emerging minds: The process of change in children's thinking.* New York: Oxford University Press.

Silver, Eric; Cirincione, Carmen; & Steadman, Henry J. (1994). Demythologizing inaccurate perceptions of the insanity defense. *Law and Human Behavior, 18,* 63–70.

Silverman, Loyd, & Weinberger, Joel (1985). Mommy and I are one: Implications for psychotherapy. *American Psychologist, 40,* 1296–1308.

Silverstein, Brett, & Perlick, Deborah (1995). *The cost of competence: Why inequality causes depression, eating disorders, and illness in women.* New York: Oxford University Press.

Silverstein, Brett; Peterson, Barbara; & Perdue, Lauren (1986). Some correlates of the thin standard of bodily attractiveness in women. *International Journal of Eating Disorders, 5,* 145–155.

Simon, Herbert A. (1973). The structure of ill-structured problems. *Artificial Intelligence, 4,* 181–202.

Simon, William, & Gagnon, John H. (1986). Sexual scripts: Permanence and change. *Archives of Sexual Behavior, 15,* 97–120.

Sims, Ethan A. (1974). Studies in human hyperphagia. In G. Bray & J. Bethune (eds.), *Treatment and management of obesity.* New York: Harper & Row.

Sinclair, Robert C.; Hoffman, Curt; Mark, Melvin M.; Martin, Leonard L.; & Pickering, Tracie L. (1994). Construct accessibility and the misattribution of arousal: Schachter and Singer revisited. *Psychological Science, 5,* 15–19.

Singer, Jerome L. (1984). The private personality. *Personality and Social Psychology Bulletin, 10,* 7–30.

Singer, Jerome L., & Singer, Dorothy G. (1988). Some hazards of growing up in a television environment: Children's aggression and restlessness. In S. Oskamp (ed.), *Applied social psychology annual: Vol. 8. Television as a social issue.* Newbury Park, CA: Sage.

Singer, Margaret T.; Temerlin, Maurice K.; & Langone, Michael D. (1990). Psychotherapy cults. *Cultic Studies Journal, 7,* 101–125.

Skinner, B. F. (1938). *The behavior of organisms: An experimental analysis.* New York: Appleton-Century-Crofts.

Skinner, B. F. (1948). Superstition in the pigeon. *Journal of Experimental Psychology, 38,* 168–172.

Skinner, B. F. (1948/1976). *Walden two.* New York: Macmillan.

Skinner, B. F. (1956). A case history in the scientific method. *American Psychologist, 11,* 221–233.

Skinner, B. F. (1961, November). Teaching machines. *Scientific American,* 91–102.

Skinner, B. F. (1968). *The technology of teaching.* New York: Appleton-Century-Crofts.

Skinner, B. F. (1972). The operational analysis of psychological terms. In B. F. Skinner, *Cumulative record* (3rd ed.). New York: Appleton-Century-Crofts.

Skinner, B. F. (1983). *A matter of consequences.* New York: Knopf.

Skinner, B. F. (1990). Can psychology be a science of mind? *American Psychologist, 45,* 1206–1210.

Skinner, Ellen A. (1996). A guide to constructs of control. *Journal of Personality and Social Psychology, 71,* 549–570.

Skinner, J. B.; Erskine, A.; Pearce, S. A.; Rubenstein, I.; et al. (1990). The evaluation of a cognitive behavioural treatment programme in outpatients with chronic pain. *Journal of Psychosomatic Research, 34,* 13–19.

Skreslet, Paula (1987, November 30). The prizes of first grade. *Newsweek,* 8.

Slade, Pauline (1984). Premenstrual emotional changes in normal women: Fact or fiction? *Journal of Psychosomatic Research, 28,* 1–7.

Slobin, Daniel I. (1970). Universals of grammatical development in children. In G. B. Flores d'Arcais & W. J. M. Levelt (eds.), *Advances in psycholinguistics.* Amsterdam, Netherlands: North-Holland.

Slobin, Daniel I. (ed.) (1985). *The cross-linguistic study of language acquisition* (Vols. 1 and 2). Hillsdale, NJ: Erlbaum.

Slobin, Daniel I. (ed.) (1991). *The cross-linguistic study of language acquisition* (Vol. 3). Hillsdale, NJ: Erlbaum.

Smelser, Neil J.; Vasconcellos, John; & Mecca, Andrew (eds.) (1989). *The social importance of self-esteem.* Berkeley: University of California Press.

Smith, Barbara A.; Fillion, Thomas J.; & Blass, Elliott M. (1990). Orally mediated sources of calming in 1- to 3-day-old human infants. *Developmental Psychology, 26,* 731–737.

Smith, Carlyle (1995). Sleep states and memory processes. *Behavioural Brain Research, 69,* 137–145.

Smith, Craig A., & Ellsworth, Phoebe C. (1987). Patterns of appraisal and emotion related to taking an exam. *Journal of Personality and Social Psychology, 52,* 475–488.

Smith, Craig A.; Haynes, Kelly N.; Lazarus, Richard S.; & Pope, Lois K. (1993). In search of the "hot" cognitions: Attributions, appraisals, and their relation to emotion. *Journal of Personality and Social Psychology, 65,* 916–929.

Smith, James F., & Kida, Thomas (1991). Heuristics and biases: Expertise and task realism in auditing. *Psychological Bulletin, 109,* 472–489.

Smith, M. Brewster (1994). Selfhood at risk: Postmodern perils and the perils of postmodernism. *American Psychologist, 49,* 405–411.

Smith, Mary Lee; Glass, Gene; & Miller, Thomas I. (1980). *The benefits of psychotherapy.* Baltimore, MD: Johns Hopkins University Press.

Smith, N.; Tsimpli, I.-M., & Ouhalla, J. (1993). Learning the impossible: The acquisition of possible and impossible languages by a polyglot savant. *Lingua, 91,* 279–347.

Smith, Peter B., & Bond, Michael H. (1993/1994). *Social psychology across cultures: Analysis and perspectives.* Boston: Allyn & Bacon.

Smith, Timothy W.; Limon, Jeffery P.; Gallo, Linda C.; & Ngu, Le Q. (1996). Interpersonal control and cardiovascular reactivity: Goals, behavioral expression, and the moderating effects of sex. *Journal of Personality and Social Psychology, 70,* 1012–1024.

Smith, Timothy W.; Sanders, Jill D.; & Alexander, James F. (1990). What does the Cook and Medley Hostility Scale measure? Affect, behavior, and attributions in the marital context. *Journal of Personality and Social Psychology, 58,* 699–708.

Smither, Robert D. (1994). *The psychology of work and human performance* (2nd ed.). New York: HarperCollins.

Snarey, John R. (1985). Cross-cultural universality of social-moral development: A critical review of Kohlbergian research. *Psychological Bulletin, 97,* 202–232.

Snodgrass, Mary Ann (1987). The relationships of differential loneliness, intimacy, and characterological attributional style to duration of loneliness. In M. Hojat & R. Crandall (eds.), *Loneliness: Theory, research, and applications* (Special Issue of the *Journal of Social Behavior and Personality*), *2,* 173–186.

Snodgrass, Sara E. (1985). Women's intuition: The effect of subordinate role on interpersonal sensitivity. *Journal of Personality and Social Psychology, 49,* 146–155.

Snodgrass, Sara E. (1992). Further effects of role versus gender on interpersonal sensitivity. *Journal of Personality and Social Psychology, 62,* 154–158.

Snow, Barry R; Pinter, Isaac; Gusmorino, Paul; Jimenez, Arthur; Rosenblum, Andrew; & Adelglass, Howard (1986). *Sex differences in chronic pain: Incidence and causal mechanisms.* Paper presented at the annual meeting of the American Psychological Association, Washington, DC.

Snow, Margaret E.; Jacklin, Carol N.; & Maccoby, Eleanor (1983). Sex-of-child differences in father-child interaction at one year of age. *Child Development, 54,* 227–232.

Snyder, C. R. (1989). Reality negotiation: From excuses to hope and beyond. [Special Issue: Self-illusions: When are they adaptive?] *Journal of Social and Clinical Psychology, 8,* 130–157.

Snyder, C. R. (1990). Self-handicapping processes and sequelae: On the taking of a psychological dive. In R. L. Higgins, C. R. Snyder, & S. C. Berglas (eds.), *Self-handicapping: The paradox that isn't.* New York: Plenum.

Snyder, C. R.; Higgins, Raymond L.; & Stucky, Rita J. (1983). *Excuses: Masquerades in search of grace.* New York: Wiley-Interscience.

Snyder, C. R., & Shenkel, Randee J. (1975, March). The P. T. Barnam effect. *Psychology Today,* 52–54.

Snyder, Robert A. (1993, Spring). The glass ceiling for women: Things that don't cause it and things that won't break it. *Human Resource Development Quarterly,* 97–106.

Solomon, Jennifer C. (1996). Humor and aging well: A laughing matter or a matter of laughing? [Special Issue: Aging well in contemporary society: II. Choices and processes.] *American Behavioral Scientist, 39,* 249–271.

Solomon, Paul R. (1979). Science and television commercials: Adding relevance to the research methodology course. *Teaching of Psychology, 6,* 26–30.

Solomon, Robert C. (1994). *About love.* Lanham, MD: Littlefield Adams.

Sommer, Robert (1969). *Personal space: The behavioral basis of design.* Englewood Cliffs, NJ: Prentice-Hall.

Sommer, Robert (1977, January). Toward a psychology of natural behavior. *APA Monitor.* (Reprinted in *Readings in psychology 78/79.* Guilford, CT: Dushkin, 1978.)

Sontag, Susan (1978). *Illness as metaphor.* New York: Farrar, Straus & Giroux.

Sorce, James F.; Emde, Robert N.; Campos, Joseph; & Klinnert, Mary D. (1985). Maternal emotional signaling: Its effect on the visual cliff behavior of 1-year-olds. *Developmental Psychology, 21,* 195–200.

Spangler, William D., & House, Robert J. (1991). Presidential effectiveness and the leadership motive profile. *Journal of Personality and Social Psychology, 60,* 439–455.

Spanos, Nicholas P. (1991). A sociocognitive approach to hypnosis. In S. J. Lynn & J. W. Rhue (eds.), *Theories of hypnosis: Current models and perspectives.* New York: Guilford Press.

Spanos, Nicholas P. (1996). *Multiple identities and false memories: A sociocognitive perspective.* Washington, DC: American Psychological Association.

Spanos, Nicholas P.; Burgess, Cheryl A.; Roncon, Vera; Wallace-Capretta, Suzanne; & Cross, Patricia (1993). Surreptitiously observed hypnotic responding in simulators and in skill-trained and untrained high hypnotizables. *Journal of Personality and Social Psychology, 65,* 391–398.

Spanos, Nicholas P.; DuBreuil, Susan C.; & Gabora, Natalie J. (1991). Four month follow-up of skill training induced enhancements in hypnotizability. *Contemporary Hypnosis, 8,* 25–32.

Spanos, Nicholas P.; Menary, Evelyn; Gabora, Natalie J.; DuBreuil, Susan C.; & Dewhirst, Bridget (1991). Secondary identity enactments during hypnotic past-life regression: A sociocognitive perspective. *Journal of Personality and Social Psychology, 61,* 308–320.

Spanos, Nicholas P.; Stenstrom, Robert J.; & Johnson, Joseph C. (1988). Hypnosis, placebo, and suggestion in the treatment of warts. *Psychosomatic Medicine, 50,* 245–260.

Spearman, Charles (1927). *The abilities of man.* London: Macmillan.

Spelke, Elizabeth S.; Breinlinger, Karen; Macomber, Janet; & Jacobson, Kristen (1992). Origins of knowledge. *Psychological Review, 99,* 605–632.

Speltz, Matthew L.; Greenberg, Mark T.; & Deklyen, Michelle (1990). Attachment in preschoolers with disruptive behavior: A comparison of clinic-referred and nonproblem children. *Development and Psychopathology, 2,* 31–46.

Spence, Janet T. (1985). Gender identity and its implications for concepts of masculinity and femininity. In T. Sonderegger (ed.), *Nebraska Symposium on Motivation.* Lincoln: University of Nebraska Press.

Spencer, M. B., & Dornbusch, Sanford M. (1990). Ethnicity. In S. S. Feldman & G. R. Elliott (eds.), *At the threshold: The developing adolescent.* Cambridge, MA: Harvard University Press.

Sperling, George (1960). The information available in brief visual presentations. *Psychological Monographs, 74*(498).

Sperry, Roger W. (1964). The great cerebral commissure. *Scientific American, 210*(1), 42–52.

Sperry, Roger W. (1982). Some effects of disconnecting the cerebral hemispheres. *Science, 217,* 1223–1226.

Spiegel, D.; Bloom, J. R.; Kraemer, H. C.; Gottheil, E. (1989, October 14). Effect of psychosocial treatment on survival of patients with metastatic breast cancer. *Lancet,* 2(8668), 888–891.

Spilich, George J.; June, Lorraine; & Renner, Judith (1992). Cigarette smoking and cognitive performance. *British Journal of Addiction, 87,* 113–126.

Spitzer, Robert L., & Williams, Janet B. (1988). Having a dream: A research strategy for DSM-IV. *Archives of General Psychiatry, 45,* 871–874.

Spitzer, W. O.; Skovron, M. L.; Salmi, L. R.; et al. (1995). Scientific monograph of the Quebec Task Force on Whiplash-Associated Disorders: Redefining "whiplash" and its management. *Spine, 20,* 1S–73S.

Sporer, Siegfried L.; Penrod, Steven; Read, Don; & Cutler, Brian (1995). Choosing, confidence, and accuracy: A meta-analysis of the confidence-accuracy relation in eyewitness identification studies. *Psychological Bulletin, 118,* 315–327.

Sprecher, Susan; Sullivan, Quintin; & Hatfield, Elaine (1994). Mate selection preferences: Gender differences examined in a national sample. *Journal of Personality and Social Psychology, 66,* 1074–1080.

Spring, Bonnie; Chiodo, June; & Bowen, Deborah J. (1987). Carbohydrates, tryptophan, and behavior: A methodological review. *Psychological Bulletin, 102,* 234–256.

Squire, Larry R. (1987). *Memory and the brain.* New York: Oxford University Press.

Squire, Larry R.; Ojemann, Jeffrey G.; Miezin, Francis M.; et al. (1992). Activation of the hippocampus in normal humans: A functional anatomical study of memory. *Proceedings of the National Academy of Science, 89,* 1837–1841.

Squire, Larry R., & Zola-Morgan, Stuart (1991). The medial temporal lobe memory system. *Science, 253,* 1380–1386.

Staats, Carolyn K., & Staats, Arthur W. (1957). Meaning established by classical conditioning. *Journal of Experimental Psychology, 54,* 74–80.

Stam, Henderikus J. (1989). From symptom relief to cure: Hypnotic interventions in cancer. In N. P. Spanos & J. F. Chaves (eds.), *Hypnosis: The cognitive-behavioral perspective.* Buffalo, NY: Prometheus Books.

Stanovich, Keith (1996). *How to think straight about psychology* (4th ed.). New York: HarperCollins.

Stanton, Annette L., & Snider, Pamela R. (1993). Coping with a breast cancer diagnosis: A prospective study. *Health Psychology, 12,* 16–23.

Staples, Brent (1994). *Parallel time.* New York: Pantheon.

Staples, Susan L. (1996). Human response to environmental noice: Psychological research and public policy. *American Psychologist, 51,* 143–150.

Stapley, Janice C., & Haviland, Jeannette M. (1989). Beyond depression: Gender differences in normal adolescents' emotional experiences. *Sex Roles, 20,* 295–308.

***State of New Hampshire* v. *Joel Hungerford* (St. 94 45 7)** & ***State* v. *John Morahan* (St. 93 1734 6)** Superior Court, Northern District of Hillsborough County, State of New Hampshire. Notice of Decision, May 23, 1995.

Stattin, Haken, & Magnusson, David (1990). *Pubertal maturation in female development.* Hillsdale, NJ: Erlbaum.

Staub, Ervin (1990). The psychology and culture of torture and torturers. In P. Suedfeld (ed.), *Psychology and torture.* Washington, DC: Hemisphere.

Staub, Ervin (1996). Cultural-social roots of violence. *American Psychologist, 51,* 117–132.

Steele, Claude M. (1994, October 31). Bizarre black IQ claims abetted by media. *San Francisco Chronicle,* op-ed page.

Steinberg, Laurence D. (1990). Interdependence in the family: Autonomy, conflict and harmony in the parent-adolescent relationship. In S. S. Feldman & G. R. Elliott (eds.), *At the threshold: The developing adolescent.* Cambridge, MA: Harvard University Press.

Steiner, Robert A. (1989). *Don't get taken!* El Cerrito, CA: Wide-Awake Books.

Stempel, Jennifer J.; Beckwith, Bill E.; & Petros, Thomas V. (1986). *The effects of alcohol on the speed of memory retrieval.* Paper presented at the annual meeting of the American Psychological Association, Washington, DC.

Stenberg, Craig R., & Campos, Joseph (1990). The development of anger expressions in infancy. In N. Stein, B. Leventhal, & T. Trabasso (eds.), *Psychological and biological approaches to emotion.* Hillsdale, NJ: Erlbaum.

Stephan, K. M.; Fink, G. R.; Passingham, R. E.; et al. (1995). Functional anatomy of the mental representation of upper movements in healthy subjects. *Journal of Neurophysiology, 73,* 373–386.

Stephan, Walter (1985). Intergroup relations. In G. Lindzey & E. Aronson (eds.), *Handbook of social psychology* (Vol. 2). New York: Random House.

Stephan, Walter G.; Ageyev, Vladimir; Coates-Shrider, Lisa; Stephan, Cookie W.; & Abalakina, Marina (1994). On the relationship between stereotypes and prejudice: An international study. *Personality and Social Psychology Bulletin, 20,* 277–284.

Stephan, Walter, & Brigham, John C. (1985). Intergroup contact: Introduction. *Journal of Social Issues, 41*(3), 1–8.

Stephens, Mitchell (1991, September 20). The death of reading. *The Los Angeles Times Magazine,* 10, 12, 16, 42, 44.

Stern, Daniel (1985). *The interpersonal world of the infant.* New York: Basic Books.

Sternberg, Robert J. (1986). *Intelligence applied: Understanding and increasing your intellectual skills.* San Diego: Harcourt Brace Jovanovich.

Sternberg, Robert J. (1988). *The triarchic mind: A new theory of human intelligence.* New York: Viking.

Sternberg, Robert J. (1994, Spring). Love is a story. *The General Psychologist, 30,* 1–11.

Sternberg, Robert J.; Okagaki, Lynn; & Jackson, Alice S. (1990). Practical intelligence for success in school. *Educational Leadership, 48,* 35–39.

Sternberg, Robert J., & Wagner, Richard K. (1989). Individual differences in practical knowledge and its acquisition. In P. Ackerman, R. J. Sternberg, & R. Glaser (eds.), *Individual differences.* New York: Freeman.

Sternberg, Robert J.; Wagner, Richard K.; & Okagaki, Lynn (1993). Practical intelligence: The nature and role of tacit knowledge in work and at school. In H. Reese & J. Puckett (eds.), *Advances in lifespan development.* Hillsdale, NJ: Erlbaum.

Sternberg, Robert J.; Wagner, Richard K.; Williams, Wendy M.; & Horvath, Joseph A. (1995). Testing common sense. *American Psychologist, 50,* 912–927.

Stevenson, Harold W.; Chen, Chuansheng; & Lee, Shin-ying (1993, January 1). Mathematics achievement of Chinese, Japanese, and American children: Ten years later. *Science, 259,* 53–58.

Stevenson, Harold W., & Stigler, James W. (1992). *The learning gap.* New York: Summit.

Stickler, Gunnar B.; Salter, Margery; Broughton, Daniel D.; & Alario, Anthony (1991). Parents' worries about children compared to actual risks. *Clinical Pediatrics, 30,* 522–528.

Stimpson, Catharine (1996, Winter). Women's studies and its discontents. *Dissent, 43,* 67–75.

Stoch, M. B., & Smythe, P. M. (1963). Does undernutrition during infancy inhibit brain growth and subsequent intellectual development? *Archives of Diseases in Childbood, 38,* 546–552.

Stoerig, Petra (1993). Sources of blindsight. *Science, 261,* 493.

Stoll, Andrew L.; Tohen, Mauricio; & Baldessarini, Ross J. (1993). Increasing frequency of the diagnosis of obsessive-compulsive disorder: A reply. *American Journal of Psychiatry, 150,* 682–683.

Storm, Christine, & Storm, Tom (1987). A taxonomic study of the vocabulary of emotions. *Journal of Personality and Social Psychology, 53,* 805–816.

Strack, Fritz; Martin, Leonard L.; & Stepper, Sabine (1988). Inhibiting and facilitating conditions of the human smile: A nonobtrusive test of the facial-feedback hypothesis. *Journal of Social and Personality Psychology, 54,* 768–777.

Straus, Murray A. (1991). Discipline and deviance: Physical punishment of children and violence and other crime in adulthood. *Social Problems, 38*(2), 133–154.

Streissguth, A. P.; Aase, J. M.; Clarren, S. K.; Randels, S. P.; LaDue, R. A.; & Smith, D. F. (1991). Fetal alcohol syndrome in adolescents and adults. *Journal of the American Medical Association, 265,* 1961–1967.

Strickland, Bonnie R. (1965). The prediction of social action from a dimension of internal-external control. *Journal of Social Psychology, 66,* 353–358.

Strickland, Bonnie R. (1989). Internal-external control expectancies: From contingency to creativity. *American Psychologist, 44,* 1–12.

Strickland, Bonnie R. (1995). Research on sexual orientation and human development: A commentary. *Developmental Psychology, 31,* 137–140.

Strickland, Tony L.; Lin, Keh-Ming; Fu, Paul; Anderson, Dora; & Zheng, Yanping (1995). Comparison of lithium ratio between African-American and Caucasian bipolar patients. *Biological Psychiatry, 37,* 325–330.

Strickland, Tony L.; Ranganath, Vijay; Lin, Keh-Ming; Poland, Russell E.; et al. (1991). Psychopharmacological considerations in the treatment of black American populations. *Psychopharmacology Bulletin, 27,* 441–448.

Stroebe, Wolfgang; Stroebe, Margaret; Abakoumkin, Georgios; & Schut, Henk (1996). The role of loneliness and social support in adjustment to loss: A test of attachment versus stress theory. *Journal of Personality and Social Psychology, 70,* 1241–1249.

Strong, Bryan, & DeVault, Christine (1994). *Human sexuality.* Mountain View, CA: Mayfield.

Strupp, Hans H. (1982). The outcome problem in psychotherapy: Contemporary perspectives. In J. H. Harvey & M. M. Parks (eds.), *Psychotherapy research and behavior change: Vol. 1. The APA Master Lecture Series.* Washington, DC: American Psychological Association.

Strupp, Hans H., & Binder, Jeffrey (1984). *Psychotherapy in a new key.* New York: Basic Books.

Stunkard, Albert J. (ed.) (1980). *Obesity.* Philadelphia: Saunders.

Stunkard, Albert J.; Harris, J. R.; Pedersen, N. L.; & McClearn, G. E. (1990, May 24). The body-mass index of twins who have been reared apart. *New England Journal of Medicine, 322,* 1483–1487.

Sue, Stanley (1991). Ethnicity and culture in psychological research and practice. In J. Goodchilds (ed.), *Psychological perspectives on human diversity in America.* Washington, DC: American Psychological Association.

Sue, Stanley, & Zane, Nolan (1987). The role of culture and cultural techniques in psychotherapy: A critique and reformulation. *American Psychologist, 42,* 37–45.

Suedfeld, Peter (1975). The benefits of boredom: Sensory deprivation reconsidered. *American Scientist, 63*(1), 60–69.

Suedfeld, Peter; Little, B. R.; Rank, A. D.; Rank, D. S.; & Ballard, E. (1986). Television and adults: Thinking, personality and attitudes. In T. M. Williams (ed.), *The impact of television: A natural experiment in three communities.* San Diego: Academic Press.

Sulloway, Frank J. (1992). *Freud, biologist of the mind: Beyond the psychoanalytic legend* (rev. ed.). Cambridge, MA: Harvard University Press.

Summerville, Mary B.; Kaslow, Nadine J.; & Doepke, Karla J. (1996). Psychopathology and cognitive and family functioning in suicidal African-American adolescents. *Current Directions in Psychological Science, 5,* 7–11.

Sundstrom, Eric; De Meuse, Kenneth P.; & Futrell, David (1990). Work teams: Applications and effectiveness. *American Psychologist, 45,* 120–133.

Suomi, Stephen J. (1987). Genetic and maternal contributions to individual differences in rhesus monkey biobehavioral development. In N. Krasnegor, E. Blass, M. Hofer, & W. Smotherman (eds.), *Perinatal development: A psychobiological perspective.* New York: Academic Press.

Suomi, Stephen J. (1989). Primate separation models of affective disorders. In J. Madden (ed.), *Adaptation, learning, and affect.* New York: Raven Press.

Suomi, Stephen J. (1991). Uptight and laid-back monkeys: Individual differences in the response to social challenges. In S. Branch, W. Hall, & J. E. Dooling (eds.), *Plasticity of development.* Cambridge, MA: MIT Press.

Super, Charles A., & Harkness, Sara (1994). The developmental niche. In W. J. Lonner & R. Malpass (eds.), *Psychology and culture.* Needham Heights, MA: Allyn & Bacon.

Susman, Elizabeth J.; Inoff-Germain, Gale; Nottelmann, Editha D.; et al. (1987). Hormones, emotional dispositions, and aggressive attributes in young adolescents. *Child Development, 58,* 1114–1134.

Susser, Ezra; Neugebauer, Richard; Hoek, Hans W.; Brown, Alan S.; et al. (1996). Schizophrenia after prenatal famine: Further evidence. *Archives of General Psychiatry, 53,* 25–31.

Swain, Scott (1989). Covert intimacy: Closeness in men's friendships. In B. J. Risman & P. Schwartz (eds.), *Gender in intimate relationships.* Belmont, CA: Wadsworth.

Sweat, Jane A., & Durm, Mark W. (1993, Winter). Psychics: Do police departments really use them? *Skeptical Inquirer, 17,* 148–158.

Swedo, Susan E., & Rapoport, Judith L. (1991). Trichotillomania [hair-pulling]. *Journal of Child Psychology and Psychiatry and Allied Disciplines, 32,* 401–409.

Symons, Donald (1979). *The evolution of human sexuality.* New York: Oxford University Press.

Szasz, Thomas (1961/1967). *The myth of mental illness.* New York: Dell Delta.

Taffel, Ronald (1990, September/October). The politics of mood. *Family Therapy Networker,* 49–53, 72.

Tajfel, Henri; Billig, M. G.; Bundy, R. P.; & Flament, C. (1971). Social categorization and intergroup behavior. *European Journal of Social Psychology, 1,* 149–178.

Tajfel, Henri, & Turner, John C. (1986). The social identity theory of intergroup behavior. In S. Worchel & W. G. Austin (eds.), *Psychology of intergroup relations.* Chicago: Nelson-Hall.

Tangney, June P. (1992). *Constructive vs. destructive responses to anger: The moderating roles of shame and guilt across the lifespan.* Paper presented at the annual meeting of the International Congress of Psychology, Brussels, Belgium.

Tangney, June P.; Wagner, Patricia E.; Hill-Barlow, Deborah; Marschall, Donna E.; & Gramzow, Richard (1996). Relation of shame and guilt to constructive versus destructive responses to anger across the lifespan. *Journal of Personality and Social Psychology, 70,* 797–809.

Tanur, Judith M. (ed.). (1992). *Questions about questions: Inquiries into the cognitive basis of surveys.* New York: Russell Sage Foundation.

Tartter, Vivien C. (1986). *Language processes.* New York: Holt, Rinehart and Winston.

Taub, David M. (1984). *Primate paternalism.* New York: Van Nostrand Reinhold.

Tavris, Carol (1987, January). How to succeed in business abroad. *Signature,* 86–87, 110–113.

Tavris, Carol (1989). *Anger: The misunderstood emotion* (2nd ed.). New York: Simon & Schuster/Touchstone.

Tavris, Carol (1992). *The mismeasure of woman.* New York: Simon & Schuster/Touchstone.

Taylor, Donald M., & Porter, Lana E. (1994). A multicultural view of stereotyping. In W. J. Lonner & R. Malpass (eds.), *Psychology and culture.* Needham Heights, MA: Allyn & Bacon.

Taylor, Shelley E. (1989). *Positive illusions: Creative self-deception and the healthy mind.* New York: Basic Books.

Taylor, Shelley E. (1995). *Health psychology* (3rd ed.). New York: McGraw Hill.

Taylor, Shelley E., & Brown, Jonathon D. (1988). Illusion and well-being: A social psychological perspective on mental health. *Psychological Bulletin, 103,* 193–210.

Taylor, Shelley E., & Brown, Jonathon D. (1994). Positive illusions and well-being revisited: Separating fact from fiction. *Psychological Bulletin, 116,* 21–27.

Taylor, Shelley E.; Lichtman, Rosemary R.; & Wood, Joanne V. (1984). Attributions, beliefs about control, and adjustment to breast cancer. *Journal of Personality and Social Psychology, 46,* 489–502.

Taylor, Shelley E., & Lobel, Marci (1989). Social comparison activity under threat: Downward evaluation and upward contacts. *Psychological Review, 96,* 569–575.

Taylor, Shelley E.; Peplau, Letitia A.; & Sears, David O. (1997). *Social psychology* (9th ed.). Englewood Cliffs, NJ: Prentice-Hall.

Taylor, Shelley E.; Repetti, Rena; & Seeman, Teresa (1997). Health psychology: What is an unhealthy environment and how does it get under the skin? *Annual Review of Psychology* (Vol. 48). Palo Alto, CA: Annual Reviews.

Tellegen, Auke (1993). Folk concepts and psychological concepts of personality and personality disorder. *Psychological Inquiry, 4,* 122–130.

Tellegen, Auke; Lykken, David T.; Bouchard, Thomas J., Jr.; et al. (1988). Personality similarity in twins reared apart and together. *Journal of Personality and Social Psychology, 54,* 1031–1039.

Terman, Lewis M., & Oden, Melita H. (1959). *Genetic studies of genius: Vol. 5. The gifted group at mid-life.* Stanford, CA: Stanford University Press.

Terrace, H. S. (1985). In the beginning was the "name." *American Psychologist, 40,* 1011–1028.

Terry, Deborah J. (1994). Determinants of coping: The role of stable and situational factors. *Journal of Personality and Social Psychology, 66,* 895–910.

Teyler, T. J., & DiScenna, P. (1987). Long-term potentiation. *Annual Review of Neuroscience, 10,* 131–161.

Thibodeau, Ruth, & Aronson, Elliot (1992). Taking a closer look: Reasserting the role of the self-concept in dissonance theory. *Personality and Social Psychology Bulletin, 18,* 591–602.

Thiriart, Philippe (1991, Winter). Acceptance of personality test results. *Skeptical Inquirer, 15,* 161–165.

Thoma, Stephen J. (1986). Estimating gender differences in the comprehension and preference of moral issues. *Developmental Review, 6,* 165–180.

Thomas, Alexander, & Chess, Stella (1984). Genesis and evolution of behavioral disorders: From infancy to early adult life. *American Journal of Psychiatry, 141,* 1–9.

Thomas, Sandra P. (1993). Introduction. In S. P. Thomas (ed.), *Women and anger.* New York: Springer.

Thompson, Richard F. (1983). Neuronal substrates of simple associative learning: Classical conditioning. *Trends in Neurosciences, 6,* 270–275.

Thompson, Richard F. (1986). The neurobiology of learning and memory. *Science, 233,* 941–947.

Thompson, Suzanne C.; Collins, Mary A.; Newcomb, Michael D.; & Hunt, William (1996). On fighting versus accepting stressful circumstances: Primary and secondary control among HIV-positive men in prison. *Journal of Personality and Social Psychology, 70,* 1307–1317.

Thompson, Suzanne C.; Nanni, Christopher; & Levine, Alexandra (1994). Primary versus secondary and central versus consequence-related control in HIV-positive men. *Journal of Personality and Social Psychology, 67,* 540–547.

Thorndike, Edward L. (1898). Animal intelligence: An experimental study of the associative processes in animals. *Psychological Review Monograph Supplement, 2* (Whole No. 8).

Thornhill, Randy (1980). Rape in *Panorpa* scorpion-flies and a general rape hypothesis. *Animal Behavior, 28,* 52–59.

Tiefer, Leonore (1995). *Sex is not a natural act and other essays.* Boulder, CO: Westview Press.

Tillman, Jane G.; Nash, Michael R.; & Lerner, Paul M. (1994). Does trauma cause dissociative pathology? In S. Lynn & J. Rhue (eds.), *Dissociation: Clinical and theoretical perspectives.* New York: Guilford Press.

Tolman, Edward C. (1938). The determiners of behavior at a choice point. *Psychological Review, 45,* 1–35.

Tolman, Edward C. (1948). Cognitive maps in rats and men. *Psychological Review, 55,* 189–208.

Tolman, Edward C., & Honzik, Chase H. (1930). Introduction and removal of reward and maze performance in rats. *University of California Publications in Psychology, 4,* 257–275.

Tomkins, Silvan S. (1981). The role of facial response in the experience of emotion: A reply to Tourangeau and Ellsworth. *Journal of Personality and Social Psychology, 40,* 355–357.

Torrey, E. Fuller (1988). *Surviving schizophrenia* (rev. ed.). New York: Harper & Row.

Torrey, E. Fuller; Bowler, Ann E.; Taylor, Edward H.; & Gottesman, Irving I. (1994). *Schizophrenia and manic-depressive disorder.* New York: Basic Books.

Tougas, Francine; Brown, Rupert; Beaton, Ann M.; & Joly, Stéphane (1995). Neosexism: Plus ça change, plus c'est pareil. *Personality and Social Psychology Bulletin, 21,* 842–849.

Tranel, Daniel, & Damasio, Antonio (1985). Knowledge without awareness: An autonomic index of facial recognition by prosopagnosics. *Science, 228,* 1453–1454.

Traub, James (1993, June 7). The hearts and minds of City College. *The New Yorker,* 42–53.

Triandis, Harry C. (1994). *Culture and social behavior.* New York: McGraw-Hill.

Triandis, Harry C. (1995). *Individualism and collectivism.* Boulder, CO: Westview Press.

Triandis, Harry C. (1996). The psychological measurement of cultural syndromes. *American Psychologist, 51,* 407–415.

Trichopoulos, Dimitrios; Li, F. P.; & Hunter, D. J. (1996, September). What causes cancer? *Scientific American, 275,* 80–87.

Trimble, Joseph E., & Medicine, Beatrice (1993). Diversification of American Indians: Forming an indigenous perspective. In U. Kim & J. W. Berry (eds.), *Indigenous psychologies: Research and experience in cultural context.* Newbury Park, CA: Sage.

Trivers, Robert (1972). Parental investment and sexual selection. In B. Campbell (ed.), *Sexual selection and the descent of man.* New York: Aldine de Gruyter.

Tronick, Edward Z. (1989). Emotions and emotional communication in infants. *American Psychologist, 44,* 112–119.

Tronick, Edward Z.; Morelli, Gilda A.; & Ivey, Paula K. (1992). The Efe forager infant and toddler's pattern of social relationships: Multiple and simultaneous. [Special Section: Cross-cultural studies of development.] *Developmental Psychology, 28,* 568–577.

Tucker, Don M., & Frederick, S. L. (1989). Emotion and brain lateralization. In H. Wagner & A. Manstead (eds.), *Handbook of social psychophysiology.* Chichester, England: Wiley.

Tulving, Endel (1985). How many memory systems are there? *American Psychologist, 40,* 385–398.

Tulving, Endel, & Schacter, Daniel L. (1990). Priming and human memory systems. *Science, 247,* 301–305.

Tversky, Amos, & Kahneman, Daniel (1973). Availability: A heuristic for judging frequency and probability. *Cognitive Psychology, 5,* 207–232.

Tversky, Amos, & Kahneman, Daniel (1981). The framing of decisions and the psychology of choice. *Science, 211,* 453–458.

Tversky, Amos, & Kahneman, Daniel (1986). Rational choice and the framing of decisions. *Journal of Business, 59,* S251–S278.

Twenge, Jean M. (1996). *Attitudes toward women, 1970–1995: A meta-analysis.* Paper presented at the annual meeting of the American Psychological Association, Toronto, Canada.

Tzischinsky, Orna; Pal, I.; Epstein, Rachel; Dagan, Y.; & Lavie, Peretz (1992). The importance of timing in melatonin administration in a blind man. *Journal of Pineal Research, 12,* 105–108.

Uchida, K., & Toya, S. (1996). Grafting of genetically manipulated cells into adult brain: Toward graft-gene therapy. *Keio Journal of Medicine* (Japan), *45,* 81–89.

Uchino, Bert N.; Cacioppo, John T.; & Kiecolt-Glaser, Janice K. (1996). The relationship between social support and physiological processes: A review with emphasis on underlying mechanisms and implications for health. *Psychological Bulletin, 119,* 488–531.

Uchino, Bert N.; Cacioppo, John T.; Malarkey, William; & Glaser, Ronald (1995). Individual differences in cardiac sympathetic control predict endocrine and immune responses to acute psychological stress. *Journal of Personality and Social Psychology, 69,* 736–743.

Unger, Rhoda (1990). Imperfect reflections of reality: Psychology constructs gender. In R. T. Hare-Mustin & J. Marecek (eds.), *Making a difference: Psychology and the construction of gender.* New Haven, CT: Yale University Press.

Usher, JoNell A., & Neisser, Ulric (1993). Childhood amnesia and the beginnings of memory for four early life events. *Journal of Experimental Psychology: General, 122,* 155–165.

Vaillant, George E. (1983). *The natural history of alcoholism: Causes, patterns, and paths to recovery.* Cambridge, MA: Harvard University Press.

Vaillant, George E. (ed.) (1992). *Ego mechanisms of defense.* Washington, DC: American Psychiatric Press.

Vaillant, George E. (1995). *The natural history of alcoholism revisited.* Cambridge, MA: Harvard University Press.

Valenstein, Elliot (1986). *Great and desperate cures: The rise and decline of psychosurgery and other radical treatments for mental illness.* New York: Basic Books.

Valkenburg, Patti M., & van der Voort, Tom H. A. (1994). Influence of TV on daydreaming and creative imagination: A review of research. *Psychological Bulletin, 116,* 316–339.

Van Cantfort, Thomas E., & Rimpau, James B. (1982). Sign language studies with children and chimpanzees. *Sign Language Studies, 34,* 15–72.

Vandenberg, Brian (1985). Beyond the ethology of play. In A. Gottfried & C. C. Brown (eds.), *Play interactions.* Lexington, MA: Lexington Books.

Vandenberg, Brian (1993). Existentialism and development. *American Psychologist, 48,* 296–297.

van de Vijver, F., & Leung, K. (1996). *Methods and data analysis for cross-cultural research.* Thousand Oaks, CA: Sage.

Van Lancker, Diana R., & Kempler, Daniel (1987). Comprehension of familiar phrases by left- but not by right-hemisphere damaged patients. *Brain and Language, 32,* 265–277.

Vasquez, Melba J. T., & Barón, Augustine, Jr. (1988). The psychology of the Chicano experience: A sample course structure. In P. Bronstein & K. Quina (eds.), *Teaching a psychology of people.* Washington, DC: American Psychological Association.

Viken, Richard J.; Rose, Richard J.; Kaprio, Jaakko; & Koskenvuo, Markku (1994). A developmental genetic analysis of adult personality: Extraversion and neuroticism from 18 to 59 years of age. *Journal of Personality and Social Psychology, 66,* 722–730.

Vila, J., & Beech, H. R. (1980). Premenstrual symptomatology: An interaction hypothesis. *British Journal of Social and Clinical Psychology, 19,* 73–80.

Vinokur, Amiram D., & van Ryn, Michelle (1993). Social support and undermining in close relationships: Their independent effects on the mental health of unemployed persons. *Journal of Personality and Social Psychology, 65,* 350–359.

Vokey, John R., & Read, J. Don (1985). Subliminal messages: Between the devil and the media. *American Psychologist, 40,* 1231–1239.

Von Lang, Jochen, & Sibyll, Claus (eds.) (1984). *Eichmann interrogated: Transcripts from the archives of the Israeli police.* New York: Random House.

Voyer, Daniel; Voyer, Susan; & Bryden, M. P. (1995). Magnitude of sex differences in spatial abilities: A meta-analysis and consideration of critical variables. *Psychological Bulletin, 117,* 250–270.

Wadden, Thomas A.; Foster, G. D.; Letizia, K. A.; & Mullen, J. L. (1990, August 8). Long-term effects of dieting on resting metabolic rate in obese outpatients. *Journal of the American Medical Association, 264,* 707–711.

Wagemaker, Herbert, Jr., & Cade, Robert (1978). Hemodialysis in chronic schizophrenic patients. *Southern Medical Journal, 71,* 1463–1465.

Wagenaar, Willem A. (1986). My memory: A study of autobiographical memory over six years. *Cognitive Psychology, 18,* 225–252.

Wakefield, Jerome C. (1992). The concept of mental disorder: On the boundary between biological facts and social values. *American Psychologist, 47,* 373–388.

Walker, Alice, & Parmar, Pratibha (1995). *Warrior marks: Female genital mutilation and the sexual binding of women.* Fort Worth, TX: Harcourt Brace.

Walker, Anne (1994). Mood and well-being in consecutive menstrual cycles: Methodological and theoretical implications. *Psychology of Women Quarterly, 18,* 271–290.

Walker, Edward L. (1970). Relevant psychology is a snark. *American Psychologist, 25,* 1081–1086.

Walker, Lawrence J. (1989). A longitudinal study of moral reasoning. *Child Development, 60,* 157–166.

Walker, Lawrence J.; de Vries, Brian; & Trevethan, Shelley D. (1987). Moral stages and moral orientations in real-life and hypothetical dilemmas. *Child Development, 58,* 842–858.

Wallbott, Harald G.; Ricci-Bitti, Pio; & Bänninger-Huber, Eva (1986). Nonverbal reactions to emotional experiences. In K. R. Scherer, H. G. Wallbott, & A. B. Summerfield (eds.), *Experiencing emotion: A cross-cultural study.* Cambridge, England: Cambridge University Press.

Waller, Niels G. (1996). Evaluating the structure of personality. In C. R. Cloninger (ed.), *Personality and psychopathology.* Washington, DC: American Psychiatric Press.

Waller, Niels G.; Kojetin, Brian A.; Bouchard, Thomas J., Jr.; Lykken, David T.; & Tellegen, Auke (1990). Genetic and environmental influences on religious interests, attitudes, and values: A study of twins reared apart and together. *Psychological Science, 1,* 138–142.

Waller, Niels G., & Shaver, Phillip (1994). The importance of nongenetic influences on romantic love styles: A twin-family study. *Psychological Science, 5,* 268–274.

Walter, John L., & Peller, Jane E. (1993). *Becoming solution-focused in brief therapy.* New York: Brunner/Mazel.

Wang, Alvin Y.; Thomas, Margaret H.; & Ouellette, Judith A. (1992). The keyword mnemonic and retention of second-language vocabulary words. *Journal of Educational Psychology, 84,* 520–528.

Ward, L. Monique (1994). *Preschoolers' awareness of associations between gender and societal status.* Paper presented at the annual meeting of the American Psychological Association, Los Angeles.

Wark, Gillian R., & Krebs, Dennis (1996). Gender and dilemma differences in real-life moral judgment. *Developmental Psychology, 32,* 220–230.

Warren, Gayle H., & Raynes, Anthony E. (1972). Mood changes during three conditions of alcohol in-take. *Quarterly Journal of Studies on Alcohol, 33,* 979–989.

Washburn, David A., & Rumbaugh, Duane M. (1991). Ordinal judgments of numerical symbols by macaques *(Macaca mulatta). Psychological Science, 2,* 190–193.

Waters, Everett; Merrick, Susan K.; Albersheim, Leah J.; & Treboux, Dominique (1995). *Attachment security from infancy to early adulthood: A 20-year-longitudinal study.* Paper presented at the annual meeting of the Society for Research in Child Development, Indianapolis.

Watson, David, & Clark, Lee Anna (1992). On traits and temperament: General and specific factors of emotional experience and their relation to the five-factor model. *Journal of Personality, 60,* 441–476.

Watson, John B. (1913). Psychology as the behaviorist views it. *Psychological Review, 20,* 158–177.

Watson, John B. (1925). *Behaviorism.* New York: Norton.

Watson, John B., & Rayner, Rosalie (1920). Conditioned emotional reactions. *Journal of Experimental Psychology, 3,* 1–14.

Webb, Wilse B., & Cartwright, Rosalind D. (1978). Sleep and dreams. In M. Rosenzweig & L. Porter (eds.), *Annual Review of Psychology, 29,* 223–252.

Webster, Richard (1995). *Why Freud was wrong.* New York: Basic Books.

Wechsler, David (1955). *Manual for the Wechsler Adult Intelligence Scale.* New York: Psychological Corporation.

Wechsler, Henry; Davenport, Andrea; Dowdall, George; Moeykens, Barbara; et al. (1994). Health and behavioral consequences of binge drinking in college: A national survey of students at 140 campuses. *Journal of the American Medical Association, 272,* 1672–1677.

Weder, Alan B., & Schork, Nicholas J. (1994). Adaptation, allometry, and hypertension. *Hypertension, 24,* 145–156.

Wegner, Daniel M. (1994). Ironic processes of mental control. *Psychological Review, 101,* 34–57.

Wegner, Daniel M., & Gold, Daniel B. (1995). Fanning old flames: Emotional and cognitive effects of suppressing thoughts of a past relationship. *Journal of Personality and Social Psychology, 68,* 782–792.

Wegner, Daniel M.; Schneider, David J.; Carter, Samuel R., III; & White, Teri L. (1987). Paradoxical effects of thought suppression. *Journal of Personality and Social Psychology, 53,* 5–13.

Weil, Andrew T. (1972/1986). *The natural mind: A new way of looking at drugs and the higher consciousness.* Boston: Houghton Mifflin.

Weil, Andrew T. (1974a, June). Parapsychology: Andrew Weil's search for the true Geller. *Psychology Today,* 45–50.

Weil, Andrew T. (1974b, July). Parapsychology: Andrew Weil's search for the true Geller—Part II. The letdown. *Psychology Today,* 74–78, 82.

Weinberger, David R. (1995, August 26). From neuropathology to neurodevelopment. *Lancet, 346,* 552–557.

Weiner, Bernard (1986). *An attributional theory of motivation and emotion.* New York: Springer-Verlag.

Weiner, Bernard; Figueroa-Muñoz, Alice; & Kakihara, Craig (1991). The goals of excuses and communication strategies related to causal perceptions. *Personality and Social Psychology Bulletin, 17,* 4–13.

Weiskrantz, L. (1992). Unconscious vision: The strange phenomenon of blindsight. *Sciences, 32,* 22.

Weiss, Bahr; Dodge, Kenneth A.; Bates, John E.; & Petitt, Gregory S. (1992). Some consequences of early harsh discipline: Child aggression and a maladaptive social information processing style. *Child Development, 63,* 1321–1335.

Weisz, John R.; Rothbaum, Fred M.; & Blackburn, Thomas C. (1984). Standing out and standing in: The psychology of control in America and Japan. *American Psychologist, 39,* 955–969.

Weisz, John R.; Weiss, Bahr; Alicke, Mark D.; & Klotz, M. L. (1987). Effectiveness of psychotherapy with children and adolescents: A meta-analysis for clinicians. *Journal of Consulting and Clinical Psychology, 55,* 542–549.

Weisz, John R.; Weiss, Bahr; Han, Susan S.; Granger, Douglas A.; & Morton, Todd (1995). Effects of psychotherapy with children and adolescents revisited: A meta-analysis of treatment outcome studies. *Psychological Bulletin, 117,* 450–468.

Weitzenhoffer, André M. (1995). *Catalepsy tests: Their implications for a science of hypnotism.* Paper presented at the annual meeting of the American Psychological Association, New York.

Wellenkamp, Jane (1995). Cultural similarities and differences regarding emotional disclosure: Some examples from Indonesia and the Pacific. In J. W. Pennebaker (ed.), *Emotion, disclosure, and health.* Washington, DC: American Psychological Association.

Wells, Gary L.; Luus, C. A. Elizabeth; & Windschitl, Paul D. (1994). Maximizing the utility of eyewitness identification evidence. *Current Directions in Psychological Science, 3,* 194–197.

Wender, Paul H., & Klein, Donald F. (1981). *Mind, mood, and medicine: A guide to the new biopsychiatry.* New York: Farrar, Straus & Giroux.

Werner, Emmy E. (1989). High-risk children in young adulthood: A longitudinal study from birth to 32 years. *American Journal of Orthopsychiatry, 59,* 72–81.

Werner, Emmy E., & Smith, Ruth S. (1982). *Vulnerable but invincible: A longitudinal study of resilient children and youth.* New York: McGraw-Hill.

West, Melissa O., & Prinz, Ronald J. (1987). Parental alcoholism and childhood psychopathology. *Psychological Bulletin, 102,* 204–218.

Westermeyer, Joseph (1995). Cultural aspects of substance abuse and alcoholism: Assessment and management. *Psychiatric Clinics of North America, 18,* 589–605.

Wheeler, Anthony (1990, Fall). Biological cycles and rhythms vs. biorhythms. *Skeptical Inquirer,* 75–82.

Wheeler, Douglas L.; Jacobson, John W.; Paglieri, Raymond A.; & Schwartz, Allen A. (1993). An experimental assessment of facilitated communication. *Mental Retardation, 31,* 49–59.

Whisman, Mark A. (1993). Mediators and moderators of change in cognitive therapy of depression. *Psychological Bulletin, 114,* 248–265.

Whitam, Frederick L.; Diamond, Milton; & Martin, James (1993). Homosexual orientation in twins: A report on 61 pairs and 3 triplet sets. *Archives of Sexual Behavior, 22,* 187–206.

White, Michael, & Epston, David (1990). *Narrative means to therapeutic ends.* New York: Norton.

White, Robert W. (1959). Motivation reconsidered: The concept of competence. *Psychological Review, 66,* 297–333.

White, Sheldon H., & Pillemer, David B. (1979). Childhood amnesia and the development of a socially accessible memory system. In J. F. Kihlstrom & F. J. Evans (eds.), *Functional disorders of memory.* Hillsdale, NJ: Erlbaum.

Whitehurst, Grover J.; Arnold, David S.; Epstein, Jeffery N.; Angell, Andrea L.; Smith, Meagan; & Fischel, Janet E. (1994). A picture book reading intervention in day care and home for children from low-income families. *Developmental Psychology, 30,* 679–689.

Whitehurst, Grover J.; Falco, F. L.; Lonigan, C. J.; Fischel, J. E.; et al. (1988). Accelerating language development through picture book reading. *Developmental Psychology, 24,* 552–559.

Whiting, Beatrice B., & Edwards, Carolyn P. (1988). *Children of different worlds: The formation of social behavior.* Cambridge, MA: Harvard University Press.

Whiting, Beatrice, & Whiting, John (1975). *Children of six cultures.* Cambridge, MA: Harvard University Press.

Widner, H.; Tetrud, J.; Rehncrona, S.; et al. (1993). Fifteen months' follow-up on bilateral embryonic mesencephalic grafts in two cases of severe MPTP-induced Parkinsonism. *Advances in Neurology, 60,* 729–733.

Widom, Cathy S. (1989). Does violence beget violence? A critical examination of the literature. *Psychological Bulletin, 106,* 3–28.

Wiggins, Jerry S. (ed.) (1996). *The five-factor model of personality: Theoretical perspectives.* New York: Guilford Press.

Williams, Kipling D., & Karau, Steven J. (1991). Social loafing and social compensation: The effects of expectations of co-worker performance. *Journal of Personality and Social Psychology, 61,* 570–581.

Williams, Linda M. (1994). Recall of childhood trauma: A prospective study of women's memories of child sexual abuse. *Journal of Consulting and Clinical Psychology, 62,* 1167–1176.

Williams, Redford B., Jr. (1989). *The trusting heart.* New York: Random House.

Williams, Redford B., Jr.; Barefoot, John C.; & Shekelle, Richard B. (1985). The health consequences of hostility. In M. A. Chesney & R. H. Rosenman (eds.), *Anger and hostility in cardiovascular and behavioral disorders.* New York: Hemisphere.

Williams, Walter (1986). *The spirit and the flesh: Sexual diversity in American Indian culture.* Boston: Beacon Press.

Williams, Wendy M.; Blythe, Tina; White, Noel; Li, Jin; et al. (1996). *Practical intelligence for school.* New York: HarperCollins.

Willie, Charles V.; Rieker, Patricia P.; Kramer, Bernard M.; & Brown, Bertram S. (eds.) (1995). *Mental health, racism, and sexism* (rev. ed.). Pittsburgh: University of Pittsburgh Press.

Willis, Sherry L. (1987). Cognitive training and everyday competence. In K. W. Schaie (ed.), *Annual review of gerontology and geriatrics* (Vol. 7). New York: Springer.

Wilner, Daniel; Walkley, Rosabelle; & Cook, Stuart (1955). *Human relations in interracial housing.* Minneapolis: University of Minnesota Press.

Wilson, Edward O. (1975). *Sociobiology: The new synthesis.* Cambridge, MA: Belknap/Harvard University Press.

Wilson, Edward O. (1978). *On human nature.* Cambridge, MA: Harvard University Press.

Wilson, Edward O. (1994). *Naturalist.* Washington, DC: Island Press.

Wilson, G. Terence, & Fairburn, Christopher G. (1993). Cognitive treatments for eating disorders. [Special Section: Recent developments in cognitive and constructivist psychotherapies.] *Journal of Consulting and Clinical Psychology, 61,* 261–269.

Windholz, George, & Lamal, P. A. (1985). Köhler's insight revisited. *Teaching of Psychology, 12,* 165–167.

Winick, Myron; Meyer, Knarig Katchadurian; & Harris, Ruth C. (1975). Malnutrition and environmental enrichment by early adoption. *Science, 190,* 1173–1175.

Winnicott, D. W. (1957/1990). *Home is where we start from.* New York: Norton.

Winter, David G. (1993). Power, affiliation, and war: Three tests of a motivational model. *Journal of Personality and Social Psychology, 65*, 532–545.

Wispé, Lauren G., & Drambarean, Nicholas C. (1953). Physiological need, word frequency, and visual duration thresholds. *Journal of Experimental Psychology, 46*, 25–31.

Witelson, Sandra F.; Glazer, I. I., & Kigar, D. L. (1994). Sex differences in numerical density of neurons in human auditory association cortex. *Society for Neuroscience Abstracts, 30* (Abstr. No. 582.12).

Wittchen, Hans-Ulrich; Kessler, Ronald C.; Zhao, Shanyang; & Abelson, Jamie (1995). Reliability and clinical validity of UM-CIDI DSM-III R generalized anxiety disorder. *Journal of Psychiatric Research, 29*, 95–110.

Wood, James M.; Nezworski, Teresa; & Stejskal, William J. (1996). The comprehensive system for the Rorschach: A critical examination. *Psychological Science, 7*, 3–10.

Wood, Wendy; Lundgren, Sharon; Ouellette, Judith A.; Busceme, Shelly; & Blackstone, Tamela (1994). Minority influence: A meta-analytic review of social influence processes. *Psychological Bulletin, 115*, 323–345.

Woodward, Amanda L.; Markman, Ellen M.; & Fitzsimmons, Colleen M. (1994). Rapid word learning in 13- and 18-month-olds. *Developmental Psychology, 30*, 553–566.

Wooley, Susan; Wooley, O. Wayne; & Dyrenforth, Susan (1979). Theoretical, practical, and social issues in behavioral treatments of obesity. *Journal of Applied Behavior Analysis, 12*, 3–25.

Wright, Daniel B. (1993). Recall of the Hillsborough disaster over time: Systematic biases of "flashbulb" memories. *Applied Cognitive Psychology, 7*, 129–138.

Wright, R. L. D. (1976). *Understanding statistics: An informal introduction for the behavioral sciences.* New York: Harcourt Brace Jovanovich.

Wu, Tzu-chin; Tashkin, Donald P.; Djahed, Behnam; & Rose, Jed E. (1988). Pulmonary hazards of smoking marijuana as compared with tobacco. *New England Journal of Medicine, 318*, 347–351.

Wurtman, Richard J. (1982). Nutrients that modify brain function. *Scientific American, 264*(4), 50–59.

Wurtman, Richard J., & Lieberman, Harris R. (eds.) (1982–1983). Research strategies for assessing the behavioral effects of foods and nutrients. *Journal of Psychiatric Research, 17*(2) [whole issue].

Wuthnow, Robert (1995). *Sharing the journey: Support groups and America's new quest for community.* New York: Free Press.

Wyatt, Gail E., & Mickey, M. Ray (1987). Ameliorating the effects of child sexual abuse: An exploratory study of support by parents and others. *Journal of Interpersonal Violence, 2*, 403–414.

Wylie, Mary S. (1993, September/October). The shadow of a doubt. *The Family Therapy Networker, 17*, 18–29, 70, 73.

Yalom, Irvin D. (1989). *Love's executioner and other tales of psychotherapy.* New York: Basic Books.

Yalom, Irvin D. (1995). *The theory and practice of group psychotherapy* (4th ed.). New York: Basic Books.

Yang, Kuo-shu, & Bond, Michael H. (1990). Exploring implicit personality theories with indigenous or imported constructs: The Chinese case. *Journal of Personality and Social Psychology, 58*, 1087–1095.

Yapko, Michael (1994). *Suggestions of abuse: True and false memories of childhood sexual trauma.* New York: Simon & Schuster.

Yazigi, R. A.; Odem, R. R.; & Polakoski, K. L. (1991, October 9). Demonstration of specific binding of cocaine to human spermatozoa. *Journal of the American Medical Association, 266*(14), 1956–1959.

Yee, Albert H.; Fairchild, Halford H.; Weizmann, Fredric; & Wyatt, Gail E. (1993). Addressing psychology's problems with race. *American Psychologist, 48*, 1132–1140.

Yoder, Janice D., & Kahn, Arnold S. (1993). Working toward an inclusive psychology of women. *American Psychologist, 48*, 846–850.

Yoken, Carol, & Berman, Jeffrey S. (1984). Does paying a fee for psychotherapy alter the effectiveness of treatment? *Journal of Consulting and Clinical Psychology, 52*, 254–260.

Young, Malcolm P., & Yamane, Shigeru (1992). Sparse population coding of faces in the inferotemporal cortex. *Science, 256*, 1327–1331.

Young-Eisendrath, Polly (1993). *You're not what I expected: Learning to love the opposite sex.* New York: Morrow.

Yu, C. E.; Oshima, J.; Fu, Y. H.; Wijsman, E. M.; et al. (1996, April 12). Positional cloning of the Werner's syndrome gene. *Science, 272*, 258–262.

Zahn-Waxler, Carolyn (1996). Environment, biology, and culture: Implications for adolescent development. *Developmental Psychology, 32*, 571–573.

Zahn-Waxler, Carolyn; Kochanska, Grazyna; Krupnick, Janice; & McKnew, Donald (1990). Patterns of guilt in children of depressed and well mothers. *Developmental Psychology, 26*, 51–59.

Zajonc, Robert B. (1968). Attitudinal effects of mere exposure. *Journal of Personality and Social Psychology, 9, Monograph Supplement 2*, 1–27.

Zajonc, Robert B., & Markus, Gregory B. (1975). Birth order and intellectual development. *Psychological Review, 82*, 74–88.

Zellman, Gail, & Goodchilds, Jacqueline (1983). Becoming sexual in adolescence. In E. R. Allgeier & N. B. McCormick (eds.), *Changing boundaries: Gender roles and sexual behavior.* Palo Alto, CA: Mayfield.

Zhang, Yiying; Proenca, Ricardo; Maffei, Margherita; et al. (1994). Positional cloning of the mouse obese gene and its human homologue. *Nature, 372*(6505), 425–432.

Zilbergeld, Bernie (1983). *The shrinking of America: Myths of psychological change.* Boston: Little, Brown.

Zilbergeld, Bernie (1992). *The new male sexuality.* New York: Bantam.

Zillmann, Dolf (1983). Transfer of excitation in emotional behavior. In J. T. Cacioppo & R. E. Petty (eds.), *Social psychophysiology: A sourcebook.* New York: Guilford Press.

Zimbardo, Philip G. (1970). The human choice: Individuation, reason, and order versus deindividuation, impulse, and chaos. In W. J. Arnold & D. Levine (eds.), *Nebraska Symposium on Motivation, 1969.* Lincoln: University of Nebraska Press.

Zimbardo, Philip (1996). Reflections on the Stanford prison experiment 25 years later: Genesis, transformations, and positive consequences. Paper presented at the annual meeting of the American Psychological Association, Toronto, Canada.

Zimbardo, Philip G., & Leippe, M. R. (1991). *The psychology of attitude change and social influence.* New York: McGraw-Hill.

Zinberg, Norman (1974). The search for rational approaches to heroin use. In P. G. Bourne (ed.), *Addiction.* New York: Academic Press.

Zivian, Marilyn, & Darjes, Richard (1983). Free recall by in-school and out-of-school adults: Performance and metamemory. *Developmental Psychology, 19*, 513–520.

Zonderman, Alan B.; Costa, Paul T., Jr.; & McCrae, Robert R. (1989, September 1). Depression as a risk for cancer morbidity and mortality in a nationally representative sample. *Journal of the American Medical Association, 262*, 1191–1195.

Zuckerman, Marvin (1990). Some dubious premises in research and theory on racial differences: Scientific, social, and ethical issues. *American Psychologist, 45*, 1297–1303.

Zuckerman, Marvin (1995). Good and bad humors: Biochemical bases of personality and its disorders. *Psychological Science, 6*, 325–332.

CREDITS

TEXT, TABLE, AND FIGURE CREDITS

CHAPTER 2 Figure 2.2, from R. L. Wright, "Correlations in understanding statistics," *Understanding Statistics: An Informal Introduction for the Behavioral Sciences.* © 1976 by Harcourt Brace & Company. Reprinted by permission of the publisher / Figure 2.5, from Sapolsky, "Opinion" illustration, 1987; courtesy of Discover magazine, © 1987.
CHAPTER 3 Page 88, from Steven Pinker, *The Language of Instinct.* © 1994 by Steven Pinker. Reprinted by permission of William Morrow and Company, Inc. / Figure 3.3, from Arnold Sameroff and Ronald Seifer, "Intelligent quotient scores of 4-year-old children: Social-environmental risk factors," *Pediatrics*, 79, pp. 343–350. Reprinted by permission of the authors / Figure 3.4, from J. Horgan, "Get smart, take a test: A long-term rise in IQ scores baffles intelligence experts," *Scientific American*, November 1995. © 1995 by Scientific American, Inc. Reprinted by permission of Scientific American, Inc. All rights reserved.
CHAPTER 4 Figure 4.6, Orietta Agostoni / p. 148, from Richard Restack, "Is Free Will a Fraud?" *Science Digest*, 91 (10), October 1983. Reprinted by permission of Science Digest.
CHAPTER 5 Figure 5.1, from Jessica McFarlane, Carol Lynn Martin, and Tannis M. Williams, "Mood changes in men and women," *Psychology of Women Quarterly*, 12 (1988), pp. 201–223. Reprinted by permission of Cambridge University Press / Figure 5.3, from Dennis Kelly, "Physiology of sleep and dreaming," *Principles of Neural Science.* © 1981 by Elsevier Science Publishing Company. Reprinted by permission of the publisher / p. 195, from Edith Fiore, *Encounters: A Psychologist Reveals Case Studies of Abduction by Extraterrestrials.* © 1989 by Edith Fiore. Reprinted by permission of Bantam Doubleday Dell Publishing Group, Inc.
CHAPTER 6 Figure 6.2, from Tom N. Cornsweet, "Information processing in human visual systems,"*The SRI Journal*, Issue 5, January 1969. © 1969 by SRI Journal. Reprinted by permission of SRI International / Table 6.1, from "Sound intensity levels in the environment." Reprinted by permission of the American Academy of Otolaryngology-Head and Neck Surgery, Washington, D C / Figure 6.13, from Bartoshuk and Reedy, "Relationships among papillae, taste pores, and 6-n-propylthiouracil (PROP) suprathreshold taste sensitivity," *Chemical Senses*, 18, pp. 618–619. Reprinted by permission of Oxford University Press.
CHAPTER 7 Figure 7.2, from Ivan P. Pavlov, "Acquisition and extinction of a salivary response," *Conditioned Reflexes.* Copyright 1927. Reprinted by permission of Oxford University Press / Figure 7.5, from B. F. Skinner, "Teaching machines," *Scientific American*, November 1961. © 1961 by Scientific American, Inc. Reprinted by permission. All rights reserved / Figure 7.6, from Carl Cheney, "A rat's route," *Learning and Behavior.* © 1979 by Wadsworth Publishing Co., Inc. Reprinted by permission of the publisher / p. 277, from Paul Chance, "Knock wood," *Psychology Today*, October, 1988. © 1988 by P. T. Partners, L. P. Reprinted by permission of Psychology Today Magazine / Figure 7.8, from E. C. Tolman and C. H. Honzik, "Introduction and removal of reward and maze performance in rats," *Psychology*, 4 (1930). Reprinted by permission of University of California Publications / Figure 7.7, from David Greene and Mark R. Lepper, "Turning play into work," *Psychology Today*, September 1974. © 1974 by Sussex Publishers, Inc. Reprinted by permission of Psychology Today Magazine.
CHAPTER 8 p. 303, from Sylvia Scribner, "Modes of thinking and ways of speaking: Culture and logic reconsidered," *Thinking: Readings in Cognitive Science*, 1977. Reprinted by permission of Cambridge University Press / Table 8.1, from Kathleen Galotti, "Two kinds of reasoning,"*Psychological Bulletin*, 105, 1989. © 1989 by the American Psychological Association. Reprinted by permission / p. 308, from Patricia King and Karen Kitchener, *Developing Reflective Judgment: Understanding and Promoting Intellectual Growth and Critical Thinking in Adolescents and Adults.* © 1994 by Jossey-Bass Inc., Publishers. Reprinted by permission / Table 8.2, from Lewis M. Terman and Maud A. Merrill, Sample items, from *Stanford-Binet Intelligence Scale.* © 1973 by Houghton Mifflin Co. Reprinted by permission of Riverside Publishing Co. / Figure 8.2, from Lee J. Cronbach, "Performance tasks on the Weschler tests," *Essentials of Psychological Testing*, 4th edition, p. 208. © 1984 by HarperCollins Publishers. Reprinted by permission / Table 8.3, from Lee J. Cronbach, "Verbal items similar to those on the WISC-R and WAIS-R," *Essentials of Psychological Testing*, 4th edition, p. 208. © 1984 by HarperCollins Publishers. Reprinted by permission.
CHAPTER 9 Figure 9.3, from Elizabeth Loftus, "Serial position effect," *Memory*, p. 25. © 1980 by Addison Wesley Publishing Co. Reprinted by permission / Figure 9.4, from Michael G. Wessell, "Retention in short term memory,"*Cognitive Psychology*, p. 98. © 1982 by Harper & Row, Publishers, Inc. Reprinted by permission / Figure 9.8, from Hermann Ebbinghaus, *Memory: A Contribution to Experimental Psychology.* © 1964 by Dover Publications, Inc. Reprinted by permission / Figure 9.8, from Marigold Linton, "I remember it well," *Psychology Today.* © 1979 by Sussex Publishers, Inc. Reprinted by permission of Psychology Today Magazine.
CHAPTER 10 Figure 10.1, from Keith Oatley and Jennifer Jenkins, "Chimeric faces," *Understanding Emotions.* © 1996 by Keith Oatley and Jennifer Jenkins. Reprinted by permission of Blackwell Publishers / p. 393, from Debi Howell, "Detecting the dirty lie" (interview with Paul Ekman), *This World*, 7, August 8, 1993. Reprinted by permission of the author / Figure 10.3, from Jane Gillham et al., "Prevention of depressive sSymptoms in school children: A two year follow-up," *Psychological Science*, 6, 1995, pp. 343–351. © 1995 by Psychological Science. Reprinted by permission of Cambridge University Press.
CHAPTER 11 p. 424, from Robert Sternberg, "Love is a story," *General Psychologist*, 30. © 1994. Reprinted by permission of the author.
CHAPTER 12 Figure 12.1, from Jerome Kagan and William James Hall, *Galen's Prophecy.* © 1994 by BasicBooks Inc. Reprinted by permission of BasicBooks, a division of HarperCollins Publishers, Inc. / p. 467, from Sigmund Freud, *The Ego and the Id*, trans. By James Strachey. © 1960 by James Strachey. Reprinted by permission of W. W. Norton and Co., Inc. / pp. 477–478, drawing recreated by Daniel John Del Ben / p. 486, from C. R. Snyder and Randee J. Shenkel, "The P. T. Barnum effect," *Psychology Today.* © 1989 by Sussex Publishers. Reprinted by permission of Permission of Psychology Today Magazine.
CHAPTER 13 Table 13.1, from Helen Bee, *The Developing Child.* © 1989 by Harper & Row, Publishers, Inc. Reprinted by permission of Harper & Row, Publishers / Table 13.2, from Paul H. Mussen et al., *Child Development and Personality.* © 1984 by Harper & Row, Publishers, Inc. Reprinted by permission of Harper & Row, Publishers / Figure 13.3, from René Baillargeon, "How do infants learn about the physical world?" *Current Directions in Psychological Science*, Vol. 5 (1994). Reprinted by permission of Cambridge University Press and the author / p. 506, from Daniel Slobin, *Psycholinguistics.* © 1979 by Addison Wesley Longman Publishers. Reprinted by permission of Addison Wesley Longman Publishers / Figure 13.4, from Kay Bussey and Albert Bandura, "Gender-

linked activities," *Child Development*, 63. © The Society for Research in Child Development, Inc. Reprinted by permission / Figure 13.5, from "U. S. child poverty is far above the European level," *San Francisco Chronicle*, September 23, 1993. © 1993 by the San Francisco Chronicle. Reprinted by permission.
CHAPTER 14 Figure 14.1, from David Holmes, "Fitness and health," *Abnormal Psychology*. © 1991 by Addison Wesley Longman Publishers. Reprinted by permission of Addison Wesley Longman Publishers / Figure 14.2, from David Holmes, "Fitness and health," *Abnormal Psychology*. © 1991 by Addison Wesley Longman Publishers. Reprinted by permission of Addison Wesley Longman Publishers.
CHAPTER 15 Figure 15.2, Robert Hare, "Antisocial personality disorder," *Journal of Psychology*, 1965, p. 369, Fig. 1–A. © 1965. Reprinted by permission of the Helen Dwight Reid Educational Foundation. Published by Heldref Publications, 1319 Eighteenth St., N. W., Washington, D C, 20036-1802 / p. 603, from Stanton Peele, Archie Brodsky, and Mary Arnold, *The Truth About Addiction and Recovery*. © 1991 by Stanton Peele, Archie Brodsky, and Mary Arnold. Reprinted by permission of Simon & Schuster, Inc. / p. 583, from Eugen Bleuler, *Dementia Praecox or the Group of Schizophrenias*, 1950, International Universities Press, Madison, CT. Reprinted by permission.
CHAPTER 16 Figure 16.2, from Monica McGoldrick and Randy Gerson, "O'Neill family—repetitive functioning patterns," *Genograms in Family Assessment*. © 1985 by Monica McGoldrick and Randy Gerson. Reprinted by permission of W. W. Norton & Company, Inc. / Figure 16.3, from Kenneth Howard et al., "The dose-effect relationship in psychotherapy," *American Psychologist*, 41, February 1986, p. 160. © 1986 by the American Psychological Association. Reprinted by permission of the publisher and the author / Figure 16.4, from Robert Hobson, "Psychotherapy in action," *Forms of Feeling*, pp. 11–13, 1985. © 1985. Reprinted by permission of Tavistock Publications (Hampshire, England).
CHAPTER 17 Page 660, from Stanley Milgram, *Obedience to Authority*. © 1974 by Stanley Milgram. Reprinted by permission of HarperCollins Publishers / p. 685, from Eva Fogelman, *Conscience & Courage: Rescuers of Jews During the Holocaust*. © 1994 by Eva Fogelman. Reprinted by permission of Bantam Doubleday Dell Publishing Group, Inc.
CHAPTER 18 Table 18.1, from Edward T. Hall and Mildred Hall, *Understanding Cultural Differences*. © 1990 by Edward T. Hall and Mildred Hall. Reprinted by permission of Intercultural Press, Yarmouth, ME / p. 706, from Nancy Mairs, "On being a cripple," *Plaintext: Deciphering A Woman's Life*. © 1986 by University of Arizona Press. Reprinted by permission of University of Arizona Press. / p. 725, from Sheldon Harnick, "Merry Little Minuet." © 1958 by Alley Music Corp. and Trio Music Co., Inc. Reprinted by permission.

PHOTOGRAPHS AND CARTOONS

Unless otherwise acknowledged, all photographs are the property of Addison Wesley Educational Publishers, Inc. Page abbreviations are as follows: (T) top, (C) center, (B) bottom, (L) left, (R) right.
CHAPTER OPENERS Page 2 © Allen Wallace/Photonica / p. 40 © Les Jorgensen/ Photonica / p. 80, © Mellisa Zexter / p. 118 © John Rizzo/Photonica / p. 160, © Ann Cutting/Photonica / p. 202 © Allen Wallace/Photonica / p. 252 © Arthur Tress/ Photonica / p. 296 "Alexandra" © 1995 Petra Karadimas / p. 338 © Barbara Singer/ Photonica / p. 382 © Jon Riley/Tony Stone Images / p. 414 © Taki Mikuri/Photonica / p. 450 © Jaimie Lyle Gordon / p. 490 © Rieder & Walsh/Photonica / p. 540 © Mya Kramer/Photonica / p. 572 © Melissa Zexter / p. 616 © Mya Kramer/Photonica / p. 652 Arthur Tress/Photonica / p. 690 © Susan Christenson
CHAPTER 1 Page 4 ©AFF/AFS Amsterdam, The Netherlands / p. 6 (L) William Thompson/The Picture Cube / p. 6 (TL) Mark E. Gibson/The Stock Market / p. 6 (TR) Kevin Vesel/Adventure Photo / p. 6 (B) Matthew Neal McVay/Tony Stone Images / p. 10 Hand-colored for Addison Wesley Educational Publishers, Inc. by Cheryl Kucharzak / p. 11 Archives of the History of American Psychology / p. 12 Harvard University Archives / pp. 13, 14, 15, 16, 17, 19 © bpk, Berlin, Gemäldegalerie / p. 23 © Punch/Rothco / p. 25 (L) Roe Di Bon / p. 25 (R) Michael Newman/PhotoEdit / p. 27 (L) Steve Skloot/Photo Researchers / p. 27 (R) Ed Kashi / p. 29 The "BIZARRO"cartoon by Dan Piraro is reprinted by permission of Chronicle Features, San Francisco, California / p. 32 (L) Stuart Franklin/Magnum Photos / p. 32 (R) A. Crickmay/International Stock Photography Ltd / p. 33 (L) Courtesy of André Kole Productions / p. 33 (R) Tannenbaum/ Sygma / p. 34 (L) Dennis Brack/Black Star / p. 34 (R) Courtesy of Natural Nectar Corp / p. 35 (L) Daniel Lainé / p. 35 (R) Deborah Davis/PhotoEdit / p. 36 *Bent Offerings* by Don Addis. By permission of Don Addis and Creators Syndicate
CHAPTER 2 Page 42 Alan Carey/The Image Works / p. 43 (L) Charles Moore/Black Star / p. 43 (R) Dan McCoy/Rainbow / p. 47 (T) Figure 2.1 Jose L. Pelaez/The Stock Market / p. 47 (B) Figure 2.1 Herbert L. Stormont/Unicorn Stock Photos / p. 49 From Susan Curtiss, *Genie: A Modern Day Wild Child*, Academic Press, used by permission. / p. 50 Copyright © 1990 Los Angeles Times Photo / p. 51 J. Guichard/Sygma / p. 54 Copyright 1994, Los Angeles Times Syndicate. Reprinted with permission. / p. 59 Joseph Schuyler/Stock Boston / p. 66 *Miss Peach* by Mell Lazarus. By permission of Mell Lazarus and Creators Syndicate / p. 72 Hank Morgan/Rainbow / p. 74 Jeff Greenberg/The Image Works
CHAPTER 3 Page 82 Richard Hutchings/Photo Researchers / p. 83 (T) Biophoto Associates/Photo Researchers / p. 83 (B) Jan Halaska/Photo Researchers / p. 86 Copyright British Museum / p. 87 (BOTH) Breck P. Kent / p. 88 (T) Harlow Primate Laboratory, University of Wisconsin / p. 88 (BL) Laura Dwight / p. 88 (BR) Chuck Fishman/Woodfin Camp & Associates / p. 90 David Young-Wolff/PhotoEdit / p. 91 *The Far Side* cartoon by Gary Larson is reprinted by permission of Chronicle Features, San Francisco, CA. All rights reserved. / p. 94 Alex Webb/Magnum Photos / p. 95 Art Wolfe/Tony Stone Images / p. 99 Peter Byron / p. 101 Bob Kramer/The Picture Cube / p. 102 (TL) Dennis Stock/Magnum Photos / p. 102 (TR) Victor Englebert/Photo Researchers / p. 106 Dan Bosler/Tony Stone Images / p. 107 (L) Shelly Katz / p. 107 (R) Lawrence Migdale/Photo Researchers/
CHAPTER 4 Page 120 Howard Sochurek/The Stock Market / p. 122 Roe Di Bona / p. 126 Biophoto Associates/Photo Researchers / p. 127 Figure 4.6 Orietta Agostoni / p. 134 (T) Dan McCoy/Rainbow / p. 134 (B) Fritz Goro, *Life* Magazine, Time Warner Inc. / p. 135 Figure 4.8a Courtesy of Dr. Michael E. Phelps and Dr. John C. Mazziotta, UCLA School of Medicine / p. 135 Figure 4.8b Richard Haier, Department of Psychiatry, University of California, Irvine / p. 136 (T) Figure 4.9 Howard Sochurek / p. 136 (B) Figure 4.10 Alan Gevins, EEG Systems Laboratory, San Francisco / p. 142 Sidney Harris / p. 143 (L) Figure 4.14 Warren Anatomical Museum, Harvard Medical School / p. 143 (R) Figure 4.14 from Damasio, Hanna; Grabowski, Thomas; Frank, Randall; Galaburda, Albert M.; Damasio, Antonio R. "The return of Phineas Gage: Clues about the brain from the skull of a famous patient." *Science*, 264, May 20, 1994, 1102–1105. Courtesy Hanna Damasio, M.D. / p. 148 Sidney Harris / p. 149 Courtesy of Natural Nectar Corp. / p. 151 (BOTH) Howard Sochurek / p. 153 Copyright © 1992 The Time Inc. Magazine Company. Reprinted by permission. / p. 154 Figure 4.17 B. A. Shaywitz, et al., 1995 NMR/Yale Medical School
CHAPTER 5 Page 162 The Granger Collection, New York / p. 164 (BOTH) Tom Ives/Sygma / p. 165 Chris Steele Perkins/Magnum Photos / p. 172 (T) AP/Wide World / p. 172 (BL) Melissa Hays English/Photo Researchers / p. 172 (BR) Earl Roberge/Photo Researchers / p. 175 (BOTH) Walter Chandoha / p. 178 (ALL) J. Allan Hobson/Photo Researchers / p. 182 (L) Adam Woolfitt/Woodfin Camp & Associates / p. 182 (C) Tibor Hirsch/Photo Researchers / p. 182 (R) Collection of Ronald K. Siegel / p. 185 (BOTH) Omikron/Photo Researchers / p. 187 (L) Paula Lerner/The Picture Cube / p. 187 (R) Tom McCarthy/Unicorn Stock Photos / p. 189 National Library of Medicine / p. 192 AP/Wide World / p. 194 Ernest Hilgard, Stanford University / p. 196 Sidney Harris
CHAPTER 6 Page 204 from R. L. Gregory and J. C. Wallace, "Recovery from early blindness," *Experimental Psychological Society Monograph No. 2* (Cambridge, 1963) / p. 208 (BOTH) Gary Retherford / p. 210 Figure 6.2 from Tom N. Cornsweet, "Information processing in human visual systems." Reprinted by permission from Issue 5, *The SRI Journal*. © January 1969, SRI International / p. 211 (L) B. Nation/Sygma / p. 211 (R) Tony O'Brien / p. 212 Michael Beasley/Tony Stone Images / p. 218 Figure 6.6 © 1998 the Josef and Anni Albers Foundation/Artists Rights Society (ARS), New York / p. 219 Figure 6.7 Ron James / p. 222 Figure 6.9a Erik Svensson/The Stock Market / p. 222 Figure 6.9b J. Williamson/Photo Researchers / p. 222 Figure 6.9c Roy Schneider/The Stock Market / p. 222 Figure 6.9d Nicholas DeSciosa/Photo Researchers / p. 222 Figure 6.9e Milt & Joan Mann/Cameramann International Ltd. / p. 222 Figure 6.9f Larry Fleming/The Image Works / p. 222 Figure 6.9g Barrie Rokeach / p. 223 The "BIZARRO" cartoon by Dan Piraro is reprinted by permission of Chronicle Features, San Francisco, California / p. 229 Molly Webster/© 1982 *Discover* Magazine / p. 231 Figure 6.13 from "Genetic and pathological taste variation: What can we learn from animal models and human disease?" by Linda M. Bartoshuk. *The Molecular Basis of Smell and Taste Transduction*, Ciba Foundation Symposium 179. © Ciba Foundation 1993, published 1993 by John Wiley & Sons Ltd. / p. 234 Arthur Tress/Photo Researchers / p. 236 (L) Dan Helms/Duomo / p. 236 (R) Barbara Morgan, *Martha Graham, Letter to the World (Kick)*. 1940. Gelatin-silver print, 14 3/4 x 18 3/8." Collection, The Museum of Modern Art, New York. John Spencer Fund. © Barbara Morgan-Willard and Barbara Morgan Archives / p. 238 Figure 6.16 Enrico Ferorelli / p. 240 (BOTH) AP/Wide World / p. 241 Tony Schwartz / p. 246 (BOTH) Culver Pictures. Hand-colored for Addison Wesley Educational Publishers, Inc. by Cheryl Kucharzak
CHAPTER 7 Page 254 SuperStock / p. 255 The Granger Collection, New York / p. 260 Cameramann/The Image Works / p. 266 *Dominion Post*. Courtesy Julie S. Vargas / p. 268 Gérard Lacz/Animals Animals / p. 271 (T) *Jester*, Columbia / p. 271 (B) Figure 7.4 Joe McNally / p. 275 Randy Taylor/Sygma / p. 278 Ira Wyman/Sygma / p. 279 David Young-Wolff/PhotoEdit / p. 280 Lee Snider/The Image Works / p. 286 Adam Woolfitt / p. 291 Figure 7.9 R. Epstein, "Insight in the Pigeon," Epstein et al., 1984
CHAPTER 8 Page 298 Gala/SuperStock / p. 299 Cary Wolinsky/Stock Boston / p. 300 (L) M. Pelletier/Sygma / p. 300 (C) Peter Marlow/Sygma / p. 300 (R) Benaroch/Lazic/

Facelly/Sipa Press / p. 301 (T) Grapes-Michaud/Photo Researchers / p. 306 Jim Pickerell/Black Star / p. 307 Malcolm Hancock / p. 315 Prouser/Sipa Press / p. 316 C. Taylor Crothers / p. 318 Bob Daemmrich/Stock Boston / p. 321 National Archives / p. 322 Sidney Harris / p. 323 Richard Hutchings/Photo Researchers / p. 325 (TL) Tom Queally/Shooting Star / p. 325 (TC) Bruce Roberts/Photo Researchers / p. 325 (TR) Peter Vadnai/The Stock Market / p. 325 (B) Harvey Lloyd/The Stock Market / p. 329 Jeff Foott / p. 331 (T) Elizabeth Rubert / p. 331 (B) Michael Goldman/Sisyphus

CHAPTER 9 Page 340 Photofest / p. 341 Bonnie J. Olsen / p. 344 (BOTH) UPI/Corbis-Bettmann / p. 345 (BOTH) Elizabeth F. Loftus / p. 347 (T) Tony Freeman/PhotoEdit / p. 347 (B) Copyright © 1985, 1958 by Robert L. May Co. Reprinted by permission of Modern Curriculum Press, Inc. / p. 349 Karen Preuss/The Image Works / p. 351 Bill Pierce/*Time* Magazine / p. 352 Ed Carlin/The Picture Cube / p. 353 Richard Hutchings/Photo Researchers / p. 354 Hank DeLespinasse/The Image Bank / p. 355 Jerry Jacka / p. 361 Chromosohm/Stock Boston / p. 364 Figure 9.7 Larry R. Squire, Veterans Affairs Medical Center, San Diego, CA / p. 365 Wasyl Szrodzinski/Photo Researchers / p. 366 Sidney Harris / p. 368 (BOTH) Elizabeth F. Loftus / p. 372 The Museum of Modern Art/Film Stills Archive / p. 373 Carolyn Rovee-Collier / p. 375 Robert S. Oakes © National Geographic Society / p. 377 Sidney Harris

CHAPTER 10 Page 384 AP/Wide World / p. 385 (L) William Karel/Sygma / p. 385 (R) Tannenbaum/Sygma / p. 386 (TL) Figure 10.1 Barry Lewis/Network/Matrix / p. 386 (TCL) Figure 10.1 Erika Stone / p. 386 (TCR) Figure 10.1 Laura Dwight / p. 386 (TR) Figure 10.1 Francie Manning/The Picture Cube / p. 386 (BL) Figure 10.1 John Giordano/SABA / p. 386 (BC) Figure 10.1 Bridgeman/Art Resource, NY / p. 386 (BR) Figure 10.1 The New York Public Library, Astor, Lenox and Tilden Foundations / p. 387 A. Knudsen/Sygma / p. 388 (T) Heidi Stetson Mario / p. 388 (B) David Matsumoto, Department of Psychology, San Francisco State University / p. 393 Sidney Harris / p. 395 Duomo / p. 397 Christie's Images/SuperStock / p. 399 Laura Dwight / p. 401 Philip J. Griffiths/Magnum Photos / p. 402 David Austen/Stock Boston / p. 403 Universitätsbibliothek, Heidelberg / p. 405 (T) Figure 10.4 Adapted from Bernieri, Davis, Rosenthal, and Knee (1991) / p. 405 (B) Tom McCarthy/The Picture Cube / p. 407 W. Hill/The Image Works / p. 408 (L) Michael O'Brien / p. 408 (R) Joel Gordon Photography / p. 409 From *Rich and Poor* by Jim Goldberg. © 1985 Jim Goldberg. Reprinted with permission of Random House.

CHAPTER 11 Page 416 Focus On Sports / p. 417 (L) Ann Goolkasian/The Picture Cube / p. 417 (R) Linda Bartlett/Folio / p. 418 Figure 11.1 Harlow Primate Laboratory, University of Wisconsin / p. 419 Elizabeth Crews / p. 422 Reprinted with permission from *Los Angeles* Magazine, October 1988, © *Los Angeles* Magazine; all rights reserved. / p. 423 Harry Groom/Photo Researchers / p. 426 Bruce Ayres/Tony Stone Images / p. 428 (L) Photofest / p. 428 (R) The poster "The Rape of the Sabine Women" was created by the Pi Kappa Phi fraternity in 1987 to raise sexual abuse awareness among its undergraduate members. / p. 429 Les Van/Unicorn Stock Photos / p. 430 Eric Kroll / p. 432 (L) Deborah Davis/PhotoEdit / p. 432 (R) Zigy Kaluzny/Tony Stone Images / p. 437 David Young-Wolff/PhotoEdit / p. 438 (L) Rick Friedman/Black Star / p. 438 (CL) American Foundation for the Blind Helen Keller Archives / p. 438 (CR) Flip Shulke/Black Star / p. 438 (R) Dennis Brack/Black Star / p. 439 (L) Owen Franken/ Sygma / p. 439 (CL) Marvin Koner/Black Star / p. 439 (CR) Duran/Giansanti/Perrin/ Sygma / p. 439 (R) Carol Halebian/Gamma-Liaison / p. 441 Spencer Grant/The Picture Cube/

CHAPTER 12 Page 452 (T) Fred Prouser/Sipa Press / p. 452 (B) Photofest / p. 453 (B) Ed Kashi / p. 456 Figure 12.1 Michael Siluk/The Image Works / p. 457 Rob Nelson/Black Star / p. 460 Figure 12.2 Evan Byrne, Laboratory of Comparative Ethnology, National Institute of Child Health and Human Development / p. 462 Herman Kokojan/Black Star / p. 464 Lisa Quinones/Black Star / p. 470 Innervisions / p. 472 John Kelly/The Image Bank / p. 473 Photofest / p. 474 Donna Day/Tony Stone Images / p. 476 S. Franklin/Sygma / p. 479 From Rorschach, *Psychodiagnostik*, Verlag Hans Huber Bern. Copyright 1921, renewed 1948 / p. 481 AP/Wide World / p. 485 Catherine Ursillo/Photo Researchers

CHAPTER 13 Page 492 National Portrait Gallery, London / p. 494 Sally & Richard Greenhill / p. 495 J. Guichard/Sygma / p. 496 Figure 13.1 Marina Raith/Gruner & Jahr / p. 497 Dorris Pinney Brenner / p. 501 (L) Figure 13.2 Mimi Forsyth/Monkmeyer / p. 501 (R) Figure 13.2 Marcia Weinstein / p. 503 (BOTH) Jackie Curtis / p. 504 Mandal Ranjiz/Photo Researchers / p. 505 Erika Stone / p. 508 (T) Laura Dwight / p. 508 (B) Lawrence Migdale/Stock Boston / p. 509 Margo Granitsas/Photo Researchers / p. 512 Sandra Lousada/Collections / p. 515 (L) Laura Dwight / p. 515 (R) Erika Stone / p. 518 (L) Tony Freeman/PhotoEdit / p. 518 (R) Robert Brenner/PhotoEdit / p. 519 (L) Diane M. Lowe/Stock Boston / p. 519 (R) Betsy Lee / p. 521 Richard Hutchings/Photo Researchers / p. 522 (L) Phil McCarten/PhotoEdit / p. 522 (C) Aneal Vohra/The Picture Cube / p. 522 (R) Jeff Greenberg/Unicorn Stock Photos / p. 526 (L) Lauren Freudmann/Rainbow / p. 526 (C) Dan McCoy/Rainbow / p. 526 (R) Ken Fisher/Tony Stone Images / p. 529 Tom McCarthy/The Picture Cube / p. 531 (L) Rhoda Sidney/PhotoEdit / p. 531 (R) Barbara Alper/Stock Boston

CHAPTER 14 Page 542 Bruce Ayres/Tony Stone Images / p. 543 (L) Stephen Agricola/The Image Works / p. 543 (R) Michael Greenlar/The Image Works / p. 544 Manfred Kage/Peter Arnold, Inc. / p. 546 (L) Mark Richards/PhotoEdit / p. 546 (R) Jeffrey Markowitz/Sygma / p. 547 Stanley Rice/Monkmeyer / p. 549 Tom Sobolik/Black Star / p. 552, 553 National Baseball Library & Archive, Cooperstown, NY / p. 554 Philip Jones Griffiths/Magnum Photos / p. 555 Roy Roper/Zuma Images / p. 557 John Griffen/The Image Works / p. 558 Bruce Ayres/Tony Stone Images / p. 559 Malcolm Hancock / p. 561 The Kobal Collection / p. 563 Fujifotos/The Image Works / p. 566 The Museum of Modern Art/Film Stills Archive / p. 567 Culver Pictures

CHAPTER 15 Page 574 Erich Lessing/Art Resource, NY / p. 575 (L) Fujifotos/The Image Works / p. 575 (C) Art Wolfe/Tony Stone Images / p. 575 (R) Les Stone/Sygma / p. 578 Sophia Smith Collection, Smith College / pp. 582, 584 Philipp Bourseiller/Gamma-Liaison / p. 585 Hand-colored for Addison Wesley Educational Publishers, Inc. by Cheryl Kucharzak / p. 586 Alfred Gescheidt/The Image Bank / p. 587 Figure 15.1 Courtesy of Dr. Michael E. Phelps and Dr. John C. Mazziotta, UCLA School of Medicine / p. 591 (T) Corbis-Betmann. Hand-colored for Addison Wesley Educational Publishers, Inc. by Cheryl Kucharzak / p. 591 (BL) AP/Wide World / p. 591 (BR) Karen Garber/*The Corning Leader*/Sipa Press / p. 595 Photofest/Jagarts / p. 601 Carol Lee/The Picture Cube / p. 602 David Young-Wolff/Tony Stone Images / p. 607 Figure 15.3 Al Vercoutere, Malibu, CA 608 Dick Bell/*Insight* Magazine / p. 609 Figure 15.4 Howard Sochurek

CHAPTER 16 Page 618 Spencer Eth, M. D. / p. 619 (BOTH) Alvin H. Perlmutter Inc. / p. 622 Figure 16.1 from Schwartz, J. M.; Stoessel, P. W.; Baxter, L. R. Jr.; Martin, K. M.; Phelps, M. E. "Systematic changes in cerebral glucose metabolic rate after successful behavior modification treatment of obsessive-compulsive disorder." *Archives of General Psychiatry*, 1996 Feb., 53 (2):109–113. © 1996 American Medical Association. Photo by Jeffrey M. Schwartz, M. D. / p. 623 Corbis-Bettmann / p. 626 Erich Lessing/Art Resource, NY/ 628 Camerique/H. Armstrong Roberts / p. 630 (BOTH) Alan D. Entin, Ph. D. / p. 636 (BOTH) Christopher Morris/Black Star / p. 641 Figure 16.4 from "Psychotherapy in action: How one therapist reached a withdrawn boy," in *Forms of Feeling* by Robert Hobson. Reprinted by permission of Tavistock Publications. / p. 643 (T) Courtesy Dr. Giuseppe Costantino / p. 643 (B) Xan Lopez

CHAPTER 17 Page 654 Courtesy of Friends of Le Chambon / p. 655 Ulrike Welsch/Photo Researchers / p. 656 Michael Greenlar/Black Star / p. 659 (BOTH) Figure 17.1 Copyright 1965 by Stanley Milgram. From the film *Obedience*, distributed by Pennsylvania State University, PCR / p. 660 Copyright 1965 by Stanley Milgram. From the film *Obedience*, distributed by Pennsylvania State University, PCR / p. 662 David. A. Harvey © National Geographic Society / p. 663 Bob Krist/Tony Stone Images / p. 668 From *Newsweek*, October 28, 1996 © 1996, Newsweek, Inc. All rights reserved. Reprinted by permission. Photos: (left) Nina Berman/ Sipa Press; (right) Nick Cardillicchio / p. 670 Attorney General, Ontario, Canada / p. 671 Sankei Shimbun / p. 673 (L) Alex Webb/Magnum Photos / p. 673 (R) Guy Marshall Anderson, *Life* Magazine © Time Inc. / p. 675 Dr. Philip G. Zimbardo / p. 677 (L) Evan Agostini/Gamma-Liaison / p. 677 (R) AP/Wide World / p. 678 Sidney Harris / p. 681 (ALL) from *Intergroup Conflict and Cooperation: The Robbers Cave Experiiment*, by Sherif, Harvey, White, Hood, and Sherif. Institute of Group Relations, University of Oklahoma, Norman, 1961. Courtesy Muzafer Sherif. / p. 682 AP/Wide World / p. 683 Shelly Katz / p. 684 Sygma

CHAPTER 18 Page 692 James W. Terry/Sipa Press / p. 694 Lionel Delevingne/Stock Boston / p. 695 (L) M. Dalmasso/Gamma-Liaison / p. 695 (R) Shahn Kermani/Gamma-Liaison / p. 698 (T) Robert Azzi/Woodfin Camp & Associates / p. 698 (BL) AP/Wide World / p. 698 (BR) Gary Conner/PhotoEdit / p. 702 (L) Wally McNamee/Woodfin Camp & Associates / p. 702 (R) Timothy Egan/Woodfin Camp & Associates / p. 704 AP/Wide World / p. 705 Eve Fowler / p. 708 (L) National Anthropological Archives/Smithsonian Institution / p. 711 Denver Public Library, Western History Department / p. 712 (T) Stephen Ferry/Gamma-Liaison / p. 712 (B) Tom McCarthy/The Picture Cube / p. 714 Penny Tweedie/Woodfin Camp & Associates / p. 715 (ALL) from Sam Keen, *Faces of the Enemy: Reflections of the Hostile Imagination.* Copyright © 1986 by Sam Keen. All rights reserved. Reprinted by permission of HarperCollins Publishers Inc. / p. 716 (TL) Collection of The New-York Historical Society / p. 716 (BL) Culver Pictures / p. 716 (R) Julie Marcotte/Stock Boston / p. 717 (L) UPI/Corbis-Bettmann / p. 717 (TR) N. Calante/Gamma-Liaison / p. 717 (BR) Steve Kagan/Photo Researchers / p. 718 (L) Bob Daemmrich/Sygma / p. 718 (TR) Library of Congress / p. 718 (BR) Corbis-Bettmann / p. 719 (L) Dana Stone, Richmond, VA / p. 719 (R) Michael Schwarz/Gamma-Liaison / p. 723 (L) Don Wright, *The Palm Beach Post* / p. 723 (R) Drawing by C. Headrick. Courtesy Patricia G. Divine, University of Wisconsin-Madison / p. 726 (BOTH) from *I Dream of Peace.* Copyright © 1994 UNICEF. First published throughout the world in the English language in 1994 by HarperCollins Publishers, Inc.

AUTHOR INDEX

SUBJECT INDEX

Page numbers followed by an *i* refer to illustrations and those followed by a *t* refer to tables.

Dedicated To

Arthur J. Moore
Walter D. Jones
Perla Rizzo
Woman Of The Star

Table of Contents

Spouses. And Lovers Briefly Imagined As........ 79

Separations & Alienations. The Usual Run Of 231

The Poet's Blogging

From www.zolencalonovels.com

I think I have a problem. A serious problem. Honest to God. I say it's about this anthology of poems; my wife says it's about me.

It is about *this*: I have always loved poetry. I always wanted to be a poet. I never looked down on the profession just because of Edgar Guest or ee cummings. And I remained determined to write even when my father told me that all poets were faggots, and my mother wailed that, though my father was wrong to call every poet a queer, they were certainly all atheists, and alcoholics, too.

Because of the wisdom imparted to me by my parents, I never dared tell a soul of my poetic ambition. Outside of school, I never read a single poem nor owned a single poetry book. If you found me in a bookstore, I can assure you it would be nowhere near the poetry racks.

Thus, as a miserable isolate did I begin to file little bits of poem in a folder I kept in a series of bottom desk drawers. I tracked my life with those poems for a long while, so long that the folder got cumbersome and stuff started falling out.

I bought a computer to format the poems and sort them by topic. Shortly afterward, the miracle occurred. I looked down one day at about three-hundred pages of neatly printed blocks of short sentences handsomely decorated by a bunch of white space, and said to myself: "By God, this looks like a book!" And yes, my ego won over me. I came out of the closet.

I drove to the city, strode boldly into a bookstore, and purchased twelve books of poetry written by the most bastardized surnames I could find—which is to say, the most revered of the world's contemporary poets. I also tuned my car radio to National Public Radio and left it on when voices—trained, I think, through self-stimulating conversations with oneself over long Minnesota winters—Aspartamed the air with verse.

And yes, I read all the books, and I listened to all the voices; every book, every recitation, hour after hour, day after day until . . . .

You guessed it. I overdosed. I went into treatment. And I came to know the piteous error of my ways.

I wallowed in self-contempt for a while. Then I moved to rue. Then I just felt lost. I watched Planet Of The Apes videos. Somehow they made me feel at home with the world of modern poem . . . and I was not even one of the apes.

But that small solace did not last. I called myself contrary, insolent, even aesthetically illiterate. I tried again to read the poets, to re-read, to open to new horizons of meaning and metaphor, rhythm, meter, beat, shades of sound and tone and verbal textures, to senses of height, depth, color, liquidity—oh so many of which qualities so perfectly illuminated the insides and undersides of things only a roach, worm, or amoeba might normally enjoy. And, most impressively, all alliterated as predictably as a consonant pinned beneath the cat's paw on my computer keyboard.

I could take it no more! In desperation, I went philosophical. I told myself: So much better not to know so much than to know so much that is so gauche.

I reasoned Buddhistically: Once the old monk attains the pinnacle of the mountain of knowledge, he is only expected to come back down and join the multitudes in the marketplace—not substitute himself for a paddle in a Los Angeles sewage aeration pond.

I decided to clean myself up. I threw out all of my chapbooks of contemporary poem. Then I threw out all my modern poetry books. I threw out all of my literature books, too. I went so far as to write 'Emily Dickinson sux' on the bathroom stall of the convenience store down the street. I even etched my ex-wife's phone number next to it as if mathematics, after all, might prove reality.

But in my ears continued to ring alliterations. I wondered if Gerard Manley Hopkins or Hart Crane gone mad had been reborn—one in each of my auditory canals. I planned trips to Ohio, Illinois, and Indiana State Universities to implode with my mental illness among the poets confined there.

Instead, I wound up at the local sushi bar. After a few slimy selections of sushi flipped succinctly past my fatally languished tongue, I found myself at practice with the popular *FISH* methodology of modern verse—whereby an intensely alliterating *S* carries the mantric beauty of the poem as an *H* dovetails to assure the listener of the sweet passivity of the author; this, while a carefully controlled *F* dots the metric landscape with a passion the equivalent of a dead flounder falling out of a tree.

To say the least, my poetic license with the *FISH* methodology did not work for any of my bar companions any more than it has ever worked for me, although I would guess that most academics in the field of modern poetry might defend it as sensually gratifying and pregnant with possibility, though carrying a potential for limpness when handled by the premature.

And speaking of limp, that's how I find myself today. I've written a truckload of poems only to learn that I don't write like a real poet should. I get angry sometimes and make the words I write yell out. And I know I'm a little rough with feminine portrayals because nobody ever told me how to do it, and all the women I ever dated—until I got married—were absolute nymphomaniacs. I don't recall using words like *dermatologist* or *photocopier* in my verse, either, although I won't say I might never use the term *meteorological* for some sly reason. And . . . Oh, God! I just remembered! I don't have a style. I hardly recognize myself from poem to poem. And I'm especially embarrassed by the senseless short ones; and by the fat ones that I can't remember what they mean.

So with these apologies having finally driven me to my point, it is this: I have written my life for you, fair reader. Yes, you—not me. And for a mere pittance of consideration, I would ask you, from my anthology, to pick out just one of my chapbooks—one, the title of which sets a little flight to your fancy, or dares you a little bit, or that you think a little wacky—and read it. Then, what the hell, if it doesn't suit you, and if you haven't bent the pages up too much with your anguish or soiled them with your tears, give it to a friend as a present.

There. You have it. Dare to try one. And remember, if you don't enjoy it, don't blame yourself for wasting perfectly good money on a poetry book. Blame me. And at the worst, make a friend happy this Christmas.

Zolen Caló

Stupored Revelations.

And Insights Therefrom

The First Chapbook Of Poem By

Zolen Caló

Table of Contents

Stupored Revelations. And Insights Therefrom

I must say to you, dear reader, that I am ashamed to have written this chapbook concerning stupored revelations. Oh! If only I could have kept it smaller.

I rationalize, however, and defend my writings on the basis that stupor is a preferred state for almost all religious denominations after six o'clock on any church night and all day on Sundays, for all legislative bodies after the work-a-week lunch hour, and for almost all artists and drug addicts before 5:30 a.m. and after 8:30 a.m. on any given day.

Honestly, if you have never experienced one of these states of stupor you should not open further into this pathetic chapbook. But if you do, I would suggest that you move ahead with an eye toward insight. Because insight does so often come from stupor—it is just that the stupored cannot remember the resplendent cognition. I, however, *did* slobber over a piece of paper or foam into a recorder for almost twenty years to glean the vivid insights I no longer remember having, so that I might share them with you here.

Now, I don't know if you are stupored or how stupored you are. But read on. I honestly believe you will come to realize, as have I, exactly how stupored you really are.

The Krystal Diner Crowd

The early morning Krystal crowd
Sits as if within a shroud
Still hanging from the night;
Their broth of coffee cooling there,
They watch the sun rise on some dare
They face another day;
(Swells their will in habits that
Flush them from ailed habitats
And post them there?)

We younger mammals of the haunt
Sip our brew as nonchalant
Passengers among those few;
But pressed the awkward way we are
'Twixt whim of man and mystic star,
We hurry lest we dwell too long.

The Willow's Vigil

From my window I watch the willow weeping;
She does not weep for me.
That delicately dangling tree takes her drooping
    branches
And, with early morning dew-time tears, she
Wets the soil from which a mad humanity,
    long witnessed,
Rushes, unwarned, like
Often looking backward weeping we.

Untouched Destiny

Moving out beyond our scope
We know of other worlds;
Pinned by our past and the
Limits of our mind, though,
We claim mere recognition.

Tied and bound, we struggle with
The smaller life we lead
While there beyond our future lies
Our untouched destiny.

An Existential Dilemma

Into its deprivation
I author my own ecstasy -
In the abundance of which
I invent my own pain.

And watching for that
Ever elusive romance
That cradles so carefully
The balance of those two,
I wait as if a tiger
And gauge the opportunity.

The Woman Driver

She drives too fast -
Leans too heavily upon the gas.
Some counterpoint within that tiny body boiling
Wipes away timidities,
And with temerity, she tears along
The roadway.

Perhaps that rapid pace
Tends to keep her in her place
At other times,
So that when reaching, she doesn't tend too far,
Or care too much.

Her Blue Shoes

Your blue shoes
Carry you places
I cannot go,
Even as I move along
Beside you.

Except that time in Louisville
When the sense of being here
Was lost in all of what was there.

It could have been
Your blue shoes I wore
For that one second;
Or it could have been
The one's I didn't know
I owned.

A Greater Dreamer's Scheme

The time is too much gone.
The bear's begun to rub his eyes,
And I - too tried and grown,
And with this winter coming on -
Wonder of my turn - even

Watch the way the noblest trees
Show through their hearts: they
Fruitless points against cold offense -
No help from mother, jury, friend;
Victims of a gray reality -
Still they greet their births again.

But I, treading along fresher lines
(As drawn by many of the greater minds),
Find a rabbit's path of doings here;
And waiting, I pretend the dog,
Stifled biter of reality, harklessly barking
Lest in occasional rabid outreach make a tear, I
Stumble blinded with my madness pathward,
Harshly judged,
A victim of some Greater Dreamer's scheme.

Must Own A Cadillac

Uncle had a Cadillac.
It was big and very black.
When I was four, I looked up high
And eyed that Cadillac in the sky.

When I was grown I got a car,
Black as night around a star.
I still hold to that same tack,
But I've never owned a Cadillac.

What this says of that small child,
Who eyed that car with starry smile,
Does not intrigue *my* random mind -
Though perplex spinal of our kind.

Ulysses Again

He wanders through the ruins;
Bits and pieces of remains intrigue him.
He scrambles them;
He toils;
His hands break and scar
Every day, every day.

And then what was
Becomes a garden
That enjoyed, he,
Too old to survive his own creation,
Leaves behind for those who
Did not share his pain:
A promise fit for spoil,
Again.

Moon Sighting

She said, "Look out and see the moon."
"Where is it tonight?" I asked.
"Over Ron and Kathy's house,"
Her reply came, too soon tapered.

It was then we came to know,
Glanced between us in the shadows,
How magnificent moons now
Hung above city houses,
As if the egos there
Possessed some pull,
Some greater power.

I Can't Do It

What's it like
To be inside
A heart so wide?

I come out tried.
I get so tired.
I wish I could.
But I can't do it.

Caulk Of Unwieldy Fantasy

Thinking, as we fall beneath the sun,
Of this aberration we've become:
Unsung greened void, seraned of sky,
With earthen patchwork tiles
Glued to crust of bubbling cauldron
First our birth, now our moil;

We of flesh and reason are
Caulk of unwieldy fantasy -
Detailing that we call reality,
Breathing in; partaking;
Recording excesses;
Giving logic to that diminished;
Studying of evolution;
Wondering of the seed; and
Gauging this store of our nutrition -
This fertile cause we tread so well
As though pond water were our home
Now as once it was;
Fearful that this freak of life
That dooms us shy of purer logic,
Might be our promise, too.

The Oneself

Powerless love.
Undiscovered touch.
Unlinked bond
Bound by one's
Own voluntary
Limitations.

On Execution

If there were humor in execution,
Either a lot would get done
Or many people would die.

Token of One, Icon of Naught

Come up ether, put me my way,
I, cast in a sconce of human decay
Where no ego dares purpose
For no reason at all
Except to be big or maybe just small.

Sometimes I feel so much of the whole
Before jerked back, made part of the dole;
A spiritual wafer my means to connect
Short of pure fusion and clear intersect.

I would wish to know Godhead
With me in its might
Unburdened of judging its ways wrong or right;
To wake and define that in what I sought
Is a token of truth from an icon of naught.

Run, Run, Run

I was trained for the 26-mile marathon,
And life turned out to be a little
        hundred-yard dash.
Says something of my ambition and
        this undefined rash
To run.

Run, run;
While others rest and others walk,
And some sit and others talk;
Those whose booties lie before,
Unlike this purblind soul of mine,
Where booty found is merely booty found,
And duty bound I run,
Run, run,
Run, run, run.

Breadths

Come back!
I demand
And she laughs.

So in this smaller cosmos go
We humans;
Conditioned,
Or maybe simply supposing,
We seek some cumbersome freedom.

And the gardens that we grow,
The paths that we make,
Unfold in those unequal ways
We make more equal
By restriction of their breadths.

Cosmos Considered

Ants outside my window
Winding on the ledge,
Hustling off to somewhere
From somewhere
They have been.

It's there that life is cosmos,
I think, and drop my heart
Into a darkened pocket
That knows not
Place nor part

Paradigms

Boxes and tape
And packing crates
Taught and remembered for
Passing grades,
Manifestations of insanity
Taught in childhood school for free;

Become circles and lines
And paradigms,
All continuumed in time,
Wonderful models of reality
Applied by humans who cannot see.

A Human Definition

The ultimate fantasy
That are we,
Searching the definitions
We become.

Pulpwood Nigger High

The loaded truck, leaning,
Reeled down the hill toward us,
Bark flipping off the logs upon its back
Into the knee-high grass along the shoulders.
That pulpwood nigger, somehow hungry for
 company,
Braked it down for two high-white thumbs up
 in the sky.

Clawed into the spring-ripped bench beside him,
The only greeting came his grunt
As tools and chain fell seat to floor.
His blackness added to the darkness of
The crusty, grease-swabbed cab
While red-puffed eyes exchanged with ours
 fatigue and ponder,
And wonder, too, as the gear-gruelled tractor
Took again command of road - went forth - he
 driving.

I pulled a number from my jeans.
The driver's eyes went squint before the flick
 of flame,
Then widened to surprise as Todd and I shuffled
'Twixt ourselves (we smoked) that honeysuckle
 weed.

Toke, breathe; toke, three; his thick black hand
struck out and,
Nearly automatically, the roach passed to his
touch,
Fingers - thumb and fore.

At dusk he stopped and bought us wine
We shared from paper cup.

The Forces

That which is -
That which was -
That which still might be:

The forces of language
Which dictate man's present
Accrued from an enfabled past,
From which he predicts his destiny.

Of The Human

To endure anything for a dream,
To dream indeed,
Is the mark.

I: Laid Out In Definition

Oh, Me! Oh, Muse!
In you two surely lies the answer
To the What
To the I
To the Am.

And as certainly as I
Tap you,
Lay myself in definition
Before you,
In so much I become you
And no longer need you
For that reply:
One which, in seed, I carry -
And one which, in word, I am
Most inhumanly supposed to know.

Fingers Through The Sand

An everywhere impalpable puppet,
It buffs against the elements.
But worn and wasted,
It becomes again what it was at first,
The sand.

I think I might clutch it,
And scoop it wildly -
Toss it merrily into the air
Or kick at it hatefully with my feet.
Indeed, I do contemplate it,
As do I accede to have myself contemplated
        upon it -
This, as I pretend to rule it
And mandate myself king of it.

Ah! So am I stubborn. And later,
Collecting my history among my ruins,
I stumble onto what has been
Is nothing more than fingers through
The sand.

It's Only A Stick

Sometimes in mirrors
The chatter is fun,
But after the discourse
That person is gone.

There's no resolution,
Just like there's no rhyme;
A meter's a stick
That beats out the time.

Remembered, The Idealist

We killed him,
Yet we loved him.
In many ways so much like us,
He scared us,
And we killed him.
He would have taken our resources
To take away injustice,
And he would have given justice back
So greatly, it would have been unjust.
He would have made us equal;
And he and I - they told us how to do it -
We killed him.

It was as if that chestnut mane, his grin,
His every blemish,
So pronounced and strong, so young,
Became obtrusive.
Could he not see he promised us
Less of everything for his sense of level?
As if hills should be planed and valleys filled
And water run through channels straight
        and long?
That scared us.
The whole thing scared us.
And we killed him.

Maybe too young to be a statesman,
He could have been, and possibly was an ass.
But we found for sure he was a man
When we killed him –
When we left him there, saying of him,
No, we did not hate him;
Yes, we feared him.
But we loved him.
We could only shake our heads in grief
The day we killed him.

The Flight Of Eros

It was at the last of the night.
We'd just blown our luck with two women in
        a pickup truck.
(They were hot, but angry, too.)

I was squatting, chatting outside the window
        of his car
When he hurried me away as if he had some
        new pursuit.
Was when I saw Eros as lonely, too.

An Addict's Denial

Tonight I talk across the room;
I know that what I say
Neither will I remember, nor
Blame myself for, since
The addict that I am
To whatever is not the norm -
Modified by alcohol or pills of
Esoteric and sometimes unknown
Substance -
Will seek answers uncommon to the
Human condition
With evidence of the perversions
Inspired by its law.

Encounter At Hooligan's

Bald-headed, he,
Stripped of his most secret defense,
He, drunken,
He, stander of bars,
Brawler of brawls,
Big, tall and intimidating, he,
Wished upon us so timid
His anger.

And we,
Equally as sotten,
Wrapping our arms around his
Broad and widely breaching shoulders,
We, holding him like the babe he was,
We, explaining ourselves in a way
He did not so anticipate,
We won him to our way.

Then he, hugging,
Unexpectedly,
He told us how we meant to him
Something he did not know.
And so saying, he let us go
Unscathed, embraced,
At Hooligan's.

We, Nail Bearers

Being free in these human
Entrapments only suits the hardy.
We, more fragile, tested, fall
To wait.

And as it goes,
Beatitudes however beautiful
Do not sustain us in our
Dilemma here.

So, wait, then await, we do.
We await.
We await the next,
The other, some other, some thing,
Which becomes in time the coming;
And turning inward,
Our belief coagulates
That Animus there;

So that we pray, we bow in the direction
It cometh.
We believe in the Greater,
The Almightier,
Salvation visible from an Ascension -
Frantically, then ferociously we believe -
We *believe* -
Until those nails we bear
Become the cross He bore.

To Know So Much

The relativity of right and wrong,
The mingling tone of black and white -
Rewards of disciplined study
(I suppose) have made me bright,
But wretched:

To know that apples may sum
With oranges,
To know the cosmos through a pyramid,
To see existence as a circle,
Does nothing for my mood.

To know the Greatest Spirit changes,
That the greatest bard was not all man,
That time kills all pain but does not
Itself endure,
Makes me brood.

But to know the alphabet
Only by nursery-rhyme style;
To sit for hours with casual companions
Talk-talk chattering away like rivets;
To take a lover of frail emotion;
Or find no surplus of my daily toil,
Would be no better either.

Some Demon Seed

This seed
Some demon must have placed young.
Deep in this frame
It threatens to break its bonds
And grow:
This rage,
This seething command it carries
To hurt,
To hurt.

Preferring others,
Still it is satisfied upon itself to crush;
Restrained,
It grows stronger;
Channeled,
It is thrilled;
Drunken,
With me it sleeps.

So toast the great rounds,
My friends,
Stand and give cheer;
Sing the wine's choruses
And keep me in beer.

Making Friendly Faces

He was one who, though befriending,
Enjoyed no friends.
All, pleased to be friendly to him,
Cared not to be to him partisan -
Though his money bought them pleasure;
His efforts, gain.

And he, having never learned that
Elusive art of friendship would,
After the smiles, handshakes, casual touches,
Rounds completed,
Catch himself at the last of night
All smiled up, touched over, shook out,
Making friendly faces to the
Mirror beyond the bar.

Mass Metaphysics

Talk to The Wind.
Listen to The Word.
Walk in The Image.
Chirp like a bird.

Earth's Rotation

As Achieved By Those Who Dictate Knowledge

More profess to know than are
There those who possess knowing:
Ancillary proof that Hell is filled,
And Earth's rotation is propelled
By a means of agitation
Caused by *professors*
Captured within Satan's backlog.

Spouses.
And Lovers Briefly Imagined As

The Second Chapbook Of Poem By

Zolen Caló

Table of Contents

Spouses. And Lovers Briefly Imagined As

I love my spouse. Actually, I love all of my spouses. As a matter of fact, I love all of my lovers briefly imagined as spouses. Now, I know these statements make me sound like an extremely virile person . . . and I will not disagree with that impression any more than would you about yourself.

That is why you took up this chapbook: You are virile. Just don't be embarrassed at yourself because you are. Sex, even an occasional interpersonal relationship, are fine when viewed within a one-hundred year post-revisionist context . . . which should put you, and everyone you had it with, dead.

But then there is love. How it muddies waters and splatters the sides of even the most durably painted time machines. But that's alright: To imagine love. To remember love. To be loved. To love. Yes, it's wonderful. So, fill yourself up! Read on.

Woman Of The Star

She on my arm is like the depths of space,
Open and forever widening, she surrounds me.
I shall never seek another star
Nor be teased by the cradle of a quarter moon.
We together form the circle,
Forever moving, and outside of which
There is no more perfect place to go.

Since 1778
(During the War of the Bavarian Succession)

Others were more beautiful
But I, your beau of night,
Vexed by the line of your courtiers,
Unwilling to await my dance, sought elsewhere.
Then, when you left angrily,
Charging me with infidelity,
I came to be enraged and called you names.

You married me the next year.
The magic of the twinkle in your eyes
Brought our child while
The roar of envy and survival
Called me away to war.

How I died, I can't remember;
Except to say with arms outstretched
You kissed my lips one day before I went.

And of you I knew no more;
Until the dream last night when,
Upon a cobbled street before the
Slender rims of horse-drawn coach,
You came to me as if two hundred years
Had never marred those rare two months
Which launched us into love.

Her Ether

That hand like silk caressing rage,
Those arms so thin and smooth,
That opened throat, so opened wide,
That sudden love,
Oh my, oh my.

Those cheeks, indeed compelling, high,
Risen into phantom eye,
That cloudless mane in which I lie
Enslaved by muse,
Oh my, oh my.

Those bee-stung lips, that begging breast,
That body fine with not one fault,
I will never question why
In her caress,
Oh my, oh my.

Her Music Room

Sitting in her music room
(She doesn't play well),
Rocking in her wicker chair,
Watching as she plays there,
The melody is all her own
As if her fingertips had grown
A keyboard.

And in that melody she makes
Of soft and sensuous mistakes,
I find myself there.

That Quarter Moon

I will never nestle
In the cradle of
A quarter moon
Again.
I did that once
And found
A love undreamt.

And now that love,
Though changed,
With memory old
And the facts of time
Accrued,
I am pleased to find
No threat can shake me -
No force can push me
From that one first time
In the cradle of
That quarter moon.

Waiting For Her

Waiting for her
Who will not come;
How she is, I do not know:
Somewhere aware,
Lover beware,
Dancing along like
Skis on snow.

The Perfume Bottle

The vanity kept them
Years after she was done.
Black as coal and onyx
There came to be just one.
And on the shelf
In antique shop
Some novice stopped to smell,
And in his heart
Her perfumed life
Came as that for sale.

But in that bottle lingered
A woman's body smooth,
Like glass and ice
And sacrifice
Along La Vene La Rue.

There was not another option
As he paid the price as said -
The bottle bought to set
Before his greatest lover's bed.
And in his arms again she grew
To be what she had been:
That woman first whose scent
Had caused
Both motherhood and sin.

Behind Me Or Beyond

My memories of you,
Though dulled by time, I find
In some ways sharpened
By age.

Your caresses,
Tender then and now,
Still do not escape me.
Your lips
Still penetrate and please me.
Your breath along my cheeks
Still warms me.

Is it behind me or beyond me,
And is it your way, too,
Still to taste, to love me,
Like I taste
And still love you.

How Came Her

How was it that I,
A creature of higher needs,
Sensed such heightened beauty
In these filthy streets of
Tegucigalpa?

How, beneath the smoke
And stench of diesel
Burned by speeding bus
Just careened through narrow corridor,
Did it come, some apprehension,
And then, through,
How came her, too?

The Nymph's Revisitation

(Since July 1878 - Near the close of the Congress Of Berlin)

I did not know you,
Yet sensed your love at twenty feet extreme.
And after a distant exchange of greetings,
After we approached, then passed,
I stopped, paused, thought uncertainly, and
Called after you as if you knew I would.

You turned. You delayed. And appearing -
With whimsical smile - to hide starved delight,
Accepted what I thought myself was
An invitation blunt, though stammered.

That night, met before that small café,
Stranger to stranger we embraced like lovers
never lost.
Lip to lips I recalled your kiss from a
Thousand times ago; your breast upon
My chest so many times re-seemed.

And after we dined,
Promises for the morrow, then, good-byes,
I worried of that next reunion -
Might it be one other hundred years.

Around My Shoulders

You passed out on me.
It didn't matter.
I awakened you
Into a smile.

Your arms around my
Shoulders,
Drunken though you were,
Prepared me for the worst
And for the best.

Mildew Memories

As a child my room set on the north side near
the lake
Where, tree riddled with moist breeze, the
dampness always stayed.
And hidden underneath my bed, behind the
desk,
All around the closet and inside my unworn
shoes,
That sneaky mildew grew.

That white of powdered stuff others said they
scorned
Became for me a way of verve - a central scent of
being,
Yet another thing lived with that knew no
restraint;
And something missed when gone when I
left home as
A young man.

Now living close with her in this high and drier
region,
Where mildew seldom pokes its growth except in
darkest cellar,
With luck one morn I found no fairer substitute
Than she, herself, my deepest love divine, my
cherished,
My softest and, oh! most wonderful.

Then kissing that fairest skin from breast to
breast,
I wandered backward toward the lowness of my
one-time home
Where, kissing those memories, her deepest
longings came with mine,
Bursting from that warm and thrusting ecstasy I
kissed around,
That dampened, gracious, muskied mound.

Home

Kinda snuck in and twisted me around was
    what she did.
Dug a hole in my back lot and made a home.
And I didn't even know it 'til the time was
    come around,
What a place to sleep could mean to love.

After All This Time

After all this time I'm in love
For the first time;
And after thinking all the love I'd had
Was real.

I've opened all this pounding brew inside
To that one great foolish fact.
The stops are gone.
Nothing matters now!

I Had Been Given

When at the close of the day
I lit the fire,
The old house beamed yellowly.
Through the crispness of the frost outside
The moon raged in its fullness.
That mostly crystalline power seemed
To feed a body of satisfied stars which,
Like so many bright bobblers,
Quivered in a heavenly wake.

And as we lay down,
Pulling the covers over our heads,
The softened light licked at her face.
And her eyes were so precious,
Her smile so warm,
That I saw more than the romance of
the moment,
More than the tenderness of the hour,
More than the love of the past few years.

It was that moment above all others since,
That I knew,
I had been given.

Arboretum Seattle

Canoe, old shoe,
Standing in the grass sole high.
She, bubble undefined, she,
Of the smile, calls.

I stand back, reserved and shy,
And like the frost of dry champagne,
I watch her 'til she's gone,
Then chase her.

Slight Embrace

In that
Slight embrace,
Tenuous though
It always was,
We held it for a moment,
Didn't we.

Truest Love

For dogs
To sleep beside me,
That's worth money.

For my
Truest love
To rest beside me,
That's worth fate.

So be gone
You sly-damned fortune!
I lie between
My truest love
And dogs.

San Francisco

San Francisco
You don't mean love.
You could be
Seattle or St. Paul.
Many miles away
I have my troth.
And she,
Oh, she,
Is my city,
My life,
My San Francisco,
My love.

Into Our Own

Be kind to your web-footed friends,
She sang and I followed.

We peered out at the pigeons in the cold.
Her laughter ran around us like my
        arms around her side
As we turned in rare joy into the warmth
        of our own.

June Illusion

The very best of life is its illusions.
The greatest illusion of life is love.
I am great in my love for you
Since June.

The Most

Even when we've had the most
Of clabbering crowds, demanding hosts,
Sleepless nights, guilt's cool ghosts,
And needs not met, unseen, denied;
There's room for love.

Foolish

As hard as I try
To bring her nigh,
It makes me sigh
The way words fly
When I get high.

(She'll tell me bye
If I
Don't watch my foolish ways).

Sisters

Their thighs run around me
Like silk on wool;
Their fingers cast upon my torso
The love they pull me into, theirs;
And breasts upon the ribs they robbed,
Sweep away the blemish of my being.

So is it, I with them:
The other never knowing
That they sometimes meet,
When her other sleeps
Upon my shoulder.

The Revelers

Bury my craw
At old Lockjaw;
And you can tickle me,
Just don't paw.

The fat's got gone
'Cause we done fried;
And when the other night she cried,
I didn't know why.

That Vamp, La Rue

Your allurements told me so
Long before I knew,
But I dared reach because (in heart)
I wanted to.

Myself, I now not badger that
Your tease did not come true.
For once I dodged entrapment by
That vamp they call La Rue.

The Blue Mist Motel

It only happened once at the Blue Mist Motel.
It was after the swaps of frustrated affection
That we both left for home with our
        respective decisions;
The blue sky outside settled silently
Into the misty dampness of the night.

Flowers Of The Moment

Rose garden, what brings you to the curb,
Wasting with the residues of wind and speeding
car.
Tossed away, your crushed and battered petals
Do not show the warmth that brought you there.

Bouquleted and ribboned, she,
With saddest smile, flung you to the street.
She had promised again tomorrow,
As after subtle touches he stepped away,
And she prepared in parking lot
For husband, child, and home.

A Dream Come True

She flipped the sheets to the end of the bed,
Arose, slipped a blouse over her head,
Turned, and looked at him and said,
"You're a dream come true."
She said,
"You're a dream come true."
He could have said the same thing too.
Each, staring past the other, knew.

A Sense Of Urgency

It was quick:
But it did not undo
That sense of urgency
Which would not desert us.

One Married Man

Were it not for me
She would not weep.
Some cry:
Aloud,
Then muffled in the sheets.

She does not know
The prize is taken.
Some prize:

A married man,
Alone,
With her love,
Without her honor,
Alone,
A married man.

Street Corner

Red light. Raining corner.
Wiping, through the windshield wiper
He saw, through the glass,
That person whose face,
Not related, never seen,
Drew from him
Memories he never told.

More Than Eggplant?

Eggplant's getting old,
But maybe there's another way to make it.
She says we've tried everything,
But even the newest's aging.

And talking later,
What about our loving?
Maybe there's another way to make it.

All Of You

It is you I love.
You.
You have that way
About you.
Maybe you
Are more of too many;
But there with you,
You carry that essence
That is you.

Let's not describe it.
Let's leave it -
That magic that you are.

And when the night comes,
When the sleep comes,
Be warranted it will be
You
Who sleeps inside me.
You,
Who, with the others
Whom,
So quietly, so deeply,
I have come,
Even though I have gone,
To love.

She, My Light

Without her.
The lights out.
I cannot turn them on
Without her -
She of the brightness
And the life.

The darkness,
This house,
Awaiting her light.
I await her;
Here without her
I await.
I will await
My light.

Summer In Georgia

Summer in Georgia,
Sun in my room,
Shade hints a softness
Of song in your name.

One time sung somewhere
Too far away,
It works wonders now
On joy and on shame.

Simply Being Here.
Plain Dumb

The Third Chapbook Of Poem By

Zolen Caló

Table of Contents

Simply Being Here. Plain Dumb

Honestly. Who wants to be here on Planet Earth? I mean, like you are standing at the ticket booth in an air-conditioned bus station and you could go either to *Women's Endless Conversation And Massage Heaven* or to *Men's Ultimate No-Talk, No-Foreplay Orgasm Zone*, both located far beyond the realm of our galaxy where not even your bitchiest aunt or your most self-righteous uncle might bump into you and reveal your activity to your divorced Scientologist mother and pedophiliac father who are in a custody battle over your suicidal, racially motivated, serial killer twin. Yet you stick your face close to the grill and chirp into the ticket master's face: "I'll take a passage to Planet Earth, please."

Well, give me a break! Give yourself a break! There is nothing wrong with not being here. Nothing at all. But, well, too late, I sigh. You and I now hold a great deal in common. And that is, by and large, simply being here.

You disagree. You actually believe all those people who come up with all those reasons for themselves, and for you, getting their irrational anuses stuck in this place. Most psychologists have reasons, too, but they clique up and keep it simple. They say being here constitutes a time structuring challenge for the organism—that's you and me. Some few philosophers dare call it a search for meaning. Meaning? Don't get me off on that shit! Right now, I call it plain dumb. And that's alright, I tell myself. Simply being here is often as productive as is not being here. Anyway, take a rest from having been here so long. Read on.

Animal

How is it, animal,
That home, like pulse,
Makes you its slave;
Your destiny driven
By nothing but a sense of place,
And blood,
And habitat.

Pulling Horn

I love those big riggers pulling down that horn -
Candied cab runs behind its blasts,
Growling after screaming storm it's tossed.
A message from some sky high trucker
That their kind, too, drive hard.

The Back Lot

Company's comin'!
Find Papa's cane,
Grab him his jug,
The back gate's jarred
And this Fall day's achin' for him.

They've round the bend
And in full view!
He'd better hurry, that old man!
The time he fell, nasty cuss,
Spoiled our day, the day, his day, cussin'!

Think he was born that way.
Some says nature's in it.
Family name, others feel.
Don't ask Pa; He tells it plain:
Has better friends out back there.

"Why come in neighbor!
Sit and rest your bones.
Coffee? Cake? And Papa?
He's out right now.
And of, Amy? How's she?"

Papa knows when the company's gone;
When the sun's fell down;
When it's chilly, what makes 'im warm;
His big back lot takes care of its own.
And the gate's jarred. He'll be home.

The Race To Ken's Tavern

What have I here?
This impulse to chase fast cars:
Insanely, in glee, I run them
Like dogs run hares and foxes;

Relegated to the boxes as I am,
I cannot contain these surprise appointments
To run,
To break,
To burst,
To scale and to scathe . . .

Until my ferment mellows,
The music stops,
The band breaks,
The bartender wakes me,
And in the morning I return to work.

Dick Davis

When I was young
I pushed Dick Davis into the wall.
It was Sunday school.
That bastard,

Even in sitting down then
At teacher's charge,
I don't know why I did it.

But that bastard, Dick Davis;
He deserved it.
And to this day,
By God,
I'm proud.

If I Knew Henry

They crowded steeply into the small room -
There, few chairs; it seemed unplanned.
The body lie in state only feet away as
She, his wife, cried, mute, into her
handkerchief.

He moved past the unfamiliar hugs,
The whispers, and the garish wreaths,
Took her hand, breathed words of momentary
comfort,
Then squeezed up to the fore to speak.

The grievers held an awkward silence
He came to comprehend as he slowly spoke:
"If I knew Henry, I would proudly say . . . ."
His voice fell away behind a somber smile
As he told the story of an old man never known
To kindred weepers not sure had ever lived.

A Mouse

Not even a muse
Arouses me tonight.
A mouse might be better.
Like some clumsy elephant
Lifting an unlikely weight,
My environment stagnates,
Then frightens me.

This Desert

Like too many cigars,
It becomes stale and tasteless:
This life I lead -
This desert I make fertile
By my dreams.

In Osierfield

He stood behind the counter,
A pharmacist whom my wife had dare let
touch her.
I had known of it, that affair, but once she chose
to claim it
To me in words - those words (merely tear-
muffled sounds come hardly as utterance)
Cut through the chains of my restraints like
surgeon's knife,
And I fell unto their power, utterly berserk.

So there in Osierfield stood he this night, that
Worn out old druggist bankrupted by his wives,
But having filled my wife, a simple girl, with his
Last hopes of age - he, of Osierfield, barely a
Point of place alongside a remote Georgia road,
Found his life brought to an end with no one
to know;

But I, knowing I should take my life right there
With his; I went irresolute and dropped the
Barrel of my gun from ear, turned, and fled -
My life not ended, no, but as good as dead,
Like him I killed in Osierfield.

A Design Of Desire

The wanting, waiting: Desire.
Even after prayers are prayed,
Demands are met,
That slack is filled,
Human, I,
Linger onward, stretch upward,
Stoop and stumble so
That almost by design
I might haply fall,
And rise to search again.

Taxis

Taxis: A symbol of the city.
Tired and worn like old worn tires,
Something like the city:
Tight; and worn like tired old ways
Tried by those who wish ecstatic
Backseat moments, vaguely lived
And so assorted, with some other souls
Merged with towers, and the tacky taxis
In the tired and old worn city.

Reading Late At Night

The knock:
He collects for dystrophy.
I deny him.

It being late,
Enraged at the intrusion
I retreat
To my couch,
My slick and weekly magazines,
My illusions of
My world.

My neighbors bear the brunt -
The next appeal.
I doze, dream,
Do not think;
Sleep among the sleepless;
They without end.
Amen. Amen.

The Baby

An airborne babe in rain arriving.
A silken sheath denied.
A seeping awe of one reality,
A pain, a cough,
A reminder,
A speck on turtled plain.

Mostly spirit,
A cream and colored pattern
Seeking spirit,
In cradled hands it sleeps
With unremembered dreams.

Beginning only primes the end
That's it's begun as searcher.
Sought, there is beginning only.
Primers pass with words and wonder.

Growing upward,
Outward, inward,
Spinning to a stop, where,
No one knows;
It, tall and blindly walks.

After A Mutual Disappointment

Out of pace with nature
Seems to be the way with us.
In a stumbling, lonely game of fate
We don't know how to play.

Home Fame

I always hoped for fame -
Until I found my birthplace burned
And statues wouldn't look just right in
Pantry Pride's new parking lot.

What, then, of my homeplaces:
Divided into ten years each,
Two equally pleasing but somehow
        squalid boxes.
(How might they make a learned choice
Of which ten years aided most
My grandiose fling toward fame?)
And later, was it the trailer,
Or that little house of brick veneer
That threw my genius into highest gear.

Oh, dear.

What luckless transitions these
Jostled times have put me through.
How can they someday celebrate my wisdom,
Void of permanent place
Where, with humble table, sturdy chair,
Dimmest light and time-scarred page
My mind would wander to laws that shaped
        mankind.

Seems, "Where he drank his wine and slept,"
Would more adeptly frame my scattered fame
In time.

The Test

I don't know where in hell I am,
And don't know where in hell I go.

I'm just sure that being here
Is someone's dirty trick -
Concocted after some delusion
That a test of human spirit
Could occur in such confusion.

The Day We Played The Niggers

Charlotte sat upon the hood, dripping hot.
I could almost see it in the crotch
Of her worn and dusty jeans
As we waited, the day we played the niggers.
The sun came bright, the sand deep,
The leaf-shorn trees could not cast shadows,
So we squinted as we watched them
Gather ‘cross the lineless, sandspurred field.

There were ten of them and ten of us.
Tennis shoes shielding sweat-scarred socks
Then thin and gray like powdery turf they
beat upon;
Multicolored jersey remains from high school
football fame
Mingling as if again under lights and cheers;
We ground our teeth as we found our points
upon the sand.

“Charlotte says t’ git her one a’ them fat-lipped,
Dirty niggers,” Buck grinned at me and spat.
“Yeah! Let’s kill a fuckin’ nigger!” we all laughed
and spat, and shouted
Hoarsely down the field, “We’re kickin’!”

Their high foreheads and swollen black lashes
Pressed down around the hate in their eyes.
We could not hear their curses through the grimace
of their lips,
But we knew they were there as the ball sailed
skyward
And we charged each other with gargoylean growls:

A race war under a pigskin.

I hit one so hard I thought my elbow went clear
to the back of his brain.
I saw Charlotte's hot, wet womanhood in my
hands as
He fell like a crumpled brown bag of bones
and too-roughed leather;
And the knees and the elbows of his fellows as
they trampled me to the ground
Felt painless in their revenge.

I was still down when he kicked me in the ribs,
The play half up the field and him spitting from
his bleeding mouth upon my face.
He kicked me again and, raging, roared,
"Git up, nigger! Git up!"
I, darkened, flew up with fist out front and hard,
And staring hatefully into that bloodied mouth,
Into those furrowed eyes where rage had been -
but now a sudden curiosity played - then,
With a nod I said instead, kind of quizzical like,
"You gonna be okay?"
And, shrugging, he said, "Yeah, I guess I may."

We swatted at the dust and dirt, the earth that
caked those things about us uniform,
Then walked on down the field to the scrimmage
Where the others who watched us waited.

Unlike A Dimple

Out of cigarettes,
Out of beer,
Out of luck and out of cheer.

Just because it comes a rhyme
Doesn't mean it's simple -
Like a dimple.
Brother Dave grew more than one,
And surely he had no more fun.

Making Ice Cream

The whole damned thing
Works in a circle:

The crank goes round
So the gears go round
So the cream goes round
In the can going round.

And the keg goes round
If I don't hold to it.

Now let's not talk
About the keg going round.
Let's just hold on to it.

Homo Sapiens

Math describes him.
He, himself, defines him.
Yet neither the grand sum
Nor the comprehensive definition
Can either create or contain him.

As raw as the forces
Of brawn and spawning,
He moves, as yet, untamed.

At the Office, Late at Night; Dinner With the Spouse & Kids Missed, Headache, Still Indigested From Lunch, No One Nearby, Not Even a Secretary; Just Me, Myself, Alone; Thinking How Those Others of Ninety-Five Percent of Earth's Population Probably Envy Me

Where is it, that challenge for me - I,
One who has begun to sense the sucking out
That shapes the void that commonplace
        becomes?
Just tell me - I tell myself - what partiality
Do I earn from tying my own shoes?
Or from owning shoes? I, one of a few who can
        afford fine shoes?
And why shoes? do I ask in my confusion.

Oh! Here am I - building my time
Like a Babeled carpenter - building;
Pretending as if for the first time
A sprawling, derelict edifice
Designed for and aimed toward
A Godhead moved *once* more.

Religion

Pre-packaged self actualization
For the embattled common man.

An Enlargement Of Potency

As if on glass on linoleum tile
I tread like a crocodile
Conscious of the sound of my movement:
Here where want realizes need -
I have made it to the purchase place.

The highly fuckable debutante
Standing by the counter front
Forces me to query long and hard
Of the wares she oversees.

I soon select not skip right there
Since down the corridor in the glare
I spy somewhat fairer merchandise
I believe I can afford.

I leave the place, my needs full.
Six sets of cuff links, nine sweaters, wool,
Lend proof to my opinion that each visit there
Enlarges so robustly
The plumb of my potency here.

The Thunderstorm

I see it from the mountaintop;
I feel it in the gorge;
Today the thing belongs to me;
Tomorrow, perhaps, to George.

Though They May Return

I beat the brown-out,
Feigned through the blue fog;
And though they may return,
There are other things
To capture me today!

A Poem Reader's Discovery

Words she reads,
But doesn't understand,
Yet clings to;

As if in those phrases -
Sophisticated consonance, high alliteration,
Vacuous vowels pretending -
She might find some hidden meaning;

As if that burden that defeats her,
That wells so deeply from within her
She cannot gauge its source,
Might somehow gain in definition
And let her rest.

Instead, she finds those poems,
So taut with rhythm,
Laden with learnéd allusions
That tease at the essence
Of all that life should be,
Leave her breast as empty
As when she first began.

Station

A potential for station;
Unheeded,
Unaided,
It grows
Or goes away -
That's all.

With Child

Here too long.
Some country where
The last chance is
A child.

And I,
Suddenly,
Watching the cook
Push the lid down tight
On a cesto of fresh pollo,
Can see her fat
With babe,
That slim, trim,
Exquisite body,
Stretched with age
Not of her own
But of that anew.

The magnitude of her beauty
Increases every day
For me.

Normal Working Man

I keep tryin' to get on with the airlines;
If I could that would be just fine;
My wife and kids and a lot of tryin'
Would be well satisfied.

Workin' in the factory here
Ain't nearly where I should be
After years of farm boy livin'
Where 'Tulip' meets 'Walkin' Tree'.

I quit here once or twice before
Lookin' for something else,
But I couldn't find no other callin'
So I came on back to this.

The pay's no good and the work's real hard,
But the hours ain't awful long,
And it's a roof to shelter the well-made plans
Of a man whose youth ain't gone.

So I spend spare time with the Salvation Army
Helpin' 'em form a band,
And I tell my wife and I tell my kids
I'm a normal workin' man.

Soldiers Of The Way

Secrets that we bring home -
Wild cats we cannot share -
Boil inside a cauldron
Rapaciously admerged;
While outside, we confide
(In hopes that we confound),
We're soldiers of The Way,
And save the higher ground.

You Think

You don't like me
Because you think I
Don't like you.

So you have a problem,
While I.... Ah! I
Remain merely unlikable.

Water Soak

Bouncing bathtub
Water soak
Rising over houses smoke:
Dirt that's stronger than pure soap,
It's us.

Grab the rig, rag;
Human sinew's in the gag;
Harking honker rise us up and over
(Rover ran before the car)
Passing things.

In our pith, epitaph;
Looking up can't solve the path;
Living longer won't shrink the wrath
We first knew.

So some are sold,
Some are told,
And bathtub water running cold
Is hard to soap
Us clean.

Lacking Fame

I wear funny hats
Because I can't afford fast cars.
And my wife, whom I stole with
Promise of poetic fame,
Tries hard now but does not achieve
Belief in me.
My dog, keeping up a dialogue
With one several blocks away,
Makes me want to kill them both,
The nearest first.

And everyone can write;
Just like a dog can bark - at will;
So does it seem a shame
That fame somehow makes words
Truer look.
Even now my dog risks death by
Saying nothing I can understand.
And though I, myself, sometimes say
Things so well,
Lacking fame,
My wife takes greater pleasure
In the dog.

Tootsie's, Nashville, Tennessee

I dropped by Tootsie's Orchid Lounge of
 Nashville, Tennessee,
Where all those great, great country greats had
 stumbled long ago
From wailing Opry House, behind, to quench
 their burning thirsts
(Their Schlitz's shaped like tall, glass, deadly
 .45's
Around which passersby did penance as, on
 crowded nights
Their seats they would concede to those more
 sequined and infallible).

In that ancient palace, doors guarded now by
 beggar throes alone,
Only billboard faces, autographed, capturing
 that older scene,
The old man played harmonica, slumped upon
 the bar, his feet on stools.

And later he lied about his TV spot with Sullivan
 who
Though very dead, planned a super special for
 the coming Fall.
He palated a preeminence he had never known
 in the shadows of fame long gone.

And like him, I lingered in those shadows then;
While, now, stayed certainly distant but even
with him still,
I journey at the tables of those who reached
their peaks,
Merely peering in my sampling from the ever-
shuffled aisles
Left for those like him and me
At Tootsie's, Nashville, Tennessee.

Separations & Alienations.
The Usual Run Of

The Fourth Chapbook Of Poem By

Zolen Caló

Table of Contents

Separations & Alienations. The Usual Run Of

What is it about the human race? I mean, what have we become of late? Are we all itinerants? Vagrants? I didn't even know that people moved until I finished high school. Of course, since high school I've lived in twenty-seven habitations within twelve cities in two hemispheres, so I cannot pretend to be old fashioned.

As a matter of fact, I know how to virtual time things in a couple of ways in order to be there without really being there. And I can email Punjabia in Kashmir and tell her what a spoiled bitch she is without the slightest fear that she will tear my eyeballs out or, worse, drag the diamond tip of her donkey wand across the paint job of my new military personnel carrier regardless of how much I exploited her.

Oh! And, ah! I sense you think this somewhat funny, right? Well, I do write a little comically sometimes to hide my fear, anxiety, obsessiveness, hypochondria, hostility, and depression. In truth, separations and alienations have always figured with me to be tragic—even with the assholes I've run from.

But now, I find I should—in order not to interrupt the fantasia of prevalent human thought—replace this engorgement of loss with a new, more buoyant point of view. Hence, separations and alienations become ***the usual run of.*** A little more upbeat, carrying a casual matter-of-factness, wouldn't you say? Wisely tough, right? But, hmm, it still feels the same to me. It feels the same to you, too, doesn't it. That's why you should read on. Read on, dear reader.

Those Gone Too

Whatever happened to the nightly news?
Certain subtle things gone,
Suddenly missed and totaled,
Point to those greater things abused,
And now gone, too.

Tolls

I was in Macon this morning
And now it's Memphis, Tennessee;
And it's so sad these same changes
Take the tolls they take
In lonely human hides,
And tender human hearts which,
Too soon,
Have nothing to share.

The Accountant

I sat and thought last night:
I love you in a way that's
Fearful;
And fearful I might act with
This senseless frenzy that dictates me,
Like some bumbling accountant
I count instead my pennies now,
And risk the abundance of our future.

Emptiness

There's something in empty stadiums
And vacant parking lots downtown
That makes me, one who growls at crowds,
Remember emptiness is all around.

From the Window Sill

I was propped at a corner with a drink on
    the bar
When she advanced from a table and some
    friends near the door;
And stumbling over my feet she laughed and
    smiled and said,
"I've seen you many times. Who are you?"

And from telling her, our story grew
Until that one stumble became her fall,
As now she stares out over windowsill
At the world that passed her by.

Empty Stare

The crib is empty.
The nurse, her magazine read,
Washes her hands
(Of the whole affair).

Waiting for the pain to strike
(In the room next door),
He gazes out the window;
She looks down at the floor.

If only there could be some blame;
If only one would face the shame,
Their eyes could turn a focus
Instead of empty stare.

That Said

Saying,
She busied herself in her words;
Until what was said
Became what was.

So doors close.
And, unopened,
They remain as fruitless reminders
Of words said,
And frail humans separated.

Airport Goodbye

She left me in the morning.
Some way to go:
Airport kiss goodbye
Under neon; steward's eye.

It wasn't 'til I set in Reno,
Coffee sobered, sleepless eyes,
I realized goodbye kiss
So shy, had really meant
Goodbye.
Goodbye.
Goodbye, goodbye.

It Was All Arranged

You wanted me to be what you wanted me to be
Until I was it,
And then you didn't want me to be that
Anymore.

And all of a sudden you didn't want to do
Anything but what you wanted to do,
Which had nothing to do with what I was
        trying to do.

So tell me who
Started this roundabout runaround
Where, when it's almost found,
A mind's been changed.

And I was just thinking it was all arranged.

You, Sad, Too?

Does he trouble you,
This new man?
Does he make you wish
You'd suffered?

You almost took the plunge
Toward my way.
Would that have made you
Sad, too -
My way?

Might Break On Cold Butter

Just bought glass knives.
Might break on cold butter;
Much like these ceramic souls of ours,
Broken - one upon the other.

Telephones

Tell me
How the night goes:
Telephones
And spacuumed wires.

Further words
From the traveler:
With laughs,
And promises,
And time
To assure
The lie.

Twice-Widened Separation

What I was doing wasn't half so bad
Until you decided to do something too;

And then that twice-widened separation grew
Into these missives from far away,
That, though delivered, don't reach,
And leave us groping ceaselessly.

My Last Lover

It's done.
It's been no fun:
Telling you lies
So you'd leave me.

Sometimes a home
Beats a telephone.
And I'm gone.
Don't call me.

The Righteous

I might have stood being close to you
Had you shown me *my* silly ways.
Instead, now, with old songs and random
        sayings,
I murk here as if misunderstood -
Scalded by your anger and your anguish,
Yet suffering as righteously as do you,
Certain that this flawed and gaudy frame
Did not deserve the social exclusion
You wrought upon it.

I might have stood being close to you
Had we shared *your* silly ways.
But righteously,
You suppositioned the trait of betrayal was
At that moment, despite your wanderous errs,
Legally and exclusively yours.

Our Love Plan

Why did you do what you did?
You didn't have to.
Then, that was years before
You met me.

If you had planned your life
Like I did,
Then you would have known,
Though I didn't,
It would have one day come
To this
Anyway.

A Human Situation

She waited for the moment
The best cut would feel good,
And she made it.

He would have done the same
Could he have faked it, there,

Where, in self defense,
Misunderstood, he and she of
Two strong people struggled,
Forging commentary to appease
Those friends who, in their huddles,
Moderated.

Disassociated, a pair of personalities,
So strong that each must
Complain of the other's imperfections,
Found, in so doing, an end to the best
Of human situations.

A Hold On Sunny Weather

It was gone:
That feeling over the wires
When there was promise.
Knowing today - talking -
That I would see you
Someday again,
Would have made all the difference.

Instead, there was no meaning
Beyond our words themselves.
Like two strangers in the park
Who would never re-convene,
We could hope for nothing better
Than a hold on sunny weather.

Rogers Vs. Rogers

It was Rogers versus Rogers
On the docket that they drew.
There, insensibly,
Two so much alike, opposing:
Something akin to brothers bickering;
But in this case, too much for keeps,
The division stands more starkly.

There, two, who knew too well the reasons,
Must stand and either lie or slay.
And what might have died only painfully,
Now, leashless, rages brutally.

That Pain Now Gone

Was it the pain
That kept us close
Ever since that first night
You, smiling, drew from your bags
That richly golden gown,
Now browned and hiding helplessly
Behind new closet fineries?

Was it the pain
That sent us alone together singing
Tunes that told our dreams
And bound our wounds
While we found newer ways
Toward better things?

Did the pain
That kept us raging -
Past tin plates and plastic cups -
That wore that once-prized gown to rags -
That moved us to peaks together
We thought we'd never know . . .

Did that pain now gone,
Soothed in newer lingerie,
Patterned sheets, linen tablecloths,
A watch bought guiltlessly,
Countless restaurants and tips,
Too large, laid carelessly,
Do this?

Quite Well

It's a hazy day in Milledgeville.
A year ago I planted a garden that wouldn't
grow.
Had the haze been here and the humidity high
like it is -
Not so dry as then -
The thing would have grown
Quite well.

I think this weather change
Says something about my human nature -
Seeing in that dryness of a year ago today,
Now, two parted human souls,
New lessons learned and circumstance
Could circumvent
Quite well.

First Love Gone Out

I had one love to give. And I gave it away.
And that one love gone out could hardly come
again -
Adjudged, as it was by me, *The Only.*

Now some can spread their love around:
Can pick those tiny bits of feelings
Left from other loves gone by,
Until that patched and mended spirit
grows again.

I don't know but what that's not the right way;
But when it's gone, when there are no pieces
For patches to mend,
Where is the start anew?
How do these tutored and logical steps
Win back that first love's consideration;
Or lusty snatches
Bring back that first tenderness?

It does not seem to be some other lover's say
As to where that painful muse might stay.
He's grabbed his bags and gone;
And laughing at himself in pity now,
He journeys down some long and lonely
back road
In between what was, and might have been.

No Longer Lovers

We used to be lovers,
And we used to be friends,
And we worked along closely
In a time without end.

And regrets that come lately
And the sadness of soon
Are only poor tidings
From the years we had hewn;

Because we're no longer lovers
And we're no longer friends;
It's a long time to never,
When one won't see one again.

Laugh Of Tears

It had been a year.
He had dropped back by to get his last few
    things.
"The hedge has grown real good," he said,
"The gum tree will cover the whole back yard
In three or so more years."
He paused.
His eyes - a long forgotten twinkle there -
Fell upon the stretches of their fruit trees.
"I wish I had a goddam peach," he said.

The frown across her face dropped away.
She laughed wildly.
A laugh of tears.

The Shirts She Bought

Even in the shirts she bought me
I feel the rage of error wrought:
Counting those patterned tissues
Hanging there in stark remindment,
I remember seven years,
And since, our separation.

It was us both.

But it is I who wear the shirts she bought
While loving, then fearing, then hating me.
And I alone eye the details,
Count the words, juggle the meanings;
And pretending to forgive my poorer ways,
Pray to begin again.

Too Late Desperation

Lying in her living room,
All alone in deep despair
Over where to go,
What to do.

She's been lying there so long,
Doesn't know where she went wrong,
Lying softly, crying softly,
Tussled, mourning,
Waiting, still.

When she met him years ago,
Then she laughed and didn't know
He was a poor boy
Looking for joy,
Too.

Were We Wrong?

Bobby was your son,
Not mine.
Still is, of course.
I guess that's so.

And thinking back about you,
Red hair and velvet eyes:
Is he grown now?
Were we wrong, now?
It's been so long now.

The Bar Sitter

She sits in bars,
Quietly smiling, sometimes not,
But mostly staring absently
Into the darkness of the corner
Past the band.

Promising her womanhood,
She sometimes earns a drink
With which, sipping slowly, she, clutching,
Tries to gauge
A new companion's dreams.

She doesn't seem to have the skills
For reading fleeting things
Like dreams,
And so she turns them to her fancy,
After which she shrugs them, emptied,
Into the darkness of the corner
Past the band.

The Bar Sitter's Companions

Her musky depths promised
For a single drink, brings others;
Until at end of night
Her promises are like so many melting cubes
Stacked back in wasted glasses.

These the tender of the bar -
As if some well-appointed angel
Guarding those behindhand hours -
Scuttles one by one,
As she so delicately
(As with the needs of her companions)
Shuffles them aside.

Her tragedy hidden and the bar closing down,
She coyly refuses their final offers,
Saying she has some other way home;
And there she will sit
As she studies the shadows,
And the lights all go out
And she walks home alone.

The Bar Sitter's Tender

He locks the door behind her every night,
And will pause to watch her in her flight
Across the street toward cab.
He'd ceased his offers long ago
To drive her home himself.

But having taken a final glass -
Her latest friend being stepped away;
The band's equipment nearly packed -
Last night he dared try once more softly:
"Sybil, might I take you home?"

Her smile shone suburban as she nodded
slightly,
And turned away into the darkness
Of the corner past the band.

Heroes

I once heard a story
About a man who did.

Somehow it came out morbid;
Although he always bid
On happenstance, heroes,
And time as heal to pain.
Yet he suffered with his errors;
Sought solace in the rain.

The Neurotic's Party Pang *

The telephone that never rang,
The guests that never came,
They sat in mute surprise,
The fear that might arise
Was there.**

* This occurs approximately 564 million times every weekend worldwide.

** This has never occurred naturally in the history of humankind when booze was served.

Fucked Over And Furloughed

"I'll protect you, Mr. Small,
(As long as the profits don't fall),"
He said with a smile and a pat of my back;
And that was better than business sense to me.
And all the things he said were great.
It was the things he didn't that opened the gate
That let me out of my job.

Still, friends, it's something to find that
Tuesday mornings, too, have
Their own quiet specialty for
Milking thoughts of starting over.

A Geographic Cure

"Georgia - But Will Consider All Others"
Lingers flatly on the page.
Another vitae teases at my age
And roof.

Where all my days I've toiled and played,
Now one phrase denies.
It, dully, blending with other words and
Letters of little consequence,
Speaks to that common penchant
For a geographic cure.

The Runaway

Lost agoddammgin'!
But three lights and a right
And I'll be heading with the wind
Home the way I was the first time.

Well, I made two, ran one, and took a left -
Nobody gives directions good -
Then turned in to turn around,
But couldn't, so I didn't,
And instead kept going the way I was going,
Wrong.

I kept driving until the country
Approached on either side
(I had nothing to do with all of that),
And when I read the other day
That my mother died,
I wanted, but I couldn't,
Go back and say goodbye.

That Macon Night

That Macon night
When we were bound
Was like no other
Night around.

The sky ranged clear
And cool to cheek;
Who cares that what
We went to seek
Lay in different pastures.

Senseless Questions.

Exacerbation By

The Fifth Chapbook Of Poem By

Zolen Caló

Table of Contents

Senseless Questions. Exacerbation By

Something about me compels me to ask questions—questions to which science is not privy and that no human should ever be able to answer. That makes such questions senseless. But if you have paused to read this introduction, then you understand that senseless questions exist and that they are extremely exacerbating as well.

Oh! You're not sure? Try this problem: How many times have you arisen in the middle of the night, gone to the bathroom, and on your way back to bed asked yourself, "What the hell am I doing with my life?" That is a very senseless question. But there are millions more of them. I would suggest that ninety-five percent of all questions you ask that start with *why* are senseless questions which are exacerbating you.

Now, my psychiatrist has confirmed to me that being exacerbated, even exacerbating, is not a thing over which humans should feel guilt. Therefore, to the extent exacerbation is part and parcel of the global pathology of senseless questions, you are here in a realm where others understand you, and you should feel no fault as you read on.

Within The Realm

That most true
Is our existence.

Yet within the realm of
Modern human reason,
May not that assumption, too,
Be left to question?

My Timely Rotations

Soft sun, bored orb,
The same this day as most everyday,
Is it glad to arrive at work?
If so or if not,
Why still do I marvel at each rotation of
its magic
When routinely I perform such timely rotations
On my own?

Steam

Steam curling past a window
On a cold day outside.
Twirling wisps of curls of steam,
Past a sash of glass that ripples,
Warping symmetry of leafless trees outside.

Steam.
Hot air teasing, moving, twisting;
Breath of winter's wayward wife,
Merged in movement with rippling glass,
Lingered, twirled, tasted and gone,
Loved by just a few,
Is that only me, my friend,
Or might it be you, too?

The Final Exam

By the very definition of infinity
Does there exist a finite ultimacy?

Our Nocturnal Way

The mushrooms on the back lawn smoked.
We didn't know until one night when,
Inadvertently,
The light of our auto's head beam
Caught them at an angle.

We yarned of what phenomenon
Brought that musty smoke from mushroom top;
What the magnitude of our discovery?

Until the next day when,
Mushrooms growing as quiet as mute,
We stood above, compelled to kick a one or two
But, like true scientists, simply observing,
Not interfering,
Acting only when not involved in
Wondering at all times carefully,
We did not know that we were smoking,
Perhaps burning,
And surely going
Our own nocturnal way.

The Evolution Of Thought

Naranz, walking on the seventh moon,
Far above the reddened orb, his home,
Thought of words and rhythms.

He, there, the Great Naranz,
Teasing with the Vital Thoughts,
Groping for a way to say,
Could he know bards long before
Had self-indulged the same wan way?

Ulysses Confounded

I come the equivocator, the equilibrator,
Pressed by my search from knowing,
To knowledge.
Usuried by ideas of which I once had no idea,
Here am I:
Stagnant in my every movement,
Doomed in the very throes of search for
    salvation,
Realizing that even as I step
There are reasons for not doing so.

Yes, a confounded Ulysses am I -
Lost of humanity while in search of a deeper
humanness,
Finder in that larger optimism
A greater dissatisfaction that what we would be,
We cannot,
And what we will be, we have already been.

So there it follows
That even as I grasp, I haven't the power to
    reach;
And as I seek to become again what I was at first
I'm evidenced it was a mere illusion.
(Were it more, only occasional artifacts tease.)

I am as limited as the oceans by their depths
And the emperor mountains by their peaks;
And I, as mortal,
Having passed those arches where-through
 gleam those untraveled worlds,
Have found their margins curried and
 misunderstood.

So do I beat against these faded limits as if they
 were my hell?
Or do I turn away like some pilgrim upon a
 country path,
And tread as if the treads themselves were a
 noble pilgrimage:
Either wayward animus, or clandestine destiny.

Sugar Cookies

Sugar cookies baking,
My baby's home!
Summer time in Georgia;
Why was I ever gone?
Mother's on the doorstep,
Father's in the yard,
Brothers playing football
Never heard the car.

I stand, look it over,
This scene I've always known;
I'll eat her sugar cookies;
A kiss, and I'll be gone.

Would it have been so different,
Would it have been so wise,
Had I stayed home in Georgia,
Been ruled by night-pink skies?
Don't ask me - I'm a star freak
Streaked with blue and gray,
But wishing for those cookies
Every night and every day.

The Impact Of Troglodytes Upon Our Precious Innocents

Who ruled
When Neanderthal and Cro-Magnon
Walked the earth
Together?
More rhetoric
As per troglodytes
From you, once more,
Poor dear?

That that one time
Has come again
Upon us now,
Would that one answer
Absolve their indignities,
Acquit your bitterness,
Assuage your fears,
Open you to your purer
Potential?

Along The Road To Osierfield

I've caught them in the headlights at roadside -
Sometimes just one, alone and very big,
With crown as wide as the way-sign that
Reads *Osierfield:* just a bit ahead.

And most times I see them in twos or threes -
Less of antlers all around, the larger ones
frozen,
The smaller ones running back into the woods.

Many times their truck-struck corpses lie
beside this
Old county highway through these toe-hold
tracts
Said dominated by man but mostly ruled by
deer, who -
Confused by the doings of the human and his
machinations,
His ways and his rules for right of way -
Find themselves wrought with injury or death,
Depending upon each crossing's make of mind
Where that first step taken, irrevocable in
consequence,
Headlines a lifetime of more or less of same.

But why the hell do I ponder deer at crossings?
Is there not enough complexity with this night's
drive?
I must be careful; and if I make it to Osierfield,
What will I do once I kill him?

Maybe He Loved Her, Too

I craved the way she looked at me
From the corners of her eyes, lids narrowed,
I could never be sure.

Her jeans clung closely to her hips,
A tender, damp gardenia
Tucked temptingly into the buckle of her belt.

My spirit modulated to her words,
Her husky voice run down my chest
A thick desire: my face draped by her hair.

She kept the tavern soft and glowing
Like the smoothness in her cheeks -
Those, too, I felt next to mine.

And he beside me at the bar,
Whose eyes held her every move, like mine,
Did he think she looked at him?

Maybe he loved her, too.

Español

With this new language
I've finally made it
To the point where I can make
Passes at camareras.

Some new language;
Same old decadence.

Pero son asi guapas,
Son ellas, no?

Two Neighbors

Look my way, neighbor!
Oh! How I could love you!
Dare you know?
Or do you bring about your garden there
Without compromise;
Without meaning beyond the work itself?

Encounter In A Doorway

I said 'hello',
Lowered my eyes,
And squeezed past you
Through the threshold.

I'm sorry you do not
Like me.
I don't know what I did,
Or what to do about it.

Enigma

Is this a pock
Where lovers lost
Tease against forgotten troths?
May be.
Yet by definition, "who"
Is but oneself,
Or all,
Then two.

What Went On There

Her husband was a welder -
He could have built big ships.
And she fed little mouths
At the school up the road.

Dryly peninsular,
Her house behind the school
Puffed a sandy road as guard -
Spokes sank unwarily
Into that thick dry heat.

We never knew her well -
That wire-rimmed, narrow face.

Her husband came up once,
His shed behind their house
Awaiting his return,
His tools like her dishes.

We would always ride past
After school, afternoons,
Pedaling our Schwins in wonder
As to what went on there.

Those Greater Movements

From whence did you come, old man -
You with your cur?
Tell me how you treat her;
And why should she love you
And serve you so well?
Tells me you have ready magic
Hidden in your heart;
Conveyed into your hands.

You prove there is a secret, then,
In those greater movements.

The Golfing Party

Terry hit the ball
Long and hard;
Paul drove the rubber long and deep;
Mickey dribbled carelessly;
And me?

I stand above the tee
Pensively awaiting
My next move -
This body,
This determination:
Where will it go,
Where will it stop,
Who will it touch,
When will it end?

A Sexual Inclination

You broke records
As you *Did It*
With meaning and without;
So where is it now that
You're young still, but alone?

Did that fine fantasy
Rule you as
Some seasonal turn
Stalks the grasses?

When you grow old
Will it seem to you then
That those tired sinews
Won you heaven
A few times while
You built yourself a hell?

Riding Bicycles

Riding bicycles in the rain,
Stuck up, down, on again;
Wet, water, soaked your daughter;
Said they never knew us.

Back roads all the same -
Soft, slushy, mud-hole sane;
Double time, slow and far;
Said they only saw us.

No uptown here, out of town,
County road, standing rain;
Skinny tires, skinny wires,
Rain, plain sopped;
Who are we?

The Motive

The talk of the town lay down a mourning head.
The grueling crowd whispered of the shame.
And little boys and girls and anxious dogs
Ran to that place of cruel exchange,
As if in their haste they might come to learn,
Or even understand, the motive.

A Misintention?

The wild wind weeps,
The desert sweeps,
The arching faults grieve,
The aching earth heaves.

And of Him, and you, and me,
We - far from that wrath -
Survive, astonished by
This thinkable misintention.

A Past Life

Could I have lived in Alabama,
Father of a preacher's son,
Pounding on the pulpit tops,
Using God as if He were a gun?

That could be, a muse tells me:
A living hell of *Thy* and *Thee*
Now come again to live the sound
Of rain and thunder all around.

My God

Whose decision?
Whose time?
Whose locus?
Whose rhyme?

And in this riddle,
So kind and so cruel,
Reading these minds,
Even You suffer, too?

The Clinger

When mother dies,
When father dies,
When brother dies,
When I die;
What then,
When,
Who first,
How,
And, oh, Jesus,
Why?

Church-Night Supper Gloom

Talking over Your intention,
Most find a way to make a mention
Of some once dried and sandied text
Of indecision.
There some call You, *Love*, Lord, others, *Rage*;
Crass Indifference or *Singular Praise.*

And shown this damnedest pathway
To Your many-mansioned soul,
I've tried to believe;
And You've tried to relieve, haven't You, Lord?
Some call it deliverance
But its hardly reprieve;

You're too much confusion,
Too much shame,
Too much delusion,
Too much blame, right now.

And is indigestion Your concoction?
So, how do You feel?

What One Is, Not

All that I am
Is here before me;
And much of what I'm not.
It's that *What*
That I am not
That so disturbs me.

Some might say,
"It's the majority."
Others kindly say,
"Only a minority."
And they - in mind
Being me apparently
(Given a removal of space and time
And the latitudes
Of learnéd tradition) -
Could know, or could not,
That which it is or which is not
The *What* or *What Not* of me;

The ultimate answer to which, of course,
Only I should be
Most privy,
Though be it one to which I only,
Quite incapably,
Could currently respond.

Generation To Generation

There is crying.
I hear no sound,
See no tears,
But there is crying all around.

I cry out, too.
It comes so deep
As if it were not me -
Not being so disposed,
I believe I know.

But still inside
It comes,
As if from generation
To generation:
In the mind,
In the genes -
An animus:
That crying to be,
To become,
To know that I,
I, have been.

Just One Thing True

Do I make it?
Is it shaped despite me?
Does it fall as mal passant
And serendipitous jollity?
Surely! There is something chosen
In my destiny.

Oh! Or, may there be, in larger mode,
That Thing distinctly other,
That huge and bold accrual -
Some fierce cognizance -
Just some Thing, one Thing,
True.

You're Too Much

Your mom's not what
She seems to be
As she struggles
For your better years;

She simply seeks some man
She hopes might help her
Put you there.

But they, those men,
Though loving her, perhaps,
Cannot meet that
First demand:
That's you.
It's you, young man -
Too good,
Too pure,
Too much
To take in hand.

Sunset Beyond El Hatillo

When the sun sets beyond
El Hatillo -
The cameled mountains
Behind me there -
The noise of children
After-hours fills
The early nighttime air.

For those who struggle
Toward a proper place
Yet read this work so weak
On grace,
Might they ask, "Is it just she,
Or is there room in
What Might Be for me?"

Inside You

I've never been there;
I won't ever be.

But is it scarier
Than being me?

The Philosopher

Quality without question,
The old slogan goes;
But questions of no quality,
Mulched the row he-hoed.

Ricky Walker's Daddy

Ricky Walker's daddy
Led the horse we rode around the pecan trees
At the party.
He was
A thin-shouldered, pot-bellied man
With thick glasses and a wide smile
Just like Ricky's.
He wore
Khaki pants and khaki shirt,
Well-worn boots and pockets rimmed with pens
Where he worked at the pecan plant,
Was the way Ricky told of him.

And we liked him.
He always grinned and made us all feel warm.
What else behind those thick fat glasses
We weren't old enough to ponder.

Then Ricky moved - not many miles away,
But in our world of city blocks and true-blood
        schools,
A different world.
He came to see me only once
Before his father went away.
(My mother in discreet adult described quite
        vaguely.)

Now whether that grinning man died
Or really went away
Is beyond me to this very day.

Is he now some pecan king?
Or king and kingdom of some
Damp tin habitat underground?

Or could he be like we have grown to be?
Deniers of wounds,
Runners of expectations,
Blame givers and awful blame takers,
Futile fixers of things that will not work;
Abandoners.
Like Ricky in some-odd thousand three,
And me, every opportunity.

Aging.
And Memories Resultant Of

The Sixth Chapbook Of Poem By

Zolen Caló

Table of Contents

Aging. And Memories Resultant Of

What an amazing experience—this aging! You may not believe it, but I grow one arthritic joint every month. This means that at Death's dreary moment I should lie dysfunctional with around 1,300 excruciatingly painful points of connection throughout my body. But that is not the end of aging. Beyond living one's days in the lobby of a physician's office, there come these things one thinks in retrospect. Ah! And can they be so good! But, oh! Can they ever be so bad!

As for the good and bad, sure, I try to chop off the bad. And, as I get older I tend to think more toward the positive as my brain frantically self-debilitates itself in order to please me.

But all of this is not to say that I am old. I still tear the spark plug wires out of my wife's car when I find it parked at the local bar at three a.m. with her nowhere to be found. And I still goggle the shapelier girls until they give me the finger. And, until last month when I missed my partner's hand and sent her reeling over the dance floor railing onto the table of a party of six, I danced away each weekend as lithely as a butterfly.

But forgive me. I fail to explain my purpose: I do not write of the awareness of aging here. I write of the concept of aging; and of the past—of memories, of conserving the memories one has. And no matter how old you are, you should remember: Aging is not something upon which you will someday embark. It is something which by now has embarked upon you. Read on, dear reader, and weep.

An Advanced Primate's Prayer

Moon tone,
Tomeful gnome of the heavens,
Arch deacon of eternity,
Grown with it,
And definer of it,
Part and parcel of forever,
Gaugeless by less than all that is,
I pray you,
Do not wane so blandly
Upon my fate.

When She Was Little

When she was little
She crouched on one knee in the grass.
Sister watched
As Daddy fixed the bike.

And, when,
Teeth bared in wildest joy,
Mane tossed to fleeting breeze,
Tiny pedal-harnessed nines propelling,
She raced into a future
Unguessed of growth's great dreads.

Jumping Board

It was hot,
And we, barefoot,
Rushed out from the stoop into the yard,
Mama yelling:
Papa would be home.

Our bare feet burned upon the sand;
The sun beat upon
Our bare and simple backs;
Somewhere there was grass and shade;
We sought it.

And arguing among ourselves,
We pulled the board upon the block,
Balanced it,
Took each a side, each an end,
And sprang high, high,
As high as the fence, high
We flew,
Jumping board.

Then Papa, Oh!
(To escape his wrath
We would do anything);
Surprising us with his gruff facade,
Stepped from inside the dark garage,
And broke into a smile.

A man of wide but throttled dreams,
He saw in us his broader scheme,
And took the plank.
His rank and weight
That made us fly,
His strength that made us part of sky,

To us his spring was part of why
We with cries of wildest glee
Bent our knees, dared the leap,
Cleared the fence . . .
Then fled the nest;
Sought to hang upon
Some winsome rainbows.

And so, as older men, wizened now,
Still we wonder that,
Having sprung,
He's not here too.

To Be Near

He tried for fifty years to touch her.
With hands and words,
His body sometimes close to hers,
Grinning face and face sincere,
He tried every way
But was never near enough.

And with the warmth abandoning
Her frail and lonely body
There by him on the bed,
Fists gnarled and paled eyes swelling,
He wailed against the limits of humanity
As he clutched her nearly
And failed again.

Running In The Dark

Running in the dark like the stark crazy kid
That I was;
Terrified 'til my heart cried,
Head high,
Running toward the house
Where cover was
From that unknown villain
(Lurking near the clothesline shed somewhere
    or beyond),
Who, with vanishing powers still strong to
    this day,
Stirred me to spirited stints of speed
I have not since paralleled.

Blue Fog

The waning comes
As if on wings
Exercising,
Slowly priming,
Still approaching,
In a blue fog.

Had the trees
Not already missed
Their leaves,
There would be none now,
Standing starkly
In a blue fog.

Engaged or lost,
The years
Like wings and
Winter's trees
Have wrapped me
In a blue fog.

On Being Older

Sometimes it happens -
The mirror don't speak,
Standing before it
Still half-asleep.

Women don't look,
Nobody cares,
Walking through life
Upon fossilized stares.

Somebody comes,
Lone body goes:
Relationship's fled
On tippy toes.

Oh! For a soft cheek
To mine, soft again,
With love and caresses
On a day in the rain.

Look Back Now

From somewhere, calling me, telling me,
Whispering,
Some older age says look back now,
Before,
At a later date then looking,
That wrinkled Satan of success,
Grappling over shoulder blades,
Grins and caws,
"You missed me!"

Man's Pants Now

The little boy looked like fairy come home
In suspendered blue pants and blazing shirt,
And toes in tiny scuffing shoes
He couldn't touch for turning over.
Too much distance to it.

And touching that barely blemished soul
Would have been the best thing I could do:
Thinking foiled it all.

Some vague fear of nature's heights
Must surge with tutored growth;
Some quiet concern in tripping over;
Seems walking in these man's pants now
Puts too much distance to it.

The Punt Return

He was six and picked up sticks
With tiny Cousin Ellen near the big oak tree.
Cousins Bud and Sam and all their friends
Of ten battled with the pigskin not far away.
He would pause and watch those boys,
Knees and elbows lacerate, lips tight and shins
bruised blue,
Crushing one upon the other, or upon the earth,
In chase of ball that won them pain or fleeting
joy.

And when the punt came, high and fast,
Over startled Safety's head, alive, and speaking
to him,
Bobbing at his feet among the acorns near
the tree,
He clutched it like the animal
He was young enough to know he was,
And ran.

The fescued turf braced his feet and sped him
Past the tangled arms and legs above him;
Through the hole, along the ditch,
Down the sideline, madly, he returned it;
Then trace narrowed, gap closed,
Bodies sprang at him like shrieking leopards,
and,
Amidst growls he did not know were his or
theirs,
Slammed him to the ground.

They took the ball and laughed and punted over.
He spit away the dirt and weeds.
Cousin Ellen pulled him to the tree and brushed
his clothes.
And even as her tiny hands swept him,
Even as her young consolements echoed in
his ears,
He stood numbed by strengths he'd never
known:
Be it pre-determined,
Or had he harrowed destiny with that ball,
He only knew that he would run again.

The Answered

The father grinned,
"They're your dogs, Ronnie,
Bought 'em just for you.
I remember I once had some
Hound dogs, too."

And smiling,
Tears locked forever
Behind rouged and swollen cheeks,
Mother, too, remembers dreams.

1022 Augusta Avenue

Sit you, Augusta Avenue,
There, ten twenty-two,
Having not thought since of me,
Your transient thief:
I who once robbed you
Of every ounce of life,
While you ignored, yet, excessively,
Baited me.

Those ages you count only
In repairs or disrepair;
Those days so etched within my mind,
You do not care.
Some other faces, other souls,
Make you now their habitat -
Still not too much of life
For you to bond or bind.

Though old we both grow,
The room I have for you
Expands against
Much shorter days;
While you, abject nurturer,
Give your room to others
Who - careless now -
Will, too, someday watch you
Through another window.

All I Need

If anger stirs ambition,
I'm living in a rage
With some awful premonition
Of unhappiness in age.

Those younger years
When all my fears
Could save the best in me,
Have dropped like early apples,
And, like them
Bitter from that early start,
Too premature to ripen,
I rage onward wanting all things
When all I need is love.

Meager Life

All of the things I wanted to do, left me.
All of the things I thought I could do, fooled me.
And watching my meager life grow meager,
I'm agonized in things that might have been.

Fool Way

They tell me I'm a fighter
And I guess I'm what they say,
Fighting like some goddamned fool
Every minute, every day.

But I wish they'd called me sissy,
Or dull, or fart, or fay, so
I could have been whatever,
And gone my own fool way.

Career Prayer

There will be no more
Trips to Augusta.
Though afraid, I went
That way and it fetched
Sheer shock; tragedy.

Why did I not stay here
In Deepstep and
Wreak against that
Low and savage salary?

Ambition!
Oh thou wert me.
And future now,
Waiting now
Seems so bleak;
My sons, they ache,
Like my wife, for me:
I, who mistook
Opportunity for reality.

So I turn and hide;
Decide I will subscribe
To the logic
Of security.
Family and me,
We will seek no more
Augustas now to
Blight our legacies.

We Weren't Even Friends

He leaned against a heavier haunch
Than when I had last seen him.
The boyish voice was still the high-pitched
 same,
The chuckle, his giggle aged.
(Was odd, the drink he would have quaffed
At some more tender age
Now flattened in the plastic cup in hand.)
(It was I in high school football camp
Who took the blame for smuggled beer,
While, with that liquid cheer in head,
He danced in laughter with the rest
Along the moon-paned lines of cleat-torn
 scrimmage field.)

Those Gypsy curls had bounced around
Behind his wide white smile as we embraced:
"You goddamned dog!" I roared at him in
 fondest memory,
And told her at my arm how great of one-time
 friends we'd been.
And he, still beaming, yet suddenly naive as
 when years ago we parted,
Denied:
"Hell! I don't know! We had that
Party the summer going to the sixth,
And played a little ball together in Clayton's
 class, is all."

How is it that that time, too, couldn't count
Toward friendship.
Must that fleeting thing meet some span
        of years -
Some formal recognition - to warrant measure?
Seems lacking that,
After all these years, we weren't even friends.

At Forty, Then Sixty

When I'm forty, and sixty, too,
Whatever will they think of you?

That Partial Ponder

In our aging
Do we find unwritten
Something that we know
But do not comprehend?

What is this mellow mood
That depletes us -
That for which we did not ask.
The passion gone,
We find a need much greater.

I ask *you*. *I* do not know.
Some time ago,
Some ravaged people
Must have asked
The same unanswered.
So you and I discover
Only as we struggle
With that which others
Later, may come to know.

An ever-growing interpretation -
One to which we are merely parcel;
But no less diminished
Is our partial ponder.

Of that, take heed;
That in these spots of aging,
In these wrinkled eyes reflected,
You share with me the revelation
We not yet know,
Or dare not recognize
At this time.

Some Child's Collard Story

She's sleeping.
Cold has her down.
Logging little lover surrendered
To collard fever going round.

She blames it all on Fall.
He sent his nasty breath
Beneath the front porch door,
Swirled into the kitchen
Stunning flowers I had picked.

That sneaky, cold-toed wisp
Must've kissed her weakened throat,
Sleeping like she does each night -
Uncovered, bathed in body's heat.

Maybe now she'll relish spring
A little more next year -
I tell her - but still beware of
Pumpkin's turn: that time when
Fall's cleared throat conceives to
Do tough work on collards
And flowers that I picked.

Somewhat Otherwise

Nature builds within its creatures
A preference for pairs;
But I have done it somewhat otherwise:
Alone. In groups. With people like you;
And, having fucked, I
Guess I've been fucked, too.

This Rhyme

My clock just won't keep time.
This rhyme of life intends
To pass me by.

More Desperate Hands

Darin pissed me off.
I punched him.
His nose ran blood
Down his skinny chest.

Poor soul.
As grown man now
I've come to feel
Like him.

Karen Of My School

She was like rubbish unsorted -
Her father a millhand, her mother a whore.

At school we played together.
None worried enough to watch
While we shared our baseness
Drawing circles on our knuckles,
Making faces in the sand.

When older, in my turning,
I found that she was gone,
I tried to understand a loss
I was not presumed to know.

Our Winter's Wonderland

No winter wonderland for us, I see,
Burdened with decisions we may never make,
Watching our aging on the other's face,
Busy defining chores and obligations.

Maybe we can make the turn, maybe not;
Loving is an age and we are aging,
But aging is a grace and we are raging.

A Midlife Drama

Burned up or bored out,
Who puts it how?
As a zombied stagger,
Or as a fattened cow?
Searching for nothing
That all seem to seek,
While the cologne that I wear,
Fades into reek.

Taken for granted
By you, and me, too,
Would there be a difference
If I bought a tattoo?
How long must I suffer
With success in my life,
While all of these years
I've thrived on the strife?

This Later Age

She scurries.
She cuts at her flowers busily;

The morning sun breaks in;

Unaware that in this later age,
She hurries busily
Lest she remember him.

A Type Of Dismay

First bunch of rain
With the sun shining
Since
I was just a little boy.

Of all the awful places,
It came in Alabama.

(Betcha' there'll be a rainbow,
Too.)

Intuit Of One Disconnected

How new:
To hurt for others.
How strange.
My druthers
Were such another way
Until today.
Some understood arousal
Hit me -
Something with this age.

Is it anew, or again, or
An awakening? Which,
Still, the same pain;
Still inside: the aching;
But this time, it's not mine.
That same old pain
So differently realized.

Cerebration At The River Styx

The thing I find most amazing of aging
Is the facility of wait -
One way to say the pace of progress
I draw down before me,
My errors now pure stupidity instead
Of brilliance unfolded from confusion.

Should I have rushed it on with drugs
A decade or so ago?
Intake and uptake *inhabitors* or *prodictors*
meant to
Seduce me to this nearside bank of
A peculiarly differentiated River Styx of mind,
I not yet accrued of violence toward myself?

Whether so or whether not,
I wonder of my purpose as I wait here now,
This theater in the round - set upon the edge of
an obscure line in time -
From atop which I squint both ways,
Either return or passage, uninvited.

Arrears I glumly watch the transgressions of
my present kind,
(I could have died there, I tell myself,
And sometimes I wish I had - or were -
Given that the good they die young, and all.)
Their audacious rambles, driven by hedonistic
reason,

A complete embarrassment to me, in that I
see me:
My badness overrunning in my memory those
few saintly moments
Of conduct I impulsively achieved.

So do I sometimes try to prepare, to set my
thoughts to the proper mental tone
For when the boat comes to carry me over yon;
But all I can think is that Heaven has no trees
and Hell has no water -
And knowing, too, that my struggle should be
here with me
Where the air thins but the pressure grows,
I wonder where I left the telephone, and
At the laundry, have I forgotten clothes.

An Adult's Desire

Little baby, pretty baby,
Hang your head on Daddy's arm,
Cry your little tears or tell your little cheers,
Little baby rock-a-bye.

Sometimes getting up isn't easy,
Sometimes going to bed is hard,
But wait a minute little learner,
A little hug will make it right.

Just keep your eyes in Daddy's eyes,
Keep your heart a new surprise,
Pretty baby rest, don't be afraid,
Little baby rock-a-bye.

Back Upon That Dream

Today I turned my back
Upon that dream.
Better that I did, she said,
Than to kill myself.
It almost killed me, anyway.
Almost ruined our love affair.
Surely broke me, and -
I have reason to believe -
Drove me mad.

So.
I will guard my words in public
And batten my thoughts behind
My study door.
I will get work;
And model success once more.
But I might disclose to those green few
Yet unmet the scathe of failure,
That far behind my eyes
So dutifully astute,
I conspire to turn again
Back upon that dream.

A Tenuous Brush With.
Enlightenment

The Partial Seventh Chapbook Of Poem By

Zolen Caló

Table of Contents

A Tenuous Brush With. Enlightenment

Do you intend to purchase this chapbook without having consulted the other six? Then, you must be a quick learner—which makes you exactly like me: Skip the shit, get to the sewer. Find for yourself that fertile thought is not intended to begin here, but to end here.

No, I don't blame you. You don't want to start with the weighty, digestible nuggets that my first six chapbooks modestly present. You prefer instead to dive into this deep, wide, dark, and odorous canal. Go for it. Fill yourself with the mix of wisdom and waste that makes this chapbook; and in the end, if you find you don't know quite what kind of shit you have filled yourself up with, don't worry. You can always drop back and grapple with a more solid set of stools.

Anyway. This is a very short book as chapbooks go. Why? Because what there is to share about enlightenment might fill a single line as thoroughly as it might fill a library entire. Further, I, personally, do not know enlightenment. I simply journey toward it. Every once in a while the light of it operates at a frequency low enough to get my attention and I scramble to scribble—I should say, inscribe—my findings. Thus, my production is both limited and brief.

As for you, you come to this tedious chapbook as one of a rare few. If you go away with dissatisfaction, please know that I have done my best. And go, instead, to create your own words. Remember that the words you find here were, at first, solely my words to me; and that by your words to you, you grow the most valuable link to whatever might be that wondrous state of enlightenment we both seek. So, then, go. And know that I will follow, and will seek you.

A Gift Of Grace

It arrives as it comes:
As if traversing the branches of trees
From the far side of a forest.

The Transformation

Kiss the little boy goodbye,
Turn and do not question why.
Like Margaret sadly grieving
Over Golden Grove un-leaving,
In such must my little laddie lie.

Houses

A house is a hard thing to build, they say,
And I believe them.
And now I know about that night of nights
When me and my old man, when he was young,
And I was young then, too,
Were building on our house like old and new
men do;
And Aunt walked in and said,
"Morris, your papa's dead."

The air stood shackled, chains and pain,
'Til he turned his head to hide his tears from me
'Cause he'd told me men don't cry.
Still, I saw that dampness before it could dry
Upon his tried and downied cheeks;
Saw him peer from inside where he was at
the time,
And say like a man,
"We'll be at Granny's soon."

And he finished the final touches and put up the
tools;
Got me into my new green suit, and he into
his blue,
And pushed me silently along the path
Toward the car out back.

And on the way to Granny's house he ruffled my
hair once
And said,
"Son, a house is a hard thing to build."
And I believe him.

The Importance Of Darkness

There is more darkness than light.
If not,
There would be no need for brightness;
And when it shone,
A spot would be no spot at all:
That patch, a concept not recorded,
Not arrived,
Therefore not gone.

Plato's Statue's Stare

Plato stares.
His marble eyes,
As if the ages
Had some greater secret,
Hide.
What did he know?
Or did the newness of it all
Award to him, unwittingly,
His heritaged respect?

Or Shakespeare,
That bastard bard
Who stole the greatest and the best
Of lines,
Was it his time?
Or did his genius
Pull those tarts ephemeral from
Early Stratford dews?

In the wealth of such a past -
Barred from us for our repast
Invention of the richest lines
And rhymes and wisdom -
Must we only re-discover?
Just re-make? Merely remember?
Or do we, new to happenstance,
Cut our gums upon the wisdom
Of some future herd,
When, upon whom then,
Like Plato stares,
Will we.

Slow Light

All that I am,
Slow light,
Is all that you,
Slow light,
Are.

The Limit

I think I found the limit now,
This point as far I go,
Stretched beyond imagination
Like Colorado snow.

I thought I would be President
Or saint or some kind King.
Instead I find the limit
A passive inner ring.

I cannot go beyond it,
No one will ever know.
Like dying and beginning
In deepest, whitest snow.

Dover's Bluff Nigger Blues

It must've been the real Dover's Bluff nigger
blues
He played that summer day.
Tuned Cross C, squatted in afternoon dimness,
His dobroe scratched his songs -
Orleans to Dothan, to Dover's Bluff Georgia
nigger blues.

His back he bent; it twisted down over red
guitar.
With eyes drooped, fatigued, as red as,
He peered at us two white boys like he
didn't know,
Didn't know his fingers,
Didn't know the bluff's sands changed, like his
fingers,
Didn't know we came as younger fingers
reaching
To some old worn nigger frowning, playing
Dover's Bluff nigger blues in *C*.

The unused pool set empty; weeds grew deeply
in its cracks.
We left down by that path,
Fingers crushing gnats from the corners of our
eyes.

The Art Of Knowing

A slight fog aligned along a lightly traveled
roadway.
Or is it dust?
Or is it ether?
Or a dew-like derivative?
Or simply smoke?
Or the haze of day abridged?
Or the great cloak of distance brought up short?
Or the quality of the photography of the eye?
Or merely the particles from sun's rising,
draining grainily back to earth?

I, for one, cannot say.
The art of knowing flows like a delta
With streams of exotic insights
That thrill, then baffle me.

Poetry Today

Determined to bring the coffee and banana
Of a stale morning breakfast
Into meaning,
Raising the inconsequential to the
Acceptable,
Thinking to prove that rhyme, measure, and
        alliteration
Add no richness to thought, much like
Toast is really better without jelly,
And low fat pop-tarts, indeed, are really little
Nectars of life
Neatly self-contained and almost crumbless,
Like a popular poem.

When I Owned Ducks

I've seen water
Roll down a duck's back.
Deep water or rain,
I, too, will survive.

The Floors I Wax

In between the floors I wax,
Something about the wood that lives -
A closeness to the forests felled
Still brings a musty scent of life
Amidst the stillness.

Some blend to bended bodies toiling,
Building, caring for,
Makes such shows of current strength, and,
Sadly later, surprise mortality,
Counterpointing contretemps.

A Chalice

Stars.
Freckles of a greater
Temporality.

Mars.
Merely a name,
Nearby.

Me.
A choice of time and space?
Or a chalice
Of that one thing?

Music Of The Mind

As if from a hill he looked to the land he loved
Stretching out like fingers hedged by brook;
And the power of that place of longing surged up
like music -
The same as that conducted flawless in
his mind:
It was one of those worn and wasted songs from
long ago,
Remembered now, fresh and perfect.

Where was he? Who? How would he turn?
Each measure came with different rule;
each tone -
Everything choice or indecision, trial or
deconstruction,
The relentless sense of a reality pressing,
And the occasional stirs of music of the mind.

A Crossroad Finally Denied

Sometimes I want to pause here and say,
"What if I dared this recurrent cross way?"
Three choices me beckon, but only
One I trust, though those others (unswept
Of folk-story dust) I see clearly lead somewhere,
If I shift my design, and aggregate essence
of human
Into mythical sign.

In such sense of had taken old runs here or
there -
Suffered insanity of heart torn and tear -
I think I've managed to live my gall,
Sprung high with my vigor to be beaten and all;
Still, I really could do it just once more again:
By a dubious turn, seek that inane.

But tonight I feel moonshine simple and slick
From a white face of wonder unapt at such
trick.
So I take the course homebound where she
and they wait
And thank God for reprieve come soon or come
late.

God's Grand Ordinance

A vulture upon the road
Silently saving tax dollars
By cleaning
Another messy aftermath of man
With his car.

As accursed as a snake,
Doomed to the living of a life
Larger predators would prefer as not,
He thanklessly hides the garbage
And thereby fills one more dark spot
In God's grand ordinance,
His Plan.

In The Beyond

Distilled right down,
We're a bunch of
Goddammed light,
Aren't we, now?

It's true.
I love you
No longer speaks
In the intemporal,
Nor in the beyond.

Perhaps

And at the party,
Before eight guests more,
He asked me,
Unaccompanied as I was,
The significance in the language of
The phrase 'tal vez'.

"The significance is yours,"
I did not reply,
Being privy to the same
Respect he did not show to me.

So what, that in this
Foreign land,
Where every syllable of
My idiom is
Valued like a jewel,
Some self-enamored cock
Must try to prove my
Knowledge of two simple words
More basic to the life I lead
Than food.

Small Success

She could flat grow okra -
From her little plot it grew high,
Like trees.

It was in that small success
She took her stature,
And claimed her place.

Small Success

He could flat grow okra -
From his little plot it grew high,
Like trees.

It was in that small success
He took his stature,
And claimed his place.

No Postcards

One thing I learned
In transformation:
I can't help you
When I cannot help myself.

So good luck, my friend.
And let's not quibble with postcards.

The Victim

She, victim of expectation,
Wearing so well that party's spirit,
Her movements marked by
Thin, thrusting shoulders
And buttery mane
Gliding through impatient crowd;
Her smile, wide and inviting
While her eyes melt back the olives
In martinic glasses.

And afterward,
She, peeled away and sliding
Quietly into sleep,
Thinks those thoughts denied her daily.
Those where, there, Greeks tread,
Great armies clash,
Dark women move,
And heartbreak threatens
While harrowed children squeal;
This, as prim ladies tuck umbrellas;
Their horses strain at carts in
        mud-flushed streets,
And lovers quarrel
And lovers sleep;

And unexpectedly,
That victim of expectation
Finds herself growing,
And reaching; she,
Waiting to be reached

A Metapoetic Of Modern Poem

Words.
Short words.
Short words squeezed
Into incoherent sentences
Like a scatter plot
Of urine droplets
Upon a toilet lid, not lifted.

Or shocklets of repulsivity,
Like your baby shot against the wall
As a gooey midnight blob and forgotten;
With, of course, God's will, or lack of,
Smack dab in the middle:
A big question mark,
Fatigued.

Oh! Give me a poem with intent sublime,
Run around with a little rhyme,
Or set off by a hungry kiss
Whereby recalled is love's last bliss.

El Suerte

"Tiene suerte,
Es verdad,"
He said upon his
leaving.
And did I deny?
Oh, no.
El suerte is upon me.

But that brought
To yo mismo,
Does it make me all I am?
I could not speak my reply
As he clenched my
Contribution
And departed.

Yet, manana.
When the next sun sets
Over this small tract
Of existence,
I could be him.
And, es verdad:
My difference will accrue
With the very fact
Of this simple
Realization.

This Time

That time I blew it.
Everybody saw,
Everybody knew.
This time I'll do it.
This time I'll do it right.

Milky Way Watcher

I'm a Milky Way watcher
Every night, every night,
I'm a wandering way watcher
Every night;
I'm a chocolate bar eater,
A creamy caramel seeker
Every night.

And when the day comes
Some have found their way home;
I wish it were me;
I wish I were grown;
But Milky Way watchers,
Dreaming cream swatchers,
Forever reaching,
Keep seeking every night.

About Zolen Caló

Defined by Romanian, Austrian, and Spanish ancestry transplanted into the New World by hopelessly migratory kin, the child **Zolen Caló** awoke into a dilemma caused by genetics faced off against opportunity. He merged the two and came to find nourishment in both books and travel. After he worked his way through southern U.S. universities, studying the liberal arts and discovering his inefficiencies in all things political, he took up his "hazardous adventures of a domestic sort."

He has consolidated his search for lore into seven novels and, most powerfully, into the seven chapbooks of poem presented here under the title of **Earth, Dirt, And Dust**.

He now writes daily, both fiction and poetry, wonders why he does, and avows to himself that you, his readers, will come to know a little of him and much about yourselves, through an acculturated appetite for his poems.

He is owned by a wife, a mother in law, six cats, two dogs, a goat, two ganders, and the Muse (the Thoroughbred and Criollo stallions jumped the fence a few weeks back and were last seen near the airport).

Other Books by Zolen Caló

Ali Zán and True Love
Fingers Through the Sand
The Quixote Imbroglio
Memory Work
He, Recalled
Nearly Diamond
Just Another Georgia Romance

www.zolencalonovels.com

Printed in the United States
208585BV00002B/4/A